National Security Law Documents

National Security Law Documents

Second Edition

John Norton Moore

Guy B. Roberts

Robert F. Turner

Carolina Academic Press

Durham, North Carolina

ISBN 1-59460-024-4
LCCN 2005937552

Carolina Academic Press
700 Kent Street
Durham, North Carolina 27701
Telephone (919) 489-7486
Fax (919) 493-5668
www.cap-press.com

Printed in the United States of America

Contents

Part III
Arms Control, Disarmament, Non-Proliferation and Confidence-Building

A. Multilateral Arms Control and Disarmament Agreements

B. National Security and Human Rights

C. Cyber Threats

Part V
Domestic Law and National Security

A. The National Security Process

B. Homeland Security and Counterterrorism

C. The Constitutional Framework for the Division of Powers between the Congress and the President

1. Treaty Power

2. War Powers

3. Executive Privilege

D. Access to Information

E. Intelligence and Counter-Intelligence

F. Foreign Assistance

G. Emergency Preparedness

Preface

Four years have passed since horrendous terrorist attacks demonstrated that a post-Cold War America continues to face serious threats to its national security. Not surprisingly, the consequences of this realization included a dramatic increase in interest in various aspects of national security law—a legal specialty area pioneered here at the University of Virginia School of Law more than three decades ago. Most law schools now offer at least one course or seminar in this area, and the Association of American Law Schools has now designated national security law as a recognized specialty. Conflicts in Afghanistan and Iraq have brought once esoteric provisions of the 1949 Geneva Conventions to the front pages, while the USA PATRIOT Act has led some to fear even for the civil liberties of Americans in the global war on terrorism. In sum, today these issues are every bit as important as they were at the height of the Cold War.

When two of the editors of this volume co-founded the Center for National Security Law twenty-five years ago, Virginia remained the only law school teaching national security law, and one of our first priorities was to prepare teaching materials so that others could join us in teaching this new field. First published in 1990, with a new edition released in 2005, *National Security Law* remains the most comprehensive text on the subject, featuring contributions from both leading scholars across American (and around the world) and key present and former practitioners.

The first edition of *National Security Law Documents* was published in 1995 to provide a convenient collection of primary documents for students and to serve as a free-standing desk reference for practitioners. In addition to excerpts from key treaties, statutes, executive orders, and other legal instruments, the volume also includes such important non-legal documents as President George Washington's *Farewell Address* and George Kennan's *Long Telegram*.

Like the casebook, *National Security Law Documents* is comprehensive and interdisciplinary in its approach. It includes key documents concerning U.S. foreign policy, institutional modes of conflict management, norms concerning the initiation of coercion, human rights, war crimes, international terrorism, arms control, separation of constitutional powers, and intelligence—to name but a few of the included topics. The editors believe that *National Security Law Documents* represents the most useful collection of documents relating to the field of national security law available today in a single volume.

Through the wonders of the Internet, most of the documents excerpted in this volume are now available online. Readers will find URLs included in most of the footnotes. A list of selected key Web sites is also appended.

John Norton Moore
Guy B. Roberts
Robert F. Turner

December 3, 2005
Charlottesville, Virginia

Acknowledgments

The second edition of *National Security Law Documents* is the product of the efforts of many, and the editors wish to express appreciation to all those who worked diligently on both the first edition and this major revision.

Our editorial assistants have spent many hours researching and collecting official documents, inputting data, proofreading, and otherwise working to make sure this edition is comprehensively and accurately updated. For these fine efforts we thank Judith A. Ellis, David M. Edinger, Elyse H. Hunter, and Joanna C. Murdick. A number of Center student research assistants have also helped in the task of collecting and preparing documents for inclusion; and for this work we are grateful to Alexander B. Patterson, Cameron N. Brown, and Ji Lee. Ms. Donna Ganoe, the Center's Executive Administrator since 1987, has also been particularly helpful in overseeing and coordinating the editorial and student assistants.

Additionally, Taylor Fitchett and research librarians Rob (Robert C.) Richards and Ben Doherty at the Morris Law Library at the University of Virginia School of Law have provided crucial assistance in cite-checking the footnotes, and to them we are deeply indebted.

The second edition of *National Security Law Documents* builds on the first edition which was published in 1995. We continue to be grateful to the many people who labored extensively to produce it: Frederick S. Tipson, the former Chief Council to the Senate Foreign Relations Committee, Susan Broadwater-Chen, Freda Berman, Irum Hassan-Khan, Kathy Wood, Kay Wood, and student research assistants Suzanne Anselmo, Bill Aniskovich, Julia Bunck, Matt Cuscias, Mark Hoch, Paula Hopping, Thomas Plochan, Patty Summers, and Robert Vander Lugt.

The Editors

John Norton Moore is the Walter L. Brown Professor of Law at the University of Virginia School of Law where he teaches numerous international and national security law courses. He also directs the University's Center for National Security Law and the Center for Oceans Law & Policy and was the Director of the Graduate Law Program at Virginia for more than twenty years. Viewed by many as the founder of the field of national security law, Professor Moore chaired the American Bar Association's prestigious Standing Committee on Law and National Security for four terms. He is the author or editor of 32 books and more than 175 scholarly articles and served for two decades on the editorial board of the *American Journal of International Law.* He is currently an honorary editor of the *Journal.* He is a member of the Council on Foreign Relations, on the Board of Directors of Freedom House, the American Law Institute, the American Society of International Law, the Order of the Coif, Phi Beta Kappa, and numerous other professional and honorary organizations. His most recent books include *Solving the War Puzzle* (2004) and *Civil Litigation Against Terrorism* (ed. 2004).

In addition to his scholarly career, Professor Moore has a distinguished record of public service. Among seven Presidential appointments, he has served two terms as the Senate-confirmed Chairman of the Board of Directors of the United States Institute of Peace and, as the first Chairman, set up this new agency. He also served as the Counselor on International Law to the Department of State, as Ambassador and Deputy Special Representative of the President to the Law of the Sea Conference, Chairman of the National Security Council Interagency Task Force on the Law of the Sea, and as a member of the United States' legal team before the International Court of Justice in the *Gulf of Maine* and *Paramilitary Activities* cases (a Deputy Agent for the United States in the *Paramilitary Activities* case). Professor Moore served as a Member of the Director of Central Intelligence's Historical Review Board from 1998–2002.

In the past, he has served as a Consultant to both the President's Intelligence Oversight Board and the Arms Control and Disarmament Agency. He has also been a member of the National Advisory Committee on Oceans and Atmosphere, the United States Delegation to the Conference on Security and Cooperation in Europe, the United States Delegation to the United Nations General Assembly, and the Presidential Delegation of the United States to observe the 1984 elections in El Salvador. In 1990, he served, with the Deputy Attorney-General of the United States, as the Co-Chairman of the United States-USSR talks on the Rule of Law. He also served as the legal advisor to the Kuwait Representative to the United Nations Iraq-Kuwait Boundary Demarcation Commission, and as a consultant to the OSS Society.

Guy B. Roberts is the Deputy Assistant Secretary General for Weapons of Mass Destruction Policy and Director, Nuclear Policy Planning Directorate for the North Atlantic Treaty Organization (NATO). In that capacity he is responsible for developing policy on issues related to combating the proliferation of weapons of mass destruction and overseeing NATO's nuclear deterrence posture. Prior to his current position Mr. Roberts was the Principal Director for Negotiations Policy in the Office of the Secretary of Defense. In that capacity he was responsible for advising the Assistant Secretary for International Security Policy and other senior DoD officials on the entire range of United States arms control and non-proliferation policies, and for implementing policy guidance and Defense Department positions for current and emerging proliferation issues in multilateral arms control and disarmament fora. Prior to that Mr. Roberts was the Associate Counsel (Arms Control) for the Department of the Navy. His responsibilities included reviewing all departmental programs to ensure compliance with international treaty obligations and to advise the Chief of Naval Operations and the Secretary of the Navy on arms control and nonproliferation issues.

Mr. Roberts also served for twenty-five years in the United States Marine Corps before retiring with the rank of Colonel. During that time he held a number of positions including representing the Department of Defense at the United Nations Conference on Disarmament and the International Atomic Energy Agency, and serving as the senior legal advisor for major combatant commands. He has also participated in numerous negotiations with foreign governments on military issues, served as a prosecutor and defense counsel in courts-martial, and was an infantry company and platoon commander.

Mr. Roberts received his law degree from the University of Denver, and he holds master's degrees in international and comparative law from Georgetown University and in international relations from the University of Southern California. He also has a master's degree in strategic studies from the Naval War College where he graduated with highest distinction and won the Stephen B. Luce Award for academic achievement. He is admitted to practice in Colorado, California, Arizona and before the Military Court of Criminal Appeals and the U.S. Supreme Court. Mr. Roberts has written extensively on nonproliferation, arms control, terrorism and law of war issues.

Robert F. Turner holds both professional and academic doctorates from the University of Virginia School of Law, where in 1981 he co-founded the Center for National Security Law with Professor Moore. A former Army Captain who served twice in Vietnam, he left the military in 1971 to accept a position at the Hoover Institution on War, Revolution and Peace at Stanford University, where he was a Public Affairs Fellow and Associate Editor of the *Yearbook on International Communist Affairs*. His extensive federal government service includes five years as national security adviser to Senator Robert P. Griffin, a member of the Foreign Relations Committee, and subsequent assignments as Special Assistant to the Under Secretary of Defense for Policy, Counsel to the President's Intelligence Oversight Board at the White House, and Principal Deputy Assistant Secretary of State for Legislative and Intergovernmental Affairs. He served as the first President of the congressionally established U.S. Institute of Peace and during 1994–95 held the Charles H. Stockton Chair of International Law at the U.S. Naval War College. He has also been a Distinguished Lecturer at the U.S. Military Academy at West Point and a Silverman Lecturer at the U.S. Supreme Court Historical Society.

In addition to teaching advanced national security law seminars with Professor Moore at the Law School, for many years Professor Turner also taught International Law, U.S. Foreign Policy, Foreign Policy and the Law, and a seminar on the Vietnam War in what is now Virginia's Woodrow Wilson Department of Politics. Each summer he runs the Center's National Security Law Institute for training law professors and government attorneys who wish to teach or practice in this growing new field. A former three-term Chairman of both the ABA Standing Committee on Law and National Security and the Committee on Executive-Congressional Relations of the ABA Section of International Law and Practice, for many years he served as editor of the ABA *National Security Law Report.* Turner has testified before more than a dozen committees of Congress, is the author or editor of more than a dozen books and has published in numerous law reviews and professional journals. He has contributed to the editorial pages of the *New York Times, Wall Street Journal, USA Today, Washington Post,* and most other major American newspapers, and is a member of the Council on Foreign Relations and the Committee on the Present Danger.

Alphabetical List of Documents

National Security Law Documents

Part I
Introduction

A. The Goals of United States Foreign Policy and Their Relation to National Security

WASHINGTON, FAREWELL ADDRESS*

UNITED STATES, *September 17, 1796*

Friends and Fellow-Citizens:

The period for a new election of a citizen to administer the Executive Government of the United States being not far distant, and the time actually arrived when your thoughts must be employed in designating the person who is to be clothed with that important trust, it appears to me proper, especially as it may conduce to a more distinct expression of the public voice, that I should now apprise you of the resolution I have formed to decline being considered among the number of those out of whom a choice is to be made.

. . . .

The unity of government which constitutes you one people is also now dear to you. It is justly so, for it is a main pillar in the edifice of your real independence, the support of your tranquility at home, your peace abroad, of your safety, of your prosperity, of that very liberty which you so highly prize. But as it is easy to foresee that from different causes and from different quarters much pains will be taken, many artifices employed, to weaken in your minds the conviction of this truth, as this is the point in your political fortress against which the batteries of internal and external enemies will be most constantly and actively (though often covertly and insidiously) directed, it is of infinite moment that you should properly estimate the immense value of your national union to your collective and individual happiness; that you should cherish a cordial, habitual, and immovable attachment to it; accustoming yourselves to think and speak of it as of the palladium of your political safety and prosperity; watching for its preservation with jealous anxiety; discountenancing whatever may suggest even a suspicion that it can in any event be abandoned, and indignantly frowning upon the first dawning of every attempt to alienate any portion of our country from the rest or to enfeeble the sacred ties which now link together the various parts.

. . . .

It is important, likewise, that the habits of thinking in a free country should inspire caution in those intrusted with its administration to confine themselves within their respective constitutional spheres, avoiding in the exercise of the powers of one department to encroach upon another. The spirit of encroachment tends to consolidate the powers of all the departments in one, and thus to create, whatever the form of government, a real despotism. A just estimate of that love of power and proneness to abuse it which predominates in the human heart is sufficient to satisfy us of the truth of this position. The necessity of reciprocal checks in the exercise of political power, by dividing and distributing it into different depositories, and constituting each the guardian of the public weal against invasions by the others, has been evinced by experiments ancient and modern, some of them in our country and under our own eyes. To preserve them must be as necessary as to institute them. If in the opinion of the people the distribution or modification of the constitutional powers be in any particular wrong, let it be corrected by an amendment in the way which the Constitution designates. But let there

* George Washington, Farewell Address (Sept. 17, 1796), *in* 1 A COMPILATION OF THE MESSAGES AND PAPERS OF THE PRESIDENTS 205, 207, 211–15 (James D. Richardson ed., 1897).

be no change by usurpation; for though this in one instance may be the instrument of good, it is the customary weapon by which free governments are destroyed. The precedent must always greatly overbalance in permanent evil any partial or transient benefit which the use can at any time yield.

Of all the dispositions and habits which lead to political prosperity, religion and morality are indispensable supports. In vain would that man claim the tribute of patriotism who should labor to subvert these great pillars of human happiness—these firmest props of the duties of men and citizens. The mere politician, equally with the pious man, ought to respect and to cherish them. A volume could not trace all their connections with private and public felicity. Let it simply be asked, Where is the security for property, for reputation, for life, if the sense of religious obligation desert the oaths which are the instruments of investigation in courts of justice? And let us with caution indulge the supposition that morality can be maintained without religion. Whatever may be conceded to the influence of refined education on minds of peculiar structure, reason and experience both forbid us to expect that national morality can prevail in exclusion of religious principle.

It is substantially true that virtue or morality is a necessary spring of popular government. The rule indeed extends with more or less force to every species of free government. Who that is a sincere friend to it can look with indifference upon attempts to shake the foundation of the fabric? Promote, then, as an object of primary importance, institutions for the general diffusion of knowledge. In proportion as the structure of a government gives force to public opinion, it is essential that public opinion should be enlightened.

As a very important source of strength and security, cherish public credit. One method of preserving it is to use it as sparingly as possible, avoiding occasions of expense by cultivating peace, but remembering also that timely disbursements to prepare for danger frequently prevent much greater disbursements to repel it; avoiding likewise the accumulation of debt, not only by shunning occasions of expense, but by vigorous exertions in time of peace to discharge the debts which unavoidable wars have occasioned, not ungenerously throwing upon posterity the burthen which we ourselves ought to bear. The execution of these maxims belongs to your representatives; but it is necessary that public opinion should cooperate. To facilitate to them the performance of their duty it is essential that you should practically bear in mind that toward the payment of debts there must be revenue; that to have revenue there must be taxes; that no taxes can be devised which are not more or less inconvenient and unpleasant; that the intrinsic embarrassment inseparable from the selection of the proper objects (which is always a choice of difficulties), ought to be a decisive motive for a candid construction of the conduct of the Government in making it, and for a spirit of acquiescence in the measures for obtaining revenue which the public exigencies may at any time dictate.

Observe good faith and justice toward all nations. Cultivate peace and harmony with all. Religion and morality enjoin this conduct. And can it be that good policy does not equally enjoin it? It will be worthy of a free, enlightened, and at no distant period a great nation to give to mankind the magnanimous and too novel example of a people always guided by an exalted justice and benevolence. Who can doubt that in the course of time and things the fruits of such a plan would richly repay any temporary advantages which might be lost by a steady adherence to it? Can it be that Providence has not connected the permanent felicity of a nation with its virtue? The experiment, at least, is recommended by every sentiment which ennobles human nature. Alas!—is it rendered impossible by its vices?

In the execution of such a plan nothing is more essential than that permanent, inveterate antipathies against particular nations and passionate attachments for others should be excluded, and that in place of them just and amicable feelings toward all should be cultivated. The nation which indulges toward another an habitual hatred or an habitual fondness is in some degree a slave. It is a slave to its animosity or to its affection, either of which is sufficient to lead it astray from its duty and its interest. Antipathy in one nation against another disposes each more readily to offer insult and injury, to lay hold of slight causes of umbrage, and to be haughty and intractable when accidental or trifling occasions of dispute occur.

Hence frequent collisions, obstinate, envenomed, and bloody contests. The nation prompted by ill will and resentment sometimes impels to war the government contrary to the best calculations of policy. The government sometimes participates in the national propensity, and adopts through passion what reason would reject. At other times it makes the animosity of the nation subservient to projects of hostility, instigated by pride, ambition, and other sinister and pernicious motives. The peace often, sometimes perhaps the liberty, of nations has been the victim.

So, likewise, a passionate attachment of one nation for another produces a variety of evils. Sympathy for the favorite nation, facilitating the illusion of an imaginary common interest in cases where no real common interest exists, and infusing into one the enmities of the other, betrays the former into a participation in the quarrels and wars of the latter without adequate inducement or justification. It leads also to concessions to the favorite nation of privileges denied to others, which is apt doubly to injure the nation making the concessions by unnecessarily parting with what ought to have been retained, and by exciting jealousy, ill will, and a disposition to retaliate in the parties from whom equal privileges are withheld; and it gives to ambitious, corrupted, or deluded citizens (who devote themselves to the favorite nation) facility to betray or sacrifice the interests of their own country without odium, sometimes even with popularity, gilding with the appearances of a virtuous sense of obligation, a commendable deference for public opinion, or a laudable zeal for public good the base or foolish compliances of ambition, corruption, or infatuation.

As avenues to foreign influence in innumerable ways, such attachments are particularly alarming to the truly enlightened and independent patriot. How many opportunities do they afford to tamper with domestic factions, to practice the arts of seduction, to mislead public opinion, to influence or awe the public councils! Such an attachment of a small or weak toward a great and powerful nation dooms the former to be a satellite of the latter. Against the insidious wiles of foreign influence (I conjure you to believe me, fellow-citizens) the jealousy of a free people ought to be constantly awake, since history and experience prove that foreign influence is one of the most baneful foes of republican government. But that jealousy, to be useful, must be impartial, else it becomes the instrument of the very influence to be avoided, instead of a defense against it. Excessive partiality for one foreign nation and excessive dislike of another cause those whom they actuate to see danger only on one side, and serve to veil and even second the arts of influence on the other. Real patriots who may resist the intrigues of the favorite are liable to become suspected and odious, while its tools and dupes usurp the applause and confidence of the people to surrender their interests.

The great rule of conduct for us in regard to foreign nations is, in extending our commercial relations to have with them as little political connection as possible. So far as we have already formed engagements let them be fulfilled with perfect good faith. Here let us stop.

Europe has a set of primary interests which to us have none or a very remote relation. Hence she must be engaged in frequent controversies, the causes of which are essentially foreign to our concerns. Hence, therefore, it must be unwise in us to implicate ourselves by artificial ties in the ordinary vicissitudes of her politics or the ordinary combinations and collisions of her friendships or enmities.

Our detached and distant situation invites and enables us to pursue a different course. If we remain one people, under an efficient government, the period is not far off when we may defy material injury from external annoyance; when we may take such an attitude as will cause the neutrality we may at any time resolve upon to be scrupulously respected; when belligerent nations, under the impossibility of making acquisitions upon us, will not lightly hazard the giving us provocation; when we may choose peace or war, as our interest, guided by justice, shall counsel.

Why forgo the advantages of so peculiar a situation? Why quit our own to stand upon foreign ground? Why, by interweaving our destiny with that of any part of Europe, entangle our peace and prosperity in the toils of European ambition, rivalship, interest, humor, or caprice?

It is our true policy to steer clear of permanent alliances with any portion of the foreign world, so far, I mean, as we are now at liberty to do it; for let me not be understood as capable of patronizing infidelity to existing engagements. I hold the maxim no less applicable to public than to private affairs that honesty is always the best policy. I repeat, therefore, let those engagements be observed in their genuine sense. But in my opinion it is unnecessary and would be unwise to extend them.

Taking care always to keep ourselves by suitable establishments on a respectable defensive posture, we may safely trust to temporary alliances for extraordinary emergencies.

Harmony, liberal intercourse with all nations are recommended by policy, humanity, and interest. But even our commercial policy should hold an equal and impartial hand, neither seeking nor granting exclusive favors or preferences; consulting the natural course of things; diffusing and diversifying by gentle means the streams of commerce, but forcing nothing; establishing with powers so disposed, in order to give trade a stable course, to define the rights of our merchants, and to enable the Government to support them, conventional rules of intercourse, the best that present circumstances and mutual opinion will permit, but temporary and liable to be from time to time abandoned or varied as experience and circumstances shall dictate; constantly keeping in view that it is folly in one nation to look for disinterested favors from another; that it must pay with a portion of its independence for whatever it may accept under that character; that by such acceptance it may place itself in the condition of having given equivalents for nominal favors, and yet of being reproached with ingratitude for not giving more. There can be no greater error than to expect or calculate upon real favors from nation to nation. It is an illusion which experience must cure, which a just pride ought to discard.

In offering to you, my countrymen, these counsels of an old and affectionate friend I dare not hope they will make the strong and lasting impression I could wish—that they will control the usual current of the passions or prevent our nation from running the course which has hitherto marked the destiny of nations. But if I may even flatter myself that they may be productive of some partial benefit, some occasional good—that they may now and then recur to moderate the fury of party spirit, to warn against the mischiefs of foreign intrigue, to guard against the impostures of pretended patriotism—this hope will be a full recompense for the solicitude for your welfare by which they have been dictated.

MONROE DOCTRINE*

At the proposal of the Russian Imperial Government, made through the minister of the Emperor residing here, a full power and instructions have been transmitted to the minister of the United States at St. Petersburg to arrange by amicable negotiation the respective rights and interests of the two nations on the northwest coast of this continent. A similar proposal had been made by His Imperial Majesty to the Government of Great Britain, which has likewise been acceded to. The Government of the United States has been desirous by this friendly proceeding of manifesting the great value which they have invariably attached to the friendship of the Emperor and their solicitude to cultivate the best understanding with his Government. In the discussions to which this interest has given rise and in the arrangements by which they may terminate the occasion has been judged proper for asserting, as a principle in which the rights and interests of the United States are involved, that the American continents, by the free and independent condition which they have assumed and maintain, are henceforth not to be considered as subjects for future colonization by any European powers.

. . . .

---

* James Monroe, Seventh Annual Message (Dec. 2, 1823), in 2 A Compilation of the Messages and Papers of the Presidents 776, 778, 786–88 (James D. Richardson ed., 1897). In a letter to James Monroe dated October 24, 1823, Thomas Jefferson wrote:

The question presented by the letters you have sent me, is the most momentous which has ever been offered to my contemplation since that of Independence. That made us a nation, this sets our compass and points the course which we are to steer through the ocean of time opening on us. And never could we embark on it under circumstances more auspicious. Our first and fundamental maxim should be, never to entangle ourselves in the broils of Europe. Our second, never to suffer Europe to intermeddle with cis-Atlantic affairs. America, North, and South, has a set of interests distinct from those of Europe, and peculiarly her own. She should therefore have a system of her own, separate and apart from that of Europe. While the last is laboring to become the domicile of despotism, our endeavor should surely be, to make our hemisphere that of freedom. One nation, most of all, could disturb us in this pursuit; she now offers to lead, aid, and accompany us in it. By acceding to her proposition, we detach her from the bands, bring her mighty weight into the scale of free government, and emancipate a continent at one stroke which might otherwise linger long in doubt and difficulty, Great Britain is the nation which can do us the most harm of any one, or all on earth; and with her on our side we need not fear the whole world. With her then, we should most sedulously cherish a cordial friendship; and nothing would tend more to knit our affections than to be fighting once more, side by side, in the same cause. Not that I would purchase even her amity at the price of taking part in her wars. But the war in which the present proposition might engage us, should that be its consequence, is not her war, but ours. Its object is to introduce and establish the American system, of keeping out of our land all foreign powers, of never permitting those of Europe to intermeddle with the affairs of our nations. It is to maintain our own principle, not to depart from it. And if, to facilitate this, we can effect a division in the body of the European powers, and draw over to our side its most powerful member, surely we should do it. But I am clearly of Mr. Canning's opinion, that it will prevent instead of provoking war. With Great Britain withdrawn from their scale and shifted into that of our two continents, all Europe combined would not undertake such a war. For how would they propose to get at either enemy without superior fleets? Nor is the occasion to be slighted which this proposition offers, of declaring our protest against the atrocious violations of the rights of nations, by the interference of any one in the internal affairs of another, so flagitiously begun by Bonaparte, and now continued by the equally lawless Alliance, calling itself Holy.

. . . .

In 15 The Writings of Thomas Jefferson 477, 477–78 (Albert Ellery Bergh, ed., 1907).

It was stated at the commencement of the last session that a great effort was then making in Spain and Portugal to improve the condition of the people of those countries, and that it appeared to be conducted with extraordinary moderation. It need scarcely be remarked that the result has been so far very different from what was then anticipated. Of events in that quarter of the globe, with which we have so much intercourse and from which we derive our origin, we have always been anxious and interested spectators. The citizens of the United States cherish sentiments the most friendly in favor of the liberty and happiness of their fellow-men on that side of the Atlantic. In the wars of the European powers in matters relating to themselves we have never taken any part, nor does it comport with our policy so to do. It is only when our rights are invaded or seriously menaced that we resent injuries or make preparation for our defense. With the movements in this hemisphere we are of necessity more immediately connected, and by causes which must be obvious to all enlightened and impartial observers. The political system of the allied powers is essentially different in this respect from that of America. This difference proceeds from that which exists in their respective Governments; and to the defense of our own, which has been achieved by the loss of so much blood and treasure, and matured by the wisdom of their most enlightened citizens, and under which we have enjoyed unexampled felicity, this whole nation is devoted. We owe it, therefore, to candor and to the amicable relations existing between the United States and those powers to declare that we should consider any attempt on their part to extend their system to any portion of this hemisphere as dangerous to our peace and safety. With the existing colonies or dependencies of any European power we have not interfered and shall not interfere. But with the Governments who have declared their independence and maintained it, and whose independence we have, on great consideration and on just principles, acknowledged, we could not view any interposition for the purpose of oppressing them, or controlling in any other manner their destiny, by any European power in any other light than as the manifestation of an unfriendly disposition toward the United States. In the war between those new Governments and Spain we declared our neutrality at the time of their recognition, and to this we have adhered, and shall continue to adhere, provided no change shall occur which, in the judgment of the competent authorities of this Government, shall make a corresponding change on the part of the United States indispensable to their security.

The late events in Spain and Portugal shew that Europe is still unsettled. Of this important fact no stronger proof can be adduced than that the allied powers should have thought it proper, on any principle satisfactory to themselves, to have interposed by force in the internal concerns of Spain. To what extent such interposition may be carried, on the same principle, is a question in which all independent powers whose governments differ from theirs are interested, even those most remote, and surely none more so than the United States. Our policy in regard to Europe, which was adopted at an early stage of the wars which have so long agitated that quarter of the globe, nevertheless remains the same, which is, not to interfere in the internal concerns of any of its powers; to consider the government de facto as the legitimate government for us; to cultivate friendly relations with it, and to preserve those relations by a frank, firm, and manly policy, meeting in all instances the just claims of every power, submitting to injuries from none. But in regard to those continents circumstances are eminently and conspicuously different. It is impossible that the allied powers should extend their political system to any portion of either continent without endangering our peace and happiness; nor can anyone believe that our southern brethren, if left to themselves, would adopt it of their own accord. It is equally impossible, therefore, that we should behold such interposition in any form with indifference. If we look to the comparative strength and resources of Spain and those new Governments, and their distance from each other, it must be obvious that she can never subdue them. It is still the true policy of the United States to leave the parties to themselves, in the hope that other powers will pursue the same course.

....

CLARK, MEMORANDUM ON THE MONROE DOCTRINE*

The Monroe Doctrine was announced by President Monroe in his annual message of December 2, 1823. The President had two main situations in mind: that which existed on the northwest coast of this continent where Russia was proposing to extend her control; and that which existed with reference to the Spanish colonies in the Western Hemisphere which had thrown off the Spanish yoke and as to which there was some agitation in Europe for cooperation among certain European powers to resubject these Spanish colonies to Spanish or other monarchical rule. But the President seems also to have had in mind, in a relation other than that incident to colonization, the whole Western Hemisphere, outside of the United States.

As to our northwest coast—President Monroe first called attention to the desire of Russia "to arrange by amicable negotiation the respective rights and interests of the two nations on the northwest coast of this continent" as to which she had made a similar proposal to Great Britain and then affirmed the friendly disposition of the United States towards Russia and our solicitude to cultivate "the best understanding" with the Government of the Emperor of Russia. He then declared:

> ...the occasion has been judged proper for asserting, as a principle in which the rights and interests of the United States are involved, that the American continents, by the free and independent condition which they have assumed and maintained, are henceforth not to be considered as subjects for future colonization by any European powers.[i]

Later in his message, President Monroe called attention to the unsettled condition of European affairs, particularly with reference to Spain and Portugal, where the result which attended an effort to improve the people was not such as had been anticipated; and to the friendly sentiments entertained by the United States towards the liberty and happiness of their fellow men on the European side of the Atlantic, though we had never participated in their wars, "nor does it comport with our policy to do so." President Monroe then continued:

> ...It is only when our rights are invaded or seriously menaced that we resent injuries or make preparation for our defense. With the movements in this hemisphere we are of necessity more immediately connected, and by causes which must be obvious to all enlightened and impartial observers. The political system of the allied powers is essentially different in this respect from that of America. This difference proceeds from that which exists in their respective Governments; and to the defense of our own, which has been achieved by the loss of so much blood and treasure, and matured by the wisdom of their most enlightened citizens, and under which we have enjoyed unexampled felicity, this whole nation is devoted. We owe it, therefore, to candor and to the amicable relations existing between the United States and those powers to declare that we should consider any attempt on their part to extend their system to any portion of this hemisphere as dangerous to our peace and safety. With the existing colonies or dependencies of any European

* J. Reuben Clark, Memorandum On The Monroe Doctrine 3–6, 230–31 (Government Printing Office 1930) (Dec. 17, 1928). (Original footnotes included as endnotes).

> power we have not interfered and shall not interfere. But with the Governments who have declared their independence and maintained it, and whose independence we have, on great consideration and on just principles, acknowledged, we could not view any interposition for the purpose of oppressing them, or controlling in any other manner their destiny, by any European power in any other light than as the manifestation of an unfriendly disposition towards the United States.[ii]

Finally, after calling attention to our neutrality in the war between Spain and her colonies, to which we should continue to adhere "provided no change shall occur which, in the judgment of the competent authorities of this Government, shall make a corresponding change on the part of the United States indispensable in their security"; to the interposition "by force" of the allied powers "in the internal concerns of Spain"; to our policy, with reference to European wars, "not to interfere in the internal concerns of any of its powers; to consider the government *de facto* as the legitimate government for us; to cultivate friendly relations with it, and to preserve those relations by a frank, firm, and manly policy, meeting in all instances the just claims of every power, submitting to injuries from none," President Monroe further declared,

> But in regard to those continents circumstances are eminently and conspicuously different. It is impossible that the allied powers should extend their political system to any portion of either continent without endangering our peace and happiness; nor can anyone believe that our southern brethren, if left to themselves, would adopt it of their own accord. It is equally impossible, therefore, that we should behold such interposition in any form with indifference... It is still the true policy of the United States to leave the parties to themselves, in the hope that other powers will pursue the same course.[iii]

The Six Prime Points of the Doctrine

An analysis of these declarations reveals that six prime matters are covered by President Monroe's message.

1. The "*American continents*" were not subject to colonization by *any European power*. This in terms certainly includes North and South America. Impliedly, colonization is considered antagonistic or detrimental to the "free and independent conditions which they" (the "American continents") "have assumed and maintained." The "rights and interests" of the United States were involved in this principle.

2. The United States would consider any attempt on the part of the "*allied powers*" to extend their system to any part of "*this hemisphere as dangerous to our peace and safety.*"

   This in terms covered the "allied powers," at this time, Austria, France, Russia, and Prussia; it covered the whole Western Hemisphere, those parts occupied by the Spanish colonies and other parts; it was aimed at the allied "system."

3. "With the existing colonies or dependencies of any European power we have not interfered and shall not interfere."

It would seem, having in mind the sentence following and the expressions..., that this sentence might be interpreted as indicating we would not have had, at that time, any objection to reconquest by Spain of the colonies which had gained and maintained their independence and which we had recognized. This is not clear beyond doubt, because later in his message, President Monroe declared that while it had become evident, looking at the comparative strength and resources of Spain and those colonial governments and their distance from each other, that Spain could never subdue them, yet we would leave the parties to themselves. (Of course later we took a definite position against reannexation or reconquest by Spain.)

> 4. With reference to Spanish colonies which had declared and maintained their independence, and which we had recognized, the United States "could not view any interposition for the purpose of oppressing them or of controlling in any other manner their destiny, *by any European power*, in any other light than as the manifestation of an *unfriendly disposition towards the United States*."

This declaration related to all European powers, not specifically excluding Spain; it specifically referred to the revolted Spanish colonies; it went beyond the reassumption of control over them by Spain or the extension to them of the allied "system"; it covered interposition in their affairs not only for the purpose of oppressing them, but for the purpose of controlling in any other manner their destiny by *any European power*.

> 5. Specifically, the United States declared that it was "impossible that the *allied powers* should extend their political *system to any part of either continent* without *endangering our peace and happiness*." It was equally impossible that we should behold "such interposition" by the allied powers in any form with indifference.

This being directed against the *allied powers*, did not, *ex vi termini*, include Spain, and at this time Great Britain was not counted within the group that was popularly so designated.

> 6. It was still "the true policy of the United States" to leave the parties, that is, the revolted colonies and Spain, to themselves to adjust their difficulties as they saw fit.

This was the Monroe Doctrine. Under it future colonization by European powers was to be regarded as antagonistic or detrimental to the free and independent condition of these continents; the extension of the allied "system" to any part of this hemisphere was considered dangerous to our peace and safety; interposition by any European power, for the purpose of oppressing or controlling the destiny of the rebelled Spanish colonies which we had recognized was to be regarded as a manifestation of an unfriendly disposition towards the United States; our peace and happiness would be endangered should the allied powers extend their political system to any part of either continent, and the interposition of those powers in any form could not be viewed with indifference; the true policy of the United States was to leave Spain and her rebelled colonies to adjust their difficulties between themselves.

The Doctrine was thus one of self-preservation for the United States.

The provisions of the declaration fall obviously into two classes: those relating to "future colonization *by any European power*" on the "American continents"; and those relating to political operations, through the formula "interposition for the purpose of oppressing them, or controlling in any other manner their destiny" seems sufficiently broad to cover other than purely political "interpositions." The distinctly political inhibitions run against the allied powers, and "to any portion of this hemisphere," or, as stated in the second formula, "to any part of either continent"; the inhibitions as to "interposition" run against "any European power," and in terms relate to Spanish American "governments who have declared their independence and maintained it, and whose independence we have, on great consideration and just principles, acknowledged."

In this memorandum no attempt is made to trace separately the development of these different classes of inhibitions, nor to identify, as belonging to the one class or the other, the occasions on which the Doctrine or its underlying principles have been invoked by this Government.

The reason these matters were regarded by President Monroe and his Cabinet as antagonistic and detrimental, as dangerous to our peace and safety, as a manifestation of an unfriendly disposition towards the United States or as endangering our peace and happiness, is best understood when we consider the historical facts—the circumstances which at that time were in the minds of Monroe, Adams, Calhoun, Jefferson, and Madison. For it was the views and discussions of these men which lay behind and which shaped and framed the announcement which President Monroe made to the world, as well as determined the terms in which the declaration was couched.

....

"Roosevelt's Corollary" of the Monroe Doctrine

In his message to Congress of December 3, 1860, President Buchanan dealt with the situation in Mexico and the obligation of this Government "to exert its power to avenge and redress the wrongs of our citizens and to afford them protection in Mexico," and with the request which he had made in his previous annual message for authority to use "a sufficient military force to penetrate into the interior, where the Government of Miramon was to be found." President Buchanan then declared he might have been able, if such authority had been granted, to avoid the "entire abandonment of our fellow citizens who had gone to Mexico under the faith of treaties to the systematic injustice, cruelty, and oppression of Miramon's Government. Besides, it is almost certain that the simple authority to employ this force would of itself have accomplished all our objects without striking a single blow." He then continued:

> In addition—and I deem this a most important consideration—European governments would have been deprived of all pretext to interfere in the territorial and domestic concerns of Mexico. We should thus have been relieved from the obligation of resisting, even by force should this become necessary, any attempt by these governments to deprive our neighboring republic of portions of her territory—a duty from which we could not shrink without abandoning the traditional and established policy of the American people.[iv]

In his note of November 26, 1895, replying to Mr. Olney's note of July 20, 1895, regarding the boundary dispute between Great Britain and Venezuela, Lord Salisbury, speaking of Mr. Olney's contention that the Monroe Doctrine justified the United States in demanding that boundary disputes between a Latin American State and the coterminous colony of a European power, be settled by arbitration, declared:

> Whatever may be the authority of the doctrine laid down by President Monroe, there is nothing in his language to show that he ever thought of claiming this novel prerogative for the United States. It is admitted that he did not seek to assert a protectorate over Mexico, or the States of Central and South America. Such a claim would have imposed upon the United States the duty of answering for the conduct of these States, and consequently the responsibility of controlling it. His sagacious foresight would have led him energetically to deprecate the addition of so serious a burden to those which the

> rulers of the United States have to bear. It follows of necessity that if the Government of the United States will not control the conduct of these communities, neither can it undertake to protect them from the consequences attaching to any misconduct of which they may be guilty towards other nations. If they violate in any way the rights of another State, or of its subjects, it is not alleged that the Monroe Doctrine will assure them the assistance of the United States in escaping from any reparation which they may be bound by international law to give. Mr. Olney expressly disclaims such an inference from the principles he lays down.[v]

In his annual message of December 6, 1904, President Roosevelt made the following statements:

> It is not true that the United States feels any land hunger or entertains any projects as regards the other nations of the Western Hemisphere save such as are for their welfare. All that this country desires is to see the neighboring countries stable, orderly, and prosperous. Any country whose people conduct themselves well can count upon our hearty friendship. If a nation shows that it knows how to cat with reasonable efficiency and decency in social and political matters, if it keeps order and pays its obligations, it need fear no interference from the United States. Chronic wrongdoing. Or an impotence which results in a general loosening of the ties of civilized society, may in America, as elsewhere, ultimately require intervention by some civilized nation, and in the Western Hemisphere the adherence of the United States to the Monroe Doctrine may force the United States, however reluctantly, in flagrant cases of wrongdoing or impotence, to the exercise of an international police power. If every country washed by the Caribbean Sea would show the progress in stable and just civilization which with the aid of the Platt amendment Cuba has shown since our troops left the island, and which so many of the republics in both Americas are constantly and brilliantly showing, all question of interference by this Nation with their affairs would be at an end. Our interests and those of our southern neighbors are in reality identical. They have great natural riches, and if within their borders the reign of law and justice obtains, prosperity is sure to come to them. While they thus obey the primary laws of civilized society they may rest assured that they will be treated by us in a spirit of cordial and helpful sympathy. We would interfere with them only in the last resort, and then only if it became evident that their inability or unwillingness to do justice at home and abroad had violated the rights of the United States or had invited foreign aggression to the detriment of the entire body of American nations. It is a mere truism to say that every nation, whether in America or anywhere else, which desires to maintain its freedom, its independence, must ultimately realize that the right of such independence can not be separated from the responsibility of making good use of it.
>
> In asserting the Monroe Doctrine, in taking such steps as we have taken in regard to Cuba, Venezuela, and Panama, and in endeavoring to circumscribe the theater of war in the far East, and to secure the open door in China, we have acted in our own interest as well as in the interest of humanity at large.[vi]

---

i. Richardson's Messages and Papers of the Presidents, vol. II, p. 209.
ii. Richardson's Messages and Papers of the Presidents, vol. II, p. 218.

iii. *Ibid.*, p. 219.
iv. RICHARDSON'S MESSAGES AND PAPERS OF THE PRESIDENTS, vol. V, p. 646.
v. Moore, *International Law Digest*, vol. VI, p. 562.
vi. *Messages and Papers of the Presidents* (1917 ed.), vol. XVI, pp. 7053–7054. 61497—30—17.

HULL, CANONS OF INTERNATIONAL CONDUCT*

I have been receiving from many sources inquiries and suggestions arising out of disturbed situations in various parts of the world.

Unquestionably there are in a number of regions tensions and strains which on their face involve only countries that are near neighbors but which in ultimate analysis are of inevitable concern to the whole world. Any situation in which armed hostilities are in progress or are threatened is a situation wherein rights and interests of all nations either are or may be seriously affected. There can be no serious hostilities anywhere in the world which will not one way or another affect interests or rights or obligations of this country. I therefore feel warranted in making—in fact, I feel it a duty to make—a statement of this Government's position in regard to international problems and situations with respect to which this country feels deep concern.

This country constantly and consistently advocates maintenance of peace. We advocate national and international self-restraint. We advocate abstinence by all nations from use of force in pursuit of policy and from interference in the internal affairs of other nations. We advocate adjustment of problems in international relations by processes of peaceful negotiation and agreement. We advocate faithful observance of international agreements. Upholding the principle of the sanctity of treaties, we believe in modification of provisions of treaties when need therefor arises, by orderly processes carried out n a spirit of mutual helpfulness and accommodation. We believe in respect by all nations for the rights of others and performance by all nations of established obligations. We stand for revitalizing and strengthening of international law. We advocate steps toward promotion of economic security and stability the world over. We advocate lowering or removing of excessive barriers in international trade. We seek effective equality of commercial opportunity and we urge upon all nations application of the principle of equality of treatment. We believe in limitation and reduction of armament. Realizing the necessity for maintaining armed forces adequate for national security, we are prepared to reduce or to increase our own armed forces in proportion to reductions or increases made by other countries. We avoid entering into alliances or entangling commitments but we believe in cooperative effort by peaceful and practicable means in support of the principles hereinbefore stated.

---

* Statement by the Secretary of State (July 16, 1937), *in* U.S. DEP'T OF STATE, PUBL'N 1983, PEACE AND WAR: UNITED STATES FOREIGN POLICY 1931–1941, at 370–71 (1943), *available at* http://www.mtholyoke.edu/acad/intrel/interwar/hull27.htm.

KENNAN, THE LONG TELEGRAM*

Background Note

In February 1946 the Department of State sent a telegram to George Kennan, the U.S. Chargé d'Affairs in Moscow, which stated in part:

"We should welcome receiving from you an interpretive analysis of what we may expect in the way of future implementation of these announced policies...." In response, Kennan sent the following message—which exerted a tremendous influence on American thinking and quickly became known as "The Long Telegram."—Eds.

The Chargée in the Soviet Union (Kennan) to the Secretary of State

SECRET Moscow, February 22, 1946—9 p.m.
[Received February 22—3: 52 p.m.]

Answer to Dept's 284, Feb 3,[i] involves questions so intricate, so delicate, so strange to our form of thought, and so important to analysis of our international environment that I cannot compress answers into single brief message without yielding to what I feel would be dangerous degree of over-simplification. I hope, therefore, Dept will bear with me if I submit in answer to this question five parts, subjects of which will be roughly as follows:

(1) Basic features of post-war Soviet outlook.

(2) Background of this outlook.

(3) Its projection in practical policy on official level.

(4) Its projection on unofficial level.

(5) Practical deductions from standpoint of U.S. policy.

I apologize in advance for this burdening of telegraphic channel; but questions involved are of such urgent importance, particularly in view of recent events, that our answers to them, if they deserve attention at all, seem to me to deserve it at once. There follows:

Part 1: Basic Features of Post War Soviet Outlook, as Put Forward by Official Propaganda Machine, Are as Follows:

(a) U.S.S.R. still lives in antagonistic "capitalist encirclement" with which in the long run there can be no permanent peaceful coexistence. As stated by Stalin in 1927 to a delegation of American workers:

> "In course of further development of international revolution there will emerge two centers of world significance: a socialist center, drawing to itself the countries which tend toward socialism, and a capitalist center, drawing to itself the countries that incline toward capitalism. Battle between these two centers for command of world economy will decide fate of capitalism and of communism in entire world."

---

* Telegram from George Kennan to the State Dep't (Feb. 22, 1946), *in* ORIGINS OF THE COLD WAR 17–31 (Kenneth M. Jensen ed., rev. ed. 1993). (Original footnote included as endnote).

(b) Capitalist world is beset with internal conflicts, inherent in nature of capitalist society. These conflicts are insoluble by means of peaceful compromise. Greatest of them is that between England and U.S.

(c) Internal conflicts of capitalism inevitably generate wars. Wars thus generated may be of two kinds: intra-capitalist wars between two capitalist states, and wars of intervention against socialist world. Smart capitalists, vainly seeking escape from inner conflicts of capitalism, incline toward latter.

(d) Intervention against U.S.S.R., while it would be disastrous to those who undertook it, would cause renewed delay in progress of Soviet socialism and must therefore be forestalled at all costs.

(e) Conflicts between capitalist states, though likewise fraught with danger for U.S.S.R., nevertheless hold out great possibilities for advancement of socialist cause, particularly if U.S.S.R. remains militarily powerful, ideologically monolithic and faithful to its present brilliant leadership.

(f) It must be borne in mind that capitalist world is not all bad. In addition to hopelessly reactionary and bourgeois elements, it includes (1) certain wholly enlightened and positive elements united in acceptable communistic parties and (2) certain other elements (now described for tactical reasons as progressive or democratic) whose reactions, aspirations and activities happen to be "objectively" favorable to interests of U.S.S.R. These last must be encouraged and utilized for Soviet purposes.

(g) Among negative elements of bourgeois-capitalist society, most dangerous of all are those whom Lenin called false friends of the people, namely moderate-socialist or social-democratic leaders (in other words, non-Communist left-wing). These are more dangerous than out-and-out reactionaries, for latter at least march under their true colors, whereas moderate left-wing leaders confuse people by employing devices of socialism to serve interests of reactionary capital.

So much for premises. To what deductions do they lead from standpoint of Soviet policy? To following:

(a) Everything must be done to advance relative strength of U.S.S.R. as factor in international society. Conversely, no opportunity muost be missed to reduce strength and influence, collectively as well as individually, of capitalist powers.

(b) Soviet efforts, and those of Russia's friends abroad, must be directed toward deepening and exploiting of differences and conflicts between capitalist powers. If these eventually deepen into an "imperialist" war, this war must be turned into revolutionary upheavals within the various capitalist countries.

(c) "Democratic-progressive" elements abroad are to be utilized to maximum to bring pressure to bear on capitalist governments along lines agreeable to Soviet interests.

(d) Relentless battle must be waged against socialist and social-democratic leaders abroad.

Part 2: Background of Outlook

Before examining ramifications of this party line in practice there are certain aspects of it to which I wish to draw attention.

First, it does not represent natural outlook of Russian people. Latter are, by and large, friendly to outside world, eager for experience of it, eager to measure against it talents they are conscious of possessing, eager above all to live in peace and enjoy fruits of their own labor. Party line only represents thesis which official propaganda machine puts forward with great skill and persistence to a public often remarkably resistant in the stronghold of its innermost thoughts. But party line is binding for outlook and conduct of people who make up apparatus of power—party, secret police and Government—and it is exclusively with these that we have to deal.

Second, please note that premises on which this party line is based are for most part simply not true. Experience has shown that peaceful and mutually profitable coexistence of capitalist and socialist states is entirely possible. Basic internal conflicts in advanced countries are no longer primarily those arising out of capitalist ownership of means of production, but are ones arising from advanced urbanism and industrialism as such, which Russia has thus far been spared not by socialism but only by her own backwardness. Internal rivalries of capitalism do not always generate wars; and not all wars are attributable to this cause. To speak of possibility of intervention against U.S.S.R. today, after elimination of Germany and Japan and after example of recent war, is sheerest nonsense. If not provoked by forces of intolerance and subversion "capitalist" world of today is quite capable of living at peace with itself and with Russia. Finally, no sane person has reason to doubt sincerity of moderate socialist leaders in Western countries. Nor is it fair to deny success of their efforts to improve conditions for working population whenever, as in Scandinavia, they have been given chance to show what they could do.

Falseness of those premises, every one of which predates recent war, was amply demonstrated by that conflict itself. Anglo-American differences did not turn out to be major differences of Western World. Capitalist countries, other than those of Axis, showed no disposition to solve their differences by joining in crusade against U.S.S.R. Instead of imperialist war turning into civil wars and revolution, U.S.S.R. found itself obliged to fight side by side with capitalist powers for an avowed community of aim.

Nevertheless, all these theses, however baseless and disproven, are being boldly put forward again today. What does this indicate? It indicates that Soviet party line is not based on any objective analysis of situation beyond Russia's borders; that it has, indeed, little to do with conditions outside of Russia; that it arises mainly from basic inner-Russian necessities which existed before recent war and exist today.

At bottom of Kremlin's neurotic view of world affairs is traditional and instinctive Russian sense of insecurity. Originally, this was insecurity of a peaceful agricultural people trying to live on vast exposed plain in neighborhood of fierce nomadic peoples. To this was added, as Russia came into contact with economically advanced West, fear of more competent, more powerful, more highly organized societies in that area. But this latter type of insecurity was one which afflicted Russian rulers rather than Russian people; for Russian rulers have invariably sensed that their rule was relatively archaic in form, fragile and artificial in its psychological foundations, unable to stand comparison or contact with political systems of Western countries. For this reason they have always feared foreign penetration, feared direct contact between Western world and their own, feared what would happen if Russians learned truth about world without or if foreigners learned truth about world within. And they have learned to seek security only in patient but deadly struggle for total destruction of rival power, never in compacts and compromises with it.

It was no coincidence that Marxism, which had smouldered ineffectively for half a century in Western Europe, caught hold and blazed for the first time in Russia. Only in this land which had never known a friendly neighbor or indeed any tolerant equilibrium of separate powers, either internal or international, could a doctrine thrive which viewed economic conflicts of society as insoluble by peaceful means. After establishment of Bolshevist regime, Marxist dogma, rendered even more truculent and intolerant by Lenin's interpretation, became a perfect vehicle for sense of insecurity with which Bolsheviks, even more than previous Russian rulers, were afflicted. In this dogma, with its basic altruism of purpose, they found justification for their instinctive fear of outside world, for the dictatorship without which they did not know how to rule, for cruelties they did not dare not to inflict, for sacrifice they felt bound to demand. In the name of Marxism they sacrificed every single ethical value in their methods and tactics. Today they cannot dispense with it. It is fig leaf of their moral and intellectual respectability. Without it they would stand before history, at best, as only the last of that long succession of cruel and wasteful Russian rulers who have relentlessly forced country on to ever new heights of military power in order to guarantee external security of their internally weak regimes. This is why Soviet purposes must always be solemnly clothed in trappings of Marxism, and why no one should underrate importance of dogma in Soviet affairs. Thus Soviet leaders are driven [by?] necessities of their own past and present position to put forward which [apparent omission] outside world as evil, hostile and menacing, but as bearing within itself germs of creeping disease and destined to be wracked with growing internal convulsions until it is given final *coup de grace* by rising power of socialism and yields to new and better world. This thesis provides justification for that increase of military and police power of Russian state, for that isolation of Russian population from outside world, and for that fluid and constant pressure to extend limits of Russian police power which are together the natural and instinctive urges of Russian rulers. Basically this is only the steady advance of uneasy Russian nationalism, a centuries old movement in which conceptions of offense and defense are inextricably confused. But in new guise of international Marxism, with its honeyed promises to a desperate and war-torn outside world, it is more dangerous and insidious than ever before.

It should not be thought from above that Soviet party line is necessarily disingenuous and insincere on part of all those who put it forward. Many of them are too ignorant of outside world and mentally too dependent to question [apparent omission] self-hypnotism, and who have no difficulty making themselves believe what they find it comforting and convenient to believe. Finally we have the unsolved mystery as to who, if anyone, in this great land actually receives accurate and unbiased information about outside world. In atmosphere of oriental secretiveness and conspiracy which pervades this Government, possibilities for distorting or poisoning sources and currents of information are infinite. The very disrespect of Russians for objective truth—indeed, their disbelief in its existence—leads them to view all stated facts as instruments for furtherance of one ulterior purpose or another. There is good reason to suspect that this Government is actually a conspiracy within a conspiracy; and I for one am reluctant to believe that Stalin himself receives anything like an objective picture of outside world. Here there is ample scope for the type of subtle intrigue at which Russians are past masters. Inability of foreign governments to place their case squarely before Russian policy makers—extent to which they are delivered up in their relations with Russia to good graces of obscure and unknown advisors whom they never see and cannot influence—this to my mind is most disquieting feature of diplomacy in Moscow, and one which Western statesmen would do well to keep in mind if they would understand nature of difficulties encountered here.

Part 3: Projection of Soviet Outlook in Practical Policy on Official Level

We have now seen nature and background of Soviet program. What may we expect by way of its practical implementation?

Soviet policy, as Department implies in its query under reference, is conducted on two planes: (1) official plane represented by actions undertaken officially in name of Soviet Government; and (2) subterranean plane of actions undertaken by agencies for which Soviet Government does not admit responsibility.

Policy promulgated on both planes will be calculated to serve basic policies (a) to (d) outlined in part 1. Actions taken on different planes will differ considerably, but will dovetail into each other in purpose, timing and effect.

On official plane we must look for following:

(a) Internal policy devoted to increasing in every way strength and prestige of Soviet state: intensive military-industrialization; maximum development of armed forces; great displays to impress outsiders; continued secretiveness about internal matters, designed to conceal weaknesses and to keep opponents in the dark.

(b) Wherever it is considered timely and promising, efforts will be made to advance official limits of Soviet power. For the moment, these efforts are restricted to certain neighboring points conceived of here as being of immediate strategic necessity, such as northern Iran, Turkey, possibly Bornholm. However, other points may at any time come into question, if and as concealed Soviet political power is extended to new areas. Thus a "friendly" Persian Government might be asked to grant Russia a port on Persian Gulf. Should Spain fall under Communist control, question of Soviet base at Gibraltar Strait might be activated. But such claims will appear on official level only when unofficial preparation is complete.

(c) Russians will participate officially in international organizations where they see opportunity of extending Soviet power or of inhibiting or diluting power of others. Moscow sees in UNO not the mechanism for a permanent and stable world society founded on mutual interest and aims of all nations, but an arena in which aims just mentioned can be favorably pursued. As long as UNO is considered here to serve this purpose, Soviets will remain with it. But if at any time they come to conclusion that it is serving to embarrass or frustrate their aims for power expansion and if they see better prospects for pursuit of these aims along other lines, they will not hesitate to abandon UNO. This would imply, however, that they felt themselves strong enough to split unity of other nations by their withdrawal to render UNO ineffective as a threat to their aims or security, and to replace it with an international weapon more effective from their viewpoint. Thus Soviet attitude toward UNO will depend largely on loyalty of other nations to it, and on degree of vigor, decisiveness and cohesion with which theose nations defend in UNO the peaceful and hopeful concept of international life, which that organization represents to our way of thinking. I reiterate, Moscow has no abstract devotion to UNO ideals. Its attitude to that organization will remain essentially pragmatic and tactical.

(d) Toward colonial areas and backward or dependent peoples, Soviet policy, even on official plane, will be directed toward weakening of power and influence and contacts of advanced Western nations, on theory that in so far as this policy is successful, there will be created a vacuum which will favor Communist-Soviet penetration. Soviet pressure for participation in trusteeship arrangements thus represents, in my opinion, a desire to be in a position to complicate and inhibit exertion of Western influence at such points rather than to provide major channel for exerting of Soviet power. Latter motive is not lacking, but for this Soviets prefer to rely on other channels than official trusteeship arrangements. Thus we may expect to find Soviets asking for admission everywhere to trusteeship or similar arrangements and using levers thus acquired to weaken Western influence among such peoples.

(e) Russians will strive energetically to develop Soviet representation in, and official ties with, countries in which they sense strong possibilities of opposition to Western centers of power. This applies to such widely separated points as Germany, Argentina, Middle Eastern countries, etc.

(f) In international economic matters, Soviet policy will really be dominated by pursuit of autarchy for Soviet Union and Soviet-dominated adjacent areas taken together. That, however, will be underlying policy. As far as official line is concerned, position is not yet clear. Soviet Government has shown strange reticence since termination hostilities on subject foreign trade. If large-scale long term credits should be forthcoming, I believe Soviet Government may eventually again do lip service, as it did in 1930's to desirability of building up international economic exchanges in general. Otherwise I think it possible Soviet foreign trade may be restricted largely to Soviet's own security sphere, including occupied areas in Germany, and that a cold official shoulder may be turned to principle of general economic collaboration among nations.

(g) With respect to cultural collaboration, lip service will likewise be rendered to desirability of deepening cultural contacts between peoples, but this will not in practice be interpreted in any way which could weaken security position of Soviet peoples. Actual manifestations of Soviet policy in this respect will be restricted to arid channels of closely shepherded official visits and functions, with superabundance of vodka and speeches and dearth of permanent effects.

(h) Beyond this, Soviet official relations will take what might be called "correct" course with individual foreign governments, with great stress being laid on prestige of Soviet Union and its representatives and with punctilious attention to protocol, as distinct from good manners.

Part 4: Following May Be Said as to What We May Expect by Way of Implementation of Basic Soviet Policies on Unofficial, or Subterranean Plane, i.e. on Plane for Which Soviet Government Accepts no Responsibility

Agencies utilized for promulgation of policies on this plane are following:

1. Inner central core of Communist Parties in other countries. While many of persons who compose this category may also appear and act in unrelated public capacities, they are in reality working closely together as an underground operating directorate of world communism, a concealed Comintern tightly coordinated and directed by Moscow. It is important to remember that this inner core is actually working on underground lines, despite legality of parties with which it is associated.

2. Rank and file of Communist parties. Note distinction is drawn between these and persons defined in paragraph 1. This distinction has become much sharper in recent years. Whereas formerly foreign Communist Parties represented a curious (and from Moscow's standpoint often inconvenient) mixture of conspiracy and legitimate activity, now the conspiratorial element has been neatly concentrated in inner circle and ordered underground, while rank and file—no longer even taken into confidence about realities of movement—are thrust forward as bona fide internal partisans of certain political tendencies within their respective countries, genuinely innocent of conspiratorial connection with foreign states. Only in certain countries where communists are numerically strong do they now regularly appear and act as a body. As a rule they are used to penetrate, and to influence or dominate, as case may be, other organizations less likely to be suspected of being tools of Soviet Government, with a view to accomplishing their

purposes through [apparent omission] organizations, rather than by direct action as a separate political party.

3. A wide variety of national associations or bodies which can be dominated or influenced by such penetration. These include: labor unions, youth leagues, women's organizations, racial societies, religious societies, social organizations, cultural groups, liberal magazines, publishing houses, etc.

4. International organizations which can be similarly penetrated through influence over various national components. Labor, youth and women's organizations are prominent among them. Particular, almost vital, importance is attached in this connection to international labor movement. In this, Moscow sees possibility of sidetracking Western governments in world affairs and building up international lobby capable of compelling governments to take actions favorable to Soviet interests in various countries and of paralyzing actions disagreeable to U.S.S.R.

5. Russian Orthodox Church, with its foreign branches, and through it the Eastern Orthodox Church in general.

6. Pan-Slav movement and other movements (Azerbaijan, Armenian, Turcoman, etc.) based on racial groups within Soviet Union.

7. Governments or governing groups willing to lend themselves to Soviet purposes in one degree or another, such as present Bulgarian and Yugoslav governments, North Persian regime, Chinese Communists, etc. Not only propaganda machines but actual policies of these regimes can be placed extensively at disposal of U.S.S.R.

It may be expected that component parts of this far-flung apparatus will be utilized in accordance with their individual suitability, as follows:

(a) To undermine general political and strategic potential of major Western Powers. Efforts will be made in such countries to disrupt national self-confidence, to hamstring measures of national defense, to increase social and industrial unrest, to stimulate all forms of disunity. All persons with grievances, whether economic or racial, will be urged to seek redress not in mediation and compromise, but in defiant violent struggle for destruction of other elements of society. Here poor will be set against rich, black against white, young against old, newcomers against established residents, etc.

(b) On unofficial plane particularly violent efforts will be made to weaken power and influence of Western Powers of [on] colonial backward, or dependent peoples. On this level, no holds will be barred. Mistakes and weaknesses of Western colonial administration will be mercilessly exposed and exploited. Liberal opinion in Western countries will be mobilized to weaken colonial policies. Resentment among dependent peoples will be stimulated. And while latter are being encouraged to seek independence [from] Western Powers, Soviet dominated puppet political machines will be undergoing preparation to take over domestic power in respective colonial areas when independence is achieved.

(c) Where individual governments stand in path of Soviet purposes pressure will be brought for their removal from office. This can happen where governments directly oppose Soviet foreign policy aims (Turkey, Iran), where they seal their territories off against Communist penetration (Switzerland, Portugal), or where they compete too strongly, (like Labor Government in England), for moral domination among elements which it is important for Communists to dominate. (Sometimes, two of these elements are present in a single case. Then Communist opposition becomes particularly shrill and savage. [])

(d) In foreign countries Communists will, as a rule, work toward destruction of all forms of personal independence, economic, political or moral. Their system can handle only individuals who have been brought into complete dependence on higher power. Thus, persons who are financially independent—such as individual businessmen, estate owners, successful farmers, artisans—and all those who exercise local leadership or have local prestige,—such as popular local clergymen or political figures,—are anathema. It is not by chance that even in U.S.S.R. local officials are kept constantly on move from one job to another, to prevent their taking root.

(e) Everything possible will be done to set major Western Powers against each other. Anti-British talk will be plugged among Americans, anti-American talk among British. Continentals, including Germans, will be taught to abhor both Anglo-Saxon powers. Where suspicions exist, they will be fanned; where not, ignited. No effort will be spared to discredit and combat all efforts which threaten to lead to any sort of unity or cohesion among other [apparent omission] from which Russia might be excluded. Thus, all forms of international organization not amenable to Communist penetration and control, whether it be the Catholic [apparent omission] international economic concerns, or the international fraternity of royalty and aristocracy, must expect to find themselves under fire from many, and often [apparent omission].

(f) In general, all Soviet efforts on unofficial international plane will be negative and destructive in character, designed to tear down sources of strength beyond reach of Soviet control. This is only in line with basic Soviet instinct that there can be no compromise with rival power and that constructive work can start only when Communist power is dominant. But behind all this will be applied insistent, unceasing pressure for penetration and command of key positions in administration and especially in police apparatus of foreign countries. The Soviet regime is a police regime par excellence, reared in the dim half world of Tsarist police intrigue, accustomed to think primarily in terms of police power. This should never be lost sight of in gaunging Soviet motives.

Part 5: [Practical Deductions From Standpoint of U.S. Policy]

In summary, we have here a political force committed fanatically to the belief that with U.S. there can be no permanent *modus vivendi* that it is desirable and necessary that the internal harmony of our society be disrupted, our traditional way of life be destroyed, the international authority of our state be broken, if Soviet power is to be secure. This political force has complete power of disposition over energies of one of world's greatest peoples and resources of world's richest national territory, and is borne along by deep and powerful currents of Russian nationalism. In addition, it has an elaborate and far-flung apparatus for exertion of its influence in other countries, an apparatus of amazing flexibility and versatility, managed by people whose experience and skill in underground methods are presumably without parallel in history. Finally, it is seemingly inaccessible to considerations of reality in its basic reactions. For it, the vast fund of objective fact about human society is not, as with us, the measure against which outlook is constantly being tested and re-formed, but a grab bag from which individual items are selected arbitrarily and tendenciously to bolster an outlook already preconceived. This is admittedly not a pleasant picture. Problem of how to cope with this force in [is] undoubtedly greatest task our diplomacy has ever faced and probably greatest it will ever have to face. It should be point of departure from which our political general staff work at present juncture should proceed. It should be approached with same thoroughness and care as solution of major strategic problem in war, and, if necessary, with no smaller outlay in planning effort. I cannot attempt to suggest all answers here. But I would like to record my conviction that problem is within our power to solve—and that without recourse to any general military conflict. And in support of this conviction there are certain observations of a more encouraging nature I should like to make:

(1) Soviet power, unlike that of Hitlerite Germany, is neither schematic nor adventurinstic. It does not work by fixed plans. It does not take unnecessary risks. Impervious to logic of reason, and it is highly sensitive to logic of force. For this reason it can easily withdraw—and usually does when strong resistance is encountered at any point. Thus, if the adversary has sufficient force and makes clear his readiness to use it, he rarely has to do so. If situations are properly handled there need be no prestige-engaging showdowns.

(2) Gauged against Western world as a whole, Soviets are still by far the weaker force. Thus, their success will really depend on degree of cohesion, firmness and vigor which Western world can muster. And this is factor which it is within our power to influence.

(3) Success of Soviet system, as form of internal power, is not yet finally proven. It has yet to be demonstrated that it can survive supreme test of successive transfer of power from one individual or group to another. Lenin's death was first such transfer, and its effects wracked Soviet state for 15 years. After Stalin's death or retirement will be second. But even this will not be final test. Soviet internal system will now be subjected, by virtue of recent territorial expansions, to series of additional strains which once proved severe tax on Tsardom. We here are convinced that never since termination of civil war have mass of Russian people been emotionally farther removed from doctrines of Communist Party than they are today. In Russia, party has now become a great and—for the moment—highly successful apparatus of dictatorial administration, but it has ceased to be a source of emotional inspiration. Thus, internal soundness and permanence of movement need not yet be regarded as assured.

(4) All Soviet propaganda beyond Soviet security sphere is basically negative and destructive. It should therefore be relatively easy to combat it by any intelligent and really constructive program.

For those reasons I think we may approach calmly and with good heart problem of how to deal with Russia. As to how this approach should be made, I only wish to advance, by way of conclusion, following comments:

(1) Our first step must be to apprehend, and recognize for what it is, the nature of the movement with which we are dealing. We must study it with same courage, detachment, objectivity, and same determination not to be emotionally provoked or unseated by it, with which doctor studies unruly and unreasonable individual.

(2) We must see that our public is educated to realities of Russian situation. I cannot over-emphasize importance of this. Press cannot do this alone. It must be done mainly by Government, which is necessarily more experienced and better informed on practical problems involved. In this we need not be deterred by [ugliness?] of picture. I am convinced that there would be far less hysterical anti-Sovietism in our country today if realities of this situation were better understood by our people. There is nothing as dangerous or as terrifying as the unknown. It may also be argued that to reveal more information on our difficulties with Russia would reflect unfavorably on Russian-American relations. I feel that if there is any real risk here involved, it is one which we should have courage to face, and sooner the better. But I cannot see what we would be risking. Our stake in this country, even coming on heels of tremendous demonstrations of our friendship for Russian people, is remarkably small. We have here no investments to guard, no actual trade to lose, virtually no citizens to protect, few cultural contacts to

preserve. Our only stake lies in what we hope rather than what we have; and I am convinced we have better chance of realizing those hopes if our public is enlightened and if our dealings with Russians are placed entirely on realistic and matter-of-fact basis.

(3) Much depends on health and vigor of our own society. World communism is like malignant parasite which feeds only on diseased tissue. This is point at which domestic and foreign policies meets Every courageous and incisive measure to solve internal problems of our own society, to improve self-confidence, discipline, morale and community spirit of our own people, is a diplomatic victory over Moscow worth a thousand diplomatic notes and joint communiqués. If we cannot abandon fatalism and indifference in face of deficiencies of our own society, Moscow will profit—Moscow cannot help profiting by them in its foreign policies.

(4) We must formulate and put forward for other nations a much more positive and constructive picture of sort of world we would like to see than we have put forward in past. It is not enough to urge people to develop political processes similar to our own. Many foreign peoples, in Europe at least, are tired and frightened by experiences of past, and are less interested in abstract freedom than in security. They are seeking guidance rather than responsibilities. We should be better able than Russians to give them this. And unless we do, Russians certainly will.

(5) Finally we must have courage and self-confidence to cling to our own methods and conceptions of human society. After all, the greatest danger that can befall us in coping with this problem of Soviet communism, is that we shall allow ourselves to become like those with whom we are coping.

KENNAN

---

i. In this telegram the State Department informed the chargé: "We should welcome receiving from you an interpretive analysis of what we may expect in the way of future implementation of these announced policies..." (861.00/2-1246). The policies referred to were those contained in the pre-election speeches of Stalin and his associates.

TRUMAN, THE TRUMAN DOCTRINE, SPECIAL MESSAGE TO THE CONGRESS ON GREECE AND TURKEY, MARCH 12, 1947*

[As delivered in person before a joint session]

Mr. President, Mr. Speaker, Members of the Congress of the United States:

The gravity of the situation which confronts the world today necessitates my appearance before a joint session of the Congress.

The foreign policy and the national security of this country are involved.

One aspect of the present situation, which I wish to present to you at this time for your consideration and decision, concerns Greece and Turkey.

The United States has received from the Greek Government an urgent appeal for financial and economic assistance. Preliminary reports from the American Economic Mission now in Greece and reports from the American Ambassador in Greece corroborate the statement of the Greek Government that assistance is imperative if Greece is to survive as a free nation.

I do not believe that the American people and the Congress wish to turn a deaf ear to the appeal of the Greek Government.

. . . .

The very existence of the Greek state is today threatened by the terrorist activities of several thousand armed men, led by Communists, who defy the government's authority at a number of points, particularly along the northern boundaries. A Commission appointed by the United Nations Security Council is at present investigating disturbed conditions in northern Greece, and alleged border violations along the frontier between Greece on the one hand and Albania, Bulgaria, and Yugoslavia on the other.

Meanwhile, the Greek Government is unable to cope with the situation. The Greek army is small and poorly equipped. It needs supplies and equipment if it is to restore the authority of the government throughout Greek territory. Greece must have assistance if it is to become a self-supporting and self-respecting democracy.

The United States must supply that assistance. We have already extended to Greece certain types of relief and economic aid, but these are inadequate.

There is no other country to which democratic Greece can turn.

No other nation is willing and able to provide the necessary support for a democratic Greek government.

The British Government, which has been helping Greece, can give no further financial or economic aid after March 31. Great Britain finds itself under the necessity of reducing or liquidating its commitments in several parts of the world, including Greece.

---

* Harry S. Truman, Special Message to the Congress on Greece and Turkey: The Truman Doctrine (March 12, 1947), *in* 1947 PUBLIC PAPERS OF THE PRESIDENTS OF THE UNITED STATES, HARRY S. TRUMAN 176–80 (1963), *available at* http://www.yale.edu/lawweb/avalon/trudoc.htm.

We have considered how the United Nations might assist in this crisis. But the situation is an urgent one requiring immediate action and the United Nations and its related organizations are not in a position to extend help of the kind that is required.

It is important to note that the Greek Government has asked for our aid in utilizing effectively the financial and other assistance we may give to Greece, and in improving its public administration. It is of the utmost importance that we supervise the use of any funds made available to Greece; in such a manner that each dollar spent will count toward making Greece self-supporting, and will help to build an economy in which a healthy democracy can flourish.

No government is perfect. One of the chief virtues of a democracy, however, is that its defects are always visible and under democratic processes can be pointed out and corrected. The Government of Greece is not perfect. Nevertheless it represents eighty-five per cent of the members of the Greek Parliament who were chosen in an election last year. Foreign observers, including 692 Americans, considered this election to be a fair expression of the views of the Greek people.

The Greek Government has been operating in an atmosphere of chaos and extremism. It has made mistakes. The extension of aid by this country does not mean that the United States condones everything that the Greek Government has done or will do. We have condemned in the past, and we condemn now, extremist measures of the right or the left. We have in the past advised tolerance, and we advise tolerance now.

Greece's neighbor, Turkey, also deserves our attention.

The future of Turkey as an independent and economically sound state is clearly no less important to the freedom-loving peoples of the world than the future of Greece. The circumstances in which Turkey finds itself today are considerably different from those of Greece. Turkey has been spared the disasters that have beset Greece. And during the war, the United States and Great Britain furnished Turkey with material aid. Nevertheless, Turkey now needs our support.

Since the war Turkey has sought financial assistance from Great Britain and the United States for the purpose of effecting that modernization necessary for the maintenance of its national integrity.

That integrity is essential to the preservation of order in the Middle East.

The British government has informed us that, owing to its own difficulties can no longer extend financial or economic aid to Turkey.

As in the case of Greece, if Turkey is to have the assistance it needs, the United States must supply it. We are the only country able to provide that help.

I am fully aware of the broad implications involved if the United States extends assistance to Greece and Turkey, and I shall discuss these implications with you at this time.

One of the primary objectives of the foreign policy of the United States is the creation of conditions in which we and other nations will be able to work out a way of life free from coercion. This was a fundamental issue in the war with Germany and Japan. Our victory was won over countries which sought to impose their will, and their way of life, upon other nations.

To insure the peaceful development of nations, free from coercion, the United States has taken a leading part in establishing the United Nations, The United Nations is designed to make possible lasting freedom and independence for all its members. We shall not realize our objectives, however, unless we are willing to help free peoples to maintain their free institutions and their national integrity against aggressive movements that seek to impose upon them totalitarian regimes. This is no more than a frank recognition that totalitarian regimes imposed on free peoples, by direct or indirect aggression, undermine the foundations of international peace and hence the security of the United States.

The peoples of a number of countries of the world have recently had totalitarian regimes forced upon them against their will. The Government of the United States has made frequent protests against coercion and intimidation, in violation of the Yalta agreement, in Poland, Rumania, and Bulgaria. I must also state that in a number of other countries there have been similar developments.

At the present moment in world history nearly every nation must choose between alternative ways of life. The choice is too often not a free one.

One way of life is based upon the will of the majority, and is distinguished by free institutions, representative government, free elections, guarantees of individual liberty, freedom of speech and religion, and freedom from political oppression.

The second way of life is based upon the will of a minority forcibly imposed upon the majority. It relies upon terror and oppression, a controlled press and radio; fixed elections, and the suppression of personal freedoms.

I believe that it must be the policy of the United States to support free peoples who are resisting attempted subjugation by armed minorities or by outside pressures.

I believe that we must assist free peoples to work out their own destinies in their own way.

I believe that our help should be primarily through economic and financial aid which is essential to economic stability and orderly political processes.

The world is not static, and the status quo is not sacred. But we cannot allow changes in the status quo in violation of the Charter of the United Nations by such methods as coercion, or by such subterfuges as political infiltration. In helping free and independent nations to maintain their freedom, the United States will be giving effect to the principles of the Charter of the United Nations.

It is necessary only to glance at a map to realize that the survival and integrity of the Greek nation are of grave importance in a much wider situation. If Greece should fall under the control of an armed minority, the effect upon its neighbor, Turkey, would be immediate and serious. Confusion and disorder might well spread throughout the entire Middle East.

Moreover, the disappearance of Greece as an independent state would have a profound effect upon those countries in Europe whose peoples are struggling against great difficulties to maintain their freedoms and their independence while they repair the damages of war.

It would be an unspeakable tragedy if these countries, which have struggled so long against overwhelming odds, should lose that victory for which they sacrificed so much. Collapse of free institutions and loss of independence would be disastrous not only for them but for the world. Discouragement and possibly failure would quickly be the lot of neighboring peoples striving to maintain their freedom and independence.

Should we fail to aid Greece and Turkey in this fateful hour, the effect will be far reaching to the West as well as to the East.

We must take immediate and resolute action.

I therefore ask the Congress to provide authority for assistance to Greece and Turkey in the amount of $400,000,000 for the period ending June 30, 1948. In requesting these funds, I have taken into consideration the maximum amount of relief assistance which would be furnished to Greece out of the $350,000,000 which I recently requested that the Congress authorize for the prevention of starvation and suffering in countries devastated by the war.

In addition to funds, I ask the Congress to authorize the detail of American civilian and military personnel to Greece and Turkey, at the request of those countries, to assist in the tasks of reconstruction, and for the purpose of supervising the use of such financial and material assistance as may be furnished. I recommend that authority also be provided for the instruction and training of selected Greek and Turkish personnel.

Finally, I ask that the Congress provide authority which will permit the speediest and most effective use, in terms of needed commodities, supplies, and equipment, of such funds as may be authorized.

If further funds, or further authority, should be needed for purposes indicated in this message, I shall not hesitate to bring the situation before the Congress. On this subject the Executive and Legislative branches of the Government must work together.

This is a serious course upon which we embark.

I would not recommend it except that the alternative is much more serious. The United States contributed $341,000,000,000 toward winning World War II. This is an investment in world freedom and world peace.

The assistance that I am recommending for Greece and Turkey amounts to little more than one tenth of one per cent of this investment. It is only common sense that we should safeguard this investment and make sure that it was not in vain.

The seeds of totalitarian regimes are nurtured by misery and want. They spread and grow in the evil soil of poverty and strife. They reach their full growth when the hope of a people for a better life has died. We must keep that hope alive.

The free peoples of the world look to us for support in maintaining their freedoms.

If we falter in our leadership, we may endanger the peace of the world—and we shall surely endanger the welfare of our own nation.

Great responsibilities have been placed upon us by the swift movement of events.

I am confident that the Congress will face these responsibilities squarely.

MARSHALL PLAN*

.... [T]he people of this country are distant from the troubled areas of the earth and it is hard for them to comprehend the plight and consequent reaction of the long-suffering peoples, and the effect of those reactions on their governments in connection with our efforts to promote peace in the world.

....

There is a phase of this matter which is both interesting and serious. The farmer has always produced the foodstuffs to exchange with the city dweller for the other necessities of life. This division of labor is the basis of modern civilization. At the present time it is threatened with breakdown. The town and city industries are not producing adequate goods to exchange with the food-producing farmer. Raw materials and fuel are in short supply. Machinery is lacking or worn out. The farmer or the peasant cannot find the goods for sale which he desires to purchase. So the sale of his farm produce for money which he cannot use seems to him unprofitable transaction. He, therefore, has withdrawn many fields from crop cultivation and is using them for grazing. He feeds more grain to stock and finds for himself and his family an ample supply of food, however short he may be on clothing and the other ordinary gadgets of civilization. Meanwhile people in the cities are short of food and fuel. So the governments are forced to use their foreign money and credits to procure these necessities abroad. This process exhausts funds which are urgently needed for reconstruction. Thus a very serious situation is rapidly developing which bodes no good for the world. The modern system of the division of labor upon which the exchange of products is based is in danger of breaking down.

The truth of the matter is that Europe's requirements for the next 3 or 4 years of foreign food and other essential products—principally from America—are so much greater than her present ability to pay that she must have substantial additional help, or face economic, social, and political deterioration of a very grave character.

The remedy lies in breaking the vicious circle and restoring the confidence of the European people in the economic future of their own countries and of Europe as a whole. The manufacturer and the farmer throughout wide areas must be able and willing to exchange their products for currencies the continuing value of which is not open to question.

Aside from the demoralizing effect on the world at large and the possibilities of disturbances arising as a result of the desperation of the people concerned, the consequences to the economy of the United States should be apparent to all. It is logical that the United States should do whatever it is able to do to assist in the return of normal economic health in the world, without which there can be no political stability and no assured peace. Our policy is directed not against any country or doctrine but against hunger, poverty, desperation, and chaos. Its purpose should be the revival of working economy in the world so as to permit the emergence of political and social conditions in which free institutions can exist. Such assistance, I am convinced, must not be on a piecemeal basis as various crises develop. Any assistance that this Government may render in the future should provide a cure rather than a mere palliative. Any government

---

* George C. Marshall, Secretary of State, Remarks at Harvard University (June 5, 1947), *in* 93 Cong. Rec. A3248 (1947), *available at* http://usinfo.state.gov/usa/infousa/facts/democrac/57.htm.

that is willing to assist in the task of recovery will find full cooperation, I am sure, on the part of the United States Government. Any government which maneuvers to block the recovery of other countries cannot expect help from us. Furthermore, governments, political parties, or groups which seek to perpetuate human misery in order to profit therefrom politically or otherwise will encounter the opposition of the United States.

It is already evident that, before the United States Government can proceed much further in its efforts to alleviate the situation and help start the European world on its way to recovery, there must be some agreement among the countries of Europe as to the requirements of the situation and the part those countries themselves will take in order to give proper effect to whatever action might be undertaken by this Government. It would be neither fitting nor efficacious for this Government to undertake to draw up unilaterally a program designed to place Europe on its feet economically. This is the business of the Europeans. The initiative, I think, must come from Europe. The role of this country should consist of friendly aid in the drafting of a European program so far as it may be practical for us to do so. The program should be a joint one, agreed to by a number, if not all European nations.

An essential part of any successful action on the part of the United States is an understanding on the part of the people of America of the character of the problem and the remedies to be applied. Political passion and prejudice should have no part. With foresight, and a willingness on the part of our people to face up to the vast responsibilities which history has clearly placed upon our country, the difficulties I have outlined can and will be overcome.

George C. Marshall,
Secretary of State

NSC 68[1]
(SOVIET UNION NUCLEAR CAPABILITIES)

Background Note

NSC 68 was written in response to a presidential request for policy recommendations following disclosure that the Soviet Union had probably achieved a successful nuclear explosion in August 1949. It was never formally approved by President Truman; but the doctrine set forth in the memorandum had a great influence on U.S. national security policy—particularly following the invasion of South Korea in June 1950. Although originally highly classified, the essence of the document was made public long before it was officially declassified by Henry Kissinger in 1975. The excerpts which follow are drawn from a longer text originally published in the Naval War College Review.—Eds.

I. Background of the Present Crisis

Within the past thirty-five years the world has experienced two global wars of tremendous violence. It has witnessed two revolutions—the Russian and the Chinese—of extreme scope and intensity. It has also seen the collapse of five empires—the Ottoman, the Austro-Hungarian, German, Italian and Japanese—and the drastic decline of two major imperial systems, the British and the French. During the span of one generation, the international distribution of power has been fundamentally altered. For several centuries it had proved impossible for any one nation to gain such preponderant strength that a coalition of other nations could not in time face it with greater strength. The international scene was marked by recurring periods of violence and war, but a system of sovereign and independent states was maintained, over which no state was able to achieve hegemony.

Two complex sets of factors have now basically altered this historical distribution of power. First, the defeat of Germany and Japan and the decline of the British and French Empires have interacted with the development of the United States ,and the Soviet Union in such a way that power has increasingly gravitated to these two centers. Second, the Soviet Union, unlike previous aspirants to hegemony, is animated by a new fanatic faith, antithetical to our own, and seeks to impose its absolute authority over the rest of the world. Conflict has, therefore, become endemic and is waged, on the part of the Soviet Union, by violent or non-violent methods in accordance with the dictates of expediency. With the development of increasingly terrifying weapons of mass destruction, every individual faces the ever-present possibility of annihilation should the conflict enter the phase of total war.

On the one hand, the people of the world yearn for relief from the anxiety arising from the risk of atomic war. On the other hand, any substantial further extension of the area under the domination of the Kremlin would raise the possibility that no coalition adequate to confront the Kremlin with greater strength could be assembled. It is in this context that this Republic and its citizens in the ascendancy of their strength stand in their deepest peril.

The issues that face us are momentous, involving the fulfillment or destruction not only of this Republic but of civilization itself. They are issues which will not await our

1. A Report to the President Pursuant to the President's Directive of January 31, 1950 (April 7, 1950), *reprinted in* NSC-68: Forging the Strategy of Containment 36 (S. Nelson Drew ed., 1996), *available at* http://purl.access.gpo.gov/GPO/LPS53185.

deliberations. With conscience and resolution this Government and the people it represents must now take new and fateful decisions.

II. Fundamental Purpose of the United States

The fundamental purpose of the United States is laid down in the Preamble to the Constitution: "...to form a more perfect Union, establish justice, insure domestic Tranquility, provide for the common defence, promote the general Welfare, and secure the Blessings of Liberty to ourselves and our Posterity." In essence, the fundamental purpose is to assure the integrity and vitality of our free society, which is founded upon the dignity and worth of the individual.

Three realities emerge as a consequence of this purpose: Our determination to maintain the essential elements of individual freedom, as set forth in the Constitution and Bill of Rights; our determination to create conditions under which our free and democratic system can live and prosper; and our determination to fight if necessary to defend our way of life, for which as in the Declaration of Independence, "with a firm reliance on the protection of Divine Providence, we mutually pledge to each other our lives, our Fortunes, and our sacred Honor."

III. Fundamental Design of the Kremlin

The fundamental design of those who control the Soviet Union and the international communist movement is to retain and solidify their absolute power, first in the Soviet Union and second in the areas now under their control. In the minds of the Soviet leaders, however, achievement of this design requires the dynamic extension of their authority and the ultimate elimination of any effective opposition to their authority.

The design, therefore, calls for the complete subversion or forcible destruction of the machinery of government and structure of society in the countries of the non-Soviet world and their replacement by an apparatus and structure subservient to and controlled from the Kremlin. To that end Soviet efforts are now directed toward the domination of the Eurasian land mass. The United States, as the principal center of power in the non-Soviet world and the bulwark of opposition to Soviet expansion, is the principal enemy whose integrity and vitality must be subverted or destroyed by one means or another if the Kremlin is to achieve its fundamental design.

IV. The Underlying Conflict in the Realm of Ideas and Values Between the U.S. Purpose and the Kremlin Design

A. NATURE OF CONFLICT

The Kremlin regards the United States as the only major threat to the achievement of its fundamental design. There is a basic conflict between the idea of freedom under a government of laws, and the idea of slavery under the grim oligarchy of the Kremlin, which has come to a crisis with the polarization of power described in Section 1, and the exclusive possession of atomic weapons by the two protagonists. The idea of freedom, moreover, is peculiarly and intolerably subversive of the idea of slavery. But the converse is not true. The implacable purpose of the slave state to eliminate the challenge of freedom has placed the two great powers at opposite poles. It is this fact which gives the present polarization of power the quality of crisis.

The free society values the individual as an end in himself, requiring of him only that measure of self-discipline and self-restraint which make the rights of each individual compatible with the rights of every other individual. The freedom of the individual has as its counterpart, therefore, the negative responsibility of the individual not to exercise his freedom in ways inconsistent with the freedom of other individuals and the positive responsibility to make constructive use of his freedom in the building of a just society.

From this idea of freedom with responsibility derives the marvelous diversity, the deep tolerance, the lawfulness of the free society. This is the explanation of the strength of free men. It constitutes the integrity and the vitality of a free and democratic system. The free society attempts to create and maintain an environment in which every individual has the opportunity to realize his creative powers. It also explains why the free society tolerates those within it who would use their freedom to destroy it. By the same token, in relations between nations, the prime reliance of the free society is on the strength and appeal of its idea, and it feels no compulsion sooner or later to bring all societies into conformity with it.

For the free society does not fear, it welcomes, diversity. It derives its strength from its hospitality even to antipathetic ideas. It is a market for free trade in ideas, secure in its faith that free men will take the best wares, and grow to a fuller and better realization of their powers in exercising their choice.

The idea of freedom is the most contagious idea in history, more contagious than the idea of submission to authority. For the breadth of freedom cannot be tolerated in a society which has come under the domination of an individual or group of individuals with a will to absolute power. Where the despot holds absolute power—the absolute power of the absolutely powerful will—all other wills must be subjugated in an act of willing submission, a degradation willed by the individual upon himself under the compulsion of a perverted faith. It is the first article of this faith that he finds and can only find the meaning of his existence in serving the ends of the system. The system becomes God, and submission to the will of God becomes submission to the will of the system. It is not enough to yield outwardly to the system—even Gandhian non-violence is not acceptable—for the spirit of resistance and the devotion to a higher authority might then remain, and the individual would not be wholly submissive.

The same compulsion which demands total power over all men within the Soviet state without a single exception, demands total power over all Communist Parties and all states under Soviet domination. Thus Stalin has said that the theory and tactics of Leninism as expounded by the Bolshevik party are mandatory for the proletarian parties of all countries. A true internationalist is defined as one who unhesitatingly upholds the position of the Soviet Union and in the satellite states true patriotism is love of the Soviet Union. By the same token the "peace policy" of the Soviet Union, described at a Party Congress as "a more advantageous form of fighting capitalism," is a device to divide and immobilize the non-Communist world, and the peace the Soviet Union seeks is the peace of total conformity to Soviet policy.

The antipathy of slavery to freedom explains the iron curtain, the isolation, the autarchy of the society whose end is absolute power. The existence and persistence of the idea of freedom is a permanent and continuous threat to the foundation of the slave society; and it therefore regards as intolerable the long continued existence of freedom in the world. What is new, what makes the continuing crisis, is the polarization of power which now inescapably confronts the slave society with the free.

The assault on free institutions is world-wide now, and in the context of the present polarization of power a defeat of free institutions anywhere is a defeat everywhere. The shock we sustained in the destruction of Czechoslovakia was not in the measure of

Czechoslovakia's material importance to us. In a material sense, her capabilities were already at Soviet disposal. But when the integrity of Czechoslovak institutions was destroyed, it was in the intangible scale of values that we registered a loss more damaging than the material loss we had already suffered.

Thus unwillingly our free society finds itself mortally challenged by the Soviet system. No other value system is so wholly irreconcilable with ours, so implacable in its purpose to destroy ours, so capable of turning to its own uses the most dangerous and divisive trends in our own society, no other so skillfully and powerfully evokes the elements of irrationality in human nature everywhere, and no other has the support of a great and growing center of military power.

B. OBJECTIVES

The objectives of a free society are determined by its fundamental values and by the necessity for maintaining the material environment in which they flourish. Logically and in fact, therefore, the Kremlin's challenge to the United States is directed not only to our values but to our physical capacity to protect their environment. It is a challenge which encompasses both peace and war and our objectives in peace and war must take account of it.

1. Thus we must make ourselves strong, both in the way in which we affirm our values in the conduct of our national life, and in the development of our military and economic strength.

2. We must lead in building a successfully functioning political and economic system in the free world. It is only by practical affirmation, abroad as well as at home, of our essential values, that we can preserve our own integrity, in which lies the real frustration of the Kremlin design.

3. But beyond thus affirming our values our policy and actions must be such as to foster a fundamental change in the nature of the Soviet system, a change toward which the frustration of the design is the first and perhaps the most important step. Clearly it will not only be less costly but more effective if this change occurs to a maximum extent as a result of internal forces in Soviet society.

. . . .

All these objectives of a free society are equally valid and necessary in peace and war. But every consideration of devotion to our fundamental values and to our national security demands that we seek to achieve them by the strategy of the cold war. It is only by developing the moral and material strength of the free world that the Soviet regime will become convinced of the falsity of its assumptions and that the pre-conditions for workable agreements can be created. By practically demonstrating the integrity and vitality of our system the free world widens the area of possible agreement and thus can hope gradually to bring about a Soviet acknowledgement of realities which in sum will eventually constitute a frustration of the Soviet design. Short of this, however, it might be possible to create a situation which will induce the Soviet Union to accommodate itself, with or without the conscious abandonment of its design, to coexistence on tolerable terms with the non-Soviet world. Such a development would be a triumph for the idea of freedom and democracy. It must be an immediate objective of United States policy.

. . . .

C. MEANS

The free society is limited in its choice of means to achieve its ends.

Compulsion is the negation of freedom, except when it is used to enforce the rights common to all. The resort to force, internally or externally, is therefore a last resort for a free society. The act is permissible only when one individual or groups of individuals within it threaten the basic rights of other individuals or when another society seeks to impose its will upon it. The free society cherishes and protects as fundamental the rights of the minority against the will of a majority, because these rights are the inalienable rights of each and every individual.

The resort to force, to compulsion, to the imposition of its will is therefore a difficult and dangerous act for a free society, which is warranted only in the face of even greater dangers. The necessity of the act must be clear and compelling; the act must commend itself to the overwhelming majority as an inescapable exception to the basic idea of freedom; or the regenerative capacity of free men after the act has been performed will be endangered.

The Kremlin is able to select whatever means are expedient in seeking to carry out its fundamental design. Thus it can make the best of several possible worlds, conducting the struggle on those levels where it considers it profitable and enjoying the benefits of a pseudo-peace on those levels where it is not ready for a contest. At the ideological or psychological level, in the struggle for men's minds, the conflict is worldwide. At the political and economic level, within states and in the relations between states, the struggle for power is being intensified. And at the military level, the Kremlin has thus far been careful not to commit a technical breach of the peace, although using its vast forces to intimidate its neighbors, and to support an aggressive foreign policy, and not hesitating through its agents to resort to arms in favorable circumstances. The attempt to carry out its fundamental design is being pressed, therefore, with all means which are believed expedient in the present situation, and the Kremlin has inextricably engaged us in the conflict between its design and our purpose.

We have no such freedom of choice, and least of all in the use of force. Resort to war is not only a last resort for a free society, but it is also an act which cannot definitively end the fundamental conflict in the realm of ideas. The idea of slavery can only be overcome by the timely and persistent demonstration of the superiority of the idea of freedom. Military victory alone would only partially and perhaps only temporarily affect the fundamental conflict, for although the ability of the Kremlin to threaten our security might be for a time destroyed, the resurgence of totalitarian forces and the re-establishment of the Soviet system or its equivalent would not be long delayed unless great progress were made in the fundamental conflict.

Practical and ideological considerations therefore both impel us to the conclusion that we have no choice but to demonstrate the superiority of the idea of freedom by its constructive application, and to attempt to change the world situation by means short of war in such a way as to frustrate the Kremlin design and hasten the decay of the Soviet system.

For us the role of military power is to serve the national purpose by deterring an attack upon us while we seek by other means to create an environment in which our free society can flourish, and by fighting, if necessary, to defend the integrity and vitality of our free society and to defeat any aggressor. The Kremlin uses Soviet military power to back up and serve the Kremlin design. It does not hesitate to use military force aggressively if that course is expedient in the achievement of its design. The differences between our fundamental purpose and the Kremlin design, therefore, are reflected in our respective attitudes toward and use of military force.

. . . .

But if war comes, what is the role of force? Unless we so use it that the Russian people can perceive that our effort is directed against the regime and its power for aggression, and not against their own interests, we will unite the regime and the people in the kind of last ditch fight in which no underlying problems are solved, new ones are created, and where our basic principles are obscured and compromised. If we do not in the application of force demonstrate the nature of our objectives we will, in fact, have compromised from the outset our fundamental purpose. In the words of the *Federalist* (No. 28) "The means to be employed must be proportioned to the extent of the mischief." The mischief may be a global war or it may be a Soviet campaign for limited objectives. In either case we should take no avoidable initiative which would cause it to become a war of annihilation, and if we have the forces to defeat a Soviet drive for limited objectives it may well be to our interest not to let it become a global war. Our aim in applying force must be to compel the acceptance of terms consistent with our objectives, and our capabilities for the application of force should, therefore, within the limits of what we can sustain over the long pull, be congruent to the range of tasks which we may encounter.

V. Soviet Intentions and Capabilities

A. POLITICAL AND PSYCHOLOGICAL

The Kremlin's design for world domination begins at home. The first concern of a despotic oligarchy is that the local base of its power and authority be secure. The massive fact of the iron curtain isolating the Soviet peoples from the outside world, the repeated political purges within the U.S.S.R. and the institutionalized crimes of the MVD [the Soviet Ministry of Internal Affairs] are evidence that the Kremlin does not feel secure at home and that "the entire coercive force of the socialist state" is more than ever one of seeking to impose its absolute authority over "the economy, manner of life, and consciousness of people" (Vyshinski, *The Law of the Soviet State,* p. 74). Similar evidence in the satellite states of Eastern Europe leads to the conclusion that this same policy, in less advanced phases, is being applied to the Kremlin's colonial areas.

Being a totalitarian dictatorship, the Kremlin's objectives in these policies is the total subjective submission of the peoples now under its control. The concentration camp is the prototype of the society which these policies are designed to achieve, a society in which the personality of the individual is so broken and perverted that he participates affirmatively in his own degradation.

The Kremlin's policy toward areas not under its control is the elimination of resistance to its will and the extension of its influence and control. It is driven to follow this policy because it cannot, for the reasons set forth in Chapter IV, tolerate the existence of free societies; to the Kremlin the most mild and inoffensive free society is an affront, a challenge and a subversive influence. Given the nature of the Kremlin, and the evidence at hand, it seems clear that the ends toward which this policy is directed are the same as those where its control has already been established.

The means employed by the Kremlin in pursuit of this policy are limited only by considerations of expediency. Doctrine is not a limiting factor; rather it dictates the employment of violence, subversion, and deceit, and rejects moral considerations. In any event, the Kremlin's conviction of its own infallibility has made its devotion to theory so subjective that past or present pronouncements as to doctrine offer no reliable guide to future actions. The only apparent restraints on resort to war are, therefore, calculations of practicality.

With particular reference to the United States, the Kremlin's strategic and tactical policy is affected by its estimate that we are not only the greatest immediate obstacle which stands between it and world domination, we are also the only power which could release forces in the free and Soviet worlds which could destroy it. The Kremlin's policy toward us is consequently animated by a peculiarly virulent blend of hatred and fear. Its strategy has been one of attempting to undermine the complex of forces, in this country and in the rest of the free world, on which our power is based. In this it has both adhered to doctrine and followed the sound principle of seeking maximum results with minimum risks and commitments. The present application of this strategy is a new form of expression for traditional Russian caution. However, there is no justification in Soviet theory or practice for predicting that, should the Kremlin become convinced that it could cause our downfall by one conclusive blow, it would not seek that solution.

In considering the capabilities of the Soviet world, it is of prime importance to remember that, in contrast to ours, they are being drawn upon close to the maximum possible extent. Also in contrast to us, the Soviet world can do more with less—it has a lower standard of living, its economy requires less to keep it functioning, and its military machine operates effectively with less elaborate equipment and organization.

....

The ideological pretensions of the Kremlin are another great source of strength. Its identification of the Soviet system with communism, its peace campaigns and its championing of colonial peoples may be viewed with apathy, if not cynicism, by the oppressed totalitariat of the Soviet world, but in the free world these ideas find favorable responses in vulnerable segments of society. They have found a particularly receptive audience in Asia, especially as the Asiatics have been impressed by what has been plausibly portrayed to them as the rapid advance of the U.S.S.R. from a backward society to a position of great world power. Thus, in its pretensions to being (a) the source of a new universal faith and (b) the model "scientific" society, the Kremlin cynically identifies itself with the genuine aspirations of large numbers of people, and places itself at the head of an international crusade with all of the benefits which derive therefrom.

Finally, there is a category of capabilities, strictly speaking neither institutional nor ideological, which should be taken into consideration. The extraordinary flexibility of Soviet tactics is certainly a strength. It derives from the utterly amoral and opportunistic conduct of Soviet policy. Combining this quality with the elements of secrecy, the Kremlin possesses a formidable capacity to act with the widest tactical latitude, with stealth, and with speed.

The greatest vulnerability of the Kremlin lies in the basic nature of its relations with the Soviet people.

That relationship is characterized by universal suspicion, fear, and denunciation. It is a relationship in which the Kremlin relies, not only for its power but its very survival, on intricately devised mechanisms of coercion. The Soviet monolith is held together by the iron curtain around it and the iron bars within it, not by any force of natural cohesion. These artificial mechanisms of unity have never been intelligently challenged by a strong outside force. The full measure of their vulnerability is therefore not yet evident.

The Kremlin's relations with its satellites and their peoples is likewise a vulnerability. Nationalism still remains the most potent emotional-political force. The well-known ills of colonialism are compounded, however, by the excessive demands of the Kremlin that its satellites accept not only the imperial authority of Moscow but that they believe in and proclaim the ideological primacy and infallibility of the Kremlin. These excessive requirements can be made good only through extreme coercion. The result is that if a satellite feels able to effect its independence of the Kremlin, as Tito was able to do, it is likely to break away.

In short, Soviet ideas and practices run counter to the best and potentially the strongest instincts of men, and deny their most fundamental aspirations. Against an adversary which effectively affirmed the constructive and hopeful instincts of men and was capable of fulfilling their fundamental aspirations, the Soviet system might prove to be fatally weak.

. . . .

B. ECONOMIC

The Kremlin has no economic intentions unrelated to its overall policies. Economics in the Soviet world is not an end in itself The Kremlin's policy, in so far as it has to do with economics, is to utilize economic processes to contribute to the overall strength, particularly the war-making capacity of the Soviet system. The material welfare of the totalitariat is severely subordinated to the interest of the system.

As for capabilities, even granting optimistic Soviet reports of production, the total economic strength of the U.S.S.R. compares with that of the U.S. as roughly one to four. This is reflected not only in gross national product (1949: U.S.S.R. $65 billion; U.S. $250 billion), but in production of key commodities in 1949:

. . . .

Assuming the maintenance of present policies, while a large U.S. advantage is likely to remain, the Soviet Union will be steadily reducing the discrepancy between its overall economic strength and that of the U.S. by continuing to devote proportionately more to capital investment than the U.S.

But a full-scale effort by the U.S. would be capable of precipitately altering this trend. The U.S.S.R. today is on a near maximum production basis. No matter what efforts Moscow might make, only a relatively slight change in the rate of increase in overall production could be brought about. In the U.S., on the other hand, a very rapid absolute expansion could be realized. The fact remains, however, that so long as the Soviet Union is virtually mobilized, and the United States has scarcely begun to summon up its forces, the greater capabilities of the U.S. are to that extent inoperative in the struggle for power. Moreover, as the Soviet attainment of an atomic capability has demonstrated, the totalitarian state, at least in time of peace, can focus its efforts on any given project far more readily than the democratic state.

. . . .

C. MILITARY

The Soviet Union is developing the military capacity to support its design for world domination. The Soviet Union actually possesses armed forces far in excess of those necessary to defend its national territory. These armed forces are probably not yet considered by the Soviet Union to be sufficient to initiate a war which would involve the United States. This excessive strength, coupled now with an atomic capability, provides the Soviet Union with great coercive power for use in time of peace in furtherance of its objectives and serves as a deterrent to the victims of its aggression from taking any action in opposition to its tactics which would risk war.

Should a major war occur in 1950 the Soviet Union and its satellites are considered by the Joint Chiefs of Staff to be in a sufficiently advanced state of preparation immediately to undertake and carry out the following campaigns.

a. To overrun Western Europe, with the possible exception of the Iberian and Scandinavian Peninsulas; to drive toward the oil-bearing areas of the Near and Middle East; and to consolidate Communist gains in the Far East;

b. To launch air attacks against the British Isles and air and sea attacks against the lines of communications of the Western Powers in the Atlantic and the Pacific;

c. To attack selected targets with atomic weapons, now including the likelihood of such attacks against targets in Alaska, Canada, and the United States. Alternatively, this capability, coupled with other actions open to the Soviet Union, might deny the United Kingdom as an effective base of operations for allied forces. It also should be possible for the Soviet Union to prevent any allied "Normandy" type amphibious operations intended to force a reentry into the continent of Europe.

After the Soviet Union completed its initial campaigns and consolidated its positions in the Western European area, it could simultaneously conduct:

a. Full-scale air and limited sea operations against the British Isles;

b. Invasions of the Iberian and Scandinavian Peninsulas;

c. Further operations in the Near and Middle East, continued air operations against the North American continent, and air and sea operations against Atlantic and Pacific lines of communication; and

d. Diversionary attacks in other areas.

During the course of the offensive operations listed in the second and third paragraphs above, the Soviet Union will have an air defense capability with respect to the vital areas of its own and its satellites' territories which can oppose but cannot prevent allied air operations against these areas.

....

We do not know accurately what the Soviet atomic capability is but the Central Intelligence Agency intelligence estimates, concurred in by State, Army, Navy, Air Force, and Atomic Energy Commission, assign to the Soviet Union a production capability giving it a fission bomb stockpile within the following ranges:

By mid-1950	10–20
By mid-1951	25–45
By mid-1952	45–90
By mid-1953	70–135
By mid-1954	200

This estimate is admittedly based on incomplete coverage of Soviet activities and represents the production capabilities of known or deducible Soviet plants. If others exist, as is possible, this estimate could lead us into a feeling of superiority in our atomic stockpile that might be dangerously misleading, particularly with regard to the timing of a possible Soviet offensive. On the other hand, if the Soviet Union experiences operating difficulties, this estimate would be reduced. There is some evidence that the Soviet Union is acquiring certain materials essential to research on and development of thermonuclear weapons.

The Soviet Union now has aircraft able to deliver the atomic bomb. Our Intelligence estimates assign to the Soviet Union an atomic bomber capability already in excess of that needed to deliver available bombs. We have at present no evaluated estimate regarding the Soviet accuracy of delivery on target. It is believed that the Soviets cannot deliver their bombs on target with a degree of accuracy comparable to ours, but a planning estimate might well place it at 40–60 percent of bombs sortied. For planning purposes, therefore, the date the Soviets possess an atomic stockpile of 200 bombs would be a critical date for the United States, for the delivery of 100 atomic bombs on targets in the United States would seriously damage this country.

At the time the Soviet Union has a substantial atomic stockpile and if it is assumed that it will strike a strong surprise blow and if it is assumed further that its atomic attacks will be met with no more effective defense opposition than the United States and its allies have programmed, results of those attacks could include:

a. Laying waste to the British Isles and thus depriving the Western Powers of their use as a base;

b. Destruction of the vital centers and of the communications of Western Europe, thus precluding effective defense by the Western Powers; and

c. Delivering devastating attacks on certain vital centers of the United States and Canada.

The possession by the Soviet Union of a thermonuclear capability in addition to this substantial atomic stockpile would result in tremendously increased damage.

During this decade, the defensive capabilities of the Soviet Union will probably be strengthened, particularly by the development and use of modern aircraft, aircraft warning and communications devices, and defensive guided missiles.

VI. U.S. Intentions and Capabilities—Actual and Potential

A. POLITICAL AND PSYCHOLOGICAL

Our overall policy at the present time may be described as one designed to foster a world environment in which the American system can survive and flourish. It therefore rejects the concept of isolation and affirms the necessity of our positive participation in the world community.

This broad intention embraces two subsidiary policies. One is a policy which we would probably pursue even if there were no Soviet threat. It is a policy of attempting to develop a healthy international community. The other is the policy of "containing" the Soviet system. These two policies are closely interrelated and interact on one another. Nevertheless, the distinction between them is basically valid and contributes to a clearer understanding of what we are trying to do.

The policy of striving to develop a healthy international community is the long-term constructive effort which we are engaged in. It was this policy which gave rise to our vigorous sponsorship of the United Nations. It is of course the principal reason for our long continuing endeavors to create and now develop the Inter-American system. It, as much as containment, underlay our efforts to rehabilitate Western Europe. Most of our international economic activities can likewise be explained in terms of this policy.

In a world of polarized power, the policies designed to develop a healthy international community are more than ever necessary to our own strength.

As for the policy of "containment," it is one which seeks by all means short of war to (1) block further expansion of Soviet power, (2) expose the falsities of Soviet pretensions, (3) induce a retraction of the Kremlin's control and influence, and (4) in general, so foster the seeds of destruction within the Soviet system that the Kremlin is brought at least to the point of modifying its behavior to conform to generally accepted international standards.

It was and continues to be cardinal in this policy that we possess superior overall power in ourselves or in dependable combination with other likeminded nations. One of the most important ingredients of power is military strength. In the concept of "containment," the maintenance of a strong military posture is deemed to be essential for two reasons: (1) as an ultimate guarantee of our national security and (2) as an indispensable backdrop to the conduct of the policy of "containment." Without superior aggregate military strength, in being and readily mobilizable, a policy of "containment"—which is in effect a policy of calculated and gradual coercion—is no more than a policy of bluff.

At the same time, it is essential to the successful conduct of a policy of "containment" that we always leave open the possibility of negotiation with the U.S.S.R. A diplomatic freeze—and we are in one now—tends to defeat the very purposes of "containment" because it raises tensions at the same time that it makes Soviet retractions and adjustments in the direction of moderated behavior more difficult. It also tends to inhibit our initiative and deprives us of opportunities for maintaining a moral ascendancy in our struggle with the Soviet system.

In "containment" it is desirable to exert pressure in a fashion which will avoid so far as possible directly challenging Soviet prestige, to keep open the possibility for the U.S.S.R. to retreat before pressure with a minimum loss of face and to secure political advantage from the failure of the Kremlin to yield or take advantage of the openings we leave it.

We have failed to implement adequately these two fundamental aspects of "containment." In the face of obviously mounting Soviet military strength ours has declined relatively. Partly as a byproduct of this, but also for other reasons, we now find ourselves at a diplomatic impasse with the Soviet Union, with the Kremlin growing bolder, with both of us holding on grimly to what we have, and with ourselves facing difficult decisions.

In examining our capabilities it is relevant to ask at the outset—capabilities for what? The answer cannot be stated solely in the negative terms of resisting the Kremlin design. It includes also our capabilities to attain the fundamental purpose of the United States, and to foster a world environment in which our free society can survive and flourish.

Potentially we have these capabilities. We know we have them in the economic and military fields. Potentially we also have them in the political and psychological fields. The vast majority of Americans are confident that the system of values which animates our society—the principles of freedom, tolerance, the importance of the individual, and the supremacy of reason over will—are valid and more vital than the ideology which is the fuel of Soviet dynamism. Translated into terms relevant to the lives of other peoples—our system of values can become perhaps a powerful appeal to millions who now seek or find in authoritarianism a refuge from anxieties, bafflement, and insecurity.

Essentially, our democracy also possesses a unique degree of unity. Our society is fundamentally more cohesive than the Soviet system, the solidarity of which is artificially created through force, fear, and favor. This means that expressions of national consensus in our society are soundly and solidly based. It means that the possibility of revolution in this country is fundamentally less than that in the Soviet system.

These capabilities within us constitute a great potential force in our international relations. The potential within us of bearing witness to the values by which we live holds promise for a dynamic manifestation to the rest of the world of the vitality of our system. The essential tolerance of our world outlook, our generous and constructive impulses, and the absence of covetousness in our international relations are assets of potentially enormous influence.

These then are our potential capabilities. Between them and our capabilities currently being utilized is a wide gap of unactualized power. In sharp contrast is the situation of the Soviet world. Its capabilities are inferior to those of our allies and to our own. But they are mobilized close to the maximum possible extent.

The full power which resides within the American people will be evoked only through the traditional democratic process: This process requires, firstly, that sufficient information regarding the basic political, economic, and military elements of the present situation be made publicly available so that an intelligent popular opinion may be formed. Having achieved a comprehension of the issues now confronting this Republic, it will then be possible for the American people and the American Government to arrive at a consensus. Out of this common view will develop a determination of the national will and a solid resolute expression of that will. The initiative in this process lies with the Government.

The democratic way is harder than the authoritarian way because, in seeking to protect and fulfill the individual, it demands of him understanding, judgment, and positive participation in the increasingly complex and exacting problems of the modern world. It demands that he exercise discrimination: that while pursuing through free inquiry the search for truth he knows when he should commit an act of faith; that he distinguish between the necessity for tolerance and the necessity for just suppression. A free society is vulnerable in that it is easy for people to lapse into excesses—the excesses of a permanently open mind wishfully waiting for evidence that evil design may become noble purpose, the excess of faith becoming prejudice, the excess of tolerance degenerating into indulgence of conspiracy and the excess of resorting to suppression when more moderate measures are not only more appropriate but more effective.

In coping with dictatorial governments acting in secrecy and with speed, we are also vulnerable in that the democratic process necessarily operates in the open and at a deliberate tempo. Weaknesses in our situation are readily apparent and subject to immediate exploitation. This Government therefore cannot afford in the face of the totalitarian challenge to operate on a narrow margin of strength. A democracy can compensate for its natural vulnerability only if it maintains clearly superior overall power in its most inclusive sense.

The very virtues of our system likewise handicap us in certain respects in our relations with our allies. While it is a general source of strength to us that our relations with our allies are conducted on a basis of persuasion and consent rather than compulsion and capitulation, it is also evident that dissent among us can become a vulnerability. Sometimes the dissent has its principal roots abroad in situations about which we can do nothing. Sometimes it arises largely out of certain weaknesses within ourselves, about which we can do something—our native impetuosity and a tendency to expect too much from people widely divergent from us.

The full capabilities of the rest of the free world are a potential increment to our own capabilities. It may even be said that the capabilities of the Soviet world, specifically the capabilities of the masses who have nothing to lose but their Soviet chains, are a potential which can be enlisted on our side.

Like our own capabilities, those of the rest of the free world exceed the capabilities of the Soviet system. Like our own they are far from being effectively mobilized and employed in the struggle against the Kremlin design. This is so because the rest of the free world lacks a sense of unity, confidence, and common purpose. This is true in even the most homogeneous and advanced segment of the free world—Western Europe.

As we ourselves demonstrate power, confidence, and a sense of moral and political direction, so those same qualities will be evoked in Western Europe. In such a situation, we may also anticipate a general improvement in the political tone in Latin America, Asia, and Africa and the real beginnings of awakening among the Soviet totalitariat.

In the absence of affirmative decision on our part, the rest of the free world is almost certain to become demoralized. Our friends will become more than a liability to us; they can eventually become a positive increment to Soviet power.

In sum, the capabilities of our allies are, in an important sense, a function of our own. An affirmative decision to summon up the potential within ourselves would evoke the potential strength within others and add it to our own.

B. ECONOMIC

1. *Capabilities.* In contrast to the war economy of the Soviet world (cf. Ch. V-B), the American economy (and the economy of the free world as a whole) is at present directed to the provision of rising standards of living. The military budget of the United States represents 6 to 7 percent of its gross national product (as against 13.8 percent for the Soviet Union). Our North Atlantic Treaty [NAT] allies devoted 4.8 percent of their national product to military purposes in 1949.

This difference in emphasis between the two economies means that the readiness of the free world to support a war effort is tending to decline relative to that of the Soviet Union. There is little direct investment in production facilities for military end-products and in dispersal. There are relatively few men receiving military training and a relatively low rate of production of weapons. However, given time to convert to a war effort, the capabilities of the United States economy and also of the Western European economy would be tremendous. In the light of Soviet military capabilities, a question which may be of decisive importance in the event of war is the question whether there will be time to mobilize our superior human and material resources for a war effort (cf. Chs. VIII and IX).

The capability of the American economy to support a build-up of economic and military strength at home and to assist a build-up abroad is limited not, as in the case of the Soviet Union, so much by the ability to produce as by the decision on the proper allocation of resources to this and other purposes. Even Western Europe could afford to assign a substantially larger proportion of its resources to defense, if the necessary foundation in public understanding and will could be laid, and if the assistance needed to meet its dollar deficit were provided.

....

The Soviet Union is now allocating nearly 40 percent of its gross available resources to military purposes and investment, much of which is in war-supporting industries. It is estimated that even in an emergency the Soviet Union could not increase this proportion to much more than 50 percent, or by one-fourth. The United States, on the other hand, is allocating only about 20 percent of its resources to defense and investment (or 22 percent including foreign assistance), and little of its investment outlays are directed to war-supporting industries. In an emergency the United States could allocate more than 50 percent of its resources to military purposes and foreign assistance, or five to six times as much as at present.

....

With a high level of economic activity, the United States could soon attain a gross national product of $300 billion per year, as was pointed out in the President's Economic Report (January 1950). Progress in this direction would permit, and might itself be aided by, a buildup of the economic and military strength of the United States and the free world; furthermore, if a dynamic expansion of the economy were achieved, the necessary build-up could be accomplished without a decrease in the national standard of living because the required resources could be obtained by siphoning off a part of the annual increment in the gross national product. These are facts of fundamental importance in considering the courses of action open to the United States (cf. Ch. IX).

2. *Intentions.* Foreign economic policy is a major instrument in the conduct of United States foreign relations. It is an instrument which can powerfully influence the world environment in ways favorable to the security and welfare of this country. It is also an instrument which, if unwisely formulated and employed, can do actual harm to our national interests. It is an instrument uniquely suited to our capabilities, provided we have the tenacity of purpose and the understanding requisite to a realization of its potentials. Finally, it is an instrument peculiarly appropriate to the cold war.

The preceding analysis has indicated that an essential element in a program to frustrate the Kremlin design is the development of a successfully functioning system among the free nations. It is clear that economic conditions are among the fundamental determinants of the will and the strength to resist subversion and aggression.

United States foreign economic policy has been designed to assist in the building of such a system and such conditions in the free world. The principal features of this policy can be summarized as follows:

1. assistance to Western Europe in recovery and the creation of a viable economy (the European Recovery Program);

2. assistance to other countries because of their special needs arising out of the war or the cold war and our special interests in or responsibility for meeting them (grant assistance to Japan, the Philippines, and Korea, loans and credits by the Export-Import Bank, the International Monetary Fund, and the International Bank to Indonesia, Yugoslavia, Iran, etc.);

3. assistance in the development of underdeveloped areas (the Point IV program and loans and credits to various countries, overlapping to some extent with those mentioned under 2);

4. military assistance to the North Atlantic Treaty countries, Greece, Turkey, etc.;

5. restriction of East-West trade in items of military importance to the East;

6. purchase and stockpiling of strategic materials; and

7. efforts to reestablish an international economy based on multilateral trade, declining trade barriers, and convertible currencies (the GATT-ITO program, the Reciprocal Trade Agreements program, the IMF-IBRD program, and the program now being developed to solve the problem of the United States balance of payments).

. . . .

Several conclusions seem to emerge. First, the Soviet Union is widening the gap between its preparedness for war and the unpreparedness of the free world for war. It is devoting a far greater *proportion* of its resources to military purposes than are the free nations and, in significant components of military power, a greater *absolute* quantity of resources. Second, the Communist success in China, taken with the politico-economic situation in the rest of South and South-East Asia, provides a springboard for a further incursion in this troubled area. Although Communist China faces serious economic problems which may impose some strains on the Soviet economy, it is probable that the social and economic problems faced by the free nations in this area present more than offsetting opportunities for Communist expansion. Third, the Soviet Union holds positions in Europe which, if it maneuvers skillfully, could be used to do great damage to the Western European economy and to the maintenance of the Western orientation of certain countries, particularly Germany and Austria. Fourth, despite (and in part because of) the Titoist' defection, the Soviet Union has accelerated its efforts to integrate satellite economy with its own and to increase the degree of autarchy within the areas under its control.

Fifth, meanwhile, Western Europe, with American (and Canadian) assistance, has achieved a record level of production. However, it faces the prospect of a rapid tapering off of American assistance without the possibility of achieving, by its own efforts, a satisfactory equilibrium with the dollar area. It has also made very little progress toward "economic integration," which would in the long run tend to improve its productivity and to provide an economic environment conducive to political stability. In particular, the movement toward economic integration does not appear to be rapid enough to provide Western Germany with adequate economic opportunities in the West. The United Kingdom still faces economic problems which may require a moderate but politically difficult decline in the British standard of living or more American assistance than is contemplated. At the same time, a strengthening of the British position is needed if the stability of the Commonwealth is not to be impaired and if it is to be a focus of resistance to Communist expansion in South and South-East Asia. Improvement of the British position is also vital in building up the defensive capabilities of Western Europe.

Sixth, throughout Asia the stability of the present moderate governments, which are more in sympathy with our purposes than any probable successor regimes would be, is doubtful. The problem is only in part an economic one. Assistance in economic development is important as a means of holding out to the peoples of Asia some prospect of improvement in standards of living under their present governments. But probably more important are a strengthening of central institutions, an improvement in administration, and generally a development of an economic and social structure within which the peoples of Asia can make more effective use of their great human and material resources.

Seventh, and perhaps most important, there are indications of a let-down of United States efforts under the pressure of the domestic budgetary situation, disillusion resulting from excessively optimistic expectations about the duration and results of our assistance programs, and doubts about the wisdom of continuing to strengthen the free nations as against preparedness measures in light of the intensity of the cold war.

Eighth, there are grounds for predicting that the United States and other free nations will within a period of a few years at most experience a decline in economic activity of serious proportions unless more positive governmental programs are developed than are now available.

In short, as we look into the future, the programs now planned will not meet the requirements of the free nations. The difficulty does not lie so much in the inadequacy or misdirection of policy as in the inadequacy of planned programs, in terms of timing or impact, to achieve our objectives. The risks inherent in this situation are set forth in the following chapter and a course of action designed to reinvigorate our efforts in order to reverse the present trends and to achieve our fundamental purpose is outlined in Chapter IX.

C. MILITARY

The United States now possesses the greatest military potential of any single nation in the world. The military weaknesses of the United States vis-à-vis the Soviet Union, however, include its numerical inferiority in forces in being and in total manpower. Coupled with the inferiority of forces in being, the United States also lacks tenable positions from which to employ its forces in event of war and munitions power in being and readily available.

It is true that the United States armed forces are now stronger than ever before in other times of apparent peace; it is also true that there exists a sharp disparity between our actual military strength and our commitments. The relationship of our strength to our present commitments, however, is not alone the governing factor. The world situation, as well as commitments, should govern; hence, our military strength more properly should be related to the world situation confronting us. When our military strength is related to the world situation and balanced against the likely exigencies of such a situation, it is clear that our military strength is becoming dangerously inadequate.

....

If the potential military capabilities of the United States and its allies were rapidly and effectively developed, sufficient forces could be produced probably to deter war, or if the Soviet Union chooses war, to withstand the initial Soviet attacks, to stabilize supporting attacks, and to retaliate in turn with even greater impact on the Soviet capabilities. From the military point of view alone, however, this would require not only the generation of the necessary military forces but also the development and stockpiling of improved weapons of all types.

Under existing peacetime conditions, a period of from two to three years is required to produce a material increase in military power. Such increased power could be provided in a somewhat shorter period in a declared period of emergency or in wartime through a full-out national effort. Any increase in military power in peacetime, however, should be related both to its probable military role in war, to the implementation of immediate and long-term United States foreign policy vis-à-vis the Soviet Union, and to the realities of the existing situation. If such a course of increasing our military power is adopted now, the United States would have the capability of eliminating the disparity between its military strength and the exigencies of the situation we face; eventually of gaining the initiative in the "cold" war and of materially delaying if not stopping the Soviet offensives in war itself.

VII. Present Risks

A. GENERAL

It is apparent from the preceding sections that the integrity and vitality of our system is in greater jeopardy than ever before in our history. Even if there were no Soviet Union we would face the great problem of the free society, accentuated many fold in this industrial age, of reconciling order, security, the need for participation, with the requirement of freedom. We would face the fact that in a shrinking world the absence of order among nations is becoming less and less tolerable. The Kremlin design seeks to impose order among nations by means which would destroy our free and democratic system. The Kremlin's possession of atomic weapons puts new power behind its design, and increases the jeopardy to our system. It adds new strains to the uneasy equilibrium-without-order which exists in the world and raises new doubts in men's minds whether the world will long tolerate this tension without moving toward some kind of order, on somebody's terms.

The risks we face are of a new order of magnitude, commensurate with the total struggle in which we are engaged. For a free society there is never total victory, since freedom and democracy are never wholly attained, are always in the process of being attained. But defeat at the hands of the totalitarian is total defeat. These risks crowd in on us, in a shrinking world of polarized power, so as to give us no choice, ultimately, between meeting them effectively or being overcome by them.

B. SPECIFIC

It is quite clear from Soviet theory and practice that the Kremlin seeks to bring the free world under its dominion by the methods of the cold war. The preferred technique is to subvert by infiltration and intimidation. Every institution of our society is an instrument which it is sought to stultify and turn against our purposes. Those that touch most closely our material and moral strength are obviously the prime targets, labor unions, civic enterprises, schools, churches, and all media for influencing opinion. The effort is not so much to make them serve obvious Soviet ends as to prevent them from serving our ends, and thus to make them sources of confusion in our economy, our culture, and our body politic. The doubts and diversities that in terms of our values are part of the merit of a free system, the weaknesses and the problems that are peculiar to it, the rights and privileges that free men enjoy, and the disorganization and destruction left in the wake of the last attack on our freedoms, all are but opportunities for the Kremlin to do its evil work. Every advantage is taken of the fact that our means of prevention and retaliation are limited by those principles and scruples which are precisely the ones that give our freedom and democracy its meaning for us. None of our scruples deter those whose only code is "morality is that which serves the revolution."

....

At the same time the Soviet Union is seeking to create overwhelming military force, in order to back up infiltration with intimidation. In the only terms in which it understands strength, it is seeking to demonstrate to the free world that force and the will to use it are on the side of the Kremlin, that those who lack it are decadent and doomed. In local incidents it threatens and encroaches both for the sake of local gains and to increase anxiety and defeatism in all the free world.

The possession of atomic weapons at each of the opposite poles of power, and the inability (for different reasons) of either side to place any trust in the other, puts a premium on a surprise attack against us. It equally puts a premium on a more violent and ruthless prosecution of its design by cold war, especially if the Kremlin is sufficiently objective to realize the improbability of our prosecuting a preventive war. It also puts a premium on piecemeal aggression against others, counting on our unwillingness to engage in atomic war unless we are directly attacked. We run all these risks and the added risk of being confused and immobilized by our inability to weigh and choose, and pursue a firm course based on a rational assessment of each.

The risk that we may thereby be prevented or too long delayed in taking all needful measures to maintain the integrity and vitality of our system is great. The risk that our allies will lose their determination is greater. And the risk that in this manner a descending spiral of too little and too late, of doubt and recrimination, may present us with ever narrower and more desperate alternatives, is the greatest risk of all. For example, it is clear that our present weakness would prevent us from offering effective resistance at any of several vital pressure points. The only deterrent we can present to the Kremlin is the evidence we give that we may make any of the critical points which we cannot hold the occasion for a global war of annihilation.

The risk of having no better choice than to capitulate or precipitate a global war at any of a number of pressure points is bad enough in itself, but it is multiplied by the weakness it imparts to our position in the cold war. Instead of appearing strong and resolute we are continually at the verge of appearing and being alternately irresolute and desperate; yet it is the cold war which we must win, because both the Kremlin design, and our fundamental purpose give it the first priority.

The frustration of the Kremlin design, however, cannot be accomplished by us alone, as will appear from the analysis in Chapter IX, B. Strength at the center, in the United States, is only the first of two essential elements. The second is that our allies and potential allies do not as a result of a sense of frustration or of Soviet intimidation drift into a course of neutrality eventually leading to Soviet domination. If this were to happen in Germany the effect upon Western Europe and eventually upon us might be catastrophic.

But there are risks in making ourselves strong. A large measure of sacrifice and discipline will be demanded of the American people. They will be asked to give up some of the benefits which they have come to associate with their freedoms. Nothing could be more important than that they fully understand the reasons for this. The risks of a superficial understanding or of an inadequate appreciation of the issues are obvious and might lead to the adoption of measures which in themselves would jeopardize the integrity of our system. At any point in the process of demonstrating our will to make good our fundamental purpose, the Kremlin may decide to precipitate a general war, or in testing us, may go too far. These are risks we will invite by making ourselves strong, but they are lesser risks than those we seek to avoid. Our fundamental purpose is more likely to be defeated from lack of the will to maintain it, than from any mistakes we may make or assault we may undergo because of asserting that will. No people in history have preserved their freedom who thought that by not being strong enough to protect themselves they might prove inoffensive to their enemies.

....

IX. Possible Courses of Action

Introduction. Four possible courses of action by the United States in the present situation can be distinguished. They are:

a. Continuation of current policies, with current and currently projected programs for carrying out these policies;

b. Isolation;

c. War; and

d. A more rapid building up of the political, economic, and military strength of the free world than provided under a, with the purpose of reaching, if possible, a tolerable state of order among nations without war and of preparing to defend ourselves in the event that the free world is attacked.

The role of negotiation. Negotiation must be considered in relation to these courses of action. A negotiator always attempts to achieve an agreement which is somewhat better than the realities of his fundamental position would justify and which is, in any case, not worse than his fundamental position requires. This is as true in relations among sovereign states as in relations between individuals. The Soviet Union possesses several advantages over the free world in negotiations on any issue:

a. It can and does enforce secrecy on all significant facts about conditions within the Soviet Union, so that it can be expected to know more about the realities of the free world's position than the free world knows about its position;

b. It does not have to be responsive in any important sense to public opinion;

c. It does not have to consult and agree with any other countries on the terms it will offer and accept; and

d. It can influence public opinion in other countries while insulating the peoples under its control.

These are important advantages. Together with the unfavorable trend of our power position, they militate, as is shown in Section A below, against successful negotiation of a general settlement at this time. For although the United States probably now possesses, principally in atomic weapons, a force adequate to deliver a powerful blow upon the Soviet Union and to open the road to victory in a long war, it is not sufficient by itself to advance the position of the United States in the cold war.

The problem is to create such political and economic conditions in the free world, backed by force sufficient to inhibit Soviet attack, that the Kremlin will accommodate itself to these conditions, gradually withdraw, and eventually change its policies drastically. It has been shown in Chapter VIII that truly effective control of atomic energy would require such an opening up of the Soviet Union and such evidence in other ways of its good faith and its intent to co-exist in peace as to reflect or at least initiate a change in the Soviet system.

Clearly under present circumstances we will not be able to negotiate a settlement which calls for a change in the Soviet system. What, then, is the role of negotiation?

In the first place, the public in the United States and in other free countries will require, as a condition to firm policies and adequate programs directed to the frustration of the Kremlin design, that the free world be continuously prepared to negotiate agreements with the Soviet Union on equitable terms. It is still argued by many people here and abroad that equitable agreements with the Soviet Union are possible, and this view will gain force if the Soviet Union begins to show signs of accommodation, even on unimportant issues.

. . . .

A sound negotiating position is, therefore, an essential element in the ideological conflict. For some time after a decision to build up strength, any offer of, or attempt at, negotiation of a general settlement along the lines of the Berkeley speech by the Secretary of State could be only a tactic.[2] Nevertheless, concurrently with a decision and a

2. The Secretary of State listed seven areas in which the Soviet Union could modify its behavior in such a way as to permit co-existence in reasonable security. These were:

start on building up the strength of the free world, it may be desirable to pursue this tactic both to gain public support for the program and to minimize the immediate risks of war. It is urgently necessary for the United States to determine its negotiating position and to obtain agreement with its major allies on the purposes and terms of negotiation.

In the second place, assuming that the United States in cooperation with other free countries decides and acts to increase the strength of the free world and assuming that the Kremlin chooses the path of accommodation, it will from time to time be necessary and desirable to negotiate on various specific issues with the Kremlin as the area of possible agreement widens.

The Kremlin will have three major objectives in negotiations with the United States. The first is to eliminate the atomic capabilities of the United States; the second is to prevent the effective mobilization of the superior potential of the free world in human and material resources; and the third is to secure a withdrawal of United States forces from, and commitments to, Europe and Japan. Depending on its evaluation of its own strengths and weaknesses as against the West's (particularly the ability and will of the West to sustain its efforts), it will or will not be prepared to make important concessions to achieve these major objectives. It is unlikely that the Kremlin's evaluation is such that it would now be prepared to make significant concessions.

The objectives of the United States and other free countries in negotiations with the Soviet Union (apart from the ideological objectives discussed above) are to record, in a formal fashion which will facilitate the consolidation and further advance of our position, the process of Soviet accommodation to the new political, psychological, and economic conditions in the world which will result from adoption of the fourth course of action and which will be supported by the increasing military strength developed as an integral part of that course of action. In short, our objectives are to record, where desirable, the gradual withdrawal of the Soviet Union and to facilitate that process by making negotiation, if possible, always more expedient than resort to force.

It must be presumed that for some time the Kremlin will accept agreements only if it is convinced that by acting in bad faith whenever and wherever there is an opportunity to do so with impunity, it can derive greater advantage from the agreements than the free world. For this reason, we must take care that any agreements are enforceable or that they are not susceptible of violation without detection and the possibility of effective countermeasures.

This further suggests that we will have to consider carefully the order in which agreements can be concluded. Agreement on the control of atomic energy would result in a relatively greater disarmament of the United States than of the Soviet Union, even assuming considerable progress in building up the strength of the free world in conven-

---

1. Treaties of peace with Austria, Germany, Japan and relaxation of pressures in the Far East;
2. Withdrawal of Soviet forces and influence from satellite area;
3. Cooperation in the United Nations;
4. Control of atomic energy and of conventional armaments;
5. Abandonment of indirect aggression;
6. Proper treatment of official representatives of the U.S.;

Increased access to the Soviet Union of persons and ideas from other countries. [Footnote in the source text. For the text of the address delivered by Secretary Acheson at the University of California, Berkeley, on March 16, 1950, concerning United States—Soviet relations, see Department of State *Bulletin*, March 27, 1950, pp. 473–478.]

tional forces and weapons. It might be accepted by the Soviet Union as part of a deliberate design to move against Western Europe and other areas of strategic importance with conventional forces and weapons. In this event, the United States would find itself at war, having previously disarmed itself in its most important weapon, and would be engaged in a race to redevelop atomic weapons.

. . . .

In the third place, negotiation will play a part in the building up of the strength of the free world, apart from the ideological strength discussed above. This is most evident in the problems of Germany, Austria, and Japan. In the process of building up strength, it may be desirable for the free nations, without the Soviet Union, to conclude separate arrangements with Japan, Western Germany, and Austria which would enlist the energies and resources of these countries in support of the free world. This will be difficult unless it has been demonstrated by attempted negotiation with the Soviet Union that the Soviet Union is not prepared to accept treaties of peace which would leave these countries free, under adequate safeguards, to participate in the United Nations and in regional or broader associations of states consistent with the United Nations' Charter and providing security and adequate opportunities for the peaceful development of their political and economic life.

This demonstrates the importance, from the point of view of negotiation as well as for its relationship to the building up of the strength of the free world (see Section D below), of the problem of closer association—on a regional or a broader basis—among the free countries.

In conclusion, negotiation is not a possible separate course of action but rather a means of gaining support for a program of building strength, of recording, where necessary and desirable, progress in the cold war, and of facilitating further progress while helping to minimize the risks of war. Ultimately, it is our objective to negotiate a settlement with the Soviet Union (or a successor state or states) on which the world can place reliance as an enforceable instrument of peace. But it is important to emphasize that such a settlement can only record the progress which the free world will have made in creating a political and economic system in the world so successful that the frustration of the Kremlin's design for world domination will be complete. The analysis in the following sections indicates that the building of such a system requires expanded and accelerated programs for the carrying out of current policies.

A. THE FIRST COURSE—CONTINUATION OF CURRENT POLICIES, WITH CURRENT AND CURRENTLY PROJECTED PROGRAMS FOR CARRYING OUT THESE POLICIES

1. *Military aspects.* On the basis of current programs, the United States has a large potential military capability but an actual capability which, though improving, is declining relative to the U.S.S.R., particularly in light of its probable fission bomb capability and possible thermonuclear bomb capability. The same holds true for the free world as a whole relative to the Soviet world as a whole. If war breaks out in 1950 or in the next few years, the United States and its allies, apart from a powerful atomic blow, will be compelled to conduct delaying actions, while building up their strength for a general offensive. A frank evaluation of the requirements, to defend the United States and its vital interests and to support a vigorous initiative in the cold war, on the one hand, and of present capabilities, on the other, indicates that there is a sharp and growing disparity between them.

A review of Soviet policy shows that the military capabilities, actual and potential, of the United States and the rest of the free world, together with the apparent determination of the free world to resist further Soviet expansion, have not induced the Kremlin to relax its pressures generally or to give up the initiative in the cold war. On the contrary, the Soviet Union has consistently pursued a bold foreign policy, modified only when it's probing revealed a determination and an ability of the free world to resist encroachment upon it. The relative military capabilities of the free world are declining, with the result that its determination to resist may also decline and that the security of the United States and the free world as a whole will be jeopardized.

From the military point of view, the actual and potential capabilities of the United States, given a continuation of current and projected programs, will become less and less effective as a war deterrent. Improvement of the state of readiness will become more and more important not only to inhibit the launching of war by the Soviet Union but also to support a national policy designed to reverse the present ominous trends in international relations. A building up of the military capabilities of the United States and the free world is a pre-condition to the achievement of the objectives outlined in this report and to the protection of the United States against disaster.

Fortunately, the United States military establishment has been developed into a unified and effective force as a result of the policies laid down by the Congress and the vigorous carrying out of these policies by the Administration in the fields of both organization and economy. It is, therefore, a base upon which increased strength can be rapidly built with maximum efficiency and economy.

2. *Political aspects.* The Soviet Union is pursuing the initiative in the conflict with the free world. Its atomic capabilities, together with its successes in the Far East, have led to an increasing confidence on its part and to an increasing nervousness in Western Europe and the rest of the free world. We cannot be sure, of course, how vigorously the Soviet Union will pursue its initiative, nor can we be sure of the strength or weakness of the other free countries in reacting to it. There are, however, ominous signs of further deterioration in the Far East. There are also some indications that a decline in morale and confidence in Western Europe may be expected. In particular, the situation in Germany is unsettled. Should the belief or suspicion spread that the free nations are not now able to prevent the Soviet Union from taking, if it chooses, the military actions outlined in Chapter V, the determination of the free countries to resist probably would lessen and there would be an increasing temptation for them to seek a position of neutrality.

Politically, recognition of the military implications of a continuation of present trends will mean that the United States and especially other free countries will tend to shift to the defensive, or to follow a dangerous policy of bluff, because the maintenance of a firm initiative in the cold war is closely related to aggregate strength in being and readily available.

This is largely a problem of the incongruity of the current actual capabilities of the free world and the threat to it, for the free world has an economic and military potential far superior to the potential of the Soviet Union and its satellites. The shadow of Soviet force falls darkly on Western Europe and Asia and supports a policy of encroachment. The free world lacks adequate means—in the form of forces in being—to thwart such expansion locally. The United States will therefore be confronted more frequently with the dilemma of reacting totally to a limited extension of Soviet control or of not reacting at all (except with ineffectual protests and half measures). Continuation of present trends is likely to lead, therefore, to a gradual withdrawal under the direct or indirect pressure of the Soviet Union, until we discover one day that we have sacrificed positions of vital interest. In other words, the United States would have chosen, by lack of the necessary decisions and actions, to fall back to isolation in the Western Hemisphere. This course would at best result in only a relatively brief truce and would be ended either by our capitulation or by a defensive war—on unfavorable terms from unfavorable positions—against a Soviet Empire compromising all or most of Eurasia. (See Section B.)

3. *Economic and social aspects.* As was pointed out in Chapter VI, the present foreign economic policies and programs of the United States will not produce a solution to the problem of international economic equilibrium, notably the problem of the dollar gap, and will not create an economic base conducive to political stability in many important free countries.

The European Recovery Program has been successful in assisting the restoration and expansion of production in Western Europe and has been a major factor in checking the dry rot of Communism in Western Europe. However, little progress has been made toward the resumption by Western Europe of a position of influence in world affairs commensurate with its potential strength. Progress in this direction will require integrated political, economic, and military policies and programs, which are supported by the United States and the Western European countries and which will probably require a deeper participation by the United States than has been contemplated.

....

4. *Negotiation.* In short, by continuing along its present course the free world will not succeed in making effective use of its vastly superior political, economic, and military potential to build a tolerable state of order among nations. On the contrary, the political, economic, and military situation of the free world is already unsatisfactory and will become less favorable unless we act to reverse present trends.

This situation is one which militates against successful negotiations with the Kremlin—for the terms of agreements on important pending issues would reflect present realities and would therefore be unacceptable, if not disastrous, to the United States and the rest of the free world. Unless a decision had been made and action undertaken to build up the strength, in the broadest sense, of the United States and the free world, an attempt to negotiate a general settlement on terms acceptable to us would be ineffective and probably long drawn out, and might thereby seriously delay the necessary measures to build up our strength.

....

B. THE SECOND COURSE—ISOLATION

Continuation of present trends, it has been shown above, will lead progressively to the withdrawal of the United States from most of its present commitments in Europe and Asia and to our isolation in the Western Hemisphere and its approaches. This would result not from a conscious decision but from a failure to take the actions necessary to bring our capabilities into line with our commitments and thus to a withdrawal under pressure. This pressure might come from our present Allies, who will tend to seek other "solutions" unless they have confidence in our determination to accelerate our efforts to build a successfully functioning political and economic system in the free world.

There are some who advocate a deliberate decision to isolate ourselves. Superficially, this has some attractiveness as a course of action, for it appears to bring our commitments and capabilities into harmony by reducing the former and by concentrating our present, or perhaps even reduced, military expenditures on the defense of the United States.

This argument overlooks the relativity of capabilities. With the United States in an isolated position, we would have to face the probability that the Soviet Union would quickly dominate most of Eurasia, probably without meeting armed resistance. It would thus acquire a potential far superior to our own, and would promptly proceed to develop this potential with the purpose of eliminating our power, which would, even in isolation, remain as a challenge to it and as an obstacle to the imposition of its kind of order in the world. There is no way to make ourselves inoffensive to the Kremlin except by complete submission to its will. Therefore isolation would in the end condemn us to capitulate or to fight alone and on the defensive, with drastically limited offensive and retaliatory capabilities in comparison with the Soviet Union. (These are the only possibilities, unless we are prepared to risk the future on the hazard that the Soviet Empire, because of over-extension or other reasons, will spontaneously destroy itself from within.)

The argument also overlooks the imponderable, but nevertheless drastic, effects on our belief in ourselves and in our way of life of a deliberate decision to isolate ourselves. As the Soviet Union came to dominate free countries, it is clear that many Americans would feel a deep sense of responsibility and guilt for having abandoned their former friends and allies. As the Soviet Union mobilized the resources of Eurasia, increased its relative military capabilities, and heightened its threat to our security, some would be tempted to accept "peace" on its terms, while many would seek to defend the United States by creating a regimented system which would permit the assignment of a tremendous part of our resources to defense. Under such a state of affairs our national morale would be corrupted and the integrity and vitality of our system subverted.

Under this course of action, there would be no negotiation, unless on the Kremlin's terms, for we would have given up everything of importance.

It is possible that at some point in the course of isolation, many Americans would come to favor a surprise attack on the Soviet Union and the area under its control, in a desperate attempt to alter decisively the balance of power by an overwhelming blow with modern weapons of mass destruction. It appears unlikely that the Soviet Union would wait for such an attack before launching one of its own. But even if it did and even if our attack were successful, it is clear that the United States would face appalling tasks in establishing a tolerable state of order among nations after such a war and after Soviet occupation of all or most of Eurasia for some years. These tasks appear so enormous and success so unlikely that reason dictates an attempt to achieve our objectives by other means.

C. THE THIRD COURSE—WAR

Some Americans favor a deliberate decision to go to war against the Soviet Union in the near future. It goes without saying that the idea of "preventive" war—in the sense of a military attack not provoked by a military attack upon us or our allies—is generally unacceptable to Americans. Its supporters argue that since the Soviet Union is in fact at war with the free world now and that since the failure of the Soviet Union to use all-out military force is explainable on grounds of expediency, we are at war and should conduct ourselves accordingly. Some further argue that the free world is probably unable, except under the crisis of war, to mobilize and direct its resources to the checking and rolling back of the Kremlin's drive for world dominion. This is a powerful argument in the light of history, but the considerations against war are so compelling that the free world must demonstrate that this argument is wrong. The case for war is premised on the assumption that the United States could launch and sustain an attack of sufficient impact to gain a decisive advantage for the free world in a long war and perhaps to win an early decision.

The ability of the United States to launch effective offensive operations is now limited to attack with atomic weapons. A powerful blow could be delivered upon the Soviet Union, but it is estimated that these operations alone would not force or induce the Kremlin to capitulate and that the Kremlin would still be able to use the forces under its control to dominate most or all of Eurasia. This would probably mean a long and difficult struggle during which the free institutions of Western Europe and many freedom-loving people would be destroyed and the regenerative capacity of Western Europe dealt a crippling blow.

Apart from this, however, a surprise attack upon the Soviet Union, despite the provocativeness of recent Soviet behavior, would be repugnant to many Americans. Although the American people would probably rally in support of the war effort, the shock of responsibility for a surprise attack would be morally corrosive. Many would doubt that it was a "just war" and that all reasonable possibilities for a peaceful settlement had been explored in good faith. Many more, proportionately, would hold such views in other countries, particularly in Western Europe and particularly after Soviet occupation, if only because the Soviet Union would liquidate articulate opponents. It would, therefore, be difficult after such a war to create a satisfactory international order among nations. Victory in such a war would have brought us little if at all closer to victory in the fundamental ideological conflict.

These considerations are no less weighty because they are imponderable, and they rule out an attack unless it is demonstrably in the nature of a counter-attack to a blow which is on its way or about to be delivered. (The military advantages of landing the first blow become increasingly important with modern weapons, and this is a fact which requires us to be on the alert in order to strike with our full weight as soon as we are attacked, and, if possible, before the Soviet blow is actually delivered.) If the argument of Chapter IV is accepted, it follows that there is no "easy" solution and that the only sure victory lies in the frustration of the Kremlin design by the steady development of the moral and material strength of the free world and its projection into the Soviet world in such a way as to bring about an internal change in the Soviet system.

D. THE REMAINING COURSE OF ACTION—A RAPID BUILD-UP OF POLITICAL, ECONOMIC, AND MILITARY STRENGTH IN THE FREE WORLD

A more rapid build-up of political, economic, and military strength and thereby of confidence in the free world than is now contemplated is the only course which is consistent with progress toward achieving our fundamental purpose. The frustration of the Kremlin design requires the free world to develop a successfully functioning political and economic system and a vigorous political offensive against the Soviet Union. These, in turn, require an adequate military shield under which they can develop. It is necessary to have the military power to deter, if possible, Soviet expansion, and to defeat, if necessary, aggressive Soviet or Soviet-directed actions of a limited or total character. The potential strength of the free world is great; its ability to develop these military capabilities and its will to resist Soviet expansion will be determined by the wisdom and will with which it undertakes to meet its political and economic problems.

1. *Military aspects.* It has been indicated in Chapter VI that U.S. military capabilities are strategically more defensive in nature than offensive and are more potential than actual. It is evident, from an analysis of the past and of the trend of weapon development, that there is now and will be in the future no absolute defense. The history of war also

indicates that a favorable decision can only be achieved through offensive action. Even a defensive strategy, if it is to be successful, calls not only for defensive forces to hold vital positions while mobilizing and preparing for the offensive, but also for offensive forces to attack the enemy and keep him off balance.

The two fundamental requirements which must be met by forces in being or readily available are support of foreign policy and protection against disaster. To meet the second requirement, the forces in being or readily available must be able, at a minimum, to perform certain basic tasks:

a. To defend the Western Hemisphere and essential allied areas in order that their war-making capabilities can be developed;

b. To provide and protect a mobilization base while the offensive forces required for victory are being built up;

c. To conduct offensive operations to destroy vital elements of the Soviet war-making capacity, and to keep the enemy off balance until the full offensive strength of the United States and its allies can be brought to bear;

d. To defend and maintain the lines of communication and base areas necessary to the execution of the above tasks; and

e. To provide such aid to allies as is essential to the execution of their role in the above tasks.

In the broadest terms, the ability to perform these tasks requires a build-up of military strength by the United States and its allies to a point at which the combined strength will be superior for at least these tasks, both initially and throughout a war, to the forces that can be brought to bear by the Soviet Union and its satellites. In specific terms, it is not essential to match item for item with the Soviet Union, but to provide an adequate defense against air attack on the United States and Canada and an adequate defense against air and surface attack on the United Kingdom and Western Europe, Alaska, the Western Pacific, Africa, and the Near and Middle East, and on the long lines of communication to these areas. Furthermore, it is mandatory that in building up our strength, we enlarge upon our technical superiority by an accelerated exploitation of the scientific potential of the United States and our allies.

Forces of this size and character are necessary not only for protection against disaster but also to support our foreign policy. In fact, it can be argued that larger forces in being and readily available are necessary to inhibit a would-be aggressor than to provide the nucleus of strength and the mobilization base on which the tremendous forces required for victory can be built....

Moreover, the United States and the other free countries do not now have the forces in being and readily available to defeat local Soviet moves with local action, but must accept reverses or make these local moves the occasion for war—for which we are not prepared. This situation makes for great uneasiness among our allies, particularly in Western Europe, for whom total war means, initially, Soviet occupation. Thus, unless our combined strength is rapidly increased, our allies will tend to become increasingly reluctant to support a firm foreign policy on our part and increasingly anxious to seek other solutions, even though they are aware that appeasement means defeat. An important advantage in adopting the fourth course of action lies in its psychological impact—the revival of confidence and hope in the future....

2. *Political and economic aspects.* The immediate objectives—to the achievement of which such a build-up of strength is a necessary though not a sufficient

condition—are a renewed initiative in the cold war and a situation to which the Kremlin would find it expedient to accommodate itself, first by relaxing tensions and pressures and then by gradual withdrawal. The United States cannot alone provide the resources required for such a build-up of strength. The other free countries must carry their part of the burden, but their ability and determination to do it will depend on the action the United States takes to develop its own strength and on the adequacy of its foreign political and economic policies. Improvement in political and economic conditions in the free world, as has been emphasized above, is necessary as a basis for building up the will and the means to resist and for dynamically affirming the integrity and vitality of our free and democratic way of life on which our ultimate victory depends.

At the same time, we should take dynamic steps to reduce the power and influence of the Kremlin inside the Soviet Union and other areas under its control. The objective would be the establishment of friendly regimes not under Kremlin domination. Such action is essential to engage the Kremlin's attention, keep it off balance, and force an increased expenditure of Soviet resources in counteraction. In other words, it would be the current Soviet cold war technique used against the Soviet Union.

A program for rapidly building up strength and improving political and economic conditions will place heavy demands on our courage and intelligence; it will be costly; it will be dangerous. But half-measures will be more costly and more dangerous, for they will be inadequate to prevent and may actually invite war. Budgetary considerations will need to be subordinated to the stark fact that our very independence as a nation may be at stake.

A comprehensive and decisive program to win the peace and frustrate the Kremlin design should be so designed that it can be sustained for as long as necessary to achieve our national objectives. It would probably involve:

1. The development of an adequate political and economic framework for the achievement of our long-range objectives.

2. A substantial increase in expenditures for military purposes adequate to meet the requirements for the tasks listed in Section D-1.

3. A substantial increase in military assistance programs, designed to foster cooperative efforts, which will adequately and efficiently meet the requirements of our allies for the tasks referred to in Section D-l-e.

4. Some increase in economic assistance programs and recognition of the need to continue these programs until their purposes have been accomplished.

5. A concerted attack on the problem of the United States balance of payments, along the lines already approved by the President.

6. Development of programs designed to build and maintain confidence among other peoples in our strength and resolution, and to wage overt psychological warfare calculated to encourage mass defections from Soviet allegiance and to frustrate the Kremlin design in other ways.

7. Intensification of affirmative and timely measures and operations by covert means in the fields of economic warfare and political and psychological warfare with a view to fomenting and supporting unrest and revolt in selected strategic satellite countries.

8. Development of internal security and civilian defense programs.

9. Improvement and intensification of intelligence activities.

10. Reduction of Federal expenditures for purposes other than defense and foreign assistance, if necessary by the deferment of certain desirable programs.

11. Increased taxes.

Essential as prerequisites to the success of this program would be (a) consultations with Congressional leaders designed to make the program the object of non-partisan legislative support, and (b) a presentation to the public of a full explanation of the facts and implications of present international trends.

The program will be costly, but it is relevant to recall the disproportion between the potential capabilities of the Soviet and non-Soviet worlds (cf. Chapters V and VI). The Soviet Union is currently devoting about 40 percent of available resources (gross national product plus reparations, equal in 1949 to about $65 billion) to military expenditures (14 percent) and to investment (26 percent), much of which is in war-supporting industries. In an emergency the Soviet Union could increase the allocation of resources to these purposes to about 50 percent, or by one-fourth.

The United States is currently devoting about 22 percent of its gross national product ($255 billion in 1949) to military expenditures (6 percent), foreign assistance (2 percent), and investment (14 percent), little of which is in war-supporting industries....

....

This comparison between the potentials of the Soviet Union and the United States also holds true for the Soviet world and the free world and is of fundamental importance in considering the courses of action open to the United States.

The comparison gives renewed emphasis to the fact that the problems faced by the free countries in their efforts to build a successfully functioning system lie not so much in the field of economics as in the field of politics. The building of such a system may require more rapid progress toward the closer association of the free countries in harmony with the concept of the United Nations. It is clear that our long-range objectives require a strengthened United Nations, or a successor organization, to which the world can look for the maintenance of peace and order in a system based on freedom and justice. It also seems clear that a unifying ideal of this kind might awaken and arouse the latent spiritual energies of free men everywhere and obtain their enthusiastic support for a positive program for peace going far beyond the frustration of the Kremlin design and opening vistas to the future that would outweigh short-run sacrifices.

....The immediate goal of our efforts to build a successfully functioning political and economic system in the free world backed by adequate military strength is to postpone and avert the disastrous situation which, in light of the Soviet Union's probable fission bomb capability and possible thermonuclear bomb capability, might arise in 1954 on a continuation of our present programs. By acting promptly and vigorously in such a way that this date is, so to speak, pushed into the future, we would permit time for the process of accommodation, withdrawal and frustration to produce the necessary changes in the Soviet system. Time is short, however, and the risks of war attendant upon a decision to build up strength will steadily increase the longer we defer it.

CONCLUSIONS AND RECOMMENDATIONS

Conclusions

The foregoing analysis indicates that the probable fission bomb capability and possible thermonuclear bomb capability of the Soviet Union have greatly intensified the

Soviet threat to the security of the United States. This threat is of the same character as that described in NSC 20/4 (approved by the President on November 24, 1948) but is more immediate than had previously been estimated. In particular, the United States now faces the contingency that within the next four or five years the Soviet Union will possess the military capability of delivering a surprise atomic attack of such weight that the United States must have substantially increased general air, ground, and sea strength, atomic capabilities, and air and civilian defenses to deter war and to provide reasonable assurance, in the event of war, that it could survive the initial blow and go on to the eventual attainment of its objectives. In return, this contingency requires the intensification of our efforts in the fields of intelligence and research and development.

Allowing for the immediacy of the danger, the following statement of Soviet threats, contained in NSC 20/4, remains valid:

> "14. The gravest threat to the security of the United States within the foreseeable future stems from the hostile designs and formidable power of the U.S.S.R., and from the nature of the Soviet system.
>
> "15. The political, economic, and psychological warfare which the U.S.S.R. is now waging has dangerous potentialities for weakening the relative world position of the United States and disrupting its traditional institutions by means short of war, unless sufficient resistance is encountered in the policies of this and other non-communist countries.
>
> "16. The risk of war with the U.S.S.R. is sufficient to warrant, in common prudence, timely and adequate preparation by the United States.
>
> > "a. Even though present estimates indicate that the Soviet leaders probably do not intend deliberate armed action involving the United States at this time, the possibility of such deliberate resort to war cannot be ruled out.
> >
> > "b. Now and for the foreseeable future there is a continuing danger that war will arise either through Soviet miscalculation of the determination of the United States to use all the means at its command to safeguard its security, through Soviet misinterpretation of our intentions, or through U.S. miscalculation of Soviet reactions to measures which we might take.
>
> "17. Soviet domination of the potential power of Eurasia, whether achieved by armed aggression or by political and subversive means, would be strategically and politically unacceptable to the United States.
>
> "18. The capability of the United States either in peace or in the event of war to cope with threats to its security or to gain its objectives would be severely weakened by internal development, important among which are:
>
> > "a. Serious espionage, subversion and sabotage, particularly by concerted and well-directed communist activity.
> >
> > "b. Prolonged or exaggerated economic instability.
> >
> > "c. Internal political and social disunity.
> >
> > "d. Inadequate or excessive armament or foreign aid expenditures.
> >
> > "e. An excessive or wasteful usage of our resources in time of peace.
> >
> > "f. Lessening of U.S. prestige and influence through vacillation of appeasement or lack of skill and imagination in the conduct of its foreign policy or by shirking world responsibilities.

"g. Development of a false sense of security through a deceptive change in Soviet tactics."

....

The analysis also confirms that our objectives with respect to the Soviet Union, in time of peace as well as in time of war, as stated in NSC 20/4 (para. 19), are still valid, as are the aims and measures stated therein (paras. 20 and 21). Our current security programs and strategic plans are based upon these objectives, aims, and measures:

"19.

"a. To reduce the power and influence of the U.S.S.R. to limits which no longer constitute a threat to the peace, national independence, and stability of the world family of nations.

"b. To bring about a basic change in the conduct of international relations by the government in power in Russia, to conform with the purposes and principles set forth in the UN Charter.

"In pursuing these objectives, due care must be taken to avoid permanently impairing our economy and the fundamental values and institutions inherent in our way of life.

"20. We should endeavor to achieve our general objectives by methods short of war through the pursuit of the following aims:

"a. To encourage and promote the gradual retraction of undue Russian power and influence from the present perimeter areas around traditional Russian boundaries and the emergence of the satellite countries as entities independent of the U.S.S.R.

"b. To encourage the development among the Russian peoples of attitudes which may help to modify current Soviet behavior and permit a revival of the national life of groups evidencing the ability and determination to achieve and maintain national independence.

"c. To eradicate the myth by which people remote from Soviet military influence are held in a position of subservience to Moscow and to cause the world at large to see and understand the true nature of the U.S.S.R. and the Soviet-directed world communist party, and to adopt a logical and realistic attitude toward them.

"d. To create situations which will compel the Soviet Government to recognize the practical undesirability of acting on the basis of its present concepts and the necessity of behaving in accordance with precepts of international conduct, as set forth in the purposes and principles of the UN Charter.

"21. Attainment of these aims requires that the United States:

"a. Develop a level of military readiness which can be maintained as long as necessary as a deterrent to Soviet aggression, as indispensable support to our political attitude toward the U.S.S.R., as a source of encouragement to nations resisting Soviet political aggression, and as an adequate basis for immediate military commitments and for rapid mobilization should war prove unavoidable.

"b. Assure the internal security of the United States against dangers of sabotage, subversion, and espionage.

"c. Maximize our economic potential, including the strengthening of our peacetime economy and the establishment of essential reserves readily available in the event of war.

"d. Strengthen the orientation toward the United States of the non-Soviet nations; and help such of those nations as are able and willing to make an important contribution to U.S. security, to increase their economic and political stability and their military capability.

"e. Place the maximum strain on the Soviet structure of power and particularly on the relationships between Moscow and the satellite countries.

"f. Keep the U.S. public fully informed and cognizant of the threats to our national security so that it will be prepared to support the measures which we must accordingly adopt."

In the light of present and prospective Soviet atomic capabilities, the action which can be taken under present programs and plans, however, becomes dangerously inadequate, in both timing and scope, to accomplish the rapid progress toward the attainment of the United States political, economic, and military objectives which is now imperative.

A continuation of present trends would result in a serious decline in the strength of the free world relative to the Soviet Union and its satellites. This unfavorable trend arises from the inadequacy of current programs and plans rather than from any error in our objectives and aims. These trends lead in the direction of isolation, not by deliberate decision but by lack of the necessary basis for a vigorous initiative in the conflict with the Soviet Union.

Our position as the center of power in the free world places a heavy responsibility upon the United States for leadership. We must organize and enlist the energies and resources of the free world in a positive program for peace which will frustrate the Kremlin design for world domination by creating a situation in the free world to which the Kremlin will be compelled to adjust. Without such a cooperative effort, led by the United States, we will have to make gradual withdrawals under pressure until we discover one day that we have sacrificed positions of vital interest.

It is imperative that this trend be reversed by a much more rapid and concerted build-up of the actual strength of both the United States and the other nations of the free world. The analysis shows that this will be costly and will involve significant domestic financial and economic adjustments.

The execution of such a build-up, however, requires that the United States have an affirmative program beyond the solely defensive one of countering the threat posed by the Soviet Union. This program must light the path to peace and order among nations in a system based on freedom and justice, as contemplated in the Charter of the United Nations. Further, it must envisage the political and economic measures with which and the military shield behind which the free world can work to frustrate the Kremlin design by the strategy of the cold war; for every consideration of devotion to our fundamental values and to our national security demands that we achieve our objectives by the strategy of the cold war, building up our military strength in order that it may not have to be used. The only sure victory lies in the frustration of the Kremlin design by the steady development of the moral and material strength of the free world and its projection into the Soviet world in such a way as to bring about an internal change in the Soviet system. Such a positive program—harmonious with our fundamental national purpose and our objectives—is necessary if we are to regain and retain the initiative and to win and hold the necessary popular support and cooperation in the United States and the rest of the free world.

This program should include a plan for negotiation with the Soviet Union, developed and agreed with our allies and which is consonant with our objectives. The United States and its allies, particularly the United Kingdom and France, should always be ready to negotiate with the Soviet Union on terms consistent with our objectives. The present world situation, however, is one which militates against successful negotiations with the Kremlin—for the terms of agreements on important pending issues would reflect present realities and would therefore be unacceptable, if not disastrous, to the United States and the rest of the free world. After a decision and a start on building up the strength of the free world has been made, it might then be desirable for the United States to take an initiative in seeking negotiations in the hope that it might facilitate the process of accommodation by the Kremlin to the new situation. Failing that, the unwillingness of the Kremlin to accept equitable terms or its bad faith in observing them would assist in consolidating popular opinion in the free world in support of the measures necessary to sustain the build-up.

In summary, we must, by means of a rapid and sustained build-up of the political, economic, and military strength of the free world, and by means of an affirmative program intended to wrest the initiative from the Soviet Union, confront it with convincing evidence of the determination and ability of the free world to frustrate the Kremlin design of a world dominated by its will. Such evidence is the only means short of war which eventually may force the Kremlin to abandon its present course of action and to negotiate acceptable agreements on issues of major importance.

The whole success of the proposed program hangs ultimately on recognition by this Government, the American people, and all free peoples, that the cold war is in fact a real war in which the survival of the free world is at stake. Essential prerequisites to success are consultations with Congressional leaders designed to make the program the object of non-partisan legislative support, and a presentation to the public of a full explanation of the facts and implications of the present international situation. The prosecution of the program will require of us all the ingenuity, sacrifice, and unity demanded by the vital importance of the issue and the tenacity to persevere until our national objectives have been attained.

Recommendations

That the President:

a. Approve the foregoing Conclusions.

b. Direct the National Security Council, under the continuing direction of the President, and with the participation of other Departments and Agencies as appropriate, to coordinate and insure the implementation of the Conclusions herein on an urgent and continuing basis for as long as necessary to achieve our objectives. For this purpose, representatives of the member Departments and Agencies, the Joint Chiefs of Staff or their deputies, and other Departments and Agencies as required should be constituted as a revised and strengthened staff organization under the National Security Council to develop coordinated programs for consideration by the National Security Council.

VANCE, HUMAN RIGHTS AND FOREIGN POLICY*

I speak today about the resolve of this Administration to make the advancement of human rights a central part of our foreign policy.

Many here today have long been advocates of human rights within our own society. And throughout our nation that struggle for civil rights continues.

In the early years of our civil rights movement, many Americans treated the issue as a "Southern" problem. They were wrong. It was and is a problem for all of us.

Now, as a nation, we must not make a comparable mistake. Protection of human rights is a challenge for *all* countries, not just for a few.

Our human rights policy must be understood in order to be effective. So today I want to set forth the substance of that policy and the results we hope to achieve.

Our concern for human rights is built upon ancient values. It looks with hope to a world in which liberty is not just a great cause, but the common condition. In the past, it may have seemed sufficient to put our name to international documents that spoke loftily of human rights. That is not enough. We will go to work, alongside other people and governments, to protect and enhance the dignity of the individual.

Let me define what we mean by "human rights."

First, there is the right to be free from governmental violation of the integrity of the person. Such violations include torture; cruel, inhuman, or degrading treatment or punishment; and arbitrary arrest or imprisonment. And they include denial of fair public trial and invasion of the home.

Second, there is the right to the fulfillment of such vital needs as food, shelter, health care, and education. We recognize that the fulfillment of this right will depend, in part, upon the stage of a nation's economic development. But we also know that this right can be violated by a government's action or inaction—for example, through corrupt official processes which divert resources to an elite at the expense of the needy of through indifference to the plight of the poor.

Third, there is the right to enjoy civil and political liberties: freedom of thought, of religion, of assembly; freedom of speech; freedom of press; freedom of movement both within and outside one's own country; freedom to take part in government.

Our policy is to promote all these rights. They are all recognized in the Universal Declaration of Human Rights, a basic document which the United States helped fashion and which the United Nations approved in 1948. There may be disagreement on the priorities these rights deserve. But I believe that, with work, all of these rights can become complementary and mutually reinforcing.

The philosophy of our human rights policy is revolutionary in the intellectual sense, reflecting our nation's origin and progressive values. As Archibald MacLeish wrote during our Bicentennial a year ago: "...the cause of human liberty is now the one great revolutionary cause...."

* Cyrus R. Vance, Secretary of State, Address at the Law Day Ceremonies at the University of Georgia School of Law (April 30, 1977), *in* 76 DEP'T ST. BULL. 505–08 (1977).

President Carter put it this way in his speech before the United Nations:

> All the signatories of the United Nations Charter have pledged themselves to observe and to respect basic human rights. Thus, no member of the United Nations can claim that mistreatment of its citizens is solely its own business. Equally, no member can avoid its responsibilities to review and to speak when torture or unwarranted deprivation occurs in any part of the world.

Since 1945, international practice has confirmed that a nation's obligation to respect human rights is a matter of concern in international law.

Our obligation under the United Nations Charter is written into our own legislation. For example, our Foreign Assistance Act now reads: "...a principal goal of the foreign policy of the United States is to promote the increased observance of internationally recognized human rights by all countries."

In these ways, our policy is in keeping with our tradition, our international obligations, and our laws.

In pursuing a human rights policy, we must always keep in mind the limits of our power and of our wisdom. A sure formula for defeat of our goals would be a rigid, hubristic attempt to impose our values on others. A doctrinaire plan of action would be as damaging as indifference.

We must be realistic. Our country can only achieve our objectives if we shape what we do to the case at hand. In each instance, we will consider these questions as we determine whether and how to act:

1. First, we will ask ourselves, what is the nature of the case that confronts us? For example:

What kinds of violations or deprivations are there? What is their extent?

Is there a pattern to the violations? If so, is the trend toward concern for human rights or away from it?

What is the degree of control and responsibility of the government involved?

And finally, is the government willing to permit independent outside investigation?

2. A second set of questions concerns the prospects for effective action:

Will our action be useful in promoting the overall cause of human rights?

Will it actually improve the specific conditions at hand? Or will it be likely to make things worse instead?

Is the country involved receptive to our interest and efforts?

Will others work with us, including official and private international organizations dedicated to furthering human rights?

Finally, does our sense of values and decency demand that we speak out or take action anyway, even though there is only a remote chance of making our influence felt?

3. We will ask a third set of questions in order to maintain a sense of perspective:

Have we steered away from the self-righteous and strident, remembering that our own record is not unblemished?

Have we been sensitive to genuine security interests, realizing that outbreak of armed conflict or terrorism could in itself pose a serious threat to human rights?

> Have we considered *all* the rights at stake? If, for instance, we reduce aid to a government which violates the political rights of its citizens, do we not risk penalizing the hungry and poor, who bear no responsibility for the abuses of their government?

If we are determined to act, the means available range from quiet diplomacy in its many forms, through public pronouncements, to withholding of assistance. Whenever possible, we will use positive steps of encouragement and inducement. Our strong support will go to countries that are working to improve the human condition. We will always try to act in concert with other countries, through international bodies.

In the end, a decision whether and how to act in the cause of human rights is a matter for informed and careful judgment. No mechanistic formula produces an automatic answer.

It is not our purpose to intervene in the internal affairs of other countries, but as the President has emphasized, no member of the United Nations can claim that violation of internationally protected human rights is solely its own affair. It is our purpose to shape our policies in accord with our beliefs and to state them without stridency or apology when we think it is desirable to do so.

Our policy is to be applied within our own society as well as abroad. We welcome constructive criticism at the same time as we offer it.

No one should suppose that we are working in a vacuum. We place great weight on joining with others in the cause of human rights.

The U.N. system is central to this cooperative endeavor. That is why the President stressed the pursuit of human rights in his speech before the General Assembly last month. That is why he is calling for U.S. ratification of four important human rights covenants and conventions and why we are trying to strengthen the human rights machinery within the United Nations.

....

The United States is seeking increased consultation with other nations for joint programs on economic assistance and more general efforts to promote human rights. We are working to assure that our efforts reach out to all, with particular sensitivity to the problems of women.

....

The United States looks to use of economic assistance—whether bilateral or through international financial institutions—as a means to foster basic human rights.

> —We have proposed a 20 percent increase in U.S. foreign economic assistance for fiscal year 1978.
>
> —We are expanding the program of the Agency for International Development for "New Initiatives in Human Rights" as a complement to present efforts to get the benefits of our aid to those most in need abroad.
>
> —The programs of the United States Information Agency and the State Department's Bureau of Educational and Cultural Affairs stress support for law in society, a free press, freedom of communication, an open educational system, and respect for ethnic diversity.

This Administration's human rights policy has been framed in collaboration and consultation with Congress and private organizations. We have taken steps to assure firsthand contact, consultation, and observation when Members of Congress travel abroad to review human rights conditions.

We are implementing current laws that bring human rights considerations directly into our decisions in several international financial institutions. At the same time, we are working with the Congress to find the most effective way to fulfill our parallel commitment to international cooperation in economic development.

In accordance with human rights provisions of legislation governing our security assistance programs, we recently announced cuts in military aid to several countries.

. . . .

All these initiatives to further human rights abroad would have a hollow ring if we were not prepared to improve our own performance at home. So we have removed all restrictions on our citizens' travel abroad and are proceeding with plans to liberalize our visa policies.

We support legislation and administrative action to expand our refugee and asylum policies and to permit more victims of repressive regimes to enter the United States. During this last year, the United States spent some $475 million on assistance to refugees around the world, and we accepted 31,000 refugees for permanent resettlement in this country.

What results can we expect from all these efforts?

We may justifiably seek a rapid end to such gross violations as those cited in our law: "torture or cruel, inhuman, or degrading treatment or punishment, (or) prolonged detention without charges...." Just last week our Ambassador at the United Nations, Andrew Young, suggested a series of new ways to confront the practice of torture around the world.

The promotion of other human rights is a broader challenge. The results may be slower in coming but are no less worth pursuing. And we intend to let other countries know where we stand.

We recognize that many nations of the world are organized on authoritarian rather than democratic principles—some large and powerful, others struggling to raise the lives of their people above bare subsistence levels. We can nourish no illusions that a call to the banner of human rights will bring sudden transformations in authoritarian societies.

We are embarked on a long journey. But our faith in the dignity of the individual encourages us to believe that people in every society, according to their own traditions, will in time give their own expression to this fundamental aspiration.

Our belief is strengthened by the way the Helsinki principles and the U.N. Declaration of Human Rights have found resonance in the hearts of people of many countries. Our task is to sustain this faith by our example and our encouragement.

In his inaugural address three months ago, President Carter said, "Because we are free we can never be indifferent to the fate of freedom elsewhere." Again, at a meeting of the Organization of American States two weeks ago, he said, "You will find this country...eager to stand beside those nations which respect human rights and which promote democratic ideals."

We seek these goals because they are right—and because we, too, will benefit. Our own well-being, and even our security, are enhanced in a world that shares common freedoms and in which prosperity and economic justice create the conditions for peace. And let us remember that we always risk paying a serious price when we become identified with repression.

REAGAN, ADDRESS TO MEMBERS OF THE BRITISH PARLIAMENT*

My Lord Chancellor, Mr. Speaker:

. . . .

In an ironic sense Karl Marx was right. We are witnessing today a great revolutionary crisis, a crisis where the demands of the economic order are conflicting directly with those of the political order. But the crisis is happening not in the free, non-Marxist West, but in the home of Marxist-Leninism, the Soviet Union. It is the Soviet Union that runs against the tide of history by denying human freedom and human dignity to its citizens. It also is in deep economic difficulty. The rate of growth in the national product has been steadily declining since the fifties and is less than half of what it was then.

The dimensions of this failure are astounding: A country which employs one-fifth of its population in agriculture is unable to feed its own people. Were it not for the private sector, the tiny private sector tolerated in Soviet agriculture, the country might be on the brink of famine. These private plots occupy a bare three percent of the arable land but account for nearly one-quarter of Soviet farm output and nearly one-third of meat products and vegetables. Overcentralized, with little or no incentives, year after year the Soviet system pours its best resource into the making of instruments of destruction. The constant shrinkage of economic growth combined with the growth of military production is putting a heavy strain on the Soviet people. What we see here is a political structure that no longer corresponds to its economic base, a society where productive forces are hampered by political ones.

The decay of the Soviet experiment should come as no surprise to us. Wherever the comparisons have been made between free and closed societies—West Germany and East Germany, Austria and Czechoslovakia, Malaysia and Vietnam—it is the democratic countries what are prosperous and responsive to the needs of their people. And one of the simple but overwhelming facts of our time is this: Of all the millions of refugees we've seen in the modern world, their flight is always away from, not toward the Communist world. Today on the NATO line, our military forces face east to prevent a possible invasion. On the other side of the line, the Soviet forces also face east to prevent their people from leaving.

The hard evidence of totalitarian rule has caused in mankind an uprising of the intellect and will. Whether it is the growth of the new schools of economics in America or England or the appearance of the so-called new philosophers in France, there is one unifying thread running through the intellectual work of these groups—rejection of the arbitrary power of the state, the refusal to subordinate the rights of the individual to the superstate, the realization that collectivism stifles all the best human impulses.

Since the exodus from Egypt, historians have written of those who sacrificed and struggled for freedom—the stand at Thermopylae, the revolt of Spartacus, the storming of the Bastille, the Warsaw uprising in World War II. More recently we've seen evi-

* Ronald Reagan, Address to Members of the British Parliament (June 8, 1982), *in* 1982 Public Papers of the Presidents of the United States, Ronald Reagan 742–48 (1983), *available at* http://millercenter.virginia.edu/scripps/diglibrary/prezspeeches/reagan/rwr_1982_0608.html.

dence of this same human impulse in one of the developing nations in Central America. For months and months the world news media covered the fighting in El Salvador. Day after day we were treated to stories and film slanted toward the brave freedom-fighters battling oppressive government forces in behalf of the silent, suffering people of that tortured country.

And then one day those silent, suffering people were offered a chance to vote, to choose the kind of government they wanted. Suddenly the freedom-fighters in the hills were exposed for what they really are—Cuban-backed guerrillas who want power for themselves, and their backers, not democracy for the people. They threatened death to any who voted, and destroyed hundreds of buses and trucks to keep the people from getting to the polling places. But on election day, the people of El Salvador, an unprecedented 1.4 million of them, braved ambush and gunfire, and trudged for miles to vote for freedom.

They stood for hours in the hot sun waiting for their turn to vote. Members of our Congress who went there as observers told me of a woman who was wounded by rifle fire on the way to the polls, who refused to leave the line to have her wound treated until after she had voted. A grandmother, who had been told by the guerrillas she would be killed when she returned from the polls, and she told the guerrillas, "You can kill me, you can kill my family, kill my neighbors, but you can't kill us all.'" The real freedom-fighters of El Salvador turned out to be the people of that country—the young, the old, the in-between.

....

The objective I propose is quite simple to state: to foster the infrastructure of democracy, the system of a free press, unions, political parties, universities, which allows a people to choose their own way to develop their own culture, to reconcile their own differences through peaceful means.

This is not cultural imperialism, it is providing the means for genuine self-determination and protection for diversity. Democracy already flourishes in countries with very different cultures and historical experiences. It would be cultural condescension, or worse, to say that any people prefer dictatorship to democracy. Who would voluntarily choose not to have the right to vote, decide to purchase government propaganda handouts instead of independent newspapers, prefer government to worker-controlled unions, opt for land to be owned by the state instead of those who till it, want government repression of religious liberty, a single political party instead of a free choice, a rigid cultural orthodoxy instead of democratic tolerance and diversity?

Since 1917 the Soviet Union has given covert political training and assistance to Marxist-Leninists in many countries. Of course, it also has promoted the use of violence and subversion by these same forces. Over the past several decades, West European and other Social Democrats, Christian Democrats, and leaders have offered open assistance to fraternal, political, and social institutions to bring about peaceful and democratic progress. Appropriately, for a vigorous new democracy, the Federal Republic of Germany's political foundations have become a major force in this effort.

We in America now intend to take additional steps, as many of our allies have already done, toward realizing this same goal. The chairmen and other leaders of the national Republican and Democratic Party organizations are initiating a study with the bipartisan American political foundation to determine how the United States can best contribute as a nation to the global campaign for democracy now gathering force. They will have the cooperation of congressional leaders of both parties, along with representatives of business, labor, and other major institutions in our society. I look forward to receiving their recommendations and to working with these institutions and the Congress in the common task of strengthening democracy throughout the world.

It is time that we committed ourselves as a nation—in both the public and private sectors—to assisting democratic development.

We plan to consult with leaders of other nations as well. There is a proposal before the Council of Europe to invite parliamentarians from democratic countries to a meeting next year in Strasbourg. That prestigious gathering could consider ways to help democratic political movements.

This November in Washington there will take place an international meeting on free elections. And next spring there will be a conference of world authorities on constitutionalism and self-government hosted by the Chief Justice of the United States. Authorities from a number of developing and developed countries—judges, philosophers, and politicians with practical experience—have agreed to explore how to turn principle into practice and further the rule of law.

At the same time, we invite the Soviet Union to consider with us how the competition of ideas and values—which it is committed to support—can be conducted on a peaceful and reciprocal basis. For example, I am prepared to offer President Brezhnev an opportunity to speak to the American people on our television if he will allow me the same opportunity with the Soviet people. We also suggest that panels of our newsmen periodically appear on each other's television to discuss major events.

Now, I don't wish to sound overly optimistic, yet the Soviet Union is not immune from the reality of what is going on in the world. It has happened in the past—a small ruling elite either mistakenly attempts to ease domestic unrest through greater repression and foreign adventure, or it chooses a wiser course. It begins to allow its people a voice in their own destiny. Even if this latter process is not realized soon, I believe the renewed strength of the democratic movement, complemented by a global campaign for freedom, will strengthen the prospects for arms control and a world at peace.

I have discussed on other occasions, including my address on May 9th, the elements of Western policies toward the Soviet Union to safeguard our interests and protect the peace. What I am describing now is a plan and a hope for the long term—the march of freedom and democracy which will leave Marxism-Leninism on the ash-heap of history as it has left other tyrannies which stifle the freedom and muzzle the self-expression of the people. And that's why we must continue our efforts to strengthen NATO even as we move forward with our Zero-Option initiative in the negotiations on intermediate-range forces and our proposal for a one-third reduction in strategic ballistic missile warheads.

Our military strength is a prerequisite to peace, but let it be clear we maintain this strength in the hope it will never be used, for the ultimate determinant in the struggle that's now going on in the world will not be bombs and rockets, but a test of wills and ideas, a trial of spiritual resolve, the values we hold, the beliefs we cherish, the ideals to which we are dedicated.

....

[T]he task I've set forth will long outlive our own generation. But together, we too have come through the worst. Let us now begin a major effort to secure the best—a crusade for freedom that will engage the faith and fortitude of the next generation. For the sake of peace and justice, let us move toward a world in which all people are at last free to determine their own destiny.

Thank you.

Part II

The International Law of Conflict Management: Institutional Modes of Conflict Management

A. Global International Organizations

WILSON, "FOURTEEN POINTS" SPEECH*

....

We entered this war because violations of right had occurred which touched us to the quick and made the life of our own people impossible unless they were corrected and the world secured once for all against their recurrence. What we demand in this war, therefore, is nothing peculiar to ourselves. It is that the world be made fit and safe to live in; and particularly that it be made safe for every peace-loving nation which, like our own, wishes to live its own life, determine its own institutions, be assured of justice and fair dealing by the other peoples of the world as against force and selfish aggression. All the peoples of the world are in effect partners in this interest, and for our own part we see very clearly that unless justice be done to others it will not be done to us.

The program of the world's peace, therefore, is our program; and that program, the only possible program, as we see it, is this:

I. Open covenants of peace, openly arrived at, after which there shall be no private international understandings of any kind but diplomacy shall proceed always frankly and in the public view.

II. Absolute freedom of navigation upon the seas, outside territorial waters, alike in peace and in war, except as the seas may be closed in whole or in part by international action for the enforcement of international covenants.

III. The removal, so far as possible, of all economic barriers and the establishment of an equality of trade conditions among all the nations consenting to the peace and associating themselves for its maintenance.

IV. Adequate guarantees given and taken that national armaments will be reduced to the lowest point consistent with domestic safety.

V. A free, open-minded, and absolutely impartial adjustment of all colonial claims, based upon a strict observance of the principle that in determining all such questions of sovereignty the interests of the populations concerned must have equal weight with the equitable claims of the government whose title is to be determined.

VI. The evacuation of all Russian territory and such a settlement of all questions affecting Russia as will secure the best and freest cooperation of the other nations of the world in obtaining for her an unhampered and unembarrassed opportunity for the independent determination of her own political development and national policy and assure her of a sincere welcome into the society of free nations under institutions of her own choosing; and, more than a welcome, assistance also of every kind that she may need and may herself desire. The treatment accorded Russia by her sister nations in the months to come will be the acid test of their good will, of their comprehension of her needs as distinguished from their own interests, and of their intelligent and unselfish sympathy.

---

* Woodrow Wilson, Address to Congress on War Aims and Peace Terms (Jan. 8, 1918), *in* 18 A Compilation of the Messages and Papers of the Presidents 8421 (James D. Richardson ed., n.d.), *available at* http://www.yale.edu/lawweb/avalon/wilson14.htm.

VII. Belgium, the whole world will agree, must be evacuated and restored, without any attempt to limit the sovereignty which she enjoys in common with all other free nations. No other single act will serve as this will serve to restore confidence among the nations in the laws which they have themselves set and determined for the government of their relations with one another. Without this healing act the whole structure and validity of international law is forever impaired.

VIII. All French territory should be freed and the invaded portions restored, and the wrong done to France by Prussia in 1871 in the matter of Alsace-Lorraine, which has unsettled the peace of the world for nearly fifty years, should be righted, in order that peace may once more be made secure in the interest of all.

IX. A readjustment of the frontiers of Italy should be effected along clearly recognizable lines of nationality.

X. The peoples of Austria-Hungary, whose place among the nations we wish to see safeguarded and assured, should be accorded the freest opportunity of autonomous development.

XI. Rumania, Serbia, and Montenegro should be evacuated; occupied territories restored; Serbia accorded free and secure access to the sea; and the relations of the several Balkan states to one another determined by friendly counsel along historically established lines of allegiance and nationality; and international guarantees of the political and economic independence and territorial integrity of the several Balkan states should be entered into.

XII. The Turkish portions of the present Ottoman Empire should be assured a secure sovereignty, but the other nationalities which are now under Turkish rule should be assured an undoubted security of life and an absolutely unmolested opportunity of an autonomous development, and the Dardanelles should be permanently opened as a free passage to the ships and commerce of all nations under international guarantees.

XIII. An independent Polish state should be erected which should include the territories inhabited by indisputably Polish populations, which should be assured a free and secure access to the sea, and whose political and economic independence and territorial integrity should be guaranteed by international covenant.

XIV. A general association of nations must be formed under specific covenants for the purpose of affording mutual guarantees of political independence and territorial integrity to great and small states alike.

....

TREATY OF VERSAILLES*

Versailles, June 28, 1919

. . . .

Part I

THE COVENANT OF THE LEAGUE OF NATIONS.

THE HIGH CONTRACTING PARTIES,

In order to promote international co-operation and to achieve international peace and security by the acceptance of obligations not to resort to war, by the prescription of open, just and honourable relations between nations, by the firm establishment of the understandings of international law as the actual rule of conduct among Governments, and by the maintenance of justice and a scrupulous respect for all treaty obligations in the dealings of organised peoples with one another,

Agree to this Covenant of the League of Nations.

Article 1. The original Members of the League of Nations shall be those of the Signatories which are named in the Annex to this Covenant and also such of those other States named in the Annex as shall accede without reservation to this Covenant. Such accession shall be effected by a Declaration deposited with the Secretariat within two months of the coming into force of the Covenant Notice thereof shall be sent to all other Members of the League.

Any fully self-governing State, Dominion, or Colony not named in the Annex may become a Member of the League if its admission is agreed to by two-thirds of the Assembly provided that it shall give effective guarantees of its sincere intention to observe its international obligations, and shall accept such regulations as may be prescribed by the League in regard to its military, naval, and air forces and armaments. . . .

Article 2. The action of the League under this Covenant shall be effected through the instrumentality of an Assembly and of a Council, with a permanent Secretariat.

Article 3. The Assembly shall consist of Representatives of the Members of the League.

The Assembly shall meet at stated intervals and from time to time as occasion may require at the Seat of the League or at such other place as may be decided upon.

The Assembly may deal at its meetings with any matter within the sphere of action of the League or affecting the peace of the world.

At meetings of the Assembly each Member of the League shall have one vote, and may not have more than three Representatives.

Article 4. The Council shall consist of Representatives of the Principal Allied and Associated Powers, together with Representatives of four other Members of the League.

---

* Treaty of Peace Between the British Empire, France, Italy, Japan and the United States (the Principal Allied and Associated Powers), and Belgium, Bolivia, Brazil, China, Cuba, Czechoslovakia, Ecuador, Greece, Guatemala, Haiti, the Hedjaz, Honduras, Liberia, Nicaragua, Panama, Peru, Poland, Portugal, Roumania, the Serb-Croat-Slovene State, Siam, and Uruguay, and Germany pt. 1, June 28, 1919, 225 Consol. T.S. 188, 195, 2 Bevans 43, 48 (entered into force Jan. 10, 1920) [hereinafter Treaty of Versailles], *available at* 225 CTS 195; 13 AJIL Supp. 128, 361 (entered into force 10 January 1920). Also available online at <http://www.yale.edu/lawweb/avalon/imt/parti.htm>.

These four Members of the League shall be selected by the Assembly from time to time in its discretion. Until the appointment of the Representatives of the four Members of the League first selected by the Assembly, Representatives of Belgium, Brazil, Spain, and Greece shall be members of the Council.

....

The Council may deal at its meetings with any matter within the sphere of action of the League or affecting the peace of the world.

Any Member of the League not represented on the Council shall be invited to send a Representative to sit as a member at any meeting of the Council during the consideration of matters specially affecting the interests of that Member of the League.

At meetings of the Council, each Member of the League represented on the Council shall have one vote, and may have not more than one Representative.

....

Article 8. The Members of the League recognise that the maintenance of peace requires the reduction of national armaments to the lowest point consistent with national safety and the enforcement by common action of international obligations.

The Council, taking account of the geographical situation and circumstances of each State, shall formulate plans for such reduction for the consideration and action of the several Governments.

Such plans shall be subject to reconsideration and revision at least every ten years.

After these plans shall have been adopted by the several Governments, the limits of armaments therein fixed shall not be exceeded without the concurrence of the Council.

The Members of the League agree that the manufacture by private enterprise of munitions and implements of war is open to grave objections. The Council shall advise how the evil effects attendant upon such manufacture can be prevented, due regard being had to the necessities of those Members of the League which are not able to manufacture the munitions and implements of war necessary for their safety.

The Members of the League undertake to interchange full and frank information as to the scale of their armaments, their military, naval, and air programmes and the condition of such of their industries as are adaptable to war-like purposes.

....

Article 10. The Members of the League undertake to respect and preserve as against external aggression the territorial integrity and existing political independence of all Members of the League. In case of any such aggression or in case of any threat or danger of such aggression the Council shall advise upon the means by which this obligation shall be fulfilled.

Article 11. Any war or threat of war, whether immediately affecting any of the Members of the League or not, is hereby declared a matter of concern to the whole League, and the League shall take any action that may be deemed wise and effectual to safeguard the peace of nations. In case any such emergency should arise the Secretary General shall on the request of any Member of the League forthwith summon a meeting of the Council.

It is also declared to be the friendly right of each Member of the League to bring to the attention of the Assembly or of the Council any circumstance whatever affecting international relations which threatens to disturb international peace or the good understanding between nations upon which peace depends.

Article 12. The Members of the League agree that if there should arise between them any dispute likely to lead to a rupture, they will submit the matter either to arbitration or to inquiry by the Council, and they agree in no case to resort to war until three months after the award by the arbitrators or the report by the Council.

In any case under this Article the award of the arbitrators shall be made within a reasonable time, and the report of the Council shall be made within six months after the submission of the dispute.

Article 13. The Members of the League agree that whenever any dispute shall arise between them which they recognise to be suitable for submission to arbitration and which cannot be satisfactorily settled by diplomacy, they will submit the whole subject-matter to arbitration.

Disputes as to the interpretation of a treaty, as to any question of international law, as to the existence of any fact which if established would constitute a breach of any international obligation, or as to the extent and nature of the reparation to be made or any such breach, are declared to be among those which are generally suitable for submission to arbitration.

For the consideration of any such dispute the court of arbitration to which the case is referred shall be the Court agreed on by the parties to the dispute or stipulated in any convention existing between them.

The Members of the League agree that they will carry out in full good faith any award that may be rendered, and that they will not resort to war against a Member of the League which complies therewith. In the event of any failure to carry out such an award, the Council shall propose what steps should be taken to give effect thereto.

Article 14. The Council shall formulate and submit to the Members of the League for adoption plans for the establishment of a Permanent Court of International Justice. The Court shall be competent to hear and determine any dispute of an international character which the parties thereto submit to it. The Court may also give an advisory opinion upon any dispute or question referred to it by the Council or by the Assembly.

Article 15. If there should arise between Members of the League any dispute likely to lead to a rupture, which is not submitted to arbitration in accordance with Article 13, the Members of the League agree that they will submit the matter to the Council. Any party to the dispute may effect such submission by giving notice of the existence of the dispute to the Secretary General, who will make all necessary arrangements for a full investigation and consideration thereof.

For this purpose the parties to the dispute will communicate to the Secretary General, as promptly as possible, statements of their case with all the relevant facts and papers, and the Council may forthwith direct the publication thereof.

The Council shall endeavour to effect a settlement of the dispute, and if such efforts are successful, a statement shall be made public giving such facts and explanations regarding the dispute and the terms of settlement thereof as the Council may deem appropriate.

If the dispute is not thus settled, the Council either unanimously or by a majority vote shall make and publish a report containing a statement of the facts of the dispute and the recommendations which are deemed just and proper in regard thereto.

Any Member of the League represented on the Council may make public a statement of the facts of the dispute and of its conclusions regarding the same.

If a report by the Council is unanimously agreed to by the members thereof other than the Representatives of one or more of the parties to the dispute, the Members of the League agree that they will not go to war with any party to the dispute which complies with the recommendations of the report.

If the Council fails to reach a report which is unanimously agreed to by the members thereof, other than the Representatives of one or more of the parties to the dispute, the Members of the League reserve to themselves the right to take such action as they shall consider necessary for the maintenance of right and justice.

If the dispute between the parties is claimed by one of them, and is found by the Council, to arise out of a matter which by international law is solely within the domestic jurisdiction of that party, the Council shall so report, and shall make no recommendation as to its settlement.

The Council may in any case under this Article refer the dispute to the Assembly. The dispute shall be so referred at the request of either party to the dispute, provided that such request be made within fourteen days after the submission of the dispute to the Council.

In any case referred to the Assembly, all the provisions of this Article and of Article 12 relating to the action and powers of the Council shall apply to the action and powers of the Assembly, provided that a report made by the Assembly, if concurred in by the Representatives of those Members of the League represented on the Council and of a majority of the other Members of the League, exclusive in each case of the Representatives of the parties to the dispute shall have the same force as a report by the Council concurred in by all the members thereof other than the Representatives of one or more of the parties to the dispute.

Article 16. Should any Member of the League resort to war in disregard of its covenants under Articles 12, 13, or 15, it shall *ipso facto* be deemed to have committed an act of war against all other Members of the League, which hereby undertake immediately to subject it to the severance of all trade or financial relations, the prohibition of all intercourse between their nations and the nationals of the covenant-breaking State, and the prevention of all financial, commercial, or personal intercourse between the nationals of the covenant-breaking State and the nationals of any other State, whether a Member of the League or not.

It shall be the duty of the Council in such case to recommend to the several Governments concerned what effective military, naval, or air force the Members of the League shall severally contribute to the armed forces to be used to protect the covenants of the League.

The Members of the League agree, further, that they will mutually support one another in the financial and economic measures which are taken under this Article, in order to minimise the loss and inconvenience resulting from the above measures, and that they will mutually support one another in resisting any special measures aimed at one of their number by the covenant-breaking State, and that they will take the necessary steps to afford passage through their territory to the forces of any of the Members of the League which are co-operating to protect the covenants of the League.

Any Member of the League which has violated any covenant of the League may be declared to be no longer a Member of the League by a vote of the Council concurred in by the Representatives of all the other Members of the League represented thereon.

Article 17. In the event of a dispute between a Member of the League and a State which is not a Member of the League, or between States not Members of the League, the State or States, not Members of the League shall be invited to accept the obligations of membership in the League for the purposes of such dispute, upon such conditions as the Council may deem just. If such invitation is accepted, the provisions of Articles 12 to 16 inclusive shall be applied with such modifications as may be deemed necessary by the Council.

Upon such invitation being given the Council shall immediately institute an inquiry into the circumstances of the dispute and recommend such action as may seem best and most effectual in the circumstances.

If a State so invited shall refuse to accept the obligations of membership in the League for the purposes of such dispute, and shall resort to war against a Member of the League, the provisions of Article 16 shall be applicable as against the State taking such action.

If both parties to the dispute when so invited refuse to accept the obligations of membership in the League for the purpose of such dispute, the Council may take such measures and make such recommendations as will prevent hostilities and will result in the settlement of the dispute.

....

Article 21. Nothing in this Covenant shall be deemed to affect the validity of international engagements, such as treaties of arbitration or regional understandings like the Monroe doctrine, for securing the maintenance of peace.

....

Article 23. Subject to and in accordance with the provisions of international conventions existing or hereafter to be agreed upon, the Members of the League:

a. will endeavour to secure and maintain fair and humane conditions of labour for men, women, and children, both in their own countries and in all countries to which their commercial and industrial relations extend, and for that purpose will establish and maintain the necessary international organisations;

b. undertake to secure just treatment of the native inhabitants of territories under their control;

c. will entrust the League with the general supervision over the execution of agreements with regard to the traffic in women and children, and the traffic in opium and other dangerous drugs;

d. will entrust the League with the general supervision of the trade in arms and ammunition with the countries in which the control of this traffic is necessary in the common interest;

e. will make provision to secure and maintain freedom of communications and of transit and equitable treatment for the commerce of all Members of the League. In this connection, the special necessities of the regions devastated during the war of 1914–1918 shall be borne in mind;

f. will endeavour to take steps in matters of international concern for the prevention and control of disease.

....

ANNEX.

I. ORIGINAL MEMBERS OF THE LEAGUE OF NATIONS SIGNATORIES OF THE TREATY OF PEACE.

UNITED STATES OF AMERICA	HAITI
BELGIUM	HEDJAZ
BOLIVIA	HONDURAS
BRAZIL	ITALY
BRITISH EMPIRE	JAPAN
CANADA	LIBERIA
AUSTRALIA	NICARAGUA
SOUTH AFRICA	PANAMA
NEW ZEALAND	PERU
INDIA	POLAND
CHINA	PORTUGAL
CUBA	ROUMANIA
ECUADOR	SERB-CROAT-SLOVENE STATE
FRANCE	SIAM
FRANCE GREECE	CZECHO-SLOVAKIA
GUATEMALA	URUGUAY

CHARTER OF THE UNITED NATIONS[1]

WE, THE PEOPLES OF THE UNITED NATIONS,

DETERMINED

to save succeeding generations from the scourge of war, which twice in our lifetime has brought untold sorrow to mankind, and

to reaffirm faith in fundamental human rights, in the dignity and worth of the human person, in the equal rights of men and women and of nations large and small, and

to establish conditions under which justice and respect for the obligations arising from treaties and other sources of international law can be maintained, and

to promote social progress and better standards of life in larger freedom,

AND FOR THESE ENDS

to practice tolerance and live together in peace with one another as good neighbours, and

to unite our strength to maintain international peace and security, and

to ensure, by the acceptance of principles and the institution of methods, that armed force shall not be used, save in the common interest, and

to employ international machinery for the promotion of the economic and social advancement of all peoples,

HAVE RESOLVED TO COMBINE OUR EFFORTS TO ACCOMPLISH THESE AIMS.

Accordingly, our respective Governments, through representatives assembled in the city of San Francisco, who have exhibited their full powers found to be in good and due form, have agreed to the present Charter of the United Nations and do hereby establish an international organization to be known as the United Nations.

CHAPTER I
PURPOSES AND PRINCIPLES

Article 1. The Purposes of the United Nations are:

1. To maintain international peace and security, and to that end: to take effective collective measures for the prevention and removal of threats to the peace, and for the suppression of acts of aggression or other breaches of the peace, and to bring about by peaceful means, and in conformity with the principles of justice and international law, adjustment or settlement of international disputes or situations which might lead to a breach of the peace;

2. To develop friendly relations among nations based on respect for the principle of equal rights and self-determination of peoples, and to take other appropriate measures to strengthen universal peace;

3. To achieve international co-operation in solving international problems of an economic, social, cultural, or humanitarian character, and in promoting and encouraging

1. Charter of the United Nations, June 26, 1945, 59 Stat. 1031, 3 Bevans 1153 (entered into force Oct. 24, 1945), *available at* http://www.un.org/aboutun/charter/.

respect for human rights and for fundamental freedoms for all without distinction as to race, sex, language, or religion; and

4. To be a centre for harmonizing the actions of nations in the attainment of these common ends.

Article 2. The Organization and its Members, in pursuit of the Purposes stated in Article 1, shall act in accordance with the following Principles.:

1. The Organization is based on the principle of the sovereign equality of all its Members.

2. All Members, in order to ensure to all of them the rights and benefits resulting from membership, shall fulfill in good faith the obligations assumed by them in accordance with the present Charter.

3. All Members shall settle their international disputes by peaceful means in such a manner that international peace and security, and justice, are not endangered.

4. All Members shall refrain in their international relations from the threat or use of force against the territorial integrity or political independence of any state, or in any other manner inconsistent with the Purposes of the United Nations.

5. All Members shall give the United Nations every assistance in any action it takes in accordance with the present Charter, and shall refrain from giving assistance to any state against which the United Nations is taking preventive or enforcement action.

6. The Organization shall ensure that states which are not Members of the United Nations act in accordance with these Principles so far as may be necessary for the maintenance of international peace and security.

7. Nothing contained in the present Charter shall authorize the United Nations to intervene in matters which are essentially within the domestic jurisdiction of any state or shall require the Members to submit such matters to settlement under the present Charter; but this principle shall not prejudice the application of enforcement measures under Chapter VII.

CHAPTER II
MEMBERSHIP

Article 3. The original Members of the United Nations shall be the states which, having participated in the United Nations Conference on International Organization at San Francisco, or having previously signed the Declaration by United Nations of 1 January 1942, sign the present Charter and ratify it in accordance with Article 110.

Article 4. 1. Membership in the United Nations is open to all other peace-loving states which accept the obligations contained in the present Charter and, in the judgment of the Organization, are able and willing to carry out these obligations.

2. The admission of any such state to membership in the United Nations will be effected by a decision of the General Assembly upon the recommendation of the Security Council.

Article 5. A Member of the United Nations against which preventive or enforcement action has been taken by the Security Council may be suspended from the exercise of the rights and privileges of membership by the General Assembly upon the recommendation of the Security Council. The exercise of these rights and privileges may be restored by the Security Council.

Article 6. A Member of the United Nations which has persistently violated the Principles contained in the present Charter may be expelled from the Organization by the General Assembly upon the recommendation of the Security Council.

CHAPTER III
ORGANS

Article 7. 1. There are established as the principal organs of the United Nations:

- a General Assembly
- a Security Council
- an Economic and Social Council
- a Trusteeship Council
- an International Court of Justice
- and a Secretariat.

2. Such subsidiary organs as may be found necessary may be established in accordance with the present Charter.

Article 8. The United Nations shall place no restrictions on the eligibility of men and women to participate in any capacity and under conditions of equality in its principal and subsidiary organs.

CHAPTER IV
THE GENERAL ASSEMBLY

COMPOSITION

Article 9. 1. The General Assembly shall consist of all the Members of the United Nations.

2. Each Member shall have not more than five representatives in the General Assembly.

FUNCTIONS and POWERS

Article 10. The General Assembly may discuss any questions or any matters within the scope of the present Charter or relating to the powers and functions of any organs provided for in the present Charter, and, except as provided in Article 12, may make recommendations to the Members of the United Nations or to the Security Council or to both on any such questions or matters.

Article 11. The General Assembly may consider the general principles of co-operation in the maintenance of international peace and security, including the principles governing disarmament and the regulation of armaments, and may make recommendations with regard to such principles to the Members or to the Security Council or to both.

1. The General Assembly may discuss any questions relating to the maintenance of international peace and security brought before it by any Member of the United Nations, or by the Security Council, or by a state which is not a Member of the United Nations in accordance with Article 35, paragraph 2, and, except as provided in Article 12, may make recommendations with regard to any such questions to the state or states concerned or to the Security Council or to both. Any such question on which action is necessary shall be referred to the Security Council by the General Assembly either before or after discussion.

2. The General Assembly may call the attention of the Security Council to situations which are likely to endanger international peace and security.

3. The powers of the General Assembly set forth in this Article shall not limit the general scope of Article 10.

Article 12. 1. While the Security Council is exercising in respect of any dispute or situation the functions assigned to it in the present Charter, the General Assembly shall not make any recommendation with regard to that dispute or situation unless the Security Council so requests.

2. The Secretary-General, with the consent of the Security Council, shall notify the General Assembly at each session of any matters relative to the maintenance of international peace and security which are being dealt with by the Security Council and shall similarly notify the General Assembly, or the Members of the United Nations if the General Assembly is not in session, immediately the Security Council ceases to deal with such matters.

Article 13. 1. The General Assembly shall initiate studies and make recommendations for the purpose of:

a. promoting international co-operation in the political field and encouraging the progressive development of international law and its codification;

b. promoting international co-operation in the economic, social, cultural, educational, and health fields, and assisting in the realization of human rights and fundamental freedoms for all without distinction as to race, sex, language, or religion.

1. The further responsibilities, functions and powers of the General Assembly with respect to matters mentioned in paragraph 1 (b) above are set forth in Chapters IX and X.

Article 14. Subject to the provisions of Article 12, the General Assembly may recommend measures for the peaceful adjustment of any situation, regardless of origin, which it deems likely to impair the general welfare or friendly relations among nations, including situations resulting from a violation of the provisions of the present Charter setting forth the Purposes and Principles of the United Nations.

....

VOTING

Article 18. 1. Each member of the General Assembly shall have one vote.

2. Decisions of the General Assembly on important questions shall be made by a two-thirds majority of the members present and voting. These questions shall include: recommendations with respect to the maintenance of international peace and security, the election of the non-permanent members of the Security Council, the election of the members of the Economic and Social Council, the election of members of the Trusteeship Council in accordance with paragraph 1 (c) of Article 86, the admission of new Members to the United Nations, the suspension of the rights and privileges of membership, the expulsion of Members, questions relating to the operation of the trusteeship system, and budgetary questions.

3. Decisions on other questions, including the determination of additional categories of questions to be decided by a two-thirds majority, shall be made by a majority of the members present and voting.

....

CHAPTER V
THE SECURITY COUNCIL

COMPOSITION

Article 23. 1. The Security Council shall consist of fifteen Members of the United Nations. The Republic of China, France, the Union of Soviet Socialist Republics, the United Kingdom of Great Britain and Northern Ireland, and the United States of America shall be permanent members of the Security Council. The General Assembly shall elect ten other Members of the United Nations to be non-permanent members of the Security Council, due regard being specially paid, in the first instance to the contribution of Members of the United Nations to the maintenance of international peace and security and to the other purposes of the Organization, and also to equitable geographical distribution.

2. The non-permanent members of the Security Council shall be elected for a term of two years. In the first election of the non-permanent members after the increase of the membership of the Security Council from eleven to fifteen, two of the four additional members shall be chosen for a term of one year. A retiring member shall not be eligible for immediate re-election.

3. Each member of the Security Council shall have one representative.

FUNCTIONS and POWERS

Article 24. 1. In order to ensure prompt and effective action by the United Nations, its Members confer on the Security Council primary responsibility for the maintenance of international peace and security, and agree that in carrying out its duties under this responsibility the Security Council acts on their behalf.

2. In discharging these duties the Security Council shall act in accordance with the Purposes and Principles of the United Nations. The specific powers granted to the Security Council for the discharge of these duties are laid down in Chapters VI, VII, VIII, and XII.

3. The Security Council shall submit annual and, when necessary, special reports to the General Assembly for its consideration.

Article 25. The Members of the United Nations agree to accept and carry out the decisions of the Security Council in accordance with the present Charter.

Article 26. In order to promote the establishment and maintenance of international peace and security with the least diversion for armaments of the world's human and economic resources, the Security Council shall be responsible for formulating, with the assistance of the Military Staff Committee referred to in Article 47, plans to be submitted to the Members of the United Nations for the establishment of a system for the regulation of armaments.

VOTING

Article 27. 1. Each member of the Security Council shall have one vote.

2. Decisions of the Security Council on procedural matters shall be made by an affirmative vote of nine members.

3. Decisions of the Security Council on all other matters shall be made by an affirmative vote of nine members including the concurring votes of the permanent members; provided that, in decisions under Chapter VI, and under paragraph 3 of Article 52, a party to a dispute shall abstain from voting.

PROCEDURE

Article 28. 1. The Security Council shall be so organized as to be able to function continuously. Each member of the Security Council shall for this purpose be represented at all times at the seat of the Organization.

2. The Security Council shall hold periodic meetings at which each of its members may, if it so desires, be represented by a member of the government or by some other specially designated representative.

3. The Security Council may hold meetings at such places other than the seat of the Organization as in its judgment will best facilitate its work.

Article 29. The Security Council may establish such subsidiary organs as it deems necessary for the performance of its functions.

Article 30. The Security Council shall adopt its own rules of procedure, including the method of selecting its President.

Article 31. Any Member of the United Nations which is not a member of the Security Council may participate, without vote, in the discussion of any question brought before the Security Council whenever the latter considers that the interests of that Member are specially affected.

Article 32. Any Member of the United Nations which is not a member of the Security Council or any state which is not a Member of the United Nations, if it is a party to a dispute under consideration by the Security Council, shall be invited to participate, without vote, in the discussion relating to the dispute. The Security Council shall lay down such conditions as it deems just for the participation of a state which is not a Member of the United Nations.

CHAPTER VI
PACIFIC SETTLEMENT OF DISPUTES

Article 33. 1. The parties to any dispute, the continuance of which is likely to endanger the maintenance of international peace and security, shall, first of all, seek a solution by negotiation, enquiry, mediation, conciliation, arbitration, judicial settlement, resort to regional agencies or arrangements, or other peaceful means of their own choice.

2. The Security Council shall, when it deems necessary, call upon the parties to settle their dispute by such means.

Article 34. The Security Council may investigate any dispute, or any situation which might lead to international friction or give rise to a dispute, in order to determine whether the continuance of the dispute or situation is likely to endanger the maintenance of international peace and security.

Article 35. 1. Any Member of the United Nations may bring any dispute, or any situation of the nature referred to in Article 34, to the attention of the Security Council or of the General Assembly.

2. A state which is not a Member of the United Nations may bring to the attention of the Security Council or of the General Assembly any dispute to which it is a party if it accepts in advance, for the purposes of the dispute, the obligations of pacific settlement provided in the present Charter.

3. The proceedings of the General Assembly in respect of matters brought to its attention under this Article will be subject to the provisions of Articles 11 and 12.

Article 36. 1. The Security Council may, at any stage of a dispute of the nature referred to in Article 33 or of a situation of like nature, recommend appropriate procedures or methods of adjustment.

2. The Security Council should take into consideration any procedures for the settlement of the dispute which have already been adopted by the parties.

3. In making recommendations under this Article the Security Council should also take into consideration that legal disputes should as a general rule be referred by the parties to the International Court of Justice in accordance with the provisions of the Statute of the Court.

Article 37. 1. Should the parties to a dispute of the nature referred to in Article 33 fail to settle it by the means indicated in that Article, they shall refer it to the Security Council.

2. If the Security Council deems that the continuance of the dispute is in fact likely to endanger the maintenance of international peace and security, it shall decide whether to take action under Article 36 or to recommend such terms of settlement as it may consider appropriate.

Article 38. Without prejudice to the provisions of Articles 33 to 37, the Security Council may, if all the parties to any dispute so request, make recommendations to the parties with a view to a pacific settlement of the dispute.

CHAPTER VII
ACTION WITH RESPECT TO THREATS TO THE PEACE, BREACHES OF THE PEACE, AND ACTS OF AGGRESSION

Article 39. The Security Council shall determine the existence of any threat to the peace, breach of the peace, or act of aggression and shall make recommendations, or decide what measures shall be taken in accordance with Articles 41 and 42, to maintain or restore international peace and security.

Article 40. In order to prevent an aggravation of the situation, the Security Council may, before making the recommendations or deciding upon the measures provided for in Article 39, call upon the parties concerned to comply with such provisional measures as it deems necessary or desirable. Such provisional measures shall be without prejudice to the rights, claims, or position of the parties concerned. The Security Council shall duly take account of failure to comply with such provisional measures.

Article 41. The Security Council may decide what measures not involving the use of armed force are to be employed to give effect to its decisions, and it may call upon the Members of the United Nations to apply such measures. These may include complete or partial interruption of economic relations and of rail, sea, air, postal, telegraphic, radio, and other means of communication, and the severance of diplomatic relations.

Article 42. Should the Security Council consider that measures provided for in Article 41 would be inadequate or have proved to be inadequate, it may take such action by air, sea, or land forces as may be necessary to maintain or restore international peace and security. Such action may include demonstrations, blockade, and other operations by air, sea, or land forces of Members of the United Nations.

Article 43. 1. All Members of the United Nations, in order to contribute to the maintenance of international peace and security, undertake to make available to the Security Council, on its call and in accordance with a special agreement or agreements, armed forces, assistance, and facilities, including rights of passage, necessary for the purpose of maintaining international peace and security.

2. Such agreement or agreements shall govern the numbers and types of forces, their degree of readiness and general location, and the nature of the facilities and assistance to be provided.

3. The agreement or agreements shall be negotiated as soon as possible on the initiative of the Security Council. They shall be concluded between the Security Council and Members or between the Security Council and groups of Members and shall be subject to ratification by the signatory states in accordance with their respective constitutional processes.

Article 44. When the Security Council has decided to use force it shall, before calling upon a Member not represented on it to provide armed forces in fulfillment of the obligations assumed under Article 43, invite that Member, if the Member so desires, to participate in the decisions of the Security Council concerning the employment of contingents of that Member's armed forces.

Article 45. In order to enable the United Nations to take urgent military measures, Members shall hold immediately available national air-force contingents for combined international enforcement action. The strength and degree of readiness of these contingents and plans for their combined action shall be determined within the limits laid down in the special agreement or agreements referred to in Article 43, by the Security Council with the assistance of the Military Staff Committee.

Article 46. Plans for the application of armed force shall be made by the Security Council with the assistance of the Military Staff Committee.

Article 47. 1. There shall be established a Military Staff Committee to advise and assist the Security Council on all questions relating to the Security Council's military requirements for the maintenance of international peace and security, the employment and command of forces placed at its disposal, the regulation of armaments, and possible disarmament.

2. The Military Staff Committee shall consist of the Chiefs of Staff of the permanent members of the Security Council or their representatives. Any Member of the United Nations not permanently represented on the Committee shall be invited by the Committee to be associated with it when the efficient discharge of the Committee's responsibilities requires the participation of that Member in its work.

3. The Military Staff Committee shall be responsible under the Security Council for the strategic direction of any armed forces placed at the disposal of the Security Council. Questions relating to the command of such forces shall be worked out subsequently.

4. The Military Staff Committee, with the authorization of the Security Council and after consultation with appropriate regional agencies, may establish regional sub-committees.

Article 48. 1. The action required to carry out the decisions of the Security Council for the maintenance of international peace and security shall be taken by all the Members of the United Nations or by some of them, as the Security Council may determine.

2. Such decisions shall be carried out by the Members of the United Nations directly and through their action in the appropriate international agencies of which they are members.

Article 49. The Members of the United Nations shall join in affording mutual assistance in carrying out the measures decided upon by the Security Council.

Article 50. If preventive or enforcement measures against any state are taken by the Security Council, any other state, whether a Member of the United Nations or not, which finds itself confronted with special economic problems arising from the carrying out of those measures shall have the right to consult the Security Council with regard to a solution of those problems.

Article 51.[2] Nothing in the present Charter shall impair the inherent right of individual or collective self-defence if an armed attack occurs against a Member of the United Nations, until the Security Council has taken measures necessary to maintain international peace and security. Measures taken by Members in the exercise of this right of self-defence shall be immediately reported to the Security Council and shall not in any way affect the authority and responsibility of the Security Council under the present Charter to take at any time such action as it deems necessary in order to maintain or restore international peace and security.

CHAPTER VIII
REGIONAL ARRANGEMENTS

Article 52. 1. Nothing in the present Charter precludes the existence of regional arrangements or agencies for dealing with such matters relating to the maintenance of international peace and security as are appropriate for regional action provided that such arrangements or agencies and their activities are consistent with the Purposes and Principles of the United Nations.

2. The Members of the United Nations entering into such arrangements or constituting such agencies shall make every effort to achieve pacific settlement of local disputes through such regional arrangements or by such regional agencies before referring them to the Security Council.

3. The Security Council shall encourage the development of pacific settlement of local disputes through such regional arrangements or by such regional agencies either on the initiative of the states concerned or by reference from the Security Council.

4. This Article in no way impairs the application of Articles 34 and 35.

Article 53. 1. The Security Council shall, where appropriate, utilize such regional arrangements or agencies for enforcement action under its authority. But no enforcement action shall be taken under regional arrangements or by regional agencies without the authorization of the Security Council, with the exception of measures against any enemy state, as defined in paragraph 2 of this Article, provided for pursuant to Article 107 or in regional arrangements directed against renewal of aggressive policy on the part of any such state, until such time as the Organization may, on request of the Governments concerned, be charged with the responsibility for preventing further aggression by such a state.

2. The term enemy state as used in paragraph 1 of this Article applies to any state which during the Second World War has been an enemy of any signatory of the present Charter.

---

2. As debate has occurred over the scope of the term "armed attack" as found in the English, Spanish and Chinese texts, it is important to note that the words "armed Aggression" appear in the French and Russian texts which are equally authentic under the Charter.

Article 54. The Security Council shall at all times be kept fully informed of activities undertaken or in contemplation under regional arrangements or by regional agencies for the maintenance of international peace and security.

. . . .

CHAPTER XIV
THE INTERNATIONAL COURT OF JUSTICE

Article 92. The International Court of Justice shall be the principal judicial organ of the United Nations. It shall function in accordance with the annexed Statute, which is based upon the Statute of the Permanent Court of International Justice and forms an integral part of the present Charter.

Article 93. 1. All Members of the United Nations are *ipso facto* parties to the Statute of the International Court of Justice.

2. A state which is not a Member of the United Nations may become a party to the Statute of the International Court of Justice on conditions to be determined in each case by the General Assembly upon the recommendation of the Security Council.

Article 94. 1. Each Member of the United Nations undertakes to comply with the decision of the International Court of Justice in any case to which it is a party.

2. If any party to a case fails to perform the obligations incumbent upon it under a judgment rendered by the Court, the other party may have recourse to the Security Council, which may, if it deems necessary, make recommendations or decide upon measures to be taken to give effect to the judgment.

Article 95. Nothing in the present Charter shall prevent Members of the United Nations from entrusting the solution of their differences to other tribunals by virtue of agreements already in existence or which may be concluded in the future.

Article 96. 1. The General Assembly or the Security Council may request the International Court of Justice to give an advisory opinion on any legal question.

2. Other organs of the United Nations and specialized agencies, which may at any time be so authorized by the General Assembly, may also request advisory opinions of the Court on legal questions arising within the scope of their activities.

CHAPTER XV
THE SECRETARIAT

Article 97. The Secretariat shall comprise a Secretary-General and such staff as the Organization may require. The Secretary-General shall be appointed by the General Assembly upon the recommendation of the Security Council. He shall be the chief administrative officer of the Organization.

Article 98. The Secretary-General shall act in that capacity in all meetings of the General Assembly, of the Security Council, of the Economic and Social Council, and of the Trusteeship Council, and shall perform such other functions as are entrusted to him by these organs. The Secretary-General shall make an annual report to the General Assembly on the work of the Organization.

Article 99. The Secretary-General may bring to the attention of the Security Council any matter which in his opinion may threaten the maintenance of international peace and security.

Article 100. 1. In the performance of their duties the Secretary-General and the staff shall not seek or receive instructions from any government or from any other authority external to the Organization. They shall refrain from any action which might reflect on their position as international officials responsible only to the Organization.

2. Each Member of the United Nations undertakes to respect the exclusively international character of the responsibilities of the Secretary-General and the staff and not to seek to influence them in the discharge of their responsibilities.

Article 101. 1. The staff shall be appointed by the Secretary-General under regulations established by the General Assembly.

2. Appropriate staffs shall be permanently assigned to the Economic and Social Council, the Trusteeship Council, and, as required, to other organs of the United Nations. These staffs shall form a part of the Secretariat.

3. The paramount consideration in the employment of the staff and in the determination of the conditions of service shall be the necessity of securing the highest standards of efficiency, competence, and integrity. Due regard shall be paid to the importance of recruiting the staff on as wide a geographical basis as possible.

CHAPTER XVI
MISCELLANEOUS PROVISIONS

Article 102. 1. Every treaty and every international agreement entered into by any Member of the United Nations after the present Charter comes into force shall as soon as possible be registered with the Secretariat and published by it.

2. No party to any such treaty or international agreement which has not been registered in accordance with the provisions of paragraph 1 of this Article may invoke that treaty or agreement before any organ of the United Nations.

Article 103. In the event of a conflict between the obligations of the Members of the United Nations under the present Charter and their obligations under any other international agreement, their obligations under the present Charter shall prevail.

Article 104. The Organization shall enjoy in the territory of each of its Members such legal capacity as may be necessary for the exercise of its functions and the fulfillment of its purposes.

Article 105. 1. The Organization shall enjoy in the territory of each of its Members such privileges and immunities as are necessary for the fulfillment of its purposes.

2. Representatives of the Members of the United Nations and officials of the Organization shall similarly enjoy such privileges and immunities as are necessary for the independent exercise of their functions in connectxion with the Organization.

3. The General Assembly may make recommendations with a view to determining the details of the application of paragraphs 1 and 2 of this Article or may propose conventions to the Members of the United Nations for this purpose.

UNITING FOR PEACE RESOLUTION*

The General Assembly,

. . . .

Conscious that failure of the Security Council to discharge its responsibilities on behalf of all the Member States, particularly those responsibilities referred to in the two preceding paragraphs, does not relieve Member States of their obligations or the United Nations of its responsibility under the Charter to maintain international peace and security,

. . . .

A

1. *Resolves* that if the Security Council, because of lack of unanimity of the permanent members, fails to exercise its primary responsibility for the maintenance of international peace and security in any case where there appears to he a threat to the peace, breach of the peace, or act of aggression, the General Assembly shall consider the matter immediately with a view to making appropriate recommendations to Members for collective measures, including in the case of a breach of the peace or act of aggression the use of armed force when necessary, to maintain or restore international peace and security. If not in session at the time, the General Assembly may meet in emergency special session within twenty-four hours of the request therefor. Such emergency special session shall be called if requested by the Security Council on the vote of any seven members, or by a majority of the Members of the United Nations;

2. *Adopts* for this purpose the amendments to ifs rules of procedure set forth in the annex to the present resolution;

B

3. *Establishes* a Peace Observation Commission which, for the calendar years 1951 and 1952, shall be composed of fourteen Members, namely: China, Colombia, Czechoslovakia, France, India, Iraq, Israel, New Zealand, Pakistan, Sweden, the Union of Soviet Socialist Republics, the United Kingdom of Great Britain and Northern Ireland, the United States of America and Uruguay, and which could observe and report on the situation in any area where there exists international tension the continuance of which is likely to endanger the maintenance of international peace and security. Upon the invitation or with the consent of the State into whose territory the Commission would go, the General Assembly, or the Interim Committee when the Assembly is riotnot in session, may utilize the Commission if the Security Council is not exercising the functions assigned to it by the Charter with respect to the matter in question. Decisions to utilize the Commission shall be made on the affirmative vote of two-thirds of the members present and voting. The Security Council may also utilize the Commission in accordance with its authority under the Charter;

4. *Decides* that the Commission shall have authority in its discretion to appoint subcommissions and to utilize the services of observers to assist it in the performance of its functions;

---

* G.A. Res. 377 (V), at 10, U.N. GAOR, 5th Sess., Supp. No. 20, U.N. Doc. A/1775 (Nov. 3, 1950), *available at* G.A. Res. 377(v) 5 UN GAOR Supp. (No. 20) at 10, UN Doc. A/1775 (1950). Also available online at <http://www.un.org/documents/ga/res/5/ares5.htm>.

5. *Recommends* to all governments and authorities that they co-operate with the Commission and assist it in the performance of its functions;

6. *Requests* the Secretary-General to provide the necessary staff and facilities, utilizing, where directed by the Commission, the United Nations Panel of Field Observers envisaged in General Assembly resolution 297 B (IV);

C

7. *Invites* each Member of the United Nations to survey its resources in order to determine the nature and scope of the assistance it may be in a position to render in support of any recommendations of the Security Council or of the General Assembly for the restoration of international peace and security:

8. *Recommends* to the States Members of the United Nations that each Member maintain within its national armed forces elements so trained, organized and equipped that they could promptly be made available, in accordance with its constitutional processes, for service as a United Nations unit or units, upon recommendation by the Security Council or the General Assembly, without prejudice to the use of such elements in exercise of the right of individual or collective self-defence recognized in Article 51 of the Charter:

9. *Invites* the Members of the United Nations to inform the Collective Measures Committee provided for in paragraph 11 as soon as possible of the measures taken in implementation of the preceding paragraph;

10. *Requests* the Secretary-General to appoint, with the approval of the Committee provided for in paragraph 11, a panel of military experts who could be made available, on request, to Member States wishing to obtain technical advice regarding the organization, training, and equipment for prompt service as United Nations units of the elements referred to in paragraph 8;

D

11. *Establishes* a Collective Measures Committee consisting of fourteen Members, namely: Australia, Belgium, Brazil, Burma, Canada, Egypt, France, Mexico, Philippines, Turkey, the United Kingdom of Great Britain and Northern Ireland, the United States of America, Venezuela and Yugoslavia, and directs the Committee, in consultation with the Secretary-General and with such Member States as the Committee finds appropriate, to study and make a report to the Security Council and the General Assembly, not later than 1 September 1951, on methods, including those in section C of the present resolution, which might be used to maintain and strengthen international peace and security in accordance with the Purposes and Principles of the Charter, taking account of collective self-defence and regional arrangements (Articles 51 and 52 of the Charter);

12. *Recommends* to all Member States that they cooperate with the Committee and assist it in the performance of its functions:

13. *Requests* the Secretary-General to furnish the staff and facilities necessary for the effective accomplishment of the purposes set forth in sections C and D of the present resolution;

E

14. *Is fully conscious* that, in adopting the proposals set forth above, enduring peace will not he secured solely by collective security arrangements against breaches of inter-

national peace and acts of aggression, but that a genuine and lasting peace depends also upon the observance of all the Principles and Purposes established in the Charter of the United Nations, upon the implementation of the resolutions of the Security Council, the General Assembly and other principal organs of the United Nations intended to achieve the maintenance of international peace and security, and especially upon respect for and observance of human rights and fundamental freedoms for all and on the establishment and maintenance of conditions of economic and social well-being in all countries; and accordingly

15. *Urges* Member States to respect fully, and to intensify, joint action, in co-operation with the United Nations, to develop and stimulate universal respect for and observance of human rights and fundamental freedoms, and to intensify individual and collective efforts to achieve conditions of economic stability and social progress, particularly through the development of under-developed countries and areas.

[Annex omitted.]

B. Alliances, Collective Security and Regional Arrangements

ACT OF CHAPULTEPEC*

WHEREAS:

The peoples of the Americas, animated by a profound love of justice, remain sincerely devoted to the principles of international law;

It is their desire that such principles, not withstanding the present difficult circumstances, may prevail with even greater force in future international relations;

The inter-American conferences have repeatedly proclaimed certain fundamental principles, but these must be reaffirmed and proclaimed at a time when the juridical bases of the community of nations are being re-established;

The new situation in the world makes more imperative than ever the union and solidarity of the American peoples, for the defense of their rights and the maintenance of international peace;

The American states have been incorporating in their international law, since 1890, by means of conventions, resolutions and declarations, the following principles:

a) The proscription of territorial conquest and the non-recognition of all acquisitions made by force (First International Conference of American States, 1890);

b) The condemnation of intervention by one State in the internal or external affairs of another (Seventh International Conference of American States, 1933, and Inter-American Conference for the Maintenance of Peace, 1936);

c) The recognition that every war or threat of war affects directly or indirectly all civilized peoples, and endangers the great principles of liberty and justice which constitute the American ideal and the standard of American international policy (Inter-American Conference for the Maintenance of Peace, 1936);

d) The system of mutual consultation in order to find means of peaceful cooperation in the event of war or threat of war between American countries (Inter-American Conference for the Maintenance of Peace, 1936);

e) The recognition that every act susceptible of disturbing the peace of America affects each and every one of the American nations and justifies the initiation of the procedure of consultation (Inter-American Conference for the Maintenance of Peace, 1936);

f) The adoption of conciliation, unrestricted arbitration, or the application of international justice, in the solution of any difference or dispute between American nations, whatever its nature or origin. (Inter-American Conference for the Maintenance of Peace, 1936);

g) The recognition that respect for the personality, sovereignty and independence of each American State constitutes the essence of international order supported by continental solidarity, which historically has been expressed and sustained by declarations and treaties in force (Eighth International Conference of American States, 1938);

h) The affirmation that respect for and the faithful observance of treaties constitutes the indispensable rule for the development of peaceful relations between

---

* Act of Chapultepec, Mar. 8, 1945, 60 Stat. 1831, 1837, 3 Bevans 1024 (entered into force Mar. 8, 1945), *available at* http://www.yale.edu/lawweb/avalon/intdip/interam/chapul.htm.

States, and that treaties can only be revised by agreement of the contracting parties (Declaration of American Principles, Eighth International Conference of American States, 1938);

i) The proclamation that in case the peace, security or territorial integrity of any American republic is threatened by acts of any nature that may impair them, they proclaim their common concern and their determination to make effective their solidarity, coordinating their respective sovereign wills by means of the procedure of consultation, using the measures which in each case the circumstances may make advisable (Declaration of Lima, Eighth International Conference of American States, 1938);

j) The declaration that any attempt on the part of a non-American State against the integrity or inviolability of the territory, the sovereignty or the political independence of an American State shall be considered as an act of aggression against all the American States (Declaration XV of the Second Meeting of the Ministers of Foreign Affairs, Habana, 1940);

The furtherance of these principles, which the American States have constantly practised in order to assure peace and solidarity between the nations of the Continent, constitutes an effective means of contributing to the general system of world security and of facilitating its establishment;

The security and solidarity of the Continent are affected to the same extent by an act of aggression against any of the American States by a non-American State, as by an act of aggression of an American State against one or more American States;

Part I. Declaration

The Governments Represented at the Inter-American Conference on Problems of War and Peace

DECLARE:

1. That all sovereign States are juridically equal among themselves.

2. That every State has the right to the respect of its individuality and independence, on the part of the other members of the international community.

3. That every attack of a State against the integrity or the inviolability of the territory, or against the sovereignty or political independence of an American State, shall, conformably to Part III hereof, be considered as an act of aggression against the other States which sign this Act. In any case invasion by armed forces of one State into the territory of another trespassing boundaries established by treaty and demarcated in accordance therewith shall constitute an act of aggression.

4. That in case acts of aggression occur or there may be reasons to believe that an aggression is being prepared by any other State against the integrity and inviolability of the territory, or against the sovereignty or political independence of an American State, the States signatory to this Act will consult amongst themselves in order to agree upon the measures it may be advisable to take.

5. That during the war, and until the treaty recommended in Part II hereof is concluded, the signatories of this Act recognize that such threats and acts of aggression, as indicated in paragraphs Third and Fourth above, constitute an interference with the war effort of the United Nations, calling for such procedures, within the scope of their constitutional powers of a general nature and for war, as may be found necessary, in-

cluding: recall of chiefs of diplomatic missions; breaking of diplomatic relations; breaking of consular relations; breaking of postal, telegraphic, telephonic, radio-telephonic relations; interruption of economic, commercial and financial relations; use of armed force to prevent or repel aggression.

6. That the principles and procedure contained in this Declaration shall become effective immediately, inasmuch as any act of aggression or threat of aggression during the present state of war interferes with the war effort of the United Nations to obtain victory. Henceforth, and to the end that the principles and procedures herein stipulated shall conform with the constitutional processes of each Republic, the respective Governments shall take the necessary steps to perfect this instrument in order that it shall be in force at all times.

Part II. Recommendation

The Inter-American Conference on Problems of War and Peace

RECOMMENDS:

That for the purpose of meeting threats or acts of aggression against any American Republic following the establishment of peace, the Governments of the American Republics consider the conclusion, in accordance with their constitutional processes, of a treaty establishing procedures whereby such threats or acts may be met by the use, by all or some of the signatories of said treaty of any one or more of the following measures: recall of chiefs of diplomatic missions; breaking of diplomatic relations; breaking of consular relations; breaking of postal, telegraphic, telephonic, radio-telephonic relations; interruption of economic, commercial and financial relations; use of armed force to prevent or repel aggression.

Part III

The above Declaration and Recommendation constitute a regional arrangement for dealing with such matters relating to the maintenance of international peace and security as are appropriate for regional action in this Hemisphere. The said arrangement, and the pertinent activities and procedures, shall be consistent with the purposes and principles of the general international organization, when established.

This agreement shall be known as the "Act of Chapultepec."

INTER-AMERICAN TREATY OF RECIPROCAL ASSISTANCE[1] (RIO TREATY)

In the name of their Peoples, the Governments represented at the Inter-American Conference for the Maintenance of Continental Peace and Security, desirous of consolidating and strengthening their relations of friendship and good neighborliness, and considering:

That Resolution VIII of the Inter-American Conference on Problems of War and Peace,[2] which met in Mexico City, recommended the conclusion of a treaty to prevent and repeal threats and acts of aggression against any of the countries of America;

That the High Contracting Parties reiterate their will to remain united in an inter-American system consistent with the purposes and principles of the United Nations, and reaffirm the existence of the agreement which they have concluded concerning those matters relating to the maintenance of international peace and security which are appropriate for regional action;

That the High Contracting Parties reaffirm their adherence to the principles of inter-American solidarity and cooperation, and especially to those set forth in the preamble and declarations of the Act of Chapultepec, all of which should be understood to be accepted as standards of their mutual relations and as the juridical basis of the Inter-American System;

That the American States propose, in order to improve the procedures for the pacific settlement of their controversies, to conclude the treaty concerning the "Inter-American Peace System" envisaged in Resolutions IX[3] and XXXIX[4] of the Inter-American Conference on Problems of War and Peace,

That the obligation of mutual assistance and common defense of the American Republics is essentially related to their democratic ideals and to their will to cooperate permanently in the fulfillment of the principles and purposes of a policy of peace;

That the American regional community affirms as a manifest truth that juridical organization is a necessary prerequisite of security and peace, and that peace is founded on justice and moral order and, consequently, on the international recognition and protection of human rights and freedoms, on the indispensable well-being of the people, and on the effectiveness of democracy for the international realization of justice and security,

Have resolved, in conformity with the objectives stated above, to conclude the following Treaty, in order to assure peace, through adequate means, to provide for effec-

---

1. Inter-American Treaty of Reciprocal Assistance, *opened for signature* Sept. 2, 1947, 62 Stat. 1681, 21 U.N.T.S. 77 (entered into force Dec. 3, 1948), *available at* http://www.yale.edu/lawweb/avalon/decade/decad061.htm.

2. Act of Chapultepec, Mar. 8, 1945, 60 Stat. 1831, 1837, 1840, 3 Bevans 1024, 1027 (entered into force Mar. 8, 1945), *available at* http://www.yale.edu/lawweb/avalon/intdip/interam/chapul.htm.

3. The Inter-American System. Arrangements Between the United States of America and Other American Republics Embodied in Resolution IX of the Final Act of the Inter-American Conference on Problems of War and Peace, Mar. 8, 1945, 60 Stat. 1847, 3 Bevans 1028 (entered into force Mar. 8, 1945).

4. U.S. Dep't of State, Publ'n No. 2497, Conference Series No. 85, Report of the Delegation of the United States of America to the Inter-American Conference on Problems of War and Peace, Mexico City, Mexico, February 21–March 8, 1945, at 107 (1946).

tive reciprocal assistance to meet armed attacks against any American State, and in order to deal with threats of aggression against any of them:

Article 1. The High Contracting Parties formally condemn war and undertake in their international relations not to resort to the threat or the use of force in any manner inconsistent with the provisions of the Charter of the United Nations or of this Treaty.

Article 2. As a consequence of the principle set forth in the preceding Article, the High Contracting Parties undertake to submit every controversy which may arise between them to methods of peaceful settlement and to endeavor to settle any such controversy among themselves by means of the procedures in force in the Inter-American System before referring it to the General Assembly or the Security Council of the United Nations.

Article 3. 1. The High Contracting Parties agree that an armed attack by any State against an American State shall be considered as an attack against all the American States and, consequently, each one of the said Contracting Parties undertakes to assist in meeting the attack in the exercise of the inherent right of individual or collective self-defense recognized by Article 51 of the Charter of the United Nations.

2. On the request of the State or States directly attacked and until the decision of the Organ of Consultation of the Inter-American System, each one of the Contracting Parties may determine the immediate measures which it may individually take in fulfillment of the obligation contained in the preceding paragraph and in accordance with the principle of continental solidarity. The Organ of Consultation shall meet without delay for the purpose of examining those measures and agreeing upon the measures of a collective character that should be taken.

3. The provisions of this Article shall be applied in case of any armed attack which takes place within the region described in Article 4 or within the territory of an American State. When the attack takes place outside of the said areas, the provisions of Article 6 shall be applied.

4. Measures of self-defense provided for under this Article may be taken until the Security Council of the United Nations has taken the measures necessary to maintain international peace and security.

Article 4. The region to which this Treaty refers is bounded as follows: beginning at the North Pole; thence due south to a point 74 degrees north latitude, 10 degrees west longitude; thence by a rhumb line to a point 47 degrees 30 minutes north latitude, 50 degrees west longitude; thence by a rhumb line to a point 35 degrees north latitude, 60 degrees west longitude; thence due south to a point in 20 degrees north latitude; thence by a rhumb line to a point 5 degrees north latitude, 24 degrees west longitude; thence due south to the South Pole; thence due north to a point 30 degrees south latitude, 90 degrees west longitude; thence by a rhumb line to a point on the Equator at 97 degrees west longitude; thence by a rhumb line to a point 15 degrees north latitude, 120 degrees west longitude; thence by a rhumb line to a point 50 degrees north latitude, 170 degrees east longitude; thence due north to a point in 54 degrees north latitude; thence by a rhumb line to a point 65 degrees 30 minutes north latitude, 168 degrees 58 minutes 5 seconds west longitude: thence due north to the North Pole.

Article 5. The High Contracting Parties shall immediately send to the Security Council of the United Nations, in conformity with Articles 51 and 54 of the Charter of the United Nations, complete information concerning the activities undertaken or in contemplation in the exercise of the right of self-defense or for the purpose of maintaining inter-American peace and security.

Article 6. If the inviolability or the integrity of the territory or the sovereignty or political independence of any American State should be affected by an aggression which is not an armed attack or by an extracontinental or intra-continental conflict, or by any other fact or situation that might endanger the peace of America, the Organ of Consultation shall meet immediately in order to agree on the measures which must be taken in case of aggression to assist the victim of the aggression or, in any case, the measures which should be taken for the common defense and for the maintenance of the peace and security of the Continent.

Article 7. In the case of a conflict between two or more American States, without prejudice to the right of self-defense in conformity with Article 51 of the Charter of the United Nations, the High Contracting Parties, meeting in consultation shall call upon the contending States to suspend hostilities and restore matters to the status quo ante bellum, and shall take in addition all other necessary measures to reestablish or maintain inter-American peace and security and for the solution of the conflict by peaceful means. The rejection of the pacifying action will be considered in the determination of the aggressor and in the application of the measures which the consultative meeting may agree upon.

Article 8. For the purposes of this Treaty, the measures on which the Organ of Consultation may agree will comprise one or more of the following: recall of chiefs of diplomatic missions; breaking of diplomatic relations; breaking of consular relations; partial or complete interruption of economic relations or of rail, sea, air, postal, telegraphic, telephonic, and radiotelephonic or radiotelegraphic communications; and use of armed force.

Article 9. In addition to other acts which the Organ of Consultation may characterize as aggression, the following shall be considered as such:

a. Unprovoked armed attack by a State against the territory, the people, or the land, sea or air forces of another State;

b. Invasion, by the armed forces of a State, of the territory of an American State, through the trespassing of boundaries demarcated in accordance with a treaty, judicial decision, or, arbitral award, or, in the absence of frontiers thus demarcated, invasion affecting a region which is under the effective jurisdiction of another State.

Article 10. None of the provisions of this Treaty shall be construed as impairing the rights and obligations of the High Contracting Parties under the Charter of the United Nations.

....

NORTH ATLANTIC TREATY[1]

The Parties to this Treaty reaffirm their faith in the purposes and principles of the Charter of the United Nations and their desire to live in peace with all peoples and all governments.

They are determined to safeguard the freedom, common heritage and civilisation of their peoples, founded on the principles of democracy, individual liberty and the rule of law.

They seek to promote stability and well-being in the North Atlantic area.

They are resolved to unite their efforts for collective defence and for the preservation of peace and security. They therefore agree to this North Atlantic Treaty:

Article 1. The Parties undertake, as set forth in the Charter of the United Nations, to settle any international dispute in which they may be involved by peaceful means in such a manner that international peace and security and justice are not endangered, and to refrain in their international relations from the threat or use of force in any manner inconsistent with the purposes of the United Nations.

Article 2. The Parties will contribute toward the further development of peaceful and friendly international relations by strengthening their free institutions, by bringing about a better understanding of the principles upon which these institutions are founded, and by promoting conditions of stability and well-being. They will seek to eliminate conflict in their international economic policies and will encourage economic collaboration between any or all of them.

Article 3. In order more effectively to achieve the objectives of this Treaty, the Parties, separately and jointly, by means of continuous and effective self-help and mutual aid, will maintain and develop their individual and collective capacity to resist armed attack.

Article 4. The Parties will consult together whenever, in the opinion of any of them, the territorial integrity, political independence or security of any of the Parties is threatened.

Article 5. The Parties agree that an armed attack against one or more of them in Europe or North America shall be considered an attack against them all and consequently they agree that, if such an armed attack occurs, each of them, in exercise of the right of individual or collective self-defence recognised by Article 51 of the Charter of the United Nations, will assist the Party or Parties so attacked by taking forthwith, individually and in concert with the other Parties, such action as it deems necessary, including the use of armed force, to restore and maintain the security of the North Atlantic area.

Any such armed attack and all measures taken as a result thereof shall immediately be reported to the Security Council. Such measures shall be terminated when the Security Council has taken the measures necessary to restore and maintain international peace and security.

---

1. North Atlantic Treaty Between the United States of America and Other Governments, Apr. 4, 1949, 63 Stat. 2241, 34 U.N.T.S. 243 (entered into force Aug. 24, 1949) [hereinafter North Atlantic Treaty], *available at* http://www.nato.int/docu/basictxt/treaty.htm.

Article 6.[2] For the purpose of Article 5, an armed attack on one or more of the Parties is deemed to include an armed attack:

—on the territory of any of the Parties in Europe or North America, on the Algerian Departments of France, on the territory of or on the Islands under the jurisdiction of any of the Parties in the North Atlantic area north of the Tropic of Cancer;

—on the forces, vessels, or aircraft of any of the Parties, when in or over these territories or any other area in Europe in which occupation forces of any of the Parties were stationed on the date when the Treaty entered into force or the Mediterranean Sea or the North Atlantic area north of the Tropic of Cancer.

Article 7. This Treaty does not affect, and shall not be interpreted as affecting in any way the rights and obligations under the Charter of the Parties which are members of the United Nations, or the primary responsibility of the Security Council for the maintenance of international peace and security.

Article 8. Each Party declares that none of the international engagements now in force between it and any other of the Parties or any third State is in conflict with the provisions of this Treaty, and undertakes not to enter into any international engagement in conflict with this Treaty.

Article 9. The Parties hereby establish a Council, on which each of them shall be represented, to consider matters concerning the implementation of this Treaty. The Council shall be so organised as to be able to meet promptly at any time. The Council shall set up such subsidiary bodies as may be necessary; in particular it shall establish immediately a defence committee which shall recommend measures for the implementation of Articles 3 and 5.

Article 10. The Parties may, by unanimous agreement, invite any other European State in a position to further the principles of this Treaty and to contribute to the security of the North Atlantic area to accede to this Treaty. Any State so invited may become a Party to the Treaty by depositing its instrument of accession with the Government of the United States of America. The Government of the United States of America will inform each of the Parties of the deposit of each such instrument of accession.

Article 11. This Treaty shall be ratified and its provisions carried out by the Parties in accordance with their respective constitutional processes....

....

2. For an amendment of article 6, see Protocol to the North Atlantic Treaty on the Accession of Greece and Turkey, *opened for signature* Oct. 17, 1951, 3 U.S.T. 43, 44–47, 126 U.N.T.S. 350, 350–353 (entered into force Feb. 15, 1952).

CHARTER OF THE ORGANIZATION OF AMERICAN STATES[1] (REVISED)

IN THE NAME OF THEIR PEOPLES, THE STATES REPRESENTED AT THE NINTH INTERNATIONAL CONFERENCE OF AMERICAN STATES,

Convinced that the historic mission of America is to offer to man a land of liberty and a favorable environment for the development of his personality and the realization of his just aspirations;

Conscious that that mission has already inspired numerous agreements, whose essential value lies in the desire of the American peoples to live together in peace and, through their mutual understanding and respect for the sovereignty of each one, to provide for the betterment of all, in independence, in equality and under law;

Convinced that representative democracy is an indispensable condition for the stability, peace and development of the region;

Confident that the true significance of American solidarity and good neighborliness can only mean the consolidation on this continent, within the framework of democratic institutions, of a system of individual liberty and social justice based on respect for the essential rights of man;

Persuaded that their welfare and their contribution to the progress and the civilization of the world will increasingly require intensive continental cooperation;

Resolved to persevere in the noble undertaking that humanity has conferred upon the United Nations, whose principles and purposes they solemnly reaffirm;

Convinced that juridical organization is a necessary condition for security and peace founded on moral order and on justice; and

In accordance with Resolution IX of the Inter-American Conference on Problems of War and Peace, held in Mexico City,

HAVE AGREED upon the following:

PART ONE
CHAPTER I
NATURE AND PURPOSES

Article 1. The American States establish by this Charter the international organization that they have developed to achieve an order of peace and justice, to promote their solidarity, to strengthen their collaboration, and to defend their sovereignty, their territorial integrity, and their independence. Within the United Nations, the Organization of American States is a regional agency.

---

1. Charter of the Organization of American States, Apr. 30, 1948, 2 U.S.T. 2394, 119 U.N.T.S. 3 (entered into force Dec. 13, 1951) (with reservations), *amended by* Protocol of Amendment to the Charter of the Organization of American States, Feb. 27, 1967, 21 U.S.T. 607, 21 U.N.T.S. 266 (entered into force Feb. 27, 1970) [hereinafter Protocol of Buenos Aires], *available at* http://www.oas.org/main/main.asp?sLang=E&sLink=../../documents/eng/documents.asp.

The Organization of American States has no powers other than those expressly conferred upon it by this Charter, none of whose provisions authorizes it to intervene in matters that are within the internal jurisdiction of the Member States.

Article 2. The Organization of American States, in order to put into practice the principles on which it is founded and to fulfill its regional obligations under the Charter of the United Nations, proclaims the following essential purposes:

a) To strengthen the peace and security of the continent;

b) To promote and consolidate representative democracy, with due respect for the principle of nonintervention;

c) To prevent possible causes of difficulties and to ensure the pacific settlement of disputes that may arise among the Member States;

d) To provide for common action on the part of those States in the event of aggression;

e) To seek the solution of political, juridical, and economic problems that may arise among them;

a. To promote, by cooperative action, their economic, social, and cultural development;

g) To eradicate extreme poverty, which constitutes an obstacle to the full democratic development of the peoples of the hemisphere; and

h) To achieve an effective limitation of conventional weapons that will make it possible to devote the largest amount of resources to the economic and social development of the Member States.

CHAPTER II
PRINCIPLES

Article 3. The American States reaffirm the following principles:

a) International law is the standard of conduct of States in their reciprocal relations;

b) International order consists essentially of respect for the personality, sovereignty, and independence of States, and the faithful fulfillment of obligations derived from treaties and other sources of international law;

c) Good faith shall govern the relations between States;

d) The solidarity of the American States and the high aims which are sought through it require the political organization of those States on the basis of the effective exercise of representative democracy;

e) Every State has the right to choose, without external interference, its political, economic, and social system and to organize itself in the way best suited to it, and has the duty to abstain from intervening in the affairs of another State. Subject to the foregoing, the American States shall cooperate fully among themselves, independently of the nature of their political, economic, and social systems;

f) The elimination of extreme poverty is an essential part of the promotion and consolidation of representative democracy and is the common and shared responsibility of the American States;

g) The American States condemn war of aggression: victory does not give rights;

h) An act of aggression against one American State is an act of aggression against all the other American States;

i) Controversies of an international character arising between two or more American States shall be settled by peaceful procedures;

j) Social justice and social security are bases of lasting peace;

k) Economic cooperation is essential to the common welfare and prosperity of the peoples of the continent;

l) The American States proclaim the fundamental rights of the individual without distinction as to race, nationality, creed, or sex;

m) The spiritual unity of the continent is based on respect for the cultural values of the American countries and requires their close cooperation for the high purposes of civilization;

n) The education of peoples should be directed toward justice, freedom, and peace.

CHAPTER III
MEMBERS

Article 4. All American States that ratify the present Charter are Members of the Organization.

Article 5. Any new political entity that arises from the union of several Member States and that, as such, ratifies the present Charter, shall become a Member of the Organization. The entry of the new political entity into the Organization shall result in the loss of membership of each one of the States which constitute it.

Article 6. Any other independent American State that desires to become a Member of the Organization should so indicate by means of a note addressed to the Secretary General, in which it declares that it is willing to sign and ratify the Charter of the Organization and to accept all the obligations inherent in membership, especially those relating to collective security expressly set forth in Articles 28 and 29 of the Charter.

. . . .

Article 9. A Member of the Organization whose democratically constituted government has been overthrown by force may be suspended from the exercise of the right to participate in the sessions of the General Assembly, the Meeting of Consultation, the Councils of the Organization and the Specialized Conferences as well as in the commissions, working groups and any other bodies established.

a) The power to suspend shall be exercised only when such diplomatic initiatives undertaken by the Organization for the purpose of promoting the restoration of representative democracy in the affected Member State have been unsuccessful;

b) The decision to suspend shall be adopted at a special session of the General Assembly by an affirmative vote of two-thirds of the Member States;

c) The suspension shall take effect immediately following its approval by the General Assembly;

d) The suspension notwithstanding, the Organization shall endeavor to undertake additional diplomatic initiatives to contribute to the re-establishment of representative democracy in the affected Member State;

e) The Member which has been subject to suspension shall continue to fulfill its obligations to the Organization;

f) The General Assembly may lift the suspension by a decision adopted with the approval of two-thirds of the Member States;

g) The powers referred to in this article shall be exercised in accordance with this Charter.

CHAPTER IV
FUNDAMENTAL RIGHTS AND DUTIES OF STATES

Article 10. States are juridically equal, enjoy equal rights and equal capacity to exercise these rights, and have equal duties. The rights of each State depend not upon its power to ensure the exercise thereof, but upon the mere fact of its existence as a person under international law.

Article 11. Every American State has the duty to respect the rights enjoyed by every other State in accordance with international law.

Article 12. The fundamental rights of States may not be impaired in any manner whatsoever.

Article 13. The political existence of the State is independent of recognition by other States. Even before being recognized, the State has the right to defend its integrity and independence, to provide for its preservation and prosperity, and consequently to organize itself as it sees fit, to legislate concerning its interests, to administer its services, and to determine the jurisdiction and competence of its courts. The exercise of these rights is limited only by the exercise of the rights of other States in accordance with international law.

Article 14. Recognition implies that the State granting it accepts the personality of the new State, with all the rights and duties that international law prescribes for the two States.

Article 15. The right of each State to protect itself and to live its own life does not authorize it to commit unjust acts against another State.

Article 16. The jurisdiction of States within the limits of their national territory is exercised equally over all the inhabitants, whether nationals or aliens.

Article 17. Each State has the right to develop its cultural, political, and economic life freely and naturally. In this free development, the State shall respect the rights of the individual and the principles of universal morality.

Article 18. Respect for and the faithful observance of treaties constitute standards for the development of peaceful relations among States. International treaties and agreements should be public.

Article 19. No State or group of States has the right to intervene, directly or indirectly, for any reason whatever, in the internal or external affairs of any other State. The foregoing principle prohibits not only armed force but also any other form of interference or attempted threat against the personality of the State or against its political, economic, and cultural elements.

Article 20. No State may use or encourage the use of coercive measures of an economic or political character in order to force the sovereign will of another State and obtain from it advantages of any kind.

Article 21. The territory of a State is inviolable; it may not be the object, even temporarily, of military occupation or of other measures of force taken by another State, directly or indirectly, on any grounds whatever. No territorial acquisitions or special advantages obtained either by force or by other means of coercion shall be recognized.

Article 22. The American States bind themselves in their international relations not to have recourse to the use of force, except in the case of self defense in accordance with existing treaties or in fulfillment thereof.

Article 23. Measures adopted for the maintenance of peace and security in accordance with existing treaties do not constitute a violation of the principles set forth in Articles 19 and 21.

CHAPTER V
PACIFIC SETTLEMENT OF DISPUTES

Article 24. International disputes between Member States shall be submitted to the peaceful procedures set forth in this Charter.

This provision shall not be interpreted as an impairment of the rights and obligations of the Member States under Articles 34 and 35 of the Charter of the United Nations.

Article 25. The following are peaceful procedures: direct negotiation, good offices, mediation, investigation and conciliation, judicial settlement, arbitration, and those which the parties to the dispute may especially agree upon at any time.

Article 26. In the event that a dispute arises between two or more American States which, in the opinion of one of them, cannot be settled through the usual diplomatic channels, the parties shall agree on some other peaceful procedure that will enable them to reach a solution.

Article 27. A special treaty will establish adequate means for the settlement of disputes and will determine pertinent procedures for each peaceful means such that no dispute between American States may remain without definitive settlement within a reasonable period of time.

CHAPTER VI
COLLECTIVE SECURITY

Article 28. Every act of aggression by a State against the territorial integrity or the inviolability of the territory or against the sovereignty or political independence of an American State shall be considered an act of aggression against the other American States.

Article 29. If the inviolability or the integrity of the territory or the sovereignty or political independence of any American State should be affected by an armed attack or by an act of aggression that is not an armed attack, or by an extracontinental conflict, or by a conflict between two or more American States, or by any other fact or situation that might endanger the peace of America, the American States, in furtherance of the principles of continental solidarity or collective self-defense, shall apply the measures and procedures established in the special treaties on the subject.

CHAPTER VII
INTEGRAL DEVELOPMENT

Article 30. The Member States, inspired by the principles of inter-American solidarity and cooperation, pledge themselves to a united effort to ensure international social justice in their relations and integral development for their peoples, as conditions essential to peace and security. Integral development encompasses the economic, social, educational, cultural, scientific, and technological fields through which the goals that each country sets for accomplishing it should be achieved.

Article 31. Inter-American cooperation for integral development is the common and joint responsibility of the Member States, within the framework of the democratic principles and the institutions of the interAmerican system. It should include the economic, social, educational, cultural, scientific, and technological fields, support the achievement of national objectives of the Member States, and respect the priorities established by each country in its development plans, without political ties or conditions.

Article 32. Inter-American cooperation for integral development should be continuous and preferably channeled through multilateral organizations, without prejudice to bilateral cooperation between Member States.

The Member States shall contribute to inter-American cooperation for integral development in accordance with their resources and capabilities and in conformity with their laws.

Article 33. Development is a primary responsibility of each country and should constitute an integral and continuous process for the establishment of a more just economic and social order that will make possible and contribute to the fulfillment of the individual.

Article 34. The Member States agree that equality of opportunity, the elimination of extreme poverty, equitable distribution of wealth and income and the full participation of their peoples in decisions relating to their own development are, among others, basic objectives of integral development. To achieve them, they likewise agree to devote their utmost efforts to accomplishing the following basic goals:

a) Substantial and self-sustained increase of per capita national product;

b) Equitable distribution of national income;

c) Adequate and equitable systems of taxation;

d) Modernization of rural life and reforms leading to equitable and efficient land-tenure systems, increased agricultural productivity, expanded use of land, diversification of production and improved processing and marketing systems for agricultural products; and the strengthening and expansion of the means to attain these ends;

e) Accelerated and diversified industrialization, especially of capital and intermediate goods;

f) Stability of domestic price levels, compatible with sustained economic development and the attainment of social justice;

g) Fair wages, employment opportunities, and acceptable working conditions for all;

h) Rapid eradication of illiteracy and expansion of educational opportunities for all;

i) Protection of man's potential through the extension and application of modern medical science;

j) Proper nutrition, especially through the acceleration of national efforts to increase the production and availability of food;

k) Adequate housing for all sectors of the population;

l) Urban conditions that offer the opportunity for a healthful, productive, and full life;

m) Promotion of private initiative and investment in harmony with action in the public sector; and

n) Expansion and diversification of exports.

Article 35. The Member States should refrain from practicing policies and adopting actions or measures that have serious adverse effects on the development of other Member States.

Article 36. Transnational enterprises and foreign private investment shall be subject to the legislation of the host countries and to the jurisdiction of their competent courts and to the international treaties and agreements to which said countries are parties, and should conform to the development policies of the recipient countries.

Article 37. The Member States agree to join together in seeking a solution to urgent or critical problems that may arise whenever the economic development or stability of any Member State is seriously affected by conditions that cannot be remedied through the efforts of that State.

Article 38. The Member States shall extend among themselves the benefits of science and technology by encouraging the exchange and utilization of scientific and technical knowledge in accordance with existing treaties and national laws.

Article 39. The Member States, recognizing the close interdependence between foreign trade and economic and social development, should make individual and united efforts to bring about the following:

a) Favorable conditions of access to world markets for the products of the developing countries of the region, particularly through the reduction or elimination, by importing countries, of tariff and non-tariff barriers that affect the exports of the Member States of the Organization, except when such barriers are applied in order to diversify the economic structure, to speed up the development of the less developed Member States, and intensify their process of economic integration, or when they are related to national security or to the needs of economic balance;

b) Continuity in their economic and social development by means of:

i. Improved conditions for trade in basic commodities through international agreements, where appropriate; orderly marketing procedures that avoid the disruption of markets, and other measures designed to promote the expansion of markets and to obtain dependable incomes for producers, adequate and dependable supplies for consumers, and stable prices that are both remunerative to producers and fair to consumers;

ii. Improved international financial cooperation and the adoption of other means for lessening the adverse impact of sharp fluctuations in export earnings experienced by the countries exporting basic commodities;

iii. Diversification of exports and expansion of export opportunities for manufactured and semimanufactured products from the developing countries; and

iv. Conditions conducive to increasing the real export earnings of the Member States, particularly the developing countries of the region, and to increasing their participation in international trade.

....

Article 45. The Member States, convinced that man can only achieve the full realization of his aspirations within a just social order, along with economic development and true peace, agree to dedicate every effort to the application of the following principles and mechanisms:

a) All human beings, without distinction as to race, sex, nationality, creed, or social condition, have a right to material well-being and to their spiritual development, under circumstances of liberty, dignity, equality of opportunity, and economic security;

b) Work is a right and a social duty, it gives dignity to the one who performs it, and it should be performed under conditions, including a system of fair wages, that ensure life, health, and a decent standard of living for the worker and his family, both during his working years and in his old age, or when any circumstance deprives him of the possibility of working;

c) Employers and workers, both rural and urban, have the right to associate themselves freely for the defense and promotion of their interests, including the right to collective bargaining and the workers' right to strike, and recognition of the juridical personality of associations and the protection of their freedom and independence, all in accordance with applicable laws;

d) Fair and efficient systems and procedures for consultation and collaboration among the sectors of production, with due regard for safeguarding the interests of the entire society;

e) The operation of systems of public administration, banking and credit, enterprise, and distribution and sales, in such a way, in harmony with the private sector, as to meet the requirements and interests of the community;

f) The incorporation and increasing participation of the marginal sectors of the population, in both rural and urban areas, in the economic, social, civic, cultural, and political life of the nation, in order to achieve the full integration of the national community, acceleration of the process of social mobility, and the consolidation of the democratic system. The encouragement of all efforts of popular promotion and cooperation that have as their purpose the development and progress of the community;

g) Recognition of the importance of the contribution of organizations such as labor unions, cooperatives, and cultural, professional, business, neighborhood, and community associations to the life of the society and to the development process;

h) Development of an efficient social security policy; and

i) Adequate provision for all persons to have due legal aid in order to secure their rights.

Article 46. The Member States recognize that, in order to facilitate the process of Latin American regional integration, it is necessary to harmonize the social legislation of the developing countries, especially in the labor and social security fields, so that the rights of the workers shall be equally protected, and they agree to make the greatest efforts possible to achieve this goal.

. . . .

PART TWO
CHAPTER VIII
THE ORGANS

Article 53. The Organization of American States accomplishes its purposes by means of:

a) The General Assembly;

b) The Meeting of Consultation of Ministers of Foreign Affairs;

c) The Councils;

d) The Inter-American Juridical Committee;

e) The Inter-American Commission on Human Rights;

f) The General Secretariat;

g) The Specialized Conferences; and

h) The Specialized Organizations.

There may be established, in addition to those provided for in the Charter and in accordance with the provisions thereof, such subsidiary organs, agencies, and other entities as are considered necessary.

CHAPTER IX
THE GENERAL ASSEMBLY

Article 54. The General Assembly is the supreme organ of the Organization of American States. It has as its principal powers, in addition to such others as are assigned to it by the Charter, the following:

a) To decide the general action and policy of the Organization, determine the structure and functions of its organs, and consider any matter relating to friendly relations among the American States;

b) To establish measures for coordinating the activities of the organs, agencies, and entities of the Organization among themselves, and such activities with those of the other institutions of the interAmerican system;

c) To strengthen and coordinate cooperation with the United Nations and it's specialized agencies;

d) To promote collaboration, especially in the economic, social, and cultural fields, with other international organizations whose purposes are similar to those of the Organization of American States;

e) To approve the program-budget of the Organization and determine the quotas of the Member States;

f) To consider the reports of the Meeting of Consultation of Ministers of Foreign Affairs and the observations and recommendations presented by the Permanent Council with regard to the reports that should be presented by the other organs and entities, in accordance with the provisions of Article 91.f, as well as the reports of any organ which may be required by the General Assembly itself;

g) To adopt general standards to govern the operations of the General Secretariat; and

h) To adopt its own rules of procedure and, by a two-thirds vote, its agenda.

The General Assembly shall exercise its powers in accordance with the provisions of the Charter and of other inter-American treaties.

....

CHAPTER X
THE MEETING OF CONSULTATION OFMINISTERS OF FOREIGN AFFAIRS

Article 61. The Meeting of Consultation of Ministers of Foreign Affairs shall be held in order to consider problems of an urgent nature and of common interest to the American States, and to serve as the Organ of Consultation.

Article 62. Any Member State may request that a Meeting of Consultation be called. The request shall be addressed to the Permanent Council of the Organization, which shall decide by an absolute majority whether a meeting should be held.

Article 63. The agenda and regulations of the Meeting of Consultation shall be prepared by the Permanent Council of the Organization and submitted to the Member States for consideration.

Article 64. If, for exceptional reasons, a Minister of Foreign Affairs is unable to attend the meeting, he shall be represented by a special delegate.

Article 65. In case of an armed attack on the territory of an American State or within the region of security delimited by the treaty in force, the Chairman of the Permanent Council shall without delay call a meeting of the Council to decide on the convocation of the Meeting of Consultation, without prejudice to the provisions of the Inter-American Treaty of Reciprocal Assistance with regard to the States Parties to that instrument.

Article 66. An Advisory Defense Committee shall be established to advise the Organ of Consultation on problems of military cooperation that may arise in connection with the application of existing special treaties on collective security.

Article 67. The Advisory Defense Committee shall be composed of the highest military authorities of the American States participating in the Meeting of Consultation. Under exceptional circumstances the Governments may appoint substitutes. Each State shall be entitled to one vote.

Article 68. The Advisory Defense Committee shall be convoked under the same conditions as the Organ of Consultation, when the latter deals with matters relating to defense against aggression.

Article 69. The Committee shall also meet when the General Assembly or the Meeting of Consultation or the Governments, by a two-thirds majority of the Member States, assign to it technical studies or reports on specific subjects.

. . . .

CHAPTER XII
THE PERMANENT COUNCIL OF THE ORGANIZATION

Article 80. The Permanent Council of the Organization is composed of one representative of each Member State, especially appointed by the respective Government, with the rank of ambassador. Each Government may accredit an acting representative, as well as such alternates and advisers as it considers necessary.

Article 81. The office of Chairman of the Permanent Council shall be held by each of the representatives, in turn, following the alphabetic order in Spanish of the names of their respective countries. The office of Vice Chairman shall be filled in the same way, following reverse alphabetic order. The Chairman and the Vice Chairman shall hold office for a term of not more than six months, which shall be determined by the statutes.

Article 82. Within the limits of the Charter and of interAmerican treaties and agreements, the Permanent Council takes cognizance of any matter referred to it by the General Assembly or the Meeting of Consultation of Ministers of Foreign Affairs.

Article 83. The Permanent Council shall serve provisionally as the Organ of Consultation in conformity with the provisions of the special treaty on the subject.

Article 84. The Permanent Council shall keep vigilance over the maintenance of friendly relations among the Member States, and for that purpose shall effectively assist them in the peaceful settlement of their disputes, in accordance with the following provisions.

Article 85. In accordance with the provisions of this Charter, any party to a dispute in which none of the peaceful procedures provided for in the Charter is under way may resort to the Permanent Council to obtain its good offices. The Council, following the provisions of the preceding article, shall assist the parties and recommend the procedures it considers suitable for peaceful settlement of the dispute.

Article 86. In the exercise of its functions and with the consent of the parties to the dispute, the Permanent Council may establish ad hoc committees.

The ad hoc committees shall have the membership and the mandate that the Permanent Council agrees upon in each individual case, with the consent of the parties to the dispute.

Article 87. The Permanent Council may also, by such means as it deems advisable, investigate the facts in the dispute, and may do so in the territory of any of the parties, with the consent of the Government concerned.

Article 88. If the procedure for peaceful settlement of disputes recommended by the Permanent Council or suggested by the pertinent ad hoc committee under the terms of its mandate is not accepted by one of the parties, or one of the parties declares that the procedure has not settled the dispute, the Permanent Council shall so inform the General Assembly, without prejudice to its taking steps to secure agreement between the parties or to restore relations between them.

Article 89. The Permanent Council, in the exercise of these functions, shall take its decisions by an affirmative vote of two thirds of its Members, excluding the parties to the dispute, except for such decisions as the rules of procedure provide shall be adopted by a simple majority.

Article 90. In performing their functions with respect to the peaceful settlement of disputes, the Permanent Council and the respective ad hoc committee shall observe the provisions of the Charter and the principles and standards of international law, as well as take into account the existence of treaties in force between the parties.

....

CHAPTER XIV
THE INTER-AMERICAN JURIDICAL COMMITTEE

Article 99. The purpose of the Inter-American Juridical Committee is to serve the Organization as an advisory body on juridical matters; to promote the progressive development and the codification of international law; and to study juridical problems related to the integration of the developing countries of the Hemisphere and, insofar as may appear desirable, the possibility of attaining uniformity in their legislation.

Article 100. The Inter-American Juridical Committee shall undertake the studies and preparatory work assigned to it by the General Assembly, the Meeting of Consultation of Ministers of Foreign Affairs, or the Councils of the Organization. It may also, on its own initiative, undertake such studies and preparatory work as it considers advisable, and suggest the holding of specialized juridical conferences.

Article 101. The Inter-American Juridical Committee shall be composed of eleven jurists, nationals of Member States, elected by the General Assembly for a period of four years from panels of three candidates presented by Member States. In the election, a system shall be used that takes into account partial replacement of membership and, insofar as possible, equitable geographic representation. No two Members of the Committee may be nationals of the same State.

Vacancies that occur for reasons other than normal expiration of the terms of office of the Members of the Committee shall be filled by the Permanent Council of the Organization in accordance with the criteria set forth in the preceding paragraph.

Article 102. The Inter-American Juridical Committee represents all of the Member States of the Organization, and has the broadest possible technical autonomy.

. . . .

PART THREE
CHAPTER XIX
THE UNITED NATIONS

Article 131. None of the provisions of this Charter shall be construed as impairing the rights and obligations of the Member States under the Charter of the United Nations.

[Chapters XX–XXII have been deleted].

RESERVATIONS MADE AT THE TIME OF RATIFICATION

NOTE—The original Charter was signed April 30, 1948, for the Argentine Republic, Bolivia, Brazil, Chile, Colombia, Costa Rica, Cuba,[2] the Dominican Republic, Ecuador, El Salvador, Guatemala, Haiti, Honduras, Mexico, Nicaragua, Panama, Paraguay, Peru, the United States of America, Uruguay, and Venezuela and the following reservations were made at the time of ratifying:

Guatemala

None of the stipulations of the present Charter of the Organization of American States may be considered as an impediment to Guatemala's assertion of its rights over the territory of Belize by such means as at any time it may deem advisable.[3]

Peru

With the reservation that the principles of inter-American solidarity and cooperation and essentially those set forth in the preamble and declarations of the Act of Chapultepec constitute standards for the mutual relations between the American States and juridical bases on the inter-American system.

United States

That the Senate give its advice and consent to ratification of the Charter with the reservation that none of its provisions shall be considered as enlarging the powers of the Federal Government of the United States or limiting the powers of the several states of the Federal Union with respect to any matters recognized under the Constitution as being within the reserved powers of the several states.

. . . .

---

2. The present Government in Cuba is excluded from participation in the Inter-American system by Res. VI, at 12, Eighth Meeting of Consultation of Ministers of Foreign Affairs Acting as Organ of Consultation in Application of the Inter-American Treaty of Reciprocal Assistance, OAS OR, OAS Doc. OE A/Ser. C/II.8 (English) (Jan. 22–31, 1962).

3. With respect to this reservation, the Pan American Union consulted the signatory governments—to ascertain whether they found it acceptable or not—in accordance with the procedure established by O.A.S. Res. XXIX, 2, Eighth International Conference of American States, Lima, Peru, Dec. 9–27, 1938, *Final Act, reprinted in* THE INTERNATIONAL CONFERENCES OF AMERICAN STATES 1889–1928, at 256 (James Brown Scott ed., Supp. 1940). At the request of the Government of Guatemala, this consultation was accompanied by a formal declaration of that Government to the effect that its reservation did not imply any alteration in the Charter of the Organization of American States, and that Guatemala is ready to act at all times within the bounds of international agreements to which it is a party. In view of this declaration, the States that previously did not find the reservation acceptable expressed their acceptance.

Protocol of Amendment to the Charter of the Organization of American States ("Protocol of Cartagena de Indias")[4]

Signed at Cartagena de Indias, Colombia, on December 5, 1985, at the Fourteenth Special Session of the General Assembly; Entered into force November 16, 1988.[5]

IN THE NAME OF THEIR PEOPLES, THE AMERICAN STATES REPRESENTED AT THE FOURTEENTH SPECIAL SESSION OF THE GENERAL ASSEMBLY, MEETING IN CARTAGENA DE INDIAS, COLOMBIA, HAVE AGREED UPON THE FOLLOWING PROTOCOL OF AMENDMENT TO THE CHARTER OF THE ORGANIZATION OF AMERICAN STATES

Article I. The text of the Preamble to the Charter of the Organization of American States is modified to read as follows:

IN THE NAME OF THEIR PEOPLES, THE STATES REPRESENTED AT THE NINTH INTERNATIONAL CONFERENCE OF AMERICAN STATES,

CONVINCED that the historic mission of America is to offer to man a land of liberty and a favorable environment for the development of his personality and the realization of his just aspirations;

CONSCIOUS that that mission has already inspired numerous agreements, whose essential value lies in the desire of the American peoples to live together in peace and, through their mutual understanding and respect for the sovereignty of each one, to provide for the betterment of all, in independence, in equality and under law;

CONVINCED that representative democracy is an indispensable condition for the stability, peace and development of the region;

CONFIDENT that the true significance of American solidarity and good neighborliness can only mean the consolidation on this continent, within the framework of democratic institutions, of a system of individual liberty and social justice based on respect for the essential rights of man;

PERSUADED that their welfare and their contribution to the progress and the civilization of the world will increasingly require intensive continental cooperation;

RESOLVED to persevere in the noble undertaking that humanity has conferred upon the United Nations, whose principles and purposes they solemnly reaffirm;

---

4. Protocol of Amendment to the Charter of the Organization of American States, Dec. 5, 1985, O.A.S.T.S. No. 66 (entered into force Nov. 16, 1988) [hereinafter Protocol of Cartagena de Indias].

On December 15, 1992, the OAS voted to reform the Charter of the OAS by permitting the suspension of member-nations that fail to maintain democratic rule. The vote on this reform was 30 to 1, with 1 abstention. Mexico voted against the reform and gave as its reason that the measure would be an intrusion in the internal affairs of Member Nations.

The reform measure provides that if a Member Country's government is replaced by force then that country would have its rights, including its participation in the OAS General Assembly and individual consultation with all other OAS commissions revoked. This revocation would occur only after diplomatic measures to reinstate democratic rule fail. Any suspension of this type would require two-thirds of the Members of the OAS agree and if a suspension occurs it can only be lifted by a two-thirds majority vote. This is the first revision to the OAS Charter since 1985. The proposed revision still must be ratified by two-thirds of the Parliaments and Congress of the Member countries.

In 1993, the General Assembly met in Managua, Nicaragua which resulted in several proposals to further amend the OAS Charter. These proposals would make social justice and elimination of poverty essential components of the OAS's mission. These amendments have not yet been incorporated into the Charter.

5. As of this date this Protocol of Amendment is not yet in force for the United States of America.

Convinced that juridical organization is a necessary condition for security and peace founded on moral order and on justice; and

In Accordance with Resolution IX of the Inter-American Conference on Problems of War and Peace, held in Mexico City,

ARTICLE II. The texts of the following articles of the Charter of the Organization of American States are amended to read as follows:

Article 1. The American States establish by this Charter the international organization that they have developed to achieve an order of peace and justice, to promote their solidarity, to strengthen their collaboration, and to defend their sovereignty, their territorial integrity, and their independence. Within the United Nations, the Organization of American States is a regional agency.

The Organization of American States has no powers other than those expressly conferred upon it by this Charter, none of whose provisions authorizes it to intervene in matters that are within the internal jurisdiction of the Member States.

Article 2. The Organization of American States, in order to put into practice the principles on which it is founded and to fulfill its regional obligations under the Charter of the United Nations, proclaims the following essential purposes:

a) To strengthen the peace and security of the continent;

b) To promote and consolidate representative democracy, with due respect for the principle of nonintervention;

c) To prevent possible causes of difficulties and to ensure the pacific settlement of disputes that may arise among the Member States;

d) To provide for common action on the part of those States in the event of aggression;

e) To seek the solution of political, juridical, and economic problems that may arise among them;

f) To promote, by cooperative action, their economic, social and cultural development, and

g) To achieve an effective limitation of conventional weapons that will make it possible to devote the largest amount of resources to the economic and social development of the Member States.

Article 3. The American States reaffirm the following principles:

a) International law is the standard of conduct of States in their reciprocal relations;

b) International order consists essentially of respect for the personality, sovereignty, and independence of States, and the faithful fulfillment of obligations derived from treaties and other sources of international law;

c) Good faith shall govern the relations between States;

d) The solidarity of the American States and the high aims which are sought through it require the political organization of those States on the basis of the effective exercise of representative democracy;

e) Every State has the right to choose, without external interference, its political, economic, and social system and to organize itself in the way best suited to it, and has the duty to abstain from intervening in the affairs of another State. Subject to the foregoing, the American States shall cooperate fully among themselves, independently of the nature of their political, economic, and social systems;

f) The American States condemn war of aggression: victory does not give rights;

g) An act of aggression against one American State is an act of aggression against all the other American States;

h) Controversies of an international character arising between two or more American States shall be settled by peaceful procedures;

i) Social justice and social security are bases of lasting peace;

j) Economic cooperation is essential to the common welfare and prosperity of the peoples of the continent;

k) The American States proclaim the fundamental rights of the individual without distinction as to race, nationality, creed, or sex;

l) The spiritual unity of the continent is based on respect for the cultural values of the American countries and requires their close cooperation for the high purposes of civilization;

m) The education of peoples should be directed toward justice, freedom and peace.

Article 8. The Permanent Council shall not make any recommendation nor shall the General Assembly take any decision with respect to a request for admission on the part of a political entity whose territory became subject, in whole or in part, prior to December 18, 1964, the date set by the First Special Inter-American Conference, to litigation or claim between an extracontinental country and one or more Member States of the Organization, until the dispute has been ended by some peaceful procedure. This article shall remain in effect until December 10, 1990.

Article 23. International disputes between Member States shall be submitted to the peaceful procedures set forth in this Charter.

This provision shall not be interpreted as an impairment of the rights and obligations of the Member States under Articles 34 and 35 of the Charter of the United Nations.

Article 26. A special treaty will establish adequate means for the settlement of disputes and will determine pertinent procedures for each peaceful means such that no dispute between American States may remain without definitive settlement within a reasonable period of time.

Article 29. The Member States, inspired by the principles of Inter-American solidarity and cooperation, pledge themselves to a united effort to ensure international social justice in their relations and integral development for their peoples, as conditions essential to peace and security. Integral development encompasses the economic, social, educational, cultural, scientific and technological fields through which the goals that each country sets for accomplishing it should be achieved.

Article 34. The Member States should refrain from practicing policies and adopting actions or measures that have serious adverse effects on the development of other Member States.

....

Article 52. The General Assembly is the supreme organ of the Organization of American States. It has as its principal powers, in addition to such others as are assigned to it by the Charter, the following:

a) To decide the general action and policy of the Organization, determine the structure and functions of its organs, and consider any matter relating to friendly relations among the American States;

b) To establish measures for coordinating the activities of the organs, agencies, and entities of the Organization among themselves, and such activities with those of the other institutions of the inter-American system;

c) To strengthen and coordinate cooperation with the United Nations and its specialized agencies;

d) To promote collaboration, especially in the economic, social, and cultural fields, with other international organizations whose purposes are similar to those of the Organization of American States;

e) To approve the program-budget of the Organization and determine the quotas of the Member States;

f) To consider the reports of the Meeting of Consultation of Ministers of Foreign Affairs and the observations and recommendations presented by the Permanent Council with regard to the reports that should be presented by the other organs and entities, in accordance with the provisions of paragraph f) of Article 91, as well as the reports of any organ which may be required by the General Assembly itself;

g) To adopt general standards to govern the operations of the General Secretariat; and

h) To adopt its own rules of procedure and, by a two-thirds vote, its agenda.

The General Assembly shall exercise its powers in accordance with the provisions of the Charter and of other Inter-American treaties.

Article 63. In case of an armed attack on the territory of an American State or within the region of security delimited by the treaty in force, the Chairman of the Permanent Council shall without delay call a meeting of the Council to decide on the convocation of the Meeting of Consultation, without prejudice to the provisions of the Inter-American Treaty of Reciprocal Assistance with regard to the States Parties to that instrument.

. . . .

SOUTHEAST ASIA COLLECTIVE DEFENSE TREATY* (MANILA PACT)

....

Article 4. 1. Each Party recognizes that aggression by means of armed attack in the treaty area against any of the Parties or against any State or territory which the Parties by unanimous agreement may hereafter designate, would endanger its own peace and safety, and agrees that it will in that event act to meet the common danger in accordance with its constitutional processes. Measures taken under this paragraph shall be immediately reported to the Security Council of the United Nations.

2. If, in the opinion of any of the Parties, the inviolability or the integrity of the territory or the sovereignty or political independence of any Party in the treaty area or of any other State or territory to which the provisions of paragraph 1 of this Article from time to time apply is threatened in any way other than by armed attack or is affected or threatened by any fact or situation which might endanger the peace of the area, the Parties shall consult immediately in order to agree on the measures which should be taken for the common defense.

3. It is understood that no action on the territory of any State designated by unanimous agreement under paragraph 1 of this Article or on any territory so designated shall be taken except at the invitation or with the consent of the government concerned.

....

* Southeast Asia Collective Defense Treaty, Sept. 8, 1954, 6 U.S.T. 81, 209 U.N.T.S. 28 (entered into force Feb. 19, 1955), *available at* http://www.yale.edu/lawweb/avalon/intdip/usmulti/usmu003.htm.

PROTOCOL RELATING TO THE ESTABLISHMENT OF THE PEACE AND SECURITY COUNCIL OF THE AFRICAN UNION*

WE, the Heads of State and Government of the Member States of the African Union;

CONSIDERING the Constitutive Act of the African Union and the Treaty establishing the African Economic Community, as well as the Charter of the United Nations;

RECALLING the Declaration on the establishment, within the Organization of African Unity (OAU), of a Mechanism for Conflict Prevention, Management and Resolution, adopted by the 29th Ordinary Session of the Assembly of Heads of State and Government of the OAU, held in Cairo, Egypt, from 28 to 30 June 1993;

RECALLING also Decision AHG/Dec. 160 (XXXVII) adopted by the 37th Ordinary Session of the Assembly of Heads of State and Government of the OAU, held in Lusaka, Zambia, from 9 to 11 July 2001, by which the Assembly decided to incorporate the Central Organ of the OAU Mechanism for Conflict Prevention, Management and Resolution as one of the organs of the Union, in accordance with Article 5(2) of the Constitutive Act of the African Union, and, in the regard, requested the Secretary-General to undertake a review of the structures, procedures and working methods of the Central Organ, including the possibility of changing its name;

MINDFUL of the provisions of the Charter of the United Nations, conferring on the Security Council primary responsibility for the maintenance of international peace and security, as well as the provisions of the Charter on the role of regional arrangements or agencies in the maintenance of international peace and security, and the need to forge closer cooperation and partnership between the United Nations, other international organizations and the African Union, in the promotion and maintenance of peace, security and stability in Africa;

ACKNOWLEDGING the contribution of African Regional Mechanisms for Conflict Prevention, Management and Resolution in the maintenance and promotion of peace, security and stability on the Continent and the need to develop formal coordination and cooperation arrangements between these Regional Mechanisms and the African Union;

RECALLING Decisions AHG/Dec.141 (XXXV) and AHG/Dec.142 (XXXV) on Unconstitutional Changes of Government, adopted by the 35th Ordinary Session of the Assembly of Heads of State and Government of the OAU held in Algiers, Algeria, from 12 to 14 July 1999, and Declaration AHG/Decl.5 (XXXVI) on the Framework for an OAU Response to Unconstitutional Changes of Government, adopted by the 36th Ordinary Session of the Assembly of Heads of State and Government of the OAU, held in Lomé, Togo, from 10 to 12 July 2000;

REAFFIRMING our commitment to Solemn Declaration AHG/Decl.4 (XXXVI) on the Conference on Security, Stability, Development and Cooperation in Africa (CSSDCA), adopted by the 36th Ordinary Session of the Assembly of Heads of State and Government of the OAU, held in Lomé, Togo, from 10 to 12 Jury 2000, as well as Declaration AHG/Decl.1 (XXXVII) on the New Partnership for Africa's Development

---

* Protocol Relating to the Establishment of the Peace and Security Council of the African Union, July 9, 2002, *available at* http://www.africa-union.org (entered into force Dec. 26, 2003).

(NEPAD), which was adopted by the 37th Ordinary Session of the Assembly of Heads of State and Government of the OAU, held in Lusaka, Zambia, from 9 to 11 July 2001,;

AFFIRMING our further commitment to Declaration AHG/Decl.2 (XXX) on the Code of Conduct for Inter-African Relations, adopted by the 30th Ordinary Session of the Assembly of Heads of State and Government of the OAU, held in Tunis, Tunisia, from 13 to 15 June 1994, as well as the Convention on the Prevention and Combating of Terrorism, adopted by the 35th Ordinary Session of the Assembly of Heads of State and Government of the OAU held in Algiers, Algeria, from 12 to 14 July 1999;

CONCERNED about the continued prevalence of armed conflicts in Africa and the fact that no single internal factor has contributed more to socioeconomic decline on the Continent and the suffering of the civilian population than the scourge of conflicts within and between our States;

CONCERNED ALSO by the fact that conflicts have forced millions of our people, including women and children, into a drifting life as refugees and internally displaced persons, deprived of their means of livelihood, human dignity and hope;

CONCERNED FURTHER about the scourge of landmines in the Continent and

RECALLING, in this respect, the Plan of Action on a Landmine Free Africa, adopted by the 1st Continental Conference of African Experts on Anti-Personnel Mines, held in Kempton Park, South Africa, from 17 to 19 May 1997, and endorsed by the 66th Ordinary Session of the OAU Council of Ministers, held in Harare, Zimbabwe, from 26 to 30 May 1997, as well as subsequent decisions adopted by the OAU on this issue;

CONCERNED ALSO about the impact of the illicit proliferation, circulation and trafficking of small arms and light weapons in threatening peace and security in Africa and undermining efforts to improve the living standards of African peoples and

RECALLING, in this respect, the Declaration on the Common African Position on the Illicit Proliferation, Circulation and Trafficking of Small Arms and Light Weapons, adopted by the OAU Ministerial Conference held in Bamako, Mali, from 30 November to 1 December 2000, as well as all subsequent OAU decisions on this issue;

AWARE that the problems caused by landmines and the illicit proliferation, circulation and trafficking of small arms and light weapons constitute a serious impediment to Africa's social and economic development, and that they can only be resolved within the framework of increased and well coordinated continental cooperation;

AWARE ALSO of the fact that the development of strong democratic institutions and culture, observance of human rights and the rule of law, as well as the implementation of post-conflict recovery programmes and sustainable development policies, are essential for the promotion of collective security, durable peace and stability, as well as for the prevention of conflicts;

DETERMINED to enhance our capacity to address the scourge of conflicts on the Continent and to ensure that Africa, through the African Union, plays a central role in bringing about peace, security and stability on the Continent;

DESIROUS of establishing an operational structure for the effective implementation of the decisions taken in the areas of conflict prevention, peace-making, peace support operations and intervention, as well as peace-building and post-conflict reconstruction, in accordance with the authority conferred in that regard by Article 5(2) of the Constitutive Act of the African Union;

HEREBY AGREE ON THE FOLLOWING:

Article 1. Definitions. For the purpose of this Protocol:

a) "Protocol" shall mean the present Protocol;

b) "Cairo Declaration" shall mean the Declaration on the Establishment, within the OAU, of the Mechanism for Conflict Prevention, Management and Resolution;

c) "Lomé Declaration" shall mean the Declaration on the Framework for an OAU Response to Unconstitutional Changes of Government;

d) "Constitutive Act" shall mean the Constitutive Act of the African Union;

e) "Union" shall mean the African Union;

f) "Assembly" shall mean the Assembly of Heads of State and Government of the African Union;

g) "Commission" shall mean the Commission of the African Union;

h) "Regional Mechanisms" shall mean the African Regional Mechanisms for Conflict Prevention, Management and Resolution;

i) "Member States" shall mean Member States of the African Union.

Article 2. Establishment, nature and structure. 1. There is hereby established, pursuant to Article 5(2) of the Constitutive Act, a Peace and Security Council within the Union, as a standing decision-making organ for the prevention, management and resolution of conflicts. The Peace and Security Council shall be a collective security and early-warning arrangement to facilitate timely and efficient response to conflict and crisis situations in Africa.

2. The Peace and Security Council shall be supported by the Commission, a Panel of the Wise, a Continental Early Warning System, an African Standby Force and a Special Fund.

Article 3. Objectives. The objectives for which the Peace and Security Council is established shall be to:

a. promote peace, security and stability in Africa, in order to guarantee the protection and preservation of life and property, the well-being of the African people and their environment, as well as the creation of conditions conducive to sustainable development;

b. anticipate and prevent conflicts. In circumstances where conflicts have occurred, the Peace and Security Council shall have the responsibility to undertake peace-making and peace-building functions for the resolution of these conflicts;

c. promote and implement peace-building and post-conflict reconstruction activities to consolidate peace and prevent the resurgence of violence;

d. co-ordinate and harmonize continental efforts in the prevention and combating of international terrorism in all its aspects;

e. develop a common defence policy for the Union, in accordance with article 4(d) of the Constitutive Act;

f. promote and encourage democratic practices, good governance and the rule of law, protect human rights and fundamental freedoms, respect for the sanctity of human life and international humanitarian law, as part of efforts for preventing conflicts.

Article 4. Principles. The Peace and Security Council shall be guided by the principles enshrined in the Constitutive Act, the Charter of the United Nations and the Universal Declaration of Human Rights. It shall, in particular, be guided by the following principles:

a. peaceful settlement of disputes and conflicts;

b. early responses to contain crisis situations so as to prevent them from developing into full-blown conflicts;

c. respect for the rule of law, fundamental human rights and freedoms, the sanctity of human life and international humanitarian law;

d. interdependence between socio-economic development and the security of peoples and States;

e. respect for the sovereignty and territorial integrity of Member States;

f. non interference by any Member State in the internal affairs of another;

g. sovereign equality and interdependence of Member States;

h. inalienable right to independent existence;

i. respect of borders inherited on achievement of independence;

j. the right of the Union to intervene in a Member State pursuant to a decision of the Assembly in respect of grave circumstances, namely war crimes, genocide and crimes against humanity, in accordance with Article 4(h) of the Constitutive Act;

k. the right of Member States to request intervention from the Union in order to restore peace and security, in accordance with Article 4(j) of the Constitutive Act.

Article 5. Composition. 1. The Peace and Security Council shall be composed of fifteen Members elected on the basis of equal rights, in the following manner:

a. ten Members elected for a term of two years; and

b. five Members elected for a term of three years in order to ensure continuity.

2. In electing the Members of the Peace and Security Council, the Assembly shall apply the principle of equitable regional representation and rotation, and the following criteria with regard to each prospective Member State:

a. commitment to uphold the principles of the Union;

b. contribution to the promotion and maintenance of peace and security in Africa—in this respect, experience in peace support operations would be an added advantage;

c. capacity and commitment to shoulder the responsibilities entailed in membership;

d. participation in conflict resolution, peace-making and peace-building at regional and continental levels;

e. willingness and ability to take up responsibility for regional and continental conflict resolution initiatives;

f. contribution to the Peace Fund and/or Special Fund created for specific purpose;

g. respect for constitutional governance, in accordance with the Lomé Declaration, as well as the rule of law and human rights;

h. having sufficiently staffed and equipped Permanent Missions at the Headquarters of the Union and the United Nations, to be able to shoulder the responsibilities which go with the membership; and

j. commitment to honor financial obligations to the Union.

3. A retiring Member of the Peace and Security Council shall be eligible for immediate re-election.

4. There shall be a periodic review by the Assembly to assess the extent to which the Members of the Peace and Security Council continue to meet the requirements spelt out in article 5 (2) and to take action as appropriate.

Article 6. *Functions.* The Peace and Security Council shall perform functions in the following areas:

a. promotion of peace, security and stability in Africa;

b. early warning and preventive diplomacy;

c. peace-making, including the use of good offices, mediation, conciliation and enquiry;

d. peace support operations and intervention, pursuant to article 4 (h) and (j) of the Constitutive Act;

e. peace-building and post-conflict reconstruction;

f. humanitarian action and disaster management;

g. any other function as may be decided by the Assembly.

Article 7. *Powers.* 1. In conjunction with the Chairperson of the Commission, the Peace and Security Council shall:

a. anticipate and prevent disputes and conflicts, as well as policies that may lead to genocide and crimes against humanity;

b. undertake peace-making and peace-building functions to resolve conflicts where they have occurred;

c. authorize the mounting and deployment of peace support missions;

d. lay down general guidelines for the conduct of such missions, including the mandate thereof, and undertake periodic reviews of these guidelines;

e. recommend to the Assembly, pursuant to Article 4(h) of the Constitutive Act, intervention, on behalf of the Union, in a Member State in respect of grave circumstances, namely war crimes, genocide and crimes against humanity, as defined in relevant international conventions and instruments;

f. approve the modalities for intervention by the Union in a Member State, following a decision by the Assembly, pursuant to article 4(j) of the Constitutive Act;

g. institute sanctions whenever an unconstitutional change of Government takes place in a Member State, as provided for in the Lomé Declaration;

h. implement the common defense policy of the Union;

i. ensure the implementation of the OAU Convention on the Prevention and Combating of Terrorism and other relevant international, continental and regional conventions and instruments and harmonize and coordinate efforts at regional and continental levels to combat international terrorism;

j. promote close harmonization, co-ordination and co-operation between Regional Mechanisms and the Union in the promotion and maintenance of peace, security and stability in Africa;

k. promote and develop a strong "partnership for peace and security" between the Union and the United Nations and its agencies, as well as with other relevant international organizations;

l. develop policies and action required to ensure that any external initiative in the field of peace and security on the continent takes place within the framework of the Union's objectives and priorities;

m. follow-up, within the framework of its conflict prevention responsibilities, the progress towards the promotion of democratic practices, good governance, the rule of law, protection of human rights and fundamental freedoms, respect for the sanctity of human life and international humanitarian law by Member States;

n. promote and encourage the implementation of OAU/AU, UN and other relevant international Conventions and Treaties on arms control and disarmament;

o. examine and take such appropriate action within its mandate in situations where the national independence and sovereignty of a Member State is threatened by acts of aggression, including by mercenaries;

p. support and facilitate humanitarian action in situations of armed conflicts or major natural disasters;

q. submit, through its Chairperson, regular reports to the Assembly on its activities and the state of peace and security in Africa; and

r. decide on any other issue having implications for the maintenance of peace, security and stability on the Continent and exercise powers that may be delegated to it by the Assembly, in accordance with Article 9 (2) of the Constitutive Act.

2. The Member States agree that in carrying out its duties under the present Protocol, the Peace and Security Council acts on their behalf.

3. The Member States agree to accept and implement the decisions of the Peace and Security Council, in accordance with the Constitutive Act.

4. The Member States shall extend full cooperation to, and facilitate action by the Peace and Security Council for the prevention, management and resolution of crises and conflicts, pursuant to the duties entrusted to it under the present Protocol.

Article 8. Procedure.

Organization and meetings

1. The Peace and Security Council shall be so organized as to be able to function continuously. For this purpose, each Member of the Peace and Security Council shall, at all times, be represented at the Headquarters of the Union.

2. The Peace and Security Council shall meet at the level of Permanent Representatives, Ministers or Heads of State and Government. It shall convene as often as required at the level of Permanent Representatives, but at least twice a month. The Ministers and the Heads of State and Government shall meet at least once a year, respectively.

3. The meetings of the Peace and Security Council shall be held at the Headquarters of the Union.

4. In the event a Member State invites the Peace and Security Council to meet in its country, provided that two-thirds of the Peace and Security Council members agree, that Member State shall defray the additional expenses incurred by the Commission as a result of the meeting being held outside the Headquarters of the Union.

Subsidiary bodies and sub-committees

5. The Peace and Security Council may establish such subsidiary bodies as it deems necessary for the performance of its functions. Such subsidiary bodies may include ad hoc committees for mediation, conciliation or enquiry, consisting of an individual State or group of States. The Peace and Security Council shall also seek such military, legal and other forms of expertise as it may require for the performance of its functions.

Chairmanship

6. The chair of the Peace and Security Council shall be held in turn by the Members of the Peace and Security Council in the alphabetical order of their names. Each Chairperson shall hold office for one calendar month.

Agenda

7. The provisional agenda of the Peace and Security Council shall be determined by the Chairperson of the Peace and Security Council on the basis of proposals submitted by the Chairperson of the Commission and Member States. The inclusion of any item in the provisional agenda may not be opposed by a Member State.

Quorum

8. The number of Members required to constitute a quorum shall be two-thirds of the total membership of the Peace and Security Council.

Conduct of business

9. The Peace and Security Council shall hold closed meetings. Any Member of the Peace and Security Council which is party to a conflict or a situation under consideration by the Peace and Security Council shall not participate either in the discussion or in the decision making process relating to that conflict or situation, Such Member shall be invited to present its case to the Peace and Security Council as appropriate, and shall, thereafter, withdraw from the proceedings.

10. The Peace and Security Council may decide to hold open meetings. In this regard:

a. any Member State which is not a Member of the Peace and Security Council, if it is party to a conflict or a situation under consideration by the Peace and Security Council, shall be invited to present its case as appropriate and shall participate, without the right to vote, in the discussion;

b. any Member State which is not a Member of the Peace and Security Council may be invited to participate, without the right to vote, in the discussion of any question brought before the Peace and Security Council whenever that Member State considers that its interests are especially affected;

c. any Regional Mechanism, international organization or civil society organization involved and/or interested in a conflict or a situation under consideration by the Peace and Security Council may be invited to participate, without the right to vote, in the discussion relating to that conflict or situation.

11. The Peace and Security Council may hold informal consultations with parties concerned by or interested in a conflict or a situation under its consideration, as well as

with Regional Mechanisms, international organizations and civil society organizations as may be needed for the discharge of its responsibilities.

Voting

12. Each Member of the Peace and Security Council shall have one vote.

13. Decisions of the Peace and Security Council shall generally be guided by the principle of consensus. In cases where consensus cannot be reached, the Peace and Security Council shall adopt its decisions on procedural matters by a simple majority, while decisions on all other matters shall be made by a two-thirds majority vote of its Members voting.

Rules of procedure

14. The Peace and Security Council shall submit its own rules of procedure, including on the convening of its meetings, the conduct of business, the publicity and records of meetings and any other relevant aspect of its work, for consideration and approval by the Assembly.

Article 9. *Entry points and modalities for action.* 1. The Peace and Security Council shall take initiatives and action it deems appropriate with regard to situations of potential conflict, as well as to those that have already developed into full-blown conflicts. The Peace and Security Council shall also take all measures that are required in order to prevent a conflict for which a settlement has already been reached from escalating.

2. To that end, the Peace and Security Council shall use its discretion to effect entry, whether through the collective intervention of the Council itself, or through its Chairperson and/or the Chairperson of the Commission, the Panel of the Wise, and/or in collaboration with the Regional Mechanisms.

Article 10. *The role of the chairperson of the commission.* 1. The Chairperson of the Commission shall, under the authority of the Peace and Security Council, and in consultation with all parties involved in a conflict, deploy efforts and take all initiatives deemed appropriate to prevent, manage and resolve conflicts.

2. To this end, the Chairperson of the Commission:

a. shall bring to the attention of the Peace and Security Council any matter, which, in his/her opinion, may threaten peace, security and stability in the Continent;

b. may bring to the attention of the Panel of the Wise any matter which, in his/her opinion, deserves their attention;

c. may, at his/her own initiative or when so requested by the Peace and Security Council, use his/her good offices, either personally or through special envoys, special representatives, the Panel of the Wise or the Regional Mechanisms, to prevent potential conflicts, resolve actual conflicts and promote peace-building and post-conflict reconstruction.

3. The Chairperson of the Commission shall also:

a. ensure the implementation and follow-up of the decisions of the Peace and Security Council, including mounting and deploying peace support missions authorized by the Peace and Security Council. In this respect, the Chairperson of the Commission shall keep the Peace and Security Council informed of developments relating to the functioning of such missions. All problems likely to affect the continued and effective functioning of these missions shall be referred to the Peace and Security Council, for its consideration and appropriate action;

b. ensure the implementation and follow-up of the decisions taken by the Assembly in conformity with Article 4 (h) and (j) of the Constitutive Act;

c. prepare comprehensive and periodic reports and documents, as required, to enable the Peace Security Council and its subsidiary bodies to perform their functions effectively.

4. In the exercise of his/her functions and powers, the Chairperson of the Commission shall be assisted by the Commissioner in charge of Peace and Security, who shall be responsible for the affairs of the Peace and Security Council. The Chairperson of the Commission shall rely on human and material resources available at the Commission, for servicing and providing support to the Peace and Security Council. In this regard, a Peace and Security Council Secretariat shall be established within the Directorate dealing with conflict prevention, management and resolution.

Article 11. Panel of the wise. 1. In order to support the efforts of the Peace and Security Council and those of the Chairperson of the Commission, particularly in the area of conflict prevention, a Panel of the Wise shall be established.

2. The Panel of the Wise shall be composed of five highly respected African personalities from various segments of society who have made outstanding contribution to the cause of peace, security and development on the continent. They shall be selected by the Chairperson of the Commission after consultation with the Member States concerned, on the basis of regional representation and appointed by the Assembly to serve for a period of three years.

3. The Panel of the Wise shall advise the Peace and Security Council and the Chairperson of the Commission on all issues pertaining to the promotion, and maintenance of peace, security and stability in Africa.

4. At the request of the Peace and Security Council or the Chairperson of the Commission, or at its own initiative, the Panel of the Wise shall undertake such action deemed appropriate to support the efforts of the Peace and Security Council and those of the Chairperson of the Commission for the prevention of conflicts, and to pronounce itself on issues relating to the promotion and maintenance of peace, security and stability in Africa.

5. The Panel of the Wise shall report to the Peace and Security Council and, through the Peace and Security Council, to the Assembly.

6. The Panel of the Wise shall meet as may be required for the performance of its mandate. The Panel of the Wise shall normally hold its meetings at the Headquarters of the Union. In consultation with the Chairperson of the Commission, the Panel of the Wise may hold meetings at such places other than the Headquarters of the Union.

7. The modalities for the functioning of the Panel of the Wise shall be worked out by the Chairperson of the Commission and approved by the Peace and Security Council.

8. The allowances of members of the Panel of the Wise shall be determined by the Chairperson of the Commission in accordance with the Financial Rules and Regulations of the Union.

Article 12. Continental early warning system. 1. In order to facilitate the anticipation and prevention of conflicts, a Continental Early Warning System to be known as the Early Warning System shall be established.

2. The Early Warning System shall consist of:

a. an observation and monitoring centre, to be known as "The Situation Room", located at the Conflict Management Directorate of the Union, and responsible for data collection and analysis on the basis of an appropriate early warning indicators module; and

b. observation and monitoring units of the Regional Mechanisms to be linked directly through appropriate means of communications to the Situation Room, and which shall collect and process data at their level and transmit the same to the Situation Room.

3. The Commission shall also collaborate with the United Nations, its agencies, other relevant international organizations, research centers, academic institutions and NGOs, to facilitate the effective functioning of the Early Warning System.

4. The Early Warning System shall develop an early warning module based on clearly defined and accepted political, economic, social, military and humanitarian indicators, which shall be used to analyze developments within the continent and to recommend the best course of action.

5. The Chairperson of the Commission shall use the information gathered through the Early Warning System timeously to advise the Peace and Security Council on potential conflicts and threats to peace and security in Africa and recommend the best course of action. The Chairperson of the Commission shall also use this information for the execution of the responsibilities and functions entrusted to him/her under the present Protocol.

6. The Member States shall commit themselves to facilitate early action by the Peace and Security Council and or the Chairperson of the Commission based on early warning information.

7. The Chairperson of the Commission shall, in consultation with Member States, the Regional Mechanisms, the United Nations and other relevant institutions, work out the practical details for the establishment of the Early Warning System and take all the steps required for its effective functioning.

***Article 13.** African standby force.*

Composition

1. In order to enable the Peace and Security Council perform its responsibilities with respect to the deployment of peace support missions and intervention pursuant to article 4 (h) and (j) of the Constitutive Act, an African Standby Force shall be established. Such Force shall be composed of standby multidisciplinary contingents, with civilian and military components in their countries of origin and ready for rapid deployment at appropriate notice.

2. For that purpose, the Member States shall take steps to establish standby contingents for participation in peace support missions decided on by the Peace and Security Council or intervention authorized by the Assembly. The strength and types of such contingents, their degree of readiness and general location shall be determined in accordance with established African Union Peace Support Standard Operating Procedures (SOPs), and shall be subject to periodic reviews depending on prevailing crisis and conflict situations.

Mandate

3. The African Standby Force shall, *inter alia,* perform functions in the following areas:

a. observation and monitoring missions;

b. other types of peace support missions;

c. intervention in a Member State in respect of grave circumstances or at the request of a Member State in order to restore peace and security, in accordance with Article 4(h) and (j) of the Constitutive Act;

d. preventive deployment in order to prevent (i) a dispute or a conflict from escalating, (ii) an ongoing violent conflict from spreading to neighboring areas or States, and (iii) the resurgence of violence after parties to a conflict have reached an agreement.;

e. peace-building, including post-conflict disarmament and demobilization;

f. humanitarian assistance to alleviate the suffering of civilian population in conflict areas and support efforts to address major natural disasters; and

g. any other functions as may be mandated by the Peace and Security Council or the Assembly.

4. In undertaking these functions, the African Standby Force shall, where appropriate, cooperate with the United Nations and its Agencies, other relevant international organizations and regional organizations, as well as with national authorities and NGOs.

5. The detailed tasks of the African Standby Force and its modus operandi for each authorized mission shall be considered and approved by the Peace and Security Council upon recommendation of the Commission.

Chain of Command

6. For each operation undertaken by the African Standby Force, the Chairperson of the Commission shall appoint a Special Representative and a Force Commander, whose detailed roles and functions shall be spelt out in appropriate directives, in accordance with the Peace Support Standing Operating Procedures.

7. The Special Representative shall, through appropriate channels, report to the Chairperson of the Commission. The Force Commander shall report to the Special Representative. Contingent Commanders shall report to the Force Commander, while the civilian components shall report to the Special Representative.

Military Staff Committee

8. There shall be established a Military Staff Committee to advise and assist the Peace and Security Council in all questions relating to military and security requirements for the promotion and maintenance of peace and security in Africa.

9. The Military Staff Committee shall be composed of Senior Military Officers of the Members of the Peace and Security Council. Any Member State not represented on the Military Staff Committee may be invited by the Committee to participate in its deliberations when it is so required for the efficient discharge of the Committee's responsibilities.

10. The Military Staff Committee shall meet as often as required to deliberate on matters referred to it by the Peace and Security Council.

11. The Military Staff Committee may also meet at the level of the Chief of Defence Staff of the Members of the Peace and Security Council to discuss questions relating to the military and security requirements for the promotion and maintenance of peace and security in Africa. The Chiefs of Defence Staff shall submit to the Chairperson of the Commission recommendations on how to enhance Africa's peace support capacities.

12. The Chairperson of the Commission shall take all appropriate steps for the convening of and follow-up of the meetings of the Chiefs of Defence Staff of Members of the Peace and Security Council.

Training

13. The Commission shall provide guidelines for the training of the civilian and military personnel of national standby contingents at both operational and tactical levels. Training on International Humanitarian Law and International Human Rights Law, with particular emphasis on the rights of women and children, shall be an integral part of the training of such personnel

14. To that end, the Commission shall expedite the development and circulation of appropriate Standing Operating Procedures to *inter-alia:*

a. support standardization of training doctrines, manuals and programmes for national and regional schools of excellence;

b. co-ordinate the African Standby Force training courses, command and staff exercises, as well as field training exercises.

15. The Commission shall, in collaboration with the United Nations, undertake periodic assessment of African peace support capacities.

16. The Commission shall, in consultation with the United Nations Secretariat, assist in the co-ordination of external initiatives in support of the African Standby Force capacity-building in training, logistics, equipment, communications and funding.

Role of Member States

17. In addition to their responsibilities as stipulated under the present Protocol:

a. troop contributing countries States shall immediately, upon request by the Commission, following an authorization by the Peace and Security Council or the Assembly, release the standby contingents with the necessary equipment for the operations envisaged under Article 9 (3) of the present Protocol;

b. Member States shall commit themselves to make available to the Union all forms of assistance and support required for the promotion and maintenance of peace, security and stability on the Continent, including rights of passage through their territories.

Article 14. Peace building.

Institutional Capacity for Peace-building

1. In post-conflict situations, the Peace and Security Council shall assist in the restoration of the rule of law, establishment and development of democratic institutions and the preparation, organization and supervision of elections in the concerned Member State.

Peace-building during Hostilities

2. In areas of relative peace, priority shall be accorded to the implementation of policy designed to reduce degradation of social and economic conditions arising from conflicts.

Peace-building at the End of Hostilities

3. To assist Member States that have been adversely affected by violent conflicts, the Peace and Security Council shall undertake the following activities:

a. consolidation of the peace agreements that have been negotiated;

b. establishment of conditions of political, social and economic reconstruction of the society and Government institutions;

c. implementation of disarmament, demobilization and reintegration programmes, including those for child soldiers;

d. resettlement and reintegration of refugees and internally displaced persons;

e. assistance to vulnerable persons, including children, the elderly, women and other traumatized groups in the society.

Article 15. *Humanitarian action.* 1. The Peace and Security Council shall take active part in coordinating and conducting humanitarian action in order to restore life to normalcy in the event of conflicts or natural disasters.

2. In this regard, the Peace and Security Council shall develop its own capacity to efficiently undertake humanitarian action.

3. The African Standby Force shall be adequately equipped to undertake humanitarian activities in their mission areas under the control of the Chairperson of the Commission.

4. The African Standby Force shall facilitate the activities of the humanitarian agencies in the mission areas.

Article 16. *Relationship with regional mechanisms for conflict prevention, management and resolution.* 1. The Regional Mechanisms are part of the overall security architecture of the Union, which has the primary responsibility for promoting peace, security and stability in Africa. In this respect, the Peace and Security Council and the Chairperson of the Commission, shall:

a) harmonize and coordinate the activities of Regional Mechanisms in the field of peace, security and stability to ensure that these activities are consistent with the objectives and principles of the Union;

b) work closely with Regional Mechanisms, to ensure effective partnership between them and the Peace and Security Council in the promotion and maintenance of peace, security and stability. The modalities of such partnership shall be determined by the comparative advantage of each and the prevailing circumstances.

2. The Peace and Security Council shall, in consultation with Regional Mechanisms, promote initiatives aimed at anticipating and preventing conflicts and, in circumstances where conflicts have occurred, peacemaking and peace-building functions.

3. In undertaking these efforts, Regional Mechanisms concerned shall, through the Chairperson of the Commission, keep the Peace and Security Council fully and continuously informed of their activities and ensure that these activities are closely harmonized and coordinated with the activities of Peace and Security Council. The Peace and Security Council shall, through the Chairperson of the Commission, also keep the Regional Mechanisms fully and continuously informed of its activities.

4. In order to ensure close harmonization and coordination and facilitate regular exchange of information, the Chairperson of the Commission shall convene periodic meetings, but at least once a year, with the Chief Executives and/or the officials in charge of peace and security within the Regional Mechanisms.

5. The Chairperson of the Commission shall take the necessary measures, where appropriate, to ensure the full involvement of Regional Mechanisms in the establishment and effective functioning of the Early Warning System and the African Standby Force.

6. Regional Mechanisms shall be invited to participate in the discussion of any question brought before the Peace and Security Council whenever that question is being addressed by a Regional Mechanism is of special interest to that Organization.

7. The Chairperson of the Commission shall be invited to participate in meetings and deliberations of Regional Mechanisms.

8. In order to strengthen coordination and cooperation, the Commission shall establish liaison offices to the Regional Mechanisms. The Regional Mechanisms shall be encouraged to establish liaison offices to the Commission.

9. On the basis of the above provisions, a Memorandum of Understanding on Cooperation shall be concluded between the Commission and the Regional Mechanisms.

Article 17. *Relationship with the United Nations and other international organizations.* 1. In the fulfillment of its mandate in the promotion and maintenance of peace, security and stability in Africa, the Peace and Security Council shall cooperate and work closely with the United Nations Security Council, which has the primary responsibility for the maintenance of international peace and security. The Peace and Security Council shall also cooperate and work closely with other relevant UN Agencies in the promotion of peace, security and stability in Africa.

2. Where necessary, recourse will be made to the United Nations to provide the necessary financial, logistical and military support for the African Unions' activities in the promotion and maintenance of peace, security and stability in Africa, in keeping with the provisions of Chapter VIII of the UN Charter on the role of Regional Organizations in the maintenance of international peace and security.

3. The Peace and Security Council and the Chairperson of the Commission shall maintain close and continued interaction with the United Nations Security Council, its African members, as well as with the Secretary-General, including holding periodic meetings and regular consultations on questions of peace, security and stability in Africa.

4. The Peace and Security Council shall also cooperate and work closely with other relevant international organizations on issues of peace, security and stability in Africa. Such organizations may be invited to address the Peace and Security Council on issues of common interest, if the latter considers that the efficient discharge of its responsibilities does so require.

Article 18. *Relationship with the pan-African parliament.* 1. The Mechanism shall maintain close working relations with the Pan-African Parliament in furtherance of peace, security and stability in Africa.

2. The Peace and Security Council shall, whenever so requested by the Pan African Parliament, submit, through the Chairperson of the Commission, reports to the Pan-African Parliament, in order to facilitate the discharge by the latter of its responsibilities relating to the maintenance of peace, security and stability in Africa.

3. The Chairperson of the Commission shall present to the Pan-African Parliament an annual report on the state of peace and security in the continent. The Chairperson of the Commission shall also take all steps required to facilitate the exercise by the Pan-African Parliament of its powers, as stipulated in Article 11 (5) of the Protocol to the Treaty establishing the African Economic Community relating to the Pan-African Parliament, as well as in Article 11 (9) in so far as it relates to the objective of promoting peace, security and stability as spelt out in Article 3 (5) of the said Protocol.

Article 19. *Relationship with the African commission on human and peoples' rights.* The Peace and Security Council shall seek close cooperation with the African Commission on Human and Peoples' Rights in all matters relevant to its objectives and mandate. The Commission on Human and Peoples' Rights shall bring to the attention of the Peace and Security Council any information relevant to the objectives and mandate of the Peace and Security Council.

Article 20. Relations with civil society organizations. The Peace and Security Council shall encourage non-governmental organizations, community-based and other civil society organizations, particularly women's organizations, to participate actively in the efforts aimed at promoting peace, security and stability in Africa. When required, such organizations may be invited to address the Peace and Security Council.

Article 21. Funding.

Peace Fund

1. In order to provide the necessary financial resources for peace support missions and other operational activities related to peace and security, a Special Fund, to be known as the Peace Fund, shall be established. The operations of the Peace Fund shall be governed by the relevant Financial Rules and Regulations of the Union.

2. The Peace Fund shall be made up of financial appropriations from the regular budget of Union, including arrears of contributions, voluntary contributions from Member States and from other sources within Africa, including the private sector, civil society and individuals, as well as through appropriate fund raising activities.

3. The Chairperson of the Commission shall raise and accept voluntary contributions from sources outside Africa, in conformity with the objectives and principles of the Union.

4. There shall also be established, within the Peace Fund, a revolving Trust Fund. The appropriate amount of the revolving Trust Fund shall be determined by the relevant Policy Organs of the Union upon recommendation by the Peace and Security Council.

Assessment of Cost of Operations and Pre-financing

5. When required, and following a decision by the relevant Policy Organs of the Union, the cost of the operations envisaged under Article 13 (3) of the present Protocol shall be assessed to Member States based on the scale of their contributions to the regular budget of the Union.

6. The States contributing contingents may be invited to bear the cost of their participation during the first three (3) months.

7. The Union shall refund the expenses incurred by the concerned contributing States within a maximum period of six (6) months and then proceed to finance the operations.

Article 22. Final provisions.

Status of the Protocol in relation to the Cairo Declaration

1. The present Protocol shall replace the Cairo Declaration.

2. The provisions of this Protocol shall supercede the resolutions and decisions of the OAU relating to the Mechanism for Conflict Prevention, Management and Resolution in Africa, which are in conflict with the present Protocol.

Signature, Ratification and Accession

3. The present Protocol shall be open for signature, ratification or accession by the Member States of the Union in accordance with their respective constitutional procedures.

4. The instruments of ratification shall be deposited with the Chairperson Commission.

Entry into Force

5. The present Protocol shall enter into force upon the deposit of the instruments of ratification by a simple majority of the Member States of the Union.

Amendments

6. Any amendment or revision of the present Protocol shall be in accordance with the provisions of Article 32 of the Constitutive Act.

Depository Authority

7. This Protocol and all instruments of ratification shall be deposited with the Chairperson of the Commission, who shall transmit certified true copies to all Member States and notify them of the dates of deposit of the instruments of ratification by the Member States and shall register it with the United Nations and any other Organization as may be decided by the Union.

Adopted by the 1st Ordinary Session of the Assembly of the African Union, Durban, 9 July 2002.

1. People's Democratic Republic of Algeria
2. Republic of Angola
3. Republic of Benin
4. Republic of Botswana
5. Burkina Faso
6. Republic of Burundi
7. Republic of Cameroon
8. Republic of Cape Verde
9. Central African Republic
10. Republic of Chad
11. Islamic Federal Republic of the Comoros
12. Republic of the Congo
13. Republic of Côte d'lvoire
14. Democratic Republic of Congo
15. Republic of Djibouti
16. Arab Republic of Egypt
17. State of Eritrea
18. Federal Democratic Republic of Ethiopia
19. Republic of Equatorial Guinea
20. Republic of Gabon
21. Republic of The Gambia
22. Republic of Ghana
23. Republic of Guinea
24. Republic of Guinea Bissau
25. Republic of Kenya
26. Kingdom of Lesotho
27. Republic of Liberia
28. Great Socialist People's Libyan Arab Jamahiriya

29. Republic of Madagascar
30. Republic of Malawi
31. Republic of Mali
32. Islamic Republic of Mauritania
33. Republic of Mauritius
34. Republic of Mozambique
35. Republic of Namibia
36. Republic of Niger
37. Federal Republic of Nigeria
38. Republic of Rwanda
39. Sahrawi Arab Democratic Republic
40. Republic of Sao Tome and Principe
41. Republic of Senegal
42. Republic of Seychelles
43. Republic of Sierra Leone
44. Republic of Somalia
45. Republic of South Africa
46. Republic of Sudan
47. Kingdom of Swaziland
48. United Republic of Tanzania
49. Republic of Togo
50. Republic of Tunisia
51. Republic of Uganda
52. Republic of Zambia
53. Republic of Zimbabwe

C. The Machinery for the Peaceful Resolution of Disputes

STATUTE OF THE INTERNATIONAL COURT OF JUSTICE[1]

Article 1. The International Court of Justice established by the Charter of the United Nations as the principal judicial organ of the United Nations shall be constituted and shall function in accordance with the provisions of the present Statute.

CHAPTER I—ORGANIZATION OF THE COURT

Article 2. The Court shall be composed of a body of independent judges, elected regardless of their nationality from among persons of high moral character, who possess the qualifications required in their respective countries for appointment to the highest judicial offices, or are jurisconsults of recognized competence in international law.

Article 3. 1. The Court shall consist of fifteen members, no two of whom may be nationals of the same state.

2. A person who for the purposes of membership in the Court could be regarded as a national of more than one state shall be deemed to be a national of the one in which he ordinarily exercises civil and political rights.

Article 4. 1. The members of the Court shall be elected by the General Assembly and by the Security Council from a list of persons nominated by the national groups in the Permanent Court of Arbitration, in accordance with the following provisions.

2. In the case of Members of the United Nations not represented in the Permanent Court of Arbitration, candidates shall be nominated by national groups appointed for this purpose by their governments under the same conditions as those prescribed for members of the Permanent Court of Arbitration by Article 44 of the Convention of The Hague of 1907 for the pacific settlement of international disputes.

3. The conditions under which a state which is a party to the present Statute but is not a Member of the United Nations may participate in electing the members of the Court shall, in the absence of a special agreement, be laid down by the General Assembly upon recommendation of the Security Council.

....

CHAPTER II—COMPETENCE OF THE COURT

Article 34.

1. Only states may be parties in cases before the Court.

---

1. Statute of the International Court of Justice, June 26, 1945, 59 Stat. 1031, 1055, 3 Bevans 1153, 1179, *available at* http://www.icj-cij.org/icjwww/ibasicdocuments/ibasictext/ibasicstatute.htm#Article_1, (entered into force Oct. 24, 1945). *See also* Declaration by the President of the United States of America Respecting Recognition by the United States of America of the Compulsory Jurisdiction of the International Court of Justice, Aug. 14, 1946, 61 Stat. 1218, 1 U.N.T.S. 9 (including the Connally Reservation) [hereinafter Declaration of the United States' Recognition of Compulsory Jurisdiction].

2. The Court, subject to and in conformity with its Rules, may request of public international organizations information relevant to cases before it, and shall receive such information presented by such organizations on their own initiative.

3. Whenever the construction of the constituent instrument of a public international organization or of an international convention adopted thereunder is in question in a case before the Court, the Registrar shall so notify the public international organization concerned and shall communicate to it copies of all the written proceedings.

Article 35.

1. The Court shall be open to the states parties to the present Statute.

2. The conditions under which the Court shall be open to other states shall, subject to the special provisions contained in treaties in force, be laid down by the Security Council, but in no case shall such conditions place the parties in a position of inequality before the Court.

3. When a state which is not a Member of the United Nations is a party to a case, the Court shall fix the amount which that party is to contribute towards the expenses of the Court. This provision shall not apply if such state is bearing a share of the expenses of the Court

Article 36. 1. The jurisdiction of the Court comprises all cases which the parties refer to it and all matters specially provided for in the Charter of the United Nations or in treaties and conventions in force.

2. The states parties to the present Statute may at any time declare that they recognize as compulsory *ipso facto* and without special agreement, in relation to any other state accepting the same obligation, the jurisdiction of the Court in all legal disputes concerning:

a. the interpretation of a treaty;

b. any question of international law;

c. the existence of any fact which, if established, would constitute a breach of an international obligation;

d. the nature or the extent of the reparation to be made for the breach of an international obligation.

. . . .

Article 38. 1. The Court, whose function is to decide in accordance with international law such disputes as are submitted to it, shall apply:

a. international conventions, whether general or particular, establishing rules expressly recognized by the contesting states;

b. international custom, as evidence of a general practice accepted as law;

c. the general principles of law recognized by civilized nations;

d. subject to the provisions of Article 59, judicial decisions and the teachings of the most highly qualified publicists of the various nations, as subsidiary means for the determination of rules of law.

2. This provision shall not prejudice the power of the Court to decide a case *ex aequo et bono*, if the parties agree thereto.

. . . .

CHAPTER III—PROCEDURE

. . . .

Article 59. The decision of the Court has no binding force except between the parties and in respect of that particular case.

. . . .

CHAPTER IV—ADVISORY OPINIONS

Article 65. 1. The Court may give an advisory opinion on any legal question at the request of whatever body may be authorized by or in accordance with the Charter of the United Nations to make such a request.

2. Questions upon which the advisory opinion of the Court is asked shall be laid before the Court by means of a written request containing an exact statement of the question upon which an opinion is required, and accompanied by all documents likely to throw light upon the question.

Article 66. 1. The Registrar shall forthwith give notice of the request for an advisory opinion to all states entitled to appear before the Court.

2. The Registrar shall also, by means of a special and direct communication, notify any state entitled to appear before the Court or international organization considered by the Court, or, should it not be sitting, by the President, as likely to be able to furnish information on the question, that the Court will be prepared to receive, within a time limit to be fixed by the President, written statements, or to hear, at a public sitting to be held for the purpose, oral statements relating to the question.

3. Should any such state entitled to appear before the Court have failed to receive the special communication referred to in paragraph 2 of this Article, such state may express a desire to submit a written statement or to be heard; and the Court will decide.

4. States and organizations having presented written or oral statements or both shall be permitted to comment on the statements made by other states or organizations in the form, to the extent, and within the time limits which the Court, or, should it not be sitting, the President, shall decide in each particular case. Accordingly, the Registrar shall in due time communicate any such written statements to states and organizations having submitted similar statements.

Article 67. The Court shall deliver its advisory opinions in open court, notice having been given to the Secretary-General and to the representatives of Members of the United Nations, of other states and of international organizations immediately concerned.

Article 68. In the exercise of its advisory functions the Court shall further be guided by the provisions of the present Statute which apply in contentious cases to the extent to which it recognizes them to be applicable.

. . . .

a. Declaration of the United States Recognition of Compulsory Jurisdiction[2] (with "Connally" Reservation)

Declaration by the President of the United States signed August 14, 1946

---

2. Declaration by the President of the United States of America Respecting Recognition by the United States of America of the Compulsory Jurisdiction of the International Court of Justice, Aug. 14, 1946, 61 Stat. at 1218, 1 U.N.T.S. at 9 (including the Connally Reservation).

Senate advice and consent to deposit August 2, 1946

Deposited with the United Nations August 26, 1946

I, Harry S. Truman, President of the United States of America, declare on behalf of the United States of America, under Article 36, paragraph 2, of the Statute of the International Court of Justice, and in accordance with the Resolution of August 2, 1946,[3] of the Senate of the United States of America (two-thirds of the Senators present concurring therein), that the United States of America recognizes as compulsory *ipso facto* and without special agreement, in relation to any other state accepting the same obligation, the jurisdiction of the International Court of Justice in all legal disputes hereafter arising concerning:

a. the interpretation of a treaty;

b. any question of international law;

c. the existence of any fact which, if established, would constitute a breach of an international obligation;

d. the nature or extent of the reparation to be made for the breach of an international obligation;

Provided, that this declaration shall not apply to:

a. disputes the solution of which the parties shall entrust to other tribunals by virtue of agreements already in existence or which may be concluded in the future; or

b. disputes with regard to matters which are essentially within the domestic jurisdiction of the United States of America as determined by the United States[4] of America; or

c. disputes arising under a multilateral treaty, unless (1) all parties to the treaty affected by the decision are also parties to the case before the Court, or (2) the United States of America specially agrees to jurisdiction; and

Provided further, that this declaration shall remain in force for a period of five years and thereafter until the expiration of six months after notice may be given to terminate this declaration.

Done at Washington this fourteenth day of August 1946.

Harry S. Truman

b. United States Modification Respecting Compulsory Jurisdiction 6 April 1984

I have the honor on behalf of the Government of the United States of America to refer to the Declaration of my Government of August 26, 1946, concerning the acceptance of the United States of America of the compulsory jurisdiction of the International Court of Justice, and to state that the aforesaid Declaration shall not apply to disputes with any Central American State or arising out of or related to events in Central America, any of which disputes shall be settled in such manner as the parties to them may agree.

Notwithstanding the terms of the aforesaid Declaration, this *proviso* shall take effect immediately and shall remain in force for two years, so as to foster the continuing re-

---

3. S. Res. 196, 79th Cong., 92 Cong. Rec. 10706 (1946) (enacted).
4. The Words "as determined by the United States" are often termed the "Connally Reservation."

gional dispute settlement process which seeks negotiated solution to the interrelated political, economic and security problems of Central America.

(*signed*) George Shultz,
Secretary of State of the United States of America.

c. United States Termination of Declaration Respecting Compulsory Jurisdiction

Dear Mr. Secretary-General: I[5] have the honor on behalf of the Government of the United States of America to refer to the declaration of my Government of 26 August 1946, as modified by my note of 6 April 1984, concerning the acceptance by the United States of America of the compulsory jurisdiction of the International Court of Justice, and to state that the aforesaid declaration is hereby terminated, with effect six months from the date hereof.

Sincerely yours,

(*signed*) George P. Shultz,
Secretary of State of the
United States of America

5. Letter from George P. Schultz, U.S. Sec'y of State, to Javier Perez de Cuellar, U.N. Sec'y Gen. (Oct. 7, 1985), Dep't St. Bull., Jan. 1986, at 67.

D. The Lawfulness of the Use of Force in International Relations: Norms Concerning the Initiation of Coercion

KELLOGG-BRIAND PACT[1] (PACT OF PARIS)[2]

. . . .

THE PRESIDENT OF THE GERMAN REICH, THE PRESIDENT OF THE UNITED STATES OF AMERICA, HIS MAJESTY THE KING OF THE BELGIANS, THE PRESIDENT OF THE FRENCH REPUBLIC, HIS MAJESTY THE KING OF GREAT BRITAIN IRELAND AND THE BRITISH DOMINIONS BEYOND THE SEAS, EMPEROR OF INDIA, HIS MAJESTY THE KING OF ITALY, HIS MAJESTY THE EMPEROR OF JAPAN, THE PRESIDENT OF THE REPUBLIC OF POLAND THE PRESIDENT OF THE CZECHOSLOVAK REPUBLIC,

Deeply sensible of their solemn duty to promote the welfare of mankind;

---

1. Treaty Between the United States and Other Powers Providing for the Renunciation of War as an Instrument of National Policy, Aug. 27, 1928, 46 Stat. 2343, 94 L.N.T.S. 57 (entered into force July 25, 1929) [hereinafter Kellogg-Briand Peace Pact or Pact of Paris], *available at* http://www.yale.edu/lawweb/avalon/imt/kbpact.htm.

2. A note from the United States to each of the Governments invited to sign the Pact clarifies the scope of the Pact, and shows that the right of self-defense is retained under the Pact:

> There is nothing in the American draft of an anti-war treaty which restricts or impairs in any way the right of self-defence. That right is inherent in every sovereign State and is implicit in every treaty. Every nation is free at all times and regardless of treaty provisions to defend its territory from attack or invasion and it alone is competent to decide whether circumstances require recourse to war in self-defence. If it has a good case, the world will applaud and not condemn its action. Express recognition by treaty of this inalienable right, however, gives rise to the same difficulty encountered in any effort to define aggression. It is the identical question approached from the other side. Inasmuch as no treaty provision can add to the natural right of self-defence, it is not in the interest of peace that a treaty should stipulate a juristic conception of self-defence since it is far too easy for the unscrupulous to mould events to accord with an agreed definition.

Note of the Government of the United States to the Governments of Australia, Belgium, Canada, Czechoslovakia, France, Germany, Great Britain, India, Irish Free State, Italy, Japan, New Zealand, Poland, and South Africa (June 23, 1928) (internal quotation marks and citation omitted), *in* U.S. Dep't of State, The General Pact for the Renunciation of War: Text of the Pact as Signed, Notes and Other Papers 36, 36-37 (1928), *quoted in* The Secretary-General, *Report by the Secretary-General*, 64, *delivered to the General Assembly*, U.N. Doc. A/2211 (Oct. 3, 1952).

Secretary of State Kellogg addressed the same issue in a letter to French Ambassador Claudel:

> If, however, such a declaration were accompanied by definitions of the word "aggressor" and by exceptions and qualifications stipulating when nations would be justified in going to war, its effect would be very greatly weakened and its positive value as a guaranty of peace virtually destroyed. The ideal which inspires the effort so sincerely and so hopefully put forward by your Government and mine is arresting and appealing just because of its purity and simplicity; and I cannot avoid the feeling that if governments should publicly acknowledge that they can only deal with this ideal in a technical spirit and must insist upon the adoption of reservations impairing, if not utterly destroying the true significance of their common endeavours, they would be, in effect only recording their impotence, to the keen disappointment of mankind in general.

Letter of Frank B. Kellogg, U.S. Sec'y of State, to Paul Claudel, French Ambassador to the U.S. (Feb. 27, 1928), *in* U.S. Dep't of State, The General Pact for the Renunciation of War: Text of the Pact as Signed, Notes and Other Papers 12, 14 (1928), *quoted in* The Secretary-General, *Report by the Secretary-General*, 62 n.48, *delivered to the General Assembly*, U.N. Doc. A/2211 (Oct. 3, 1952).

Persuaded that the time has, come when a frank renunciation of war as an instrument of national policy should be made to the end that the peaceful and friendly relations now existing between their peoples may be perpetuated;

Convinced that all changes in their relations with one another should be sought only by pacific means and be the result of a peaceful and orderly process, and that any signatory Power which shall hereafter seek to promote its national interests by resort to war should be denied the benefits furnished by this Treaty;

Hopeful that, encouraged by their example, all the other nations of the world will join in this humane endeavor and by adhering to the present Treaty as soon as it comes into force bring their peoples within the scope of its beneficent provisions, thus uniting the civilized nations of the world in a common renunciation of war as an instrument of their national policy;

Have decided to conclude a Treaty....

Article 1. The High Contracting Parties solemnly declare in the names of their respective peoples that they condemn recourse to war for the solution of international controversies, and renounce it, as an instrument of national policy in their relations with one another.

Article 2. The High Contracting Parties agree that the settlement or solution of all disputes or conflicts of whatever nature or of whatever origin they may be, which may arise among them, shall never be sought except by pacific means.

Article 3. The present Treaty shall be ratified by the High Contracting Parties named in the Preamble in accordance with their respective constitutional requirements, and shall take effect as between them as soon as all their several instruments of ratification shall have been deposited at Washington.

This Treaty shall, when it has come into effect as prescribed in the preceding paragraph, remain open as long as may be necessary for adherence by all the other Powers of the world. Every instrument evidencing the adherence of a Power shall be deposited at Washington and the Treaty shall immediately upon such deposit become effective as; between the Power thus adhering and the other Powers parties hereto.

It shall be the duty of the Government of the United States to furnish each Government named in the Preamble and every Government subsequently adhering to this Treaty with a certified copy of the Treaty and of every instrument of ratification or adherence. It shall also be the duty of the Government of the United States telegraphically to notify such Governments immediately upon the deposit with it of each instrument of ratification or adherence.

IN FAITH WHEREOF the respective Plenipotentiaries have signed this Treaty in the French and English languages both texts having equal force, and hereunto affix their seals.

DONE at Paris, the twenty-seventh day of August in the year one thousand nine hundred and twenty-eight.

....

DECLARATION ON THE INADMISSIBILITY OF INTERVENTION IN THE DOMESTIC AFFAIRS OF STATES AND THE PROTECTION OF THEIR INDEPENDENCE AND SOVEREIGNTY*

The General Assembly,

Deeply concerned at the gravity of the international situation and the increasing threat to universal peace due to armed intervention and other direct or indirect forms of interference threatening the sovereign personality and the political independence of States,

Considering that the United Nations, in accordance with their aim to eliminate war, threats to the peace and acts of aggression, created an Organization, based on the sovereign equality of States, whose friendly relations would be based on respect for the principle of equal rights and self-determination of peoples and on the obligation of its Members to refrain from the threat or use of force against the territorial integrity or political independence of any State,

Recognizing that, in fulfillment of the principle of self-determination, the General Assembly, in the Declaration on the Granting of Independence to Colonial Countries and Peoples contained in resolution 1514 (XV) of 14 December 1960, stated its conviction that all peoples have an inalienable right to complete freedom, the exercise of their sovereignty and the integrity of their national territory, and that, by virtue of that right, they freely determine their political status and freely pursue their economic, social and cultural development,

Recalling that in the Universal Declaration of Human Rights the General Assembly proclaimed that recognition of the inherent dignity and of the equal and inalienable rights of all members of the human family is the foundation of freedom, justice and peace in the world, without distinction of any kind,

Reaffirming the principle of non-intervention, proclaimed in the charters of the Organization of American States, the League of Arab States and the Organization of African Unity and affirmed at the conferences held at Montevideo. Buenos Aires, Chapultepec and Bogotá, as well as in the decisions of the Asian-African Conference at Bandung, the First Conference of Heads of State or Government of Non-Aligned Countries at Belgrade, in the Programme for Peace and International Cooperation adopted at the end of the Second Conference of Heads of State or Government of Non-Aligned Countries at Cairo, and in the declaration on subversion adopted at Accra by the Heads of State and Government of the African States,

Recognizing that full observance of the principle of the non-intervention of States in the internal and external affairs of other States is essential to the fulfillment of the purposes and principles of the United Nations,

* G.A. Res. 2131 (XX), at 11, U.N. GAOR, 20th Sess., Supp. No. 14, U.N. Doc. A/6014 (Dec. 21, 1965), *available at* http://www.un.org/documents/ga/res/20/ares20.htm.

Considering that armed intervention is synonymous with aggression and, as such, is contrary to the basic principles on which peaceful international co-operation between States should be built,

Considering further that direct intervention, subversion and all forms of indirect intervention are contrary to these principles and, consequently, constitute a violation of the Charter of the United Nations,

Mindful that violation of the principle of non-intervention poses a threat to the independence, freedom and normal political, economic, social and cultural development of countries, particularly those which have freed themselves from colonialism, and can pose a serious threat to the maintenance of peace,

Fully aware of the imperative need to create appropriate conditions which would enable all States, and in particular the developing countries, to choose without duress or coercion their own political, economic and social institutions,

In the light of the foregoing considerations, solemnly declares:

1. No State has the right to intervene, directly or indirectly, for any reason whatever, in the internal or external affairs of any other State. Consequently, armed intervention and all other forms of interference or attempted threats against the personality of the State or against its political, economic and cultural elements, are condemned.

2. No State may use or encourage the use of economic, political or any other type of measures to coerce another State in order to obtain from it the subordination of the exercise of its sovereign rights or to secure from it advantages of any kind. Also, no State shall organize, assist, foment, finance, incite or tolerate subversive, terrorist or armed activities directed towards the violent overthrow of the regime of another State, or interfere in civil strife in another State.

3. The use of force to deprive peoples of their national identity constitutes a violation of their inalienable rights and of the principle of non-intervention.

4. The strict observance of these obligations is an essential condition to ensure that nations live together in peace with one another, since the practice of any form of intervention not only violates the spirit and letter of the Charter of the United Nations but also leads to the creation of situations which threaten international peace and security.

5. Every State has an inalienable right to choose its political, economic, social and cultural systems, without interference in any form by another State.

6. All States shall respect the right of self-determination and independence of peoples and nations, to be freely exercised without any foreign pressure, and with absolute respect for human rights and fundamental freedoms. Consequently, all States shall contribute to the complete elimination of racial discrimination and colonialism in all its forms and manifestations.

7. For the purpose of the present Declaration, the term "State" covers both individual States and groups of States.

8. Nothing in this Declaration shall be construed as affecting in any manner the relevant provisions of the Charter of the United Nations relating to the maintenance of international peace and security, in particular those contained in Chapters VI, VII and VIII.

....

DECLARATION ON PRINCIPLES OF INTERNATIONAL LAW CONCERNING FRIENDLY RELATIONS AND CO-OPERATION AMONG STATES IN ACCORDANCE WITH THE CHARTER OF THE UNITED NATIONS*

The General Assembly,

*Recalling*its resolutions 1815 (XVII) of 18 December 1962, 1966 (XVIII) of 16 December 1963, 2103 (XX) of 20 December 1965, 2181 (XXI) of 12 December 1966, 2327 (XXII) of 18 December 1967, 2463 (XXIII) of 20 December 1968 and 2533 (XXIV) of 8 December 1969, in which it affirmed the importance of the progressive development and codification of the principles of international law concerning friendly relations and co-operation among States,

Having considered the report of the Special Committee on Principles of International Law concerning Friendly Relations and Co-operation among States, which met in Geneva from 31 March to 1 May 1970,

Emphasizing the paramount importance of the Charter of the United Nations for the maintenance of international peace and security and for the development of friendly relations and co-operation among States,

Deeply convinced that the adoption of the Declaration on Principles of International Law concerning Friendly Relations and Co-operation among States in accordance with the Charter of the United Nations on the occasion of the twenty-fifth anniversary of the United Nations would contribute to the strengthening of world peace and constitute a landmark in the development of international law and of relations among States, in promoting the rule of law among nations and particularly the universal application of the principles embodied in the Charter,

Considering the desirability of the wide dissemination of the text of the Declaration,

1. *Approves* the Declaration on Principles of International Law concerning Friendly Relations and Cooperation among States in accordance with the Charter of the United Nations, the text of which is annexed to the present resolution;

2. *Expresses its appreciation* to the Special Committee on Principles of International Law concerning Friendly Relations and Co-operation among States for its work resulting in the elaboration of the Declaration;

3. *Recommends* that all efforts be made so that the Declaration becomes generally known.

....

* G.A. Res. 2625 (XXV), at 121, U.N. GAOR, 25th Sess., Supp. No. 28, U.N. Doc. A/8028 (Oct. 24, 1970).

Annex
Declaration on Principles of International Law Concerning Friendly Relations and Co-operation Among States In Accordance with the Charter of the United Nations

Preamble

The General Assembly,

Reaffirming in the terms of the Charter of the United Nations that the maintenance of international peace and security and the development of friendly relations and co-operation between nations are among the fundamental purposes of the United Nations,

Recalling that the peoples of the United Nations are determined to practise tolerance and live together in peace with one another as good neighbours,

Bearing in mind the importance of maintaining and strengthening international peace founded upon freedom, equality, justice and respect for fundamental human rights and of developing friendly relations among nations irrespective of their political, economic and social systems or the levels of their development,

Bearing in mind also the paramount importance of the Charter of the United Nations in the promotion of the rule of law among nations,

Considering that the faithful observance of the principles of international law concerning friendly relations and co-operation among States and the fulfillment in good faith of the obligations assumed by States, in accordance with the Charter, is of the greatest importance for the maintenance of international peace and security and for the implementation of the other purposes of the United Nations,

Noting that the great political, economic and social changes and scientific progress which have taken place in the world since the adoption of the Charter give increased importance to these principles and to the need for their more effective application in the conduct of States wherever carried on,

Recalling the established principle that outer space, including the Moon and other celestial bodies, is not subject to national appropriation by claim of sovereignty, by means of use or occupation, or by any other means, and mindful of the fact that consideration is being given in the United Nations to the question of establishing other appropriate provisions similarly inspired,

Convinced that the strict observance by States of the obligation not to intervene in the affairs of any other State is an essential condition to ensure that nations live together in peace with one another, since the practice of any form of intervention not only violates the spirit and letter of the Charter, but also leads to the creation of situations which threaten international peace and security,

Recalling the duty of States to refrain in their international relations from military, political, economic or any other form of coercion aimed against the political independence or territorial integrity of any State,

Considering it essential that all States shall refrain in their international relations from the threat or use of force against the territorial integrity or political independence of any State, or in any other manner inconsistent with the purposes of the United Nations,

Considering it equally essential that all States shall settle their international disputes by peaceful means in accordance with the Charter,

Reaffirming, in accordance with the Charter, the basic importance of sovereign equality and stressing that the purposes of the United Nations can be implemented only if States enjoy sovereign equality and comply fully with the requirements of this principle in their international relations,

Convinced that the subjection of peoples to alien subjugation, domination and exploitation constitutes a major obstacle to the promotion of international peace and security,

Convinced that the principle of equal rights and self-determination of peoples constitutes a significant contribution to contemporary international law, and that its effective application is of paramount importance for the promotion of friendly relations among States, based on respect for the principle of sovereign equality,

Convinced in consequence that any attempt aimed at the partial or total disruption of the national unity and territorial integrity of a State or country or at its political independence is incompatible with the purposes and principles of the Charter.

Considering the provisions of the Charter as a whole and taking into account the role of relevant resolutions adopted by the competent organs of the United Nations relating to the content of the principles,

Considering that the progressive development and codification of the following principles:

(a) The principle that States shall refrain in their international relations from the threat or use of force against the territorial integrity or political independence of any State, or in any other manner inconsistent with the purposes of the United Nations,

(b) The principle that States shall settle their international disputes by peaceful means in such a manner that international peace and security and justice are not endangered,

(c) The duty not to intervene in matters within the domestic jurisdiction of any State, in accordance with the Charter,

(d) The duty of States to co-operate with one another in accordance with the Charter,

(e) The principle of equal rights and self-determination of peoples,

(f) The principle of sovereign equality of States,

(g) The principle that States shall fulfill in good faith the obligations assumed by them in accordance with the Charter, so as to secure their more effective application within the international community, would promote the realization of the purposes of the United Nations,

Having considered the principles of international law relating to friendly relations and co-operation among States,

1. Solemnly proclaims the following principles:

The principle that States shall refrain in their international relations from the threat or use of force against the territorial integrity or political independence of any State, or in any other manner inconsistent with the purposes of the United Nations

Every State has the duty to refrain in its international relations from the threat or use of force against the territorial integrity or political independence of any State, or in any other manner inconsistent with the purposes of the United Nations. Such a threat or use of force constitutes a violation of international law and the Charter of the United Nations and shall never be employed as a means of settling international issues.

A war of aggression constitutes a crime against the peace, for which there is responsibility under international law.

In accordance with the purposes and principles of the United Nations, States have the duty to refrain from propaganda for wars of aggression.

Every State has the duty to refrain from the threat or use of force to violate the existing international boundaries of another State or as a means of solving international disputes, including territorial disputes and problems concerning frontiers of States.

Every State likewise has the duty to refrain from the threat or use of force to violate international lines of demarcation, such as armistice lines, established by or pursuant to an international agreement to which it is a party or which it is otherwise bound to respect. Nothing in the foregoing shall be construed as prejudicing the positions of the parties concerned with regard to the status and effects of such lines under their special regimes or as affecting their temporary character.

States have a duty to refrain from acts of reprisal involving the use of force.

Every State has the duty to refrain from any forcible action which deprives peoples referred to in the elaboration of the principle of equal rights and self-determination of their right to self-determination and freedom and independence.

Every State has the duty to refrain from organizing or encouraging the organization of irregular forces or armed bands, including mercenaries, for incursion into the territory of another State.

Every State has the duty to refrain from organizing, instigating, assisting or participating in acts of civil strife or terrorist acts in another State or acquiescing in organized activities within its territory directed towards the commission of such acts, when the acts referred to in the present paragraph involve a threat or use of force.

The territory of a State shall not be the object of military occupation resulting from the use of force in contravention of the provisions of the Charter. The territory of a State shall not be the object of acquisition by another State resulting from the threat or use of force. No territorial acquisition resulting from the threat or use of force shall be recognized as legal. Nothing in the foregoing shall be construed as affecting:

(a) Provisions of the Charter or any international agreement prior to the Charter regime and valid under international law; or

(b) The powers of the Security Council under the Charter.

All States shall pursue in good faith negotiations for the early conclusion of a universal treaty on general and complete disarmament under effective international control and strive to adopt appropriate measures to reduce international tensions and strengthen confidence among States.

All States shall comply in good faith with their obligations under the generally recognized principles and rules of international law with respect to the maintenance of international peace and security, and shall endeavour to make the United Nations security system based on the Charter more effective.

Nothing in the foregoing paragraphs shall be construed as enlarging or diminishing in any way the scope of the provisions of the Charter concerning cases in which the use of force is lawful.

The principle that States shall settle their international disputes by peaceful means in such a manner that international peace and security and justice are not endangered

Every State shall settle its international disputes with other States by peaceful means in such a manner that international peace and security and justice are not endangered.

States shall accordingly seek early and just settlement of their international disputes by negotiation, inquiry, mediation, conciliation, arbitration, judicial settlement, resort to regional agencies or arrangements or other peaceful means of their choice. In seeking such a settlement the parties shall agree upon such peaceful means as may be appropriate to the circumstances and nature of the dispute.

The parties to a dispute have the duty, in the event of failure to reach a solution by any one of the above peaceful means, to continue to seek a settlement of the dispute by other peaceful means agreed upon by them.

States parties to an international dispute, as well as other States, shall refrain from any action which may aggravate the situation so as to endanger the maintenance of international peace and security, and shall act in accordance with the purposes and principles of the United Nations.

International disputes shall be settled on the basis of the sovereign equality of States and in accordance with the principle of free choice of means. Recourse to, or acceptance of, a settlement procedure freely agreed to by States with regard to existing or future disputes to which they are parties shall not be regarded as incompatible with sovereign equality.

Nothing in the foregoing paragraphs prejudices or derogates from the applicable provisions of the Charter, in particular those relating to the pacific settlement of international disputes.

The principle concerning the duty not to intervene in matters within the domestic jurisdiction of any State, in accordance with the Charter

No State or group of States has the right to intervene, directly or indirectly, for any reason whatever, in the internal or external affairs of any other State. Consequently, armed intervention and all other forms of interference or attempted threats against the personality of the State or against its political, economic and cultural elements, are in violation of international law.

No State may use or encourage the use of economic, political or any other type of measures to coerce another State in order to obtain from it the subordination of the exercise of its sovereign rights and to secure from it advantages of any kind. Also, no State shall organize, assist, foment, finance, incite or tolerate subversive, terrorist or armed activities directed towards the violent overthrow of the regime of another State, or interfere in civil strife in another State.

The use of force to deprive peoples of their national identity constitutes a violation of their inalienable rights and of the principle of non-intervention.

Every State has an inalienable right to choose its political, economic, social and cultural systems, without interference in any form by another State.

Nothing in the foregoing paragraphs shall be construed as affecting the relevant provisions of the Charter relating to the maintenance of international peace and security.

The duty of States to co-operate with one another in accordance with the Charter

States have the duty to co-operate with one another, irrespective of the differences in their political, economic and social systems, in the various spheres of international relations, in order to maintain international peace and security and to promote international economic stability and progress, the general welfare of nations and international co-operation free from discrimination based on such differences.

To this end:

(a) States shall co-operate with other States in the maintenance of international peace and security;

(b) States shall co-operate in the promotion of universal respect for, and observance of, human rights and fundamental freedoms for all, and in the elimination of all forms of racial discrimination and all forms of religious intolerance;

(c) States shall conduct their international relations in the economic, social, cultural, technical and trade fields in accordance with the principles of sovereign equality and non-intervention;

(d) States Members of the United Nations have the duty to take joint and separate action in co-operation with the United Nations in accordance with the relevant provisions of the Charter.

States should co-operate in the economic, social and cultural fields as well as in the field of science and technology and for the promotion of international cultural and educational progress. States should co-operate in the promotion of economic growth throughout the world, especially that of the developing countries.

The principle of equal rights and self-determination of peoples

By virtue of the principle of equal rights and self-determination of peoples enshrined in the Charter of the United Nations, all peoples have the right freely to determine, without external interference, their political status and to pursue their economic, social and cultural development, and every State has the duty to respect this right in accordance with the provisions of the Charter.

Every State has the duty to promote, through joint and separate action, realization of the principle of equal rights and self-determination of peoples, in accordance with the provisions of the Charter, and to render assistance to the United Nations in carrying out the responsibilities entrusted to it by the Charter regarding the implementation of the principle, in order:

(a) *To* promote friendly relations and co-operation among States; and

(b) To bring a speedy end to colonialism, having due regard to the freely expressed will of the peoples concerned;

and bearing in mind that subjection of peoples to alien subjugation, domination and exploitation constitutes a violation of the principle, as well as a denial of fundamental human rights, and is contrary to the Charter.

Every State has the duty to promote through joint and separate action universal respect for and observance of human rights and fundamental freedoms in accordance with the Charter.

The establishment of a sovereign and independent State, the free association or integration with an independent State or the emergence into any other political status freely determined by a people constitute modes of implementing the right of self-determination by that people.

Every State has the duty to refrain from any forcible action which deprives peoples referred to above in the elaboration of the present principle of their right to self-determination and freedom and independence. In their actions against, and resistance to, such forcible action in pursuit of the exercise of their right to self-determination, such peoples are entitled to seek and to receive support in accordance with the purposes and principles of the Charter.

The territory of a colony or other Non-Self-Governing Territory has, under the Charter, a status separate and distinct from the territory of the State administering it; and such separate and distinct status under the Charter shall exist until the people of the colony or Non-Self-Governing Territory have exercised their right of self-determination in accordance with the Charter, and particularly its purposes and principles.

Nothing in the foregoing paragraphs shall be construed as authorizing or encouraging any action which would dismember or impair, totally or in part, the territorial integrity or political unity of sovereign and independent States conducting themselves in compliance with the principle of equal rights and self-determination of peoples as described above and thus possessed of a government representing the whole people belonging to the territory without distinction as to race, creed or colour.

Every State shall refrain from any action aimed at the partial or total disruption of the national unity and territorial integrity of any other State or country.

The principle of sovereign equality of States

All States enjoy sovereign equality. They have equal rights and duties and are equal members of the international community, notwithstanding differences of an economic, social, political or other nature.

In particular, sovereign equality includes the following elements:

(a) States are juridically equal;

(b) Each State enjoys the rights inherent in full sovereignty;

(c) Each State has the duty to respect the personality of other States;

(d) The territorial integrity and political independence of the State are inviolable;

(e) Each State has the right freely to choose and develop its political, social, economic and cultural systems;

(f) Each State has the duty to comply fully and in good faith with its international obligations and to live in peace with other States.

The principle that States shall fulfill in good faith the obligations assumed by them in accordance with the Charter

Every State has the duty to fulfill in good faith the obligations assumed by it in accordance with the Charter of the United Nations.

Every State has the duty to fulfill in good faith its obligations under the generally recognized principles and rules of international law.

Every State has the duty to fulfill in good faith its obligations under international agreements valid under the generally recognized principles and rules of international law.

Where obligations arising under international agreements are in conflict with the obligations of Members of the United Nations under the Charter of the United Nations, the obligations under the Charter shall prevail.

General Part

2. *Declares* that:

In their interpretation and application the above principles are interrelated and each principle should be construed in the context of the other principles.

Nothing in this Declaration shall be construed as prejudicing in any manner the provisions of the Charter or the rights and duties of Member States under the Charter or the rights of peoples under the Charter, taking into account the elaboration of these rights in this Declaration.

3. *Declares further* that:

The principles of the Charter which are embodied in this Declaration constitute basic principles of international law, and consequently appeals to all States to be guided by these principles in their international conduct and to develop their mutual relations on the basis of the strict observance of these principles.

DEFINITION OF AGGRESSION RESOLUTION* (DRAFT PROPOSAL)

C. *Draft proposal submitted by Australia, Canada, Italy, Japan, the United Kingdom of Great Britain and Northern Ireland and the United States of America*

The General Assembly,

Conscious that a primary purpose of the United Nations is to maintain international peace and security, and, to that end, to take effective collective measures for the prevention and removal of threats to the peace, and for the suppression of acts of aggression or other breaches of the peace,

Recalling that Article 39 of the Charter of the United Nations provides that the Security Council shall determine the existence of any threat to the peace, breach of the peace, or act of aggression and shall make recommendations, or decide what measures shall be taken in accordance with Articles 41 and 42, to maintain or restore international peace and security,

Reaffirming that all States shall settle their international disputes by peaceful means in such a manner that international peace and security, and justice, are not endangered,

Believing that, although the question of whether an act of aggression has been committed must be considered in the light of all the circumstances of each particular case, a generally accepted definition of aggression may nevertheless provide guidance for such consideration,

Being of the view that such a definition of aggression may accordingly facilitate the processes of the United Nations and encourage States to fulfill in good faith their obligations under the Charter of the United Nations,

Adopts the following definition:

I. Under the Charter of the United Nations, "aggression" is a term to be applied by the Security Council when appropriate in the exercise of its primary responsibility for the maintenance of international peace and security under Article 24 and its functions under Article 39.

II. The term "aggression" is applicable, without prejudice to a finding of threat to the peace or breach of the peace, to the use of force in international relations, overt or covert, direct or indirect, by a State against the territorial integrity or political independence of any other State, or in any other manner inconsistent with the purposes of the United Nations. Any act which would constitute aggression by or against a State likewise constitutes aggression when committed by a State or other political entity delimited by international boundaries or internationally agreed lines of demarcation against any State or other political entity so delimited and not subject to its authority.

---

* Draft Proposal Submitted by Australia, Canada, Italy, Japan, the United Kingdom of Great Britain and Northern Ireland and the United States of America, U.N. Doc. A/AC.134/L.17 & Adds. 1-2 (Mar. 23 & 26, 1969, & July 16, 1970), *in* U.N. Special Comm. on the Question of Defining Aggression, *Report of the Special Committee on the Question of Defining Aggression*, at 11, U.N. Doc. A/9019 (Apr. 25-May 30, 1973).

III. The use of force in the exercise of the inherent right of individual or collective self defence, or pursuant to decisions of or authorization by competent United Nations organs or regional organizations consistent with the Charter of the United Nations, does not constitute aggression.

IV. The uses of force which may constitute aggression include, but are not necessarily limited to, a use of force by a State as described in paragraph II.

A. In order to:

(1) Diminish the territory or alter the boundaries of another State;

(2) Alter internationally agreed lines of demarcation;

(3) Disrupt or interfere with the conduct of the affairs of another State;

(4) Secure changes in the Government of another State; or

(5) Inflict harm or obtain concessions of any sort;

B. By such means as:

(1) Invasion by its armed forces of territory under the jurisdiction of another State;

(2) Use of its armed forces in another State in violation of the fundamental conditions of permission for their presence, or maintaining them there beyond the termination of permission;

(3) Bombardment by its armed forces of territory under the jurisdiction of another State;

(4) Inflicting physical destruction on another State through the use of other forms of armed force;

(5) Carrying out deliberate attacks on the armed forces, ships or aircraft of another State;

(6) Organizing, supporting or directing armed bands or irregular or volunteer forces that make incursions or infiltrate into another State;

(7) Organizing, supporting or directing violent civil strife or acts of terrorism in another State; or

(8) Organizing, supporting or directing subversive activities aimed at the violent overthrow of the Government of another State.

U.S. AND SOVIET COMMENTS ON DEFINITION OF AGGRESSION*

Mr. Rosenstock (United States of America) acknowledged the patience and spirit of compromise of members of the Committee which had made it possible to achieve a draft definition of aggression. He saw no objection to the draft text going forward to the General Assembly, even though it was by no means perfect. Indeed, even a legally perfect definition might do more harm than good if given too much emphasis. The text that had been produced was a recommendation of the General Assembly for use by the Security Council. The law concerning the use of force was found in the Charter and in the Declaration on Friendly Relations, as was underlined by the preambular affirmation. It would, however, misconstrue and frustrate the purposes of Chapter VII of the Charter if the Council were led by the draft definition to delay urgent action under Chapter VII while it debated whether an act of aggression had occurred, if a finding of a threat to the peace or breach of the peace would more effectively activate the collective security mechanism of the Charter.

The second and fourth preambular paragraphs of the draft definition recalled that the term "act of aggression" with which the text dealt was that contained in Article 39 of the Charter and thus reflected a primary responsibility of the Security Council. The third preambular paragraph emphasized the importance of the peaceful settlement of disputes, of negotiation, inquiry and conciliation to avoid the escalation of differences between States. For such methods to be effective, and if the principle of the sovereign equality of States was to be maintained, the possibility of referring disputes to binding third party settlement must be an available option for all States as against every other State.

The fifth preambular paragraph, while recognizing the dangers which would flow from an illegal use of force amounting to aggression, correctly stated the view that not every act of force in violation of the Charter constituted aggression.

The right of all peoples to equal rights and self-determination was stated in the sixth preambular paragraph; the final clause of the paragraph reaffirmed the principle that the right of self-determination did not imply the legitimation of action which would disrupt the territorial integrity of a State which conducts itself in compliance with the principle of equal rights and self-determination and thus possesses a government representing the people belonging to the territory.

Article 1 contained a general statement which must be understood in the light of other articles. It properly made no distinction based on the means of armed force used, and the phrase "as set out in this definition" indicated that not all illegal uses of armed force could be denominated acts of aggression.

In article 2, the definition suggested the considerations which the Security Council should bear in mind in determining whether an act of aggression had occurred. The Council would be well advised to take account of which State first used force and to give

* Views Expressed by Members of the Special Committee at the Concluding Stage of the Special Committee's Session (1974), *in* U.N. Special Comm. on the Question of Defining Aggression, *Report of the Special Committee on the Question of Defining Aggression*, at 22-24, 36-37, U.N. Doc. A/9619 (Mar. 11-Apr. 12, 1974) (relating the comments of the representatives of the United States and the Soviet Union).

due weight to all relevant circumstances. It had been agreed that it was unnecessary to make special reference to the intent or purpose (including the proof of *animus*) of the States involved, that notion being covered by the phrase "other relevant circumstances." He understood the article to mean that the first use of armed force by a State in contravention of the Charter was only *prima facie* evidence of an act of aggression; the Security Council might or might not in the particular case find that there had actually been an act of aggression. If the Security Council did not make a finding of an act of aggression, the Council must be presumed not to have found the *prima facie* evidence persuasive. That interpretation accorded with the Council's *modus operandi*, which was to consider whether a finding under Article 39 of the Charter would be justified—rather than determining that it would not be justified. This definition accordingly could only be reasonably interpreted in the light of the whole history of the Council's method of operation and, of course, in any event could not alter the intent of Article 39 of the Charter.

Article 3 of the draft definition gave certain familiar examples of the use of force which the Security Council might reasonably consider, in the manner set forth in article 2, as potential acts of aggression. The scope of the list made it clear that no distinction was made as to the means employed or the directness or otherwise of their use. There was no suggestion that article 3 was intended to be an exhaustive list of all illicit uses of force which might constitute acts of aggression; indeed, article 4 expressly stipulated that article 3 was not exhaustive.

The first paragraph of article 5 said in effect that illicit activities were those for which there was no justification; that was a useful addition to the extent that it represented a further safeguard against misuse of the definition.

The second paragraph of article 5 noted the continued validity of the principles set which formed the basis of the trials following the Second World War, enunciated in the Moscow Declaration of 1943, the London Agreement of 1945 and the Charter of the International Military Tribunal for the Far East. The second sentence noted that States were responsible for their wrongful acts.

The third paragraph of the article, while being a formulation of the Stimson Doctrine and of the relevant principles of the Declaration on Friendly Relations, did not alter or extend existing international law with regard to the consequences for States or individuals involved in acts of aggression.

Articles 6 and 7 were classic rulings clauses which by their very nature did not function to create rights but merely to provide express assurance with regard to rules not being dealt with. Article 6 merely recalled that the purpose of the definition was to elucidate the means by which certain types of illicit conduct on the part of States might be determined to constitute aggression, rather than to examine cases in which the use of force might be lawful. That was, indeed, already clear from the text of article 2.

Article 7 expressly affirmed that the definition defined aggression and not the right of self-determination. His Government was always ready to support any text which reasonably reaffirmed the right of all peoples to self-determination and it could therefore accept a formulation which did not speak of the use of force but of actions in accordance with the principles of the Charter and the Declaration on Friendly Relations. Thus, the article did not legitimize acts of armed force by a State, which would otherwise constitute aggression. Even if it mentioned the use of force (which it did not), the article would not constitute an assertion that such use by a State in those circumstances was legal. Rather, it might amount to a recommendation to the Security Council, in considering a particular case, to bear in mind the purposes of the States involved, when considering whether a particular illegal activity should be denominated an act of aggression under Article 39 of the Charter.

Article 8 reaffirmed the need to construe each part of the definition in the context of all other relevant parts. That was particularly true in the case of articles 1 to 4, which formed an integrated whole.

. . . .

Mr. Kolesnik (Union of Soviet Socialist Republics) expressed satisfaction with the results of the Special Committee's work: the draft definition of aggression was generally regarded as an acceptable compromise, and its adoption by the General Assembly would represent a victory for international diplomacy and the forces of peace. The definition would help the Security Council in its difficult task of determining the existence of acts of aggression and taking appropriate action under the Charter. Like all compromises, the draft definition did not completely satisfy certain delegations. During the seven years of work by the Special Committee, the Soviet delegation, actively participating in the formulation of a definition of aggression, had consistently upheld the United Nations Charter and had constantly sought to insert wording consistent with the Charter. His delegation reserved the right to present its definitive views at the twenty-ninth session of the General Assembly; in the meantime he would offer a preliminary evaluation of the definition, basing himself on the Charter.

The preamble of the draft definition reflected a political will to see an end to wars of aggression and the illegal use of force. Without wishing to minimize the importance of the other provisions of the preamble, he stressed the paramount importance of the sixth, seventh and ninth paragraphs.

Article 1 was a concise version of the Charter provisions regarding the illegal use of armed force. In a spirit of compromise, his delegation had agreed to the use of the word "sovereignty" in the text, on the understanding that, in the context of the article, violation of the sovereignty of a State meant the use of armed force against territorial integrity and political independence.

Article 2 was a key provision which had given rise to wide disagreement. There had been much discussion whether to include the phrase "in contravention of the Charter," and his delegation had maintained that unless those words were included, State acts committed in strict conformity with the Charter of the United Nations could be regarded as acts of aggression within the meaning of the article. There must be no room for misunderstandings in such an important document as the definition of aggression, and the opposing views put forward by some delegations were unconvincing. The Charter definitely sanctioned the use of force in well-known specific cases, and any disregard of its provisions would not help the cause of peace. The Security Council was the only United Nations organ empowered to determine the existence of acts of aggression. His delegation was pleased that that fact had been brought out in the definition. It had also wanted to ensure that the wording of the definition should not leave open the possibility of branding an innocent party as an aggressor. That was the idea underlying the statement in article 2 that the Security Council might in conformity with the Charter conclude that a determination that an act of aggression had been committed would not be justified in light of other circumstances which might be taken into account by the Security Council. Aggression was a grave international crime, and in investigating any armed conflict, the Security Council must carefully analyse all consequences for the course of peace. His delegation attached great importance to the intentions of the States parties to a conflict. Some delegations had not wished to see the question of intent dealt with in article 2, but his delegation felt that the Security Council, if it was to adopt correct decisions, must analyze the intentions of the States involved, since a careful study of intentions would make it easier for the Council to identify the true aggressor.

With regard to article 3, he stressed that nothing in the wording of paragraph (g) could be construed as casting doubt on the legitimacy of national liberation struggles, guerrilla warfare or resistance movements. There was a certain connexion between that paragraph and article 7. His delegation attached great weight to the fact that not a single delegation, during the drafting of the definition, had expressed opposition to the right of peoples to self-determination. But it was no longer sufficient to recognize that right without also recognizing the elements comprised in it: the right of peoples to take up arms against the colonialists. Peoples engaged in that struggle had a right to seek and receive political and material aid. Not only was the armed struggle of colonial peoples and people under the domination of racist régimes legitimate, but the aid which they received from many States was equally so.

One of the important elements of the draft definition concerned the question of responsibility for aggression. His delegation had agreed as a compromise that article 5 should be reworded to take account of the provisions of article 6 of the consolidated text; nevertheless, he felt that there was no solid grounds for the distinction made between "a war of aggression" and "aggression" in article 5. Not only a war of aggression but any other act of aggression was a crime against international peace. Any act of aggression must engage international responsibility. His delegation's concept of responsibility for aggression was based in particular on the Charter of the Nuremberg Military Tribunal: there was no difference between "international responsibility" and "responsibility under international law," since the former presupposed the latter, i.e. responsibility for acts designated as crimes in relevant international legal instruments.

With regard to article 5, he agreed that no consideration of whatever nature could serve as a justification for aggression. The Special Committee had not intended to extend the concept of aggression, much less replace it by the concept of interference by a State in the domestic affairs of another State. Such interference was certainly prohibited under contemporary international law, but it could not be placed on the same footing as aggression.

The international legal doctrine followed by the U.S.S.R. was based on the fact that the United Nations Charter was a code of conduct for sovereign States. Strict compliance with the Charter was necessary if the aims of the Organization, namely, the establishment and maintenance of international peace, were to be achieved, and it was for that reason that his Government regarded article 6 as being of such significance.

The definition of aggression was the culmination of unceasing efforts by the Government and the U.S.S.R. Lenin, the founder of the Soviet State, had proclaimed as the Soviet ideal an end to war, peace between peoples and the cessation of pillage and violence. The Soviet Government had put forward a definition of aggression in 1933, and since that time relations between peoples had become more friendly through the application of the principle of peaceful coexistence, but the structure of peace was not yet complete. In conclusion, he praised the part played by the third world countries in the preparation of the draft definition of aggression and paid a tribute to the Chairman and officers of the Special Committee.

UN SECURITY COUNCIL RESOLUTION 678* (IRAQ AND KUWAIT)

The Security Council,

. . . .

Noting that, despite all efforts by the United Nations, Iraq refuses to comply with its obligation to implement resolution 660 (1990) and the above-mentioned subsequent relevant resolutions, in flagrant contempt of the Security Council,

Mindful of its duties and responsibilities under the Charter of the United Nations for the maintenance and preservation of international peace and security,

Determined to secure full compliance with its decisions,

Acting under Chapter VII of the Charter,

1. *Demands* that Iraq comply fully with resolution 660 (1990) and all subsequent relevant resolutions, and decides, while maintaining all its decisions, to allow Iraq one final opportunity, as a pause of goodwill, to do so;

2. *Authorizes* Member States co-operating with the Government of Kuwait, unless Iraq on or before 15 January 1991 fully implements, as set forth in paragraph 1 above, the above-mentioned resolutions, to use all necessary means to uphold and implement resolution 660 (1990) and all subsequent relevant resolutions and to restore international peace and security in the area;

3. *Requests* all States to provide appropriate support for the actions undertaken in pursuance of paragraph 2 of the present resolution;

4. *Requests* the States concerned to keep the Security Council regularly informed on the progress of actions undertaken pursuant to paragraphs 2 and 3 of the present resolution;

5. *Decides* to remain seized of the matter.

---

* S.C. Res. 678, U.N. Doc. S/RES/678 (Nov. 29, 1990), *available at* http://www.un.org/Docs/scres/1990/scres90.htm.

UN SECURITY COUNCIL RESOLUTION 687* (IRAQ AND KUWAIT)

The Security Council,

. . . .

Welcoming the restoration to Kuwait of its sovereignty, independence and territorial integrity and the return of its legitimate Government,

Affirming the commitment of all Member States to the sovereignty, territorial integrity and political independence of Kuwait and Iraq, and noting the intention expressed by the Member States cooperating with Kuwait under paragraph 2 of resolution 678 (1990) to bring their military presence in Iraq to an end as soon as possible consistent with paragraph 8 of resolution 686 (1991),

Reaffirming the need to be assured of Iraq's peaceful intentions in the light of its unlawful invasion and occupation of Kuwait,

Taking note of the letter dated 27 February 1991 from the Deputy Prime Minister and Minister for Foreign Affairs of Iraq addressed to the President of the Security Council and of his letters of the same date addressed to the President of the Council and to the Secretary-General, and those letters dated 3 March and 5 March he addressed to them, pursuant ot Resolution 686 (1991),

Noting that Iraq and Kuwait, as independent sovereign States, signed at Baghdad on 4 October 1963 "Agreed Minutes Between the State of Kuwait and the Republic of Iraq Regarding the Restoration of Friendly Relations, Recognition and Related Matters", thereby recognizing formally the boundary between Iraq and Kuwait and the allocation of islands, which were registered with the United Nations in accordance with Article 102 of the Charter of the United Nations and in which Iraq recognized the independence and complete sovereignty of the State of Kuwait within its borders as specified and accepted in the letter of the Prime Minister of Iraq dated 21 July 1932, and as accepted by the Ruler of Kuwait in his letter dated 10 August 1932,

Conscious of the need for demarcation of the said boundary,

Conscious also of the statements by Iraq threatening to use weapons in violation of its obligations under the Geneva Protocol for the Prohibition of the Use in War of Asphyxiating, Poisonous or Other Gases, and of Bacteriological Methods of Warfare, signed at Geneva on 17 June 1925, and of its prior use of chemical weapons and affirming that grave consequences would follow any further use by Iraq of such weapons,

Recalling that Iraq has subscribed to the Declaration adopted by all States participating in the Conference of States Parties to the 1925 Geneva Protocol and Other Interested States, held in Paris from 7 to 11 January 1989, establishing the objective of universal elimination of chemical and biological weapons,

Recalling also that Iraq has signed the Convention on the Prohibition of the Development, Production and Stockpiling of Bacteriological (Biological) and Toxin Weapons and on Their Destruction, of 10 April 1972,

---

* S.C. Res. 687, U.N. Doc. S/RES/687 (Apr. 3, 1991), *available at* http://www.un.org/Docs/scres/1991/scres91.htm.

Noting the importance of Iraq ratifying this Convention,

Noting also the importance of all States adhering to this Convention and encouraging its forthcoming Review Conference to reinforce the authority, efficiency and universal scope of the convention,

Stressing the importance of an early conclusion by the Conference on Disarmament of its work on a Convention on the Universal Prohibition of Chemical Weapons and of universal adherence thereto,

Aware of the use by Iraq of ballistic missiles in unprovoked attacks and therefore of the need to take specific measures in regard to such missiles located in Iraq,

Concerned by the reports in the hands of Member States that Iraq has attempted to acquire materials for a nuclear-weapons programme contrary to its obligations under the Treaty on the Non-Proliferation of Nuclear Weapons of 1 July 1968,

Recalling the objective of the establishment of a nuclear-weapons-free zone in the region of the Middle East,

Conscious of the threat that all weapons of mass destruction pose to peace and security in the area and of the need to work towards the establishment in the Middle East of a zone free of such weapons,

Conscious also of the objective of achieving balanced and comprehensive control of armaments in the region,

Conscious further of the importance of achieving the objectives noted above using all available means, including a dialogue among the States of the region,

Noting that resolution 686 (1991) marked the lifting of the measures imposed by resolution 661 (1990) in so far as they applied to Kuwait,

Noting also that despite the progress being made in fulfilling the obligations of resolution 686 (1991), many Kuwaiti and third country nationals are still not accounted for and property remains unreturned,

Recalling the International Convention against the Taking of Hostages, opened for signature at New York on 18 December 1979, which categorizes all acts of taking hostages as manifestations of international terrorism,

Deploring threats made by Iraq during the recent conflict to make use of terrorism against targets outside Iraq and the taking of hostages by Iraq,

Taking note with grave concern of the reports of the Secretary-General of 20 March 1991 and 28 March 1991, and conscious of the necessity to meet urgently the humanitarian needs in Kuwait and Iraq,

Bearing in mind its objective of restoring international peace and security in the area as set out in recent resolutions of the Security Council,

Conscious of the need to take the following measures acting under Chapter VII of the Charter,

1. *Affirms* all thirteen resolutions noted above, except as expressly changed below to achieve the goals of this resolution, including a formal cease-fire;

A

2. *Demands* that Iraq and Kuwait respect the inviolability of the international boundary and the allocation of islands set out in the "Agreed Minutes Between the State of

Kuwait and the Republic of Iraq Regarding the Restoration of Friendly Relations, Recognition and Related Matters", signed by them in the exercise of their sovereignty at Baghdad on 4 October 1963 and registered with the United Nations and published by the United Nations in document 7063, United Nations, Treaty Series, 1964;

3. *Calls upon* the Secretary-General to lend his assistance to make arrangements with Iraq and Kuwait to demarcate the boundary between Iraq and Kuwait, drawing on appropriate material, including the map transmitted by Security Council document S/22412 and to report back to the Security Council within one month;

4. *Decides* to guarantee the inviolability of the above-mentioned international boundary and to take as appropriate all necessary measures to that end in accordance with the Charter of the United Nations;

B

5. *Requests* the Secretary-General, after consulting with Iraq and Kuwait, to submit within three days to the Security Council for its approval a plan for the immediate deployment of a United Nations observer unit to monitor the Khor Abdullah and a demilitarized zone, which is hereby established, extending ten kilometres into Iraq and five kilometres into Kuwait from the boundary referred to in the "Agreed Minutes Between the State of Kuwait and the Republic of Iraq Regarding the Restoration of Friendly Relations, Recognition and Related Matters" of 4 October 1963; to deter violations of the boundary through its presence in and surveillance of the demilitarized zone; to observe any hostile or potentially hostile action mounted from the territory of one State to the other; and for the Secretary-General to report regularly to the Security Council on the operations of the unit, and immediately if there are serious violations of the zone or potential threats to peace;

6. *Notes* that as soon as the Secretary-General notifies the Security Council of the completion of the deployment of the United Nations observer unit, the conditions will be established for the Member States cooperating with Kuwait in accordance with resolution 678 (1990) to bring their military presence in Iraq to an end consistent with resolution 686 (1991);

C

7. *Invites* Iraq to reaffirm unconditionally its obligations under the Geneva Protocol for the Prohibition of the Use in War of Asphyxiating, Poisonous or Other Gases, and of Bacteriological Methods of Warfare, signed at Geneva on 17 June 1925, and to ratify the Convention on the Prohibition of the Development, Production and Stockpiling of Bacteriological (Biological) and Toxin Weapons and on Their Destruction, of 10 April 1972;

8. *Decides* that Iraq shall unconditionally accept the destruction, removal, or rendering harmless, under international supervision, of:

(a) All chemical and biological weapons and all stocks of agents and all related subsystems and components and all research, development, support and manufacturing facilities;

(b) All ballistic missiles with a range greater than 150 kilometres and related major parts, and repair and production facilities;

9. *Decides also*, for the implementation of paragraph 8 above, the following:

(a) Iraq shall submit to the Secretary-General, within fifteen days of the adoption of the present resolution, a declaration of the locations, amounts and types of all items specified in paragraph 8 and agree to urgent, on-site inspection as specified below;

(b) The Secretary-General, in consultation with the appropriate Governments and, where appropriate, with the Director-General of the World Health Organization, within forty-five days of the passage of the present resolution, shall develop, and submit to the Council for approval, a plan calling for the completion of the following acts within forty-five days of such approval:

(i) The forming of a Special Commission, which shall carry out immediate on-site inspection of Iraq's biological, chemical and missile capabilities, based on Iraq's declarations and the designation of any additional locations by the Special Commission itself;

(ii) The yielding by Iraq of possession to the Special Commission for destruction, removal or rendering harmless, taking into account the requirements of public safety, of all items specified under paragraph 8 (a) above, including items at the additional locations designated by the Special Commission under paragraph 9 (b) (i) above and the destruction by Iraq, under the supervision of the Special Commission, of all its missile capabilities, including launchers, as specified under paragraph 8 (b) above;

(iii) The provision by the Special Commission of the assistance and cooperation to the Director-General of the International Atomic Energy Agency required in paragraphs 12 and 13 below;

10. *Decides further* that Iraq shall unconditionally undertake not to use, develop, construct or acquire any of the items specified in paragraphs 8 and 9 above and requests the Secretary-General, in consultation with the Special Commission, to develop a plan for the future ongoing monitoring and verification of Iraq's compliance with this paragraph, to be submitted to the Security Council for approval within one hundred and twenty days of the passage of this resolution;

11. *Invites* Iraq to reaffirm unconditionally its obligations under the Treaty on the Non-Proliferation of Nuclear Weapons of 1 July 1968;

12. *Decides* that Iraq shall unconditionally agree not to acquire or develop nuclear weapons or nuclear-weapons-usable material or any subsystems or components or any research, development, support or manufacturing facilities related to the above; to submit to the Secretary-General and the Director-General of the International Atomic Energy Agency within fifteen days of the adoption of the present resolution a declaration of the locations, amounts, and types of all items specified above; to place all of its nuclear-weapons-usable materials under the exclusive control, for custody and removal, of the International Atomic Energy Agency, with the assistance and cooperation of the Special Commission as provided for in the plan of the Secretary-General discussed in paragraph 9 (b) above; to accept, in accordance with the arrangements provided for in paragraph 13 below, urgent on-site inspection and the destruction, removal or rendering harmless as appropriate of all items specified above; and to accept the plan discussed in paragraph 13 below for the future ongoing monitoring and verification of its compliance with these undertakings;

13. *Requests* the Director-General of the International Atomic Energy Agency, through the Secretary-General, with the assistance and cooperation of the Special Commission as provided for in the plan of the Secretary-General in paragraph 9 (b) above,

to carry out immediate on-site inspection of Iraq's nuclear capabilities based on Iraq's declarations and the designation of any additional locations by the Special Commission; to develop a plan for submission to the Security Council within forty-five days calling for the destruction, removal, or rendering harmless as appropriate of all items listed in paragraph 12 above; to carry out the plan within forty-five days following approval by the Security Council; and to develop a plan, taking into account the rights and obligations of Iraq under the Treaty on the Non-Proliferation of Nuclear Weapons of 1 July 1968, for the future ongoing monitoring and verification of Iraq's compliance with paragraph 12 above, including an inventory of all nuclear material in Iraq subject to the Agency's verification and inspections to confirm that Agency safeguards cover all relevant nuclear activities in Iraq, to be submitted to the Security Council for approval within one hundred and twenty days of the passage of the present resolution;

14. *Notes* that the actions to be taken by Iraq in paragraphs 8, 9, 10, 11, 12 and 13 of the present resolution represent steps towards the goal of establishing in the Middle East a zone free from weapons of mass destruction and all missiles for their delivery and the objective of a global ban on chemical weapons;

D

15. *Requests* the Secretary-General to report to the Security Council on the steps taken to facilitate the return of all Kuwaiti property seized by Iraq, including a list of any property that Kuwait claims has not been returned or which has not been returned intact;

E

16. *Reaffirms* that Iraq, without prejudice to the debts and obligations of Iraq arising prior to 2 August 1990, which will be addressed through the normal mechanisms, is liable under international law for any direct loss, damage, including environmental damage and the depletion of natural resources, or injury to foreign Governments, nationals and corporations, as a result of Iraq's unlawful invasion and occupation of Kuwait;

17. *Decides* that all Iraqi statements made since 2 August 1990 repudiating its foreign debt are null and void, and demands that Iraq adhere scrupulously to all of its obligations concerning servicing and repayment of its foreign debt;

18. *Decides also* to create a fund to pay compensation for claims that fall within paragraph 16 above and to establish a Commission that will administer the fund;

19. *Directs* the Secretary-General to develop and present to the Security Council for decision, no later than thirty days following the adoption of the present resolution, recommendations for the fund to meet the requirement for the payment of claims established in accordance with paragraph 18 above and for a programme to implement the decisions in paragraphs 16, 17 and 18 above, including:

administration of the fund;

mechanisms for determining the appropriate level of Iraq's contribution to the fund based on a percentage of the value of the exports of petroleum and petroleum products from Iraq not to exceed a figure to be suggested to the Council by the Secretary-General, taking into account the requirements of the people of Iraq, Iraq's payment capacity as assessed in conjunction with the international financial institutions taking into consideration external debt service, and the needs of the Iraqi economy; arrangements for ensuring that payments are made to the fund; the process by which funds will be allocated and claims paid; appropriate procedures for evaluating losses, listing claims and verifying their validity and resolving disputed claims in respect of Iraq's liability as specified in paragraph 16 above; and the composition of the Commission designated above;

F

20. *Decides,* effective immediately, that the prohibitions against the sale or supply to Iraq of commodities or products, other than medicine and health supplies, and prohibitions against financial transactions related thereto contained in resolution 661 (1990) shall not apply to foodstuffs notified to the Security Council Committee established by resolution 661 (1990) concerning the situation between Iraq and Kuwait or, with the approval of that Committee, under the simplified and accelerated "no-objection" procedure, to materials and supplies for essential civilian needs as identified in the report of the Secretary-General dated 20 March 1991, and in any further findings of humanitarian need by the Committee;

21. *Decides* that the Security Council shall review the provisions of paragraph 20 above every sixty days in the light of the policies and practices of the Government of Iraq, including the implementation of all relevant resolutions of the Security Council, for the purpose of determining whether to reduce or lift the prohibitions referred to therein;

22. *Decides also* that upon the approval by the Security Council of the programme called for in paragraph 19 above and upon Council agreement that Iraq has completed all actions contemplated in paragraphs 8, 9, 10, 11, 12 and 13 above, the prohibitions against the import of commodities and products originating in Iraq and the prohibitions against financial transactions related thereto contained in resolution 661 (1990) shall have no further force or effect;

23. *Decides further* that, pending action by the Security Council under paragraph 22 above, the Security Council Committee established by resolution 661 (1990) shall be empowered to approve, when required to assure adequate financial resources on the part of Iraq to carry out the activities under paragraph 20 above, exceptions to the prohibition against the import of commodities and products originating in Iraq;

24. *Decides* that, in accordance with resolution 661 (1990) and subsequent related resolutions and until a further decision is taken by the Security Council, all States shall continue to prevent the sale or supply, or the promotion or facilitation of such sale or supply, to Iraq by their nationals, or from their territories or using their flag vessels or aircraft, of:

(a) Arms and related *matèrìel* of all types, specifically including the sale or transfer through other means of all forms of conventional military equipment, including for paramilitary forces, and spare parts and components and their means of production, for such equipment;

(b) Items specified and defined in paragraphs 8 and 12 above not otherwise covered above;

(c) Technology under licensing or other transfer arrangements used in the production, utilization or stockpiling of items specified in subparagraphs (a) and (b) above;

(d) Personnel or materials for training or technical support services relating to the design, development, manufacture, use, maintenance or support of items specified in subparagraphs (a) and (b) above;

25. *Calls upon* all States and international organizations to act strictly in accordance with paragraph 24 above, notwithstanding the existence of any contracts, agreements, licenses or any other arrangements;

26. *Requests the* Secretary-General, in consultation with appropriate Governments, to develop within sixty days, for the approval of the Security Council, guidelines to facilitate full international implementation of paragraphs 24 and 25 above and paragraph 27 below, and to make them available to all States and to establish a procedure for updating these guidelines periodically;

27. *Calls upon* all States to maintain such national controls and procedures and to take such other actions consistent with the guidelines to be established by the Security Council under paragraph 26 above as may be necessary to ensure compliance with the terms of paragraph 24 above, and calls upon international organizations to take all appropriate steps to assist in ensuring such full compliance;

28. *Agrees* to review its decisions in paragraphs 22, 23, 24 and 25 above, except for the items specified and defined in paragraphs 8 and 12 above, on a regular basis and in any case one hundred and twenty days following passage of the present resolution, taking into account Iraq's compliance with the resolution and general progress towards the control of armaments in the region;

29. *Decides* that all States, including Iraq, shall take the necessary measures to ensure that no claim shall lie at the instance of the Government of Iraq, or of any person or body in Iraq, or of any person claiming through or for the benefit of any such person or body, in connection with any contract or other transaction where its performance was affected by reason of the measures taken by the Security Council in resolution 661 (1990) and related resolutions;

G

30. *Decides* that, in furtherance of its commitment to facilitate the repatriation of all Kuwaiti and third country nationals, Iraq shall extend all necessary cooperation to the International Committee of the Red Cross, providing lists of such persons, facilitating the access of the International Committee of the Red Cross to all such persons wherever located or detained and facilitating the search by the International Committee of the Red Cross for those Kuwaiti and third country nationals still unaccounted for;

31. *Invites* the International Committee of the Red Cross to keep the Secretary-General apprised as appropriate of all activities undertaken in connection with facilitating the repatriation or return of all Kuwaiti and third country nationals or their remains present in Iraq on or after 2 August 1990;

H

32. *Requires* Iraq to inform the Security Council that it will not commit or support any act of international terrorism or allow any organization directed towards commission of such acts to operate within its territory and to condemn unequivocally and renounce all acts, methods and practices of terrorism;

I

33. *Declares* that, upon official notification by Iraq to the Secretary-General and to the Security Council of its acceptance of the provisions above, a formal cease-fire is effective between Iraq and Kuwait and the Member States cooperating with Kuwait in accordance with resolution 678 (1990);

34. *Decides* to remain seized of the matter and to take such further steps as may be required for the implementation of the present resolution and to secure peace and security in the area.

UN SECURITY COUNCIL RESOLUTION 1441* (IRAQ NONCOMPLIANCE)

The Security Council,

....

Recognizing the threat Iraq's non-compliance with Council resolutions and proliferation of weapons of mass destruction and long-range missiles poses to international peace and security,

Recalling that its resolution 678 (1990) authorized Member States to use all necessary means to uphold and implement its resolution 660 (1990) of 2 August 1990 and all relevant resolutions subsequent to resolution 660 (1990) and to restore international peace and security in the area,

Further recalling that its resolution 687 (1991) imposed obligations on Iraq as a necessary step for achievement of its stated objective of restoring international peace and security in the area,

Deploring the fact that Iraq has not provided an accurate, full, final, and complete disclosure, as required by resolution 687 (1991), of all aspects of its programmes to develop weapons of mass destruction and ballistic missiles with a range greater than one hundred and fifty kilometres, and of all holdings of such weapons, their components and production facilities and locations, as well as all other nuclear programmes, including any which it claims are for purposes not related to nuclear-weapons-usable material,

....

Deploring also that the Government of Iraq has failed to comply with its commitments pursuant to resolution 687 (1991) with regard to terrorism, pursuant to resolution 688 (1991) to end repression of its civilian population and to provide access by international humanitarian organizations to all those in need of assistance in Iraq, and pursuant to resolutions 686 (1991), 687 (1991), and 1284 (1999) to return or cooperate in accounting for Kuwaiti and third country nationals wrongfully detained by Iraq, or to return Kuwaiti property wrongfully seized by Iraq,

Recalling that in its resolution 687 (1991) the Council declared that a ceasefire would be based on acceptance by Iraq of the provisions of that resolution, including the obligations on Iraq contained therein,

Determined to ensure full and immediate compliance by Iraq without conditions or restrictions with its obligations under resolution 687 (1991) and other relevant resolutions and recalling that the resolutions of the Council constitute the governing standard of Iraqi compliance,

....

*Determ*ined to secure full compliance with its decisions,

Acting under Chapter VII of the Charter of the United Nations

---

* S.C. Res. 1441, U.N. Doc. S/RES/1441 (Nov. 8, 2002), *available at* http://www.un.org/Docs/scres/2002/sc2002.htm.

1. *Decides* that Iraq has been and remains in material breach of its obligations under relevant resolutions, including resolution 687 (1991), in particular through Iraq's failure to cooperate with United Nations inspectors and the IAEA, and to complete the actions required under paragraphs 8 to 13 of resolution 687 (1991);

2. *Decides*, while acknowledging paragraph 1 above, to afford Iraq, by this resolution, a final opportunity to comply with its disarmament obligations under relevant resolutions of the Council; and accordingly decides to set up an enhanced inspection regime with the aim of bringing to full and verified completion the disarmament process established by resolution 687 (1991) and subsequent resolutions of the Council;

3. *Decides* that, in order to begin to comply with its disarmament obligations, in addition to submitting the required biannual declarations, the Government of Iraq shall provide to UNMOVIC, the IAEA, and the Council, not later than 30 days from the date of this resolution, a currently accurate, full, and complete declaration of all aspects of its programmes to develop chemical, biological, and nuclear weapons, ballistic missiles, and other delivery systems such as unmanned aerial vehicles and dispersal systems designed for use on aircraft, including any holdings and precise locations of such weapons, components, subcomponents, stocks of agents, and related material and equipment, the locations and work of its research, development and production facilities, as well as all other chemical, biological, and nuclear programmes, including any which it claims are for purposes not related to weapon production or material;

4. *Decides* that false statements or omissions in the declarations submitted by Iraq pursuant to this resolution and failure by Iraq at any time to comply with, and cooperate fully in the implementation of, this resolution shall constitute a further material breach of Iraq's obligations and will be reported to the Council for assessment....

....

E. Human Rights for Contexts of Violence: Norms Concerning the Conduct of Hostilities

INSTRUCTIONS FOR THE GOVERNMENT OF ARMIES OF THE UNITED STATES IN THE FIELD* (LIEBER CODE)

SECTION I
Martial Law—Military jurisdiction—Military necessity—Retaliation

....

Article 11. The law of war does not only disclaim all cruelty and bad faith concerning engagements concluded with the enemy during the war, but also the breaking of stipulations solemnly contracted by the belligerents in time of peace, and avowedly intended to remain in force in case of war between the contracting powers.

It disclaims all extortions and other transactions for individual gain; all acts of private revenge, or connivance at such acts.

Offenses to the contrary shall be severely punished, and especially so if committed by officers.

....

Article 14. Military necessity, as understood by modern civilized nations, consists in the necessity of those measures which are indispensable for securing the ends of the war, and which are lawful according to the modern law and usages of war.

Article 15. Military necessity admits of all direct destruction of life or limb of armed enemies, and of other persons whose destruction is incidentally unavoidable in the armed contests of the war; it allows of the capturing of every armed enemy, and every enemy of importance to the hostile government, or of peculiar danger to the captor; it allows of all destruction of property, and obstruction of the ways and channels of traffic, travel, or communication, and of all withholding of sustenance or means of life from the enemy; of the appropriation of whatever an enemy's country affords necessary for the subsistence and safety of the army, and of such deception as does not involve the breaking of good faith either positively pledged, regarding agreements entered into during the war, or supposed by the modern law of war to exist. Men who take up arms against one another in public war do not cease on this account to be moral beings, responsible to one another and to God.

Article 16. Military necessity does not admit of cruelty—that is, the infliction of suffering for the sake of suffering or for revenge, nor of maiming or wounding except in fight, nor of torture to extort confessions. It does not admit of the use of poison in any way, nor of the wanton devastation of a district. It admits of deception, but disclaims acts of perfidy; and, in general, military necessity does not include any act of hostility which makes the return to peace unnecessarily difficult.

---

* U.S. DEP'T OF WAR, GEN. ORDERS 100, INSTRUCTIONS FOR THE GOVERNMENT OF ARMIES OF THE UNITED STATES IN THE FIELD (Apr. 24, 1863), *reprinted in* RICHARD SHELLY HARTIGAN, LIEBER'S CODE AND THE LAW OF WAR 45 (1983), *available at* http://www.yale.edu/lawweb/avalon/lieber.htm#sec1. Francis Lieber drafted this code on the law of land warfare as a guide for operations for the Union armies.

Article 17. War is not carried on by arms alone. It is lawful to starve the hostile belligerent, armed or unarmed, so that it leads to the speedier subjection of the enemy.

Article 18. When a commander of a besieged place expels the noncombatants, in order to lessen the number of those who consume his stock of provisions, it is lawful, though an extreme measure, to drive them back, so as to hasten on the surrender.

Article 19. Commanders, whenever admissible, inform the enemy of their intention to bombard a place, so that the noncombatants, and especially the women and children, may be removed before the bombardment commences. But it is no infraction of the common law of war to omit thus to inform the enemy. Surprise may be a necessity.

Article 20. Public war is a state of armed hostility between sovereign nations or governments. It is a law and requisite of civilized existence that men live in political, continuous societies, forming organized units, called states or nations, whose constituents bear, enjoy, suffer, advance and retrograde together, in peace and in war.

Article 21. The citizen or native of a hostile country is thus an enemy, as one of the constituents of the hostile state or nation, and as such is subjected to the hardships of the war.

Article 22. Nevertheless, as civilization has advanced during the last centuries, so has likewise steadily advanced, especially in war on land, the distinction between the private individual belonging to a hostile country and the hostile country itself, with its men in arms. The principle has been more and more acknowledged that the unarmed citizen is to be spared in person, property, and honor as much as the exigencies of war will admit.

Article 23. Private citizens are no longer murdered, enslaved, or carried off to distant parts, and the inoffensive individual is as little disturbed in his private relations as the commander of the hostile troops can afford to grant in the overruling demands of a vigorous war.

Article 24. The almost universal rule in remote times was, and continues to be with barbarous armies, that the private individual of the hostile country is destined to suffer every privation of liberty and protection, and every disruption of family ties. Protection was, and still is with uncivilized people, the exception.

Article 25. In modern regular wars of the Europeans, and their descendants in other portions of the globe, protection of the inoffensive citizen of the hostile country is the rule; privation and disturbance of private relations are the exceptions.

Article 26. Commanding generals may cause the magistrates and civil officers of the hostile country to take the oath of temporary allegiance or an oath of fidelity to their own victorious government or rulers, and they may expel everyone who declines to do so. But whether they do so or not, the people and their civil officers owe strict obedience to them as long as they hold sway over the district or country, at the peril of their lives.

Article 27. The law of war can no more wholly dispense with retaliation than can the law of nations, of which it is a branch. Yet civilized nations acknowledge retaliation as the sternest feature of war. A reckless enemy often leaves to his opponent no other means of securing himself against the repetition of barbarous outrage.

Article 28. Retaliation will, therefore, never be resorted to as a measure of mere revenge, but only as a means of protective retribution, and moreover, cautiously and unavoidably; that is to say, retaliation shall only be resorted to after careful inquiry into the real occurrence, and the character of the misdeeds that may demand retribution.

Unjust or inconsiderate retaliation removes the belligerents farther and farther from the mitigating rules of regular war, and by rapid steps leads them nearer to the internecine wars of savages.

Article 29. Modern times are distinguished from earlier ages by the existence, at one and the same time, of many nations and great governments related to one another in close intercourse.

Peace is their normal condition; war is the exception. The ultimate object of all modern war is a renewed state of peace.

The more vigorously wars are pursued, the better it is for humanity. Sharp wars are brief.

Article 30. Ever since the formation and coexistence of modern nations, and ever since wars have become great national wars, war has come to be acknowledged not to be its own end, but the means to obtain great ends of state, or to consist in defense against wrong; and no conventional restriction of the modes adopted to injure the enemy is any longer admitted; but the law of war imposes many limitations and restrictions on principles of justice, faith, and honor.

SECTION II

Public and private property of the enemy—Protection of persons, and especially of women, of religion, the arts and sciences—Punishment of crimes against the inhabitants of hostile countries.

Article 31. A victorious army appropriates all public money, seizes all public movable property until further direction by its government, and sequesters for its own benefit or of that of its government all the revenues of real property belonging to the hostile government or nation. The title to such real property remains in abeyance during military occupation, and until the conquest is made complete.

Article 32. A victorious army, by the martial power inherent in the same, may suspend, change, or abolish, as far as the martial power extends, the relations which arise from the services due, according to the existing laws of the invaded country, from one citizen, subject, or native of the same to another.

The commander of the army must leave it to the ultimate treaty of peace to settle the permanency of this change.

Article 33. It is no longer considered lawful—on the contrary, it is held to be a serious breach of the law of war—to force the subjects of the enemy into the service of the victorious government, except the latter should proclaim, after a fair and complete conquest of the hostile country or district, that it is resolved to keep the country, district, or place permanently as its own and make it a portion of its own country.

Article 34. As a general rule, the property belonging to churches, to hospitals, or other establishments of an exclusively charitable character, to establishments of education, or foundations for the promotion of knowledge, whether public schools, universities, academies of learning or observatories, museums of the fine arts, or of a scientific character such property is not to be considered public property in the sense of paragraph 31; but it may be taxed or used when the public service may require it.

Article 35. Classical works of art, libraries, scientific collections, or precious instruments, such as astronomical telescopes, as well as hospitals, must be secured against all avoidable injury, even when they are contained in fortified places whilst besieged or bombarded.

Article 36. If such works of art, libraries, collections, or instruments belonging to a hostile nation or government, can be removed without injury, the ruler of the conquering state or nation may order them to be seized and removed for the benefit of the said nation. The ultimate ownership is to be settled by the ensuing treaty of peace.

In no case shall they be sold or given away, if captured by the armies of the United States, nor shall they ever be privately appropriated, or wantonly destroyed or injured.

Article 37. The United States acknowledge and protect, in hostile countries occupied by them, religion and morality; strictly private property; the persons of the inhabitants, especially those of women: and the sacredness of domestic relations. Offenses to the contrary shall be rigorously punished.

This rule does not interfere with the right of the victorious invader to tax the people or their property, to levy forced loans, to billet soldiers, or to appropriate property, especially houses, lands, boats or ships, and churches, for temporary and military uses.

Article 38. Private property, unless forfeited by crimes or by offenses of the owner, can be seized only by way of military necessity, for the support or other benefit of the army or of the United States.

If the owner has not fled, the commanding officer will cause receipts to be given, which may serve the spoliated owner to obtain indemnity.

Article 39. The salaries of civil officers of the hostile government who remain in the invaded territory, and continue the work of their office, and can continue it according to the circumstances arising out of the war—such as judges, administrative or police officers, officers of city or communal governments—are paid from the public revenue of the invaded territory, until the military government has reason wholly or partially to discontinue it. Salaries or incomes connected with purely honorary titles are always stopped.

Article 40. There exists no law or body of authoritative rules of action between hostile armies, except that branch of the law of nature and nations which is called the law and usages of war on land.

Article 41. All municipal law of the ground on which the armies stand, or of the countries to which they belong, is silent and of no effect between armies in the field.

Article 42. Slavery, complicating and confounding the ideas of property, (that is of a thing,) and of personality, (that is of humanity,) exists according to municipal or local law only. The law of nature and nations has never acknowledged it. The digest of the Roman law enacts the early dictum of the pagan jurist, that "so far as the law of nature is concerned, all men are equal." Fugitives escaping from a country in which they were slaves, villains, or serfs, into another country, have, for centuries past, been held free and acknowledged free by judicial decisions of European countries, even though the municipal law of the country in which the slave had taken refuge acknowledged slavery within its own dominions.

Article 43. Therefore, in a war between the United States and a belligerent which admits of slavery, if a person held in bondage by that belligerent be captured by or come as a fugitive under the protection of the military forces of the United States, such person is immediately entitled to the rights and privileges of a freeman. To return such person into slavery would amount to enslaving a free person, and neither the United States nor any officer under their authority can enslave any human being. Moreover, a person so made free by the law of war is under the shield of the law of nations, and the former owner or State can have, by the law of postliminy, no belligerent lien or claim of service.

Article 44. All wanton violence committed against persons in the invaded country, all destruction of property not commanded by the authorized officer, all robbery, all pillage or sacking, even after taking a place by main force, all rape, wounding, maiming, or killing of such inhabitants, are prohibited under the penalty of death, or such other severe punishment as may seem adequate for the gravity of the offense.

A soldier, officer or private, in the act of committing such violence, and disobeying a superior ordering him to abstain from it, may be lawfully killed on the spot by such superior.

Article 45. All captures and booty belong, according to the modern law of war, primarily to the government of the captor.

Prize money, whether on sea or land, can now only be claimed under local law.

Article 46. Neither officers nor soldiers are allowed to make use of their position or power in the hostile country for private gain, not even for commercial transactions otherwise legitimate. Offenses to the contrary committed by commissioned officers will be punished with cashiering or such other punishment as the nature of the offense may require; if by soldiers, they shall be punished according to the nature of the offense.

Article 47. Crimes punishable by all penal codes, such as arson, murder, maiming, assaults, highway robbery, theft, burglary, fraud, forgery, and rape, if committed by an American soldier in a hostile country against its inhabitants, are not only punishable as at home, but in all cases in which death is not inflicted, the severer punishment shall be preferred.

SECTION III
Deserters — Prisoners of war — Hostages — Booty on the battle-field.

Article 48. Deserters from the American Army, having entered the service of the enemy, suffer death if they fall again into the hands of the United States, whether by capture, or being delivered up to the American Army; and if a deserter from the enemy, having taken service in the Army of the United States, is captured by the enemy, and punished by them with death or otherwise, it is not a breach against the law and usages of war, requiring redress or retaliation.

Article 49. A prisoner of war is a public enemy armed or attached to the hostile army for active aid, who has fallen into the hands of the captor, either fighting or wounded, on the field or in the hospital, by individual surrender or by capitulation.

All soldiers, of whatever species of arms; all men who belong to the rising en masse of the hostile country; all those who are attached to the army for its efficiency and promote directly the object of the war, except such as are hereinafter provided for; all disabled men or officers on the field or elsewhere, if captured; all enemies who have thrown away their arms and ask for quarter, are prisoners of war, and as such exposed to the inconveniences as well as entitled to the privileges of a prisoner of war.

Article 50. Moreover, citizens who accompany an army for whatever purpose, such as sutlers, editors, or reporters of journals, or contractors, if captured, may be made prisoners of war, and be detained as such.

The monarch and members of the hostile reigning family, male or female, the chief, and chief officers of the hostile government, its diplomatic agents, and all persons who are of particular and singular use and benefit to the hostile army or its government, are, if captured on belligerent ground, and if unprovided with a safe conduct granted by the captor's government, prisoners of war.

Article 51. If the people of that portion of an invaded country which is not yet occupied by the enemy, or of the whole country, at the approach of a hostile army, rise, under a duly authorized levy en masse to resist the invader, they are now treated as public enemies, and, if captured, are prisoners of war.

Article 52. No belligerent has the right to declare that he will treat every captured man in arms of a levy en masse as a brigand or bandit. If, however, the people of a country, or any portion of the same, already occupied by an army, rise against it, they are violators of the laws of war, and are not entitled to their protection.

Article 53. The enemy's chaplains, officers of the medical staff, apothecaries, hospital nurses and servants, if they fall into the hands of the American Army, are not prisoners of war, unless the commander has reasons to retain them. In this latter case; or if, at their own desire, they are allowed to remain with their captured companions, they are treated as prisoners of war, and may be exchanged if the commander sees fit.

Article 54. A hostage is a person accepted as a pledge for the fulfillment of an agreement concluded between belligerents during the war, or in consequence of a war. Hostages are rare in the present age.

Article 55. If a hostage is accepted, he is treated like a prisoner of war, according to rank and condition, as circumstances may admit.

Article 56. A prisoner of war is subject to no punishment for being a public enemy, nor is any revenge wreaked upon him by the intentional infliction of any suffering, or disgrace, by cruel imprisonment, want of food, by mutilation, death, or any other barbarity.

Article 57. So soon as a man is armed by a sovereign government and takes the soldier's oath of fidelity, he is a belligerent; his killing, wounding, or other warlike acts are not individual crimes or offenses. No belligerent has a right to declare that enemies of a certain class, color, or condition, when properly organized as soldiers, will not be treated by him as public enemies.

Article 58. The law of nations knows of no distinction of color, and if an enemy of the United States should enslave and sell any captured persons of their army, it would be a case for the severest retaliation, if not redressed upon complaint.

The United States cannot retaliate by enslavement; therefore death must be the retaliation for this crime against the law of nations.

Article 59. A prisoner of war remains answerable for his crimes committed against the captor's army or people, committed before he was captured, and for which he has not been punished by his own authorities.

All prisoners of war are liable to the infliction of retaliatory measures.

Article 60. It is against the usage of modern war to resolve, in hatred and revenge, to give no quarter. No body of troops has the right to declare that it will not give, and therefore will not expect, quarter; but a commander is permitted to direct his troops to give no quarter, in great straits, when his own salvation makes it impossible to cumber himself with prisoners.

Article 61. Troops that give no quarter have no right to kill enemies already disabled on the ground, or prisoners captured by other troops.

Article 62. All troops of the enemy known or discovered to give no quarter in general, or to any portion of the army, receive none.

Article 63. Troops who fight in the uniform of their enemies, without any plain, striking, and uniform mark of distinction of their own, can expect no quarter.

Article 64. If American troops capture a train containing uniforms of the enemy, and the commander considers it advisable to distribute them for use among his men, some striking mark or sign must be adopted to distinguish the American soldier from the enemy.

Article 65. The use of the enemy's national standard, flag, or other emblem of nationality, for the purpose of deceiving the enemy in battle, is an act of perfidy by which they lose all claim to the protection of the laws of war.

Article 66. Quarter having been given to an enemy by American troops, under a misapprehension of his true character, he may, nevertheless, be ordered to suffer death if, within three days after the battle, it be discovered that he belongs to a corps which gives no quarter.

Article 67. The law of nations allows every sovereign government to make war upon another sovereign state, and, therefore, admits of no rules or laws different from those of regular warfare, regarding the treatment of prisoners of war, although they may belong to the army of a government which the captor may consider as a wanton and unjust assailant.

Article 68. Modern wars are not internecine wars, in which the killing of the enemy is the object. The destruction of the enemy in modern war, and, indeed, modern war itself, are means to obtain that object of the belligerent which lies beyond the war.

Unnecessary or revengeful destruction of life is not lawful.

Article 69. Outposts, sentinels, or pickets are not to be fired upon, except to drive them in, or when a positive order, special or general, has been issued to that effect.

Article 70. The use of poison in any manner, be it to poison wells, or food, or arms, is wholly excluded from modern warfare. He that uses it puts himself out of the pale of the law and usages of war.

Article 71. Whoever intentionally inflicts additional wounds on an enemy already wholly disabled, or kills such an enemy, or who orders or encourages soldiers to do so, shall suffer death, if duly convicted, whether he belongs to the Army of the United States, or is an enemy captured after having committed his misdeed.

. . . .

Article 75. Prisoners of war are subject to confinement or imprisonment such as may be deemed necessary on account of safety, but they are to be subjected to no other intentional suffering or indignity. The confinement and mode of treating a prisoner may be varied during his captivity according to the demands of safety.

Article 76. Prisoners of war shall be fed upon plain and wholesome food, whenever practicable, and treated with humanity.

They may be required to work for the benefit of the captor's government, according to their rank and condition.

Article 77. A prisoner of war who escapes may be shot or otherwise killed in his flight; but neither death nor any other punishment shall be inflicted upon him simply for his attempt to escape, which the law of war does not consider a crime. Stricter means of security shall be used after an unsuccessful attempt at escape.

If, however, a conspiracy is discovered, the purpose of which is a united or general escape, the conspirators may be rigorously punished, even with death; and capital punishment may also be inflicted upon prisoners of war discovered to have plotted rebellion against the authorities of the captors, whether in union with fellow prisoners or other persons.

Article 78. If prisoners of war, having given no pledge nor made any promise on their honor, forcibly or otherwise escape, and are captured again in battle after having rejoined their own army, they shall not be punished for their escape, but shall be treated as simple prisoners of war, although they will be subjected to stricter confinement.

Article 79. Every captured wounded enemy shall be medically treated, according to the ability of the medical staff.

Article 80. Honorable men, when captured, will abstain from giving to the enemy information concerning their own army, and the modern law of war permits no longer the use of any violence against prisoners in order to extort the desired information or to punish them for having given false information.

SECTION IV
Partisans—Armed enemies not belonging to the hostile army—Scouts—Armed prowlers—War-rebels

Article 81. Partisans are soldiers armed and wearing the uniform of their army, but belonging to a corps which acts detached from the main body for the purpose of making inroads into the territory occupied by the enemy. If captured, they are entitled to all the privileges of the prisoner of war.

Article 82. Men, or squads of men, who commit hostilities, whether by fighting, or inroads for destruction or plunder, or by raids of any kind, without commission, without being part and portion of the organized hostile army, and without sharing continuously in the war, but who do so with intermitting returns to their homes and avocations, or with the occasional assumption of the semblance of peaceful pursuits, divesting themselves of the character or appearance of soldiers—such men, or squads of men, are not public enemies, and, therefore, if captured, are not entitled to the privileges of prisoners of war, but shall be treated summarily as highway robbers or pirates.

Article 83. Scouts, or single soldiers, if disguised in the dress of the country or in the uniform of the army hostile to their own, employed in obtaining information, if found within or lurking about the lines of the captor, are treated as spies, and suffer death.

Article 84. Armed prowlers, by whatever names they may be called, or persons of the enemy's territory, who steal within the lines of the hostile army for the purpose of robbing, killing, or of destroying bridges, roads or canals, or of robbing or destroying the mail, or of cutting the telegraph wires, are not entitled to the privileges of the prisoner of war.

Article 85. War-rebels are persons within an occupied territory who rise in arms against the occupying or conquering army, or against the authorities established by the same. If captured, they may suffer death, whether they rise singly, in small or large bands, and whether called upon to do so by their own, but expelled, government or not. They are not prisoners of war; nor are they if discovered and secured before their conspiracy has matured to an actual rising or armed violence.

SECTION V
Safe-conduct — Spies — War-traitors — Captured messengers — Abuse of the flag of truce

Article 86. All intercourse between the territories occupied by belligerent armies, whether by traffic, by letter, by travel, or in any other way, ceases. This is the general rule, to be observed without special proclamation.

Exceptions to this rule, whether by safe-conduct, or permission to trade on a small or large scale, or by exchanging mails, or by travel from one territory into the other, can take place only according to agreement approved by the government, or by the highest military authority.

Contraventions of this rule are highly punishable.

Article 87. Ambassadors, and all other diplomatic agents of neutral powers, accredited to the enemy, may receive safe-conducts through the territories occupied by the belligerents, unless there are military reasons to the contrary, and unless they may reach the place of their destination conveniently by another route. It implies no international affront if the safe-conduct is declined. Such passes are usually given by the supreme authority of the State, and not by subordinate officers.

Article 88. A spy is a person who secretly, in disguise or under false pretense, seeks information with the intention of communicating it to the enemy.

The spy is punishable with death by hanging by the neck, whether or not he succeed in obtaining the information or in conveying it to the enemy.

Article 89. If a citizen of the United States obtains information in a legitimate manner, and betrays it to the enemy, be he a military or civil officer, or a private citizen, he shall suffer death.

Article 90. A traitor under the law of war, or a war-traitor, is a person in a place or district under Martial Law who, unauthorized by the military commander, gives information of any kind to the enemy, or holds intercourse with him.

Article 91. The war-traitor is always severely punished. If his offense consists in betraying to the enemy anything concerning the condition, safety, operations, or plans of the troops holding or occupying the place or district, his punishment is death.

. . . .

Article 101. While deception in war is admitted as a just and necessary means of hostility, and is consistent with honorable warfare, the common law of war allows even capital punishment for clandestine or treacherous attempts to injure an enemy, because they are so dangerous, and it is difficult to guard against them.

Article 102. The law of war, like the criminal law regarding other offenses, makes no difference on account of the difference of sexes, concerning the spy, the war-traitor, or the war-rebel.

Article 103. Spies, war-traitors, and war-rebels are not exchanged according to the common law of war. The exchange of such persons would require a special cartel, authorized by the government, or, at a great distance from it, by the chief commander of the army in the field.

Article 104. A successful spy or war-traitor, safely returned to his own army, and afterwards captured as an enemy, is not subject to punishment for his acts as a spy or war-traitor, but he may be held in closer custody as a person individually dangerous.

SECTION VI
Exchange of prisoners—Flags of truce—Flags of protection

....

SECTION VII
Parole

....

SECTION VIII
Armistice—Capitulation

....

SECTION IX
Assassination

Article 148. The law of war does not allow proclaiming either an individual belonging to the hostile army, or a citizen, or a subject of the hostile government, an outlaw, who may be slain without trial by any captor, any more than the modern law of peace allows such intentional outlawry; on the contrary, it abhors such outrage. The sternest retaliation should follow the murder committed in consequence of such proclamation, made by whatever authority. Civilized nations look with horror upon offers of rewards for the assassination of enemies as relapses into barbarism.

SECTION X
Insurrection—Civil War—Rebellion

....

HAGUE CONVENTION IV*
RESPECTING THE LAWS AND CUSTOMS OF WAR ON LAND

BY THE PRESIDENT OF THE UNITED STATES OF AMERICA

A PROCLAMATION.

Whereas a Convention respecting the laws and customs of war on land was concluded and signed at The Hague on October 18, 1907, by respective Plenipotentiaries of the United States of America, Germany, the Argentine Republic, Austria-Hungary, Belgium, Bolivia, Brazil, Bulgaria, Chile, Colombia, Cuba, Denmark, the Dominican Republic, Ecuador, France, Great Britain, Greece, Guatemala, Haiti, Italy, Japan, Luxembourg, Mexico, Montenegro, Norway, Panama, Paraguay, the Netherlands, Peru, Persia, Portugal, Roumania, Russia, Salvador, Serbia, Siam, Sweden, Switzerland, Turkey, Uruguay, and Venezuela, the original of which Convention, being in the French language, is word for word as follows:

[The French text has been omitted here.]

IV.

CONVENTION RESPECTING THE LAWS AND CUSTOMS OF WAR ON LAND

Seeing that, while seeking means to preserve peace and prevent armed conflicts between nations, it is likewise necessary to bear in mind the case where the appeal to arms has been brought about by events which their care was unable to avert;

Animated by the desire to serve, even in this extreme case, the interests of humanity and the ever progressive needs of civilization;

Thinking it important, with this object, to revise the general laws and customs of war, either with a view to defining them with greater precision or to confining them within such limits as would mitigate their severity as far as possible;

Have deemed it necessary to complete and explain in certain particulars the work of the First Peace Conference, which, following on the Brussels Conference of 1874, and inspired by the ideas dictated by a wise and generous forethought, adopted provisions intended to define and govern the usages of war on land.

According to the views of the High Contracting Parties, these provisions, the wording of which has been inspired by the desire to diminish the evils of war, as far as military requirements permit, are intended to serve as a general rule of conduct for the belligerents in their mutual relations and in their relations with the inhabitants.

It has not, however, been found possible at present to concert regulations covering all the circumstances which arise in practice;

---

* CONVENTION BETWEEN THE UNITED STATES AND OTHER POWERS RESPECTING THE LAWS AND CUSTOMS OF WAR ON LAND, OCT. 18, 1907, 36 Stat. 2277, 1 Bevans 631 (entered into force Jan. 26, 1910), *available at* http://www.yale.edu/lawweb/avalon/lawofwar/hague04.htm.

On the other hand, the High Contracting Parties clearly do not intend that unforeseen cases should, in the absence of a written undertaking, be left to the arbitrary judgment of military commanders.

Until a more complete code of the laws of war has been issued, the High Contracting Parties deem it expedient to declare that, in cases not included in the Regulations adopted by them, the inhabitants and the belligerents remain under the protection and the rule of the principles of the law of nations, as they result from the usages established among civilized peoples, from the laws of humanity, and the dictates of the public conscience.

They declare that it is in this sense especially that Articles 1 and 2 of the Regulations adopted must be understood.

The High Contracting Parties, wishing to conclude afresh Convention to this effect, have appointed the following as their Plenipotentiaries:

(List of Plenipotentiaries)

Who, after having deposited their full powers, found in good and due form, have agreed upon the following:

Article 1. The Contracting Powers shall issue instructions to their armed land forces which shall be in conformity with the Regulations respecting the laws and customs of war on land, annexed to the present Convention.

Article 2. The provisions contained in the Regulations referred to in Article 1, as well as in the present Convention, do not apply except between Contracting Powers, and then only if all the belligerents are parties to the Convention.

Article 3. A belligerent party which violates the provisions of the said Regulations shall, if the case demands, be liable to pay compensation. It shall be responsible for all acts committed by persons forming part of its armed forces.

....

ANNEX TO THE CONVENTION

Regulations respecting the laws and customs of war on land

SECTION I—ON BELLIGERENTS
CHAPTER I—*The Qualifications of Belligerents*

Article 1. The laws, rights, and duties of war apply not only to armies, but also to militia and volunteer corps fulfilling the following conditions:

To be commanded by a person responsible for his subordinates;

To have a fixed distinctive emblem recognizable at a distance;

To carry arms openly; and

To conduct their operations in accordance with the laws and customs of war.

In countries where militia or volunteer corps constitute the army, or form part of it, they are included under the denomination "army."

Article 2. The inhabitants of a territory which has not been occupied, who, on the approach of the enemy, spontaneously take up arms to resist the invading troops without having had time to organize themselves in accordance with Article 1, shall be regarded as belligerents if they carry arms openly and if they respect the laws and customs of war.

Article 3. The armed forces of the belligerent parties may consist of combatants and non-combatants. In the case of capture by the enemy, both have a right to be treated as prisoners of war.

CHAPTER II—*Prisoners of War*

Article 4. Prisoners of war are in the power of the hostile Government, but not of the individuals or corps who capture them.

They must be humanely treated.

All their personal belongings, except arms, horses, and military papers, remain their property.

Article 5. Prisoners of war may be interned in a town, fortress, camp, or other place, and bound not to go beyond certain fixed limits, but they cannot be confined except as in indispensable measure of safety and only while the circumstances which necessitate the measure continue to exist.

Article 6. The State may utilize the labour of prisoners of war according to their rank and aptitude, officers excepted. The tasks shall not be excessive and shall have no connection with the operations of the war.

Prisoners may be authorized to work for the public service, for private persons, or on their own account.

Work done for the State is paid for at the rates in force for work of a similar kind done by soldiers of the national army, or, if there are none in force, at a rate according to the work executed.

When the work is for other branches of the public service or for private persons the conditions are settled in agreement with the military authorities.

The wages of the prisoners shall go towards improving their position, and the balance shall be paid them on their release, after deducting the cost of their maintenance.

Article 7. The Government into whose hands prisoners of war have fallen is charged with their maintenance.

In the absence of a special agreement between the belligerents, prisoners of war shall be treated as regards board, lodging, and clothing on the same footing as the troops of the Government who captured them.

....

Article 18. Prisoners of war shall enjoy complete liberty in the exercise of their religion, including attendance at the services of whatever church they may belong to, on the sole condition that they comply with the measures of order and police issued by the military authorities.

....

Article 20. After the conclusion of peace, the repatriation of prisoners of war shall be carried out as quickly as possible.

CHAPTER III—*The Sick and Wounded*

Article 21. The obligations of belligerents with regard to the sick and wounded are governed by the Geneva Convention.

SECTION II—HOSTILITIES

CHAPTER I—*Means of Injuring the Enemy, Sieges, and Bombardments*

Article 22. The right of belligerents to adopt means of injuring the enemy is not unlimited.

Article 23. In addition to the prohibitions provided by special Conventions, it is especially forbidden—

To employ poison or poisoned weapons;

To kill or wound treacherously individuals belonging to the hostile nation or army;

To kill or wound an enemy who, having laid down his arms, or having no longer means of defence, has surrendered at discretion;

To declare that no quarter will be given;

To employ arms, projectiles, or material calculated to cause unnecessary suffering;

To make improper use of a flag of truce, of the national flag or of the military insignia and uniform of the enemy, as well as the distinctive badges of the Geneva Convention;

To destroy or seize the enemy's property, unless such destruction or seizure be imperatively demanded by the necessities of war;

To declare abolished, suspended, or inadmissible in a court of law the rights and actions of the nationals of the hostile party. A belligerent is likewise forbidden to compel the nationals of the hostile party to take part in the operations of war directed against their own country, even if they were in the belligerent's service before the commencement of the war.

Article 24. Ruses of war and the employment of measures necessary for obtaining information about the enemy and the country are considered permissible.

Article 25. The attack or bombardment, by whatever means, of towns, villages, dwellings, or buildings which are undefended is prohibited.

Article 26. The officer in command of an attacking force must, before commencing a bombardment, except in cases of assault, do all in his power to warn the authorities.

Article 27. In sieges and bombardments all necessary steps must be taken to spare, as far as possible, buildings dedicated to religion, art, science, or charitable purposes, historic monuments, hospitals, and places where the sick and wounded are collected, provided they are not being used at the time for military purposes.

It is the duty of the besieged to indicate the presence of such buildings or places by distinctive and visible signs, which shall be notified to the enemy beforehand.

Article 28. The pillage of a town or place, even when taken by assault, is prohibited.

CHAPTER II—*Spies*

Article 29. A person can only be considered a spy when, acting clandestinely or on false pretences, he obtains or endeavours to obtain information in the zone of operations of a belligerent, with the intention of communicating it to the hostile party.

Thus, soldiers not wearing a disguise who have penetrated into the zone of operations of the hostile army, for the purpose of obtaining information, are not considered spies. Similarly, the following are not considered spies: Soldiers and civilians, carrying out their mission openly, entrusted with the delivery of despatches intended either for their own army or for the enemy's army. To this class belong likewise persons sent in balloons for the purpose of carrying despatches and, generally, of maintaining communications between the different parts of an army or a territory.

Article 30. A spy taken in the act shall not be punished without previous trial.

Article 31. A spy who, after rejoining the army to which he belongs, is subsequently captured by the enemy, is treated as a prisoner of war, and incurs no responsibility for his previous acts of espionage.

CHAPTER III—*Flags of Truce*

Article 32. A person is regarded as a parlementaire who has been authorized by one of the belligerents to enter into communication with the other, and who advances bearing a white flag. He has a right to inviolability, as well as the trumpeter, bugler or drummer, the flag-bearer and interpreter who may accompany him.

Article 33. The commander to whom a parlementaire is sent is not in all cases obliged to receive him.

He may take all the necessary steps to prevent the parlementaire taking advantage of his mission to obtain information.

In case of abuse, he has the right to detain the parlementaire temporarily.

....

CHAPTER IV—*Capitulations*

....

CHAPTER V—*Armistices*

....

SECTION III—MILITARY AUTHORITY OVER THE TERRITORY OF THE HOSTILE STATE

Article 42. Territory is considered occupied when it is actually placed under the authority of the hostile army.

The occupation extends only to the territory where such authority has been established and can be exercised.

Article 43. The authority of the legitimate power having in fact passed into the hands of the occupant, the latter shall take all the measures in his power to restore, and ensure, as far as possible, public order and safety, while respecting, unless absolutely prevented, the laws in force in the country.

Article 44. A belligerent is forbidden to force the inhabitants of territory occupied by it to furnish information about the army of the other belligerent, or about its means of defense.

Article 45. It is forbidden to compel the inhabitants of occupied territory to swear allegiance to the hostile Power.

Article 46. Family honour and rights, the lives of persons, and private property, as well as religious convictions and practice, must be respected.

Private property cannot be confiscated.

Article 47. Pillage is formally forbidden.

....

HAGUE CONVENTION V* RESPECTING THE RIGHTS AND DUTIES OF NEUTRAL POWERS AND PERSONS IN CASE OF WAR ON LAND

V.

CONVENTION RESPECTING THE RIGHTS AND DUTIES OF NEUTRAL POWERS AND PERSONS IN CASE OF WAR ON LAND

....

CHAPTER I — *The Rights and Duties of Neutral Powers*

Article 1. The territory of neutral Powers is inviolable.

Article 2. Belligerents are forbidden to move troops or convoys of either munitions of war or supplies across the territory of a neutral Power.

Article 3. Belligerents are likewise forbidden to:

(a) Erect on the territory of a neutral Power a wireless telegraphy station or other apparatus for the purpose of communicating with belligerent forces on land or sea;

(b) Use any installation of this kind established by them before the war on the territory of a neutral Power for purely military purposes, and which has not been opened for the service of public messages.

Article 4. Corps of combatants cannot be formed nor recruiting agencies opened on the territory of a neutral Power to assist the belligerents.

Article 5. A neutral Power must not allow any of the acts referred to in Articles 2 to 4 to occur on its territory.

It is not called upon to punish acts in violation of its neutrality unless the said acts have been committed on its own territory.

Article 6. The responsibility of a neutral Power is not engaged by the fact of persons crossing the frontier separately to offer their services to one of the belligerents.

Article 7. A neutral Power is not called upon to prevent the export or transport, on behalf of one or other of the belligerents, of arms, munitions of war, or, in general, of anything which can be of use to an army or a fleet.

Article 8. A neutral Power is not called upon to forbid or restrict the use on behalf of the belligerents of telegraph or telephone cables or of wireless telegraphy apparatus belonging to it or to companies or private individuals.

---

* Convention Between the United States and Other Powers Respecting the Rights and Duties of Neutral Powers and Persons in Case of War on Land, Oct. 18, 1907, 36 Stat. 2310, 1 Bevans 654 (centered into force Jan. 26, 1910), *available at* http://www.yale.edu/lawweb/avalon/lawofwar/hague05.htm.

Article 9. Every measure of restriction or prohibition taken by a neutral Power in regard to the matters referred to in Articles 7 and 8 must be impartially applied by it to both belligerents.

A neutral Power must see to the same obligation being observed by companies or private individuals owning telegraph or telephone cables or wireless telegraphy apparatus.

Article 10. The fact of a neutral Power resisting, even by force, attempts to violate its neutrality cannot be regarded as a hostile act.

CHAPTER II—*Belligerents Interned and Wounded Tended in Neutral Territory*

....

CHAPTER III—*Neutral Persons*

Article 16. The nationals of a State which is not taking part in the war are considered as neutrals.

Article 17. A neutral cannot avail himself of his neutrality

(a) If he commits hostile acts against a belligerent;

(b) If he commits acts in favor of a belligerent, particularly if he voluntarily enlists in the ranks of the armed force of one of the parties. In such a case, the neutral shall not be more severely treated by the belligerent as against whom he has abandoned his neutrality than a national of the other belligerent State could be for the same act.

....

HAGUE CONVENTION IX RESPECTING BOMBARDMENT BY NAVAL FORCES IN TIME OF WAR*

IX.

CONVENTION CONCERNING BOMBARDMENT BY NAVAL FORCES IN TIME OF WAR

....

Animated by the desire to realize the wish expressed by the First Peace Conference respecting the bombardment by naval forces of undefended ports, towns, and villages;

Whereas it is expedient that bombardments by naval forces should be subject to rules of general application which would safeguard the rights of the inhabitants and assure the preservation of the more important buildings, by applying as far as possible to this operation of war the principles of the Regulation of 1899 respecting the laws and customs of land war;

Actuated, accordingly, by the desire to serve the interests of humanity and to diminish the severity and disasters of war;

Have resolved to conclude a Convention to this effect, and have, for this purpose, appointed the following as their Plenipotentiaries:

(List of Plenipotentiaries)

Who, after depositing their full powers, found in good and due form, have agreed upon the following provisions:

CHAPTER I—*The Bombardment of Undefended Ports, Towns, Villages, Dwellings, or Buildings*

Article 1. The bombardment by naval forces of undefended ports, towns, villages, dwellings, or buildings is forbidden.

A place cannot be bombarded solely because automatic submarine contact mines are anchored off the harbour.

Article 2. Military works, military or naval establishments, depots of arms or war materiel, workshops or plant which could be utilized for the needs of the hostile fleet or army, and the ships of war in the harbour, are not, however, included in this prohibition. The commander of a naval force may destroy them with artillery, after a summons followed by a reasonable time of waiting, if all other means are impossible, and when the local authorities have not themselves destroyed them within the time fixed.

He incurs no responsibility for any unavoidable damage which may be caused by a bombardment under such circumstances.

---

* Convention Between the United States and Other Powers Concerning Bombardment by Naval Forces in Time of War, Oct. 18, 1907, 36 Stat. 2351, 1 Bevans 681 (entered into force Jan. 26, 1910), *available at* http://www.yale.edu/lawweb/avalon/lawofwar/hague09.htm.

If for military reasons immediate action is necessary, and no delay can be allowed the enemy, it is understood that the prohibition to bombard the undefended town holds good, as in the case given in paragraph 1, and that the commander shall take all due measures in order that the town may suffer as little harm as possible.

Article 3. After due notice has been given, the bombardment of undefended ports, towns, villages, dwellings, or buildings may be commenced, if the local authorities, after a formal summons has been made to them, decline to comply with requisitions for provisions or supplies necessary for the immediate use of the naval force before the place in question.

These requisitions shall be in proportion to the resources of the place. They shall only be demanded in the name of the commander of the said naval force, and they shall, as far as possible, be paid for in cash; if not, they shall be evidenced by receipts.

Article 4. Undefended ports, towns, villages, dwellings, or buildings may not be bombarded on account of failure to pay money contributions.

CHAPTER II—*General Provisions*

Article 5. In bombardments by naval forces all the necessary measures must be taken by the commander to spare as far as possible sacred edifices, buildings used for artistic, scientific, or charitable purposes, historic monuments, hospitals, and places where the sick or wounded are collected, on the understanding that they are not used at the same time for military purposes.

It is the duty of the inhabitants to indicate such monuments, edifices, or places by visible signs, which shall consist of large, stiff rectangular panels divided diagonally into two coloured triangular portions, the upper portion black, the lower portion white.

Article 6. If the military situation permits, the commander of the attacking naval force, before commencing the bombardment, must do his utmost to warn the authorities.

Article 7. A town or place, even when taken by storm, may not be pillaged.

CHAPTER III—*Final Provisions*

....

HAGUE CONVENTION XIII CONCERNING THE RIGHTS AND DUTIES OF NEUTRAL POWERS IN NAVAL WAR*

XIII.

CONVENTION CONCERNING THE RIGHTS AND DUTIES OF NEUTRAL POWERS IN NAVAL WAR

With a view to harmonizing the divergent views which, in the event of naval war, are still held on the relations between neutral Powers and belligerent Powers, and to anticipating the difficulties to which such divergence of views might give rise;

Seeing that, even if it is not possible at present to concert measures applicable to all circumstances which may in practice occur, it is nevertheless undeniably advantageous to frame, as far as possible, rules of general application to meet the case where war has unfortunately broken out;

Seeing that, in cases not covered by the present Convention, it is expedient to take into consideration the general principles of the law of nations;

Seeing that it is desirable that the Powers should issue detailed enactments to regulate the results of the attitude of neutrality when adopted by them;

Seeing that it is, for neutral Powers, an admitted duty to apply these rules impartially to the several belligerents;

Seeing that, in this category of ideas, these rules should not, in principle, be altered, in the course of the war, by a neutral Power, except in a case where experience has shown the necessity for such change for the protection of the rights of that Power;

Have agreed to observe the following common rules, which cannot however modify provisions laid down in existing general treaties, and have appointed as their Plenipotentiaries, namely:

(List of Plenipotentiaries)

Who, after having deposited their full powers, found in good and due form, have agreed upon the following provisions:

Article 1. Belligerents are bound to respect the sovereign rights of neutral Powers and to abstain, in neutral territory or neutral waters, from any act which would, if knowingly permitted by any Power, constitute a violation of neutrality.

Article 2. Any act of hostility, including capture and the exercise of the right of search, committed by belligerent war-ships in the territorial waters of a neutral Power, constitutes a violation of neutrality and is strictly forbidden.

---

* CONVENTION BETWEEN THE UNITED STATES AND OTHER POWERS CONCERNING THE RIGHTS AND DUTIES OF NEUTRAL POWERS IN NAVAL WAR, OCT. 18, 1907, 36 Stat. 2415, 1 Bevans 723 (entered into force Jan. 26, 1910), *available at* http://www.yale.edu/lawweb/avalon/lawofwar/hague13.htm.

Article 3. When a ship has been captured in the territorial waters of a neutral Power, this Power must employ, if the prize is still within its jurisdiction, the means at its disposal to release the prize with its officers and crew, and to intern the prize crew.

If the prize is not in the jurisdiction of the neutral Power, the captor Government, on the demand of that Power, must liberate the prize with its officers and crew.

Article 4. A prize court cannot be set up by a belligerent on neutral territory or on a vessel in neutral waters.

Article 5. Belligerents are forbidden to use neutral ports and waters as a base of naval operations against their adversaries, and in particular to erect wireless telegraphy stations or any apparatus for the purpose of communicating with the belligerent forces on land or sea.

Article 6. The supply, in any manner, directly or indirectly, by a neutral Power to a belligerent Power, of war-ships, ammunition, or war material of any kind whatever, is forbidden.

Article 7. A neutral Power is not bound to prevent the export or transit, for the use of either belligerent, of arms, ammunition, or, in general, of anything which could be of use to an army or fleet.

Article 8. A neutral Government is bound to employ the means at its disposal to prevent the fitting out or arming of any vessel within its jurisdiction which it has reason to believe is intended to cruise, or engage in hostile operations, against a Power with which that Government is at peace. It is also bound to display the same vigilance to prevent the departure from its jurisdiction of any vessel intended to cruise, or engage in hostile operations, which had been adapted entirely or partly within the said jurisdiction for use in war.

Article 9. A neutral Power must apply impartially to the two belligerents the conditions, restrictions, or prohibitions made by it in regard to the admission into its ports, roadsteads, or territorial waters, of belligerent war-ships or of their prizes.

Nevertheless, a neutral Power may forbid a belligerent vessel which has failed to conform to the orders and regulations made by it, or which has violated neutrality, to enter its ports or roadsteads.

Article 10. The neutrality of a Power is not affected by the mere passage through its territorial waters of war-ships or prizes belonging to belligerents.

Article 11. A neutral Power may allow belligerent war-ships to employ its licensed pilots.

Article 12. In the absence of special provisions to the contrary in the legislation of a neutral Power, belligerent war-ships are not permitted to remain in the ports, roadsteads, or territorial waters of the said Power for more than twenty-four hours, except in the cases covered by the present Convention.

Article 13. If a Power which has been informed of the outbreak of hostilities learns that a belligerent war-ship is in one of its ports or roadsteads, or in its territorial waters, it must notify the said ship to depart within twenty-four hours or within the time prescribed by local regulations.

Article 14. A belligerent war-ship may not prolong its stay in a neutral port beyond the permissible time except on account of damage or stress of weather. It must depart as soon as the cause of the delay is at an end.

The regulations as to the question of the length of time which these vessels may remain in neutral ports, roadsteads, or waters, do not apply to war-ships devoted exclusively to religious, scientific, or philanthropic purposes.

Article 15. In the absence of special provisions to the contrary in the legislation of a neutral Power, the maximum number of warships belonging to a belligerent which may be in one of the ports or roadsteads of that Power simultaneously shall be three.

Article 16. When war-ships belonging to both belligerents are present simultaneously in a neutral port or roadstead, a period of not less than twenty-four hours must elapse between the departure of the ship belonging to one belligerent and the departure of the ship belonging to the other.

The order of departure is determined by the order of arrival, unless the ship which arrived first is so circumstanced that an extension of its stay is permissible.

A belligerent war-ship may not leave a neutral port or roadstead until twenty-four hours after the departure of a merchant ship flying the flag of its adversary.

Article 17. In neutral ports and roadsteads belligerent war-ships may only carry out such repairs as are absolutely necessary to render them seaworthy, and may not add in any manner whatsoever to their fighting force. The local authorities of the neutral Power shall decide what repairs are necessary, and these must be carried out with the least possible delay.

Article 18. Belligerent war-ships may not make use of neutral ports, roadsteads, or territorial waters for replenishing or increasing their supplies of war material or their armament, or for completing their crews.

Article 19. Belligerent war-ships may only revictual in neutral ports or roadsteads to bring up their supplies to the peace standard.

Similarly these vessels may only ship sufficient fuel to enable them to reach the nearest port in their own country. They may, on the other hand, fill up their bunkers built to carry fuel, when in neutral countries which have adopted this method of determining the amount of fuel to be supplied.

If, in accordance with the law of the neutral Power, the ships are not supplied with coal within twenty-four hours of their arrival, the permissible duration of their stay is extended by twenty-four hours.

Article 20. Belligerent war-ships which have shipped fuel in a port belonging to a neutral Power may not within the succeeding three months replenish their supply in a port of the same Power.

Article 21. A prize may only be brought into a neutral port on account of unseaworthiness, stress of weather, or want of fuel or provisions.

It must leave as soon as the circumstances which justified its entry are at an end. If it does not, the neutral Power must order it to leave at once; should it fail to obey, the neutral Power must employ the means at its disposal to release it with its officers and crew and to intern the prize crew.

Article 22. A neutral Power must, similarly, release a prize brought into one of its ports under circumstances other than those referred to in Article 21.

Article 23. A neutral Power may allow prizes to enter its ports and roadsteads, whether under convoy or not, when they are brought there to be sequestrated pending the decision of a Prize Court. It may have the prize taken to another of its ports.

If the prize is convoyed by a war-ship, the prize crew may go on board the convoying ship.

If the prize is not under convoy, the prize crew are left at liberty.

Article 24. If, notwithstanding the notification of the neutral Power, a belligerent ship of war does not leave a port where it is not entitled to remain, the neutral Power is entitled to take such measures as it considers necessary to render the ship incapable of taking the sea during the war, and the commanding officer of the ship must facilitate the execution of such measures.

When a belligerent ship is detained by a neutral Power, the officers and crew are likewise detained.

The officers and crew thus detained may be left in the ship or kept either on another vessel or on land, and may be subjected to the measures of restriction which it may appear necessary to impose upon them. A sufficient number of men for looking after the vessel must, however, be always left on board.

The officers may be left at liberty on giving their word not to quit the neutral territory without permission.

Article 25. A neutral Power is bound to exercise such surveillance as the means at its disposal allow to prevent any violation of the provisions of the above Articles occurring in its ports or roadsteads or in its waters.

Article 26. The exercise by a neutral Power of the rights laid down in the present Convention can under no circumstances be considered as an unfriendly act by one or other belligerent who has accepted the articles relating thereto.

Article 27. The Contracting Powers shall communicate to each other in due course all laws, proclamations, and other enactments regulating in their respective countries the status of belligerent war-ships in their ports and waters, by means of a communication addressed to the Government of the Netherlands, and forwarded immediately by that Government to the other Contracting Powers.

....

GENEVA CONVENTION FOR THE AMELIORATION OF THE CONDITION OF THE WOUNDED AND SICK IN ARMED FORCES IN THE FIELD[1] (FIRST GENEVA CONVENTION)

CHAPTER I — *General provisions*

Article 1. The High Contracting Parties undertake to respect and to ensure respect for the present Convention in all circumstances.

Article 2. In addition to the provisions which shall be implemented in peacetime, the present Convention shall apply to all cases of declared war or of any other armed conflict which may arise between two or more of the High Contracting Parties, even if the state of war is not recognized by one of them.

The Convention shall also apply to all cases of partial or total occupation of the territory of a High Contracting Party, even if the said occupation meets with no armed resistance.

Although one of the Powers in conflict may not be a party to the present Convention, the Powers who are parties thereto shall remain bound by it in their mutual relations. They shall furthermore be bound by the Convention in relation to the said Power, if the latter accepts and applies the provisions thereof.

Article 3. In the case of armed conflict not of an international character occurring in the territory of one of the High Contracting Parties, each Party to the conflict shall be bound to apply, as a minimum, the following provisions:

(1) Persons taking no active part in the hostilities, including members of armed forces who have laid down their arms and those placed *hors de combat* by sickness, wounds, detention, or any other cause, shall in all circumstances be treated humanely, without any adverse distinction founded on race, colour, religion or faith, sex, birth or wealth, or any other similar criteria.

To this end, the following acts are and shall remain prohibited at any time and in any place whatsoever with respect to the above-mentioned persons:

(a) violence to life and person, in particular murder of all kinds, mutilation, cruel treatment and torture;

(b) taking of hostages;

(c) outrages upon personal dignity, in particular humiliating and degrading treatment;

(d) the passing of sentences and the carrying out of executions without previous judgment pronounced by a regularly constituted court, affording all the judicial guarantees which are recognized as indispensable by civilized peoples.

---

1. Geneva Convention for the Amelioration of the Condition of the Wounded and Sick in Armed Forces in the Field, Aug. 12, 1949, 6 U.S.T. 3114, 75 U.N.T.S. 31 (entered into force Oct. 21, 1950), *available at* http://www.icrc.org/ihl.nsf/WebART?OpenView&Start=1&Count=150&Expand=53#53.

(2) The wounded and sick shall be collected and cared for.

An impartial humanitarian body, such as the International Committee of the Red Cross, may offer its services to the Parties to the conflict.

The Parties to the conflict should further endeavour to bring into force, by means of special agreements, all or part of the other provisions of the present Convention.

The application of the preceding provisions shall not affect the legal status of the Parties to the conflict.[2]

Article 4. Neutral Powers shall apply by analogy the provisions of the present Convention to the wounded and sick, and to members of the medical personnel and to chaplains of the armed forces of the Parties to the conflict, received or interned in their territory, as well as to dead persons found.

Article 5. For the protected persons who have fallen into the hands of the enemy, the present Convention shall apply until their final repatriation.

Article 6. In addition to the agreements expressly provided for in Articles 10, 15, 23, 28, 31, 36, 37 and 52, the High Contracting Parties may conclude other special agreements for all matters concerning which they may deem it suitable to make separate provision. No special agreement shall adversely affect the situation of the wounded and sick, of members of the medical personnel or of chaplains, as defined by the present Convention, nor restrict the rights which it confers upon them.

Wounded and sick, as well as medical personnel and chaplains, shall continue to have the benefit of such agreements as long as the Convention is applicable to them, except where express provisions to the contrary are contained in the aforesaid or in subsequent agreements, or where more favourable measures have been taken with regard to them by one or other of the Parties to the conflict.

Article 7. Wounded and sick, as well as members of the medical personnel and chaplains, may in no circumstances renounce in part or in entirety the rights secured to them by the present Convention, and by the special agreements referred to in the foregoing Article, if such there be.

....

Article 9. The provisions of the present Convention constitute no obstacle to the humanitarian activities which the International Committee of the Red Cross or any other impartial humanitarian organization may, subject to the consent of the Parties to the conflict concerned, undertake for the protection of wounded and sick, medical personnel and chaplains, and for their relief.

....

CHAPTER II—*Wounded and sick*

Article 12. Members of the armed forces and other persons mentioned in the following Article, who are wounded or sick, shall be respected and protected in all circumstances.

They shall be treated humanely and cared for by the Party to the conflict in whose power they may be, without any adverse distinction founded on sex, race, nationality, religion, political opinions, or any other similar criteria. Any attempts upon their lives,

2. Articles 1–3, known as the mini-Geneva Convention, are identical in all four conventions.

or violence to their persons, shall be strictly prohibited; in particular, they shall not be murdered or exterminated, subjected to torture or to biological experiments; they shall not willfully be left without medical assistance and care, nor shall conditions exposing them to contagion or infection be created.

Only urgent medical reasons will authorize priority in the order of treatment to be administered.

Women shall be treated with all consideration due to their sex.

The Party to the conflict which is compelled to abandon wounded or sick to the enemy shall, as far as military considerations permit, leave with them a part of its medical personnel and material to assist in their care.

Article 13. The present Convention shall apply to the wounded and sick belonging to the following categories:

(1) Members of the armed forces of a Party to the conflict as well as members of militias or volunteer corps forming part of such armed forces.

(2) Members of other militias and members of other volunteer corps, including those of organized resistance movements, belonging to a Party to the conflict and operating in or outside their own territory, even if this territory is occupied, provided that such militias or volunteer corps, including such organized resistance movements, fulfill the following conditions:

(a) that of being commanded by a person responsible for his subordinates;

(b) that of having a fixed distinctive sign recognizable at a distance;

(c) that of carrying arms openly;

(d) that of conducting their operations in accordance with the laws and customs of war.

(3) Members of regular armed forces who profess allegiance to a Government or an authority not recognized by the Detaining Power.

(4) Persons who accompany the armed forces without actually being members thereof, such as civil members of military aircraft crews, war correspondents, supply contractors, members of labour units or of services responsible for the welfare of the armed forces, provided that they have received authorization from the armed forces which they accompany.

(5) Members of crews, including masters, pilots and apprentices of the merchant marine and the crews of civil aircraft of the Parties to the conflict, who do not benefit by more favourable treatment under any other provisions in international law.

(6) Inhabitants of a non-occupied territory who on the approach of the enemy spontaneously take up arms to resist the invading forces, without having had time to form themselves into regular armed units, provided they carry arms openly and respect the laws and customs of war.

Article 14. Subject to the provisions of Article 12, the wounded and sick of a belligerent who fall into enemy hands shall be prisoners of war, and the provisions of international law concerning prisoners of war shall apply to them.

Article 15. At all times, and particularly after an engagement, Parties to the conflict shall, without delay, take all possible measures to search for and collect the wounded and sick, to protect them against pillage and ill-treatment, to ensure their adequate care, and to search for the dead and prevent their being despoiled.

Whenever circumstances permit, an armistice or a suspension of fire shall be arranged, or local arrangements made, to permit the removal, exchange and transport of the wounded left on the battlefield.

Likewise, local arrangements may be concluded between Parties to the conflict for the removal or exchange of wounded and sick from a besieged or encircled area, and for the passage of medical and religious personnel and equipment on their way to that area.

Article 16. Parties to the conflict shall record as soon as possible, in respect of each wounded, sick or dead person of the adverse Party falling into their hands, any particulars which may assist in his identification.

These records should if possible include:

(a) designation of the Power on which he depends;

(b) army, regimental, personal or serial number;

(c) surname;

(d) first name or names;

(e) date of birth;

(f) any other particulars shown on his identity card or disc;

(g) date and place of capture or death;

(h) particulars concerning wounds or illness, or cause of death.

As soon as possible the above mentioned information shall be forwarded to the Information Bureau described in Article 122 of the Geneva Convention relative to the Treatment of Prisoners of War of August 12, 1949, which shall transmit this information to the Power on which these persons depend through the intermediary of the Protecting Power and of the Central Prisoners of War Agency.

Parties to the conflict shall prepare and forward to each other through the same bureau, certificates of death or duly authenticated lists of the dead. They shall likewise collect and forward through the same bureau one half of a double identity disc, last wills or other documents of importance to the next of kin, money and in general all articles of an intrinsic or sentimental value, which are found on the dead. These articles, together with unidentified articles, shall be sent in sealed packets, accompanied by statements giving all particulars necessary for the identification of the deceased owners, as well as by a complete list of the contents of the parcel.

Article 17. Parties to the conflict shall ensure that burial or cremation of the dead, carried out individually as far as circumstances permit, is preceded by a careful examination, if possible by a medical examination, of the bodies, with a view to confirming death, establishing identity and enabling a report to be made. One half of the double identity disc, or the identity disc itself if it is a single disc, should remain on the body.

Bodies shall not be cremated except for imperative reasons of hygiene or for motives based on the religion of the deceased. In case of cremation, the circumstances and reasons for cremation shall be stated in detail in the death certificate or on the authenticated list of the dead.

They shall further ensure that the dead are honourably interred, if possible according to the rites of the religion to which they belonged, that their graves are respected, grouped if possible according to the nationality of the deceased, properly maintained and marked so that they may always be found. For this purpose, they shall organize at the commencement of hostilities an Official Graves Registration Service, to allow subsequent exhumations and to ensure the identification of bodies, whatever the site of the graves, and the possible transportation to the home country. These provisions shall likewise apply to the ashes, which shall be kept by the Graves Registration Service until proper disposal thereof in accordance with the wishes of the home country.

As soon as circumstances permit, and at latest at the end of hostilities, these Services shall exchange, through the Information Bureau mentioned in the second paragraph of Article 16, lists showing the exact location and markings of the graves together with particulars of the dead interred therein.

....

CHAPTER III—*Medical units and establishments*

Article 19. Fixed establishments and mobile medical units of the Medical Service may in no circumstances be attacked, but shall at all times be respected and protected by the Parties to the conflict. Should they fall into the hands of the adverse Party, their personnel shall be free to pursue their duties, as long as the capturing Power has not itself ensured the necessary care of the wounded and sick found in such establishments and units.

The responsible authorities shall ensure that the said medical establishments and units are, as far as possible, situated in such a manner that attacks against military objectives cannot imperil their safety.

Article 20. Hospital ships entitled to the protection of the Geneva Convention for the Amelioration of the Condition of Wounded, Sick and Shipwrecked Members of Armed Forces at Sea of August 12, 1949, shall not be attacked from the land.

Article 21. The protection to which fixed establishments and mobile medical units of the Medical Service are entitled shall not cease unless they are used to commit, outside their humanitarian duties, acts harmful to the enemy. Protection may, however, cease only after a due warning has been given, naming, in all appropriate cases, a reasonable time limit and after such warning has remained unheeded.

Article 22. The following conditions shall not be considered as depriving a medical unit or establishment of the protection guaranteed by Article 19:

(1) That the personnel of the unit or establishment are armed, and that they use the arms in their own defence, or in that of the wounded and sick in their charge.

(2) That in the absence of armed orderlies, the unit or establishment is protected by a picket or by sentries or by an escort.

(3) That small arms and ammunition taken from the wounded and sick and not yet handed to the proper service, are found in the unit or establishment.

(4) That personnel and material of the veterinary service are found in the unit or establishment, without forming an integral part thereof.

(5) That the humanitarian activities of medical units and establishments or of their personnel extend to the care of civilian wounded or sick.

....

CHAPTER IV—*Personnel*

Article 24. Medical personnel exclusively engaged in the search for, or the collection, transport or treatment of the wounded or sick, or in the prevention of disease, staff exclusively engaged in the administration of medical units and establishments, as well as chaplains attached to the armed forces, shall be respected and protected in all circumstances.

....

CHAPTER V—*Buildings and material*

Article 33. The material of mobile medical units of the armed forces which fall into the hands of the enemy, shall be reserved for the care of wounded and sick.

The buildings, material and stores of fixed medical establishments of the armed forces shall remain subject to the laws of war, but may not be diverted from their purpose as long as they are required for the care of wounded and sick. Nevertheless, the commanders of forces in the field may make use of them, in case of urgent military necessity, provided that they make previous arrangements for the welfare of the wounded and sick who are nursed in them.

The material and stores defined in the present Article shall not be intentionally destroyed.

....

CHAPTER VI—*Medical transports*

Article 35. Transports of wounded and sick or of medical equipment shall be respected and protected in the same way as mobile medical units.

Should such transports or vehicles fall into the hands of the adverse Party, they shall be subject to the laws of war, on condition that the Party to the conflict who captures them shall in all cases ensure the care of the wounded and sick they contain.

The civilian personnel and all means of transport obtained by requisition shall be subject to the general rules of international law.

Article 36. Medical aircraft, that is to say, aircraft exclusively employed for the removal of wounded and sick and for the transport of medical personnel and equipment, shall not be attacked, but shall be respected by the belligerents, while flying at heights, times and on routes specifically agreed upon between the belligerents concerned.

They shall bear, clearly marked, the distinctive emblem prescribed in Article 38, together with their national colours, on their lower, upper and lateral surfaces. They shall be provided with any other markings or means of identification that may be agreed upon between the belligerents upon the outbreak or during the course of hostilities.

Unless agreed otherwise, flights over enemy or enemy-occupied territory are prohibited. Medical aircraft shall obey every summons to land. In the event of a landing thus imposed, the aircraft with its occupants may continue its flight after examination, if any.

In the event of an involuntary landing in enemy or enemy-occupied territory, the wounded and sick, as well as the crew of the aircraft shall be prisoners of war. The medical personnel shall be treated according to Article 24, and the Articles following.

....

CHAPTER VII—*The distinctive emblem*

Article 38. As a compliment to Switzerland, the heraldic emblem of the red cross on a white ground, formed by reversing the Federal colours, is retained as the emblem and distinctive sign of the Medical Service of armed forces.

Nevertheless, in the case of countries which already use as emblem, in place of the red cross, the red crescent or the red lion and sun on a white ground, those emblems are also recognized by the terms of the present Convention.

. . . .

CHAPTER VIII—*Execution of the convention*

Article 45. Each Party to the conflict, acting through its commanders-in-chief, shall ensure the detailed execution of the preceding Articles and provide for unforeseen cases, in conformity with the general principles of the present Convention.

Article 46. Reprisals against the wounded, sick, personnel, buildings or equipment protected by the Convention are prohibited.

Article 47. The High Contracting Parties undertake, in time of peace as in time of war, to disseminate the text of the present Convention as widely as possible in their respective countries, and, in particular, to include the study thereof in their programmes of military and, if possible, civil instruction, so that the principles thereof may become known to the entire population, in particular to the armed fighting forces, the medical personnel and the chaplains.

. . . .

CHAPTER IX—*Repression of abuses and infractions*

Article 49. The High Contracting Parties undertake to enact any legislation necessary to provide effective penal sanctions for persons committing, or ordering to be committed, any of the grave breaches of the present Convention defined in the following Article.

Each High Contracting Party shall be under the obligation to search for persons alleged to have committed, or to have ordered to be committed, such grave breaches, and shall bring such persons, regardless of their nationality, before its own courts. It may also, if it prefers, and in accordance with the provisions of its own legislation, hand such persons over for trial to another High Contracting Party concerned, provided such High Contracting Party has made out a *prima facie* case.

Each High Contracting Party shall take measures necessary for the suppression of all acts contrary to the provisions of the present Convention other than the grave breaches defined in the following Article.

In all circumstances, the accused persons shall benefit by safeguards of proper trial and defence, which shall not be less favourable than those provided by Article 105 and those following of the Geneva Convention relative to the Treatment of Prisoners of War of August 12, 1949.

Article 50. Grave breaches to which the preceding Article relates shall be those involving any of the following acts, if committed against persons or property protected by the Convention: willful killing, torture or inhuman treatment, including biological experiments, willfully causing great suffering or serious injury to body or health, and extensive destruction and appropriation of property, not justified by military necessity and carried out unlawfully and wantonly.

Article 51. No High Contracting Party shall be allowed to absolve itself or any other High Contracting Party of any liability incurred by itself or by another High Contracting Party in respect of breaches referred to in the preceding Article.

Article 52. At the request of a Party to the conflict, an enquiry shall be instituted, in a manner to be decided between the interested Parties, concerning any alleged violation of the Convention.

If agreement has not been reached concerning the procedure for the enquiry, the Parties should agree on the choice of an umpire who will decide upon the procedure to be followed.

Once the violation has been established, the Parties to the conflict shall put an end to it and shall repress it with the least possible delay.

Article 53. The use by individuals, societies, firms or companies either public or private, other than those entitled thereto under the present Convention, of the emblem or the designation "Red Cross" or "Geneva Cross", or any sign or designation constituting an imitation thereof, whatever the object of such use, and irrespective of the date of its adoption, shall be prohibited at all times.

By reason of the tribute paid to Switzerland by the adoption of the reversed Federal colours, and of the confusion which may arise between the arms of Switzerland and the distinctive emblem of the Convention, the use by private individuals, societies or firms, of the arms of the Swiss Confederation, or of marks constituting an imitation thereof, whether as trademarks or commercial marks, or as parts of such marks, or for a purpose contrary to commercial honesty, or in circumstances capable of wounding Swiss national sentiment, shall be prohibited at all times.

. . . .

GENEVA CONVENTION RELATIVE TO THE TREATMENT OF PRISONERS OF WAR* (THIRD GENEVA CONVENTION)

....

PART I
GENERAL PROVISIONS

....

Article 4.

A. Prisoners of war, in the sense of the present Convention, are persons belonging to one of the following categories, who have fallen into the power of the enemy:

(1) Members of the armed forces of a Party to the conflict, as well as members of militias or volunteer corps forming part of such armed forces.

(2) Members of other militias and members of other volunteer corps, including those of organized resistance movements, belonging to a Party to the conflict and operating in or outside their own territory, even if this territory is occupied, provided that such militias or volunteer corps, including such organized resistance movements, fulfill the following conditions:

(a) that of being commanded by a person responsible for his subordinates;

(b) that of having a fixed distinctive sign recognizable at a distance;

(c) that of carrying arms openly;

(d) that of conducting their operations in accordance with the laws and customs of war.

(3) Members of regular armed forces who profess allegiance to a government or an authority not recognized by the Detaining Power.

(4) Persons who accompany the armed forces without actually being members thereof, such as civilian members of military aircraft crews, war correspondents, supply contractors, members of labour units or of services responsible for the welfare of the armed forces, provided that they have received authorization, from the armed forces which they accompany, who shall provide them for that purpose with an identity card similar to the annexed model.

(5) Members of crews, including masters, pilots and apprentices, of the merchant marine and the crews of civil aircraft of the Parties to the conflict, who do not benefit by more favourable treatment under any other provisions of international law.

(6) Inhabitants of a non-occupied territory, who on the approach of the enemy spontaneously take up arms to resist the invading forces, without having had time to form themselves into regular armed units, provided they carry arms openly and respect the laws and customs of war.

---

* Geneva Convention Relative to the Treatment of Prisoners of War, Aug. 12, 1949, 6 U.S.T. 3316, 75 U.N.T.S. 135 (entered into force Oct. 21, 1950), *available at* http://www.yale.edu/lawweb/avalon/lawofwar/geneva03.htm.

B. The following shall likewise be treated as prisoners of war under the present Convention:

(1) Persons belonging, or having belonged, to the armed forces of the occupied country, if the occupying Power considers it necessary by reason of such allegiance to intern them, even though it has originally liberated them while hostilities were going on outside the territory it occupies, in particular where such persons have made an unsuccessful attempt to rejoin the armed forces to which they belong and which are engaged in combat, or where they fail to comply with a summons made to them with a view to internment.

(2) The persons belonging to one of the categories enumerated in the present Article, who have been received by neutral or non-belligerent Powers on their territory and whom these Powers are required to intern under international law, without prejudice to any more favourable treatment which these Powers may choose to give and with the exception of Articles 8, 10, 15, 30, fifth paragraph, 58–67, 92, 126 and, where diplomatic relations exist between the Parties to the conflict and the neutral or non-belligerent Power concerned, those Articles concerning the Protecting Power. Where such diplomatic relations exist, the Parties to a conflict on whom these persons depend shall be allowed to perform towards them the functions of a Protecting Power as provided in the present Convention, without prejudice to the functions which these Parties normally exercise in conformity with diplomatic and consular usage and treaties.

C. This Article shall in no way affect the status of medical personnel and chaplains as provided for in Article 33 of the present Convention.

Article 5. The present Convention shall apply to the persons referred to in Article 4 from the time they fall into the power of the enemy and until their final release and repatriation.

Should any doubt arise as to whether persons, having committed a belligerent act and having fallen into the hands of the enemy, belong to any of the categories enumerated in Article 4, such persons shall enjoy the protection of the present Convention until such time as their status has been determined by a competent tribunal.

....

PART II
GENERAL PROTECTION OF PRISONERS OF WAR

Article 12. Prisoners of war are in the hands of the enemy Power, but not of the individuals or military units who have captured them. Irrespective of the individual responsibilities that may exist, the Detaining Power is responsible for the treatment given them.

Prisoners of war may only be transferred by the Detaining Power to a Power which is a party to the Convention and after the Detaining Power has satisfied itself of the willingness and ability of such transferee Power to apply the Convention. When prisoners of war are transferred under such circumstances, responsibility for the application of the Convention rests on the Power accepting them while they are in its custody.

Nevertheless, if that Power fails to carry out the provisions of the Convention in any important respect, the Power by whom the prisoners of war were transferred shall, upon being notified by the Protecting Power, take effective measures to correct the situation or shall request the return of the prisoners of war. Such requests must be complied with.

Article 13. Prisoners of war must at all times be humanely treated. Any unlawful act or omission by the Detaining Power causing death or seriously endangering the health of a prisoner of war in its custody is prohibited, and will be regarded as a serious breach of the present Convention. In particular, no prisoner of war may be subjected to physical mutilation or to medical or scientific experiments of any kind which are not justified by the medical, dental or hospital treatment of the prisoner concerned and carried out in his interest.

Likewise, prisoners of war must at all times be protected, particularly against acts of violence or intimidation and against insults and public curiosity.

Measures of reprisal against prisoners of war are prohibited.

Article 14. Prisoners of war are entitled in all circumstances to respect for their persons and their honour.

Women shall be treated with all the regard due to their sex and shall in all cases benefit by treatment as favourable as that granted to men.

Prisoners of war shall retain the full civil capacity which they enjoyed at the time of their capture. The Detaining Power may not restrict the exercise, either within or without its own territory, of the rights such capacity confers except in so far as the captivity requires.

Article 15. The Power detaining prisoners of war shall be bound to provide free of charge for their maintenance and for the medical attention required by their state of health.

Article 16. Taking into consideration the provisions of the present Convention relating to rank and sex, and subject to any privileged treatment which may be accorded to them by reason of their state of health, age or professional qualifications, all prisoners of war shall be treated alike by the Detaining Power, without any adverse distinction based on race, nationality, religious belief or political opinions, or any other distinction founded on similar criteria.

PART III
CAPTIVITY

SECTION I—BEGINNING OF CAPTIVITY

Article 17. Every prisoner of war, when questioned on the subject, is bound to give only his surname, first names and rank, date of birth, and army, regimental, personal or serial number, or failing this, equivalent information.

If he willfully infringes this rule, he may render himself liable to a restriction of the privileges accorded to his rank or status.

Each Party to a conflict is required to furnish the persons under its jurisdiction who are liable to become prisoners of war, with an identity card showing the owner's surname, first names, rank, army, regimental, personal or serial number or equivalent information, and date of birth. The identity card may, furthermore, bear the signature or the fingerprints, or both, of the owner, and may bear, as well, any other information the Party to the conflict may wish to add concerning persons belonging to its armed forces. As far as possible the card shall measure 6.5 x 10 cm. and shall be issued in duplicate. The identity card shall be shown by the prisoner of war upon demand, but may in no case be taken away from him.

No physical or mental torture, nor any other form of coercion, may be inflicted on prisoners of war to secure from them information of any kind whatever. Prisoners of war who refuse to answer may not be threatened, insulted, or exposed to unpleasant or disadvantageous treatment of any kind. Prisoners of war who, owing to their physical or mental condition, are unable to state their identity, shall be handed over to the medical service. The identity of such prisoners shall be established by all possible means, subject to the provisions of the preceding paragraph.

The questioning of prisoners of war shall be carried out in a language which they understand.

Article 18. All effects and articles of personal use, except arms, horses, military equipment and military documents, shall remain in the possession of prisoners of war, likewise their metal helmets and gas masks and like articles issued for personal protection. Effects and articles used for their clothing or feeding shall likewise remain in their possession, even if such effects and articles belong to their regulation military equipment.

At no time should prisoners of war be without identity documents. The Detaining Power shall supply such documents to prisoners of war who possess none.

Badges of rank and nationality, decorations and articles having above all a personal or sentimental value may not be taken from prisoners of war.

Sums of money carried by prisoners of war may not be taken away from them except by order of an officer, and after the amount and particulars of the owner have been recorded in a special register and an itemized receipt has been given, legibly inscribed with the name, rank and unit of the person issuing the said receipt. Sums in the currency of the Detaining Power, or which are changed into such currency at the prisoner's request, shall be placed to the credit of the prisoner's account as provided in Article 64.

The Detaining Power may withdraw articles of value from prisoners of war only for reasons of security; when such articles are withdrawn, the procedure laid down for sums of money impounded shall apply.

Such objects, likewise sums taken away in any currency other than that of the Detaining Power and the conversion of which has not been asked for by the owners, shall be kept in the custody of the Detaining Power and shall be returned in their initial shape to prisoners of war at the end of their captivity.

Article 19. Prisoners of war shall be evacuated, as soon as possible after their capture, to camps situated in an area far enough from the combat zone for them to be out of danger.

Only those prisoners of war who, owing to wounds or sickness, would run greater risks by being evacuated than by remaining where they are, may be temporarily kept back in a danger zone.

Prisoners of war shall not be unnecessarily exposed to danger while awaiting evacuation from a fighting zone.

Article 20. The evacuation of prisoners of war shall always be effected humanely and in conditions similar to those for the forces of the Detaining Power in their changes of station.

The Detaining Power shall supply prisoners of war who are being evacuated with sufficient food and potable water, and with the necessary clothing and medical attention. The Detaining Power shall take all suitable precautions to ensure their safety during evacuation, and shall establish as soon as possible a list of the prisoners of war who are evacuated.

If prisoners of war must, during evacuation, pass through transit camps, their stay in such camps shall be as brief as possible.

SECTION II—INTERNMENT OF PRISONERS OF WAR

CHAPTER I—*General observations*

Article 21. The Detaining Power may subject prisoners of war to internment. It may impose on them the obligation of not leaving, beyond certain limits, the camp where they are interned, or if the said camp is fenced in, of not going outside its perimeter. Subject to the provisions of the present Convention relative to penal and disciplinary sanctions, prisoners of war may not be held in close confinement except where necessary to safeguard their health and then only during the continuation of the circumstances which make such confinement necessary.

Prisoners of war may be partially or wholly released on parole or promise, in so far as is allowed by the laws of the Power on which they depend. Such measures shall be taken particularly in cases where this may contribute to the improvement of their state of health. No prisoner of war shall be compelled to accept liberty on parole or promise.

Upon the outbreak of hostilities, each Party to the conflict shall notify the adverse Party of the laws and regulations allowing or forbidding its own nationals to accept liberty on parole or promise. Prisoners of war who are paroled or who have given their promise in conformity with the laws and regulations so notified, are bound on their personal honour scrupulously to fulfill, both towards the Power on which they depend and towards the Power which has captured them, the engagements of their paroles or promises. In such cases, the Power on which they depend is bound neither to require nor to accept from them any service incompatible with the parole or promise given.

Article 22. Prisoners of war may be interned only in premises located on land and affording every guarantee of hygiene and healthfulness. Except in particular cases which are justified by the interest of the prisoners themselves, they shall not be interned in penitentiaries.

Prisoners of war interned in unhealthy areas, or where the climate is injurious for them, shall be removed as soon as possible to a more favourable climate.

The Detaining Power shall assemble prisoners of war in camps or camp compounds according to their nationality, language and customs, provided that such prisoners shall not be separated from prisoners of war belonging to the armed forces with which they were serving at the time of their capture, except with their consent.

Article 23. No prisoner of war may at any time be sent to, or detained in areas where he may be exposed to the fire of the combat zone, nor may his presence be used to render certain points or areas immune from military operations.

Prisoners of war shall have shelters against air bombardment and other hazards of war, to the same extent as the local civilian population. With the exception of those engaged in the protection of their quarters against the aforesaid hazards, they may enter such shelters as soon as possible after the giving of the alarm. Any other protective measure taken in favour of the population shall also apply to them.

Detaining Powers shall give the Powers concerned, through the intermediary of the Protecting Powers, all useful information regarding the geographical location of prisoner of war camps.

Whenever military considerations permit, prisoner of war camps shall be indicated in the day-time by the letters PW or PG, placed so as to be clearly visible from the air. The Powers concerned may, however, agree upon any other system of marking. Only prisoner of war camps shall be marked as such.

Article 24. Transit or screening camps of a permanent kind shall be fitted out under conditions similar to those described in the present Section, and the prisoners therein shall have the same treatment as in other camps.

....

CHAPTER VI—*Discipline*

Article 39. Every prisoner of war camp shall be put under the immediate authority of a responsible commissioned officer belonging to the regular armed forces of the Detaining Power. Such officer shall have in his possession a copy of the present Convention; he shall ensure that its provisions are known to the camp staff and the guard and shall be responsible, under the direction of his government, for its application.

Prisoners of war, with the exception of officers, must salute and show to all officers of the Detaining Power the external marks of respect provided for by the regulations applying in their own forces.

Officer prisoners of war are bound to salute only officers of a higher rank of the Detaining Power; they must, however, salute the camp commander regardless of his rank.

Article 40. The wearing of badges of rank and nationality, as well as of decorations, shall be permitted.

Article 41. In every camp the text of the present Convention and its Annexes and the contents of any special agreement provided for in Article 6, shall be posted, in the prisoners' own language, in places where all may read them. Copies shall be supplied, on request, to the prisoners who cannot have access to the copy which has been posted.

Regulations, orders, notices and publications of every kind relating to the conduct of prisoners of war shall be issued to them in a language which they understand. Such regulations, orders and publications shall be posted in the manner described above and copies shall be handed to the prisoners' representative. Every order and command addressed to prisoners of war individually must likewise be given in a language which they understand.

Article 42. The use of weapons against prisoners of war, especially against those who are escaping or attempting to escape, shall constitute an extreme measure, which shall always be preceded by warnings appropriate to the circumstances.

CHAPTER VII—*Rank of prisoners of war*

Article 43. Upon the outbreak of hostilities, the Parties to the conflict shall communicate to one another the titles and ranks of all the persons mentioned in Article 4 of the present Convention, in order to ensure equality of treatment between prisoners of equivalent rank. Titles and ranks which are subsequently created shall form the subject of similar communications.

The Detaining Power shall recognize promotions in rank which have been accorded to prisoners of war and which have been duly notified by the Power on which these prisoners depend.

Article 44. Officers and prisoners of equivalent status shall be treated with the regard due to their rank and age.

In order to ensure service in officers' camps, other ranks of the same armed forces who, as far as possible, speak the same language, shall be assigned in sufficient numbers, account being taken of the rank of officers and prisoners of equivalent status. Such orderlies shall not be required to perform any other work.

Supervision of the mess by the officers themselves shall be facilitated in every way.

Article 45. Prisoners of war other than officers and prisoners of equivalent status shall be treated with the regard due to their rank and age.

Supervision of the mess by the prisoners themselves shall be facilitated in every way.

CHAPTER VIII—*Transfer of prisoners of war after their arrival in camp*

....

SECTION III—LABOUR OF PRISONERS OF WAR

Article 49. The Detaining Power may utilize the labour of prisoners of war who are physically fit, taking into account their age, sex, rank and physical aptitude, and with a view particularly to maintaining them in a good state of physical and mental health.

Non-commissioned officers who are prisoners of war shall only be required to do supervisory work. Those not so required may ask for other suitable work which shall, so far as possible, be found for them.

If officers or persons of equivalent status ask for suitable work, it shall be found for them, so far as possible, but they may in no circumstances be compelled to work.

Article 50. Besides work connected with camp administration, installation or maintenance, prisoners of war may be compelled to do only such work as is included in the following classes:

(a) agriculture;

(b) industries connected with the production or the extraction of raw materials, and manufacturing industries, with the exception of metallurgical, machinery and chemical industries; public works and building operations which have no military character or purpose;

(c) transport and handling of stores which are not military in character or purpose;

(d) commercial business, and arts and crafts;

(e) domestic service;

(f) public utility services having no military character or purpose.

Should the above provisions be infringed, prisoners of war shall be allowed to exercise their right of complaint, in conformity with Article 78.

Article 51. Prisoners of war must be granted suitable working conditions, especially as regards accommodation, food, clothing and equipment; such conditions shall not be inferior to those enjoyed by nationals of the Detaining Power employed in similar work; account shall also be taken of climatic conditions.

The Detaining Power, in utilizing the labour of prisoners of war, shall ensure that in areas in which such prisoners are employed, the national legislation concerning the protection of labour, and, more particularly, the regulations for the safety of workers, are duly applied.

Prisoners of war shall receive training and be provided with the means of protection suitable to the work they will have to do and similar to those accorded to the nationals of the Detaining Power. Subject to the provisions of Article 52, prisoners may be submitted to the normal risks run by these civilian workers.

Conditions of labour shall in no case be rendered more arduous by disciplinary measures.

Article 52. Unless he be a volunteer, no prisoner of war may be employed on labour which is of an unhealthy or dangerous nature.

No prisoner of war shall be assigned to labour which would be looked upon as humiliating for a member of the Detaining Power's own forces.

The removal of mines or similar devices shall be considered as dangerous labour.

Article 53. The duration of the daily labour of prisoners of war, including the time of the journey to and fro, shall not be excessive, and must in no case exceed that permitted for civilian workers in the district, who are nationals of the Detaining Power and employed on the same work.

Prisoners of war must be allowed, in the middle of the day's work, a rest of not less than one hour. This rest will be the same as that to which workers of the Detaining Power are entitled, if the latter is of longer duration. They shall be allowed in addition a rest of twenty-four consecutive hours every week, preferably on Sunday or the day of rest in their country of origin. Furthermore, every prisoner who has worked for one year shall be granted a rest of eight consecutive days, during which his working pay shall be paid him.

If methods of labour such as piece work are employed, the length of the working period shall not be rendered excessive thereby.

Article 54. The working pay due to prisoners of war shall be fixed in accordance with the provisions of Article 62 of the present Convention.

Prisoners of war who sustain accidents in connection with work, or who contract a disease in the course, or in consequence of their work, shall receive all the care their condition may require. The Detaining Power shall furthermore deliver to such prisoners of war a medical certificate enabling them to submit their claims to the Power on which they depend, and shall send a duplicate to the Central Prisoners of War Agency provided for in Article 123.

Article 55. The fitness of prisoners of war for work shall be periodically verified by medical examinations at least once a month. The examinations shall have particular regard to the nature of the work which prisoners of war are required to do.

If any prisoner of war considers himself incapable of working, he shall be permitted to appear before the medical authorities of his camp. Physicians or surgeons may recommend that the prisoners who are, in their opinion, unfit for work, be exempted therefrom.

Article 56. The organization and administration of labour detachments shall be similar to those of prisoner of war camps.

Every labour detachment shall remain under the control of and administratively part of a prisoner of war camp. The military authorities and the commander of the said camp shall be responsible, under the direction of their government, for the observance of the provisions of the present Convention in labour detachments.

The camp commander shall keep an up-to-date record of the labour detachments dependent on his camp, and shall communicate it to the delegates of the Protecting

Power, of the International Committee of the Red Cross, or of other agencies giving relief to prisoners of war, who may visit the camp.

Article 57. The treatment of prisoners of war who work for private persons, even if the latter are responsible for guarding and protecting them, shall not be inferior to that which is provided for by the present Convention. The Detaining Power, the military authorities and the commander of the camp to which such prisoners belong shall be entirely responsible for the maintenance, care, treatment, and payment of the working pay of such prisoners of war.

Such prisoners of war shall have the right to remain in communication with the prisoners' representatives in the camps on which they depend.

. . . .

SECTION VI—RELATIONS BETWEEN PRISONERS OF WAR AND THE AUTHORITIES

CHAPTER I—*Complaints of prisoners of war respecting the conditions of captivity*

Article 78. Prisoners of war shall have the right to make known to the military authorities in whose power they are, their requests regarding the conditions of captivity to which they are subjected.

They shall also have the unrestricted right to apply to the representatives of the Protecting Powers either through their prisoners' representative or, if they consider it necessary, direct, in order to draw their attention to any points on which they may have complaints to make regarding their conditions of captivity.

These requests and complaints shall not be limited nor considered to be a part of the correspondence quota referred to in Article 71. They must be transmitted immediately. Even if they are recognized to be unfounded, they may not give rise to any punishment.

Prisoners' representatives may send periodic reports on the situation in the camps and the needs of the prisoners of war to the representatives of the Protecting Powers.

. . . .

CHAPTER III—*Penal and disciplinary sanctions*

I. General Provisions

Article 82. A prisoner of war shall be subject to the laws, regulations and orders in force in the armed forces of the Detaining Power; the Detaining Power shall be justified in taking judicial or disciplinary measures in respect of any offence committed by a prisoner of war against such laws, regulations or orders. However, no proceedings or punishments contrary to the provisions of this Chapter shall be allowed.

If any law, regulation or order of the Detaining Power shall declare acts committed by a prisoner of war to be punishable, whereas the same acts would not be punishable if committed by a member of the forces of the Detaining Power, such acts shall entail disciplinary punishments only.

Article 83. In deciding whether proceedings in respect of an offence alleged to have been committed by a prisoner of war shall be judicial or disciplinary, the Detaining Power shall ensure that the competent authorities exercise the greatest leniency and adopt, wherever possible, disciplinary rather than judicial measures.

Article 84. A prisoner of war shall be tried only by a military court, unless the existing laws of the Detaining Power expressly permit the civil courts to try a member of the armed forces of the Detaining Power in respect of the particular offence alleged to have been committed by the prisoner of war.

In no circumstances whatever shall a prisoner of war be tried by a court of any kind which does not offer the essential guarantees of independence and impartiality as generally recognized, and, in particular, the procedure of which does not afford the accused the rights and means of defence provided for in Article 105.

Article 85. Prisoners of war prosecuted under the laws of the Detaining Power for acts committed prior to capture shall retain, even if convicted, the benefits of the present Convention.

Article 86. No prisoner of war may be punished more than once for the same act or on the same charge.

Article 87. Prisoners of war may not be sentenced by the military authorities and courts of the Detaining Power to any penalties except those provided for in respect of members of the armed forces of the said Power who have committed the same acts.

When fixing the penalty, the courts or authorities of the Detaining Power shall take into consideration, to the widest extent possible, the fact that the accused, not being a national of the Detaining Power, is not bound to it by any duty of allegiance, and that he is in its power as the result of circumstances independent of his own will. The said courts or authorities shall be at liberty to reduce the penalty provided for the violation of which the prisoner of war is accused, and shall therefore not be bound to apply the minimum penalty prescribed.

Collective punishment for individual acts, corporal punishment, imprisonment in premises without daylight and, in general, any form of torture or cruelty, are forbidden.

No prisoner of war may be deprived of his rank by the Detaining Power, or prevented from wearing his badges.

Article 88. Officers, non-commissioned officers and men who are prisoners of war undergoing a disciplinary or judicial punishment, shall not be subjected to more severe treatment than that applied in respect of the same punishment to members of the armed forces of the Detaining Power of equivalent rank.

A woman prisoner of war shall not be awarded or sentenced to a punishment more severe, or treated whilst undergoing punishment more severely, than a woman member of the armed forces of the Detaining Power dealt with for a similar offence.

In no case may a woman prisoner of war be awarded or sentenced to a punishment more severe, or treated whilst undergoing punishment more severely, than a male member of the armed forces of the Detaining Power dealt with for a similar offence.

Prisoners of war who have served disciplinary or judicial sentences may not be treated differently from other prisoners of war.

II. Disciplinary Sanctions

Article 89. The disciplinary punishments applicable to prisoners of war are the following:

(1) A fine which shall not exceed 50 per cent of the advances of pay and working pay which the prisoner of war would otherwise receive under the provisions of Articles 60 and 62 during a period of not more than thirty days.

(2) Discontinuance of privileges granted over and above the treatment provided for by the present Convention.

(3) Fatigue duties not exceeding two hours daily.

(4) Confinement.

The punishment referred to under (3) shall not be applied to officers.

In no case shall disciplinary punishments be inhuman, brutal or dangerous to the health of prisoners of war.

Article 90. The duration of any single punishment shall in no case exceed thirty days. Any period of confinement awaiting the hearing of a disciplinary offence or the award of disciplinary punishment shall be deducted from an award pronounced against a prisoner of war.

The maximum of thirty days provided above may not be exceeded, even if the prisoner of war is answerable for several acts at the same time when he is awarded punishment, whether such acts are related or not.

The period between the pronouncing of an award of disciplinary punishment and its execution shall not exceed one month.

When a prisoner of war is awarded a further disciplinary punishment, a period of at least three days shall elapse between the execution of any two of the punishments, if the duration of one of these is ten days or more.

Article 91.

The escape of a prisoner of war shall be deemed to have succeeded when:

(1) he has joined the armed forces of the Power on which he depends, or those of an allied Power;

(2) he has left the territory under the control of the Detaining Power, or of an ally of the said Power;

(3) he has joined a ship flying the flag of the Power on which he depends, or of an allied Power, in the territorial waters of the Detaining Power, the said ship not being under the control of the last named Power.

Prisoners of war who have made good their escape in the sense of this Article and who are recaptured, shall not be liable to any punishment in respect of their previous escape.

Article 92. A prisoner of war who attempts to escape and is recaptured before having made good his escape in the sense of Article 91 shall be liable only to a disciplinary punishment in respect of this act, even if it is a repeated offence.

A prisoner of war who is recaptured shall be handed over without delay to the competent military authority.

Article 88, fourth paragraph, notwithstanding, prisoners of war punished as a result of an unsuccessful escape may be subjected to special surveillance. Such surveillance must not affect the state of their health, must be undergone in a prisoner of war camp, and must not entail the suppression of any of the safeguards granted them by the present Convention.

Article 93. Escape or attempt to escape, even if it is a repeated offence, shall not be deemed an aggravating circumstance if the prisoner of war is subjected to trial by judicial proceedings in respect of an offence committed during his escape or attempt to escape.

In conformity with the principle stated in Article 83, offences committed by prisoners of war with the sole intention of facilitating their escape and which do not entail any violence against life or limb, such as offences against public property, theft without intention of self-enrichment, the drawing up or use of false papers, or the wearing of civilian clothing, shall occasion disciplinary punishment only.

Prisoners of war who aid or abet an escape or an attempt to escape shall be liable on this count to disciplinary punishment only.

Article 94. If an escaped prisoner of war is recaptured, the Power on which he depends shall be notified thereof in the manner defined in Article 122, provided notification of his escape has been made.

Article 95. A prisoner of war accused of an offence against discipline shall not be kept in confinement pending the hearing unless a member of the armed forces of the Detaining Power would be so kept if he were accused of a similar offence, or if it is essential in the interests of camp order and discipline.

Any period spent by a prisoner of war in confinement awaiting the disposal of an offence against discipline shall be reduced to an absolute minimum and shall not exceed fourteen days.

The provisions of Articles 97 and 98 of this Chapter shall apply to prisoners of war who are in confinement awaiting the disposal of offences against discipline.

Article 96. Acts which constitute offences against discipline shall be investigated immediately.

Without prejudice to the competence of courts and superior military authorities, disciplinary punishment may be ordered only by an officer having disciplinary powers in his capacity as camp commander, or by a responsible officer who replaces him or to whom he has delegated his disciplinary powers.

In no case may such powers be delegated to a prisoner of war or be exercised by a prisoner of war.

Before any disciplinary award is pronounced, the accused shall be given precise information regarding the offences of which he is accused, and given an opportunity of explaining his conduct and of defending himself. He shall be permitted, in particular, to call witnesses and to have recourse, if necessary, to the services of a qualified interpreter. The decision shall be announced to the accused prisoner of war and to the prisoners' representative.

A record of disciplinary punishments shall be maintained by the camp commander and shall be open to inspection by representatives of the Protecting Power.

Article 97. Prisoners of war shall not in any case be transferred to penitentiary establishments (prisons, penitentiaries, convict prisons, etc.) to undergo disciplinary punishment therein.

All premises in which disciplinary punishments are undergone shall conform to the sanitary requirements set forth in Article 25. A prisoner of war undergoing punishment shall be enabled to keep himself in a state of cleanliness, in conformity with Article 29.

Officers and persons of equivalent status shall not be lodged in the same quarters as non-commissioned officers or men.

Women prisoners of war undergoing disciplinary punishment shall be confined in separate quarters from male prisoners of war and shall be under the immediate supervision of women.

Article 98. A prisoner of war undergoing confinement as a disciplinary punishment, shall continue to enjoy the benefits of the provisions of this Convention except in so far as these are necessarily rendered inapplicable by the mere fact that he is confined. In no case may he be deprived of the benefits of the provisions of Articles 78 and 126.

A prisoner of war awarded disciplinary punishment may not be deprived of the prerogatives attached to his rank.

Prisoners of war awarded disciplinary punishment shall be allowed to exercise and to stay in the open air at least two hours daily.

They shall be allowed, on their request, to be present at the daily medical inspections. They shall receive the attention which their state of health requires and, if necessary, shall be removed to the camp infirmary or to a hospital.

They shall have permission to read and write, likewise to send and receive letters. Parcels and remittances of money however, may be withheld from them until the completion of the punishment; they shall meanwhile be entrusted to the prisoners' representative, who will hand over to the infirmary the perishable goods contained in such parcels.

III. Judicial Proceedings

Article 99. No prisoner of war may be tried or sentenced for an act which is not forbidden by the law of the Detaining Power or by international law, in force at the time the said act was committed.

No moral or physical coercion may be exerted on a prisoner of war in order to induce him to admit himself guilty of the act of which he is accused.

No prisoner of war may be convicted without having had an opportunity to present his defence and the assistance of a qualified advocate or counsel.

Article 100. Prisoners of war and the Protecting Powers shall be informed as soon as possible of the offences which are punishable by the death sentence under the laws of the Detaining Power.

Other offences shall not thereafter be made punishable by the death penalty without the concurrence of the Power on which the prisoners of war depend.

The death sentence cannot be pronounced on a prisoner of war unless the attention of the court has, in accordance with Article 87, second paragraph, been particularly called to the fact that since the accused is not a national of the Detaining Power, he is not bound to it by any duty of allegiance, and that he is in its power as the result of circumstances independent of his own will.

Article 101. If the death penalty is pronounced on a prisoner of war, the sentence shall not be executed before the expiration of a period of at least six months from the date when the Protecting Power receives, at an indicated address, the detailed communication provided for in Article 107.

Article 102. A prisoner of war can be validly sentenced only if the sentence has been pronounced by the same courts according to the same procedure as in the case of members of the armed forces of the Detaining Power, and if, furthermore, the provisions of the present Chapter have been observed.

Article 103. Judicial investigations relating to a prisoner of war shall be conducted as rapidly as circumstances permit and so that his trial shall take place as soon as possible.

A prisoner of war shall not be confined while awaiting trial unless a member of the armed forces of the Detaining Power would be so confined if he were accused of a similar offence, or if it is essential to do so in the interests of national security. In no circumstances shall this confinement exceed three months.

Any period spent by a prisoner of war in confinement awaiting trial shall be deducted from any sentence of imprisonment passed upon him and taken into account in fixing any penalty.

The provisions of Articles 97 and 98 of this Chapter shall apply to a prisoner of war whilst in confinement awaiting trial.

Article 104. In any case in which the Detaining Power has decided to institute judicial proceedings against a prisoner of war, it shall notify the Protecting Power as soon as possible and at least three weeks before the opening of the trial. This period of three weeks shall run as from the day on which such notification reaches the Protecting Power at the address previously indicated by the latter to the Detaining Power.

The said notification shall contain the following information:

(1) Surname and first names of the prisoner of war, his rank, his army, regimental, personal or serial number, his date of birth, and his profession or trade, if any;

(2) Place of internment or confinement;

(3) Specification of the charge or charges on which the prisoner of war is to be arraigned, giving the legal provisions applicable;

(4) Designation of the court which will try the case, likewise the date and place fixed for the opening of the trial.

The same communication shall be made by the Detaining Power to the prisoners' representative.

If no evidence is submitted, at the opening of a trial, that the notification referred to above was received by the Protecting Power, by the prisoner of war and by the prisoners' representative concerned, at least three weeks before the opening of the trial, then the latter cannot take place and must be adjourned.

Article 105. The prisoner of war shall be entitled to assistance by one of his prisoner comrades, to defence by a qualified advocate or counsel of his own choice, to the calling of witnesses and, if he deems necessary, to the services of a competent interpreter. He shall be advised of these rights by the Detaining Power in due time before the trial.

Failing a choice by the prisoner of war, the Protecting Power shall find him an advocate or counsel, and shall have at least one week at its disposal for the purpose. The Detaining Power shall deliver to the said Power, on request, a list of persons qualified to present the defence. Failing a choice of an advocate or counsel by the prisoner of war or the Protecting Power, the Detaining Power shall appoint a competent advocate or counsel to conduct the defence.

The advocate or counsel conducting the defence on behalf of the prisoner of war shall have at his disposal a period of two weeks at least before the opening of the trial, as well as the necessary facilities to prepare the defence of the accused. He may, in particular, freely visit the accused and interview him in private. He may also confer with any witnesses for the defence, including prisoners of war. He shall have the benefit of these facilities until the term of appeal or petition has expired.

Particulars of the charge or charges on which the prisoner of war is to be arraigned, as well as the documents which are generally communicated to the accused by virtue of the laws in force in the armed forces of the Detaining Power, shall be communicated to the accused prisoner of war in a language which he understands, and in good time before the opening of the trial. The same communication in the same circumstances shall be made to the advocate or counsel conducting the defence on behalf of the prisoner of war.

The representatives of the Protecting Power shall be entitled to attend the trial of the case, unless, exceptionally, this is held *in camera* in the interest of State security. In such a case the Detaining Power shall advise the Protecting Power accordingly.

Article 106. Every prisoner of war shall have, in the same manner as the members of the armed forces of the Detaining Power, the right of appeal or petition from any sentence pronounced upon him, with a view to the quashing or revising of the sentence or the reopening of the trial. He shall be fully informed of his right to appeal or petition and of the time limit within which he may do so.

Article 107. Any judgment and sentence pronounced upon a prisoner of war shall be immediately reported to the Protecting Power in the form of a summary communication, which shall also indicate whether he has the right of appeal with a view to the quashing of the sentence or the reopening of the trial. This communication shall likewise be sent to the prisoners' representative concerned. It shall also be sent to the accused prisoner of war in a language he understands, if the sentence was not pronounced in his presence. The Detaining Power shall also immediately communicate to the Protecting Power the decision of the prisoner of war to use or to waive his right of appeal.

Furthermore, if a prisoner of war is finally convicted or if a sentence pronounced on a prisoner of war in the first instance is a death sentence, the Detaining Power shall as soon as possible address to the Protecting Power a detailed communication containing:

(1) the precise wording of the finding and sentence;

(2) a summarized report of any preliminary investigation and of the trial, emphasizing in particular the elements of the prosecution and the defence;

(3) notification, where applicable, of the establishment where the sentence will be served.

The communications provided for in the foregoing sub-paragraphs shall be sent to the Protecting Power at the address previously made known to the Detaining Power.

Article 108. Sentences pronounced on prisoners of war after a conviction has become duly enforceable, shall be served in the same establishments and under the same conditions as in the case of members of the armed forces of the Detaining Power. These conditions shall in all cases conform to the requirements of health and humanity.

A woman prisoner of war on whom such a sentence has been pronounced shall be confined in separate quarters and shall be under the supervision of women.

In any case, prisoners of war sentenced to a penalty depriving them of their liberty shall retain the benefit of the provisions of Articles 78 and 126 of the present Convention. Furthermore, they shall be entitled to receive and despatch correspondence, to receive at least one relief parcel monthly, to take regular exercise in the open air, to have the medical care required by their state of health, and the spiritual assistance they may desire. Penalties to which they may be subjected shall be in accordance with the provisions of Article 87, third paragraph.

. . . .

GENEVA CONVENTION RELATIVE TO THE PROTECTION OF CIVILIAN PERSONS IN TIME OF WAR* (FOURTH GENEVA CONVENTION)

. . . .

PART I
GENERAL PROVISIONS

. . . .

Article 4. Persons protected by the Convention are those who, at a given moment and in any manner whatsoever, find themselves, in case of a conflict or occupation, in the hands of a Party to the conflict or Occupying Power of which they are not nationals.

Nationals of a State which is not bound by the Convention are not protected by it. Nationals of a neutral State who find themselves in the territory of a belligerent State, and nationals of a co-belligerent State, shall not be regarded as protected persons while the State of which they are nationals has normal diplomatic representation in the State in whose hands they are.

The provisions of Part II are, however, wider in application, as defined in Article 13.

Persons protected by the Geneva Convention for the Amelioration of the Condition of the Wounded and Sick in Armed Forces in the Field of 12 August 1949, or by the Geneva Convention for the Amelioration of the Condition of Wounded, Sick and Shipwrecked Members of Armed Forces at Sea of 12 August 1949, or by the Geneva Convention relative to the Treatment of Prisoners of War of 12 August 1949, shall not be considered as protected persons within the meaning of the present Convention.

Article 5. Where in the territory of a Party to the conflict, the latter is satisfied that an individual protected person is definitely suspected of or engaged in activities hostile to the security of the State, such individual person shall not be entitled to claim such rights and privileges under the present Convention as would, if exercised in the favour of such individual person, be prejudicial to the security of such State.

Where in occupied territory an individual protected person is detained as a spy or saboteur, or as a person under definite suspicion of activity hostile to the security of the Occupying Power, such person shall, in those cases where absolute military security so requires, be regarded as having forfeited rights of communication under the present Convention.

In each case, such persons shall nevertheless be treated with humanity and, in case of trial, shall not be deprived of the rights of fair and regular trial prescribed by the present Convention. They shall also be granted the full rights and privileges of a protected person under the present Convention at the earliest date consistent with the security of the State or Occupying Power, as the case may be.

---

* Geneva Convention Relative to the Protection of Civilian Persons in Time of War, Aug. 12, 1949, 6 U.S.T. 3516, 75 U.N.T.S. 287 (entered into force Oct. 21, 1950), *available at* http://www.yale.edu/lawweb/avalon/lawofwar/geneva07.htm.

Article 6. The present Convention shall apply from the outset of any conflict or occupation mentioned in Article 2.

In the territory of Parties to the conflict, the application of the present Convention shall cease on the general close of military operations.

In the case of occupied territory, the application of the present Convention shall cease one year after the general close of military operations; however, the Occupying Power shall be bound, for the duration of the occupation, to the extent that such Power exercises the functions of government in such territory, by the provisions of the following Articles of the present Convention: 1 to 12, 27, 29 to 34, 47, 49, 51, 52, 53, 59, 61 to 77, 143.

Protected persons whose release, repatriation or re-establishment may take place after such dates shall meanwhile continue to benefit by the present Convention.

....

Article 12. In cases where they deem it advisable in the interest of protected persons, particularly in cases of disagreement between the Parties to the conflict as to the application or interpretation of the provisions of the present Convention, the Protecting Powers shall lend their good offices with a view to settling the disagreement.

For this purpose, each of the Protecting Powers may, either at the invitation of one Party or on its own initiative, propose to the Parties to the conflict a meeting of their representatives, and in particular of the authorities responsible for protected persons, possibly on neutral territory suitably chosen. The Parties to the conflict shall be bound to give effect to the proposals made to them for this purpose. The Protecting Powers may, if necessary, propose for approval by the Parties to the conflict a person belonging to a neutral Power, or delegated by the International Committee of the Red Cross, who shall be invited to take part in such a meeting.

PART II
GENERAL PROTECTION OF POPULATIONS AGAINST CERTAIN CONSEQUENCES OF WAR

Article 13. The provisions of Part II cover the whole of the populations of the countries in conflict, without any adverse distinction based, in particular, on race, nationality, religion or political opinion, and are intended to alleviate the sufferings caused by war.

Article 14. In time of peace, the High Contracting Parties and, after the outbreak of hostilities, the Parties thereto, may establish in their own territory and, if the need arises, in occupied areas, hospital and safety zones and localities so organized as to protect from the effects of war, wounded, sick and aged persons, children under fifteen, expectant mothers and mothers of children under seven.

Upon the outbreak and during the course of hostilities, the Parties concerned may conclude agreements on mutual recognition of the zones and localities they have created. They may for this purpose implement the provisions of the Draft Agreement annexed to the present Convention, with such amendments as they may consider necessary.

The Protecting Powers and the International Committee of the Red Cross are invited to lend their good offices in order to facilitate the institution and recognition of these hospital and safety zones and localities.

Article 15. Any Party to the conflict may, either direct or through a neutral State or some humanitarian organization, propose to the adverse Party to establish, in the regions where fighting is taking place, neutralized zones intended to shelter from the effects of war the following persons, without distinction:

(a) wounded and sick combatants or non-combatants;

(b) civilian persons who take no part in hostilities, and who, while they reside in the zones, perform no work of a military character.

When the Parties concerned have agreed upon the geographical position, administration, food supply and supervision of the proposed neutralized zone, a written agreement shall be concluded and signed by the representatives of the Parties to the conflict. The agreement shall fix the beginning and the duration of the neutralization of the zone.

Article 16. The wounded and sick, as well as the infirm, and expectant mothers, shall be the object of particular protection and respect.

As far as military considerations allow, each Party to the conflict shall facilitate the steps taken to search for the killed and wounded, to assist the shipwrecked and other persons exposed to grave danger, and to protect them against pillage and ill-treatment.

Article 17. The Parties to the conflict shall endeavour to conclude local agreements for the removal from besieged or encircled areas, of wounded, sick, infirm, and aged persons, children and maternity cases, and for the passage of ministers of all religions, medical personnel and medical equipment on their way to such areas.

Article 18. Civilian hospitals organized to give care to the wounded and sick, the infirm and maternity cases, may in no circumstances be the object of attack but shall at all times be respected and protected by the Parties to the conflict.

States which are Parties to a conflict shall provide all civilian hospitals with certificates showing that they are civilian hospitals and that the buildings which they occupy are not used for any purpose which would deprive these hospitals of protection in accordance with Article 19.

Civilian hospitals shall be marked by means of the emblem provided for in Article 38 of the Geneva Convention for the Amelioration of the Condition of the Wounded and Sick in Armed Forces in the Field of 12 August 1949, but only if so authorized by the State.

The Parties to the conflict shall, in so far as military considerations permit, take the necessary steps to make the distinctive emblems indicating civilian hospitals clearly visible to the enemy land, air and naval forces in order to obviate the possibility of any hostile action.

In view of the dangers to which hospitals may be exposed by being close to military objectives, it is recommended that such hospitals be situated as far as possible from such objectives.

Article 19. The protection to which civilian hospitals are entitled shall not cease unless they are used to commit, outside their humanitarian duties, acts harmful to the enemy. Protection may, however, cease only after due warning has been given, naming, in all appropriate cases, a reasonable time limit and after such warning has remained unheeded. The fact that sick or wounded members of the armed forces are nursed in these hospitals, or the presence of small arms and ammunition taken from such combatants which have not yet been handed to the proper service, shall not be considered to be acts harmful to the enemy.

Article 20. Persons regularly and solely engaged in the operation and administration of civilian hospitals, including the personnel engaged in the search for, removal and transporting of and caring for wounded and sick civilians, the infirm and maternity cases shall be respected and protected.

In occupied territory and in zones of military operations, the above personnel shall be recognizable by means of an identity card certifying their status, bearing the photograph of the holder and embossed with the stamp of the responsible authority, and also by means of a stamped, water-resistant armlet which they shall wear on the left arm while carrying out their duties. This armlet shall be issued by the State and shall bear the emblem provided for in Article 38 of the Geneva Convention for the Amelioration of the Condition of the Wounded and Sick in Armed Forces in the Field of 12 August 1949.

Other personnel who are engaged in the operation and administration of civilian hospitals shall be entitled to respect and protection and to wear the armlet, as provided in and under the conditions prescribed in this Article, while they are employed on such duties. The identity card shall state the duties on which they are employed.

The management of each hospital shall at all times hold at the disposal of the competent national or occupying authorities an up-to-date list of such personnel.

Article 21. Convoys of vehicles or hospital trains on land or specially provided vessels on sea, conveying wounded and sick civilians, the infirm and maternity cases, shall be respected and protected in the same manner as the hospitals provided for in Article 18, and shall be marked, with the consent of the State, by the display of the distinctive emblem provided for in Article 38 of the Geneva Convention for the Amelioration of the Condition of the Wounded and Sick in Armed Forces in the Field of 12 August 1949.

Article 22. Aircraft exclusively employed for the removal of wounded and sick civilians, the infirm and maternity cases or for the transport of medical personnel and equipment, shall not be attacked, but shall be respected while flying at heights, times and on routes specifically agreed upon between all the Parties to the conflict concerned.

They may be marked with the distinctive emblem provided for in Article 38 of the Geneva Convention for the Amelioration of the Condition of the Wounded and Sick in Armed Forces in the Field of 12 August 1949.

Unless agreed otherwise, flights over enemy or enemy occupied territory are prohibited.

Such aircraft shall obey every summons to land. In the event of a landing thus imposed, the aircraft with its occupants may continue its flight after examination, if any.

Article 23. Each High Contracting Party shall allow the free passage of all consignments of medical and hospital stores and objects necessary for religious worship intended only for civilians of another High Contracting Party, even if the latter is its adversary. It shall likewise permit the free passage of all consignments of essential foodstuffs, clothing and tonics intended for children under fifteen, expectant mothers and maternity cases.

The obligation of a High Contracting Party to allow the free passage of the consignments indicated in the preceding paragraph is subject to the condition that this Party is satisfied that there are no serious reasons for fearing:

(a) that the consignments may be diverted from their destination,

(b) that the control may not be effective, or

(c) that a definite advantage may accrue to the military efforts or economy of the enemy through the substitution of the above-mentioned consignments for goods which would otherwise be provided or produced by the enemy or through the release of such material, services or facilities as would otherwise be required for the production of such goods.

The Power which allows the passage of the consignments indicated in the first paragraph of this Article may make such permission conditional on the distribution to the persons benefited thereby being made under the local supervision of the Protecting Powers.

Such consignments shall be forwarded as rapidly as possible, and the Power which permits their free passage shall have the right to prescribe the technical arrangements under which such passage is allowed.

Article 24. The Parties to the conflict shall take the necessary measures to ensure that children under fifteen, who are orphaned or are separated from their families as a result of the war, are not left to their own resources, and that their maintenance, the exercise of their religion and their education are facilitated in all circumstances. Their education shall, as far as possible, be entrusted to persons of a similar cultural tradition.

The Parties to the conflict shall facilitate the reception of such children in a neutral country for the duration of the conflict with the consent of the Protecting Power, if any, and under due safeguards for the observance of the principles stated in the first paragraph.

They shall, furthermore, endeavour to arrange for all children under twelve to be identified by the wearing of identity discs, or by some other means.

Article 25. All persons in the territory of a Party to the conflict, or in a territory occupied by it, shall be enabled to give news of a strictly personal nature to members of their families, wherever they may be, and to receive news from them. This correspondence shall be forwarded speedily and without undue delay.

If, as a result of circumstances, it becomes difficult or impossible to exchange family correspondence by the ordinary post, the Parties to the conflict concerned shall apply to a neutral intermediary, such as the Central Agency provided for in Article 140, and shall decide in consultation with it how to ensure the fulfillment of their obligations under the best possible conditions, in particular with the cooperation of the National Red Cross (Red Crescent, Red Lion and Sun) Societies.

If the Parties to the conflict deem it necessary to restrict family correspondence, such restrictions shall be confined to the compulsory use of standard forms containing twenty-five freely chosen words, and to the limitation of the number of these forms despatched to one each month.

Article 26. Each Party to the conflict shall facilitate enquiries made by members of families dispersed owing to the war, with the object of renewing contact with one another and of meeting, if possible. It shall encourage, in particular, the work of organizations engaged on this task provided they are acceptable to it and conform to its security regulations.

PART III
STATUS AND TREATMENT OF PROTECTED PERSONS

SECTION I—PROVISIONS COMMON TO THE TERRITORIES OF THE PARTIES TO THE CONFLICT AND TO OCCUPIED TERRITORIES

Article 27. Protected persons are entitled, in all circumstances, to respect for their persons, their honour, their family rights, their religious convictions and practices, and their manners and customs. They shall at all times be humanely treated, and shall be protected especially against all acts of violence or threats thereof and against insults and public curiosity.

Women shall be especially protected against any attack on their honour, in particular against rape, enforced prostitution, or any form of indecent assault.

Without prejudice to the provisions relating to their state of health, age and sex, all protected persons shall be treated with the same consideration by the Party to the conflict in whose power they are, without any adverse distinction based, in particular, on race, religion or political opinion.

However, the Parties to the conflict may take such measures of control and security in regard to protected persons as may be necessary as a result of the war.

Article 28. The presence of a protected person may not be used to render certain points or areas immune from military operations.

Article 29. The Party to the conflict in whose hands protected persons may be, is responsible for the treatment accorded to them by its agents, irrespective of any individual responsibility which may be incurred.

Article 30. Protected persons shall have every facility for making application to the Protecting Powers, the International Committee of the Red Cross, the National Red Cross (Red Crescent, Red Lion and Sun) Society of the country where they may be, as well as to any organization that might assist them.

These several organizations shall be granted all facilities for that purpose by the authorities, within the bounds set by military or security considerations.

Apart from the visits of the delegates of the Protecting Powers and of the International Committee of the Red Cross, provided for by Article 143, the Detaining or Occupying Powers shall facilitate, as much as possible, visits to protected persons by the representatives of other organizations whose object is to give spiritual aid or material relief to such persons.

Art. 31. No physical or moral coercion shall be exercised against protected persons, in particular to obtain information from them or from third parties.

Article 32. The High Contracting Parties specifically agree that each of them is prohibited from taking any measure of such a character as to cause the physical suffering or extermination of protected persons in their hands. This prohibition applies not only to murder, torture, corporal punishments, mutilation and medical or scientific experiments not necessitated by the medical treatment of a protected person, but also to any other measures of brutality whether applied by civilian or military agents.

Article 33. No protected person may be punished for an offence he or she has not personally committed. Collective penalties and likewise all measures of intimidation or of terrorism are prohibited.

Pillage is prohibited.

Reprisals against protected persons and their property are prohibited.

Article 34. The taking of hostages is prohibited.

. . . .

SECTION III—OCCUPIED TERRITORIES

Article 47. Protected persons who are in occupied territory shall not be deprived, in any case or in any manner whatsoever, of the benefits of the present Convention by any change introduced, as the result of the occupation of a territory, into the institutions or government of the said territory, nor by any agreement concluded between the authorities of the occupied territories and the Occupying Power, nor by any annexation by the latter of the whole or part of the occupied territory.

Article 48. Protected persons who are not nationals of the Power whose territory is occupied, may avail themselves of the right to leave the territory subject to the provisions of Article 35, and decisions thereon shall be taken in accordance with the procedure which the Occupying Power shall establish in accordance with the said Article.

Article 49. Individual or mass forcible transfers, as well as deportations of protected persons from occupied territory to the territory of the Occupying Power or to that of any other country, occupied or not, are prohibited, regardless of their motive.

Nevertheless, the Occupying Power may undertake total or partial evacuation of a given area if the security of the population or imperative military reasons so demand. Such evacuations may not involve the displacement of protected persons outside the bounds of the occupied territory except when for material reasons it is impossible to avoid such displacement. Persons thus evacuated shall be transferred back to their homes as soon as hostilities in the area in question have ceased.

The Occupying Power undertaking such transfers or evacuations shall ensure, to the greatest practicable extent, that proper accommodation is provided to receive the protected persons, that the removals are effected in satisfactory conditions of hygiene, health, safety and nutrition, and that members of the same family are not separated.

The Protecting Power shall be informed of any transfers and evacuations as soon as they have taken place.

The Occupying Power shall not detain protected persons in an area particularly exposed to the dangers of war unless the security of the population or imperative military reasons so demand.

The Occupying Power shall not deport or transfer parts of its own civilian population into the territory it occupies.

Article 50. The Occupying Power shall, with the cooperation of the national and local authorities, facilitate the proper working of all institutions devoted to the care and education of children.

The Occupying Power shall take all necessary steps to facilitate the identification of children and the registration of their parentage. It may not, in any case, change their personal status, nor enlist them in formations or organizations subordinate to it.

Should the local institutions be inadequate for the purpose, the Occupying Power shall make arrangements for the maintenance and education, if possible by persons of their own nationality, language and religion, of children who are orphaned or separated from their parents as a result of the war and who cannot be adequately cared for by a near relative or friend.

A special section of the Bureau set up in accordance with Article 136 shall be responsible for taking all necessary steps to identify children whose identity is in doubt. Particulars of their parents or other near relatives should always be recorded if available.

The Occupying Power shall not hinder the application of any preferential measures in regard to food, medical care and protection against the effects of war which may have been adopted prior to the occupation in favour of children under fifteen years, expectant mothers, and mothers of children under seven years.

Article 51. The Occupying Power may not compel protected persons to serve in its armed or auxiliary forces. No pressure or propaganda which aims at securing voluntary enlistment is permitted.

The Occupying Power may not compel protected persons to work unless they are over eighteen years of age, and then only on work which is necessary either for the needs of the army of occupation, or for the public utility services, or for the feeding, sheltering, clothing, transportation or health of the population of the occupied country. Protected persons may not be compelled to undertake any work which would involve them in the obligation of taking part in military operations. The Occupying Power may not compel protected persons to employ forcible means to ensure the security of the installations where they are performing compulsory labour.

The work shall be carried out only in the occupied territory where the persons whose services have been requisitioned are. Every such person shall, so far as possible, be kept in his usual place of employment. Workers shall be paid a fair wage and the work shall be proportionate to their physical and intellectual capacities. The legislation in force in the occupied country concerning working conditions, and safeguards as regards, in particular, such matters as wages, hours of work, equipment, preliminary training and compensation for occupational accidents and diseases, shall be applicable to the protected persons assigned to the work referred to in this Article.

In no case shall requisition of labour lead to a mobilization of workers in an organization of a military or semi-military character.

Article 52. No contract, agreement or regulation shall impair the right of any worker, whether voluntary or not and wherever he may be, to apply to the representatives of the Protecting Power in order to request the said Power's intervention.

All measures aiming at creating unemployment or at restricting the opportunities offered to workers in an occupied territory, in order to induce them to work for the Occupying Power, are prohibited.

Article 53. Any destruction by the Occupying Power of real or personal property belonging individually or collectively to private persons, or to the State, or to other public authorities, or to social or cooperative organizations, is prohibited, except where such destruction is rendered absolutely necessary by military operations.

Article 54. The Occupying Power may not alter the status of public officials or judges in the occupied territories, or in any way apply sanctions to or take any measures of coercion or discrimination against them, should they abstain from fulfilling their functions for reasons of conscience.

This prohibition does not prejudice the application of the second paragraph of Article 51. It does not affect the right of the Occupying Power to remove public officials from their posts.

Article 55. To the fullest extent of the means available to it, the Occupying Power has the duty of ensuring the food and medical supplies of the population; it should, in particular, bring in the necessary foodstuffs, medical stores and other articles if the resources of the occupied territory are inadequate.

The Occupying Power may not requisition foodstuffs, articles or medical supplies available in the occupied territory, except for use by the occupation forces and administration personnel, and then only if the requirements of the civilian population have been taken into account. Subject to the provisions of other international Conventions, the Occupying Power shall make arrangements to ensure that fair value is paid for any requisitioned goods.

The Protecting Power shall, at any time, be at liberty to verify the state of the food and medical supplies in occupied territories, except where temporary restrictions are made necessary by imperative military requirements.

Article 56. To the fullest extent of the means available to it, the public Occupying Power has the duty of ensuring and maintaining, with the cooperation of national and local authorities, the medical and hospital establishments and services, public health and hygiene in the occupied territory, with particular reference to the adoption and application of the prophylactic and preventive measures necessary to combat the spread of contagious diseases and epidemics. Medical personnel of all categories shall be allowed to carry out their duties.

If new hospitals are set up in occupied territory and if the competent organs of the occupied State are not operating there, the occupying authorities shall, if necessary, grant them the recognition provided for in Article 18. In similar circumstances, the occupying authorities shall also grant recognition to hospital personnel and transport vehicles under the provisions of Articles 20 and 21.

In adopting measures of health and hygiene and in their implementation, the Occupying Power shall take into consideration the moral and ethical susceptibilities of the population of the occupied territory.

Article 57. The Occupying Power may requisition civilian hospitals of hospitals only temporarily and only in cases of urgent necessity for the care of military wounded and sick, and then on condition that suitable arrangements are made in due time for the care and treatment of the patients and for the needs of the civilian population for hospital accommodation.

The material and stores of civilian hospitals cannot be requisitioned so long as they are necessary for the needs of the civilian population.

Article 58. The Occupying Power shall permit ministers of religion to give spiritual assistance to the members of their religious communities.

The Occupying Power shall also accept consignments of books and articles required for religious needs and shall facilitate their distribution in occupied territory.

Article 59. If the whole or part of the population of an occupied territory is inadequately supplied, the Occupying Power shall agree to relief schemes on behalf of the said population, and shall facilitate them by all the means at its disposal.

Such schemes, which may be undertaken either by States or by impartial humanitarian organizations such as the International Committee of the Red Cross, shall consist, in particular, of the provision of consignments of foodstuffs, medical supplies and clothing.

All Contracting Parties shall permit the free passage of these consignments and shall guarantee their protection.

A Power granting free passage to consignments on their way to territory occupied by an adverse Party to the conflict shall, however, have the right to search the consignments, to regulate their passage according to prescribed times and routes, and to be reasonably satisfied through the Protecting Power that these consignments are to be used for the relief of the needy population and are not to be used for the benefit of the Occupying Power.

Article 60. Relief consignments shall in no way relieve the Occupying Power of any of its responsibilities under Articles 55, 56 and 59. The Occupying Power shall in no way whatsoever divert relief consignments from the purpose for which they are intended, except in cases of urgent necessity, in the interests of the population of the occupied territory and with the consent of the Protecting Power.

Article 61. The distribution of the relief consignments referred to in the foregoing Articles shall be carried out with the cooperation and under the supervision of the Protecting Power. This duty may also be delegated, by agreement between the Occupying Power and the Protecting Power, to a neutral Power, to the International Committee of the Red Cross or to any other impartial humanitarian body.

Such consignments shall be exempt in occupied territory from all charges, taxes or customs duties unless these are necessary in the interests of the economy of the territory. The Occupying Power shall facilitate the rapid distribution of these consignments.

All Contracting Parties shall endeavour to permit the transit and transport, free of charge, of such relief consignments on their way to occupied territories.

Article 62. Subject to imperative reasons of security, protected persons in occupied territories shall be permitted to receive the individual relief consignments sent to them.

Article 63. Subject to temporary and exceptional measures imposed for urgent reasons of security by the Occupying Power:

(a) recognized National Red Cross (Red Crescent, Red Lion and Sun) Societies shall be able to pursue their activities in accordance with Red Cross principles, as defined by the International Red Cross Conferences. Other relief societies shall be permitted to continue their humanitarian activities under similar conditions;

(b) the Occupying Power may not require any changes in the personnel or structure of these societies, which would prejudice the aforesaid activities.

The same principles shall apply to the activities and personnel of special organizations of a non-military character, which already exist or which may be established, for the purpose of ensuring the living conditions of the civilian population by the maintenance of the essential public utility services, by the distribution of relief and by the organization of rescues.

Article 64. The penal laws of the occupied territory shall remain in force, with the exception that they may be repealed or suspended by the Occupying Power in cases where they constitute a threat to its security or an obstacle to the application of the present Convention.

Subject to the latter consideration and to the necessity for ensuring the effective administration of justice, the tribunals of the occupied territory shall continue to function in respect of all offences covered by the said laws.

The Occupying Power may, however, subject the population of the occupied territory to provisions which are essential to enable the Occupying Power to fulfill its obligations under the present Convention, to maintain the orderly government of the territory, and to ensure the security of the Occupying Power, of the members and property of the occupying forces or administration, and likewise of the establishments and lines of communication used by them.

Article 65. The penal provisions enacted by the Occupying Power shall not come into force before they have been published and brought to the knowledge of the inhabitants in their own language. The effect of these penal provisions shall not be retroactive.

Article 66. In case of a breach of the penal provisions promulgated by it by virtue of the second paragraph of Article 64 the Occupying Power may hand over the accused to its properly constituted, non-political military courts, on condition that the said courts sit in the occupied country. Courts of appeal shall preferably sit in the occupied country.

Article 67. The courts shall apply only those provisions of law which were applicable prior to the offence, and which are in accordance with general principles of law, in particular the principle that the penalty shall be proportionate to the offence. They shall take into consideration the fact the accused is not a national of the Occupying Power.

Article 68. Protected persons who commit an offence which is solely intended to harm the Occupying Power, but which does not constitute an attempt on the life or limb of members of the occupying forces or administration, nor a grave collective danger, nor seriously damage the property of the occupying forces or administration or the installations used by them, shall be liable to internment or simple imprisonment, provided the duration of such internment or imprisonment is proportionate to the offence committed. Furthermore, internment or imprisonment shall, for such offences, be the only measure adopted for depriving protected persons of liberty. The courts provided for under Article 66 of the present Convention may at their discretion convert a sentence of imprisonment to one of internment for the same period.

The penal provisions promulgated by the Occupying Power in accordance with Articles 64 and 65 may impose the death penalty on a protected person only in cases where the person is guilty of espionage, of serious acts of sabotage against the military installations of the Occupying Power or of intentional offences which have caused the death of one or more persons, provided that such offences were punishable by death under the law of the occupied territory in force before the occupation began.

The death penalty may not be pronounced on a protected person unless the attention of the court has been particularly called to the fact that since the accused is not a national of the Occupying Power, he is not bound to it by any duty of allegiance.

In any case, the death penalty may not be pronounced on a protected person who was under eighteen years of age at the time of the offence.

Article 69. In all cases the duration of the period during which a protected person accused of an offence is under arrest awaiting trial or punishment shall be deducted from any period of imprisonment of awarded.

Article 70. Protected persons shall not be arrested, prosecuted or convicted by the Occupying Power for acts committed or for opinions expressed before the occupation, or during a temporary interruption thereof, with the exception of breaches of the laws and customs of war.

Nationals of the occupying Power who, before the outbreak of hostilities, have sought refuge in the territory of the occupied State, shall not be arrested, prosecuted, convicted or deported from the occupied territory, except for offences committed after the outbreak of hostilities, or for offences under common law committed before the outbreak of hostilities which, according to the law of the occupied State, would have justified extradition in time of peace.

Article 71. No sentence shall be pronounced by the competent courts of the Occupying Power except after a regular trial.

Accused persons who are prosecuted by the Occupying Power shall be promptly informed, in writing, in a language which they understand, of the particulars of the charges preferred against them, and shall be brought to trial as rapidly as possible. The Protecting Power shall be informed of all proceedings instituted by the Occupying Power against protected persons in respect of charges involving the death penalty or imprisonment for two years or more; it shall be enabled, at any time, to obtain information regarding the state of such proceedings. Furthermore, the Protecting Power shall be entitled, on request, to be furnished with all particulars of these and of any other proceedings instituted by the Occupying Power against protected persons.

The notification to the Protecting Power, as provided for in the second paragraph above, shall be sent immediately, and shall in any case reach the Protecting Power three weeks before the date of the first hearing. Unless, at the opening of the trial, evidence is submitted that the provisions of this Article are fully complied with, the trial shall not proceed. The notification shall include the following particulars:

(a) description of the accused;

(b) place of residence or detention;

(c) specification of the charge or charges (with mention of the penal provisions under which it is brought);

(d) designation of the court which will hear the case;

(e) place and date of the first hearing.

Article 72. Accused persons shall have the right to present evidence necessary to their defence and may, in particular, call witnesses. They shall have the right to be assisted by a qualified advocate or counsel of their own choice, who shall be able to visit them freely and shall enjoy the necessary facilities for preparing the defence.

Failing a choice by the accused, the Protecting Power may provide him with an advocate or counsel. When an accused person has to meet a serious charge and the Protecting Power is not functioning, the Occupying Power, subject to the consent of the accused, shall provide an advocate or counsel.

Accused persons shall, unless they freely waive such assistance, be aided by an interpreter, both during preliminary investigation and during the hearing in court. They shall have at any time the right to object to the interpreter and to ask for his replacement.

Article 73. A convicted person shall have the right of appeal provided for by the laws applied by the court. He shall be fully informed of his right to appeal or petition and of the time limit within which he may do so.

The penal procedure provided in the present Section shall apply, as far as it is applicable, to appeals. Where the laws applied by the Court make no provision for appeals, the convicted person shall have the right to petition against the finding and sentence to the competent authority of the Occupying Power.

Article 74. Representatives of the Protecting Power shall have the right to attend the trial of any protected person, unless the hearing has, as an exceptional measure, to be held in camera in the interests of the security of the Occupying Power, which shall then notify the Protecting Power. A notification in respect of the date and place of trial shall be sent to the Protecting Power.

Any judgment involving a sentence of death, or imprisonment for two years or more, shall be communicated, with the relevant grounds, as rapidly as possible to the Protecting Power. The notification shall contain a reference to the notification made under Article 71 and, in the case of sentences of imprisonment, the name of the place where the sentence is to be served. A record of judgments other than those referred to above shall be kept by the court and shall be open to inspection by representatives of the Protecting Power. Any period allowed for appeal in the case of sentences involving the death penalty, or imprisonment of two years or more, shall not run until notification of judgment has been received by the Protecting Power.

Article 75. In no case shall persons condemned to death be deprived of the right of petition for pardon or reprieve.

No death sentence shall be carried out before the expiration of a period of at least six months from the date of receipt by the Protecting Power of the notification of the final judgment confirming such death sentence, or of an order denying pardon or reprieve.

The six months period of suspension of the death sentence herein prescribed may be reduced in individual cases in circumstances of grave emergency involving an organized threat to the security of the Occupying Power or its forces, provided always that the Protecting Power is notified of such reduction and is given reasonable time and opportunity to make representations to the competent occupying authorities in respect of such death sentences.

Article 76. Protected persons accused of offences shall be detained in the occupied country, and if convicted they shall serve their sentences therein. They shall, if possible, be separated from other detainees and shall enjoy conditions of food and hygiene which will be sufficient to keep them in good health, and which will be at least equal to those obtaining in prisons in the occupied country.

They shall receive the medical attention required by their state of health.

They shall also have the right to receive any spiritual assistance which they may require.

Women shall be confined in separate quarters and shall be under the direct supervision of women.

Proper regard shall be paid to the special treatment due to minors.

Protected persons who are detained shall have the right to be visited by delegates of the Protecting Power and of the International Committee of the Red Cross, in accordance with the provisions of Article 143.

Such persons shall have the right to receive at least one relief parcel monthly.

Article 77. Protected persons who have been accused of offences or convicted by the courts in occupied territory, shall be handed over at the close of occupation, with the relevant records, to the authorities of the liberated territory.

Article 78. If the Occupying Power considers it necessary, for imperative reasons of security, to take safety measures concerning protected persons, it may, at the most, subject them to assigned residence or to internment.

Decisions regarding such assigned residence or internment shall be made according to a regular procedure to be prescribed by the Occupying Power in accordance with the provisions of the present Convention. This procedure shall include the right of appeal for the parties concerned. Appeals shall be decided with the least possible delay. In the event of the decision being upheld, it shall be subject to periodical review, if possible every six months, by a competent body set up by the said Power.

Protected persons made subject to assigned residence and thus required to leave their homes shall enjoy the full benefit of Article 39 of the present Convention.

. . . .

PROTOCOL ADDITIONAL TO THE GENEVA CONVENTIONS OF 12 AUGUST 1949, AND RELATING TO THE PROTECTION OF VICTIMS OF INTERNATIONAL ARMED CONFLICTS* (PROTOCOL I)

....

Preamble

The High Contracting Parties,

Proclaiming their earnest wish to see peace prevail among peoples,

Recalling that every State has the duty, in conformity with the Charter of the United Nations, to refrain in its international relations from the threat or use of force against the sovereignty, territorial integrity or political independence of any State, or in any other manner inconsistent with the purposes of the United Nations.

Believing it necessary nevertheless to reaffirm and develop the provisions protecting the victims of armed conflicts and to supplement measures intended to reinforce their application,

Expressing their conviction that nothing in this Protocol or in the Geneva Conventions of 12 August 1949 can be construed as legitimizing or authorizing any act of aggression or any other use of force inconsistent with the Charter of the United Nations,

Reaffirming further that the provisions of the Geneva Conventions of 12 August 1949 and of this Protocol must be fully applied in all circumstances to all persons who are protected by those instruments, without any adverse distinction based on the nature or origin of the armed conflict or on the causes espoused by or attributed to the Parties to the conflicts,

Have agreed on the following:

PART I
GENERAL PROVISIONS

Article 1. General principles and scope of application.

1. The High Contracting Parties undertake to respect and to ensure respect for this Protocol in all circumstances.

2. In cases not covered by this Protocol or by other international agreements, civilians and combatants remain under the protection and authority of the principles of international law derived from established custom, from the principles of humanity and from the dictates of public conscience.

---

* Protocol Additional to the Geneva Conventions of 12 August 1949, and Relating to the Protection of Victims of International Armed Conflicts (Protocol I), June 8, 1977, 1125 U.N.T.S. 3, 16 I.L.M. 1391 (entered into force Dec. 7, 1978), *available at* http://www.unhchr.ch/html/menu3/b/93.htm.

3. This Protocol, which supplements the Geneva Conventions of 12 August 1949 for the protection of war victims, shall apply in the situations referred to in Article 2 common to those Conventions.

4. The situations referred to in the preceding paragraph include armed conflicts in which peoples are fighting against colonial domination and alien occupation and against racist regimes in the exercise of their right of self-determination, as enshrined in the Charter of the United Nations and the Declaration on Principles of International Law concerning Friendly Relations and Co-operation among States in accordance with the Charter of the United Nations.

Article 2. Definitions

For the purposes of this Protocol:

(a) "First Convention", "Second Convention", "Third Convention" and "Fourth Convention" mean, respectively, the Geneva Convention for the Amelioration of the Condition of the Wounded and Sick in Armed Forces in the Field of 12 August 1949; the Geneva Convention for the Amelioration of the Condition of Wounded, Sick and Shipwrecked Members of Armed Forces at Sea of 12 August 1949; the Geneva Convention Relative to the Treatment of Prisoners of War of 12 August 1949; the Geneva Convention Relative to the Protection of Civilian Persons in Time of War of 12 August 1949; "the Conventions" means the four Geneva Conventions of 12 August 1949; for the protection of war victims;

(b) "Rules of international law applicable in armed conflict" means the rules applicable in armed conflict set forth in international agreements to which the Parties to the conflict are Parties and the generally recognized principles and rules of international law which are applicable to armed conflict;

(c) "Protecting Power" means a neutral or other State not a Party to the conflict which has been designated by a Party to the conflict and accepted by the adverse Party and has agreed to carry out the functions assigned to a Protecting Power under the Conventions and this Protocol;

(d) "Substitute" means an organization acting in place of a Protecting Power in accordance with Article 5.

Article 3. Beginning and end of application

Without prejudice to the provisions which are applicable at all times:

(a) The Conventions and this Protocol shall apply from the beginning of any situation referred to in Article 1 of this Protocol;

(b) The application of the Conventions and of this Protocol shall cease, in the territory of Parties to the conflict, on the general close of military operations and, in the case of occupied territories, on the termination of the occupation, except, in either circumstance, for those persons whose final release, repatriation or re-establishment takes place thereafter. These persons shall continue to benefit from the relevant provisions of the Conventions and of this Protocol until their final release, repatriation or re-establishment.

Article 4. Legal status of the Parties to the conflict

The application of the Conventions and of this Protocol, as well as the conclusion of the agreements provided for therein, shall not affect the legal status of the Parties to the conflict. Neither the occupation of a territory nor the application of the Conventions and this Protocol shall affect the legal status of the territory in question.

Article 5. Appointment of Protecting Powers and of their substitute

....

PART II
WOUNDED, SICK AND SHIPWRECKED

SECTION I—GENERAL PROTECTION

Article 8. Terminology

For the purposes of this Protocol:

(a) "Wounded" and "sick" mean persons, whether military or civilian, who, because of trauma, disease or other physical or mental disorder or disability, are in need of medical assistance or care and who refrain from any act of hostility. These terms also cover maternity cases, new-born babies and other persons who may be in need of immediate medical assistance or care, such as the infirm or expectant mothers, and who refrain from any act of hostility;

(b) "Shipwrecked" means persons, whether military or civilian, who are in peril at sea or in other waters as a result of misfortune affecting them or the vessel or aircraft carrying them and who refrain from any act of hostility. These persons, provided that they continue to refrain from any act of hostility, shall continue to be considered shipwrecked during their rescue until they acquire another status under the Conventions or this Protocol;

(c) "Medical personnel" means those persons assigned, by a Party to the conflict, exclusively to the medical purposes enumerated under subparagraph (e) or to the administration of medical units or to the operation or administration of medical transports. Such assignments may be either permanent or temporary. The term includes:

(i) Medical personnel of a Party to the conflict, whether military or civilian, including those described in the First and Second Conventions, and those assigned to civil defence organizations;

(ii) Medical personnel of national Red Cross (Red Crescent, Red Lion and Sun) Societies and other national voluntary aid societies duly recognized and authorized by a Party to the conflict;

(iii) Medical personnel of medical units or medical transports described in Article 9, paragraph 2;

(d) "Religious personnel" means military or civilian persons, such as chaplains, who are exclusively engaged in the work of their ministry and attached:

(i) To the armed forces of a Party to the conflict;

(ii) To medical units or medical transports of a Party to the conflict;

(iii) To medical units or medical transports described in Article 9, paragraph 2; or

(iv) To civil defence organizations of a Party to the conflict.

The attachment of religious personnel may be either permanent or temporary, and the relevant provisions mentioned under sub-paragraph (k) apply to them;

(e) "Medical units" means establishments and other units, whether military or civilian, organized for medical purposes, namely the search for, collection, transportation, diagnosis or treatment-including first-aid treatment-of the wounded, sick and shipwrecked, or for the prevention of disease. The term includes, for example, hospitals and other similar units, blood transfusion centres, preventive medicine centres and institutes, medical depots and the medical and pharmaceutical stores of such units. Medical units may be fixed or mobile, permanent or temporary;

(f) "Medical transportation" means the conveyance by land, water or air of the wounded, sick, shipwrecked, medical personnel, religious personnel, medical equipment or medical supplies protected by the Conventions and by this Protocol;

(g) "Medical transports" means any means of transportation. whether military or civilian, permanent or temporary, as signed exclusively to medical transportation and under the control of a competent authority of a Party to the conflict;

(h) "Medical vehicles" means any medical transports by land;

(i) "Medical ships and craft" means any medical transports by water;

(j) "Medical aircraft" means any medical transports by air;

(k) "Permanent medical personnel", "permanent medical units" and "permanent medical transports" mean those assigned exclusively to medical purposes for an indeterminate period. "Temporary medical personnel", "temporary medical units" and "temporary medical transports" mean those devoted exclusively to medical purposes for limited periods during the whole of such periods. Unless otherwise specified, the terms "medical personnel", " medical units" and "medical transports" cover both permanent and temporary categories;

(l) "Distinctive emblem" means the distinctive emblem of the red cross, red crescent or red lion and sun on a white ground when used for the protection of medical units and transports, or medical and religious personnel, equipment or supplies;

(m) "Distinctive signal" means any signal or message specified for the identification exclusively of medical units or transports in Chapter III of Annex I to this Protocol.

Article 9. Field of application

1. This Part, the provisions of which are intended to ameliorate the condition of the wounded, sick and shipwrecked, shall apply to all those affected by a situation referred to in Article 1, without any adverse distinction founded on race, colour, sex, language, religion or belief, political or other opinion, national or social origin, wealth, birth or other status, or on any other similar criteria.

2. The relevant provisions of Articles 27 and 32 of the First Convention shall apply to permanent medical units and transports (other than hospital ships, to which Article 25 of the Second Convention applies) and their personnel made available to a Party to the conflict for humanitarian purposes:

(a) By a neutral or other State which is not a Party to that conflict;

(b) By a recognized and authorized aid society of such a State;

(c) By an impartial international humanitarian organization.

Article 10. Protection and care

1. All the wounded, sick and shipwrecked, to whichever Party they belong, shall be respected and protected.

2. In all circumstances they shall be treated humanely and shall receive, to the fullest extent practicable and with the least possible delay, the medical care and attention required by their condition. There shall be no distinction among them founded on any grounds other than medical ones.

Article 11. Protection of persons

1. The physical or mental health and integrity of persons who are in the power of the adverse Party or who are interned, detained or otherwise deprived of liberty as a result of a situation referred to in Article I shall not be endangered by any unjustified act or omission. Accordingly, it is prohibited to subject the persons described in this Article to any medical procedure which is not indicated by the state of health of the person concerned and which is not consistent with generally accepted medical standards which would be applied under similar medical circumstances to persons who are nationals of the Party conducting the procedure and who are in no way deprived of liberty.

2. It is, in particular, prohibited to carry out on such persons, even with their consent:

(a) Physical mutilations;

(b) Medical or scientific experiments;

(c) Removal of tissue or organs for transplantation,

except where these acts are justified in conformity with the conditions provided for in paragraph 1.

3. Exceptions to the prohibition in paragraph 2 (c) may be made only in the case of donations of blood for transfusion or of skin for grafting, provided that they are given voluntarily and without any coercion or inducement, and then only for therapeutic purposes, under conditions consistent with generally accepted medical standards and controls designed for the benefit of both the donor and the recipient.

4. Any willful act or omission which seriously endangers the physical or mental health or integrity of any person who is in the power of a Party other than the one on which he depends and which either violates any of the prohibitions in paragraphs 1 and 2 or fails to comply with the requirements of paragraph 3 shall be a grave breach of this Protocol.

5. The persons described in paragraph I have the right to refuse any surgical operation. In case of refusal, medical personnel shall endeavour to obtain a written statement to that effect, signed or acknowledged by the patient.

6. Each Party to the conflict shall keep a medical record for every donation of blood for transfusion or skin for grafting by persons referred to in paragraph 1, if that donation is made under the responsibility of that Party. In addition, each Party to the conflict shall endeavour to keep a record of all medical procedures undertaken with respect to any person who is interned, detained or otherwise deprived of liberty as a result of a situation referred to in Article 1. These records shall be available at all times for inspection by the Protecting Power.

Article 12. Protection of medical units

1. Medical units shall be respected and protected at all times and shall not be the object of attack.

2. Paragraph I shall apply to civilian medical units, provided that they:

(a) Belong to one of the Parties to the conflict;

(b) Are recognized and authorized by the competent authority of one of the Parties to the conflict; or

(c) Are authorized in conformity with Article 9, paragraph 2, of this Protocol or Article 27 of the First Convention.

3. The Parties to the conflict are invited to notify each other of the location of their fixed medical units. The absence of such notification shall not exempt any of the Parties from the obligation to comply with the provisions of paragraph 1.

4. Under no circumstances shall medical units be used in an attempt to shield military objectives from attack. Whenever possible, the Parties to the conflict shall ensure that medical units are so sated that attacks against military objectives do not imperil their safety.

Article 13. Discontinuance of protection of civilian medical units

1. The protection to which civilian medical units are entitled shall not cease unless they are used to commit, outside their humanitarian function, acts harmful to the enemy. Protection may, however, cease only after a warning has been given setting, whenever appropriate, a reasonable time-limit, and after such warning has remained unheeded.

2. The following shall not be considered as acts harmful to the enemy;

(a) That the personnel of the unit are equipped with light individual weapons for their own defence or for that of the wounded and sick in their charge;

(b) That the unit is guarded by a picket or by sentries or by an escort;

(c) That small arms and ammunition taken from the wounded and sick, and not yet handed to the proper service, are found in the units;

(d) That members of the armed forces or other combatants are in the unit for medical reasons.

. . . .

PART III
METHODS AND MEANS OF WARFARE
COMBATANT AND PRISONER-OF-WAR STATUS

SECTION I—METHODS AND MEANS OF WARFARE

Article 35. Basic rules

1. In any armed conflict, the right of the Parties to the conflict to choose methods or means of warfare is not unlimited.

2. It is prohibited to employ weapons, projectiles and material and methods of warfare of a nature to cause superfluous injury or unnecessary suffering.

3. It is prohibited to employ methods or means of warfare which are intended, or may be expected, to cause widespread, long-term and severe damage to the natural environment.

Article 36. New weapons

In the study, development, acquisition or adoption of a new weapon, means or method of warfare, a High Contracting Party is under an obligation to determine whether its employment would, in some or all circumstances, be prohibited by this Protocol or by any other rule of international law applicable to the High Contracting Party.

Article 37. Prohibition of perfidy

1. It is prohibited to kill, injure or capture an adversary by resort to perfidy. Acts inviting the confidence of an adversary to lead him to believe that he is entitled to, or is obliged to accord, protection under the rules of international law applicable in armed conflict, with intent to betray that confidence, shall constitute perfidy. The following acts are examples of perfidy:

(a) The feigning of an intent to negotiate under a flag of truce or of a surrender;

(b) The feigning of an incapacitation by wounds or sickness;

(c) The feigning of civilian, non-combatant status; and

(d) The feigning of protected status by the use of signs, emblems or uniforms of the United Nations or of neutral or other States not Parties to the conflict.

2. Ruses of war are not prohibited. Such ruses are acts which are intended to mislead an adversary or to induce him to act recklessly but which infringe no rule of international law applicable in armed conflict and which are not perfidious because they do not invite the confidence of an adversary with respect to protection under that law. The following are examples of such ruses: the use of camouflage, decoys, mock operations and misinformation.

Article 38. Recognized emblems

1. It is prohibited to make improper use of the distinctive emblem of the red cross, red crescent or red lion and sun or of other emblems, signs or signals provided for by the Conventions or by this Protocol. It is also prohibited to misuse deliberately in an armed conflict other internationally recognized protective emblems, signs or signals, including the flag of truce, and the protective emblem of cultural property.

2. It is prohibited to make use of the distinctive emblem of the United Nations, except as authorized by that Organization.

Article 39. Emblems of nationality

1. It is prohibited to make use in an armed conflict of the flags or military emblems, insignia or uniforms of neutral or other States not Parties to the conflict.

2. It is prohibited to make use of the flags or military emblems, insignia or uniforms of adverse Parties while engaging in attacks or in order to shield, favour, protect or impede military operations.

3. Nothing in this Article or in Article 37, paragraph 1 (d), shall affect the existing generally recognized rules of international law applicable to espionage or to the use of flags in the conduct of armed conflict at sea.

Article 40. Quarter

It is prohibited to order that there shall be no survivors, to threaten an adversary therewith or to conduct hostilities on this basis.

Article 41. Safeguard of an enemy hors de combat

1. A person who is recognized or who, in the circumstances, should be recognized to be *hors de combat* shall not be made the object of attack.

2. A person is *hors de combat* if:

(a) He is in the power of an adverse Party;

(b) He clearly expresses an intention to surrender; or

(c) He has been rendered unconscious or is otherwise incapacitated by wounds or sickness, and therefore is incapable of defending himself; provided that in any of these cases he abstains from any hostile act and does not attempt to escape.

3. When persons entitled to protection as prisoners of war have fallen into the power of an adverse Party under unusual conditions of combat which prevent their evacuation as provided for in Part m, Section I, of the Third Convention, they shall be released and all feasible precautions shall be taken to ensure their safety.

Article 42. Occupants of aircraft

1. No person parachuting from an aircraft in distress shall be made the object of attack during his descent.

2. Upon reaching the ground in territory controlled by an adverse Party, a person who has parachuted from an aircraft in distress shall be given an opportunity to surrender before being made the object of attack, unless it is apparent that he is engaging in a hostile act.

3. Airborne troops are not protected by this Article.

SECTION II—COMBATANT AND PRISONER-OF-WAR STATUS

Article 43. Armed forces

1. The armed forces of a Party to a conflict consist of all organized armed forces, groups and units which are under a command responsible to that Party for the conduct of its subordinates, even if that Party is represented by a government or an authority not recognized by an adverse Party. Such armed forces shall be subject to an internal disciplinary system which, inter alia, shall enforce compliance with the rules of international law applicable in armed conflict.

2. Members of the armed forces of a Party to a conflict (other than medical personnel and chaplains covered by Article 33 of the Third Convention) are combatants, that is to say, they have the right to participate directly in hostilities.

3. Whenever a Party to a conflict incorporates a paramilitary or armed law enforcement agency into its armed forces it shall so notify the other Parties to the conflict.

Article 44. Combatants and prisoners of war

1. Any combatant, as defined in Article 43, who falls into the power of an adverse Party shall be a prisoner of war.

2. While all combatants are obliged to comply with the rules of international law applicable in armed conflict, violations of these rules shall not deprive a combatant of his right to be a combatant or, if he falls into the power of an adverse Party, of his right to be a prisoner of war, except as provided in paragraphs 3 and 4.

3. In order to promote the protection of the civilian population from the effects of hostilities, combatants are obliged to distinguish themselves from the civilian population while they are engaged in an attack or in a military operation preparatory to an attack. Recognizing, however, that there are situations in armed conflicts where, owing to the nature of the hostilities an armed combatant cannot so distinguish himself, he shall retain his status as a combatant, provided that, in such situations, he carries his arms openly:

(a) During each military engagement, and

(b) During such time as he is visible to the adversary while he is engaged in a military deployment preceding the launching of an attack in which he is to participate.

Acts which comply with the requirements of this paragraph shall not be considered as perfidious within the meaning of Article 37, paragraph 1 (c).

4. A combatant who falls into the power of an adverse Party while failing to meet the requirements set forth in the second sentence of paragraph 3 shall forfeit his right to be a prisoner of war, but he shall, nevertheless, be given protections equivalent in all respects to those accorded to prisoners of war by the Third Convention and by this Protocol. This protection includes protections equivalent to those accorded to prisoners of war by the Third Convention in the case where such a person is tried and punished for any offences he has committed.

5. Any combatant who falls into the power of an adverse Party while not engaged in an attack or in a military operation preparatory to an attack shall not forfeit his rights to be a combatant and a prisoner of war by virtue of his prior activities.

6. This Article is without prejudice to the right of any person to be a prisoner of war pursuant to Article 4 of the Third Convention.

7. This Article is not intended to change the generally accepted practice of States with respect to the wearing of the uniform by combatants assigned to the regular, uniformed armed units of a Party to the conflict.

8. In addition to the categories of persons mentioned in Article 13 of the First and Second Conventions, all members of the armed forces of a Party to the conflict, as defined in Article 43 of this Protocol, shall be entitled to protection under those Conventions if they are wounded or sick or, in the case of the Second Convention, shipwrecked at sea or in other waters.

Article 45. Protection of persons who have taken part in hostilities

1. A person who takes part in hostilities and falls into the power of an adverse Party shall be presumed to be a prisoner of war, and therefore shall be protected by the Third Convention, if he claims the status of prisoner of war, or if he appears to be entitled to such status, or if the Party on which he depends claims such status on his behalf by notification to the detaining Power or to the Protecting Power. Should any doubt arise as to whether any such person is entitled to the status of prisoner of war, he shall continue to have such status and, therefore, to be protected by the Third Convention and this Protocol until such time as his status has been determined by a competent tribunal.

2. If a person who has fallen into the power of an adverse Party is not held as a prisoner of war and is to be tried by that Party for an offence arising out of the hostilities, he shall have the right to assert his entitlement to prisoner-of-war status before a judicial tribunal and to have that question adjudicated. Whenever possible under the applicable procedure, this adjudication shall occur before the trial for the offence. The representatives of the Protecting Power shall be entitled to attend the proceedings in which that question is adjudicated, unless, exceptionally, the proceedings are held in camera in the interest of State security. In such a case the detaining Power shall advise the Protecting Power accordingly.

3. Any person who has taken part in hostilities, who is not entitled to prisoner-of-war status and who does not benefit from more favourable treatment in accordance with the Fourth Convention shall have the right at all times to the protection of Article 75 of this Protocol. In occupied territory, an such person, unless he is held as a spy, shall also be entitled, notwithstanding Article 5 of the Fourth Convention, to his rights of communication under that Convention.

Article 46. Spies

1. Notwithstanding any other provision of the Conventions or of this Protocol, any member of the armed forces of a Party to the conflict who falls into the power of an adverse Party while engaging in espionage shall not have the right to the status of prisoner of war and may be treated as a spy.

2. A member of the armed forces of a Party to the conflict who, on behalf of that Party and in territory controlled by an adverse Party, gathers or attempts to gather information shall not be considered as engaging in espionage if, while so acting, he is in the uniform of his armed forces.

3. A member of the armed forces of a Party to the conflict who is a resident of territory occupied by an adverse Party and who, on behalf of the Party on which he depends, gathers or attempts to gather information of military value within that territory shall not be considered as engaging in espionage unless he does so through an act of false pretences or deliberately in a clandestine manner. Moreover, such a resident shall not lose his right to the status of prisoner of war and may not be treated as a spy unless he is captured while engaging in espionage.

4. A member of the armed forces of a Party to the conflict who is not a resident of territory occupied by an adverse Party and who has engaged in espionage in that territory shall not lose his right to the status of prisoner of war and may not be treated as a spy unless he is captured before he has rejoined the armed forces to which he belongs.

Article 47. Mercenaries

1. A mercenary shall not have the right to be a combatant or a prisoner of war.

2. A mercenary is any person who:

(a) Is specially recruited locally or abroad in order to fight in an armed conflict;

(b) Does, in fact, take a direct part in the hostilities;

(c) Is motivated to take part in the hostilities essentially by the desire for private gain and, in fact, is promised, by or on behalf of a Party to the conflict, material compensation substantially in excess of that promised or paid to combatants of similar ranks and functions in the armed forces of that Party;

(d) Is neither a national of a Party to the conflict nor a resident of territory controlled by a Party to the conflict;

(e) Is not a member of the armed forces of a Party to the conflict; and

(f) Has not been sent by a State which is not a Party to the conflict on official duty as a member of its armed forces.

PART IV
CIVILIAN POPULATION

SECTION I—GENERAL PROTECTION AGAINST EFFECTS OF HOSTILITIES

CHAPTER 1—*Basic rule and field of application*

Article 48. Basic rule

In order to ensure respect for and protection of the civilian population and civilian objects, the Parties to the conflict shall at all times distinguish between the civilian population and combatants and between civilian objects and military objectives and accordingly shall direct their operations only against military objectives.

Article 49. Definition of attacks and scope of application

1. "Attacks" means acts of violence against the adversary, whether in offence or in defence.

2. The provisions of this Protocol with respect to attacks apply to all attacks in whatever territory conducted, including the national territory belonging to a Party to the conflict but under the control of an adverse Party.

3. The provisions of this Section apply to any land, air or sea warfare which may affect the civilian population, individual civilians or civilian objects on land. They further apply to all attacks from the sea or from the air against objectives on land but do not otherwise affect the rules of international law applicable in armed conflict at sea or in the air.

4. The provisions of this Section are additional to the rules concerning humanitarian protection contained in the Fourth Convention, particularly in Part II thereof, and in other international agreements binding upon the High Contracting Parties, as well as to other rules of international law relating to the protection of civilians and civilian objects on land, at sea or in the air against the effects of hostilities.

CHAPTER II—*Civilians and civilian population*

Article 50. Definition of civilians and civilian population

1. A civilian is any person who does not belong to one of the categories of persons referred to in Article 4 A (1), (2), (3) and (6) of the Third Convention and in Article 43 of this Protocol. In case of doubt whether a person is a civilian, that person shall be considered to be a civilian.

2. The civilian population comprises all persons who are civilians.

3. The presence within the civilian population of individuals who do not come within the definition of civilians does not deprive the population of its civilian character.

Article 51. Protection of the civilian population

1. The civilian population and individual civilians shall enjoy general protection against dangers arising from military operations. To give effect to this protection, the following rules, which are additional to other applicable rules of international law, shall be observed in circumstances.

2. The civilian population as such, as well as individual civilians, shall not be the object of attack. Acts or threats of violence the primary purpose of which is to spread terror among the civilian population are prohibited.

3. Civilians shall enjoy the protection afforded by this Section, unless and for such time as they take a direct part in hostilities.

4. Indiscriminate attacks are prohibited. Indiscriminate attacks are:

(a) Those which are not directed at a specific military objective;

(b) Those which employ a method or means of combat which cannot be directed at a specific military objective; or

(c) Those which employ a method or means of combat the effects of which cannot be limited as required by this Protocol; and consequently, in each such case, are of a nature to strike military objectives and civilians or civilian objects without distinction.

5. Among others, the following types of attacks are to be considered as indiscriminate:

(a) An attack by bombardment by any methods or means which treats as a single military objective a number of clearly separated and distinct military objectives located in a city, town, village or other area containing a similar concentration of civilians or civilian objects; and

(b) An attack which may be expected to cause incidental loss of civilian life, injury to civilians, damage to civilian objects, or a combination thereof, which would be excessive in relation to the concrete and direct military advantage anticipated.

6. Attacks against the civilian population or civilians by way of reprisals are prohibited.

7. The presence or movements of the civilian population or individual civilians shall not be used to render certain points or areas immune from military operations, in particular in attempts to shield military objectives from attacks or to shield, favour or impede military operations. The Parties to the conflict shall not direct the movement of the civilian population or individual civilians in order to attempt to shield military objectives from attacks or to shield military operations.

8. Any violation of these prohibitions shall not release the Parties to the conflict from their legal obligations with respect to the civilian population and civilians, including the obligation to take the precautionary measures provided for in Article 57.

CHAPTER III—*Civilian objects*

Article 52. General protection of civilian objects

1. Civilian objects shall not be the object of attack or of reprisals. Civilian objects are all objects which are not military objectives as defined in paragraph 2.

2. Attacks shall be limited strictly to military objectives. In so far as objects are concerned, military objectives are limited to those objects which by their nature, location, purpose or use make an effective contribution to military action and whose total or partial destruction, capture or neutralization, in the circumstances ruling at the time, offers a definite military of advantage.

3. In case of doubt whether an object which is normally dedicated to civilian purposes, such as a place of worship, a house or other dwelling or a school, is being used to make an effective contribution to military action, it shall be presumed not to be so used.

Article 53. Protection of cultural objects and of places of worship

Without prejudice to the provisions of the Hague Convention for the Protection of Cultural Property in the Event of Armed Conflict of 14 May 1954, and of other relevant international instruments, it is prohibited:

(a) To commit any acts of hostility directed against the historic monuments, works of art or places of worship which constitute the cultural or spiritual heritage of peoples;

(b) To use such objects in support of the military effort;

(c) To make such objects the object of reprisals.

Article 54. Protection of objects indispensable to the survival of the civilian population

1. Starvation of civilians as a method of warfare is prohibited.

2. It is prohibited to attack, destroy, remove or render useless objects indispensable to the survival of the civilian population, such as foodstuffs, agricultural areas for the production of foodstuffs, crops, livestock, drinking water installations and supplies and irrigation works, for the specific purpose of denying them for their sustenance value to the civilian population or to the adverse Party, whatever the motive, whether in order to starve out civilians, to cause them to move away, or for any other motive.

3. The prohibitions in paragraph 2 shall not apply to such of the objects covered by it as are used by an adverse Party:

(a) As sustenance solely for the members of its armed forces; or

(b) If not as sustenance, then in direct support of military action, provided, however, that in no event shall actions against these objects be taken which may be expected to leave the civilian population with such inadequate food or water as to cause its starvation or force its movement.

4. These objects shall not be made the object of reprisals.

5. In recognition of the vital requirements of any Party to the conflict in the defence of its national territory against invasion, derogation from the prohibitions contained in paragraph 2 may be made by a Party to the conflict within such territory under its own control where required by imperative military necessity.

Article 55. Protection of the natural environment

1. Care shall be taken in warfare to protect the natural environment against widespread, long-term and severe damage. This protection includes a prohibition of the use of methods or means of warfare which are intended or may be expected to cause such damage to the natural environment and thereby to prejudice the health or survival of the population.

2. Attacks against the natural environment by way of reprisals are prohibited.

Article 56. Protection of works and installations containing dangerous forces

1. Works or installations containing dangerous forces, namely dams, dykes and nuclear electrical generating stations, shall not be made the object of attack, even where these objects are military objectives, if such attack may cause the release of dangerous forces and consequent severe losses among the civilian population. Other military objectives located at or in the vicinity of these works or installations shall not be made the object of attack if such attack may cause the release of dangerous forces from the works or installations and consequent severe losses among the civilian population.

2. The special protection against attack provided by paragraph 1 shall cease:

(a) For a dam or a dyke only if it is used for other than its normal function and in regular, significant and direct support of military operations and if such attack is the only feasible way to terminate such support;

(b) For a nuclear electrical generating station only if it provides electric power in regular, significant and direct support of military operations and if such attack is the only feasible way to terminate such support;

(c) For other military objectives located at or in the vicinity of these works or installations only if they are used in regular, significant and direct support of military operations and if such attack is the only feasible way to terminate such support.

3. In all cases, the civilian population and individual civilians shall remain entitled to all the protection accorded them by international law, including the protection of the

precautionary measures provided for in Article 57. If the protection ceases and any of the works, installations or military objectives mentioned in paragraph I is attacked, all practical precautions shall be taken to avoid the release of the dangerous forces.

4. It is prohibited to make any of the works, installations or military objectives mentioned in paragraph 1 the object of reprisals.

5. The Parties to the conflict shall endeavour to avoid locating any military objectives in the vicinity of the works or installations mentioned in paragraph 1. Nevertheless, installations erected for the sole purpose of defending the protected works or installations from attack are permissible and shall not themselves be made the object of attack, provided that they are not used in hostilities except for defensive actions necessary to respond to attacks against the protected works or installations and that their armament is limited to weapons capable only of repelling hostile action against the protected works or installations.

6. The High Contracting Parties and the Parties to the conflict are urged to conclude further agreements among themselves to provide additional protection for objects containing dangerous forces.

7. In order to facilitate the identification of the objects protected by this article, the Parties to the conflict may mark them with a special sign consisting of a group of three bright orange circles placed on the same axis, as specified in Article 16 of Annex I to this Protocol. The absence of such marking in no way relieves any Party to the conflict of its obligations under this Article.

CHAPTER IV—*Precautionary measures*

Article 57. Precautions in attack

1. In the conduct of military operations, constant care shall be taken to spare the civilian population, civilians and civilian objects.

2. With respect to attacks, the following precautions shall be taken:

(a) Those who plan or decide upon an attack shall:

(i) Do everything feasible to verify that the objectives to be attacked are neither civilians nor civilian objects and are not subject to special protection but are military objectives within the meaning of paragraph 2 of Article 52 and that it is not prohibited by the provisions of this Protocol to attack them;

(ii) Take all feasible precautions in the choice of means and methods of attack with a view to avoiding, and in any event to minimizing, incidental loss of civilian life, injury to civilians and damage to civilian objects;

(iii) Refrain from deciding to launch any attack which may be expected to cause incidental loss of civilian life, injury to civilians, damage to civilian objects, or a combination thereof, which would be excessive in relation to the concrete and direct military advantage anticipated;

(b) An attack shall be cancelled or suspended if it becomes apparent that the objective is not a military one or is subject to special protection or that the attack may be expected to cause incidental loss of civilian life, injury to civilians, damage to civilian objects, or a combination thereof, which would be excessive in relation to the concrete and direct military advantage anticipated;

(c) Effective advance warning shall be given of attacks which may affect the civilian population, unless circumstances do not permit.

3. When a choice is possible between several military objectives for obtaining a similar military advantage, the objective to be selected shall be that the attack on which may be expected to cause the least danger to civilian lives and to civilian objects.

4. In the conduct of military operations at sea or in the air, each Party to the conflict shall, in conformity with its rights and duties under the rules of international law applicable in armed conflict, take all reasonable precautions to avoid losses of civilian lives and damage to civilian objects.

5. No provision of this Article may be construed as authorizing any attacks against the civilian population, civilians or civilian objects.

Article 58. Precautions against the effects of attacks

The Parties to the conflict shall, to the maximum extent feasible:

(a) Without prejudice to Article 49 of the Fourth Convention, endeavour to remove the civilian population, individual civilians and civilian objects under their control from the vicinity of military objectives;

(b) Avoid locating military objectives within or near densely populated areas;

(c) Take the other necessary precautions to protect the civilian population, individual civilians and civilian objects under their control against the dangers resulting from military operations.

CHAPTER V—LOCALITIES AND ZONES UNDER SPECIAL PROTECTION

Article 59. Non-defended localities

1. It is prohibited for the Parties to the conflict to attack, by any means whatsoever, non-defended localities.

2. The appropriate authorities of a Party to the conflict may declare as a non-defended locality any inhabited place near or in a zone where armed forces are in contact which is open for occupation by an adverse Party. Such a locality shall fulfill the following conditions:

(a) All combatants, as well as mobile weapons and mobile military equipment must have been evacuated;

(b) No hostile use shall be made of fixed military installations or establishments;

(c) No acts of hostility shall be committed by the authorities or by the population; and

(d) No activities in support of military operations shall be undertaken.

....

Article 60. Demilitarized zones

....

SECTION III—TREATMENT OF PERSONS IN THE POWER OF A PARTY TO THE CONFLICT

CHAPTER 1—*Field of application and protection of persons and objects*

....

Article 75. Fundamental guarantees

1. In so far as they are affected by a situation referred to in Article 1 of this Protocol, persons who are in the power of a Party to the conflict and who do not benefit from more favourable treatment under the Conventions or under this Protocol shall be treated humanely in all circumstances and shall enjoy, as a minimum, the protection provided by this Article without any adverse distinction based upon race, colour, sex, language, religion or belief, political or other opinion, national or social origin, wealth, birth or other status, or on any other similar criteria. Each Party shall respect the person, honour, convictions and religious practices of all such persons.

2. The following acts are and shall remain prohibited at any time and in any place whatsoever, whether committed by civilian or by military agents:

(a) Violence to the life, health, or physical or mental well-being of persons, in particular:

(i) Murder;

(ii) Torture of all kinds, whether physical or mental;

(iii) Corporal punishment ; and

(iv) Mutilation;

(b) Outrages upon personal dignity, in particular humiliating and degrading treatment, enforced prostitution and any form of indecent assault;

(c) The taking of hostages;

(d) Collective punishments; and

(e) Threats to commit any of the foregoing acts.

3. Any person arrested, detained or interned for actions related to the armed conflict shall be informed promptly, in a language he understands, of the reasons why these measures have been taken. Except in cases of arrest or detention for penal offences, such persons shall be released with the minimum delay possible and in any event as soon as the circumstances justifying the arrest, detention or internment have ceased to exist.

4. No sentence may be passed and no penalty may be executed on a person found guilty of a penal offence related to the armed conflict except pursuant to a conviction pronounced by an impartial and regularly constituted court respecting the generally recognized principles of regular judicial procedure, which include the following:

(a) The procedure shall provide for an accused to be informed without delay of the particulars of the offence alleged against him and shall afford the accused before and during his trial all necessary rights and means of defence;

(b) No one shall be convicted of an offence except on the basis of individual penal responsibility;

(c) No one shall be accused or convicted of a criminal offence on account of any act or omission which did not constitute a criminal offence under the national or international law to which he was subject at the time when it was committed; nor shall a heavier penalty be imposed than that which was applicable at the time when the criminal offence was committed; if, after the commission of the offence, provision is made by law for the imposition of a lighter penalty, the offender shall benefit thereby;

(d) Anyone charged with an offence is presumed innocent until proved guilt according to law;

(e) Anyone charged with an offence shall have the right to be tried in his presence;

(f) No one shall be compelled to testify against himself or to confess guilt;

(g) Anyone charged with an offence shall have the right to examine, or have examined, the witnesses against him and to obtain the attendance and examination of witnesses on his behalf under the same conditions as witnesses against him;

(h) No one shall be prosecuted or punished by the same Party for an offence in respect of which a final judgment acquitting or convicting that person has been previously pronounced under the same law and judicial procedure;

(i) Anyone prosecuted for an offence shall have the right to have the judgment pronounced publicly; and

(j) A convicted person shall be advised on conviction of his judicial and other remedies and of the time-limits within which they may be exercised.

5. Women whose liberty has been restricted for reasons related to the armed conflict shall be held in quarters separated from men's quarters. They shall be under the immediate supervision of women. Nevertheless, in cases where families are detained or interned, they shall, whenever possible, be held in the same place and accommodated as family units.

6. Persons who are arrested, detained or interned for reasons related to the armed conflict shall enjoy the protection provided by this Article until their final release, repatriation or re-establishment, even after the end of the armed conflict.

7. In order to avoid any doubt concerning the prosecution and trial of persons accused of war crimes or crimes against humanity, the following principles shall apply:

> (a) Persons who are accused of such crimes should be submitted for the purpose of prosecution and trial in accordance with the applicable rules of international law; and
>
> (b) Any such persons who do not benefit from more favourable treatment under the Conventions or this Protocol shall be accorded the treatment provided by this Article, whether or not the crimes of which they are accused constitute grave breaches of the Conventions or of this Protocol.

8. No provision of this Article may be construed as limiting or infringing any other more favourable provision granting greater protection, under any applicable rules of international law, to persons covered by paragraph 1.

....

PART V
EXECUTION OF THE CONVENTIONS AND OF THIS PROTOCOL

SECTION I—GENERAL PROVISIONS

Article 80. Measures for execution

1. The High Contracting Parties and the Parties to the conflict shall without delay take all necessary measures for the execution of their obligations under the Conventions and this Protocol.

2. The High Contracting Parties and the Parties to the conflict shall give orders and instructions to ensure observance of the Conventions and this Protocol, and shall supervise their execution.

Article 81. Activities of the Red Cross and other humanitarian organizations

1. The Parties to the conflict shall grant to the International Committee of the Red Cross all facilities within their power so as to enable it to carry out the humanitarian

functions assigned to it by the Conventions and this Protocol in order to ensure protection and assistance to the victims of conflicts; the International Committee of the Red Cross may also carry out any other humanitarian activities in favour of these victims, subject to the consent of the Parties to the conflict concerned.

2. The Parties to the conflict shall grant to their respective Red Cross (Red Crescent, Red Lion and Sun) organizations the facilities necessary for carrying out their humanitarian activities in favour of the victims of the conflict, in accordance with the provisions of the Conventions and this Protocol and the fundamental principles of the Red Cross as formulated by the International Conferences of the Red Cross.

3. The High Contracting Parties and the Parties to the conflict shall facilitate in every possible way the assistance which Red Cross (Red Crescent, Red Lion and Sun) organizations and the League of Red Cross Societies extend to the victims of conflicts in accordance with the provisions of the Conventions and this Protocol and with the fundamental principles of the Red Cross as formulated by the International Conferences of the Red Cross.

4. The High Contracting Parties and the Parties to the conflict shall, as far as possible, make facilities similar to those mentioned in paragraphs 2 and 3 available to the other humanitarian organizations referred to in the Conventions and this Protocol which are duly authorized by the respective Parties to the conflict and which perform their humanitarian activities in accordance with the provisions of the Conventions and this Protocol.

Article 82. Legal advisers in armed forces

The High Contracting Parties at all times, and the Parties to the conflict in time of armed conflict, shall ensure that legal advisers are available, when necessary, to advise military commanders at the appropriate level on the application of the Conventions and this Protocol and on the appropriate instruction to be given to the armed forces on this subject.

Article 83. Dissemination

1. The High Contracting Parties undertake, in time of peace as in time of armed conflict, to disseminate the Conventions and this Protocol as widely as possible in their respective countries and, in particular, to include the study thereof in their programmes of military instruction and to encourage the study thereof by the civilian population, so that those instruments may become known to the armed forces and to the civilian population.

2. Any military or civilian authorities who, in time of armed conflict, assume responsibilities in respect of the application of the Conventions and this Protocol shall be fully acquainted with the text thereof.

. . . .

SECTION II—REPRESSION OF BREACHES OF THE CONVENTIONS AND OF THIS PROTOCOL

Article 85. Repression of breaches of this Protocol

1. The provisions of the Conventions relating to the repression of breaches and grave breaches, supplemented by this Section, shall apply to the repression of breaches and grave breaches of this Protocol.

2. Acts described as grave breaches in the Conventions are grave breaches of this Protocol if committed against persons in the power of an adverse Party protected by Ar-

ticles 44, 45 and 73 of this Protocol, or against the wounded, sick and shipwrecked of the adverse Party who are protected by this Protocol, or against those medical or religious personnel, medical units or medical transports which are under the control of the adverse Party and are protected by this Protocol.

3. In addition to the grave breaches defined in Article 11, the following acts shall be regarded as grave breaches of this Protocol, when committed willfully, in violation of the relevant provisions of this Protocol, and causing death or serious injury to body or health:

(a) Making the civilian population or individual civilians the object of attack;

(b) Launching an indiscriminate attack affecting the civilian population or civilian objects in the knowledge that such attack will cause excessive loss of life, injury to civilians or damage to civilian objects, as defined in Article 57, paragraph 2 (a) (iii);

(c) Launching an attack against works or installations containing dangerous forces in the knowledge that such attack will cause excessive loss of life, injury to civilians or damage to civilian objects, as defined in Article 57, paragraph 2 (a) (iii);

(d) Making non-defended localities and demilitarized zones the object of attack;

(e) Making a person the object of attack in the knowledge that he is *hors de combat*;

(f) The perfidious use, in violation of Article 37, of the distinctive emblem of the red cross, red crescent or red lion and sun or of other protective signs recognized by the Conventions or this Protocol.

4. In addition to the grave breaches defined in the preceding paragraphs and in the Conventions, the following shall be regarded as grave breaches of this Protocol, when committed wilfully and in violation of the Conventions of the Protocol;

(a) The transfer by the Occupying Power of parts of its own civilian population into the territory it occupies, or the deportation or transfer of all or parts of the population of the occupied territory within or outside this territory, in violation of Article 49 of the Fourth Convention;

(b) Unjustifiable delay in the repatriation of prisoners of war or civilians;

(c) Practices of apartheid and other inhuman and degrading practices involving outrages upon personal dignity, based on racial discrimination;

(d) Making the clearly-recognized historic monuments, works of art or places of worship which constitute the cultural or spiritual heritage of peoples and to which special protection has been given by special arrangement, for example, within the framework of a competent international organization, the object of attack, causing as a result extensive destruction thereof, where there is no evidence of the violation by the adverse Party of Article 53, sub-paragraph (b), and when such historic monuments, works of art and places of worship are not located in the immediate proximity of military objectives:

(e) Depriving a person protected by the Conventions or referred to in paragraph 2 of this Article of the rights of fair and regular trial.

5. Without prejudice to the application of the Conventions and of this Protocol, grave breaches of these instruments shall be regarded as war crimes.

Article 86. Failure to act

. . . .

2. The fact that a breach of the Conventions or of this Protocol was committed by a subordinate does not absolve his superiors from penal or disciplinary responsibility, as the case may be, if they knew, or had information which should have enabled them to conclude in the circumstances at the time, that he was committing or was going to commit such a breach and if they did not take all feasible measures within their power to prevent or repress the breach.

Article 87. Duty of commanders

1. The High Contracting Parties and the Parties to the conflict shall require military commanders, with respect to members of the armed forces under their command and other persons under their control, to prevent and, where necessary, to suppress and to report to competent authorities breaches of the Conventions and of this Protocol.

2. In order to prevent and suppress breaches, High Contracting Parties and Parties to the conflict shall require that, commensurate with their level of responsibility, commanders ensure that members of the armed forces under their command are aware of their obligations under the Conventions and this Protocol.

3. The High Contracting Parties and Parties to the conflict shall require any commander who is aware that subordinates or other persons under his control are going to commit or have committed a breach of the Conventions or of this Protocol, to initiate such steps as are necessary to prevent such violations of the Conventions or this Protocol, and, where appropriate, to initiate disciplinary or penal action against violators thereof.

. . . .

PROTOCOL ADDITIONAL TO THE GENEVA CONVENTIONS OF 12 AUGUST 1949, AND RELATING TO THE PROTECTION OF VICTIMS OF NON-INTERNATIONAL ARMED CONFLICTS* (PROTOCOL II)

Preamble

The High Contracting Parties,

Recalling that the humanitarian principles enshrined in Article 3 common to the Geneva Conventions of 12 August 1949 constitute the foundation of respect for the human person in cases of armed conflict not of an international character,

Recalling furthermore that international instruments relating to human rights offer a basic protection to the human person,

Emphasizing the need to ensure a better protection for the victims of those armed conflicts,

Recalling that, in cases not covered by the law in force, the human person remains under the protection of the principles of humanity and the dictates of the public conscience,

Have agreed on the following:

PART I
SCOPE OF THIS PROTOCOL

Article 1. Material field of application

1. This Protocol, which develops and supplements Article 3 common to the Geneva Conventions of 12 August 1949 without modifying its existing conditions of application, shall apply to all armed conflicts which are not covered by Article 1 of the Protocol Additional to the Geneva Conventions of 12 August 1949, and relating to the Protection of Victims of International Armed Conflicts (Protocol I) and which take place in the territory of a High Contracting Party between its armed forces and dissident armed forces or other organized armed groups which, under responsible command, exercise such control over a part of its territory as to enable them to carry out sustained and concerted military operations and to implement this Protocol.

2. This Protocol shall not apply to situations of internal disturbances and tensions, such as riots, isolated and sporadic acts of violence and other acts of a similar nature, as not being armed conflicts.

---

* Protocol Additional to the Geneva Conventions of 12 August 1949, and Relating to the Protection of Victims of Non-International Armed Conflicts (Protocol II), June 8, 1977, S. TREATY DOC. No. 100-2, at 7, 1125 U.N.T.S. 609 (entered into force Dec. 7, 1978), *available at* http://www.unhchr.ch/html/menu3/b/94.htm.

Article 2. Personal field of application

1. This Protocol shall be applied without any adverse distinction founded on race, colour, sex, language, religion or belief, political or other opinion, national or social origin, wealth, birth or other status, or on any other similar criteria (hereinafter referred to as "adverse distinction") to all persons affected by an armed conflict as defined in Article 1.

2. At the end of the armed conflict, all the persons who have been deprived of their liberty or whose liberty has been restricted for reasons related to such conflict, as well as those deprived of their liberty or whose liberty is restricted after the conflict for the same reasons, shall enjoy the protection of Articles 5 and 6 until the end of such deprivation or restriction of liberty.

Article 3. Non-intervention

1. Nothing in this Protocol shall be invoked for the purpose of affecting the sovereignty of a State or the responsibility of the government, by all legitimate means, to maintain or re-establish law and order in the State or to defend the national unity and territorial integrity of the State.

2. Nothing in this Protocol shall be invoked as a justification for intervening, directly or indirectly, for any reason whatever, in the armed conflict or in the internal or external affairs of the High Contracting Party in the territory of which that conflict occurs.

PART II
HUMANE TREATMENT

Article 4. Fundamental guarantees

1. All persons who do not take a direct part or who have ceased to take part in hostilities, whether or not their liberty has been restricted, are entitled to respect for their person, honour and convictions and religious practices. They shall in all circumstances be treated humanely, without any adverse distinction. It is prohibited to order that there shall be no survivors.

2. Without prejudice to the generality of the foregoing, the following acts against the persons referred to in paragraph I are and shall remain prohibited at any time and in any place whatsoever:

(a) Violence to the life, health and physical or mental well-being of persons, in particular murder as well as cruel treatment such as torture, mutilation or any form of corporal punishment;

(b) Collective punishments;

(c) Taking of hostages;

(d) Acts of terrorism;

(e) Outrages upon personal dignity, in particular humiliating and degrading treatment, rape, enforced prostitution and any form of indecent assault;

(f) Slavery and the slave trade in all their forms;

(g) Pillage;

(h) Threats to commit any of the foregoing acts.

3. Children shall be provided with the care and aid they require, and in particular:

(a) They shall receive an education, including religious and moral education, in keeping with the wishes of their parents, or in the absence of parents, of those responsible for their care;

(b) All appropriate steps shall be taken to facilitate the reunion of families temporarily separated;

(c) Children who have not attained the age of fifteen years shall neither be recruited in the armed forces or groups nor allowed to take part in hostilities;

(d) The special protection provided by this Article to children who have not attained the age of fifteen years shall remain applicable to them if they take a direct part in hostilities despite the provisions of sub-paragraph (c) and are captured;

(e) Measures shall be taken, if necessary, and whenever possible with the consent of their parents or persons who by law or custom are primarily responsible for their care, to remove children temporarily from the area in which hostilities are taking place to a safer area within the country and ensure that they are accompanied by persons responsible for their safety and well-being.

Article 5. Persons whose liberty has been restricted

1. In addition to the provisions of Article 4, the following provisions shall be respected as a minimum with regard to persons deprived of their liberty for reasons related to the armed conflict, whether they are interned or detained:

(a) The wounded and the sick shall be treated in accordance with Article 7;

(b) The persons referred to in this paragraph shall, to the same extent as the local civilian population, be provided with food and drinking water and be afforded safeguards as regards health and hygiene and protection against the rigours of the climate and the dangers of the armed conflict;

(c) They shall be allowed to receive individual or collective relief;

(d) They shall be allowed to practise their religion and, if requested and appropriate, to receive spiritual assistance from persons, such as chaplains, performing religious functions;

(e) They shall, if made to work, have the benefit of working conditions and safeguards similar to those enjoyed by the local civilian population.

2. Those who are responsible for the internment or detention of the persons referred to in paragraph I shall also, within the limits of their capabilities, respect the following provisions relating to such persons:

(a) Except when men and women of a family are accommodated together, women shall be held in quarters separated from those of men and shall be under the immediate supervision of women;

(b) They shall be allowed to send and receive letters and cards, the number of which may be limited by the competent authority if it deems necessary;

(c) Places of internment and detention shall not be located close to the combat zone. The persons referred to in paragraph 1 shall be evacuated when the places where they are interned or detained become particularly exposed to danger arising out of the armed conflict, if their evacuation can be carried out under adequate conditions of safety;

(d) They shall have the benefit of medical examinations;

(e) Their physical or mental health and integrity shall not be endangered by an unjustified act or omission. Accordingly, it is prohibited to subject the persons described in this Article to any medical procedure which is not indicated by the state of health of the person concerned, and which is not consistent with the generally accepted medical standards applied to free persons under similar medical circumstances.

3. Persons who are not covered by paragraph 1 but whose liberty has been restricted in any way whatsoever for reasons related to the armed conflict shall be treated humanely in accordance with Article 4 and with paragraphs 1 (a), (c) and (d), and 2 (b) of this Article.

4. If it is decided to release persons deprived of their liberty, necessary measures to ensure their safety shall be taken by those so deciding.

Article 6. Penal prosecutions

1. This Article applies to the prosecution and punishment of criminal offences related to the armed conflict.

2. No sentence shall be passed and no penalty shall be executed on a person found guilty of an offence except pursuant to a conviction pronounced by a court offering the essential guarantees of independence and impartiality. In particular:

(a) The procedure shall provide for an accused to be informed without delay of the particulars of the offence alleged against him and shall afford the accused before and during his trial all necessary rights and means of defence;

(b) No one shall be convicted of an offence except on the basis of individual penal responsibility;

(c) No one shall be held guilty of any criminal offence on account of any act or omission which did not constitute a criminal offence, under the law, at the time when it was committed; nor shall a heavier penalty be imposed than that which was applicable at the time when the criminal offence was committed; if, after the commission of the offence, provision is made by law for the imposition of a lighter penalty, the offender shall benefit thereby;

(d) Anyone charged with an offence is presumed innocent until proved guilty according to law;

(e) Anyone charged with an offence shall have the right to be tried in his presence;

(f) No one shall be compelled to testify against himself or to confess guilt.

3. A convicted person shall be advised on conviction of his judicial and other remedies and of the time-limits within which they may be exercised.

4. The death penalty shall not be pronounced on persons who were under the age of eighteen years at the time of the offence and shall not be carried out on pregnant women or mothers of young children.

5. At the end of hostilities, the authorities in power shall endeavour to grant the broadest possible amnesty to persons who have participated in the armed conflict, or those deprived of their liberty for reasons related to the armed conflict, whether they are interned or detained.

PART III
WOUNDED, SICK AND SHIPWRECKED

Article 7. Protection and care

1. All the wounded, sick and shipwrecked, whether or not they have taken part in the armed conflict, shall be respected and protected.

2. In all circumstances they shall be treated humanely and shall receive, to the fullest extent practicable and with the least possible delay, the medical care and attention required by their condition. There shall be no distinction among them founded on any grounds other than medical ones.

Article 8. Search

Whenever circumstances permit, and particularly after an engagement, all possible measures shall be taken, without delay, to search for and collect the wounded, sick and shipwrecked, to protect them against pillage and ill-treatment, to ensure their adequate care, and to search for the dead, prevent their being despoiled, and decently dispose of them.

Article 9. Protection of medical and religious personnel

1. Medical and religious personnel shall be respected and protected and shall be granted all available help for the performance of their duties. They shall not be compelled to carry out tasks which are not compatible with their humanitarian mission.

2. In the performance of their duties medical personnel may not be required to give priority to any person except on medical grounds.

Article 10. General protection of medical duties

1. Under no circumstances shall any person be punished for having carried out medical activities compatible with medical ethics, regardless of the person benefiting therefrom.

2. Persons engaged in medical activities shall neither be compelled to perform acts or to carry out work contrary to, nor be compelled to refrain from acts required by, the rules of medical ethics or other rules designed for the benefit of the wounded and sick, or this Protocol.

3. The professional obligations of persons engaged in medical activities regarding information which they may acquire concerning the wounded and sick under their care shall, subject to national law, be respected.

4. Subject to national law, no person engaged in medical activities may be penalized in any way for refusing or failing to give information concerning the wounded and sick who are, or who have been, under his care.

Article 11. Protection of medical units and transports

1. Medical units and transports shall be respected and protected at all times and shall not be the object of attack.

2. The protection to which medical units and transports are entitled shall not cease unless they are used to commit hostile acts, outside their humanitarian function. Protection may, however, cease only after a warning has been given setting, whenever appropriate, a reasonable time-limit, and after such warning has remained unheeded.

Article 12. The distinctive emblem

Under the direction of the competent authority concerned, the distinctive emblem of the red cross, red crescent or red lion and sun on a white ground shall be displayed by medical and religious personnel and medical units, and on medical transports. It shall be respected in all circumstances. It shall not be used improperly.

PART IV
CIVILIAN POPULATION

Article 13. Protection of the civilian population

1. The civilian population and individual civilians shall enjoy general protection against the dangers arising from military operations. To give effect to this protection, the following rules shall be observed in all circumstances.

2. The civilian population as such, as well as individual civilians, shall not be the object of attack. Acts or threats of violence the primary purpose of which is to spread terror among the civilian population are prohibited.

3. Civilians shall enjoy the protection afforded by this Part, unless and for such time as they take a direct part in hostilities.

Article 14. Protection of objects indispensable to the survival of the civilian population

Starvation of civilians as a method of combat is prohibited. It is therefore prohibited to attack, destroy, remove or render useless, for that purpose, objects indispensable to the survival of the civilian population, such as foodstuffs, agricultural areas for the production of foodstuffs, crops, livestock, drinking water installations and supplies and irrigation works.

Article 15. Protection of works and installations containing dangerous forces

Works or installations containing dangerous forces, namely dams, dykes and nuclear electrical generating stations, shall not be made the object of attack, even where these objects are military objectives, if such attack may cause the release of dangerous forces and consequent severe losses among the civilian population.

Article 16. Protection of cultural objects and of places of worship

Without prejudice to the provisions of The Hague Convention for the Protection of Cultural Property in the Event of Armed Conflict of 14 May 1954, it is prohibited to commit any acts of hostility directed against historic monuments, works of art or places of worship which constitute the cultural or spiritual heritage of peoples, and to use them in support of the military effort.

Article 17. Prohibition of forced movement of civilians

1. The displacement of the civilian population shall not be ordered for reasons related to the conflict unless the security of the civilians involved or imperative military reasons so demand. Should such displacements have to be carried out, all possible measures shall be taken in order that the civilian population may be received under satisfactory conditions of shelter, hygiene, health, safety and nutrition.

2. Civilians shall not be compelled to leave their own territory for reasons connected with the conflict.

Article 18. Relief societies and relief actions

1. Relief societies located in the territory of the High Contracting Party, such as Red Cross (Red Crescent, Red Lion and Sun) organizations, may offer their services for the performance of their traditional functions in relation to the victims of the armed conflict. The civilian population may, even on its own initiative, offer to collect and care for the wounded, sick and shipwrecked.

2. If the civilian population is suffering undue hardship owing to a lack of the supplies essential for its survival, such as foodstuffs and medical supplies, relief actions for the civilian population which are of an exclusively humanitarian and impartial nature

and which are conducted without any adverse distinction shall be undertaken subject to the consent of the High Contracting Party concerned.

. . . .

CONVENTION ON PROHIBITIONS OR RESTRICTIONS ON THE USE OF CERTAIN CONVENTIONAL WEAPONS WHICH MAY BE DEEMED TO BE EXCESSIVELY INJURIOUS OR TO HAVE INDISCRIMINATE EFFECTS* (CCCW)

The High Contracting Parties,

Recalling that every State has the duty, in conformity with the Charter of the United Nations, to refrain in its international relations from the threat or use of force against the sovereignty, territorial integrity or political independence of any State, or in any other manner inconsistent with the purposes of the United Nations,

Further recalling the general principle of the protection of the civilian population against the effects of hostilities,

Basing themselves on the principle of international law that the right of the parties to an armed conflict to choose methods or means of warfare is not unlimited, and on the principle that prohibits the employment in armed conflicts of weapons, projectiles and material and methods of warfare of a nature to cause superfluous injury or unnecessary suffering,

Also recalling that it is prohibited to employ methods or means of warfare which are intended, or may be expected, to cause widespread, long-term and severe damage to the natural environment,

Confirming their determination that in cases not covered by this Convention and its annexed Protocols or by other international agreements, the civilian population and the combatants shall at all times remain under the protection and authority of the principles of international law derived from established custom, from the principles of humanity and from the dictates of public conscience,

Desiring to contribute to international detente, the ending of the arms race and the building of confidence among States, and hence to the realization of the aspiration of all peoples to live in peace,

Recognizing the importance of pursuing every effort which may contribute to progress towards general and complete disarmament under strict and effective international control,

Reaffirming the need to continue the codification and progressive development of the rules of international law applicable in armed conflict,

Wishing to prohibit or restrict further the use of certain conventional weapons and believing that the positive results achieved in this area may facilitate the main talks on

---

* Convention on Prohibitions or Restrictions on the Use of Certain Conventional Weapons Which May Be Deemed to Be Excessively Injurious or to Have Indiscriminate Effects, Oct. 10, 1980, S. Treaty Doc. Nos. 103-25, at 6, 105-1, at 37, 1342 U.N.T.S. 137 (entered into force Dec. 2, 1983), *available at* http://disarmament.un.org:8080/TreatyStatus.nsf/44e6eeabc9436b78852568770078d9c0/3ce9f6e537ca47dd852568770079dd9b?OpenDocument.

disarmament with a view to putting an end to the production, stockpiling and proliferation of such weapons,

Emphasizing the desirability that all States become parties to this Convention and its annexed Protocols, especially the militarily significant States,

Bearing in mind that the General Assembly of the United Nations and the United Nations Disarmament Commission may decide to examine the question of a possible broadening of the scope of the prohibitions and restrictions contained in this Convention and its annexed Protocols,

Further bearing in mind that the Committee on Disarmament may decide to consider the question of adopting further measures to prohibit or restrict the use of certain conventional weapons,

Have agreed as follows:

Article 1. Scope of application. This Convention and its annexed Protocols shall apply in the situations referred to in Article 2 common to the Geneva Conventions of 12 August 1949 for the Protection of War Victims, including any situation described in paragraph 4 of Article 1 of Additional Protocol I to these Conventions.

Article 2. Relations with other international agreements. Nothing in this Convention or its annexed Protocols shall be interpreted as detracting from other obligations imposed upon the High Contracting Parties by international humanitarian law applicable in armed conflict.

Article 3. Signature. This Convention shall be open for signature by all States at United Nations Headquarters in New York for a period of twelve months from 10 April 1981.

Article 4. Ratification, acceptance, approval or accession. 1. This Convention is subject to ratification, acceptance or approval by the Signatories. Any State which has not signed this Convention may accede to it.

2. The instrument of ratification, acceptance, approval or accession shall be deposited with the Depositary.

3. Expressions of consent to be bound by any of the Protocols annexed to this Convention shall be optional for each State, provided that at the time of the deposit of its instrument of ratification, acceptance or approval of this Convention or of accession thereto, that State shall notify the Depositary of its consent to be bound by any two or more of these Protocols.

4. At any time after the deposit of its instrument of ratification, acceptance or approval of this Convention or of accession thereto, a State may notify the Depositary of its consent to be bound by any annexed Protocol by which it is not already bound.

5. Any Protocol by which a High Contracting Party is bound shall for that Party form an integral part of this Convention.

Article 5. Entry into force. 1. This Convention shall enter into force six months after the date of deposit of the twentieth instrument of ratification, acceptance, approval or accession.

2. For any State which deposits its instrument of ratification, acceptance, approval or accession after the date of the deposit of the twentieth instrument of ratification, acceptance, approval or accession, this Convention shall enter into force six months after the date on which that State has deposited its instrument of ratification, acceptance, approval or accession.

3. Each of the Protocols annexed to this Convention shall enter into force six months after the date by which twenty States have notified their consent to be bound by it in accordance with paragraph 3 or 4 of Article 4 of this Convention.

4. For any State which notifies its consent to be bound by a Protocol, annexed to this Convention after the date by which twenty States have notified their consent to be bound by it, the Protocol shall enter into force six months after the date on which that State has notified its consent so to be bound.

Article 6. *Dissemination.* The High Contracting Parties undertake, in time of peace as in time of armed conflict, to disseminate this Convention and those of its annexed Protocols by which they are bound as widely as possible in their respective countries and, in particular, to include the study thereof in their programmes of military instruction, so that those instruments may become known to their armed forces.

Article 7. *Treaty relations upon entry into force of this Convention.* 1. When one of the parties to a conflict is not bound by an annexed Protocol, the parties bound by this Convention and that annexed Protocol shall remain bound by them in their mutual relations.

2. Any High Contracting Party shall be bound by this Convention and any Protocol annexed thereto which is in force for it, in any situation contemplated by Article 1, in relation to any State which is not a party to this Convention or bound by the relevant annexed Protocol, if the latter accepts and applies this Convention or the relevant Protocol, and so notifies the Depositary.

3. The Depositary shall immediately inform the High Contracting Parties concerned of any notification received under paragraph 2 of this Article.

4. This Convention, and the annexed Protocols by which a High Contracting Party is bound, shall apply with respect to an armed conflict against that High Contracting Party of the type referred to in Article 1, paragraph 4, of Additional Protocol I to the Geneva Conventions of 12 August 1949 for the Protection of War Victims:

(a) where the High Contracting Party is also a party to Additional Protocol I and an authority referred to in Article 96, paragraph 3, of that Protocol has undertaken to apply the Geneva Conventions and Additional Protocol I in accordance with Article 96, paragraph 3, of the said Protocol, and undertakes to apply this Convention and the relevant annexed Protocols in relation to that conflict; or

(b) where the High Contracting Party is not a party to Additional Protocol I and an authority of the type referred to in subparagraph (a) above accepts and applies the obligations of the Geneva Conventions and of this Convention and the relevant annexed Protocols in relation to that conflict. Such an acceptance and application shall have in relation to that conflict the following effects:

(i) the Geneva Conventions and this Convention and its relevant annexed Protocols are brought into force for the parties to the conflict with immediate effect;

(ii) the said authority assumes the same rights and obligations as those which have been assumed by a High Contracting Party to the Geneva Conventions, this Convention and its relevant annexed Protocols; and

(iii) the Geneva Conventions, this Convention and its relevant annexed Protocols are equally binding upon all parties to the conflict.

The High Contracting Party and the authority may also agree to accept and apply the obligations of Additional Protocol I to the Geneva Conventions on a reciprocal basis.

Article 8. Review and amendments. 1. (a) At any time after the entry into force of this Convention any High Contracting Party may propose amendments to this Convention or any annexed Protocol by which it is bound. Any proposal for an amendment shall be communicated to the Depositary, who shall notify it to all the High Contracting Parties and shall seek their views on whether a conference should be convened to consider the proposal. If a majority, that shall not be less than eighteen of the High Contracting Parties, so agree, he shall promptly convene a conference to which all High Contracting Parties shall be invited. States not parties to this Convention shall be invited to the conference as observers.

(b) Such a conference may agree upon amendments which shall be adopted and shall enter into force in the same manner as this Convention and the annexed Protocols, provided that amendments to this Convention may be adopted only by the High Contracting Parties and that amendments to a specific annexed Protocol may be adopted only by the High Contracting Parties which are bound by that Protocol.

2. (a) At any time after the entry into force of this Convention any High Contracting Party may propose additional protocols relating to other categories of conventional weapons not covered by the existing annexed Protocols. Any such proposal for an additional protocol shall be communicated to the Depositary, who shall notify it to all the High Contracting Parties in accordance with subparagraph 1 (a) of this Article. If a majority, that shall not be less than eighteen of the High Contracting Parties, so agree, the Depositary shall promptly convene a conference to which all States shall be invited.

(b) Such a conference may agree, with the full participation of all States represented at the conference, upon additional protocols which shall be adopted in the same manner as this Convention, shall be annexed thereto and shall enter into force as provided in paragraphs 3 and 4 of Article 5 of this Convention.

3. (a) If, after a period of ten years following the entry into force of this Convention, no conference has been convened in accordance with subparagraph 1 (a) or 2 (a) of this Article, any High Contracting Party may request the Depositary to convene a conference to which all High Contracting Parties shall be invited to review the scope and operation of this Convention and the Protocols annexed thereto and to consider any proposal for amendments of this Convention or of the existing Protocols. States not Parties to this Convention shall be invited as observers to the conference. The conference may agree upon amendments which shall be adopted and enter into force in accordance with subparagraph 1 (b) above.

(b) At such conference consideration may also be given to any proposal for additional protocols relating to other categories of conventional weapons not covered by the existing annexed Protocols. All States represented at the conference may participate fully in such consideration. Any additional protocols shall be adopted in the same manner as this Convention, shall be annexed thereto and shall enter into force as provided in paragraphs 3 and 4 of Article 5 of this Convention.

(c) Such a conference may consider whether provision should be made for the convening of a further conference at the request of any High Contracting Party if, after a similar period to that referred to in subparagraph 3 (a) of this Article, no conference has been convened in accordance with subparagraph 1 (a) or 2 (a) of this Article.

Article 9. *Denunciation.* 1. Any High Contracting Party may denounce this Convention or any of its annexed Protocols by so notifying the Depositary.

2. Any such denunciation shall only take effect one year after receipt by the Depositary of the notification of denunciation. If, however, on the expiry of that year the denouncing High Contracting Party is engaged in one of the situations referred to in Article 1, the Party shall continue to be bound by the obligations of this Convention and of the relevant annexed Protocols until the end of the armed conflict or occupation and, in any case, until the termination of operations connected with the final release, repatriation or reestablishment of the person protected by the rules of international law applicable in armed conflict, and in the case of any annexed Protocol containing provisions concerning situations in which peace-keeping, observation or similar functions are performed by United Nations forces or missions in the area concerned, until the termination of those functions.

3. Any denunciation of this Convention shall be considered as also applying to all annexed Protocols by which the denouncing High Contracting Party is bound.

4. Any denunciation shall have effect only in respect of the denouncing High Contracting Party.

5. Any denunciation shall not affect the obligations already incurred, by reason of an armed conflict, under this Convention and its annexed Protocols by such denouncing High Contracting Party in respect of any act committed before this denunciation becomes effective.

Article 10. *Depositary.* 1. The Secretary-General of the United Nations shall be the Depositary of this Convention and of its annexed Protocols.

2. In addition to his usual functions, the Depositary shall inform all States of:

(a) signatures affixed to this Convention under Article 3;

(b) deposits of instruments of ratification, acceptance or approval of or accession to this Convention deposited under Article 4;

(c) notifications of consent to be bound by annexed Protocols under Article 4;

(d) the dates of entry into force of this Convention and of each of its annexed Protocols under Article 5; and

(e) notifications of denunciation received under article 9, and their effective date.

Article 11. *Authentic texts.* The original of this Convention with the annexed Protocols, of which the Arabic, Chinese, English, French, Russian and Spanish texts are equally authentic, shall be deposited with the Depositary, who shall transmit certified true copies thereof to all States.

Protocol on Non-Detectable Fragments (Protocol I)

It is prohibited to use any weapon the primary effect of which is to injure by fragments which in the human body escape detection by X-rays.

Protocol on Prohibitions or Restrictions on the Use of Mines, Booby-Traps and Other Devices (Protocol II)

Article 1. *Material scope of application.* This Protocol relates to the use on land of the mines, booby-traps and other devices defined herein, including mines laid to interdict beaches, waterway crossings or river crossings, but does not apply to the use of anti-ship mines at sea or in inland waterways.

Article 2. *Definitions.* For the purpose of this Protocol:

1. "Mine" means any munition placed under, on or near the ground or other surface area and designed to be detonated or exploded by the presence, proximity or contact of a person or vehicle, and "remotely delivered mine" means any mine so defined delivered by artillery, rocket, mortar or similar means or dropped from an aircraft.

2. "Booby-trap" means any device or material which is designed, constructed or adapted to kill or injure and which functions unexpectedly when a person disturbs or approaches an apparently harmless object or performs an apparently safe act.

3. "Other devices" means manually-emplaced munitions and devices designed to kill, injure or damage and which are actuated by remote control or automatically after a lapse of time.

4. "Military objective" means, so far as objects are concerned, any object which by its nature, location, purpose or use makes an effective contribution to military action and whose total or partial destruction, capture or neutralization, in the circumstances ruling at the time, offers a definite military advantage.

5. "Civilian objects" are all objects which are not military objectives as defined in paragraph 4.

6. "Recording" means a physical, administrative and technical operation designed to obtain, for the purpose of registration in the official records, all available information facilitating the location of minefields, mines and booby-traps.

Article 3. *General restrictions on the use of mines, booby-traps and other devices.* 1. This Article applies to:

(a) mines;

(b) booby-traps; and

(c) other devices.

2. It is prohibited in all circumstances to direct weapons to which this Article applies, either in offence, defence or by way of reprisals, against the civilian population as such or against individual civilians.

3. The indiscriminate use of weapons to which this Article applies is prohibited. Indiscriminate use is any placement of such weapons:

(a) which is not on, or directed at, a military objective; or

(b) which employs a method or means of delivery which cannot be directed at a specific military objective; or

(c) which may be expected to cause incidental loss of civilian life, injury to civilians, damage to civilian objects, or a combination thereof, which would be excessive in relation to the concrete and direct military advantage anticipated.

4. All feasible precautions shall be taken to protect civilians from the effects of weapons to which this Article applies. Feasible precautions are those precautions which are practicable or practically possible taking into account all circumstances ruling at the time, including humanitarian and military considerations.

Article 4. *Restrictions on the use of mines other than remotely delivered mines, booby-traps and other devices in populated areas.* 1. This Article applies to:

(a) mines other than remotely delivered mines;

(b) booby-traps; and

(c) other devices.

2. It is prohibited to use weapons to which this Article applies in any city, town, village or other area containing a similar concentration of civilians in which combat between ground forces is not taking place or does not appear to be imminent, unless either:

(a) they are placed on or in the close vicinity of a military objective belonging to or under the control of an adverse party; or

(b) measures are taken to protect civilians from their effects, for example, the posting of warning signs, the posting of sentries, the issue of warnings or the provision of fences.

Article 5. *Restrictions on the use of remotely delivered mines.* 1. The use of remotely delivered mines is prohibited unless such mines are only used within an area which is itself a military objective or which contains military objectives, and unless:

(a) their location can be accurately recorded in accordance with Article 7(1)(a); or

(b) an effective neutralizing mechanism is used on each such mine, that is to say, a self-actuating mechanism which is designed to render a mine harmless or cause it to destroy itself when it is anticipated that the mine will no longer serve the military purpose for which it was placed in position, or a remotely-controlled mechanism which is designed to render harmless or destroy a mine when the mine no longer serves the military purpose for which it was placed in position.

2. Effective advance warning shall be given of any delivery or dropping of remotely delivered mines which may affect the civilian population, unless circumstances do not permit.

Article 6. *Prohibition on the use of certain booby-traps.* 1. Without prejudice to the rules of international law applicable in armed conflict relating to treachery and perfidy, it is prohibited in all circumstances to use:

(a) any booby-trap in the form of an apparently harmless portable object which is specifically designed and constructed to contain explosive material and to detonate when it is disturbed or approached; or

(b) booby-traps which are in any way attached to or associated with:

(i) internationally recognized protective emblems, signs or signals;

(ii) sick, wounded or dead persons;

(iii) burial or cremation sites or graves;

(iv) medical facilities, medical equipment, medical supplies or medical transportation;

(v) children's toys or other portable objects or products specially designed for the feeding, health, hygiene, clothing or education of children;

(vi) food or drink;

(vii) kitchen utensils or appliances except in military establishments, military locations or military supply depots;

(viii) objects clearly of a religious nature;

(ix) historic monuments, works of art or places or worship which constitute the cultural or spiritual heritage of peoples;

(x) animals or their carcasses.

2. It is prohibited in all circumstances to use any booby-trap which is designed to cause superfluous injury or unnecessary suffering.

Article 7. *Recording and publication of the location of minefields, mines and booby-traps.* 1. The parties to a conflict shall record the location of:

(a) all pre-planned minefields laid by them; and

(b) all areas in which they have made large-scale and pre-planned use of booby-traps.

2. The parties shall endeavour to ensure the recording of the location of all other minefields, mines and booby-traps which they have laid or placed in position.

3. All such records shall be retained by the parties who shall:

(a) immediately after the cessation of active hostilities:

(i) take all necessary and appropriate measures, including the use of such records, to protect civilians from the effects of minefields, mines and booby-traps; and either

(ii) in cases where the forces of neither party are in the territory of the adverse party, make available to each other and to the Secretary-General of the United Nations all information in their possession concerning the location of minefields, mines and booby-traps in the territory of the adverse party; or

(iii) once complete withdrawal of the forces of the parties from the territory of the adverse party has taken place, make available to the adverse party and to the Secretary-General of the United Nations all information in their possession concerning the location of minefields, mines and booby-traps in the territory of the adverse party;

(b) when a United Nations force or mission performs functions in any area, make available to the authority mentioned in Article 8 such information as is required by that Article;

(c) whenever possible, by mutual agreement, provide for the release of information concerning the location of minefields, mines and booby-traps, particularly in agreements governing the cessation of hostilities.

Article 8. *Protection of United Nations forces and missions from the effects of minefields, mines and booby-traps.* 1. When a United Nations force or mission performs functions of peace-keeping, observation or similar functions in any area, each party to the conflict shall, if requested by the head of the United Nations force or mission in that area, as far as it is able:

(a) remove or render harmless all mines or booby-traps in that area;

(b) take such measures as may be necessary to protect the force or mission from the effects of minefields, mines and booby-traps while carrying out its duties; and

(c) make available to the head of the United Nations force or mission in that area, all information in the party's possession concerning the location of minefields, mines and booby-traps in that area.

2. When a United Nations fact-finding mission performs functions in any area, any party to the conflict concerned shall provide protection to that mission except where, because of the size of such mission, it cannot adequately provide such protection. In that case it shall make available to the head of the mission the information in its possession concerning the location of minefields, mines and booby-traps in that area.

Article 9. International co-operation in the removal of minefields, mines and booby-traps. After the cessation of active hostilities, the parties shall endeavour to reach agreement, both among themselves and, where appropriate, with other States and with international organizations, on the provision of information and technical and material assistance—including, in appropriate circumstances, joint operations—necessary to remove or otherwise render ineffective minefields, mines and booby-traps placed in position during the conflict.

....

Protocol on Prohibitions or Restrictions on the Use of Incendiary Weapons (Protocol III)

Article 1. Definitions. For the purpose of this Protocol:

1. "Incendiary weapon" means any weapon or munition which is primarily designed to set fire to objects or to cause burn injury to persons through the action of flame, heat, or a combination thereof, produced by a chemical reaction of a substance delivered on the target.

(a) Incendiary weapons can take the form of, for example, flame throwers, fougasses, shells, rockets, grenades, mines, bombs and other containers of incendiary substances.

(b) Incendiary weapons do not include:

(i) Munitions which may have incidental incendiary effects, such as illuminants, tracers, smoke or signalling systems;

(ii) Munitions designed to combine penetration, blast or fragmentation effects with an additional incendiary effect, such as armour-piercing projectiles, fragmentation shells, explosive bombs and similar combined-effects munitions in which the incendiary effect is not specifically designed to cause burn injury to persons, but to be used against military objectives, such as armoured vehicles, aircraft and installations or facilities.

2. "Concentration of civilians" means any concentration of civilians, be it permanent or temporary, such as in inhabited parts of cities, or inhabited towns or villages, or as in camps or columns of refugees or evacuees, or groups of nomads.

3. "Military objective" means, so far as objects are concerned, any object which by its nature, location, purpose or use makes an effective contribution to military action and whose total or partial destruction capture or neutralization, in the circumstances ruling at the time, offers a definite military advantage.

4. "Civilian objects" are all objects which are not military objectives as defined in paragraph 3.

5. "Feasible precautions" are those precautions which are practicable or practically possible taking into account all circumstances ruling at the time, including humanitarian and military considerations.

Article 2. Protection of civilians and civilian objects. 1. It is prohibited in all circumstances to make the civilian population as such, individual civilians or civilian objects the object of attack by incendiary weapons.

2. It is prohibited in all circumstances to make any military objective located within a concentration of civilians the object of attack by air-delivered incendiary weapons.

3. It is further prohibited to make any military objective located within a concentration of civilians the object of attack by means of incendiary weapons other than air-delivered incendiary weapons, except when such military objective is clearly separated from the concentration of civilians and all feasible precautions are taken with a view to limiting the incendiary effects to the military objective and to avoiding, and in any event to minimizing, incidental loss of civilian life, injury to civilians and damage to civilian objects.

4. It is prohibited to make forests or other kinds of plant cover the object of attack by incendiary weapons except when such natural elements are used to cover, conceal or camouflage combatants or other military objectives, or are themselves military objectives.

ADDITIONAL PROTOCOL TO THE CONVENTION ON PROHIBITIONS OR RESTRICTIONS ON THE USE OF CERTAIN CONVENTIONAL WEAPONS WHICH MAY BE DEEMED TO BE EXCESSIVELY INJURIOUS OR TO HAVE INDISCRIMINATE EFFECTS: PROTOCOL ON BLINDING LASER WEAPONS*

Article 1. It is prohibited to employ laser weapons specifically designed, as their sole combat function or as one of their combat functions, to cause permanent blindness to unenhanced vision, that is to the naked eye or to the eye with corrective eyesight devices. The High Contracting Parties shall not transfer such weapons to any State or non-State entity.

Article 2. In the employment of laser systems, the High Contracting Parties shall take all feasible precautions to avoid the incidence of permanent blindness to unenhanced vision. Such precautions shall include training of their armed forces and other practical measures.

Article 3. Blinding as an incidental or collateral effect of the legitimate military employment of laser systems, including laser systems used against optical equipment, is not covered by the prohibition of this Protocol.

Article 4. For the purpose of this Protocol "permanent blindness" means irreversible and uncorrectable loss of vision which is seriously disabling with no prospect of recovery. Serious disability is equivalent to visual acuity of less than 20/200 Snellen measured using both eyes.

. . . .

* Additional Protocol to the Convention on Prohibitions or Restrictions on the Use of Certain Conventional Weapons Which May Be Deemed to Be Excessively Injurious or to Have Indiscriminate Effects, Oct. 13, 1995, S. Treaty Doc. No. 105-1, at 60, 2024 U.N.T.S. 164, 167 (entered into force July 30, 1998), *available at* http://www.fas.org/nuke/control/ccw/text/protocol4.htm.

DEPARTMENT OF DEFENSE DIRECTIVE NUMBER 5100.77 LAW OF WAR PROGRAM*

SUBJECT: DoD Law of War Program

References:

(a) DoD Directive 5100.77, "DoD Law of War Program," July 10, 1979 (hereby canceled)

(b) DoD Directive 2310.1, "DoD Program for Enemy Prisoners of War (EPOW) and other Detainees (Short Title: DoD Enemy POW Detainee Program)," August 18, 1994

(c) DoD Directive 5000.1, "Defense Acquisition," March 15, 1996

(d) Hague Convention No. IV, "Respecting the Laws and Customs of War on Land," October 18, 1907

(e) through (1), see enclosure 1

1. <u>REISSUANCE AND PURPOSE</u>

This Directive:

. . . .

1.2. Expands the responsibilities of the Secretary of the Army as the DoD Executive Agent for the investigation and reporting of reportable incidents.

1.3. Establishes the DoD Law of War Working Group.

2. <u>APPLICABILITY AND SCOPE</u>

2.1. This Directive applies to the Office of the Secretary of Defense, the Military Departments, the Chairman of the Joint Chiefs of Staff, the Combatant Commands, the Defense Agencies, and the DoD Field Activities (hereafter referred to collectively as "the DoD Components").

2.2. In implementation of this Directive, reference (b) addresses the DoD program for care and treatment of enemy prisoners of war (EPW), retained persons, and detainees. A reportable incident (as defined in subsection 3.2., below) involving possible, suspected, or alleged violations of the protections afforded EPWs, retained persons, or detainees is included in the scope of this Directive.

2.3. In further implementation of this Directive, that part of the law of war relating to legal reviews of the development, acquisition, and procurement of weapons and weapon systems for the DoD Components is addressed in DoD Directive 5000.1 (reference (c)) and in related guidance pertaining to Special Access Programs.

3. <u>DEFINITIONS</u>

3.1. <u>Law of War</u>. That part of international law that regulates the conduct of armed hostilities. It is often called the law of armed conflict. The law of war encompasses all

---

* U.S. Dep't of Def., Dir. 5100.77, DoD Law of War Program (December 9, 1998), *available at* http://www.dtic.mil/whs/directives/corres/html/510077.htm.

international law for the conduct of hostilities binding on the United States or its individual citizens, including treaties and international agreements to which the United States is a party, and applicable customary international law.

3.2. Reportable Incident. A possible, suspected, or alleged violation of the law of war.

4. POLICY

It is DoD policy to ensure that:

4.1. The law of war obligations of the United States are observed and enforced by the DoD Components.

4.2. An effective program to prevent violations of the law of war is implemented by the DoD Components.

4.3. All reportable incidents committed by or against U.S. or enemy persons are promptly reported, thoroughly investigated, and, where appropriate, remedied by corrective action.

4.4. All reportable incidents committed by or against allied persons, or by or against other persons during a conflict to which the U.S. is not a party, are reported through command channels for ultimate transmission to appropriate U.S. Agencies, allied governments, or other appropriate authorities. Once it has been determined that U.S. persons are not involved in a reportable incident, an additional U.S. investigation shall be continued only at the direction of the appropriate Combatant Commander. On-scene commanders shall ensure that measures are taken to preserve evidence of reportable incidents pending turnover to U.S., allied, or other appropriate authorities.

5. RESPONSIBILITIES

5.1. The General Counsel of the Department of Defense shall:

5.1.1. Provide overall legal guidance in the Department of Defense on the Law of War Program, to include review of policies developed under or relating to the program, coordination of special legislative proposals and other legal matters with other Federal Departments and Agencies, and resolution of disagreements on questions of law.

5.1.2. Establish a DoD Law of War Working Group consisting of representatives from the General Counsel of the Department of Defense (GC, DoD), the Legal Counsel to the Chairman of the Joint Chiefs of Staff, the International and Operational Law Division of the Office of the Judge Advocate General of each Military Department, and the Operational Law Branch of the Office of the Staff Judge Advocate to the Commandant of the Marine Corps. The DoD Law of War Working Group shall develop and coordinate law of war initiatives and issues, manage other law of war matters as they arise, and provide advice to the General Counsel on legal matters covered by this Directive.

5.1.3. Coordinate and monitor the Military Departments' plans and policies for training and education in the law of war.

5.2. The Under Secretary of Defense for Policy shall:

5.2.1. Exercise primary staff responsibility for the DoD Law of War Program.

5.2.2. Ensure that the Assistant Secretary of Defense (International Security Affairs) shall provide overall development, coordination, approval, and promulgation of major DoD policies and plans, including final coordination of such proposed policies and plans with DoD Components and other Federal Departments and Agencies as necessary, and final coordination of DoD positions on international negotiations on the law of war and U.S. signature or ratification of law of war treaties.

5.3. The Heads of the DoD Components shall:

5.3.1. Ensure that the members of their Components comply with the law of war during all armed conflicts, however such conflicts are characterized, and with the principles and spirit of the law of war during all other operations.

5.3.2. Institute and implement effective programs to prevent violations of the law of war, including law of war training and dissemination, as required by references (d) through (h).

5.3.3. Ensure that qualified legal advisers are immediately available at all levels of command to provide advice about law of war compliance during planning and execution of exercises and operations; and institute and implement programs to comply with the reporting requirements established in section 6., below.

5.4. The Assistant Secretary of Defense for Public Affairs shall monitor the public affairs aspects of the DoD Law of War Program and provide public affairs guidance, as appropriate, to the DoD Components.

5.5. The Secretaries of the Military Departments shall develop internal policies and procedures consistent with this Directive in support of the DoD Law of War Program to:

5.5.1. Provide directives, publications, instructions, and training so that the principles and rules of the law of war will be known to members of their respective Departments, the extent of such knowledge to be commensurate with each individual's duties and responsibilities.

5.5.2. Ensure that programs are implemented in their respective Military Departments to prevent violations of the law of war, emphasizing any types of violations that have been reported under this Directive.

5.5.3. Provide for the prompt reporting and investigation of reportable incidents committed by or against members of their respective Military Departments, or persons accompanying them, in accordance with directives issued under paragraph 5.8.4., below.

5.5.4. Where appropriate, provide for disposition, under the Uniform Code of Military Justice (reference (i)), of cases involving alleged violations of the law of war by members of their respective Military Departments who are subject to court-martial jurisdiction.

5.5.5. Provide for the central collection of reports and investigations of reportable incidents alleged to have been committed by or against members of their respective Military Departments, or persons accompanying them.

5.5.6. Ensure that all reports of reportable incidents are forwarded to the Secretary of the Army in his or her capacity as the DoD Executive Agent under subsection 5.6., below.

5.6. The Secretary of the Army, as the Executive Agent for the Secretary of Defense for reportable incidents, shall act for the Secretary of Defense in developing and coordinating plans and policies for, and in supervising the execution of, the investigation of reportable incidents and, subject to DoD 8910.1-M (reference (j)), the collection, recording, and reporting of information concerning reportable incidents. This authority is separate from and subject to the responsibilities assigned the Combatant Commanders in subsections 4.4., above, and 5.8., below, and the responsibilities assigned the Secretaries of the Military Departments in subsection 5.5., above.

5.7. The Chairman of the Joint Chiefs of Staff shall:

5.7.1. Provide appropriate guidance to the Commanders of the Combatant Commands, consistent with 10 U.S.C. 163 (a)(2) (reference (k)), conforming with the policies and procedures in this Directive. This guidance will include direction on the collection and investigation of reports of enemy violations of the law of war.

5.7.2. Designate a primary point of contact in his organization to administer activities under this Directive.

5.7.3. Issue and review appropriate plans, policies, directives, and rules of engagement, as necessary, ensuring their consistency with the law of war obligations of the United States.

5.7.4. Ensure that plans, policies, directives, and rules of engagement issued by the Commanders of the Combatant Commands are consistent with this Directive and the law of war.

5.8. The Commanders of the Combatant Commands shall:

5.8.1. Institute effective programs within their respective commands to prevent violations of the law of war and ensure that their commands' plans, policies, directives, and rules of engagement are subject to periodic review and evaluation, particularly in light of any violations reported.

5.8.2. Implement guidance from the Chairman of the Joint Chiefs of Staff for the collection and investigation of reports of enemy violations of the law of war.

5.8.3. Designate the command legal adviser to supervise the administration of those aspects of this program dealing with possible, suspected, or alleged enemy violations of the law of war.

5.8.4. Issue directives to ensure that reportable incidents involving U.S. or enemy persons are reported promptly to appropriate authorities, are thoroughly investigated, and the results of such investigations are promptly forwarded to the applicable Military Department or other appropriate authorities.

5.8.5. Determine the extent and manner in which a reportable incident not involving U.S. or enemy persons will be investigated by U.S. forces and ensure that such incidents are reported promptly to appropriate U.S. Agencies, allied governments, or other appropriate authorities.

5.8.6. Ensure all plans, policies, directives, and rules of engagement issued by the command and its subordinate commands and components are reviewed by legal advisers to ensure their consistency with this Directive and the law of war.

5.8.7. Ensure that law of war training and dissemination programs of subordinate commands and components are consistent with this Directive and the law of war obligations of the United States.

5.9. The Assistant Secretary of Defense for Command, Control, Communications and Intelligence shall ensure that the Director, Defense Intelligence Agency, shall provide information from the intelligence community to the Secretary of the Army and to the Commanders of the Combatant Commands, consistent with their respective obligations under subsections 5.6. and 5.8., above, concerning reportable incidents perpetrated against captured or detained U.S. persons, or committed by or against U.S. allies, or committed by or against other persons during a conflict to which the United States is not a party.

6. INFORMATION REQUIREMENTS

6.1. Reports of Incidents. All military and civilian personnel assigned to or accompanying a DoD Component shall report reportable incidents through their chain of command. Such reports also may also be made through other channels, such as the military police, a judge advocate, or an Inspector General. Reports that are made to officials other than those specified in this subsection shall, nonetheless, be accepted and immediately forwarded through the recipient's chain of command.

6.2. Initial Report. The commander of any unit that obtains information about a reportable incident shall immediately report the incident through command channels to higher authority. The initial report shall be made through the most expeditious means available.

6.3. Higher authorities receiving an initial report shall:

6.3.1. Request a formal investigation by the cognizant military investigation authority.

6.3.2. Submit a report of any reportable incident, by the most expeditious means available, through command channels, to the responsible Combatant Commander. Normally, an OPREP-3 report, established in Joint Pub 1-03.6, Joint Reporting System, Event/Incident Reports (E/IR), will be required. Copies of the E/IR shall be provided to the DoD Component officials designated by the Heads of the DoD Components concerned.

6.3.3. Submit a report, in accordance with DoD Instruction 5240.4 (reference (l)), concerning any criminal case, regardless of the allegation, that has received, is expected to receive, or which, if disclosed, could reasonably be expected to receive, significant media interest.

6.4. The Combatant Commander shall report, by the most expeditious means available, all reportable incidents to the Chairman of the Joint Chiefs of Staff, the Secretary of Defense, and the Secretary of the Army in his role as the Executive Agent under subsection 5.6., above.

6.5. DoD Notifications. Notifications of a reportable incident shall be forwarded to the Chairman of the Joint Chiefs of Staff; the GC, DoD; the Assistant Secretary of Defense for Public Affairs; and the Inspector General of the Department of Defense, who will inform their counterparts in any Military Service or Department concerned.

6.6. Information Requirements. The Event/Incident Reports referred to in this Directive and further described in reference (l) are exempt from licensing in accordance with paragraph 5.4.2. of DoD 8910.1-M (reference (j)).

....

Signature of John J. Hamre, Deputy Secretary of Defense

[enclosures, references continued]

F. War Crimes and the Nuremberg Principles: The Ascription of Personal Responsibility for Knowing Violation of the Major Norms of Conflict Management

LONDON CHARTER*

....

WHEREAS the United Nations have from time to time made declarations of their intention that War Criminals shall be brought to justice;

AND WHEREAS the Moscow Declaration of the 30th October 1943, on German atrocities in Occupied Europe stated that those German Officers and men and members of the Nazi Party who have been responsible for or have taken a consenting part in atrocities and crimes will be sent back to the countries in which their abominable deeds were done in order that they may be judged and punished according to the laws of these liberated countries and of the free Governments that will be created therein;

AND WHEREAS this Declaration was stated to be without prejudice to the case of major criminals whose offenses have no particular geographical location and who will be punished by the joint decision of the Governments of the Allies;

Now THEREFORE the Government of the United States of America, the Provisional Government of the French Republic, the Government of the United Kingdom of Great Britain and Northern Ireland and the Government of the Union of Soviet Socialist Republics (hereinafter called "the Signatories") acting in the interests of all the United Nations and by their representatives duly authorized thereto have concluded this Agreement.

Article 1. There shall be established after consultation with the Control Council for Germany an International Military Tribunal for the trial of war criminals whose offenses have no particular geographical location whether they be accused individually or in their capacity as members of organizations or groups or in both capacities.

Article 2. The constitution, jurisdiction and functions of the International Military Tribunal shall be those set out in the Charter annexed to this Agreement, which Charter shall form an integral part of this Agreement.

Article 3. Each of the Signatories shall take the necessary steps to make available for the investigation of the charges and trial the major war criminals detained by them who are to be tried by the International Military Tribunal. The Signatories shall also use their best endeavors to make available for investigation of the charges against and the trial before the International Military Tribunal such of the major war criminals as are not in the territories of any of the Signatories.

Article 4. Nothing in this Agreement shall prejudice the provisions established by the Moscow Declaration concerning the return of war criminals to the countries where they committed their crimes.

---

* Agreement by the Government of the United States of America, the Provisional Government of the French Republic, the Government of the United Kingdom of Great Britain and Northern Ireland and the Government of the Union of Soviet Socialist Republics for the Prosecution and Punishment of the Major War Criminals of the European Axis, Aug. 8, 1945, 59 Stat. 1544, 82 U.N.T.S. 279 (entered into force Aug. 8, 1945), *available at* http://www.yale.edu/lawweb/avalon/imt/jackson/jack60.htm. *See also* Charter of the International Tribunal for the Far East, Jan. 19, 1946, T.I.A.S. No. 1589, 4 Bevans 27 (entered into force Jan. 19, 1946) (amended Apr. 26, 1946).

Article 5. Any Government of the United Nations may adhere to this Agreement by notice given through the diplomatic channel to the Government of the United Kingdom, who shall inform the other signatory and adhering Governments of each such adherence.

Article 6. Nothing in this Agreement shall prejudice the jurisdiction or the powers of any national or occupation court established or to be established in any allied territory or in Germany for the trial of war criminals.

Article 7. This Agreement shall come into force on the day of signature and shall remain in force for the period of one year and shall continue thereafter, subject to the right of any Signatory to give, through the diplomatic channel, one month's notice of intention to terminate it. Such termination shall not prejudice any proceedings already taken or any findings already made in pursuance of this Agreement.

IN WITNESS WHEREOF the Undersigned have signed the present Agreement.

Donne in quadruplicate in London this 8th day of August 1945 each in English, French and Russian, and each text to have equal authenticity.

CHARTER OF THE INTERNATIONAL MILITARY TRIBUNAL

I. CONSTITUTION OF THE INTERNATIONAL MILITARY TRIBUNAL

Article 1. In pursuance of the Agreement signed on the 8th day of August 1945 by the Government of the United States of America, the Provisional Government of the French Republic, the Government of the United Kingdom of Great Britain and Northern Ireland and the Government of the Union of Soviet Socialist Republics, there shall be established an International Military Tribunal (hereinafter called "the Tribunal") for the just and prompt trial and punishment of the major war criminals of the European Axis.

Article 2. The Tribunal shall consist of four members, each with an alternate. One member and one alternate shall be appointed by each of the Signatories. The alternates shall, so far as they are able, be present at all sessions of the Tribunal. In case of illness of any member of the Tribunal or his incapacity for some other reason to fulfill his functions, his alternate shall take his place.

Article 3. Neither the Tribunal, its members nor their alternates can be challenged by the prosecution, or by the Defendants or their Counsel. Each Signatory may replace its member of the Tribunal or his alternate for reasons of health or for other good reasons, except that no replacement may take place during a Trial, other than by an alternate.

Article 4. (a) The presence of all four members of the Tribunal or the alternate for any absent member shall be necessary to constitute the quorum.

(b) The members of the Tribunal shall, before any trial begins, agree among themselves upon the selection from their number of a President, and the President shall hold office during that trial, or as may otherwise be agreed by a vote of not less than three members. The principle of rotation of presidency for successive trials is agreed. If, however, a session of the Tribunal takes place on the territory of one of the four Signatories, the representative of that Signatory on the Tribunal shall preside.

(c) Save as aforesaid the Tribunal shall take decisions by a majority vote and in case the votes are evenly divided, the vote of the President shall be decisive: provided always that convictions and sentences shall only be imposed by affirmative votes of at least three members of the Tribunal.

Article 5. In case of need and depending on the number of the matters to be tried, other Tribunals may be set up; and the establishment, functions, and procedure of each Tribunal shall be identical, and shall be governed by this Charter.

II. JURISDICTION AND GENERAL PRINCIPLES

Article 6. The Tribunal established by the Agreement referred to in Article 1 hereof for the trial and punishment of the major war criminals of the European Axis countries shall have the power to try and punish persons who, acting in the interests of the European Axis countries, whether as individuals or as members of organizations, committed any of the following crimes.

The following acts, or any of them, are crimes coming within the jurisdiction of the Tribunal for which there shall be individual responsibility:

(a) *Crimes against peace:* namely, planning, preparation, initiation or waging of a war of aggression, or a war in violation of international treaties, agreements or assurances, or participation in a common plan or conspiracy for the accomplishment of any of the foregoing;

(b) *War Crimes:* namely, violations of the laws or customs of war. Such violations shall include, but not be limited to, murder, ill-treatment or deportation to slave labor or for any other purpose of civilian population of or in occupied territory, murder or ill-treatment of prisoners of war or persons on the seas, killing of hostages, plunder of public or private property, wanton destruction of cities, towns or villages, or devastation not justified by military necessity;

(c) *Crimes against humanity:* namely, murder, extermination, enslavement, deportation, and other inhumane acts committed against any civilian population, before or during the war; or persecutions on political, racial or religious grounds in execution of or in connection with any crime within the jurisdiction of the Tribunal, whether or not in violation of the domestic law of the country where perpetrated.

Leaders, organizers, instigators and accomplices participating in the formulation or execution of a common plan or conspiracy to commit any of the foregoing crimes are responsible for all acts performed by any persons in execution of such plan.

Article 7. The official position of defendants, whether as Heads of State or responsible officials in Government Departments, shall not be considered as freeing them from responsibility or mitigating punishment.

Article 8. The fact that the Defendant acted pursuant to order of his Government or of a superior shall not free him from responsibility, but may be considered in mitigation of punishment if the Tribunal determines that justice so requires.

Article 9. At the trial of any individual member of any group or organization the Tribunal may declare (in connection with any act of which the individual may be convicted) that the group or organization of which the individual was a member was a criminal organization.

....

Article 10. In cases where a group or organization is declared criminal by the Tribunal, the competent national authority of any Signatory shall have the right to bring individuals to trial for membership therein before national, military or occupation courts. In any such case the criminal nature of the group or organization is considered proved and shall not be questioned.

Article 11. Any person convicted by the Tribunal may be charged before a national, military or occupation court, referred to in Article 10 of this Charter, with a crime other than of membership in a criminal group or organization and such court may, after convicting him, impose upon him punishment independent of and additional to the punishment imposed by the Tribunal for participation in the criminal activities of such group or organization.

Article 12. The Tribunal shall have the right to take proceedings against a person charged with crimes set out in Article 6 of this Charter in his absence, if he has not been found or if the Tribunal, for any reason, finds it necessary, in the interests of justice, to conduct the hearing in his absence.

Article 13. The Tribunal shall draw up rules for its procedure. These rules shall not be inconsistent with the provisions of this Charter.

III. COMMITTEE FOR THE INVESTIGATION AND PROSECUTION OF MAJOR WAR CRIMINALS

Article 14. Each Signatory shall appoint a Chief Prosecutor for the investigation of the charges against and the prosecution of major war criminals.

The Chief Prosecutors shall act as a committee for the following purposes:

(a) to agree upon a plan of the individual work of each of the Chief Prosecutors and his staff,

(b) to settle the final designation of major war criminals to be tried by the Tribunal,

(c) to approve the Indictment and the documents to be submitted therewith,

(d) to lodge the Indictment and the accompanying documents with the Tribunal,

(e) to draw up and recommend to the Tribunal for its approval draft rules of procedure, contemplated by Article 13 of this Charter. The Tribunal shall have power to accept, with or without amendments, or to reject, the rules so recommended.

The Committee shall act in all the above matters by a majority vote and shall appoint a Chairman as may be convenient and in accordance with the principle of rotation: provided that if there is an equal division of vote concerning the designation of a Defendant to be tried by the Tribunal, or the crimes with which he shall be charged, that proposal will be adopted which was made by the party which proposed that the particular Defendant be tried, or the particular charges be preferred against him.

Article 15. The Chief Prosecutors shall individually, and acting in collaboration with one another, also undertake the following duties:

(a) investigation, collection and production before or at the Trial of all necessary evidence,

(b) the preparation of the Indictment for approval by the Committee in accordance with paragraph (c) of Article 14 hereof,

(c) the preliminary examination of all necessary witnesses and of the Defendants,

(d) to act as prosecutor at the Trial,

(e) to appoint representatives to carry out such duties as may be assigned to them,

(f) to undertake such other matters as may appear necessary to them for the purposes of the preparation for and conduct of the Trial.

It is understood that no witness or Defendant detained by any Signatory shall be taken out of the possession of that Signatory without its assent.

IV. FAIR TRIAL FOR DEFENDANTS

Article 16. In order to ensure fair trial for the Defendants, the following procedure shall be followed:

(a) The Indictment shall include full particulars specifying in detail the charges against the Defendants. A copy of the Indictment and of all the documents lodged with the Indictment, translated into a language which he understands, shall be furnished to the Defendant at a reasonable time before the Trial.

(b) During any preliminary examination or trial of a Defendant he shall have the right to give any explanation relevant to the charges made against him.

(c) A preliminary examination of a Defendant and his Trial shall be conducted in, or translated into, a language which the Defendant understands.

(d) A defendant shall have the right to conduct his own defense before the Tribunal or to have the assistance of Counsel.

(e) A defendant shall have the right through himself or through his Counsel to present evidence at the Trial in support of his defense, and to cross-examine any witness called by the Prosecution.

V. POWERS OF THE TRIBUNAL AND CONDUCT OF THE TRIAL

Article 17. The Tribunal shall have the power:

(a) to summon witnesses to the Trial and to require their attendance and testimony and to put questions to them,

(b) to interrogate any Defendant,

(c) to require the production of documents and other evidentiary material,

(d) to administer oaths to witnesses,

(e) to appoint officers for the carrying out of any task designated by the Tribunal including the power to have evidence taken on commission.

Article 18. The Tribunal shall:

(a) confine the Trial strictly to an expeditious hearing of the issues raised by the charges,

(b) take strict measures to prevent any action which will cause unreasonable delay, and rule out irrelevant issues and statements of any kind whatsoever,

(c) deal summarily with any contumacy, imposing appropriate punishment, including exclusion of any Defendant or his Counsel from some or all further proceedings, but without prejudice to the determination of the charges.

Article 19. The Tribunal shall not be bound by technical rules of evidence. It shall adopt and apply to the greatest possible extent expeditious and non-technical procedure, and shall admit any evidence which it deems to have probative value.

Article 20. The Tribunal may require to be informed of the nature of any evidence before it is offered so that it may rule upon the relevance thereof.

Article 21. The Tribunal shall not require proof of facts of common knowledge but shall take judicial notice thereof. It shall also take judicial notice of official governmental documents and reports of the United Nations, including the acts and documents of the committees set up in the various allied countries for the investigation of war crimes, and the records and findings of military or other Tribunals of any of the United Nations.

. . . .

Article 24. The proceedings at the Trial shall take the following course:

(a) The Indictment shall be read in court.

(b) The Tribunal shall ask each Defendant whether he pleads "guilty" or "not guilty".

(c) The prosecution shall make an opening statement.

(d) The Tribunal shall ask the prosecution and the defense what evidence (if any) they wish to submit to the Tribunal, and the Tribunal shall rule upon the admissibility of any such evidence.

(e) The witnesses for the Prosecution shall be examined and after that the witnesses for the Defense. Thereafter such rebutting evidence as may be held by the Tribunal to be admissible shall be called by either the Prosecution or the Defense.

(f) The Tribunal may put any question to any witness and to any Defendant, at any time.

(g) The prosecution and the Defense shall interrogate and may cross-examine any witnesses and any Defendant who gives testimony.

(h) The Defense shall address the court.

(i) The Prosecution shall address the court.

(j) Each Defendant may make a statement to the Tribunal.

(k) The Tribunal shall deliver judgment and pronounce sentence.

Article 25. All official documents shall be produced, and all court proceedings conducted, in English, French and Russian, and in the language of the Defendant. So much of the record and of the proceedings may also be translated into the language of any country in which the Tribunal is sitting, as the Tribunal considers desirable in the interests of justice and public opinion.

VI. JUDGMENT AND SENTENCE

Article 26. The Judgment of the Tribunal as to the guilt or the innocence of any Defendant shall give the reasons on which it is based, and shall be final and not subject to review.

Article 27. The Tribunal shall have the right to impose upon a Defendant, on conviction, death or such other punishment as shall be determined by it to be just.

Article 28. In addition to any punishment imposed by it, the Tribunal shall have the right to deprive the convicted person of any stolen property and order its delivery to the Control Council for Germany.

Article 29. In case of guilt, sentences shall be carried out in accordance with the orders of the Control Council for Germany, which may at any time reduce or otherwise alter the sentences, but may not increase the severity thereof. If the Control Council for Germany, after any Defendant has been convicted and sentenced, discovers fresh evidence which, in its opinion, would found a fresh charge against him, the Council shall report accordingly to the Committee established under Article 14 hereof, for such action as they may consider proper having regard to the interests of justice.

VII. EXPENSES

Article 30. The Expenses of the Tribunal and of the Trials, shall be charged by the Signatories against the funds allotted for maintenance of the Control Council for Germany.

....

NUREMBERG TRIALS FINAL REPORT: CONTROL COUNCIL LAW NO. 10*

Punishment of Persons Guilty of War Crimes, Crimes Against Peace and Against Humanity

In order to give effect to the terms of the Moscow Declaration of 30 October 1943 and the London Agreement of 8 August 1945, and the Charter issued pursuant thereto and in order to establish a uniform legal basis in Germany for the prosecution of war criminals and other similar offenders, other than those dealt with by the International Military Tribunal, the Control Council enacts as follows:

Article I. The Moscow Declaration of 30 October 1943 "Concerning Responsibility of Hitlerites for Committed Atrocities" and the London Agreement of 8 August 1945 "Concerning Prosecution and Punishment of Major War Criminals of European Axis" are made integral parts of this Law. Adherence to the provisions of the London Agreement by any of the United Nations, as provided for in Article V of that Agreement, shall not entitle such Nation to participate or interfere in the operation of this Law within the Control Council area of authority in Germany.

Article II. 1. Each of the following acts is recognized as a crime:

(a) Crimes against Peace. Initiation of invasions of other countries and wars of aggression in violation of international laws and treaties, including but not limited to planning, preparation, initiation or waging a war of aggression, or a war of violation of international treaties, agreements or assurances, or participation in a common plan or conspiracy for the accomplishment of any of the foregoing.

(b) War Crimes. Atrocities or offenses against persons or property constituting violations of the laws or customs of war, including but not limited to, murder, ill treatment or deportation to slave labour or for any other purpose, of civilian population from occupied territory, murder or ill treatment of prisoners of war or persons on the seas, killing of hostages, plunder of public or private property, wanton destruction of cities, towns or villages, or devastation not justified by military necessity.

(c) Crimes against Humanity. Atrocities and offenses, including but not limited to murder, extermination, enslavement, deportation, imprisonment, torture, rape, or other inhumane acts committed against any civilian population, or persecutions on political, racial or religious grounds whether or not in violation of the domestic laws of the country where perpetrated.

(d) Membership in categories of a criminal group or organization declared criminal by the International Military Tribunal.

2. Any person without regard to nationality or the capacity in which he acted, is deemed to have committed a crime as defined in paragraph 1 of this Article, if he was

---

* Control Council Law No. 10, Punishment of Persons Guilty of War Crimes, Crimes Against Peace and Against Humanity, Dec. 20, 1945, 3 OFFICIAL GAZETTE OF THE CONTROL COUNCIL FOR GERMANY 50 (1946), *reprinted in* TELFORD TAYLOR, U.S. DEP'T OF ARMY, OFFICE, CHIEF OF COUNSEL FOR WAR CRIMES, FINAL REPORT TO THE SECRETARY OF THE ARMY ON THE NUERNBERG WAR CRIMES TRIALS UNDER CONTROL COUNCIL LAW NO. 10, at 250 (1949), *available at* http://www.yale.edu/lawweb/avalon/imt/imt10.htm.

(a) a principal; or

(b) was an accessory to the commission of any such crime or ordered or abetted the same; or

(c) took a consenting part therein; or

(d) was connected with plans or enterprises involving its commission; or

(e) was a member of any organization or group connected with the commission of any such crime; or

(f) with reference to paragraph 1 (a) if he held a high political, civil or military (including General Staff) position in Germany or in one of its Allies, co-belligerents or satellites or held high position in the financial, industrial or economic life of any such country.

3. Any persons found guilty of any of the crimes above mentioned may upon conviction be punished as shall be determined by the tribunal to be just. Such punishment may consist of one or more of the following:

(a) Death.

(b) Imprisonment for life or a term of years, with or without hard labor.

(c) Fine, and imprisonment with or without hard labour, in lieu thereof.

(d) Forfeiture of property.

(e) Restitution of property wrongfully acquired.

(f) Deprivation of some or all civil rights.

Any property declared to be forfeited or the restitution of which is ordered by the Tribunal shall be delivered to the Control Council for Germany, which shall decide on its disposal.

4. (a) The official position of any person, whether as Head of State or as a responsible official in a Government Department, does not free him from responsibility for a crime or entitle him to mitigation of punishment.

(b) The fact that any person acted pursuant to the order of his Government or of a superior does not free him from responsibility for a crime, but may be considered in mitigation.

5. In any trial or prosecution for a crime herein referred to, the accused shall not be entitled to the benefits of any statute of limitation in respect to the period from 30 January 1933 to 1 July 1945, nor shall any immunity, pardon or amnesty granted under the Nazi regime be admitted as a bar to trial or punishment.

....

Done at Berlin, 20 December 1945.
(Signed) Joseph T. McNarney
JOSEPH T. MCNARNEY
General, U. S. Army
(Signed) Bernard B. Montgomery
BERNARD B. MONTGOMERY
Field Marshall
(Signed) Louis Koeltz, General d'Corps de Armee
for PIEIRR KOENIG
General d'Armee

(Signed) Georgi Zhukov
GEORGI ZHUKOV
Marshall of the Soviet Union

AFFIRMATION OF THE PRINCIPLES OF INTERNATIONAL LAW RECOGNIZED BY THE CHARTER OF THE NÜRNBERG TRIBUNAL*

The General Assembly,

Recognizes the obligation laid upon it by Article 13, paragraph 1, sub-paragraph a, of the Charter, to initiate studies and make recommendations for the purpose of encouraging the progressive development of international law and its codification;

Takes note of the Agreement for the establishment of an International Military Tribunal for the prosecution and punishment of the major war criminals of the European Axis signed in London on 8 August 1945, and of the Charter annexed thereto, and of the fact that similar principles have been adopted in the Charter of the International Military Tribunal for the trial of the major war criminals in the Far East, proclaimed at Tokyo on 19 January 1946;

Therefore,

Affirms the principles of international law recognized by the Charter of the Nurnberg Tribunal and the judgment of the Tribunal;

Directs the Committee on the codification of international law established by the resolution of the General Assembly of 11 December 1946, to treat as a matter of primary importance plans for the formulation, in the context of a general codification of offences against the peace and security of mankind, or of an International Criminal Code, of the principles recognized in the Charter of the Nurnberg Tribunal and in the judgment of the Tribunal.

....

* G.A. Res. 95 (I), at 188, U.N. Doc. A/64/Add.1 (Dec. 11, 1946), *available at* http://www.un.org/documents/ga/res/1/ares1.htm .

UN SECURITY COUNCIL RESOLUTION 780* (WAR CRIMES IN THE FORMER YUGOSLAVIA)

....

The Security Council,

Reaffirming its resolution 713 (1991) of 25 September 1991 and all subsequent relevant resolutions,

Recalling paragraph 10 of its resolution 764 (1992) of 13 July 1992, in which it reaffirmed that all parties are bound to comply with the obligations under international humanitarian law and in particular the Geneva Conventions of 12 August 1949, and that persons who commit or order the commission of grave breaches of the Conventions are individually responsible in respect of such breaches,

Recalling also its resolution 771 (1992) of 13 August 1992, in which, *inter alia*, it demanded that all parties and others concerned in the former Yugoslavia, and all military forces in Bosnia and Herzegovina, immediately cease and desist from all breaches of international humanitarian law,

Expressing once again its grave alarm at continuing reports of widespread violations of international humanitarian law occurring within the territory of the former Yugoslavia and especially in Bosnia and Herzegovina, including reports of mass killings and the continuance of the practice of "ethnic cleansing",

1. *Reaffirms* its call, in paragraph 5 of resolution 771 (1992), upon States and, as appropriate, international humanitarian organizations to collate substantiated information in their possession or submitted to them relating to the violations of humanitarian law, including grave breaches of the Geneva Conventions being committed in the territory of the former Yugoslavia, and requests States, relevant United Nations bodies, and relevant organizations to make this information available within thirty days of the adoption of the present resolution and as appropriate thereafter, and to provide other appropriate assistance to the Commission of Experts referred to in paragraph 2 below;

2. *Requests* the Secretary-General to establish, as a matter of urgency, an impartial Commission of Experts to examine and analyse the information submitted pursuant to resolution 771 (1992) and the present resolution, together with such further information as the Commission of Experts may obtain through its own investigations or efforts, of other persons or bodies pursuant to resolution 771 (1992), with a view to providing the Secretary-General with its conclusions on the evidence of grave breaches of the Geneva Conventions and other violations of international humanitarian law committed in the territory of the former Yugoslavia;

3. *Also requests* the Secretary-General to report to the Council on the establishment of the Commission of Experts;

4. *Further requests* the Secretary-General to report to the Council on the conclusions of the Commission of Experts and to take account of these conclusions in any recommendations for further appropriate steps called for by resolution 771 (1992);

5. *Decides* to remain actively seized of the matter.

---

* S.C. Res. 780, U.N. Doc. S/RES/780 (Oct. 6, 1992), *available at* http://www.un.org/Docs/scres/1992/scres92.htm.

UN SECURITY COUNCIL RESOLUTION 827* (INTERNATIONAL TRIBUNAL FOR THE FORMER YUGOSLAVIA)

The Security Council,

Reaffirming its resolution 713 (1991) of 25 September 1991 and all subsequent relevant resolutions,

Having considered the report of the Secretary-General (S/25704 and Add. 1) pursuant to paragraph 2 of resolution 808 (1993),

Expressing once again its grave alarm at continuing reports of widespread and flagrant violations of international humanitarian law occurring within the territory of the former Yugoslavia, and especially in the Republic of Bosnia and Herzegovina, including reports of mass killings, massive, organized and systematic detention and rape of women, and the continuance of the practice of "ethnic cleansing", including for the acquisition and the holding of territory,

Determining that this situation continues to constitute a threat to international peace and security,

Determined to put an end to such crimes and to take effective measures to bring to justice the persons who are responsible for them,

Convinced that in the particular circumstances of the former Yugoslavia the establishment as an ad hoc measure by the Council of an international tribunal and the prosecution of persons responsible for serious violations of international humanitarian law would enable this aim to be achieved and would contribute to the restoration and maintenance of peace,

Believing that the establishment of an international tribunal and the prosecution of persons responsible for the above-mentioned violations of international humanitarian law will contribute to ensuring that such violations are halted and effectively redressed,

Noting in this regard the recommendation by the Co-Chairmen of the Steering Committee of the International Conference on the Former Yugoslavia for the establishment of such a tribunal (S/25221),

Reaffirming in this regard its decision in resolution 808 (1993) that an international tribunal shall be established for the prosecution of persons responsible for serious violations of international humanitarian law committed in the territory of the former Yugoslavia since 1991,

Considering that, pending the appointment of the Prosecutor of the International Tribunal, the Commission of Experts established pursuant to resolution 780 (1992) should continue on an urgent basis the collection of information relating to evidence of grave breaches of the Geneva Conventions and other violations of international humanitarian law as proposed in its interim report (S/25274),

Acting under Chapter VII of the Charter of the United Nations,

---

* S.C. Res. 827, U.N. Doc. S/RES/827 (May 25, 1993), *available at* http://www.un.org/Docs/scres/1993/scres93.htm.

1. *Approves* the report of the Secretary-General;

2. *Decides* hereby to establish an international tribunal for the sole purpose of prosecuting persons responsible for serious violations of international humanitarian law committed in the territory of the former Yugoslavia between 1 January 1991 and a date to be determined by the Security Council upon the restoration of peace and to this end to adopt the Statute of the International Tribunal annexed to the above-mentioned report;

3. *Requests* the Secretary-General to submit to the judges of the International Tribunal, upon their election, any suggestions received from States for the rules of procedure and evidence called for in Article 15 of the Statute of the International Tribunal;

4. *Decides* that all States shall cooperate fully with the International Tribunal and its organs in accordance with the present resolution and the Statute of the International Tribunal and that consequently all States shall take any measures necessary under their domestic law to implement the provisions of the present resolution and the Statute, including the obligation of States to comply with requests for assistance or orders issued by a Trial Chamber under Article 29 of the Statute;

5. *Urges* States and intergovernmental and non-governmental organizations to contribute funds, equipment and services to the International Tribunal, including the offer of expert personnel;

6. *Decides* that the determination of the seat of the International Tribunal is subject to the conclusion of appropriate arrangements between the United Nations and the Netherlands acceptable to the Council, and that the International Tribunal may sit elsewhere when it considers it necessary for the efficient exercise of its functions;

7. *Decides also* that the work of the International Tribunal shall be carried out without prejudice to the right of the victims to seek, through appropriate means, compensation for damages incurred as a result of violations of international humanitarian law;

8. *Requests* the Secretary-General to implement urgently the present resolution and in particular to make practical arrangements for the effective functioning of the International Tribunal at the earliest time and to report periodically to the Council;

9. *Decides* to remain actively seized of the matter.

UN SECURITY COUNCIL RESOLUTION 955* (INTERNATIONAL TRIBUNAL FOR RWANDA)

The Security Council,

Reaffirming all its previous resolutions on the situation in Rwanda,

Having considered the reports of the Secretary-General pursuant to paragraph 3 of resolution 935 (1994) of 1 July 1994 (S/1994/879 and S/1994/906), and having taken note of the reports of the Special Rapporteur for Rwanda of the United Nations Commission on Human Rights (S/1994/1157, annex I and annex II),

Expressing appreciation for the work of the Commission of Experts established pursuant to resolution 935 (1994), in particular its preliminary report on violations of international humanitarian law in Rwanda transmitted by the Secretary-General's letter of 1 October 1994 (S/1994/1125),

Expressing once again its grave concern at the reports indicating that genocide and other systematic, widespread and flagrant violations of international humanitarian law have been committed in Rwanda,

Determining that this situation continues to constitute a threat to international peace and security,

Determined to put an end to such crimes and to take effective measures to bring to justice the persons who are responsible for them,

Convinced that in the particular circumstances of Rwanda, the prosecution of persons responsible for serious violations of international humanitarian law would enable this aim to be achieved and would contribute to the process of national reconciliation and to the restoration and maintenance of peace,

Believing that the establishment of an international tribunal for the prosecution of persons responsible for genocide and the other above-mentioned violations of international humanitarian law will contribute to ensuring that such violations are halted and effectively redressed,

Stressing also the need for international cooperation to strengthen the courts and judicial system of Rwanda, having regard in particular to the necessity for those courts to deal with large numbers of suspects,

Considering that the Commission of Experts established pursuant to resolution 935 (1994) should continue on an urgent basis the collection of information relating to evidence of grave violations of international humanitarian law committed in the territory of Rwanda and should submit its final report to the Secretary-General by 30 November 1994,

Acting under Chapter VII of the Charter of the United Nations,

1. *Decides* hereby, having received the request of the Government of Rwanda (S/1994/1115), to establish an international tribunal for the sole purpose of prosecuting persons responsible for genocide and other serious violations of international humani-

* S.C. Res. 955, U.N. Doc. S/RES/955 (Nov. 8, 1994), *available at* http://www.un.org/Docs/scres/1994/scres94.htm.

tarian law committed in the territory of Rwanda and Rwandan citizens responsible for genocide and other such violations committed in the territory of neighbouring States, between 1 January 1994 and 31 December 1994 and to this end to adopt the Statute of the International Criminal Tribunal for Rwanda annexed hereto;

2. *Decides* that all States shall cooperate fully with the International Tribunal and its organs in accordance with the present resolution and the Statute of the International Tribunal and that consequently all States shall take any measures necessary under their domestic law to implement the provisions of the present resolution and the Statute, including the obligation of States to comply with requests for assistance or orders issued by a Trial Chamber under Article 28 of the Statute, and requests States to keep the Secretary-General informed of such measures;

3. *Considers* that the Government of Rwanda should be notified prior to the taking of decisions under articles 26 and 27 of the Statute;

4. *Urges* States and intergovernmental and non-governmental organizations to contribute funds, equipment and services to the International Tribunal, including the offer of expert personnel;

5. Requests the Secretary-General to implement this resolution urgently and in particular to make practical arrangements for the effective functioning of the International Tribunal, including recommendations to the Council as to possible locations for the seat of the International Tribunal at the earliest time and to report periodically to the Council;

6. *Decides* that the seat of the International Tribunal shall be determined by the Council having regard to considerations of justice and fairness as well as administrative efficiency, including access to witnesses, and economy, and subject to the conclusion of appropriate arrangements between the United Nations and the State of the seat, acceptable to the Council, having regard to the fact that the International Tribunal may meet away from its seat when it considers it necessary for the efficient exercise of its functions; and decides that an office will be established and proceedings will be conducted in Rwanda, where feasible and appropriate, subject to the conclusion of similar appropriate arrangements;

7. *Decides* to consider increasing the number of judges and Trial Chambers of the International Tribunal if it becomes necessary;

8. *Decides* to remain actively seized of the matter.

Annex

Statute of the International Tribunal for Rwanda

Having been established by the Security Council acting under Chapter VII of the Charter of the United Nations, the International Criminal Tribunal for the Prosecution of Persons Responsible for Genocide and Other Serious Violations of International Humanitarian Law Committed in the Territory of Rwanda and Rwandan citizens responsible for genocide and other such violations committed in the territory of neighbouring States, between 1 January 1994 and 31 December 1994 (hereinafter referred to as "the International Tribunal for Rwanda") shall function in accordance with the provisions of the present Statute.

Article 1. *Competence of the International Tribunal for Rwanda.* The International Tribunal for Rwanda shall have the power to prosecute persons responsible for serious violations of international humanitarian law committed in the territory of Rwanda and

Rwandan citizens responsible for such violations committed in the territory of neighbouring States, between 1 January 1994 and 31 December 1994, in accordance with the provisions of the present Statute.

Article 2. *Genocide.* 1. The International Tribunal for Rwanda shall have the power to prosecute persons committing genocide as defined in paragraph 2 of this article or of committing any of the other acts enumerated in paragraph 3 of this article.

2. Genocide means any of the following acts committed with intent to destroy, in whole or in part, a national, ethnical, racial or religious group, as such:

(a) Killing members of the group;

(b) Causing serious bodily or mental harm to members of the group;

(c) Deliberately inflicting on the group conditions of life calculated to bring about its physical destruction in whole or in part;

(d) Imposing measures intended to prevent births within the group;

(e) Forcibly transferring children of the group to another group.

3. The following acts shall be punishable:

(a) Genocide;

(b) Conspiracy to commit genocide;

(c) Direct and public incitement to commit genocide;

(d) Attempt to commit genocide;

(e) Complicity in genocide.

Article 3. *Crimes against humanity.* The International Tribunal for Rwanda shall have the power to prosecute persons responsible for the following crimes when committed as part of a widespread or systematic attack against any civilian population on national, political, ethnic, racial or religious grounds:

(a) Murder;

(b) Extermination;

(c) Enslavement;

(d) Deportation;

(e) Imprisonment;

(f) Torture;

(g) Rape;

(h) Persecutions on political, racial and religious grounds;

(i) Other inhumane acts.

Article 4. *Violations of Article 3 common to the Geneva Conventions and of Additional Protocol II.* The International Tribunal for Rwanda shall have the power to prosecute persons committing or ordering to be committed serious violations of Article 3 common to the Geneva Conventions of 12 August 1949 for the Protection of War Victims, and of Additional Protocol II thereto of 8 June 1977. These violations shall include, but shall not be limited to:

(a) Violence to life, health and physical or mental well-being of persons, in particular murder as well as cruel treatment such as torture, mutilation or any form of corporal punishment;

(b) Collective punishments;

(c) Taking of hostages;

(d) Acts of terrorism;

(e) Outrages upon personal dignity, in particular humiliating and degrading treatment, rape, enforced prostitution and any form of indecent assault;

(f) Pillage;

(g) The passing of sentences and the carrying out of executions without previous judgment pronounced by a regularly constituted court, affording all the judicial guarantees which are recognized as indispensable by civilized peoples;

(h) Threats to commit any of the foregoing acts.

Article 5. Personal jurisdiction. The International Tribunal for Rwanda shall have jurisdiction over natural persons pursuant to the provisions of the present Statute.

Article 6. Individual criminal responsibility. 1.A person who planned, instigated, ordered, committed or otherwise aided and abetted in the planning, preparation or execution of a crime referred to in articles 2 to 4 of the present Statute, shall be individually responsible for the crime.

2. The official position of any accused person, whether as Head of State or Government or as a responsible Government official, shall not relieve such person of criminal responsibility nor mitigate punishment.

3. The fact that any of the acts referred to in articles 2 to 4 of the present Statute was committed by a subordinate does not relieve his or her superior of criminal responsibility if he or she knew or had reason to know that the subordinate was about to commit such acts or had done so and the superior failed to take the necessary and reasonable measures to prevent such acts or to punish the perpetrators thereof.

4. The fact that an accused person acted pursuant to an order of a Government or of a superior shall not relieve him or her of criminal responsibility, but may be considered in mitigation of punishment if the International Tribunal for Rwanda determines that justice so requires.

Article 7. Territorial and temporal jurisdiction. The territorial jurisdiction of the International Tribunal for Rwanda shall extend to the territory of Rwanda including its land surface and airspace as well as to the territory of neighbouring States in respect of serious violations of international humanitarian law committed by Rwandan citizens. The temporal jurisdiction of the International Tribunal for Rwanda shall extend to a period beginning on 1 January 1994 and ending on 31 December 1994.

Article 8. Concurrent jurisdiction. 1. The International Tribunal for Rwanda and national courts shall have concurrent jurisdiction to prosecute persons for serious violations of international humanitarian law committed in the territory of Rwanda and Rwandan citizens for such violations committed in the territory of neighbouring States, between 1 January 1994 and 31 December 1994.

2. The International Tribunal for Rwanda shall have primacy over the national courts of all States. At any stage of the procedure, the International Tribunal for Rwanda may formally request national courts to defer to its competence in accordance with the present Statute and the Rules of Procedure and Evidence of the International Tribunal for Rwanda.

Article 9. Non bis in idem. 1. No person shall be tried before a national court for acts constituting serious violations of international humanitarian law under the present

Statute, for which he or she has already been tried by the International Tribunal for Rwanda.

2. A person who has been tried by a national court for acts constituting serious violations of international humanitarian law may be subsequently tried by the International Tribunal for Rwanda only if:

(a) The act for which he or she was tried was characterized as an ordinary crime; or

(b) The national court proceedings were not impartial or independent, were designed to shield the accused from international criminal responsibility, or the case was not diligently prosecuted.

3. In considering the penalty to be imposed on a person convicted of a crime under the present Statute, the International Tribunal for Rwanda shall take into account the extent to which any penalty imposed by a national court on the same person for the same act has already been served.

Article 10. Organization of the International Tribunal for Rwanda. The International Tribunal for Rwanda shall consist of the following organs:

(a) The Chambers, comprising two Trial Chambers and an Appeals Chamber;

(b) The Prosecutor; and

(c) A Registry.

Article 11. Composition of the Chambers. The Chambers shall be composed of eleven independent judges, no two of whom may be nationals of the same State, who shall serve as follows:

(a) Three judges shall serve in each of the Trial Chambers;

(b) Five judges shall serve in the Appeals Chamber.

Article 12. Qualification and election of judges. 1. The judges shall be persons of high moral character, impartiality and integrity who possess the qualifications required in their respective countries for appointment to the highest judicial offices. In the overall composition of the Chambers due account shall be taken of the experience of the judges in criminal law, international law, including international humanitarian law and human rights law.

2. The members of the Appeals Chamber of the International Tribunal for the Prosecution of Persons Responsible for Serious Violations of International Law Committed in the Territory of the Former Yugoslavia since 1991 (hereinafter referred to as "the International Tribunal for the Former Yugoslavia") shall also serve as the members of the Appeals Chamber of the International Tribunal for Rwanda.

3. The judges of the Trial Chambers of the International Tribunal for Rwanda shall be elected by the General Assembly from a list submitted by the Security Council, in the following manner:

(a) The Secretary-General shall invite nominations for judges of the Trial Chambers from States Members of the United Nations and non-member States maintaining permanent observer missions at United Nations Headquarters;

(b) Within thirty days of the date of the invitation of the Secretary-General, each State may nominate up to two candidates meeting the qualifications set out in paragraph 1 above, no two of whom shall be of the same nationality and neither of whom shall be of the same nationality as any judge on the Appeals Chamber;

(c) The Secretary-General shall forward the nominations received to the Security Council. From the nominations received the Security Council shall establish a list of not less than twelve and not more than eighteen candidates, taking due account of adequate representation on the International Tribunal for Rwanda of the principal legal systems of the world;

(d) The President of the Security Council shall transmit the list of candidates to the President of the General Assembly. From that list the General Assembly shall elect the six judges of the Trial Chambers. The candidates who receive an absolute majority of the votes of the States Members of the United Nations and of the non-Member States maintaining permanent observer missions at United Nations Headquarters, shall be declared elected. Should two candidates of the same nationality obtain the required majority vote, the one who received the higher number of votes shall be considered elected.

4. In the event of a vacancy in the Trial Chambers, after consultation with the Presidents of the Security Council and of the General Assembly, the Secretary-General shall appoint a person meeting the qualifications of paragraph 1 above, for the remainder of the term of office concerned.

5. The judges of the Trial Chambers shall be elected for a term of four years. The terms and conditions of service shall be those of the judges of the International Tribunal for the Former Yugoslavia. They shall be eligible for re-election.

Article 13. Officers and members of the Chambers. 1. The judges of the International Tribunal for Rwanda shall elect a President.

2. After consultation with the judges of the International Tribunal for Rwanda, the President shall assign the judges to the Trial Chambers. A judge shall serve only in the Chamber to which he or she was assigned.

3. The judges of each Trial Chamber shall elect a Presiding Judge, who shall conduct all of the proceedings of that Trial Chamber as a whole.

Article 14. Rules of procedure and evidence. The judges of the International Tribunal for Rwanda shall adopt, for the purpose of proceedings before the International Tribunal for Rwanda, the rules of procedure and evidence for the conduct of the pre-trial phase of the proceedings, trials and appeals, the admission of evidence, the protection of victims and witnesses and other appropriate matters of the International Tribunal for the Former Yugoslavia with such changes as they deem necessary.

Article 15. The Prosecutor. 1. The Prosecutor shall be responsible for the investigation and prosecution of persons responsible for serious violations of international humanitarian law committed in the territory of Rwanda and Rwandan citizens responsible for such violations committed in the territory of neighbouring States, between 1 January 1994 and 31 December 1994.

2. The Prosecutor shall act independently as a separate organ of the International Tribunal for Rwanda. He or she shall not seek or receive instructions from any Government or from any other source.

3. The Prosecutor of the International Tribunal for the Former Yugoslavia shall also serve as the Prosecutor of the International Tribunal for Rwanda. He or she shall have additional staff, including an additional Deputy Prosecutor, to assist with prosecutions before the International Tribunal for Rwanda. Such staff shall be appointed by the Secretary-General on the recommendation of the Prosecutor.

Article 16. The Registry. 1. The Registry shall be responsible for the administration and servicing of the International Tribunal for Rwanda.

2. The Registry shall consist of a Registrar and such other staff as may be required.

3. The Registrar shall be appointed by the Secretary-General after consultation with the President of the International Tribunal for Rwanda. He or she shall serve for a four-year term and be eligible for reappointment. The terms and conditions of service of the Registrar shall be those of an Assistant Secretary-General of the United Nations.

4. The staff of the Registry shall be appointed by the Secretary-General on the recommendation of the Registrar.

Article 17. Investigation and preparation of indictment. 1. The Prosecutor shall initiate investigations ex-officio or on the basis of information obtained from any source, particularly from Governments, United Nations organs, intergovernmental and non-governmental organizations. The Prosecutor shall assess the information received or obtained and decide whether there is sufficient basis to proceed.

2. The Prosecutor shall have the power to question suspects, victims and witnesses, to collect evidence and to conduct on-site investigations. In carrying out these tasks, the Prosecutor may, as appropriate, seek the assistance of the State authorities concerned.

3. If questioned, the suspect shall be entitled to be assisted by counsel of his or her own choice, including the right to have legal assistance assigned to the suspect without payment by him or her in any such case if he or she does not have sufficient means to pay for it, as well as to necessary translation into and from a language he or she speaks and understands.

4. Upon a determination that a prima facie case exists, the Prosecutor shall prepare an indictment containing a concise statement of the facts and the crime or crimes with which the accused is charged under the Statute. The indictment shall be transmitted to a judge of the Trial Chamber.

Article 18. Review of the indictment. 1. The judge of the Trial Chamber to whom the indictment has been transmitted shall review it. If satisfied that a prima facie case has been established by the Prosecutor, he or she shall confirm the indictment. If not so satisfied, the indictment shall be dismissed.

2. Upon confirmation of an indictment, the judge may, at the request of the Prosecutor, issue such orders and warrants for the arrest, detention, surrender or transfer of persons, and any other orders as may be required for the conduct of the trial.

Article 19. Commencement and conduct of trial proceedings. 1. The Trial Chambers shall ensure that a trial is fair and expeditious and that proceedings are conducted in accordance with the rules of procedure and evidence, with full respect for the rights of the accused and due regard for the protection of victims and witnesses.

2. A person against whom an indictment has been confirmed shall, pursuant to an order or an arrest warrant of the International Tribunal for Rwanda, be taken into custody, immediately informed of the charges against him or her and transferred to the International Tribunal for Rwanda.

3. The Trial Chamber shall read the indictment, satisfy itself that the rights of the accused are respected, confirm that the accused understands the indictment, and instruct the accused to enter a plea. The Trial Chamber shall then set the date for trial.

4. The hearings shall be public unless the Trial Chamber decides to close the proceedings in accordance with its rules of procedure and evidence.

Article 20. *Rights of the accused.* 1. All persons shall be equal before the International Tribunal for Rwanda.

2. In the determination of charges against him or her, the accused shall be entitled to a fair and public hearing, subject to article 21 of the Statute.

3. The accused shall be presumed innocent until proved guilty according to the provisions of the present Statute.

4. In the determination of any charge against the accused pursuant to the present Statute, the accused shall be entitled to the following minimum guarantees, in full equality:

(a) To be informed promptly and in detail in a language which he or she understands of the nature and cause of the charge against him or her;

(b) To have adequate time and facilities for the preparation of his or her defence and to communicate with counsel of his or her own choosing;

(c) To be tried without undue delay;

(d) To be tried in his or her presence, and to defend himself or herself in person or through legal assistance of his or her own choosing; to be informed, if he or she does not have legal assistance, of this right; and to have legal assistance assigned to him or her, in any case where the interests of justice so require, and without payment by him or her in any such case if he or she does not have sufficient means to pay for it;

(e) To examine, or have examined, the witnesses against him or her and to obtain the attendance and examination of witnesses on his or her behalf under the same conditions as witnesses against him or her;

(f) To have the free assistance of an interpreter if he or she cannot understand or speak the language used in the International Tribunal for Rwanda;

(g) Not to be compelled to testify against himself or herself or to confess guilt.

Article 21. *Protection of victims and witnesses.* The International Tribunal for Rwanda shall provide in its rules of procedure and evidence for the protection of victims and witnesses. Such protection measures shall include, but shall not be limited to, the conduct of in camera proceedings and the protection of the victim's identity.

Article 22. *Judgment.* 1. The Trial Chambers shall pronounce judgments and impose sentences and penalties on persons convicted of serious violations of international humanitarian law.

2. The judgment shall be rendered by a majority of the judges of the Trial Chamber, and shall be delivered by the Trial Chamber in public. It shall be accompanied by a reasoned opinion in writing, to which separate or dissenting opinions may be appended.

Article 23. *Penalties.* 1. The penalty imposed by the Trial Chamber shall be limited to imprisonment. In determining the terms of imprisonment, the Trial Chambers shall have recourse to the general practice regarding prison sentences in the courts of Rwanda.

2. In imposing the sentences, the Trial Chambers should take into account such factors as the gravity of the offence and the individual circumstances of the convicted person.

3. In addition to imprisonment, the Trial Chambers may order the return of any property and proceeds acquired by criminal conduct, including by means of duress, to their rightful owners.

Article 24. *Appellate proceedings.* 1. The Appeals Chamber shall hear appeals from persons convicted by the Trial Chambers or from the Prosecutor on the following grounds:

(a) An error on a question of law invalidating the decision; or

(b) An error of fact which has occasioned a miscarriage of justice.

2. The Appeals Chamber may affirm, reverse or revise the decisions taken by the Trial Chambers.

Article 25. *Review proceedings.* Where a new fact has been discovered which was not known at the time of the proceedings before the Trial Chambers or the Appeals Chamber and which could have been a decisive factor in reaching the decision, the convicted person or the Prosecutor may submit to the International Tribunal for Rwanda an application for review of the judgment.

Article 26. *Enforcement of sentences.* Imprisonment shall be served in Rwanda or any of the States on a list of States which have indicated to the Security Council their willingness to accept convicted persons, as designated by the International Tribunal for Rwanda. Such imprisonment shall be in accordance with the applicable law of the State concerned, subject to the supervision of the International Tribunal for Rwanda.

Article 27. *Pardon or commutation of sentences.* If, pursuant to the applicable law of the State in which the convicted person is imprisoned, he or she is eligible for pardon or commutation of sentence, the State concerned shall notify the International Tribunal for Rwanda accordingly. There shall only be pardon or commutation of sentence if the President of the International Tribunal for Rwanda, in consultation with the judges, so decides on the basis of the interests of justice and the general principles of law.

Article 28. *Cooperation and judicial assistance.* 1. States shall cooperate with the International Tribunal for Rwanda in the investigation and prosecution of persons accused of committing serious violations of international humanitarian law.

2. States shall comply without undue delay with any request for assistance or an order issued by a Trial Chamber, including, but not limited to:

(a) The identification and location of persons;

(b) The taking of testimony and the production of evidence;

(c) The service of documents;

(d) The arrest or detention of persons;

(e) The surrender or the transfer of the accused to the International Tribunal for Rwanda.

Article 29. *The status, privileges and immunities of the International Tribunal for Rwanda.* 1. The Convention on the Privileges and Immunities of the United Nations of 13 February 1946 shall apply to the International Tribunal for Rwanda, the judges, the Prosecutor and his or her staff, and the Registrar and his or her staff.

2. The judges, the Prosecutor and the Registrar shall enjoy the privileges and immunities, exemptions and facilities accorded to diplomatic envoys, in accordance with international law.

3. The staff of the Prosecutor and of the Registrar shall enjoy the privileges and immunities accorded to officials of the United Nations under articles V and VII of the Convention referred to in paragraph 1 of this article.

4. Other persons, including the accused, required at the seat or meeting place of the International Tribunal for Rwanda shall be accorded such treatment as is necessary for the proper functioning of the International Tribunal for Rwanda.

Article 30. *Expenses of the International Tribunal for Rwanda.* The expenses of the International Tribunal for Rwanda shall be expenses of the Organization in accordance with Article 17 of the Charter of the United Nations.

Article 31. *Working languages.* The working languages of the International Tribunal shall be English and French.

Article 32. *Annual report.* The President of the International Tribunal for Rwanda shall submit an annual report of the International Tribunal for Rwanda to the Security Council and to the General Assembly.

ROME STATUTE OF THE INTERNATIONAL CRIMINAL COURT*

PREAMBLE

The States Parties to this Statute,

Conscious that all peoples are united by common bonds, their cultures pieced together in a shared heritage, and concerned that this delicate mosaic may be shattered at any time,

Mindful that during this century millions of children, women and men have been victims of unimaginable atrocities that deeply shock the conscience of humanity,

Recognizing that such grave crimes threaten the peace, security and well-being of the world,

Affirming that the most serious crimes of concern to the international community as a whole must not go unpunished and that their effective prosecution must be ensured by taking measures at the national level and by enhancing international cooperation,

Determined to put an end to impunity for the perpetrators of these crimes and thus to contribute to the prevention of such crimes,

Recalling that it is the duty of every State to exercise its criminal jurisdiction over those responsible for international crimes,

Reaffirming the Purposes and Principles of the Charter of the United Nations, and in particular that all States shall refrain from the threat or use of force against the territorial integrity or political independence of any State, or in any other manner inconsistent with the Purposes of the United Nations,

Emphasizing in this connection that nothing in this Statute shall be taken as authorizing any State Party to intervene in an armed conflict or in the internal affairs of any State,

Determined to these ends and for the sake of present and future generations, to establish an independent permanent International Criminal Court in relationship with the United Nations system, with jurisdiction over the most serious crimes of concern to the international community as a whole,

Emphasizing that the International Criminal Court established under this Statute shall be complementary to national criminal jurisdictions,

Resolved to guarantee lasting respect for and the enforcement of international justice,

Have agreed as follows

PART 1. ESTABLISHMENT OF THE COURT

Article 1
The Court

An International Criminal Court ("the Court") is hereby established. It shall be a permanent institution and shall have the power to exercise its jurisdiction over persons for the most serious crimes of international concern, as referred to in this Statute, and

* (2002), http://www.un.org/law/icc/statute/english/rome_statute(e).pdf (entered into force on July 1, 2002).

shall be complementary to national criminal jurisdictions. The jurisdiction and functioning of the Court shall be governed by the provisions of this Statute.

. . . .

Article 4
Legal status and powers of the Court

1. The Court shall have international legal personality. It shall also have such legal capacity as may be necessary for the exercise of its functions and the fulfillment of its purposes.

2. The Court may exercise its functions and powers, as provided in this Statute, on the territory of any State Party and, by special agreement, on the territory of any other State.

PART 2. JURISDICTION, ADMISSIBILITY AND APPLICABLE LAW

Article 5
Crimes within the jurisdiction of the Court

1. The jurisdiction of the Court shall be limited to the most serious crimes of concern to the international community as a whole. The Court has jurisdiction in accordance with this Statute with respect to the following crimes:

(a) The crime of genocide;

(b) Crimes against humanity;

(c) War crimes;

(d) The crime of aggression.

2. The Court shall exercise jurisdiction over the crime of aggression once a provision is adopted in accordance with articles 121 and 123 defining the crime and setting out the conditions under which the Court shall exercise jurisdiction with respect to this crime. Such a provision shall be consistent with the relevant provisions of the Charter of the United Nations.

Article 6
Genocide

For the purpose of this Statute, "genocide" means any of the following acts committed with intent to destroy, in whole or in part, a national, ethnical, racial or religious group, as such:

(a) Killing members of the group;

(b) Causing serious bodily or mental harm to members of the group;

(c) Deliberately inflicting on the group conditions of life calculated to bring about its physical destruction in whole or in part;

(d) Imposing measures intended to prevent births within the group;

(e) Forcibly transferring children of the group to another group.

Article 7
Crimes against humanity

1. For the purpose of this Statute, "crime against humanity" means any of the following acts when committed as part of a widespread or systematic attack directed against any civilian population, with knowledge of the attack:

(a) Murder;

(b) Extermination;

(c) Enslavement;

(d) Deportation or forcible transfer of population;

(e) Imprisonment or other severe deprivation of physical liberty in violation of fundamental rules of international law;

(f) Torture;

(g) Rape, sexual slavery, enforced prostitution, forced pregnancy, enforced sterilization, or any other form of sexual violence of comparable gravity;

(h) Persecution against any identifiable group or collectivity on political, racial, national, ethnic, cultural, religious, gender as defined in paragraph 3, or other grounds that are universally recognized as impermissible under international law, in connection with any act referred to in this paragraph or any crime within the jurisdiction of the Court;

(i) Enforced disappearance of persons;

(j) The crime of apartheid;

(k) Other inhumane acts of a similar character intentionally causing great suffering, or serious injury to body or to mental or physical health.

2. For the purpose of paragraph 1:

(a) "Attack directed against any civilian population" means a course of conduct involving the multiple commission of acts referred to in paragraph 1 against any civilian population, pursuant to or in furtherance of a State or organizational policy to commit such attack;

(b) "Extermination" includes the intentional infliction of conditions of life, inter alia the deprivation of access to food and medicine, calculated to bring about the destruction of part of a population;

(c) "Enslavement" means the exercise of any or all of the powers attaching to the right of ownership over a person and includes the exercise of such power in the course of trafficking in persons, in particular women and children;

(d) "Deportation or forcible transfer of population" means forced displacement of the persons concerned by expulsion or other coercive acts from the area in which they are lawfully present, without grounds permitted under international law;

(e) "Torture" means the intentional infliction of severe pain or suffering, whether physical or mental, upon a person in the custody or under the control of the accused; except that torture shall not include pain or suffering arising only from, inherent in or incidental to, lawful sanctions;

(f) "Forced pregnancy" means the unlawful confinement of a woman forcibly made pregnant, with the intent of affecting the ethnic composition of any population or carrying out other grave violations of international law. This definition shall not in any way be interpreted as affecting national laws relating to pregnancy;

(g) "Persecution" means the intentional and severe deprivation of fundamental rights contrary to international law by reason of the identity of the group or collectivity;

(h) "The crime of apartheid" means inhumane acts of a character similar to those referred to in paragraph 1, committed in the context of an institutionalized regime of systematic oppression and domination by one racial group over any other racial group or groups and committed with the intention of maintaining that regime;

(i) "Enforced disappearance of persons" means the arrest, detention or abduction of persons by, or with the authorization, support or acquiescence of, a State or a political organization, followed by a refusal to acknowledge that deprivation of freedom or to give information on the fate or whereabouts of those persons, with the intention of removing them from the protection of the law for a prolonged period of time.

3. For the purpose of this Statute, it is understood that the term "gender" refers to the two sexes, male and female, within the context of society. The term "gender" does not indicate any meaning different from the above.

Article 8
War crimes

1. The Court shall have jurisdiction in respect of war crimes in particular when committed as part of a plan or policy or as part of a large-scale commission of such crimes.

2. For the purpose of this Statute, "war crimes" means:

(a) Grave breaches of the Geneva Conventions of 12 August 1949, namely, any of the following acts against persons or property protected under the provisions of the relevant Geneva Convention:

(i) Willful killing;

(ii) Torture or inhuman treatment, including biological experiments;

(iii) Willfully causing great suffering, or serious injury to body or health;

(iv) Extensive destruction and appropriation of property, not justified by military necessity and carried out unlawfully and wantonly;

(v) Compelling a prisoner of war or other protected person to serve in the forces of a hostile Power;

(vi) Willfully depriving a prisoner of war or other protected person of the rights of fair and regular trial;

(vii) Unlawful deportation or transfer or unlawful confinement;

(viii)Taking of hostages.

(b) Other serious violations of the laws and customs applicable in international armed conflict, within the established framework of international law, namely, any of the following acts:

(i) Intentionally directing attacks against the civilian population as such or against individual civilians not taking direct part in hostilities;

(ii) Intentionally directing attacks against civilian objects, that is, objects which are not military objectives;

(iii) Intentionally directing attacks against personnel, installations, material, units or vehicles involved in a humanitarian assistance or peacekeeping mission in accordance with the Charter of the United Nations, as long as they are entitled to the protection given to civilians or civilian objects under the international law of armed conflict;

(iv) Intentionally launching an attack in the knowledge that such attack will cause incidental loss of life or injury to civilians or damage to civilian objects or widespread, long-term and severe damage to the natural environment which would be clearly excessive in relation to the concrete and direct overall military advantage anticipated;

(v) Attacking or bombarding, by whatever means, towns, villages, dwellings or buildings which are undefended and which are not military objectives;

(vi) Killing or wounding a combatant who, having laid down his arms or having no longer means of defence, has surrendered at discretion;

(vii) Making improper use of a flag of truce, of the flag or of the military insignia and uniform of the enemy or of the United Nations, as well as of the distinctive emblems of the Geneva Conventions, resulting in death or serious personal injury;

(viii) The transfer, directly or indirectly, by the Occupying Power of parts of its own civilian population into the territory it occupies, or the deportation or transfer of all or parts of the population of the occupied territory within or outside this territory;

(ix) Intentionally directing attacks against buildings dedicated to religion, education, art, science or charitable purposes, historic monuments, hospitals and places where the sick and wounded are collected, provided they are not military objectives;

(x) Subjecting persons who are in the power of an adverse party to physical mutilation or to medical or scientific experiments of any kind which are neither justified by the medical, dental or hospital treatment of the person concerned nor carried out in his or her interest, and which cause death to or seriously endanger the health of such person or persons;

(xi) Killing or wounding treacherously individuals belonging to the hostile nation or army;

(xii) Declaring that no quarter will be given;

(xiii) Destroying or seizing the enemy's property unless such destruction or seizure be imperatively demanded by the necessities of war;

(xiv) Declaring abolished, suspended or inadmissible in a court of law the rights and actions of the nationals of the hostile party;

(xv) Compelling the nationals of the hostile party to take part in the operations of war directed against their own country, even if they were in the belligerent's service before the commencement of the war;

(xvi) Pillaging a town or place, even when taken by assault;

(xvii) Employing poison or poisoned weapons;

(xviii) Employing asphyxiating, poisonous or other gases, and all analogous liquids, materials or devices;

(xix) Employing bullets which expand or flatten easily in the human body, such as bullets with a hard envelope which does not entirely cover the core or is pierced with incisions;

(xx) Employing weapons, projectiles and material and methods of warfare which are of a nature to cause superfluous injury or unnecessary suffering or which are inherently indiscriminate in violation of the international law of armed conflict, provided that such weapons, projectiles and material and methods of warfare are the subject of a comprehensive prohibition and are included in an annex to this Statute, by an amendment in accordance with the relevant provisions set forth in articles 121 and 123;

(xxi) Committing outrages upon personal dignity, in particular humiliating and degrading treatment;

(xxii) Committing rape, sexual slavery, enforced prostitution, forced pregnancy, as defined in article 7, paragraph 2 (f), enforced sterilization, or any other form of sexual violence also constituting a grave breach of the Geneva Conventions;

(xxiii) Utilizing the presence of a civilian or other protected person to render certain points, areas or military forces immune from military operations;

(xxiv) Intentionally directing attacks against buildings, material, medical units and transport, and personnel using the distinctive emblems of the Geneva Conventions in conformity with international law;

(xxv) Intentionally using starvation of civilians as a method of warfare by depriving them of objects indispensable to their survival, including willfully impeding relief supplies as provided for under the Geneva Conventions;

(xxvi) Conscripting or enlisting children under the age of fifteen years into the national armed forces or using them to participate actively in hostilities.

(c) In the case of an armed conflict not of an international character, serious violations of article 3 common to the four Geneva Conventions of 12 August 1949, namely, any of the following acts committed against persons taking no active part in the hostilities, including members of armed forces who have laid down their arms and those placed hors de combat by sickness, wounds, detention or any other cause:

(i) Violence to life and person, in particular murder of all kinds, mutilation, cruel treatment and torture;

(ii) Committing outrages upon personal dignity, in particular humiliating and degrading treatment;

(iii) Taking of hostages;

(iv) The passing of sentences and the carrying out of executions without previous judgment pronounced by a regularly constituted court, affording all judicial guarantees which are generally recognized as indispensable.

(d) Paragraph 2 (c) applies to armed conflicts not of an international character and thus does not apply to situations of internal disturbances and tensions, such as riots, isolated and sporadic acts of violence or other acts of a similar nature.

(e) Other serious violations of the laws and customs applicable in armed conflicts not of an international character, within the established framework of international law, namely, any of the following acts:

(i) Intentionally directing attacks against the civilian population as such or against individual civilians not taking direct part in hostilities;

(ii) Intentionally directing attacks against buildings, material, medical units and transport, and personnel using the distinctive emblems of the Geneva Conventions in conformity with international law;

(iii) Intentionally directing attacks against personnel, installations, material, units or vehicles involved in a humanitarian assistance or peacekeeping mission in accordance with the Charter of the United Nations, as long as they are entitled to the protection given to civilians or civilian objects under the international law of armed conflict;

(iv) Intentionally directing attacks against buildings dedicated to religion, education, art, science or charitable purposes, historic monuments, hospitals and places where the sick and wounded are collected, provided they are not military objectives;

(v) Pillaging a town or place, even when taken by assault;

(vi) Committing rape, sexual slavery, enforced prostitution, forced pregnancy, as defined in article 7, paragraph 2 (f), enforced sterilization, and any other form of sexual violence also constituting a serious violation of article 3 common to the four Geneva Conventions;

(vii) Conscripting or enlisting children under the age of fifteen years into armed forces or groups or using them to participate actively in hostilities;

(viii)Ordering the displacement of the civilian population for reasons related to the conflict, unless the security of the civilians involved or imperative military reasons so demand;

(ix) Killing or wounding treacherously a combatant adversary;

(x) Declaring that no quarter will be given;

(xi) Subjecting persons who are in the power of another party to the conflict to physical mutilation or to medical or scientific experiments of any kind which are neither justified by the medical, dental or hospital treatment of the person concerned nor carried out in his or her interest, and which cause death to or seriously endanger the health of such person or persons;

(xii) Destroying or seizing the property of an adversary unless such destruction or seizure be imperatively demanded by the necessities of the conflict;

(f) Paragraph 2 (e) applies to armed conflicts not of an international character and thus does not apply to situations of internal disturbances and tensions, such as riots, isolated and sporadic acts of violence or other acts of a similar nature. It applies to armed conflicts that take place in the territory of a State when there is protracted armed conflict between governmental authorities and organized armed groups or between such groups.

3. Nothing in paragraph 2 (c) and (e) shall affect the responsibility of a Government to maintain or re-establish law and order in the State or to defend the unity and territorial integrity of the State, by all legitimate means.

Article 9
Elements of Crimes

1. Elements of Crimes shall assist the Court in the interpretation and application of articles 6, 7 and 8. They shall be adopted by a two-thirds majority of the members of the Assembly of States Parties.

2. Amendments to the Elements of Crimes may be proposed by:

(a) Any State Party;

(b) The judges acting by an absolute majority;

(c) The Prosecutor.

Such amendments shall be adopted by a two-thirds majority of the members of the Assembly of States Parties.

3. The Elements of Crimes and amendments thereto shall be consistent with this Statute.

....

Article 11
Jurisdiction ratione temporis

1. The Court has jurisdiction only with respect to crimes committed after the entry into force of this Statute.

2. If a State becomes a Party to this Statute after its entry into force, the Court may exercise its jurisdiction only with respect to crimes committed after the entry into force of this Statute for that State, unless that State has made a declaration under article 12, paragraph 3.

Article 12
Preconditions to the exercise of jurisdiction

1. A State which becomes a Party to this Statute thereby accepts the jurisdiction of the Court with respect to the crimes referred to in article 5.

2. In the case of article 13, paragraph (a) or (c), the Court may exercise its jurisdiction if one or more of the following States are Parties to this Statute or have accepted the jurisdiction of the Court in accordance with paragraph 3:

(a) The State on the territory of which the conduct in question occurred or, if the crime was committed on board a vessel or aircraft, the State of registration of that vessel or aircraft;

(b) The State of which the person accused of the crime is a national.

3. If the acceptance of a State which is not a Party to this Statute is required under paragraph 2, that State may, by declaration lodged with the Registrar, accept the exercise of jurisdiction by the Court with respect to the crime in question. The accepting State shall cooperate with the Court without any delay or exception in accordance with Part 9.

Article 13
Exercise of jurisdiction

The Court may exercise its jurisdiction with respect to a crime referred to in article 5 in accordance with the provisions of this Statute if:

(a) A situation in which one or more of such crimes appears to have been committed is referred to the Prosecutor by a State Party in accordance with article 14;

(b) A situation in which one or more of such crimes appears to have been committed is referred to the Prosecutor by the Security Council acting under Chapter VII of the Charter of the United Nations; or

(c) The Prosecutor has initiated an investigation in respect of such a crime in accordance with article 15.

Article 14
Referral of a situation by a State Party

1. A State Party may refer to the Prosecutor a situation in which one or more crimes within the jurisdiction of the Court appear to have been committed requesting the Prosecutor to investigate the situation for the purpose of determining whether one or more specific persons should be charged with the commission of such crimes.

2. As far as possible, a referral shall specify the relevant circumstances and be accompanied by such supporting documentation as is available to the State referring the situation.

....

Article 21
Applicable law

1. The Court shall apply:

(a) In the first place, this Statute, Elements of Crimes and its Rules of Procedure and Evidence;

(b) In the second place, where appropriate, applicable treaties and the principles and rules of international law, including the established principles of the international law of armed conflict;

(c) Failing that, general principles of law derived by the Court from national laws of legal systems of the world including, as appropriate, the national laws of States that would normally exercise jurisdiction over the crime, provided that those principles are not inconsistent with this Statute and with international law and internationally recognized norms and standards.

2. The Court may apply principles and rules of law as interpreted in its previous decisions.

3. The application and interpretation of law pursuant to this article must be consistent with internationally recognized human rights, and be without any adverse distinction founded on grounds such as gender as defined in article 7, paragraph 3, age, race, colour, language, religion or belief, political or other opinion, national, ethnic or social origin, wealth, birth or other status.

....

Article 25
Individual criminal responsibility

1. The Court shall have jurisdiction over natural persons pursuant to this Statute.

2. A person who commits a crime within the jurisdiction of the Court shall be individually responsible and liable for punishment in accordance with this Statute.

3. In accordance with this Statute, a person shall be criminally responsible and liable for punishment for a crime within the jurisdiction of the Court if that person:

(a) Commits such a crime, whether as an individual, jointly with another or through another person, regardless of whether that other person is criminally responsible;

(b) Orders, solicits or induces the commission of such a crime which in fact occurs or is attempted;

(c) For the purpose of facilitating the commission of such a crime, aids, abets or otherwise assists in its commission or its attempted commission, including providing the means for its commission;

(d) In any other way contributes to the commission or attempted commission of such a crime by a group of persons acting with a common purpose. Such contribution shall be intentional and shall either:

(i) Be made with the aim of furthering the criminal activity or criminal purpose of the group, where such activity or purpose involves the commission of a crime within the jurisdiction of the Court; or

(ii) Be made in the knowledge of the intention of the group to commit the crime;

(e) In respect of the crime of genocide, directly and publicly incites others to commit genocide;

(f) Attempts to commit such a crime by taking action that commences its execution by means of a substantial step, but the crime does not occur because of circumstances independent of the person's intentions. However, a person who abandons the effort to commit the crime or otherwise prevents the completion of the crime shall not be liable for punishment under this Statute for the attempt to commit that crime if that person completely and voluntarily gave up the criminal purpose.

4. No provision in this Statute relating to individual criminal responsibility shall affect the responsibility of States under international law.

Article 26
Exclusion of jurisdiction over persons under eighteen

The Court shall have no jurisdiction over any person who was under the age of 18 at the time of the alleged commission of a crime.

Article 27
Irrelevance of official capacity

1. This Statute shall apply equally to all persons without any distinction based on official capacity. In particular, official capacity as a Head of State or Government, a member of a Government or parliament, an elected representative or a government official shall in no case exempt a person from criminal responsibility under this Statute, nor shall it, in and of itself, constitute a ground for reduction of sentence.

2. Immunities or special procedural rules which may attach to the official capacity of a person, whether under national or international law, shall not bar the Court from exercising its jurisdiction over such a person.

Article 28
Responsibility of commanders and other superiors

In addition to other grounds of criminal responsibility under this Statute for crimes within the jurisdiction of the Court:

(a) A military commander or person effectively acting as a military commander shall be criminally responsible for crimes within the jurisdiction of the Court committed by forces under his or her effective command and control, or effective authority and control as the case may be, as a result of his or her failure to exercise control properly over such forces, where:

(i) That military commander or person either knew or, owing to the circumstances at the time, should have known that the forces were committing or about to commit such crimes; and

(ii) That military commander or person failed to take all necessary and reasonable measures within his or her power to prevent or repress their commission or to submit the matter to the competent authorities for investigation and prosecution.

(b) With respect to superior and subordinate relationships not described in paragraph (a), a superior shall be criminally responsible for crimes within the jurisdiction of the Court committed by subordinates under his or her effective authority and control, as a result of his or her failure to exercise control properly over such subordinates, where:

(i) The superior either knew, or consciously disregarded information which clearly indicated, that the subordinates were committing or about to commit such crimes;

(ii) The crimes concerned activities that were within the effective responsibility and control of the superior; and

(iii) The superior failed to take all necessary and reasonable measures within his or her power to prevent or repress their commission or to submit the matter to the competent authorities for investigation and prosecution.

Article 29
Non-applicability of statute of limitations

The crimes within the jurisdiction of the Court shall not be subject to any statute of limitations.

....

Article 33
Superior orders and prescription of law

1. The fact that a crime within the jurisdiction of the Court has been committed by a person pursuant to an order of a Government or of a superior, whether military or civilian, shall not relieve that person of criminal responsibility unless:

(a) The person was under a legal obligation to obey orders of the Government or the superior in question;

(b) The person did not know that the order was unlawful; and

(c) The order was not manifestly unlawful.

2. For the purposes of this article, orders to commit genocide or crimes against humanity are manifestly unlawful.

....

Article 34
Organs of the Court

The Court shall be composed of the following organs:

(a) The Presidency;

(b) An Appeals Division, a Trial Division and a Pre-Trial Division;

(c) The Office of the Prosecutor;

(d) The Registry.

....

Article 36
Qualifications, nomination and election of judges

1. Subject to the provisions of paragraph 2, there shall be 18 judges of the Court.

....

Article 72
Protection of national security information

1. This article applies in any case where the disclosure of the information or documents of a State would, in the opinion of that State, prejudice its national security interests. Such cases include those falling within the scope of article 56, paragraphs 2 and 3, article 61, paragraph 3, article 64, paragraph 3, article 67, paragraph 2, article 68, paragraph 6, article 87, paragraph 6 and article 93, as well as cases arising at any other stage of the proceedings where such disclosure may be at issue.

2. This article shall also apply when a person who has been requested to give information or evidence has refused to do so or has referred the matter to the State on the ground that disclosure would prejudice the national security interests of a State and the State concerned confirms that it is of the opinion that disclosure would prejudice its national security interests.

3. Nothing in this article shall prejudice the requirements of confidentiality applicable under article 54, paragraph 3 (e) and (f), or the application of article 73.

4. If a State learns that information or documents of the State are being, or are likely to be, disclosed at any stage of the proceedings, and it is of the opinion that disclosure would prejudice its national security interests, that State shall have the right to intervene in order to obtain resolution of the issue in accordance with this article.

5. If, in the opinion of a State, disclosure of information would prejudice its national security interests, all reasonable steps will be taken by the State, acting in conjunction with the Prosecutor, the defence or the Pre-Trial Chamber or Trial Chamber, as the case may be, to seek to resolve the matter by cooperative means. Such steps may include:

(a) Modification or clarification of the request;

(b) A determination by the Court regarding the relevance of the information or evidence sought, or a determination as to whether the evidence, though relevant, could be or has been obtained from a source other than the requested State;

(c) Obtaining the information or evidence from a different source or in a different form; or

(d) Agreement on conditions under which the assistance could be provided including, among other things, providing summaries or redactions, limitations on disclosure, use of in camera or ex parte proceedings, or other protective measures permissible under the Statute and the Rules of Procedure and Evidence.

6. Once all reasonable steps have been taken to resolve the matter through cooperative means, and if the State considers that there are no means or conditions under which the information or documents could be provided or disclosed without prejudice to its national security interests, it shall so notify the Prosecutor or the Court of the specific reasons for its decision, unless a specific description of the reasons would itself necessarily result in such prejudice to the State's national security interests.

7. Thereafter, if the Court determines that the evidence is relevant and necessary for the establishment of the guilt or innocence of the accused, the Court may undertake the following actions:

(a) Where disclosure of the information or document is sought pursuant to a request for cooperation under Part 9 or the circumstances described in paragraph 2, and the State has invoked the ground for refusal referred to in article 93, paragraph 4:

(i) The Court may, before making any conclusion referred to in subparagraph 7 (a) (ii), request further consultations for the purpose of considering the State's representations, which may include, as appropriate, hearings in camera and ex parte;

(ii) If the Court concludes that, by invoking the ground for refusal under article 93, paragraph 4, in the circumstances of the case, the requested State is not acting in accordance with its obligations under this Statute, the Court may refer the matter in accordance with article 87, paragraph 7, specifying the reasons for its conclusion; and

(iii) The Court may make such inference in the trial of the accused as to the existence or non-existence of a fact, as may be appropriate in the circumstances; or

(b) In all other circumstances:

(i) Order disclosure; or

(ii) To the extent it does not order disclosure, make such inference in the trial of the accused as to the existence or non-existence of a fact, as may be appropriate in the circumstances.

....

PART 7. PENALTIES

Article 77
Applicable penalties

1. Subject to article 110, the Court may impose one of the following penalties on a person convicted of a crime referred to in article 5 of this Statute:

(a) Imprisonment for a specified number of years, which may not exceed a maximum of 30 years; or

(b) A term of life imprisonment when justified by the extreme gravity of the crime and the individual circumstances of the convicted person.

2. In addition to imprisonment, the Court may order:

(a) A fine under the criteria provided for in the Rules of Procedure and Evidence;

(b) A forfeiture of proceeds, property and assets derived directly or indirectly from that crime, without prejudice to the rights of bona fide third parties.

....

Article 86
General obligation to cooperate

States Parties shall, in accordance with the provisions of this Statute, cooperate fully with the Court in its investigation and prosecution of crimes within the jurisdiction of the Court.

....

PART 11. ASSEMBLY OF STATES PARTIES

Article 112
Assembly of States Parties

1. An Assembly of States Parties to this Statute is hereby established. Each State Party shall have one representative in the Assembly who may be accompanied by alternates and advisers. Other States which have signed this Statute or the Final Act may be observers in the Assembly.

2. The Assembly shall:

(a) Consider and adopt, as appropriate, recommendations of the Preparatory Commission;

(b) Provide management oversight to the Presidency, the Prosecutor and the Registrar regarding the administration of the Court;

(c) Consider the reports and activities of the Bureau established under paragraph 3 and take appropriate action in regard thereto;

(d) Consider and decide the budget for the Court;

(e) Decide whether to alter, in accordance with article 36, the number of judges;

(f) Consider pursuant to article 87, paragraphs 5 and 7, any question relating to non-cooperation;

(g) Perform any other function consistent with this Statute or the Rules of Procedure and Evidence.

3. (a) The Assembly shall have a Bureau consisting of a President, two Vice-Presidents and 18 members elected by the Assembly for three-year terms.

(b) The Bureau shall have a representative character, taking into account, in particular, equitable geographical distribution and the adequate representation of the principal legal systems of the world.

(c) The Bureau shall meet as often as necessary, but at least once a year. It shall assist the Assembly in the discharge of its responsibilities.

4. The Assembly may establish such subsidiary bodies as may be necessary, including an independent oversight mechanism for inspection, evaluation and investigation of the Court, in order to enhance its efficiency and economy.

5. The President of the Court, the Prosecutor and the Registrar or their representatives may participate, as appropriate, in meetings of the Assembly and of the Bureau.

6. The Assembly shall meet at the seat of the Court or at the Headquarters of the United Nations once a year and, when circumstances so require, hold special sessions. Except as otherwise specified in this Statute, special sessions shall be convened by the Bureau on its own initiative or at the request of one third of the States Parties.

7. Each State Party shall have one vote. Every effort shall be made to reach decisions by consensus in the Assembly and in the Bureau. If consensus cannot be reached, except as otherwise provided in the Statute:

(a) Decisions on matters of substance must be approved by a two-thirds majority of those present and voting provided that an absolute majority of States Parties constitutes the quorum for voting;

(b) Decisions on matters of procedure shall be taken by a simple majority of States Parties present and voting.

8. A State Party which is in arrears in the payment of its financial contributions towards the costs of the Court shall have no vote in the Assembly and in the Bureau if the amount of its arrears equals or exceeds the amount of the contributions due from it for the preceding two full years. The Assembly may, nevertheless, permit such a State Party to vote in the Assembly and in the Bureau if it is satisfied that the failure to pay is due to conditions beyond the control of the State Party.

9. The Assembly shall adopt its own rules of procedure.

10. The official and working languages of the Assembly shall be those of the General Assembly of the United Nations.

....

PART 13. FINAL CLAUSES

Article 119
Settlement of disputes

1. Any dispute concerning the judicial functions of the Court shall be settled by the decision of the Court.

2. Any other dispute between two or more States Parties relating to the interpretation or application of this Statute which is not settled through negotiations within three months of their commencement shall be referred to the Assembly of States Parties. The Assembly may itself seek to settle the dispute or may make recommendations on further means of settlement of the dispute, including referral to the International Court of Justice in conformity with the Statute of that Court.

Article 120
Reservations

No reservations may be made to this Statute.

....

UN SECURITY COUNCIL RESOLUTION 1315* (SIERRA LEONE SPECIAL COURT)

The Security Council:

Deeply concerned at the very serious crimes committed within the territory of Sierra Leone against the people of Sierra Leone and United Nations and associated personnel and at the prevailing situation of impunity,

Commending the efforts of the Government of Sierra Leone and the Economic Community of West African States (ECOWAS) to bring lasting peace to Sierra Leone,

Noting that the Heads of State and Government of ECOWAS agreed at the 23rd Summit of the Organization in Abuja on 28 and 29 May 2000 to dispatch a regional investigation of the resumption of hostilities,

Noting also the steps taken by the Government of Sierra Leone in creating a national truth and reconciliation process, as required by Article XXVI of the Lomé Peace Agreement (S/1999/777) to contribute to the promotion of the rule of law,

Recalling that the Special Representative of the Secretary-General appended to his signature of the Lomé Agreement a statement that the United Nations holds the understanding that the amnesty provisions of the Agreement shall not apply to international crimes of genocide, crimes against humanity, war crimes and other serious violations of international humanitarian law,

Reaffirming the importance of compliance with international humanitarian law, and *reaffirming further* that persons who commit or authorize serious violations of international humanitarian law are individually responsible and accountable for those violations and that the international community will exert every effort to bring those responsible to justice in accordance with international standards of justice, fairness and due process of law,

Recognizing that, in the particular circumstances of Sierra Leone, a credible system of justice and accountability for the very serious crimes committed there would end impunity and would contribute to the process of national reconciliation and to the restoration and maintenance of peace,

Taking note in this regard of the letter dated 12 June 2000 from the President of Sierra Leone to the Secretary-General and the Suggested Framework attached to it (S/2000/786, annex),

Recognizing further the desire of the Government of Sierra Leone for assistance from the United Nations in establishing a strong and credible court that will meet the objectives of bringing justice and ensuring lasting peace,

Noting the report of the Secretary-General of 31 July 2000 (S/2000/751) and, in particular, *taking note* with appreciation of the steps already taken by the Secretary-General in response to the request of the Government of Sierra Leone to assist it in establishing a special court,

---

* S.C. Res. 1315, U.N. Doc. S/RES/1315 (Aug. 14, 2000), *available at* http://www.un.org/Docs/scres/2000/sc2000.htm.

Noting further the negative impact of the security situation on the administration of justice in Sierra Leone and the pressing need for international cooperation to assist in strengthening the judicial system of Sierra Leone,

Acknowledging the important contribution that can be made to this effort by qualified persons from West African States, the Commonwealth, other Member States of the United Nations and international organizations, to expedite the process of bringing justice and reconciliation to Sierra Leone and the region,

Reiterating that the situation in Sierra Leone continues to constitute a threat to international peace and security in the region,

1. *Requests* the Secretary-General to negotiate an agreement with the Government of Sierra Leone to create an independent special court consistent with this resolution, and *expresses* its readiness to take further steps expeditiously upon receiving and reviewing the report of the Secretary-General referred to in paragraph 6 below;

2. *Recommends* that the subject matter jurisdiction of the special court should include notably crimes against humanity, war crimes and other serious violations of international humanitarian law, as well as crimes under relevant Sierra Leonean law committed within the territory of Sierra Leone;

3. *Recommends further* that the special court should have personal jurisdiction over persons who bear the greatest responsibility for the commission of the crimes referred to in paragraph 2, including those leaders who, in committing such crimes, have threatened the establishment of and implementation of the peace process in Sierra Leone;

4. *Emphasizes* the importance of ensuring the impartiality, independence and credibility of the process, in particular with regard to the status of the judges and the prosecutors;

5. *Requests*, in this connection, that the Secretary-General, if necessary, send a team of experts to Sierra Leone as may be required to prepare the report referred to in paragraph 6 below;

6. *Requests* the Secretary-General to submit a report to the Security Council on the implementation of this resolution, in particular on his consultations and negotiations with the Government of Sierra Leone concerning the establishment of the special court, including recommendations, no later than 30 days from the date of this resolution;

7. *Requests* the Secretary-General to address in his report the questions of the temporal jurisdiction of the special court, an appeals process including the advisability, feasibility, and appropriateness of an appeals chamber in the special court or of sharing the Appeals Chamber of the International Criminal Tribunals for the Former Yugoslavia and Rwanda or other effective options, and a possible alternative host State, should it be necessary to convene the special court outside the seat of the court in Sierra Leone, if circumstances so require;

8. *Requests* the Secretary-General to include recommendations on the following:

(a) any additional agreements that may be required for the provision of the international assistance which will be necessary for the establishment and functioning of the special court;

(b) the level of participation, support and technical assistance of qualified persons from Member States of the United Nations, including in particular, member States of ECOWAS and the Commonwealth, and from the United Nations Mission in Sierra Leone that will be necessary for the efficient, independent and impartial functioning of the special court;

(c) the amount of voluntary contributions, as appropriate, of funds, equipment and services to the special court, including through the offer of expert personnel that may be needed from States, intergovernmental organizations and non-governmental organizations;

(d) whether the special court could receive, as necessary and feasible, expertise and advice from the International Criminal Tribunals for the Former Yugoslavia and Rwanda;

9. *Decides* to remain actively seized of the matter.

STATUTE OF THE INTERNATIONAL CRIMINAL TRIBUNAL FOR THE FORMER YUGOSLAVIA*

(ADOPTED 25 MAY 1993 BY RESOLUTION 827)
(AS AMENDED 13 MAY 1998 BY RESOLUTION 1166)
(AS AMENDED 30 NOVEMBER 2000 BY RESOLUTION 1329)
(AS AMENDED 17 MAY 2002 BY RESOLUTION 1411)
(AS AMENDED 14 AUGUST 2002 BY RESOLUTION 1431)
(AS AMENDED 19 MAY 2003 BY RESOLUTION 1481)

Having been established by the Security Council acting under Chapter VII of the Charter of the United Nations, the International Tribunal for the Prosecution of Persons Responsible for Serious Violations of International Humanitarian Law Committed in the Territory of the Former Yugoslavia since 1991 (hereinafter referred to as "the International Tribunal") shall function in accordance with the provisions of the present Statute.

Article 1
Competence of the International Tribunal

The International Tribunal shall have the power to prosecute persons responsible for serious violations of international humanitarian law committed in the territory of the former Yugoslavia since 1991 in accordance with the provisions of the present Statute.

Article 2
Grave breaches of the Geneva Conventions of 1949

The International Tribunal shall have the power to prosecute persons committing or ordering to be committed grave breaches of the Geneva Conventions of 12 August 1949, namely the following acts against persons or property protected under the provisions of the relevant Geneva Convention:

(a) willful killing;

(b) torture or inhuman treatment, including biological experiments;

(c) willfully causing great suffering or serious injury to body or health;

(d) extensive destruction and appropriation of property, not justified by military necessity and carried out unlawfully and wantonly;

(e) compelling a prisoner of war or a civilian to serve in the forces of a hostile power;

(f) willfully depriving a prisoner of war or a civilian of the rights of fair and regular trial;

(g) unlawful deportation or transfer or unlawful confinement of a civilian;

(h) taking civilians as hostages.

---

* (2004), http://www.un.org/icty/basic/statut/statute-april04-e.pdf.

Article 3
Violations of the laws or customs of war

The International Tribunal shall have the power to prosecute persons violating the laws or customs of war. Such violations shall include, but not be limited to:

(a) employment of poisonous weapons or other weapons calculated to cause unnecessary suffering;

(b) wanton destruction of cities, towns or villages, or devastation not justified by military necessity;

(c) attack, or bombardment, by whatever means, of undefended towns, villages, dwellings, or buildings;

(d) seizure of, destruction or willful damage done to institutions dedicated to religion, charity and education, the arts and sciences, historic monuments and works of art and science;

(e) plunder of public or private property.

Article 4
Genocide

1. The International Tribunal shall have the power to prosecute persons committing genocide as defined in paragraph 2 of this article or of committing any of the other acts enumerated in paragraph 3 of this article.

2. Genocide means any of the following acts committed with intent to destroy, in whole or in part, a national, ethnical, racial or religious group, as such:

(a) killing members of the group;

(b) causing serious bodily or mental harm to members of the group;

(c) deliberately inflicting on the group conditions of life calculated to bring about its physical destruction in whole or in part;

(d) imposing measures intended to prevent births within the group;

(e) forcibly transferring children of the group to another group.

3. The following acts shall be punishable:

(a) genocide;

(b) conspiracy to commit genocide;

(c) direct and public incitement to commit genocide;

(d) attempt to commit genocide;

(e) complicity in genocide.

Article 5
Crimes against humanity

The International Tribunal shall have the power to prosecute persons responsible for the following crimes when committed in armed conflict, whether international or internal in character, and directed against any civilian population:

(a) murder;

(b) extermination;

(c) enslavement;

(d) deportation;

(e) imprisonment;

(f) torture;

(g) rape;

(h) persecutions on political, racial and religious grounds;

(i) other inhumane acts.

Article 6
Personal jurisdiction

The International Tribunal shall have jurisdiction over natural persons pursuant to the provisions of the present Statute.

Article 7
Individual criminal responsibility

1. A person who planned, instigated, ordered, committed or otherwise aided and abetted in the planning, preparation or execution of a crime referred to in articles 2 to 5 of the present Statute, shall be individually responsible for the crime.

2. The official position of any accused person, whether as Head of State or Government or as a responsible Government official, shall not relieve such person of criminal responsibility nor mitigate punishment.

3. The fact that any of the acts referred to in articles 2 to 5 of the present Statute was committed by a subordinate does not relieve his superior of criminal responsibility if he knew or had reason to know that the subordinate was about to commit such acts or had done so and the superior failed to take the necessary and reasonable measures to prevent such acts or to punish the perpetrators thereof.

4. The fact that an accused person acted pursuant to an order of a Government or of a superior shall not relieve him of criminal responsibility, but may be considered in mitigation of punishment if the International Tribunal determines that justice so requires.

Article 8
Territorial and temporal jurisdiction

The territorial jurisdiction of the International Tribunal shall extend to the territory of the former Socialist Federal Republic of Yugoslavia, including its land surface, airspace and territorial waters. The temporal jurisdiction of the International Tribunal shall extend to a period beginning on 1 January 1991.

Article 9
Concurrent jurisdiction

1. The International Tribunal and national courts shall have concurrent jurisdiction to prosecute persons for serious violations of international humanitarian law committed in the territory of the former Yugoslavia since 1 January 1991.

2. The International Tribunal shall have primacy over national courts. At any stage of the procedure, the International Tribunal may formally request national courts to defer

to the competence of the International Tribunal in accordance with the present Statute and the Rules of Procedure and Evidence of the International Tribunal.

. . . .

Article 11
Organization of the International Tribunal

The International Tribunal shall consist of the following organs:

(a) the Chambers, comprising three Trial Chambers and an Appeals Chamber;

(b) the Prosecutor; and

(c) a Registry, servicing both the Chambers and the Prosecutor.

. . . .

Article 21
Rights of the accused

1. All persons shall be equal before the International Tribunal.

2. In the determination of charges against him, the accused shall be entitled to a fair and public hearing, subject to article 22 of the Statute.

3. The accused shall be presumed innocent until proved guilty according to the provisions of the present Statute.

4. In the determination of any charge against the accused pursuant to the present Statute, the accused shall be entitled to the following minimum guarantees, in full equality:

(a) to be informed promptly and in detail in a language which he understands of the nature and cause of the charge against him;

(b) to have adequate time and facilities for the preparation of his defence and to communicate with counsel of his own choosing;

(c) to be tried without undue delay;

(d) to be tried in his presence, and to defend himself in person or through legal assistance of his own choosing; to be informed, if he does not have legal assistance, of this right; and to have legal assistance assigned to him, in any case where the interests of justice so require, and without payment by him in any such case if he does not have sufficient means to pay for it;

(e) to examine, or have examined, the witnesses against him and to obtain the attendance and examination of witnesses on his behalf under the same conditions as witnesses against him;

(f) to have the free assistance of an interpreter if he cannot understand or speak the language used in the International Tribunal;

(g) not to be compelled to testify against himself or to confess guilt.

Article 22
Protection of victims and witnesses

The International Tribunal shall provide in its rules of procedure and evidence for the protection of victims and witnesses. Such protection measures shall include, but shall not be limited to, the conduct of in camera proceedings and the protection of the victim's identity.

. . . .

G. International Responses to Transnational Terrorism: Criminal Responsibility for Human Rights Violations in Contravention of International Norms of Conduct

TOKYO CONVENTION ON OFFENCES AND CERTAIN OTHER ACTS COMMITTED ON BOARD AIRCRAFT*

THE STATES PARTIES to this Convention,

HAVE AGREED as follows:

Chapter I — Scope of the Convention

Article 1. 1. This Convention shall apply in respect of:

a. offences against penal law;

b. acts which, whether or not they are offences, may or do jeopardize the safety of the aircraft or of persons or property therein or which jeopardize good order and discipline on board.

1. Except as provided in Chapter III, this Convention shall apply in respect of offences committed or acts done by a person on board any aircraft registered in a Contracting State, while that aircraft is in flight or on the surface of the high seas or of any other area outside the territory of any State.

2. For the purposes of this Convention, an aircraft is considered to be in flight from the moment when power is applied for the purpose of take-off until the moment when the landing run ends.

3. This Convention shall not apply to aircraft used in military, customs or police services.

Article 2. Without prejudice to the provisions of Article 4 and except when the safety of the aircraft or of persons or property on board so requires, no provision of this Convention shall be interpreted as authorizing or requiring any action in respect of offences against penal laws of a political nature or those based on racial or religious discrimination.

Chapter II — Jurisdiction

Article 3. 1. The State of registration of the aircraft is competent to exercise jurisdiction over offences and acts committed on board.

1. Each Contracting State shall take such measures as may be necessary to establish its jurisdiction as the State of registration over offences committed on board aircraft registered in such State.

2. This Convention does not exclude any criminal jurisdiction exercised in accordance with national law.

Article 4. A Contracting State which is not the State of registration may not interfere with an aircraft in flight in order to exercise its criminal jurisdiction over an offence committed on board except in the following cases:

a. the offence has effect on the territory of such State;

---

* Convention on Offences and Certain Other Acts Committed on Board Aircraft, Sept. 14, 1963, 20 U.S.T. 2941, 704 U.N.T.S. 219 (entered into force Dec. 4, 1969), *available at* http://www.unodc.org/unodc/terrorism_convention_aircraft.html.

b. the offence has been committed by or against a national or permanent resident of such State;

c. the offence is against the security of such State;

d. the offence consists of a breach of any rules or regulations relating to the flight or manoeuvre of aircraft in force in such State;

e. the exercise of jurisdiction is necessary to ensure the observance of any obligation of such State under a multilateral international agreement.

Chapter III — Powers of the Aircraft Commander

Article 5. 1. The provisions of this Chapter shall not apply to offences and acts committed or about to be committed by a person on board an aircraft in flight in the airspace of the State of registration or over the high seas or any other area outside the territory of any State unless the last point of take-off or the next point of intended landing is situated in a State other than that of registration, or the aircraft subsequently flies in the airspace of a State other than that of registration with such person still on board.

1. Notwithstanding the provisions of Article 1, paragraph 3, an aircraft shall for the purposes of this Chapter, be considered to be in flight at any time from the moment when all its external doors are closed following embarkation until the moment when any such door is opened for disembarkation. In the case of a forced landing, the provisions of this Chapter shall continue to apply with respect to offences and acts committed on board until competent authorities of a State take over the responsibility for the aircraft and for the persons and property on board.

. . . .

Article 9. 1. The aircraft commander may deliver to the competent authorities of any Contracting State in the territory of which the aircraft lands any person who he has reasonable grounds to believe has committed on board the aircraft an act which, in his opinion, is a serious offence according to the penal law of the State of registration of the aircraft.

. . . .

Chapter V — Powers and Duties of States

. . . .

Article 13. 1. Any Contracting State shall take delivery of any person whom the aircraft commander delivers pursuant to Article 9, paragraph 1.

1. Upon being satisfied that the circumstances so warrant, any Contracting State shall take custody or other measures to ensure the presence of any person suspected of an act contemplated in Article 11, paragraph 1 and of any person of whom it has taken delivery. The custody and other measures shall be as provided in the law of that State but may only be continued for such time as is reasonably necessary to enable any criminal or extradition proceedings to be instituted.

2. Any person in custody pursuant to the previous paragraph shall be assisted in communicating immediately with the nearest appropriate representative of the State of which he is a national.

3. Any Contracting State, to which a person is delivered pursuant to Article 9, paragraph 1, or in whose territory an aircraft lands following the commission of an act con-

templated in Article 11, paragraph 1, shall immediately make a preliminary enquiry into the facts.

4. When a State, pursuant to this Article, has taken a person into custody, it shall immediately notify the State of registration of the aircraft and the State of nationality of the detained person and, if it considers it advisable, any other interested State of the fact that such person is in custody and of the circumstances which warrant his detention. The State which makes the preliminary enquiry contemplated in paragraph 4 of this Article shall promptly report its findings to the said States and shall indicate whether it intends to exercise jurisdiction.

Article 14. 1. When any person has been disembarked in accordance with Article 8, paragraph 1, or delivered in accordance with Article 9, paragraph 1, or has disembarked after committing an act contemplated in Article 11, paragraph 1, and when such person cannot or does not desire to continue his journey and the State of landing refuses to admit him, that State may, if the person in question is not a national or permanent resident of that State, return him to the territory of the State of which he is a national or permanent resident or to the territory of the State in which he began his journey by air.

1. Neither disembarkation, nor delivery, not the taking of custody or other measures contemplated in Article 13, paragraph 2, nor return of the person concerned, shall be considered as admission to the territory of the Contracting State concerned for the purpose of its law relating to entry or admission of persons and nothing in this Convention shall affect the law of a Contracting State relating to the expulsion of persons from its territory.

....

Chapter VI — Other Provisions

Article 16. 1. Offences committed on aircraft registered in a Contracting State shall be treated, for the purpose of extradition, as if they had been committed not only in the place in which they have occurred but also in the territory of the State of registration of the aircraft.

2. Without prejudice to the provisions of the preceding paragraph, nothing in this Convention shall be deemed to create an obligation to grant extradition.

....

HAGUE CONVENTION FOR THE SUPPRESSION OF UNLAWFUL SEIZURE OF AIRCRAFT[1]

The States Parties to this Convention,

Considering that unlawful acts of seizure or exercise of control of aircraft in flight jeopardize the safety of persons and property, seriously affect the operation of air services, and undermine the confidence of the peoples of the world in the safety of civil aviation;

Considering that the occurrence of such acts is a matter of grave concern;

Considering that, for the purpose of deterring such acts, there is an urgent need to provide appropriate measures for punishment of offenders;

Have Agreed As Follows:

Article 1. Any person who on board an aircraft in flight:

a. unlawfully, by force or threat thereof, or by any other form of intimidation, seizes, or exercises control of, that aircraft, or attempts to perform any such act, or

b. is an accomplice of a person who performs or attempts to perform any such act commits an offence (hereinafter referred to as "the offence").

Article 2. Each Contracting State undertakes to make the offence punishable by severe penalties.

. . . .

Article 4. 1. Each Contracting State shall take such measures as may be necessary to establish its jurisdiction over the offence and any other act of violence against passengers or crew committed by the alleged offender in connection with the offence, in the following cases:

a. when the offence is committed on board an aircraft registered in that State;

b. when the aircraft on board which the offence is committed lands in its territory with the alleged offender still on board;

c. when the offence is committed on board an aircraft leased without crew to a lessee who has his principal place of business or, if the lessee has no such place of business, his permanent residence, in that State.

1. Each Contracting State shall likewise take such measures as may be necessary to establish its jurisdiction over the offence in the case where the alleged offender is present in its territory and it does not extradite him pursuant to Article 8 to any of the States mentioned in paragraph 1 of this Article.

2. This Convention does not exclude any criminal jurisdiction exercised in accordance with national law.

. . . .

Article 6. 1. Upon being satisfied that the circumstances so warrant, any Contracting State in the territory of which the offender or the alleged offender is present, shall take

1. Convention for the Suppression of Unlawful Seizure of Aircraft, Dec. 16, 1970, 22 U.S.T. 1641, 860 U.N.T.S. 105 (entered into force Oct. 14, 1971), *available at* http://www.unodc.org/unodc/en/terrorism_convention_aircraft_seizure.html.

him into custody or take other measures to ensure his presence. The custody and other measures shall be as provided in the law of that State but may only be continued for such time as is necessary to enable any criminal or extradition proceedings to be instituted.

1. Such State shall immediately make a preliminary enquiry into the facts.

2. Any person in custody pursuant to paragraph 1 of this Article shall be assisted in communicating immediately with the nearest appropriate representative of the State of which he is a national.

3. When a State, pursuant to this Article, has taken a person into custody, it shall immediately notify the State of registration of the aircraft, the State mentioned in Article 4, paragraph 1(c), the State of nationality of the detained person and, if it considers it advisable, any other interested States of the fact that such person is in custody and of the circumstances which warrant his detention. The State which makes the preliminary enquiry contemplated in paragraph 2 of this Article shall promptly report its findings to the said States and shall indicate whether it intends to exercise jurisdiction.

Article 7. The Contracting State in the territory of which the alleged offender is found shall, if it does not extradite him, be obliged, without exception whatsoever and whether or not the offence was committed in its territory, to submit the case to its competent authorities for the purpose of prosecution. Those authorities shall take their decision in the same manner as in the case of any ordinary offence of a serious nature under the law of that State.

Article 8. 1. The offence shall be deemed to be included as an extraditable offence in any extradition treaty existing between Contracting States. Contracting States undertake to include the offence as an extraditable offence in every extradition treaty to be concluded between them.

1. If a Contracting State which makes extradition conditional on the existence of a treaty receives a request for extradition from another Contracting State with which it has no extradition treaty, it may at its option consider this Convention as the legal basis for extradition in respect of the offence. Extradition shall be subject to the other conditions provided by the law of the requested State.

2. Contracting States which do not make extradition conditional on the existence of a treaty shall recognize the offence as an extraditable offence between themselves subject to the conditions provided by the law of the requested State.

3. The offence shall be treated, for the purpose of extradition between Contracting States, as if it had been committed not only in the place in which it occurred but also in the territories of the States required to establish their jurisdiction in accordance with Article 4, paragraph 1.

....

Article 10. 1. Contracting States shall afford one another the greatest measure of assistance in connection with criminal proceedings brought in respect of the offence and other acts mentioned in Article 4. The law of the State requested shall apply in all cases.

1. The provisions of paragraph 1 of this Article shall not affect obligations under any other treaty, bilateral or multilateral, which governs or will govern, in whole or in part, mutual assistance in criminal matters.

Article 12. 1. Any dispute between two or more Contracting States concerning the interpretation or application of this Convention which cannot be settled through negotiation, shall, at the request of one of them, be submitted to arbitration. If within six months from the date of the request for arbitration the Parties are unable to agree on the organization of the arbitration, any one of those Parties may refer the dispute to the International Court of Justice by request in conformity with the Statute of the Court.[2]

....

2. Statute of the International Court of Justice, June 26, 1945, 59 Stat. 1031, 1055, at 1160-61, 3 Bevans 1153, 1179 at 1186-88.

MONTREAL CONVENTION FOR THE SUPPRESSION OF UNLAWFUL ACTS AGAINST THE SAFETY OF CIVIL AVIATION*

The States Parties to the Convention

CONSIDERING that unlawful acts against the safety of civil aviation jeopardize the safety of persons and property, seriously affect the operation of air services, and undermine the confidence of the peoples of the world in the safety of civil aviation;

CONSIDERING that the occurrence of such acts is a matter of grave concern;

CONSIDERING that, for the purpose of deterring such acts, there is an urgent need to provide appropriate measures for punishment of offenders;

Have agreed as follows:

Article 1. 1. Any person commits an offence if he unlawfully and intentionally:

a. performs an act of violence against a person on board an aircraft in flight if that act is likely to endanger the safety of that aircraft; or

b. destroys an aircraft in service or causes damage to such an aircraft which renders it incapable of flight or which is likely to endanger its safety in flight; or

c. places or causes to be placed on an aircraft in service, by any means whatsoever, a device or substance which is likely to destroy that aircraft, or to cause damage to it which renders it incapable of flight, or to cause damage to it which is likely to endanger its safety in flight; or

d. destroys or damages air navigation facilities or interferes with their operation, if any such act is likely to endanger the safety of aircraft in flight; or

e. communicates information which he knows to be false, thereby endangering the safety of an aircraft in flight.

2. Any person also commits an offence if he:

a. attempts to commit any of the offences mentioned in paragraph 1 of this Article; or

b. is an accomplice of a person who commits or attempts to commit any such offence.

....

Article 3. Each Contracting State undertakes to make the offences mentioned in Article 1 punishable by severe penalties.

....

Article 5. 1. Each Contracting State shall take such measures as may be necessary to establish its jurisdiction over the offences in the following cases:

a. when the offence is committed in the territory of that State;

* Convention for the Suppression of Unlawful Acts Against the Safety of Civil Aviation, Sept. 23, 1971, 24 U.S.T. 565, 974 U.N.T.S. 177 (entered into force Jan. 26, 1973) [hereinafter Montreal Convention], *available at* http://www.unodc.org/unodc/terrorism_convention_civil_aviation.html.

b. when the offence is committed against or on board an aircraft registered in that State;

c. when the aircraft on board which the offence is committed lands in its territory with the alleged offender still on board;

d. when the offence is committed against or on board an aircraft leased without crew to a lessee who has his principal place of business or, if the lessee has no such place of business, his permanent residence, in that State.

2. Each Contracting State shall likewise take such measures as may be necessary to establish its jurisdiction over the offences mentioned in Article 1, paragraph 1 (a), (b) and (c), and in Article 1, paragraph 2, in so far as that paragraph relates to those offences, in the case where the alleged offender is present in its territory and it does not extradite him pursuant to Article 8 to any of the States mentioned in paragraph 1 of this Article.

3. This Convention does not exclude any criminal jurisdiction exercised in accordance with national law.

Article 6. 1. Upon being satisfied that the circumstances so warrant, any Contracting State in the territory of which the offender or the alleged offender is present, shall take him into custody or take other measures to ensure his presence. The custody and other measures shall be as provided in the law of that State but may only be continued for such time as is necessary to enable any criminal or extradition proceedings to be instituted.

2. Such State shall immediately make a preliminary enquiry into the facts.

3. Any person in custody pursuant to paragraph 1 of this Article shall be assisted in communicating immediately with the nearest appropriate representative of the State of which he is a national.

4. When a State, pursuant to this Article, has taken a person into custody, it shall immediately notify the States mentioned in Article 5, paragraph 1, the State of nationality of the detained person and, if it considers it advisable, any other interested State of the fact that such person is in custody and of the circumstances which warrant his detention. The State which makes the preliminary enquiry contemplated in paragraph 2 of this Article shall promptly report its findings to the said States and shall indicate whether it intends to exercise jurisdiction.

Article 7. The Contracting State in the territory of which the alleged offender is found shall, if it does not extradite him, be obliged, without exception whatsoever and whether or not the offence was committed in its territory, to submit the case to its competent authorities for the purpose of prosecution. Those authorities shall take their decision in the same manner as in the case of any ordinary offence of a serious nature under the law of that State.

Article 8. 1. The offences shall be deemed to be included as extraditable offences in any extradition treaty existing between Contracting States. Contracting States undertake to include the offences as extraditable offences in every extradition treaty to be concluded between them.

2. If a Contracting State which makes extradition conditional on the existence of a treaty receives a request for extradition from another Contracting State with which it has no extradition treaty, it may at its option consider this Convention as the legal basis for extradition in respect of the offences. Extradition shall be subject to the other conditions provided by the law of the requested State.

3. Contracting States which do not make extradition conditional on the existence of a treaty shall recognize the offences as extraditable offences between themselves subject to the conditions provided by the law of the requested State.

4. Each of the offences shall be treated, for the purpose of extradition between Contracting States, as if it had been committed not only in the place in which it occurred but also in the territories of the States required to establish their jurisdiction in accordance with Article 5, paragraph 1 (b), (c) and (d).

. . . .

CONVENTION TO PREVENT AND PUNISH THE ACTS OF TERRORISM TAKING THE FORM OF CRIMES AGAINST PERSONS AND RELATED EXTORTION THAT ARE OF INTERNATIONAL SIGNIFICANCE*

....

The Member States of the Organization of American States have agreed upon the following articles:

Article 1. The contracting states undertake to cooperate among themselves by taking all the measures that they may consider effective, under their own laws, and especially those established in this convention, to prevent and punish acts of terrorism, especially kidnapping, murder, and other assaults against the life or physical integrity of those persons to whom the state has the duty according to international law to give special protection, as well as extortion in connection with those crimes.

Article 2. For the purposes of this convention, kidnapping, murder, and other assaults against the life or personal, integrity of those persons to whom the state has the duty to give special protection according to international law, as well as extortion in connection with those crimes, shall be considered common crimes of international significance, regardless of motive.

Article 3. Persons who have been charged or convicted for any of the crimes referred to in Article 2 of this convention shall be subject to extradition under the provisions of the extradition treaties in force between the parties or, in the case of states that do not make extradition dependent on the existence of a treaty, in accordance with their own laws.

In any case, it is the exclusive responsibility of the state under whose jurisdiction or protection such persons are located to determine the nature of the acts and decide whether the standards of this convention are applicable.

....

Article 8. To cooperate in preventing and punishing the crimes contemplated in Article 2 of this convention, the contracting states accept the following obligations:

a. To take all measures within their power, and in conformity with their own laws, to prevent and impede the preparation in their respective territories of the crimes mentioned in Article 2 that are to be carried out in the territory of another contracting state;

b. To exchange information and consider effective administrative measures for the purpose of protecting the persons to whom Article 2 of this convention refers;

c. To guarantee to every person deprived of his freedom through the application of this convention every right to defend himself;

* Convention to Prevent and Punish the Acts of Terrorism Taking the Form of Crimes Against Persons and Related Extortion that Are of International Significance, Feb. 2, 1971, 27 U.S.T. 3949, 1438 U.N.T.S. 191 (entered into force Mar. 8, 1973), *available at* http://untreaty.un.org/English/Terrorism.asp.

d. To endeavor to have the criminal acts contemplated in this convention included in their penal laws, if not already so included;

e. To comply most expeditiously with the requests for extradition concerning the criminal acts contemplated in this convention.

....

CONVENTION ON THE PREVENTION AND PUNISHMENT OF CRIMES AGAINST INTERNATIONALLY PROTECTED PERSONS, INCLUDING DIPLOMATIC AGENTS*

The States Parties to this Convention,

Having in mind the purposes and principles of the Charter of the United Nations concerning the maintenance of international peace and the promotion of friendly relations and co-operation among States,

Considering that crimes against diplomatic agents and other internationally protected persons jeopardizing the safety of these persons create a serious threat to the maintenance of normal international relations which are necessary for co-operation among States,

Believing that the commission of such crimes is a matter of grave concern to the international community,

Convinced that there is an urgent need to adopt appropriate and effective measures for the prevention and punishment of such crimes,

Have agreed as follows:

Article 1. For the purposes of this Convention:

1. "Internationally protected person" means:

(a) a Head of State, including any member of a collegial body performing the functions of a Head of State under the constitution of the State concerned, a Head of Government or a Minister for Foreign Affairs, whenever any such person is in a foreign State, as well as members of his family who accompany him;

(b) any representative or official of a State or any official or other agent of an international organization of an intergovernmental character who, at the time when and in the place where a crime against him, his official premises, his private accommodation or his means of transport is committed, is entitled pursuant to international law to special protection from any attack on his person, freedom or dignity, as well as members of his family forming part of his household;

2. "Alleged offender" means a person as to whom there is sufficient evidence to determine *prima facie* that he has committed or participated in one or more of the crimes set forth in article 2.

Article 2. 1. The intentional commission of:

(a) a murder, kidnapping or other attack upon the person or liberty of an internationally protected person;

(b) a violent attack upon the official premises, the private accommodation or the means of transport of an internationally protected person likely to endanger his person or liberty;

---

* Convention on the Prevention and Punishment of Crimes Against Internationally Protected Persons, Including Diplomatic Agents, Dec. 14, 1973, 28 U.S.T. 1975, 1035 U.N.T.S. 167 (entered into force Feb. 20, 1977), *available at* http://untreaty.un.org/English/Terrorism.asp.

(c) a threat to commit any such attack;

(d) an attempt to commit any such attack; and

(e) an act constituting participation as an accomplice in any such attack; shall be made by each State Party a crime under its internal law.

2. Each State Party shall make these crimes punishable by appropriate penalties which take into account their grave nature.

3. Paragraphs 1 and 2 of this article in no way derogate from the obligations of States Parties under international law to take all appropriate measures to prevent other attacks on the person, freedom or dignity of an internationally protected person.

Article 3. 1. Each State Party shall take such measures as may be necessary to establish its jurisdiction over the crimes set forth in article 2 in the following cases:

(a) when the crime is committed in the territory of that State or on board a ship or aircraft registered in that State;

(b) when the alleged offender is a national of that State;

(c) when the crime is committed against an internationally protected person as defined in article 1 who enjoys his status as such by virtue of functions which he exercises on behalf of that State.

2. Each State Party shall likewise take such measures as may be necessary to establish its jurisdiction over these crimes in cases where the alleged offender is present in its territory and it does not extradite him pursuant to article 8 to any of the States mentioned in paragraph 1 of this article.

3. This Convention does not exclude any criminal jurisdiction exercised in accordance with internal law.

Article 4. States Parties shall co-operate in the prevention of the crimes set forth in article 2, particularly by:

(a) taking all practicable measures to prevent preparations in their respective territories for the commission of those crimes within or outside their territories;

(b) exchanging information and co-ordinating the taking of administrative and other measures as appropriate to prevent the commission of those crimes.

Article 5. 1. The State Party in which any of the crimes set forth in article 2 has been committed shall, if it has reason to believe that an alleged offender has fled from its territory, communicate to all other States concerned, directly or through the Secretary-General of the United Nations, all the pertinent facts regarding the crime committed and all available information regarding the identity of the alleged offender.

2. Whenever any of the crimes set forth in article 2 has been committed against an internationally protected person, any State Party which has information concerning the victim and the circumstances of the crime shall endeavour to transmit it, under the conditions provided for in its internal law, fully and promptly to the State Party on whose behalf he was exercising his functions.

Article 6. 1. Upon being satisfied that the circumstances so warrant, the State Party in whose territory the alleged offender is present shall take the appropriate measures under its internal law so as to ensure his presence for the purpose of prosecution or extradition. Such measures shall be notified without delay directly or through the Secretary-General of the United Nations to:

(a) the State where the crime was committed;

(b) the State or States of which the alleged offender is a national or, if he is a stateless person, in whose territory he permanently resides;

(c) the State or States of which the internationally protected person concerned is a national or on whose behalf he was exercising his functions;

(d) all other States concerned; and

(e) the international organization of which the internationally protected person concerned is an official or an agent.

2. Any person regarding whom the measures referred to in paragraph I of this article are being taken shall be entitled:

(a) to communicate without delay with the nearest appropriate representative of the State of which he is a national or which is otherwise entitled to protect his rights or, if he is a stateless person, which he requests and which is willing to protect his rights; and

(b) to be visited by a representative of that State.

Article 7. The State Party in whose territory the alleged offender is present shall, if it does not extradite him, submit, without exception whatsoever and without undue delay, the case to its competent authorities for the purpose of prosecution, through proceedings in accordance with the laws of that State.

Article 8. 1. To the extent that the crimes set forth in article 2 are not listed as extraditable offences in any extradition treaty existing between States Parties, they shall be deemed to be included as such therein. States Parties undertake to include those crimes as extraditable offences in every future extradition treaty to be concluded between them.

2. If a State Party which makes extradition conditional on the existence of a treaty receives a request for extradition from another State Party with which it has no extradition treaty, it may, if it decides to extradite, consider this Convention as the legal basis for extradition in respect of those crimes. Extradition shall be subject to the procedural provisions and the other conditions of the law of the requested State.

3. States Parties which do not make extradition conditional on the existence of a treaty shall recognize those crimes as extraditable offences between themselves subject to the procedural provisions and the other conditions of the law of the requested State.

4. Each of the crimes shall be treated, for the purpose of extradition between States Parties, as if it had been committed not only in the place in which it occurred but also in the territories of the States required to establish their jurisdiction in accordance with paragraph 1 of article 3.

. . . .

EUROPEAN CONVENTION ON THE SUPPRESSION OF TERRORISM*

The member States of the Council of Europe, signatory hereto,

Considering that the aim of the Council of Europe is to achieve a greater unity between its Members,

Aware of the growing concern caused by the increase in acts of terrorism,

Wishing to take effective measures to ensure that the perpetrators of such acts do not escape prosecution and punishment,

Convinced that extradition is a particularly effective measure for achieving this result,

Have agreed as follows:

Article 1. For the purposes of extradition between Contracting States, none of the following offences shall be regarded as a political offence or as an offence connected with a political offence or as an offence inspired by political motives:

(a) An offence within the scope of the Convention for the Suppression of Unlawful Seizure of Aircraft, signed at The Hague on 16 December 1970;

(b) An offence within the scope of the Convention for the Suppression of Unlawful Acts against the Safety of Civil Aviation, signed at Montreal on 23 September 1971;

(c) A serious offence involving an attack against the life, physical integrity or liberty of internationally protected persons, including diplomatic agents;

(d) An offence involving kidnapping, the taking of a hostage or serious unlawful detention;

(e) An offence involving the use of a bomb, grenade, rocket, automatic firearm or letter or parcel bomb if this use endangers persons;

(f) An attempt to commit any of the foregoing offences or participation as an accomplice of a person who commits or attempts to commit such an offence.

Article 2. 1. For the purposes of extradition between Contracting States, a Contracting State may decide not to regard as a political offence or as an offence connected with a political offence or as an offence inspired by political motives a serious offence involving an act of violence, other than one covered by article 1, against the life, physical integrity or liberty of a person.

2. The same shall apply to a serious offence involving an act against property, other than one covered by article 1, if the act created a collective danger for persons.

3. The same shall apply to an attempt to commit any of the foregoing offences or participation as an accomplice of a person who commits or attempts to commit such an offence.

Article 3. The provisions of all extradition treaties and arrangements applicable between Contracting States, including the European Convention on Extradition, are modified as between Contracting States to the extent that they are incompatible with this Convention.

---

* European Convention on the Suppression of Terrorism, Jan. 27, 1977, 1137 U.N.T.S. 93 (entered into force Aug. 4, 1978), *available at* http://untreaty.un.org/English/Terrorism.asp.

Article 4. For the purposes of this Convention and to the extent that any offence mentioned in article 1 or 2 is not listed as an extraditable offence in any extradition convention or treaty existing between Contracting States, it shall be deemed to be included as such therein.

Article 5. Nothing in this Convention shall be interpreted as imposing an obligation to extradite if the requested State has substantial grounds for believing that the request for extradition for an offence mentioned in article 1 or 2 has been made for the purpose of prosecuting or punishing a person on account of his race, religion, nationality or political opinion, or that that person's position may be prejudiced for any of these reasons.

Article 6. 1. Each Contracting State shall take such measures as may be necessary to establish its jurisdiction over an offence mentioned in article 1 in the case where the suspected offender is present in its territory and it does not extradite him after receiving a request for extradition from a Contracting State whose jurisdiction is based on a rule of jurisdiction existing equally in the law of the requested State.

2. This Convention does not exclude any criminal jurisdiction exercised in accordance with national law.

Article 7. A Contracting State in whose territory a person suspected to have committed an offence mentioned in article 1 is found and which has received a request for extradition under the conditions mentioned in article 6, paragraph 1, shall, if it does not extradite that person, submit the case, without exception whatsoever and without undue delay, to its competent authorities for the purpose of prosecution. Those authorities shall take their decision in the same manner as in the case of any offence of a serious nature under the law of that State.

Article 8. 1. Contracting States shall afford one another the widest measure of mutual assistance in criminal matters in connection with proceedings brought in respect of the offences mentioned in article 1 or 2. The law of the requested State concerning mutual assistance in criminal matters shall apply in all cases. Nevertheless this assistance may not be refused on the sole ground that it concerns a political offence or an offence connected with a political offence or an offence inspired by political motives.

2. Nothing in this Convention shall be interpreted as imposing an obligation to afford mutual assistance if the requested State has substantial grounds for believing that the request for mutual assistance in respect of an offence mentioned in article 1 or 2 has been made for the purpose of prosecuting or punishing a person on account of his race, religion, nationality or political opinion or that that person's position may be prejudiced for any of these reasons.

3. The provisions of all treaties and arrangements concerning mutual assistance in criminal matters applicable between Contracting States, including the European Convention on Mutual Assistance in Criminal Matters, are modified as between Contracting States to the extent that they are incompatible with this Convention.

Article 9. 1. The European Committee on Crime Problems of the Council of Europe shall be kept informed regarding the application of this Convention.

2. It shall do whatever is needful to facilitate a friendly settlement of any difficulty which may arise out of its execution.

Article 10. 1. Any dispute between Contracting States concerning the interpretation or application of this Convention, which has not been settled in the framework of article 9, paragraph 2, shall, at the request of any Party to the dispute, be referred to arbitration. Each Party shall nominate an arbitrator and the two arbitrators shall nominate a referee. If any Party has not nominated its arbitrator within the three months following the request for arbitration, he shall be nominated at the request of the other Party by the President of the European Court of Human Rights. If the latter should be a national of one of the Parties to the dispute, this duty shall be carried out by the Vice-President of the Court or, if the Vice-President is a national of one of the Parties to the dispute, by the most senior judge of the Court not being a national of one of the Parties to the dispute. The same procedure shall be observed if the arbitrators cannot agree on the choice of referee.

2. The arbitration tribunal shall lay down its own procedure. Its decisions shall be taken by majority vote. Its award shall be final.

....

Article 13. 1. Any State may, at the time of signature or when depositing its instrument of ratification, acceptance or approval, declare that it reserves the right to refuse extradition in respect of any offence mentioned in article 1 which it considers to be a political offence, an offence connected with a political offence or an offence inspired by political motives, provided that it undertakes to take into due consideration, when evaluating the character of the offence, any particularly serious aspects of the offence, including:

(a) That it created a collective danger to the life, physical integrity or liberty of persons; or

(b) That it affected persons foreign to the motives behind it; or

(c) That cruel or vicious means have been used in the commission of the offence.

....

INTERNATIONAL CONVENTION AGAINST THE TAKING OF HOSTAGES*

The States Parties to this Convention,

Having in mind the purposes and principles of the Charter of the United Nations concerning the maintenance of international peace and security and the promotion of friendly relations and co-operation among States,

Recognizing in particular that everyone has the right to life, liberty and security of person, as set out in the Universal Declaration of Human Rights and the International Covenant on Civil and Political Rights,

Reaffirming the principle of equal rights and self-determination of peoples as enshrined in the Charter of the United Nations and the Declaration on Principles of International Law concerning Friendly Relations and Co-operation among States in accordance with the Charter of the United Nations, as well as in other relevant resolutions of the General Assembly,

Considering that the taking of hostages is an offence of grave concern to the international community and that, in accordance with the provisions of this Convention, any person committing an act of hostage taking shall either be prosecuted or extradited,

Being convinced that it is urgently necessary to develop international cooperation between States in devising and adopting effective measures for the prevention, prosecution and punishment of all acts of taking of hostages as manifestations of international terrorism,

Have agreed as follows:

Article 1. 1. Any person who seizes or detains and threatens to kill, to injure or to continue to detain another person (hereinafter referred to as the "hostage") in order to compel a third party, namely, a State, an international intergovernmental organization, a natural or juridical person, or a group of persons, to do or abstain from doing any act as an explicit or implicit condition for the release of the hostage commits the offence of taking of hostages ("hostage-taking") within the meaning of this Convention.

2. Any person who:

(a) Attempts to commit an act of hostage-taking, or

(b) Participates as an accomplice of anyone who commits or attempts to commit an act of hostage-taking likewise commits an offence for the purposes of this Convention.

Article 2. Each State Party shall make the offences set forth in article 1 punishable by appropriate penalties which take into account the grave nature of those offences.

Article 3. 1. The State Party in the territory of which the hostage is held by the offender shall take all measures it considers appropriate to ease the situation of the hostage, in particular, to secure his release and, after his release, to facilitate, when relevant, his departure.

---

* International Convention Against the Taking of Hostages, Dec. 17, 1979, T.I.A.S. No. 11081, 1316 U.N.T.S. 205 (entered into force June 3, 1983), *available at* http://untreaty.un.org/English/Terrorism.asp.

2. If any object which the offender has obtained as a result of the taking of hostages comes into the custody of a State Party, that State Party shall return it as soon as possible to the hostage or the third party referred to in article 1, as the case may be, or to the appropriate authorities thereof.

Article 4. States Parties shall co-operate in the prevention of the offences set forth in article 1, particularly by:

(a) Taking all practicable measures to prevent preparations in their respective territories for the commission of those offences within or outside their territories, including measures to prohibit in their territories illegal activities of persons, groups and organizations that encourage, instigate, organize or engage in the perpetration of acts of taking of hostages;

(b) Exchanging information and co-ordinating the taking of administrative and other measures as appropriate to prevent the commission of those offences.

Article 5. 1. Each State Party shall take such measures as may be necessary to establish its jurisdiction over any of the offences set forth in article 1 which are committed:

(a) In its territory or on board a ship or aircraft registered in that State;

(b) By any of its nationals or, if that State considers it appropriate, by those stateless persons who have their habitual residence in its territory;

(c) In order to compel that State to do or abstain from doing any act; or

(d) With respect to a hostage who is a national of that State, if that State considers it appropriate.

2. Each State Party shall likewise take such measures as may be necessary to establish its jurisdiction over the offences set forth in article 1 in cases where the alleged offender is present in its territory and it does not extradite him to any of the States mentioned in paragraph 1 of this article.

3. This Convention does not exclude any criminal jurisdiction exercised in accordance with internal law.

Article 6. 1. Upon being satisfied that the circumstances so warrant, any State Party in the territory of which the alleged offender is present shall, in accordance with its laws, take him into custody or take other measures to ensure his presence for such time as is necessary to enable any criminal or extradition proceedings to be instituted. That State Party shall immediately make a preliminary inquiry into the facts.

2. The custody or other measures referred to in paragraph 1 of this article shall be notified without delay directly or through the Secretary-General of the United Nations to:

(a) The State where the offence was committed;

(b) The State against which compulsion has been directed or attempted;

(c) The State of which the natural or juridical person against whom compulsion has been directed or attempted is a national;

(d) The State of which the hostage is a national or in the territory of which he has his habitual residence;

(e) The State of Which the alleged offender is a national or, if he is a stateless person, in the territory of which he has his habitual residence;

(f) The international intergovernmental organization against which compulsion has been directed or attempted;

(g) All other States concerned.

3. Any person regarding whom the measures referred to in paragraph I of this article are being taken shall be entitled:

(a) To communicate without delay with the nearest appropriate representative of the State of which he is a national or which is otherwise entitled to establish such communication or, if he is a stateless person, the State in the territory of which he has his habitual residence;

(b) To be visited by a representative of that State.

4. The rights referred to in paragraph 3 of this article shall be exercised in conformity with the laws and regulations of the State in the territory of which the alleged offender is present subject to the proviso, however, that the said laws and regulations must enable full effect to be given to the purposes for which the rights accorded under paragraph 3 of this article are intended.

5. The provisions of paragraphs 3 and 4 of this article shall be without prejudice to the right of any State Party having a claim to jurisdiction in accordance with paragraph 1 (b) of article 5 to invite the International Committee of the Red Cross to communicate with and visit the alleged offender.

6. The State which makes the preliminary inquiry contemplated in paragraph 1 of this article shall promptly report its findings to the States or organization referred to in paragraph 2 of this article and indicate whether it intends to exercise jurisdiction.

Article 7. The State Party where the alleged offender is prosecuted shall in accordance with its laws communicate the final outcome of the proceedings to the Secretary.-General of the United Nations, who shall transmit the information to the other States concerned and the international intergovernmental organizations concerned.

Article 8. 1. The State Party in the territory of which the alleged offender is found shall, if it does not extradite him, be obliged, without exception whatsoever and whether or not the offence was committed in its territory, to submit the case to its competent authorities for the purpose of prosecution, through proceedings in accordance with the laws of that State. Those authorities shall take their decision in the same manner as in the case of any ordinary offence of a grave nature under the law of that State.

2. Any person regarding whom proceedings are being carried out in connection with any of the offences set forth in article 1 shall be guaranteed fair treatment at all stages of the proceedings, including enjoyment of all the rights and guarantees provided by the law of the State in the territory of which he is present.

Article 9. 1. A request for the extradition of an alleged offender, pursuant to this Convention, shall not be granted if the requested State Party has substantial grounds for believing:

(a) That the request for extradition for an offence set forth in article 1 has been made for the purpose of prosecuting or punishing a person on account of his race, religion, nationality, ethnic origin or political opinion; or

(b) That the person's position may be prejudiced:

(i) For any of the reasons mentioned in subparagraph (a) of this paragraph, or

(ii) For the reason that communication with him by the appropriate authorities of the State entitled to exercise rights of protection cannot be effected.

2. With respect to the offences as defined in this Convention, the provisions of all extradition treaties and arrangements applicable between States Parties are modified as between States Parties to the extent that they are incompatible with this Convention.

....

Article 13. This Convention shall not apply where the offence is committed within a single State, the hostage and the alleged offender are nationals of that State and the alleged offender is found in the territory of that State.

Article 14. Nothing in this Convention shall be construed as justifying the violation of the territorial integrity or political independence of a State in contravention of the Charter of the United Nations.

....

DRAFT CONVENTION FOR THE PREVENTION AND PUNISHMENT OF CERTAIN ACTS OF INTERNATIONAL TERRORISM*

The States Parties to this Convention—

Recalling United Nations General Assembly Resolution 2625 (XXV) proclaiming principles of international law concerning friendly relations and co-operation among States in accordance with the Charter of the United Nations;

Considering that this Resolution provides that every State has the duty to refrain from organizing, instigating, assisting or participating in terrorist acts in another State or acquiescing in organized activities within its territory directed towards the commission of such acts;

Considering the common danger posed by the spread of terrorist acts across national boundaries;

Considering that civilians must be protected from terrorist acts;

Affirming that effective measures to control international terrorism are urgently needed and require international as well as national action;

Have agreed as follows:

Article 1. 1. Any person who unlawfully kills, causes serious bodily harm or kidnaps another person, attempts to commit any such act, or participates as an accomplice of a person who commits or attempts to commit any such act, commits an offense of international significance if the act:

a. is committed or takes effect outside the territory of a State of which the alleged offender is a national; and

b. is committed or takes effect:

i. outside the territory of the State against which the act is directed, or

ii. within the territory of the State against which the act is directed and the alleged offender knows or has reason to know that a person against whom the act is directed is not a national of that State; and

c. is committed neither by nor against a member of the Armed Forces of a State in the course of military hostilities; and

d. is intended to damage the interests of or obtain concessions from a State or an international organization.

2. For the purposes of this Convention:

a. An "international organization" means an international intergovernmental organization.

b. An "alleged offender" means a person as to whom there are grounds to believe that he has committed one or more of the offenses of international significance set forth in this Article.

---

* Draft Convention for the Prevention and Punishment of Certain Acts of International Terrorism, Sept. 26, 1972, 67 DEP'T ST. BULL. 431 (1972).

c. The "Territory" of a State includes all territory under the jurisdiction or administration of the State.

Article 2. Each State Party undertakes to make the offenses set forth in Article 1 punishable by severe penalties.

Article 3. A State Party in whose territory an alleged offender is found shall, if it does not extradite him, submit, without exception whatsoever and without undue delay, the case to its competent authorities for the purpose of prosecution, through proceedings in accordance with the laws of that State.

Article 4. 1. Each State Party shall take such measures as may be necessary to establish its jurisdiction over the offenses set forth in Article 1:

a. when the offense is committed in its territory, or

b. when the offense is committed by its national

2. Each State Party shall likewise take such measures as may be necessary to establish its jurisdiction over the offenses set forth in Article 1 in the case where an alleged offender is present in its territory and the State does not extradite him to any of the States mentioned in Paragraph 1 of this Article.

3. This Convention does not exclude any criminal jurisdiction exercised in accordance with national law.

Article 5. A State Party in which one or more of the offenses set forth in Article 1 have been committed shall, if it has reason to believe an alleged offender has fled from its territory, communicate to all other States Parties all the pertinent facts regarding the offenses committed and all available information regarding the identity of the alleged offender.

Article 6. 1. The State Party in whose territory an alleged offender is found shall take appropriate measures under its internal law so as to ensure his presence for prosecution or extradition. Such measures shall be immediately notified to the States mentioned in Article 4, paragraph 1, and all other interested States.

2. Any person regarding whom the measures referred to in Paragraph 1 of this Article are being taken shall be entitled to communicate immediately with the nearest appropriate representative of the State of which he is a national and to be visited by a representative of that State.

Article 7. 1. To the extent that the offenses set forth in Article 1 are not listed as extraditable offenses in any extradition treaty existing between State Parties they shall be deemed to have been included as such therein. States Parties undertake to include those offenses as extraditable offenses in every future extradition treaty to be concluded between them.

3. If a State Party which makes extradition conditional on the existence of a treaty receives a request for extradition from another State Party with which it has no extradition treaty, it may, if it decided to extradite consider the present articles as the legal basis for extradition in respect of the offenses. Extradition shall be subject to the provisions of the law of the requested State.

4. States Parties which do not make extradition conditional upon the existence of a treaty shall recognize the offenses as extraditable offenses between themselves subject to the provisions of the law of the requested State.

5. Each of the offense shall be treated, for the purpose of extradition between States parties as if it has been committed not only in the place in which it occurred but also in

the territories of the States required to establish their jurisdiction in accordance with Article 4, Paragraph 1 (b).

6. An extradition request from the State in which the offenses were committed shall have priority over other such requests if received by the State Party in whose territory the alleged offender has been found within thirty days after the communication required in paragraph 1 of Article 6 has been made.

Article 8. Any person regarding whom proceedings are being carried out in connection with any of the offenses set forth in Article 1 shall be guaranteed fair treatment at all stages of the proceedings.

Article 9. The statutory limitation as to the time within which prosecution may be instituted for the offenses set forth in Article 1 shall be, in each State Party, that fixed for the most serious crimes under its internal law.

Article 10. 1. States Parties shall, in accordance with international and national law, endeavor to take all practicable measures for the purpose of preventing the offenses set forth in Article 1.

2. Any State Party having reason to believe that one of the offenses set forth in Article 1 may be committed shall, in accordance with its national law, furnish any relevant information in its possession to those States which it believes would be the States mentioned in Article 4, Paragraph 1, if any such offense were committed.

Article 11. 1. States Parties shall afford one another the greatest measure of assistance in connection with criminal proceedings brought in respect of the offenses set forth in Article 1, including the supply of all evidence at their disposal necessary for the proceedings.

2. The provisions of Paragraph 1 of this Article shall not affect obligations concerning mutual assistance embodied in any other treaty.

Article 12. States Parties shall consult together for the purpose of considering and implementing such other cooperative measures as may seem useful for carrying out the purposes of this Convention.

Article 13. In any case in which one or more of the Geneva Conventions of August 12, 1949, or any other convention concerning the law of armed conflicts is applicable, such conventions shall, if in conflict with any provision of this Convention, take precedence. In particular:

a. nothing in this Convention shall make an offense of any act which is permissible under the Geneva Convention Relative to the Protection of Civilian Persons in Time of War or any other international law applicable in armed conflicts; and

b. nothing in this Convention shall deprive any person of prisoner of war status if entitled to such status under the Geneva Convention Relative to the Treatment of Prisoners of War or any other applicable convention concerning respect for human rights in armed conflicts.

Article 14. In any case in which the Convention on Offenses and Certain Other Acts Committed on Board Aircraft, the Convention for the Suppression of Unlawful Seizure of Aircraft, the Convention for the Suppression of Unlawful Acts against the Safety of Civil Aviation, the Convention to Prevent and Punish the Acts of Terrorism Taking the Form of Crimes Against Person and Related Extortion that are of International Significance, or any other convention which has or may be concluded concerning the protection of civil aviation, diplomatic agents and other internationally protected persons, is applicable, such convention shall, if in conflict with any provision of this Convention, take precedence.

Article 15. Nothing in this Convention shall derogate from any obligations of the Parties under the United Nations Charter.

Article 16. 1. Any dispute between the Parties arising out of the application or interpretation of the present articles that is not settled through negotiation may be brought by any State Party to the dispute before a Conciliation Commission to be constituted in accordance in accordance with the provisions of this Article by the giving of written notice to the other State or States Party to the dispute and to the Secretary-General of the United Nations.

2. A Conciliation Commission will be composed of three members. One member shall be appointed by each party to the dispute. If there is more than one party on either side of the dispute they shall jointly appoint a member of the Conciliation Commission. These two appointments shall be made within two months of the written notice referred to in Paragraph 1. The third member, the Chairman, shall be chosen by the other two members.

3. If either side has failed to appoint its members within the time limit referred to in Paragraph 2, the Secretary-General of the United Nations shall appoint such member within a further period of two months. If no agreement is reached on the choice of the Chairman within five months of the written notice referred to in Paragraph 1, the Secretary-General shall within a further period of one month appoint as the Chairman a qualified jurist who is not a national of any State Party to the dispute.

4. Any vacancy shall be filled in the same manner as the original appointment was made.

5. The Commission shall establish its own rules of procedure and shall reach its decisions and recommendations by a majority vote. It shall be competent to ask any organ that is authorized by or in accordance with the Charter of the United Nations to request an advisory opinion from the International Court of Justice to make such a request regarding the interpretation or application of the present articles.

6. If the Commission is unable to obtain an agreement among the parties on a settlement of the dispute within six months of its initial meeting, it shall prepare as soon as possible a report of its proceedings and transmit it to the parties and to the depository. The report shall include the Commission's conclusions upon the facts and questions of law and the recommendations it has submitted to the parties in order to facilitate a settlement of the dispute. The six months time limit may be extended by a decision of the Commission.

7. This Article is without prejudice to provisions concerning the settlement of disputes contained in international agreements in force between States.

CONVENTION ON THE PHYSICAL PROTECTION OF NUCLEAR MATERIAL*

The States Parties to This Convention,

Recognizing the right of all States to develop and apply nuclear energy for peaceful purposes and their legitimate interests in the potential benefits to be derived from the peaceful application of nuclear energy,

Convinced of the need for facilitating international co-operation in the peaceful application of nuclear energy,

Desiring to avert the potential dangers posed by the unlawful taking and use of nuclear material,

Convinced that offenses relating to nuclear material are a matter of grave concern and that there is an urgent need to adopt appropriate and effective measures to ensure the prevention, detection and punishment of such offenses,

. . . .

Have agreed as follows:

. . . .

Article 2. 1. The Convention shall apply to nuclear material used for peaceful purposes while in international nuclear transport.

2. With the exception of articles 3 and 4 and paragraph 3 of article 5, this Convention shall also apply to nuclear material used for peaceful purposes while in domestic use, storage and transport.

3. Apart from the commitments expressly undertaken by States Parties in the articles covered by paragraph 2 with respect to nuclear material used for peaceful purposes while in domestic use, storage and transport, nothing in this Convention shall be interpreted as affecting the sovereign rights of a State regarding the domestic use, storage and transport of such nuclear material.

Article 3. Each State Party shall take appropriate steps within the framework of its national law and consistent with international law to ensure as far as practicable that, during international nuclear transport, nuclear material within its territory, or on board a ship or aircraft under its jurisdiction insofar as such ship or aircraft is engaged in the transport to or from that State, is protected at the levels described in Annex I.

Article 4. 1. Each State Party shall not export or authorize the export of nuclear material unless the State Party has received assurances that such material will be protected during the international nuclear transport at the levels described in Annex I.

2. Each State Party shall not import or authorize the import of nuclear material from a State not party to this Convention unless the State Party has received assurances that such material will during the international nuclear transport be protected at the levels described in Annex I.

---

* Convention on the Physical Protection of Nuclear Material, *opened for signature* Mar. 3, 1980, T.I.A.S. No. 11080, 1456 U.N.T.S. 101 (entered into force Feb. 8, 1987), *available at* http://www.state.gov/t/ac/trt/5079.htm.

3. A State Party shall not allow the transit of its territory by land or internal waterways or through its airports or seaports of nuclear material between States that are not parties to this Convention unless the State Party has received assurances as far as practicable that this nuclear material will be protected during international nuclear transport at the levels described in Annex I.

4. Each State Party shall apply within the framework of its national law the levels of physical protection described in Annex I to nuclear material being transported from a part of that State to another part of the same State through international waters or airspace.

5. The State Party responsible for receiving assurances that the nuclear material will be protected at the levels described in Annex I according to paragraphs 1 to 3 shall identify and inform in advance States which the nuclear material is expected to transit by land or internal waterways, or whose airports or seaports it is expected to enter.

....

Article 5.

....

2. In the case of theft, robbery or any other unlawful taking of nuclear material or of credible threat thereof, States Parties shall, in accordance with their national law, provide co-operation and assistance to the maximum feasible extent in the recovery and protection of such material to any State that so requests...

....

Article 6. 1. States Parties shall take appropriate measures consistent with their national law to protect the confidentiality of any information which they receive in confidence by virtue of the provisions of this Convention from another State Party or through participation in an activity carried out for the implementation of this Convention. If States Parties provide information to international organizations in confidence, steps shall be taken to ensure that the confidentiality of such information is protected.

2. States Parties shall not be required by this Convention to provide any information which they are not permitted to communicate pursuant to national law or which would jeopardize the security of the State concerned or the physical protection of nuclear material.

Article 7. 1. The intentional commission of:

(a) an act without lawful authority which constitutes the receipt, possession, use, transfer, alteration, disposal or dispersal of nuclear material and which causes or is likely to cause death or serious injury to any person or substantial damage to property;

(b) a theft or robbery of nuclear material;

(c) an embezzlement or fraudulent obtaining of nuclear material;

(d) an act constituting a demand for nuclear material by threat or use of force or by any other form of intimidation;

(e) a threat:

(i) to use nuclear material to cause death or serious injury to any person or substantial property damage, or

(ii) to commit an offense described in subparagraph (b) in order to compel a natural or legal person, international organization or State to do or to refrain from doing any act;

(f) an attempt to commit any offense described in paragraphs (a), (b) or (c); and

(g) an act which constitutes participation in any offense described in paragraphs (a) to (f) shall be made a punishable offense by each State Party under its national law.

2. Each State Party shall make the offenses described in this article punishable by appropriate penalties which take into account their grave nature.

. . . .

Article 10. The State Party in whose territory the alleged offender is present shall, if it does not extradite him, submit, without exception whatsoever and without undue delay, the case to its competent authorities for the purpose of prosecution, through proceedings in accordance with the laws of that State.

Article 11. 1. The offenses in article 7 shall be deemed to be included as extraditable offenses in any extradition Treaty existing between States Parties. States Parties undertake to include those offenses as extraditable offenses in every future extradition Treaty to be concluded between them.

. . . .

U.S.-U.K. SUPPLEMENTARY TREATY CONCERNING THE EXTRADITION TREATY*

The Government of the United States of America and the Government of the United Kingdom of Great Britain and Northern Ireland;

Desiring to make more effective the Extradition Treaty between the Contracting Parties, signed at London on 8 June 1982 (hereinafter referred to as "the Extradition Treaty");

Have resolved to conclude a Supplementary Treaty and have agreed as follows:

Article 1. For the purposes of the Extradition Treaty, none of the following offenses shall be regarded as an offense of a political character:

a. an offense within the scope of the Convention for the Suppression of Unlawful Seizure of Aircraft, opened for signature at The Hague on 16 December 1970;

b. an offense within the scope of the Convention for the Suppression of Unlawful Acts against the safety of Civil Aviation, opened for signature at Montreal on 23 September 1961;

c. an offense within the scope of the Convention on the Prevention and Punishment of Crimes against Internationally Protected Persons, including Diplomatic Agents, opened for signature at New York on 14 December 1973;

d. an offense within the scope of the International Convention against the Taking of Hostages, opened for signature at New York on 18 December 1979;

e. murder;

f. manslaughter

g. maliciously wounding or inflicting grievous bodily harm;

h. kidnapping, abduction, false imprisonment or unlawful detention, including the taking of a hostage;

i. the following offenses relating to explosives:

1. the causing of an explosion likely to endanger life or cause serious damage to property; or

2. conspiracy to cause such an explosion; or

3. the making or possession of an explosive substance by a person who intends either himself or through another person to endanger life or cause serious damage to property;

j. the following offenses relating to firearms or ammunition:

1. the possession of a firearm or ammunition by a person who intends either through himself or through another person to endanger life; or

2. the use of a firearm by a person with intent to resist or prevent the arrest or detention of himself or another person;

---

* Supplementary Treaty Concerning the Extradition Treaty Between the Government of the United States of America and the Government of the United Kingdom of Great Britain and Northern Ireland Signed at London on 8 June 1972, U.S.-U.K., June 25, 1985, T.I.A.S. No. 12050 (entered into force Dec. 23, 1986).

k. damaging property with intent to endanger life or with reckless disregard as to whether the life of another would thereby be endangered;

l. an attempt to commit any of the foregoing offenses.

Article 2. Article V, paragraph (1)(b) of the Extradition Treaty is amended to read as follows:

"(b) the prosecution for the offense for which extradition is requested has become barred by the lapse of time according to the law of the requesting Party; or"

Article 3. Article VIII, paragraph (2) of the Extradition Treaty is amended to read as follows:

"(2) A person arrested upon such an application shall be set at liberty upon the expiration of sixty days from the date of his arrest if a request for his extradition shall not have been received. This provision shall not prevent the institution of further proceedings for the extradition of the person sought if a request for extradition is subsequently received."

Article 4. This Supplementary Treaty shall apply to any offense committed before or after this Supplementary Treaty enters into force, provided that this Supplementary Treaty shall not apply to an offense committed before this Supplementary Treaty enters into force which was not an offense under the laws of both Contracting Parties at the time of its commission.

Article 5. This Supplementary Treaty shall form an integral part of the Extradition Treaty and shall apply:

a. in relation to the United Kingdom: to Great Britain and Northern Ireland, the Channel Islands, the Isle of Man and the territories for whose international relations the United Kingdom is responsible which are listed in the Annex to this Supplementary Treaty;

b. to the United States of America:

and references to the territory of a Contracting Party shall be construed accordingly.

Article 6. This Supplementary Treaty shall be subject to ratification and the instruments of ratification shall be exchanged at London as soon as possible. It shall enter into force upon the exchange of instruments of ratification. It shall be subject to termination in the same manner as the Extradition Treaty....

Annex

Anguilla
Bermuda
British Indian Ocean territory
British Virgin Islands
Cayman Islands
Falkland Islands
Falkland Islands Dependencies
Gibraltar
Hong Kong
Montserrat
Pitcairn, Henderson, Ducie and Oeno Islands

St. Helena
St. Helena Dependencies
The Sovereign Base Areas of Akrotiri and Dhekelia in the Island of Cyprus
Turks and Caicos Islands

CONVENTION FOR THE SUPPRESSION OF UNLAWFUL ACTS AGAINST THE SAFETY OF MARITIME NAVIGATION*

THE STATES PARTIES to this Convention,

HAVING IN MIND the purposes and principles of the Charter of the United Nations concerning the maintenance of international peace and security and the promotion of friendly relations and co-operation among States,

. . . .

DEEPLY CONCERNED about the world-wide escalation of acts of terrorism in all its forms, which endanger or take innocent human lives, jeopardize fundamental freedoms and seriously impair the dignity of human beings,

. . . .

CONSIDERING that the occurrence of such acts is a matter of grave concern to the international community as a whole,

. . . .

HAVE AGREED as follows:

Article 1. For the purposes of this Convention, "ship" means a vessel of any type whatsoever not permanently attached to the seabed, including dynamically supported craft, submersibles, or any other floating craft.

Article 2. 1. This Convention does not apply to:

a. a warship; or

b. a ship owned or operated by a State when being used as a naval auxiliary or for customs or police purposes; or

c. a ship which has been withdrawn from navigation or laid up.

2. Nothing in this Convention affects the immunities of warships and other government ships operated for non-commercial purposes.

Article 3. 1. Any person commits an offence if that person unlawfully and intentionally:

a. seizes or exercises control over a ship by force or threat thereof or any other form of intimidation; or

b. performs an act of violence against a person on board a ship if that act is likely to endanger the safe navigation of that ship; or

c. destroys a ship or causes damage to a ship or to its cargo which is likely to endanger the safe navigation of that ship; or

---

* Convention for the Suppression of Unlawful Acts Against the Safety of Maritime Navigation, Mar. 10, 1988, S. TREATY DOC. NO. 101-1, at 1, 1678 U.N.T.S. 221 (entered into force Mar. 1, 1992), *available at* http://www.unodc.org/unodc/terrorism_convention_maritime_navigation.html.

d. places or causes to be placed on a ship, by any means whatsoever, a device or substance which is likely to destroy that ship, or cause damage to that ship or its cargo which endangers or is likely to endanger the safe navigation of that ship; or

e. destroys or seriously damages maritime navigational facilities or seriously interferes with their operation, if any such act is likely to endanger the safe navigation of a ship; or

f. communicates information which he knows to be false, thereby endangering the safe navigation of a ship; or

g. injures or kills any person, in connection with the commission or the attempted commission of any of the offences set forth in subparagraphs (a) to (f).

2. Any person also commits an offence if that person:

a. attempts to commit any of the offences set forth in paragraph 1; or

b. abets the commission of any of the offences set forth in paragraph 1 perpetrated by any person or is otherwise an accomplice of a person who commits such an offence; or

c. threatens, with or without a condition, as is provided for under national law, aimed at compelling a physical or juridical person to do or refrain from doing any act, to commit any of the offences set forth in paragraph 1, subparagraphs (b), (c) and (e), if that threat is likely to endanger the safe navigation of the ship in question.

....

Article 5. Each State Party shall make the offences set forth in article 3 punishable by appropriate penalties which take into account the grave nature of those offences.

Article 6. 1. Each State Party shall take such measures as may be necessary to establish its jurisdiction over the offences set forth in article 3....

....

Article 10. 1. The State Party in the territory of which the offender or the alleged offender is found shall, in cases to which article 6 applies, if it does not extradite him, be obliged, without exception whatsoever and whether or not the offence was committed in its territory, to submit the case without delay to its competent authorities for the purpose of prosecution, through proceedings in accordance with the laws of that State.

....

Article 11. 1. The offences set forth in article 3 shall be deemed to be included as extraditable offences in any extradition treaty existing between any of the States Parties. States Parties undertake to include such offences as extraditable offences in every extradition treaty to be concluded between them.

....

Article 16. 1. Any dispute between two or more States Parties concerning the interpretation or application of this Convention which cannot be settled through negotiation within a reasonable time shall, at the request of one of them, be submitted to arbitration.

....

PROTOCOL FOR THE SUPPRESSION OF UNLAWFUL ACTS AGAINST THE SAFETY OF FIXED PLATFORMS LOCATED ON THE CONTINENTAL SHELF*

THE STATES PARTIES to this Protocol,

....

HAVE AGREED as follows:

Article 1. 1. The provisions of articles 5 and 7 and of articles 10 to 16 of the Convention for the Suppression of unlawful Acts against the Safety of Maritime Navigation (hereafter referred to as "the Convention") shall also apply mutatis mutandis to the offences set forth in article 2 of this Protocol where such offences are committed on board or against fixed platforms located on the continental shelf.

2. In cases where this Protocol does not apply pursuant to paragraph 1, it nevertheless applies when the offender or the alleged offender is found in the territory of a State Party other than the State in whose international waters or territorial sea the fixed platform is located.

3. For the purposes of this Protocol, "fixed platform" means an artificial island, installation or structure permanently attached to the seabed for the purpose of exploration or exploitation of resources or for other economic purposes.

Article 2. 1. Any person commits an offence if that person unlawfully and intentionally:

---

* Protocol for the Suppression of Unlawful Acts Against the Safety of Fixed Platforms Located on the Continental Shelf, Mar. 10, 1988, S. TREATY DOC. NO. 101-1, at 11, 1678 U.N.T.S. 304 (entered into force Mar. 1, 1992), *available at* http://www.unodc.org/unodc/terrorism_convention_platforms.html. The following were parties to the Protocol when it originally came into force:

Participant	*Date of deposit of the instrument of ratification, approval (AA) or accession(a)*		
Austria	28	December	1989 *a*
China	20	August	1991
France	2	December	1991 *AA*
German Democratic Republic‡	14	April	1989 *a*
Germany	6	November	1990 *a*
Hungary	9	November	1989
Italy	26	January	1990
Norway	18	April	1991
Oman	24	September	1990 *a*
Poland	25	June	1991
Seychelles	24	January	1989
Spain	7	July	1989
Sweden	13	September	1990
Trinidad and Tobago	27	July	1989 *a*
United Kingdom of Great Britain and Northern Ireland	3	May	1991

‡ Prior to the coming into effect of the accession, the German Democratic Republic acceded to the Federal Republic of Germany with the effect from 3 October 1990.

a. seizes or exercises control over a fixed platform by force or threat thereof or any other form of intimidation; or

b. performs an act of violence against a person on board a fixed platform lf that act is likely to endanger its safety; or

c. destroys a fixed platform or causes damage to it which is likely to endanger its safety; or

d. places or causes to be placed on a fixed platform, by any means whatsoever, a device or substance which is likely to destroy that fixed platform or likely to endanger its safety; or

e. injures or kills any person in connection with the commission or the attempted commission of any of the offences set forth in subparagraphs (a) to (d).

2. Any person also commits an offence if that person:

a. attempts to commit any of the offences set forth in paragraph 1; or

b. abets the commission of any such offences perpetrated by any person or is otherwise an accomplice of a person who commits such an offence; or

c. threatens, with or without a condition, as is provided for under national law, aimed at compelling a physical or juridical person to do or refrain from doing any act, to commit any of the offences set forth in paragraph 1, subparagraphs (b) and (c), lf that threat is likely to endanger the safety of the fixed platform.

Article 3. 1. Each State Party shall take such measures as may be necessary to establish its jurisdiction over the offences set forth in article 2 when the offence is committed:

a. against or on board a fixed platform while it is located on the continental shelf of that State; or

b. by a national of that State.

2. A State Party may also establish its jurisdiction over any such offence when:

a. it is committed by a stateless person whose habitual residence is in that State;

b. during its commission a national of that State is seized, threatened, injured or killed; or

c. it is committed in an attempt to compel that State to do or abstain from doing any act.

....

4. Each State Party shall take such measures as may be necessary to establish its jurisdiction over the offences set forth in article 2 in cases where the alleged offender is present in its territory and it does not extradite him to any of the States Parties which have established their jurisdiction in accordance with paragraphs 1 and 2 of this article.

5. This Protocol does not exclude any criminal jurisdiction exercised in accordance with national law.

Article 4. Nothing in this Protocol shall affect in any way the rules of international law pertaining to fixed platforms located on the continental shelf.

....

CONVENTION ON THE MARKING OF PLASTIC EXPLOSIVES FOR THE PURPOSE OF DETECTION*

THE STATES PARTIES to this Convention,

CONSCIOUS of the implications of acts of terrorism for international security;

EXPRESSING deep concern regarding terrorist acts aimed at destruction of aircraft, other means of transportation and other targets;

CONCERNED that plastic explosives have been used for such terrorist acts;

CONSIDERING that the marking of such explosives for the purpose of detection would contribute significantly to the prevention of such unlawful acts;

. . . .

HAVE AGREED as follows:

Article 1. For the purposes of this Convention:

1. "Explosives" mean explosive products, commonly known as "plastic explosives", including explosives in flexible or elastic sheet form, as described in the Technical Annex to this Convention.

2. "Detection agent" means a substance as described in the Technical Annex to this Convention which is introduced into an explosive to render it detectable.

3. "Marking" means introducing into an explosive a detection agent in accordance with the Technical Annex to this Convention.

. . . .

Article 2. Each State Party shall take the necessary and effective measures to prohibit and prevent the manufacture in its territory of unmarked explosives.

Article 3. 1. Each State Party shall take the necessary and effective measures to prohibit and prevent the movement into or out of its territory of unmarked explosives.

2. The preceding paragraph shall not apply in respect of movements for purposes not inconsistent with the objectives of this Convention, by authorities of a State Party performing military or police functions, of unmarked explosives under the control of that State Party in accordance with paragraph 1 of Article IV.

Article 4. 1. Each State Party shall take the necessary measures to exercise strict and effective control over the possession and transfer of possession of unmarked explosives which have been manufactured in or brought into its territory prior to the entry into force of this Convention in respect of that State, so as to prevent their diversion or use for purposes inconsistent with the objectives of this Convention.

2. Each State Party shall take the necessary measures to ensure that all stocks of those explosives referred to in paragraph 1 of this Article not held by its authorities performing military or police functions are destroyed or consumed for purposes not inconsis-

* Convention on the Marking of Plastic Explosives for the Purpose of Detection, Mar. 1, 1991, S. Treaty Doc. No. 103-8, at 1, 30 I.L.M. 721, 726 (1991), *available at* http://www.unodc.org/unodc/terrorism_convention_plastic_explosives.html.

tent with the objectives of this Convention, marked or rendered permanently ineffective, within a period of three years from the entry into force of this Convention in respect of that State.

....

Article 5. 1. There is established by this Convention an International Explosives Technical Commission (hereinafter referred to as "the Commission") consisting of not less than fifteen nor more than nineteen members appointed by the Council of the International Civil Aviation Organization (hereinafter referred to as "the Council") from among persons nominated by States Parties to this Convention.

....

Article 6. 1. The Commission shall evaluate technical developments relating to the manufacture, marking and detection of explosives.

2. The Commission, through the Council, shall report its findings to the States Parties and international organizations concerned....

....

UN SECURITY COUNCIL RESOLUTION 731* (LIBYA)

The Security Council,

Deeply disturbed by the world-wide persistence of acts of international terrorism in all its forms, including those in which States are directly or indirectly involved, which endanger or take innocent lives, have a deleterious effect on international relations and jeopardize the security of States,

Deeply concerned by all illegal activities directed against international civil aviation, and affirming the right of all States, in accordance with the Charter of the United Nations and relevant principles of international law, to protect their nationals from acts of international terrorism that constitute threats to international peace and security,

. . . .

Recalling the statement made on 30 December 1988 by the President of the Security Council on behalf of the members of the Council strongly condemning the destruction of Pan Am flight 103 and calling on all States to assist in the apprehension and prosecution of those responsible for this criminal act,

Deeply concerned over the results of investigations, which implicate officials of the Libyan Government and which are contained in Security Council documents that include the requests addressed to the Libyan authorities by France, the United Kingdom of Great Britain and Northern Ireland and the United States of America in connection with the legal procedures related to the attacks carried out against Pan Am flight 103 and Union de transports aériens flight 772;

Determined to eliminate international terrorism,

1. *Condemns* the destruction of Pan Am flight 103 and Union de transports aériens flight 772 and the resultant loss of hundreds of lives;

2. *Strongly deplores* the fact that the Libyan Government has not yet responded effectively to the above requests to cooperate fully in establishing responsibility for the terrorist acts referred to above against Pan Am flight 103 and Union de transports aériens flight 772;

3. *Urges* the Libyan Government immediately to provide a full and effective response to those requests so as to contribute to the elimination of international terrorism;

4. *Requests* the Secretary-General to seek the cooperation of the Libyan Government to provide a full and effective response to those requests;

5. *Urges* all States individually and collectively to encourage the Libyan Government to respond fully and effectively to those requests;

6. *Decides* to remain seized of the matter.

Adopted unanimously at its *3033rd meeting.*

(a) Letters dated 20 and 23 December 1991

---

* S.C. Res. 731, U.N. Doc. S/RES/731 (Jan. 21, 1992), *available at* http://www.un.org/Docs/scres/1992/scres92.htm.

(b) Report by the Secretary-General pursuant to paragraph ***4 of*** **Security Council resolution 731 (1992)**

(c) Further report by the Secretary-General pursuant to paragraph 4 of Security Council resolution 731 (1992)

Decisions

At its 3063rd meeting, on 31 March 1992, the Council decided to invite the representatives of Iraq, Jordan, the Libyan Arab Jamahiriya, Mauritania and Uganda to participate, without vote, in the discussion of the item entitled:

"(a) Letters dated 20 and 23 December 1991 (S/23306, S/23307, S/23308, S/23309, S/23317);

"(b) Report by the Secretary-General pursuant to paragraph 4 of resolution 731 (1992) (S23574);

"(c) Further report by the Secretary-General pursuant to paragraph 4 of Security Council resolution 731 (1992) (S/23672)."

At the same meeting, the Council also decided, at the request of the representative of Morocco, to extend an invitation to Mr. Engin Ansay, Permanent Observer of the Organization of the Islamic Conference to the United Nations, under rule 39 of the provisional rules of procedure.

UN SECURITY COUNCIL RESOLUTION 748* (LIBYA)

The Security Council,

Reaffirming its resolution 731 (1992) of 21 January 1992,

. . . .

Deeply concerned that the Libyan Government has still not provided a full and effective response to the requests in its resolution 731 (1992),

Convinced that the suppression of acts of international terrorism, including those in which States are directly or indirectly involved, is essential for the maintenance of international peace and security,

. . . .

Reaffirming that, in accordance with the principle in Article 2, paragraph 4, of the Charter of the United Nations, every State has the duty to refrain from organizing, instigating, assisting or participating in terrorist acts in another State or acquiescing in organized activities within its territory directed towards the commission of such acts, when such acts involve a threat or use of force,

Determining, in this context, that the failure by the Libyan Government to demonstrate by concrete actions its renunciation of terrorism and in particular its continued failure to respond fully and effectively to the requests in resolution 731 (1992) constitute a threat to international peace and security,

Determined to eliminate international terrorism.

. . . .

Acting under Chapter VII of the Charter,

1. *Decides* that the Libyan Government must now comply without any further delay with paragraph 3 of resolution 731 (1992) regarding the requests addressed to the Libyan authorities by France, the United Kingdom of Great Britain and Northern Ireland and the United States of America,

2. *Decides also* that the Libyan Government must commit itself definitively to cease all forms of terrorist action and all assistance to terrorist groups and that it must promptly, by concrete actions, demonstrate its renunciation of terrorism;

3. *Decides* that, on 15 April 1992, all States shall adopt the measures set out below, which shall apply until the Security Council decides that the Libyan Government has complied with paragraphs 1 and 2 above;

4. *Decides also* that all States shall:

(a) Deny permission to any aircraft to take off from, land in or overfly their territory if it is destined to land in or has taken off from the territory of Libya, unless the particular flight has been approved on grounds of significant humanitarian need by the Security Council Committee established by paragraph 9 below;

* S.C. Res. 748, U.N. Doc. S/RES/748 (Mar. 31, 1992), *available at* http://www.un.org/Docs/scres/1992/scres92.htm.

(b) Prohibit, by their nationals or from their territory, the supply of any aircraft or aircraft components to Libya, the provision of engineering and maintenance servicing of Libyan aircraft or aircraft components, the certification of airworthiness for Libyan aircraft, the payment of new claims against existing insurance contracts and the provision of new direct insurance for Libyan aircraft;

5. *Decides further* that all States shall:

(a) Prohibit any provision to Libya by their nationals or from their territory of arms and including the sale or transfer of weapons and ammunition, military vehicles and equipment, paramilitary police equipment and spare parts for the aforementioned, as well as the provision of any types of equipment, supplies and grants of licensing arrangements, for the manufacture or maintenance of the aforementioned;

(b) Prohibit any provision to Libya by their nationals or from their territory of technical advice, assistance or training related to the provision, manufacture, maintenance, or use of the items in subparagraph (a) above;

(c) Withdraw any of their officials or agents present in Libya to advise the Libyan authorities on military matters;

6. *Decides* that all States shall:

. . . .

(b) Prevent the operation of all Libyan Arab Airlines offices;

(c) Take all appropriate steps to deny entry to or expel Libyan nationals who have been denied entry to or expelled from other States because of their involvement in terrorist activities;

7. *Calls upon* all States, including States not members of the United Nations, and all international organizations, to act strictly in accordance with the provisions of the present resolution, notwithstanding the existence of any rights or obligations conferred or imposed by any international agreement or any contract entered into or any license or permit granted prior to 15 April 1992;

. . . .

INTERNATIONAL CONVENTION FOR THE SUPPRESSION OF TERRORIST BOMBINGS*

THE STATES PARTIES to this Convention,

Having in mind the purposes and principles of the Charter of the United Nations concerning the maintenance of international peace and security and the promotion of good-neighbourliness and friendly relations and cooperation among States,

Deeply concerned about the worldwide escalation of acts of terrorism in all its forms and manifestations,

....

Noting that terrorist attacks by means of explosives or other lethal devices have become increasingly widespread,

Noting also that existing multilateral legal provisions do not adequately address these attacks,

Being convinced of the urgent need to enhance international cooperation between States in devising and adopting effective and practical measures for the prevention of such acts of terrorism and for the prosecution and punishment of their perpetrators,

Considering that the occurrence of such acts is a matter of grave concern to the international community as a whole,

Noting that the activities of military forces of States are governed by rules of international law outside the framework of this Convention and that the exclusion of certain actions from the coverage of this Convention does not condone or make lawful otherwise unlawful acts, or preclude prosecution under other laws,

Have agreed as follows:

....

***Article** 2.* 1. Any person commits an offence within the meaning of this Convention if that person unlawfully and intentionally delivers, places, discharges or detonates an explosive or other lethal device in, into or against a place of public use, a State or government facility, a public transportation system or an infrastructure facility:

a. With the intent to cause death or serious bodily injury; or

b. With the intent to cause extensive destruction of such a place, facility or system, where such destruction results in or is likely to result in major economic loss.

2. Any person also commits an offence if that person attempts to commit an offence as set forth in paragraph 1 of the present article.

3. Any person also commits an offence if that person:

a. Participates as an accomplice in an offence as set forth in paragraph 1 or 2 of the present article; or

---

* International Convention for the Suppression of Terrorist Bombings, Dec. 15, 1997, S. Treaty Doc. No. 106-6, at 1, 2149 U.N.T.S. 260 (entered into force May 23, 2001), *available at* http://www.unodc.org/unodc/terrorism_convention_terrorist_bombing.html.

b. Organizes or directs others to commit an offence as set forth in paragraph 1 or 2 of the present article; or

c. In any other way contributes to the commission of one or more offences as set forth in paragraph 1 or 2 of the present article by a group of persons acting with a common purpose; such contribution shall be intentional and either be made with the aim of furthering the general criminal activity or purpose of the group or be made in the knowledge of the intention of the group to commit the offence or offences concerned.

Article 3. This Convention shall not apply where the offence is committed within a single State, the alleged offender and the victims are nationals of that State, the alleged offender is found in the territory of that State and no other State has a basis under article 6, paragraph 1 or paragraph 2, of this Convention to exercise jurisdiction, except that the provisions of articles 10 to 15 shall, as appropriate, apply in those cases.

Article 4. Each State Party shall adopt such measures as may be necessary:

a. To establish as criminal offences under its domestic law the offences set forth in article 2 of this Convention;

b. To make those offences punishable by appropriate penalties which take into account the grave nature of those offences.

Article 5. Each State Party shall adopt such measures as may be necessary, including, where appropriate, domestic legislation, to ensure that criminal acts within the scope of this Convention, in particular where they are intended or calculated to provoke a state of terror in the general public or in a group of persons or particular persons, are under no circumstances justifiable by considerations of a political, philosophical, ideological, racial, ethnic, religious or other similar nature and are punished by penalties consistent with their grave nature.

Article 6. 1. Each State Party shall take such measures as may be necessary to establish its jurisdiction over the offences set forth in article 2 when:

a. The offence is committed in the territory of that State; or

b. The offence is committed on board a vessel flying the flag of that State or an aircraft which is registered under the laws of that State at the time the offence is committed; or

c. The offence is committed by a national of that State.

2. A State Party may also establish its jurisdiction over any such offence when:

a. The offence is committed against a national of that State; or

b. The offence is committed against a State or government facility of that State abroad, including an embassy or other diplomatic or consular premises of that State; or

c. The offence is committed by a stateless person who has his or her habitual residence in the territory of that State; or

d. The offence is committed in an attempt to compel that State to do or abstain from doing any act; or

e. The offence is committed on board an aircraft which is operated by the Government of that State.

. . . .

4. Each State Party shall likewise take such measures as may be necessary to establish its jurisdiction over the offences set forth in article 2 in cases where the alleged offender is present in its territory and it does not extradite that person to any of the States Parties which have established their jurisdiction in accordance with paragraph 1 or 2 of the present article.

5. This Convention does not exclude the exercise of any criminal jurisdiction established by a State Party in accordance with its domestic law.

Article 7. 1. Upon receiving information that a person who has committed or who is alleged to have committed an offence as set forth in article 2 may be present in its territory, the State Party concerned shall take such measures as may be necessary under its domestic law to investigate the facts contained in the information.

2. Upon being satisfied that the circumstances so warrant, the State Party in whose territory the offender or alleged offender is present shall take the appropriate measures under its domestic law so as to ensure that person's presence for the purpose of prosecution or extradition.

. . . .

Article 8. 1. The State Party in the territory of which the alleged offender is present shall, in cases to which article 6 applies, if it does not extradite that person, be obliged, without exception whatsoever and whether or not the offence was committed in its territory, to submit the case without undue delay to its competent authorities for the purpose of prosecution, through proceedings in accordance with the laws of that State. Those authorities shall take their decision in the same manner as in the case of any other offence of a grave nature under the law of that State.

2. Whenever a State Party is permitted under its domestic law to extradite or otherwise surrender one of its nationals only upon the condition that the person will be returned to that State to serve the sentence imposed as a result of the trial or proceeding for which the extradition or surrender of the person was sought, and this State and the State seeking the extradition of the person agree with this option and other terms they may deem appropriate, such a conditional extradition or surrender shall be sufficient to discharge the obligation set forth in paragraph 1 of the present article.

Article 9. 1. The offences set forth in article 2 shall be deemed to be included as extraditable offences in any extradition treaty existing between any of the States Parties before the entry into force of this Convention. States Parties undertake to include such offences as extraditable offences in every extradition treaty to be subsequently concluded between them.

3. When a State Party which makes extradition conditional on the existence of a treaty receives a request for extradition from another State Party with which it has no extradition treaty, the requested State Party may, at its option, consider this Convention as a legal basis for extradition in respect of the offences set forth in article 2. Extradition shall be subject to the other conditions provided by the law of the requested State.

. . . .

4. If necessary, the offences set forth in article 2 shall be treated, for the purposes of extradition between States Parties, as if they had been committed not only in the place in which they occurred but also in the territory of the States that have established jurisdiction in accordance with article 6, paragraphs 1 and 2.

5. The provisions of all extradition treaties and arrangements between States Parties with regard to offences set forth in article 2 shall be deemed to be modified as between State Parties to the extent that they are incompatible with this Convention.

....

Article 11. None of the offences set forth in article 2 shall be regarded, for the purposes of extradition or mutual legal assistance, as a political offence or as an offence connected with a political offence or as an offence inspired by political motives.

....

Article 12. Nothing in this Convention shall be interpreted as imposing an obligation to extradite or to afford mutual legal assistance, if the requested State Party has substantial grounds for believing that the request for extradition for offences set forth in article 2 or for mutual legal assistance with respect to such offences has been made for the purpose of prosecuting or punishing a person on account of that person's race, religion, nationality, ethnic origin or political opinion or that compliance with the request would cause prejudice to that person's position for any of these reasons.

....

Article 14. Any person who is taken into custody or regarding whom any other measures are taken or proceedings are carried out pursuant to this Convention shall be guaranteed fair treatment, including enjoyment of all rights and guarantees in conformity with the law of the State in the territory of which that person is present and applicable provisions of international law, including international law of human rights.

....

Article 18. Nothing in this Convention entitles a State Party to undertake in the territory of another State Party the exercise of jurisdiction and performance of functions which are exclusively reserved for the authorities of that other State Party by its domestic law.

Article 19. 1. Nothing in this Convention shall affect other rights, obligations and responsibilities of States and individuals under international law, in particular the purposes and principles of the Charter of the United Nations and international humanitarian law.

2. The activities of armed forces during an armed conflict, as those terms are understood under international humanitarian law, which are governed by that law, are not governed by this Convention, and the activities undertaken by military forces of a State in the exercise of their official duties, inasmuch as they are governed by other rules of international law, are not governed by this Convention.

....

INTERNATIONAL CONVENTION FOR THE SUPPRESSION OF THE FINANCING OF TERRORISM*

Preamble

The States Parties to this Convention,

. . . .

Deeply concerned about the worldwide escalation of acts of terrorism in all its forms and manifestations,

. . . .

Considering that the financing of terrorism is a matter of grave concern to the international community as a whole,

Noting that the number and seriousness of acts of international terrorism depend on the financing that terrorists may obtain,

Noting also that existing multilateral legal instruments do not expressly address such financing,

Being convinced of the urgent need to enhance international cooperation among States in devising and adopting effective measures for the prevention of the financing of terrorism, as well as for its suppression through the prosecution and punishment of its perpetrators,

Have agreed as follows:

. . . .

Article 2. 1. Any person commits an offence within the meaning of this Convention if that person by any means, directly or indirectly, unlawfully and willfully, provides or collects funds with the intention that they should be used or in the knowledge that they are to be used, in full or in part, in order to carry out:

(a) An act which constitutes an offence within the scope of and as defined in one of the treaties listed in the annex; or

(b) Any other act intended to cause death or serious bodily injury to a civilian, or to any other person not taking an active part in the hostilities in a situation of armed conflict, when the purpose of such act, by its nature or context, is to intimidate a population, or to compel a Government or an international organization to do or to abstain from doing any act.

2. (a) On depositing its instrument of ratification, acceptance, approval or accession, a State Party which is not a party to a treaty listed in the annex may declare that, in the application of this Convention to the State Party, the treaty shall be deemed not to be included in the annex referred to in paragraph 1, subparagraph (a). The declaration shall cease to have effect as soon as the treaty enters into force for the State Party, which shall notify the depositary of this fact;

* International Convention for the Suppression of the Financing of Terrorism, Dec. 9, 1999, S. Treaty Doc. No. 106-49, at 1, 2178 U.N.T.S. 200 (entered into force Apr. 10, 2002), *available at* http://untreaty.un.org/English/Terrorism/Conv12.pdf.

b. When a State Party ceases to be a party to a treaty listed in the annex, it may make a declaration as provided for in this article, with respect to that treaty.

3. For an act to constitute an offence set forth in paragraph 1, it shall not be necessary that the funds were actually used to carry out an offence referred to in paragraph 1, subparagraph (a) or (b).

4. Any person also commits an offence if that person attempts to commit an offence as set forth in paragraph 1 of this article.

5. Any person also commits an offence if that person:

(a) Participates as an accomplice in an offence as set forth in paragraph 1 or 4 of this article;

(b) Organizes or directs others to commit an offence as set forth in paragraph 1 or 4 of this article;

(c) Contributes to the commission of one or more offences as set forth in paragraph 1 or 4 of this article by a group of persons acting with a common purpose. Such contribution shall be intentional and shall either:

(i) Be made with the aim of furthering the criminal activity or criminal purpose of the group, where such activity or purpose involves the commission of an offence as set forth in paragraph 1 of this article; or

(ii) Be made in the knowledge of the intention of the group to commit an offence as set forth in paragraph 1 of this article.

Article 3. This Convention shall not apply where the offence is committed within a single State, the alleged offender is a national of that State and is present in the territory of that State and no other State has a basis under article 7, paragraph 1 or 2, to exercise jurisdiction, except that the provisions of articles 12 to 18 shall, as appropriate, apply in those cases.

Article 4. Each State Party shall adopt such measures as may be necessary:

(a) To establish as criminal offences under its domestic law the offences as set forth in article 2;

(b) To make those offences punishable by appropriate penalties which take into account the grave nature of the offences.

....

Article 6. Each State Party shall adopt such measures as may be necessary, including, where appropriate, domestic legislation, to ensure that criminal acts within the scope of this Convention are under no circumstances justifiable by considerations of a political, philosophical, ideological, racial, ethnic, religious or other similar nature.

Article 7. Each State Party shall take such measures as may be necessary to establish its jurisdiction over the offences set forth in article 2....

....

Article 9. 1. Upon receiving information that a person who has committed or who is alleged to have committed an offence set forth in article 2 may be present in its territory, the State Party concerned shall take such measures as may be necessary under its domestic law to investigate the facts contained in the information.

2. Upon being satisfied that the circumstances so warrant, the State Party in whose territory the offender or alleged offender is present shall take the appropriate measures

under its domestic law so as to ensure that person's presence for the purpose of prosecution or extradition.

....

Article 10. 1. The State Party in the territory of which the alleged offender is present shall, in cases to which article 7 applies, if it does not extradite that person, be obliged, without exception whatsoever and whether or not the offence was committed in its territory, to submit the case without undue delay to its competent authorities for the purpose of prosecution, through proceedings in accordance with the laws of that State. Those authorities shall take their decision in the same manner as in the case of any other offence of a grave nature under the law of that State.

....

Article 13. None of the offences set forth in article 2 shall be regarded, for the purposes of extradition or mutual legal assistance, as a fiscal offence. Accordingly, States Parties may not refuse a request for extradition or for mutual legal assistance on the sole ground that it concerns a fiscal offence.

Article 14. None of the offences set forth in article 2 shall be regarded for the purposes of extradition or mutual legal assistance as a political offence or as an offence connected with a political offence or as an offence inspired by political motives.

....

Article 15. Nothing in this Convention shall be interpreted as imposing an obligation to extradite or to afford mutual legal assistance, if the requested State Party has substantial grounds for believing that the request for extradition for offences set forth in article 2 or for mutual legal assistance with respect to such offences has been made for the purpose of prosecuting or punishing a person on account of that person's race, religion, nationality, ethnic origin or political opinion or that compliance with the request would cause prejudice to that person's position for any of these reasons.

....

Article 17. Any person who is taken into custody or regarding whom any other measures are taken or proceedings are carried out pursuant to this Convention shall be guaranteed fair treatment, including enjoyment of all rights and guarantees in conformity with the law of the State in the territory of which that person is present and applicable provisions of international law, including international human rights law.

Article 18. 1. States Parties shall cooperate in the prevention of the offences set forth in article 2 by taking all practicable measures, *inter alia*, by adapting their domestic legislation, if necessary, to prevent and counter preparations in their respective territories for the commission of those offences within or outside their territories, including:

(a) Measures to prohibit in their territories illegal activities of persons and organizations that knowingly encourage, instigate, organize or engage in the commission of offences set forth in article 2;

(b) Measures requiring financial institutions and other professions involved in financial transactions to utilize the most efficient measures available for the identification of their usual or occasional customers, as well as customers in whose interest accounts are opened, and to pay special attention to unusual or suspicious transactions and report transactions suspected of stemming from a criminal activity....

....

UN SECURITY COUNCIL RESOLUTION 1373* (SUPPRESSING TERRORISM FINANCING)

The Security Council,

Reaffirming its resolutions 1269 (1999) of 19 October 1999 and 1368 (2001) of 12 September 2001,

Reaffirming also its unequivocal condemnation of the terrorist attacks which took place in New York, Washington, D.C. and Pennsylvania on 11 September 2001, and expressing its determination to prevent all such acts,

Reaffirming further that such acts, like any act of international terrorism, constitute a threat to international peace and security,

Reaffirming the inherent right of individual or collective self-defence as recognized by the Charter of the United Nations as reiterated in resolution 1368 (2001),

Reaffirming the need to combat by all means, in accordance with the Charter of the United Nations, threats to international peace and security caused by terrorist acts,

Deeply concerned by the increase, in various regions of the world, of acts of terrorism motivated by intolerance or extremism,

Calling on States to work together urgently to prevent and suppress terrorist acts, including through increased cooperation and full implementation of the relevant international conventions relating to terrorism,

Recognizing the need for States to complement international cooperation by taking additional measures to prevent and suppress, in their territories through all lawful means, the financing and preparation of any acts of terrorism,

Reaffirming the principle established by the General Assembly in its declaration of October 1970 (resolution 2625 (XXV)) and reiterated by the Security Council in its resolution 1189 (1998) of 13 August 1998, namely that every State has the duty to refrain from organizing, instigating, assisting or participating in terrorist acts in another State or acquiescing in organized activities within its territory directed towards the commission of such acts,

Acting under Chapter VII of the Charter of the United Nations,

1. *Decides* that all States shall:

(a) Prevent and suppress the financing of terrorist acts;

(b) Criminalize the willful provision or collection, by any means, directly or indirectly, of funds by their nationals or in their territories with the intention that the funds should be used, or in the knowledge that they are to be used, in order to carry out terrorist acts;

(c) Freeze without delay funds and other financial assets or economic resources of persons who commit, or attempt to commit, terrorist acts or participate in or facilitate the commission of terrorist acts; of entities owned or controlled directly or indirectly by such persons; and of persons and entities acting on behalf of, or at the

* S.C. Res. 1373, U.N. Doc. S/RES/1373 (Sept. 28, 2001), *available at* http://www.un.org/Docs/scres/2001/sc2001.htm.

direction of such persons and entities, including funds derived or generated from property owned or controlled directly or indirectly by such persons and associated persons and entities;

(d) Prohibit their nationals or any persons and entities within their territories from making any funds, financial assets or economic resources or financial or other related services available, directly or indirectly, for the benefit of persons who commit or attempt to commit or facilitate or participate in the commission of terrorist acts, of entities owned or controlled, directly or indirectly, by such persons and of persons and entities acting on behalf of or at the direction of such persons;

2. *Decides also* that all States shall:

(a) Refrain from providing any form of support, active or passive, to entities or persons involved in terrorist acts, including by suppressing recruitment of members of terrorist groups and eliminating the supply of weapons to terrorists;

(b) Take the necessary steps to prevent the commission of terrorist acts, including by provision of early warning to other States by exchange of information;

(c) Deny safe haven to those who finance, plan, support, or commit terrorist acts, or provide safe havens;

(d) Prevent those who finance, plan, facilitate or commit terrorist acts from using their respective territories for those purposes against other States or their citizens;

(e) Ensure that any person who participates in the financing, planning, preparation or perpetration of terrorist acts or in supporting terrorist acts is brought to justice and ensure that, in addition to any other measures against them, such terrorist acts are established as serious criminal offences in domestic laws and regulations and that the punishment duly reflects the seriousness of such terrorist acts;

(f) Afford one another the greatest measure of assistance in connection with criminal investigations or criminal proceedings relating to the financing or support of terrorist acts, including assistance in obtaining evidence in their possession necessary for the proceedings;

(g) Prevent the movement of terrorists or terrorist groups by effective border controls and controls on issuance of identity papers and travel documents, and through measures for preventing counterfeiting, forgery or fraudulent use of identity papers and travel documents;

3. *Calls* upon all States to:

(a) Find ways of intensifying and accelerating the exchange of operational information, especially regarding actions or movements of terrorist persons or networks; forged or falsified travel documents; traffic in arms, explosives or sensitive materials; use of communications technologies by terrorist groups; and the threat posed by the possession of weapons of mass destruction by terrorist groups;

(b) Exchange information in accordance with international and domestic law and cooperate on administrative and judicial matters to prevent the commission of terrorist acts;

(c) Cooperate, particularly through bilateral and multilateral arrangements and agreements, to prevent and suppress terrorist attacks and take action against perpetrators of such acts;

(d) Become parties as soon as possible to the relevant international conventions and protocols relating to terrorism, including the International Convention for the Suppression of the Financing of Terrorism of 9 December 1999;

(e) Increase cooperation and fully implement the relevant international conventions and protocols relating to terrorism and Security Council resolutions 1269 (1999) and 1368 (2001);

(f) Take appropriate measures in conformity with the relevant provisions of national and international law, including international standards of human rights, before granting refugee status, for the purpose of ensuring that the asylum-seeker has not planned, facilitated or participated in the commission of terrorist acts;

(g) Ensure, in conformity with international law, that refugee status is not abused by the perpetrators, organizers or facilitators of terrorist acts, and that claims of political motivation are not recognized as grounds for refusing requests for the extradition of alleged terrorists;

4. *Notes* with concern the close connection between international terrorism and transnational organized crime, illicit drugs, money-laundering, illegal arms-trafficking, and illegal movement of nuclear, chemical, biological and other potentially deadly materials, and in this regard *emphasizes* the need to enhance coordination of efforts on national, subregional, regional and international levels in order to strengthen a global response to this serious challenge and threat to international security;

5. *Declares* that acts, methods, and practices of terrorism are contrary to the purposes and principles of the United Nations and that knowingly financing, planning and inciting terrorist acts are also contrary to the purposes and principles of the United Nations;

6. *Decides* to establish, in accordance with rule 28 of its provisional rules of procedure, a Committee of the Security Council, consisting of all the members of the Council, to monitor implementation of this resolution, with the assistance of appropriate expertise, and *calls upon* all States to report to the Committee, no later than 90 days from the date of adoption of this resolution and thereafter according to a timetable to be proposed by the Committee, on the steps they have taken to implement this resolution;

7. *Directs* the Committee to delineate its tasks, submit a work programme within 30 days of the adoption of this resolution, and to consider the support it requires, in consultation with the Secretary-General;

8. *Expresses* its determination to take all necessary steps in order to ensure the full implementation of this resolution, in accordance with its responsibilities under the Charter;

9. *Decides* to remain seized of this matter.

UN SECURITY COUNCIL RESOLUTION 1390* (TALIBAN/AL-QAIDA ASSETS)

The Security Council,

. . . .

Reaffirming its unequivocal condemnation of the terrorist attacks which took place in New York, Washington and Pennsylvania on 11 September 2001, expressing its determination to prevent all such acts, *noting* the continued activities of Usama bin Laden and the Al-Qaida network in supporting international terrorism, and expressing its determination to root out this network,

Noting the indictments of Usama bin Laden and his associates by the United States of America for, inter alia, the 7 August 1998 bombings of the United States embassies in Nairobi, Kenya and Dar es Salaam, Tanzania,

Determining that the Taliban have failed to respond to the demands in paragraph 13 of resolution 1214 (1998) of 8 December 1998, paragraph 2 of resolution 1267 (1999) and paragraphs 1, 2 and 3 of resolution 1333 (2000),

Condemning the Taliban for allowing Afghanistan to be used as a base for terrorists training and activities, including the export of terrorism by the Al-Qaida network and other terrorist groups as well as for using foreign mercenaries in hostile actions in the territory of Afghanistan,

Condemning the Al-Qaida network and other associated terrorist groups, for the multiple criminal, terrorist acts, aimed at causing the deaths of numerous innocent civilians, and the destruction of property,

Reaffirming further that acts of international terrorism constitute a threat to international peace and security,

Acting under Chapter VII of the Charter of the United Nations,

1. *Decides* to continue the measures imposed by paragraph 8 (c) of resolution 1333 (2000) and *takes note* of the continued application of the measures imposed by paragraph 4 (b) of resolution 1267 (1999), in accordance with paragraph 2 below, and *decides* to terminate the measures imposed in paragraph 4 (a) of resolution 1267 (1999);

2. *Decides* that all States shall take the following measures with respect to Usama bin Laden, members of the Al-Qaida organization and the Taliban and other individuals, groups, undertakings and entities associated with them, as referred to in the list created pursuant to resolutions 1267 (1999) and 1333 (2000) to be updated regularly by the Committee established pursuant to resolution 1267 (1999) hereinafter referred to as "the Committee";

(a) Freeze without delay the funds and other financial assets or economic resources of these individuals, groups, undertakings and entities, including funds derived from property owned or controlled, directly or indirectly, by them or by persons acting on their behalf or at their direction, and ensure that neither these nor any other funds, financial assets or economic resources are made available, directly

* S.C. Res. 1390, U.N. Doc. S/RES/1390 (Jan. 28, 2002), *available at* http://www.un.org/Docs/scres/2002/sc2002.htm.

or indirectly, for such persons' benefit, by their nationals or by any persons within their territory;

(b) Prevent the entry into or the transit through their territories of these individuals, provided that nothing in this paragraph shall oblige any State to deny entry into or require the departure from its territories of its own nationals and this paragraph shall not apply where entry or transit is necessary for the fulfillment of a judicial process or the Committee determines on a case by case basis only that entry or transit is justified;

(c) Prevent the direct or indirect supply, sale and transfer, to these individuals, groups, undertakings and entities from their territories or by their nationals outside their territories, or using their flag vessels or aircraft, of arms and related materiel of all types including weapons and ammunition, military vehicles and equipment, paramilitary equipment, and spare parts for the aforementioned and technical advice, assistance, or training related to military activities;

3. *Decides* that the measures referred to in paragraphs 1 and 2 above will be reviewed in 12 months and that at the end of this period the Council will either allow these measures to continue or decide to improve them, in keeping with the principles and purposes of this resolution;

4. *Recalls* the obligation placed upon all Member States to implement in full resolution 1373 (2001), including with regard to any member of the Taliban and the Al-Qaida organization, and any individuals, groups, undertakings and entities associated with the Taliban and the Al-Qaida organization, who have participated in the financing, planning, facilitating and preparation or perpetration of terrorist acts or in supporting terrorist acts;

5. *Requests* the Committee to undertake the following tasks and to report on its work to the Council with its observations and recommendations;

....

8. *Urges* all States to take immediate steps to enforce and strengthen through legislative enactments or administrative measures, where appropriate, the measures imposed under domestic laws or regulations against their nationals and other individuals or entities operating on their territory, to prevent and punish violations of the measures referred to in paragraph 2 of this resolution, and to inform the Committee of the adoption of such measures, and *invites* States to report the results of all related investigations or enforcement actions to the Committee unless to do so would compromise the investigation or enforcement actions;

....

UN SECURITY COUNCIL RESOLUTION 1456[*] (COMBATING TERRORISM)

The Security Council,

Decides to adopt the attached declaration on the issue of combating terrorism.

Annex

The Security Council,

Meeting at the level of Ministers for Foreign Affairs on 20 January 2003 reaffirms that:

– terrorism in all its forms and manifestations constitutes one of the most serious threats to peace and security;

– any acts of terrorism are criminal and unjustifiable, regardless of their motivation, whenever and by whomsoever committed and are to be unequivocally condemned, especially when they indiscriminately target or injure civilians;

– there is a serious and growing danger of terrorist access to and use of nuclear, chemical, biological and other potentially deadly materials, and therefore a need to strengthen controls on these materials;

– it has become easier, in an increasingly globalized world, for terrorists to exploit sophisticated technology, communications and resources for their criminal objectives;

– measures to detect and stem the flow of finance and funds for terrorist purposes must be urgently strengthened;

– terrorists must also be prevented from making use of other criminal activities such as transnational organized crime, illicit drugs and drug trafficking, money-laundering and illicit arms trafficking;

– since terrorists and their supporters exploit instability and intolerance to justify their criminal acts the Security Council is determined to counter this by contributing to peaceful resolution of disputes and by working to create a climate of mutual tolerance and respect;

≠ terrorism can only be defeated, in accordance with the Charter of the United Nations and international law, by a sustained comprehensive approach involving the active participation and collaboration of all States, international and regional organizations, and by redoubled efforts at the national level.

* * *

The Security Council therefore calls for the following steps to be taken:

1. All States must take urgent action to prevent and suppress all active and passive support to terrorism, and in particular comply fully with all relevant resolutions of the Security Council, in particular resolutions 1373 (2001), 1390 (2002) and 1455 (2003);

2. The Security Council calls upon States to:

---

* S.C. Res. 1456, U.N. Doc. S/RES/1456 (Jan. 20, 2003), *available at* http://www.un.org/Docs/scres/2003/sc2003.htm.

(a) become a party, as a matter of urgency, to all relevant international conventions and protocols relating to terrorism, in particular the 1999 international convention for the suppression of the financing of terrorism and to support all international initiatives taken to that aim, and to make full use of the sources of assistance and guidance which are now becoming available;

(b) assist each other, to the maximum extent possible, in the prevention, investigation, prosecution and punishment of acts of terrorism, wherever they occur;

(c) cooperate closely to implement fully the sanctions against terrorists and their associates, in particular Al-Qaeda and the Taliban and their associates, as reflected in resolutions 1267 (1999), 1390 (2002) and 1455 (2003), to take urgent actions to deny them access to the financial resources they need to carry out their actions, and to cooperate fully with the Monitoring Group established pursuant to resolution 1363 (2001);

3. States must bring to justice those who finance, plan, support or commit terrorist acts or provide safe havens, in accordance with international law, in particular on the basis of the principle to extradite or prosecute;

. . . .

UN SECURITY COUNCIL RESOLUTION 1526* (FREEZING TALIBAN/AL-QAIDA ASSETS)

The Security Council,

Recalling its resolutions 1267 (1999) of 15 October 1999, 1333 (2000) of 19 December 2000, 1363 (2001) of 30 July 2001, 1373 (2001) of 28 September 2001, 1390 (2002) of 16 January 2002, 1452 (2002) of 20 December 2002, and 1455(2003) of 17 January 2003,

Underlining the obligation placed upon all Member States to implement, in full, resolution 1373 (2001), including with regard to any member of the Taliban and the Al-Qaida organization, and any individuals, groups, undertakings and entities associated with the Taliban and the Al-Qaida organization, who have participated in the financing, planning, facilitating and preparation or perpetration of terrorist acts or in supporting terrorist acts, as well as to facilitate the implementation of counter-terrorism obligations in accordance with relevant Security Council resolutions,

Reaffirming the need to combat by all means, in accordance with the Charter of the United Nations and international law, threats to international peace and security caused by terrorist acts,

Noting that, in giving effect to the measures in paragraph 4 (b) of resolution 1267 (1999), paragraph 8 (c) of resolution 1333 (2000) and paragraphs 1 and 2 of resolution 1390 (2002), full account is to be taken of the provisions of paragraphs 1 and 2 of resolution 1452 (2002),

Reiterating its condemnation of the Al-Qaida network and other associated terrorist groups for ongoing and multiple criminal terrorist acts, aimed at causing the deaths of innocent civilians, and other victims, and the destruction of property, and greatly undermining stability,

Reiterating its unequivocal condemnation of all forms of terrorism and terrorist acts,

Stressing to all States, international bodies, and regional organizations, the importance of ensuring that resources are committed, including through international partnership, to meet the ongoing threat the Al-Qaida organization and members of the Taliban, and any individuals, groups, undertakings and entities associated with them, represent to international peace and security,

Acting under Chapter VII of the Charter of the United Nations,

1. *Decides*.... with respect to Usama bin Laden, members of the Al-Qaida organization and the Taliban and other individuals, groups, undertakings and entities associated with them.... to:

(a) Freeze without delay the funds and other financial assets or economic resources of these individuals, groups, undertakings and entities, including funds derived from property owned or controlled, directly or indirectly, by them or by persons acting on their behalf or at their direction, and ensure that neither these nor any other funds, financial assets or economic resources are made available, directly

* S.C. Res. 1526, U.N. Doc. S/RES/1526 (Jan. 30, 2004), *available at* http://www.un.org/Docs/sc/unsc_resolutions04.html.

or indirectly, for such persons' benefit, by their nationals or by any persons within their territory;

(b) Prevent the entry into or the transit through their territories of these individuals, provided that nothing in this paragraph shall oblige any State to deny entry or require the departure from its territories of its own nationals and this paragraph shall not apply where entry or transit is necessary for the fulfillment of a judicial process or the Committee determines on a case-by-case basis only that entry or transit is justified;

(c) Prevent the direct or indirect supply, sale or transfer, to these individuals, groups, undertakings and entities from their territories or by their nationals outside their territories, or using their flag vessels or aircraft, of arms and related materiel of all types including weapons and ammunition, military vehicles and equipment, paramilitary equipment, and spare parts for the aforementioned and technical advice, assistance, or training related to military activities;

and *recalls* that all States shall implement the measures with respect to listed individuals and entities;

....

4. *Calls upon* States to move vigorously and decisively to cut the flows of funds and other financial assets and economic resources to individuals and entities associated with the Al-Qaida organization, Usama bin Laden and/or the Taliban, taking into account, as appropriate, international codes and standards for combating the financing of terrorism, including those designed to prevent the abuse of non-profit organizations and informal/alternative remittance systems;

....

UN SECURITY COUNCIL RESOLUTION 1540* (WEAPONS OF MASS DESTRUCTION)

The Security Council,

Affirming that proliferation of nuclear, chemical and biological weapons, as well as their means of delivery,1 constitutes a threat to international peace and security,

....

Affirming its resolve to take appropriate and effective actions against any threat to international peace and security caused by the proliferation of nuclear, chemical and biological weapons and their means of delivery, in conformity with its primary responsibilities, as provided for in the United Nations Charter,

Affirming its support for the multilateral treaties whose aim is to eliminate or prevent the proliferation of nuclear, chemical or biological weapons and the importance for all States parties to these treaties to implement them fully in order to promote international stability,

....

Gravely *concerned* by the threat of terrorism and the risk that non-State actorsi such as those identified in the United Nations list established and maintained by the Committee established under Security Council resolution 1267 and those to whom resolution 1373 applies, may acquire, develop, traffic in or use nuclear, chemical and biological weapons and their means of delivery,

Gravely concerned by the threat of illicit trafficking in nuclear, chemical, or biological weapons and their means of delivery, and related materials,[i] which adds a new dimension to the issue of proliferation of such weapons and also poses a threat to international peace and security,

....

Reaffirming the need to combat by all means, in accordance with the Charter of the United Nations, threats to international peace and security caused by terrorist acts,

Determined to facilitate henceforth an effective response to global threats in the area of non-proliferation,

Acting under Chapter VII of the Charter of the United Nations,

1. *Decides that* all States shall refrain from providing any form of support to non-State actors that attempt to develop, acquire, manufacture, possess, transport, transfer or use nuclear, chemical or biological weapons and their means of delivery;

2. *Decides also* that all States, in accordance with their national procedures, shall adopt and enforce appropriate effective laws which prohibit any non-State actor to manufacture, acquire, possess, develop, transport, transfer or use nuclear, chemical or biological weapons and their means of delivery, in particular for terrorist purposes, as

---

* S.C. Res. 1540, U.N. Doc. S/RES/1540 (Apr. 28, 2004), *available at* http://www.un.org/Docs/sc/unsc_resolutions04.html. (Original footnote included as endnote). UN Security Council Resolutions responding to terrorism in light of the attacks of September 11, 2001: 1368, 1373, 1377, 1378 (2001); 1390, 1438, 1441, 1450, 1452 (2002); 1455, 1456 (2003); 1526, 1535, 1540 (2004).

well as attempts to engage in any of the foregoing activities, participate in them as an accomplice, assist or finance them;

3. *Decides also* that all States shall take and enforce effective measures to establish domestic controls to prevent the proliferation of nuclear, chemical, or biological weapons and their means of delivery, including by establishing appropriate controls over related materials and to this end shall:

(a) Develop and maintain appropriate effective measures to account for and secure such items in production, use, storage or transport;

(b) Develop and maintain appropriate effective physical protection measures;

(c) Develop and maintain appropriate effective border controls and law enforcement efforts to detect, deter, prevent and combat, including through international cooperation when necessary, the illicit trafficking and brokering in such items in accordance with their national legal authorities and legislation and consistent with international law;

(d) Establish, develop, review and maintain appropriate effective national export and trans-shipment controls over such items, including appropriate laws and regulations to control export, transit, trans-shipment and re-export and controls on providing funds and services related to such export and trans-shipment such as financing, and transporting that would contribute to proliferation, as well as establishing end-user controls; and establishing and enforcing appropriate criminal or civil penalties for violations of such export control laws and regulations;

. . . .

5. *Decides* that none of the obligations set forth in this resolution shall be interpreted so as to conflict with or alter the rights and obligations of State Parties to the Nuclear Non-Proliferation Treaty, the Chemical Weapons Convention and the Biological and Toxin Weapons Convention or alter the responsibilities of the International Atomic Energy Agency or the Organization for the Prohibition of Chemical Weapons;

. . . .

9. *Calls upon* all States to promote dialogue and cooperation on non-proliferation so as to address the threat posed by proliferation of nuclear, chemical, or biological weapons, and their means of delivery;

10. Further to counter that threat, *calls upon* all States, in accordance with their national legal authorities and legislation and consistent with international law, to take cooperative action to prevent illicit trafficking in nuclear, chemical or biological weapons, their means of delivery, and related materials;

. . . .

---

i. Definitions for the purpose of this resolution only:

Means of delivery: missiles, rockets and other unmanned systems capable of delivering nuclear, chemical, or biological weapons, that are specially designed for such use.

Non-State actor: individual or entity, not acting under the lawful authority of any State in conducting activities which come within the scope of this resolution.

Related materials: materials, equipment and technology covered by relevant multilateral treaties and arrangements, or included on national control lists, which could be used for the design, development, production or use of nuclear, chemical and biological weapons and their means of delivery.

INTERNATIONAL CONVENTION FOR THE SUPPRESSION OF ACTS OF NUCLEAR TERRORISM*

The States Parties to this Convention,

....

Recognizing the right of all States to develop and apply nuclear energy for peaceful purposes and their legitimate interests in the potential benefits to be derived from the peaceful application of nuclear energy,

....

Deeply concerned about the worldwide escalation of acts of terrorism in all its forms and manifestations,

Recalling the Declaration on Measures to Eliminate International Terrorism annexed to General Assembly resolution 49/60 of 9 December 1994, in which, inter alia, the States Members of the United Nations solemnly reaffirm their unequivocal condemnation of all acts, methods and practices of terrorism as criminal and unjustifiable, wherever and by whomever committed, including those which jeopardize the friendly relations among States and peoples and threaten the territorial integrity and security of States,

....

Noting that acts of nuclear terrorism may result in the gravest consequences and may pose a threat to international peace and security,

....

Have agreed as follows:

....

Article 2. 1. Any person commits an offence within the meaning of this Convention if that person unlawfully and intentionally:

(a) Possesses radioactive material or makes or possesses a device:

(i) With the intent to cause death or serious bodily injury; or

(ii) With the intent to cause substantial damage to property or to the environment;

(b) Uses in any way radioactive material or a device, or uses or damages a nuclear facility in a manner which releases or risks the release of radioactive material:

(i) With the intent to cause death or serious bodily injury; or

(ii) With the intent to cause substantial damage to property or to the environment; or

---

* International Convention for the Suppression of Acts of Nuclear Terrorism, *opened for signature* Sept. 14, 2005, 44 I.L.M. 815, U.N. Gen. Assembly, Ad Hoc Comm. Established by Gen. Assembly Resolution 51/210 of 17 December 1996, *Report of the Ad Hoc Committee Established by General Assembly Resolution 51/210 of 17 December 1996: International Convention for the Suppression of Acts of Nuclear Terrorism*, at 1, U.N. Doc. A/59/766 (Apr. 4, 2005), *available at* http://untreaty.un.org/English/notpubl/English_18_15.pdf.

(iii) With the intent to compel a natural or legal person, an international organization or a State to do or refrain from doing an act.

2. Any person also commits an offence if that person:

(a) Threatens, under circumstances which indicate the credibility of the threat, to commit an offence as set forth in paragraph 1 (b) of the present article; or

(b) Demands unlawfully and intentionally radioactive material, a device or a nuclear facility by threat, under circumstances which indicate the credibility of the threat, or by use of force.

3. Any person also commits an offence if that person attempts to commit an offence as set forth in paragraph 1 of the present article.

4. Any person also commits an offence if that person:

(a) Participates as an accomplice in an offence as set forth in paragraph 1, 2 or 3 of the present article; or

(b) Organizes or directs others to commit an offence as set forth in paragraph 1, 2 or 3 of the present article; or

(c) In any other way contributes to the commission of one or more offences as set forth in paragraph 1, 2 or 3 of the present article by a group of persons acting with a common purpose; such contribution shall be intentional and either be made with the aim of furthering the general criminal activity or purpose of the group or be made in the knowledge of the intention of the group to commit the offence or offences concerned.

Article 3. This Convention shall not apply where the offence is committed within a single State, the alleged offender and the victims are nationals of that State, the alleged offender is found in the territory of that State and no other State has a basis under article 9, paragraph 1 or 2, to exercise jurisdiction, except that the provisions of articles 7, 12, 14, 15, 16 and 17 shall, as appropriate, apply in those cases.

Article 4.

....

2. The activities of armed forces during an armed conflict, as those terms are understood under international humanitarian law, which are governed by that law are not governed by this Convention, and the activities undertaken by military forces of a State in the exercise of their official duties, inasmuch as they are governed by other rules of international law, are not governed by this Convention.

3. The provisions of paragraph 2 of the present article shall not be interpreted as condoning or making lawful otherwise unlawful acts, or precluding prosecution under other laws.

4. This Convention does not address, nor can it be interpreted as addressing, in any way, the issue of the legality of the use or threat of use of nuclear weapons by States.

Article 5. Each State Party shall adopt such measures as may be necessary:

(a) To establish as criminal offences under its national law the offences set forth in article 2;

(b) To make those offences punishable by appropriate penalties which take into account the grave nature of these offences.

Article 6. Each State Party shall adopt such measures as may be necessary, including, where appropriate, domestic legislation, to ensure that criminal acts within the scope of this Convention, in particular where they are intended or calculated to provoke a state of terror in the general public or in a group of persons or particular persons, are under no circumstances justifiable by considerations of a political, philosophical, ideological, racial, ethnic, religious or other similar nature and are punished by penalties consistent with their grave nature.

Article 7. 1. States Parties shall cooperate by:

(a) Taking all practicable measures, including, if necessary, adapting their national law, to prevent and counter preparations in their respective territories for the commission within or outside their territories of the offences set forth in article 2, including measures to prohibit in their territories illegal activities of persons, groups and organizations that encourage, instigate, organize, knowingly finance or knowingly provide technical assistance or information or engage in the perpetration of those offences;

(b) Exchanging accurate and verified information in accordance with their national law and in the manner and subject to the conditions specified herein....

2. States Parties shall take appropriate measures consistent with their national law to protect the confidentiality of any information which they receive in confidence by virtue of the provisions of this Convention from another State Party or through participation in an activity carried out for the implementation of this Convention....

....

Article 10. 1. Upon receiving information that an offence set forth in article 2 has been committed or is being committed in the territory of a State Party or that a person who has committed or who is alleged to have committed such an offence may be present in its territory, the State Party concerned shall take such measures as may be necessary under its national law to investigate the facts contained in the information.

2. Upon being satisfied that the circumstances so warrant, the State Party in whose territory the offender or alleged offender is present shall take the appropriate measures under its national law so as to ensure that person's presence for the purpose of prosecution or extradition.

....

Article 11. 1. The State Party in the territory of which the alleged offender is present shall, in cases to which article 9 applies, if it does not extradite that person, be obliged, without exception whatsoever and whether or not the offence was committed in its territory, to submit the case without undue delay to its competent authorities for the purpose of prosecution, through proceedings in accordance with the laws of that State....

....

Article 12. Any person who is taken into custody or regarding whom any other measures are taken or proceedings are carried out pursuant to this Convention shall be guaranteed fair treatment, including enjoyment of all rights and guarantees in conformity with the law of the State in the territory of which that person is present and applicable provisions of international law, including international law of human rights.

Article 13. 1. The offences set forth in article 2 shall be deemed to be included as extraditable offences in any extradition treaty existing between any of the States Parties before the entry into force of this Convention....

....

Article 14. 1. States Parties shall afford one another the greatest measure of assistance in connection with investigations or criminal or extradition proceedings brought in respect of the offences set forth in article 2, including assistance in obtaining evidence at their disposal necessary for the proceedings.

....

Article 15. None of the offences set forth in article 2 shall be regarded, for the purposes of extradition or mutual legal assistance, as a political offence or as an offence connected with a political offence or as an offence inspired by political motives....

Article 16. Nothing in this Convention shall be interpreted as imposing an obligation to extradite or to afford mutual legal assistance if the requested State Party has substantial grounds for believing that the request for extradition for offences set forth in article 2 or for mutual legal assistance with respect to such offences has been made for the purpose of prosecuting or punishing a person on account of that person's race, religion, nationality, ethnic origin or political opinion or that compliance with the request would cause prejudice to that person's position for any of these reasons.

....

Article 21. The States Parties shall carry out their obligations under this Convention in a manner consistent with the principles of sovereign equality and territorial integrity of States and that of non-intervention in the domestic affairs of other States.

Article 22. Nothing in this Convention entitles a State Party to undertake in the territory of another State Party the exercise of jurisdiction and performance of functions which are exclusively reserved for the authorities of that other State Party by its national law.

Article 23. 1. Any dispute between two or more States Parties concerning the interpretation or application of this Convention which cannot be settled through negotiation within a reasonable time shall, at the request of one of them, be submitted to arbitration....

....

Part III

Arms Control, Disarmament, Non-Proliferation and Confidence-Building

A. Multilateral Arms Control and Disarmament Agreements

DECLARATION RENOUNCING THE USE, IN TIME OF WAR, OF EXPLOSIVE PROJECTILES UNDER 400 GRAMMES WEIGHT* (ST. PETERSBURG, 1868)

On the proposition of the Imperial Cabinet of Russia, an International Military Commission having assembled at St. Petersburg in order to examine the expediency of forbidding the use of certain projectiles in time of war between civilized nations, and that Commission having by common agreement fixed the technical limits at which the necessities of war ought to yield to the requirements of humanity, the Undersigned are authorized by the orders of their Governments to declare as follows:

Considering:

That the progress of civilization should have the effect of alleviating as much as possible the calamities of war;

That the only legitimate object which States should endeavour to accomplish during war is to weaken the military forces of the enemy;

That for this purpose it is sufficient to disable the greatest possible number of men;

That this object would be exceeded by the employment of arms which uselessly aggravate the sufferings of disabled men, or render their death inevitable;

That the employment of such arms would, therefore, be contrary to the laws of humanity;

The Contracting Parties engage mutually to renounce, in case of war among themselves, the employment by their military or naval troops of any projectile of a weight below 400 grammes, which is either explosive or charged with fulminating or inflammable substances.

They will invite all the States which have not taken part in the deliberations of the International Military Commission assembled at St. Petersburg by sending Delegates thereto, to accede to the present engagement.

This engagement is compulsory only upon the Contracting or Acceding Parties thereto in case of war between two or more of themselves; it is not applicable to non-Contracting Parties, or Parties who shall not have acceded to it.

It will also cease to be compulsory from the moment when, in a war between Contracting or Acceding Parties, a non-Contracting Party or a non-Acceding Party shall join one of the belligerents.

---

* Declaration Renouncing the Use, in Time of War, of Explosive Projectiles Under 400 Grammes Weight, Between Austria-Hungary, Bavaria, Belgium, Denmark, France, Great Britain, Greece, Italy, The Netherlands, Persia, Portugal, Prussia and the Northern German Confederation, Russia, Sweden-Norway, Switzerland, Turkey and Wurtemberg, Dec. 11, 1868, 38 Consol. T.S. 297, 1 AM. J. INT'L L. 95 (Supp. 1907) (entered into force Dec. 11, 1868), *available at* http://www.icrc.org/ihl.nsf/0/dbe0afb2065e0d7ec125641e0031f38c?OpenDocument.

The Contracting or Acceding Parties reserve to themselves to come hereafter to an understanding whenever a precise proposition shall be drawn up in view of future improvements which science may effect in the armament of troops, in order to maintain the principles which they have established, and to conciliate the necessities of war with the laws of humanity.

Done at St. Petersburg, 29 November (11 December) 1868.

(Here follow signatures)

NAVAL ARMAMENT LIMITATION TREATY*

The United States of America, the British Empire, France, Italy and Japan:

Desiring to contribute to the maintenance of the general peace, and to reduce the burdens of competition in armament;

Have resolved, with a view to accomplishing these purposes, to conclude a treaty to limit their respective naval armament....

....

CHAPTER I — *General provisions relating to the limitation of Naval Armament*

Article I. The Contracting Powers agree to limit their respective naval armament as provided in the present Treaty.

....

Article IV. The total capital ship replacement tonnage of each of the Contracting Powers shall not exceed in standard displacement, for the United States 525,000 tons (533,400 metric tons); for the British Empire 525,000 tons (533,400 metric tons); for France 175,000 tons (177,800 metric tons); for Italy 175,000 tons (177,800 metric tons); for Japan 315,000 tons (320,040 metric tons).

Article V. No capital ship exceeding 35,000 tons (35,560 metric tons) standard displacement shall be acquired by, or constructed by, for, or within the jurisdiction of, any of the Contracting Powers.

Article VI. No capital ship of any of the Contracting Powers shall carry a gun with a calibre in excess of 16 inches (406 millimetres).

Article VII. The total tonnage for aircraft carriers of each of the Contracting Powers shall not exceed in standard displacement, for the United States 135,000 tons (137,160 metric tons); for the British Empire 135,000 tons (137,160 metric tons); for France 60,000 tons (60,960 metric tons); for Italy 60,000 tons (60,960 metric tons); for Japan 81,000 tons (82,296 metric tons).

....

Article XIX. The United States, the British Empire and Japan agree that the status quo at the time of the signing of the present Treaty, with regard to fortifications and naval bases, shall be maintained in their respective territories and possessions specified hereunder:

(1) The insular possessions which the United States now holds or may hereafter acquire in the Pacific Ocean, except:

(a) those adjacent to the coast of the United States, Alaska and the Panama Canal Zone, not including the Aleutian Islands, and

---

* Treaty Between the United States, the British Empire, France, Italy, and Japan Agreeing to a Limitation of Naval Armament, Feb. 6, 1922, 43 Stat. 1655, 25 L.N.T.S. 201 (entered into force Aug. 17, 1923), *available at* http://www.ibiblio.org/pha/pre-war/1922/nav_lim.html. *See also* Treaty Between the United States of America and Other Powers for the Limitation and Reduction of Naval Armament, Apr. 22, 1930, 46 Stat. 2858, 112 L.N.T.S. 65 (entered into force Dec. 31, 1930), *reprinted infra*.

(b) the Hawaiian Islands;

(2) Hong Kong and the insular possessions which the British Empire now holds or may hereafter acquire in the Pacific Ocean, east of the meridian of 110° east longitude, except:

(a) those adjacent to the coast of Canada,

(b) the Commonwealth of Australia and its Territories, and

(c) New Zealand;

(3) The following insular territories and possessions of Japan in the Pacific Ocean, to wit: the Kurile Islands, the Bonin Islands, Amami-Oshima, the Loochoo Islands, Formosa and the Pescadores, and any insular territories or possessions in the Pacific Ocean which Japan may hereafter acquire.

The maintenance of the status quo under the foregoing provisions implies that no new fortifications or naval bases shall be established in the territories and possessions specified; that no measures shall be taken to increase the existing naval facilities for the repair and maintenance of naval forces, and that no increase shall be made in the coast defences of the territories and possessions above specified. This restriction, however, does not preclude such repair and replacement of worn-out weapons and equipment as is customary in naval and military establishments in time of peace.

. . . .

PROTOCOL FOR THE PROHIBITION OF THE USE IN WAR OF ASPHYXIATING, POISONOUS OR OTHER GASES, AND OF BACTERIOLOGICAL METHODS OF WARFARE*

The Undersigned Plenipotentiaries, in the name of their respective Governments:

Whereas the use in war of asphyxiating, poisonous or other gases, and of all analogous liquids, materials or devices, has been justly condemned by the general opinion of the civilized world; and

Whereas the prohibition of such use has been declared in Treaties to which the majority of Powers of the World are Parties; and

To the end that this prohibition shall be universally accepted as a part of International Law, binding alike the conscience and the practice of nations;

Declare:

That the High Contracting Parties, so far as they are not already Parties to Treaties prohibiting such use, accept this prohibition, agree to extend this prohibition to the use of bacteriological methods of warfare and agree to be bound as between themselves according to the terms of this declaration.

The High Contracting Parties will exert every effort to induce other States to accede to the present Protocol. Such accession will be notified to the Government of the French Republic, and by the latter to all signatory and acceding Powers, and will take effect on the date of the notification by the Government of the French Republic.

The present Protocol, of which the French and English texts are both authentic, shall be ratified as soon as possible. It shall bear today's date.

The ratifications of the present Protocol shall be addressed to the Government of the French Republic, which will at once notify the deposit of such ratification to each of the signatory and acceding Powers.

The instruments of ratification of and accession to the present Protocol will remain deposited in the archives of the Government of the French Republic.

The present Protocol will come into force for each signatory Power as from the date of deposit of its ratification, and, from that moment, each Power will be bound as regards other powers which have already deposited their ratifications.

IN WITNESS WHEREOF the Plenipotentiaries have signed the present Protocol.

DONE at Geneva in a single copy, this seventeenth day of June, One Thousand Nine Hundred and Twenty-Five.

---

* Protocol for the Prohibition of the Use in War of Asphyxiating, Poisonous or Other Gases, and of Bacteriological Methods of Warfare, June 17, 1925, 26 U.S.T. 571, 573, 94 L.N.T.S. 65 (entered into force Feb. 8, 1928), *available at* http://www.state.gov/t/ac/trt/4784.htm.

TREATY BETWEEN THE UNITED STATES AND OTHER POWERS FOR THE LIMITATION AND REDUCTION OF NAVAL ARMAMENT*

. . . .

PART IV

Article 22. The following are accepted as established rules of International Law:

(1) In their action with regard to merchant ships, submarines must conform to the rules of International Law to which surface vessels are subject.

(2) In particular, except in the case of persistent refusal to stop on being duly summoned, or of active resistance to visit or search, a warship, whether surface vessel or submarine, may not sink or render incapable of navigation a merchant vessel without having first placed passengers, crew and ship's papers in a place of safety. For this purpose the ship's boats are not regarded as a place of safety unless the safety of the passengers and crew is assured, in the existing sea and weather conditions, by the proximity of land, or the presence of another vessel which is in a position to take them on board.

The High Contracting Parties invite all other Powers to express their assent to the above rules.

. . . .

* Treaty Between the United States of America and Other Powers for the Limitation and Reduction of Naval Armament, art. 22, Apr. 22, 1930, 46 Stat. 2858, 2881–82, 112 L.N.T.S. 65, 88 (entered into force Dec. 31, 1930), *available at* http://www.navweaps.com/index_inro/INRO_London_Treaty_1930.htm.

ANTARCTIC TREATY*

The Governments of Argentina, Australia, Belgium, Chile, the French Republic, Japan, New Zealand, Norway, the Union of South Africa, the Union of Soviet Socialist Republics, the United Kingdom of Great Britain and Northern Ireland, and the United States of America,

Recognizing that it is in the interest of all mankind that Antarctica shall continue forever to be used exclusively for peaceful purposes and shall not become the scene or object of international discord;

Acknowledging the substantial contributions to scientific knowledge resulting from international cooperation in scientific investigation in Antarctica;

Convinced that the establishment of a firm foundation for the continuation and development of such cooperation on the basis of freedom of scientific investigation in Antarctica as applied during the International Geophysical Year accords with the interests of science and the progress of all mankind;

Convinced also that a treaty ensuring the use of Antarctica for peaceful purposes only and the continuance of international harmony in Antarctica will further the purposes and principles embodied in the Charter of the United Nations;

Have agreed as follows:

Article I. 1. Antarctica shall be used for peaceful purposes only. There shall be prohibited, inter alia, any measures of a military nature, such as the establishment of military bases and fortifications, the carrying out of military maneuvers, as well as the testing of any type of weapons.

2. The present treaty shall not prevent the use of military personnel or equipment for scientific research or for any other peaceful purposes.

. . . .

Article V. 1. Any nuclear explosions in Antarctica and the disposal there of radioactive waste material shall be prohibited.

2. In the event of the conclusion of international agreements concerning the use of nuclear energy, including nuclear explosions and the disposal of radioactive waste material, to which all of the Contracting Parties whose representatives are entitled to participate in the meetings provided for under Article IX are parties, the rules established under such agreements shall apply in Antarctica.

. . . .

* The Antarctic Treaty, Dec. 1, 1959, 12 U.S.T. 794, 795, 402 U.N.T.S. 71 (entered into force June 23, 1961), *available at* http://www.state.gov/t/ac/trt/4700.htm#treaty.

TREATY BANNING NUCLEAR WEAPON TESTS IN THE ATMOSPHERE, IN OUTER SPACE AND UNDER WATER* (PTBT)

The Governments of the United States of America, the United Kingdom of Great Britain and Northern Ireland, and the Union of Soviet Socialist Republics, hereinafter referred to as the "Original Parties",

Proclaiming as their principal aim the speediest possible achievement of an agreement on general and complete disarmament under strict international control in accordance with the objectives of the United Nations which would put an end to the armaments race and eliminate the incentive to the production and testing of all kinds of weapons, including nuclear weapons,

Seeking to achieve the discontinuance of all test explosions of nuclear weapons for all time, determined to continue negotiations to this end, and desiring to put an end to the contamination of man's environment by radioactive substances,

Have agreed as follows:

Article 1. 1. Each of the Parties to this Treaty undertakes to prohibit, to prevent, and not to carry out any nuclear weapon test explosion, or any other nuclear explosion, at any place under its jurisdiction or control:

a. in the atmosphere; beyond its limits, including outer space; or underwater, including territorial waters or high seas; or

b. in any other environment if such explosion causes radioactive debris to be present outside the territorial limits of the State under whose jurisdiction or control such explosion is conducted. It is understood in this connection that the provisions of this subparagraph are without prejudice to the conclusion of a treaty resulting in the permanent banning of all nuclear test explosions, including all such explosions underground, the conclusion of which, as the Parties have stated in the Preamble to this Treaty, they seek to achieve.

2. Each of the Parties to this Treaty undertakes furthermore to refrain from causing, encouraging, or in any way participating in, the carrying out of any nuclear weapon test explosion, or any other nuclear explosion, anywhere which would take place in any of the environments described, or have the effect referred to, in paragraph 1 of this Article.

....

* Treaty Banning Nuclear Weapon Tests in the Atmosphere, in Outer Space and Under Water, Aug. 5, 1963, 14 U.S.T. 1313, 1316, 480 U.N.T.S. 43, 45 (entered into force Oct. 10, 1963), *available at* http://www.state.gov/t/ac/trt/4797.htm.

TREATY ON THE NON-PROLIFERATION OF NUCLEAR WEAPONS[1]

The States concluding this Treaty, hereinafter referred to as the "Parties to the Treaty",

Considering the devastation that would be visited upon all mankind by a nuclear war and the consequent need to make every effort to avert the danger of such a war and to take measures to safeguard the security of peoples,

Believing that the proliferation of nuclear weapons would seriously enhance the danger of nuclear war,

In conformity with resolutions of the United Nations General Assembly calling for the conclusion of an agreement on the prevention of wider dissemination of nuclear weapons,

Undertaking to cooperate in facilitating the application of International Atomic Energy Agency safeguards on peaceful nuclear activities,

Expressing their support for research, development and other efforts to further the application, within the framework of the International Atomic Energy Agency safeguards system, of the principle of safeguarding effectively the flow of source and special fissionable materials by use of instruments and other techniques at certain strategic points,

Affirming the principle that the benefits of peaceful applications of nuclear technology, including any technological by-products which may be derived by nuclear-weapon States from the development of nuclear explosive devices, should be available for peaceful purposes to all Parties of the Treaty, whether nuclear-weapon or non-nuclear weapon States,

Convinced that, in furtherance of this principle, all Parties to the Treaty are entitled to participate in the fullest possible exchange of scientific information for, and to contribute alone or in cooperation with other States to, the further development of the applications of atomic energy for peaceful purposes,

Declaring their intention to achieve at the earliest possible date the cessation of the nuclear arms race and to undertake effective measures in the direction of nuclear disarmament,

Urging the cooperation of all States in the attainment of this objective,

Recalling the determination expressed by the Parties to the 1963 Treaty banning nuclear weapon tests in the atmosphere, in outer space and under water in its Preamble to seek to achieve the discontinuance of all test explosions of nuclear weapons for all time and to continue negotiations to this end,

Desiring to further the easing of international tension and the strengthening of trust between States in order to facilitate the cessation of the manufacture of nuclear weapons, the liquidation of all their existing stockpiles, and the elimination from national arsenals of nuclear weapons and the means of their delivery pursuant to a Treaty on general and complete disarmament under strict and effective international control,

Recalling that, in accordance with the Charter of the United Nations, States must refrain in their international relations from the threat or use of force against the territorial

1. Treaty on the Non-Proliferation of Nuclear Weapons, July 1, 1968, 21 U.S.T. 483, 484, 729 U.N.T.S. 161, 169 (entered into force Mar. 5, 1970), *available at* http://www.state.gov/t/np/trty/16281.htm#treaty.

integrity or political independence of any State, or in any other manner inconsistent with the Purposes of the United Nations, and that the establishment and maintenance of international peace and security are to be promoted with the least diversion for armaments of the worlds human and economic resources,

Have agreed as follows:

Article I. Each nuclear-weapon State Party to the Treaty undertakes not to transfer to any recipient whatsoever nuclear weapons or other nuclear explosive devices or control over such weapons or explosive devices directly, or indirectly; and not in any way to assist, encourage, or induce any non-nuclear weapon State to manufacture or otherwise acquire nuclear weapons or other nuclear explosive devices, or control over such weapons or explosive devices.

Article II. Each non-nuclear-weapon State Party to the Treaty undertakes not to receive the transfer from any transferor whatsoever of nuclear weapons or other nuclear explosive devices or of control over such weapons or explosive devices directly, or indirectly; not to manufacture or otherwise acquire nuclear weapons or other nuclear explosive devices; and not to seek or receive any assistance in the manufacture of nuclear weapons or other nuclear explosive devices.

Article III. 1. Each non-nuclear-weapon State Party to the Treaty undertakes to accept safeguards, as set forth in an agreement to be negotiated and concluded with the International Atomic Energy Agency in accordance with the Statute of the International Atomic Energy Agency[2] and the Agency's safeguards system, for the exclusive purpose of verification of the fulfillment of its obligations assumed under this Treaty with a view to preventing diversion of nuclear energy from peaceful uses to nuclear weapons or other nuclear explosive devices. Procedures for the safeguards required by this article shall be followed with respect to source or special fissionable material whether it is being produced, processed or used in any principal nuclear facility or is outside any such facility. The safeguards required by this article shall be applied to all source or special fissionable material in all peaceful nuclear activities within the territory of such State, under its jurisdiction, or carried out under its control anywhere.

2. Each State Party to the Treaty undertakes not to provide:

(a) source or special fissionable material, or

(b) equipment or material especially designed or prepared for the processing, use or production of special fissionable material, to any non-nuclear-weapon State for peaceful purposes, unless the source or special fissionable material shall be subject to the safeguards required by this article.

....

Article IV. 1. Nothing in this Treaty shall be interpreted as affecting the inalienable right of all the Parties to the Treaty to develop research, production and use of nuclear energy for peaceful purposes without discrimination and in conformity with articles I and II of this Treaty.

2. All the Parties to the Treaty undertake to facilitate, and have the right to participate in, the fullest possible exchange of equipment, materials and scientific and technological information for the peaceful uses of nuclear energy. Parties to the Treaty in a po-

2. Statute of the International Atomic Energy Agency, Oct. 26, 1956, 8 U.S.T. 1093, 1095, 276 U.N.T.S. 3 (entered into force July 29, 1957).

sition to do so shall also cooperate in contributing alone or together with other States or international organizations to the further development of the applications of nuclear energy for peaceful purposes, especially in the territories of non-nuclear-weapon States Party to the Treaty, with due consideration for the needs of the developing areas of the world.

....

Article VI. Each of the Parties to the Treaty undertakes to pursue negotiations in good faith on effective measures relating to cessation of the nuclear arms race at an early date and to nuclear disarmament, and on a Treaty on general and complete disarmament under strict and effective international control.

Article VII. Nothing in this Treaty affects the right of any group of States to conclude regional treaties in order to assure the total absence of nuclear weapons in their respective territories.

....

Article X. 1. Each Party shall in exercising its national sovereignty have the right to withdraw from the Treaty if it decides that extraordinary events, related to the subject matter of this Treaty, have jeopardized the supreme interests of its country. It shall give notice of such withdrawal to all other Parties to the Treaty and to the United Nations Security Council three months in advance. Such notice shall include a statement of the extraordinary events it regards as having jeopardized its supreme interests.

2. Twenty-five years after the entry into force of the Treaty, a conference shall be convened to decide whether the Treaty shall continue in force indefinitely, or shall be extended for an additional fixed period or periods. This decision shall be taken by a majority of the Parties to the Treaty.

....

TREATY ON THE PROHIBITION OF THE EMPLACEMENT OF NUCLEAR WEAPONS AND OTHER WEAPONS OF MASS DESTRUCTION ON THE SEABED AND THE OCEAN FLOOR AND IN THE SUBSOIL THEREOF*

The States Parties to this Treaty,

Recognizing the common interest of mankind in the progress of the exploration and use of the seabed and the ocean floor for peaceful purposes,

Considering that the prevention of a nuclear arms race on the seabed and the ocean floor serves the interests of maintaining world peace, reduces international tensions and strengthens friendly relations among States,

Convinced that this Treaty constitutes a step towards the exclusion of the seabed, the ocean floor and the subsoil thereof from the arms race,

Convinced that this Treaty constitutes a step towards a Treaty on general and complete disarmament under strict and effective international control, and determined to continue negotiations to this end,

Convinced that this Treaty will further the purposes and principles of the Charter of the United Nations, in a manner consistent with the principles of international law and without infringing the freedoms of the high seas,

Have agreed as follows:

Article I. 1. The States Parties to this Treaty undertake not to emplant or emplace on the seabed and the ocean floor and in the subsoil thereof beyond the outer limit of a seabed zone, as defined in article II, any nuclear weapons or any other types of weapons of mass destruction as well as structures, launching installations or any other facilities specifically designed for storing, testing or using such weapons.

2. The undertakings of paragraph 1 of this article shall also apply to the seabed zone referred to in the same paragraph, except that within such seabed zone, they shall not apply either to the coastal State or to the seabed beneath its territorial waters.

. . . .

Article II. For the purpose of this Treaty, the outer limit of the seabed zone referred to in article I shall be coterminous with the twelve-mile outer limit of the zone referred to in part II of the Convention on the Territorial Sea and the Contiguous Zone, signed at Geneva on April 29, 1958, and shall be measured in accordance with the provisions of part I, section II, of that Convention and in accordance with international law.

---

* Treaty on the Prohibition of the Emplacement of Nuclear Weapons and Other Weapons of Mass Destruction on the Seabed and the Ocean Floor and in the Subsoil Thereof, Feb. 11, 1971, 23 U.S.T. 701, 703, 955 U.N.T.S. 115, 116 (entered into force May 18, 1972), *available at* http://www.state.gov/t/ac/trt/5187.htm.

Article III. 1. In order to promote the objectives of and insure compliance with the provisions of this Treaty, each State Party to the Treaty shall have the right to verify through observations the activities of other States Parties to the Treaty on the seabed and the ocean floor and in the subsoil thereof beyond the zone referred to in article I, provided that observation does not interfere with such activities.

2. If after such observation reasonable doubts remain concerning the fulfillment of the obligations assumed under the Treaty, the State Party having such doubts and the State Party that is responsible for the activities giving rise to the doubts shall consult with a view to removing the doubts. If the doubts persist, the State Party having such doubts shall notify the other States Parties, and the Parties concerned shall cooperate on such further procedures for verification as may be agreed, including appropriate inspection of objects, structures, installations or other facilities that reasonably may be expected to be of a kind described in article I. The Parties in the region of the activities, including any coastal State, and any other Party so requesting, shall be entitled to participate in such consultation and cooperation. After completion of the further procedures for verification, an appropriate report shall be circulated to other Parties by the Party that initiated such procedures.

3. If the State responsible for the activities giving rise to the reasonable doubts is not identifiable by observation of the object, structure, installation or other facility, the State Party having such doubts shall notify and make appropriate inquiries of States Parties in the region of the activities and of any other State Party. If it is ascertained through these inquiries that a particular State Party is responsible for the activities, that State Party shall consult and cooperate with other Parties as provided in paragraph 2 of this article. If the identity of the State responsible for the activities cannot be ascertained through these inquiries, then further verification procedures, including inspection, may be undertaken by the inquiring State Party, which shall invite the participation of the Parties in the region of the activities, including any coastal State, and of any other Party desiring to cooperate.

4. If consultation and cooperation pursuant to paragraphs 2 and 3 of this article have not removed the doubts concerning the activities and there remains a serious question concerning fulfillment of the obligations assumed under this Treaty, a State Party may, in accordance with the provisions of the Charter of the United Nations, refer the matter to the Security Council, which may take action in accordance with the Charter.

5. Verification pursuant to this article may be undertaken by any State Party using its own means, or with the full or partial assistance of any other State Party, or through appropriate international procedures within the framework of the United Nations and in accordance with its Charter.

6. Verification activities pursuant to this Treaty shall not interfere with activities of other States Parties and shall be conducted with due regard for rights recognized under international law, including the freedoms of the high seas and the rights of coastal States with respect to the exploration and exploitation of their continental shelves.

Article IV. Nothing in this Treaty shall be interpreted as supporting or prejudicing the position of any State Party with respect to existing international conventions, including the 1958 Convention on the Territorial Sea and the Contiguous Zone, or with respect to rights or claims which such State Party may assert, or with respect to recognition or non-recognition of rights or claims asserted by any other State, related to waters off its coasts, including, inter alia, territorial seas and contiguous zones, or to the seabed and the ocean floor, including continental shelves.

Article V. The Parties to this Treaty undertake to continue negotiations in good faith concerning further measures in the field of disarmament for the prevention of an arms race on the seabed, the ocean floor and the subsoil thereof.

. . . .

CONVENTION ON THE PROHIBITION OF THE DEVELOPMENT, PRODUCTION AND STOCKPILING OF BACTERIOLOGICAL (BIOLOGICAL) AND TOXIN WEAPONS AND THEIR DESTRUCTION*

The States Parties to this Convention,

Determined to act with a view to achieving effective progress towards general and complete disarmament, including the prohibition and elimination of all types of weapons of mass destruction, and convinced that the prohibition of the development, production and stockpiling of chemical and bacteriological (biological) weapons and their elimination, through effective measures, will facilitate the achievement of general and complete disarmament under strict and effective international control,

Recognizing the important significance of the Protocol for the Prohibition of the Use in War of Asphyxiating, Poisonous or Other Gases, and of Bacteriological Methods of Warfare, signed at Geneva on June 17, 1925, and conscious also of the contribution which the said Protocol has already made, and continues to make, to mitigating the horrors of war,

Reaffirming their adherence to the principles and objectives of that Protocol and calling upon all States to comply strictly with them,

Recalling that the General Assembly of the United Nations has repeatedly condemned all actions contrary to the principles and objectives of the Geneva Protocol of June 17, 1925,

Desiring to contribute to the strengthening of confidence between peoples and the general improvement of the international atmosphere,

Desiring also to contribute to the realization of the purposes and principles of the Charter of the United Nations,

Convinced of the importance and urgency of eliminating from the arsenals of States, through effective measures, such dangerous weapons of mass destruction as those using chemical or bacteriological (biological) agents,

Recognizing that an agreement on the prohibition of bacteriological (biological) and toxin weapons represents a first possible step towards the achievement of agreement on effective measures also for the prohibition of the development, production and stockpiling of chemical weapons, and determined to continue negotiations to that end,

Determined, for the sake of all mankind, to exclude completely the possibility of bacteriological (biological) agents and toxins being used as weapons,

Convinced that such use would be repugnant to the conscience of mankind and that no effort should be spared to minimize this risk,

Have agreed as follows:

---

* Convention on the Prohibition of the Development, Production and Stockpiling of Bacteriological (Biological) and Toxin Weapons and Their Destruction, Apr. 10, 1972, 26 U.S.T. 583, 585, 1015 U.N.T.S. 163, 164 (entered into force Mar. 26, 1975), *available at* http://www.state.gov/t/ac/trt/4718.htm.

Article I. Each State Party to this Convention undertakes never in any circumstances to develop, produce, stockpile or otherwise acquire or retain:

(1) Microbial or other biological agents, or toxins whatever their origin or method of production, of types and in quantities that have no justification for prophylactic, protective or other peaceful purposes;

(2) Weapons, equipment or means of delivery designed to use such agents or toxins for hostile purposes or in armed conflict.

Article II. Each State Party to this Convention undertakes to destroy, or to divert to peaceful purposes, as soon as possible but not later than nine months after the entry into force of the Convention, all agents, toxins, weapons, equipment and means of delivery specified in article I of the Convention, which are in its possession or under its jurisdiction or control. In implementing the provisions of this article all necessary safety precautions shall be observed to protect populations and the environment.

Article III. Each State Party to this Convention undertakes not to transfer to any recipient whatsoever, directly or indirectly, and not in any way to assist, encourage, or induce any State, group of States or international organizations to manufacture or otherwise acquire any of the agents, toxins, weapons, equipment or means of delivery specified in article I of the Convention.

Article IV. Each State Party to this Convention shall, in accordance with its constitutional processes, take any necessary measures to prohibit and prevent the development, production, stockpiling, acquisition, or retention of the agents, toxins, weapons, equipment and means of delivery specified in article I of the Convention, within the territory of such State, under its jurisdiction or under its control anywhere.

Article V. The States Parties to this Convention undertake to consult one another and to cooperate in solving any problems which may arise in relation to the objective of, or in the application of the provisions of, the Convention. Consultation and cooperation pursuant to this article may also be undertaken through appropriate international procedures within the framework of the United Nations and in accordance with its Charter.

Article VI. (1) Any State Party to this Convention which finds that any other State Party is acting in breach of obligations deriving from the provisions of the Convention may lodge a complaint with the Security Council of the United Nations. Such a complaint should include all possible evidence confirming its validity, as well as a request for its consideration by the Security Council.

(2) Each State Party to this Convention undertakes to cooperate in carrying out any investigation which the Security Council may initiate, in accordance with the provisions of the Charter of the United Nations, on the basis of the complaint received by the Council. The Security Council shall inform the States Parties to the Convention of the results of the investigation.

Article VII. Each State Party to this Convention undertakes to provide or support assistance, in accordance with the United Nations Charter, to any Party to the Convention which so requests, if the Security Council decides that such Party has been exposed to danger as a result of violation of the Convention.

Article VIII. Nothing in this Convention shall be interpreted as in any way limiting or detracting from the obligations assumed by any State under the Protocol for the Prohibition of the Use in War of Asphyxiating, Poisonous or Other Gases, and of Bacteriological Methods of Warfare, signed at Geneva on June 17, 1925.

Article IX. Each State Party to this Convention affirms the recognized objective of effective prohibition of chemical weapons and, to this end, undertakes to continue negotiations in good faith with a view to reaching early agreement on effective measures for the prohibition of their development, production and stockpiling and for their destruction, and on appropriate measures concerning equipment and means of delivery specifically designed for the production or use of chemical agents for weapons purposes.

Article X. (1) The States Parties to this Convention undertake to facilitate, and have the right to participate in, the fullest possible exchange of equipment, materials and scientific and technological information for the use of bacteriological (biological) agents and toxins for peaceful purposes. Parties to the Convention in a position to do so shall also cooperate in contributing individually or together with other States or international organizations to the further development and application of scientific discoveries in the field of bacteriology (biology) for prevention of disease, or for other peaceful purposes.

(2) This Convention shall be implemented in a manner designed to avoid hampering the economic or technological development of States Parties to the Convention or international cooperation in the field of peaceful bacteriological (biological) activities, including the international exchange of bacteriological (biological) agents and toxins and equipment for the processing, use or production of bacteriological (biological) agents and toxins for peaceful purposes in accordance with the provisions of the Convention.

Article XI. Any State Party may propose amendments to this Convention. Amendments shall enter into force for each State Party accepting the amendments upon their acceptance by a majority of the States Parties to the Convention and thereafter for each remaining State Party on the date of acceptance by it.

Article XII. Five years after the entry into force of this Convention, or earlier if it is requested by a majority of Parties to the Convention by submitting a proposal to this effect to the Depositary Governments, a conference of States Parties to the Convention shall be held at Geneva, Switzerland, to review the operation of the Convention, with a view to assuring that the purposes of the preamble and the provisions of the Convention, including the provisions concerning negotiations on chemical weapons, are being realized. Such review shall take into account any new scientific and technological developments relevant to the Convention.

. . . .

CONVENTION ON THE PROHIBITION OF MILITARY OR ANY OTHER HOSTILE USE OF ENVIRONMENTAL MODIFICATION TECHNIQUES[1]

Signed in Geneva May 18, 1977
Entered into force October 5, 1978
Ratification by U.S. President December 13, 1979
U.S. ratification deposited at New York January 17, 1980

The States Parties to this Convention,

Guided by the interest of consolidating peace, and wishing to contribute to the cause of halting the arms race, and of bringing about general and complete disarmament under strict and effective international control, and of saving mankind from the danger of using new means of warfare,

Determined to continue negotiations with a view to achieving effective progress towards further measures in the field of disarmament,

Recognizing that scientific and technical advances may open new possibilities with respect to modification of the environment,

Recalling the Declaration of the United Nations Conference on the Human Environment adopted at Stockholm on 16 June 1972,

Realizing that the use of environmental modification techniques for peaceful purposes could improve the interrelationship of man and nature and contribute to the preservation and improvement of the environment for the benefit of present and future generations,

Recognizing, however, that military or any other hostile use of such techniques could have effects extremely harmful to human welfare,

Desiring to prohibit effectively military or any other hostile use of environmental modification techniques in order to eliminate the dangers to mankind from such use, and affirming their willingness to work towards the achievement of this objective,

Desiring also to contribute to the strengthening of trust among nations and to the further improvement of the international situation in accordance with the purposes and principles of the Charter of the United Nations,

Have agreed as follows:

Article I. 1. Each State Party to this Convention undertakes not to engage in military or any other hostile use of environmental modification techniques having widespread, long-lasting or severe effects as the means of destruction, damage or injury to any other State Party.

2. Each State Party to this Convention undertakes not to assist, encourage or induce any State, group of States or international organization to engage in activities contrary to the provisions of paragraph 1 of this article.

---

1. Convention on the Prohibition of Military or Any Other Hostile Use of Environmental Modification Techniques, May 18, 1977, 31 U.S.T. 333, 335, 1108 U.N.T.S. 151, 152 (entered into force Oct. 5, 1978), *available at* http://www.state.gov/t/ac/trt/4783.htm.

Article II. As used in Article I, the term "environmental modification techniques" refers to any technique for changing—through the deliberate manipulation of natural processes—the dynamics, composition or structure of the Earth, including its biota, lithosphere, hydrosphere and atmosphere, or of outer space.

Article III. 1. The provisions of this Convention shall not hinder the use of environmental modification techniques for peaceful purposes and shall be without prejudice to the generally recognized principles and applicable rules of international law concerning such use.

2. The States Parties to this Convention undertake to facilitate, and have the right to participate in, the fullest possible exchange of scientific and technological information on the use of environmental modification techniques for peaceful purposes. States Parties in a position to do so shall contribute, alone or together with other States or international organizations, to international economic and scientific co-operation in the preservation, improvement, and peaceful utilization of the environment, with due consideration for the needs of the developing areas of the world.

Article IV. Each State Party to this Convention undertakes to take any measures it considers necessary in accordance with its constitutional processes to prohibit and prevent any activity in violation of the provisions of the Convention anywhere under its jurisdiction or control.

Article V. 1. The States Parties to this Convention undertake to consult one another and to cooperate in solving any problems which may arise in relation to the objectives of, or in the application of the provisions of, the Convention. Consultation and cooperation pursuant to this article may also be undertaken through appropriate international procedures within the framework of the United Nations and in accordance with its Charter. These international procedures may include the services of appropriate international organizations, as well as of a Consultative Committee of Experts as provided for in paragraph 2 of this article.

....

Article VI. 1. Any State Party to this Convention may propose amendments to the Convention. The text of any proposed amendment shall be submitted to the Depositary who shall promptly circulate it to all States Parties.

....

Annex to the Convention
Consultative Committee of Experts

....

Understandings Regarding the Convention[2]

Understanding Relating to Article I

It is the understanding of the Committee that, for the purposes of this Convention, the terms, "widespread", "long-lasting" and "severe" shall be interpreted as follows:

2. These are not incorporated into the Convention but are part of the negotiating record and were included in the report transmitted by the CCD to the U.N. General Assembly in September 1976. *See* 1 U.N. Conference of the Comm. on Disarmament, *Report of the Conference of the Committee on Disarmament*, at 91–92, U.N. Doc. A/31/27 (1976).

(a) "widespread": encompassing an area on the scale of several hundred square kilometres;

(b) "long-lasting": lasting for a period of months, or approximately a season;

(c) "severe": involving serious or significant disruption or harm to human life, natural and economic resources or other assets.

It is further understood that the interpretation set forth above is intended exclusively for this Convention and is not intended to prejudice the interpretation of the same or similar terms if used in connection with any other international agreement.

Understanding Relating to Article II

It is the understanding of the Committee that the following examples are illustrative of phenomena that could be caused by the use of environmental modification techniques as defined in Article II of the Convention: earthquakes, tsunamis; an upset in the ecological balance of a region; changes in weather patterns (clouds, precipitation, cyclones of various types and tornadic storms); changes in climate patterns; changes in ocean currents; changes in the state of the ozone layer; and changes in the state of the ionosphere.

It is further understood that all the phenomena listed above, when produced by military or any other hostile use of environmental modification techniques, would result, or could reasonably be expected to result, in widespread, long-lasting or severe destruction, damage or injury. Thus, military or any other hostile use of environmental modification techniques as defined in Article II, so as to cause those phenomena as a means of destruction, damage or injury to another State Party, would be prohibited.

It is recognized, moreover, that the list of examples set out above is not exhaustive. Other phenomena which could result from the use of environmental modification techniques as defined in Article II could also be appropriately included. The absence of such phenomena from the list does not in any way imply that the undertaking contained in Article I would not be applicable to those phenomena, provided the criteria set out in that article were met.

Understanding Relating to Article III

It is the understanding of the Committee that this Convention does not deal with the question whether or not a given use of environmental modification techniques for peaceful purposes is in accordance with generally recognized principles and applicable rules of international law.

. . . .

U.N.G.A. RESOLUTION ON PROTECTION OF THE ENVIRONMENT IN TIMES OF ARMED CONFLICT*

The General Assembly,

Recognizing that the use of certain means and methods of warfare may have dire effects on the environment,

Recognizing also the importance of the provisions of international law applicable to the protection of the environment in times of armed conflict and, in particular, both the rules of universal applicability laid down in the Hague Convention respecting the Laws and Customs of War on Land, of 18 October 1907, with the Regulations annexed thereto, and the Geneva Convention relative to the Protection of Civilian Persons in Time of War, of 12 August 1949, and the applicable rules of the Protocol Additional to the Geneva Conventions of 12 August 1949, and relating to the Protection of Victims of International Armed Conflicts (Protocol I), of 1977, and of the Convention on the Prohibition of Military or Any Other Hostile Use of Environmental Modification Techniques, of 1976,

Expressing its deep concern about environmental damage and depletion of natural resources, including the destruction of hundreds of oil-well heads and the release and waste of crude oil into the sea, during recent conflicts,

Noting that existing provisions of international law prohibit such acts,

Stressing that destruction of the environment, not justified by military necessity and carried out wantonly, is clearly contrary to existing international law,

Concerned that the provisions of international law prohibiting such acts may not be widely disseminated and applied,

Noting the work on environmental protection carried out within the United Nations system and at meetings and symposia on the subject,

Taking note of the Final Declaration of the Second Review Conference of the Parties to the Convention on the Prohibition of Military or Any Other Hostile Use of Environmental Modification Techniques,

Taking note also of the Rio Declaration on Environment and Development, adopted at the United Nations Conference on Environment and Development at Rio de Janeiro on 14 June 1992, in particular principle 24 thereof, and other relevant decisions of the Conference,

Expressing its appreciation for the report of the Secretary-General submitted pursuant to General Assembly decision 46/417 of 9 December 1991,

Welcoming the activities of the International Committee of the Red Cross in this field, including plans to continue its consultation of experts with an enlarged basis of participation and its readiness to prepare a handbook of model guidelines for military manuals,

1. Urges States to take all measures to ensure compliance with the existing international law applicable to the protection of the environment in times of armed conflict;

* G.A. Res. 47/37, U.N. Doc. A/RES/47/37 (Nov. 25, 1992), *available at* http://www.un.org/documents/ga/res/47/a47r037.htm.

2. Appeals to all States that have not yet done so to consider becoming parties to the relevant international conventions;

3. Urges States to take steps to incorporate the provisions of international law applicable to the protection of the environment into their military manuals and to ensure that they are effectively disseminated;

4. Requests the Secretary-General to invite the International Committee of the Red Cross to report on activities undertaken by the Committee and other relevant bodies with regard to the protection of the environment in times of armed conflict, and to submit to the General Assembly at its forty-eighth session, under the item entitled "United Nations Decade of International Law", a report on activities reported by the Committee.

CONVENTION ON THE PROHIBITION OF THE DEVELOPMENT, PRODUCTION, STOCKPILING AND USE OF CHEMICAL WEAPONS AND ON THEIR DESTRUCTION*

The States Parties to this Convention,

Determined to act with a view to achieving effective progress towards general and complete disarmament under strict and effective international control, including the prohibition and elimination of all types of weapons of mass destruction,

Desiring to contribute to the realization of the purposes and principles of the Charter of the United Nations,

Recalling that the General Assembly of the United Nations has repeatedly condemned all actions contrary to the principles and objectives of the Protocol for the Prohibition of the Use in War of Asphyxiating, Poisonous or Other Gases, and of Bacteriological Methods of Warfare, signed at Geneva on 17 June 1925 (the Geneva Protocol of 1925),

Recognizing that this Convention reaffirms principles and objectives of and obligations assumed under the Geneva Protocol of 1925, and the Convention on the Prohibition of the Development, Production and Stockpiling of Bacteriological (Biological) and Toxin Weapons and on their Destruction signed at London, Moscow and Washington on 10 April 1972,

Bearing in mind the objective contained in Article IX of the Convention on the Prohibition of the Development, Production and Stockpiling of Bacteriological (Biological) and Toxin Weapons and on their Destruction,

Determined for the sake of all mankind, to exclude completely the possibility of the use of chemical weapons, through the implementation of the provisions of this Convention, thereby complementing the obligations assumed under the Geneva Protocol of 1925,

Recognizing the prohibition, embodied in the pertinent agreements and relevant principles of international law, of the use of herbicides as a method of warfare,

Considering that achievements in the field of chemistry should be used exclusively for the benefit of mankind,

---

* Convention on the Prohibition of the Development, Production, Stockpiling and Use of Chemical Weapons and on Their Destruction, *opened for signature* Jan. 13, 1993, S. TREATY DOC. No. 103-21, at 278, 1974 U.N.T.S. 45, 317 (entered into force Apr. 29, 1997), *available at* http://www.state.gov/t/np/trty/16286.htm. The Convention was signed by 125 States (including the United States) on 13 Jan. 1993 in Paris. It is based on a proposed treaty submitted by then Vice-President Bush in 1984 to the Conference on Disarmament. After eight years of negotiation in the ad hoc committee on chemical weapons, the Conference on Disarmament approved the draft convention for forwarding to the United Nations. The UN General Assembly adopted by consensus in November 1992 a resolution urging all nations to sign and become a party to the convention at the earliest opportunity.

The Convention, over 200 pages in length, contains detailed provisions on verification, the protection of confidential information, collective measures and protection against chemical weapons, and provisions for economic and technological development of chemical industries.

Desiring to promote free trade in chemicals as well as international cooperation and exchange of scientific and technical information in the field of chemical activities for purposes not prohibited under this Convention in order to enhance the economic and technological development of all States Parties,

Convinced that the complete and effective prohibition of the development, production, acquisition, stockpiling, retention, transfer and use of chemical weapons, and their destruction, represent a necessary step towards the achievement of these common objectives,

Have agreed as follows:

Article I. *General Obligations* 1. Each State Party to this Convention undertakes never under any circumstances:

(a) To develop, produce, otherwise acquire, stockpile or retain chemical weapons, or transfer, directly or indirectly, chemical weapons to anyone;

(b) To use chemical weapons;

(c) To engage in any military preparations to use chemical weapons;

(d) To assist, encourage or induce, in any way, anyone to engage in any activity prohibited to a State Party under this Convention.

2. Each State Party undertakes to destroy chemical weapons it owns or possesses, or that are located in any place under its jurisdiction or control, in accordance with the provisions of this Convention.

3. Each State Party undertakes to destroy all chemical weapons it abandoned on the territory of another State Party, in accordance with the provisions of this Convention.

4. Each State Party undertakes to destroy any chemical weapons production facilities it owns or possesses, or that are located in any place under its jurisdiction or control, in accordance with the provisions of this Convention.

5. Each State Party undertakes not to use riot control agents as a method of warfare.

Article II. *Definitions and Criteria.* For the purposes of this Convention:

1. "Chemical Weapons" means the following, together or separately:

(a) Toxic chemicals and their precursors, except where intended for purposes not prohibited under this Convention, as long as the types and quantities are consistent with such purposes;

(b) Munitions and devices, specifically designed to cause death or other harm through the toxic properties of those toxic chemicals specified in subparagraph (a), which would be released as a result of the employment of such munitions and devices;

(c) Any equipment specifically designed for use directly in connection with the employment of munitions and devices specified in subparagraph (b).

2. "Toxic Chemical" means:

Any chemical which through its chemical action on life processes can cause death, temporary incapacitation or permanent harm to humans or animals. This includes all such chemicals, regardless of their origin or of their method of production, and regardless of whether they are produced in facilities, in munitions or elsewhere.

(For the purpose of implementing this Convention, toxic chemicals which have been identified for the application of verification measures are listed in Schedules contained in the Annex on Chemicals.)

3. "Precursor" means:

Any chemical reactant which takes part at any stage in the production by whatever method of a toxic chemical. This includes any key component of a binary or multicomponent chemical system.

(For the purpose of implementing this Convention, precursors which have been identified for the application of verification measures are listed in Schedules contained in the Annex on Chemicals.)

4. "Key Component of Binary or Multicomponent Chemical Systems" (hereinafter referred to as "key component") means:

The precursor which plays the most important role in determining the toxic properties of the final product and reacts rapidly with other chemicals in the binary or multicomponent system.

5. "Old Chemical Weapons" means:

(a) Chemical weapons which were produced before 1925; or

(b) Chemical weapons produced in the period between 1925 and 1946 that have deteriorated to such extent that they can no longer be used as chemical weapons.

6. "Abandoned Chemical Weapons" means:

Chemical weapons, including old chemical weapons, abandoned by a State after 1 January 1925 on the territory of another State without the consent of the latter.

7. "Riot Control Agent" means:

Any chemical not listed in a Schedule, which can produce rapidly in humans sensory irritation or disabling physical effects which disappear within a short time following termination of exposure.

8. "Chemical Weapons Production Facility":

(a) Means any equipment, as well as any building housing such equipment, that was designed, constructed or used at any time since 1 January 1946:

(i) As part of the stage in the production of chemicals ("final technological stage") where the material flows would contain, when the equipment is in operation:

(1) Any chemical listed in Schedule 1 in the Annex on Chemicals; or

(2) Any other chemical that has no use, above 1 tonne per year on the territory of a State Party or in any other place under the jurisdiction or control of a State Party, for purposes not prohibited under this Convention, but can be used for chemical weapons purposes; or

(ii) For filling chemical weapons, including, inter alia, the filling of chemicals listed in Schedule 1 into munitions, devices or bulk storage containers; the filling of chemicals into containers that form part of assembled binary munitions and devices or into chemical submunitions that form part of assembled unitary munitions and devices, and the loading of the containers and chemical submunitions into the respective munitions and devices;

(b) Does not mean:

(i) Any facility having a production capacity for synthesis of chemicals specified in subparagraph (a) (i) that is less than 1 tonne;

(ii) Any facility in which a chemical specified in subparagraph (a) (i) is or was produced as an unavoidable by-product of activities for purposes not prohibited under this Convention, provided that the chemical does not exceed 3 percent of the total product and that the facility is subject to declaration and inspection under the Annex on Implementation and Verification (hereinafter referred to as "Verification Annex"); or

(iii) The single small-scale facility for production of chemicals listed in Schedule 1 for purposes not prohibited under this Convention as referred to in Part VI of the Verification Annex.

9. "Purposes Not Prohibited Under this Convention" means:

(a) Industrial, agricultural, research, medical, pharmaceutical or other peaceful purposes;

(b) Protective purposes, namely those purposes directly related to protection against toxic chemicals and to protection against chemical weapons;

(c) Military purposes not connected with the use of chemical weapons and not dependent on the use of the toxic properties of chemicals as a method of warfare;

(d) Law enforcement including domestic riot control purposes.

10. "Production Capacity" means:

The annual quantitative potential for manufacturing a specific chemical based on the technological process actually used or, if the process is not yet operational, planned to be used at the relevant facility. It shall be deemed to be equal to the nameplate capacity or, if the nameplate capacity is not available, to the design capacity. The nameplate capacity is the product output under conditions optimized for maximum quantity for the production facility, as demonstrated by one or more test-runs. The design capacity is the corresponding theoretically calculated product output.

11. "Organization" means the Organization for the Prohibition of Chemical Weapons established pursuant to Article VIII of this Convention.

12. For the purposes of Article VI:

(a) "Production" of a chemical means its formation through chemical reaction;

(b) "Processing" of a chemical means a physical process, such as formulation, extraction and purification, in which a chemical is not converted into another chemical;

(c) "Consumption" of a chemical means its conversion into another chemical via a chemical reaction.

Article III. *Declarations.* 1. Each State Party shall submit to the Organization, not later than 30 days after this Convention enters into force for it, the following declarations, in which it shall:

(a) With respect to chemical weapons:

(i) Declare whether it owns or possesses any chemical weapons, or whether there are any chemical weapons located in any place under its jurisdiction or control;

(ii) Specify the precise location, aggregate quantity and detailed inventory of chemical weapons it owns or possesses, or that are located in any place under its jurisdiction or control, in accordance with Part IV (A), paragraphs 1 to 3, of the Verification Annex, except for those chemical weapons referred to in sub-subparagraph (iii);

(iii) Report any chemical weapons on its territory that are owned and possessed by another State and located in any place under the jurisdiction or control of another State, in accordance with Part IV (A), paragraph 4, of the Verification Annex;

(iv) Declare whether it has transferred or received, directly or indirectly, any chemical weapons since 1 January 1946 and specify the transfer or receipt of such weapons, in accordance with Part IV (A), paragraph 5, of the Verification Annex;

(v) Provide its general plan for destruction of chemical weapons that it owns or possesses, or that are located in any place under its jurisdiction or control, in accordance with Part IV (A), paragraph 6, of the Verification Annex;

(b) With respect to old chemical weapons and abandoned chemical weapons:

(i) Declare whether it has on its territory old chemical weapons and provide all available information in accordance with Part IV (B), paragraph 3, of the Verification Annex;

(ii) Declare whether there are abandoned chemical weapons on its territory and provide all available information in accordance with Part IV (B), paragraph 8, of the Verification Annex;

(iii) Declare whether it has abandoned chemical weapons on the territory of other States and provide all available information in accordance with Part IV (B), paragraph 10, of the Verification Annex;

(c) With respect to chemical weapons production facilities:

(i) Declare whether it has or has had any chemical weapons production facility under its ownership or possession, or that is or has been located in any place under its jurisdiction or control at any time since 1 January 1946;

(ii) Specify any chemical weapons production facility it has or has had under its ownership or possession or that is or has been located in any place under its jurisdiction or control at any time since 1 January 1946, in accordance with Part V, paragraph 1, of the Verification Annex, except for those facilities referred to in sub-subparagraph (iii);

(iii) Report any chemical weapons production facility on its territory that another State has or has had under its ownership and possession and that is or has been located in any place under the jurisdiction or control of another State at any time since 1 January 1946, in accordance with Part V, paragraph 2, of the Verification Annex;

(iv) Declare whether it has transferred or received, directly or indirectly, any equipment for the production of chemical weapons since 1 January 1946 and specify the transfer or receipt of such equipment, in accordance with Part V, paragraphs 3 to 5, of the Verification Annex;

(v) Provide its general plan for destruction of any chemical weapons production facility it owns or possesses, or that is located in any place under its jurisdiction or control, in accordance with Part V, paragraph 6, of the Verification Annex;

(vi) Specify actions to be taken for closure of any chemical weapons production facility it owns or possesses, or that is located in any place under its jurisdiction or control, in accordance with Part V, paragraph 1 (i), of the Verification Annex;

(vii) Provide its general plan for any temporary conversion of any chemical weapons production facility it owns or possesses, or that is located in any place under its jurisdiction or control, into a chemical weapons destruction facility, in accordance with Part V, paragraph 7, of the Verification Annex;

(d) With respect to other facilities:

Specify the precise location, nature and general scope of activities of any facility or establishment under its ownership or possession, or located in any place under its jurisdiction or control, and that has been designed, constructed or used since 1 January 1946 primarily for development of chemical weapons. Such declaration shall include, inter alia, laboratories and test and evaluation sites;

(e) With respect to riot control agents:

Specify the chemical name, structural formula and Chemical Abstracts Service (CAS) registry number, if assigned, of each chemical it holds for riot control purposes. This declaration shall be updated not later than 30 days after any change becomes effective.

2. The provisions of this Article and the relevant provisions of Part IV of the Verification Annex shall not, at the discretion of a State Party, apply to chemical weapons buried on its territory before 1 January 1977 and which remain buried, or which had been dumped at sea before 1 January 1985.

Article IV. Chemical Weapons. 1. The provisions of this Article and the detailed procedures for its implementation shall apply to all chemical weapons owned or possessed by a State Party, or that are located in any place under its jurisdiction or control, except old chemical weapons and abandoned chemical weapons to which Part IV (B) of the Verification Annex applies.

2. Detailed procedures for the implementation of this Article are set forth in the Verification Annex.

3. All locations at which chemical weapons specified in paragraph 1 are stored or destroyed shall be subject to systematic verification through on-site inspection and monitoring with on-site instruments, in accordance with Part IV (A) of the Verification Annex.

4. Each State Party shall, immediately after the declaration under Article III, paragraph 1 (a), has been submitted, provide access to chemical weapons specified in paragraph 1 for the purpose of systematic verification of the declaration through on-site inspection. Thereafter, each State Party shall not remove any of these chemical weapons, except to a chemical weapons destruction facility. It shall provide access to such chemical weapons, for the purpose of systematic on-site verification.

5. Each State Party shall provide access to any chemical weapons destruction facilities and their storage areas, that it owns or possesses, or that are located in any place under its jurisdiction or control, for the purpose of systematic verification through on-site inspection and monitoring with on-site instruments.

6. Each State Party shall destroy all chemical weapons specified in paragraph 1 pursuant to the Verification Annex and in accordance with the agreed rate and sequence of

destruction (hereinafter referred to as "order of destruction"). Such destruction shall begin not later than two years after this Convention enters into force for it and shall finish not later than 10 years after entry into force of this Convention. A State Party is not precluded from destroying such chemical weapons at a faster rate.

7. Each State Party shall:

(a) Submit detailed plans for the destruction of chemical weapons specified in paragraph 1 not later than 60 days before each annual destruction period begins, in accordance with Part IV (A), paragraph 29, of the Verification Annex; the detailed plans shall encompass all stocks to be destroyed during the next annual destruction period;

(b) Submit declarations annually regarding the implementation of its plans for destruction of chemical weapons specified in paragraph 1, not later than 60 days after the end of each annual destruction period; and

(c) Certify, not later than 30 days after the destruction process has been completed, that all chemical weapons specified in paragraph 1 have been destroyed.

8. If a State ratifies or accedes to this Convention after the 10-year period for destruction set forth in paragraph 6, it shall destroy chemical weapons specified in paragraph 1 as soon as possible. The order of destruction and procedures for stringent verification for such a State Party shall be determined by the Executive Council.

9. Any chemical weapons discovered by a State Party after the initial declaration of chemical weapons shall be reported, secured and destroyed in accordance with Part IV (A) of the Verification Annex.

10. Each State Party, during transportation, sampling, storage and destruction of chemical weapons, shall assign the highest priority to ensuring the safety of people and to protecting the environment. Each State Party shall transport, sample, store and destroy chemical weapons in accordance with its national standards for safety and emissions.

11. Any State Party which has on its territory chemical weapons that are owned or possessed by another State, or that are located in any place under the jurisdiction or control of another State, shall make the fullest efforts to ensure that these chemical weapons are removed from its territory not later than one year after this Convention enters into force for it. If they are not removed within one year, the State Party may request the Organization and other States Parties to provide assistance in the destruction of these chemical weapons.

12. Each State Party undertakes to cooperate with other States Parties that request information or assistance on a bilateral basis or through the Technical Secretariat regarding methods and technologies for the safe and efficient destruction of chemical weapons.

13. In carrying out verification activities pursuant to this Article and Part IV (A) of the Verification Annex, the Organization shall consider measures to avoid unnecessary duplication of bilateral or multilateral agreements on verification of chemical weapons storage and their destruction among States Parties.

To this end, the Executive Council shall decide to limit verification to measures complementary to those undertaken pursuant to such a bilateral or multilateral agreement, if it considers that:

(a) Verification provisions of such an agreement are consistent with the verification provisions of this Article and Part IV (A) of the Verification Annex;

(b) Implementation of such an agreement provides for sufficient assurance of compliance with the relevant provisions of this Convention; and

(c) Parties to the bilateral or multilateral agreement keep the Organization fully informed about their verification activities.

14. If the Executive Council takes a decision pursuant to paragraph 13, the Organization shall have the right to monitor the implementation of the bilateral or multilateral agreement.

15. Nothing in paragraphs 13 and 14 shall affect the obligation of a State Party to provide declarations pursuant to Article III, this Article and Part IV (A) of the Verification Annex.

16. Each State Party shall meet the costs of destruction of chemical weapons it is obliged to destroy. It shall also meet the costs of verification of storage and destruction of these chemical weapons unless the Executive Council decides otherwise. If the Executive Council decides to limit verification measures of the Organization pursuant to paragraph 13, the costs of complementary verification and monitoring by the Organization shall be paid in accordance with the United Nations scale of assessment, as specified in Article VIII, paragraph 7.

17. The provisions of this Article and the relevant provisions of Part IV of the Verification Annex shall not, at the discretion of a State Party, apply to chemical weapons buried on its territory before 1 January 1977 and which remain buried, or which had been dumped at sea before 1 January 1985.

Article V. Chemical Weapons Production Facilities. 1. The provisions of this Article and the detailed procedures for its implementation shall apply to any and all chemical weapons production facilities owned or possessed by a State Party, or that are located in any place under its jurisdiction or control.

2. Detailed procedures for the implementation of this Article are set forth in the Verification Annex.

3. All chemical weapons production facilities specified in paragraph 1 shall be subject to systematic verification through on-site inspection and monitoring with on-site instruments in accordance with Part V of the Verification Annex.

4. Each State Party shall cease immediately all activity at chemical weapons production facilities specified in paragraph 1, except activity required for closure.

5. No State Party shall construct any new chemical weapons production facilities or modify any existing facilities for the purpose of chemical weapons production or for any other activity prohibited under this Convention.

6. Each State Party shall, immediately after the declaration under Article III, paragraph 1 (c), has been submitted, provide access to chemical weapons production facilities specified in paragraph 1, for the purpose of systematic verification of the declaration through on-site inspection.

7. Each State Party shall:

(a) Close, not later than 90 days after this Convention enters into force for it, all chemical weapons production facilities specified in paragraph 1, in accordance with Part V of the Verification Annex, and give notice thereof; and

(b) Provide access to chemical weapons production facilities specified in paragraph 1, subsequent to closure, for the purpose of systematic verification through on-site inspection and monitoring with on-site instruments in order to ensure that the facility remains closed and is subsequently destroyed.

8. Each State Party shall destroy all chemical weapons production facilities specified in paragraph 1 and related facilities and equipment, pursuant to the Verification Annex and in accordance with an agreed rate and sequence of destruction (hereinafter referred to as "order of destruction"). Such destruction shall begin not later than one year after this Convention enters into force for it, and shall finish not later than 10 years after entry into force of this Convention. A State Party is not precluded from destroying such facilities at a faster rate.

9. Each State Party shall:

(a) Submit detailed plans for destruction of chemical weapons production facilities specified in paragraph 1, not later than 180 days before the destruction of each facility begins;

(b) Submit declarations annually regarding the implementation of its plans for the destruction of all chemical weapons production facilities specified in paragraph 1, not later than 90 days after the end of each annual destruction period; and

(c) Certify, not later than 30 days after the destruction process has been completed, that all chemical weapons production facilities specified in paragraph 1 have been destroyed.

10. If a State ratifies or accedes to this Convention after the 10-year period for destruction set forth in paragraph 8, it shall destroy chemical weapons production facilities specified in paragraph 1 as soon as possible. The order of destruction and procedures for stringent verification for such a State Party shall be determined by the Executive Council.

11. Each State Party, during the destruction of chemical weapons production facilities, shall assign the highest priority to ensuring the safety of people and to protecting the environment. Each State Party shall destroy chemical weapons production facilities in accordance with its national standards for safety and emissions.

12. Chemical weapons production facilities specified in paragraph 1 may be temporarily converted for destruction of chemical weapons in accordance with Part V, paragraphs 18 to 25, of the Verification Annex. Such a converted facility must be destroyed as soon as it is no longer in use for destruction of chemical weapons but, in any case, not later than 10 years after entry into force of this Convention.

13. A State Party may request, in exceptional cases of compelling need, permission to use a chemical weapons production facility specified in paragraph 1 for purposes not prohibited under this Convention. Upon the recommendation of the Executive Council, the Conference of the States Parties shall decide whether or not to approve the request and shall establish the conditions upon which approval is contingent in accordance with Part V, Section D, of the Verification Annex.

14. The chemical weapons production facility shall be converted in such a manner that the converted facility is not more capable of being reconverted into a chemical weapons production facility than any other facility used for industrial, agricultural, research, medical, pharmaceutical or other peaceful purposes not involving chemicals listed in Schedule 1.

15. All converted facilities shall be subject to systematic verification through on-site inspection and monitoring with on-site instruments in accordance with Part V, Section D, of the Verification Annex.

16. In carrying out verification activities pursuant to this Article and Part V of the Verification Annex, the Organization shall consider measures to avoid unnecessary duplication of bilateral or multilateral agreements on verification of chemical weapons production facilities and their destruction among States Parties.

To this end, the Executive Council shall decide to limit the verification to measures complementary to those undertaken pursuant to such a bilateral or multilateral agreement, if it considers that:

(a) Verification provisions of such an agreement are consistent with the verification provisions of this Article and Part V of the Verification Annex;

(b) Implementation of the agreement provides for sufficient assurance of compliance with the relevant provisions of this Convention; and

(c) Parties to the bilateral or multilateral agreement keep the Organization fully informed about their verification activities.

17. If the Executive Council takes a decision pursuant to paragraph 16, the Organization shall have the right to monitor the implementation of the bilateral or multilateral agreement.

18. Nothing in paragraphs 16 and 17 shall affect the obligation of a State Party to make declarations pursuant to Article III, this Article and Part V of the Verification Annex.

19. Each State Party shall meet the costs of destruction of chemical weapons production facilities it is obliged to destroy. It shall also meet the costs of verification under this Article unless the Executive Council decides otherwise. If the Executive Council decides to limit verification measures of the Organization pursuant to paragraph 16, the costs of complementary verification and monitoring by the Organization shall be paid in accordance with the United Nations scale of assessment, as specified in Article VIII, paragraph 7.

Article VI. *Activities Not Prohibited Under This Convention.* 1. Each State Party has the right, subject to the provisions of this Convention, to develop, produce, otherwise acquire, retain, transfer and use toxic chemicals and their precursors for purposes not prohibited under this Convention.

2. Each State Party shall adopt the necessary measures to ensure that toxic chemicals and their precursors are only developed, produced, otherwise acquired, retained, transferred, or used within its territory or in any other place under its jurisdiction or control for purposes not prohibited under this Convention. To this end, and in order to verify that activities are in accordance with obligations under this Convention, each State Party shall subject toxic chemicals and their precursors listed in Schedules 1, 2 and 3 of the Annex on Chemicals, facilities related to such chemicals, and other facilities as specified in the Verification Annex, that are located on its territory or in any other place under its jurisdiction or control, to verification measures as provided in the Verification Annex.

. . . .

Article VII. *National Implementation Measures.*

General undertakings

1. Each State Party shall, in accordance with its constitutional processes, adopt the necessary measures to implement its obligations under this Convention. In particular, it shall:

(a) Prohibit natural and legal persons anywhere on its territory or in any other place under its jurisdiction as recognized by international law from undertaking any activity prohibited to a State Party under this Convention, including enacting penal legislation with respect to such activity;

(b) Not permit in any place under its control any activity prohibited to a State Party under this Convention; and

(c) Extend its penal legislation enacted under subparagraph (a) to any activity prohibited to a State Party under this Convention undertaken anywhere by natural persons, possessing its nationality, in conformity with international law.

2. Each State Party shall cooperate with other States Parties and afford the appropriate form of legal assistance to facilitate the implementation of the obligations under paragraph 1.

3. Each State Party, during the implementation of its obligations under this Convention, shall assign the highest priority to ensuring the safety of people and to protecting the environment, and shall cooperate as appropriate with other States Parties in this regard.

Relations between the State Party and the Organization

4. In order to fulfill its obligations under this Convention, each State Party shall designate or establish a National Authority to serve as the national focal point for effective liaison with the Organization and other States Parties. Each State Party shall notify the Organization of its National Authority at the time that this Convention enters into force for it.

5. Each State Party shall inform the Organization of the legislative and administrative measures taken to implement this Convention.

6. Each State Party shall treat as confidential and afford special handling to information and data that it receives in confidence from the Organization in connection with the implementation of this Convention. It shall treat such information and data exclusively in connection with its rights and obligations under this Convention and in accordance with the provisions set forth in the Confidentiality Annex.

7. Each State Party undertakes to cooperate with the Organization in the exercise of all its functions and in particular to provide assistance to the Technical Secretariat.

Article VIII. *The Organization.*

A. GENERAL PROVISIONS

1. The States Parties to this Convention hereby establish the Organization for the Prohibition of Chemical Weapons to achieve the object and purpose of this Convention, to ensure the implementation of its provisions, including those for international verification of compliance with it, and to provide a forum for consultation and cooperation among States Parties.

2. All States Parties to this Convention shall be members of the Organization. A State Party shall not be deprived of its membership in the Organization.

3. The seat of the Headquarters of the Organization shall be The Hague, Kingdom of the Netherlands.

4. There are hereby established as the organs of the Organization: the Conference of the States Parties, the Executive Council, and the Technical Secretariat.

5. The Organization shall conduct its verification activities provided for under this Convention in the least intrusive manner possible consistent with the timely and efficient accomplishment of their objectives. It shall request only the information and data necessary to fulfill its responsibilities under this Convention. It shall take every precaution to protect the confidentiality of information on civil and military activities and facilities coming to its knowledge in the implementation of this Convention and, in particular, shall abide by the provisions set forth in the Confidentiality Annex.

6. In undertaking its verification activities the Organization shall consider measures to make use of advances in science and technology.

. . . .

B. THE CONFERENCE OF THE STATES PARTIES

Composition, procedures and decision-making

9. The Conference of the States Parties (hereinafter referred to as "the Conference") shall be composed of all members of this Organization. Each member shall have one representative in the Conference, who may be accompanied by alternates and advisers.

10. The first session of the Conference shall be convened by the depositary not later than 30 days after the entry into force of this Convention.

11. The Conference shall meet in regular sessions which shall be held annually unless it decides otherwise.

12. Special sessions of the Conference shall be convened:

(a) When decided by the Conference;

(b) When requested by the Executive Council;

(c) When requested by any member and supported by one third of the members; or

(d) In accordance with paragraph 22 to undertake reviews of the operation of this Convention.

Except in the case of subparagraph (d), the special session shall be convened not later than 30 days after receipt of the request by the Director-General of the Technical Secretariat, unless specified otherwise in the request.

13. The Conference shall also be convened in the form of an Amendment Conference in accordance with Article XV, paragraph 2.

14. Sessions of the Conference shall take place at the seat of the Organization unless the Conference decides otherwise.

15. The Conference shall adopt its rules of procedure. At the beginning of each regular session, it shall elect its Chairman and such other officers as may be required. They shall hold office until a new Chairman and other officers are elected at the next regular session.

16. A majority of the members of the Organization shall constitute a quorum for the Conference.

17. Each member of the Organization shall have one vote in the Conference.

18. The Conference shall take decisions on questions of procedure by a simple majority of the members present and voting. Decisions on matters of substance should be taken as far as possible by consensus. If consensus is not attainable when an issue comes

up for decision, the Chairman shall defer any vote for 24 hours and during this period of deferment shall make every effort to facilitate achievement of consensus, and shall report to the Conference before the end of this period. If consensus is not possible at the end of 24 hours, the Conference shall take the decision by a two-thirds majority of members present and voting unless specified otherwise in this Convention. When the issue arises as to whether the question is one of substance or not, that question shall be treated as a matter of substance unless otherwise decided by the Conference by the majority required for decisions on matters of substance.

Powers and functions

19. The Conference shall be the principal organ of the Organization. It shall consider any questions, matters or issues within the scope of this Convention, including those relating to the powers and functions of the Executive Council and the Technical Secretariat. It may make recommendations and take decisions on any questions, matters or issues related to this Convention raised by a State Party or brought to its attention by the Executive Council.

20. The Conference shall oversee the implementation of this Convention, and act in order to promote its object and purpose. The Conference shall review compliance with this Convention. It shall also oversee the activities of the Executive Council and the Technical Secretariat and may issue guidelines in accordance with this Convention to either of them in the exercise of their functions.

21. The Conference shall:

(a) Consider and adopt at its regular sessions the report, programme and budget of the Organization, submitted by the Executive Council, as well as consider other reports;

(b) Decide on the scale of financial contributions to be paid by States Parties in accordance with paragraph 7;

(c) Elect the members of the Executive Council;

(d) Appoint the Director-General of the Technical Secretariat (hereinafter referred to as "the Director-General");

(e) Approve the rules of procedure of the Executive Council submitted by the latter;

(f) Establish such subsidiary organs as it finds necessary for the exercise of its functions in accordance with this Convention;

(g) Foster international cooperation for peaceful purposes in the field of chemical activities;

(h) Review scientific and technological developments that could affect the operation of this Convention and, in this context, direct the Director-General to establish a Scientific Advisory Board to enable him, in the performance of his functions, to render specialized advice in areas of science and technology relevant to this Convention, to the Conference, the Executive Council or States Parties. The Scientific Advisory Board shall be composed of independent experts appointed in accordance with terms of reference adopted by the Conference;

(i) Consider and approve at its first session any draft agreements, provisions and guidelines developed by the Preparatory Commission;

(j) Establish at its first session the voluntary fund for assistance in accordance with Article X;

(k) Take the necessary measures to ensure compliance with this Convention and to redress and remedy any situation which contravenes the provisions of this Convention, in accordance with Article XII.

22. The Conference shall not later than one year after the expiry of the fifth and the tenth year after the entry into force of this Convention, and at such other times within that time period as may be decided upon, convene in special sessions to undertake reviews of the operation of this Convention. Such reviews shall take into account any relevant scientific and technological developments. At intervals of five years thereafter, unless otherwise decided upon, further sessions of the Conference shall be convened with the same objective.

C. THE EXECUTIVE COUNCIL

Composition, procedure and decision-making

23. The Executive Council shall consist of 41 members. Each State Party shall have the right, in accordance with the principle of rotation, to serve on the Executive Council. The members of the Executive Council shall be elected by the Conference for a term of two years. In order to ensure the effective functioning of this Convention, due regard being specially paid to equitable geographical distribution, to the importance of chemical industry, as well as to political and security interests, the Executive Council shall be composed as follows:

(a) Nine States Parties from Africa to be designated by States Parties located in this region. As a basis for this designation it is understood that, out of these nine States Parties, three members shall, as a rule, be the States Parties with the most significant national chemical industry in the region as determined by internationally reported and published data; in addition, the regional group shall agree also to take into account other regional factors in designating these three members;

(b) Nine States Parties from Asia to be designated by States Parties located in this region. As a basis for this designation it is understood that, out of these nine States Parties, four members shall, as a rule, be the States Parties with the most significant national chemical industry in the region as determined by internationally reported and published data; in addition, the regional group shall agree also to take into account other regional factors in designating these four members;

(c) Five States Parties from Eastern Europe to be designated by States Parties located in this region. As a basis for this designation it is understood that, out of these five States Parties, one member shall, as a rule, be the State Party with the most significant national chemical industry in the region as determined by internationally reported and published data; in addition, the regional group shall agree also to take into account other regional factors in designating this one member;

(d) Seven States Parties from Latin America and the Caribbean to be designated by States Parties located in this region. As a basis for this designation it is understood that, out of these seven States Parties, three members shall, as a rule, be the States Parties with the most significant national chemical industry in the region as determined by internationally reported and published data; in addition, the regional group shall agree also to take into account other regional factors in designating these three members;

(e) Ten States Parties from among Western European and other States to be designated by States Parties located in this region. As a basis for this designation it is understood that, out of these 10 States Parties, 5 members shall, as a rule, be the States Parties with the most significant national chemical industry in the region as determined by internationally reported and published data; in addition, the regional group shall agree also to take into account other regional factors in designating these five members;

(f) One further State Party to be designated consecutively by States Parties located in the regions of Asia and Latin America and the Caribbean. As a basis for this designation it is understood that this State Party shall be a rotating member from these regions.

24. For the first election of the Executive Council 20 members shall be elected for a term of one year, due regard being paid to the established numerical proportions as described in paragraph 23.

25. After the full implementation of Articles IV and V the Conference may, upon the request of a majority of the members of the Executive Council, review the composition of the Executive Council taking into account developments related to the principles specified in paragraph 23 that are governing its composition.

26. The Executive Council shall elaborate its rules of procedure and submit them to the Conference for approval.

27. The Executive Council shall elect its Chairman from among its members.

28. The Executive Council shall meet for regular sessions. Between regular sessions it shall meet as often as may be required for the fulfillment of its powers and functions.

29. Each member of the Executive Council shall have one vote. Unless otherwise specified in this Convention, the Executive Council shall take decisions on matters of substance by a two-thirds majority of all its members. The Executive Council shall take decisions on questions of procedure by a simple majority of all its members. When the issue arises as to whether the question is one of substance or not, that question shall be treated as a matter of substance unless otherwise decided by the Executive Council by the majority required for decisions on matters of substance.

Powers and functions

30. The Executive Council shall be the executive organ of the Organization. It shall be responsible to the Conference. The Executive Council shall carry out the powers and functions entrusted to it under this Convention, as well as those functions delegated to it by the Conference. In so doing, it shall act in conformity with the recommendations, decisions and guidelines of the Conference and assure their proper and continuous implementation.

31. The Executive Council shall promote the effective implementation of, and compliance with, this Convention. It shall supervise the activities of the Technical Secretariat, cooperate with the National Authority of each State Party and facilitate consultations and cooperation among States Parties at their request.

32. The Executive Council shall:

(a) Consider and submit to the Conference the draft programme and budget of the Organization;

(b) Consider and submit to the Conference the draft report of the Organization on the implementation of this Convention, the report on the performance of its own activities and such special reports as it deems necessary or which the Conference may request;

(c) Make arrangements for the sessions of the Conference including the preparation of the draft agenda.

33. The Executive Council may request the convening of a special session of the Conference.

34. The Executive Council shall:

(a) Conclude agreements or arrangements with States and international organizations on behalf of the Organization, subject to prior approval by the Conference;

(b) Conclude agreements with States Parties on behalf of the Organization in connection with Article X and supervise the voluntary fund referred to in Article X;

(c) Approve agreements or arrangements relating to the implementation of verification activities, negotiated by the Technical Secretariat with States Parties.

35. The Executive Council shall consider any issue or matter within its competence affecting this Convention and its implementation, including concerns regarding compliance, and cases of non-compliance, and, as appropriate, inform States Parties and bring the issue or matter to the attention of the Conference.

36. In its consideration of doubts or concerns regarding compliance and cases of non-compliance, including, inter alia, abuse of the rights provided for under this Convention, the Executive Council shall consult with the States Parties involved and, as appropriate, request the State Party to take measures to redress the situation within a specified time. To the extent that the Executive Council considers further action to be necessary, it shall take, inter alia, one or more of the following measures:

(a) Inform all States Parties of the issue or matter;

(b) Bring the issue or matter to the attention of the Conference;

(c) Make recommendations to the Conference regarding measures to redress the situation and to ensure compliance.

The Executive Council shall, in cases of particular gravity and urgency, bring the issue or matter, including relevant information and conclusions, directly to the attention of the United Nations General Assembly and the United Nations Security Council. It shall at the same time inform all States Parties of this step.

D. THE TECHNICAL SECRETARIAT

37. The Technical Secretariat shall assist the Conference and the Executive Council in the performance of their functions. The Technical Secretariat shall carry out the verification measures provided for in this Convention. It shall carry out the other functions entrusted to it under this Convention as well as those functions delegated to it by the Conference and the Executive Council.

. . . .

Article IX. *Consultations, Cooperation and Fact-Finding.*

. . . .

Procedures for Challenge Inspections

8. Each State Party has the right to request an on-site challenge inspection of any facility or location in the territory or in any other place under the jurisdiction or control of any other State Party for the sole purpose of clarifying and resolving any questions concerning possible non-compliance with the provisions of this Convention, and to have this inspection conducted anywhere without delay by an inspection team designated by the Director-General and in accordance with the Verification Annex.

9. Each State Party is under the obligation to keep the inspection request within the scope of this Convention and to provide in the inspection request all appropriate information on the basis of which a concern has arisen regarding possible non-compliance with this Convention as specified in the Verification Annex. Each State Party shall refrain from unfounded inspection requests, care being taken to avoid abuse. The challenge inspection shall be carried out for the sole purpose of determining facts relating to the possible non-compliance.

10. For the purpose of verifying compliance with the provisions of this Convention, each State Party shall permit the Technical Secretariat to conduct the on-site challenge inspection pursuant to paragraph 8.

11. Pursuant to a request for a challenge inspection of a facility or location, and in accordance with the procedures provided for in the Verification Annex, the inspected State Party shall have:

(a) The right and the obligation to make every reasonable effort to demonstrate its compliance with this Convention and, to this end, to enable the inspection team to fulfill its mandate;

(b) The obligation to provide access within the requested site for the sole purpose of establishing facts relevant to the concern regarding possible non-compliance; and

(c) The right to take measures to protect sensitive installations, and to prevent disclosure of confidential information and data, not related to this Convention.

12. With regard to an observer, the following shall apply:

(a) The requesting State Party may, subject to the agreement of the inspected State Party, send a representative who may be a national either of the requesting State Party or of a third State Party, to observe the conduct of the challenge inspection.

(b) The inspected State Party shall then grant access to the observer in accordance with the Verification Annex.

(c) The inspected State Party shall, as a rule, accept the proposed observer, but if the inspected State Party exercises a refusal, that fact shall be recorded in the final report.

13. The requesting State Party shall present an inspection request for an on-site challenge inspection to the Executive Council and at the same time to the Director-General for immediate processing.

14. The Director-General shall immediately ascertain that the inspection request meets the requirements specified in Part X, paragraph 4, of the Verification Annex, and,

if necessary, assist the requesting State Party in filing the inspection request accordingly. When the inspection request fulfils the requirements, preparations for the challenge inspection shall begin.

15. The Director-General shall transmit the inspection request to the inspected State Party not less than 12 hours before the planned arrival of the inspection team at the point of entry.

16. After having received the inspection request, the Executive Council shall take cognizance of the Director-General's actions on the request and shall keep the case under its consideration throughout the inspection procedure. However, its deliberations shall not delay the inspection process.

17. The Executive Council may, not later than 12 hours after having received the inspection request, decide by a three-quarter majority of all its members against carrying out the challenge inspection, if it considers the inspection request to be frivolous, abusive or clearly beyond the scope of this Convention as described in paragraph 8. Neither the requesting nor the inspected State Party shall participate in such a decision. If the Executive Council decides against the challenge inspection, preparations shall be stopped, no further action on the inspection request shall be taken, and the States Parties concerned shall be informed accordingly.

18. The Director-General shall issue an inspection mandate for the conduct of the challenge inspection. The inspection mandate shall be the inspection request referred to in paragraphs 8 and 9 put into operational terms, and shall conform with the inspection request.

19. The challenge inspection shall be conducted in accordance with Part X or, in the case of alleged use, in accordance with Part XI of the Verification Annex. The inspection team shall be guided by the principle of conducting the challenge inspection in the least intrusive manner possible, consistent with the effective and timely accomplishment of its mission.

20. The inspected State Party shall assist the inspection team throughout the challenge inspection and facilitate its task. If the inspected State Party proposes, pursuant to Part X, Section C, of the Verification Annex, arrangements to demonstrate compliance with this Convention, alternative to full and comprehensive access, it shall make every reasonable effort, through consultations with the inspection team, to reach agreement on the modalities for establishing the facts with the aim of demonstrating its compliance.

21. The final report shall contain the factual findings as well as an assessment by the inspection team of the degree and nature of access and cooperation granted for the satisfactory implementation of the challenge inspection. The Director-General shall promptly transmit the final report of the inspection team to the requesting State Party, to the inspected State Party, to the Executive Council and to all other States Parties. The Director-General shall further transmit promptly to the Executive Council the assessments of the requesting and of the inspected States Parties, as well as the views of other States Parties which may be conveyed to the Director-General for that purpose, and then provide them to all States Parties.

22. The Executive Council shall, in accordance with its powers and functions, review the final report of the inspection team as soon as it is presented, and address any concerns as to:

(a) Whether any non-compliance has occurred;

(b) Whether the request had been within the scope of this Convention; and

(c) Whether the right to request a challenge inspection had been abused.

23. If the Executive Council reaches the conclusion, in keeping with its powers and functions, that further action may be necessary with regard to paragraph 22, it shall take the appropriate measures to redress the situation and to ensure compliance with this Convention, including specific recommendations to the Conference. In the case of abuse, the Executive Council shall examine whether the requesting State Party should bear any of the financial implications of the challenge inspection.

24. The requesting State Party and the inspected State Party shall have the right to participate in the review process. The Executive Council shall inform the States Parties and the next session of the Conference of the outcome of the process.

25. If the Executive Council has made specific recommendations to the Conference, the Conference shall consider action in accordance with Article XII.

Article X. *Assistance and Protection Against Chemical Weapons.* 1. For the purposes of this Article, "Assistance" means the coordination and delivery to States Parties of protection against chemical weapons, including, inter alia, the following: detection equipment and alarm systems; protective equipment; decontamination equipment and decontaminants; medical antidotes and treatments; and advice on any of these protective measures.

2. Nothing in this Convention shall be interpreted as impeding the right of any State Party to conduct research into, develop, produce, acquire, transfer or use means of protection against chemical weapons, for purposes not prohibited under this Convention.

3. Each State Party undertakes to facilitate, and shall have the right to participate in, the fullest possible exchange of equipment, material and scientific and technological information concerning means of protection against chemical weapons.

4. For the purposes of increasing the transparency of national programmes related to protective purposes, each State Party shall provide annually to the Technical Secretariat information on its programme, in accordance with procedures to be considered and approved by the Conference pursuant to Article VIII, paragraph 21 (i).

5. The Technical Secretariat shall establish, not later than 180 days after entry into force of this Convention and maintain, for the use of any requesting State Party, a data bank containing freely available information concerning various means of protection against chemical weapons as well as such information as may be provided by States Parties.

The Technical Secretariat shall also, within the resources available to it, and at the request of a State Party, provide expert advice and assist the State Party in identifying how its programmes for the development and improvement of a protective capacity against chemical weapons could be implemented.

6. Nothing in this Convention shall be interpreted as impeding the right of States Parties to request and provide assistance bilaterally and to conclude individual agreements with other States Parties concerning the emergency procurement of assistance.

. . . .

COMPREHENSIVE NUCLEAR TEST-BAN TREATY*

Preamble

The States Parties to this Treaty (hereinafter referred to as "the States Parties"),

Welcoming the international agreements and other positive measures of recent years in the field of nuclear disarmament, including reductions in arsenals of nuclear weapons, as well as in the field of the prevention of nuclear proliferation in all its aspects,

Underlining the importance of the full and prompt implementation of such agreements and measures,

Convinced that the present international situation provides an opportunity to take further effective measures towards nuclear disarmament and against the proliferation of nuclear weapons in all its aspects, and declaring their intention to take such measures,

Stressing therefore the need for continued systematic and progressive efforts to reduce nuclear weapons globally, with the ultimate goal of eliminating those weapons, and of general and complete disarmament under strict and effective international control,

Recognizing that the cessation of all nuclear weapon test explosions and all other nuclear explosions, by constraining the development and qualitative improvement of nuclear weapons and ending the development of advanced new types of nuclear weapons, constitutes an effective measure of nuclear disarmament and non-proliferation in all its aspects,

Further recognizing that an end to all such nuclear explosions will thus constitute a meaningful step in the realization of a systematic process to achieve nuclear disarmament,

Convinced that the most effective way to achieve an end to nuclear testing is through the conclusion of a universal and internationally and effectively verifiable comprehensive nuclear test-ban treaty, which has long been one of the highest priority objectives of the international community in the field of disarmament and non-proliferation,

Noting the aspirations expressed by the Parties to the 1963 Treaty Banning Nuclear Weapon Tests in the Atmosphere, in Outer Space and Under Water to seek to achieve the discontinuance of all test explosions of nuclear weapons for all time,

Noting also the views expressed that this Treaty could contribute to the protection of the environment,

Affirming the purpose of attracting the adherence of all States to this Treaty and its objective to contribute effectively to the prevention of the proliferation of nuclear weapons in all its aspects, to the process of nuclear disarmament and therefore to the enhancement of international peace and security,

Have agreed as follows:

---

* Comprehensive Nuclear Test-Ban Treaty, *opened for signature* Sept. 24, 1996, S. Treaty Doc. No. 105-28, at 122, 35 I.L.M. 1439, 1444 (1996), *available at* http://www.state.gov/t/np/trty/16411.htm.

Article I.

BASIC OBLIGATIONS

1. Each State Party undertakes not to carry out any nuclear weapon test explosion or any other nuclear explosion, and to prohibit and prevent any such nuclear explosion at any place under its jurisdiction or control.

2. Each State Party undertakes, furthermore, to refrain from causing, encouraging, or in any way participating in the carrying out of any nuclear weapon test explosion or any other nuclear explosion.

Article II.

THE ORGANIZATION

A. GENERAL PROVISIONS

1. The States Parties hereby establish the Comprehensive Nuclear Test-Ban Treaty Organization (hereinafter referred to as "the Organization") to achieve the object and purpose of this Treaty, to ensure the implementation of its provisions, including those for international verification of compliance with it, and to provide a forum for consultation and cooperation among States Parties.

. . . .

5. Each State Party shall cooperate with the Organization in the exercise of its functions in accordance with this Treaty. States Parties shall consult, directly among themselves, or through the Organization or other appropriate international procedures, including procedures within the framework of the United Nations and in accordance with its Charter, on any matter which may be raised relating to the object and purpose, or the implementation of the provisions, of this Treaty.

6. The Organization shall conduct its verification activities provided for under this Treaty in the least intrusive manner possible consistent with the timely and efficient accomplishment of their objectives. It shall request only the information and data necessary to fulfill its responsibilities under this Treaty. It shall take every precaution to protect the confidentiality of information on civil and military activities and facilities coming to its knowledge in the implementation of this Treaty and, in particular, shall abide by the confidentiality provisions set forth in this Treaty.

. . . .

Article III.

NATIONAL IMPLEMENTATION MEASURES

1. Each State Party shall, in accordance with its constitutional processes, take any necessary measures to implement its obligations under this Treaty. In particular, it shall take any necessary measures:

(a) To prohibit natural and legal persons anywhere on its territory or in any other place under its jurisdiction as recognized by international law from undertaking any activity prohibited to a State Party under this Treaty;

(b) To prohibit natural and legal persons from undertaking any such activity anywhere under its control; and

(c) To prohibit, in conformity with international law, natural persons possessing its nationality from undertaking any such activity anywhere.

....

Article IV.

VERIFICATION

A. GENERAL PROVISIONS

1. In order to verify compliance with this Treaty, a verification regime shall be established consisting of the following elements:

(a) An International Monitoring System;

(b) Consultation and clarification;

(c) On-site inspections; and

(d) Confidence-building measures.

At entry into force of this Treaty, the verification regime shall be capable of meeting the verification requirements of this Treaty.

2. Verification activities shall be based on objective information, shall be limited to the subject matter of this Treaty, and shall be carried out on the basis of full respect for the sovereignty of States Parties and in the least intrusive manner possible consistent with the effective and timely accomplishment of their objectives. Each State Party shall refrain from any abuse of the right of verification.

3. Each State Party undertakes in accordance with this Treaty to cooperate, through its National Authority established pursuant to Article III, paragraph 4, with the Organization and with other States Parties to facilitate the verification of compliance with this Treaty by *inter alia*:

(a) Establishing the necessary facilities to participate in these verification measures and establishing the necessary communication;

(b) Providing data obtained from national stations that are part of the International Monitoring System;

(c) Participating, as appropriate, in a consultation and clarification process;

(d) Permitting the conduct of on-site inspections; and

(e) Participating, as appropriate, in confidence-building measures.

4. All States Parties, irrespective of their technical and financial capabilities, shall enjoy the equal right of verification and assume the equal obligation to accept verification.

....

CONVENTION ON THE PROHIBITION OF THE USE, STOCKPILING, PRODUCTION AND TRANSFER OF ANTI-PERSONNEL MINES AND ON THEIR DESTRUCTION*

Preamble

The States Parties,

Determined to put an end to the suffering and casualties caused by anti-personnel mines, that kill or maim hundreds of people every week, mostly innocent and defenceless civilians and especially children, obstruct economic development and reconstruction, inhibit the repatriation of refugees and internally displaced persons, and have other severe consequences for years after emplacement,

Believing it necessary to do their utmost to contribute in an efficient and coordinated manner to face the challenge of removing anti-personnel mines placed throughout the world, and to assure their destruction,

Wishing to do their utmost in providing assistance for the care and rehabilitation, including the social and economic reintegration of mine victims,

Recognizing that a total ban of anti-personnel mines would also be an important confidence-building measure,

. . . .

Welcoming also United Nations General Assembly Resolution 51/45 S of 10 December 1996 urging all States to pursue vigorously an effective, legally-binding international agreement to ban the use, stockpiling, production and transfer of anti-personnel landmines,

Welcoming furthermore the measures taken over the past years, both unilaterally and multilaterally, aiming at prohibiting, restricting or suspending the use, stockpiling, production and transfer of anti-personnel mines,

Stressing the role of public conscience in furthering the principles of humanity as evidenced by the call for a total ban of anti-personnel mines and recognizing the efforts to that end undertaken by the International Red Cross and Red Crescent Movement, the International Campaign to Ban Landmines and numerous other non-governmental organizations around the world,

. . . .

Basing themselves on the principle of international humanitarian law that the right of the parties to an armed conflict to choose methods or means of warfare is not unlimited, on the principle that prohibits the employment in armed conflicts of weapons, projectiles and materials and methods of warfare of a nature to cause superfluous injury or unnecessary suffering and on the principle that a distinction must be made between civilians and combatants,

---

* Convention on the Prohibition of the Use, Stockpiling, Production and Transfer of Anti-Personnel Mines and on Their Destruction, Sept. 18, 1997, 2056 U.N.T.S. 215, 241 (entered into force Mar. 1, 1999), *available at* http://www.mines.gc.ca/VII/VII_AA_i-en.asp.

Have agreed as follows:

Article 1.

GENERAL OBLIGATIONS

1. Each State Party undertakes never under any circumstances:

a) To use anti-personnel mines;

b) To develop, produce, otherwise acquire, stockpile, retain or transfer to anyone, directly or indirectly, anti-personnel mines;

c) To assist, encourage or induce, in any way, anyone to engage in any activity prohibited to a State Party under this Convention.

2. Each State Party undertakes to destroy or ensure the destruction of all anti-personnel mines in accordance with the provisions of this Convention.

Article 2.

DEFINITIONS

1. "Anti-personnel mine" means a mine designed to be exploded by the presence, proximity or contact of a person and that will incapacitate, injure or kill one or more persons. Mines designed to be detonated by the presence, proximity or contact of a vehicle as opposed to a person, that are equipped with anti-handling devices, are not considered anti-personnel mines as a result of being so equipped.

2. "Mine" means a munition designed to be placed under, on or near the ground or other surface area and to be exploded by the presence, proximity or contact of a person or a vehicle.

3. "Anti-handling device" means a device intended to protect a mine and which is part of, linked to, attached to or placed under the mine and which activates when an attempt is made to tamper with or otherwise intentionally disturb the mine.

4. "Transfer" involves, in addition to the physical movement of anti-personnel mines into or from national territory, the transfer of title to and control over the mines, but does not involve the transfer of territory containing emplaced anti-personnel mines.

5. "Mined area" means an area which is dangerous due to the presence or suspected presence of mines.

Article 3.

EXCEPTIONS

1. Notwithstanding the general obligations under Article 1, the retention or transfer of a number of anti-personnel mines for the development of and training in mine detection, mine clearance, or mine destruction techniques is permitted. The amount of such mines shall not exceed the minimum number absolutely necessary for the above-mentioned purposes.

2. The transfer of anti-personnel mines for the purpose of destruction is permitted.

Article 4.

DESTRUCTION OF STOCKPILED ANTI-PERSONNEL MINES

Except as provided for in Article 3, each State Party undertakes to destroy or ensure the destruction of all stockpiled anti-personnel mines it owns or possesses, or that are under its jurisdiction or control, as soon as possible but not later than four years after the entry into force of this Convention for that State Party.

Article 5.

DESTRUCTION OF ANTI-PERSONNEL MINES IN MINED AREAS

1. Each State Party undertakes to destroy or ensure the destruction of all anti-personnel mines in mined areas under its jurisdiction or control, as soon as possible but not later than ten years after the entry into force of this Convention for that State Party.

2. Each State Party shall make every effort to identify all areas under its jurisdiction or control in which anti-personnel mines are known or suspected to be emplaced and shall ensure as soon as possible that all anti-personnel mines in mined areas under its jurisdiction or control are perimeter marked, monitored and protected by fencing or other means, to ensure the effective exclusion of civilians, until all anti-personnel mines contained therein have been destroyed. ....

3. If a State Party believes that it will be unable to destroy or ensure the destruction of all antipersonnel mines referred to in paragraph 1 within that time period, it may submit a request to a Meeting of the States Parties or a Review Conference for an extension of the deadline for completing the destruction of such anti-personnel mines, for a period of up to ten years.

....

Article 6.

INTERNATIONAL COOPERATION AND ASSISTANCE

1. In fulfilling its obligations under this Convention each State Party has the right to seek and receive assistance, where feasible, from other States Parties to the extent possible.

2. Each State Party undertakes to facilitate and shall have the right to participate in the fullest possible exchange of equipment, material and scientific and technological information concerning the implementation of this Convention. The States Parties shall not impose undue restrictions on the provision of mine clearance equipment and related technological information for humanitarian purposes.

3. Each State Party in a position to do so shall provide assistance for the care and rehabilitation, and social and economic reintegration, of mine victims and for mine awareness programs. Such assistance may be provided, inter alia, through the United Nations system, international, regional or national organizations or institutions, the International Committee of the Red Cross, national Red Cross and Red Crescent societies and their International Federation, nongovernmental organizations, or on a bilateral basis.

....

Article 9.

NATIONAL IMPLEMENTATION MEASURES

Each State Party shall take all appropriate legal, administrative and other measures, including the imposition of penal sanctions, to prevent and suppress any activity prohibited to a State Party under this Convention undertaken by persons or on territory under its jurisdiction or control.

Article 10.

SETTLEMENT OF DISPUTES

1. The States Parties shall consult and cooperate with each other to settle any dispute that may arise with regard to the application or the interpretation of this Convention. Each State Party may bring any such dispute before the Meeting of the States Parties.

2. The Meeting of the States Parties may contribute to the settlement of the dispute by whatever means it deems appropriate, including offering its good offices, calling upon the States parties to a dispute to start the settlement procedure of their choice and recommending a time-limit for any agreed procedure.

3. This Article is without prejudice to the provisions of this Convention on facilitation and clarification of compliance.

....

Article 12.

REVIEW CONFERENCES

1. A Review Conference shall be convened by the Secretary-General of the United Nations five years after the entry into force of this Convention. Further Review Conferences shall be convened by the Secretary-General of the United Nations if so requested by one or more States Parties, provided that the interval between Review Conferences shall in no case be less than five years. All States Parties to this Convention shall be invited to each Review Conference.

....

Article 17.

ENTRY INTO FORCE

1. This Convention shall enter into force on the first day of the sixth month after the month in which the 40th instrument of ratification, acceptance, approval or accession has been deposited.

2. For any State which deposits its instrument of ratification, acceptance, approval or accession after the date of the deposit of the 40th instrument of ratification, acceptance, approval or accession, this Convention shall enter into force on the first day of the sixth month after the date on which that State has deposited its instrument of ratification, acceptance, approval or accession.

....

Article 19.

RESERVATIONS

The Articles of this Convention shall not be subject to reservations.

Article 20.

DURATION AND WITHDRAWAL

1. This Convention shall be of unlimited duration.

2. Each State Party shall, in exercising its national sovereignty, have the right to withdraw from this Convention. It shall give notice of such withdrawal to all other States

Parties, to the Depositary and to the United Nations Security Council. Such instrument of withdrawal shall include a full explanation of the reasons motivating this withdrawal.

3. Such withdrawal shall only take effect six months after the receipt of the instrument of withdrawal by the Depositary. If, however, on the expiry of that six-month period, the withdrawing State Party is engaged in an armed conflict, the withdrawal shall not take effect before the end of the armed conflict.

4. The withdrawal of a State Party from this Convention shall not in any way affect the duty of States to continue fulfilling the obligations assumed under any relevant rules of international law.

....

B. Regional Arms Control and Disarmament Regimes

TREATY FOR THE PROHIBITION OF NUCLEAR WEAPONS IN LATIN AMERICA* (TREATY OF TLATELOLCO)

In the name of their peoples and faithfully interpreting their desires and aspirations, the Governments of the States which sign the Treaty for the Prohibition of Nuclear Weapons in Latin America,

Desiring to contribute, so far as lies in their power, towards ending the armaments race, especially in the field of nuclear weapons, and towards strengthening a world at peace, based on the sovereign equality of States, mutual respect and good neighbourliness,

Recalling that the United Nations General Assembly, in its Resolution 808 (IX), adopted unanimously as one of the three points of a coordinated programme of disarmament "the total prohibition of the use and manufacture of nuclear weapons and weapons of mass destruction of every type,"

Recalling that military denuclearized zones are not an end in themselves but rather a means for achieving general and complete disarmament at a later stage,

Recalling United Nations General Assembly Resolution 1911 (XVIII), which established that the measures that should be agreed upon for the denuclearization of Latin America should be taken "in the light of the principles of the Charter of the United Nations and of regional agreements,"

Recalling United Nations General Assembly Resolution 2028 (XX), which established the principle of an acceptable balance of mutual responsibilities and duties for the nuclear and non-nuclear powers, and

Recalling that the Charter of the Organization of American States proclaims that it is an essential purpose of the Organization to strengthen the peace and security of the hemisphere,

Convinced:

That the incalculable destructive power of nuclear weapons has made it imperative that the legal prohibition of war should be strictly observed in practice if the survival of civilization and of mankind itself is to be assured,

That nuclear weapons, whose terrible effects are suffered, indiscriminately and inexorably, by military forces and civilian population alike, constitute, through the persistence of the radioactivity they release, an attack on the integrity of the human species and ultimately may even render the whole earth uninhabitable,

That general and complete disarmament under effective international control is a vital matter which all the peoples of the world equally demand,

---

* Treaty for the Prohibition of Nuclear Weapons in Latin America, Feb. 14, 1967, 634 U.N.T.S. 281, 326 (entered into force Apr. 22, 1968), *available at* http://www.state.gov/t/ac/trt/4796.htm. The United States is not a party to the Treaty, but did ratify Additional Protocol I, which entered into force for the U.S. on 23 Nov. 1981, and Additional Protocol II, which entered into force for the U.S. on 12 May 1971. *See* Additional Protocol I to the Treaty for the Prohibition of Nuclear Weapons in Latin America, Feb. 14, 1967, 33 U.S.T. 1792, 1794, 634 U.N.T.S. at 360; Additional Protocol II to the Treaty for the Prohibition of Nuclear Weapons in Latin America, Feb. 14, 1967, 22 U.S.T. 754, 755, 634 U.N.T.S. at 364.

That the proliferation of nuclear weapons, which seems inevitable unless States, in the exercise of their sovereign rights, impose restrictions on themselves in order to prevent it, would make any agreement on disarmament enormously difficult and would increase the danger of the outbreak of a nuclear conflagration,

That the establishment of militarily denuclearized zones is closely linked with the maintenance of peace and security in the respective regions,

That the military denuclearization of vast geographical zones, adopted by the sovereign decision of the States comprised therein, will exercise a beneficial influence on other regions where similar conditions exist,

That the privileged situation of the signatory States, whose territories are wholly free from nuclear weapons, imposes upon them the inescapable duty of preserving that situation both in their own interest and for the good of mankind,

That the existence of nuclear weapons in any country of Latin America would make it a target for possible nuclear attacks and would inevitably set off, throughout the region, a ruinous race in nuclear weapons which would involve the unjustifiable diversion, for warlike purposes, of the limited resources required for economic and social development,

That the foregoing reasons, together with the traditional peace-loving outlook of Latin America, give rise to an inescapable necessity that nuclear energy should be used in that region exclusively for peaceful purposes, and that the Latin American countries should use their right to the greatest and most equitable possible access to this new source of energy in order to expedite the economic and social development of their peoples,

Convinced finally:

That the military denuclearization of Latin America—being understood to mean the undertaking entered into internationally in this Treaty to keep their territories forever free from nuclear weapons—will constitute a measure which will spare their peoples from the squandering of their limited resources on nuclear armaments and will protect them against possible nuclear attacks on their territories, and will also constitute a significant contribution towards preventing the proliferation of nuclear weapons and a powerful factor for general and complete disarmament, and

That Latin America, faithful to its tradition of universality, must not only endeavour to banish from its homelands the scourge of a nuclear war, but must also strive to promote the well-being and advancement of its peoples, at the same time co-operating in the fulfillment of the ideals of mankind, that is to say, in the consolidation of a permanent peace based on equal rights, economic fairness and social justice for all, in accordance with the principles and purposes set forth in the Charter of the United Nations and in the Charter of the Organization of American States.

Have agreed as follows:

Obligations

Article 1. 1. The Contracting Parties hereby undertake to use exclusively for peaceful purposes the nuclear material and facilities which are under their jurisdiction, and to prohibit and prevent in their respective territories:

(a) The testing, use, manufacture, production or acquisition by any means whatsoever of any nuclear weapons, by the Parties themselves, directly or indirectly, on behalf of anyone else or in any other way, and

(b) The receipt, storage, installation, deployment and any form of possession of any nuclear weapons, directly or indirectly, by the Parties themselves, by anyone on their behalf or in any other way.

2. The Contracting Parties also undertake to refrain from engaging in, encouraging or authorizing, directly or indirectly, or in any way participating in the testing, use, manufacture, production, possession or control of any nuclear weapon.

Definition of the Contracting Parties

Article 2. For the purposes of this Treaty, the Contracting Parties are those for whom the Treaty is in force.

Definition of Territory

Article 3. For the purposes of this Treaty, the term "territory" shall include the territorial sea, air space and any other space over which the State exercises sovereignty in accordance with its own legislation.

Zone of Application

Article 4. 1. The zone of application of this Treaty is the whole of the territories for which the Treaty is in force.

2. Upon fulfillment of the requirements of article 28, paragraph 1, the zone of application of this Treaty shall also be that which is situated in the western hemisphere within the following limits (except the continental part of the territory of the United States of America and its territorial waters): starting at a point located at 35 north latitude, 75 west longitude; from this point directly southward to a point at 30 north latitude, 75 west longitude; from there, directly eastward to a point at 30 north latitude, 50 west longitude; from there, along a loxodromic line to a point at 5 north latitude, 20 west longitude; from there directly southward to a point 60 south latitude, 20 west longitude; from there, directly westward to a point at 60 south latitude, 115 west longitude; from there, directly northward to a point at 0 latitude, 115 west longitude; from there, along a loxodromic line to a point at 35 north latitude, 150 west longitude; from there, directly eastward to a point at 35 north latitude, 75 west longitude.

Definition of Nuclear Weapons

Article 5. For the purposes of this Treaty, a nuclear weapon is any device which is capable of releasing nuclear energy in an uncontrolled manner and which has a group of characteristics that are appropriate for use for warlike purposes. An instrument that may be used for the transport or propulsion of the device is not included in this definition if it is separable from the device and not an indivisible part thereof.

. . . .

Organization

Article 7. 1. In order to ensure compliance with the obligations of this Treaty, the Contracting Parties hereby establish an international organization to be known as the "Agency for the Prohibition of Nuclear Weapons in Latin America," hereinafter referred to as "the Agency." Only the Contracting Parties shall be affected by its decisions.

2. The Agency shall be responsible for the holding of periodic or extraordinary consultations among Member States on matters relating to the purposes, measures and

procedures set forth in this Treaty and to the supervision of compliance with the obligations arising therefrom.

3. The Contracting Parties agree to extend to the Agency full and prompt cooperation in accordance with the provisions of this Treaty, of any agreements they may conclude with the Agency and of any agreements the Agency may conclude with any other international organization or body.

4. The headquarters of the Agency shall be in Mexico City.

Organs

Article 8. 1. There are hereby established as principal organs of the Agency a General Conference, a Council and a Secretariat.

2. Such subsidiary organs as are considered necessary by the General Conference may be established within the purview of this Treaty.

The General Conference

Article 9. 1. The General Conference, the supreme organ of the Agency, shall be composed of all the Contracting Parties; it shall hold regular sessions every two years, and may also hold special sessions whenever this Treaty so provides or, in the opinion of the Council, the circumstances so require.

2. The General Conference:

(a) May consider and decide on any matters or questions covered by this Treaty, within the limits thereof, including those referring to powers and functions of any organ provided for in this Treaty.

(b) Shall establish procedures for the control system to ensure observance of this Treaty in accordance with its provisions.

(c) Shall elect the Members of the Council and the General Secretary.

(d) May remove the General Secretary from office if the proper functioning of the Agency so requires.

(e) Shall receive and consider the biennial and special reports submitted by the Council and the General Secretary.

(f) Shall initiate and consider studies designed to facilitate the optimum fulfillment of the aims of this Treaty, without prejudice to the power of the General Secretary independently to carry out similar studies for submission to and consideration by the Conference.

(g) Shall be the organ competent to authorize the conclusion of agreements with Governments and other international organizations and bodies.

3. The General Conference shall adopt the Agency's budget and fix the scale of financial contributions to be paid by Member States, taking into account the systems and criteria used for the same purpose by the United Nations.

4. The General Conference shall elect its officers for each session and may establish such subsidiary organs as it deems necessary for the performance of its functions.

5. Each Member of the Agency shall have one vote. The decisions of the General Conference shall be taken by a two-thirds majority of the Members present and voting in the case of matters relating to the control system and measures referred to in article 20, the admission of new Members, the election or removal of the General Secretary,

adoption of the budget and matters related thereto. Decisions on other matters, as well as procedural questions and also determination of which questions must be decided by a two-thirds majority, shall be taken by a simple majority of the Members present and voting.

6. The General Conference shall adopt its own rules of procedure.

The Council

Article 10. 1. The Council shall be composed of five Members of the Agency elected by the General Conference from among the Contracting Parties, due account being taken of equitable geographic distribution.

2. The Members of the Council shall be elected for a term of four years. However, in the first election three will be elected for two years. Outgoing Members may not be re-elected for the following period unless the limited number of States for which the Treaty is in force so requires.

3. Each Member of the Council shall have one representative.

4. The Council shall be so organized as to be able to function continuously.

5. In addition to the functions conferred upon it by this Treaty and to those which may be assigned to it by the General Conference, the Council shall, through the General Secretary, ensure the proper operation of the control system in accordance with the provisions of this Treaty and with the decisions adopted by the General Conference.

6. The Council shall submit an annual report on its work to the General Conference as well as such special reports as it deems necessary or which the General Conference requests of it.

7. The Council shall elect its officers for each session.

8. The decisions of the Council shall be taken by a simple majority of its Members present and voting.

9. The Council shall adopt its own rules of procedure.

....

Control System

Article 12. 1. For the purpose of verifying compliance with the obligations entered into by the Contracting Parties in accordance with article 1, a control system shall be established which shall be put into effect in accordance with the provisions of articles 13–18 of this Treaty.

2. The control system shall be used in particular for the purpose of verifying:

(a) That devices, services and facilities intended for peaceful uses of nuclear energy are not used in the testing or manufacture of nuclear weapons,

(b) That none of the activities prohibited in article 1 of this Treaty are carried out in the territory of the Contracting Parties with nuclear materials or weapons introduced from abroad, and

(c) That explosions for peaceful purposes are compatible with article 18 of this Treaty.

IAEA Safeguards

Article 13. Each Contracting Party shall negotiate multilateral or bilateral agreements with the International Atomic Energy Agency for the application of its safeguards to its nuclear activities. Each Contracting Party shall initiate negotiations within a period of 180 days after the date of the deposit of its instrument of ratification of this Treaty. These agreements shall enter into force, for each Party, not later than eighteen months after the date of the initiation of such negotiations except in case of unforeseen circumstances or *force majeure.*

Reports of the Parties

Article 14. 1. The Contracting Parties shall submit to the Agency and to the International Atomic Energy Agency, for their information, semi-annual reports stating that no activity prohibited under this Treaty has occurred in their respective territories.

2. The Contracting Parties shall simultaneously transmit to the Agency a copy of any report they may submit to the International Atomic Energy Agency which relates to matters that are the subject of this Treaty and to the application of safeguards.

3. The Contracting Parties shall also transmit to the Organization of American States, for its information, any reports that may be of interest to it, in accordance with the obligations established by the Inter-American System.

. . . .

Use of Nuclear Energy for Peaceful Purposes

Article 17. Nothing in the provisions of this Treaty shall prejudice the rights of the Contracting Parties, in conformity with this Treaty, to use nuclear energy for peaceful purposes, in particular for their economic development and social progress.

Explosions for Peaceful Purposes

Article 18. 1. The Contracting Parties may carry out explosions of nuclear devices for peaceful purposes—including explosions which involve devices similar to those used in nuclear weapons—or collaborate with third parties for the same purpose, provided that they do so in accordance with the provisions of this article and the other articles of the Treaty, particularly articles 1 and 5.

2. Contracting Parties intending to carry out, or to cooperate in carrying out, such an explosion shall notify the Agency and the International Atomic Energy Agency, as far in advance as the circumstances require, of the date of the explosion and shall at the same time provide the following information:

(a) The nature of the nuclear device and the source from which it was obtained,

(b) The place and purpose of the planned explosion,

(c) The procedures which will be followed in order to comply with paragraph 3 of this article,

(d) The expected force of the device, and

(e) The fullest possible information on any possible radioactive fall-out that may result from the explosion or explosions, and measures which will be taken to avoid danger to the population, flora, fauna and territories of any other Party or Parties.

3. The General Secretary and the technical personnel designated by the Council and the International Atomic Energy Agency may observe all the preparations, including the explosion of the device, and shall have unrestricted access to any area in the vicinity of the site of the explosion in order to ascertain whether the device and the procedures fol-

lowed during the explosion are in conformity with the information supplied under paragraph 2 of this article and the other provisions of this Treaty.

4. The Contracting Parties may accept the collaboration of third parties for the purpose set forth in paragraph 1 of the present article, in accordance with paragraphs 2 and 3 thereof.

Measures in the Event of Violation of the Treaty

Article 20. 1. The General Conference shall take note of all cases in which, in its opinion, any Contracting Party is not complying fully with its obligations under this Treaty and shall draw the matter to the attention of the Party concerned, making such recommendations as it deems appropriate.

2. If, in its opinion, such non-compliance constitutes a violation of this Treaty which might endanger peace and security, the General Conference shall report thereon simultaneously to the United Nations Security Council and the General Assembly through the Secretary-General of the United Nations, and to the Council of the Organization of American States. The General Conference shall likewise report to the International Atomic Energy Agency for such purposes as are relevant in accordance with its Statute.

....

Signature

Article 25. 1. This Treaty shall be open indefinitely for signature by:

(a) All the Latin American Republics, and

(b) All other sovereign States situated in their entirety south of latitude 35° north in the western hemisphere; and, except as provided in paragraph 2 of this article, all such States which become sovereign, when they have been admitted by the General Conference.

2. The General Conference shall not take any decision regarding the admission of a political entity part or all of whose territory is the subject, prior to the date when this Treaty is opened for signature, of a dispute or claim between an extra-continental country and one or more Latin American States, so long as the dispute has not been settled by peaceful means.

....

Entry into Force

Article 28. 1. Subject to the provisions of paragraph 2 of this article, this Treaty shall enter into force among the States that have ratified it as soon as the following requirements have been met:

(a) Deposit of the instruments of ratification of this Treaty with the Depositary Government by the Governments of the States mentioned in article 25 which are in existence on the date when this Treaty is opened for signature and which are not affected by the provisions of article 25, paragraph 2;

(b) Signature and ratification of Additional Protocol I annexed to this Treaty by all extra-continental or continental States having de jure or de facto international responsibility for territories situated in the zone of application of the Treaty;

(c) Signature and ratification of the Additional Protocol II annexed to this Treaty by all powers possessing nuclear weapons;

(d) Conclusion of bilateral or multilateral agreements on the application of Safeguards System of the International Atomic Energy Agency in accordance with article 13 of this Treaty.

2. All signatory States shall have the imprescriptible right to waive, wholly or in part, the requirements laid down in the preceding paragraph. They may do so by means of a declaration which shall be annexed to their respective instrument of ratification and which may be formulated at the time of deposit of the instrument or subsequently. For those States which exercise this right, this Treaty shall enter into force upon deposit of the declaration, or as soon as those requirements have been met which have not been expressly waived.

3. As soon as this Treaty has entered into force in accordance with the provisions of paragraph 2 for eleven States, the Depositary Government shall convene a preliminary meeting of those States in order that the Agency may be set up and commence its work.

4. After the entry into force of this Treaty for all the countries of the zone, the rise of a new power possessing nuclear weapons shall have the effect of suspending the execution of this Treaty for those countries which have ratified it without waiving requirements of paragraph 1, sub-paragraph (c) of this article, and which request such suspension; the Treaty shall remain suspended until the new power, on its own initiative or upon request by the General Conference, ratifies the annexed Additional Protocol II.

....

ADDITIONAL PROTOCOL I

The undersigned Plenipotentiaries, furnished with full powers by their respective Governments,

Convinced that the Treaty for the Prohibition of Nuclear Weapons in Latin America, negotiated and signed in accordance with the recommendations of the General Assembly of the United Nations in Resolution 1911 (XVIII) of 27 November 1963, represents an important step towards ensuring the non-proliferation of nuclear weapons,

Aware that the non-proliferation of nuclear weapons is not an end in itself but, rather, a means of achieving general and complete disarmament at a later stage, and

Desiring to contribute, so far as lies in their power, towards ending the armaments race, especially in the field of nuclear weapons, and towards strengthening a world at peace, based on mutual respect and sovereign equality of States,

Have agreed as follows:

Article 1. To undertake to apply the statute of denuclearization in respect of warlike purposes as defined in articles 1, 3, 5 and 13 of the Treaty for the Prohibition of Nuclear Weapons in Latin America in territories for which, *de jure* or *de facto*, they are internationally responsible and which lie within the limits of the geographical zone established in that Treaty.

Article 2. The duration of this Protocol shall be the same as that of the Treaty for the Prohibition of Nuclear Weapons in Latin America of which this Protocol is an annex, and the provisions regarding ratification and denunciation contained in the Treaty shall be applicable to it.

Article 3. This Protocol shall enter into force, for the States which have ratified it, on the date of the deposit of their respective instruments of ratification.

IN WITNESS WHEREOF the undersigned Plenipotentiaries, having deposited their full powers, found in good and due form, sign this Protocol on behalf of their respective Governments.

ADDITIONAL PROTOCOL II

The undersigned Plenipotentiaries, furnished with full powers by their respective Governments,

Convinced that the Treaty for the Prohibition of Nuclear Weapons in Latin America, negotiated and signed in accordance with the recommendations of the General Assembly of the United Nations in Resolution 1911 (XVIII) of 27 November 1963, represents an important step towards ensuring the non-proliferation of nuclear weapons,

Aware that the non-proliferation of nuclear weapons is not an end in itself but, rather, a means of achieving general and complete disarmament at a later stage, and

Desiring to contribute, so far as lies in their power, towards ending the armaments race, especially in the field of nuclear weapons, and towards promoting and strengthening a world at peace, based on mutual respect and sovereign equality of States,

Have agreed as follows:

Article 1. The statute of denuclearization of Latin America in respect or warlike purposes, as defined, delimited and set forth in the Treaty for the Prohibition of Nuclear Weapons in Latin America of which this instrument is an annex, shall be fully respected by the Parties to this Protocol in all its express aims and provisions.

Article 2. The Governments represented by the undersigned Plenipotentiaries undertake, therefore, not to contribute in any way to the performance of acts involving a violation of the obligations of article 1 of the Treaty in the territories to which the Treaty applies in accordance with article 4 thereof.

Article 3. The Governments represented by the undersigned Plenipotentiaries also undertake not to use or threaten to use nuclear weapons against the Contracting Parties of the Treaty for the Prohibition of Nuclear Weapons in Latin America.

Article 4. The duration of this Protocol shall be the same as that of the Treaty for the Prohibition of Nuclear Weapons in Latin America of which this protocol is an annex, and the definitions of territory and nuclear weapons set forth in articles 3 and 5 of the Treaty shall be applicable to this Protocol, as well as the provisions regarding ratification, reservations, denunciation, authentic texts and registration contained in articles 26, 27, 30 and 31 of the Treaty.

Article 5. This Protocol shall enter into force, for the States which have ratified it, on the date of the deposit of their respective instruments of ratification.

IN WITNESS WHEREOF the undersigned Plenipotentiaries, having deposited their full powers, found in good and due form, sign this Additional Protocol on behalf of their respective Governments.

SOUTH PACIFIC NUCLEAR WEAPONS FREE ZONE TREATY*

Preamble

The Parties to this Treaty,

United in their commitment to a world at peace;

Gravely concerned that the continuing nuclear arms race presents the risk of nuclear war which would have devastating consequences for all people;

Convinced that all countries have an obligation to make every effort to achieve the goal of eliminating nuclear weapons, the terror which they hold for humankind and the threat which they pose to life on earth;

Believing that regional arms control measures can contribute to global efforts to reverse the nuclear arms race and promote the national security of each country in the region and the common security of all;

Determined to ensure, so far as lies within their power, that the bounty and beauty of the land and sea in their region shall remain the heritage of their peoples and their descendants in perpetuity to be enjoyed by all in peace;

Reaffirming the importance of the Treaty on the Non-Proliferation of Nuclear Weapons (NPT) in preventing the proliferation of nuclear weapons and in contributing to world security;

Noting, in particular, that Article VII of the NPT recognizes the right of any group of States to conclude regional treaties in order to assure the total absence of nuclear weapons in their respective territories;

Noting that the prohibitions of emplantation and emplacement of nuclear weapons on the seabed and the ocean floor and in the subsoil thereof contained in the Treaty on the Prohibition of the Emplacement of Nuclear Weapons and Other Weapons of Mass Destruction on the Seabed and the Ocean Floor and in the Subsoil Thereof apply in the South Pacific;

Noting also that the prohibition of testing of nuclear weapons in the atmosphere or under water, including territorial waters or high seas, contained in the Treaty Banning Nuclear Weapon Tests in the Atmosphere, in Outer Space and Under Water applies in the South Pacific;

Determined to keep the region free of environmental pollution by radioactive wastes and other radioactive matter;

---

* South Pacific Nuclear Free Zone Treaty, Aug. 6, 1985, 1445 U.N.T.S. 177, 178 (entered into force Dec. 11, 1986), *available at* http://www.state.gov/t/ac/trt/5189.htm. In 1996, Protocols 1, 2, and 3 were signed by the United States and the United Kingdom, and ratified by France, but have not yet entered into force for the U.S. or U.K. *See* South Pacific Nuclear Free Zone Treaty, Concluded at Rarotonga on 6 August 1985. Protocols 1-3, Aug. 8, 1986, 28 I.L.M. 1599, 1600, 1971 U.N.T.S. 470 (entered into force Apr. 21, 1988). Protocols 2 and 3 were ratified by China and U.S.S.R. in 1988.

Guided by the decision of the Fifteenth South Pacific Forum at Tuvalu that a nuclear free zone should be established in the region at the earliest possible opportunity in accordance with the principles set out in the communique of that meeting;

Have agreed as follows:

Article 1. Usage of Terms. For the purposes of this Treaty and its Protocols:

(a) "South Pacific Nuclear Free Zone" means the areas described in Annex 1 as illustrated by the map attached to that Annex;

(b) "territory" means internal waters, territorial sea and archipelagic waters, the seabed and subsoil beneath, the land territory and the airspace above them;

(c) "nuclear explosive device" means any nuclear weapon or other explosive device capable of releasing nuclear energy, irrespective of the purpose for which it could be used. The term includes such a weapon or device in unassembled and partly assembled forms, but does not include the means of transport or delivery of such a weapon or device if separable from and not an indivisible part of it;

(d) "stationing" means emplantation, emplacement, transportation on land or inland waters, stockpiling, storage, installation and deployment.

Article 2. Application of the Treaty. 1. Except where otherwise specified, this Treaty and its Protocols shall apply to territory within the South Pacific Nuclear Free Zone.

2. Nothing in this Treaty shall prejudice or in any way affect the rights, or the exercise of the rights, of any State under international law with regard to freedom of the seas.

Article 3. Renunciation of Nuclear Explosive Devices. Each Party undertakes:

(a) not to manufacture or otherwise acquire, possess or have control over any nuclear explosive device by any means anywhere inside or outside the South Pacific Nuclear Free Zone;

(b) not to seek or receive any assistance in the manufacture or acquisition of any nuclear explosive device;

(c) not to take any action to assist or encourage the manufacture or acquisition of any nuclear explosive device by any State.

Article 4. Peaceful Nuclear Activities. Each Party undertakes:

(a) not to provide source or special fissionable material, or equipment or material especially designed or prepared for the processing, use or production of special fissionable material for peaceful purposes to:

(i) any non-nuclear-weapon State unless subject to the safeguards required by Article III.1 of the NPT, or

(ii) any nuclear-weapon State unless subject to applicable safeguards agreements with the International Atomic Energy Agency (IAEA).

Any such provisions shall be in accordance with strict non-proliferation measures to provide assurance of exclusively peaceful non-explosive use;

(b) to support the continued effectiveness of the international non-proliferation system based on the NPT and the IAEA safeguards system.

Article 5. Prevention of Stationing of Nuclear Explosive Devices. 1. Each Party undertakes to prevent in its territory the stationing of any nuclear explosive device.

2. Each Party in the exercise of its sovereign rights remains free to decide for itself whether to allow visits by foreign ships and aircraft to its ports and airfields, transit of its airspace by foreign aircraft, and navigation by foreign ships in its territorial sea or archipelagic waters in a manner not covered by the rights of innocent passage, archipelagic sea lane passage or transit passage of straits.

Article 6. Prevention of Testing of Nuclear Explosive Devices. Each Party undertakes:

(a) to prevent in its territory the testing of any nuclear explosive device;

(b) not to take any action to assist or encourage the testing of any nuclear explosive device by any State.

Article 7. Prevention of Dumping. 1. Each Party undertakes:

(a) not to dump radioactive wastes and other radioactive matter at sea anywhere within the South Pacific Nuclear Free Zone.

(b) to prevent the dumping of radioactive wastes and other radioactive matter by anyone in its territorial sea;

(c) not to take any action to assist or encourage the dumping by anyone of radioactive wastes and other radioactive matter at sea anywhere within the South Pacific Nuclear Free Zone;

(d) to support the conclusion as soon as possible of the proposed Convention relating to the protection of the natural resources and environment of the South Pacific region and its Protocol for the prevention of pollution of the South Pacific region by dumping, with the aim of precluding dumping at sea of radioactive wastes and other radioactive matter by anyone anywhere in the region.

2. Paragraphs l(a) and l(b) of this Article shall not apply to areas of the South Pacific Nuclear Free Zone in respect of which such a Convention and Protocol have entered into force.

Article 8. Control System. 1. The Parties hereby establish a control system for the purpose of verifying compliance with their obligations under this Treaty.

2. The control system shall comprise:

(a) reports and exchange of information as provided for in Article 9;

(b) consultations as provided for in Article 10 and Annex 4 (1);

(c) the application to peaceful nuclear activities of safeguards by the IAEA as provided for in Annex 2;

(d) a complaints procedure as provided for in Annex 4.

Article 9. Reports and Exchanges of Information. 1. Each Party shall report to the Director of the South Pacific Bureau for Economic Co-operation (the Director) as soon as possible any significant event within its jurisdiction affecting the implementation of this Treaty. The Director shall circulate such reports promptly to all Parties.

2. The Parties shall endeavour to keep each other informed on matters arising under or in relation to this Treaty. They may exchange information by communicating it to the Director, who shall circulate it to all Parties.

3. The Director shall report annually to the South Pacific Forum on the status of this Treaty and matters arising under or in relation to it, incorporating reports and communications made under paragraphs 1 and 2 of this Article and matters arising under Articles 8(2)(d) and 10 and Annex 2(4).

Article 10. Consultations and Review. Without prejudice to the conduct of consultations among Parties by other means, the Director, at the request of any Party, shall convene a meeting of the Consultative Committee established by Annex 3 for consultation and co-operation on any matter arising in relation to this Treaty or for reviewing its operation.

Article 11. Amendment. The Consultative Committee shall consider proposals for amendment of the provisions of this Treaty proposed by any Party and circulated by the Director to all Parties not less than three months prior to the convening of the Consultative Committee for this purpose. Any proposal agreed upon by consensus by the Consultative Committee shall be communicated to the Director who shall circulate it for acceptance to all Parties. An amendment shall enter into force thirty days after receipt by the depositary of acceptances from all Parties.

Article 12. Signature and Ratification. 1. This Treaty shall be open for signature by any Member of the South Pacific Forum.

2. This Treaty shall be subject to ratification. Instruments of ratification shall be deposited with the Director who is hereby designated depositary of this Treaty and its Protocols.

3. If a Member of the South Pacific Forum whose territory is outside the South Pacific Nuclear Free Zone becomes a Party to this Treaty, Annex 1 shall be deemed to be amended so far as is required to enclose at least the territory of that Party within the boundaries of the South Pacific Nuclear Free Zone. The delineation of any area added pursuant to this paragraph shall be approved by the South Pacific Forum.

Article 13. Withdrawal. 1. This Treaty is of a permanent nature and shall remain in force indefinitely, provided that in the event of a violation by any Party of a provision of this Treaty essential to the achievement of the objectives of the Treaty or of the spirit of the Treaty, every other Party shall have the right to withdraw from the Treaty.

2. Withdrawal shall be effected by giving notice twelve months in advance to the Director who shall circulate such notice to all other Parties.

Article 14. Reservations. This Treaty shall not be subject to reservations.

Article 15. Entry into Force. 1. This Treaty shall enter into force on the date of deposit of the eighth instrument of ratification.

2. For a signatory which ratifies this Treaty after the date of deposit of the eighth instrument of ratification, the Treaty shall enter into force on the date of deposit of its instrument of ratification.

Article 16. Depositary Functions. The depositary shall register this Treaty and its Protocols pursuant to Article 102 of the Charter of the United Nations and shall transmit certified copies of the Treaty and its Protocols to all Members of the South Pacific Forum and all States eligible to become Party to the Protocols to the Treaty and shall notify them of signatures and ratifications of the Treaty and its Protocols.

IN WITNESS WHEREOF the undersigned, being duly authorized by their Governments, have signed this Treaty.

....

Protocol I

The Parties to this Protocol

Noting the South Pacific Nuclear Free Zone Treaty (the Treaty)

Have agreed as follows:

Article 1. Each Party undertakes to apply, in respect of the territories for which it is internationally responsible situated within the South Pacific Nuclear Free Zone, the prohibitions contained in Articles 3, 5 and 6, insofar as they related to the manufacture, stationing and testing of any nuclear explosive device within those territories, and the safeguards specified in Article 8(2)(c) and Annex 2 of the Treaty.

Article 2. Each Party may, by written notification to the depositary, indicate its acceptance from the date of such notification of any alteration to its obligation under this Protocol brought about by the entry into force of an amendment to the Treaty pursuant to Article 11 of the Treaty.

Article 3. This Protocol shall be open for signature by the French Republic, the United Kingdom of Great Britain and Northern Ireland and the United States of America.

Article 4. This Protocol shall be subject to ratification.

Article 5. This Protocol is of a permanent nature and shall remain in force indefinitely, provided that each Party shall, in exercising its national sovereignty, have the right to withdraw from this Protocol if it decides that extraordinary events, related to the subject matter of this Protocol, have jeopardized its supreme interests. It shall give notice of such withdrawal to the depositary three months in advance. Such notice shall include a statement of the extraordinary events it regards as having jeopardized its supreme interests.

Article 6. This Protocol shall enter into force for each State on the date of its deposit with the depositary of its instrument of ratification.

IN WITNESS WHEREOF the undersigned, being duly authorized by their Governments, have signed this Protocol.

. . . .

Protocol II

The Parties to this Protocol

Noting the South Pacific Nuclear Free Zone Treaty (the Treaty)

Have agreed as follows:

Article 1. Each Party undertakes not to use or threaten to use any nuclear explosive device against:

(a) Parties to the Treaty; or

(b) Any territory within the South Pacific Nuclear Free Zone for which a State that has become a Party to Protocol 1 is internationally responsible.

Article 2. Each Party undertakes not to contribute to any act of a Party to the Treaty which constitutes a violation of the Treaty, or to any act of another Party to a Protocol which constitutes a violation of a Protocol.

Article 3. Each Party may, by written notification to the depositary, indicate its acceptance from the date of such notification of any alteration to its obligation under this Protocol brought about by the entry into force of an amendment to the Treaty pursuant to Article 11 of the Treaty or by the extension of the South Pacific Nuclear Free Zone pursuant to Article 12(3) of the Treaty.

Article 4. This Protocol shall be open for signature by the French Republic, the People's Republic of China, the Union of Soviet Socialist Republics, the United Kingdom of Great Britain and Northern Ireland and the United States of America.

Article 5. This Protocol shall be subject to ratification.

Article 6. This Protocol is of a permanent nature and shall remain in force indefinitely, provided that each Party shall, in exercising its national sovereignty, have the right to withdraw from this Protocol if it decides that extraordinary events, related to the subject matter of this Protocol, have jeopardized its supreme interests. It shall give notice of such withdrawal to the depositary three months in advance. Such notice shall include a statement of the extraordinary events it regards as having jeopardized its supreme interests.

Article 7. This Protocol shall enter into force for each State on the date of its deposit with the depositary of its instrument of ratification.

IN WITNESS WHEREOF the undersigned, being duly authorized by their Governments, have signed this Protocol.

. . . .

Protocol III

The Parties to this Protocol

Noting the South Pacific Nuclear Free Zone Treaty (the Treaty)

Have agreed as follows:

Article 1. Each Party undertakes not to test any nuclear explosive device anywhere within the South Pacific Nuclear Free Zone.

Article 2. Each Party may, by written notification to the depositary, indicate its acceptance from the date of such notification of any alteration to its obligation under this Protocol brought about by the entry into force of an amendment to the Treaty pursuant to Article 11 of the Treaty or by the extension of the South Pacific Nuclear Free Zone pursuant to Article 12(3) of the Treaty.

Article 3. This Protocol shall be open for signature by the French Republic, the People's Republic of China, the Union of Soviet Socialist Republics, the United Kingdom of Great Britain and Northern Ireland and the United States of America.

Article 4. This Protocol shall be subject to ratification.

Article 5. This Protocol is of a permanent nature and shall remain in force indefinitely, provided that each Party shall, in exercising its national sovereignty, have the right to withdraw from this Protocol if it decides that extraordinary events, related to the subject matter of this Protocol, have jeopardized its supreme interests. It shall give notice of such withdrawal to the depositary three months in advance. Such notice shall include a statement of the extraordinary events it regards as having jeopardized its supreme interests.

Article 6. This Protocol shall enter into force for each State on the date of its deposit with the depositary of its instrument of ratification.

IN WITNESS WHEREOF the undersigned, being duly authorized by their Governments, have signed this Protocol.

. . . .

TREATY ON CONVENTIONAL ARMED FORCES IN EUROPE* (CFE TREATY)

The Kingdom of Belgium, the Republic of Bulgaria, Canada, the Czech and Slovak Federal Republic, the Kingdom of Denmark, the French Republic, the Federal Republic of Germany, the Hellenic Republic, the Republic of Hungary, the Republic of Iceland, the Italian Republic, the Grand Duchy of Luxembourg, the Kingdom of the Netherlands, the Kingdom of Norway, the Republic of Poland, the Portuguese Republic, Romania, the Kingdom of Spain, the Republic of Turkey, the Union of Soviet Socialist Republics, the United Kingdom of Great Britain and Northern Ireland and the United States of America, hereinafter referred to as the States Parties,

Guided by the Mandate for Negotiation on Conventional Armed Forces in Europe of January 10, 1989, and having conducted this negotiation in Vienna beginning on March 9, 1989,

Guided by the objectives and the purposes of the Conference on Security and Cooperation in Europe, within the framework of which the negotiation of this Treaty was conducted,

Recalling their obligation to refrain in their mutual relations, as well as in their international relations in general, from the threat or use of force against the territorial integrity or political independence of any State, or in any other manner inconsistent with the purposes and principles of the Charter of the United Nations,

Conscious of the need to prevent any military conflict in Europe,

Conscious of the common responsibility which they all have for seeking to achieve greater stability and security in Europe,

Striving to replace military confrontation with a new pattern of security relations among all the States Parties based on peaceful cooperation and thereby to contribute to overcoming the division of Europe,

Committed to the objectives of establishing a secure and stable balance of conventional armed forces in Europe at lower levels than heretofore, of eliminating disparities prejudicial to stability and security and of eliminating, as a matter of high priority, the capability for launching surprise attack and for initiating large-scale offensive action in Europe,

Recalling that they signed or acceded to the Treaty of Brussels of 1948, the Treaty of Washington of 1949 or the Treaty of Warsaw of 1955 and that they have the right to be or not to be a party to treaties of alliance,

Committed to the objective of ensuring that the numbers of conventional armaments and equipment limited by the Treaty within the area of application of this Treaty do not exceed 40,000 battle tanks, 60,000 armoured combat vehicles, 40,000 pieces of artillery, 13,600 combat aircraft and 4,000 attack helicopters,

Affirming that this Treaty is not intended to affect adversely the security interests of any State,

---

* Nov. 18, 1990, S. Treaty Doc. No. 102-8, at 223 (1991), 30 I.L.M. 1, *available at* http://www.state.gov/t/ac/trt/4781.htm.

Affirming their commitment to continue the conventional arms control process including negotiations, taking into account future requirements for European stability and security in the light of political developments in Europe,

Have agreed as follows:

Article I. 1. Each State Party shall carry out the obligations set forth in this Treaty in accordance with its provisions, including those obligations relating to the following five categories of conventional armed forces: battle tanks, armoured combat vehicles, artillery, combat aircraft and combat helicopters.

2. Each State Party also shall carry out the other measures set forth in this Treaty designed to ensure security and stability both during the period of reduction of conventional armed forces and after the completion of reductions.

....

Article II. 1. For the purposes of this Treaty:

(A) The term "group of States Parties" means the group of States Parties that signed the Treaty of Warsaw of 1955 consisting of the Republic of Bulgaria, the Czech and Slovak Federal Republic, the Republic of Hungary, the Republic of Poland, Romania and the Union of Soviet Socialist Republics, or the group of States Parties that signed or acceded to the Treaty of Brussels of 1948 or the Treaty of Washington of 1949 consisting of the Kingdom of Belgium, Canada, the Kingdom of Denmark, the French Republic, the Federal Republic of Germany, the Hellenic Republic, the Republic of Iceland, the Italian Republic, the Grand Duchy of Luxembourg, the Kingdom of the Netherlands, the Kingdom of Norway, the Portuguese Republic, the Kingdom of Spain, the Republic of Turkey, the United Kingdom of Great Britain and Northern Ireland and the United States of America.

(B) The term "area of application" means the entire land territory of the States Parties in Europe from the Atlantic Ocean to the Ural Mountains, which includes all the European island territories of the States Parties, including the Faroe Islands of the Kingdom of Denmark, Svalbard including Bear Island of the Kingdom of Norway, the islands of Azores and Madeira of the Portuguese Republic, the Canary Islands of the Kingdom of Spain and Franz Josef Land and Novaya Zemlya of the Union of Soviet Socialist Republics. In the case of the Union of Soviet Socialist Republics, the area of application includes all territory lying west of the Ural River and the Caspian Sea. In the case of the Republic of Turkey, the area of application includes the territory of the Republic of Turkey north and west of a line extending from the point of intersection of the Turkish border with the 39th parallel to Muradiye, Patnos, Karayazi, Tekman, Kemaliye, Feke, Ceyhan, Dogankent, Gzne and thence to the sea.

....

Article IV. 1. Within the area of application, as defined in Article II, each State Party shall limit and, as necessary, reduce its battle tanks, armoured combat vehicles, artillery, combat aircraft and attack helicopters so that, 40 months after entry into force of this Treaty and thereafter, for the group of States Parties to which it belongs, as defined in Article II, the aggregate numbers do not exceed:

(A) 20,000 battle tanks, of which no more than 16,500 shall be in active units;

(B) 30,000 armoured combat vehicles, of which no more than 27,300 shall be in active units. Of the 30,000 armoured combat vehicles, no more than 18,000 shall be armoured infantry fighting vehicles and heavy armament combat vehicles; of armoured infantry fighting vehicles and heavy armament combat vehicles, no more than 1,500 shall be heavy armament combat vehicles;

(C) 20,000 pieces of artillery, of which no more than 17,000 shall be in active units;

(D) 6,800 combat aircraft; and

(E) 2,000 attack helicopters.

Battle tanks, armoured combat vehicles and artillery not in active units shall be placed in designated permanent storage sites, as defined in Article II, and shall be located only in the area described in paragraph 2 of this Article. Such designated permanent storage sites may also be located in that part of the territory of the Union of Soviet Socialist Republics comprising the Odessa Military District and the southern part of the Leningrad Military District. In the Odessa Military District, no more than 400 battle tanks and no more than 500 pieces of artillery may be thus stored. In the southern part of the Leningrad Military District, no more than 600 battle tanks, no more than 800 armoured combat vehicles, including no more than 300 armoured combat vehicles of any type with the remaining number consisting of armoured personnel carriers, and no more than 400 pieces of artillery may be thus stored. The southern part of the Leningrad Military District is understood to mean the territory within that military district south of the line East-West 60 degrees 15 minutes northern latitude.

2. Within the area consisting of the entire land territory in Europe, which includes all the European island territories, of the Kingdom of Belgium, the Czech and Slovak Federal Republic, the Kingdom of Denmark including the Faroe Islands, the French Republic, the Federal Republic of Germany, the Republic of Hungary, the Italian Republic, the Grand Duchy of Luxembourg, the Kingdom of the Netherlands, the Republic of Poland, the Portuguese Republic including the islands of Azores and Madeira, the Kingdom of Spain including the Canary Islands, the United Kingdom of Great Britain and Northern Ireland and that part

of the territory of the Union of Soviet Socialist Republics west of the Ural Mountains comprising the Baltic, Byelorussian, Carpathian, Kiev, Moscow and Volga-Ural Military Districts, each State Party shall limit and, as necessary, reduce its battle tanks, armoured combat vehicles and artillery so that, 40 months after entry into force of this Treaty and thereafter, for the group of States Parties to which it belongs the aggregate numbers do not exceed:

(A) 15,300 battle tanks, of which no more than 11,800 shall be in active units;

(B) 24,100 armoured combat vehicles, of which no more than 21,400 shall be in active units; and

(C) 14,000 pieces of artillery, of which no more than 11,000 shall be in active units.

3. Within the area consisting of the entire land territory in Europe, which includes all the European island territories, of the Kingdom of Belgium, the Czech and Slovak Federal Republic, the Kingdom of Denmark including the Faroe Islands, the French Republic, the Federal Republic of Germany, the Republic of Hungary, the Italian Republic, the Grand Duchy of Luxembourg, the Kingdom of the Netherlands, the Republic of Poland, the United Kingdom of Great Britain and Northern Ireland and that part of the territory of the Union of Soviet Socialist Republics comprising the Baltic, Byelorussian, Carpathian and Kiev Military Districts, each State Party shall limit and, as necessary, reduce its battle tanks, armoured combat vehicles and artillery so that, 40 months after

entry into force of this Treaty and thereafter, for the group of States Parties to which it belongs the aggregate numbers in active units do not exceed:

(A) 10,300 battle tanks;

(B) 19,260 armoured combat vehicles; and

(C) 9,100 pieces of artillery; and

(D) in the Kiev Military District, the aggregate numbers in active units and designated permanent storage sites together shall not exceed:

(1) 2,250 battle tanks;

(2) 2,500 armoured combat vehicles; and

(3) 1,500 pieces of artillery.

4. Within the area consisting of the entire land territory in Europe, which includes all the European island territories, of the Kingdom of Belgium, the Czech and Slovak Federal Republic, the Federal Republic of Germany, the Republic of Hungary, the Grand Duchy of Luxembourg, the Kingdom of the Netherlands and the Republic of Poland, each State Party shall limit and, as necessary, reduce its battle tanks, armoured combat vehicles and artillery so that, 40 months after entry into force of this Treaty and thereafter, for the group of States Parties to which it belongs the aggregate numbers in active units do not exceed:

(A) 7,500 battle tanks;

(B) 11,250 armoured combat vehicles; and

(C) 5,000 pieces of artillery.

5. States Parties belonging to the same group of States Parties may locate battle tanks, armoured combat vehicles and artillery in active units in each of the areas described in this Article and Article V, paragraph 1, subparagraph (A) up to the numerical limitations applying in that area, consistent with the maximum levels for holdings notified pursuant to Article VII and provided that no State Party stations conventional armed forces on the territory of another State Party without the agreement of that State Party.

6. If a group of States Parties' aggregate numbers of battle tanks, armoured combat vehicles and artillery in active units within the area described in paragraph 4 of this Article are less than the numerical limitations set forth in paragraph 4 of this Article, and provided that no State Party is thereby prevented from reaching its maximum levels for holdings notified in accordance with Article VII, paragraphs 2, 3 and 5, then amounts equal to the difference between the aggregate numbers in each of the categories of battle tanks, armoured combat vehicles and artillery and the specified numerical limitations for that area may be located by States Parties belonging to that group of States Parties in the area described in paragraph 3 of this Article, consistent with the numerical limitations specified in paragraph 3 of this Article.

Article V. 1. To ensure that the security of each State Party is not affected adversely at any stage:

(A) within the area consisting of the entire land territory in Europe, which includes all the European island territories, of the Republic of Bulgaria, the Hellenic Republic, the Republic of Iceland, the Kingdom of Norway, Romania, the part of the Republic of Turkey within the area of application and that part of the Union of Soviet Socialist Republics comprising the Leningrad, Odessa, Transcaucasus and North Caucasus Military Districts, each State Party shall limit and, as necessary, reduce its battle tanks, armoured combat vehicles and artillery so that, 40 months after entry into force of this Treaty and thereafter, for the group of States Parties to which it belongs the aggregate numbers in active units do not exceed the difference between the overall numerical limitations set forth in Article IV, paragraph 1 and those in Article IV, paragraph 2, that is:

(1) 4,700 battle tanks;

(2) 5,900 armoured combat vehicles; and

(3) 6,000 pieces of artillery;

(B) notwithstanding the numerical limitations set forth in subparagraph (A) of this paragraph, a State Party or States Parties may on a temporary basis deploy into the territory belonging to the members of the same group of States Parties within the area described in subparagraph (A) of this paragraph additional aggregate numbers in active units for each group of States Parties not to exceed:

(1) 459 battle tanks;

(2) 723 armoured combat vehicles; and

(3) 420 pieces of artillery; and

(C) provided that for each group of States Parties no more than one-third of each of these additional aggregate numbers shall be deployed to any State Party with territory within the area described in subparagraph (A) of this paragraph, that is:

(1) 153 battle tanks;

(2) 241 armoured combat vehicles; and

(3) 140 pieces of artillery.

2. Notification shall be provided to all other States Parties no later than at the start of the deployment by the State Party or States Parties conducting the deployment and by the recipient State Party or States Parties, specifying the total number in each category of battle tanks, armoured combat vehicles and artillery deployed. Notification also shall be provided to all other States Parties by the State Party or States Parties conducting the deployment and by the recipient State Party or States Parties within 30 days of the withdrawal of those battle tanks, armoured combat vehicles and artillery that were temporarily deployed.

Article VI. With the objective of ensuring that no single State Party possesses more than approximately one-third of the conventional armaments and equipment limited by the Treaty within the area of application, each State Party shall limit and, as necessary, reduce its battle tanks, armoured combat vehicles, artillery, combat aircraft and attack helicopters so that, 40 months after entry into force of this Treaty and thereafter, the numbers within the area of application for that State Party do not exceed:

(A) 13,300 battle tanks;

(B) 20,000 armoured combat vehicles;

(C) 13,700 pieces of artillery;

(D) 5,150 combat aircraft; and

Article VII. 1. In order that the limitations set forth in Articles IV, V and VI are not exceeded, no State Party shall exceed, from 40 months after entry into force of this Treaty, the maximum levels which it has previously agreed upon within its group of

States Parties, in accordance with paragraph 7 of this Article, for its holdings of conventional armaments and equipment limited by the Treaty and of which it has provided notification pursuant to the provisions of this Article.

2. Each State Party shall provide at the signature of this Treaty notification to all other States Parties of the maximum levels for its holdings of conventional armaments and equipment limited by the Treaty. The notification of the maximum levels for holdings of conventional armaments and equipment limited by the Treaty provided by each State Party at the signature of this Treaty shall remain valid until the date specified in a subsequent notification pursuant to paragraph 3 of this Article.

3. In accordance with the limitations set forth in Articles IV, V and VI, each State Party shall have the right to change the maximum levels for its holdings of conventional armaments and equipment limited by the Treaty. Any change in the maximum levels for holdings of a State Party shall be notified by that State Party to all other States Parties at least 90 days in advance of the date, specified in the notification, on which such a change takes effect. In order not to exceed any of the limitations set forth in Articles IV and V, any increase in the maximum levels for holdings of a State Party that would otherwise cause those limitations to be exceeded shall be preceded or accompanied by a corresponding reduction in the previously notified maximum levels for holdings of conventional armaments and equipment limited by the Treaty of one or more States Parties belonging to the same group of States Parties. The notification of a change in the maximum levels for holdings shall remain valid from the date specified in the notification until the date specified in a subsequent notification of change pursuant to this paragraph.

4. Each notification required pursuant to paragraph 2 or 3 of this Article for armoured combat vehicles shall also include maximum levels for the holdings of armoured infantry fighting vehicles and heavy armament combat vehicles of the State Party providing the notification.

5. Ninety days before expiration of the 40-month period of reductions set forth in Article VIII and subsequently at the time of any notification of a change pursuant to paragraph 3 of this Article, each State Party shall provide notification of the maximum levels for its holdings of battle tanks, armoured combat vehicles and artillery with respect to each of the areas described in Article IV, paragraphs 2 to 4 and Article V, paragraph 1, subparagraph (A).

6. A decrease in the numbers of conventional armaments and equipment limited by the Treaty held by a State Party and subject to notification pursuant to the Protocol on Information Exchange shall by itself confer no right on any other State Party to increase the maximum levels for its holdings subject to notification pursuant to this Article.

7. It shall be the responsibility solely of each individual State Party to ensure that the maximum levels for its holdings notified pursuant to the provisions of this Article are not exceeded. States Parties belonging to the same group of States Parties shall consult in order to ensure that the maximum levels for holdings notified pursuant to the provisions of this Article, taken together as appropriate, do not exceed the limitations set forth in Articles IV, V and VI.

....

Article XIII. 1. For the purpose of ensuring verification of compliance with the provisions of this Treaty, each State Party shall provide notifications and exchange information pertaining to its conventional armaments and equipment in accordance with the Protocol on Information Exchange.

2. Such notifications and exchange of information shall be provided in accordance with Article XVII.

3. Each State Party shall be responsible for its own information; receipt of such information and of notifications shall not imply validation or acceptance of the information provided.

Article XIV. 1. For the purpose of ensuring verification of compliance with the provisions of this Treaty, each State Party shall have the right to conduct, and the obligation to accept, within the area of application, inspections in accordance with the provisions of the Protocol on Inspection.

2. The purpose of such inspections shall be:

(A) to verify, on the basis of the information provided pursuant to the Protocol on Information Exchange, the compliance of States Parties with the numerical limitations set forth in Articles IV, V and VI;

(B) to monitor the process of reduction of battle tanks, armoured combat vehicles, artillery, combat aircraft and attack helicopters carried out at reduction sites in accordance with Article VIII and the Protocol on Reduction; and

(C) to monitor the certification of recategorized multi-purpose attack helicopters and reclassified combat-capable trainer aircraft carried out in accordance with the Protocol on Helicopter Recategorization and the Protocol on Aircraft Reclassification, respectively.

3. No State Party shall exercise the rights set forth in paragraphs 1 and 2 of this Article in respect of States Parties which belong to the group of States Parties to which it belongs in order to elude the objectives of the verification regime.

4. In the case of an inspection conducted jointly by more than one State Party, one of them shall be responsible for the execution of the provisions of this Treaty.

5. The number of inspections pursuant to Sections VII and VIII of the Protocol on Inspection which each State Party shall have the right to conduct and the obligation to accept during each specified time period shall be determined in accordance with the provisions of Section II of that Protocol.

6. Upon completion of the 120-day residual level validation period, each State Party shall have the right to conduct, and each State Party with territory within the area of application shall have the obligation to accept, an agreed number of aerial inspections within the area of application. Such agreed numbers and other applicable provisions shall be developed during negotiations referred to in Article XVIII.

Article XV. 1. For the purpose of ensuring verification of compliance with the provisions of this Treaty, a State Party shall have the right to use, in addition to the procedures referred to in Article XIV, national or multinational technical means of verification at its disposal in a manner consistent with generally recognized principles of international law.

2. A State Party shall not interfere with national or multinational technical means of verification of another State Party operating in accordance with paragraph 1 of this Article.

3. A State Party shall not use concealment measures that impede verification of compliance with the provisions of this Treaty by national or multinational technical means of verification of another State Party operating in accordance with paragraph 1 of this

Article. This obligation does not apply to cover or concealment practices associated with normal personnel training, maintenance or operations involving conventional armaments and equipment limited by the Treaty.

Article XVI.

1. To promote the objectives and implementation of the provisions of this Treaty, the States Parties hereby establish a Joint Consultative Group.

2. Within the framework of the Joint Consultative Group, the States Parties shall:

(A) address questions relating to compliance with or possible circumvention of the provisions of this Treaty;

(B) seek to resolve ambiguities and differences of interpretation that may become apparent in the way this Treaty is implemented;

(C) consider and, if possible, agree on measures to enhance the viability and effectiveness of this Treaty;

(D) update the lists contained in the Protocol on Existing Types, as required by Article II, paragraph 2;

(E) resolve technical questions in order to seek common practices among the States Parties in the way this Treaty is implemented;

(F) work out or revise, as necessary, rules of procedure, working methods, the scale of distribution of expenses of the Joint Consultative Group and of conferences convened under this Treaty and the distribution of costs of inspections between or among States Parties;

(G) consider and work out appropriate measures to ensure that information obtained through exchanges of information among the States Parties or as a result of inspections pursuant to this Treaty is used solely for the purposes of this Treaty, taking into account the particular requirements of each State Party in respect of safeguarding information which that State Party specifies as being sensitive;

(H) consider, upon the request of any State Party, any matter that a State Party wishes to propose for examination by any conference to be convened in accordance with Article XXI; such consideration shall not prejudice the right of any State Party to resort to the procedures set forth in Article XXI; and

(I) consider matters of dispute arising out of the implementation of this Treaty.

3. Each State Party shall have the right to raise before the Joint Consultative Group, and have placed on its agenda, any issue relating to this Treaty.

4. The Joint Consultative Group shall take decisions or make recommendations by consensus. Consensus shall be understood to mean the absence of any objection by any representative of a State Party to the taking of a decision or the making of a recommendation.

5. The Joint Consultative Group may propose amendments to this Treaty for consideration and confirmation in accordance with Article XX. The Joint Consultative Group may also agree on improvements to the viability and effectiveness of this Treaty, consistent with its provisions. Unless such improvements relate only to minor matters of an administrative or technical nature, they shall be subject to consideration and confirmation in accordance with Article XX before they can take effect.

6. Nothing in this Article shall be deemed to prohibit or restrict any State Party from requesting information from or undertaking consultations with other States Parties on

matters relating to this Treaty and its implementation in channels or fora other than the Joint Consultative Group.

7. The Joint Consultative Group shall follow the procedures set forth in the Protocol on the Joint Consultative Group.

....

Article XVIII. 1. The States Parties, after signature of this Treaty, shall continue the negotiations on conventional armed forces with the same Mandate and with the goal of building on this Treaty.

2. The objective for these negotiations shall be to conclude an agreement on additional measures aimed at further strengthening security and stability in Europe, and pursuant to the Mandate, including measures to limit the personnel strength of their conventional armed forces within the area of application.

3. The States Parties shall seek to conclude these negotiations no later than the follow-up meeting of the Conference on Security and Cooperation in Europe to be held in Helsinki in 1992.

Article XIX. 1. This Treaty shall be of unlimited duration. It may be supplemented by a further treaty.

2. Each State Party shall, in exercising its national sovereignty, have the right to withdraw from this Treaty if it decides that extraordinary events related to the subject matter of this Treaty have jeopardized its supreme interests. A State Party intending to withdraw shall give notice of its decision to do so to the Depositary and to all other States Parties. Such notice shall be given at least 150 days prior to the intended withdrawal from this Treaty. It shall include a statement of the extraordinary events the State Party regards as having jeopardized its supreme interests.

3. Each State Party shall, in particular, in exercising its national sovereignty, have the right to withdraw from this Treaty if another State Party increases its holdings in battle tanks, armoured combat vehicles, artillery, combat aircraft or attack helicopters, as defined in Article II, which are outside the scope of the limitations of this Treaty, in such proportions as to pose an obvious threat to the balance of forces within the area of application.

Article XX. 1. Any State Party may propose amendments to this Treaty. The text of a proposed amendment shall be submitted to the Depositary, which shall circulate it to all the States Parties.

2. If an amendment is approved by all the States Parties, it shall enter into force in accordance with the procedures set forth in Article XXII governing the entry into force of this Treaty.

Article XXI. 1. Forty-six months after entry into force of this Treaty, and at five-year intervals thereafter, the Depositary shall convene a conference of the States Parties to conduct a review of the operation of this Treaty.

2. The Depositary shall convene an extraordinary conference of the States Parties, if requested to do so by any State Party which considers that exceptional circumstances relating to this Treaty have arisen, in particular, in the event that a State Party has announced its intention to leave its group of States Parties or to join the other group of States Parties, as defined in Article II, paragraph 1, subparagraph (A). In order to enable the other States Parties to prepare for this conference, the request shall include the reason why that State Party deems an extraordinary conference to be necessary. The

conference shall consider the circumstances set forth in the request and their effect on the operation of this Treaty. The conference shall open no later than 15 days after receipt of the request and, unless it decides otherwise, shall last no longer than three weeks.

3. The Depositary shall convene a conference of the States Parties to consider an amendment proposed pursuant to Article XX, if requested to do so by three or more States Parties. Such a conference shall open no later than 21 days after receipt of the necessary requests.

4. In the event that a State Party gives notice of its decision to withdraw from this Treaty pursuant to Article XIX, the Depositary shall convene a conference of the States Parties which shall open no later than 21 days after receipt of the notice of withdrawal in order to consider questions relating to the withdrawal from this Treaty.

Article XXII. 1. This Treaty shall be subject to ratification by each State Party in accordance with its constitutional procedures. Instruments of ratification shall be deposited with the Government of the Kingdom of the Netherlands, hereby designated the Depositary.

2. This Treaty shall enter into force 10 days after instruments of ratification have been deposited by all States Parties listed in the Preamble.

3. The Depositary shall promptly inform all States Parties of:

(A) the deposit of each instrument of ratification;

(B) the entry into force of this Treaty;

(C) any withdrawal in accordance with Article XIX and its effective date;

(D) the text of any amendment proposed in accordance with Article XX;

(E) the entry into force of any amendment to this Treaty;

(F) any request to convene a conference in accordance with Article XXI;

(G) the convening of a conference pursuant to Article XXI; and

(H) any other matter of which the Depositary is required by this Treaty to inform the States Parties.

4. This Treaty shall be registered by the Depositary pursuant to Article 102 of the Charter of the United Nations.

Article XXIII. The original of this Treaty, of which the English, French, German, Italian, Russian and Spanish texts are equally authentic, shall be deposited in the archives of the Depositary. Duly certified copies of this Treaty shall be transmitted by the Depositary to all the States Parties.

[Protocols referred to in Article 1, paragraph 3 are omitted].

WHITE HOUSE FACT SHEET: ADAPTATION OF THE TREATY ON CONVENTIONAL ARMED FORCES IN EUROPE* (CFE)

Background: The 1990 CFE Treaty

The CFE Treaty was signed in Paris on November 19, 1990 by the 22 NATO and Warsaw Pact nations. The Treaty established equal East-West limits on five key categories of conventional armaments—battle tanks, armored combat vehicles, artillery pieces, combat aircraft and attack helicopters—and thus eliminated the Warsaw Pact's longstanding numerical superiority in armor and artillery.

Subsequent to the break-up of the Soviet Union, all Soviet successor states with territory in the CFE area of application (Europe from the Atlantic to the Urals) joined the Treaty, so that Treaty Parties now number 30. Since the collapse of the Warsaw Pact, the break-up of the USSR, and NATO enlargement, the two-group structure has become obsolete.

More than 70,000 pieces of Treaty-Limited Equipment have been destroyed under the CFE Treaty and its associated documents, and thousands of intrusive on-site inspections have been conducted. The Treaty's detailed reporting and inspection requirements have provided unprecedented transparency and predictability of military forces in Europe; that will continue.

The 1999 Adapted Treaty

The Adaptation Agreement signed today updates the 1990 Treaty to create a new, highly stable, transparent set of limitations on conventional forces, and bring it in line with today's European security environment. In signing this agreement, we and the other States Parties have demonstrated our common commitment to enhancing security and stability in Europe.

- New Structure of Limitations. The Adaptation Agreement replaces the Treaty's obsolete bloc-to-bloc structure with nationally-based limits. Each state will have a national ceiling. States with territory in the CFE area of application will also have a territorial ceiling limiting the total amount of equipment that can be on their soil. This structure will, for example:
    - eliminate the outdated requirement for our new NATO allies to coordinate their equipment limits with Russia and other former Warsaw Pact countries;
    - reinforce the territorial sovereignty of individual States Parties by setting limits on a state-by-state basis; and
    - retain the principle of special restrictions on forces, including Russian forces, in the Treaty's flank region.

---

* Press Release, White House, Fact Sheet: Adaptation of the Treaty on Conventional Armed Forces in Europe (CFE) (Nov. 19, 1999), http://clinton4.nara.gov/WH/New/Europe-9911/facts/1999-11-19.html.

- Enhanced Transparency. The Adaptation Agreement builds on the original Treaty's intrusive verification and information regime. Under the adapted Treaty, States Parties will be required to provide more information than they provide on their forces currently. Quotas for mandatory on-site inspections will be increased.
- Host Nation Consent. The Adaptation Agreement strengthens requirements for host nation consent to the presence of foreign forces, including notifications to all parties as to whether such consent has been granted. These provisions address a key security concern of a number of non-NATO states, including Ukraine, Moldova, Georgia, and Azerbaijan. These requirements would not apply to NATO deployments in Kosovo because the Former Republic of Yugoslavia is not a CFE Party and, even if it were, the deployments there are authorized under the UN Charter.
- Accession Clause. The Adaptation Agreement allows for extending this stable security regime by opening it to other European states. Accession would be subject to approval by all 30 Parties.

CFE adaptation preserves NATO's ability to fulfill its post-Cold War responsibilities and is consistent with NATO's "Open Door" to potential new members. It will set new territorial ceilings at levels appropriate to peacetime stability, but allow for NATO operational flexibility to exceed these ceilings temporarily, for routine training purposes or reinforcement in a crisis. It also records the plans of a number of States Parties to adopt lower national ceilings, as a reflection of the changes in military requirements in Europe since 1990.

The CFE Final Act, also adopted by the CFE States Parties in Istanbul, contains a number of political commitments related to the adapted CFE Treaty. In particular:

- Responding to the concerns of many CFE States Parties about the implications of Russian deployments in Chechnya for CFE compliance, the Final Act includes a reaffirmation of Russia's November 1, 1999 commitment to fulfill all its obligations under the Treaty, in particular with respect to equipment levels in the flank region.
- The Final Act contains a Russian commitment to exercise restraint in its future deployments in the Kaliningrad and Pskov oblasts, which border the Baltic states.
- A number of countries in the center of Europe have committed not to increase, and in some cases, to reduce, their CFE territorial ceilings.
- The Final Act also reflects agreements between Georgia and Russia and between Moldova and Russia on withdrawals of Russian forces from their territories, reached in the last few days. These agreements were developed consistent with the adapted Treaty's enhanced provisions on host nation consent to the presence of foreign forces.

AGREEMENT ON ADAPTATION OF THE TREATY ON CONVENTIONAL ARMED FORCES IN EUROPE* (CFE TREATY)

Background Note

The 1999 Adapted CFE Treaty was signed on November 19, 1999 and updates the original Treaty to reflect the breakup of the Warsaw Pact and Soviet Union and the enlargement of NATO. The Agreement on Adaptation will enter into force when all the States Parties ratify it. The United States and NATO allies have stated that they will not ratify the agreement until Russia completes the withdrawal of its TLE from the territories of Georgia and Moldova. This Adaptation Agreement serves three major purposes:

1. To eliminate the systems of zones and groups in favor of individual ceilings for each member country;

2. To alter the geographic structure of the Treaty by eliminating "flank" zones and adapting the treaty to the Post Cold-War European Security environment;

3. To develop new means for accession to the Treaty by opening membership to all OSCE members.

—*Eds.*

The Republic of Armenia, the Republic of Azerbaijan, the Republic of Belarus, the Kingdom of Belgium, the Republic of Bulgaria, Canada, the Czech Republic, the Kingdom of Denmark, the French Republic, Georgia, the Federal Republic of Germany, the Hellenic Republic, the Republic of Hungary, the Republic of Iceland, the Italian Republic, the Republic of Kazakhstan, the Grand Duchy of Luxembourg, the Republic of Moldova, the Kingdom of the Netherlands, the Kingdom of Norway, the Republic of Poland, the Portuguese Republic, Romania, the Russian Federation, the Slovak Republic, the Kingdom of Spain, the Republic of Turkey, Ukraine, the United Kingdom of Great Britain and Northern Ireland, and the United States of America, hereinafter referred to as the States Parties,

Conscious of the fundamental changes that have occurred in Europe since the Treaty on Conventional Armed Forces in Europe was signed in Paris on 19 November 1990, hereinafter referred to as the Treaty,

Determined to sustain the key role of the Treaty as the cornerstone of European security,

Noting the fulfillment of the objective of the original Treaty of ensuring that the numbers of conventional armaments and equipment limited by the Treaty within the area of application of the Treaty would not exceed 40,000 battle tanks, 60,000 armoured combat vehicles, 40,000 pieces of artillery, 13,600 combat aircraft and 4,000 attack helicopters,

Have agreed as follows:

---

* Nov. 19, 1999, http://www.oscebih.org/documents/51-eng.pdf.

Article 1

The Preamble of the Treaty shall be deleted and replaced by:

"The Republic of Armenia, the Republic of Azerbaijan, the Republic of Belarus, the Kingdom of Belgium, the Republic of Bulgaria, Canada, the Czech Republic, the Kingdom of Denmark, the French Republic, Georgia, the Federal Republic of Germany, the Hellenic Republic, the Republic of Hungary, the Republic of Iceland, the Italian Republic, the Republic of Kazakhstan, the Grand Duchy of Luxembourg, the Republic of Moldova, the Kingdom of the Netherlands, the Kingdom of Norway, the Republic of Poland, the Portuguese Republic, Romania, the Russian Federation, the Slovak Republic, the Kingdom of Spain, the Republic of Turkey, Ukraine, the United Kingdom of Great Britain and Northern Ireland, and the United States of America, hereinafter referred to as the States Parties,

Guided by the Mandate for Negotiation on Conventional Armed Forces in Europe of 10 January 1989,

Guided by the objectives and the purposes of the Organization for (formerly Conference on) Security and Co-operation in Europe, within the framework of which the negotiation of this Treaty was conducted in Vienna,

Recalling their obligation to refrain in their mutual relations, as well as in their international relations in general, from the threat or use of force against the territorial integrity or political independence of any State, or in any other manner inconsistent with the purposes and principles of the Charter of the United Nations,

Conscious of the need to prevent any military conflict in Europe,

Conscious of the common responsibility which they all have for seeking to achieve greater stability and security in Europe, and bearing in mind their right to be or not to be a party to treaties of alliance,

Striving to develop further and consolidate a new pattern of security relations among all the States Parties based on peaceful cooperation and thereby to contribute to establishing a common and indivisible security space in Europe,

Committed to the objectives of establishing maintaining a secure, and stable and balanced overall level of conventional armed forces in Europe lower than heretofore, of eliminating disparities prejudicial to stability and security and of eliminating the capability for launching surprise attack and for initiating large-scale offensive action in Europe,

Affirming that this Treaty is not intended to affect adversely the security interests of any State,

Having taken note of the Final Act of the Conference of the States Parties to the Treaty on Conventional Armed Forces in Europe held in Istanbul from 17 to 19 November 1999, as well as of the statements made by certain States Parties concerning their political commitments referred to therein,

Affirming their commitment to continue the conventional arms control process including negotiations, taking into account the opening of the Treaty for accession by other participating States of the Organization for Security and Co-operation in Europe with territory in the geographic area between the Atlantic Ocean and the Urals Mountains as well as future requirements for European stability and security in the light of political developments in Europe,

Have agreed as follows:"

Article 2

Article I of the Treaty shall be deleted and replaced by the following:

"Article I

1. Each State Party shall carry out the obligations set forth in this Treaty in accordance with its provisions, including those obligations relating to the following five categories of conventional armed forces: battle tanks, armoured combat vehicles, artillery, combat aircraft and combat helicopters.

2. Each State Party shall also carry out the other measures set forth in this Treaty designed to ensure security and stability.

3. Conventional armaments and equipment of a State Party in the categories limited by the Treaty shall only be present on the territory of another State Party in conformity with international law, the explicit consent of the host State Party, or a relevant resolution of the United Nations Security Council. Explicit consent must be provided in advance, and must continue to be in effect as provided for in Article XIII, paragraph 1 *bis*.

4. This Treaty incorporates the Protocol on Existing Types of Conventional Armaments and Equipment, hereinafter referred to as the Protocol on Existing Types, with an Annex thereto; the Protocol on National Ceilings for Conventional Armaments and Equipment Limited by the Treaty on Conventional Armed Forces in Europe, hereinafter referred to as the Protocol on National Ceilings; the Protocol on Territorial Ceilings for Conventional Armaments and Equipment Limited by the Treaty on Conventional Armed Forces in Europe, hereinafter referred to as the Protocol on Territorial Ceilings; the Protocol on Procedures Governing the Reclassification of Specific Models or Versions of Combat-Capable Trainer Aircraft into Unarmed Trainer Aircraft, hereinafter referred to as the Protocol on Aircraft Reclassification; the Protocol on Procedures Governing the Reduction of Conventional Armaments and Equipment Limited by the Treaty on Conventional Armed Forces in Europe, hereinafter referred to as the Protocol on Reduction; the Protocol on Procedures Governing the Categorisation of Combat Helicopters and the Recategorisation of Multi-purpose Attack Helicopters, hereinafter referred to as the Protocol on Helicopter Recategorisation; the Protocol on Notification and Exchange of Information, hereinafter referred to as the Protocol on Information Exchange, with an Annex on the Format for the Exchange of Information, hereinafter referred to as the Annex on Format; the Protocol on Inspection; and the Protocol on the Joint Consultative Group.

Each of these documents constitutes an integral part of this Treaty."

Article 3

1. In Article II of the Treaty, paragraph 1, subparagraphs (A) and (G) shall be deleted.

2. In Article II of the Treaty, paragraph 1, subparagraph (B) shall be deleted and replaced by the following:

"(B) The term "area of application" means the entire land territory of the States Parties in Europe from the Atlantic Ocean to the Ural Mountains, which includes all the European island territories of the States Parties, including the Faroe Islands of the Kingdom of Denmark, Svalbard including Bear Island of the Kingdom of

Norway, the islands of Azores and Madeira of the Portuguese Republic, the Canary Islands of the Kingdom of Spain and Franz Josef Land and Novaya Zemlya of the Russian Federation.

....

Article 4

In Article III of the Treaty, paragraph 1 shall be deleted and replaced by the following:

"1. For the purposes of this Treaty, the States Parties shall apply the following counting rules:

All battle tanks, armoured combat vehicles, artillery, combat aircraft and attack helicopters, as defined in Article II, within the area of application shall be subject to the numerical limitations and other provisions set forth in Articles IV, V[,]VII, and in the Protocol on National Ceilings and the Protocol on Territorial Ceilings, with the exception of those which in a manner consistent with a State Party's normal practices:

(A) Are in the process of manufacture, including manufacturing-related testing;

(B) Are used exclusively for the purposes of research and development;

(C) Belong to historical collections;

(D) Are awaiting disposal, having been decommissioned from service in accordance with the provisions of Article IX;

(E) Are awaiting, or being refurbished for, export or re-export and are temporarily retained within the area of application. Such battle tanks, armoured combat vehicles, artillery, combat aircraft and attack helicopters shall be located elsewhere than at sites declared under the terms of Section V of the Protocol on Information Exchange or at no more than 10 such declared sites which shall have been notified in the previous year's annual information exchange. In the latter case, they shall be separately distinguishable from conventional armaments and equipment limited by the Treaty;

(F) Are, in the case of armoured personnel carriers, armoured infantry fighting vehicles (AIFVs), heavy armament combat vehicles (HACVs) or multipurpose attack helicopters, held by organisations designed and structured to perform in peacetime internal security functions; or

(G) Are in transit through the area of application from a location outside the area of application to a final destination outside the area of application, and are in the area of application for no longer than a total of seven days."

Article 5

Article IV of the Treaty shall be deleted and replaced by the following:

"Article IV

1. Within the area of application, each State Party shall limit and, as necessary, reduce its battle tanks, armoured combat vehicles, artillery, combat aircraft and attack helicopters so that the numbers do not exceed the national ceiling, the subceiling for active units and the subceiling for sub-categories established in accordance with this Article and the Protocol on National Ceilings for that State Party. The subceiling for active units shall establish the maximum number of battle tanks, armoured combat vehicles and pieces of artillery that a State Party may hold in active

units within the area of application. The subceiling for active units shall be equal to the national ceiling unless otherwise specified by the Protocol on National Ceilings. Any battle tanks, armoured combat vehicles and pieces of artillery under a national ceiling in any category in excess of the corresponding subceiling for active units shall be located in designated permanent storage sites. The subceiling for sub-categories shall establish the maximum aggregate number of armoured infantry fighting vehicles and heavy armament combat vehicles and the maximum number of heavy armament combat vehicles that a State Party may hold within the area of application in the category of armoured combat vehicles.

....

3. Each State Party shall have the right to change its national ceiling, its subceiling for active units and its subceiling for sub-categories as follows:

(A) Each State Party shall have the right, in accordance with paragraphs 4 and 6 of this Article, to increase its national ceiling, its subceiling for active units and its subceiling for sub-categories in any category or sub-category of conventional armaments and equipment limited by the Treaty. Any such increase shall be preceded or accompanied by a corresponding decrease in the national ceiling, the subceiling for active units or the subceiling for sub-categories of one or more other States Parties in the same category or sub-category, except as provided for in paragraph 6 of this Article. The State Party or States Parties undertaking the corresponding decrease in their national ceiling, subceiling for active units or subceiling for sub-categories shall notify all States Parties of their consent to the corresponding increase in the national ceiling, subceiling for active units or subceiling for sub-categories of another State Party. No national ceiling for a State Party with territory in the area of application shall exceed that State Party's territorial ceiling in the same category of conventional armaments and equipment limited by the Treaty.

(B) Each State Party shall have the right to decrease unilaterally its national ceiling, subceiling for active units or subceiling for sub-categories in any category or sub-category of conventional armaments and equipment limited by the Treaty. A unilateral decrease in the national ceiling, subceiling for active units or subceiling for sub-categories of a State Party shall by itself confer no right on any other State Party to increase its national ceiling, subceiling for active units or subceiling for sub-categories.

4. Within each five-year period between conferences of States Parties held in accordance with Article XXI, paragraph 1, each State Party shall have the right to increase its national ceiling or subceiling for active units:

(A) In the categories of battle tanks, armoured combat vehicles and artillery by no more than 40 battle tanks, 60 armoured combat vehicles and 20 pieces of artillery or 20 percent of the national ceiling established for that State Party in the Protocol on National Ceilings for battle tanks, armoured combat vehicles and artillery, whichever is greater, but in no case exceeding 150 battle tanks, 250 armoured combat vehicles and 100 pieces of artillery;

(B) In the categories of combat aircraft and attack helicopters by no more than 30 combat aircraft and 25 attack helicopters.

Each State Party shall have the right to increase its national ceiling or subceiling for active units in excess of the levels set forth in paragraph 4, subparagraphs (A) and (B) above, subject to the consent of all other States Parties.

5. A State Party intending to change its national ceiling, subceiling for active units or subceiling for sub-categories shall provide notification to all other States Parties at least 90 days in advance of the date, specified in the notification, on which such a change is to take effect. For increases subject to the consent of all other States Parties, the change shall take effect on the date specified in the notification provided that no State Party, within 60 days of the notification, objects to the change and notifies its objection to all other States Parties. A national ceiling, a subceiling for active units or a subceiling for sub-categories shall remain in effect until a change to that ceiling or subceiling takes effect.

....

Article 6

Article V of the Treaty shall be deleted and replaced by the following:

"Article V

1. Within the area of application, as defined in Article II, each State Party shall limit the total number of its battle tanks, armoured combat vehicles and artillery on its territory and of battle tanks, armoured combat vehicles and artillery of other States Parties that it permits to be present on its territory and each State Party shall limit its battle tanks, armoured combat vehicles and pieces of artillery present on the territory of other States Parties so that the overall numbers do not exceed the territorial ceilings and the territorial subceilings established in accordance with this Article and the Protocol on Territorial Ceilings, except as otherwise provided for in Article VII.

2. Battle tanks, armoured combat vehicles and artillery present on the territory of a State Party for an operation in support of peace conducted under and consistent with a resolution or a decision of the United Nations Security Council or the Organization for Security and Co-operation in Europe shall be exempt from that State Party's territorial ceiling or territorial subceiling. The duration of the presence of these battle tanks, armoured combat vehicles and artillery on the territory of a State Party shall be consistent with such a resolution or decision.

Battle tanks, armoured combat vehicles and artillery present on the territory of a State Party for an operation in support of peace pursuant to this paragraph shall be subject to notification in accordance with the Protocol on Information Exchange.

....

4. Each State Party shall have the right to change its territorial ceiling or territorial subceiling as follows:

(A) Each State Party shall have the right, in accordance with paragraph 5 of this Article, to increase its territorial ceiling or territorial subceiling for battle tanks, armoured combat vehicles and artillery in any category. Any such increase shall be preceded or accompanied by a corresponding decrease in the same category in the territorial ceiling or territorial subceiling of one or more other States Parties, subject to the provisions of the Protocol on Territorial Ceilings regarding relevant territorial ceilings and territorial subceilings. The State Party or States Parties undertaking the corresponding decrease in their territorial ceiling or territorial subceiling shall notify all States Parties of their consent to the corresponding increase in the territorial ceiling or territorial subceiling of another State Party.

(B) Each State Party shall have the right to decrease unilaterally its territorial ceiling or territorial subceiling for battle tanks, armoured combat vehicles and artillery in any category; however, no territorial ceiling in any category shall be at any time lower than the corresponding national ceiling. A unilateral decrease in the territorial ceiling or territorial subceiling of a State Party shall by itself confer no right on any other State Party to increase its territorial ceiling or territorial subceiling. Any decrease in a national ceiling under the provisions of Article IV, paragraph 6, shall result in a decrease of the corresponding territorial ceiling by an amount equal to the decrease in the national ceiling.

. . . .

6. A State Party intending to change its territorial ceiling or territorial subceiling in any category shall provide notification to all other States Parties at least 90 days in advance of the date, specified in the notification, on which such a change is to take effect. For increases subject to the consent of all other States Parties, the change shall take effect on the date specified in the notification provided that no State Party, within 60 days of the notification, objects to the change and notifies its objection to all other States Parties. A territorial ceiling, a subceiling for active units or a territorial subceiling for subcategories shall remain in effect until a change to that ceiling or subceiling takes effect."

Article 7

Article VI of the Treaty shall be deleted.

Article 8

Article VII of the Treaty shall be deleted and replaced by the following:

"Article VII

1. Each State Party shall have the right to exceed on a temporary basis, for military exercises and temporary deployments, the territorial ceilings and territorial subceilings established in the Protocol on Territorial Ceilings, subject to the provisions of this Article.

(A) Military exercises:

(1) Each State Party shall have the right to host on its territory military exercises which cause its territorial ceiling to be exceeded, and, for States Parties with a territorial subceiling, to conduct or host exercises which cause its territorial subceiling to be exceeded in accordance with the Protocol on Territorial Ceilings;

(2) The number of battle tanks, armoured combat vehicles and pieces of artillery present on the territory of a State Party in excess of its territorial ceiling or territorial subceiling for a military exercise, alone or in combination with any other military exercise or any temporary deployment on that territory, shall not exceed the number of battle tanks, armoured combat vehicles and pieces of artillery specified for each State Party in subparagraph (B), sub-subparagraph (1), of this paragraph and in the Protocol on Territorial Ceilings;

(3) A military exercise or successive military exercises notified in accordance with the Protocol on Information Exchange, that result in a territorial ceiling or a territorial subceiling being exceeded for more than 42 days shall thereafter be considered a temporary deployment as long as the territorial ceiling or territorial subceiling continues to be exceeded.

(B) Temporary deployments:

(1) Each State Party shall have the right to host on its territory temporary deployments in excess of its territorial ceiling, and, for States Parties with a territorial subceiling, to conduct or host temporary deployments in excess of their territorial subceiling. For this purpose, territorial ceilings and territorial subceilings may be exceeded, on a temporary basis, by no more than 153 battle tanks, 241 armoured combat vehicles and 140 pieces of artillery, unless otherwise set forth in the relevant provisions of the Protocol on Territorial Ceilings. In exceptional circumstances and unless otherwise set forth in the relevant provisions of the Protocol on Territorial Ceilings, a territorial ceiling may be exceeded, on a temporary basis, by no more than 459 battle tanks, 723 armoured combat vehicles and 420 pieces of artillery.

....

Article 9

Article VIII of the Treaty shall be deleted and replaced by the following:

"Article VIII

1. Any battle tanks, armoured combat vehicles, artillery, combat aircraft and attack helicopters in excess of the numerical limitations set forth in Article IV and in the Protocol on National Ceilings shall be eliminated only by means of reduction in accordance with the Protocol on Reduction, the Protocol on Helicopter Recategorisation, the Protocol on Aircraft Reclassification....

2. The categories of conventional armaments and equipment subject to reductions are battle tanks, armoured combat vehicles, artillery, combat aircraft and attack helicopters. The specific types are listed in the Protocol on Existing Types.

....

Article 14

1. In Article XIII of the Treaty, paragraph 1 shall be deleted and replaced by the following:

"1. For the purpose of ensuring verification of compliance with the provisions of this Treaty, each State Party shall provide notifications and exchange information pertaining to its conventional armaments and equipment and to the conventional armaments and equipment of other States Parties that it permits to be present on its territory, in accordance with the Protocol on Information Exchange."

2. In Article XIII of the Treaty, the following paragraph 1 *bis* shall be added:

"1. *bis* The presence of conventional armaments and equipment of a State Party on the territory of another State Party as set forth in Article V, paragraph 1, for transit as set forth in Article V, paragraph 3, for military exercises as set forth in Article VII, paragraph 1, subparagraph (A), and for temporary deployment as set forth in Article VII, paragraph 1, subparagraph (B), shall be in accordance with Article I, paragraph 3. Consent of the host State Party shall be reflected through the appropriate notifications in accordance with the Protocol on Information Exchange."

Article 15

Article XIV of the Treaty shall be deleted and replaced by the following:

"Article XIV

1. For the purpose of ensuring verification of compliance with the provisions of this Treaty, each State Party shall have the right to conduct, and the obligation to accept, within the area of application, inspections in accordance with the provisions of the Protocol on Inspection.

2. The purpose of such inspections shall be:

(A) To verify, on the basis of the information provided pursuant to the Protocol on Information Exchange, the compliance of States Parties with the numerical limitations set forth in Articles IV, V, and VII, the Protocol on National Ceilings and the Protocol on Territorial Ceilings;

(B) To monitor any reductions of battle tanks, armoured combat vehicles, artillery, combat aircraft and attack helicopters carried out at reduction sites in accordance with Article VIII and the Protocol on Reduction;

(C) To monitor the certification of recategorised multi-purpose attack helicopters and reclassified combat-capable trainer aircraft carried out in accordance with the Protocol on Helicopter Recategorisation and the Protocol on Aircraft Reclassification, respectively.

3. No State Party shall exercise the rights set forth in paragraphs 1 and 2 of this Article in order to elude the objectives of the verification regime.

4. In the case of an inspection conducted jointly by more than one State Party, one of them shall be responsible for the execution of the provisions of this Treaty.

5. The number of inspections pursuant to Sections VII and VIII of the Protocol on Inspection which each State Party shall have the right to conduct and the obligation to accept during each specified time period shall be determined in accordance with the provisions of Section II of that Protocol.

6. The number of inspections, pursuant to Section IX of the Protocol on Inspection, that each State Party shall have the right to conduct and the State Party whose territorial ceiling or territorial subceiling is temporarily exceeded shall have the obligation to accept shall be determined in accordance with the provisions of that Section.

7. Each State Party which carries out disposal of conventional armaments and equipment limited by the Treaty in excess of reduction liabilities shall provide for confirmation of the results of the disposal either by inviting an observation team or through the use of cooperative measures, in accordance with the provisions of Section XII of the Protocol on Inspection."

Article 16

In Article XVI of the Treaty, paragraph 2 shall be deleted and replaced by the following:

"2. Within the framework of the Joint Consultative Group, the States Parties shall:

(A) Address questions relating to compliance with or possible circumvention of the provisions of this Treaty;

(B) Seek to resolve ambiguities and differences of interpretation that may become apparent in the way this Treaty is implemented;

(C) Consider and, if possible, agree on measures to enhance the viability and effectiveness of this Treaty;

(D) Address, upon the request of any State Party, questions concerning the intention of any State Party to revise its national ceiling upwards under Article IV, paragraph 4, or its territorial ceiling under Article V, paragraph 5;

(E) Receive and consider the explanatory report, and any subsequent updates, provided in accordance with Article VII, paragraph 2;

(F) Update the lists contained in the Protocol on Existing Types, as required by Article II, paragraph 2;

(G) Consider measures of cooperation to enhance the verification regime of the Treaty, including through the appropriate utilisation of results of aerial inspections;

(HH) Resolve technical questions in order to seek common practices among the States Parties in the way this Treaty is implemented;

(II) Work out or revise, as necessary, rules of procedure, working methods, the scale of distribution of expenses of the Joint Consultative Group and of conferences convened under this Treaty and the distribution of costs of inspections between or among States Parties;

(JJ) Consider and work out appropriate measures to ensure that information obtained through exchanges of information among the States Parties or as a result of inspections pursuant to this Treaty is used solely for the purposes of this Treaty, taking into account the particular requirements of each State Party in respect of safeguarding information which that State Party specifies as being sensitive;

(KK) Consider, upon the request of any State Party, any matter that a State Party wishes to propose for examination by any conference to be convened in accordance with Article XXI; such consideration shall not prejudice the right of any State Party to resort to the procedures set forth in Article XXI;

(LL) Consider any request to accede to this Treaty, pursuant to Article XVIII, by acting as the body through which the States Parties may establish, and recommend approval of, the terms under which a requesting State accedes to the Treaty;

(MM) Conduct any future negotiations, if the States Parties so decide; and

(N) Consider matters of dispute arising out of the implementation of this Treaty."

....

Article 18

Article XVIII of the Treaty shall be deleted and replaced by the following:

"Article XVIII

[Placeholder for accession]

1. Any participating State of the Organization for Security and Co-operation in Europe whose land territory lies in Europe within the geographic area between the Atlantic Ocean and the Ural Mountains may submit to the Depositary a written request to accede to this Treaty.

2. The requesting State shall include in its request the following information:

(A) The designation of its existing types of conventional armaments and equipment;

(B) Its proposed national and territorial ceilings and the related subceilings for each category of armaments and equipment limited by the Treaty; and

(C) Any other information deemed relevant by the requesting State.

3. The Depositary shall notify all States Parties of the request and of the information provided by the requesting State.

4. The requesting State may modify or supplement this information. Any State Party may request additional information.

5. States Parties shall, beginning no later than 21 days after the notification pursuant to paragraph 3 of this Article, hold meetings of the Joint Consultative Group at which the States Parties shall address the request, conduct negotiations and establish the terms for accession. The requesting State may be invited to attend meetings of the Joint Consultative Group if the States Parties so decide.

6. Each request shall be considered individually by the States Parties in an expeditious manner. Any decision shall be taken by consensus.

7. The agreed terms for accession shall be enshrined in an Agreement on Accession between the States Parties and the requesting State, which shall be circulated to all States Parties and the requesting State by the Depositary and deposited in the archives of the Depositary.

8. Upon the receipt of confirmation of approval of the Agreement on Accession by all States Parties, the Depositary shall so inform all States Parties and the requesting State. The requesting State may then, subject to ratification in accordance with its constitutional procedures, submit an instrument of accession to the Treaty that shall acknowledge the terms and conditions of the Agreement on Accession.

9. This Treaty shall enter into force for the requesting State 10 days after the deposit of its instrument of accession to the Treaty with the Depositary, at which time the requesting State shall become a State Party to the Treaty."

Article 19

In Article XXI of the Treaty, paragraphs 1 and 2 shall be deleted and replaced by the following:

"1. Forty-six months after entry into force of this Treaty, and at five-year intervals thereafter, the Depositary shall convene a conference of the States Parties to conduct a review of the operation of this Treaty, to include, *inter alia*, a review of the operation and the levels of national ceilings, territorial ceilings and territorial subceilings, and related commitments, together with other Treaty elements, taking into account the need to ensure that the security of no State Party is diminished.

....

2. The Depositary shall convene an extraordinary conference of the States Parties if requested to do so by any State Party which considers that exceptional circumstances relating to this Treaty have arisen. In order to enable the other States Parties to prepare for this conference, the request shall include the reason why that State Party deems an extraordinary conference to be necessary. The conference shall consider the circumstances set forth in the request and their effect on the operation of this Treaty. The conference shall open no later than 15 days after receipt of the request and, unless it decides otherwise, shall last no longer than three weeks."

Article 20

1. In Article XXII of the Treaty, paragraph 1 shall be deleted and replaced by the following:

"1. This Treaty shall be subject to ratification by each State Party in accordance with its constitutional procedures; it shall be open for accession by new States pursuant to Article XVIII. Instruments of ratification and, in the case of accession, instruments of accession shall be deposited with the Government of the Kingdom of the Netherlands, hereby designated the Depositary."

....

Article 26

The Protocol on Notification and Exchange of Information, with an Annex on the Format for the Exchange of Information, shall be deleted and replaced by the following:

"PROTOCOL ON NOTIFICATION AND EXCHANGE OF INFORMATION

The States Parties hereby agree on procedures and provisions regarding notification and exchange of information pursuant to Article XIII of the Treaty on Conventional Armed Forces in Europe.

SECTION I. INFORMATION ON THE STRUCTURE OF EACH STATE PARTY'S LAND FORCES AND AIR AND AIR DEFENCE AVIATION FORCES WITHIN THE AREA OF APPLICATION

1. Each State Party shall provide to all other States Parties the following information about the structure of its land forces and air and air defence aviation forces within the area of application:

(A) The command organisation of its land forces, specifying the designation and subordination of all combat, combat support and combat service support formations and units at each level of command down to the level of brigade/regiment or equivalent level, including air defence formations and units subordinated at or below the military district or equivalent level. Independent units at the next level of command below the brigade/regiment level directly subordinate to formations above the brigade/regiment level (i.e., independent battalions) shall be identified, with the information indicating the formation or unit to which such units are subordinated;

(B) The command organisation of its air and air defence aviation forces, specifying the designation and subordination of formations and units at each level of command down to wing/air regiment or equivalent level. Independent units at the next level of command below the wing/air regiment level directly subordinate to formations above the wing/air regiment level (i.e., independent squadrons) shall be identified, with the information indicating the formation or unit to which such units are subordinated; and

(C) The designation and subordination of military installations as specified in Section III, paragraph 3, subparagraphs (A) and (B), of this Protocol.

SECTION II. INFORMATION ON THE OVERALL HOLDINGS IN EACH CATEGORY OF CONVENTIONAL ARMAMENTS AND EQUIPMENT LIMITED BY THE TREATY AND ON THE OVERALL HOLDINGS OF CERTAIN CONVENTIONAL ARMAMENTS AND EQUIPMENT SUBJECT TO THE TREATY

1. Each State Party shall provide to all other States Parties information on:

(A) Overall numbers and numbers by type of its holdings in each category of conventional armaments and equipment limited by the Treaty and subject to the numerical limitations set forth in the Protocol on National Ceilings;

(B) Overall numbers and numbers by type of its holdings of battle tanks, armoured combat vehicles and artillery by States Parties' territory and territory with a subceiling as countable against the numerical limitations set forth in the Protocol on Territorial Ceilings;

(C) Overall numbers and numbers by type of its holdings of combat aircraft and attack helicopters by States Parties' territory as countable against the numerical limitations set forth in the Protocol on National Ceilings;

. . . .

SECTION V. INFORMATION ON OBJECTS OF VERIFICATION AND DECLARED SITES

1. Each State Party shall provide to all other States Parties information specifying its objects of verification, including the total number and the designation of each object of verification, and enumerating its declared sites, as defined in Section I of the Protocol on Inspection. . . .

. . . .

SECTION XII. CONVENTIONAL ARMAMENTS AND EQUIPMENT IN TRANSIT THROUGH OR WITHIN THE AREA OF APPLICATION

1. Conventional armaments and equipment in the categories specified in Section III of this Protocol which entered the area of application in transit shall be reported pursuant to this Protocol only if they remain within the area of application for a period longer than seven days.

2. In the case of transit of battle tanks, armoured combat vehicles and artillery in accordance with Article V of the Treaty, each State Party undertaking such transit shall provide to all other States Parties the following information no later than the day the conventional armaments and equipment in transit enter the territory of the first transited State Party or a territory with a subceiling:

(A) Start date of the transit;

(B) Mode of transportation;

(C) First State Party transited;

(D) The categories of armaments and equipment in transit; and

(E) The State Party or the territory with a subceiling into which the conventional armaments and equipment in transit entered the area of application; or

(F) The State Party or the territory with a subceiling of origin of the conventional armaments and equipment in transit, as applicable.

. . . .

SECTION XVII. INFORMATION ON AUTHORIZATION TO MAKE USE OF A STATE PARTY'S HEADROOM

1. Each State Party with territory in the area of application shall notify all other States Parties of the entitlement authorised for use by another State Party of the headroom between its national holdings of battle tanks, armoured combat vehicles

and artillery on its territory and its territorial ceiling in those categories. Such notification shall be provided no later than the effective date of the authorisation and shall specify the maximum headroom authorised for use by a State Party, the start date and the effective duration of the authorisation. The notifying State Party shall update its notification if it modifies the authorisation.

....

SECTION XVIII. INFORMATION WHEN A TERRITORIAL CEILING OR A TERRITORIAL SUBCEILING IS TEMPORARILY EXCEEDED

1. Each State Party with territory within the area of application shall notify all other States Parties whenever its territorial ceiling or territorial subceiling is temporarily exceeded in accordance with Article VII of this Treaty.

2. Each State Party which participates with its battle tanks, armoured combat vehicles or artillery in an activity that results in exceeding either another State Party's territorial ceiling or territorial subceiling or its own territorial subceiling shall notify all other States Parties.

....

ANNEX ON THE FORMAT FOR THE EXCHANGE OF INFORMATION

....

Article 27

The Protocol on Inspection shall be deleted and replaced by the following:

"PROTOCOL ON INSPECTION

The States Parties hereby agree on procedures and other provisions governing the conduct of inspections as provided for in Article XIV of the Treaty on Conventional Armed Forces in Europe.

....

SECTION IV. NOTIFICATION OF INTENT TO INSPECT

1. The inspecting State Party shall notify the inspected State Party of its intention to carry out an inspection provided for in Article XIV of the Treaty.

In the case of inspection pursuant to Section VII of this Protocol of conventional armed forces of a State Party other than the State Party on whose territory the inspection is to be carried out, that State Party shall also be notified, regardless of whether it will be the first or a sequential inspection.

In the case of inspection pursuant to Section IX of this Protocol, the inspecting State Party shall notify the host State Party.

In the case of inspection of certification or reduction procedures carried out by a State Party on the territory of another State Party, the inspecting State Party shall simultaneously notify the host State Party and the other State Party.

....

SECTION VII. DECLARED SITE INSPECTION

1. Inspection of a declared site pursuant to this Protocol shall not be refused. Such inspections may be delayed only in cases of force majeure or in accordance

with Section II, paragraphs 7, 25 and 26, of this Protocol. In the case of force majeure the provisions of Section VI, paragraph 1, of this Protocol shall apply.

....

SECTION VIII. CHALLENGE INSPECTION WITHIN A SPECIFIED AREA

1. Each State Party shall have the right to conduct challenge inspections within specified areas in accordance with this Protocol.

....

Article 28

1. In the Protocol on the Joint Consultative Group, paragraph 3 shall be deleted and replaced by the following:

> "3. The Joint Consultative Group shall meet for regular sessions to be held two times per year, unless it decides otherwise."

....

Article 31

1. This Agreement on Adaptation shall be subject to ratification by each State Party in accordance with its constitutional procedures.

2. Instruments of ratification shall be deposited with the Depositary.

3. This Agreement on Adaptation shall enter into force 10 days after instruments of ratification have been deposited by all States Parties listed in the Preamble, after which time the Treaty shall exist only in its amended form.

....

TREATY ON OPEN SKIES*

The States concluding this Treaty, hereinafter referred to collectively as the States Parties or individually as a State Party,

Recalling the commitments they have made in the Conference on Security and Co-operation in Europe to promoting greater openness and transparency in their military activities and to enhancing security by means of confidence- and security-building measures,

Welcoming the historic events in Europe which have transformed the security situation from Vancouver to Vladivostok,

Wishing to contribute to the further development and strengthening of peace, stability and co-operative security in that area by the creation of an Open Skies regime for aerial observation,

Recognizing the potential contribution which an aerial observation regime of this type could make to security and stability in other regions as well,

Noting the possibility of employing such a regime to improve openness and transparency, to facilitate the monitoring of compliance with existing or future arms control agreements and to strengthen the capacity for conflict prevention and crisis management in the framework of the Conference on Security and Co-operation in Europe and in other relevant international institutions,

Envisaging the possible extension of the Open Skies regime into additional fields, such as the protection of the environment,

Seeking to establish agreed procedures to provide for aerial observation of all the territories of States Parties, with the intent of observing a single State Party or groups of States Parties, on the basis of equity and effectiveness while maintaining flight safety,

Noting that the operation of such an Open Skies regime will be without prejudice to States not participating in it,

Have agreed as follows:

Article I. *General Provisions.* 1. This Treaty establishes the regime, to be known as the Open Skies regime, for the conduct of observation flights by States Parties over the territories of other States Parties, and sets forth the rights and obligations of the States Parties relating thereto.

2. Each of the Annexes and their related Appendices constitutes an integral part of this Treaty.

Article II. *Definitions.* For the purposes of this Treaty:

1. The term "observed Party" means the State Party or group of States Parties over whose territory an observation flight is conducted or is intended to be conducted, from the time it has received notification thereof from an observing Party until completion of the procedures relating to that flight, or personnel acting on behalf of that State Party or group of States Parties.

---

* Treaty on Open Skies, Mar. 24, 1992, S. Treaty Doc. No. 102-37, at 2, 1992 U.S.T. LEXIS 179 (entered into force Jan. 1, 2002), *available at* http://www.state.gov/t/np/trty/18467.htm.

2. The term "observing Party" means the State Party or group of States Parties that intends to conduct or conducts an observation flight over the territory of another State Party or group of States Parties, from the time that it has provided notification of its intention to conduct an observation flight until completion of the procedures relating to that flight, or personnel acting on behalf of that State Party or group of States Parties.

3. The term "group of States Parties" means two or more States Parties that have agreed to form a group for the purposes of this Treaty.

4. The term "observation aircraft" means an unarmed, fixed wing aircraft designated to make observation flights, registered by the relevant authorities of a State Party and equipped with agreed sensors. The term "unarmed" means that the observation aircraft used for the purposes of this Treaty is not equipped to carry and employ weapons.

5. The term "observation flight" means the flight of the observation aircraft conducted by an observing Party over the territory of an observed Party, as provided in the flight plan, from the point of entry or Open Skies airfield to the point of exit or Open Skies airfield.

6. The term "transit flight" means a flight of an observation aircraft or transport aircraft conducted by or on behalf of an observing Party over the territory of a third State Party en route to or from the territory of the observed Party.

7. The term "transport aircraft" means an aircraft other than an observation aircraft that, on behalf of the observing Party, conducts flights to or from the territory of the observed Party exclusively for the purposes of this Treaty.

8. The term "territory" means the land, including islands, and internal and territorial waters, over which a State Party exercises sovereignty.

9. The term "passive quota" means the number of observation flights that each State Party is obliged to accept as an observed Party.

10. The term "active quota" means the number of observation flights that each State Party has the right to conduct as an observing Party.

11. The term "maximum flight distance" means the maximum distance over the territory of the observed Party from the point at which the observation flight may commence to the point at which that flight may terminate, as specified in Annex A to this Treaty.

12. The term "sensor" means equipment of a category specified in Article IV, paragraph 1 that is installed on an observation aircraft for use during the conduct of observation flights.

13. The term "ground resolution" means the minimum distance on the ground between two closely located objects distinguishable as separate objects.

14. The term "infra-red line-scanning device" means a sensor capable of receiving and visualizing thermal electro-magnetic radiation emitted in the invisible infra-red part of the optical spectrum by objects due to their temperature and in the absence of artificial illumination.

15. The term "observation period" means a specified period of time during an observation flight when a particular sensor installed on the observation aircraft is operating.

16. The term "flight crew" means individuals from any State Party who may include, if the State Party so decides, interpreters and who perform duties associated with the operation or servicing of an observation aircraft or transport aircraft.

17. The term "pilot-in-command" means the pilot on board the observation aircraft who is responsible for the operation of the observation aircraft, the execution of the flight plan, and the safety of the observation aircraft.

18. The term "flight monitor" means an individual who, on behalf of the observed Party, is on board an observation aircraft provided by the observing Party during the observation flight and who performs duties in accordance with Annex G to this Treaty.

19. The term "flight representative" means an individual who, on behalf of the observing Party, is on board an observation aircraft provided by the observed Party during an observation flight and who performs duties in accordance with Annex G to this Treaty.

20. The term "representative" means an individual who has been designated by the observing Party and who performs activities on behalf of the observing Party in accordance with Annex G during an observation flight on an observation aircraft designated by a State Party other than the observing Party or the observed Party.

21. The term "sensor operator" means an individual from any State Party who performs duties associated with the functioning, operation and maintenance of the sensors of an observation aircraft.

22. The term "inspector" means an individual from any State Party who conducts an inspection of sensors or observation aircraft of another State Party.

23. The term "escort" means an individual from any State Party who accompanies the inspectors of another State Party.

24. The term "mission plan" means a document, which is in a format established by the Open Skies Consultative Commission, presented by the observing Party that contains the route, profile, order of execution and support required to conduct the observation flight, which is to be agreed upon with the observed Party and which will form the basis for the elaboration of the flight plan.

25. The term "flight plan" means a document elaborated on the basis of the agreed mission plan in the format and with the content specified by the International Civil Aviation Organization, hereinafter referred to as the ICAO, which is presented to the air traffic control authorities and on the basis of which the observation flight will be conducted.

26. The term "mission report" means a document describing an observation flight completed after its termination by the observing Party and signed by both the observing and observed Parties, which is in a format established by the Open Skies Consultative Commission.

27. The term "Open Skies airfield" means an airfield designated by the observed Party as a point where an observation flight may commence or terminate.

28. The term "point of entry" means a point designated by the observed Party for the arrival of personnel of the observing Party on the territory of the observed Party.

29. The term "point of exit" means a point designated by the observed Party for departure of personnel of the observing Party from the territory of the observed Party.

30. The term "refueling airfield" means an airfield designated by the observed Party used for fuelling and servicing of observation aircraft and transport aircraft.

31. The term "alternate airfield" means an airfield specified in the flight plan to which an observation aircraft or transport aircraft may proceed when it becomes inadvisable to land at the airfield of intended landing.

32. The term "hazardous airspace" means the prohibited areas, restricted areas and danger areas, defined on the basis of Annex 2 to the Convention on International Civil Aviation, that are established in accordance with Annex 15 to the Convention on International Civil Aviation in the interests of flight safety, public safety and environmental protection and about which information is provided in accordance with ICAO provisions.

33. The term "prohibited area" means an airspace of defined dimensions, above the territory of a State Party, within which the flight of aircraft is prohibited.

34. The term "restricted area" means an airspace of defined dimensions, above the territory of a State Party, within which the flight of aircraft is restricted in accordance with specified conditions.

35. The term "danger area" means an airspace of defined dimensions within which activities dangerous to the flight of aircraft may exist at specified times.

Article III. *Quotas.*

SECTION I. GENERAL PROVISIONS

1. Each State Party shall have the right to conduct observation flights in accordance with the provisions of this Treaty.

2. Each State Party shall be obliged to accept observation flights over its territory in accordance with the provisions of this Treaty.

3. Each State Party shall have the right to conduct a number of observation flights over the territory of any other State Party equal to the number of observation flights which that other State Party has the right to conduct over it.

4. The total number of observation flights that each State Party is obliged to accept over its territory is the total passive quota for that State Party. The allocation of the total passive quota to the States Parties is set forth in Annex A, Section I to this Treaty.

5. The number of observation flights that a State Party shall have the right to conduct each year over the territory of each of the other States Parties is the individual active quota of that State Party with respect to that other State Party. The sum of the individual active quotas is the total active quota of that State Party. The total active quota of a State Party shall not exceed its total passive quota.

6. The first distribution of active quotas is set forth in Annex A, Section II to this Treaty.

7. After entry into force of this Treaty, the distribution of active quotas shall be subject to an annual review for the following calendar year within the framework of the Open Skies Consultative Commission. In the event that it is not possible during the annual review to arrive within three weeks at agreement on the distribution of active quotas with respect to a particular State Party, the previous year's distribution of active quotas with respect to that State Party shall remain unchanged.

8. Except as provided for by the provisions of Article VIII, each observation flight conducted by a State Party shall be counted against the individual and total active quotas of that State Party.

9. Notwithstanding the provisions of paragraphs 3 and 5 of this Section, a State Party to which an active quota has been distributed may, by agreement with the State Party to be overflown, transfer a part or all of its total active quota to other States Parties and shall promptly notify all other States Parties and the Open Skies Consultative Commission thereof. Paragraph 10 of this Section shall apply.

10. No State Party shall conduct more observation flights over the territory of another State Party than a number equal to 50 percent, rounded up to the nearest whole number, of its own total active quota, or of the total passive quota of that other State Party, whichever is less.

11. The maximum flight distances of observation flights over the territories of the States Parties are set forth in Annex A, Section III to this Treaty.

SECTION II. PROVISIONS FOR A GROUP OF STATES PARTIES

....

Article IV. Sensors. 1. Except as otherwise provided for in paragraph 3 of this Article, observation aircraft shall be equipped with sensors only from amongst the following categories:

(a) optical panoramic and framing cameras;

(b) video cameras with real-time display;

(c) infra-red line-scanning devices; and

(d) sideways-looking synthetic aperture radar.

8. In the event that the observation aircraft is provided by, the observing Party, the observing Party shall have the right to use an observation aircraft equipped with sensors in each sensor category that do not exceed the capability specified in paragraph 2 of this Article.

9. In the event that the observation aircraft used for an observation flight is provided by the observed Party, the observed Party shall be obliged to provide an observation aircraft equipped with sensors from each sensor category specified in paragraph 1 of this Article, at the maximum capability and in the numbers specified in paragraph 2 of this Article, subject to the provisions of Article XVIII, Section II, unless otherwise agreed by the observing and observed Parties. The package and configuration of such sensors shall be installed in such a way so as to provide coverage of the ground provided for in paragraph 2 of this Article. In the event that the observation aircraft is provided by the observed Party, the latter shall provide a sideways-looking synthetic aperture radar with a ground resolution of no worse than six metres, determined by the object separation method.

10. When designating an aircraft as an observation aircraft pursuant to Article V of this Treaty, each State Party shall inform all other States Parties of the technical information on each sensor installed on such aircraft as provided for in Annex B to this Treaty.

....

Article V. Aircraft Designation. 1. Each State Party shall have the right to designate as observation aircraft one or more types or models of aircraft registered by the relevant authorities of a State Party.

2. Each State Party shall have the right to designate types or models of aircraft as observation aircraft or add new types or models of aircraft to those designated earlier by it, provided that it notifies all other States Parties 30 days in advance thereof. The notification of the designation of aircraft of a type or model shall contain the information specified in Annex C to this Treaty.

3. Each State Party shall have the right to delete types or models of aircraft designated earlier by it, provided that it notifies all other States Parties 90 days in advance thereof.

4. Only one exemplar of a particular type and model of aircraft with an identical set of associated sensors shall be required to be offered for certification in accordance with the provisions of Annex D to this Treaty.

5. Each observation aircraft shall be capable of carrying the flight crew and the personnel specified in Article VI, Section III.

Article VI. *Choice of Observation Aircraft, General Provisions for the Conduct of Observation Flights, and Requirements for Mission Planning.*

SECTION I. CHOICE OF OBSERVATION AIRCRAFT AND GENERAL PROVISIONS FOR THE CONDUCT OF OBSERVATION FLIGHTS

1. Observation flights shall be conducted using observation aircraft that have been designated by a State Party pursuant to Article V. Unless the observed Party exercises its right to provide an observation aircraft that it has itself designated, the observing Party shall have the right to provide the observation aircraft. In the event that the observing Party provides the observation aircraft, it shall have the right to provide an aircraft that it has itself designated or an aircraft designated by another State Party. In the event that the observed Party provides the observation aircraft, the observing Party shall have the right to be provided with an aircraft capable of achieving a minimum unrefueled range, including the necessary fuel reserves, equivalent to one-half of the flight distance, as notified in accordance with paragraph 5, subparagraph (G) of this Section.

2. Each State Party shall have the right, pursuant to paragraph 1 of this Section, to use an observation aircraft designated by another State Party for observation flights. Arrangements for the use of such aircraft shall be worked out by the States Parties involved to allow for active participation in the Open Skies regime.

A. 3. States Parties having the right to conduct observation flights may co-ordinate their plans for conducting observation flights in accordance with Annex H to this Treaty. No State Party shall be obliged to accept more than one observation flight at any one time during the 96-hour period specified in paragraph 9 of this Section, unless that State Party has requested a demonstration flight pursuant to Annex F to this Treaty. In that case, the observed Party shall be obliged to accept an overlap for the observation flights of up to 24 hours. After having been notified of the results of the co-ordination of plans to conduct observation flights, each State Party over whose territory observation flights are to be conducted shall inform other States Parties, in accordance with the provisions of Annex H, whether it will exercise, with regard to each specific observation flight, its right to provide its own observation aircraft.

....

B. 5. The observing Party shall notify the observed Party of its intention to conduct an observation flight, no less than 72 hours prior to the estimated time of arrival of the observing Party at the point of entry of the observed Party. States Parties providing such notifications shall make every effort to avoid using the minimum pre-notification period over weekends....

....

8. The observing Party, when notifying the observed Party in accordance with paragraph 5 of this Section, shall simultaneously notify all other States Parties of its intention to conduct the observation flight.

9. The period from the estimated time of arrival at the point of entry until completion of the observation flight shall not exceed 96 hours, unless otherwise agreed. In the event that the observed Party requests a demonstration flight pursuant to Annex F to the Treaty, it shall extend the 96-hour period pursuant to Annex F, Section III, paragraph 4, if additional time is required by the observing Party for the unrestricted execution of the mission plan.

10. Upon arrival of the observation aircraft at the point of entry, the observed Party shall inspect the covers for sensor apertures or other devices that inhibit the operation of sensors to confirm that they are in their proper position pursuant to Annex E, unless otherwise agreed by all States Parties involved.

11. In the event that the observation aircraft is provided by the observing Party, upon the arrival of the observation aircraft at the point of entry or at the Open Skies airfield where the observation flight commences, the observed Party shall have the right to carry out the pre-flight inspection pursuant to Annex F, Section I. In the event that, in accordance with paragraph 1 of this Section, an observation aircraft is provided by the observed Party, the observing Party shall have the right to carry out the pre-flight inspection of sensors pursuant to Annex F, Section II. Unless otherwise agreed, such inspections shall terminate no less than four hours prior to the scheduled commencement of the observation flight set forth in the flight plan.

12. The observing Party shall ensure that its flight crew includes at least one individual who has the necessary linguistic ability to communicate freely with the personnel of the observed Party and its air traffic control authorities in the language or languages notified by the observed Party in accordance with paragraph 4 of this Section.

13. The observed Party shall provide the flight crew, upon its arrival at the point of entry or at the Open Skies airfield where the observation flight commences, with the most recent weather forecast and air navigation information and information on flight safety, including Notices to Airmen. Updates of such information shall be provided as requested. Instrument procedures, and information about alternate airfields along the flight route, shall be provided upon approval of the mission plan in accordance with the requirements of Section II of this Article.

14. While conducting observation flights pursuant to this Treaty, all observation aircraft shall be operated in accordance with the provisions of this Treaty and in accordance with the approved flight plan. Without prejudice to the provisions of Section II, paragraph 2 of this Article, observation flights shall also be conducted in compliance with:

(a) published ICAO standards and recommended practices; and

(b) published national air traffic control rules, procedures and guidelines on flight safety of the State Party whose territory is being overflown.

15. Observation flights shall take priority over any regular air traffic. The observed Party shall ensure that its air traffic control authorities facilitate the conduct of observation flights in accordance with this Treaty.

16. On board the aircraft the pilot-in-command shall be the sole authority for the safe conduct of the flight and shall be responsible for the execution of the flight plan.

17. The observed Party shall provide:

(a) a calibration target suitable for confirming the capability of sensors in accordance with the procedures set forth in Annex D, Section III to this Treaty, to be overflown during the demonstration flight or the observation flight upon the request of either Party, for each sensor that is to be used during the observation flight. The calibration target shall be located in the vicinity of the airfield at which the pre-flight inspection is conducted pursuant to Annex F to this Treaty;

(b) customary commercial aircraft fuelling and servicing for the observation aircraft or transport aircraft at the point of entry, at the Open Skies airfield, at any refuelling airfield, and at the point of exit specified in the flight plan, according to the specifications that are published about the designated airfield;

(c) meals and the use of accommodation for the personnel of the observing Party; and

(d) upon the request of the observing Party, further services, as may be agreed upon between the observing and observed Parties, to facilitate the conduct of the observation flight.

18. All costs involved in the conduct of the observation flight, including the costs of the recording media and the processing of the data collected by sensors, shall be reimbursed in accordance with Annex L, Section I, paragraph 9 to this Treaty.

19. Prior to the departure of the observation aircraft from the point of exit, the observed Party shall confirm that the covers for sensor apertures or other devices that inhibit the operation of sensors are in their proper position pursuant to Annex E to this Treaty.

20. Unless otherwise agreed, the observing Party shall depart from the point of exit no later than 24 hours following completion of the observation flight, unless weather conditions or the airworthiness of the observation aircraft or transport aircraft do not permit, in which case the flight shall commence as soon as practicable.

21. The observing Party shall compile a mission report of the observation flight using the appropriate format developed by the Open Skies Consultative Commission. The mission report shall contain pertinent data on the date and time of the observation flight, its route and profile, weather conditions, time and period for each sensor, the approximate amount of data collected by sensors, and the result of inspection of covers for sensor apertures or other devices that inhibit the operation of sensors in accordance with Article VII and Annex E. The mission report shall be signed by the observing and observed Parties at the point of exit and shall be provided by the observing Party to all other States Parties within seven days after departure of the observing Party from the point of exit.

SECTION II. REQUIREMENTS FOR MISSION PLANNING

. . . .

SECTION III. SPECIAL PROVISIONS

. . . .

Article VII. *Transit Flights.* 1. Transit flights conducted by an observing Party to and from the territory of an observed Party for the purposes of this Treaty shall originate on the territory of the observing Party or of another State Party.

2. Each State Party shall accept transit flights. Such transit flights shall be conducted along internationally recognized Air Traffic Services routes, unless otherwise agreed by the States Parties involved, and in accordance with the instructions of the national air traffic control authorities of each State Party whose airspace is transited. The observing

Party shall notify each State Party whose airspace is to be transited at the same time that it notifies the observed Party in accordance with Article VI.

3. The operation of sensors on an observation aircraft during transit flights is prohibited. In the event that, during the transit flight, the observation aircraft lands on the territory of a State Party, that State Party shall, upon landing and prior to departure, inspect the covers of sensor apertures or other devices that inhibit the operation of sensors to confirm that they are in their proper position.

Article VIII. *Prohibitions, Deviations From Flight Plans and Emergency Situations.*

SECTION I. PROHIBITION OF OBSERVATION FLIGHTS AND CHANGES TO MISSION PLANS

1. The observed Party shall have the right to prohibit an observation flight that is not in compliance with the provisions of this Treaty. 2. The observed Party shall have the right to prohibit an observation flight prior to its commencement in the event that the observing Party fails to arrive at the point of entry within 24 hours after the estimated time of arrival specified in the notification provided in accordance with Article VI, Section I, paragraph 5, unless otherwise agreed between the States Parties involved.

3. In the event that an observed State Party prohibits an observation flight pursuant to this Article or Annex F, it shall immediately state the facts for the prohibition in the mission plan. Within seven days the observed Party shall provide to all States Parties, through diplomatic channels, a written explanation for this prohibition in the mission report provided pursuant to Article VI, Section I, paragraph 21. An observation flight that has been prohibited shall not be counted against the quota of either State Party.

4. The observed Party shall have the right to propose changes to the mission plan as a result of any of the following circumstances:

(a) the weather conditions affect flight safety;

(b) the status of the Open Skies airfield to be used, alternate airfields, or refueling airfields prevents their use; or

(c) the mission plan is inconsistent with Article VI, Section II, paragraphs 2 and 4.

5. In the event that the observing Party disagrees with the proposed changes to the mission plan, it shall have the right to submit alternatives to the proposed changes. In the event that agreement on a mission plan is not reached within eight hours of the submission of the original mission plan, and if the observing Party considers the changes to the mission plan to be prejudicial to its rights under this Treaty with respect to the conduct of the observation flight, the observing Party shall have the right to decline to conduct the observation flight, which shall not be recorded against the quota of either State Party.

6. In the event that an observing Party declines to conduct an observation flight pursuant to this Article or Annex F, it shall immediately provide an explanation of its decision in the mission plan prior to the departure of the observing Party. Within seven days after departure of the observing Party, the observing Party shall provide to all other States Parties, through diplomatic channels, a written explanation for this decision in the mission report provided pursuant to Article VI, Section I, paragraph 21.

SECTION II. DEVIATIONS FROM THE FLIGHT PLAN

. . . .

SECTION III. EMERGENCY SITUATIONS

....

Article X. Open Skies Consultative Commission. 1. In order to promote the objectives and facilitate the implementation of the provisions of this Treaty, the States Parties hereby establish an Open Skies Consultative Commission.

2. The Open Skies Consultative Commission shall take decisions or make recommendations by consensus. Consensus shall be understood to mean the absence of any objection by any State Party to the taking of a decision or the making of a recommendation.

3. Each State Party shall have the right to raise before the Open Skies Consultative Commission, and have placed on its agenda, any issue relating to this Treaty, including any issue related to the case when the observed Party provides an observation aircraft.

4. Within the framework of the Open Skies Consultative Commission the States Parties to this Treaty shall:

(a) consider questions relating to compliance with the provisions of this Treaty;

(b) seek to resolve ambiguities and differences of interpretation that may become apparent in the way this Treaty is implemented;

(c) consider and take decisions on applications for accession to this Treaty; and

(d) agree as to those technical and administrative measures, pursuant to the provisions of this Treaty, deemed necessary following the accession to this Treaty by other States.

5. The Open Skies Consultative Commission may propose amendments to this Treaty for consideration and approval in accordance with Article XVI. The Open Skies Consultative Commission may also agree on improvements to the viability and effectiveness of this Treaty, consistent with its provisions. Improvements relating only to modification of the annual distribution of active quotas pursuant to Article III and Annex A, to updates and additions to the categories or capabilities of sensors pursuant to Article IV, to revision of the share of costs pursuant to Annex L, Section I, paragraph 9, to arrangements for the sharing and availability of data pursuant to Article IX, Sections III and IV and to the handling of mission reports pursuant to Article VI, Section I, paragraph 21, as well as to minor matters of an administrative or technical nature, shall be agreed upon within the Open Skies Consultative Commission and shall not be deemed to be amendments to this Treaty.

6. The Open Skies Consultative Commission shall request the use of the facilities and administrative support of the Conflict Prevention Centre of the Conference on Security and Co-operation in Europe, or other existing facilities in Vienna, unless it decides otherwise.

7. Provisions for the operation of the Open Skies Consultative Commission are set forth in Annex L to this Treaty.

Article XI. Notifications and Reports. The States Parties shall transmit notifications and reports required by this Treaty in written form. The States Parties shall transmit such notifications and reports through diplomatic channels or, at their choice, through other official channels, such as the communications network of the Conference on Security and Co-operation in Europe.

Article XII. Liability. A State Party shall, in accordance with international law and practice, be liable to pay compensation for damage to other States Parties, or to their natural or juridical persons or their property, caused by it in the course of the implementation of this Treaty.

Article XIII. Designation of Personnel and Privileges and Immunities.

SECTION I. DESIGNATION OF PERSONNEL

....

SECTION II. PRIVILEGES AND IMMUNITIES

1. In order to exercise their functions effectively, for the purpose of implementing this Treaty and not for their personal benefit, personnel designated in accordance with the provisions of Section I, paragraph 1 of this Article shall be accorded the privileges and immunities enjoyed by diplomatic agents pursuant to Article 29; Article 30, paragraph 2; Article 31, paragraphs 1, 2 and 3; and Articles 34 and 35 of the Vienna Convention on Diplomatic Relations of 18 April 1961, hereinafter referred to as the Vienna Convention. In addition, designated personnel shall be accorded the privileges enjoyed by diplomatic agents pursuant to Article 36, paragraph 1, subparagraph (b) of the Vienna Convention, except in relation to articles, the import or export of which is prohibited by law or controlled by quarantine regulations.

2. Such privileges and immunities shall be accorded to designated personnel for the entire period between arrival on and departure from the territory of the observed Party, and thereafter with respect to acts previously performed in the exercise of their official functions. Such personnel shall also, when transiting the territory of other States Parties, be accorded the privileges and immunities enjoyed by diplomatic agents pursuant to Article 40, paragraph 1 of the Vienna Convention.

3. The immunity from jurisdiction may be waived by the observing Party in those cases when it would impede the course of justice and can be waived without prejudice to this Treaty. The immunity of personnel who are not nationals of the observing Party may be waived only by the States Parties of which such personnel are nationals. Waiver must always be express.

4. Without prejudice to their privileges and immunities or the rights of the observing Party set forth in this Treaty, it is the duty of designated personnel to respect the laws and regulations of the observed Party.

5. The transportation means of the personnel shall be accorded the same immunities from search, requisition, attachment or execution as those of a diplomatic mission pursuant to Article

22, paragraph 3 of the Vienna Convention, except as otherwise provided for in this Treaty.

....

Article XV. Duration and Withdrawal. 1. This Treaty shall be of unlimited duration.

2. A State Party shall have the right to withdraw from this Treaty. A State Party intending to withdraw shall provide notice of its decision to withdraw to either Depositary at least six months in advance of the date of its intended withdrawal and to all other States Parties. The Depositaries shall promptly inform all other States Parties of such notice.

3. In the event that a State Party provides notice of its decision to withdraw from this Treaty in accordance with paragraph 2 of this Article, the Depositaries shall convene a

conference of the States Parties no less than 30 days and no more than 60 days after they have received such notice, in order to consider the effect of the withdrawal on this Treaty.

Article XVI. *Amendments and Periodic Review.* 1. Each State Party shall have the right to propose amendments to this Treaty. The text of each proposed amendment shall be submitted to either Depositary, which shall circulate it to all States Parties for consideration. If so requested by no less than three States Parties within a period of 90 days after circulation of the proposed amendment, the Depositaries shall convene a conference of the States Parties to consider the proposed amendment. Such a conference shall open no earlier than 30 days and no later than 60 days after receipt of the third of such requests.

2. An amendment to this Treaty shall be subject to the approval of all States Parties, either by providing notification, in writing, of their approval to a Depositary within a period of 90 days after circulation of the proposed amendment, or by expressing their approval at a conference convened in accordance with paragraph 1 of this Article. An amendment so approved shall be subject to ratification in accordance with the provisions of Article XVII, paragraph 1, and shall enter into force 60 days after the deposit of instruments of ratification by the States Parties.

3. Unless requested to do so earlier by no less than three States Parties, the Depositaries shall convene a conference of the States Parties to review the implementation of this Treaty three years after entry into force of this Treaty and at five-year intervals thereafter.

. . . .

C. Bilateral Arms Control and Disarmament Agreements between the United States and the Soviet Union Successor States

TREATY BETWEEN THE UNITED STATES OF AMERICA AND THE UNION OF SOVIET SOCIALIST REPUBLICS ON THE LIMITATION OF ANTI-BALLISTIC MISSILE SYSTEMS* (ABM TREATY)

Note

This treaty was terminated effective June 14, 2002.

The United States of America and the Union of Soviet Socialist Republics, hereinafter referred to as the Parties,

Proceeding from the premise that nuclear war would have devastating consequences for all mankind,

Considering that effective measures to limit anti-ballistic missile systems would be a substantial factor in curbing the race in strategic offensive arms and would lead to a decrease in the risk of outbreak of war involving nuclear weapons,

Proceeding from the premise that the limitation of anti-ballistic missile systems, as well as certain agreed measures with respect to the limitation of strategic offensive arms, would contribute to the creation of more favorable conditions for further negotiations on limiting strategic arms,

Mindful of their obligations under Article VI of the Treaty on the Non-Proliferation of Nuclear Weapons,

Declaring their intention to achieve at the earliest possible date the cessation of the nuclear arms race and to take effective measures toward reductions in strategic arms, nuclear disarmament, and general and complete disarmament,

Desiring to contribute to the relaxation of international tension and the strengthening of trust between States,

Have agreed as follows:

Article I. 1. Each Party undertakes to limit anti-ballistic missile (ABM) systems and to adopt other measures in accordance with the provisions of this Treaty.

2. Each Party undertakes not to deploy ABM systems for a defense of the territory of its country and not to provide a base for such a defense, and not to deploy ABM systems for defense of an individual region except as provided for in Article III of this Treaty.

Article II. 1. For the purpose of this Treaty an ABM system is a system to counter strategic ballistic missiles or their elements in flight trajectory, currently consisting of:

---

* Treaty Between the United States of America and the Union of Soviet Socialist Republics on the Limitation of Anti-Ballistic Missile Systems, U.S.-U.S.S.R., May 26, 1972, 23 U.S.T. 3435, 3437 (entered into force Oct. 3, 1972), *available at* http://www.state.gov/t/np/trty/16332.htm.

In a diplomatic note sent to Russia, Belarus, Kazakhstan, and the Ukraine on December 13, 2001, the United States exercised its option to withdraw from the treaty on six-months notice pursuant to Article XV of the treaty.

(a) ABM interceptor missiles, which are interceptor missiles constructed and deployed for an ABM role, or of a type tested in an ABM mode;

(b) ABM launchers, which are launchers constructed and deployed for launching ABM interceptor missiles; and

(c) ABM radars, which are radars constructed and deployed for an ABM role, or of a type tested in an ABM mode.

2. The ABM system components listed in paragraph 1 of this Article include those which are:

(a) operational;

(b) under construction;

(c) undergoing testing;

(d) undergoing overhaul, repair or conversion; or

(e) mothballed.

Article III. Each Party undertakes not to deploy ABM systems or their components except that:

(a) within one ABM system deployment area having a radius of one hundred and fifty kilometers and centered on the Party's national capital, a Party may deploy:

(1) no more than one hundred ABM launchers and no more than one hundred ABM interceptor missiles at launch sites, and

(2) ABM radars within no more than six ABM radar complexes, the area of each complex being circular and having a diameter of no more than three kilometers; and

(b) within one ABM system deployment area having a radius of one hundred and fifty kilometers and containing ICBM silo launchers, a Party may deploy:

(1) no more than one hundred ABM launchers and no more than one hundred ABM interceptor missiles at launch sites,

(2) two large phased-array ABM radars comparable in potential to corresponding ABM radars operational or under construction on the date of signature of the Treaty in an ABM system deployment area containing ICBM silo launchers, and

(3) no more than eighteen ABM radars each having a potential less than the potential of the smaller of the above-mentioned two large phased-array ABM radars.

Article IV. The limitations provided for in Article III shall not apply to ABM systems or their components used for development or testing, and located within current or additionally agreed test ranges. Each Party may have no more than a total of fifteen ABM launchers at test ranges.

Article V. 1. Each Party undertakes not to develop, test, or deploy ABM systems or components which are sea-based, air-based, space-based, or mobile land-based.

2. Each Party undertakes not to develop, test or deploy ABM launchers for launching more than one ABM interceptor missile at a time from each launcher, not to modify deployed launchers to provide them with such a capacity, not to develop, test, or deploy automatic or semi-automatic or other similar systems for rapid reload of ABM launchers.

Article VI. To enhance assurance of the effectiveness of the limitations on ABM systems and their components provided by the Treaty, each Party undertakes:

(a) not to give missiles, launchers, or radars, other than ABM interceptor missiles, ABM launchers, or ABM radars, capabilities to counter strategic ballistic missiles or their elements in flight trajectory, and not to test them in an ABM mode; and

(b) not to deploy in the future radars for early warning of strategic ballistic missile attack except at locations along the periphery of its national territory and oriented outward.

Article VII. Subject to the provisions of this Treaty, modernization and replacement of ABM systems or their components may be carried out.

Article VIII. ABM systems or their components in excess of the numbers or outside the areas specified in this Treaty, as well as ABM systems or their components prohibited by this Treaty, shall be destroyed or dismantled under agreed procedures within the shortest possible agreed period of time.

Article IX. To assure the viability and effectiveness of this Treaty, each Party undertakes not to transfer to other States, and not to deploy outside its national territory, ABM systems or their components limited by this Treaty.

Article X. Each Party undertakes not to assume any international obligations which would conflict with this Treaty.

Article XI. The Parties undertake to continue active negotiations for limitations on strategic offensive arms.

Article XII. 1. For the purpose of providing assurance or compliance with the provisions of this Treaty, each Party shall use national technical means of verification at its disposal in a manner consistent with generally recognized principles of international law.

2. Each Party undertakes not to interfere with the national technical means of verification of the other Party operating in accordance with paragraph 1 of this Article.

3. Each Party undertakes not to use deliberate concealment measures which impede verification by national technical means of compliance with the provisions of this Treaty. This obligation shall not require changes in current construction, assembly, conversion, or overhaul practices.

Article XIII. 1. To promote the objectives and implementation of the provisions of this Treaty, the Parties shall establish promptly a Standing Consultative Commission, within the framework of which they will:

(a) consider questions concerning compliance with the obligations assumed and related situations which may be considered ambiguous;

(b) provide on a voluntary basis such information as either Party considers necessary to assure confidence in compliance with the obligations assumed;

(c) consider questions involving unintended interference with national technical means of verification;

(d) consider possible changes in the strategic situation which have a bearing on the provisions of this Treaty;

(e) agree upon procedures and dates for destruction or dismantling of ABM systems or their components in cases provided for by the provisions of this Treaty;

(f) consider, as appropriate, possible proposals for further increasing the viability of this Treaty; including proposals for amendments in accordance with the provisions of this Treaty;

(g) consider, as appropriate, proposals for further measures aimed at limiting strategic arms.

2. The Parties through consultation shall establish, and may amend as appropriate, Regulations for the Standing Consultative Commission governing procedures, composition and other relevant matters.

Article XIV. 1. Each Party may propose amendments to this Treaty. Agreed amendments shall enter into force in accordance with the procedures governing the entry into force of this Treaty.

2. Five years after entry into force of this Treaty, and at five-year intervals thereafter, the Parties shall together conduct a review of this Treaty.

Article XV. 1. This Treaty shall be of unlimited duration.

2. Each Party shall, in exercising its national sovereignty, have the right to withdraw from this Treaty if it decides that extraordinary events related to the subject matter of this Treaty have jeopardized its supreme interests. It shall give notice of its decision to the other Party six months prior to withdrawal from the Treaty. Such notice shall include a statement of the extraordinary events the notifying Party regards as having jeopardized its supreme interests.

. . . .

DONE at Moscow on May 26, 1972, in two copies, each in the English and Russian languages, both texts being equally authentic.

Agreed Statements, Common Understandings, and Unilateral Statements Regarding the Treaty Between the United States of America and the Union of Soviet Socialist Republics on the Limitation of Anti-Ballistic Missiles

1. Agreed Statements

The document was set forth below was agreed upon and initialed by the Heads of the Delegations on May 26, 1972 (letter designations added):

AGREED STATEMENTS REGARDING THE TREATY BETWEEN THE UNITED STATES OF AMERICA AND THE UNION OF SOVIET SOCIALIST REPUBLICS ON THE LIMITATION OF ANTI-BALLISTIC MISSILE SYSTEMS

[A]

. . . .

[B]

. . . .

[C]

. . . .

[D]

In order to insure fulfillment of the obligation not to deploy ABM systems and their components except as provided in Article III of the Treaty, the Parties agree that in the event ABM systems based on other physical principles and including components capable of substituting for ABM interceptor missiles, ABM launchers, or ABM radars are created in the future, specific limitations on such systems and their components would be subject to discussion in accordance with Article XIII and agreement in accordance with Article XIV of the Treaty.

[E]

The Parties understand that Article V of the Treaty includes obligations not to develop, test or deploy ABM interceptor missiles for the delivery by each ABM interceptor missile of more than one independently guided warhead.

[F]

....

[G]

....

3. Unilateral Statements

....

B. Tested in ABM Mode

On April 7, 1972, the U.S. Delegation made the following statement:

Article II of the Joint Text Draft uses the term "tested in an ABM mode," in defining ABM components, and Article VI includes certain obligations concerning such testing. We believe that the sides should have a common understanding of this phrase. First, we would like to note that the testing provisions of the ABM Treaty are intended to apply to testing which occurs after the date of the signature of the Treaty, and not to any testing which may have occurred in the past. Next, we would amplify the remarks we have made on this subject during the previous Helsinki phase by setting forth the objectives which govern the U.S. view on the subject, namely, while prohibiting testing of non-ABM components for non-ABM purposes. To clarify our interpretation of "tested in an ABM mode," we note we would consider a launcher, missile or radar to be "tested in an ABM mode" if, for example, any of the following events occur:

(1) a launcher is used to launch an ABM interceptor missile,

(2) an interceptor missile is flight tested against a target vehicle which has a flight trajectory with characteristics of a strategic ballistic missile flight trajectory, or is flight tested in conjunction with the test of an ABM interceptor missile or an ABM radar at the same test range, or is flight tested to an altitude inconsistent with interception of targets against which air defenses are deployed,

(3) a radar makes measurements on a cooperative target vehicle of the kind referred to in item (2) above during the reentry portion of its trajectory or makes measurements in conjunction with the test of an ABM interceptor missile or an ABM radar at the same

test range. Radars are used for purposes such as range safety or instrumentation would be exempt from application of these criteria.

. . . .

INTERIM AGREEMENT BETWEEN THE UNITED STATES OF AMERICA AND THE UNION OF SOVIET SOCIALIST REPUBLICS ON CERTAIN MEASURES WITH RESPECT TO THE LIMITATION OF STRATEGIC OFFENSIVE ARMS* (SALT I)

The United States of America and the Union of Soviet Socialist Republics, hereinafter referred to as the Parties,

Convinced that the Treaty on the Limitation of Anti-Ballistic Missile Systems and this Interim Agreement on Certain Measures with Respect to the Limitation of Strategic Offensive Arms will contribute to the creation of more favorable conditions for active negotiations on limiting strategic arms as well as to the relaxation of international tension and the strengthening of trust between States,

Taking into account the relationship between strategic offensive and defensive arms,

Mindful of their obligations under Article VI of the Treaty on the Non-Proliferation of Nuclear Weapons,

Have agreed as follows:

Article I. The Parties undertake not to start construction of additional fixed land-based intercontinental ballistic missile (ICBM) launchers after July 1, 1972.

Article II. The Parties undertake not to convert land-based launchers for light ICBMs, or for ICBMs of older types deployed prior to 1964, into land-based launchers for heavy ICBMs of types deployed after that time.

Article III. The Parties undertake to limit submarine-launched ballistic missile (SLBM) launchers and modern ballistic missile submarines to the numbers operational and under construction on the date of signature of this Interim Agreement, and in addition to launchers and submarines constructed under procedures established by the Parties as replacements for an equal number of ICBM launchers of older types deployed prior to 1964 or for launchers on older submarines.

Article IV. Subject to the provisions of this Interim Agreement, modernization and replacement of strategic offensive ballistic missiles and launchers covered by this Interim Agreement may be undertaken.

Article V. 1. For the purpose of providing assurance of compliance with the provisions of this Interim Agreement, each Party shall use national technical means of verification at its disposal in a manner consistent with generally recognized principles of international law.

---

* Interim Agreement Between the United States of America and the Union of Soviet Socialist Republics on Certain Measures with Respect to the Limitation of Strategic Offensive Arms, U.S.-U.S.S.R., May 26, 1972, 23 U.S.T. 3462, 3463 (entered into force Oct. 3, 1972), *available at* http://www.fas.org/nuke/control/salt1/text/salt1.htm. This treaty, known as "SALT I," was signed in Moscow on 26 May 1972 as part of the ABM Treaty.

2. Each Party undertakes not to interfere with the national technical means of verification of the other Party operating in accordance with paragraph 1 of this Article.

3. Each Party undertakes not to use deliberate concealment measures which impede verification by national technical means of compliance with the provisions of this Interim Agreement. This obligation shall not require changes in current construction, assembly, conversion, or overhaul practices.

Article VI. To promote the objectives and implementation of the provisions of this Interim Agreement, the Parties shall use the Standing Consultative Commission established under Article XIII of the Treaty on the Limitation of Anti-Ballistic Missile Systems in accordance with the provisions of that Article.

Article VII. The Parties undertake to continue active negotiations for limitations on strategic offensive arms. The obligations provided for in this Interim Agreement shall not prejudice the scope or terms of the limitations on strategic offensive arms which may be worked out in the course of further negotiations.

Article VIII. 1. This Interim Agreement shall enter into force upon exchange of written notices of acceptance by each Party, which exchange shall take place simultaneously with the exchange of instruments of ratification of the Treaty on the Limitation of Anti-Ballistic Missile Systems.

2. This Interim Agreement shall remain in force for a period of five years unless replaced earlier by an agreement on more complete measures limiting strategic offensive arms. It is the objective of the Parties to conduct active follow-on negotiations with the aim of concluding such an agreement as soon as possible.

3. Each Party shall, in exercising its national sovereignty, have the right to withdraw from this Interim Agreement if it decides that extraordinary events related to the subject matter of this Interim Agreement have jeopardized its supreme interests. It shall give notice of its decision to the other Party six months prior to withdrawal from this Interim Agreement. Such notice shall include a statement of the extraordinary events the notifying Party regards as having jeopardized its supreme interests.

DONE at Moscow on May 26, 1972, in two copies, each in the English and Russian languages, both texts being equally authentic.

Protocol to the Interim Agreement Between the United States of America and the Union of Soviet Socialist Republics on Certain Measures with Respect to the Limitation of Strategic Offensive Arms

The United States of America and the Union of Soviet Socialist Republics, hereinafter referred to as the Parties,

Having agreed on certain limitations relating to submarine-launched ballistic missile launchers and modern ballistic missile submarines, and to replacement procedures, in the Interim Agreement,

Have agreed as follows:

The Parties understand that, under Article III of the Interim Agreement, for the period during which that Agreement remains in force:

The United States may have no more than 710 ballistic missile launchers on submarines (SLBMs) and no more than 44 modern ballistic missile submarines. The Soviet Union may have no more than 950 ballistic missile launchers on submarines and no more than 62 modern ballistic missile submarines.

Additional ballistic missile launchers on submarines up to the above-mentioned levels, in the United States—over 656 ballistic missile launchers on nuclear-powered submarines, and in the USSR—over 740 ballistic missile launchers on nuclear-powered submarines, operational and under construction, may become operational as replacements for equal numbers of ballistic missile launchers of older types deployed prior to 1964 or of ballistic missile launchers on older submarines.

The deployment of modern SLBMs on any submarine, regardless of type, will be counted against the total level of SLBMs permitted for the United States and the USSR.

This Protocol shall be considered an integral part of the Interim Agreement.

BASIC PRINCIPLES OF RELATIONS BETWEEN THE UNITED STATES OF AMERICA AND THE UNION OF SOVIET SOCIALIST REPUBLICS*

The United States of America and the Union of Soviet Socialist Republics,

Guided by their obligations under the Charter of the United Nations and by a desire to strengthen peaceful relations with each other and to place these relations on the firmest possible basis,

Aware of the need to make every effort to remove the threat of war and to create conditions which promote the reduction of tensions in the world and the strengthening of universal security and international cooperation,

Believing that the improvement of U.S.-Soviet relations and their mutually advantageous development in such areas as economics, science and culture, will meet these objectives and contribute to better mutual understanding and business-like cooperation, without in any way prejudicing the interests of third countries,

Conscious that these objectives reflect the interests of the peoples of both countries,

Have agreed as follows:

First. They will proceed from the common determination that in the nuclear age there is no alternative to conducting their mutual relations on the basis of peaceful coexistence. Differences in ideology and in the social systems of the U.S.A. and the U.S.S.R. are not obstacles to the bilateral development of normal relations based on the principles of sovereignty, equality, non-interference in internal affairs and mutual advantage.

Second. The U.S.A. and the U.S.S.R. attach major importance to preventing the development of situations capable of causing a dangerous exacerbation of their relations. Therefore, they will do their utmost to avoid military confrontations and to prevent the outbreak of nuclear war. They will always exercise restraint in their mutual relations, and will be prepared to negotiate and settle differences by peaceful means. Discussions and negotiations on outstanding issues will be conducted in spirit of reciprocity, mutual accommodation and mutual benefit.

Both sides recognize that efforts to obtain unilateral advantage at the expense of the other, directly or indirectly, are inconsistent with these objectives. The prerequisites for maintaining and strengthening peaceful relations between the U.S.A. and the U.S.S.R. are the recognition of the security interests of the Parties based on the principle of equality and the renunciation of the use of threat or force.

Third. The U.S.A. and the U.S.S.R. have a special responsibility, as do other countries which are permanent members of the United Nations Security Council, to do everything in their power so that conflicts or situations will not arise which would serve to increase international tensions. Accordingly, they will seek to promote conditions in

---

* Basic Principles of Relations Between the United States of America and the Union of Soviet Socialist Republics, U.S.-U.S.S.R., May 29, 1972, 66 DEP'T ST. BULL. 898 (June 26, 1972).

which all countries will live in peace and security and will not be subject to outside interference in their internal affairs.

Fourth. The U.S.A. and the U.S.S.R. intend to widen the juridical basis of their mutual relations and to exert the necessary efforts so that bilateral agreements which they have concluded and multilateral treaties and agreements to which they are jointly parties are faithfully implemented.

Fifth. The U.S.A. and the U.S.S.R. reaffirm their readiness to continue the practice of exchanging views on problems of mutual interest and, when necessary, to conduct such exchanges at the highest level, including meetings between leaders of the two countries.

The two governments welcome and will facilitate an increase in productive contacts between representatives of the legislative bodies of the two countries.

Sixth. The Parties will continue their efforts to limit armaments on a bilateral as well as on a multilateral basis. They will continue to make special efforts to limit strategic armaments. Whenever possible, they will conclude concrete agreements aimed at achieving these purposes.

The U.S.A. and the U.S.S.R. regard as the ultimate objective of their efforts the achievement of general and complete disarmament and the establishment of an effective system of international security in accordance with the purposes and principles of the United Nations.

Seventh. The U.S.A. and the U.S.S.R. regard commercial and economic ties as an important and necessary element in the strengthening of their bilateral relations and thus will actively promote the growth of such ties. They will facilitate cooperation between the relevant organizations and enterprises of the two countries and the conclusion of appropriate agreements and contracts, including long-term ones.

The two countries will contribute to the improvement of maritime and air communications between them.

Eighth. The two sides consider it timely and useful to develop mutual contacts and cooperation in the fields of science and technology. Where suitable, the U.S.A. and the U.S.S.R. will conclude appropriate agreements dealing with concrete cooperation in these fields.

Ninth. The two sides reaffirm their intention to deepen cultural ties with one another and to encourage fuller familiarization with each other's cultural values. They will promote improved conditions for cultural exchanges and tourism.

Tenth. The U.S.A. and the U.S.S.R. will seek to ensure that their ties and cooperation in all the above-mentioned fields and in any others in their mutual interest are built on a firm and long-term basis. To give a permanent character to these efforts, they will establish in all fields where this is feasible joint commissions or other joint bodies.

Eleventh. The U.S.A. and the U.S.S.R. make no claim for themselves and would not recognize the claims of anyone else to any special rights or advantages in world affairs. They recognize the sovereign equality of all states.

The development of U.S.-Soviet relations is not directed against third countries and their interests.

Twelfth. The basic principles set forth in this document do not affect any obligations with respect to other countries earlier assumed by the U.S.A. and the U.S.S.R.

JOINT U.S.-SOVIET STATEMENT, 24 NOVEMBER 1974 ON FURTHER LIMITATION OF STRATEGIC OFFENSIVE ARMS*

During their working meeting in the area of Vladivostok on November 23–24, 1974, General Secretary of the Central Committee of the CPSU L. I. Brezhnev and President of the U.S.A. Gerald R. Ford discussed in detail the question of further limitations of strategic offensive arms.

They reaffirmed the great significance that both the U.S.S.R. and the United States attach to the limitation of strategic offensive arms. They are convinced that a long-term agreement on this question would be a significant contribution to improving relations between the U.S.S.R. and the U.S.A. to reducing the danger of war and to enhancing world peace.

Having noted the value of previous agreements on this question, including the Interim Agreement of May 26, 1972, they reaffirm the intention to conclude a new agreement on the limitation of strategic offensive arms, to last through 1985.

As a result of the exchange of views on the substance of such a new agreement the General Secretary of the Central Committee of the CPSU and the President of the United States of America concluded that favourable prospects exist for completing the work on this agreement in 1975.

Agreement was reached that further negotiations will be based on the following provisions:

1. The new agreement will incorporate the relevant provisions of the Interim Agreement of May 26, 1972, which will remain in force until October 1977.

2. The new agreement will cover the period from October 1977 through December 31, 1985.

3. Based on the principle of equality and equal security, the new agreement will include the following limitations:

    a. both Sides will be entitled to have a certain agreed aggregate number of strategic delivery vehicles;

    b. both Sides will be entitled to have a certain agreed aggregate number of intercontinental ballistic missiles and submarine-launched ballistic missiles equipped with multiple independently targetable warheads.

4. The new agreement will include a provision for further negotiations beginning not later than 1980–1981 on the question of further limitation and possible reductions of strategic arms in the period after 1985.

5. Negotiations between the delegations of the U.S.S.R. and the U.S.A. to work out the new agreement incorporating the foregoing points will resume in Geneva in January 1975.

---

* Joint U.S.-Soviet Statement, U.S.-U.S.S.R., Nov. 24, 1974, 71 DEP'T ST. BULL. 879 (Dec. 23, 1974), *available at* http://cbw.sipri.se/intermediate/20403100.html.

TREATY BETWEEN THE UNITED STATES OF AMERICA AND THE UNION OF SOVIET SOCIALIST REPUBLICS ON THE LIMITATION OF STRATEGIC OFFENSIVE ARMS* (SALT II)

The United States of America and the Union of Soviet Socialist Republics, hereinafter referred to as the Parties,

Conscious that nuclear war would have devastating consequences for all mankind,

Proceeding from the Basic Principles of Relations Between the United States of America and the Union of Soviet Socialist Republics of May 29, 1972,

Attaching particular significance to the limitation of strategic arms and determined to continue their efforts begun with the Treaty on the Limitation of Anti-Ballistic Missile Systems and the Interim Agreement on Certain Measures with Respect to the Limitation of Strategic Offensive Arms, of May 26, 1972,

Convinced that the additional measures limiting strategic offensive arms provided for in this Treaty will contribute to the improvement of relations between the Parties, help to reduce the risk of outbreak of nuclear war and strengthen international peace and security,

Mindful of their obligations under Article VI of the Treaty on the Non-Proliferation of Nuclear Weapons,

Guided by the principle of equality and equal security,

Recognizing that the strengthening of strategic stability meets the interests of the Parties and the interests of international security,

Reaffirming their desire to take measures for the further limitation and for the further reduction of strategic arms, having in mind the goal of achieving general and complete disarmament,

Declaring their intention to undertake in the near future negotiations further to limit and further to reduce strategic offensive arms,

Have agreed as follows:

Article I. Each Party undertakes, in accordance with the provisions of this Treaty, to limit strategic offensive arms quantitatively and qualitatively, to exercise restraint in the development of new types of strategic offensive arms, and to adopt other measures provided for in this Treaty.

Article II. For the purposes of this Treaty:

1. Intercontinental ballistic missile (ICBM) launchers are land-based launchers of ballistic missiles capable of a range in excess of the shortest distance between the northeastern border of the continental part of the territory of the United States of America

* Treaty Between the United States of America and the Union of Soviet Socialist Republics on the Limitation of Strategic Offensive Arms, U.S.-U.S.S.R., June 18, 1979, S. Exec. Doc. Y, 96-1, at 37 (1979), *available at* http://www.state.gov/t/ac/trt/5195.htm. The treaty, known as "SALT II," was never ratified, but both sides observed its provisions until it was superseded by START.

and the northwestern border of the continental part of the territory of the Union of Soviet Socialist Republics, that is, a range in excess of 5,500 kilometers.

* The text of the SALT II Treaty and Protocol, as signed in Vienna, is accompanied by a set of Agreed Statements and Common Understandings, also signed by President Carter and General Secretary Brezhnev...

....

First Agreed Statement. The term "intercontinental ballistic missile launchers," as defined in paragraph 1 of Article II of the Treaty, includes all launchers which have been developed and tested for launching ICBMs. If a launcher has been developed and tested for launching an ICBM, all launchers of that type shall be considered to have been developed and tested for launching ICBMs.

....

3. Heavy bombers are considered to be:

(a) currently, for the United States of America, bombers of the B-52 and B-1 types, and for the Union of Soviet Socialist Republics, bombers of the Tupolev-95 and Myasishchev types;

(b) in the future, types of bombers which can carry out the mission of a heavy bomber in a manner similar or superior to that of bombers listed in subparagraph (a) above;

(c) types of bombers equipped for cruise missiles capable of a range in excess of 600 kilometers; and

(d) types of bombers equipped for ASBMs.

First Agreed Statement. The term "bombers," as used in paragraph 3 of Article II and other provisions of the Treaty, means airplanes of types initially constructed to be equipped for bombs or missiles.

....

Article III. 1. Upon entry into force of this Treaty, each Party undertakes to limit ICBM launchers, SLBM launchers, heavy bombers, and ASBMs to an aggregate number not to exceed 2,400.

2. Each Party undertakes to limit, from January 1, 1981, strategic offensive arms referred to in paragraph 1 of this Article to an aggregate number not to exceed 2,250, and to initiate reductions of those arms which as of that date would be in excess of this aggregate number.

3. Within the aggregate numbers provided for in paragraphs 1 and 2 of this Article and subject to the provisions of this Treaty, each Party has the right to determine the composition of these aggregates.

4. For each bomber of a type equipped for ASBMs, the aggregate numbers provided for in paragraphs 1 and 2 of this Article shall include the maximum number of such missiles for which a bomber of that type is equipped for one operational mission.

5. A heavy bomber equipped only for ASBMs shall not itself be included in the aggregate numbers provided for in paragraphs 1 and 2 of this Article.

6. Reductions of the numbers of strategic offensive arms required to comply with the provisions of paragraphs 1 and 2 of this Article shall be carried out as provided for in Article XI.

Article IV. 1. Each Party undertakes not to start construction of additional fixed ICBM launchers.

2. Each Party undertakes not to relocate fixed ICBM launchers.

3. Each Party undertakes not to convert launchers of light ICBMs, or of ICBMs of older types deployed prior to 1964, into launchers of heavy ICBMs of types deployed after that time.

4. Each Party undertakes in the process of modernization and replacement of ICBM silo launchers not to increase the original internal volume of an ICBM silo launcher by more than thirty-two percent. Within this limit each Party has the right to determine whether such an increase will be made through an increase in the original diameter or in the original depth of an ICBM silo launcher, or in both of these dimensions.

. . . .

Article V. 1. Within the aggregate numbers provided for in paragraphs 1 and 2 of Article III, each Party undertakes to limit launchers of ICBMs and SLBMs equipped with MIRVs, ASBMs equipped with MIRVs, and heavy bombers equipped for cruise missiles capable of a range in excess of 600 kilometers to an aggregate number not to exceed 1,320,455.

2. Within the aggregate number provided for in paragraph 1 of this Article, each Party undertakes to limit launchers of ICBMs and SLBMs equipped with MIRVs, and ASBMs equipped with MIRVs to an aggregate number not to exceed 1,200.

3. Within the aggregate number provided for in paragraph 2 of this Article, each Party undertakes to limit launchers of ICBMs equipped with MIRVs to an aggregate number not to exceed 820.

. . . .

Article VI. 1. The limitations provided for in this Treaty shall apply to those arms which are:

(a) operational;

(b) in the final stage of construction;

(c) in reserve, in storage, or mothballed;

(d) undergoing overhaul, repair, modernization, or conversion.

. . . .

Article VIII. 1. Each Party undertakes not to flight-test cruise missiles capable of a range in excess of 600 kilometers or ASBMs from aircraft other than bombers or to convert such aircraft into aircraft equipped for such missiles.

. . . .

Article IX. 1. Each Party undertakes not to develop, test, or deploy:

(a) ballistic missiles capable of a range in excess of 600 kilometers for installation on waterborne vehicles other than submarines, or launchers of such missiles;

. . . .

(b) fixed ballistic or cruise missile launchers for emplacement on the ocean floor, on the seabed, or on the beds of internal waters and inland waters, or in the subsoil thereof, or mobile launchers of such missiles, which move only in contact with the ocean floor, the seabed, or the beds of internal waters and inland waters, or missiles for such launchers;

. . . .

(c) systems for placing into Earth orbit nuclear weapons or any other kind of weapons of mass destruction, including fractional orbital missiles;

. . . .

(d) mobile launchers of heavy ICBMs;

(e) SLBMs which have a launch-weight greater or a throw-weight greater than that of the heaviest, in terms of either launch-weight or throw-weight, respectively, of the light ICBMs deployed by either Party as of the date of signature of this Treaty, or launchers of such SLBMs; or

. . . .

Article X. Subject to the provisions of this Treaty, modernization and replacement of strategic offensive arms may be carried out.

Article XI. 1. Strategic offensive arms which would be in excess of the aggregate numbers provided for in this Treaty as well as strategic offensive arms prohibited by this Treaty shall be dismantled or destroyed under procedures to be agreed upon in the Standing Consultative Commission.

2. Dismantling or destruction of strategic offensive arms which would be in excess of the aggregate number provided for in paragraph 1 of Article III shall begin on the date of the entry into force of this Treaty and shall be completed within the following periods from that date: four months for ICBM launchers; six months for SLBM launchers; and three months for heavy bombers.

3. Dismantling or destruction of strategic offensive arms which would be in excess of the aggregate number provided for in paragraph 2 of Article III shall be initiated no later than January 1, 1981, shall be carried out throughout the ensuing twelve-month period, and shall be completed no later than December 31, 1981.

4. Dismantling or destruction of strategic offensive arms prohibited by this Treaty shall be completed within the shortest possible agreed period of time, but not later than six months after the entry into force of this Treaty.

. . . .

Article XIV. The Parties undertake to begin, promptly after the entry into force of this Treaty, active negotiations with the objective of achieving, as soon as possible, agreement on further measures for the limitation and reduction of strategic arms. It is also the objective of the Parties to conclude well in advance of 1985 an agreement limiting strategic offensive arms to replace this Treaty upon its expiration.

Article XV. 1. For the purpose of providing assurance of compliance with the provisions of this Treaty, each Party shall use national technical means of verification at its disposal in a manner consistent with generally recognized principles of international law.

2. Each party undertakes not to interfere with the national technical means of verification of the other Party operating in accordance with paragraph 1 of this Article.

3. Each Party undertakes not to use deliberate concealment measures which impede verification by national technical means of compliance with the provisions of this Treaty. This obligation shall not require changes in current construction, assembly, conversion, or overhaul practices.

First Agreed Statement. Deliberate concealment measures, as referred to in paragraph 3 of Article XV of the Treaty, are measures carried out deliberately to hinder or deliberately to impede verification by national technical means of compliance with the provisions of the Treaty.

....

Article XVII. 1. To promote the objectives and implementation of the provisions of this Treaty, the Parties shall use the Standing Consultative Commission established by the Memorandum of Understanding Between the Government of the United States of America and the Government of the Union of Soviet Socialist Republics Regarding the Establishment of a Standing Consultative Commission of December 21, 1972.

2. Within the framework of the Standing Consultative Commission, with respect to this Treaty, the Parties will:

(a) consider questions concerning compliance with the obligations assumed and related situations which may be considered ambiguous;

(b) provide on a voluntary basis such information as either Party considers necessary to assure confidence in compliance with the obligations assumed;

(c) consider questions involving unintended interference with national technical means of verification, and questions involving unintended impeding of verification by national technical means of compliance with the provisions of this Treaty;

....

TREATY BETWEEN THE UNITED STATES OF AMERICA AND THE UNION OF SOVIET SOCIALIST REPUBLICS ON THE ELIMINATION OF THEIR INTERMEDIATE-RANGE AND SHORTER-RANGE MISSILES* (INF TREATY)

The United States of America and the Union of Soviet Socialist Republics, hereinafter referred to as the Parties,

Conscious that nuclear war would have devastating consequences for all mankind,

Guided by the objective of strengthening strategic stability,

Convinced that the measures set forth in this Treaty will help to reduce the risk of outbreak of war and strengthen international peace and security, and

Mindful of their obligations under Article VI of the Treaty on the Non-Proliferation of Nuclear Weapons,

Have agreed as follows:

Article I. In accordance with the provisions of this Treaty which includes the Memorandum of Understanding and Protocols which form an integral part thereof, each Party shall eliminate its intermediate-range and shorter-range missiles, not have such systems thereafter, and carry out the other obligations set forth in this Treaty.

Article II. For the purposes of this Treaty:

1. The term "ballistic missile" means a missile that has a ballistic trajectory over most of its flight path. The term "ground-launched ballistic missile (GLBM)" means a ground-launched ballistic missile that is a weapon-delivery vehicle.

2. The term "cruise missile" means an unmanned, self-propelled vehicle that sustains flight through the use of aerodynamic lift over most of its flight path. The term "ground-launched cruise missile (GLCM)" means a ground-launched cruise missile that is a weapon-delivery vehicle.

3. The term "GLBM launcher" means a fixed launcher or a mobile land-based transporter-erector-launcher mechanism for launching a GLBM.

4. The term "GLCM launcher" means a fixed launcher or a mobile land-based transporter-erector-launcher mechanism for launching a GLCM.

5. The term "intermediate-range missile" means a GLBM or a GLCM having a range capability in excess of 1000 kilometers but not in excess of 5500 kilometers.

---

* Treaty Between the United States of America and the Union of Soviet Socialist Republics on the Elimination of Their Intermediate-Range and Shorter-Range Missiles, U.S.-U.S.S.R., Dec. 8, 1987, S. Treaty Doc. No. 100-11, at 67 (entered into force June 1, 1988), *available at* http://www.state.gov/t/np/trty/18432.htm>. *See also* U.S. Dep't of State, Article-by-Article Analysis of the Treaty Between the United States of America and the Union of Soviet Socialist Republics on the Elimination of Their Intermediate-Range and Shorter-Range Missiles, *in id.* at 1.

6. The term "shorter-range missile" means a GLBM or a GLCM having a range capability equal to or in excess of 500 kilometers but not in excess of 1000 kilometers.

7. The term "deployment area" means a designated area within which intermediate-range missiles and launchers of such missiles may operate and within which one or more missile operating bases are located.

....

Article III. 1. For the purposes of this Treaty, existing types of intermediate-range missiles are:

(a) for the United States of America, missiles of the types designated by the United States of America as the Pershing II and the BGM-109G, which are known to the Union of Soviet Socialist Republics by the same designations; and

(b) for the Union of Soviet Socialist Republics, missiles of the types designated by the Union of Soviet Socialist Republics as the RSD-10, the R-12 and the R-14, which are known to the United States of America as the SS-20, the SS-4 and the SS-5, respectively.

2. For the purposes of this Treaty, existing types of shorter-range missiles are:

(a) for the United States of America, missiles of the type designated by the United States of America as the Pershing IA, which is known to the Union of Soviet Socialist Republics by the same designation; and

(b) for the Union of Soviet Socialist Republics, missiles of the types designated by the Union of Soviet Socialist Republics as the OTR-22 and the OTR-23, which are known to the United States of America as the SS-12 and the SS-23, respectively.

Article IV. 1. Each Party shall eliminate all its intermediate-range missiles and launchers of such missiles, and all support structures and support equipment of the categories listed in the Memorandum of Understanding associated with such missiles and launchers, so that no later than three years after entry into force of this Treaty and thereafter no such missiles, launchers, support structures or support equipment shall be possessed by either Party.

2. To implement paragraph 1 of this Article, upon entry into force of this Treaty, both Parties shall begin and continue throughout the duration of each phase, the reduction of all types of their deployed and non-deployed intermediate-range missiles and deployed and non-deployed launchers of such missiles and support structures and support equipment associated with such missiles and launchers in accordance with the provisions of this Treaty. These reductions shall be implemented in two phases so that:

(a) by the end of the first phase, that is, no later than 29 months after entry into force of this Treaty:

(i) the number of deployed launchers of intermediate-range missiles for each Party shall not exceed the number of launchers that are capable of carrying or containing at one time missiles considered by the Parties to carry 171 warheads;

(ii) the number of deployed intermediate-range missiles for each Party shall not exceed the number of such missiles considered by the Parties to carry 180 warheads;

(iii) the aggregate number of deployed and non-deployed launchers of intermediate-range missiles for each Party shall not exceed the number of launchers that are capable of carrying or containing at one time missiles considered by the Parties to carry 200 warheads;

(iv) the aggregate number of deployed and non-deployed intermediate-range missiles for each Party shall not exceed the number of such missiles considered by the Parties to carry 200 warheads; and

(v) the ratio of the aggregate number of deployed and non-deployed intermediate-range GLBMs of existing types for each Party to the aggregate number of deployed and non-deployed intermediate-range missiles of existing types possessed by that Party shall not exceed the ratio of such intermediate-range GLBMs to such intermediate-range missiles for that Party as of November 1, 1987, as set forth in the Memorandum of Understanding; and

(b) by the end of the second phase, that is, no later than three years after entry into force of this Treaty, all intermediate-range missiles of each Party, launchers of such missiles and all support structures and support equipment of the categories listed in the Memorandum of Understanding associated with such missiles and launchers, shall be eliminated.

Article V. 1. Each Party shall eliminate all its shorter-range missiles and launchers of such missiles, and all support equipment of the categories listed in the Memorandum of Understanding associated with such missiles and launchers, so that no later than 18 months after entry into force of this Treaty and thereafter no such missiles, launchers or support equipment shall be possessed by either Party.

2. No later than 90 days after entry into force of this Treaty, each Party shall complete the removal of all its deployed shorter-range missiles and deployed and non-deployed launchers of such missiles to elimination facilities and shall retain them at those locations until they are eliminated in accordance with the procedures set forth in the Protocol on Elimination. No later than 12 months after entry into force of this Treaty, each Party shall complete the removal of all its non-deployed shorter-range missiles to elimination facilities and shall retain them at those locations until they are eliminated in accordance with the procedures set forth in the Protocol on Elimination.

3. Shorter-range missiles and launchers of such missiles shall not be located at the same elimination facility. Such facilities shall be separated by no less than 1000 kilometers.

Article VI. 1. Upon entry into force of this Treaty and thereafter, neither Party shall:

(a) produce or flight-test any intermediate-range missiles or produce any stages of such missiles or any launchers of such missiles; or

(b) produce, flight-test or launch any shorter-range missiles or produce any stages of such missiles or any launchers of such missiles.

2. Notwithstanding paragraph 1 of this Article, each Party shall have the right to produce a type of GLBM not limited by this Treaty which uses a stage which is outwardly similar to, but not interchangeable with, a stage of an existing type of intermediate-range GLBM having more than one stage, providing that that Party does not produce any other stage which is outwardly similar to, but not interchangeable with, any other stage of an existing type of intermediate-range GLBM.

. . . .

Article X. 1. Each Party shall eliminate its intermediate-range and shorter-range missiles and launchers of such missiles and support structures and support equipment associated with such missiles and launchers in accordance with the procedures set forth in the Protocol on Elimination.

2. Verification by on-site inspection of the elimination of items of missile systems specified in the Protocol on Elimination shall be carried out in accordance with Article XI of this Treaty, the Protocol on Elimination and the Protocol on Inspection.

. . . .

Article XI. 1. For the purpose of ensuring verification of compliance with the provisions of this Treaty, each Party shall have the right to conduct on-site inspections. The Parties shall implement on-site inspections in accordance with this Article, the Protocol on Inspection and the Protocol on Elimination.

2. Each Party shall have the right to conduct inspections provided for by this Article both within the territory of the other Party and within the territories of basing countries.

3. Beginning 30 days after entry into force of this Treaty, each Party shall have the right to conduct inspections at all missile operating bases and missile support facilities specified in the Memorandum of Understanding other than missile production facilities, and at all elimination facilities included in the initial data update required by paragraph 3 of Article IX of this Treaty. These inspections shall be completed no later than 90 days after entry into force of this Treaty. The purpose of these inspections shall be to verify the number of missiles, launchers, support structures and support equipment and other data, as of the date of entry into force of this Treaty, provided pursuant to paragraph 3 of Article IX of this Treaty.

4. Each Party shall have the right to conduct inspections to verify the elimination, notified pursuant to paragraph 5(a) of Article IX of this Treaty, of missile operating bases and missile support facilities other than missile production facilities, which are thus no longer subject to inspections pursuant to paragraph 5(a) of this Article. Such an inspection shall be carried out within 60 days after the scheduled date of the elimination of that facility. If a Party conducts an inspection at a particular facility pursuant to paragraph 3 of this Article after the scheduled date of the elimination of that facility, then no additional inspection of that facility pursuant to this paragraph shall be permitted.

5. Each Party shall have the right to conduct inspections pursuant to this paragraph for 13 years after entry into force of this Treaty. Each Party shall have the right to conduct 20 such inspections per calendar year during the first three years after entry into force of this Treaty, 15 such inspections per calendar year during the subsequent five years, and ten such inspections per calendar year during the last five years. Neither Party shall use more than half of its total number of these inspections per calendar year within the territory of any one basing country. Each Party shall have the right to conduct:

(a) inspections, beginning 90 days after entry into force of this Treaty, of missile operating bases and missile support facilities other than elimination facilities and missile production facilities, to ascertain, according to the categories of data specified in the Memorandum of Understanding, the numbers of missiles, launchers, support structures and support equipment located at each missile operating base or missile support facility at the time of the inspection; and

(b) inspections of former missile operating bases and former missile support facilities eliminated pursuant to paragraph 8 of Article X of this Treaty other than former missile production facilities.

6. Beginning 30 days after entry into force of this Treaty, each Party shall have the right, for 13 years after entry into force of this Treaty, to inspect by means of continuous monitoring:

(a) the portals of any facility of the other Party at which the final assembly of a GLBM using stages, any of which is outwardly similar to a stage of a solid-propellant GLBM listed in Article III of this Treaty, is accomplished; or

(b) if a Party has no such facility, the portals of an agreed former missile production facility at which existing types of intermediate-range or shorter-range GLBMs were produced.

The Party whose facility is to be inspected pursuant to this paragraph shall ensure that the other Party is able to establish a permanent continuous monitoring system at that facility within six months after entry into force of this Treaty or within six months of initiation of the process of final assembly described in subparagraph (a). If, after the end of the second year after entry into force of this Treaty, neither Party conducts the process of final assembly described in subparagraph (a) for a period of 12 consecutive months, then neither Party shall have the right to inspect by means of continuous monitoring any missile production facility of the other Party unless the process of final assembly as described in subparagraph (a) is initiated again. Upon entry into force of this Treaty, the facilities to be inspected by continuous monitoring shall be: in accordance with subparagraph (b), for the United States of America, Hercules Plant Number 1, at Magna, Utah; in accordance with subparagraph (a), for the Union of Soviet Socialist Republics, the Votkinsk Machine Building Plant, Udmurt Autonomous Soviet Socialist Republic, Russian Soviet Federative Socialist Republic.

7. Each Party shall conduct inspections of the process of elimination, including elimination of intermediate-range missiles by means of launching, of intermediate-range and shorter-range missiles and launchers of such missiles and support equipment associated with such missiles and launchers carried out at elimination facilities in accordance with Article X of this Treaty and the Protocol on Elimination. Inspectors conducting inspections provided for in this paragraph shall determine that the processes specified for the elimination of the missiles, launchers and support equipment have been completed.

8. Each Party shall have the right to conduct inspections to confirm the completion of the process of elimination of intermediate-range and shorter-range missiles and launchers of such missiles and support equipment associated with such missiles and launchers eliminated pursuant to Section V of the Protocol on Elimination, and of training missiles, training missile stages, training launch canisters and training launchers eliminated pursuant to Sections II, IV and V of the Protocol on Elimination.

Article XII. 1. For the purpose of ensuring verification of compliance with the provisions of this Treaty, each Party shall use national technical means of verification at its disposal in a manner consistent with generally recognized principles of international law.

2. Neither Party shall:

(a) interfere with national technical means of verification of the other Party operating in accordance with paragraph 1 of this Article; or

(b) use concealment measures which impede verification of compliance with the provisions of this Treaty by national technical means of verification carried out in accordance with paragraph 1 of this Article. This obligation does not apply to cover or concealment practices, within a deployment area, associated with normal training, maintenance and operations, including the use of environmental shelters to protect missiles and launchers.

3. To enhance observation by national technical means of verification, each Party shall have the right until a Treaty between the Parties reducing and limiting strategic offensive arms enters into force, but in any event for no more than three years after entry into force of this Treaty, to request the implementation of cooperative measures at deployment bases for road-mobile GLBMs with a range capability in excess of 5500 kilometers, which are not former missile operating bases eliminated pursuant to paragraph 8 of Article X of this Treaty. The Party making such a request shall inform the other Party of the deployment base at which cooperative measures shall be implemented. The Party whose base is to be observed shall carry out the following cooperative measures:

(a) no later than six hours after such a request, the Party shall have opened the roofs of all fixed structures for launchers located at the base, removed completely all missiles on launchers from such fixed structures for launchers and displayed such missiles on launchers in the open without using concealment measures; and

(b) the Party shall leave the roofs open and the missiles on launchers in place until twelve hours have elapsed from the time of the receipt of a request for such an observation.

Each Party shall have the right to make six such requests per calendar year. Only one deployment base shall be subject to these cooperative measures at any one time.

Article XIII. 1. To promote the objectives and implementation of the provisions of this Treaty, the Parties hereby establish the Special Verification Commission. The Parties agree that, if either Party so requests, they shall meet within the framework of the Special Verification Commission to:

(a) resolve questions relating to compliance with the obligations assumed; and

(b) agree upon such measures as may be necessary to improve the viability and effectiveness of this Treaty.

2. The Parties shall use the Nuclear Risk Reduction Centers, which provide for continuous communication between the Parties, to:

(a) exchange data and provide notifications as required by paragraphs 3, 4, 5 and 6 of Article IX of this Treaty and the Protocol on Elimination;

(b) provide and receive the information required by paragraph 9 of Article X of this Treaty;

(c) provide and receive notifications of inspections as required by Article XI of this Treaty and the Protocol on Inspection; and

(d) provide and receive requests for cooperative measures as provided for in paragraph 3 of Article XII of this Treaty.

AGREEMENT BETWEEN THE UNITED STATES OF AMERICA AND THE UNION OF SOVIET SOCIALIST REPUBLICS ON NOTIFICATIONS OF LAUNCHES OF INTERCONTINENTAL BALLISTIC MISSILES AND SUBMARINE-LAUNCHED BALLISTIC MISSILES*

The United States of America and the Union of Soviet Socialist Republics, hereinafter referred to as the Parties,

Affirming their desire to reduce and ultimately eliminate the risk of outbreak of nuclear war, in particular, as a result of misinterpretation, miscalculation, or accident,

Believing that a nuclear war cannot be won and must never be fought,

Believing that agreement on measures for reducing the risk of outbreak of nuclear war serves the interests of strengthening international peace and security,

Reaffirming their obligations under the Agreement on Measures to Reduce the Risk of Outbreak of Nuclear War between the United States of America and the Union of Soviet Socialist Republics of September 30, 1971, the Agreement between the Government of the United States of America and the Government of the Union of Soviet Socialist Republics on the Prevention of Incidents on and over the High Seas of May 25, 1972, and the Agreement between the United States of America and the Union of Soviet Socialist Republics on the Establishment of Nuclear Risk Reduction Centers of September 15, 1987,

Have agreed as follows:

Article I. Each Party shall provide the other Party notification, through the Nuclear Risk Reduction Centers of the United States of America and the Union of Soviet Socialist Republics, no less than twenty-four hours in advance, of the planned date, launch area, and area of impact for any launch of a strategic ballistic missile: an intercontinental ballistic missile (hereinafter "ICBM") or a submarine-launched ballistic missile (hereinafter "SLBM").

Article II. A notification of a planned launch of an ICBM or an SLBM shall be valid for four days counting from the launch date indicated in such a notification. In case of postponement of the launch date within the indicated four days, or cancellation of the launch, no notification thereof shall be required.

Article III. 1. For launches of ICBMs or SLBMs from land, the notification shall indicate the area from which the launch is planned to take place.

2. For launches of SLBMs from submarines, the notification shall indicate the general area from which the missile will be launched. Such notification shall indicate either the quadrant within the ocean (that is, the ninety-degree sector encompassing approxi-

* Agreement Between the United States of America and the Union of Soviet Socialist Republics on Notifications of Launches of Intercontinental Ballistic Missiles and Submarine-Launched Ballistic Missiles, U.S.-U.S.S.R., May 31, 1988, 27 I.L.M. 1200 (entered into force May 31, 1988), *available at* http://www.state.gov/t/ac/trt/4714.htm.

mately one-fourth of the area of the ocean) or the body of water (for example, sea or bay) from which the launch is planned to take place.

3. For all launches of ICBMs or SLBMs, the notification shall indicate the geographic coordinates of the planned impact area or areas of the reentry vehicles. Such an area shall be specified either by indicating the geographic coordinates of the boundary points of the area, or by indicating the geographic coordinates of the center of a circle with a radius specified in kilometers or nautical miles. The size of the impact area shall be determined by the notifying Party at its discretion.

Article IV. The Parties undertake to hold consultations, as mutually agreed, to consider questions relating to implementation of the provisions of this Agreement, as well as to discuss possible amendments thereto aimed at furthering the implementation of the objectives of this Agreement. Amendments shall enter into force in accordance with procedures to be agreed upon.

Article V. This Agreement shall not affect the obligations of either Party under other agreements.

Article VI. This Agreement shall enter into force on the date of its signature.

The duration of this Agreement shall not be limited.

This Agreement may be terminated by either Party upon 12 months written notice to the other Party.

DONE at Moscow on May 31, 1988, in two copies, each in the English and Russian languages, both texts being equally authentic.

TREATY BETWEEN THE UNITED STATES OF AMERICA AND THE UNION OF SOVIET SOCIALIST REPUBLICS ON THE REDUCTION AND LIMITATION OF STRATEGIC OFFENSIVE ARMS* (START I)

Background Note

The Strategic Arms Reduction Treaty (START I), signed by the United States and the former Soviet Union on July 31, 1991, was finally ratified and entered into force in December 1994, after several years of sustained effort to adapt the Treaty's original bilateral implementation regime to a new multilateral context that established Belarus, Kazakhstan, Russia, and Ukraine as the legal successors to the Soviet Union for the purposes of the START I Treaty. All nuclear warheads and strategic offensive arms were subsequently removed from Belarus, Kazakhstan, and Ukraine. On December 5, 2001, the third and final phase of reductions in strategic offensive arms required by the Strategic Arms Reduction Treaty (START I Treaty) was successfully completed. The United States and Russia each now maintain fewer than the Treaty's mandated limits of 1,600 deployed strategic delivery vehicles and 6,000 accountable warheads, a reduction of some 30-to-40 percent of aggregate levels since 1994, when the Treaty entered into force. It is a Treaty unprecedented in length, complexity, and the extent of its verification regime. START I will remain in force through at least 2009, and may be amended to unlimited duration in successive five-year increments.—Eds.

The United States of America and the Union of Soviet Socialist Republics, hereinafter referred to as the Parties,

Conscious that nuclear war would have devastating consequences for all humanity, that it cannot be won and must never be fought,

Convinced that the measures for the reduction and limitation of strategic offensive arms and the other obligations set forth in this Treaty will help to reduce the risk of outbreak of nuclear war and strengthen international peace and security,

Recognizing that the interests of the Parties and the interests of international security require the strengthening of strategic stability,

Mindful of their undertakings with regard to strategic offensive arms in Article VI of the Treaty on the Non-Proliferation of Nuclear Weapons of July 1, 1968; Article XI of the Treaty on the Limitation of Anti-Ballistic Missile Systems of May 26, 1972; and the Washington Summit Joint Statement of June 1, 1990,

Have agreed as follows:

---

* U.S.-U.S.S.R., July 3, 1991, S. Treaty Doc. No. 102-20 (1991), *available at* http://www.fas.org/nuke/control/start1/.

Article I. Each Party shall reduce and limit its strategic offensive arms in accordance with the provisions of this Treaty, and shall carry out the other obligations set forth in this Treaty and its Annexes, Protocols, and Memorandum of Understanding.

Article II. 1. Each Party shall reduce and limit its ICBMs and ICBM launchers, SLBMs and SLBM launchers, heavy bombers, ICBM warheads, SLBM warheads, and heavy bomber armaments, so that seven years after entry into force of this Treaty and thereafter, the aggregate numbers, as counted in accordance with Article III of this Treaty, do not exceed:

(a) 1600, for deployed ICBMs and their associated launchers, deployed SLBMs and their associated launchers, and deployed heavy bombers, including 154 for deployed heavy ICBMs and their associated launchers;

(b) 6000, for warheads attributed to deployed ICBMs, deployed SLBMs, and deployed heavy bombers, including:

(i) 4900, for warheads attributed to deployed ICBMs and deployed SLBMs;

(ii) 1100, for warheads attributed to deployed ICBMs on mobile launchers of ICBMs;

(iii) 1540, for warheads attributed to deployed heavy ICBMs

2. Each Party shall implement the reductions pursuant to paragraph 1 of this Article in three phases, so that its strategic offensive arms do not exceed:

(a) by the end of the first phase, that is, no later than 36 months after entry into force of this Treaty, and thereafter, the following aggregate numbers:

(i) 2100, for deployed ICBMs and their associated launchers, deployed SLBMs and their associated launchers, and deployed heavy bombers;

(ii) 9150, for warheads attributed to deployed ICBMs, deployed SLBMs, and deployed heavy bombers;

(iii) 8050, warheads attributed to deployed ICBMs and deployed SLBMs;

(b) by the end of the second phase, that is, no later than 60 months after entry into force of this Treaty, and thereafter, the following aggregate numbers:

(i) 1900, for deployed ICBMs and their associated launchers, deployed SLBMs and their associated launchers, and deployed heavy bombers;

(ii) 7950, for warheads attributed to deployed ICBMs, deployed SLBMs, and deployed heavy bombers;

(iii) 6750, warheads attributed to deployed ICBMs and deployed SLBMs;

(c) by the end of the third phase, that is, no later than 84 months after entry into force of this Treaty: the aggregate numbers provided for in paragraph 1 of this Article.

3. Each Party shall limit the aggregate throw-weight of its deployed ICBMs and deployed SLBMs so that seven years after entry into force of this Treaty and thereafter such aggregate throw-weight does not exceed 3600 metric tons.

....

Article V. 1. Except as prohibited by the provisions of this Treaty, modernization and replacement of strategic offensive arms may be carried out.

2. Each Party undertakes not to:

(a) produce, flight-test, or deploy heavy ICBMs of a new type, or increase the launch weight or throw-weight of heavy ICBMs of an existing type;

(b) produce, flight-test, or deploy heavy SLBMs;

(c) produce test, or deploy mobile launchers of heavy ICBMs;

(d) produce, test, or deploy additional silo launchers of ICBMs of heavy ICBMs, except for silo launchers of heavy ICBMs that replace silo launchers of heavy ICBMs that have been eliminated in accordance with Section II of the Conversion or Elimination Protocol, provided that the limits provided for in Article II of this Treaty are not exceeded;

(e) convert launchers that are not launchers of heavy ICBMs into launchers of heavy ICBMs;

(f) produce, test, or deploy launchers of heavy SLBMs;

(g) reduce the number of warheads attributed to a heavy ICBM of an existing type.

3. Each Party undertakes not to deploy ICBMs other than in silo launchers of ICBMs, on road-mobile launchers of ICBMs, or on rail-mobile launchers of ICBMs. Each Party undertakes not to produce, test, or deploy ICBM launchers other than silo launchers of ICBMs, road-mobile launchers of ICBMs, or rail-mobile launchers of ICBMs.

4. Each Party undertakes not to deploy on a mobile launcher of ICBMs an ICBM of a type that was not specified as a type of ICBM for mobile launchers of ICBMs in accordance with paragraph 2 of Section VII of the Protocol on Notifications Relating to this Treaty, hereinafter referred to as the Notification Protocol, unless it is an ICBM to which no more than one warhead is attributed and the Parties have agreed within the framework of the Joint Compliance and Inspection Commission to permit deployment of such ICBMs on mobile launchers of ICBMs. A new type of ICBM for mobile launchers of ICBMs may cease to be considered to be a type of ICBM for mobile launchers of ICBMs if no ICBM of that type has been contained on, or flight-tested from, a mobile launcher of ICBMs.

5. Each Party undertakes not to deploy ICBM launchers of a new type of ICBM and not to deploy SLBM launchers of a new type of SLBM if such launchers are capable of launching ICBMs or SLBMs, respectively, of other types. ICBM launchers of existing types of ICBMs and SLBM launchers of existing types of SLBMs shall be incapable, without conversion, of launching ICBMs or SLBMs, respectively, of other types.

6. Each Party undertakes not to convert SLBMs into ICBMs for mobile launchers of ICBMs, or to load SLBMs on, or launch SLBMs from, mobile launchers of ICBMs.

7. Each Party undertakes not to produce, test, or deploy transporter-loaders other than transporter-loaders for ICBMs for road-mobile launchers of ICBMs attributed with one warhead.

8. Each Party undertakes not to locate deployed silo launchers of ICBMs outside ICBM bases for silo launchers of ICBMs.

9. Each Party undertakes not to locate soft-site launchers except at test ranges and space launch facilities. All existing soft-site launchers not at test ranges or space launch facilities shall be eliminated in accordance with the procedures provided for in the Conversion or Elimination Protocol no later than 60 days after entry into force of this Treaty.

10. Each Party undertakes not to:

(a) flight-test ICBMs or SLBMs of a retired or former type from other than test launchers specified for such use or launchers at space launch facilities. Except for soft-site launchers, test launchers specified for such use shall not be used to flight-test ICBMs or SLBMs of a type, any one of which is deployed;

(b) produce ICBMs for mobile launchers of ICBMs of a retired type.

11. Each Party undertakes not to convert silos used as launch control centers into silo launchers of ICBMs.

12. Each Party undertakes not to:

(a) produce, flight-test, or deploy an ICBM or SLBM with more than ten reentry vehicles;

(b) flight-test an ICBM or SLBM with a number of reentry vehicles greater than the number of warheads attributed to it, or, for an ICBM or SLBM of a retired type, with a number of reentry vehicles greater than the largest number of warheads that was attributed to any ICBM or SLBM of that type;

(c) deploy an ICBM or SLBM with a number of reentry vehicles greater than the number of warheads attributed to it;

(d) increase the number of warheads attributed to an ICBM or SLBM of an existing or new type.

13. Each Party undertakes not to flight-test or deploy an ICBM or SLBM with a number of reentry vehicles greater than the number of warheads attributed to it.[Agreed State 3]

14. Each Party undertakes not to flight-test from space launch facilities ICBMs or SLBMs equipped with reentry vehicles.

15. Each Party undertakes not to use ICBMs or SLBMs for delivering objects into the upper atmosphere or space for purposes inconsistent with existing international obligations undertaken by the Parties.

16. Each Party undertakes not to produce, test, or deploy systems for rapid reload and not to conduct rapid reload.

17. Each Party undertakes not to install SLBM launchers on submarines that were not originally constructed as ballistic missile submarines.

18. Each Party undertakes not to produce, test, or deploy:

(a) ballistic missiles with a range in excess of 600 kilometers, or launchers of such missiles, for installation on waterborne vehicles, including free-floating launchers, other than submarines. This obligation shall not require changes in current ballistic missile storage, transport, loading, or unloading practices;

(b) launchers of ballistic or cruise missiles for emplacement on or for tethering to the ocean floor, the seabed, or the beds of internal waters and inland waters, or for emplacement in or for tethering to the subsoil thereof, or mobile launchers of such missiles that move only in contact with the ocean floor, the seabed, or the beds of internal waters and inland waters, or missiles for such launchers. This obligation shall apply to all areas of the ocean floor and the seabed, including the seabed zone referred to in Articles I and II of the Treaty on the Prohibition of the Emplacement of Nuclear Weapons and Other Weapons of Mass Destruction on the Seabed and the Ocean Floor and in the Subsoil Thereof of February 11, 1971;

(c) systems, including missiles, for placing nuclear weapons or any other kinds of weapons of mass destruction into Earth orbit or a fraction of an Earth orbit;

(d) air-to-surface ballistic missiles (ASBMs);

(e) long-range nuclear ALCMs armed with two or more nuclear weapons.

19. Each Party undertakes not to:

(a) flight-test with nuclear armaments an aircraft that is not an airplane, but that has a range of 8000 kilometers or more; equip such an aircraft for nuclear armaments; or deploy such an aircraft with nuclear armaments;

(b) flight-test with nuclear armaments an airplane that was not initially constructed as a bomber, but that has a range of 8000 kilometers or more, or an integrated platform area in excess of 310 square meters; equip such an airplane for nuclear armaments; or deploy such an airplane with nuclear armaments;

(c) flight-test with long-range nuclear ALCMs an aircraft that is not an airplane, or an airplane that was not initially constructed as a bomber; equip such an aircraft or such an airplane for long-range nuclear ALCMs; or deploy such an aircraft or such an airplane with long-range nuclear ALCMs.

20. The United States of America undertakes not to equip existing or future heavy bombers for more than 20 long-range nuclear ALCMs.

21. The Union of Soviet Socialist Republics undertakes not to equip existing or future heavy bombers for more than 16 long-range nuclear ALCMs.

22. Each Party undertakes not to locate long-range nuclear ALCMs at air bases for heavy bombers equipped for nuclear armaments other than long-range nuclear ALCMs, air bases for heavy bombers equipped for non-nuclear armaments, air bases for former heavy bombers, or training facilities for heavy bombers.

23. Each Party undertakes not to base heavy bombers equipped for long-range nuclear ALCMs, heavy bombers equipped for nuclear armaments other than long-range nuclear ALCMs, or heavy bombers equipped for non-nuclear armaments at air bases at which heavy bombers of either of the other two categories are based.

24. Each Party undertakes not to convert:

(a) heavy bombers equipped for nuclear armaments other than long-range nuclear ALCMs into heavy bombers equipped for long-range nuclear ALCM, if such heavy bombers were previously equipped for long-range nuclear ALCMs;

(b) heavy bombers equipped for non-nuclear armaments into heavy bombers equipped for long-range nuclear ALCM or into heavy bombers equipped for nuclear armaments other than long-range nuclear ALCMs;

(c) training heavy bombers into heavy bombers of another category;

(d) former heavy bombers into heavy bombers.

25. Each Party undertakes not to have underground facilities accessible to ballistic missile submarines.

26. Each Party undertakes not to locate railcars at the site of a rail garrison that has been eliminated in accordance with Section IX of the Conversion or Elimination Protocol, unless such railcars have differences, observable by national technical means of verification, in length, width, or height from rail-mobile launchers of ICBMs or launch-associated railcars.

27. Each Party undertakes not to engage in any activities associated with strategic offensive arms at eliminated facilities, notification of the elimination of which has been provided in accordance with paragraph 3 of Section I of the Notification Protocol, unless notification of a new facility at the same location has been provided in accordance with paragraph 3 of Section I of the Notification Protocol. Strategic offensive arms and support equipment shall not be located at eliminated facilities except during their movement through such facilities and during visits of heavy bombers or former heavy bombers at such facilities. Missile tenders may be located at eliminated facilities only for purposes not associated with strategic offensive arms.

28. Each Party undertakes not to base strategic offensive arms subject to the limitations of this Treaty outside its national territory.

29. Each Party undertakes not to use naval vessels that were formerly declared as missile tenders to transport, store, or load SLBMs. Such naval vessels shall not be tied to a ballistic missile submarines for the purpose of supporting such a submarine if such a submarine is located within five kilometers of a submarine base.

30. Each Party undertakes not to remove from production facilities for ICBMs for mobile launchers of ICBMs, solid rocket motors with attached nozzles for the first stages of ICBMs for mobile launchers of ICBMs, except for:

(a) the removal of such motors as part of assembled first stages of ICBMs for ICBMs for mobile launchers of ICBMs that are maintained, stored, and transported in stages;

(b) the removal of such motors as part of assembled ICBMs for mobile launchers of ICBMs that are maintained, stored, and transported as assembled missiles in launch canisters or without launch canisters; and

(c) the removal of such motors as part of assembled first stages of ICBMs for mobile launchers of ICBMs that are maintained, stored, and transported as assembled missiles in launch canisters or without launch canisters, for the purpose of technical characteristics exhibitions.

Article VI. 1. Deployed road-mobile launchers of ICBMs and their associated missiles shall be based only in restricted areas. A restricted area shall not exceed five square kilometers in size and shall not overlap another restricted area. No more than ten deployed road-mobile launchers of ICBMs and their associated missiles may be based or located in a restricted area. A restricted area shall not contain deployed ICBMs for road-mobile launchers of ICBMs of more than one type of ICBM.

2. Each Party shall limit the number of fixed structures for road-mobile launchers of ICBMs within each restricted areas so that these structures shall not be capable of containing more road-mobile launchers of ICBMs than the number of road-mobile launchers of ICBMs specified for that restricted area.

3. Each restricted area shall be located within a deployment area. A deployment area shall not exceed 125,000 square kilometers in size and shall not overlap another deployment area. A deployment area shall contain no more than one ICBM base for road-mobile launchers of ICBMs.[RF MOU Annex A]

4. Deployed rail-mobile launchers of ICBMs and their associated missiles shall be based only in rail garrisons. Each Party shall have no more than seven rail garrisons. No point on a portion of track located inside a rail garrison shall be more than 20 kilometers from any entrance/exit for that rail garrison. This distance shall be measured along the tracks. A rail garrison shall not overlap another rail garrison.

5. Each rail garrison shall have no more than two rail entrances/exits. Each such entrance/exit shall have no more than two separate sets of tracks passing through it (a total of four rails).

6. Each Party shall limit the number of parking sites in each rail garrison to no more than the number of trains of standard configuration specified for that rail garrison. Each rail garrison shall have no more than five parking sites.

7. Each Party shall limit the number of fixed structures for rail-mobile launchers of ICBMs in each rail garrison to no more than the number of trains of standard configuration specified for that rail garrison. Each such structure shall contain no more than one train of standard configuration.

8. Each rail garrison shall contain no more than one maintenance facility.

9. Deployed mobile launchers of ICBMs and their associated missiles may leave restricted areas or rail garrisons only for routine movements, relocations, or dispersals. Deployed road-mobile launchers of ICBMs and their associated missiles may leave deployment areas only for relocations or operational dispersals.

10. Relocations shall be completed within 25 days. No more than 15 percent of the total number of deployed road-mobile launchers of ICBMs and their associated missiles or five such launchers and their associated missiles, whichever is greater, may be outside restricted areas at any one time for the purpose of relocation. No more than 20 percent of the total number of deployed rail-mobile launchers of ICBMs and their associated missiles or five such launchers and their associated missiles, whichever is greater, may be outside rail garrisons at any one time for the purpose of relocation.

11. No more than 50 percent of the total number of deployed rail-mobile launchers of ICBMs and their associated missiles may be engaged in routine movements at any one time.

12. All trains with deployed rail-mobile launchers of ICBMs and their associated missiles of a particular type shall be of one standard configuration. All such trains shall conform to that standard configuration except those taking part in routine movements, relocations, or dispersals, and except that portion of a train remaining within a rail garrisons after the other portion of such a train has departed for the maintenance facility associated with that rail garrison, has been relocated to another facility, or has departed the rail garrison for routine movement. Except for dispersals, notification of variations from standard configuration shall be provided in accordance with paragraphs 13, 14, and 15 of Section II of the Notification Protocol.

....

Article XI. 1. For the purpose of ensuring verification of compliance with the provisions of this Treaty, each Party shall have the right to conduct inspections and continuous monitoring activities and shall conduct exhibitions pursuant to this Article and the Inspection Protocol. Inspections, continuous monitoring activities, and exhibitions shall be conducted in accordance with the procedures provided for in the Inspection Protocol and the Conversion or Elimination Protocol.

2. Each Party shall have the right to conduct baseline data inspections at facilities to confirm the accuracy of data on the numbers and types of items specified for such facilities in the initial exchange of data provided in accordance with paragraph 1 of Section I of the Notification Protocol.

3. Each Party shall have the right to conduct data update inspections at facilities to confirm the accuracy of data on the numbers and types of items specified for such facilities in the notifications and regular exchanges of updated data provided in accordance with paragraphs 2 and 3 of Section I of the Notification Protocol.

4. Each Party shall have the right to conduct new facility inspections to confirm the accuracy of data on the numbers and types of items specified in the notifications of new facilities provided in accordance with paragraph 3 of Section I of the Notification Protocol.

5. Each Party shall have the right to conduct suspect-site inspections to confirm that covert assembly of ICBMs for mobile launchers of ICBMs or covert assembly of first stages of such ICBMs is not occurring.

6. Each Party shall have the right to conduct reentry vehicle inspections of deployed ICBMs and SLBMs to confirm that such ballistic missiles contain no more reentry vehicles than the number of warheads attributed to them.

7. Each Party shall have the right to conduct post-exercise dispersal inspections of deployed mobile launchers of ICBMs and their associated missiles to confirm that the number of mobile launchers of ICBMs and their associated missiles that are located at the inspected ICBM bases and those that have not returned to it after completion of the dispersal does not exceed the number specified for that ICBM base.

8. Each Party shall conduct or shall have the right to conduct conversion or elimination inspections to confirm the conversion or elimination of strategic offensive arms.

9. Each Party shall have the right to conduct close-out inspections to confirm that the elimination of facilities has been completed.

10. Each Party shall have the right to conduct formerly declared facility inspections to confirm that facilities, notification of the elimination of which has been provided in accordance with paragraph 3 of Section I of the Notification Protocol, are not being used for purposes inconsistent with this Treaty.

11. Each Party shall conduct technical characteristics exhibitions, and shall have the right during such exhibitions by the other Party to conduct inspections of an ICBM and an SLBM of each type, and each variant thereof, and of a mobile launcher of ICBMs and each version of such launcher for each type of ICBM for mobile launchers of ICBMs. The purpose of such exhibitions shall be to permit the inspecting Party to confirm that technical characteristics correspond to the data specified for these items. [RF MOU Annex F] [US MOU Annex F][Agreed State 25] [Early Exhibitions Agreement][Agreed State 28]

12. Each Party shall conduct distinguishability exhibitions for heavy bombers, former heavy bombers, and long-range nuclear ALCMs....

....

13. Each Party shall conduct baseline exhibitions, and shall have the right during such exhibitions by the other Party to conduct inspections, of all heavy bombers equipped for long-range nuclear ALCMs equipped for non-nuclear armaments, all training heavy bombers, and all former heavy bombers specified in the initial exchange of data provided in accordance with paragraph 1 of Section I of the Notification Protocol. The purpose of these exhibitions shall be to demonstrate to the inspecting Party that such airplanes satisfy the requirements for conversion in accordance with the Conversion or Elimination Protocol. After a long-range nuclear ALCM has been flight-tested from a heavy bomber of a type, from none of which a long-range nuclear ALCM

had previously been flight-tested, the Party conducting the flight test shall conduct baseline exhibitions, and the other Party shall have the right during such exhibitions to conduct inspections, of 30 percent of the heavy bombers equipped for long-range nuclear ALCMs of such type equipped for nuclear armaments other than long-range nuclear ALCMs at each air base specified for such heavy bombers. The purpose of these exhibitions shall be to demonstrate to the inspecting Party the presence of specified features that make each exhibited heavy bomber distinguishable from heavy bombers of the same type equipped for long-range nuclear ALCMs.

14. Each Party shall have the right to conduct continuous monitoring activities at production facilities for ICBMs for mobile launchers of ICBMs to confirm the number of ICBMs for mobile launchers of ICBMs produced.

Article XII. 1. To enhance the effectiveness of national technical means of verification, each Party shall, if the other Party makes a request in accordance with paragraph 1 of Section V of the Notification Protocol, carry out the following cooperative measures:

(a) a display in the open of the road-mobile launchers of ICBMs located within restricted areas specified by the requesting Party. The number of road-mobile launchers of ICBMs based at the restricted areas specified in each such request shall not exceed ten percent of the total number of deployed road-mobile launchers of ICBMs of the requested Party, and such launchers shall be contained within one ICBM base for road-mobile launchers of ICBMs. For each specified restricted area, the roofs of fixed structures for road-mobile launchers of ICBMs shall be open for the duration of a display. The road-mobile launchers of ICBMs located within the restricted area shall be displayed either located next to or moved halfway out of such fixed structures;

(b) a display in the open of the rail-mobile launchers of ICBMs located at parking sites specified by the requesting Party. Such launchers shall be displayed by removing the entire train from its fixed structure and locating the train within the rail garrison. The number of rail-mobile launchers of ICBMs subject to display pursuant to each such request shall include all such launchers located at no more than eight parking sites, provided that no more than two parking sites may be requested within any one rail garrison in any one request. Requests concerning specific parking sites shall include the designation for each parking site as provided for in Annex A to the Memorandum of Understanding; and

(c) a display in the open of all heavy bombers and former heavy bombers located within one air base specified by the requesting Party, except those heavy bombers and former heavy bombers that are not readily movable due to maintenance or operations. Such heavy bombers and former heavy bombers shall be displayed by removing the entire airplane from its fixed structure, if any, and locating the airplane within the air base. Those heavy bombers and former heavy bombers at the air base specified by the requesting Party that are not readily movable due to maintenance or operations shall be specified by the requested Party in a notification provided in accordance with paragraph 2 of Section V of the Notification Protocol. Such a notification shall be provided no later than 12 hours after the request for display has been made.

2. Road-mobile launchers of ICBMs, rail-mobile launchers of ICBMs, heavy bombers, and former heavy bombers subject to each request pursuant to paragraph 1 of this Article shall be displayed in open view without using concealment measures. Each Party shall have the right to make seven such requests each year, but shall not request a display at any particular ICBM base for road-mobile launchers of ICBMs, any particular parking site, or any particular air base more than two times each year. A Party shall

have the right to request, in any single request, only a display of road-mobile launchers of ICBMs, a display of rail-mobile launchers of ICBMs, or a display of heavy bombers and former heavy bombers. A display shall begin no later than 12 hours after the request is made and shall continue until 18 hours have elapsed from the time that the request was made. If the requested Party cannot conduct a display due to circumstances brought about by *force majeure*, it shall provide notification to the requesting Party in accordance with paragraph 3 of Section V of the Notification Protocol, and the display shall be cancelled. In such a case, the number of requests to which the requesting Party is entitled shall not be reduced.

3. A request for cooperative measures shall not be made for a facility that has been designated for inspection until such an inspection has been completed and the inspectors have departed the facility. A facility for which cooperative measures have been requested shall not be designated for inspection until the cooperative measures have been completed or until notification has been provided in accordance with paragraph 3 of Section V of the Notification Protocol.

....

Article XV. To promote the objectives and implementation of the provisions of this Treaty, the Parties hereby establish the Joint Compliance and Inspection Commission. The Parties agree that, if either Party so requests, they shall meet within the framework of the Joint Compliance and Inspection Commission to:

(a) resolve questions relating to compliance with the obligations assumed;

(b) agree upon such additional measures as may be necessary to improve the viability and effectiveness of this Treaty; and

(c) resolve questions related to the application of relevant provisions of this Treaty to a new kind of strategic offensive arm, after notification has been provided in accordance with paragraph 16 of Section VII of the Notification Protocol.

....

COOPERATIVE THREAT REDUCTION PROGRAM OR SOVIET NUCLEAR THREAT REDUCTION ACT OF 1991*

Background Note

In the fall of 1991, conditions in the disintegrating Soviet Union created a clear and present danger to nuclear safety. An estimated 30,000 nuclear weapons were spread among the former Soviet republics. About 3,200 strategic nuclear warheads were located outside of Russia on the territories of Belarus, Kazakhstan, and Ukraine. Political, social, and economic upheaval heightened the prospects that, unassisted, the former Soviet republics would be unable to provide for safe and secure storage or disposition of these nuclear weapons or other weapons of mass destruction. These conditions also caused concerns that former Soviet nuclear weapons scientists and engineers would export their expertise or services to rogue countries and groups.

The dangers posed by this situation in the new independent states (NIS) were becoming increasingly clear: weapons might be diverted or used in an unauthorized manner; warheads and fissile materials might be sold to countries or groups inimical to the United States; and former Soviet weapons scientists and engineers might contribute to global proliferation. The spectre that nuclear materials could be smuggled beyond Russia's borders increased expectations that it would be only a matter of time before sufficient materials to build a bomb fell into the hands of rogue states, unless immediate action was taken.

Congress responded to these conditions and associated threats by initiating the Nunn-Lugar program in November 1991. Referred to as the Cooperative Threat Reduction (CTR) program, this congressional effort provided the Department of Defense (DoD) with the authority to fund assistance to the eligible states of the former Soviet Union to dismantle and destroy weapons of mass destruction; to strengthen the security of nuclear weapons and fissile materials in connection with dismantlement; to prevent proliferation; and to help demilitarize the industrial and scientific infrastructure which has supported weapons of mass destruction in the NIS.

In accordance with Congressional direction, prior to negotiating any agreement for CTR assistance or obligating any funds, the President (delegated to the Secretary of State) must certify that the recipient nations are making progress toward compliance with criteria outlined in the legislation. In addition, DoD must notify Congress fifteen days in advance of its intent to obligate assistance funds. Negotiations, therefore, take place following Congressional notification, and when DoD is confident that sufficient funding is available to allow for program execution.

The CTR program will continue to provide Russia, Belarus, Kazakhstan, and Ukraine with destruction and dismantlement assistance directed toward accelerating strategic offensive arms elimination. The CTR program will provide assistance to enhance the safety and security of nuclear materials with emphasis on strengthening the entire chain of custody—from eliminating and dismantling the weapons, to assisting in the design and construction

---

* Soviet Nuclear Threat Reduction Act of 1991, Pub. L. No. 102-228, 105 Stat. 1693 (codified as amended at 22 U.S.C. § 2551 note (2000)), *available at* http://www.fas.org/nuke/control/ctr/docs/s3807.html.

of a fissile material storage facility in Russia, and monitoring the storage of the plutonium resulting from dismantlement.

Another key CTR project involves assisting Russia to destroy the 40,000 metric tons of declared chemical weapons agent inherited from the Soviet Union. Without substantial technical and monetary assistance from the United States and other countries, Russia will have difficulty complying with the Chemical Weapons Convention (CWC) destruction schedules.

The CTR program represents a small investment when compared to the overall size of the DoD budget and to the costs of major U.S. defense systems. The payoffs for this modest investment, just $1.27 billion since FY 1992, can be enormous: The denuclearization of Ukraine, Belarus, and Kazakhstan; accelerated Russian strategic arms reductions to START II levels; the initiation and acceleration of the destruction program for Russian chemical weapons; enhanced security, safety, and control of nuclear weapons and fissile material in Russia; progress in moving the scientific and industrial infrastructure in the NIS that has been dedicated to producing Weapons of Mass Destruction to civilian commercial activities; and increased defense and military-to-military contacts. All of this is made possible by a program whose FY 1995 budget of $400 million represented less than two-tenths of one percent of the entire DoD budget.—Eds.

Agreed to November 27, 1991

PART B—FINDINGS AND PROGRAM AUTHORITY

SEC. 211. NATIONAL DEFENSE AND SOVIET WEAPONS DESTRUCTION.

(a) Findings.—The Congress finds—

(1) that Soviet President Gorbachev has requested Western help in dismantling nuclear weapons, and President Bush has proposed United States cooperation on the storage, transportation, dismantling, and destruction of Soviet nuclear weapons;

(2) that the profound changes underway in the Soviet Union pose three types of danger to nuclear safety and stability, as follows:

(A) ultimate disposition of nuclear weapons among the Soviet Union, its republics, and any successor entities that is not conducive to weapons safety or to international stability;

(B) seizure, theft, sale, or use of nuclear weapons or components; and

(C) transfers of weapons, weapons components, or weapons know-how outside of the territory of the Soviet Union, its republics, and any successor entities, that contribute to worldwide proliferation; and

(3) that it is in the national security interests of the United States (A) to facilitate on a priority basis the transportation, storage, safeguarding, and destruction of nuclear and other weapons in the Soviet Union, its republics, and any successor entities, and (B) to assist in the prevention of weapons proliferation.

(b) Exclusions.—United States assistance in destroying nuclear and other weapons under this title may not be provided to the Soviet Union, any of its republics, or any successor entity unless the President certifies to the Congress that the proposed recipient is committed to—

(1) making a substantial investment of its resources for dismantling or destroying such weapons;

(2) forgoing any military modernization program that exceeds legitimate defense requirements and forgoing the replacement of destroyed weapons of mass destruction;

(3) forgoing any use of fissionable and other components of destroyed nuclear weapons in new nuclear weapons;

(4) facilitating United States verification of weapons destruction carried out under section 212;

(5) complying with all relevant arms control agreements; and

(6) observing internationally recognized human rights, including the protection of minorities.

SEC. 212. AUTHORITY FOR PROGRAM TO FACILITATE SOVIET WEAPONS DESTRUCTION.

(a) In General.—Notwithstanding any other provision of law, the President, consistent with the findings stated in section 211, may establish a program as authorized in subsection (b) to assist Soviet weapons destruction. Funds for carrying out this program shall be provided as specified in part C.

(b) Type of Program.—The program under this section shall be limited to cooperation among the United States, the Soviet Union, its republics, and any successor entities to—

(1) destroy nuclear weapons, chemical weapons, and other weapons,

(2) transport, store, disable, and safeguard weapons in connection with their destruction, and

(3) establish verifiable safeguards against the proliferation of such weapons.

Such cooperation may involve assistance in planning and in resolving technical problems associated with weapons destruction and proliferation. Such cooperation may also involve the funding of critical short-term requirements related to weapons destruction and should, to the extent feasible, draw upon United States technology and United States technicians.

PART C—ADMINISTRATIVE AND FUNDING AUTHORITIES

SEC. 221. ADMINISTRATION OF NUCLEAR THREAT REDUCTION PROGRAMS.

(a) Funding.—

(1) Transfer authority.—The President may, to the extent provided in an appropriations Act or joint resolution, transfer to the appropriate defense accounts from amounts appropriated to the Department of Defense for fiscal year 1992 for operation and maintenance or from balances in working capital accounts established under section 2208 of title 10, United States Code, not to exceed $400,000,000 for use in reducing the Soviet military threat under part B.

(2) Limitation.—Amounts for transfers under paragraph (1) may not be derived from amounts appropriated for any activity of the Department of Defense that the Secretary of Defense determines essential for the readiness of the Armed Forces, including amounts for—

(A) training activities; and

(B) depot maintenance activities.

(b) Department of Defense.—The Department of Defense shall serve as the executive agent for any program established under part B.

(c) Reimbursement of Other Agencies.—The Secretary of Defense may reimburse other United States Government departments and agencies under this section for costs of participation, as directed by the President, only in a program established under part B.

(d) Charges Against Funds.—The value of any material from existing stocks and inventories of the Department of Defense, or any other United States Government department or agency, that is used in providing assistance under part B to reduce the Soviet military threat may not be charged against funds available pursuant to subsection (a) to the extent that the material contributed is directed by the President to be contributed without subsequent replacement.

(e) Determination by Director of OMB.—No amount may be obligated for the program under part B unless expenditures for that program have been determined by the Director of the Office of Management and Budget to be counted against the defense category of the discretionary spending limits for fiscal year 1992 (as defined in section 601(a)(2) of the Congressional Budget Act of 1974) for purposes of part C of the Balanced Budget and Emergency Deficit Control Act of 1985.

SEC. 222. REPAYMENT ARRANGEMENTS.

(a) Reimbursement Arrangements.—Assistance provided under part B to the Soviet Union, any of its republics, or any successor entity shall be conditioned, to the extent that the President determines to be appropriate after consultation with the recipient government, upon the agreement of the recipient government to reimburse the United States Government for the cost of such assistance from natural resources or other materials available to the recipient government.

(b) Natural Resources, Etc.—The President shall encourage the satisfaction of such reimbursement arrangements through the provision of natural resources, such as oil and petroleum products and critical and strategic materials, and industrial goods. Materials received by the United States Government pursuant to this section that are suitable for inclusion in the Strategic Petroleum Reserve or the National Defense Stockpile may be deposited in the reserve or stockpile without reimbursement. Other material and services received may be sold or traded on the domestic or international market with the proceeds to be deposited in the General Fund of the Treasury.

It is the sense of the Senate that the committee of conference on House Joint Resolution 157 should consider providing the necessary authority in the conference agreement for the President to transfer funds pursuant to this title.

PART D—REPORTING REQUIREMENTS

SEC. 231. PRIOR NOTICE OF OBLIGATIONS TO CONGRESS.

Not less than 15 days before obligating any funds for a program under part B, the President shall transmit to the Congress a report on the proposed obligation. Each such report shall specify—

(1) the account, budget activity, and particular program or programs from which the funds proposed to be obligated are to be derived and the amount of the proposed obligation; and

(2) the activities and forms of assistance under part B for which the President plans to obligate such funds.

SEC. 232. QUARTERLY REPORTS ON PROGRAM.

Not later than 30 days after the end of each quarter of fiscal years 1992 and 1993, the President shall transmit to the Congress a report on the activities to reduce the Soviet military threat carried out under part B. Each such report shall set forth, for the preceding quarter and cumulatively, the following:

(1) Amounts spent for such activities and the purposes for which they were spent.

(2) The source of the funds obligated for such activities, stated specifically by program.

(3) A description of the participation of the Department of Defense, and the participation of any other United States Government department or agency, in such activities.

(4) A description of the activities carried out under part B and the forms of assistance provided under part B.

(5) Such other information as the President considers appropriate to fully inform the Congress concerning the operation of the program under part B.

. . . .

TREATY BETWEEN THE UNITED STATES OF AMERICA AND THE RUSSIAN FEDERATION ON FURTHER REDUCTION AND LIMITATION OF STRATEGIC OFFENSIVE ARMS* (START II)

Background Note

START II was signed in Moscow by U.S. President George H.W. Bush and Russian President Boris Yeltsin on January 3, 1993. The intent of START II was to reduce deployed warheads by an additional 50%. Seven years after the Treaty was signed the Russian Duma finally ratified it on April 14, 2000 but with a number of stipulations (including the continuation in force of the ABM Treaty) which were ultimately unacceptable to the United States. As a response to the U.S. withdrawal from the ABM Treaty on June 13, 2002, Russia declared that it would no longer be bound by the Treaty. Subsequent events, including the subsequent entry into force of the Moscow Treaty mandating reductions of nuclear weapons to levels far lower than anticipated by START II, makes it extremely unlikely this treaty will ever enter into force.—Eds.

The United States of America and the Russian Federation, hereinafter referred to as the Parties,

Reaffirming their obligations under the Treaty Between the United States of America and the Union of Soviet Socialist Republics on the Reduction and Limitation of Strategic Offensive Arms of July 31, 1991, hereinafter referred to as the START Treaty,

Stressing their firm commitment to the Treaty on the Non-Proliferation of Nuclear Weapons of July 1, 1968, and their desire to contribute to its strengthening,

Taking into account the commitment by the Republic of Belarus, the Republic of Kazakhstan, and Ukraine to accede to the Treaty on the Non-Proliferation of Nuclear Weapons of July 1, 1968, as non-nuclear-weapon States Parties,

Mindful of their undertakings with respect to strategic offensive arms under Article VI of the Treaty on the Non-Proliferation of Nuclear Weapons of July 1, 1968, and under the Treaty Between the United States of America and the Union of Soviet Socialist Republics on the Limitation of Anti-Ballistic Missile Systems of May 26, 1972, as well as the provisions of the Joint Understanding signed by the Presidents of the United States of America and the Russian Federation on June 17, 1992, and of the Joint Statement on a Global Protection System signed by the Presidents of the United States of America and the Russian Federation on June 17, 1992,

Desiring to enhance strategic stability and predictability, and, in doing so, to reduce further strategic offensive arms, in addition to the reductions and limitations provided for in the START Treaty,

---

* U.S.-Russ., Jan. 3, 1993, S. TREATY DOC. No. 103-1, at 32 (1993), *available at* http://www.fas.org/nuke/control/start2/.

Considering that further progress toward that end will help lay a solid foundation for a world order built on democratic values that would preclude the risk of outbreak of war,

Recognizing their special responsibility as permanent members of the United Nations Security Council for maintaining international peace and security,

Taking note of United Nations General Assembly Resolution 47/52K of December 9, 1992.

Conscious of the new realities that have transformed the political and strategic relations between the Parties, and the relations of partnership that have been established between them,

Have agreed as follows:

Article I. 1. Each Party shall reduce and limit its intercontinental ballistic missiles (ICBMs) and ICBM launchers, submarine-launched ballistic missiles (SLBMs) and SLBM launchers, heavy bombers, ICBM warheads, SLBM warheads, and heavy bomber armaments, so that no later than December 31, 2004 and thereafter, the aggregate number for each Party, as counted in accordance with Articles III and IV of this Treaty, does not exceed, for warheads attributed to deployed ICBMs, deployed SLBMs, and deployed heavy bombers, a number between 3800 and 4250 or such lower number as each Party shall decide for itself, but in no case shall such number exceed 4250.

2. Within the limitations provided for in paragraph 1 of this Article, the aggregate numbers for each Party shall not exceed:

(a) 2160, for warheads attributed to deployed SLBMs;

(b) 1200 for warheads attributed to deployed ICBMs of types to which more than one warhead is attributed; and

(c) 650, for warheads attributed to deployed heavy ICBMs.

3. Upon fulfillment of the obligations provided for in paragraph 1 of this Article, each Party shall further reduce and limit its ICBMs and ICBM launchers, SLBMs and SLBM launchers, s, ICBM warheads, SLBM warheads, and heavy bomber armaments, so that no later than December 31, 2007, and thereafter, the aggregate number for each Party, as counted in accordance with Articles III and IV of this Treaty, does not exceed, for warheads attributed to deployed ICBMs, deployed SLBMS, and deployed heavy bombers, a number between 3000 and 3500 or such lower number as each Party shall decide for itself, but in no case shall such number exceed 3500.

4. Within the limitations provided for in paragraph 3 of this Article, the aggregate numbers for each Party shall not exceed:

(a) a number between 1700 and 1750, for warheads attributed to deployed SLBMs or such lower number as each Party shall decide for itself, but in no case shall such number exceed 1750;

(b) zero, for warheads attributed to deployed ICBMs of types to which more than one warhead is attributed; and

(c) zero, for warheads attributed to deployed heavy ICBMs.

5. The process of reductions provided for in paragraphs 1 and 2 of this Article shall begin upon entry into force of this Treaty, shall be sustained throughout the reductions period provided for in paragraph 1 of this Article, and shall be completed no later than December 31, 2004. Upon completion of these reductions, the Parties shall begin fur-

ther reductions provided for in paragraphs 3 and 4 of this Article, which shall also be sustained throughout the reductions period defined in accordance with paragraphs 3 and 6 of this Article.

6. The Parties may conclude an agreement on a program of assistance for the purpose of facilitating implementation of the provisions of this Article, including for the purpose of accelerating such implementation.

Article II. 1. No later than December 31, 2007, each Party undertakes to have eliminated or to have converted to launchers of ICBMs to which one warhead is attributed all its deployed and non-deployed launchers of ICBMs to which more than one warhead is attributed under Article III of this Treaty (including test launchers and training launchers), with the exception of those launchers of ICBMs other than heavy ICBMs at space launch facilities allowed under the START Treaty, and not to have thereafter launchers of ICBMs to which more than one warhead is attributed. ICBM launchers that have been converted to launch an ICBM of a different type shall not be capable of launching an ICBM of the former type. Each Party shall carry out such elimination or conversion using the procedures provided for in the START Treaty, except as otherwise provided for in paragraph 3 of this Article.

2. The obligations provided for in paragraph 1 of this Article shall not apply to silo launchers of ICBMs on which the number of warheads has been reduced to one pursuant to paragraph 2 of Article III of this Treaty.

3. Elimination of silo launchers of heavy ICBMs, including test launchers and training launchers, shall be implemented by means of either:

(a) elimination in accordance with the procedures provided for in Section II of the Protocol on Procedures Governing the Conversion or Elimination of the Items Subject to the START Treaty; or

(b) conversion to silo launchers of ICBMs other than heavy ICBMs in accordance with the procedures provided for in the Protocol on Procedures Governing Elimination of Heavy ICBMs and on Procedures Governing Conversion of Silo Launchers of Heavy ICBMs Relating to the Treaty Between the United States of America and the Russian Federation on Further Reduction and Limitation of Strategic Offensive Arms, hereinafter referred to as the Elimination and Conversion Protocol. No more than 90 silo launchers of heavy ICBMs may be so converted.

4. Each Party undertakes not to emplace an ICBM, the launch canister of which has a diameter greater than 2.5 meters, in any silo launcher of heavy ICBMs converted in accordance with subparagraph 3(b) of this Article.

5. Elimination of launchers of heavy ICBMs at space launch facilities shall only be carried out in accordance with subparagraph 3(a) of this Article.

6. No later than December 31, 2007, each Party undertakes to have eliminated all of its deployed and non-deployed heavy ICBMs and their launch canisters in accordance with the procedures provided for in the Elimination and Conversion Protocol or by using such missiles for delivering objects into the upper atmosphere or space, and not to have such missiles or launch canisters thereafter.

7. Each Party shall have the right to conduct inspections in connection with the elimination of heavy ICBMs and their launch canisters, as well as inspections in connection with the conversion of silo launchers of heavy ICBMs. Except as otherwise pro-

vided for in the Elimination and Conversion Protocol, such inspections shall be conducted subject to the applicable provisions of the START Treaty.

8. Each Party undertakes not to transfer heavy ICBMs to any recipient whatsoever, including any other Party to the START Treaty.

9. Beginning on December 31, 2007, and thereafter, each Party undertakes not to produce, acquire, flight-test (except for flight tests from space launch facilities conducted in accordance with the provisions of the START Treaty), or deploy ICBMs to which more than one warhead is attributed under Article III of this Treaty.

Article III. 1. For the purposes of attributing warheads to deployed ICBMs and deployed SLBMs under this Treaty, the Parties shall use the provisions provided for in Article III of the START Treaty, except as otherwise provided for in paragraph 2 of this Article.

2. Each Party shall have the right to reduce the number of warheads attributed to deployed ICBMs or deployed SLBMs only of existing types, except for heavy ICBMs. Reduction in the number of warheads attributed to deployed ICBMs and deployed SLBMs of existing types that are not heavy ICBMs shall be carried out in accordance with the provisions of paragraph 5 of Article III of the START Treaty, except that:

(a) the aggregate number by which warheads are reduced may exceed the 1250 limit provided for in paragraph 5 of Article III of the START Treaty;

(b) the number by which warheads are reduced on ICBMs and SLBMS, other than the Minuteman III ICBM for the United States of America and the SS-N-18 SLBM for the Russian Federation, may at any one time exceed the limit of 500 warheads for each Party provided for in subparagraph 5(c)(i) of Article III of the START Treaty;

(c) each Party shall have the right to reduce by more than four warheads, but not by more than five warheads, the number of warheads attributed to each ICBM out of no more than 105 ICBMs of one existing type of ICBM. An ICBM to which the number of warheads attributed has been reduced in accordance with this paragraph shall only be deployed in an ICBM launcher in which an ICBM of that type was deployed as of the date of signature of the START Treaty; and

(d) the reentry vehicle platform for an ICBM or SLBM to which a reduced number of warheads is attributed is not required to be destroyed and replaced with a new reentry vehicle platform.

3. Notwithstanding the number of warheads attributed to a type of ICBM or SLBM in accordance with the START Treaty, each Party undertakes not to:

(a) produce, flight-test, or deploy an ICBM or SLBM with a number of reentry vehicles greater than the number of warheads attributed to it under this Treaty; and

(b) increase the number of warheads attributed to an ICBM or SLBM that has had the number of warheads attributed to it reduced in accordance with the provisions of this Article.

Article IV.

1. For the purposes of this Treaty, the number of warheads attributed to each deployed heavy bombers shall be equal to the number of nuclear weapons for which any heavy bomber of the same type or variant of a type is actually equipped, with the exception of heavy bombers reoriented to a conventional role as provided for in paragraph 7

of this Article. Each nuclear weapon for which a heavy bomber is actually equipped shall count as one warhead toward the limitations provided for in Article I of this Treaty. For the purpose of such counting, nuclear weapons include long-range nuclear air-launched cruise missiles (ALCMs), nuclear air-to-surface missiles with a range of less than 600 kilometers, and nuclear bombs.

2. For the purposes of this Treaty, the number of nuclear weapons for which a heavy bomber is actually equipped shall be the number specified for heavy bombers of that type and variant of a type in the Memorandum of Understanding on Warhead Attribution and Heavy Bomber Data Relating to the Treaty Between the United States of America and the Russian Federation on Further Reduction and Limitation of Strategic Offensive Arms, hereinafter referred to as the Memorandum on Attribution.

3. Each Party undertakes not to equip any heavy bomber with a greater number of nuclear weapons than the number specified for heavy bombers of that type or variant of a type in the Memorandum on Attribution.

4. No later than 180 days after entry into force of this Treaty, each Party shall exhibit one heavy bomber of each type and variant of a type specified in the Memorandum on Attribution. The purpose of the exhibition shall be to demonstrate to the other Party the number of nuclear weapons for which a heavy bomber of a given type or variant of a type is actually equipped.

5. If either Party intends to change the number of nuclear weapons specified in the Memorandum on Attribution, for which a heavy bomber of a type or variant of a type is actually equipped, it shall provide a 90-day advance notification of such intention to the other Party. Ninety days after providing such a notification, or at a later date agreed by the Parties, the Party changing the number of nuclear weapons for which a heavy bomber is actually equipped shall exhibit one heavy bomber of each such type or variant of a type. The purpose of the exhibition shall be to demonstrate to the other Party the revised number of nuclear weapons for which heavy bombers of the specified type or variant of a type are actually equipped. The number of nuclear weapons attributed to the specified type and variant of a type of heavy bomber shall change on the ninetieth day after the notification of such intent. On that day, the Party changing the number of nuclear weapons for which a heavy bomber is actually equipped shall provide to the other Party a notification of each change in data according to categories of data contained in the Memorandum on Attribution.

6. The exhibitions and inspections conducted pursuant to paragraphs 4 and 5 of this Article shall be carried out in accordance with the procedures provided for in the Protocol on Exhibitions and Inspections of Heavy Bombers Relating to the Treaty Between the United States of America and the Russian Federation on Further Reduction and Limitation of Strategic Offensive Arms, hereinafter referred to as the Protocol on Exhibitions and Inspections.

7. Each Party shall have the right to reorient to a conventional role heavy bomber equipped for nuclear armaments other than long-range nuclear ALCMS. For the purposes of this Treaty, heavy bombers reoriented to a conventional role are those heavy bombers specified by a Party from among its heavy bombers equipped for nuclear armaments other than long-range nuclear ALCMs that have never been accountable under the START Treaty as heavy bombers equipped for long-range nuclear ALCMS. The reorienting Party shall provide to the other Party a notification of its intent to reorient a heavy bomber to a conventional role no less than 90 days in advance of such re-

orientation. No conversion procedures shall be required for such a heavy bomber to be specified as a heavy bomber reoriented to a conventional role.

8. Heavy bomber reoriented to a conventional role shall be subject to the following requirements

(a) the number of such heavy bombers shall not exceed 100 at any one time;

(b) such heavy bombers shall be based separately from heavy bombers with nuclear roles;

(c) such heavy bombers shall be used only for non-nuclear missions. Such heavy bombers shall not be used in exercises for nuclear missions, and their aircrews shall not train or exercise for such missions; and

(d) heavy bombers reoriented to a conventional role shall have differences from other heavy bombers of that type or variant of a type that are observable by national technical means of verification and visible during inspection.

9. Each Party shall have the right to return to a nuclear role heavy bombers that have been reoriented in accordance with paragraph 7 of this Article to a conventional role. The Party carrying out such action shall provide to the other Party through diplomatic channels notification of its intent to return a heavy bomber to a nuclear role no less than 90 days in advance of taking such action. Such a heavy bomber returned to a nuclear role shall not subsequently be reoriented to a conventional role. Heavy bombers reoriented to a conventional role that are subsequently returned to a nuclear role shall have differences observable by national technical means of verification and visible during inspection from other heavy bombers of that type and variant of a type that have not been reoriented to a conventional role, as well as from heavy bombers of that type and variant of a type that are still reoriented to a conventional role.

10. Each Party shall locate storage areas for heavy bomber nuclear armaments no less than 100 kilometers from any air base where heavy bombers reoriented to a conventional role are based.

11. Except as otherwise provided for in this Treaty, heavy bombers reoriented to a conventional role shall remain subject to the provisions of the START Treaty, including the inspection provisions.

12. If not all heavy bombers of a given type or variant of a type are reoriented to a conventional role, one heavy bomber of each type or variant of a type of heavy bomber reoriented to a conventional role shall be exhibited in the open for the purpose of demonstrating to the other Party the differences referred to in subparagraph 8(d) of this Article. Such differences shall be subject to inspection by the other Party.

13. If not all heavy bombers of a given type or variant of a type reoriented to a conventional role are returned to a nuclear role, one heavy bomber of each type and variant of a type of heavy bomber returned to a nuclear role shall be exhibited in the open for the purpose of demonstrating to the other Party the differences referred to in paragraph 9 of this Article. Such differences shall be subject to inspection by the other Party.

14. The exhibitions and inspections provided for in paragraphs 12 and 13 of this Article shall be carried out in accordance with the procedures provided for in the Protocol on Exhibitions and Inspections.

Article V. 1. Except as provided for in this Treaty, the provisions of the START Treaty, including the verification provisions, shall be used for implementation of this Treaty.

2. To promote the objectives and implementation of the provisions of this Treaty, the Parties hereby establish the Bilateral Implementation Commission. The Parties agree that, if either Party so requests, they shall meet within the framework of the Bilateral Implementation Commission to:

(a) resolve questions relating to compliance with the obligations assumed; and

(b) agree upon such additional measures as may be necessary to improve the viability and effectiveness of this Treaty.

Article VI. 1. This Treaty, including its Memorandum on Attribution, Elimination and Conversion Protocol, and Protocol on Exhibitions and Inspections, all of which are integral parts thereof, shall be subject to ratification in accordance with the constitutional procedures of each Party. This Treaty shall enter into force on the date of the exchange of instruments of ratification, but not prior to the entry into force of the START Treaty.

2. The provisions of paragraph 8 of Article II of this Treaty shall be applied provisionally by the Parties from the date of its signature.

3. This Treaty shall remain in force so long as the START Treaty remains in force.

4. Each Party shall, in exercising its national sovereignty, have the right to withdraw from this Treaty if it decides that extraordinary events related to the subject matter of this Treaty have jeopardized its supreme interests. It shall give notice of its decision to the other Party six months prior to withdrawal from this Treaty. Such notice shall include a statement of the extraordinary events the notifying Party regards as having jeopardized its supreme interests.

Article VII. Each Party may propose amendments to this Treaty. Agreed amendments shall enter into force in accordance with the procedures governing entry into force of this Treaty.

Article VIII. This Treaty shall be registered pursuant to Article 102 of the Charter of the United Nations.

DONE at Moscow on January 3, 1993, in two copies, each in the English and Russian languages, both texts being equally authentic.

MEMORANDUM OF UNDERSTANDING ON NOTIFICATIONS OF MISSILE LAUNCHES*

The United States of America and the Russian Federation, hereinafter referred to as the Parties,

Guided by the Joint Statement of the Presidents of the United States of America and the Russian Federation on the Exchange of Information on Missile Launches and Early Warning of September 2, 1998,

Considering the obligations of the Memorandum of Agreement Between the United States of America and the Russian Federation on the Establishment of a Joint Center for the Exchange of Data from Early Warning Systems and Notifications of Missile Launches of June 4, 2000, hereinafter referred to as the JDEC Memorandum, and

Taking into account the need to minimize the consequences of a false missile attack warning and to prevent the possibility of a missile launch caused by such false warning,

Have agreed as follows:

1. This Memorandum establishes a Pre- and Post-Missile Launch Notification System, hereinafter referred to as the PLNS.

2. Each Party shall provide pre-launch and post-launch notifications for launches of ballistic missiles that meet the range or altitude criteria set forth in paragraph 4 of this Memorandum and, with rare exceptions, pre-launch and post-launch notifications for launches of space launch vehicles. Each Party, at its discretion and in support of the objectives of this Memorandum, may also provide information in a timely fashion on other launches and objects, including de-orbiting spacecraft, and geophysical experiments and other work in near-earth space that are capable of disrupting the normal operation of equipment of the early warning systems of the Parties.

. . . .

4. For ballistic missiles, each Party shall provide a notification in accordance with paragraph 2 of this Memorandum when the planned flight range is in excess of 500 kilometers or the planned apex altitude is in excess of 500 kilometers.

5. The terms and their definitions applicable to this Memorandum are provided in Appendix 1 to this Memorandum. Notifications shall be provided in accordance with the provisions of this Memorandum and in the formats set forth in Appendix 2 to this Memorandum. When a date and time are to be specified in a notification, that date and time shall be expressed in Coordinated Universal Time (UTC).

6. Each Party shall provide notifications in accordance with paragraph 2 of this Memorandum of all launches of ballistic missiles and space launch vehicles from the territory of that Party, and all other launches of ballistic missiles and space launch vehicles owned, possessed or controlled by that Party or by any corporation, partnership, joint venture, association or other legal or natural person (either government or pri-

* Memorandum of Understanding on Notifications of Missile Launches, U.S.-Russ., Dec. 16, 2000, 2000 U.S.T. LEXIS 119 (entered into force Dec. 16, 2000), *available at* http://www.state.gov/t/ac/trt/4954.htm#mou.

vate, including international organizations), organized or existing under the laws of that Party.

. . . .

8. A pre-launch notification. . . . shall set forth a launch window in connection with the notification that shall be valid for four days beginning with the date and time of the beginning of the launch window indicated in the notification. Such a pre-launch notification shall be provided no more than 30 days, but no less than 24 hours, prior to the start of the launch window. The launch window may be extended, in increments of four days. Notification of an extension shall be provided no less than one hour prior to the end of the launch window. If the launch window expires prior to a launch, a new pre-launch notification shall be provided. If simultaneous or near simultaneous launches from the same launch location are planned, a Party may provide a single pre-launch notification for all of the launches.

9. A post-launch notification . . . shall be provided not later than 48 hours after the launch.

a. For simultaneous or near simultaneous launches from the same launch location, a Party may provide one post-launch notification for all the launches or a separate post-launch notification for each launch. However, if a separate pre-launch notification has been provided for each launch, a separate post-launch notification shall be provided for each launch.

b. A cancellation notification for a launch for which a pre-launch notification has been provided shall be provided if the launch is cancelled prior to the beginning of the launch window, or did not take place in the launch window, or is postponed for more than four days. A cancellation notification for a multiple launch is not required if at least one ballistic missile of that multiple launch was successfully launched.

. . . .

8. Unless otherwise agreed by the Parties, all notifications shall be provided to the PLNS Information Center, operated as part of the Joint Data Exchange Center (JDEC) in Moscow as established by the JDEC Memorandum. The PLNS Information Center shall serve as the repository for these notifications, and shall transmit them to the Parties. Until the JDEC is fully operational, an interim repository for notifications shall be created and jointly operated under agreed procedures at a location to be determined by the Parties.

. . . .

19. This Memorandum, including its associated appendices, all of which form integral parts thereof, shall enter into force on the date of its signature. This Memorandum shall remain in force for ten years. Upon agreement by the Parties, this Memorandum may be extended for successive five-year periods.

20. A Party may withdraw from this Memorandum upon six months written notice.

Appendix 1
Terms and Their Definitions

For the purposes of this Memorandum:

a. "Space launch vehicle (SLV)" means a rocket used for delivering an object into earth orbit or outer space.

b. "Ballistic missile (BM)" means a missile that has a ballistic trajectory over most of its flight path, regardless of whether or not it is a weapon-delivery vehicle.

c. "Intercontinental ballistic missile (ICBM)" means a land-based ballistic missile that is a weapon-delivery vehicle with a range in excess of 5500 kilometers.

d. "Submarine-launched ballistic missile (SLBM)" means a ballistic missile that is a weapon-delivery vehicle with a range in excess of 600 kilometers launched from a submarine.

e. "Earth's ellipsoid" means a mathematical model of the surface of the earth. The standard for this model will be agreed by the Parties.

f. "Launch window" means the four-day interval of time during which the ballistic missile launch is scheduled to take place and starting with the day and time specified in a notification.

g. "Day" means a 24-hour period measured from the specific event to be notified, when applied to timing of notifications in this Memorandum.

h. "Payload" means everything that separates from the last propulsion stage of a ballistic missile, except for the previous propulsion stages.

i. "Range" means the maximum distance measured along the surface of the earth's ellipsoid from the point of launch of a ballistic missile to the point of impact of the last element of its payload.

j. "Apex altitude" means the distance measured along the normal to the earth's ellipsoid from its surface to the apex of the flight trajectory of a missile.

k. "Launch azimuth" means the angle formed by the projection of the flight trajectory of a missile onto the surface of the earth's ellipsoid and the North direction, measured clockwise in degrees.

l. "Geophysical experiment" means activities conducted in near-earth space that are capable of causing changes in the environment of radio wave propagation, leading to a disruption or cessation of the operation of the early warning systems of the Parties.

m. "Spacecraft" means a vehicle with special equipment and intended for flights into or in outer space for military, commercial (economic) or research (scientific) purposes.

....

Appendix 2

....

f. Revised Launch Window Start Time: time revised launch window begins. Four digits (HHMM) indicate the time.

HH is a number from 00 to 23 that indicates the hour; and MM is a number from 00 to 59 that indicates the minute.

g. For SLVs and for ballistic missiles for which there is no payload impact area: launch azimuth.

h. For ICBMs and SLBMs and for ballistic missiles for which there is a payload impact area: the geographic coordinates of the planned impact area of the payload. This area shall be specified either by the geographic coordinates of four boundary points, or by the geographic coordinates of the center of a circle with a radius specified in kilometers or nautical miles. The notifying Party shall determine at its discretion the size of the impact area.

i. Indication of a single or multiple launch.

j. End of: Notification ID using the unique identification number—PLN/PP/YYYY/xxx/zzz/02-n.

Data Format 3. Post-Launch Notification: A post-launch notification confirming that a launch has occurred shall be made using Data Format 3 and shall include the following data elements:

a. Notification ID: PLN/PP/YYYY/xxx/zzz/03. PLN is a prefix which identifies that the notification is related to the PLNS; PP is a Country Identification Code; YYYY indicates the calendar year; xxx is a number from 001 to 500 that represents the PLNS-generated sequential ID number; zzz is a number from 001 to 999 that represents the sequential number of the launch, this field is used to identify all notifications associated with a specific launch; and 03 is the notification format number.

b. Reference: Reference to the most recent precursor notification (Data Format 1 or Data Format 2) for the launch that has taken place, using the notification's unique identification number.

c. Launch Date: Reported date of launch. Eight digits (DDMMYYYY) indicate the date. DD is a number from 01 to 31 that indicates the day of the month; MM is a number from 01 to 12 that indicates the calendar month; and YYYY indicates the calendar year.

d. Launch Time: Reported time of launch. Four digits (HHMM) indicate the time. HH is a number from 00 to 23 that indicates the hour; and MM is a number from 00 to 59 that indicates the minute.

e. Number of missiles launched.

f. End of: Notification ID using the unique identification number—PLN/PP/YYYY/xxx/zzz/03.

Data Format 4. Launch Cancellation Notification: A notification canceling a previously notified launch shall be made using Data Format 4 and shall include the following data elements:

a. Notification ID: PLN/PP/YYYY/xxx/zzz/04. PLN is a prefix which identifies that the notification is related to the PLNS; PP is a Country Identification Code; YYYY indicates the calendar year; xxx is a number from 001 to 500 that represents the specific PLNS-generated sequential ID number; zzz is a number from 001 to 999 that represents the sequential number of the launch, this field is used to identify all notifications associated with a specific launch; and 04 is the notification format number.

b. Reference: Reference to the most recent precursor notification (Data Format 1 or Data Format 2) for the launch that has been canceled, using the notification's unique identification number.

c. End of: Notification ID using the unique identification number—PLN/PP/YYYY/xxx/zzz/04.

. . . .

Appendix 3
System Implementation

. . . .

Appendix 4
Security Management

. . . .

TREATY BETWEEN THE UNITED STATES OF AMERICA AND THE RUSSIAN FEDERATION ON STRATEGIC OFFENSIVE REDUCTIONS* (SORT/MOSCOW TREATY)

The United States of America and the Russian Federation, hereinafter referred to as the Parties,

Embarking upon the path of new relations for a new century and committed to the goal of strengthening their relationship through cooperation and friendship,

Believing that new global challenges and threats require the building of a qualitatively new foundation for strategic relations between the Parties,

Desiring to establish a genuine partnership based on the principles of mutual security, cooperation, trust, openness, and predictability,

Committed to implementing significant reductions in strategic offensive arms,

Proceeding from the Joint Statements by the President of the United States of America and the President of the Russian Federation on Strategic Issues of July 22, 2001 in Genoa and on a New Relationship between the United States and Russia of November 13, 2001 in Washington,

Mindful of their obligations under the Treaty Between the United States of America and the Union of Soviet Socialist Republics on the Reduction and Limitation of Strategic Offensive Arms of July 31, 1991, hereinafter referred to as the START Treaty,

Mindful of their obligations under Article VI of the Treaty on the Non-Proliferation of Nuclear Weapons of July 1, 1968, and

Convinced that this Treaty will help to establish more favorable conditions for actively promoting security and cooperation, and enhancing international stability,

Have agreed as follows:

Article I. Each Party shall reduce and limit strategic nuclear warheads, as stated by the President of the United States of America on November 13, 2001 and as stated by the President of the Russian Federation on November 13, 2001 and December 13, 2001 respectively, so that by December 31, 2012 the aggregate number of such warheads does not exceed 1700–2200 for each Party. Each Party shall determine for itself the composition and structure of its strategic offensive arms, based on the established aggregate limit for the number of such warheads.

Article II. The Parties agree that the START Treaty remains in force in accordance with its terms.

Article III. For purposes of implementing this Treaty, the Parties shall hold meetings at least twice a year of a Bilateral Implementation Commission.

---

* Treaty Between the United States of America and the Russian Federation on Strategic Offensive Reductions, U.S.-Russ., May 24, 2002, S. Treaty Doc. No. 107-8, at 1 (entered into force June 1, 2003), *available at* http://www.state.gov/t/ac/trt/18016.htm.

Article IV. 1. This Treaty shall be subject to ratification in accordance with the constitutional procedures of each Party. This Treaty shall enter into force on the date of the exchange of instruments of ratification.

2. This Treaty shall remain in force until December 31, 2012 and may be extended by agreement of the Parties or superseded earlier by a subsequent agreement.

3. Each Party, in exercising its national sovereignty, may withdraw from this Treaty upon three months written notice to the other Party.

Article V. This Treaty shall be registered pursuant to Article 102 of the Charter of the United Nations.

Done at Moscow on May 24, 2002, in two copies, each in the English and Russian languages, both texts being equally authentic.

JOINT DECLARATION ON THE NEW STRATEGIC RELATIONSHIP TO THE TREATY ON STRATEGIC OFFENSIVE REDUCTIONS[1] (U.S.A. AND RUSSIAN FEDERATION)

The United States of America and the Russian Federation,

....

Declare as follows:

A Foundation for Cooperation

We are achieving a new strategic relationship. The era in which the United States and Russia saw each other as an enemy or strategic threat has ended. We are partners and we will cooperate to advance stability, security, and economic integration, and to jointly counter global challenges and to help resolve regional conflicts.

To advance these objectives the United States and Russia will continue an intensive dialogue on pressing international and regional problems, both on a bilateral basis and in international fora, including in the UN Security Council, the G-8, and the OSCE. Where we have differences, we will work to resolve them in a spirit of mutual respect.

We will respect the essential values of democracy, human rights, free speech and free media, tolerance, the rule of law, and economic opportunity.

We recognize that the security, prosperity, and future hopes of our peoples rest on a benign security environment, the advancement of political and economic freedoms, and international cooperation.

The further development of U.S.-Russian relations and the strengthening of mutual understanding and trust will also rest on a growing network of ties between our societies and peoples. We will support growing economic interaction between the business communities of our two countries and people-to-people and cultural contacts and exchanges.

Political Cooperation

The United States and Russia are already acting as partners and friends in meeting the new challenges of the 21st century; affirming our Joint Statement of October 21, 2001, our countries are already allied in the global struggle against international terrorism.

The United States and Russia will continue to cooperate to support the Afghan people's efforts to transform Afghanistan into a stable, viable nation at peace with itself and its neighbors. Our cooperation, bilaterally and through the United Nations, the 'Six-Plus-Two' diplomatic process, and in other multilateral fora, has proved important to our success so far in ridding Afghanistan of the Taliban and al-Qaida.

In Central Asia and the South Caucasus, we recognize our common interest in promoting the stability, sovereignty, and territorial integrity of all the nations of this re-

1. U.S.-Russia Joint Declaration, U.S.-Russ., May 24, 2002, Press Release, White House, Office of the Press Sec'y, Text of U.S.-Russia Joint Declaration (May 24, 2002) (on file with editor), *available at* http://www.state.gov/p/eur/rls/or/2002/10469.htm.

gion. The United States and Russia reject the failed model of "Great Power" rivalry that can only increase the potential for conflict in those regions. We will support economic and political development and respect for human rights while we broaden our humanitarian cooperation and cooperation on counterterrorism and counternarcotics.

The United States and Russia will cooperate to resolve regional conflicts, including those in Abkhazia and Nagorno-Karabakh, and the Transnistrian issue in Moldova. We strongly encourage the Presidents of Azerbaijan and Armenia to exhibit flexibility and a constructive approach to resolving the conflict concerning Nagorno-Karabakh. As two of the Co-Chairmen of the OSCE's Minsk Group, the United States and Russia stand ready to assist in these efforts.

On November 13, 2001, we pledged to work together to develop a new relationship between NATO and Russia that reflects the new strategic reality in the Euro-Atlantic region. We stressed that the members of NATO and Russia are increasingly allied against terrorism, regional instability, and other contemporary threats. We therefore welcome the inauguration at the May 28, 2002 NATO-Russia summit in Rome of a new NATO-Russia Council, whose members, acting in their national capacities and in a manner consistent with their respective collective commitments and obligations, will identify common approaches, take joint decisions, and bear equal responsibility, individually and jointly, for their implementation. In this context, they will observe in good faith their obligations under international law, including the UN Charter, provisions and principles contained in the Helsinki Final Act and the OSCE Charter for European Security. In the framework of the NATO-Russia Council, NATO member states and Russia will work as equal partners in areas of common interest. They aim to stand together against common threats and risks to their security.

As co-sponsors of the Middle East peace process, the United States and Russia will continue to exert joint and parallel efforts, including in the framework of the "Quartet," to overcome the current crisis in the Middle East, to restart negotiations, and to encourage a negotiated settlement. In the Balkans, we will promote democracy, ethnic tolerance, self-sustaining peace, and long-term stability, based on respect for the sovereignty and territorial integrity of the states in the region and United Nations Security Council resolutions. The United States and Russia will continue their constructive dialogue on Iraq and welcome the continuation of special bilateral discussions that opened the way for UN Security Council adoption of the Goods Review List.

Recalling our Joint Statement of November 13, 2001 on counternarcotics cooperation, we note that illegal drug trafficking poses a threat to our peoples and to international security, and represents a substantial source of financial support for international terrorism. We are committed to intensifying cooperation against this threat, which will bolster both the security and health of the citizens of our countries.

The United States and Russia remain committed to intensifying cooperation in the fight against transnational organized crime. In this regard, we welcome the entry into force of the Treaty on Mutual Legal Assistance in Criminal Matters on January 31, 2002.

. . . .

****

Preventing the Spread of Weapons of Mass Destruction: Non-Proliferation and International Terrorism

The United States and Russia will intensify joint efforts to confront the new global challenges of the twenty-first century, including combating the closely linked threats of international terrorism and the proliferation of weapons of mass destruction and their means of delivery. We believe that international terrorism represents a particular danger to international stability as shown once more by the tragic events of September 11, 2001. It is imperative that all nations of the world cooperate to combat this threat decisively. Toward this end, the United States and Russia reaffirm our commitment to work together bilaterally and multilaterally.

The United States and Russia recognize the profound importance of preventing the spread of weapons of mass destruction and missiles. The specter that such weapons could fall into the hands of terrorists and those who support them illustrates the priority all nations must give to combating proliferation.

To that end, we will work closely together, including through cooperative programs, to ensure the security of weapons of mass destruction and missile technologies, information, expertise, and material. We will also continue cooperative threat reduction programs and expand efforts to reduce weapons-usable fissile material. In that regard, we will establish joint experts groups to investigate means of increasing the amount of weapons-usable fissile material to be eliminated, and to recommend collaborative research and development efforts on advanced, proliferation-resistant nuclear reactor and fuel cycle technologies. We also intend to intensify our cooperation concerning destruction of chemical weapons.

The United States and Russia will also seek broad international support for a strategy of proactive nonproliferation, including by implementing and bolstering the Treaty on the Non-Proliferation of Nuclear Weapons and the conventions on the prohibition of chemical and biological weapons. The United States and Russia call on all countries to strengthen and strictly enforce export controls, interdict illegal transfers, prosecute violators, and tighten border controls to prevent and protect against proliferation of weapons of mass destruction.

Missile Defense, Further Strategic Offensive Reductions, New Consultative Mechanism on Strategic Security

The United States and Russia proceed from the Joint Statements by the President of the United States of America and the President of the Russian Federation on Strategic Issues of July 22, 2001 in Genoa and on a New Relationship Between the United States and Russia of November 13, 2001 in Washington.

The United States and Russia are taking steps to reflect, in the military field, the changed nature of the strategic relationship between them.

The United States and Russia acknowledge that today's security environment is fundamentally different than during the Cold War.

In this connection, the United States and Russia have agreed to implement a number of steps aimed at strengthening confidence and increasing transparency in the area of missile defense, including the exchange of information on missile defense programs and tests in this area, reciprocal visits to observe missile defense tests, and observation aimed at familiarization with missile defense systems. They also intend to take the steps necessary to bring a joint center for the exchange of data from early warning systems into operation.

The United States and Russia have also agreed to study possible areas for missile defense cooperation, including the expansion of joint exercises related to missile defense, and the exploration of potential programs for the joint research and development of missile defense technologies, bearing in mind the importance of the mutual protection of classified information and the safeguarding of intellectual property rights.

The United States and Russia will, within the framework of the NATO-Russia Council, explore opportunities for intensified practical cooperation on missile defense for Europe.

The United States and Russia declare their intention to carry out strategic offensive reductions to the lowest possible levels consistent with their national security requirements and alliance obligations, and reflecting the new nature of their strategic relations.

A major step in this direction is the conclusion of the Treaty Between the United States of America and the Russian Federation on Strategic Offensive Reductions.

In this connection, both sides proceed on the basis that the Treaty Between the United States of America and the Union of Soviet Socialist Republics on the Reduction and Limitation of Strategic Offensive Arms of July 31,1991, remains in force in accordance with its terms and that its provisions will provide the foundation for providing confidence, transparency, and predictability in further strategic offensive reductions, along with other supplementary measures, including transparency measures, to be agreed.

The United States and Russia agree that a new strategic relationship between the two countries, based on the principles of mutual security, trust, openness, cooperation, and predictability requires substantive consultation across a broad range of international security issues. To that end we have decided to:

- establish a Consultative Group for Strategic Security to be chaired by Foreign Ministers and Defense Ministers with the participation of other senior officials. This group will be the principal mechanism through which the sides strengthen mutual confidence, expand transparency, share information and plans, and discuss strategic issues of mutual interest; and

- seek ways to expand and regularize contacts between our two countries' Defense Ministries and Foreign Ministries, and our intelligence agencies.

[Signatures omitted]

Moscow
May 24, 2002.

December 13, 2001

Text of Diplomatic Notes Sent to Russia, Belarus, Kazakhstan and Ukraine on U.S. Withdrawal from the ABM Treaty.[2]

The following is the text of diplomatic notes sent to Russia, Belarus, Kazakhstan, and Ukraine on December 13, 2001:

> The Embassy of the United States of America has the honor to refer to the Treaty between the United States of America and the Union of Soviet Socialist Republics (USSR) on the Limitation of Anti-Ballistic Missile Systems signed at Moscow May 26, 1972.
>
> Article XV, paragraph 2, gives each Party the right to withdraw from the Treaty if it decides that extraordinary events related to the subject matter of the treaty have jeopardized its supreme interests.

---

2. Press Release, Richard Boucher, Spokesman, U.S. Dep't of State, Text of Diplomatic Notes Sent to Russia, Belarus, Kazakhstan and Ukraine (Dec. 14, 2001) (on file with editor), *available at* http://www.state.gov/r/pa/prs/ps/2001/6859.htm.

The United States recognizes that the Treaty was entered into with the USSR, which ceased to exist in 1991. Since then, we have entered into a new strategic relationship with Russia that is cooperative rather than adversarial, and are building strong relationships with most states of the former USSR.

Since the Treaty entered into force in 1972, a number of state and non-state entities have acquired or are actively seeking to acquire weapons of mass destruction. It is clear, and has recently been demonstrated, that some of these entities are prepared to employ these weapons against the United States. Moreover, a number of states are developing ballistic missiles, including long-range ballistic missiles, as a means of delivering weapons of mass destruction. These events pose a direct threat to the territory and security of the United States and jeopardize its supreme interests. As a result, the United States has concluded that it must develop, test, and deploy anti-ballistic missile systems for the defense of its national territory, of its forces outside the United States, and of its friends and allies.

Pursuant to Article XV, paragraph 2, the United States has decided that extraordinary events related to the subject matter of the Treaty have jeopardized its supreme interests. Therefore, in the exercise of the right to withdraw from the Treaty provided in Article XV, paragraph 2, the United States hereby gives notice of its withdrawal from the Treaty. In accordance with the terms of the Treaty, withdrawal will be effective six months from the date of this notice.

December 13, 2001

A Statement Made by Russian President Vladimir Putin on December 13, 2001, Regarding the Decision of the Administration of the United States of America to Withdraw from the Antiballistic Missile Treaty of 1972.[3]

The U.S. Administration today announced that it will withdraw from the 1972 ABM Treaty in six months' time.

The Treaty does indeed allow each of the parties to withdraw from it under exceptional circumstances. The leadership of the United States has spoken about it repeatedly and this step has not come as a surprise to us. But we believe this decision to be mistaken.

As is known, Russia, like the United States and unlike other nuclear powers, has long possessed an effective system to overcome anti-missile defense. So, I can say with full confidence that the decision made by the President of the United States does not pose a threat to the national security of the Russian Federation.

At the same time our country elected not to accept the insistent proposals on the part of the U.S. to jointly withdraw from the ABM Treaty and did everything it could to preserve the Treaty. I still think that this is a correct and valid position. Russia was guided above all by the aim of preserving and strengthening the international legal foundation in the field of disarmament and non-proliferation of mass destruction weapons.

The ABM Treaty is one of the supporting elements of the legal system in this field. That system was created through joint efforts during past decades.

---

3. Vladimir Putin, President, Russian Federation, Statement (Dec. 13, 2001), *in President Vladimir Putin's Statement on ABM Treaty*, Official Kremlin Int'l News Broad., Dec. 14, 2001 (LEXIS, News Library, Allnws File).

It is our conviction that the development of the situation in the present world dictates a certain logic of actions.

Now that the world has been confronted with new threats one cannot allow a legal vacuum to be formed in the sphere of strategic stability. One should not undermine the regimes of non-proliferation of mass destruction weapons.

I believe that the present level of bilateral relations between the Russian Federation and the U.S. should not only be preserved but should be used for working out a new framework of strategic relations as soon as possible.

Along with the problem of anti-missile defense a particularly important task under these conditions is putting a legal seal on the achieved agreements on further radical, irreversible and verifiable cuts of strategic offensive weapons, in our opinion to the level of 1,500–2,200 nuclear warheads for each side.

In conclusion I would like to note that Russia will continue to adhere firmly to its course in world affairs aimed at strengthening strategic stability and international security.

D. United States Arms Control and Disarmament Initiatives and Programs

BARUCH PLAN*

My Fellow Members of the United Nations Atomic Energy Commission, and My Fellow Citizens of the World:

We are here to make a choice between the quick and the dead.

That is our business.

Behind the black portent of the new atomic age lies a hope which, seized upon with faith, can work our salvation. If we fail, then we have damned every man to be the slave of Fear. Let us not deceive ourselves: We must elect World Peace or World Destruction.

Science has torn from nature a secret so vast in its potentialities that our minds cower from the terror it creates. Yet terror is not enough to inhibit the use of the atomic bomb. The terror created by weapons has never stopped man from employing them. For each new weapon a defense has been produced, in time. But now we face a condition in which adequate defense does not exist.

Science, which gave us this dread power, shows that it can be made a giant help to humanity, but science does not show us how to prevent its baleful use. So we have been appointed to obviate that peril by finding a meeting of the minds and the hearts of our peoples. Only in the will of mankind lies the answer.

It is to express this will and make it effective that we have been assembled. We must provide the mechanism to assure that atomic energy is used for peaceful purposes and preclude its use in war. To that end, we must provide immediate, swift, and sure punishment of those who violate the agreements that are reached by the nations. Penalization is essential if peace is to be more than a feverish interlude between wars. And, too, the United Nations can prescribe individual responsibility and punishment on the principles applied at Nuremberg by the Union of Soviet Socialist Republics, the United Kingdom, France and the United States—a formula certain to benefit the world's future.

In this crisis, we represent not only our governments but, in a larger way, we represent the peoples of the world. We must remember that the peoples do not belong to the governments but that the governments belong to the peoples. We must answer their demands; we must answer the world's longing for peace and security.

In that desire the United States shares ardently and hopefully. The search of science for the absolute weapon has reached fruition in this country. But she stands ready to proscribe and destroy this instrument—to lift its use from death to life—if the world will join in a pact to that end.

In our success lies the promise of a new life, freed from the heart-stopping fears that now beset the world. The beginning of victory for the great ideals for which millions have bled and died lies in building a workable plan. Now we approach fulfillment of the

---

* Bernard Mannes Baruch, U.S. Representative to the U.N. Atomic Energy Comm'n, The Baruch Plan: Statement to the United Nations Atomic Energy Commission (June 14, 1946), *in* 1 U.S. DEP'T OF STATE, PUBL'N NO. 7008, DOCUMENTS ON DISARMAMENT: 1945–1959, at 7–16 (1960), *available at* http://www.nuclearfiles.org/menu/key-issues/nuclear-weapons/issues/arms-control-disarmament/baruch-plan_1946-06-14.htm>.

aspirations of mankind. At the end of the road lies the fairer, better, surer life we crave and mean to have.

Only by a lasting peace are liberties and democracies strengthened and deepened. War is their enemy. And it will not do to believe that any of us can escape war's devastation. Victor, vanquished, and neutrals alike are affected physically, economically and morally.

Against the degradation of war we can erect a safeguard. That is the guerdon for which we reach. Within the scope for the formula we outline here there will be found, to those who seek it, the essential elements of our purpose. Others will see only emptiness. Each of us carries his own mirror in which is reflected hope—or determined desperation—courage or cowardice.

There is a famine throughout the world today. It starves men's bodies. But there is a greater famine—the hunger of men's spirit. That starvation can be cured by the conquest of fear, and the substitution of hope, from which springs faith—faith in each other, faith that we want to work together toward salvation, and determination that those who threaten the peace and safety shall be punished.

The peoples of these democracies gathered here have a particular concern with our answer, for their peoples hate war. They will have a heavy exaction to make of those who fail to provide an escape. They are not afraid of an internationalism that protects; they are unwilling to be fobbed off by mouthings about narrow sovereignty, which is today's phrase for yesterday's isolation.

The basis of a sound foreign policy, in this new age, for all the nations here gathered, is that anything that happens, no matter where or how, which menaces the peace of the world, or the economic stability, concerns each and all of us.

That roughly, may be said to be the central theme of the United Nations. It is with that thought we begin consideration of the most important subject that can engage mankind - life itself.

Let there be no quibbling about the duty and the responsibility of this group and of the governments we represent. I was moved, in the afternoon of my life, to add my effort to gain the world's quest, by the broad mandate under which we were created. The resolution of the General Assembly, passed January 24, 1946 in London reads:

"Section V. Terms of References of the Commission

"The Commission shall proceed with the utmost despatch and enquire into all phases of the problem, and make such recommendations from time to time with respect to them as it finds possible. In particular the Commission shall make specific proposals:

"(a) For extending between all nations the exchange of basic scientific information for peaceful ends;

"(b) For control of atomic energy to the extent necessary to ensure its use only for peaceful purposes;

"(c) For the elimination from national armaments of atomic weapons and of all other major weapons adaptable to mass destruction;

"(d) For effective safeguards by way of inspection and other means to protect complying States against the hazards of violations and evasions.

"The work of the Commission should proceed by separate stages, the successful completion of each of which will develop the necessary confidence of the world before the next stage is undertaken...."

....

The United States proposes the creation of an International Atomic Development Authority, to which should be entrusted all phases of the development and use of atomic energy, starting with the raw material and including:

1. Managerial control or ownership of all atomic-energy, activities potentially dangerous to world security.

2. Power to control, inspect, and license all other atomic activities.

3. The duty of fostering the beneficial uses of atomic energy.

4. Research and development responsibilities of an affirmative character intended to put the Authority in the forefront of atomic knowledge and thus to enable it to comprehend, and therefore to detect, misuse of atomic energy. To be effective, the Authority must itself be the world's leader in the field of atomic knowledge and development and thus supplement its legal authority with the great power inherent in possession of leadership in knowledge.

I offer this as a basis for beginning our discussion.

But I think the peoples we serve would not believe—and without faith nothing counts—that a treaty, merely outlawing possession or use of the atomic bomb, constitutes effective fulfillment of the instructions to this Commission. Previous failures have been recorded in trying the method of simple renunciation, unsupported by effective guaranties of security and armament limitation. No one would have faith in that approach alone.

Now, if ever, is the time to act for the common good. Public opinion supports a world movement toward security. If I read the signs aright, the peoples want a program not composed merely of pious thoughts but of enforceable sanctions—an international law with teeth in it.

We of this nation, desirous of helping to bring peace to the world and realizing the heavy obligations upon us arising from our possession of the means of producing the bomb and from the fact that it is part of our armament, are prepared to make our full contribution toward effective control of atomic energy.

When an adequate system for control of atomic energy, including the renunciation of the bomb as a weapon, has been agreed upon and put into effective operation and condign punishments set up for violations of the rules of control which are to be stigmatized as international crimes, we propose that:

1. Manufacture of atomic bombs shall stop;

2. Existing bombs shall be disposed of pursuant to the terms of the treaty; and

3. The Authority shall be in possession of full information as to the know-how for the production of atomic energy.

Let me repeat, so as to avoid misunderstanding: My country is ready to make its full contribution toward the end we seek, subject of course to our constitutional processes and to an adequate system of control becoming fully effective, as we finally work it out.

Now as to violations: In the agreement, penalties of as serious a nature as the nations may wish and as immediate and certain in their execution as possible should be fixed for:

1. Illegal possession or use of an atomic bomb;

2. Illegal possession, or separation, of atomic material suitable for use in an atomic bomb;

3. Seizure of any plant or other property belonging to or licensed by the Authority;

4. Willful interference with the activities of the Authority;

5. Creation or operation of dangerous projects in a manner contrary to, or in the absence of, a license granted by the international control body.

. . . .

The bomb does not wait upon debate. To delay may be to die. The time between violation and preventive action or punishment would be all too short for extended discussion as to the course to be followed.

. . . .

But before a country is ready to relinquish any winning weapons it must have more than words to reassure it. It must have a guarantee of safety, not only against the offenders in the atomic area but against the illegal users of other weapons—bacteriological, biological, gas—perhaps—why not!—against war itself.

In the elimination of war lies our solution, for only then will nations cease to compete with one another in the production and use of dread 'secret' weapons which are evaluated solely by their capacity to kill. This devilish program takes us back not merely to the Dark Ages but from cosmos to chaos. If we succeed in finding a suitable way to control atomic weapons, it is reasonable to hope that we may also preclude the use of other weapons adaptable to mass destruction. When a man learns to say "A" he can, if he chooses, learn the rest of the alphabet too.

Let this be anchored in our minds:

Peace is never long preserved by weight of metal or by an armament race. Peace can be made tranquil and secure only by understanding and agreement fortified by sanctions. We must embrace international cooperation or international disintegration.

Science has taught us how to put the atom to work. But to make it work for good instead of for evil lies in the domain dealing with the principles of human duty. We are now facing a problem more of ethics than of physics.

The solution will require apparent sacrifice in pride and in position, but better pain as the price of peace than death as the price of war.

I now submit the following measures as representing the fundamental features of a plan which would give effect to certain of the conclusions with I have epitomized.

1. *General.* The Authority should set up a thorough plan for control of the field of atomic energy, through various forms of ownership, dominion, licenses, operation, inspection, research, and management by competent personnel. After this is provided for, there should be as little interference as may be with the economic plans and the present private, corporate and state relationships in the several countries involved.

2. *Raw Materials.* The Authority should have as one of its earliest purposes to obtain and maintain complete and accurate information on world supplies of uranium and thorium and to bring them under its dominion. The precise pattern of control for various types of deposits of such materials will have to depend upon the geological, mining, refining and economic facts involved in different situations.

The Authority should conduct continuous surveys so that it will have the most complete knowledge of the world geology of uranium and thorium. Only after all current information on world sources of uranium and thorium is known to us all can equitable plans be made for their productions, refining, and distribution.

3. *Primary Production Plants.* The Authority should exercise complete managerial control of the production of fissionable materials in dangerous quantities and must own and control the product of these plants.

4. *Atomic Explosives.* The Authority should be given sole and exclusive right to conduct research in the field of atomic explosives. Research activities in the field of atomic explosives are essential in order that the Authority may keep in the forefront of knowledge in the field of atomic energy and fulfill the objective of preventing illicit manufacture of bombs. Only by maintaining its position as the best-informed agency will the Authority be able to determine the line between intrinsically dangerous and non-dangerous activities.

5. *Strategic Distribution of Activities and Materials.* The activities entrusted exclusively to the Authority because they are intrinsically dangerous to security should be distributed throughout the world. Similarly, stockpiles of raw materials and fissionable materials should not be centralized.

6. *Non-Dangerous Activities.* A function of the Authority should be promotion of the peacetime benefits of atomic energy.

Atomic research (except in explosives), the use of research reactors, the production of radioactive tracers by means of non-dangerous reactors, the use of such tracers, and to some extent the production of power should be open to nations and their citizens under reasonable licensing arrangements from the Authority. Denatured materials, whose use we know also requires suitable safeguards, should be furnished for such purposes by the Authority under lease or other arrangement. Denaturing seems to have been overestimated by the public as a safety measure.

7. *Definition of Dangerous and Non-Dangerous Activities.* Although a reasonable dividing line can be drawn between dangerous and non-dangerous activities, it is not hard and fast. Provision should, therefore, be made to assure constant re-examination of the questions and to permit revision of the dividing line as changing conditions and new discoveries may require.

8. *Operations of Dangerous Activities.* Any plant dealing with uranium or thorium after it once reaches the potential of dangerous use must be not only subject to the most rigorous and competent inspection by the Authority, but its actual operation shall be under the management, supervision, and control of the Authority.

9. *Inspection.* By assigning intrinsically dangerous activities exclusively to the Authority, the difficulties of inspection are reduced. If the Authority is the only agency which may lawfully conduct dangerous activities, then visible operation by others than the Authority will constitute an unambiguous danger signal, Inspection will also occur in connection with the licensing functions of the Authority.

10. *Freedom of Access.* Adequate ingress and egress for all qualified representatives of the Authority must be assured. Many of the inspection activities of the Authority

should grow out of and be incidental to, its other functions. Important measures of inspection will be associated with the tight control of raw materials, for this is a keystone of the plan. The continuing activities of prospecting, survey, and research in relation to raw materials will be designed not only to serve the affirmative development functions of the Authority but also to assure that no surreptitious operations are conducted in the raw-materials field by nations or their citizens.

11. *Personnel.* The personnel of the Authority should be recruited on a basis of proven competence but also so far as possible on an international basis.

12. *Progress by Stages.* A primary step in the creation of the system of control is the setting forth, in comprehensive terms, of the functions, responsibilities, powers, and limitations of the Authority. Once a charter for the Authority has been adopted, the Authority and the system of control for which it will be responsible will require time to become fully organized and effective. The plan of control will, therefore, have to come into effect in successive stages. These should be specifically fixed in the charter or means should be otherwise set forth in the charter for transitions from one stage to another, as contemplated in the resolution of the United Nations Assembly which created this Commission.

13. *Disclosures.* In the deliberations of the United Nations Commission on Atomic Energy, the United States is prepared to make available the information essential to a reasonable understanding of the proposals which it advocates. Further disclosures must be dependent, in the interests of all, upon the effective ratification of the treaty. When the Authority is actually created, the United States will join the other nations in making available the further information essential to that organization for the performance of its functions. As the successive stages of international control are reached, the United States will be prepared to yield, to the extent required by each stage, national control of activities in this field to the Authority.

14. *International Control.* There will be questions about the extent of control to be allowed to national bodies, when the Authority is established. Purely national authorities for control and development of atomic energy should to the extent necessary for the effective operation of the Authority be subordinate to it. This is neither an endorsement nor a disapproval of the creation of national authorities. The Commission should evolve a clear demarcation of the scope of duties and responsibilities of such national authorities.

And now I end. I have submitted an outline for present discussion. Our consideration will be broadened by the criticism of the United States proposals and by the plans of the other nations, which, it is to be hoped, will be submitted at their early convenience. I and my associates of the United States Delegation will make available to each member of this body books and pamphlets, including the Acheson-Lilienthal report, recently made by the United States Department of State, and the McMahon Committee Monograph No. I entitled "Essential Information on Atomic Energy" relating to the McMahon bill recently passed by the United States Senate, which may prove of value in assessing the situation.

All of us are consecrated to making an end of gloom and hopelessness. It will not be an easy job. The way is long and thorny, but supremely worth traveling. All of us want to stand erect, with our faces to the sun, instead of being forced to burrow into the earth, like rats.

The pattern of salvation must be worked out by all for all.

The light at the end of the tunnel is dim, but our path seems to grow brighter as we actually begin our journey. We cannot yet light the way to the end. However, we hope the suggestions of my Government will be illuminating.

Let us keep in mind the exhortation of Abraham Lincoln, whose words, uttered at a moment of shattering national peril, form a complete text for our deliberation. I quote, paraphrasing slightly:

"We cannot escape history. We of this meeting will be remembered in spite of ourselves. No personal significance or insignificance can spare one or another of us. The fiery trial through which we are passing will light us down in honor or dishonor to the latest generation.

"We say we are for Peace. The world will not forget that we say this. We know how to save Peace. The world knows that we do. We, even we here, hold the power and have the responsibility.

"We shall nobly save, or meanly lose, the last, best hope of earth. The way is plain, peaceful, generous, just—a way which, if followed, the world will forever applaud."

My thanks for your attention.

U.S. NUCLEAR TESTING POLICY*

Background

For more than four decades, a strong nuclear deterrent has ensured U.S. security and helped preserve freedom. As long as nuclear weapons play a critical role in U.S. national security strategy, they must continue to be tested underground to ensure their safety, reliability, effectiveness, and survivability. In this context, the United States and Soviet Union ratified two nuclear testing treaties and verification protocols in December 1990.

Nuclear Testing Talks

Nuclear testing talks between the United States and the Soviet Union began in Geneva in November 1987, when the two countries agreed to negotiate effective verification protocols for two existing but then unratified treaties—the Threshold Test Ban Treaty (1974), which covers tests of nuclear weapons, and the Peaceful Nuclear Explosions Treaty (1976), which covers the use of nuclear explosives for peaceful purposes such as excavations. The treaties ban individual nuclear explosions—whether for testing nuclear weapons or for peaceful purposes—with a yield exceeding 150 kilotons (150,000 tons of TNT). However, neither treaty could be verified effectively in its original form. Following six rounds of talks, the negotiating teams completed work in May 1990 on these verification protocols, which were signed at the Washington summit, May 30 - June 3, 1990. The TTBT and PNET entered into force when Secretary Baker and Foreign Minister Shevardnadze exchanged instruments of ratification in Houston on December 11, 1990.

Effective Verification

The two protocols, which contain similar provisions, provide for effective verification and compliance with the treaties. The protocols give each side the right to employ hydrodynamic yield measurement, on-site inspection, and seismic monitoring in the territory of the testing party. Each side will have the right to use these methods in the measurement of explosions whose planned yields exceed agreed levels.

For effective verification of compliance with these treaties, the United States requires and has achieved the right to make direct, on-site hydrodynamic yield measurements of all Soviet tests exceeding 50 kilotons. The U.S. hydrodynamic method is CORRTEX (continuous refectonmetry for radius vs. time experiment), the most accurate, non-intrusive technique the United States has identified. This verification method determines the yield of a nuclear test by measuring, at the detonation site, the speed of a supersonic shock wave in the earth caused by the detonation. The speed of the shock wave is determined by measuring the rate at which it crushes a coaxial cable buried near the explosive device.

Seismic monitoring is the traditional method of calculating the strength of an explosion. Seismic monitors measure the explosion's shock waves as they move through the earth.

Why Testing is Essential

Underground nuclear testing is necessary to maintain the credibility of the U.S. deterrent by ensuring that nuclear weapons are:

---

* *Gist: US Nuclear Testing Policy*, 2 Dep't St. Dispatch 626, 626–27 (Aug. 19, 1991).

- **Safe**—Testing permits improvements to be made in safety and security features of nuclear weapons.
- **Reliable**—Testing is needed to detect deterioration or other potentially serioU.S. problems that may arise in stockpiled weapons.
- **Effective**—Testing enables the United States to modernize weapons as needed in relation to improvement and growth in Soviet military capabilities.
- **Survivability**—Testing allows the United States to ensure that military and command and control equipment are survivable.

WATER DEVELOPMENT APPROPRIATIONS ACT §507[1]

. . . .

Sec. 507

(a) Hereafter, funds made available by this Act or any other Act for fiscal year 1993 or for any other fiscal year may be available for conducting a test of a nuclear explosive device only if the conduct of that test is permitted in accordance with the provisions of this section

(b) No underground test of a nuclear weapon may be conducted by the United States after September 30, 1992 and before July 1, 1993.

(c) On and after July 1, 1993 and before January 1, 1997, an underground test of a nuclear weapon may be conducted by the United States—

(1) only if—

(A) the President has submitted the annual report required under subsection (d);

(B) 90 days have elapsed after the submittal of that report in accordance with that subsection; and

(C) Congress has not agreed to a joint resolution described in subsection (d)(3) within that 90-day period; and

(2) only if the test is conducted during the period covered by this report.

(d) (1) Not later than March 1, of a each year beginning after 1992, the President shall submit to the Committees on Armed Services and Appropriations of the Senate and the House of Representatives, in classified and unclassified forms, a report containing the following matters:

(A) A schedule for resumption of the Nuclear Testing Talks with Russia.

(B) A plan for achieving a multilateral comprehensive ban on the testing of nuclear weapons on or before September 30, 1996.

(C) An assessment of the number and type of nuclear warheads that will remain in the United States stockpile of active nuclear weapons on September 30, 1996.

(D) For each fiscal year after fiscal year 1992, an assessment of the number and type of nuclear warheads that will remain in the United States stockpile of nuclear weapons and that—

(i) will not be in the United States stockpile of active nuclear weapons.

(ii) will remain under the control of the Department of Defense; and

(iii) will not be transferred to the Department of Energy for dismantlement.

---

1. Energy and Water Development Appropriations Act, 1993 § 507, 106 Stat. 1315, 1343–45 (1992).

(E) A description of the safety features of each warhead that is covered by an assessment referred to in subparagraph (C) or (D).

(F) A plan for installing one or more modern safety features in each warhead identified in the assessment referred to in subparagraph (C), as determined after an analysis of the costs and benefits of installing such features in the warhead, should have one or more such features.

(G) An assessment of the number and type of nuclear weapons tests, not to exceed 5 tests in any period covered by an annual report under this paragraph and a total of 15 tests in the 4-fiscal year period beginning with fiscal year 1993, that are necessary in order to ensure the safety of each nuclear warhead in which one or more modern safety features are installed pursuant to the plan referred to in subparagraph (F).

(H) A schedule, in accordance with subparagraph (G), for conducting at the Nevada test site, each of the tests enumerated in the assessment pursuant of subparagraph (G).

(2) The first annual report shall cover the period beginning on the date on which a resumption of testing of nuclear weapons is permitted under subsection (c) and ending on September 30, 1994. Each annual report thereafter shall cover the fiscal year following the fiscal year in which the report is submitted.

(3) For the purposes of paragraph (1) "joint resolution" means only a joint resolution introduced after the date on which the Committees referred to in that paragraph receive the report required by that paragraph the matter after the resolving clause of which is as follows: "The Congress disapproves the report of the President on nuclear weapons testing dated ." (the blank space being appropriately filled in).

(4) No report is required under this subsection after 1996.

(e) (1) Except as provided in paragraphs (2) and (3), during a period covered by an annual report submitted pursuant to subsection (d), nuclear weapons may be tested only as follows:

(A) Only those nuclear explosive devices in which modern safety features have been installed pursuant to the plan referred to in subsection (d)(1)(F) may be tested.

(B) Only the number and types of tests specified in the report pursuant to subsection (d)(1)(G) may be conducted.

(2) (A) One test of the reliability of a nuclear weapon other than one referred to in paragraph (1)(A) may b conducted during any period covered by an annual report, but only if—

(i) within the first 60 days after the beginning of that period, the President certifies to Congress that it is vital to the national security interests of the United States to test the reliability of such nuclear weapon; and

(ii) within the 60-day period beginning on the date that Congress receives the certification, Congress does not agree to a joint resolution described in subparagraph (B).

(B) For the purposes of subparagraph (A), "joint resolution" means only a joint resolution introduced after the date on which the Congress receives the certification referred to in that subparagraph the matter after the resolving clause of which is as follows: "The Congress disapproves the testing of a nuclear weapon covered by the certification of the President dated ." (the blank space being appropriately filled in).

(3) The President may authorize the United Kingdom to conduct in the United States, within the period covered by an annual report, one test of a nuclear weapon if the President determines that it is in the national interests of the United States to do so. Such a test shall be considered as one of the tests within the maximum number of tests that the United States is permitted to conduct during that period under paragraph (1)(B).

(f) No underground test of nuclear weapons may be conducted by the United States after September 30, 1996, unless a foreign state conducts a nuclear test after this date, at which time the prohibition on United States nuclear testing is lifted.

(g) In the computation of the 90-day period referred to in subsection (c)(1) and the 60-day period referred to in subsection (e)(2)(A)(ii), the days on which either the House is not in session because of an adjournment of more than 3 days to a day certain shall be excluded.

....

The President's Statement on Signing the Act

On October 2, the President signed the Energy and Water Development Appropriations Act which provides funding for the Department of Energy (including the superconducting super collider). Among the Bill's provisions were new limits on U.S. Nuclear Testing, including:

— A nine-month moratorium (through June 30, 1993);

— No tests permitted after September 30, 1996, unless another State conducts a nuclear test after that date, at which time the prohibition on U.S. testing would be lifted;

— Limits on the number of tests (5 per fiscal year, and a total of 15 during the 3 years and 3 months from July 1, 1993 through September 30, 1996);

....

— An allowance of one test per year for the U.K. to count against the U.S. ceiling. U.K. tests would not be bound by he same purpose or technical constraints placed on U.S. tests (see below); No U.K. testing in the U.S. after September 30, 1996, unless another State conducts a nuclear test after this date (as in second tick. above);

— Limits on the purpose of tests (all must be "necessary to ensure safety" of active stockpile weapons, except that one test of the reliability of a nuclear weapon may be conducted each year. If the President certifies that such a test is vital to the national security);

— A requirement that devices tested must include at least one "modern safety feature"—insensitive high explosive, a fire resistant pit, or an enhanced detonation safety (ENDS) system—except for reliability tests;

The legislation also requires that the Administration report to Congress on "A schedule for the resumption of the nuclear testing talks with Russia" and "A plan for achieving a multilateral comprehensive ban" on testing by the end of FY 96 (i.e., by the time the U.S. ends its own testing).

Finally, the legislation involves Congress more directly in the approval process for future testing. By giving Congress 90 days to veto the Administration's annual testing program, as well as the power to separately to disapprove any test proposed under the reliability exception. A new Presidential Report (Due March 1), presenting the proposed test program for the next fiscal year must also account to Congress for progress on the arms control undertakings noted above, and the installation of modern safety devices on all active stockpile weapons, as well as a current inventory of all weapons held by DoD.

On October 2, the President released a statement concerning the new law that included the following remarks on the nuclear testing portions:[2]

> I must, however, note a number of objectionable provisions in the Act. Specifically, Section 507 of H.R. 5373, which concerns nuclear testing, is highly objectionable. It may prevent the United States from conducting underground nuclear tests that are necessary to maintain a safe and reliable nuclear deterrent. This provision unwisely restricts the number and purpose of U.S. nuclear tests and will make future U.S. nuclear testing dependent on actions by another country, rather than on our own national security requirements. Despite the dramatic reductions in nuclear arsenals, the United States continues to rely on nuclear deterrence as an essential element of our national security. We must ensure that our forces are as safe and reliable as possible. To do so, we must continue to conduct a minimal number of underground nuclear tests, regardless of the actions of other countries. Therefore, I will work for new legislation to permit the conduct of a modest number of necessary underground nuclear tests.
>
> In July 1992, I adopted a new nuclear testing policy to reflect the changes in the international security environment and in the size and nature of our nuclear deterrent. That policy imposed strict new limits on the purpose, number, and yield of U.S. nuclear tests, consistent with our national security and safety requirements and with our international obligations. It remains the soundest approach to U.S. nuclear testing.

Policy Statement on Nuclear Testing[3]

We have witnessed and participated in dramatic changes in the international security environment over the past several years which are leading to monumental changes in the size and composition of the nuclear forces of the United States and the new states that have replaced the former Soviet Union. The START Treaty, the Presidents nuclear initiative of last September, and the June 17, 1992 Joint Understanding on further strategic nuclear reductions will lower the number of our nuclear forces to less than one-third the 1990 level.

Despite these reductions, nuclear weapons and nuclear deterrence will continue to be an important element of the U.S. national security strategy. As long as this is the case, the U.S. must conduct a modest number of nuclear weapons tests to ensure the safety and credibility of our forces.

Testing is essential to monitor, improve, and maintain the safety of the stockpile. Nuclear testing is required to introduce recommended modern safety features in all existing weapon types and to maintain confidence in the performance of the modified weapons. In addition, there will be a continuing requirement for testing to ensure that the weapons in the stockpile remain safe.

---

2. George Bush, Statement on Signing the Energy and Water Development Appropriations Act, 1993, 2 Pub. Papers 1736, 1737 (Oct. 2, 1992).

3. July 10, 1992.

As the size of the stockpile and number of weapons types decrease, it is also increasingly important to ensure that the remaining weapons meet their performance specifications, and that our military forces are capable of functioning despite exposure to nuclear effects. Nuclear testing remains critical to evaluating and maintaining the reliability of our forces.

The United States has already significantly reduced the number of nuclear tests it conducts. We now conduct only about one-third as many tests as we did in the early 1980s, and about one-quarter the average level of the 1970s.

To reflect the changes in the international security environment and in the size and nature of our nuclear deterrent, the President has decided to modify U.S. testing policy:

We are hopeful that successful results from the Congressionally-directed Test Ban Readiness Program and a continuously improving international security environment would make it possible to reduce even further the number and/or yield of tests in the future. We do not plan further discussions with the Russians on incorporating safety improvements into nuclear weapons and on the requirements for nuclear testing to ensure safety and reliability.

These U.S. steps fulfill the U.S. commitment to a "step-by-step" approach to nuclear testing limits. When that approach was developed in 1986, it envisaged a long process of incremental changes. The new international environment has allowed us instead to implement rapidly major changes in U.S. policy and practice regarding the number, purpose, and yield of our tests. Further limits now would be inconsistent with the need to maintain a safe and reliable deterrent.

E. Non-Proliferation and Counter-Proliferation Initiatives

NUCLEAR SUPPLIERS GROUP AND ZANGGER COMMITTEE

The Nuclear Suppliers Group (NSG) is a group of countries which supply nuclear materials and related equipment and technology to other countries with nascent nuclear programs. The NSG partners agree to contribute to the nonproliferation of nuclear weapons through the implementation of a number of guidelines for the export of nuclear materials and related equipment and technology. The NSG currently consists of 44 member states and is widely considered to be an effective export control arrangement in support of the Nuclear Non-Proliferation Treaty (NPT).

The NSG was created following the explosion in 1974 of a nuclear device by India. As a result it became obvious that nuclear technology transferred ostensibly for peaceful purposes could be misused and contribute to a clandestine nuclear weapon program.

Nuclear supplier states decided to create the NSG as a consultative mechanism and a forum for establishing an agreed set of guidelines by which nuclear supplier states would adhere to and would hopefully limit the use of the knowledge and technology provided to peaceful nuclear activities.

The first set of NSG Guidelines (Part 1) governs exports of nuclear materials and equipment which require the application of International Atomic Energy Agency (IAEA) safeguards at the recipient facility.[1] The Part 1 nuclear control list is called the "Trigger List" because the export of such items "triggers" the requirement for IAEA safeguards.

Part 1 was published in 1978 by the International Atomic Energy Agency (IAEA). It established requirements for:

1. Assurances from recipient governments that IAEA safeguards would be fully agreed to and implements and that the technology and equipment provided would not be used for explosive purposes;

2. Ensuring that the equipment and materials provided would have adequate physical protection; and

3. In the case of particularly sensitive facilities, technology and weapons-usable material, as designated by the Guidelines, they would be provided with extra security and protection.

In 1992 the NSG established a second set of guidelines (Part 2) for transfers of nuclear-related dual-use equipment, material and technology (items which have both nuclear and non-nuclear applications) that could make a significant contribution to an unsafeguarded nuclear fuel cycle or nuclear explosive activity.[2]

---

1. *See* Int'l Atomic Energy Agency, *Guidelines for Nuclear Transfers, in Communications Received from Certain Member States Regarding Guidelines for the Export of Nuclear Material, Equipment and Technology*, IAEA Doc. INFCIRC/254/Rev.7/Part 1 (Feb. 23, 2005), *available at* http://www.nuclearsuppliersgroup.org/PDF/infcirc254r7p1-050223.pdf.

2. *See* Int'l Atomic Energy Agency, *Guidelines for Transfers of Nuclear-Related Dual-Use Equipment, Materials, Software, and Related Technology, in Communications Received from Certain Member States Regarding Guidelines for Transfers of Nuclear-Related Dual-Use Equipment, Materials, Software and Related Technology*, IAEA Doc. INFCIRC/254/Rev.6/Part 2 (Feb. 23, 2005), *available at* http://www.nuclearsuppliersgroup.org/PDF/infcirc254r6p2-050223.pdf.

Both Parts 1 and 2 of the NSG Guidelines aim to ensure that nuclear trade for peaceful purposes does not contribute to the proliferation of nuclear weapons or explosive devices while not hindering such trade. Members pursue these aims through voluntary adherence to the Guidelines which are adopted by consensus and through exchanges of information on developments of nuclear proliferation concern.

The NSG meets periodically either in plenary session, as a consultative body, or in working groups or committees to strengthen information sharing, propose amendments to Part 1 and 2 of the Guidelines, consider requests for membership to the Group, discuss new initiatives to ensure compliance with obligations under the NPT.

For example, in 2004 the NSG met to consider establishing the adherence to the Additional Protocol (a modification to the standard IAEA safeguards agreement requiring, among other things, more intrusive inspection mechanisms to further ensure there is no diversion to a clandestine nuclear weapons program), and the suspension of cooperation with any nation found by the IAEA to be in non-compliance with its safeguards obligations. Since the NSG operates on the basis of consensus all partners have to agree before any new proposal is adopted. These proposals have not yet been approved.

Supporting the work of the NSG is another export control group called the Zangger Committee[3] or sometimes the "NPT Exporters Committee." This group grew out of a series of informal meetings among NPT member supplier to reach a common understanding on:

> (a) the definition of what constituted "equipment or material especially designed or prepared for the processing, use or production of special fissionable material" (as it was not defined anywhere in the Treaty);
>
> (b) the conditions and procedures that would govern exports of such equipment or material in order to meet the obligations of article III, paragraph 2 of the NPT, on a basis of fair commercial competition. In essence the Zangger Committee provides interpretative guidance to NPT states parties on article II, paragraph 2,[4] which mandates that states parties should not export, directly or indirectly, nuclear material and equipment to non-nuclear-weapon States unless the export is subject to IAEA safeguards.

The Zangger Committee currently has 35 members, all of which are members of the NSG. The Committee meetings periodically and its decisions are not legally binding upon its members. All decisions of the Committee are made by consensus.

The members of the Committee have reached basic "understandings" for procedures for the export of materials and equipment described in article III, paragraph 2.[5] The Zangger Committee Understandings provide for three conditions of supply:

---

3. Named after Professor Claude Zangger of Switzerland who charged the initial meetings.

4. NPT Article III, paragraph 2 provides:

> Each State Party to the Treaty undertakes not to provide: (a) source or special fissionable material, or (b) equipment or material especially designed or prepared for the processing, use, or production of special fissionable material, to any non-nuclear-weapon State for peaceful purposes, unless the source or special fissionable material shall be subject to the safeguards required by this article.

Treaty on the Non-Proliferation of Nuclear Weapons art. III, para. 2, July 1, 1968, 21 U.S.T. 483, 488, 729 U.N.T.S. 161, 172 (entered into force Mar. 5, 1970).

5. *See* Int'l Atomic Energy Agency, *Consolidated Trigger List, in Communications of 15 November 1999 Received from Member States Regarding the Export of Nuclear Material and of Certain Categories of Equipment and Other Material*, at 2–37, IAEA Doc. INFCIRC/209/Rev.2 (Mar. 9, 2000), *available at* http://www.iaea.org/Publications/Documents/Infcircs/2000/infcirc209r2.pdf.

(a) For exports to non-nuclear-weapon States, source or special fissionable material either directly transferred, or produced, processed, or used in the facility for which the transferred item is intended, shall not be diverted to nuclear weapons or other nuclear explosive devices;

(b) For exports to non-nuclear-weapon States, such source or special fissionable material, as well as transferred equipment and non-nuclear material, shall be subject to IAEA safeguards agreement;

(c) Source or special fissionable material, and equipment and non-nuclear material shall not be re-exported to a non-nuclear-weapon State unless the recipient State accepts safeguards on the re-exported item.

The understandings have been formally accepted by individual States members of the Committee in an exchange of notes among themselves. These amounted to unilateral declarations that the Understandings would be given effect through respective domestic export control legislation. These unilateral declarations are subsequently communicated to all member states of the IAEA through IAEA publications. These understandings became known as the "trigger list" since the export of listed items "triggers" IAEA safeguards. The Committee meets periodically to consider revisions to the trigger list. To date there have been eight modifications to the list.—Eds.

For more information on The Nuclear Suppliers Group see http://www.state.gov/t/np/rls/fs/34729.htm.

For more information on the Zangger Committee see http://www.zanggercommittee.org/Zangger/NPT/default.htm.

AUSTRALIA GROUP[1] (CHEMICAL WEAPONS)

The Australia Group (AG) was formed in 1984 in response to the use of chemical weapons in the Iran-Iraq war. It is an informal, politically binding arrangement of currently 34 like-minded states who share information for the purpose of controlling the export of chemical precursors, biological agents and related equipment and technology which could be used for chemical or biological weapons. Members of the Australia Group meet twice a year for the purpose of making the measures already taken by members more effective, including through the exchange of information, harmonizing measures already taken and, where necessary, considering additional and complementary national measures. All decisions are taken by consensus.

The AG currently controls 54 chemical weapons precursors; dual-use chemical manufacturing equipment and related technology; plan and animal pathogens; biological agents, and dual-use biological equipment. In addition, the AG has agreed to "catch-all" controls which can apply to any transfer if deemed to be of proliferation concern, and the partners have agreed to a "no undercut policy" which means that once an item has been denied to an end-user no other partner will provide the item to that entity.

Controls and limits on exports by these countries are based on an agreed set of guidelines, which all partners apply in considering whether or not to grant an export for an item on the control lists of the Australia Group. This is consistent with the obligations under the Biological Weapons Convention and the Chemical Weapons Convention to ensure that states do not contribute to or participate in activities inconsistent with the legal and political obligations under those conventions banning biological and chemical weapons.

Australia Group Guidelines[2]

1. The purpose of these Guidelines is to limit the risks of proliferation and terrorism involving chemical and biological weapons (CBW) by controlling transfers that could contribute to CBW activities by states or non-state actors, consistent with Article III of the Biological Weapons Convention, Article I of the Chemical Weapons Convention, and all relevant United Nations Security Council Resolutions. In accordance with Article X of the Biological Weapons Convention and Article XI of the Chemical Weapons Convention, these Guidelines are not intended to impede chemical or biological trade or international cooperation that could not contribute to CBW activities or terrorism. These Guidelines, including the.... Australia Group (AG) control lists and subsequent amendments thereto, form the basis for controlling transfers to any destination beyond the Government's national jurisdiction or control of materials, equipment, and technology that could contribute to CBW activities.... [T]hese Guidelines [will be implemented] in accordance with.... national legislation.

2. These Guidelines will be applied to each transfer of any item in the AG control lists. However, it is a matter for the Government's discretion to determine whether and to

---

1. *See* Australia Group—Home Page, http://www.australiagroup.net/

2. Australia Group, *Guidelines for Transfers of Sensitive Chemical or Biological Items* (June 2004), *available at* http://www.australiagroup.net/en/guidelines.html.

what extent to apply expedited licensing measures in the case of transfers to destinations it judges possess consistently excellent non-proliferation credentials. Vigilance will be exercised in the consideration of all transfers of items on the AG control lists. Transfers will be denied if the Government judges, on the basis of all available, persuasive information, evaluated according to factors including those in paragraph 3, that the controlled items are intended to be used in a chemical weapons or biological weapons program, or for CBW terrorism, or that a significant risk of diversion exists. It is understood that the decision to transfer remains the sole and sovereign judgment of the Government.

3. In fulfilling the purposes of these Guidelines, national export control legislation, including enforcement and sanctions for violations, plays an important role.

4. To fulfill the purposes of these Guidelines, the evaluation of export applications will take into account the following non-exhaustive list of factors:

a) Information about proliferation and terrorism involving CBW, including any proliferation or terrorism-related activity, or about involvement in clandestine or illegal procurement activities, of the parties to the transaction;

b) The capabilities and objectives of the chemical and biological activities of the recipient state;

c) The significance of the transfer in terms of

(1) the appropriateness of the stated end-use, including any relevant assurances submitted by the recipient state or end-user, and

(2) the potential development of CBW;

d) The assessment of the end-use of the transfer, including whether a transfer has been previously denied to the end-user, whether the end-user has diverted for unauthorized purposes any transfer previously authorized, and, to the extent possible, whether the end-user is capable of securely handling and storing the item transferred;

e) The extent and effectiveness of the export control system in the recipient state as well as any intermediary states;

f) The applicability of relevant multilateral agreements, including the BTWC and CWC.

5. In a manner consistent with its national legislation and practices, the Government should, before authorizing a transfer of an AG-controlled item, either

a) satisfy itself that goods are not intended for re-export;

b) satisfy itself that, if re-exported, the goods would be controlled by the recipient government pursuant to these guidelines; or

c) obtain satisfactory assurances that its consent will be secured prior to any retransfer to a third country.

6. The objective of these Guidelines should not be defeated by the transfer of any non-controlled item containing one or more controlled components where the controlled component(s) are the principal element of the item and can feasibly be removed or used for other purposes. (In judging whether the controlled component(s) are to be considered the principal element, the Government will weigh the factors of quantity, value, and technological know-how involved and other special circumstances that might establish the controlled component or components as the principal element of the item being procured.) The objective of these Guidelines also should not be defeated

by the transfer of a whole plant, on any scale, that has been designed to produce any CBW agent or AG-controlled precursor chemical.

7. The Government reserves the discretion to:

a) apply additional conditions for transfer that it may consider necessary;

b) apply these guidelines to items not on the AG control lists; and

c) apply measure to restrict exports for other reasons of public policy consistent with its treaty obligations.

8. In furtherance of the effective operation of the Guidelines, the Government will, as necessary and appropriate, exchange relevant information with other governments applying the same Guidelines.

9. The Government encourages the adherence of all states to these Guidelines in the interest of international peace and security.

....

Further Provisions Applicable to Australia Group Participants

In addition, participants in the Australia Group, consistent with their obligations under the BTWC and CWC and in accordance with their national legislation have, after careful consideration, decided also to give equal respect to the following provisions.

Catch-All

1. Participant states will ensure that their regulations require the following:

a) an authorization for the transfer of non-listed items where the exporter is informed by the competent authorities of the Participant State in which it is established that the items in question may be intended, in their entirety or part, for use in connection with chemical or biological weapons activities;

b) that if the exporter is aware that non-listed items are intended to contribute to such activities it must notify the authorities referred to above, which will decide whether or not it is expedient to make the export concerned subject to authorization.

2. Participant states are encouraged to share information on these measures on a regular basis, and to exchange information on catch-all denials relevant for the purpose of the AG.

No Undercut Policy

3. In accordance with the Group's agreed procedures, a license for an export that is essentially identical to one denied by another AG participant will only be granted after consultations with that participant, provided it has not expired or been rescinded. Essentially identical is defined as being the same biological agent or chemical or, in the case of dual-use equipment, equipment that has the same or similar specifications and performance being sold to the same consignee. The terms of the Group's 'no undercut policy' do not apply to denials of items under national catch-all provisions.

Common Approaches

4. AG participants implement these Guidelines in accordance with the Group's agreed common approaches on end-user undertakings and chemical mixtures.

....

MISSILE TECHNOLOGY CONTROL REGIME[1]

The MTCR was formed in 1987 to restrict proliferation of delivery vehicles (that can carry a 500 kilogram payload at least 300 kilometers) capable of delivering weapons of mass destruction. It is politically binding and operates by consensus. MTCR partners agree to common export control guidelines and meet periodically to agree on items to control and share "denial" information. At publication there were 34 MTCR partner states.

Guidelines for Sensitive Missile-Relevant Transfers[2]

1. The purpose of these Guidelines is to limit the risks of proliferation of weapons of mass destruction (i.e. nuclear, chemical and biological weapons), by controlling transfers that could make a contribution to delivery systems (other than manned aircraft) for such weapons. The Guidelines are also intended to limit the risk of controlled items and their technology falling into the hands of terrorist groups and individuals. The Guidelines are not designed to impede national space programs or international cooperation in such programs as long as such programs could not contribute to delivery systems for weapons of mass destruction. These Guidelines, including the attached Annex, form the basis for controlling transfers to any destination beyond the Government's jurisdiction or control of all delivery systems (other than manned aircraft) capable of delivering weapons of mass destruction, and of equipment and technology relevant to missiles whose performance in terms of payload and range exceeds stated parameters. Restraint will be exercised in the consideration of all transfers of items within the Annex and all such transfers will be considered on a case-by-case basis. The Government will implement the Guidelines in accordance with national legislation.

2. The Annex consists of two categories of items, which term includes equipment and technology. Category I items, all of which are in Annex items 1 and 2, are those items of greatest sensitivity. If a Category I item is included in a system, that system will also be considered as Category I, except when the incorporated item cannot be separated, removed or duplicated. Particular restraint will be exercised in the consideration of Category I transfers regardless of their purpose, and there will be a strong presumption to deny such transfers. Particular restraint will also be exercised in the consideration of transfers of any items in the Annex, or of any missiles (whether or not in the Annex), if the Government judges, on the basis of all available, persuasive information, evaluated according to factors including those in paragraph 3, that they are intended to be used for the delivery of weapons of mass destruction, and there will be a strong presumption to deny such transfers. Until further notice, the transfer of Category I production facilities will not be authorized. The transfer of other Category I items will be authorized only on rare occasions and where the Government (A) obtains binding government-to-government undertakings embodying the assurances from the recipient government called for in paragraph 5 of these Guidelines and (B) assumes responsibility for taking all steps necessary to ensure that the item is put only to its stated end-use. It is understood that the decision to transfer remains the sole and sovereign judgment of the Government.

---

1. *See* Missile Technology Control Regime, *available at* http://www.mtcr.info/english/index.html.
2. Missile Techn. Control Regime, *Guidelines for Sensitive Missile-Relevant Transfers, available at* http://www.mtcr.info/english/guidetext.htm.

3. In the evaluation of transfer applications for Annex items, the following factors will be taken into account:

A. Concerns about the proliferation of weapons of mass destruction;

B. The capabilities and objectives of the missile and space programs of the recipient state;

C. The significance of the transfer in terms of the potential development of delivery systems (other than manned aircraft) for weapons of mass destruction;

D. The assessment of the end use of the transfers, including the relevant assurances of the recipient states referred to in sub paragraphs 5.A and 5.B below;

E. The applicability of relevant multilateral agreements.

F. The risk of controlled items falling into the hands of terrorist groups and individuals.

4. The transfer of design and production technology directly associated with any items in the Annex will be subject to as great a degree of scrutiny and control as will the equipment itself, to the extent permitted by national legislation.

5. Where the transfer could contribute to a delivery system for weapons of mass destruction, the Government will authorize transfers of items in the Annex only on receipt of appropriate assurances from the government of the recipient state that:

A. The items will be used only for the purpose stated and that such use will not be modified nor the items modified or replicated without the prior consent of the Government;

B. Neither the items nor replicas nor derivatives thereof will be retransferred without the consent of the Government.

6. In furtherance of the effective operation of the Guidelines, the Government will, as necessary and appropriate, exchange relevant in formation with other governments applying the same Guidelines.

7. The Government will:

A. provide that its national export controls require an authorization for the transfer of non-listed items if the exporter has been informed by the competent authorities of the Government that the items may be intended, in their entirety or part, for use in connection with delivery systems for weapons of mass destruction other than manned aircraft;

B. and, if the exporter is aware that non-listed items are intended to contribute to such activities, in their entirety or part, provide, to the extent compatible with national export controls, for notification by the exporter to the authorities referred to above, which will decide whether or not it is appropriate to make the export concerned subject to authorization.

8. The adherence of all States to these Guidelines in the interest of international peace and security would be welcome.

MEMORANDUM OF DISAPPROVAL FOR THE OMNIBUS EXPORT AMENDMENTS ACT[1]

I am withholding my approval of H.R. 4653, the "Omnibus Export Amendments Act of 1990." Although this legislation contains constructive provisions, it would severely constrain Presidential authority in carrying out foreign policy.

I agree with the principal goals of this bill, which include improved export controls for, and sanctions against the use of, chemical and biological weapons; sanctions on Iraq; missile technology sanctions; and reauthorization of the Export Administration Act. Indeed, I have recently signed into law provisions on missile technology sanctions and sanctions against Iraq comparable to those contained in this bill. H.R. 4653, however, contains elements that I believe would undermine these objectives and our ability to act quickly, decisively, and multilaterally at a time when we must be able to do so. These provisions unduly interfere with the President's constitutional responsibilities for carrying out foreign policy. Rather than signing the bill, I am directing action under existing authorities to accomplish the bill's principal goals.

I am pleased that the Congress endorses my goal of stemming the dangerous proliferation of chemical and biological weapons. The Administration has worked closely with the Congress to design appropriate and effective legislation to improve our ability to impose sanctions on the nations that use such weapons and any companies that contribute to their spread. Indeed, the Administration supported the House version of the sanctions provision. Throughout discussions with the Congress, my Administration insisted that any such legislation should not harm cooperation with our partners and should respect the President's constitutional responsibilities. Unfortunately, as reported from conference, H.R. 4653 does not safeguard those responsibilities, nor does it meet our broader foreign policy goals.

The major flaw in H.R. 4653 is not the requirement of sanctions, but the rigid way in which they are imposed. The mandatory imposition of unilateral sanctions as provided in this bill would harm U.S. economic interests and provoke friendly countries who are essential to our efforts to resist Iraqi aggression. If there is one lesson we have all learned in Operation Desert Shield, it is that multilateral support enhances the effectiveness of sanctions.

Because of my deep concern about the serious threat posed by chemical and biological weapons, I have signed an Executive order directing the imposition of the sanctions contained in this bill and implementing new chemical and biological weapon export controls. This Executive order goes beyond H.R. 4653 in some respects. It sets forth a clear set of stringent sanctions, while encouraging negotiations with our friends and allies. It imposes an economic penalty on companies that contribute to the spread of these weapons and on countries that actually use such weapons or are making preparations to do so. At the same time, it allows the President necessary flexibility in implementing these sanctions and penalties. Furthermore, the Executive order reaffirms my determination to achieve early conclusion of a verifiable global convention to prevent the production and use of chemical weapons.

---

1. George Bush, Memorandum of Disapproval for the Omnibus Export Amendments Act of 1990, 2 Pub. Papers 1619, 1619–21 (Nov. 16, 1990), *available at* http://bushlibrary.tamu.edu/research/papers/1990/90111616.html.

The Executive order also directs the establishment of enhanced proliferation controls, carefully targeted on exports, projects, and countries of concern. On this issue, as with other important export control matters, my goal is to pursue effective, multilateral export controls that send the clear message that the United States will not tolerate violations of international law.

I am also concerned that other features of H.R. 4653 would hamper our efforts to improve the effectiveness of export controls. In the rapidly changing situation in Eastern Europe, and in bilateral relationships with the Soviet Union, we have demonstrated the ability to adjust, in cooperation with our allies, export controls on high technology to reflect the new strategic relationships. Last May I asked our allies to liberalize dramatically our multilateral export controls. Negotiations designed to liberalize trade to encourage democratic institutions and open market economies will continue. Our multilateral export controls have contributed significantly to the positive changes brought about in West-East relations. The micromanagement of export controls mandated by H.R. 4653 can only damage these ongoing efforts.

In other areas, H.R. 4653 would be harmful to closely linked U.S. economic and foreign policy interests. For example, under section 128 of the bill there would be extraterritorial application of U.S. law that could force foreign subsidiaries of U.S. firms to choose between violating U.S. or host country laws.

Other sections of H.R. 4653 contain useful provisions that will be implemented as soon as possible. However, additional legal authority is not required to make our export control system reflect the economic and national security realities of today's world. In response to recent world events, I am directing Executive departments and agencies to implement the following changes:

—By June 1, 1991, the United States will eliminate all dual-use export licenses under section 5 of the Export Administration Act to members of the export control group known as CoCom, consistent with multilateral arrangements. In addition, all re-export licenses under section 5 to and from CoCom will be eliminated, consistent with multilateral arrangements.

—By June 1, 1991, the United States will remove from the U.S. munitions list all items contained on the CoCom dual-use list unless significant U.S. national security interests would be jeopardized.

—By January 1, 1991, U.S. review of export licenses subject to CoCom Favorable Consideration and National Discretion procedures will be reduced to 30 and 15 days, respectively.

—By January 1, 1991, new interagency procedures will be instituted to make dual-use export license decisions more predictable and timely.

—By January 1, 1991, the Secretary of State will initiate negotiations to ensure that supercomputer export controls are multilateral in nature and not undermined by the policies of other supplier countries. By June 1, 1991, in consultation with industry, we will devise and publish a method to index supercomputer license conditions to reflect rapid advances in the industry and changes in strategic concerns.

—By January 1, 1991, we will significantly increase the threshold for Distribution Licenses to free world destinations and ensure that at least annually these thresholds are adjusted to reflect changes in technology and are consistent with international relationships, including changing requirements to stem the proliferation of missile technology and nuclear, chemical and biological weapons.

In summary, H.R. 4653 contains serious and unacceptable flaws that would hamper our efforts to prevent the proliferation of weapons of mass destruction and to ease restrictions on the legitimate sale of dual-use goods to acceptable users. Rather than sign this bill, I have chosen to take a series of steps under existing authorities to ensure that mutually shared objectives are met in a timely and effective manner. I will work with the Congress, upon its return, to enact an appropriate extension of the Export Administration Act.

George Bush

FACT SHEET ON ENHANCED PROLIFERATION INITIATIVE[2]

Responding to the President's call in his speech before the UN General Assembly to "redouble our efforts to stem the spread" of missile technology as well as nuclear, chemical, and biological weapons, an interagency study proposed a series of measures designed to ensure that these weapons and the technology to make them do not fall into the wrong hands. The "Enhanced Proliferation Control Initiative" includes the following elements:

1. The United States shall adopt worldwide export controls on 50 precursors for chemical weapons and shall urge all nations that manufacture these chemicals to adopt equivalent controls.

2. Export licenses shall be required for proposed exports of potentially chemical-weapon-related industrial facilities, and related designs and technology.

3. Export licenses shall be required for any export destined for publicly-listed company, ministry, project, or other entity that is engaged in activities of proliferation concern.

4. Export licenses shall be required when an exporter knows or is informed by the U.S. Government that a proposed export may be destined for a project of proliferation concern. (A similar regulation applies to exports of possible nuclear weapon concerns).

5. Current regulations shall be supplemented by control lists of (i) dual-use equipment and technology related to chemical weapons, biological weapons, and missiles, and (ii) countries to which such equipment and technology shall be controlled.

6. Civil and criminal penalties shall be imposed upon U.S. citizens who knowingly participate in activities that promote the spread of missile technology and chemical weapons. (Similar penalties already apply in the areas of nuclear and biological weapons).

These measures will implement portions of Executive Order No. 12735, issued by President Bush on November 16, 1990, to combat the spread of chemical and biological weapons. Close consultations with members of Congress and American industry will now be required to ensure effective implementation of these measures by February 16.

The United States will seek the widest and earliest multilateral concurrence in these measures, recognizing that the support of other supplier nations is essential to effective export controls.

---

2. Press Release, White House, Office of the Press Sec'y, Fact Sheet: Enhanced Proliferation Initiative (Dec. 13, 1990) (on file with editor), *reprinted in New Export Control Procedures*, J. Com., Mar. 1, 1991, at 4A.

SOVIET-UNITED STATES JOINT STATEMENT ON NON-PROLIFERATION JUNE 4, 1990*

The United States of America and the Union of Soviet Socialist Republics oppose the proliferation of nuclear weapons, chemical weapons, missiles capable of carrying such weapons, and certain other missiles and missile technologies. The more nations that possess such weapons, the more difficult it will be to realize the desire of people everywhere to achieve effective arms control and disarmament measures and to reduce the threat of war. Weapons proliferation can provoke or intensify insecurity and hostility among nations, and threatens mankind with warfare of unprecedented destructiveness.

Our discussions over the past months point the way to a new era in relations between our two countries. We have taken major steps toward concluding agreements to reduce our own strategic nuclear arsenals, to bring limits on nuclear testing into force, and to reach a global ban on chemical weapons. Together with the nations of Europe, we are taking unprecedented steps to reduce existing conventional weaponry as part of a process of building a lasting structure of European security. The progress we are making and the commitments we have made in these bilateral and multilateral arms control efforts clearly demonstrate that arms reductions can contribute to increased security, even when there have been long-standing and deep-seated differences between countries.

The historic steps we have taken to improve U.S.-Soviet relations and to cooperate in the interests of international stability create the possibility of even closer and more concrete cooperation in the areas of nuclear, chemical, and missile non-proliferation.

With these considerations in mind, The United States and the Soviet Union:

• Declare their commitment to preventing the proliferation of nuclear weapons, chemical weapons, and missiles capable of carrying such weapons and certain other missiles and missile technologies, in particular those subject to the provisions of the Missile Technology Control Regime (MTCR);

• Agree to work closely together and with other members of the international community to develop and to put into action concrete measures against the proliferation of these types of weapons; and

• Call on other nations to join in a renewed commitment to effective non-proliferation measures as a means of securing international peace and stability and as a step toward the effective limitation worldwide of nuclear weapons, chemical weapons, missiles, and missile technology.

The two sides have taken specific actions to advance these commitments.

---

* Joint Statement on Non-Proliferation, U.S.-U.S.S.R., June 4, 1990, Press Release, White House, Joint Statement on Non-Proliferation (June 4, 1990) (on file with editor), *reprinted in Joint Statement on Non-Proliferation as Released by the White House, Monday, June 4, 1990*, FED. NEWS SERV., June 4, 1990 (LEXIS, News Library, Allnws File), *available at* http://bushlibrary.tamu.edu/research/papers/1990/90060400.html.

Nuclear Weapons Non-Proliferation

In order to prevent the proliferation of nuclear weapons, the United States and the Soviet Union:

• Reaffirm their steadfast and long-lasting commitment to prevent the proliferation of nuclear weapons and to strengthen the international nuclear weapons non-proliferation regime;

• Reaffirm their strong support for the Treaty on the Non-Proliferation of Nuclear Weapons (NPT) and agree that it continues to make an invaluable contribution to global and regional security and stability;

• Urge all countries which have not yet done so to adhere to the NPT;

• Urge all NPT parties to implement scrupulously their International Atomic Energy Agency (IAEA) safeguards obligations under the Treaty;

• Affirm their intention to cooperate together and with other Treaty parties to ensure a successful 1990 Review Conference on the Treaty on the Non-Proliferation of Nuclear Weapons which would reaffirm support for the objectives of the Treaty and its importance to international security and stability;

• Support the Treaty for the Prohibition of Nuclear Weapons in Latin America (the Treaty of Tlatelolco) and urge all countries in the region to bring it into force at an early date;

• Reiterate their continuing commitment to strengthening the IAEA, whose unique system of safeguards has contributed to the widespread peaceful use of nuclear energy for social and economic development;

• Support increased international cooperation in the peaceful uses of nuclear energy under IAEA safeguards;

• Call on all non-nuclear-weapons states with unsafeguarded nuclear activities to place these activities under international safeguards;

• Agree on the need for stringent controls over exports of nuclear-related material, equipment and technology, to ensure that they will not be misused for nuclear explosive purposes, and urge all other nations capable of exporting nuclear-related technology to apply similarly strict controls;

• Continue to support efforts to improve and strengthen the international nuclear export control regime;

• Support discussions among states in regions of nuclear proliferation concern for the purpose of achieving concrete steps to reduce the risk of nuclear proliferation, and, in particular, join in calling on the nations of the Middle East, Southern Africa, and South Asia to engage in and pursue such discussions;

• Agree to continue their regular, constructive bilateral consultations on nuclear weapons non-proliferation.

Missile and Missile Technology Non-Proliferation

In order to stem the proliferation of missiles and missile technology, the United States and the Soviet Union:

• Have signed the Treaty between the United States of America and the Union of Soviet Socialist Republics on the Elimination of Their Intermediate-Range and Shorter-

Range Missiles, demonstrating that controls on—indeed the elimination of—such missiles can enhance national security;

• Reaffirm their intention that the START Treaty be signed by the end of the year;

• Affirm their support for the objectives of the Missile Technology Control Regime, covering missiles, and certain equipment and technology relating to missiles capable of delivering at least 500 kilograms of payload to a range of at least 300 kilometers and they call on all nations that have not done so to observe the spirit and the guidelines of this regime;

• Are taking measures to restrict missile proliferation on a worldwide basis, including export controls and other internal procedures;

• Have instituted bilateral consultations to exchange information concerning such controls and procedures and identify specific measures to prevent missile proliferation;

• Agree to work to stop missile proliferation, particularly in regions of tension, such as the Middle East;

• To this end, affirm their intent to explore regional initiatives to reduce the threat of missile proliferation, including the possibility of offering their good offices to promote such initiatives;

• Recall that they favor international economic cooperation including cooperation aimed at peaceful space exploration, as long as such cooperation could not contribute to missile proliferation;

• Appeal to all countries—to exporters of missiles and missile technology as well as purchasers—to exercise restraint, and express their willingness to continue their respective dialogues with other countries on the non-proliferation of missiles and missile technology.

• Are resolved, on their part, to continue to work to strengthen such international restraint with respect to missile and missile technology proliferation.

Chemical Weapons Non-proliferation

In order to stem the use and proliferation of chemical weapons, the United States and the Soviet Union:

• Declare that a multilateral, effectively verifiable chemical weapons convention banning the development, production and use of chemical weapons and eliminating all stocks on a global basis is the best long-term solution to the threat to international security posed by the use and spread of chemical weapons, and that non-proliferation measures are considered a step toward achieving such a convention;

• Will intensify their cooperation to expedite the negotiations in Geneva with the view to resolving outstanding issues as soon as possible and to finalizing the draft convention at the earliest date;

• Have instituted bilateral confidence building measures, including chemical weapons data exchange and reciprocal site visits;

• Have just signed a trailblazing agreement on destruction and non-production of chemical weapons and on measures to facilitate the multilateral convention on chemical weapons;

• Commit themselves, in that agreement to take practical measures to encourage all chemical weapons-capable states to become parties to the multilateral convention;

• Having declared their possession of chemical weapons, urge other states possessing chemical weapons to declare their possession, to commit to their destruction, and to begin immediately to address, through research and cooperation, the need for chemical weapons destruction capability;

• State that they themselves will not proliferate chemical weapons;

• Have instituted export controls to stem the proliferation of chemical weapons. These measures are not intended to hinder or discriminate against legitimate peaceful chemical activities;

• Have agreed to conduct bilateral discussions to improve the effectiveness of their respective export controls to stem the proliferation of chemical weapons;

• Conduct regular bilateral consultations to broaden bilateral cooperation, including the reciprocal exchange of information on the problems of chemical weapons proliferation;

• Confirm their intent to pursue political and diplomatic actions, where specific cases give rise to concerns about the production, use or spread of chemical weapons;

• Join with other nations in multilateral efforts to coordinate export controls, exchange information, and broaden international cooperation to stem the proliferation of chemical weapons;

• Reaffirm their support for the 1925 Geneva Protocol banning the use of chemical weapons in violation of international law;

• Are taking steps to strengthen the 1925 Geneva Protocol by:

— Encouraging states that are not parties to accede;

— Confirming their intention to provide active support to the United Nations Secretary General in conducting investigations of reported violations of the Protocol;

— Affirming their intention to consider the imposition of sanctions against violators of the Protocol, including those under Chapter VII of the United Nations Charter;

— Agreeing to consult promptly in the event of a violation of the Protocol to discuss possible bilateral and multilateral actions against the offender, as well as appropriate assistance to the victims of such violation;

• Agree that the presence and further proliferation of chemical weapons in areas of tension, such as the Middle East, is particularly dangerous. The two countries therefore affirm their intent to explore regional initiatives in the Middle East and other areas, including the possibility of offering their good offices to promote such initiatives as:

— Efforts to broaden awareness of the dangers of chemical weapons proliferation and its negative impact on implementation of the multilateral convention on chemical weapons;

— Bilateral or multilateral efforts to stem chemical weapons proliferation, including the renunciation of the production of chemical weapons;

— Efforts to destroy chemical weapons in advance of the multilateral convention on chemical weapons, as the United States and the Soviet Union are doing.

The United States and the Soviet Union call on all nations of the world that have not already done so to join them in taking comparable, effective measures to stem chemical weapons proliferation.

EXECUTIVE ORDER 12938* (PROLIFERATION OF WEAPONS OF MASS DESTRUCTION)

By the authority vested in me as President by the Constitution and the laws of the United States of America, including the International Emergency Economic Powers Act (50 U.S.C. 1701 et seq.), the National Emergencies Act (50 U.S.C. 1601 et seq.), the Arms Export Control Act, as amended (22 U.S.C. 2751 et seq.), Executive Orders Nos. 12851 and 12924, and section 301 of title 3, United States Code,

I, WILLIAM J. CLINTON, President of the United States of America, find that the proliferation of nuclear, biological, and chemical weapons ("weapons of mass destruction") and of the means of delivering such weapons, constitutes an unusual and extraordinary threat to the national security, foreign policy, and economy of the United States, and hereby declare a national emergency to deal with that threat.

Accordingly, I hereby order:

Section 1. *International Negotiations.* It is the policy of the United States to lead and seek multilaterally coordinated efforts with other countries to control the proliferation of weapons of mass destruction and the means of delivering such weapons. Accordingly, the Secretary of State shall cooperate in and lead multilateral efforts to stop the proliferation of weapons of mass destruction and their means of delivery.

Sec. 2. *Imposition of Controls.* As provided herein, the Secretary of State and the Secretary of Commerce shall use their respective authorities, including the Arms Export Control Act and the International Emergency Economic Powers Act, to control any exports, to the extent they are not already controlled by the Department of Energy and the Nuclear Regulatory Commission, that either Secretary determines would assist a country in acquiring the capability to develop, produce, stockpile, deliver, or use weapons of mass destruction or their means of delivery. The Secretary of State shall pursue early negotiations with foreign governments to adopt effective measures comparable to those imposed under this order.

Sec. 3. *Department of Commerce Controls.* (a) The Secretary of Commerce shall prohibit the export of any goods, technology, or services subject to the Secretary's export jurisdiction that the Secretary of Commerce determines, in consultation with the Secretary of State, the Secretary of Defense, and other appropriate officials, would assist a foreign country in acquiring the capability to develop, produce, stockpile, deliver, or use weapons of mass destruction or their means of delivery. The Secretary of State shall pursue early negotiations with foreign governments to adopt effective measures comparable to those imposed under this section.

(b) Subsection (a) of this section will not apply to exports relating to a particular category of weapons of mass destruction (i.e., nuclear, chemical, or biological weapons) if their destination is a country with whose government the United States has entered into

* Exec. Order No. 12938, 3 C.F.R. 950 (1995), *amended by* Exec. Order No. 13094, 3 C.F.R. 200 (1999), Exec. Order No. 13128, 3 C.F.R. 199 (2000), and Exec. Order No. 13382, 70 Fed. Reg. 38,567 (July 1, 2005), *available at* http://www.archives.gov/federal-register/executive-orders/1994.html. Executive Order 13382 is published below as Doc. 3:44.

a bilateral or multilateral arrangement for the control of that category of weapons of mass destruction-related goods (including delivery systems) and technology, or maintains domestic export controls comparable to controls that are imposed by the United States with respect to that category of goods and technology, or that are otherwise deemed adequate by the Secretary of State.

(c) The Secretary of Commerce shall require validated licenses to implement this order and shall coordinate any license applications with the Secretary of State and the Secretary of Defense.

(d) The Secretary of Commerce, in consultation with the Secretary of State, shall take such actions, including the promulgation of rules, regulations, and amendments thereto, as may be necessary to continue to regulate the activities of United States persons in order to prevent their participation in activities that could contribute to the proliferation of weapons of mass destruction or their means of delivery, as provided in the Export Administration Regulations, set forth in Title 15, Chapter VII, Subchapter C, of the Code of Federal Regulations, Parts 768 to 799 inclusive.

Sec. 4. *Sanctions Against Foreign Persons.* (a) In addition to the sanctions imposed on foreign persons as provided in the National Defense Authorization Act for Fiscal Year 1991 and the Chemical and Biological Weapons Control and Warfare Elimination Act of 1991, sanctions also shall be imposed on a foreign person with respect to chemical and biological weapons proliferation if the Secretary of State determines that the foreign person on or after the effective date of this order or its predecessor, Executive Order No. 12735 of November 16, 1990, knowingly and materially contributed to the efforts of any foreign country, project, or entity to use, develop, produce, stockpile, or otherwise acquire chemical or biological weapons.

(b) No department or agency of the United States Government may procure or enter into any contract for the procurement of, any goods or services from any foreign person described in subsection (a) of this section. The Secretary of the Treasury shall prohibit the importation into the United States of products produced by that foreign person.

(c) Sanctions pursuant to this section may be terminated or not imposed against foreign persons if the Secretary of State determines that there is reliable evidence that the foreign person concerned has ceased all activities referred to in subsection (a).

(d) The Secretary of State and the Secretary of the Treasury may provide appropriate exemptions for procurement contracts necessary to meet U.S. operational military requirements or requirements under defense production agreements, sole source suppliers, spare parts, components, routine servicing and maintenance of products, and medical and humanitarian items. They may provide exemptions for contracts in existence on the date of this order under appropriate circumstances.

Sec. 5. *Sanctions Against Foreign Countries.* (a) In addition to the sanctions imposed on foreign countries as provided in the Chemical and Biological Weapons Control and Warfare Elimination Act of 1991, sanctions also shall be imposed on a foreign country as specified in subsection (b) of this section, if the Secretary of State determines that the foreign country has, on or after the effective date of this order or its predecessor, Executive Order No. 12735 of November 16, 1990, (1) used chemical or biological weapons in violation of international law; (2) made substantial preparations to use chemical or biological weapons in violation of international law; or (3) developed, produced, stockpiled, or otherwise acquired chemical or biological weapons in violation of international law.

(b) The following sanctions shall be imposed on any foreign country identified in subsection (a)(1) of this section unless the Secretary of State determines, on grounds of significant foreign policy or national security, that any individual sanction should not be applied. The sanctions specified in this section may be made applicable to the countries identified in subsections (a)(2) or (a)(3) when the Secretary of State determines that such action will further the objectives of this order pertaining to proliferation. The sanctions specified in subsection (b)(2) below shall be imposed with the concurrence of the Secretary of the Treasury.

(1) Foreign Assistance. No assistance shall be provided to that country under the Foreign Assistance Act of 1961, or any successor act, or the Arms Export Control Act, other than assistance that is intended to benefit the people of that country directly and that is not channeled through governmental agencies or entities of that country.

(2) Multilateral Development Bank Assistance. The United States shall oppose any loan or financial or technical assistance to that country by international financial institutions in accordance with section 701 of the International Financial Institutions Act (22 U.S.C. 262d).

(3) Denial of Credit or Other Financial Assistance. The United States shall deny to that country any credit or financial assistance by any department, agency, or instrumentality of the United States Government.

(4) Prohibition of Arms Sales. The United States Government shall not, under the Arms Export Control Act, sell to that country any defense articles or defense services or issue any license for the export of items on the United States Munitions List.

(5) Exports of National Security-Sensitive Goods and Technology. No exports shall be permitted of any goods or technologies controlled for national security reasons under the Export Administration Regulations.

(6) Further Export Restrictions. The Secretary of Commerce shall prohibit or otherwise substantially restrict exports to that country of goods, technology, and services (excluding agricultural commodities and products otherwise subject to control).

(7) Import Restrictions. Restrictions shall be imposed on the importation into the United States of articles (that may include petroleum or any petroleum product) that are the growth, product, or manufacture of that country.

(8) Landing Rights. At the earliest practicable date, the Secretary of State shall terminate, in a manner consistent with international law, the authority of any air carrier that is controlled in fact by the government of that country to engage in air transportation (as defined in section 101(10) of the Federal Aviation Act of 1958 (49 U.S.C. App. 1301(10)).

Sec. 6. *Duration.* Any sanctions imposed pursuant to sections 4 or 5 of this order shall remain in force until the Secretary of State determines that lifting any sanction is in the foreign policy or national security interests of the United States or, as to sanctions under section 4 of this order, until the Secretary has made the determination under section 4(c).

Sec. 7. *Implementation.* The Secretary of State, the Secretary of the Treasury, and the Secretary of Commerce are hereby authorized and directed to take such actions, including the promulgation of rules and regulations, as may be necessary to carry out the purposes of this order. These actions, and in particular those in sections 4 and 5 of this order, shall be made in consultation with the Secretary of Defense and, as appropriate, other agency heads and shall be implemented in accordance with procedures established pursuant to Executive Order No. 12851. The Secretary concerned may redelegate any of these functions to other officers in agencies of the Federal Government. All heads of departments and agencies of the United States Government are directed to take all appropriate measures within their authority to carry out the provisions of this order, including the suspension or termination of licenses or other authorizations.

Sec. 8. *Preservation of Authorities.* Nothing in this order is intended to affect the continued effectiveness of any rules, regulations, orders, licenses, or other forms of administrative action issued, taken, or continued in effect heretofore or hereafter under the authority of the International Economic Emergency Powers Act, the Export Administration Act, the Arms Export Control Act, the Nuclear Non-proliferation Act, Executive Order No. 12730 of September 30, 1990, Executive Order No. 12735 of November 16, 1990, Executive Order No. 12924 of August 18, 1994, and Executive Order No. 12930 of September 29, 1994.

Sec. 9. *Judicial Review.* This order is not intended to create, nor does it create, any right or benefit, substantive or procedural, enforceable at law by a party against the United States, its agencies, officers, or any other person.

Sec. 10. *Revocation of Executive Orders Nos. 12735 and 12930.* Executive Order No. 12735 of November 16, 1990, and Executive Order No. 12930 of September 29, 1994, are hereby revoked.

Sec. 11. *Effective Date.* This order is effective immediately.

This order shall be transmitted to the Congress and published in the Federal Register.

William J. Clinton
The White House
November 14, 1994

PROLIFERATION SECURITY INITIATIVE[1] (WEAPONS OF MASS DESTRUCTION)

The Proliferation Security Initiative (PSI) announced by President Bush in Krakow, Poland on May 31,2003, is a multinational response to the growing challenge posed by the proliferation of weapons of mass destruction (WMD), their delivery systems, and related materials worldwide. The increasingly aggressive efforts by proliferators to circumvent existing nonproliferation norms, and to profit from such trade, require new and stronger actions by the international community. PSI activities will be consistent with national legal authorities and existing international treaties and regimes. It will involve all states that have a stake in nonproliferation and the ability and willingness to take steps to stop the flow of such items at sea, in the air, or on land.

The Initiative is consistent with and a critical step in the implementation of the UN Security Council Presidential Statement of January 1992, which states that the proliferation of WMD constitutes a threat to international peace and security, and underlines the need for member states of the UN to prevent proliferation.

Eleven nations are participating as the PSI core group: Australia, France, Germany, Italy, Japan, Netherlands, Poland, Portugal, Spain, U.K. and the United States. The PSI will utilize existing national and international legal authorities and seek to strengthen these authorities to meet today's WMD proliferation challenges.

Proliferation Security Initiative Statement of Interdiction Principles[2]

The Proliferation Security Initiative (PSI) is a response to the growing challenge posed by the proliferation of weapons of mass destruction (WMD), their delivery systems, and related materials worldwide. The PSI builds on efforts by the international community to prevent proliferation of such items, including existing treaties and regimes. It is consistent with and a step in the implementation of the United Nations Security Council Presidential Statement of January 1992, which states that the proliferation of all WMD constitutes a threat to international peace and security, and underlines the need for member states of the U.N. to prevent proliferation. The PSI is also consistent with recent statements of the G8 and the European Union, establishing that more coherent and concerted efforts are needed to prevent the proliferation of WMD, their delivery systems, and related materials. PSI participants are deeply concerned about this threat and of the danger that these items could fall into the hands of terrorists, and are committed to working together to stop the flow of these items to and from states and non-state actors of proliferation concern.

The PSI seeks to involve in some capacity all states that have a stake in nonproliferation and the ability and willingness to take steps to stop the flow of such items at sea, in the air, or on land. The PSI also seeks cooperation from any state whose vessels, flags, ports, territorial waters, airspace, or land might be used for proliferation purposes by

---

1. *See* Press Release, U.S. Dep't of State, Bureau of Nonproliferation, The Proliferation Security Initiative (July 8, 2004) (on file with editor), *available at* http://www.state.gov/t/np/rls/other/34726.htm.

2. Press Release, White House, Office of the Press Sec'y, Fact Sheet: Proliferation Security Initiative: Statement of Interdiction Principles (Sept. 4, 2003) (on file with editor), *available at* http://www.state.gov/t/np/rls/fs/23764.htm.

states and non-state actors of proliferation concern. The increasingly aggressive efforts by proliferators to stand outside or to circumvent existing nonproliferation norms, and to profit from such trade, requires new and stronger actions by the international community. We look forward to working with all concerned states on measures they are able and willing to take in support of the PSI, as outlined in the following set of "Interdiction Principles."

Interdiction Principles for the Proliferation Security Initiative

PSI participants are committed to the following interdiction principles to establish a more coordinated and effective basis through which to impede and stop shipments of WMD, delivery systems, and related materials flowing to and from states and non-state actors of proliferation concern, consistent with national legal authorities and relevant international law and frameworks, including the United Nations Security Council. They call on all states concerned with this threat to international peace and security to join in similarly committing to:

1) Undertake effective measures, either alone or in concert with other states, for interdicting the transfer or transport of WMD, their delivery systems, and related materials to and from states and non-state actors of proliferation concern. "States or non-state actors of proliferation concern" generally refers to those countries or entities that the PSI participants involved establish should be subject to interdiction activities because they are engaged in proliferation through: (1) efforts to develop or acquire chemical, biological, or nuclear weapons and associated delivery systems; or (2) transfers (either selling, receiving, or facilitating) of WMD, their delivery systems, or related materials.

2) Adopt streamlined procedures for rapid exchange of relevant information concerning suspected proliferation activity, protecting the confidential character of classified information provided by other states as part of this initiative, dedicate appropriate resources and efforts to interdiction operations and capabilities, and maximize coordination among participants in interdiction efforts.

3) Review and work to strengthen their relevant national legal authorities where necessary to accomplish these objectives, and work to strengthen when necessary relevant international laws and frameworks in appropriate ways to support these commitments.

4) Take specific actions in support of interdiction efforts regarding cargoes of WMD, their delivery systems, or related materials, to the extent their national legal authorities permit and consistent with their obligations under international law and frameworks, to include:

a) Not to transport or assist in the transport of any such cargoes to or from states or non-state actors of proliferation concern, and not to allow any persons subject to their jurisdiction to do so.

b) At their own initiative, or at the request and good cause shown by another state, to take action to board and search any vessel flying their flag in their internal waters or territorial seas, or areas beyond the territorial seas of any other state, that is reasonably suspected of transporting such cargoes to or from states or non-state actors of proliferation concerns, and to seize such cargoes that are identified.

c) To seriously consider providing consent under the appropriate circumstances to the boarding and searching of its own flag vessels by other states, and to the seizure of such WMD-related cargoes in such vessels that may be identified by such states.

d) To take appropriate actions to:

(1) stop and/or search in their internal waters, territorial seas, or contiguous zones (when declared) vessels that are reasonably suspected of carrying such cargoes to or from states or non-state actors of proliferation concern and to seize such cargoes that are identified; and

(2) enforce conditions on vessels entering or leaving their ports, internal waters, or territorial seas that are reasonably suspected of carrying such cargoes, such as requiring that such vessels be subject to boarding, search, and seizure of such cargoes prior to entry.

e) At their own initiative or upon the request and good cause shown by another state, to

(1) require aircraft that are reasonably suspected of carrying such cargoes to or from states or non-state actors of proliferation concern and that are transiting their airspace to land for inspection and seize any such cargoes that are identified; and/or

(2) deny aircraft reasonably suspected of carrying such cargoes transit rights through their airspace in advance of such flights.

f) If their ports, airfields, or other facilities are used as transshipment points for shipment of such cargoes to or from states or non-state actors of proliferation concern, to inspect vessels, aircraft, or other modes of transport reasonably suspected of carrying such cargoes, and to seize such cargoes that are identified.

EXECUTIVE ORDER 13382* (BLOCKING PROPERTY OF WMD PROLIFERATORS)

By the authority vested in me as President by the Constitution and the laws of the United States of America, including the International Emergency Economic Powers Act (50 U.S.C. 1701 et seq.) (IEEPA), the National Emergencies Act (50 U.S.C. 1601 et seq.), and section 301 of title 3, United States Code,

I, George W. Bush, President of the United States of America, in order to take additional steps with respect to the national emergency described and declared in Executive Order 12938 of November 14, 1994, regarding the proliferation of weapons of mass destruction and the means of delivering them, and the measures imposed by that order, as expanded by Executive Order 13094 of July 28, 1998, hereby order:

Section 1. (a) Except to the extent provided in section 203(b)(1), (3), and (4) of IEEPA (50 U.S.C. 1702(b)(1), (3), and (4)), or in regulations, orders, directives, or licenses that may be issued pursuant to this order, and notwithstanding any contract entered into or any license or permit granted prior to the effective date of this order, all property and interests in property of the following persons, that are in the United States, that hereafter come within the United States, or that are or hereafter come within the possession or control of United States persons, are blocked and may not be transferred, paid, exported, withdrawn, or otherwise dealt in:

(i) the persons listed in the Annex to this order;

(ii) any foreign person determined by the Secretary of State, in consultation with the Secretary of the Treasury, the Attorney General, and other relevant agencies, to have engaged, or attempted to engage, in activities or transactions that have materially contributed to, or pose a risk of materially contributing to, the proliferation of weapons of mass destruction or their means of delivery (including missiles capable of delivering such weapons), including any efforts to manufacture, acquire, possess, develop, transport, transfer or use such items, by any person or foreign country of proliferation concern;

(iii) any person determined by the Secretary of the Treasury, in consultation with the Secretary of State, the Attorney General, and other relevant agencies, to have provided, or attempted to provide, financial, material, technological or other support for, or goods or services in support of, any activity or transaction described in paragraph (a)(ii) of this section, or any person whose property and interests in property are blocked pursuant to this order; and

(iv) any person determined by the Secretary of the Treasury, in consultation with the Secretary of State, the Attorney General, and other relevant agencies, to be owned or controlled by, or acting or purporting to act for or on behalf of, directly or indirectly, any person whose property and interests in property are blocked pursuant to this order.

(b) Any transaction or dealing by a United States person or within the United States in property or interests in property blocked pursuant to this order is prohibited, includ-

---

* Exec. Order No. 13,382, 70 F.R. 38,567 (June 28, 2005), *available at* http://www.archives.gov/federal-register/executive-orders/2005.html.

ing, but not limited to, (i) the making of any contribution or provision of funds, goods, or services by, to, or for the benefit of, any person whose property and interests in property are blocked pursuant to this order, and (ii) the receipt of any contribution or provision of funds, goods, or services from any such person.

(c) Any transaction by a United States person or within the United States that evades or avoids, has the purpose of evading or avoiding, or attempts to violate any of the prohibitions set forth in this order is prohibited.

(d) Any conspiracy formed to violate the prohibitions set forth in this order is prohibited.

Section 2. For purposes of this order:

(a) the term "person" means an individual or entity;

(b) the term "entity" means a partnership, association, trust, joint venture, corporation, group, subgroup, or other organization; and

(c) the term "United States person" means any United States citizen, permanent resident alien, entity organized under the laws of the United States or any jurisdiction within the United States (including foreign branches), or any person in the United States.

Section 3. I hereby determine that the making of donations of the type of articles specified in section 203(b)(2) of IEEPA (50 U.S.C. 1702(b)(2)) by, to, or for the benefit of, any person whose property and interests in property are blocked pursuant to this order would seriously impair my ability to deal with the national emergency declared in Executive Order 12938, and I hereby prohibit such donations as provided by section 1 of this order.

Section 4. Section 4(a) of Executive Order 12938, as amended, is further amended to read as follows:

"Sec. 4. *Measures Against Foreign Persons.*

(a) Determination by Secretary of State; Imposition of Measures. Except to the extent provided in section 203(b) of the International Emergency Economic Powers Act (50 U.S.C. 1702(b)), where applicable, if the Secretary of State, in consultation with the Secretary of the Treasury, determines that a foreign person, on or after November 16, 1990, the effective date of Executive Order 12735, the predecessor order to Executive Order 12938, has engaged, or attempted to engage, in activities or transactions that have materially contributed to, or pose a risk of materially contributing to, the proliferation of weapons of mass destruction or their means of delivery (including missiles capable of delivering such weapons), including any efforts to manufacture, acquire, possess, develop, transport, transfer, or use such items, by any person or foreign country of proliferation concern, the measures set forth in subsections (b), (c), and (d) of this section shall be imposed on that foreign person to the extent determined by the Secretary of State, in consultation with the implementing agency and other relevant agencies. Nothing in this section is intended to preclude the imposition on that foreign person of other measures or sanctions available under this order or under other authorities."

Section 5. For those persons whose property and interests in property are blocked pursuant to section 1 of this order who might have a constitutional presence in the United States, I find that because of the ability to transfer funds or other assets instantaneously, prior notice to such persons of measures to be taken pursuant to this order would render these measures ineffectual. I therefore determine that for these measures to be effective in addressing the national emergency declared in Executive Order 12938, as amended, there need be no prior notice of a listing or determination made pursuant to section 1 of this order.

Section 6. The Secretary of the Treasury, in consultation with the Secretary of State, is hereby authorized to take such actions, including the promulgation of rules and regulations, and to employ all powers granted to the President by IEEPA as may be necessary to carry out the purposes of this order. The Secretary of the Treasury may redelegate any of these functions to other officers and agencies of the United States Government, consistent with applicable law. All agencies of the United States Government are hereby directed to take all appropriate measures within their authority to carry out the provisions of this order and, where appropriate, to advise the Secretary of the Treasury in a timely manner of the measures taken.

Section 7. The Secretary of the Treasury, in consultation with the Secretary of State, is hereby authorized to determine, subsequent to the issuance of this order, that circumstances no longer warrant the inclusion of a person in the Annex to this order and that the property and interests in property of that person are therefore no longer blocked pursuant to section 1 of this order.

Section 8. This order is not intended to, and does not, create any right or benefit, substantive or procedural, enforceable at law or in equity by any party against the United States, its departments, agencies, instrumentalities, or entities, its officers or employees, or any other person.

Section 9. (a) This order is effective at 12:01 a.m. eastern daylight time on June 29, 2005.

(b) This order shall be transmitted to the Congress and published in the Federal Register.

George W. Bush
THE WHITE HOUSE,
June 28, 2005.

ANNEX

Korea Mining Development Trading Corporation
Tanchon Commercial Bank
Korea Ryonbong General Corporation
Aerospace Industries Organization
Shahid Hemmat Industrial Group
Shahid Bakeri Industrial Group
Atomic Energy Organization of Iran
Scientific Studies and Research Center

F. Confidence-Building, Transparency and Risk Reduction

1. Multilateral

INTERNATIONAL CODE OF CONDUCT AGAINST BALLISTIC MISSILE PROLIFERATION* (THE HAGUE CONFERENCE, OPENING STATEMENT)

The Hague 25–26 November 2002
Opening Statement by the Netherlands Minister of Foreign Affairs

. . . .

Ballistic Missile proliferation is not limited to a particular region; its risks affect us all.

I wish to extend a special welcome to the representative of the Secretary-General of the United Nations. International peace and security are matters of global concern and the world's single-most important organisation in dealing with them are the United Nations. The increasing threat posed by the proliferation of weapons of mass destruction, their means of delivery and the possibility of these weapons falling into the hands of terrorists, forces the UN to try and find global answers where it can, and stimulate regional responses where needed. The Code itself also underlines the role and responsibility of the United Nations in this respect.

Why have ballistic missiles become the focus of so much attention and why is it urgent that we act in trying to better control them? Ballistic Missiles have been around ever since World War II. For most of the Cold War, ballistic missiles, in particular those with strategic ranges, were confined to a limited number of states. Since then, however, both their geographical spread and their average ranges have increased rapidly. Ballistic missiles have a number of characteristics that require special attention. They are rapidly deployable, reach their targets in a very short time-span, they are difficult to defend against and, for all of these reasons, create strategic leverage, all the more so when combined with weapons of mass destruction. These characteristics make the unimpeded spread of ballistic missiles a prime source for destabilising regional power equations. Through the almost inherent link with weapons of mass destruction ballistic missile proliferation has also become a major threat to international peace and security at large.

The present Code is not the only initiative to stem the proliferation of ballistic missiles. An Increasing number of countries have policies in place to prevent systems, key components or relevant technologies from falling into the hands of proliferators or even terrorists. Within the U.N., last year a panel of experts conducted in-depth discussions on the issue of missiles, including that of missile proliferation, leading to a report to the General Assembly. This multi-faceted engagement of the international community with the ballistic missile issue is proof of the growing realisation that regional stability and international security stand to gain from norm building, proper non-proliferation conduct, transparency and confidence building measures.

In 1999 a number of countries, including the Netherlands, took the initiative to elaborate a politically binding instrument that would draw up norms regarding ballistic

---

* Jaap de Hoop Scheffer, Neth. Minister of Foreign Affairs, Opening Statement at the Launching Conference for the International Code of Conduct Against Ballistic Missile Proliferation, The Hague, Neth. (Nov. 25, 2002), *available at* http://projects.sipri.se/expcon/hcoc-netmin.htm.

missiles capable of delivering weapons of mass destruction. Because of the urgency of the problem, an approach had to be taken that would provide early results and at the same time create a political instrument that would be able to attract as many countries as possible. The European Union has been supportive of this initiative from the very beginning. Last year, the European Union decided to prepare the then draft Code of Conduct for universal adherence and committed itself to get the instrument up and running before the end of the year 2002. The ensuing process, conducted in a spirit of transparency and inclusiveness, resulted in a final text that you have all received and which will be brought into effect today.

As I indicated in my invitation to you to come to The Hague, the present Code is a first step and, I should add, a modest one. For all the importance that we attach to it, the Code of Conduct needs to be followed up by other initiatives, in the UN and elsewhere. I express the hope that the Code will be the nucleus of an expanding framework of non-proliferation measures in the field of ballistic missiles. Most of all I hope that the entire international community will be united in working towards that goal.

I thank you for your attention.

INTERNATIONAL CODE OF CONDUCT AGAINST BALLISTIC MISSILE PROLIFERATION* (ICOC)

Preamble

The Subscribing States:

....

Believing that an International Code of Conduct against Ballistic Missile Proliferation will contribute to the process of strengthening existing national and international security arrangements and disarmament and non-proliferation objectives and mechanisms;

Recognising that subscribing States may wish to consider engaging in co-operative measures among themselves to this end;

1. Adopt this International Code of Conduct against Ballistic Missile Proliferation (hereinafter referred to as 'the Code');

2. Resolve to respect the following Principles:

a) Recognition of the need comprehensively to prevent and curb the proliferation of Ballistic Missile systems capable of delivering weapons of mass destruction and the need to continue pursuing appropriate international endeavours, including through the Code:

b) Recognition of the importance of strengthening, and gaining wider adhere to, multilateral disarmament and non-proliferation mechanisms;

c) Recognition that adherence to, and full compliance with, international arms control, disarmament and non-proliferation norms help build confidence as to the peaceful intentions of states;

d) Recognition that participation in this Code is voluntary and open to all States;

....

f) Recognition that states should not be excluded from utilising the benefits space for peaceful purposes, but that, in reaping such benefits and in conducting related cooperation, they must not contribute to the proliferation of Ballistic Missiles capable of delivering weapons of mass destruction;

g) Recognition that Space Launch Vehicle programmes should not be used to conceal Ballistic Missile programmes;

h) Recognition of the necessity of appropriate transparency measures on Ballistic Missile programmes and Space Launch Vehicle programmes in order to increase confidence and to promote non-proliferation of Ballistic Missiles and Ballistic Missile technology;

3. Resolve to implement the following General Measures:

---

* International Code of Conduct Against Ballistic Missile Proliferation, Nov. 25, 2002, *available at* http://projects.sipri.se/expcon/hcocfinal.htm.

a) To ratify, accede to or otherwise abide by:

• the Treaty on Principles Governing the Activities of States in the Exploration and Use of Outer Space, including the Moon and Other Celestial Bodies (1967),

• the Convention on International Liability for Damage Caused by Space Objects (1972), and

• the Convention on Registration of Objects Launched into Outer Space (1974);

b) To curb and prevent the proliferation of Ballistic Missiles capable of delivering weapons of mass destruction, both at a global and regional level, through multilateral, bilateral and national endeavours:

c) To exercise maximum possible restraint in the development, testing and deployment of Ballistic Missiles capable of delivering weapons of mass destruction including, where possible, to reduce national holdings of such missiles, in the interest of global and regional peace and security;

d) To exercise the necessary vigilance in the consideration of assistance to Space Launch Vehicle programmes in any other country so as to prevent contributing to delivery systems for weapons of mass destruction, considering that such programmes may be used to conceal Ballistic Missile programmes;

e) Not to contribute to, support or assist any Ballistic Missile programme in countries which might be developing or acquiring weapons of mass destruction in contravention of norms established by, and of those countries' obligations under, international disarmament and non-proliferation treaties;

4. Resolve to implement the following:

a) Transparency measures as follows, with an appropriate and sufficient degree of detail to increase confidence and to promote non-proliferation of Ballistic Missiles capable of delivering weapons of mass destruction:

i) With respect to Ballistic Missile programmes to:

• make an annual declaration providing an outline of their Ballistic Missile policies.

Examples of openness in such declarations might be relevant information on Ballistic Missile systems and land (test-) launch sites;

• provide annual information on the number and generic class of Ballistic Missiles launched during the preceding year, as declared in conformity with the pre-launch notification mechanism referred to hereunder, in tiret iii);

ii) With respect to expendable Space Launch Vehicle programmes, and consistent with commercial and economic confidentiality principles, to:

• make an annual declaration providing an outline of their Space Launch Vehicle policies and land (test-) launch sites;

• provide annual information on the number and generic class of Space Launch Vehicles launched during the preceding year, as declared in conformity with the pre-launch notification mechanism referred to hereunder, in tiret iii);

- consider, on a voluntary basis (including on the degree of access permitted), inviting international observers to their land (test-) launch sites;

iii) With respect to their Ballistic Missile and Space Launch Vehicle programmes to:

- exchange pre-launch notifications on their Ballistic Missile and Space Launch Vehicle launches and test flights. These notifications should include such information as the generic class of the Ballistic Missile or Space Launch Vehicle, the planned launch notification window, the launch area and the planned direction;

b) Subscribing States could, as appropriate and on a voluntary basis, develop bilateral or regional transparency measures, in addition to those above.

c) Implementation of the above Confidence Building Measures does not set justification for the programmes to which these Confidence Building Measures apply;

. . . .

INTERNATIONAL CODE OF CONDUCT AGAINST BALLISTIC MISSILE PROLIFERATION* (THE HAGUE CONFERENCE, BOLTON REMARKS)

John R. Bolton, Under Secretary for Arms Control and International Security
Remarks at the Launching Conference for the International Code of Conduct Against Ballistic Missile ProliferationThe Hague, The Netherlands
November 25, 2002

(Remarks as delivered)

Mr. Chairman, Ministers, Ambassadors, Distinguished Delegates:

I am honored to represent the United States of America as an initial Subscribing State to the International Code of Conduct against Ballistic Missile Proliferation (ICOC). The entry into effect today of the ICOC marks an important contribution to the international effort against the proliferation of ballistic missiles capable of delivering weapons of mass destruction (WMD)—an effort that the United States has always strongly supported.

The large number of countries that have subscribed to the ICOC and are represented here is a concrete demonstration that the international community has recognized and is looking for additional ways to address the proliferation of the most threatening means of delivery for weapons of mass destruction. It is no accident that the dangerous proliferation of ballistic missiles occurs predominantly in parallel with programs for nuclear, chemical, and biological weapons. International concern about such ballistic missile programs is heightened by the fact that weapons of mass destruction programs also often exist in parallel with support for terrorist groups. Viewed in this context, it is clear why the proliferation of ballistic missiles threatens international peace and security on a worldwide basis.

The United States regards the proliferation of ballistic missiles capable of delivering WMD as a direct threat to the U.S., our deployed forces, our friends and allies, and our interests in key regions of the world.

The United States sees the International Code of Conduct against Ballistic Missile Proliferation as an important addition to the wide range of tools available to countries to impede and roll back this proliferation threat. One element of our strategy is multilateral efforts against missile proliferation, such as the ICOC and the Missile Technology Control Regime (MTCR). Another important element is missile defense. We view our missile defense efforts as complementary to, and consistent with the objectives of, the ICOC and the MTCR. Each seeks in different ways to protect us from the dangers posed by WMD and ballistic missile proliferation. We are now in the process of discussing with allies and friends, including the Russian Federation, cooperation on missile defense programs because our nation is hardly alone in needing the additional pro-

* John R. Bolton, U.S. Dep't of State, Under Sec'y for Arms Control & Int'l Sec., Remarks at the Launching Conference for the International Code of Conduct Against Ballistic Missile Proliferation, The Hague, Neth. (Nov. 25, 2002), *available at* http://www.state.gov/t/us/rm/15488.htm.

tection that such programs can provide. Missile defenses, the MTCR, and the ICOC play important roles in deterring and reducing missile proliferation, and the United States will be ready to work with members of the ICOC, and of the MTCR, to ensure that these complementary efforts are mutually reinforcing.

While an important new addition to the broad arsenal of nonproliferation measures, it is no secret that the ICOC has its limitations. For example, in taking on the political commitment pursuant to the ICOC to "exercise maximum possible restraint in the development, testing and deployment of Ballistic Missiles capable of delivering weapon of mass destruction," the United States—like other countries—understands this commitment as not limiting our right to take steps in these areas necessary to meet our national security requirements consistent with U.S. national security strategy. This includes our ability to maintain our deterrent umbrella for our friends and allies, and the capabilities necessary to defeat aggression involving WMD attacks. But all Subscribing States will have the opportunity to discuss these issues in detail, and to participate in consensus decisions to evolve the text.

Most of this implementation work will concern the ICOC's requirements for pre-launch notification of Subscribing States' ballistic missile and space-launch vehicle launches and test flights. The United States intends to make pre-launch notifications and annual declarations pursuant to the ICOC based upon current U.S. proposals in its negotiations with the Russian Federation on a Pre-Launch Notification System, including on the question of which launches are to be notified. For example, the United States reserves the right in circumstances of war to launch ballistic missiles and space-launch vehicles without prior notification.

Once implementation is completed, the notifications and annual declarations that the United States provides pursuant to the ICOC will be based upon the U.S.-Russian Pre-Launch Notification System, to be established in connection with the U.S.-Russian Joint Data Exchange Center. Over the longer term, we agree with the Russian Federation that the bilateral U.S.-Russian system should be multilateralized. We hope, in turn, that such a multilateralized system might provide the mechanism by which all ICOC Subscribing States exchange pre-launch notifications. We plan to keep all Subscribing States informed on the progress of the implementation of the U.S.-Russia agreement on launch notification, and on the implications and opportunities that a multilateralized U.S.-Russia Pre-Launch Notification System can present for the ICOC.

Some have been concerned that the ICOC is simply a political declaration and not "legally binding." But surely the real issue is not the nature of the commitment, but the extent of the political will to comply with the Code that signatories demonstrate. Too often in the arms control and nonproliferation fields, countries make a great public flourish about adhering to codes and conventions, and then, quietly and deceptively, do precisely the opposite in private.

In the context of the Biological Weapons Convention (BWC), for example, we know that several member states are violating their commitments to the treaty. To expose some of these violators to the international community, we have named publicly states the U.S. Government knows to be pursuing the production of biological warfare agents in violation of the BWC—including Iraq, North Korea, Iran and Libya, as well as Cuba, which we believe has at least a limited, developmental offensive biological warfare R&D [research and development] effort, and which has provided dual-use biotechnology to other rogue states.

Even as we speak, we face a grave threat to the integrity of the Non-Proliferation Treaty. North Korea brazenly admitted last month to having a program to enrich uranium for nuclear weapons. This egregious violation of its treaty commitments threatens the security of all nations, as well as the continued credibility of the Non-Proliferation Treaty.

Surely, none of us wants this disdain and disregard to happen to the new ICOC. That is why we are not concerned about the states that have chosen not to subscribe to the Code. Far better to know who is actually prepared to live under its terms, and who is not. Far better to know who is truly serious about stopping the proliferation of ballistic missile technology and the risk that such technology could be used to carry weapons of mass destruction against innocent civilian populations.

In conclusion, Mr. Chairman, the United States places great value on the International Code of Conduct against Ballistic Missile Proliferation and has high confidence in its future potential. We pledge our full support to you and our fellow Subscribing States in the demanding tasks ahead. Thank you.

[End]

2. Bilateral Efforts between the U.S. and the Soviet Union or Successor States

MEMORANDUM OF UNDERSTANDING BETWEEN THE UNITED STATES OF AMERICA AND THE UNION OF SOVIET SOCIALIST REPUBLICS REGARDING THE ESTABLISHMENT OF A DIRECT COMMUNICATIONS LINK*

For use in time of emergency the Government of the United States of America and the Government of the Union of Soviet Socialist Republics have agreed to establish as soon as technically feasible a direct communications link between the two Governments.

Each Government shall be responsible for the arrangements for the link on its own territory. Each Government shall take the necessary steps to ensure continuous functioning of the link and prompt delivery to its head of government of any communications received by means of the link from the head of government of the other party.

Arrangements for establishing and operating the link are set forth in the Annex which is attached hereto and forms an integral part hereof.

DONE in duplicate in the English and Russian languages at Geneva, Switzerland, this 20th day of June, 1963.

[Signatures omitted].

Annex
To the Memorandum of Understanding Between the United States of America and the Union of Soviet Socialist Republics Regarding the Establishment of a Direct Communications Link

The direct communications link between Washington and Moscow established in accordance with the Memorandum, and the operation of such link, shall be governed by the following provisions:

1. The direct communications link shall consist of:

a. Two terminal points with telegraph-teleprinter equipment between which communications shall be directly exchanged;

b. One full-time duplex wire telegraph circuit, routed Washington-London-Copenhagen-Stockholm-Helsinki-Moscow, which shall be used for the transmission of messages;

c. One full-time duplex radiotelegraph circuit, routed Washington-Tangier-Moscow, which shall be used for service communications and for coordination of operations between the two terminal points.

---

* Memorandum of Understanding Between the United States of America and the Union of Soviet Socialist Republics Regarding the Establishment of a Direct Communications Link, U.S.-U.S.S.R., June 20, 1963, 14 U.S.T. 826 (entered into force June 20, 1963), *amended by* Agreement Between the United States of America and the Union of Soviet Socialist Republics on Measures to Improve the USA-USSR Direct Communications Link, U.S.-U.S.S.R., Sept. 30, 1971, 22 U.S.T. 1598 (entered into force Sept. 30, 1971), *amended by* Direct Communications Link: Agreement Amending the Agreement of September 30, 1971, U.S-U.S.S.R., Mar. 20 & Apr. 29, 1975, 26 U.S.T. 564 (entered into force Apr. 29, 1975), *available at* http://www.state.gov/t/ac/trt/4785.htm.

If experience in operating the direct communications link should demonstrate that the establishment of an additional wire telegraph circuit is advisable, such circuit may be established by mutual agreement between authorized representatives of both Governments.

2. In case of interruption of the wire circuit, transmission of messages shall be effected via the radio circuit, and for this purpose provision shall be made at the terminal points for the capability of prompt switching of all necessary equipment from one circuit to another.

3. The terminal points of the link shall be so equipped as to provide for the transmission and reception of messages from Moscow to Washington in the Russian language and from Washington to Moscow in the English language. In this connection, the U.S.S.R. shall furnish the United States four sets of telegraph terminal equipment, including page printers, transmitters, and reperforators, with one years supply of spare parts and all necessary special tools, test equipment, operating instructions, and other technical literature, to provide for transmission and reception of messages in the Russian language.

The United States shall furnish the Soviet Union four sets of telegraph terminal equipment, including page printers, transmitters, and reperforators, with one years supply of spare parts and all necessary special tools, test equipment, operating instructions and other technical literature, to provide for transmission and reception of messages in the English language.

The equipment described in this paragraph shall be exchanged directly between the parties without any payment being required therefor.

4. The terminal points of the direct communications link shall be provided with encoding equipment. For the terminal point in the U.S.S.R., four sets of such equipment (each capable of simplex operation), with one years supply of spare parts, with all necessary special tools, test equipment, operating instructions and other technical literature, and with all necessary blank tape, shall be furnished by the United States to the U.S.S.R. against payment of the cost thereof by the U.S.S.R.

. . . .

5. The United States and the U.S.S.R. shall designate the agencies responsible for the arrangements regarding the direct communications link, for its technical maintenance, continuity and reliability, and for the timely transmission of messages.

Such agencies may, by mutual agreement, decide matters and develop instructions relating to the technical maintenance and operation of the direct communications link and effect arrangements to improve the operation of the link.

. . . .

7. The costs of the direct communications link shall be borne as follows:

a. The U.S.S.R. shall pay the full cost of leasing the portion of the telegraph circuit from Moscow to Helsinki and 50 percent of the cost of leasing the portion of the telegraph circuit from Helsinki to London. The United States shall pay the full cost of leasing the portion of the telegraph circuit from Washington to London and 50 percent of the cost of leasing the portion of the telegraph circuit from London to Helsinki.

b. Payment of the cost of leasing the radio telegraph circuit between Washington and Moscow shall be effected without any transfer of payments between the parties. The U.S.S.R. shall bear the expenses relating to the transmission of messages from Moscow to Washington. The United States shall bear the expenses relating to the transmission of messages from Washington to Moscow.

AGREEMENT BETWEEN THE GOVERNMENT OF THE UNITED STATES OF AMERICA AND THE GOVERNMENT OF THE UNION OF SOVIET SOCIALIST REPUBLICS ON THE PREVENTION OF INCIDENTS ON AND OVER THE HIGH SEAS*

Signed at Moscow May 25, 1972
Entered into force May 25, 1972

The Government of the United States of America and the Government of the Union of Soviet Socialist Republics,

Desiring to assure the safety of navigation of the ships of their respective armed forces on the high seas and flight of their military aircraft over the high seas, and

Guided by the principles and rules of international law,

Have decided to conclude this Agreement and have agreed as follows:

Article I. For the purpose of this Agreement, the following definitions shall apply:

1. "Ship" means:

(a) A warship belonging to the naval forces of the Parties bearing the external marks distinguishing warships of its nationality, under the command of an officer duly commissioned by the government and whose name appears in the Navy list, and manned by a crew who are under regular naval discipline;

(b) Naval auxiliaries of the Parties, which include all naval ships authorized to fly the naval auxiliary flag where such a flag has been established by either Party.

2. "Aircraft" means all military manned heavier-than-air and lighter-than-air craft, excluding space craft.

3. "Formation" means an ordered arrangement of two or more ships proceeding together and normally maneuvered together.

Article II. The Parties shall take measures to instruct the commanding officers of their respective ships to observe strictly the letter and spirit of the International Regulations for Preventing Collisions at Sea, hereinafter referred to as the Rules of the Road. The Parties recognize that their freedom to conduct operations on the high seas is based on the principles established under recognized international law and codified in the 1958 Geneva Convention on the High Seas.

Article III. 1. In all cases ships operating in proximity to each other, except when required to maintain course and speed under the Rules of the Road, shall remain well clear to avoid risk of collision.

* Agreement Between the Government of the United States of America and the Union of Soviet Socialist Republics on the Prevention of Incidents on and over the High Seas, U.S.-U.S.S.R., May 25, 1972, 23 U.S.T. 1168 (entered into force May 25, 1972), *available at* http://www.state.gov/t/ac/trt/4791.htm.

2. Ships meeting or operating in the vicinity of a formation of the other Party shall, while conforming to the Rules of the Road, avoid maneuvering in a manner which would hinder the evolutions of the formation.

3. Formations shall not conduct maneuvers through areas of heavy traffic where internationally recognized traffic separation schemes are in effect.

4. Ships engaged in surveillance of other ships shall stay at a distance which avoids the risk of collision and also shall avoid executing maneuvers embarrassing or endangering the ships under surveillance. Except when required to maintain course and speed under the Rules of the Road, a surveillant shall take positive early action so as, in the exercise of good seamanship, not to embarrass or endanger ships under surveillance.

5. When ships of both Parties maneuver in sight of one another, such signals (flag, sound, and light) as are prescribed by the Rules of the Road, the International Code of Signals, or other mutually agreed signals, shall be adhered to for signaling operations and intentions.

6. Ships of the Parties shall not simulate attacks by aiming guns, missile launchers, torpedo tubes, and other weapons in the direction of a passing ship of the other Party, not launch any object in the direction of passing ships of the other Party, and not use searchlights or other powerful illumination devices to illuminate the navigation bridges of passing ships of the other Party.

7. When conducting exercises with submerged submarines, exercising ships shall show the appropriate signals prescribed by the International Code of Signals to warn ships of the presence of submarines in the area.

8. Ships of one Party when approaching ships of the other Party conducting operations as set forth in Rule 4 (c) of the Rules of the Road, and particularly ships engaged in launching or landing aircraft as well as ships engaged in replenishment underway, shall take appropriate measures not to hinder maneuvers of such ships and shall remain well clear.

Article IV. Commanders of aircraft of the Parties shall use the greatest caution and prudence in approaching aircraft and ships of the other Party operating on and over the high seas, in particular, ships engaged in launching or landing aircraft, and in the interest of mutual safety shall not permit: simulated attacks by the simulated use of weapons against aircraft and ships, or performance of various aerobatics over ships, or dropping various objects near them in such a manner as to be hazardous to ships or to constitute a hazard to navigation.

Article V. 1. Ships of the Parties operating in sight of one another shall raise proper signals concerning their intent to begin launching or landing aircraft.

2. Aircraft of the Parties flying over the high seas in darkness or under instrument conditions shall, whenever feasible, display navigation lights.

Article VI. Both Parties shall:

1. Provide through the established system of radio broadcasts of information and warning to mariners, not less than 3 to 5 days in advance as a rule, notification of actions on the high seas which represent a danger to navigation or to aircraft in flight.

2. Make increased use of the informative signals contained in the International Code of Signals to signify the intentions of their respective ships when maneuvering in proximity to one another. At night, or in conditions of reduced visibility, or under conditions of lighting and such distances when signal flags are not distinct, flashing light

should be used to inform ships of maneuvers which may hinder the movements of others or involve a risk of collision.

3. Utilize on a trial basis signals additional to those in the International Code of Signals, submitting such signals to the Intergovernmental Maritime Consultative Organization for its consideration and for the information of other States.

Article VII. The Parties shall exchange appropriate information concerning instances of collision, incidents which result in damage, or other incidents at sea between ships and aircraft of the Parties. The United States Navy shall provide such information through the Soviet Naval Attaché in Washington and the Soviet Navy shall provide such information through the United States Naval Attaché in Moscow.

Article VIII. This Agreement shall enter into force on the date of its signature and shall remain in force for a period of three years. It will thereafter be renewed without further action by the Parties for successive periods of three years each.

This Agreement may be terminated by either Party upon six months written notice to the other Party.

Article IX. The Parties shall meet within one year after the date of the signing of this Agreement to review the implementation of its terms. Similar consultations shall be held thereafter annually, or more frequently as the Parties may decide.

Article X. The Parties shall designate members to form a Committee which will consider specific measures in conformity with this Agreement. The Committee will, as a particular part of its work, consider the practical workability of concrete fixed distances to be observed in encounters between ships, aircraft, and ships and aircraft. The Committee will meet within six months of the date of signature of this Agreement and submit its recommendations for decision by the Parties during the consultations prescribed in Article IX.

DONE in duplicate on the 25th day of May 1972 in Moscow in the English and Russian languages each being equally authentic.

. . . .

STANDING CONSULTATIVE COMMISSION ON ARMS LIMITATION*

MEMORANDUM OF UNDERSTANDING BETWEEN THE GOVERNMENT OF THE UNITED STATES OF AMERICA AND THE GOVERNMENT OF THE UNION OF SOVIET SOCIALIST REPUBLICS REGARDING THE ESTABLISHMENT OF A STANDING CONSULTATIVE COMMISSION

I

The Government of the United States of America and the Government of the Union of Soviet Socialist Republics hereby establish a Standing Consultative Commission.

II

The Standing Consultative Commission shall promote the objectives and implementation of the provisions of the Treaty between the USA and the USSR on the Limitation of Anti-Ballistic Missile Systems of May 26, 1972, the Interim Agreement between the USA and the USSR on Certain Measures with Respect to the Limitation of Strategic Offensive Arms of May 26, 1972, and the Agreement on Measures to Reduce the Risk of Outbreak of Nuclear War between the USA and the USSR of September 30, 1971, and shall exercise its competence in accordance with the provisions of Article XIII of said Treaty, Article VI of said Interim Agreement, and Article 7 of said Agreement on Measures.

III

Each Government shall be represented on the Standing Consultative Commission by a Commissioner and a Deputy Commissioner, assisted by such staff as it deems necessary.

IV

The Standing Consultative Commission shall hold periodic sessions on dates mutually agreed by the Commissioners but no less than two times per year. Sessions shall also be convened as soon as possible, following reasonable notice, at the request of either Commissioner.

V

The Standing Consultative Commission shall establish and approve Regulations governing procedures and other relevant matters and may amend them as it deems appropriate.

VI

The Standing Consultative Commission will meet in Geneva. It may also meet at such other places as may be agreed.

Done in Geneva, on December 21, 1972, in two copies, each in the English and Russian languages, both texts being equally authentic.

---

* Memorandum of Understanding Between the Government of the United States of America and the Government of the Union of Soviet Socialist Republics Regarding the Establishment of a Standing Consultative Commission, U.S.-U.S.S.R., Dec. 21, 1972, 24 U.S.T. 238, 239 (entered into force Dec. 21, 1972), *available at* http://www.fas.org/nuke/control/abmt/text/abm_mou.htm.

AGREEMENT BETWEEN THE UNITED STATES OF AMERICA AND THE UNION OF SOVIET SOCIALIST REPUBLICS TO EXPAND THE U.S.-U.S.S.R. DIRECT COMMUNICATIONS LINK*

The Department of State, referring to the Memorandum of Understanding between the United States of America and the Union of Soviet Socialist Republics regarding the Establishment of a Direct Communications Link, signed June 20, 1963; to the Agreement on Measures to Improve the Direct Communications Link, signed September 30, 1971; and to the exchange of views between the two parties in Moscow and Washington during which it was deemed desirable to arrange for facsimile communication in addition to the current teletype Direct Communications Link, proposes that for this purpose the parties shall:

1. Establish and maintain three transmission links employing INTELSAT and STATSIONAR satellites and cable technology with secure orderwire circuit for operational monitoring. In this regard:

(a) Each party shall provide communications circuits capable of simultaneously transmitting and receiving 4800 bits per second.

(b) Operation of facsimile communication shall begin with the test operation over the INTELSAT satellite channel as soon as development, procurement and delivery of the necessary equipment by the sides are completed.

(c) Facsimile communication via STATSIONAR shall be established after transition of the Direct Communications Link teletype circuit from MOLNIYA to STATSIONAR using mutually agreeable transition procedures and after successful tests of facsimile communication via INTELSAT and cable.

2. Employ agreed-upon information security devices to assure secure transmission of facsimile materials. In this regard:

(a) The information security devices shall consist of microprocessors that will combine the digital facsimile output with buffered random data read from standard 5¼ inch floppy disks. The American side shall provide a specification describing the key data format and necessary keying material resident on a floppy disk for both parties until such time as the Soviet side develops this capability. Beyond that time, each party shall provide necessary keying material to the other.

(b) The American side shall provide to the Soviet side the floppy disk drives integral to the operation of the microprocessor.

(c) The necessary security devices as well as spare parts for the said equipment shall be provided by the American side to the Soviet side in return for payment of costs thereof by the Soviet side.

---

* Direct Communications Link: Agreement Between the United States of America and the Union of Soviet Socialist Republics, U.S.-U.S.S.R., July 17, 1984, T.I.A.S. No. 11428 (entered into force July 17, 1984), *available at* http://www.state.gov/t/ac/trt/4786.htm.

3. Establish and maintain at each operating end of the Direct Communications Link facsimile terminals of the same make and model. In this regard:

(a) Each party shall be responsible for the acquisition, installation, operation and maintenance of its own facsimile machines, the related information security devices, and local transmission circuits appropriate to the implementation of this understanding, except as otherwise specified.

(b) A Group III facsimile unit which meets CCITT Recommendations T.4 and T.30 and operates at 4800 bits per second shall be used for this purpose.

....

4. Establish and maintain secure orderwire communications necessary for coordination of facsimile operation....

....

5. Ensure the exchange of information necessary for the operation and maintenance of the facsimile system.

6. Take all possible measures to assure the continuous, secure and reliable operation of the facsimile equipment, information security devices and communications links including orderwire, for which each party is responsible in accordance with this agreement.

The Department of State also proposes that the parties, in consideration of the continuing advances in information and communications technology, conduct reviews as necessary regarding questions concerning improvement of the Direct Communications Link and its technical maintenance.

It is also proposed to note that the Memorandum of Understanding between the United States of America and the Union of Soviet Socialist Republics regarding the Establishment of a Direct Communications Link, signed on June 20, 1963, with the Annex thereto; the Agreement between the United States of America and the Union of the Soviet Socialist Republics on Measures to Improve the Direct Communications Link, with the Annex thereto, signed on September 30, 1971; those Understandings, with Attached Annexes, reached between the United States and Union of Soviet Republics, Shall constitute an agreement, effective on the date of the Embassy's reply.

Department of StateWashington, July 17, 1984

AGREEMENT BETWEEN THE UNITED STATES OF AMERICA AND THE UNION OF SOVIET SOCIALIST REPUBLICS ON THE ESTABLISHMENT OF NUCLEAR RISK REDUCTION CENTERS*

The United States of America and the Union of Soviet Socialist Republics, hereinafter referred to as the Parties,

Affirming their desire to reduce and ultimately eliminate the risk of outbreak of nuclear war, in particular, as a result of misinterpretation, miscalculation, or accident,

Believing that a nuclear war cannot be won and must never be fought,

Believing that agreement on measures for reducing the risk of outbreak of nuclear war serves the interests of strengthening international peace and security,

Reaffirming their obligations under the Agreement on Measures to Reduce the Risk of Outbreak of Nuclear War between the United States of America and the Union of Soviet Socialist Republics of September 30, 1971, and the Agreement between the Government of the United States of America and the Government of the Union of Soviet Socialist Republics on the Prevention of Incidents on and over the High Seas of May 25, 1972,

Have agreed as follows:

Article 1. Each Party shall establish, in its capital, a national Nuclear Risk Reduction Center that shall operate on behalf of and under the control of its respective Government.

Article 2. The Parties shall use the Nuclear Risk Reduction Centers to transmit notifications identified in Protocol I which constitutes an integral part of this Agreement.

In the future, the list of notifications transmitted through the Centers may be altered by agreement between the Parties, as relevant new agreements are reached.

Article 3. The Parties shall establish a special facsimile communications link between their national Nuclear Risk Reduction Centers in accordance with Protocol II which constitutes an integral part of this Agreement.

Article 4. The Parties shall staff their national Nuclear Risk Reduction Centers as they deem appropriate, so as to ensure their normal functioning.

Article 5. The Parties shall hold regular meetings between representatives of the Nuclear Risk Reduction Centers at least once each year to consider matters related to the functioning of such Centers.

Article 6. This Agreement shall not affect the obligations of either Party under other agreements.

Article 7. This Agreement shall enter into force on the date of its signature.

The duration of this Agreement shall not be limited.

---

* Agreement Between the United States of America and the Union of Soviet Socialist Republics on the Establishment of Nuclear Risk Reduction Centers, U.S.-U.S.S.R., Sept. 15, 1987, DEP'T ST. BULL., Nov. 1987, at 34, 34–35 (entered into force Sept. 15, 1987), *available at* http://www.state.gov/t/ac/trt/5179.htm.

This Agreement may be terminated by either Party upon 12 months written notice to the other Party.

DONE at Washington on September 15, 1987, in two copies, each in the English and Russian languages, both texts being equally authentic.

[Signatures omitted]

....

MEMORANDUM OF UNDERSTANDING BETWEEN THE GOVERNMENT OF THE UNION OF SOVIET SOCIALIST REPUBLICS AND THE GOVERNMENT OF THE UNITED STATES OF AMERICA REGARDING A BILATERAL VERIFICATION EXPERIMENT AND DATA EXCHANGE RELATED TO PROHIBITION OF CHEMICAL WEAPONS*

The Government of the Union of Soviet Socialist Republics and the Government of the United States of America,

Determined to facilitate the process of negotiation, signature and ratification of a comprehensive, effectively verifiable, and truly global convention of the prohibition and destruction of chemical weapons,

Convinced that increased openness about their chemical weapons capabilities is essential for building the confidence necessary for early completion of the convention,

Desiring also to gain experience in the procedures and measures for verification of the convention,

Having agreed as follows:

I. GENERAL PROVISIONS

1. As set forth below, the two sides shall conduct a bilateral verification experiment and data exchange related to the prohibition of chemical weapons.

2. The bilateral verification experiment and data exchange shall be conducted in two phases. In Phase I, the two sides shall exchange general data on their chemical weapons capabilities and carry out a series of visits to relevant facilities. In Phase II, the two sides shall exchange detailed data and perform on-site inspection to verify the accuracy of those data.

3. The bilateral verification experiment and data exchange is intended to facilitate the process of negotiation, signature and ratification of a comprehensive, effectively verifiable and truly global convention on the prohibition and destruction of chemical weapons by:

(1) enabling each side to gain confidence in the data on chemical weapons capabilities that will be provided under the provisions of the convention;

(2) enabling each side to gain confidence in the inspection procedures that will be used to verify compliance with the convention; and

* Memorandum of Understanding Between the Government of the United States of America and the Government of the Union of Soviet Socialist Republics Regarding a Bilateral Verification Experiment and Data Exchange Related to Prohibition of Chemical Weapons, U.S.-U.S.S.R., Sept. 23, 1989, DEP'T ST. BULL., Nov. 1989, at 18, 18–20 (entered into force Sept. 23, 1989), *available at* http://cbw.sipri.se/intermediate/20207110.html.

(3) facilitating the elaboration of the provisions of the convention.

4. Terms used in this Memorandum shall have the same meaning as in the draft convention text under negotiation by the Conference on Disarmament. The draft convention text that is current as of the date of the exchange of data shall be used.

5. Data shall be current as of the date of the exchange, and shall encompass all sites and facilities specified below, wherever they are located.

6. Each side shall take appropriate steps to protect the confidentiality of the data it receives. Each side undertakes not to divulge this data without the explicit consent of the side that provided the data.

....

V. VERIFICATION

1. Each side shall use its own national means to evaluate Phase I data and Phase II data.

2. During Phase I, the sides shall hold consultations to discuss the information that has been presented and visits that have been exchanged. The sides will co-operate in clarifying ambiguous situations.

3. During Phase II, each side shall have the opportunity to verify Phase I and Phase II data by means of on-site inspections. The purpose of these inspections shall be to verify the accuracy of the data that has been exchanged and to gain confidence that the signature and ratification of the convention will take place on the basis of up-to-date and verified data on the chemical weapons capability of the sides.

4. Prior to the initialing of the convention, each side shall have the opportunity to select and inspect at its discretion up to five facilities from the list of chemical weapons storage facilities and chemical weapons production facilities declared by the other side. During Phase I, the sides will consider whether each side may inspect not less (sic) than half of the declared facilities of the other side if their number is more than 10. Should either side as of the date of the Phase II exchange possess a single small-scale facility for production of Schedule 1 chemicals, it shall be subject to an additional inspection.

Each side shall also have the opportunity to carry out up to five challenge inspections, as specified below. All inspections shall be carried out within the agreed four months from the date of the declaration pertaining to Phase II, referred to in Section IV.

5. While the signed convention is being considered by their respective legislative bodies, each side shall have the opportunity to request from the other side, and to obtain from it, updated data. Each side shall have the opportunity to conduct up to five challenge inspections, as specified below. During this process, the two sides will consult with their respective legislative bodies, as appropriate, in accordance with their constitutional requirements.

For each side, these inspections shall be carried out within a four-month period, beginning with the date that it conducts its first inspection. The sides shall consult and agree on the dates when the first inspection will be conducted by each side. The dates shall be chosen to ensure that the inspections shall be conducted by both sides at approximately the same time. Once the inspections begin, the sides may, by mutual consent, extend the four-month periods for an additional specified period.

6. Inspections of declared facilities, as well as challenge inspections, shall be conducted in accordance with the corresponding provisions of the draft convention, taking into account that these inspections are being carried out on a bilateral basis and do not

involve the bodies that will be established under the convention. If necessary, the two sides shall supplement the provisions of the draft convention by mutually-agreed procedures.

7. Challenge inspections may be made at any location or facility of the other side, as provided for in the draft convention text, except that, for the purposes of this Memorandum and without creating a precedent, challenge inspections at facilities not on the territory of the sides may be made only at military facilities of a side in a limited number of countries; the sides will agree later on these specific countries.

8. Challenge inspections conducted pursuant to this Memorandum shall be conducted in a manner consistent with the domestic law of the side being inspected and shall be based on a recognition by both sides of the need to resolve concerns and build confidence.

9. To clarify questions related to the data provided during Phase I and Phase II, the two sides shall employ normal diplomatic channels, specifically-designated representatives, or such other means as may be agreed upon.

....

CHARTER FOR AMERICAN-RUSSIAN PARTNERSHIP AND FRIENDSHIP*

The United States of America and the Russian Federation,

Striving to provide a solid and enduring basis for American-Russian relations of partnership and friendship;

Believing that the advancement of the well-being, prosperity, and security of a democratic Russian Federation and the United States of America are vitally interrelated;

Declaring their determination to observe strictly democratic principles and practices, including the rule of law and respect for human rights and fundamental freedoms, including the rights of persons belonging to minorities;

Recognizing the importance of the rights of the individual in building a just and prosperous society;

Reaffirming their commitment to the purposes and principles of the United Nations charter, the Helsinki Final Act, and subsequent CSCE [Conference on Security and Cooperation in Europe] documents;

Desiring to build a democratic peace that unites the entire community of democratic nations;

Noting their special responsibility as permanent members of the United Nations Security Council for maintaining international peace and security;

Wishing to promote the development of free markets, economic recovery and growth, and closer economic cooperation, trade, and investment;

Have established the following Charter for American-Russian Partnership and Friendship:

Democracy and Partnership

The United States of America and the Russian Federation reaffirm their commitment to the ideals of democracy, to the primacy of the rule of law, and to respect for human rights and fundamental freedoms. The United States of America fully supports the Russian Federation's efforts to build a democratic state and society founded on the rule of law and respect for fundamental human rights. Beginning with mutual trust and respect as the basis for their relations, they are developing relations of partnership and friendship.

The United States of America and the Russian Federation will cooperate closely in the international arena in the interest of advancing and defending common democratic values and human rights and fundamental freedoms.

The United States of America and the Russian Federation intend to expand and intensify a comprehensive dialogue at various levels on both bilateral and international issues.

---

* A Charter for American-Russian Partnership and Friendship, U.S.-Russ., June 17, 1992, 3 DEP'T ST. DISPATCH 490 (June 22, 1992), *available at* http://fas.org/spp/starwars/offdocs/b920617k.htm.

Given the crucial importance of contacts between the President of the United States of America and the President of the Russian Federation for defining the basic directions of bilateral relations and also in terms of global cooperation and stability, Summit meetings will be held on a regular basis.

The United States of America and the Russian Federation express their determination to promote confidence and enhance understanding between their peoples. They proceed on the assumption that an expansion of contacts between citizens will help ensure the irreversibility of the new quality of American-Russian relations.

For this purpose, they intend to facilitate the establishment of direct contacts between citizens and political, social, labor, religious, and other organizations.

The United States of America and the Russian Federation are prepared to facilitate the work of each other's diplomats, journalists, businessmen, scientists, and other citizens by reaching agreement in opening their lands to travel, by lifting other travel restrictions, and by expanding their consulates.

The United States of America and the Russian Federation place particular emphasis on developing appropriate contacts between all levels of government—federal, regional, and local—and between private sector and voluntary organizations.

The United States of America intends to continue cooperation toward strengthening democratic institutions and a rule of law state in Russia; including developing an independent judiciary and institutionalizing guarantees for respect of individual rights.

International Peace and Security

The United States of America and the Russian Federation reiterate their determination to build a democratic peace, one founded on the twin pillars of political and economic freedom. The United States of America and the Russian Federation recognize the critical importance that democracy's success in Russia and the other former Soviet republics can have on international peace and security.

The United States of America and the Russian Federation, proceeding from the basis of mutual trust and respect and a common commitment to democracy and economic freedom and reaffirming the Camp David Declaration of February 1992; the November 1990 Charter of Paris, the December 1991, March 1992 and June 1992 communiqués of the North Atlantic Cooperation Council, and the April 1992 communiqué of the Defense Ministers' Meeting, once again declare that they do not regard each other as adversaries and are developing relations of partnership and friendship.

Consistent with the United Nations Charter and other treaty obligations, the United States of America and the Russian Federation confirm their commitments to settle disputes between them by peaceful means and to refrain from the threat or use of force against the territorial integrity and political independence of each other.

Beginning on the basis of their shared democratic values, the United States of America and the Russian Federation will unite in their efforts toward strengthening international peace and security, preventing and settling regional conflicts, and solving global problems.

While working toward a democratic peace, the United States of America and the Russian Federation realize that the end of the Cold War has not meant the end of insecurity and conflict in Europe. Ethnic tensions, territorial disputes, and international rivalries already threaten to turn an opportunity for peace into yet another phase of European turmoil.

The United States of America and the Russian Federation reaffirm their respect for the independence and sovereignty and the existing borders of the CSCE-participating states, including the new independent states, and recognize that border changes can be made only by peaceful and consensual means, in accordance with the rules of international law and the principles of CSCE.

Like the other nations of the Euro-Atlantic Community, the United States of America and the Russian Federation cannot accept another phase of European instability. They therefore intend to lend both support and leadership to the effort to spare this community further tragedies like that which has befallen the peoples of Yugoslavia. The need is clear: International means of collective engagement must be devised and strengthened to help prevent conflicts by addressing their root causes, to help resolve disputes before they become violent, to help mediate an end to conflicts wherever they occur, and to help keep the peace once it is established.

Therefore, mechanisms for conflict prevention, management, and settlement and European peacekeeping capabilities must be strengthened if we are to adequately cope with future conflicts. To this end, the United States of America and the Russian Federation support the following initiatives:

- The creation of a CSCE special representative to help strengthen efforts to address ethnic antagonisms and the treatment of minorities.
- The strengthening of means within CSCE to provide for more effective international dispute prevention, management, and settlement.
- The creation of a credible Euro-Atlantic peacekeeping capability, based on CSCE political authority, which allows for the use of the capacities of NACC, NATO, and WEU to prepare, support, and manage operations for CSCE as well as allows for the contribution of forces and resources from any and all CSCE states.

With the security of North America and Europe inseparable, the United States of America and the Russian Federation support the strengthening of the Euro-Atlantic Community, believing that security is indivisible from Vancouver to Vladivostok. The parties share a vision of such a Euro-Atlantic Community as being open to cooperation with all democratic societies. A prominent role for institutions like NACC, NATO, and WEU along with CSCE contributes uniquely to Euro-Atlantic security. The potential of other institutions and mechanisms, including the Commonwealth of Independent States, in support of security and peace in the area is also noted.

The United States of America and the Russian Federation believe that strengthening confidence and stability in Asia and the Pacific region in cooperation with other states will also promote global security. The parties are prepared to cooperate on these goals. They aim at a fuller utilization of the potential of economic-commercial cooperation in this region of the world, particularly in view of the geographic positions of the United States of America and Russia.

Noting the progress in the resolution of long-standing conflicts, promotion of democracy and human rights, and advancement of economic freedom and prosperity in vast areas of Latin America, Africa, and Asia, the United States of America and the Russian Federation stress the necessity to continue this process. Both sides are ready to contribute to tapping the new-potential for peace, to putting an end to conflicts, to bolstering mutual confidence and trust, and to enhancing democracy—which forms the basis of an enduring peace in all parts of the world.

With the aim of coordinating crisis prevention activities, the United States of America and the Russian Federation recognize the critical importance of maintaining open lines of communication and exchange. The United States of America and the Russian Federation recognize the importance of the United Nations Security Council and intend to maintain communications with other members of the Security Council to prevent, manage, and resolve crises. The United States and the Russian Federation recognize the prominent role of the United Nations in solving major international problem. They welcome in particular the contribution of the United Nations to peace and security, including the strengthening of UN peace-keeping.

The United States of America and the Russian Federation are prepared to work together toward further arms control and disarmament with the aim of promoting stability through implementation with all countries involved of the treaties on conventional forces in Europe and on the reduction and limitation of strategic offensive arms and by carrying out respective U.S. and Russian unilateral and complementary nuclear initiatives. They are committed to discuss further steps which might improve stability and result in further reductions of nuclear and conventional weapons, the global elimination of chemical weapons, and the promotion of confidence-building and crisis prevention measures.

The United States of America and the Russian Federation are prepared to cooperate in the matter of eliminating nuclear warheads and chemical weapons subject to destruction within the framework of treaty obligations and unilateral and complementary initiatives.

The United States of America and the Russian Federation believe that non-proliferation of weapons of mass destruction is a critical priority. Both parties will work towards strengthening and improving the non-proliferation regimes of weapons of mass destruction, including nuclear, biological, and chemical-weapons; of missiles and missile technology; as well as of destabilizing conventional weapons in accordance with international rules and agreements.

In this regard, the United States of America and the Russian Federation, in a separate statement, have expressed their determination to cooperate in exploring the potential to create a Ballistic Missile Early Warning Center and to cooperate in the development of ballistic missile defense capabilities and technologies.

In view of the potential for building a strategic partnership between the United States of America and the Russian Federation, the parties intend to accelerate defense cooperation between their military establishments including: intensifying contacts at all levels; expanding activities that encourage doctrinal and operational openness; establishing expanded exchange and liaison programs; exchanging ideas on fostering proper civil-military relations in a democratic society. The parties will also pursue cooperation in peacekeeping, counter-terrorism, and counter-narcotics missions.

. . . .

3. Joint Declarations

CONFERENCE ON SECURITY AND CO-OPERATION IN EUROPE: FINAL ACT*

The Conference on Security and Co-operation in Europe, which opened at Helsinki on 3 July 1973 and continued at Geneva from 18 September 1973 to 21 July 1975, was concluded at Helsinki on 1 August 1975 by the High Representatives of Austria, Belgium, Bulgaria, Canada, Cyprus, Czechoslovakia, Denmark, Finland, France, the German Democratic Republic, the Federal Republic of Germany, Greece, the Holy See, Hungary, Iceland, Ireland, Italy, Liechtenstein, Luxembourg, Malta, Monaco, the Netherlands, Norway, Poland, Portugal, Romania, San Marino, Spain, Sweden, Switzerland, Turkey, the Union of Soviet Socialist Republics, the United Kingdom, the United States of America and Yugoslavia.

....

Motivated by the political will, in the interest of peoples, to improve and intensify their relations and to contribute in Europe to peace, security, justice and cooperation as well as to rapprochement among themselves and with the other States of the world,

Determined, in consequence, to give full effect to the results of the Conference and to assure, among their States and throughout Europe, the benefits deriving from those results and thus to broaden, deepen and make continuing and lasting the process of détente,

The High Representatives of the participating States have solemnly adopted the following:

Questions relating to Security in Europe

The States participating in the Conference on Security and Co-operation in Europe,

Reaffirming their objective of promoting better relations among themselves and ensuring conditions in which their people can live in true and lasting peace free from any threat to or attempt against their security;

Convinced of the need to exert efforts to make détente both a continuing and an increasingly viable and comprehensive process, universal in scope, and that the implementation of the results of the Conference on Security and Cooperation in Europe will be a major contribution to this process;

Considering that solidarity among peoples, as well as the common purpose of the participating States in achieving the aims as set forth by the Conference on Security and Cooperation in Europe, should lead to the development of better and closer relations among them in all fields and thus to overcoming the confrontation stemming from the character of their past relations, and to better mutual understanding;

---

* Conference on Security and Co-operation in Europe, July 3, 1973-Aug. 1, 1975, *Final Act*, CSCE Doc. No. CSCE/III/PV.7 (Aug. 1, 1975), *reprinted in* 73 DEP'T ST. BULL. 323, 323-50 (Sept. 1, 1975), *available at* http://www.osce.org/documents/mcs/1975/08/4044_en.pdf. A European conference on security and cooperation was proposed as early as 1954. However a prerequisite to the success of the Conference, the implementation of the Final Quadripartite Protocol on Berlin, was not completed until June 3, 1972. Multilateral prepatory talks for the Conference began in November 1972. The Conference formally opened in July 1973; the working session began in September 1973 and ended in July 1975, after the preparation of this final document. The document, which was signed by the thirty-five nations participating in the Conference, has no legally binding effect.

Mindful of their common history and recognizing that the existence of elements common to their traditions and values can assist them in developing their relations, and desiring to search, fully taking into account the individuality and diversity of their positions and views, for possibilities of joining their efforts with a view to overcoming distrust and increasing confidence, solving the problems that separate them and cooperating in the interest of mankind;

Recognizing the indivisibility of security in Europe as well as their common interest in the development of cooperation throughout Europe and among selves and expressing their intention to pursue efforts accordingly;

Recognizing the close link between peace and security in Europe and in the world as a whole and conscious of the need for each of them to make its contribution to the strengthening of world peace and security and to the promotion of fundamental rights, economic and social progress and well-being for all peoples;

Have adopted the following:

(a) Declaration on Principles Guiding Relations between Participating States

The participating States,

Reaffirming their commitment to peace, security and justice and the continuing development of friendly relations and co-operation;

Recognizing that this commitment, which reflects the interest and aspirations of peoples, constitutes for each participating State a present and future responsibility, heightened by experience of the past;

Reaffirming, in conformity with their membership in the United Nations and in accordance with the purposes and principles of the United Nations, their full and active support for the United Nations and for the enhancement of its role and effectiveness in strengthening international peace, security and justice, and in promoting the solution of international problems, as well as the development of friendly relations and cooperation among States;

Expressing their common adherence to the principles which are set forth below and are in conformity with the Charter of the United Nations, as well as their common will to act, in the application of these principles, in conformity with the purposes and principles of the Charter of the United Nations;

Declare their determination to respect and put into practice, each of them in its relations with all other participating States, irrespective of their political, economic or social systems as well as of their size, geographical location or level of economic development, the following principles, which all are of primary significance, guiding their mutual relations:

I. *Sovereign Equality, Respect for the Rights Inherent in Sovereignty*

The participating States will respect each other's sovereign equality and individuality as well as all the rights inherent in and encompassed by its sovereignty, including in particular the right of every State to juridical equality, to territorial integrity and to freedom and political independence. They will also respect each other's right freely to choose and develop its political, social, economic and cultural systems as well as its right to determine its laws and regulations.

Within the framework of international law, all the participating States have equal rights and duties. They will respect each other's right to define and conduct as it wishes its relations with other States in accordance with international law and in the spirit of the present Declaration. They consider that their frontiers can be changed, in accordance with international law, by peaceful means and by agreement. They also have the right to belong or not to belong to international organizations, to be or not to be a party to bilateral or multilateral treaties including the right to be or not to be a party to treaties of alliance; they also have the right to neutrality.

II. *Refraining From the Threat or Use of Force*

The participating States will refrain in their mutual relations, as well as in their international relations in general, from the threat or use of force against the territorial integrity or political independence of any State, or in any other manner inconsistent with the purposes of the United Nations and with the present Declaration. No consideration may be invoked to serve to warrant resort to the threat or use of force in contravention of this principle.

Accordingly, the participating States will refrain from any acts constituting a threat of force or direct or indirect use of force against another participating State. Likewise they will refrain from any manifestation of force for the purpose of inducing another participating State to renounce the full exercise of its sovereign rights. Likewise they will also refrain in their mutual relations from any act of reprisal by force.

No such threat or use of force will be employed as a means of settling disputes, or questions likely to give rise to disputes, between them.

III. *Inviolability of Frontiers*

The participating States regard as inviolable all one another's frontiers as well as the frontiers of all States in Europe and therefore they will refrain now and in the future from assaulting these frontiers.

Accordingly, they will also refrain from any demand for, or act of, seizure and usurpation of part or all of the territory of any participating State.

IV. *Territorial Integrity of States*

The participating States will respect the territorial integrity of each of the participating States.

Accordingly, they will refrain from any action inconsistent with the purposes and principles of the Charter of the United Nations against the territorial integrity, political independence or the unity of any participating State, and in particular from any such action constituting a threat or use of force.

The participating States will likewise refrain from making each other's territory the object of military occupation or other direct or indirect measures of force in contravention of international law, or the object of acquisition by means of such measures or the threat of them. No such occupation or acquisition will be recognized as legal.

V. *Peaceful Settlement of Disputes*

The participating States will settle disputes among them by peaceful means in such a manner as not to endanger international peace and security, and justice.

They will endeavour in good faith and a spirit of cooperation to reach a rapid and equitable solution on the basis of international law.

For this purpose they will use such means as negotiation, enquiry, mediation, conciliation, arbitration, judicial settlement or other peaceful means of their own choice including any settlement procedure agreed to in advance of disputes to which they are parties.

In the event of failure to reach a solution by any of the above peaceful means, the parties to a dispute will continue to seek a mutually agreed way to settle the dispute peacefully.

Participating States, parties to a dispute among them, as well as other participating States, will refrain from any action which might aggravate the situation to such a degree as to endanger the maintenance of international peace and security and thereby make a peaceful settlement of the dispute more difficult.

VI. *Non-Intervention in Internal Affairs*

The participating States will refrain from any intervention, direct or indirect, individual or collective, in the internal or external affairs falling within the domestic jurisdiction of another participating State, regardless of their mutual relations.

They will accordingly refrain from any form of armed intervention or threat of such intervention against another participating State. They will likewise in all circumstances refrain from any other act of military, or of political, economic or other coercion designed to subordinate to their own interest the exercise by another participating State of the rights inherent in its sovereignty and thus to secure advantages of any kind.

Accordingly, they will, inter alia, refrain from direct or indirect assistance to terrorist activities, or to subversive or other activities directed towards the violent overthrow of the regime of another participating State.

VII. *Respect for Human Rights and Fundamental Freedoms, Including the Freedom of Thought, Conscience, Religion or Belief*

The participating States will respect human rights and fundamental freedoms, including the freedom of thought, conscience, religion or belief, for all without distinction as to race, sex, language or religion.

They will promote and encourage the effective exercise of civil, political, economic, social, cultural and other rights and freedoms all of which derive from the inherent dignity of the human person and are essential for his free and full development.

Within this framework the participating States will recognize and respect the freedom of the individual to profess and practice, alone or in community with others, religion or belief acting in accordance with the dictates of his own conscience.

The participating States on whose territory national minorities exist will respect the right of persons belonging to such minorities to equality before the law, will afford them the full opportunity for the actual enjoyment of human rights and fundamental freedoms and will, in this manner, protect their legitimate interests in this sphere.

The participating States recognize the universal significance of human rights and fundamental freedoms, respect for which is an essential factor for the peace, justice and well-being necessary to ensure the development of friendly relations and co-operation among themselves as among all States.

They will constantly respect these rights and freedoms in their mutual relations and will endeavour jointly and separately, including in co-operation with the United Nations, to promote universal and effective respect for them.

They confirm the right of the individual to know and act upon his rights and duties in this field.

In the field of human rights and fundamental freedoms, the participating States will act in conformity with the purposes and principles of the Charter of the United Nations and with the Universal Declaration of Human Rights. They will also fulfill their obligations as set forth in the international declarations and agreements in this field, including inter alia the International Covenants on Human Rights, by which they may be bound.

VIII. *Equal Rights and Self-Determination of Peoples*

The participating States will respect the equal rights of peoples and their right to self-determination, acting at all times in conformity with the purposes and principles of the Charter of the United Nations and with the relevant norms of international law, including those relating to territorial integrity of States.

By virtue of the principle of equal rights and self-determination of peoples, all peoples always have the right, in full freedom, to determine, when and as they wish, their internal and external political status, without external interference, and to pursue as they wish their political, economic, social and cultural development.

The participating States reaffirm the universal significance of respect for and effective exercise of equal rights and self-determination of peoples for the development of friendly relations among themselves as among all States; they also recall the importance of the elimination of any form of violation of this principle.

IX. *Co-operation Among States*

The participating States will develop their co-operation with one another and with all States in all fields in accordance with the purposes and principles of the Charter of the United Nations. In developing their co-operation the participating States will place special emphasis on the fields as set forth within the framework of the Conference on Security and Co-operation in Europe, with each of them making its contribution in conditions of full equality.

They will endeavour, in developing their co-operation as equals, to promote mutual understanding and confidence, friendly and good-neighbourly relations among themselves, international peace, security and justice. They will equally endeavour, in developing their cooperation, to improve the well-being of peoples and contribute to the fulfillment of their aspirations through, inter alia, the benefits resulting from increased mutual knowledge and from progress and achievement in the economic, scientific, technological, social, cultural and humanitarian fields. They will take steps to promote conditions favourable to making these benefits available to all; they will take into account the interest of all in the narrowing of differences in the levels of economic development, and in particular the interest of developing countries throughout the world.

They confirm that governments, institutions, organizations and persons have a relevant and positive role to play in contributing toward the achievement of these aims of their cooperation.

They will strive, in increasing their cooperation as set forth above, to develop closer relations among themselves on an improved and more enduring basis for the benefit of peoples.

X. *Fulfillment in Good Faith of Obligations Under International Law*

The participating States will fulfill in good faith their obligations under international law, both those obligations arising from the generally recognized principles and rules of international law and those obligations arising from treaties or other agreements, in conformity with international law, to which they are parties.

In exercising their sovereign rights, including the right to determine their laws and regulations, they will conform with their legal obligations under international law; they will furthermore pay due regard to and implement the provisions in the Final Act of the Conference on Security and Cooperation in Europe.

The participating States confirm that in the event of a conflict between the obligations of the members of the United Nations under the Charter of the United Nations and their obligations under any treaty or other international agreement, their obligations under the Charter will prevail, in accordance with Article 103 of the Charter of the United Nations.

All the principles set forth above are of primary significance and, accordingly, they will be equally and unreservedly applied, each of them being interpreted taking into account the others.

The participating States express their determination fully to respect and apply these principles, as set forth in the present Declaration, in all aspects, to their mutual relations and cooperation in order to ensure to each participating State the benefits resulting from the respect and application of these principles by all.

The participating States, paying due regard to the principles above and, in particular, to the first sentence of the tenth principle, "Fulfillment in good faith of obligations under international law", note that the present Declaration does not affect their rights and obligations, nor the corresponding treaties and other agreements and arrangements.

The participating States express the conviction that respect for these principles will encourage the development of normal and friendly relations and the progress of co-operation among them in all fields. They also express the conviction that respect for these principles will encourage the development of political contacts among them which in time would contribute to better mutual understanding of their positions and views.

The participating States declare their intention to conduct their relations with all other States in the spirit of the principles contained in the present Declaration.

(b) Matters Related to Giving Effect to Certain of the Above Principles

(i) **The participating States,**

Reaffirming that they will respect and give effect to refraining from the threat or use of force and convinced of the necessity to make it an effective norm of international life,

Declare that they are resolved to respect and carry out, in their relations with one another, *inter ali*a, the following provisions which are in conformity with the Declaration on Principles Guiding Relations between Participating States:

—To give effect and expression, by all the ways and forms which they consider appropriate, to the duty to refrain from the threat or use of force in their relations with one another.

—To refrain from any use of armed forces inconsistent with the purposes and principles of the Charter of the United Nations and the provisions of the Declaration on Principles Guiding Relations between Participating States, against another participating State, in particular from invasion of or attack on its territory.

—To refrain from any manifestation of force for the purpose of inducing another participating State to renounce the full exercise of its sovereign rights.

—To refrain from any act of economic coercion designed to subordinate to their own interest the exercise by another participating State of the rights inherent in its sovereignty and thus to secure advantages of any kind.

—To take effective measures which by their scope and by their nature constitute steps towards the ultimate achievement of general and complete disarmament under strict and effective international control.

—To promote, by all means which each of them considers appropriate, a climate of confidence and respect among peoples consonant with their duty to refrain from propaganda for wars of aggression or for any threat or use of force inconsistent with the purposes of the United Nations and with the Declaration on Principles Guiding Relations between Participating States, against another participating State.

—To make every effort to settle exclusively by peaceful means any dispute between them, the continuance of which is likely to endanger the maintenance of international peace and security in Europe, and to seek, first of all, a solution through the peaceful means set forth in Article 33 of the United Nations Charter.

—To refrain from any action which could hinder the peaceful settlement of disputes between the participating States.

(ii) **The participating States,**

Reaffirming their determination to settle their disputes as set forth in the Principle of Peaceful Settlement of Disputes;

Convinced that the peaceful settlement of disputes is a complement to refraining from the threat or use of force, both being essential though not exclusive factors for the maintenance and consolidation of peace and security;

Desiring to reinforce and to improve the methods at their disposal for the peaceful settlement of disputes;

1. Are resolved to pursue the examination and elaboration of a generally acceptable method for the peaceful settlement of disputes aimed at complementing existing methods, and to continue to this end to work upon the "Draft Convention on a European System for the Peaceful Settlement of Disputes" submitted by Switzerland during the second stage of the Conference on Security and Co-operation in Europe, as well as other proposals relating to it and directed towards the elaboration of such a method.

2. Decide that, on the invitation of Switzerland, a meeting of experts of all the participating States will be convoked in order to fulfill the mandate described in paragraph 1 above within the framework and under the procedures of the follow-up to the Conference laid down in the chapter "Follow-up to the Conference".

3. This meeting of experts will take place after the meeting of the representatives appointed by the Ministers of Foreign Affairs of the participating States, scheduled according to the chapter "Follow-up to the Conference" for 1977; the results of the work of this meeting of experts will be submitted to Governments.

2.

Document on Confidence-Building Measures and Certain Aspects of Security and Disarmament

The participating States,

Desirous of eliminating the causes of tension that may exist among them and thus of contributing to the strengthening of peace and security in the world;

Determined to strengthen confidence among them and thus to contribute to increasing stability and security in Europe;

Determined further to refrain in their mutual relations, as well as in their international relations in general, from the threat or use of force against the territorial integrity or political independence of any State, or in any other manner inconsistent with the purposes of the United Nations and with the Declaration on Principles Guiding Relations between Participating States as adopted in this Final Act;

Recognizing the need to contribute to reducing the dangers of armed conflict and of misunderstanding or miscalculation of military activities which could give rise to apprehension, particularly in a situation where the participating States lack clear and timely information about the nature of such activities;

Taking into account considerations relevant to efforts aimed at lessening tension and promoting disarmament;

Recognizing that the exchange of observers by invitation at military manoeuvres will help to promote contacts and mutual understanding;

Having studied the question of prior notification of major military movements in the context of confidence-building;

Recognizing that there are other ways in which individual States can contribute further to their common objectives;

Convinced of the political importance of prior notification of major military manoeuvres for the promotion of mutual understanding and the strengthening of confidence, stability and security;

Accepting the responsibility of each of them to promote these objectives and to implement this measure, in accordance with the accepted criteria and modalities, as essentials for the realization of these objectives;

Recognizing that this measure deriving from political decision rests upon a voluntary basis;

Have adopted the following:

I

Prior Notification of Major Military Manoeuvres

They will notify their major military manoeuvres to all other participating States through usual diplomatic channels in accordance with the following provisions:

Notification will be given of major military manoeuvres exceeding a total of 25,000 troops, independently or combined with any possible air or naval components (in this context the word "troops" includes amphibious and airborne troops). In the case of independent manoeuvres of amphibious or airborne troops, or of combined manoeuvres involving them, these troops will be included in this total. Furthermore, in the case of combined manoeuvres which do not reach the above total but which involve land forces together with significant numbers of either amphibious or airborne troops, or both, notification can also be given.

Notification will be given of major military manoeuvres which take place on the territory, in Europe, of any participating State as well as, if applicable, in the adjoining sea area and air space.

In the case of a participating State whose territory extends beyond Europe, prior notification need be given only of manoeuvres which take place in an area within 250 kilometres from its frontier facing or shared with any other European participating State, the participating State need not, however, give notification in cases in which that area is also contiguous to the participating State's frontier facing or shared with a non-European non-participating State. Notification will be given 21 days or more in advance of the start of the manoeuvre or in the case of a manoeuvre arranged at shorter notice at the earliest possible opportunity prior to its starting date.

Notification will contain information of the designation, if any, the general purpose of and the States involved in the manoeuvre, the type or types and numerical strength of the forces engaged, the area and estimated time-frame of its conduct. The participating States will also, if possible, provide additional relevant information, particularly that related to the components of the forces engaged and the period of involvement of these forces.

Prior Notification of Other Military Manoeuvres

The participating States recognize that they can contribute further to strengthening confidence and increasing security and stability, and to this end may also notify smaller-scale military manoeuvres to other participating States, with special regard for those near the area of such manoeuvres.

To the same end, the participating States also recognize that they may notify other military manoeuvres conducted by them.

Exchange of Observers

The participating States will invite other participating States, voluntarily and on a bilateral basis, in a spirit of reciprocity and goodwill towards all participating States, to send observers to attend military manoeuvres.

The inviting State will determine in each case the number of observers, the procedures and conditions of their participation, and give other information which it may consider useful. It will provide appropriate facilities and hospitality.

The invitation will be given as far ahead as is conveniently possible through usual diplomatic channels.

Prior Notification of Major Military Movements

In accordance with the Final Recommendations of the Helsinki Consultations the participating States studied the question of prior-notification of major military movements as a measure to strengthen confidence.

Accordingly, the participating States recognize that they may, at their own discretion and with a view to contributing to confidence-building, notify their major military movements.

In the same spirit, further consideration will be given by the States participating in the Conference on Security and Cooperation in Europe to the question of prior notification of major military movements, bearing in mind, in particular, the experience gained by the implementation of the measures which are set forth in this document.

Other Confidence-Building Measures

The participating States recognize that there are other means by which their common objectives can be promoted.

In particular, they will, with due regard to reciprocity and with a view to better mutual understanding, promote exchanges by invitation among their military delegations.

....

II

Questions Relating to Disarmament

The participating States recognize the interest of all of them in efforts aimed at lessening military confrontation and promoting disarmament which are designed to complement political détente in Europe and to strengthen their security. They are convinced of the necessity to take effective measures in these fields which by their scope and by their nature constitute steps towards the ultimate achievement of general and complete disarmament under strict and effective international control, and which should result in strengthening peace and security throughout the world.

III

General Considerations

Having considered the views expressed on various subjects related to the strengthening of security in Europe through joint efforts aimed at promoting détente and disarmament, the participating States, when engaged in such efforts, will, in this context, proceed, in particular, from the following essential considerations:

— The complementary nature of the political and military aspects of security;

— The interrelation between the security of each participating State and security in Europe as a whole and the relationship which exists, in the broader context of world security, between security in Europe and security in the Mediterranean area;

— Respect for the security interests of all States participating in the Conference on Security and Co-operation in Europe inherent in their sovereign equality;

— The importance that participants in negotiating fora see to it that information about relevant developments, progress and results is provided on an appropriate basis to other States participating in the Conference on Security and Co-operation in Europe and, in return, the justified interest of any of those States in having their views considered.

Co-operation in the Field of Economics,
of Science and Technology and of the Environment

....

Questions relating to Security and
Co-operation in the Mediterranean

....

Co-operation in Humanitarian and Other Fields

....

Follow-up to the Conference

The participating States,

Having considered and evaluated the progress made at the Conference on Security and Co-operation in Europe,

Considering further that, within the broader context of the world, the Conference is an important part of the process of improving security and developing co-operation in Europe and that its results will contribute significantly to this process,

Intending to implement the provisions of the Final Act of the Conference in order to give full effect to its results and thus to further the process of improving security and developing co-operation in Europe,

Convinced that, in order to achieve the aims sought by the Conference, they should make further unilateral, bilateral and multilateral efforts and continue, in the appropriate forms set forth below, the multilateral process initiated by the Conference,

1. *Declare their resolve*, in the period following the Conference, to pay due regard to and implement the provisions of the Final Act of the Conference:

   (a) unilaterally, in all cases which lend themselves to such action;

   (b) bilaterally, by negotiations with other participating States;

   (c) multilaterally, by meetings of experts of the participating States, and also within the framework of existing international organizations, such as the United Nations Economic Commission for Europe and UNESCO, with regard to educational, scientific and cultural co-operation;

2. *Declare furthermore their resolve* to continue the multilateral process initiated by the Conference:

   (a) by proceeding to a thorough exchange of views both on the implementation of the provisions of the Final Act and of the tasks defined by the Conference, as well as, in the context of the questions dealt with by the latter, on the deepening of their mutual relations, the improvement of security and the development of co-operation in Europe, and the development of the process of détente in the future;

   (b) by organizing to these ends meetings among their representatives, beginning with a meeting at the level of representatives appointed by the Ministers of foreign Affairs. This meeting will define the appropriate modalities for the holding of other meetings which could include further similar meetings and the possibility of a new Conference;

3. The first of the meetings indicated above will be held at Belgrade in 1977. A preparatory meeting to organize this meeting will be held at Belgrade on 15 June 1977. The preparatory meeting will decide on the date, duration, agenda and other modalities of the meeting of representatives appointed by the Ministers of Foreign Affairs;

....

CHARTER OF PARIS FOR A NEW EUROPE*

A NEW ERA OF DEMOCRACY, PEACE AND UNITY

We, the Heads of State or Government of the States participating in the Conference on Security and Cooperation in Europe, have assembled in Paris at a time of profound change and historic expectations. The era of confrontation and division of Europe has ended. We declare that henceforth our relations will be founded on respect and co-operation.

Europe is liberating itself from the legacy of the past. The courage of men and women, the strength of the will of the peoples and the power of the ideas of the Helsinki Final Act have opened a new era of democracy, peace and unity in Europe.

Ours is a time for fulfilling the hopes and expectations our peoples have cherished for decades: steadfast commitment to democracy based on human rights and fundamental freedoms; prosperity through economic liberty and social justice; and equal security for all our countries.

The Ten Principles of the Final Act will guide us towards this ambitious future, just as they have lighted our way towards better relations for the past fifteen years. Full implementation of all CSCE commitments must form the basis for the initiatives we are now taking to enable our nations to live in accordance with their aspirations.

Human Rights, Democracy and Rule of Law

We undertake to build, consolidate and strengthen democracy as the only system of government of our nations. In this endeavor, we will abide by the following:

Human rights and fundamental freedoms are the birthright of all human beings, are inalienable and are guaranteed by law. Their protection and promotion is the first responsibility of government. Respect for them is an essential safeguard against an over-mighty State. Their observance and full exercise are the foundation of freedom, justice and peace.

Democratic government is based on the will of the people, expressed regularly through free and fair elections. Democracy has as its foundation respect for the human person and the rule of law. Democracy is the best safeguard of freedom of expression, tolerance of all groups of society, and equality of opportunity for each person.

Democracy, with its representative and pluralist character, entails accountability to the electorate, the obligation of public authorities to comply with the law and justice administered impartially. No one will be above the law.

We affirm that, without discrimination, every individual has the right to:

freedom of thought, conscience and religion or belief,

freedom of expression,

freedom of association and peaceful assembly,

freedom of movement;

no one will be:

---

* Charter of Paris for a New Europe, Nov. 21, 1990, 2 Dep't St. Dispatch 1, 1-10 (Supp. Mar. 1991), 30 I.L.M. 193 (1991), *available at* http://www.state.gov/t/ac/trt/4721.htm.

subject to arbitrary arrest or detention,

subject to torture or other cruel, inhuman or degrading treatment or punishment;

everyone also has the right:

to know and act upon his rights,

to participate in free and fair elections,

to fair and public trial if charged with an offense,

to own property alone or in association and to exercise individual enterprise,

to enjoy his economic, social and cultural rights.

We affirm that the ethnic, cultural, linguistic and religious identity of national minorities will be protected and that persons belonging to national minorities have the right freely to express, preserve, and develop that identity without any discrimination and in full equality before the law.

We will ensure that everyone will enjoy recourse to effective remedies, national or international, against any violation of his rights. Full respect for these precepts is the bedrock on which we will seek to construct the new Europe. Our States will cooperate and support each other with the aim of making democratic gains irreversible.

Economic Liberty and Responsibility

Economic liberty, social justice and environmental responsibility are indispensable for prosperity.

The free will of the individual, exercised in democracy and protected by the rule of law, forms the necessary basis for successful economic and social development. We will promote economic activity which respects and upholds human dignity.

Freedom and political pluralism are necessary elements in our common objective of developing market economies towards sustainable economic growth, prosperity, social justice, expanding employment and efficient use of economic resources. The success of the transition to market economy by countries making efforts to this effect is important and in the interest of us all. It will enable us to share a higher level of prosperity which is our common objective. We will cooperate to this end.

Preservation of the environment is a shared responsibility of all our nations. While supporting national and regional efforts in this field, we must also look to the pressing need for joint action on a wider scale.

Friendly Relations Among Participating States

Now that a new era is dawning in Europe, we are determined to expand and strengthen friendly relations and cooperation among the States of Europe, the United States of America and Canada, and to promote friendship among our peoples.

To uphold and promote democracy, peace and unity in Europe, we solemnly pledge our full commitment to the Ten Principles of the Helsinki Final Act. We affirm the continuing validity of the Ten Principles and our determination to put them into practice. All the Principles apply equally and unreservedly, each of them being interpreted taking into account the others. They form the basis for our relations.

In accordance with our obligations under the Charter of the United Nations and commitments under the Helsinki Final Act, we renew our pledge to refrain from the threat or use of force against the territorial integrity or political independence of any

State, or from acting in any other manner inconsistent with the principles or purposes of those documents. We recall that non-compliance with obligations under the Charter of the United Nations constitutes a violation of international law.

We reaffirm or commitment to settle disputes by peaceful means. We decide to develop mechanisms for the prevention and resolution of conflicts among the participating States.

With the ending of the division of Europe, we will strive for a new quality in our security relations while fully respecting each other's freedom of choice in that respect. Security is indivisible and the security of every participating State is inseparably linked to that of all the others. We therefore pledge to cooperate in strengthening confidence and security among us and in promoting arms control and disarmament.

We welcome the joint Declaration of Twenty-Two States on the improvement of their relations.

Our relations will rest on our common adherence to democratic values and to human rights and fundamental freedoms. We are convinced that in order to strengthen peace and security among our States, the advancement of democracy, and respect for and effective exercise of human rights, are indispensable. We reaffirm the equal rights of peoples and their right to self-determination in conformity with the Charter of the United Nations and with the relevant norms of international law, including those relating to territorial integrity of States.

We are determined to enhance political consultation and to widen cooperation to solve economic, social, environmental, cultural and humanitarian problems. This common resolve and our growing interdependence will help to overcome the mistrust of decades, to increase stability and to build a united Europe.

We want Europe to be a source of peace, open to dialogue and to cooperation with other countries, welcoming exchanges and involved in the search for common responses to the challenges of the future.

Security

Friendly relations among us will benefit from the consolidation of democracy and improved security.

We welcome the signature of the Treaty on Conventional Armed Forces in Europe by twenty-two participating States, which will lead to lower levels of armed forces. We endorse the adoption of a substantial new set of Confidence- and Security-building Measures which will lead to increased transparency and confidence among all participating States. These are important steps towards enhanced stability and security in Europe.

The unprecedented reduction in armed forces resulting from the Treaty on Conventional Armed Forces in Europe, together with new approaches to security and cooperation within the CSCE process, will lead to a new perception of security in Europe and a new dimension in our relations. In this context we fully recognize the freedom of States to choose their own security arrangements.

....

GUIDELINES FOR THE FUTURE

Proceeding from our firm commitment to the full implementation of all CSCE principles and provisions, we now resolve to give a new impetus to a balanced and comprehensive development of our cooperation in order to address the needs and aspirations of our peoples.

Human Dimension

We declare our respect for human rights and fundamental freedoms to be irrevocable. We will fully implement and build upon the provisions relating to the human dimension of the CSCE.

Proceeding from the Document of the Copenhagen Meeting of the Conference on the Human Dimension, we will cooperate to strengthen democratic institutions and to promote the application of the rule of law. To that end, we decide to convene a seminar of experts in Oslo from 4 to 15 November 1991.

Determined to foster the rich contribution of national minorities to the life of our societies, we undertake further to improve their situation. We reaffirm our deep conviction that friendly relations among our peoples, as well as peace, justice, stability and democracy, require that the ethnic, cultural, linguistic and religious identity of national minorities be protected and conditions for the promotion of that identity be created. We declare that questions related to national minorities can only be satisfactorily resolved in a democratic political framework. We further acknowledge that the rights of persons belonging to national minorities must be fully respected as part of universal human rights. Being aware of the urgent need for increased cooperation on, as well as better protection of, national minorities, we decide to convene a meeting of experts on national minorities to be held in Geneva from 1 to 19 July 1991.

We express our determination to combat all forms of racial and ethnic hatred, anti-Semitism, xenophobia and discrimination against anyone as well as persecution on religious and ideological grounds.

In accordance with our CSCE commitments, we stress that free movement and contacts among our citizens as well as the free flow of information and ideas are crucial for the maintenance and development of free societies and flourishing cultures. We welcome increased tourism and visits among our countries.

. . . .

Security

The changing political and military environment in Europe opens new possibilities for common efforts in the field of military security. We will build on the important achievements attained in the Treaty on Conventional Armed Forces in Europe and in the Negotiations on Confidence- and Security-Building Measures. We undertake to continue the CSBM negotiations under the same mandate, and to seek to conclude them no later than the Follow-up Meeting of the CSCE to be held in Helsinki in 1992. We also welcome the decision of the participating States concerned to continue the CFE negotiation under the same mandate and to seek to conclude it no later than the Helsinki Follow-up Meeting. Following a period for national preparations, we look forward to a more structured co-operation among all participating States on security matters, and to discussions and consultations among the thirty-four participating States aimed at establishing by 1992, from the conclusion of the Helsinki Follow-up Meeting, new negotiations on disarmament and confidence and security building open to all participating States.

We call for the earliest possible conclusion of the Convention on an effectively verifiable, global and comprehensive ban on chemical weapons, and we intend to be original signatories to it.

We reaffirm the importance of the Open Skies initiative and call for the successful conclusion of the negotiations as soon as possible.

Although the threat of conflict in Europe has diminished, other dangers threaten the stability of our societies. We are determined to cooperate in defending democratic institutions against activities which violate the independence, sovereign equality or territorial integrity of the participating States. These include illegal activities involving outside pressure, coercion and subversion.

We unreservedly condemn, as criminal, all acts, methods and practices of terrorism and express our determination to work for its eradication both bilaterally and through multilateral cooperation. We will also join together in combating illicit trafficking in drugs.

Being aware that an essential complement to the duty of States to refrain from the threat or use of force is the peaceful settlement of disputes, both being essential factors for the maintenance and consolidation of international peace and security, we will not only seek effective ways of preventing, through political means, conflicts which may yet emerge, but also define, in conformity with international law, appropriate mechanisms for the peaceful resolution of any disputes which may arise. Accordingly, we undertake to seek new forms of cooperation in this area, in particular a range of methods for the peaceful settlement of disputes, including mandatory third-party involvement. We stress that full use should be made in this context of the opportunity of the meeting on the peaceful settlement of disputes which will be convened in Valletta at the beginning of 1991. The Council of Ministers for Foreign Affairs will take into account the Report of the Valletta Meeting.

Economic Co-operation

....

We reaffirm the need to continue to support democratic countries in transition towards the establishment of market economy and the creation of the basis for self-sustained economic and social growth, as already undertaken by the Group of twenty-four countries. We further underline the necessity of their increased integration, involving the acceptance of disciplines as well as benefits, into the international economic and financial system.

We consider that increased emphasis on economic cooperation within the CSCE process should take into account the interests of developing participating States.

We recall the link between respect for and promotion of human rights and fundamental freedoms and scientific progress. Cooperation in the field of science and technology will play an essential role in economic and social development. Therefore, it must evolve towards a greater sharing of appropriate scientific and technological information and knowledge with a view to overcoming the technological gap which exists among the participating States. We further encourage the participating States to work together in order to develop human potential and the spirit of free enterprise.

....

NEW STRUCTURES AND INSTITUTIONS OF THE CSCE PROCESS

Our common efforts to consolidate respect for human rights, democracy and the rule of law, to strengthen peace and to promote unity in Europe require a new quality of political dialogue and cooperation and thus development of the structures of the CSCE.

The intensification of our consultations at all levels is of prime importance in shaping our future relations. To this end, we decide on the following:

We, the Heads of State or Government, shall meet next time in Helsinki on the occasion of the CSCE Follow-up Meeting 1992. Thereafter, we will meet on the occasion of subsequent follow-up meetings.

Our Ministers for Foreign Affairs will meet, as a Council, regularly and at least once a year. These meetings will provide the central forum for political consultations within the CSCE process. The Council will consider issues relevant to the Conference on Security and Cooperation in Europe and take appropriate decisions.

The first meeting of the Council will take place in Berlin. A Committee of Senior Officials will prepare the meetings of the Council and carry out its decisions. The Committee will review current issues and may take appropriate decisions, including in the form of recommendations to the Council.

Additional meetings of the representatives of the participating States may be agreed upon to discuss questions of urgent concern.

The Council will examine the development of provisions for convening meetings of the Committee of Senior Officials in emergency situations. Meetings of other Ministers may also be agreed by the participating States. In order to provide administrative support for these consultations we establish a Secretariat in Prague.

Follow-up meetings of the participating States will be held, as a rule, every two years to allow the participating States to take stock of developments, review the implementation of their commitments and consider further steps in the CSCE process.

We decide to create a Conflict Prevention Center in Vienna to assist the Council in reducing the risk of conflict.

We decide to establish an Office for Free Elections in Warsaw to facilitate contacts and the exchange of information on elections within participating States.

Recognizing the important role parliamentarians can play in the CSCE process, we call for greater parliamentary involvement in the CSCE, in particular through the creation of a CSCE parliamentary assembly, involving members of parliaments from all participating States. To this end, we urge that contacts be pursued at parliamentary level to discuss the field of activities, working methods and rules of procedure of such a CSCE parliamentary structure, drawing on existing experience and work already undertaken in this field.

We ask our Ministers for Foreign Affairs to review this matter on the occasion of their first meeting as a Council.

***

....

***

The original of the Charter of Paris for a New Europe, drawn up in English, French, German, Italian, Russian and Spanish, will be transmitted to the Government of the French Republic, which will retain it in its archives. Each of the participating States will receive from the Government of the French Republic a true copy of the Charter of Paris.

The text of the Charter of Paris will be published in each participating State, which will disseminate it and make it known as widely as possible.

The Government of the French Republic is requested to transmit to the Secretary-General of the United Nations the text of the Charter of Paris for a New Europe, which is not eligible for registration under Article 102 of the Charter of the United Nations, with a view to its circulation to all the members of the Organization as an official document of the United Nations.

....

Done at Paris,
on 21 November 1990,

SUPPLEMENTARY DOCUMENT TO GIVE EFFECT TO CERTAIN PROVISIONS CONTAINED IN THE CHARTER OF PARIS FOR A NEW EUROPE

Procedures and organizational modalities relating to certain provisions contained in the Charter of Paris for a New Europe, signed in Paris on 21 November 1990, are set out below.

I. INSTITUTIONAL ARRANGEMENTS

A. THE COUNCIL

1. The Council, consisting of Ministers of Foreign Affairs of the participating States, provides the central forum for regular political consultations within the CSCE process.

2. The Council will:

— consider issues relevant to the Conference on Security and Cooperation in Europe and take appropriate decisions;

— prepare the meetings of Heads of State or Government of the participating States and implement tasks defined and decisions taken by these meetings.

3. The Council will hold meetings regularly and at least once a year.

4. The participating States may agree to hold additional meetings of the Council.

5. The Chair throughout each meeting of the Council will be taken by the representative of the host country.

6. An agenda for the meetings of the Council, including proposals for the venue—on a basis of rotation—and date of the next meeting, will be prepared by the Committee of Senior Officials.

B. THE COMMITTEE OF SENIOR OFFICIALS

1. A Committee of Senior officials will prepare the work of the Council, carry out its decisions, review current issues and consider future work of the CSCE including its relations with other international fora.

2. In order to prepare the agenda of the meetings of the Council, the Committee will identify the issues for discussion on the basis of suggestions submitted by the participating States. The Committee will finalize a draft agenda shortly before the meeting of the Council.

3. Each participating State will establish a point of contact which will be used to transmit suggestions for the work of the Committee to the Secretariat for collection and circulation and to facilitate communication between the Secretariat and each participating State.

4. Each meeting of the Committee will be chaired by the representative of the State whose Foreign Minister had been Chairman at the preceding Council meeting. Meetings will be convened by the Chairman of the Committee after consultation with the participating States.

Meetings of the Committee will be held at the seat of the Secretariat and will not exceed two days, unless otherwise agreed. Meetings immediately preceding a meeting of the Council will be held at the venue of the Council meeting.

5. Due to practical considerations, the first meeting of the Committee will be held in Vienna from 28 to 29 January 1991. It will be chaired by the representative of Yugoslavia.

C. EMERGENCY MECHANISM

The Council will discuss the possibility of establishing a mechanism for convening meetings of the Committee of Senior Officials in emergency situations.

D. FOLLOW-UP MEETINGS

Follow-up meetings of the participating States will be held as a rule every two years. Their duration will not exceed three months, unless otherwise agreed.

E. THE CSCE SECRETARIAT

....

F. THE CONFLICT PREVENTION CENTER (CPC)

1. The Conflict Prevention Center (CPC) will assist the Council in reducing the risk of conflict. The Center's functions and structure are described below.

2. During its initial stage of operations the Center's role will consist in giving support to the implementation of CSBMs such as:

— mechanism for consultation and cooperation as regards unusual military activities;

— annual exchange of military information;

— communications network;

— annual implementation assessment meetings;

— cooperation as regards hazardous incidents of a military nature.

3. The Center might assume other functions and the above tasks are without prejudice to any additional tasks concerning a procedure for the conciliation of disputes as well as broader tasks relating to dispute settlement, which may be assigned to it in the future by the Council of the Foreign Ministers.

Consultative Committee

4. The Consultative Committee, composed of representatives from all participating States, will be responsible to the Council. As a rule, these representatives will be the Heads of Delegation to the CSBM negotiations until the Helsinki Follow-up Meeting.

The Consultative Committee will:

— hold the meetings of the participating States which may be convened under the mechanism on unusual military activities;

— hold the annual implementation assessment meetings;

— prepare seminars on military doctrine and such other seminars as may be agreed by the participating States;

— supervise the Secretariat of the Center;

— provide the forum for discussion and clarification, as necessary, of information exchanged under agreed CSBMS;

— have overall responsibility for the communications network within the mandate of the CPC.

....

G. THE OFFICE FOR FREE ELECTIONS

1. The function of the Office for Free Elections will be to facilitate contacts and the exchange of information on elections within participating States. The Office will thus foster the implementation of paragraphs 6, 7 and 8 of the Document of the Copenhagen Meeting of the Conference on the Human Dimension of the CSCE (the relevant provisions are contained in Annex 1).

....

II. MEETINGS OF EXPERTS

....

OAS GENERAL ASSEMBLY RESOLUTION 1080* (ON DEMOCRACY)

REPRESENTATIVE DEMOCRACY

Approved at the June 5, 1991 OAS General Assembly creating a new mechanism for convening foreign ministers in response to a coup d'etat or interruption of a legitimate, elected government.

Whereas:

The Preamble of the Charter of the OAS establishes that representative democracy is an indispensable condition for the stability, peace, and development of the region;

Under the provisions of the Charter, one of the basic purposes of the OAS is to promote and consolidate representative democracy, with due respect for the principle of non-intervention;

Due respect must be accorded to the policies of each member country in regard to the recognition of states and governments;

In view of the widespread existence of democratic governments in the Hemisphere, the principle, enshrined in the Charter, that the solidarity of the American states and the high aims which it pursues require the political organization of those states to be based on effective exercise of representative democracy must be made operative; and

The region still faces serious political, social, and economic problems that may threaten the stability of democratic governments,

The General Assembly Resolves:

1. To instruct the Secretary General to call for the immediate convocation of a meeting of the Permanent Council in the event of any occurrences giving rise to the sudden or irregular interruption of the democratic political institutional process or of the legitimate exercise of power by the democratically elected government in any of the Organization's member states, in order, within the framework of the Charter, to examine the situation, decide on and convene and ad hoc meeting of the Ministers of Foreign Affairs, or a special session of the General Assembly, all of which must take place within a ten-day period.

2. To state that the purpose of the ad hoc meeting of Ministers of Foreign Affairs or the special session of the General Assembly shall be to look into the events collectively and adopt any decisions deemed appropriate, in accordance with the Charter and international law.

3. To instruct the Permanent Council to devise a set of proposals that will serve as incentives to preserve and strengthen democratic systems, based on international solidarity and cooperation, and to apprise the General Assembly thereof at its twenty-second regular session.

The vote on this resolution was unanimous 34–0.

---

* O.A.S. G.A. Res. 1080, O.A.S. Doc. AG/RES. 1080 (XXI-O/91) (June 5, 1991), *reprinted in* 2 Dep't St. Dispatch 750 (Oct. 7, 1991), *available at* http://www.oas.org/juridico/english/agres 1080.htm.

VIENNA DOCUMENT 1999 OF THE NEGOTIATIONS ON CONFIDENCE AND SECURITY-BUILDING MEASURES*

(1) Representatives of the participating States of the Organization for Security and Co-operation in Europe (OSCE), Albania, Andorra, Armenia, Austria, Azerbaijan, Belarus, Belgium, Bosnia and Herzegovina, Bulgaria, Canada, Croatia, Cyprus, the Czech Republic, Denmark, Estonia, Finland, France, Georgia, Germany, Greece, the Holy See, Hungary, Iceland, Ireland, Italy, Kazakhstan, Kyrgyzstan, Latvia, Liechtenstein, Lithuania, Luxembourg, Malta, Moldova, Monaco, the Netherlands, Norway, Poland, Portugal, Romania, the Russian Federation, San Marino, the Slovak Republic, Slovenia, Spain, Sweden, Switzerland, Tajikistan, the former Yugoslav Republic of Macedonia, Turkey, Turkmenistan, Ukraine, the United Kingdom, the United States of America, Uzbekistan and Yugoslavia[i] met in Vienna in accordance with the provisions relating to the Conference on Confidence- and Security-Building Measures and Disarmament in Europe contained in the Concluding Documents of the Madrid, Vienna and Helsinki Follow-up Meetings of the OSCE.

(2) The Negotiations were conducted from 1989 to 1999.

(3) The participating States recalled that the aim of the Conference on Confidence- and Security-Building Measures and Disarmament in Europe is, as a substantial and integral part of the multilateral process initiated by the Conference on Security and Co-operation in Europe, to undertake, in stages, new, effective and concrete actions designed to make progress in strengthening confidence and security and in achieving disarmament, so as to give effect and expression to the duty of States to refrain from the threat or use of force in their mutual relations as well as in their international relations in general.

(4) The participating States recognized that the mutually complementary confidence and security-building measures which are adopted in the present document and which are in accordance with the mandates of the Madrid,[ii] Vienna and Helsinki Follow-up Meetings of the CSCE serve by their scope and nature and by their implementation to strengthen confidence and security among the participating States.

(5) The participating States recalled the declaration on Refraining from the Threat or Use of Force contained in paragraphs (9) to (27) of the Document of the Stockholm Conference and stressed its continuing validity as seen in the light of the Charter of Paris for a New Europe.

(6) On 17 November 1990, the participating States adopted the Vienna Document 1990, which built upon and added to the confidence- and security-building measures contained in the Document of the Stockholm Conference 1986. On 4 March 1992, the participating States adopted the Vienna Document 1992, which built upon and added to the confidence- and security-building measures contained in the Vienna Document 1990. On 28 November 1994, the participating States similarly adopted the Vienna Document 1994.

(7) In fulfillment of the Charter of Paris for a New Europe of November 1990 and the Programme for Immediate Action, set out in the Helsinki Document 1992, they

---

* Nov. 16, 1999, http://www.defenselink.mil/acq/acic/treaties/vienna/text.htm#intro. (Original footnotes included as endnotes).

continued the CSBM negotiations under the same mandate, and have adopted the present document which integrates a set of new confidence- and security-building measures with measures previously adopted.

(8) The participating States have adopted the following:

I. ANNUAL EXCHANGE OF MILITARY INFORMATION

INFORMATION ON MILITARY FORCES

(9) The participating States will exchange annually information on their military forces concerning the military organization, manpower and major weapon and equipment systems, as specified below, in the zone of application for confidence- and security-building measures (CSBMs). Participating States which have no military forces to be reported will so inform all other participating States.

(10) The information will be provided in an agreed format to all other participating States not later than 15 December of each year. It will be valid as of 1 January of the following year and will include:

(10.1)1. Information on the command organization of those military forces referred to under points 2 and 3 specifying the designation and subordination of all formations[iii] and units[iv] at each level of command down to and including brigade/regiment or equivalent level. The information will be designed in such a way as to distinguish units from formations.

(10.1.1) Each participating State providing information on military forces will include a statement indicating the total number of units contained therein and the resultant annual evaluation quota as provided for in paragraph (109).

(10.2)2. For each formation and combat unit[v] of land forces down to and including brigade/regiment or equivalent level the information will indicate:

(10.2.1) - the designation and subordination;

(10.2.2) - whether it is active or non-active;[vi]

(10.2.3) - the normal peacetime location of its headquarters indicated by exact geographic terms and/or co-ordinates;

(10.2.4) - the peacetime authorized personnel strength;

(10.2.5) - the major organic weapon and equipment systems, specifying the numbers of each type of:

(10.2.5.1) - battle tanks;

(10.2.5.2) - helicopters;

(10.2.5.3) - armoured combat vehicles (armoured personnel carriers, armoured infantry fighting vehicles, heavy armament combat vehicles);

(10.2.5.4) - armoured personnel carrier look-alikes and armoured infantry fighting vehicle look-alikes;

(10.2.5.5) - anti-tank guided missile launchers permanently/integrally mounted on armoured vehicles;

(10.2.5.6) - self-propelled and towed artillery pieces, mortars and multiple rocket launchers (100 mm calibre and above);

(10.2.5.7) - armoured vehicle launched bridges.

(10.3) For planned increases in personnel strength above that reported under paragraph (10.2.4) for more than 21 days by more than 1,000 troops for each active combat unit and by more than 3,000 troops for each active formation, excluding personnel increases in the formation's subordinate formations and/or combat units subject to separate reporting under paragraph (10.2); as well as

(10.3.1) for each non-active formation and non-active combat unit which is planned to be temporarily activated for routine military activities or for any other purpose with more than 2,000 troops for more than 21 days;

(10.3.2) the following additional information will be provided in the annual exchange of military information:

(10.3.2.1) - designation and subordination of the formation or combat unit;

(10.3.2.2) - purpose of the increase or activation;

(10.3.2.3) - for active formations and combat units the planned number of troops exceeding the personnel strength indicated under paragraph (10.2.4) or for non-active formations and combat units the number of troops involved during the period of activation;

(10.3.2.4) - start and end dates of the envisaged increase in personnel strength or activation;

(10.3.2.5) - planned location/area of activation;

(10.3.2.6) - the numbers of each type of the major weapon and equipment systems as listed in paragraphs (10.2.5.1) to (10.2.5.7) which are planned to be used during the period of the personnel increase or activation.

(10.3.3) In cases where the information required under paragraphs (10.3) to (10.3.2.6) cannot be provided in the annual exchange of military information, or in cases of changes in the information already provided, the required information will be communicated at least 42 days prior to such a personnel increase or temporary activation taking effect or, in cases when the personnel increase or temporary activation is carried out without advance notice to the troops involved, at the latest at the time the increase or the activation has taken effect.

(10.4) For each amphibious formation and amphibious combat unit[vii] permanently located in the zone of application down to and including brigade/regiment or equivalent level, the information will include the items as set out above.

(10.5)3. For each air formation and air combat unit[viii] of the air forces, air defence aviation and of naval aviation permanently based on land down to and including wing/air regiment or equivalent level, the information will include:

(10.5.1) - the designation and subordination;

(10.5.2) - the normal peacetime location of the headquarters indicated by exact geographic terms and/or co-ordinates;

(10.5.3) - the normal peacetime location of the unit indicated by the air base or military airfield on which the unit is based, specifying:

(10.5.3.1) - the designation or, if applicable, name of the air base or military airfield; and

(10.5.3.2) - its location indicated by exact geographic terms and/or co-ordinates;

(10.5.4) - the peacetime authorized personnel strength;[ix]

(10.5.5) - the numbers of each type of:

(10.5.5.1) - combat aircraft;

(10.5.5.2) - helicopters organic to the formation or unit.

DATA RELATING TO MAJOR WEAPON AND EQUIPMENT SYSTEMS

(11) The participating States will exchange data relating to their major weapon and equipment systems as specified in the provisions on Information on Military Forces within the zone of application for CSBMs.

(11.1) Data on existing weapon and equipment systems, if not already provided, will be provided once to all other participating States at the time of the entry into force of this document.

(11.2) Data on new types or versions of major weapon and equipment systems will be provided by each State when its deployment plans for the systems concerned are provided for the first time in accordance with paragraphs (13) and (14) below or, at the latest, when it deploys the systems concerned for the first time in the zone of application for CSBMs. If a participating State has already provided data on the same new type or version, other participating States may, if appropriate, certify the validity of those data as far as their system is concerned and indicate the national nomenclature if different.

(11.3) Participating States will inform each other when a type or version of a major weapon and equipment system is no longer in service with their armed forces.

INFORMATION ON PLANS FOR THE DEPLOYMENT OF MAJOR WEAPON AND EQUIPMENT SYSTEMS

(13) The participating States will exchange annually information on their plans for the deployment of major weapon and equipment systems as specified in the provisions on Information on Military Forces within the zone of application for CSBMs.

(14) The information will be provided in an agreed format to all other participating States not later than 15 December of each year. It will cover plans for the following year and will include:

(14.1) - the type and name of the weapon/equipment systems to be deployed;

(14.2) - the total number of each weapon/equipment system;

(14.3) - whenever possible, the number of each weapon/equipment system planned to be allocated to each formation or unit;

(14.4) - the extent to which the deployment will add to or replace existing weapon/equipment systems.

II. DEFENCE PLANNING[x]

EXCHANGE OF INFORMATION

(15) General provisions

The participating States will exchange annually information as specified below in paragraphs (15.1) to (15.4), to provide transparency about each OSCE participating State's intentions in the medium to long term as regards size, structure, training and equipment of its armed forces, as well as defence policy, doctrines and budgets related thereto, based on their national practice and providing the background for a dialogue among the participating States, including the date on which the military budget for the forthcoming fiscal year was approved by the competent national authorities and the identification of those authorities. The information will be provided to all other participating States not later than three months after the military budget, referred to in paragraph (15.4.1), has been approved by the competent national authorities.

Participating States which, for whatever reasons, will not be able to meet the deadline required above will give notification of the delay, while explaining the reasons, and provide an envisaged date for the actual submission.

Participating States which do not have armed forces and therefore have no information to provide in accordance with this chapter of the Vienna Document will so inform all other participating States.

This NIL report will be provided together with the Annual Exchange of Military Information (paragraph (9)) not later than 15 December of each year for the following year.

(15.1) Defence policy and doctrine

In a written statement participating States will address:

(15.1.1) - their defence policy, including military strategy/doctrine as well as changes occurring thereto;

(15.1.2) - their national procedures for defence planning, the stages of defence planning, the institutions involved in the decision-making process as well as changes occurring thereto;

(15.1.3) - their current personnel policy and the most substantial changes in it.

If the information under this point has remained the same, participating States may refer to the previously exchanged information.

(15.2) Force planning

In a written statement participating States will address in the form of a general description:

(15.2.1) - The size, structure, personnel, major weapon and equipment systems of their armed forces;

(15.2.2) - The deployment of their armed forces and the envisaged changes thereto;

(15.2.3) - In view of the reorganization of the defence structure in a number of participating States, similar information will be provided on other forces, including paramilitary forces, on a voluntary basis and as appropriate;

(15.2.3.1) - The scope and the status of the information on such forces will be reviewed after their status has been further defined, in the process of reorganization;

(15.2.4) - The training programmes for their armed forces and planned changes thereto in the forthcoming years;

(15.2.5) - The procurement of major equipment and major military construction programmes on the basis of the categories as set out in the United Nations Instrument mentioned in paragraph (15.3), either ongoing or starting in the forthcoming years, if planned, and the implications of such projects, accompanied by explanations, where appropriate;

(15.2.6) - The realization of the intentions previously reported under this paragraph.

In order to facilitate the understanding of the information provided, the participating States are encouraged to use illustrative charts and maps, wherever applicable.

(15.2.7) If no changes are foreseen, this should be stated where applicable.

(15.3) Information on previous expenditures

Participating States will report their defence expenditures of the preceding fiscal year (i.e., the most recent fiscal year for which figures are available) on the basis of the categories as set out in the United Nations "Instrument for Standardized International Reporting of Military Expenditures" adopted on 12 December 1980.

They will provide, in addition, any appropriate clarification, if necessary, as to possible discrepancies between expenditures and previously reported budgets, and information on the relation of the military budget to the gross national product (GNP) as a percentage.

(15.4) Information on budgets

The written statement will be supplemented with the following information, where available (i.e., relevant and releasable facts, figures and/or estimates under consideration in the national procedures for defence planning described in paragraph (15.1.2)):

....

CLARIFICATION, REVIEW AND DIALOGUE

(15.5) Request for clarification

To increase transparency, each participating State may ask any other participating State for clarification of the information provided. Questions should be submitted within a period of two months following the receipt of a participating State's information. Participating States will make every effort to answer such questions fully and promptly. It should be understood that these exchanges are informational only. The questions and replies may be transmitted to all other participating States.

(15.6) Annual discussion meetings

Without prejudice to the possibility of having ad hoc discussions on the information and clarification provided, the participating States will hold each year a meeting for a focused and structured dialogue to discuss the issues relating to defence planning. The Annual Implementation Assessment Meeting as foreseen in Chapter XI of the Vienna Document could be used for the purpose. Such discussions may extend to the methodology of defence planning and the implications originating from the information provided.

(15.7) OSCE High-level military doctrine seminars

The participating States are also encouraged to hold periodic high-level military doctrine seminars similar to those already held.

(15.8) Study visits

To increase knowledge of national defence planning procedures and promote dialogue, each participating State may arrange study visits for representatives of other OSCE participating States to meet with officials at the institutions involved in defence planning and appropriate bodies such as government agencies (planning, finance, economy), ministry of defence, general staff and relevant parliamentary committees.

Such exchanges could be organized within the framework of military contacts and co-operation.

POSSIBLE ADDITIONAL INFORMATION

(15.9) Participating States are encouraged to provide any other factual and documentary information relating to their defence planning. This may include:

(15.9.1) - the list and, if possible, the texts of major publicly available documents, in any of the OSCE working languages, reflecting their defence policy, military strategies and doctrines;

(15.9.2) - any other publicly available documentary reference material on their plans relating to paragraphs (15.1) and (15.2), e.g., military documents and/or "white papers".

(15.10) This documentary information may be provided to the Conflict Prevention Centre (CPC) which will distribute lists of received information and make it available upon request.

III. REDUCTION

MECHANISM FOR CONSULTATION AND CO-OPERATION AS REGARDS UNUSUAL MILITARY ACTIVITIES

(16) Participating States will, in accordance with the following provisions, consult and co-operate with each other about any unusual and unscheduled activities of their military forces outside their normal peacetime locations which are militarily significant, within the zone of application for CSBMs and about which a participating State expresses its security concern.

(16.1) The participating State which has concerns about such an activity may transmit a request for an explanation to another participating State where the activity is taking place.

(16.1.1) The request will state the cause, or causes, of the concern and, to the extent possible, the type and location, or area, of the activity.

(16.1.2) The reply will be transmitted within not more than 48 hours.

(16.1.3) The reply will give answers to questions raised, as well as any other relevant information in order to explain the activity in question and dispel the concern.

(16.1.4) The request and the reply will be transmitted to all other participating States without delay.

(16.2) The requesting State, after considering the reply provided, may then request a meeting with the responding State to discuss the matter.

....

CO-OPERATION AS REGARDS HAZARDOUS INCIDENTS OF A MILITARY NATURE

(17) Participating States will co-operate by reporting and clarifying hazardous incidents of a military nature within the zone of application for CSBMs in order to prevent possible misunderstandings and mitigate the effects on another participating State.

....

VOLUNTARY HOSTING OF VISITS TO DISPEL CONCERNS ABOUT MILITARY ACTIVITIES

(18) In order to help to dispel concerns about military activities in the zone of application for CSBMs, participating States are encouraged to invite other participating States to take part in visits to areas on the territory of the host State in which there may be cause for such concerns. Such invitations will be without prejudice to any action taken under paragraphs (16) to (16.3).

....

IV. CONTACTS

VISITS TO AIR BASES

(19) Each participating State with air combat units reported under paragraph (10) will arrange visits for representatives of all other participating States to one of its nor-

mal peacetime air bases[xi] on which such units are located in order to provide the visitors with the opportunity to view activity at the air base, including preparations to carry out the functions of the air base, and to gain an impression of the approximate number of air sorties and type of missions being flown.

....

(28) The visitors will have the opportunity to communicate with commanders and troops, including those of support/logistic units located at the air base. They will be provided with the opportunity to view all types of aircraft located at the air base.

(29) At the close of the visit, the State arranging the visit will provide an opportunity for the visitors to meet together and also with State officials and senior air base personnel to discuss the course of the visit.

....

(30) PROGRAMME OF MILITARY CONTACTS AND CO-OPERATION

MILITARY CONTACTS

(30.1) To improve further their mutual relations in the interest of strengthening the process of confidence- and security-building, the participating States will, on a voluntary basis and as appropriate, promote and facilitate:

(30.1.1) - exchanges and visits between members of the armed forces at all levels, especially those between junior officers and commanders;

(30.1.2) - contacts between relevant military institutions, especially between military units;

(30.1.3) - exchanges of visits of naval vessels and air force units;

(30.1.4) - reservation of places in military academies and schools and on military training courses for members of the armed forces from the participating States;

(30.1.5) - use of the language facilities of military training institutions for the foreign-language instruction of members of the armed forces from the participating States and the organization of language courses in military training institutions for military foreign-language instructors from the participating States;

(30.1.6) - exchanges and contacts between academics and experts in military studies and related areas;

(30.1.7) - participation and contribution by members of the armed forces of the participating States, as well as civil experts in security matters and defence policy, to academic conferences, seminars, symposia and study visits;

(30.1.8) - issuing of joint academic publications on security and defence issues;

(30.1.9) - sporting and cultural events between members of their armed forces.

MILITARY CO-OPERATION

Joint military exercises and training

(30.2) The participating States will conduct, on a voluntary basis and as appropriate, joint military training and exercises to work on tasks of mutual interest.

Visits to military facilities, to military formations and observation of certain military activities

(30.3) In addition to the provisions of the Vienna Document regarding visits to air bases, each participating State will arrange for representatives of all other participating States to visit one of its military facilities or military formations, or to observe military activities below thresholds specified in Chapter VI. These events will provide the visitors or observers with the opportunity to view activity of that military facility, observe the training of that military formation or observe the conduct of that military activity.

....

DEMONSTRATION OF NEW TYPES OF MAJOR WEAPON AND EQUIPMENT SYSTEMS

(31) The first participating State which deploys with its military forces in the zone of application a new type of major weapon and equipment system as specified in the provisions on Information on Military Forces will arrange at the earliest opportunity, but not later than one year after deployment has started, a demonstration for representatives of all other participating States,[xii] which may coincide with other events stipulated in this document.

....

V. PRIOR NOTIFICATION OF CERTAIN MILITARY ACTIVITIES

(38) The participating States will give notification in writing in accordance with the provisions of paragraphs (151) and (152) to all other participating States 42 days or more in advance of the start of notifiable[xiii] military activities in the zone of application for CSBMs.

(39) Notification will be given by the participating State on whose territory the activity in question is planned to take place (host State) even if the forces of that State are not engaged in the activity or their strength is below the notifiable level. This will not relieve other participating States of their obligation to give notification, if their involvement in the planned military activity reaches the notifiable level.

....

VI. OBSERVATION OF CERTAIN MILITARY ACTIVITIES

(47) The participating States will invite observers from all other participating States to the following notifiable military activities:

(47.1) - The engagement of formations of land forces[xiv] of the participating States in the same exercise activity conducted under a single operational command independently or in combination with any possible air or naval components.

(47.2) - The engagement of military forces in an amphibious landing, heliborne landing or parachute assault in the zone of application for CSBMs.

....

VII. ANNUAL CALENDARS

(61) Each participating State will exchange, with all other participating States, an annual calendar of its military activities subject to prior notification,[xv] within the zone of application for CSBMs, forecast for the subsequent calendar year. A participating State which is to host military activities subject to prior notification conducted by any other participating State(s) will include these activities in its annual calendar. It will be transmitted every year in writing, in accordance with the provisions of paragraphs (151) and (152), not later than 15 November for the following year.

(62) If a participating State does not forecast any military activity subject to prior notification, it will so inform all other participating States in the same manner as prescribed for the exchange of annual calendars.

....

VIII. CONSTRAINING PROVISIONS

(67) The following provisions will apply to military activities subject to prior notification7:

(67.1) No participating State will carry out within three calendar years more than one military activity subject to prior notification, involving more than 40,000 troops or 900 battle tanks or 2,000 ACVs or 900 self-propelled and towed artillery pieces, mortars and multiple rocket launchers (100 mm calibre and above).

(67.2) No participating State will carry out within one calendar year more than six military activities subject to prior notification each one involving more than 13,000 troops or 300 battle tanks or 500 ACVs or 300 self-propelled and towed artillery pieces, mortars and multiple rocket launchers (100 mm calibre and above) but not more than 40,000 troops or 900 battle tanks or 2,000 ACVs or 900 self-propelled and towed artillery pieces, mortars and multiple rocket launchers (100 mm calibre and above).

....

IX. COMPLIANCE AND VERIFICATION

(72) According to the Madrid mandate, the confidence- and security-building measures to be agreed upon "will be provided with adequate forms of verification which correspond to their content".

(73) The participating States recognize that national technical means can play a role in monitoring compliance with agreed confidence- and security-building measures.

INSPECTION

(74) In accordance with the provisions contained in this document each participating State has the right to conduct inspections on the territory of any other participating State within the zone of application for CSBMs. The inspecting State may invite other participating States to participate in an inspection.

(75) Any participating State will be allowed to address a request for inspection to another participating State within the zone of application for CSBMs.

(76) No participating State will be obliged to accept on its territory within the zone of application for CSBMs more than three inspections per calendar year.

(76.1) When a participating State has accepted three inspections in a calendar year, it will so inform all other participating States.

(77) No participating State will be obliged to accept more than one inspection per calendar year from the same participating State.

(78) An inspection will not be counted if, due to *force majeure*, it cannot be carried out.

(78.1) If the inspecting State is prevented from carrying out an inspection due to *force majeure*, it shall explain in detail the reasons without delay.

....

(80) The participating State which requests an inspection will be permitted to designate for inspection on the territory of another State within the zone of application for CSBMs, a specific area. Such an area will be referred to as the "specified area". The specified area will comprise terrain where notifiable military activities are conducted or where another participating State believes a notifiable military activity is taking place. The specified area will be defined and limited by the scope and scale of notifiable military activities but will not exceed that required for an army level military activity.

(81) In the specified area the inspection team accompanied by the representatives of the receiving State will be permitted access, entry and unobstructed survey, except for areas or sensitive points to which access is normally denied or restricted, military and other defence installations, as well as naval vessels, military vehicles and aircraft. The number and extent of the restricted areas should be as limited as possible. Areas where notifiable military activities can take place will not be declared restricted areas, except for certain permanent or temporary military installations which, in territorial terms, should be as small as possible, and consequently those areas will not be used to prevent inspection of notifiable military activities. Restricted areas will not be employed in a way inconsistent with the agreed provisions on inspection.

(82) Within the specified area, the forces of participating States other than the receiving State will also be subject to the inspection. Representatives of these forces will co-operate with the receiving State during the inspection.

(83) Inspection will be permitted on the ground, from the air, or both.

(84) The representatives of the receiving State will accompany the inspection team, including when it is in land vehicles and an aircraft from the time of their first employment until the time they are no longer in use for the purposes of inspection.

. . . .

(91) There will be no more than four inspectors in an inspection team. The inspecting State may invite other participating States to participate in an inspection. The inspection team may consist of nationals from up to three participating States. The inspection team will be headed by a national of the inspecting State, which will have at least as many inspectors in the team as any invited State. The inspection team will be under the responsibility of the inspecting State, against whose quota the inspection is counted. While conducting the inspection, the inspection team may divide into two subteams.

. . . .

(93) The participating States will ensure that troops, other armed personnel and officials in the specified area are adequately informed regarding the presence, status and functions of inspectors and, if applicable, auxiliary personnel. The receiving State will ensure that no action is taken by its representatives which could endanger inspectors and, if applicable, auxiliary personnel. In carrying out their duties, inspectors and, if applicable, auxiliary personnel will take into account safety concerns expressed by representatives of the receiving State.

. . . .

X. REGIONAL MEASURES

(138) The participating States are encouraged to undertake, including on the basis of separate agreements, in a bilateral, multilateral or regional context, measures to increase transparency and confidence.

(139) Taking into account the regional dimension of security, participating States, on a voluntary basis, may therefore complement OSCE-wide confidence- and security-building measures through additional politically or legally binding measures, tailored to specific regional needs.

....

(142) Such measures should:

(142.1) - be in accordance with the basic OSCE principles, as enshrined in its documents;

(142.2) - contribute to strengthening the security and stability of the OSCE area, including the concept of the indivisibility of security;

(142.3) - add to existing transparency and confidence;

(142.4) - complement, not duplicate nor replace, existing OSCE-wide CSBMs or arms control agreements;

(142.5) - be in accordance with international laws and obligations;

(142.6) - be consistent with the Vienna Document;

(142.7) - not be detrimental to the security of third parties in the region.

(143) Agreed regional CSBMs form part of the OSCE-wide web of interlocking and mutually reinforcing agreements. Negotiation and implementation within the OSCE area of regional or other agreements not binding on all OSCE participating States are a matter of direct interest to all participating States. Participating States are therefore encouraged to inform the Forum for Security Co-operation (FSC) of the regional CSBM initiatives undertaken and agreements reached, as well as of their implementation, when appropriate. The FSC could be the repository of regional CSBM agreements.

(144) There are a wide range of possible measures which could serve regional needs, such as:

(144.1) - exchange of information on defence planning, military strategy and doctrine as far as they refer to a particular regional context;

(144.2) - further development of the provisions with regard to risk reduction;

(144.3) - enhancement of the existing mechanism for consultation and co-operation as regards unusual military activities conducted by participating States;

(144.4) - joint training courses and manoeuvres;

(144.5) - intensification of military contacts and co-operation, particularly in border areas;

(144.6) - establishment of cross-border communications networks;

(144.7) - reduction of the thresholds for military activities, in particular with regard to border areas;

(144.8) - reduction of the thresholds for notifications and observations of certain military activities that a State is allowed to carry out in a given period, particularly in border areas;

(144.9) - agreement on additional inspection and evaluation visits by neighbouring States, especially in border areas;

(144.10) - increase in the size of evaluation teams and agreement to multinational evaluation teams;

(144.11) - creation of bi-national or regional verification agencies to co-ordinate "out of the region" verification activities.

. . . .

IMPLEMENTATION

. . . .

(158) The measures adopted in this document are politically binding and will come into force on 1 January 2000, unless specified otherwise.

Istanbul, 16 November 1999

ANNEX I

Under the terms of the Madrid mandate, the zone of application for CSBMs is defined as follows:

"On the basis of equality of rights, balance and reciprocity, equal respect for the security interests of all OSCE participating States, and of their respective obligations concerning confidence- and security-building measures and disarmament in Europe, these confidence- and security-building measures will cover the whole of Europe as well as the adjoining sea area[xvi] and air space. They will be of military significance and politically binding and will be provided with adequate forms of verification which correspond to their content.

As far as the adjoining sea area and air space is concerned, the measures will be applicable to the military activities of all the participating States taking place there whenever these activities affect security in Europe as well as constitute a part of activities taking place within the whole of Europe as referred to above, which they will agree to notify. Necessary specifications will be made through the negotiations on the confidence- and security-building measures at the Conference.

Nothing in the definition of the zone given above will diminish obligations already undertaken under the Final Act. The confidence- and security-building measures to be agreed upon at the Conference will also be applicable in all areas covered by any of the provisions in the Final Act relating to confidence-building measures and certain aspects of security and disarmament.

. . . .

i. On 13 December 1992 the CSCE Committee of Senior Officials agreed to maintain in force its decision of 8 July 1992 to suspend the participation of Yugoslavia in the CSCE and review it as appropriate.

ii. The zone of application for CSBMs under the terms of the Madrid mandate is set out in Annex I.

iii. In this context, formations are armies, corps and divisions and their equivalents.

iv. In this context, units are brigades, regiments and their equivalents.

v. In this context, combat units are infantry, armoured, mechanized, motorized rifle, artillery, combat engineer and army aviation units. Those combat units which are airmobile or airborne will also be included.

vi. In this context, non-active formations or combat units are those manned from zero to fifteen percent of their authorized combat strength. This term includes low strength formations and units.

vii. Combat units as defined above.

viii. In this context, air combat units are units, the majority of whose organic aircraft are combat aircraft.

ix. As an exception, this information need not be provided on air defence aviation units.

x. The application of the measures relating to defence planning is not restricted by the zone of application for CSBMs set out in Annex I.

xi. In this context, the term normal peacetime air base is understood to mean the normal peacetime location of the air combat unit indicated by the air base or military airfield on which the unit is based.

xii. This provision will not apply if another participating State has already arranged a demonstration of the same type of major weapon and equipment system.

xiii. In this document, the term notifiable means subject to notification.

xiv. In this context , the term land forces includes amphibious, airmobile or heliborne forces and airborne forces.

xv. As defined in the provisions on Prior Notification of Certain Military Activities.

xvi. In this context, the notion of adjoining sea area is understood to refer also to ocean areas adjoining Europe.

Wherever the term "the zone of application for CSBMs" is used in this document, the above definition will apply. The following understanding will apply as well:

The commitments undertaken in letters to the Chairman-in-Office of the OSCE Council by Armenia, Azerbaijan, Belarus, Kazakhstan, Kyrgyzstan, Moldova, Tajikistan, Turkmenistan, Ukraine and Uzbekistan on 29 January 1992 have the effect of extending the application of CSBMs in the Vienna Document 1992 to the territories of the above-mentioned States insofar as their territories were not covered already by the above.

The former Yugoslav Republic of Macedonia, which had observer status at the time when the Vienna Document 1994 was negotiated, has been a participating State since 12 October 1995, and Andorra has been a participating State since 25 April 1996.

As a consequence, "the zone of application for CSBMs" as defined in this annex extends, as of the given dates, to the territories of the above-mentioned States.

Part IV

National Security and Other International Legal Issues

A. Law of the Sea

THIRD UNITED NATIONS LAW OF THE SEA CONVENTION*

....

SECTION 3. INNOCENT PASSAGE IN THE TERRITORIAL SEA
SUBSECTION A. RULES APPLICABLE TO ALL SHIPS

Article 17. *Right of innocent passage.* Subject to this Convention, ships of all States, whether coastal or land-locked, enjoy the right of innocent passage through the territorial sea.

Article 18. *Meaning of passage.* 1. Passage means navigation through the territorial sea for the purpose of:

(a) traversing that sea without entering internal waters or calling at a roadstead or port facility outside internal waters; or

(b) proceeding to or from internal waters or a call at such roadstead or port facility.

2. Passage shall be continuous and expeditious. However, passage includes stopping and anchoring, but only in so far as the same are incidental to ordinary navigation or are rendered necessary by *force majeure* or distress or for the purpose of rendering assistance to persons, ships or aircraft in danger or distress.

Article 19. Meaning of innocent passage. 1. Passage is innocent so long as it is not prejudicial to the peace, good order or security of the coastal State. Such passage shall take place in conformity with this Convention and with other rules of international law.

2. Passage of a foreign ship shall be considered to be prejudicial to the peace, good order or security of the coastal State if in the territorial sea it engages in any of the following activities:

(a) any threat or use of force against the sovereignty, territorial integrity or political independence of the coastal State, or in any other manner in violation of the principles of international law embodied in the Charter of the United Nations;

(b) any exercise or practice with weapons of any kind;

(c) any act aimed at collecting information to the prejudice of the defence or security of the coastal State;

(d) any act of propaganda aimed at affecting the defence or security of the coastal State;

(e) the launching, landing or taking on board of any aircraft;

(f) the launching, landing or taking on board of any military device;

---

* United Nations Convention on the Law of the Sea, arts. 17–21, 23–32, 34–42, 44–50, 52–54, 86–92, 95–96, 98–108, 110–111, 297–299, Dec. 10, 1982, 1833 U.N.T.S. 3 (entered into force on Nov. 16, 1994), *available at* http://www.un.org/Depts/los/convention_agreements/texts/unclos/unclos_e.pdf.

(g) the loading or unloading of any commodity, currency or person contrary to the customs, fiscal, immigration or sanitary laws and regulations of the coastal State;

(h) any act of willful and serious pollution contrary to this Convention;

(i) any fishing activities;

(j) the carrying out of research or survey activities;

(k) any act aimed at interfering with any systems of communication or any other facilities or installations of the coastal State;

(l) any other activity not having a direct bearing on passage.

Article 20. *Submarines and other underwater vehicles.* In the territorial sea, submarines and other underwater vehicles are required to navigate on the surface and to show their flag.

Article 21. *Laws and regulations of the coastal State relating to innocent passage.* 1. The coastal State may adopt laws and regulations, in conformity with the provisions of this Convention and other rules of international law, relating to innocent passage through the territorial sea, in respect of all or any of the following:

(a) the safety of navigation and the regulation of maritime traffic;

(b) the protection of navigational aids and facilities and other facilities or installations;

(c) the protection of cables and pipelines;

(d) the conservation of the living resources of the sea;

(e) the prevention of infringement of the fisheries laws and regulations of the coastal State;

(f) the preservation of the environment of the coastal State and the prevention, reduction and control of pollution thereof;

(g) marine scientific research and hydrographic surveys;

(h) the prevention of infringement of the customs, fiscal, immigration or sanitary laws and regulations of the coastal State.

2. Such laws and regulations shall not apply to the design, construction, manning or equipment of foreign ships unless they are giving effect to generally accepted international rules or standards.

3. The coastal State shall give due publicity to all such laws and regulations.

4. Foreign ships exercising the right of innocent passage through the territorial sea shall comply with all such laws and regulations and all generally accepted international regulations relating to the prevention of collisions at sea.

Article 22. *Sea lanes and traffic separation schemes in the territorial sea.* 1. The coastal State may, where necessary having regard to the safety of navigation, require foreign ships exercising the right of innocent passage through its territorial sea to use such sea lanes and traffic separation schemes as it may designate or prescribe for the regulation of the passage of ships.

2. In particular, tankers, nuclear-powered ships and ships carrying nuclear or other inherently dangerous or noxious substances or materials may be required to confine their passage to such sea lanes.

3. In the designation of sea lanes and the prescription of traffic separation schemes under this article, the coastal State shall take into account:

(a) the recommendations of the competent international organization;

(b) any channels customarily used for international navigation;

(c) the special characteristics of particular ships and channels; and

(d) the density of traffic.

4. The coastal State shall clearly indicate such sea lanes and traffic separation schemes on charts to which due publicity shall be given.

Article 23. *Foreign nuclear-powered ships and ships carrying nuclear or other inherently dangerous or noxious substances.* Foreign nuclear-powered ships and ships carrying nuclear or other inherently dangerous or noxious substances shall, when exercising the right of innocent passage through the territorial sea, carry documents and observe special precautionary measures established for such ships by international agreements.

Article 24. *Duties of the coastal State.* 1. The coastal State shall not hamper the innocent passage of foreign ships through the territorial sea except in accordance with this Convention. In particular, in the application of this Convention or of any laws or regulations adopted in conformity with this Convention, the coastal State shall not:

(a) impose requirements on foreign ships which have the practical effect of denying or impairing the right of innocent passage; or

(b) discriminate in form or in fact against the ships of any State or against ships carrying cargoes to, from or on behalf of any State.

2. The coastal State shall give appropriate publicity to any danger to navigation, of which it has knowledge, within its territorial sea.

Article 25. Rights of protection of the coastal State. 1. The coastal State may take the necessary steps in its territorial sea to prevent passage which is not innocent.

2. In the case of ships proceeding to internal waters or a call at a port facility outside internal waters, the coastal State also has the right to take the necessary steps to prevent any breach of the conditions to which admission of those ships to internal waters or such a call is subject.

3. The coastal State may, without discrimination in form or in fact among foreign ships, suspend temporarily in specified areas of its territorial sea the innocent passage of foreign ships if such suspension is essential for the protection of its security, including weapons exercises. Such suspension shall take effect only after having been duly published.

Article 26. *Charges which may be levied upon foreign ships.* 1. No charge may be levied upon foreign ships by reason only of their passage through the territorial sea.

2. Charges may be levied upon a foreign ship passing through the territorial sea as payment only for specific services rendered to the ship. These charges shall be levied without discrimination.

SUBSECTION B. RULES APPLICABLE TO MERCHANT SHIPS AND GOVERNMENT SHIPS OPERATED FOR COMMERCIAL PURPOSES

Article 27. *Criminal jurisdiction on board a foreign ship.* 1. The criminal jurisdiction of the coastal State should not be exercised on board a foreign ship passing through the territorial sea to arrest any person or to conduct any investigation in connection with any crime committed on board the ship during its passage, save only in the following cases:

(a) if the consequences of the crime extend to the coastal State;

(b) if the crime is of a kind to disturb the peace of the country or the good order of the territorial sea;

(c) if the assistance of the local authorities has been requested by the master of the ship or by a diplomatic agent or consular officer of the flag State; or

(d) if such measures are necessary for the suppression of illicit traffic in narcotic drugs or psychotropic substances.

2. The above provisions do not affect the right of the coastal State to take any steps authorized by its laws for the purpose of an arrest or investigation on board a foreign ship passing through the territorial sea after leaving internal waters.

....

Article 28. *Civil jurisdiction in relation to foreign ships.* 1. The coastal State should not stop or divert a foreign ship passing through the territorial sea for the purpose of exercising civil jurisdiction in relation to a person on board the ship.

2. The coastal State may not levy execution against or arrest the ship for the purpose of any civil proceedings, save only in respect of obligations or liabilities assumed or incurred by the ship itself in the course or for the purpose of its voyage through the waters of the coastal State.

3. Paragraph 2 is without prejudice to the right of the coastal State, in accordance with its laws, to levy execution against or to arrest, for the purpose of any civil proceedings, a foreign ship lying in the territorial sea, or passing through the territorial sea after leaving internal waters.

SUBSECTION C. RULES APPLICABLE TO WARSHIPS AND OTHER GOVERNMENT SHIPS OPERATED FOR NON-COMMERCIAL PURPOSES

Article 29. *Definition of warships.* For the purposes of this Convention, "warship" means a ship belonging to the armed forces of a State bearing the external marks distinguishing such ships of its nationality, under the command of an officer duly commissioned by the government of the State and whose name appears in the appropriate service list or its equivalent, and manned by a crew which is under regular armed forces discipline.

Article 30. *Non-compliance by warships with the laws and regulations of the coastal State.* If any warship does not comply with the laws and regulations of the coastal State concerning passage through the territorial sea and disregards any request for compliance therewith which is made to it, the coastal State may require it to leave the territorial sea immediately.

Article 31. *Responsibility of the flag State for damage caused by a warship or other government ship operated for non-commercial purposes.* The flag State shall bear international responsibility for any loss or damage to the coastal State resulting from the non-compliance by a warship or other government ship operated for non-commercial purposes with the laws and regulations of the coastal State concerning passage through the territorial sea or with the provisions of this Convention or other rules of international law.

Article 32. *Immunities of warships and other government ships operated for non-commercial purposes.* With such exceptions as are contained in subsection A and in articles

30 and 31, nothing in this Convention affects the immunities of warships and other government ships operated for non-commercial purposes.

. . . .

PART III
STRAITS USED FOR INTERNATIONAL NAVIGATION
SECTION 1. GENERAL PROVISIONS

Article 34. *Legal status of waters forming straits used for international navigation.* 1. The regime of passage through straits used for international navigation established in this Part shall not in other respects affect the legal status of the waters forming such straits or the exercise by the States bordering the straits of their sovereignty or jurisdiction over such waters and their air space, bed and subsoil.

2. The sovereignty or jurisdiction of the States bordering the straits is exercised subject to this Part and to other rules of international law.

Article 35. *Scope of this Part.* Nothing in this Part affects:

(a) any areas of internal waters within a strait, except where the establishment of a straight baseline in accordance with the method set forth in article 7 has the effect of enclosing as internal waters areas which had not previously been considered as such;

(b) the legal status of the waters beyond the territorial seas of States bordering straits as exclusive economic zones or high seas; or

(c) the legal regime in straits in which passage is regulated in whole or in part by long-standing international conventions in force specifically relating to such straits.

Article 36. *High seas routes or routes through exclusive economic zones through straits used for international navigation.* This Part does not apply to a strait used for international navigation if there exists through the strait a route through the high seas or through an exclusive economic zone of similar convenience with respect to navigational and hydrographical characteristics; in such routes, the other relevant Parts of this Convention, including the provisions regarding the freedoms of navigation and overflight, apply.

SECTION 2. TRANSIT PASSAGE

Article 37. *Scope of this section.* This section applies to straits which are used for international navigation between one part of the high seas or an exclusive economic zone and another part of the high seas or an exclusive economic zone.

Article 38. *Right of transit passage.* 1. In straits referred to in article 37, all ships and aircraft enjoy the right of transit passage, which shall not be impeded; except that, if the strait is formed by an island of a State bordering the strait and its mainland, transit passage shall not apply if there exists seaward of the island a route through the high seas or through an exclusive economic zone of similar convenience with respect to navigational and hydrographical characteristics.

2. Transit passage means the exercise in accordance with this Part of the freedom of navigation and overflight solely for the purpose of continuous and expeditious transit of the strait between one part of the high seas or an exclusive economic zone and another part of the high seas or an exclusive economic zone. However, the requirement of

continuous and expeditious transit does not preclude passage through the strait for the purpose of entering, leaving or returning from a State bordering the strait, subject to the conditions of entry to that State.

3. Any activity which is not an exercise of the right of transit passage through a strait remains subject to the other applicable provisions of this Convention.

Article 39. *Duties of ships and aircraft during transit passage.* 1. Ships and aircraft, while exercising the right of transit passage, shall:

(a) proceed without delay through or over the strait;

(b) refrain from any threat or use of force against the sovereignty, territorial integrity or political independence of States bordering the strait, or in any other manner in violation of the principles of international law embodied in the Charter of the United Nations;

(c) refrain from any activities other than those incident to their normal modes of continuous and expeditious transit unless rendered necessary by *force majeure* or by distress;

(d) comply with other relevant provisions of this Part.

2. Ships in transit passage shall:

(a) comply with generally accepted international regulations, procedures and practices for safety at sea, including the International Regulations for Preventing Collisions at Sea;

(b) comply with generally accepted international regulations, procedures and practices for the prevention, reduction and control of pollution from ships.

3. Aircraft in transit passage shall:

(a) observe the Rules of the Air established by the International Civil Aviation Organization as they apply to civil aircraft; state aircraft will normally comply with such safety measures and will at all times operate with due regard for the safety of navigation;

(b) at all times monitor the radio frequency assigned by the competent internationally designated air traffic control authority or the appropriate international distress radio frequency.

Article 40. *Research and survey activities.* During transit passage, foreign ships, including marine scientific research and hydrographic survey ships, may not carry out any research or survey activities without the prior authorization of the States bordering straits.

Article 41. *Sea lanes and traffic separation schemes in straits used for international navigation.* 1. In conformity with this Part, States bordering straits may designate sea lanes and prescribe traffic separation schemes for navigation in straits where necessary to promote the safe passage of ships.

2. Such States may, when circumstances require, and after giving due publicity thereto, substitute other sea lanes or traffic separation schemes for any sea lanes or traffic separation schemes previously designated or prescribed by them.

3. Such sea lanes and traffic separation schemes shall conform to generally accepted international regulations.

4. Before designating or substituting sea lanes or prescribing or substituting traffic separation schemes, States bordering straits shall refer proposals to the competent inter-

national organization with a view to their adoption. The organization may adopt only such sea lanes and traffic separation schemes as may be agreed with the States bordering the straits, after which the States may designate, prescribe or substitute them.

5. In respect of a strait where sea lanes or traffic separation schemes through the waters of two or more States bordering the strait are being proposed, the States concerned shall cooperate in formulating proposals in consultation with the competent international organization.

6. States bordering straits shall clearly indicate all sea lanes and traffic separation schemes designated or prescribed by them on charts to which due publicity shall be given.

7. Ships in transit passage shall respect applicable sea lanes and traffic separation schemes established in accordance with this article.

Article 42. *Laws and regulations of States bordering straits relating to transit passage.* 1. Subject to the provisions of this section, States bordering straits may adopt laws and regulations relating to transit passage through straits, in respect of all or any of the following:

(a) the safety of navigation and the regulation of maritime traffic, as provided in article 41;

(b) the prevention, reduction and control of pollution, by giving effect to applicable international regulations regarding the discharge of oil, oily wastes and other noxious substances in the strait;

(c) with respect to fishing vessels, the prevention of fishing, including the stowage of fishing gear;

(d) the loading or unloading of any commodity, currency or person in contravention of the customs, fiscal, immigration or sanitary laws and regulations of States bordering straits.

2. Such laws and regulations shall not discriminate in form or in fact among foreign ships or in their application have the practical effect of denying, hampering or impairing the right of transit passage as defined in this section.

3. States bordering straits shall give due publicity to all such laws and regulations.

4. Foreign ships exercising the right of transit passage shall comply with such laws and regulations.

5. The flag State of a ship or the State of registry of an aircraft entitled to sovereign immunity which acts in a manner contrary to such laws and regulations or other provisions of this Part shall bear international responsibility for any loss or damage which results to States bordering straits.

....

Article 44. *Duties of States bordering straits.* States bordering straits shall not hamper transit passage and shall give appropriate publicity to any danger to navigation or overflight within or over the strait of which they have knowledge. There shall be no suspension of transit passage.

SECTION 3. INNOCENT PASSAGE

Article 45. *Innocent passage.* 1. The regime of innocent passage, in accordance with Part II, section 3, shall apply in straits used for international navigation:

(a) excluded from the application of the regime of transit passage under article 38, paragraph 1; or

(b) between a part of the high seas or an exclusive economic zone and the territorial sea of a foreign State.

2. There shall be no suspension of innocent passage through such straits.

PART IV
ARCHIPELAGIC STATES

Article 46. *Use of terms.* For the purposes of this Convention:

(a) "archipelagic State" means a State constituted wholly by one or more archipelagos and may include other islands;

(b) "archipelago" means a group of islands, including parts of islands, interconnecting waters and other natural features which are so closely interrelated that such islands, waters and other natural features form an intrinsic geographical, economic and political entity, or which historically have been regarded as such.

Article 47. *Archipelagic baselines.* 1. An archipelagic State may draw straight archipelagic baselines joining the outermost points of the outermost islands and drying reefs of the archipelago provided that within such baselines are included the main islands and an area in which the ratio of the area of the water to the area of the land, including atolls, is between 1 to 1 and 9 to 1.

2. The length of such baselines shall not exceed 100 nautical miles, except that up to 3 per cent of the total number of baselines enclosing any archipelago may exceed that length, up to a maximum length of 125 nautical miles.

3. The drawing of such baselines shall not depart to any appreciable extent from the general configuration of the archipelago.

4. Such baselines shall not be drawn to and from low-tide elevations, unless lighthouses or similar installations which are permanently above sea level have been built on them or where a low-tide elevation is situated wholly or partly at a distance not exceeding the breadth of the territorial sea from the nearest island.

5. The system of such baselines shall not be applied by an archipelagic State in such a manner as to cut off from the high seas or the exclusive economic zone the territorial sea of another State.

6. If a part of the archipelagic waters of an archipelagic State lies between two parts of an immediately adjacent neighbouring State, existing rights and all other legitimate interests which the latter State has traditionally exercised in such waters and all rights stipulated by agreement between those States shall continue and be respected.

7. For the purpose of computing the ratio of water to land under paragraph l, land areas may include waters lying within the fringing reefs of islands and atolls, including that part of a steep-sided oceanic plateau which is enclosed or nearly enclosed by a chain of limestone islands and drying reefs lying on the perimeter of the plateau.

8. The baselines drawn in accordance with this article shall be shown on charts of a scale or scales adequate for ascertaining their position. Alternatively, lists of geographical coordinates of points, specifying the geodetic datum, may be substituted.

9. The archipelagic State shall give due publicity to such charts or lists of geographical coordinates and shall deposit a copy of each such chart or list with the Secretary-General of the United Nations.

Article 48. *Measurement of the breadth of the territorial sea, the contiguous zone, the exclusive economic zone and the continental shelf.* The breadth of the territorial sea, the contiguous zone, the exclusive economic zone and the continental shelf shall be measured from archipelagic baselines drawn in accordance with article 47.

Article 49. *Legal status of archipelagic waters, of the air space over archipelagic waters and of their bed and subsoil.* 1. The sovereignty of an archipelagic State extends to the waters enclosed by the archipelagic baselines drawn in accordance with article 47, described as archipelagic waters, regardless of their depth or distance from the coast.

2. This sovereignty extends to the air space over the archipelagic waters, as well as to their bed and subsoil, and the resources contained therein.

3. This sovereignty is exercised subject to this Part.

4. The regime of archipelagic sea lanes passage established in this Part shall not in other respects affect the status of the archipelagic waters, including the sea lanes, or the exercise by the archipelagic State of its sovereignty over such waters and their air space, bed and subsoil, and the resources contained therein.

Article 50. *Delimitation of internal waters.* Within its archipelagic waters, the archipelagic State may draw closing lines for the delimitation of internal waters, in accordance with articles 9, 10 and 11.

. . . .

Article 52. *Right of innocent passage.* 1. Subject to article 53 and without prejudice to article 50, ships of all States enjoy the right of innocent passage through archipelagic waters, in accordance with Part II, section 3.

2. The archipelagic State may, without discrimination in form or in fact among foreign ships, suspend temporarily in specified areas of its archipelagic waters the innocent passage of foreign ships if such suspension is essential for the protection of its security. Such suspension shall take effect only after having been duly published.

Article 53. *Right of archipelagic sea lanes passage.* 1. An archipelagic State may designate sea lanes and air routes there above, suitable for the continuous and expeditious passage of foreign ships and aircraft through or over its archipelagic waters and the adjacent territorial sea.

2. All ships and aircraft enjoy the right of archipelagic sea lanes passage in such sea lanes and air routes.

3. Archipelagic sea lanes passage means the exercise in accordance with this Convention of the rights of navigation and overflight in the normal mode solely for the purpose of continuous, expeditious and unobstructed transit between one part of the high seas or an exclusive economic zone and another part of the high seas or an exclusive economic zone.

4. Such sea lanes and air routes shall traverse the archipelagic waters and the adjacent territorial sea and shall include all normal passage routes used as routes for international navigation or overflight through or over archipelagic waters and, within such routes, so far as ships are concerned, all normal navigational channels, provided that duplication of routes of similar convenience between the same entry and exit points shall not be necessary.

5. Such sea lanes and air routes shall be defined by a series of continuous axis lines from the entry points of passage routes to the exit points. Ships and aircraft in archipelagic sea lanes passage shall not deviate more than 25 nautical miles to either side of such

axis lines during passage, provided that such ships and aircraft shall not navigate closer to the coasts than 10 per cent of the distance between the nearest points on islands bordering the sea lane.

6. An archipelagic State which designates sea lanes under this article may also prescribe traffic separation schemes for the safe passage of ships through narrow channels in such sea lanes.

. . . .

12. If an archipelagic State does not designate sea lanes or air routes, the right of archipelagic sea lanes passage may be exercised through the routes normally used for international navigation.

Article 54. *Duties of ships and aircraft during their passage, research and survey activities, duties of the archipelagic State and laws and regulations of the archipelagic State relating to archipelagic sea lanes passage.* Articles 39, 40, 42 and 44 apply *mutatis mutandis* to archipelagic sea lanes passage.

PART V
EXCLUSIVE ECONOMIC ZONE

. . . .

Article 56. *Rights, jurisdiction and duties of the coastal State in the exclusive economic zone.* 1. In the exclusive economic zone, the coastal State has:

(a) sovereign rights for the purpose of exploring and exploiting, conserving and managing the natural resources, whether living or non-living, of the waters superjacent to the seabed and of the seabed and its subsoil, and with regard to other activities for the economic exploitation and exploration of the zone, such as the production of energy from the water, currents and winds;

(b) jurisdiction as provided for in the relevant provisions of this Convention with regard to:

(i) the establishment and use of artificial islands, installations and structures;

(ii) marine scientific research;

(iii) the protection and preservation of the marine environment;

(c) other rights and duties provided for in this Convention.

2. In exercising its rights and performing its duties under this Convention in the exclusive economic zone, the coastal State shall have due regard to the rights and duties of other States and shall act in a manner compatible with the provisions of this Convention.

3. The rights set out in this article with respect to the seabed and subsoil shall be exercised in accordance with Part VI.

Article 57. *Breadth of the exclusive economic zone.* The exclusive economic zone shall not extend beyond 200 nautical miles from the baselines from which the breadth of the territorial sea is measured.

Article 58. *Rights and duties of other States in the exclusive economic zone.* 1. In the exclusive economic zone, all States, whether coastal or land-locked, enjoy, subject to the relevant provisions of this Convention, the freedoms referred to in article 87 of navigation and overflight and of the laying of submarine cables and pipelines, and other internationally lawful uses of the sea related to these freedoms, such as those associated with the operation of ships, aircraft and submarine cables and pipelines, and compatible with the other provisions of this Convention.

2. Articles 88 to 115 and other pertinent rules of international law apply to the exclusive economic zone in so far as they are not incompatible with this Part.

3. In exercising their rights and performing their duties under this Convention in the exclusive economic zone, States shall have due regard to the rights and duties of the coastal State and shall comply with the laws and regulations adopted by the coastal State in accordance with the provisions of this Convention and other rules of international law in so far as they are not incompatible with this Part.

Article 59. *Basis for the resolution of conflicts regarding the attribution of rights and jurisdiction in the exclusive economic zone.* In cases where this Convention does not attribute rights or jurisdiction to the coastal State or to other States within the exclusive economic zone, and a conflict arises between the interests of the coastal State and any other State or States, the conflict should be resolved on the basis of equity and in the light of all the relevant circumstances, taking into account the respective importance of the interests involved to the parties as well as to the international community as a whole.

....

PART VII

HIGH SEAS

SECTION 1. GENERAL PROVISIONS

Article 86. *Application of the provisions of this Part.* The provisions of this Part apply to all parts of the sea that are not included in the exclusive economic zone, in the territorial sea or in the internal waters of a State, or in the archipelagic waters of an archipelagic State. This article does not entail any abridgement of the freedoms enjoyed by all States in the exclusive economic zone in accordance with article 58.

Article 87. *Freedom of the high seas.* 1. The high seas are open to all States, whether coastal or land-locked. Freedom of the high seas is exercised under the conditions laid down by this Convention and by other rules of international law. It comprises, *inter alia*, both for coastal and land-locked States:

(a) freedom of navigation;

(b) freedom of overflight;

(c) freedom to lay submarine cables and pipelines, subject to Part VI;

(d) freedom to construct artificial islands and other installations permitted under international law, subject to Part VI;

(e) freedom of fishing, subject to the conditions laid down in section 2;

(f) freedom of scientific research, subject to Parts VI and XIII.

2. These freedoms shall be exercised by all States with due regard for the interests of other States in their exercise of the freedom of the high seas, and also with due regard for the rights under this Convention with respect to activities in the Area.

Article 88. *Reservation of the high seas for peaceful purposes.* The high seas shall be reserved for peaceful purposes.

Article 89. *Invalidity of claims of sovereignty over the high seas.* No State may validly purport to subject any part of the high seas to its sovereignty.

Article 90. *Right of navigation.* Every State, whether coastal or land-locked, has the right to sail ships flying its flag on the high seas.

Article 91. *Nationality of ships.* 1. Every State shall fix the conditions for the grant of its nationality to ships, for the registration of ships in its territory, and for the right to fly its flag. Ships have the nationality of the State whose flag they are entitled to fly. There must exist a genuine link between the State and the ship.

2. Every State shall issue to ships to which it has granted the right to fly its flag documents to that effect.

Article 92. *Status of ships.* 1. Ships shall sail under the flag of one State only and, save in exceptional cases expressly provided for in international treaties or in this Convention, shall be subject to its exclusive jurisdiction on the high seas. A ship may not change its flag during a voyage or while in a port of call, save in the case of a real transfer of ownership or change of registry.

2. A ship which sails under the flags of two or more States, using them according to convenience, may not claim any of the nationalities in question with respect to any other State, and may be assimilated to a ship without nationality.

. . . .

Article 95. *Immunity of warships on the high seas.* Warships on the high seas have complete immunity from the jurisdiction of any State other than the flag State.

Article 96. *Immunity of ships used only on government non-commercial service.* Ships owned or operated by a State and used only on government non-commercial service shall, on the high seas, have complete immunity from the jurisdiction of any State other than the flag State.

. . . .

Article 98. *Duty to render assistance.* 1. Every State shall require the master of a ship flying its flag, in so far as he can do so without serious danger to the ship, the crew or the passengers:

(a) to render assistance to any person found at sea in danger of being lost;

(b) to proceed with all possible speed to the rescue of persons in distress, if informed of their need of assistance, in so far as such action may reasonably be expected of him;

(c) after a collision, to render assistance to the other ship, its crew and its passengers and, where possible, to inform the other ship of the name of his own ship, its port of registry and the nearest port at which it will call.

2. Every coastal State shall promote the establishment, operation and maintenance of an adequate and effective search and rescue service regarding safety on and over the sea and, where circumstances so require, by way of mutual regional arrangements cooperate with neighbouring States for this purpose.

Article 99. *Prohibition of the transport of slaves.* Every State shall take effective measures to prevent and punish the transport of slaves in ships authorized to fly its flag and to prevent the unlawful use of its flag for that purpose. Any slave taking refuge on board any ship, whatever its flag, shall *ipso facto* be free.

Article 100. *Duty to cooperate in the repression of piracy.* All States shall cooperate to the fullest possible extent in the repression of piracy on the high seas or in any other place outside the jurisdiction of any State.

Article 101. Definition of piracy. Piracy consists of any of the following acts:

(a) any illegal acts of violence or detention, or any act of depredation, committed for private ends by the crew or the passengers of a private ship or a private aircraft, and directed:

(i) on the high seas, against another ship or aircraft, or against persons or property on board such ship or aircraft;

(ii) against a ship, aircraft, persons or property in a place outside the jurisdiction of any State;

(b) any act of voluntary participation in the operation of a ship or of an aircraft with knowledge of facts making it a pirate ship or aircraft;

(c) any act of inciting or of intentionally facilitating an act described in subparagraph (a) or (b).

Article 102. Piracy by a warship, government ship or government aircraft whose crew has mutinied. The acts of piracy, as defined in article 101, committed by a warship, government ship or government aircraft whose crew has mutinied and taken control of the ship or aircraft are assimilated to acts committed by a private ship or aircraft.

Article 103. Definition of a pirate ship or aircraft. A ship or aircraft is considered a pirate ship or aircraft if it is intended by the persons in dominant control to be used for the purpose of committing one of the acts referred to in article 101. The same applies if the ship or aircraft has been used to commit any such act, so long as it remains under the control of the persons guilty of that act.

Article 104. Retention or loss of the nationality of a pirate ship or aircraft. A ship or aircraft may retain its nationality although it has become a pirate ship or aircraft. The retention or loss of nationality is determined by the law of the State from which such nationality was derived.

Article 105. Seizure of a pirate ship or aircraft. On the high seas, or in any other place outside the jurisdiction of any State, every State may seize a pirate ship or aircraft, or a ship or aircraft taken by piracy and under the control of pirates, and arrest the persons and seize the property on board. The courts of the State which carried out the seizure may decide upon the penalties to be imposed, and may also determine the action to be taken with regard to the ships, aircraft or property, subject to the rights of third parties acting in good faith.

Article 106. Liability for seizure without adequate grounds. Where the seizure of a ship or aircraft on suspicion of piracy has been effected without adequate grounds, the State making the seizure shall be liable to the State the nationality of which is possessed by the ship or aircraft for any loss or damage caused by the seizure.

Article 107. Ships and aircraft which are entitled to seize on account of piracy. A seizure on account of piracy may be carried out only by warships or military aircraft, or other ships or aircraft clearly marked and identifiable as being on government service and authorized to that effect.

Article 108. Illicit traffic in narcotic drugs or psychotropic substances. 1. All States shall cooperate in the suppression of illicit traffic in narcotic drugs and psychotropic substances engaged in by ships on the high seas contrary to international conventions.

2. Any State which has reasonable grounds for believing that a ship flying its flag is engaged in illicit traffic in narcotic drugs or psychotropic substances may request the cooperation of other States to suppress such traffic.

....

Article 110. Right of visit. 1. Except where acts of interference derive from powers conferred by treaty, a warship which encounters on the high seas a foreign ship, other than a ship entitled to complete immunity in accordance with articles 95 and 96, is not justified in boarding it unless there is reasonable ground for suspecting that:

(a) the ship is engaged in piracy;

(b) the ship is engaged in the slave trade;

(c) the ship is engaged in unauthorized broadcasting and the flag State of the warship has jurisdiction under article 109;

(d) the ship is without nationality; or

(e) though flying a foreign flag or refusing to show its flag, the ship is, in reality, of the same nationality as the warship.

2. In the cases provided for in paragraph 1, the warship may proceed to verify the ship's right to fly its flag. To this end, it may send a boat under the command of an officer to the suspected ship. If suspicion remains after the documents have been checked, it may proceed to a further examination on board the ship, which must be carried out with all possible consideration.

3. If the suspicions prove to be unfounded, and provided that the ship boarded has not committed any act justifying them, it shall be compensated for any loss or damage that may have been sustained.

4. These provisions apply *mutatis mutandis* to military aircraft.

5. These provisions also apply to any other duly authorized ships or aircraft clearly marked and identifiable as being on government service.

Article 111. Right of hot pursuit. 1. The hot pursuit of a foreign ship may be undertaken when the competent authorities of the coastal State have good reason to believe that the ship has violated the laws and regulations of that State. Such pursuit must be commenced when the foreign ship or one of its boats is within the internal waters, the archipelagic waters, the territorial sea or the contiguous zone of the pursuing State, and may only be continued outside the territorial sea or the contiguous zone if the pursuit has not been interrupted. It is not necessary that, at the time when the foreign ship within the territorial sea or the contiguous zone receives the order to stop, the ship giving the order should likewise be within the territorial sea or the contiguous zone. If the foreign ship is within a contiguous zone, as defined in article 33, the pursuit may only be undertaken if there has been a violation of the rights for the protection of which the zone was established.

2. The right of hot pursuit shall apply *mutatis mutandis* to violations in the exclusive economic zone or on the continental shelf, including safety zones around continental shelf installations, of the laws and regulations of the coastal State applicable in accordance with this Convention to the exclusive economic zone or the continental shelf, including such safety zones.

3. The right of hot pursuit ceases as soon as the ship pursued enters the territorial sea of its own State or of a third State.

4. Hot pursuit is not deemed to have begun unless the pursuing ship has satisfied itself by such practicable means as may be available that the ship pursued or one of its boats or other craft working as a team and using the ship pursued as a mother ship is

within the limits of the territorial sea, or, as the case may be, within the contiguous zone or the exclusive economic zone or above the continental shelf. The pursuit may only be commenced after a visual or auditory signal to stop has been given at a distance which enables it to be seen or heard by the foreign ship.

5. The right of hot pursuit may be exercised only by warships or military aircraft, or other ships or aircraft clearly marked and identifiable as being on government service and authorized to that effect.

6. Where hot pursuit is effected by an aircraft:

(a) the provisions of paragraphs 1 to 4 shall apply *mutatis mutandis*;

(b) the aircraft giving the order to stop must itself actively pursue the ship until a ship or another aircraft of the coastal State, summoned by the aircraft, arrives to take over the pursuit, unless the aircraft is itself able to arrest the ship. It does not suffice to justify an arrest outside the territorial sea that the ship was merely sighted by the aircraft as an offender or suspected offender, if it was not both ordered to stop and pursued by the aircraft itself or other aircraft or ships which continue the pursuit without interruption.

7. The release of a ship arrested within the jurisdiction of a State and escorted to a port of that State for the purposes of an inquiry before the competent authorities may not be claimed solely on the ground that the ship, in the course of its voyage, was escorted across a portion of the exclusive economic zone or the high seas, if the circumstances rendered this necessary.

8. Where a ship has been stopped or arrested outside the territorial sea in circumstances which do not justify the exercise of the right of hot pursuit, it shall be compensated for any loss or damage that may have been thereby sustained.

. . . .

SECTION 3. LIMITATIONS AND EXCEPTIONS TO APPLICABILITY OF SECTION 2

Article 297. *Limitations on applicability of section 2.* 1. Disputes concerning the interpretation or application of this Convention with regard to the exercise by a coastal State of its sovereign rights or jurisdiction provided for in this Convention shall be subject to the procedures provided for in section 2 in the following cases:

(a) when it is alleged that a coastal State has acted in contravention of the provisions of this Convention in regard to the freedoms and rights of navigation, overflight or the laying of submarine cables and pipelines, or in regard to other internationally lawful uses of the sea specified in article 58;

(b) when it is alleged that a State in exercising the aforementioned freedoms, rights or uses has acted in contravention of this Convention or of laws or regulations adopted by the coastal State in conformity with this Convention and other rules of international law not incompatible with this Convention; or

(c) when it is alleged that a coastal State has acted in contravention of specified international rules and standards for the protection and preservation of the marine environment which are applicable to the coastal State and which have been established by this Convention or through a competent international organization or diplomatic conference in accordance with this Convention.

2. (a) Disputes concerning the interpretation or application of the provisions of this Convention with regard to marine scientific research shall be settled in accordance with section 2, except that the coastal State shall not be obliged to accept the submission to such settlement of any dispute arising out of:

(i) the exercise by the coastal State of a right or discretion in accordance with article 246; or

(ii) a decision by the coastal State to order suspension or cessation of a research project in accordance with article 253.

(b) A dispute arising from an allegation by the researching State that with respect to a specific project the coastal State is not exercising its rights under articles 246 and 253 in a manner compatible with this Convention shall be submitted, at therequest of either party, to conciliation under Annex V, section 2, provided that the conciliation commission shall not call in question the exercise by the coastal State of its discretion to designate specific areas as referred to in article 246, paragraph 6, or of its discretion to withhold consent in accordance with article 246, paragraph 5.

3. (a) Disputes concerning the interpretation or application of the provisions of this Convention with regard to fisheries shall be settled in accordance with section 2, except that the coastal State shall not be obliged to accept the submission to such settlement of any dispute relating to its sovereign rights with respect to the living resources in the exclusive economic zone or their exercise, including its discretionary powers for determining the allowable catch, its harvesting capacity, the allocation of surpluses to other States and the terms and conditions established in its conservation and management laws and regulations.

(b) Where no settlement has been reached by recourse to section 1 of this Part, a dispute shall be submitted to conciliation under Annex V, section 2, at the request of any party to the dispute, when it is alleged that:

(i) a coastal State has manifestly failed to comply with its obligations to ensure through proper conservation and management measures that the maintenance of the living resources in the exclusive economic zone is not seriously endangered;

(ii) a coastal State has arbitrarily refused to determine, at the request of another State, the allowable catch and its capacity to harvest living resources with respect to stocks which that other State is interested in fishing; or

(iii) a coastal State has arbitrarily refused to allocate to any State, under articles 62, 69 and 70 and under the terms and conditions established by the coastal State consistent with this Convention, the whole or part of the surplus it has declared to exist.

(c) In no case shall the conciliation commission substitute its discretion for that of the coastal State.

(d) The report of the conciliation commission shall be communicated to the appropriate international organizations.

(e) In negotiating agreements pursuant to articles 69 and 70, States Parties, unless they otherwise agree, shall include a clause on measures which they shall take in order to minimize the possibility of a disagreement concerning the interpretation or application of the agreement, and on how they should proceed if a disagreement nevertheless arises.

Article 298. *Optional exceptions to applicability of section 2.* 1. When signing, ratifying or acceding to this Convention or at any time thereafter, a State may, without prejudice to the obligations arising under section 1, declare in writing that it does not accept any one or more of the procedures provided for in section 2 with respect to one or more of the following categories of disputes:

(a) (i) disputes concerning the interpretation or application of articles 15, 74 and 83 relating to sea boundary delimitations, or those involving historic bays or titles, provided that a State having made such a declaration shall, when such a dispute arises subsequent to the entry into force of this Convention and where no agreement within a reasonable period of time is reached in negotiations between the parties, at the request of any party to the dispute, accept submission of the matter to conciliation under Annex V, section 2; and provided further that any dispute that necessarily involves the concurrent consideration of any unsettled dispute concerning sovereignty or other rights over continental or insular land territory shall be excluded from such submission;

(ii) after the conciliation commission has presented its report, which shall state the reasons on which it is based, the parties shall negotiate an agreement on the basis of that report; if these negotiations do not result in an agreement, the parties shall, by mutual consent, submit the question to one of the procedures provided for in section 2, unless the parties otherwise agree;

(iii) this subparagraph does not apply to any sea boundary dispute finally settled by an arrangement between the parties, or to any such dispute which is to be settled in accordance with a bilateral or multilateral agreement binding upon those parties;

(b) disputes concerning military activities, including military activities by government vessels and aircraft engaged in non-commercial service, and disputes concerning law enforcement activities in regard to the exercise of sovereign rights or jurisdiction excluded from the jurisdiction of a court or tribunal under article 297, paragraph 2 or 3;

(c) disputes in respect of which the Security Council of the United Nations is exercising the functions assigned to it by the Charter of the United Nations, unless the Security Council decides to remove the matter from its agenda or calls upon the parties to settle it by the means provided for in this Convention.

2. A State Party which has made a declaration under paragraph 1 may at any time withdraw it, or agree to submit a dispute excluded by such declaration to any procedure specified in this Convention.

3. A State Party which has made a declaration under paragraph 1 shall not be entitled to submit any dispute falling within the excepted category of disputes to any procedure in this Convention as against another State Party, without the consent of that party.

4. If one of the States Parties has made a declaration under paragraph 1(a), any other State Party may submit any dispute falling within an excepted category against the declarant party to the procedure specified in such declaration.

5. A new declaration, or the withdrawal of a declaration, does not in any way affect proceedings pending before a court or tribunal in accordance with this article, unless the parties otherwise agree.

6. Declarations and notices of withdrawal of declarations under this article shall be deposited with the Secretary-General of the United Nations, who shall transmit copies thereof to the States Parties.

Article 299*. Right of the parties to agree upon a procedure.* 1. A dispute excluded under article 297 or excepted by a declaration made under article 298 from the dispute settlement procedures provided for in section 2 may be submitted to such procedures only by agreement of the parties to the dispute.

2. Nothing in this section impairs the right of the parties to the dispute to agree to some other procedure for the settlement of such dispute or to reach an amicable settlement.

STATEMENT OF THE PRESIDENT ON THE UN LAW OF THE SEA CONVENTION*

The United States has long been a leader in developing customary and conventional law of the sea. Our objectives have consistently been to provide a legal order that will, among other things, facilitate peaceful, international uses of the oceans and provide for equitable and effective management and conservation of marine resources. The United States also recognizes that all nations have an interest in these issues.

Last July I announced that the United States will not sign the United Nations Law of the Sea Convention that was opened for signature on 10 December. We have taken this step because several major problems in the Convention's deep sea-bed mining provisions are contrary to the interests and principles of industrialized nations and would not help attain the aspirations of developing countries.

The United States does not stand alone in those concerns. Some important allies and friends have not signed the Convention. Even some signatory States have raised concerns about these problems.

However, the Convention also contains provisions with respect to traditional uses of the oceans which generally confirm existing maritime law and practice and fairly balance the interests of all States.

Today I am announcing three decisions to promote and protect the oceans interests of the United States in a manner consistent with those fair and balanced results in the Convention and international law.

First, the United States is prepared to accept and act in accordance with the balance of interests relating to traditional uses of the oceans—such as navigation and overflight. In this respect, the United States will recognize the rights of other States in the waters off their coasts, as reflected in the Convention, so long as the rights and freedoms of the United States and others under international law are recognized by such coastal States.

Second, the United States will exercise and assert its navigation and overflight rights and freedoms on a world-wide basis in a manner that is consistent with the balance of interests reflected in the Convention. The United States will not, however, acquiesce in unilateral acts of other States designed to restrict the rights and freedoms of the international community in navigation and overflight and other related high seas uses.

Third, I am proclaiming today an exclusive economic zone in which the United States will exercise sovereign rights in living and non-living resources within 200 nautical miles of its coast. This will provide United States jurisdiction for mineral resources out to 200 nautical miles that are not on the continental shelf. Recently discovered deposits there could be an important future source of strategic minerals.

Within this zone all nations will continue to enjoy the high-seas rights and freedoms that are not resource-related, including the freedoms of navigation and overflight. My Proclamation does not change existing United States policies concerning the continen-

* United States Oceans Policy, Statement by the President, 19 Weekly Comp. Pres. Docs. 383 (Mar. 10, 1983), *available at* http://www.un.org/Depts/los/LEGISLATIONANDTREATIES/PDFFILES/USA_1983_Statement.pdf.

tal shelf, marine mammals and fisheries, including highly migratory species of tuna which are not subject to United States jurisdiction. The United States will continue efforts to achieve international agreements for the effective management of these species. The Proclamation also reinforces this Government's policy of promoting the United States fishing industry.

While international law provides for a right of jurisdiction over marine scientific research within such a zone, the Proclamation does not assert this right. I have elected not to do so because of the United States interest in encouraging marine scientific research and avoiding any unnecessary burdens. The United States will nevertheless recognize the right of other coastal States to exercise jurisdiction over marine scientific research within 200 nautical miles of their coasts, if that jurisdiction is exercised reasonably in a manner consistent with international law.

The Exclusive Economic Zone established today will also enable the United States to take limited additional steps to protect the marine environment. In this connection, the United States will continue to work through the International Maritime Organization and other appropriate international organizations to develop uniform international measures for the protection of the marine environment while imposing no unreasonable burdens on commercial shipping.

The policy decisions I am announcing today will not affect the application of existing United States law concerning the high seas or existing authorities of any United States government agency.

In addition to the above policy steps, the United States will continue to work with other countries to develop a regime, free of unnecessary political and economic restraints, for mining deep sea-bed minerals beyond national jurisdiction. Deep sea-bed mining remains a lawful exercise of the freedom of the high seas open to all nations. The United States will continue to allow its firms to explore for and, when the market permits, exploit these resources.

The Administration looks forward to working with the Congress on legislation to implement these new policies.

JOINT STATEMENT BY THE UNITED STATES OF AMERICA AND THE UNION OF SOVIET SOCIALIST REPUBLICS ON INTERNATIONAL LAW GOVERNING INNOCENT PASSAGE*

Since 1986, representatives of the United States of America and the Union of Soviet Socialist Republics have been conducting friendly and constructive discussions of certain international legal aspects of traditional uses of the oceans, in particular, navigation.

The governments are guided by the provisions of the 1982 United Nations Convention on the Law of the Sea, which, with respect to traditional uses of the oceans, generally constitute international law and practice and balance fairly the interests of all States. They recognize the need to encourage all States to harmonize their internal laws, regulations and practices with those provisions.

The governments consider it useful to issue the attached uniform interpretation of the Rules of International Law Governing Innocent Passage. Both Governments have agreed to take necessary steps to conform their internal laws, regulations and practices with this understanding of the rules.

Uniform Interpretation of Rules
Of International Law Governing
Innocent Passage

1. The relevant rules of international law governing innocent passage of ships in the territorial sea are stated in the 1982 United Nations Convention on the Law of the Sea (Convention of 1982), particularly in Part II, Section 3.

2. All ships, including warships, regardless of cargo, armament or means of propulsion, enjoy the right of innocent passage through the territorial sea in accordance with international law, for which neither prior notification nor authorization is required.

3. Article 19 of the Convention of 1982 sets out in paragraph 2 an exhaustive list of activities that would render passage not innocent. A ship passing through the territorial sea that does not engage in any of those activities is in innocent passage.

4. A coastal State which questions whether the particular passage of a ship through its territorial sea is innocent shall inform the ship of the reason why it questions the innocence of passage, and provide the ship an opportunity to clarify its intentions or correct its conduct in a reasonably short period of time.

5. Ships exercising the right of innocent passage shall comply with all laws and regulations of the coastal State adopted in conformity with relevant rules of international law as reflected in Articles 21, 22, 23, and 25 of the Convention of 1982. These include the laws and regulations requiring ships exercising the right of innocent passage through its territorial sea to use such sea lanes and traffic separation schemes as it may prescribe where needed to protect safety of navigation. In areas where no such sea lanes

* Joint Statement with Attached Uniform Interpretation of Rules of International Law Governing Innocent Passage, U.S.S.R.-U.S., Sept. 23, 1989, 28 I.L.M. 1444, *available at* http://www.basicint.org/pubs/Research/04PSIapp.pdf.

or traffic separation schemes have been prescribed, ships nevertheless enjoy the right of innocent passage.

6. Such laws and regulations of the coastal State may not have the practical effect of denying or impairing the exercise of the right of innocent passage as set forth in Article 24 of the Convention of 1982.

7. If a warship engages in conduct which violates such laws or regulations or renders its passage not innocent and does not take corrective action upon request, the coastal State may require it to leave the territorial sea, as set forth in Article 30 of the Convention of 1982. In such case the warship shall do so immediately.

8. Without prejudice to the exercise of the rights of coastal and flag States, all differences which may arise regarding a particular case of passage of ships through the territorial sea shall be settled through diplomatic channels or other agreed means.

1. Special Claims

INTERDICTION OF THE DELIVERY OF OFFENSIVE WEAPONS TO CUBA PRESIDENTIAL PROCLAMATION 3504, OCTOBER 23, 1962*

NOW, THEREFORE, I, JOHN F. KENNEDY, President of the United States of America, acting under and by virtue of the authority conferred upon me by the Constitution and statutes of the United States, in accordance with the aforementioned resolutions of the United States Congress and of the Organ of Consultation of the American Republics, and to defend the security of the United States, do hereby proclaim that the forces under my command are ordered, beginning at 2:00 P.M. Greenwich time October 24, 1962, to interdict, subject to the instructions herein contained, the delivery of offensive weapons and associated material to Cuba.

For the purposes of this Proclamation, the following are declared to be prohibited material:

Surface-to-surface missiles; bomber aircraft; bombs, air-to-surface rockets and guided missiles; warheads for any of the above weapons; mechanical or electronic equipment to support or operate the above items; and any other classes of material hereafter designed by the Secretary of Defense for the purpose of effectuating this Proclamation.

To enforce this order, the Secretary of Defense shall take appropriate measures to prevent the delivery of prohibited material to Cuba, employing the land, sea, and air forces of the United States in cooperation with any forces that may be made available by other American States.

....

Any vessel or craft which may be proceeding toward Cuba may be intercepted and may be directed to identify itself, its cargo, equipment and stores and its ports of call, to stop, to lie to, to submit to visit and search, or to proceed as directed. Any vessel or craft which fails or refuses to respond to or comply with directions shall be subject to being taken into custody. Any vessel or craft which it is believed is en route to Cuba and may be carrying prohibited material or may itself constitute such material shall, wherever possible, be directed to proceed to another destination of its own choice and shall be taken into custody shall be sent into a port of the United States for appropriate disposition.

In carrying out this order, force shall not be used except in case of failure or refusal to comply with directions, or with regulations or directives of the Secretary of Defense issued hereunder, after reasonable efforts have been made to communicate them to the vessel or craft, or in case of self-defense. In any case, force shall be used only to the extent necessary.

* 3 C.F.R. 232, at 233–34 (1959–63 Comp.); 77 Stat. 958.

DECLARATION OF A MARITIME EXCLUSION ZONE*

From 0400 Greenwich Mean Time on Monday April 12, 1982, a maritime exclusion zone will be established around the Falkland Islands. The outer limits of this zone is a circle of 200 nautical mile radius from [point described by latitude and longitude coordinates], which is approximately the center of the Falkland Islands.

From the time indicated, any Argentine warships and Argentine naval auxiliaries found within this zone will be treated as hostile and are liable to be attacked by British forces.

This measure is without prejudice to the right of the United Kingdom to take whatever additional measures may be needed in exercise of its right of self-defense under Article 51 of the United Nations Charter.

DECLARATION OF A TOTAL EXCLUSION ZONE†

From 11 a.m. GMT on April 30, 1982, a Total Exclusion Zone (TEZ) will be established around the Falkland Islands. The Outer limit of this zone will be the same as for the MEZ established on April 12....

From the time indicated the exclusion zone will apply not only to Argentine warships and naval auxiliaries but also to any other ship, whether naval or merchant vessel, which is operating in support of the illegal occupation of the Falkland Islands by Argentine forces.

* *Parliament April 7, 1982*, TIMES (London), Apr. 8, 1982, at 6, col. 8.

† Henry Stanhope, *Task Force Puts on the Pressure*, TIMES (London), Apr. 29, 1982, at 1.

B. National Security and Human Rights

UNIVERSAL DECLARATION OF HUMAN RIGHTS*

Preamble

Whereas recognition of the inherent dignity and of the equal and inalienable rights of all members of the human family is the foundation of freedom, justice and peace in the world,

Whereas disregard and contempt for human rights have resulted in barbarous acts which have outraged the conscience of mankind, and the advent of a world in which human beings shall enjoy freedom of speech and belief and freedom from fear and want has been proclaimed as the highest aspiration of the common people,

Whereas it is essential, if man is not to be compelled to have recourse, as a last resort, to rebellion against tyranny and oppression, that human rights should be protected by the rule of law,

Whereas it is essential to promote the development of friendly relations between nations,

Whereas the peoples of the United Nations have in the Charter reaffirmed their faith in fundamental human rights, in the dignity and worth of the human person and in the equal rights of men and women and have determined to promote social progress and better standards of life in larger freedom,

Whereas Member States have pledged themselves to achieve, in co-operation with the United Nations, the promotion of universal respect for and observance of human rights and fundamental freedoms,

Whereas a common understanding of these rights and freedoms is of the greatest importance for the full realization of this pledge,

Now, therefore,

The General Assembly

Proclaims this Universal Declaration of Human Rights as a common standard of achievement for all peoples and all nations, to the end that every individual and every organ of society, keeping this Declaration constantly in mind, shall strive by teaching and education to promote respect for these rights and freedoms and by progressive measures, national and international, to secure their universal and effective recognition and observance, both among the peoples of Member States themselves and among the peoples of territories under their jurisdiction.

Article 1. All human beings are born free and equal in dignity and rights. They are endowed with reason and conscience and should act towards one another in a spirit of brotherhood.

Article 2. Everyone is entitled to all the rights and freedoms set forth in this Declaration, without distinction of any kind, such as race, colour, sex, language, religion, political or other opinion, national or social origin, property, birth or other status.

---

* G.A. Res. 217A(III), U.N. Doc. A/810 at 71 (1948), *available at* http://www.unhchr.ch/udhr/index.htm.

Furthermore, no distinction shall be made on the basis of the political, jurisdictional or international status of the country or territory to which a person belongs, whether it be independent, trust, non-self-governing or under any other limitation of sovereignty.

Article 3. Everyone has the right to life, liberty and the security of person.

Article 4. No one shall be held in slavery or servitude; slavery and the slave trade shall be prohibited in all their forms.

Article 5. No one shall be subjected to torture or to cruel, inhuman or degrading treatment or punishment.

Article 6. Everyone has the right to recognition everywhere as a person before the law.

Article 7. All are equal before the law and are entitled without any discrimination to equal protection of the law. All are entitled to equal protection against any discrimination in violation of this Declaration and against any incitement to such discrimination.

Article 8. Everyone has the right to an effective remedy by the competent national tribunals for acts violating the fundamental rights granted him by the constitution or by law.

Article 9. No one shall be subjected to arbitrary arrest, detention or exile.

Article 10. Everyone is entitled in full equality to a fair and public hearing by an independent and impartial tribunal, in the determination of his rights and obligations and of any criminal charge against him.

Article 11. 1. Everyone charged with a penal offence has the right to be presumed innocent until proved guilty according to law in a public trial at which he has had all the guarantees necessary for his defence.

2. No one shall be held guilty of any penal offence on account of any act or omission which did not constitute a penal offence, under national or international law, at the time when it was committed. Nor shall a heavier penalty be imposed than the one that was applicable at the time the penal offence was committed.

Article 12. No one shall be subjected to arbitrary interference with his privacy, family, home or correspondence, nor to attacks upon his honour and reputation. Everyone has the right to the protection of the law against such interference or attacks.

Article 13. 1. Everyone has the right to freedom of movement and residence within the borders of each State.

2. Everyone has the right to leave any country, including his own, and to return to his country.

Article 14. 1. Everyone has the right to seek and to enjoy in other countries asylum from persecution.

2. This right may not be invoked in the case of prosecutions genuinely arising from nonpolitical crimes or from acts contrary to the purposes and principles of the United Nations.

Article 15. 1. Everyone has the right to a nationality.

2. No one shall be arbitrarily deprived of his nationality nor denied the right to change his nationality.

Article 16. 1. Men and women of full age, without any limitation due to race, nationality or religion, have the right to marry and to found a family. They are entitled to equal rights as to marriage, during marriage and at its dissolution.

2. Marriage shall be entered into only with the free and full consent of the intending spouses.

3. The family is the natural and fundamental group unit of society and is entitled to protection by society and the State.

Article 17. 1. Everyone has the right to own property alone as well as in association with others.

2. No one shall be arbitrarily deprived of his property.

Article 18. Everyone has the right to freedom of thought, conscience and religion; this right includes freedom to change his religion or belief, and freedom, either alone or in community with others and in public or private, to manifest his religion or belief in teaching, practice, worship and observance.

Article 19. Everyone has the right to freedom of opinion and expression; this right includes freedom to hold opinions without interference and to seek, receive and impart information and ideas through any media and regardless of frontiers.

Article 20. 1. Everyone has the right to freedom of peaceful assembly and association.

2. No one may be compelled to belong to an association.

Article 21. 1. Everyone has the right to take part in the government of his country, directly or through freely chosen representatives.

2. Everyone has the right of equal access to public service in his country.

3. The will of the people shall be the basis of the authority of government; this will shall be expressed in periodic and genuine elections which shall be by universal and equal suffrage and shall be held by secret vote or by equivalent free voting procedures.

Article 22. Everyone, as a member of society, has the right to social security and is entitled to realization, through national effort and international co-operation and in accordance with the organization and resources of each State, of the economic, social and cultural rights indispensable for his dignity and the free development of his personality.

Article 23. 1. Everyone has the right to work, to free choice of employment, to just and favourable conditions of work and to protection against unemployment.

2. Everyone, without any discrimination, has the right to equal pay for equal work.

3. Everyone who works has the right to just and favourable remuneration ensuring for himself and his family an existence worthy of human dignity, and supplemented, if necessary, by other means of social protection.

4. Everyone has the right to form and to join trade unions for the protection of his interests.

Article 24. Everyone has the right to rest and leisure, including reasonable limitation of working hours and periodic holidays with pay.

Article 25. 1. Everyone has the right to a standard of living adequate for the health and well-being of himself and of his family, including food, clothing, housing and medical care and necessary social services, and the right to security in the event of unemployment, sickness, disability, widowhood, old age or other lack of livelihood in circumstances beyond his control.

2. Motherhood and childhood are entitled to special care and assistance. All children, whether born in or out of wedlock, shall enjoy the same social protection.

Article 26. 1. Everyone has the right to education. Education shall be free, at least in the elementary and fundamental stages. Elementary education shall be compulsory. Technical and professional education shall be made generally available and higher education shall be equally accessible to all on the basis of merit.

2. Education shall be directed to the full development of the human personality and to the strengthening of respect for human rights and fundamental freedoms. It shall promote understanding, tolerance and friendship among all nations, racial or religious groups, and shall further the activities of the United Nations for the maintenance of peace.

3. Parents have a prior right to choose the kind of education that shall be given to their children.

Article 27. 1. Everyone has the right freely to participate in the cultural life of the community, to enjoy the arts and to share in scientific advancement and its benefits.

2. Everyone has the right to the protection of the moral and material interests resulting from any scientific, literary or artistic production of which he is the author.

Article 28. Everyone is entitled to a social and international order in which the rights and freedoms set forth in this Declaration can be fully realized.

Article 29. 1. Everyone has duties to the community in which alone the free and full development of his personality is possible.

2. In the exercise of his rights and freedoms, everyone shall be subject only to such limitations as are determined by law solely for the purpose of securing due recognition and respect for the rights and freedoms of others and of meeting the just requirements of morality, public order and the general welfare in a democratic society.

3. These rights and freedoms may in no case be exercised contrary to the purposes and principles of the United Nations.

Article 30. Nothing in this Declaration may be interpreted as implying for any State, group or person any right to engage in any activity or to perform any act aimed at the destruction of any of the rights and freedoms set forth herein.

Hundred and eighty-third plenary meeting,
10 December 1948.

CONVENTION ON THE PREVENTION AND PUNISHMENT OF THE CRIME OF GENOCIDE*

The General Assembly

Approves the annexed Convention on the Prevention and Punishment of the Crime of Genocide and proposes it for signature and ratification or accession in accordance with its article XI.

Hundred and seventy-ninth plenary meeting,
9 December 1948.

ANNEX

TEXT OF THE CONVENTION

The Contracting Parties,

Having considered the declaration made by the General Assembly of the United Nations in its resolution 96(I) dated 11 December 1946 that genocide is a crime under international law, contrary to the spirit and aims of the United Nations and condemned by the civilized world;

Recognizing that at all periods of history genocide has inflicted great losses on humanity; and

Being convinced that, in order to liberate mankind from such an odious scourge, international cooperation is required;

Hereby agree as hereinafter provided.

Article I. The Contracting Parties confirm that genocide, whether committed in time of peace or in time of war, is a crime under international law which they undertake to prevent and to punish.

Article II. In the present Convention, genocide means any of the following acts committed with intent to destroy, in whole or in part, a national, ethnical, racial or religious group, as such:

(a) Killing members of the group;

(b) Causing serious bodily or mental harm to members of the group ;

(c) Deliberately inflicting on the group conditions of life calculated to bring about its physical destruction in whole or in part;

(d) Imposing measures intended to prevent births within the group ;

(e) Forcibly transferring children of the group to another group.

Article III. The following acts shall be punishable:

(a) Genocide;

(b) Conspiracy to commit genocide;

(c) Direct and public incitement to commit genocide;

* Dec. 9, 1948, 78 U.N.T.S. 277 (entered into force on Jan. 12, 1957), *available at* http://www.un.org/documents/ga/res/3/ares3.htm.

(d) Attempt to commit genocide;

(e) Complicity in genocide.

Article IV. Persons committing genocide or any of the other acts enumerated in article III shall be punished, whether they are constitutionally responsible rulers, public officials or private individuals.

Article V. The Contracting Parties undertake to enact, in accordance with their respective Constitutions, the necessary legislation to give effect to the provisions of the present Convention and, in particular, to provide effective penalties for persons guilt of genocide or any of the other acts enumerate in article III.

Article VI. Persons charged with genocide or any of the other acts enumerated in article III shall be tried by a competent tribunal of the State in the territory of which the act was committed, or by such international penal tribunal as may have jurisdiction with respect to those Contracting Parties which shall have accepted its jurisdiction.

Article VII. Genocide and the other acts enumerated in article III shall not be considered as political crimes for the purpose of extradition.

The Contracting Parties pledge themselves in such cases to grant extradition in accordance with their laws and treaties in force.

Article VIII. Any Contracting Party may call upon the competent organs of the United Nations to take such action under the Charter of the United Nations as they consider appropriate for the prevention and suppression of acts of genocide or any of the other acts enumerated in article III.

....

EUROPEAN CONVENTION FOR THE PROTECTION OF HUMAN RIGHTS AND FUNDAMENTAL FREEDOMS OF NOVEMBER 4, 1950*

The Governments signatory hereto, being Members of the Council of Europe,

Considering the Universal Declaration of Human Rights proclaimed by the General Assembly of the United Nations on 10th December 1948;

Considering that this Declaration aims at securing the universal and effective recognition and observance of the Rights therein declared;

Considering that the aim of the Council of Europe is the achievement of greater unity between its Members and that one of the methods by which that aim is to be pursued is the maintenance and further realisation of Human Rights and Fundamental Freedoms;

Reaffirming their profound belief in those Fundamental Freedoms which are the foundation of justice and peace in the world and are best maintained on the one hand by an effective political democracy and on the other by a common understanding and observance of the Human Rights upon which they depend;

Being resolved, as the Governments of European countries which are likeminded and have a common heritage of political traditions, ideals, freedom and the rule of law, to take the first steps for the collective enforcement of certain of the Rights stated in the Universal Declaration;

Have agreed as follows:

Article 1. Obligation to respect human rights. The High Contracting Parties shall secure to everyone within their jurisdiction the rights and freedoms defined in Section 1 of this Convention.

SECTION I—RIGHTS AND FREEDOMS

Article 2. Right to life. 1. Everyone's right to life shall be protected by law. No one shall be deprived of his life intentionally save in the execution of a sentence of a court following his conviction of a crime for which this penalty is provided by law.

2. Deprivation of life shall not be regarded as inflicted in contravention of this Article when it results from the use of force which is no more than absolutely necessary:

(a) in defence of any person from unlawful violence;

(b) in order to effect a lawful arrest or to prevent the escape of a person lawfully detained;

(c) in action lawfully taken for the purpose of quelling a riot or insurrection.

Article 3. Prohibition of torture. No one shall be subjected to torture or to inhuman or degrading treatment or punishment.

---

* Europ. T.S. 5, *amended by* Protocol No. 11, May 11, 1994, Europ. T.S. 155 (the convention entered into force on Sept. 3, 1953; Protocol No. 11 entered into force on Nov. 1, 1998) (as of Sept. 13, 2005, there were 45 ratifications or accessions to the convention), *available at* http://conventions.coe.int/treaty/EN/cadreprincipal.htm.

Article 4. Prohibition of slavery and forced labour. 1. No one shall be held in slavery or servitude.

2. No one shall be required to perform forced or compulsory labour.

3. For the purpose of this Article the term "forced or compulsory labour" shall not include;

(a) any work required to be done in the ordinary course of detention imposed according to the provisions of Article 5 of this Convention or during conditional release from such detention;

(b) any service of a military character or, in case of conscientious objectors in countries where they are recognized, service exacted instead of compulsory military service;

(c) any service exacted in case of an emergency or calamity threatening the life or well-being of the community;

(d) any work or service which forms part of normal civic obligations.

Article 5. Right to liberty and security. 1. Everyone has the right to liberty and security of person. No one shall be deprived of his liberty save in the following cases and in accordance with a procedure prescribed by law:

(a) the lawful detention of a person after conviction by a competent court;

(b) the lawful arrest or detention;

(c) the lawful arrest or detention of a person effected for the purpose of bringing him before the competent legal authority on reasonable suspicion of having committed an offence or when it is reasonably considered necessary to prevent his committing an offence or fleeing after having done so;

(d) the detention of a minor by lawful order for the purpose of educational supervision or his lawful detention for the purpose of bringing him before the competent legal authority;

(e) the lawful detention of persons for the prevention of the spreading of infectious diseases, of persons of unsound mind, alcoholics, drug addicts or vagrants;

(f) the lawful arrest or detention of a person to prevent his effecting an unauthorized entry into the country or of a person against whom action is being taken with a view to deportation or extradition.

2. Everyone who is arrested shall be informed promptly, in a language which he understands, of the reasons for his arrest and of any charge against him.

3. Everyone arrested or detained in accordance with the provisions of paragraph 1(c) of this Article shall be brought promptly before a judge or other officer authorised by law to exercise judicial power and shall be entitled to trial within a reasonable time or to release pending trial. Release may be conditioned by guarantees to appear to trial.

4. Everyone who is deprived of his liberty by arrest or detention shall be entitled to take proceedings by which the lawfulness of his detention shall be decided speedily by a court and his release ordered if the detention is not lawful.

5. Everyone who has been the victim of arrest or detention in contravention of the provisions of this Article shall have an enforceable right to compensation.

Article 6. Right to a fair trial. 1. In the determination of his civil rights and obligations or of any criminal charge against him, everyone is entitled to a fair and public hearing within a reasonable time by an independent and impartial tribunal established by law. Judgment shall be pronounced publicly but the press and public may be excluded from all or part of the trial in the interests of morals, public order or national security in a democratic society, where the interests of juveniles or the protection of the private life of the parties so require, or to the extent strictly necessary in the opinion of the court in special circumstances where publicity would prejudice the interests of justice.

2. Everyone charged with a criminal offence shall be presumed innocent until proved guilty according to law.

3. Everyone charged with a criminal offence has the following minimum rights:

(a) to be informed promptly, in a language which he understands and in detail, of the nature and cause of the accusation against him;

(b) to have adequate time and facilities for the preparation of his defence;

(c) to defend himself in person or through legal assistance of his own choosing or, if he has not sufficient means to pay for legal assistance, to be given it free when the interests of justice so require;

(d) to examine or have examined witnesses against him and to obtain the attendance and examination of witnesses on his behalf under the same conditions as witnesses against him;

(e) to have the free assistance of an interpreter if he cannot understand or speak the language used in court.

Article 7. No punishment without law. 1. No one shall be held guilty of any criminal offence on account of any act or omission which did not constitute a criminal offence under national or international law at the time when it was committed. Nor shall a heavier penalty be imposed than the one that was applicable at the time the criminal offence was committed.

2. This Article shall not prejudice the trial and punishment of any person for any act or omission which, at the time when it was committed, was criminal according to the general principles of law recognized by civilised nations.

Article 8. Right to respect for private and family life. 1. Everyone has the right to respect for his private and family life, his home and his correspondence.

2. There shall be no interference by a public authority with the exercise of this right except such as is in accordance with the law and is necessary in a democratic society in the interests of national security, public safety or the economic well-being of the country, for the prevention of disorder or crime, for the protection of health or morals, or for the protection of the rights and freedoms of others.

Article 9. Freedom of thought, conscience and religion. 1. Everyone has the right to freedom of thought, conscience and religion; this right includes freedom to change his religion or belief and freedom, either alone or in community with others and in public or private, to manifest his religion or belief, in worship, teaching, practice and observance.

2. Freedom to manifest one's religion or beliefs shall be subject only to such limitations as are prescribed by law and are necessary in a democratic society in the interests of public safety, for the protection of public order, health or morals, or for the protection of the rights and freedoms of others.

Article 10. Freedom of expression. 1. Everyone has the right to freedom of expression. This right shall include freedom to hold opinions and to receive and impart information and ideas without interference by public authority and regardless of frontiers. This Article shall not prevent States from requiring the licensing of broadcasting, television or cinema enterprises.

2. The exercise of these freedoms, since it carries with it duties and responsibilities, may be subject to such formalities, conditions, restrictions or penalties as are prescribed by law and are necessary in a democratic society, in the interests of national security, territorial integrity or public safety, for the prevention of disorder or crime, for the protection of health or morals, for the protection of the reputation or rights of others, for preventing the disclosure of information received in confidence, or for maintaining the authority and impartiality of the judiciary.

Article 11. Freedom of assembly and association. 1. Everyone has the right to freedom of peaceful assembly and to freedom of association with others, including the right to form and to join trade unions for the protection of his interests.

2. No restrictions shall be placed on the exercise of these rights other than such as are prescribed by law and are necessary in a democratic society in the interests of national security or public safety, for the prevention of disorder or crime, for the protection of health or morals or for the protection of the rights and freedoms of others. This Article shall not prevent the imposition of lawful restrictions on the exercise of these rights by members of the armed forces, of the police or of the administration of the State.

Article 12. Right to marry. Men and women of marriageable age have the right to marry and to found a family, according to the national laws governing the exercise of this right.

Article 13. Right to an effective remedy. Everyone whose rights and freedoms as set forth in this Convention are violated shall have an effective remedy before a national authority notwithstanding that the violation has been committed by persons acting in an official capacity.

Article 14. Prohibition of discrimination. The enjoyment of the rights and freedoms set forth in this Convention shall be secured without discrimination on any ground such as sex, race, colour, language, religion, political or other opinion, national or social origin, association with a national minority, property, birth or other status.

Article 15. Derogation in time of emergency. 1. In time of war or other public emergency threatening the life of the nation any High Contracting Party may take measures derogating from its obligations under this Convention to the extent strictly required by the exigencies of the situation, provided that such measures are not inconsistent with its other obligations under international law.

2. No derogation from Article 2, except in respect of deaths resulting from lawful acts of war, or from Article 3, 4 (paragraph 1) and 7 shall be made under this provision.

3. Any High Contracting Party availing itself of this right of derogation shall keep the Secretary-General of the Council of Europe fully informed of the measures which it has taken and the reasons therefor. It shall also inform the Secretary-General of the Council of Europe when such measures have ceased to operate and the provisions of the Convention are again being fully executed.

Article 16. Restrictions on political activity of aliens. Nothing in Articles 10, 11 and 14 shall be regarded as preventing the High Contracting Parties from imposing restrictions on the political activity of aliens.

Article 17. Prohibition of abuse of rights. Nothing in this Convention may be interpreted as implying for any State, group or person any right to engage in any activity or perform any act aimed at the destruction of any of the rights and freedoms set forth herein or at their limitation to a greater extent than is provided for in the Convention.

Article 18. Limitation on use of restrictions on rights. The restrictions permitted under this Convention to the said rights and freedoms shall not be applied for any purpose other than those for which they have been prescribed.

....

U.S. SENATE ADVISE AND CONSENT OF THE GENOCIDE CONVENTION*

Resolved (two thirds of the Senators present and concurring therein), That the Senate advise and consent to the ratification of the International Convention on the Prevention and Punishment of the Crime of Genocide, adopted unanimously by the General Assembly of the United Nations in Paris on December 9, 1948 (Executive O, Eighty-first Congress, first session), *Provided that:*

I. The Senate's advise and consent is subject to the following reservations:

(1) That with reference to Article IX of the Convention, before any dispute to which the United States is a party may be submitted to the jurisdiction of the International Court of Justice under this article, the specific consent of the United States is required in each case.

(2) That nothing in the Convention requires or authorizes legislation or other action by the United States of America prohibited by the Constitution of the United States as interpreted by the United States.

II. The Senate's advise and consent is subject to the following understandings, which shall apply to the obligations of the United States under this Convention:

(1) That the term "intent to destroy, in whole or in part, a national, ethnical, racial, or religious group as such" appearing in Article II means the specific intent to destroy, in whole or substantial part, a national, ethnical, racial or religious group as such by the acts specified in Article II.

(2) That the term "mental harm" in Article II(b) means permanent impairment of mental faculties through drugs, torture or similar techniques.

(3) That the pledge to grant extradition in accordance with a state's laws and treaties in force found in Article VII extends only to acts which are criminal under laws of both the requesting and the requested state and nothing in Article VI affects the right of any state to bring to trial before its own tribunals any of its nationals for acts committed outside a state.

(4) That acts in the course of armed conflicts committed without the specific intent required by Article II are not sufficient to constitute genocide as defined by this Convention.

(5) That with regard to the reference to an international penal tribunal in Article VI of the Convention, the United States declares that it reserves the right to effect its participation in any such tribunal only by a treaty entered into specifically for that purpose with the advice and consent of the Senate.

III. The Senate's advice and consent is subject to the following declaration:

That the President will not deposit the instrument of ratification until after the implementing legislation referred to in Article V has been enacted.

* S. Exec. Rep. No. 99-2, at 26–27 (1985).

CONVENTION AGAINST TORTURE AND OTHER CRUEL, INHUMAN OR DEGRADING TREATMENT OR PUNISHMENT*

The States Parties to this Convention,

Considering that, in accordance with the principles proclaimed in the Charter of the United Nations, recognition of the equal and inalienable rights of all members of the human family is the foundation of freedom, justice and peace in the world,

Recognizing that those rights derive from the inherent dignity of the human person,

Considering the obligation of States under the Charter, in particular Article 55, to promote universal respect for, and observance of, human rights and fundamental freedoms,

Having regard to article 5 of the Universal Declaration of Human Rights and article 7 of the International Covenant on Civil and Political Rights, both of which provide that no one may be subjected to torture or to cruel, inhuman or degrading treatment or punishment,

Having regard also to the Declaration on the Protection of All Persons from Being Subjected to Torture and Other Cruel, Inhuman or Degrading Treatment or Punishment, adopted by the General Assembly on 9 December 1975 (resolution 3452 (XXX)),

Desiring to make more effective the struggle against torture and other cruel, inhuman or degrading treatment or punishment throughout the world,

Have agreed as follows:

Part I

Article 1. 1. For the purposes of this Convention, torture means any act by which severe pain or suffering, whether physical or mental, is intentionally inflicted on a person for such purposes as obtaining from him or a third person information or a confession, punishing him for an act he or a third person has committed or is suspected of having committed, or intimidating or coercing him or a third person, or for any reason based on discrimination of any kind, when such pain or suffering is inflicted by or at the instigation of or with the consent or acquiescence of a public official or other person acting in an official capacity. It does not include pain or suffering arising only from, inherent in or incidental to lawful sanctions.

2. This article is without prejudice to any international instrument or national legislation which does or may contain provisions of wider application.

Article 2. 1. Each State Party shall take effective legislative, administrative, judicial or other measures to prevent acts of torture in any territory under its jurisdiction.

2. No exceptional circumstances whatsoever, whether a state of war or a threat or war, internal political instability or any other public emergency, may be invoked as a justification of torture.

---

* Dec. 10, 1984, S. Treaty Doc. No. 100-20, at 19 (1988), 1465 U.N.T.S. 85 (entered into force on June 16, 1987), *available at* http://www.hrweb.org/legal/cat.html.

3. An order from a superior officer or a public authority may not be invoked as a justification of torture.

Article 3. 1. No State Party shall expel, return ("refouler") or extradite a person to another State where there are substantial grounds for believing that he would be in danger of being subjected to torture.

2. For the purpose of determining whether there are such grounds, the competent authorities shall take into account all relevant considerations including, where applicable, the existence in the State concerned of a consistent pattern of gross, flagrant or mass violations of human rights.

Article 4. 1. Each State Party shall ensure that all acts of torture are offences under its criminal law. The same shall apply to an attempt to commit torture and to an act by any person which constitutes complicity or participation in torture.

2. Each State Party shall make these offences punishable by appropriate penalties which take into account their grave nature.

Article 5. 1. Each State Party shall take such measures as may be necessary to establish its jurisdiction over the offences referred to in article 4 in the following cases:

(a) When the offences are committed in any territory under its jurisdiction or on board a ship or aircraft registered in that State;

(b) When the alleged offender is a national of that State;

(c) When the victim was a national of that State if that State considers it appropriate.

2. Each State Party shall likewise take such measures as may be necessary to establish its jurisdiction over such offences in cases where the alleged offender is present in any territory under its jurisdiction and it does not extradite him pursuant to article 8 to any of the States mentioned in Paragraph 1 of this article.

3. This Convention does not exclude any criminal jurisdiction exercised in accordance with internal law.

Article 6. 1. Upon being satisfied, after an examination of information available to it, that the circumstances so warrant, any State Party in whose territory a person alleged to have committed any offence referred to in article 4 is present, shall take him into custody or take other legal measures to ensure his presence. The custody and other legal measures shall be as provided in the law of that State but may be continued only for such time as is necessary to enable any criminal or extradition proceedings to be instituted.

2. Such State shall immediately make a preliminary inquiry into the facts.

3. Any person in custody pursuant to paragraph 1 of this article shall be assisted in communicating immediately with the nearest appropriate representative of the State of which he is a national, or, if he is a stateless person, to the representative of the State where he usually resides.

4. When a State, pursuant to this article, has taken a person into custody, it shall immediately notify the States referred to in article 5, paragraph 1, of the fact that such person is in custody and of the circumstances which warrant his detention. The State which makes the preliminary inquiry contemplated in paragraph 2 of this article shall promptly report its findings to the said State and shall indicate whether it intends to exercise jurisdiction.

Article 7. 1. The State Party in territory under whose jurisdiction a person alleged to have committed any offence referred to in article 4 is found, shall in the cases contemplated in article 5, if it does not extradite him, submit the case to its competent authorities for the purpose of prosecution.

2. These authorities shall take their decision in the same manner as in the case of any ordinary offence of a serious nature under the law of that State. In the cases referred to in article 5, paragraph 2, the standards of evidence required for prosecution and conviction shall in no way be less stringent than those which apply in the cases referred to in article 5, paragraph 1.

3. Any person regarding whom proceedings are brought in connection with any of the offences referred to in article 4 shall be guaranteed fair treatment at all stages of the proceedings.

Article 8. 1. The offences referred to in article 4 shall be deemed to be included as extraditable offences in any extradition treaty existing between States Parties. States Parties undertake to include such offences as extraditable offences in every extradition treaty to be concluded between them.

2. If a State Party which makes extradition conditional on the existence of a treaty receives a request for extradition from another State Party with which it has no extradition treaty, it may consider this Convention as the legal basis for extradition in respect of such offenses. Extradition shall be subject to the other conditions provided by the law of the requested State.

3. States Parties which do not make extradition conditional on the existence of a treaty shall recognize such offences as extraditable offences between themselves subject to the conditions provided by the law of the requested state.

4. Such offences shall be treated, for the purpose of extradition between States Parties, as if they had been committed not only in the place in which they occurred but also in the territories of the States required to establish their jurisdiction in accordance with article 5, paragraph 1.

Article 9. 1. States Parties shall afford one another the greatest measure of assistance in connection with civil proceedings brought in respect of any of the offences referred to in article 4, including the supply of all evidence at their disposal necessary for the proceedings.

2. States Parties shall carry out their obligations under paragraph 1 of this article in conformity with any treaties on mutual judicial assistance that may exist between them.

Article 10. 1. Each State Party shall ensure that education and information regarding the prohibition against torture are fully included in the training of law enforcement personnel, civil or military, medical personnel, public officials and other persons who may be involved in the custody, interrogation or treatment of any individual subjected to any form of arrest, detention or imprisonment.

2. Each State Party shall include this prohibition in the rules or instructions issued in regard to the duties and functions of any such persons.

Article 11. Each State Party shall keep under systematic review interrogation rules, instructions, methods and practices as well as arrangements for the custody and treatment of persons subjected to any form of arrest, detention or imprisonment in any territory under its jurisdiction, with a view to preventing any cases of torture.

Article 12. Each State Party shall ensure that its competent authorities proceed to a prompt and impartial investigation, wherever there is reasonable ground to believe that an act of torture has been committee in any territory under its jurisdiction.

Article 13. Each State Party shall ensure that any individual who alleges he has been subjected to torture in any territory under its jurisdiction has the right to complain to and to have his case promptly and impartially examined by its competent authorities. Steps shall be taken to ensure that the complainant and witnesses are protected against all ill-treatment or intimidation as a consequence of his complaint or any evidence given.

Article 14. 1. Each State Party shall ensure in its legal system that the victim of an act of torture obtains redress and has an enforceable right to fair and adequate compensation including the means for as full rehabilitation as possible. In the event of the death of the victim as a result of an act of torture, his dependents shall be entitled to compensation.

2. Nothing in this article shall affect any right of the victim or other person to compensation which may exist under national law.

Article 15. Each State Party shall ensure that any statement which is established to have been made as a result of torture shall not be invoked as evidence in any proceedings, except against a person accused of torture as evidence that the statement was made.

Article 16. 1. Each State Party shall undertake to prevent in any territory under its jurisdiction other acts of cruel, inhuman or degrading treatment or punishment which do not amount to torture as defined in article 1, when such acts are committed by or at the instigation of or with the consent or acquiescence of a public official or other person acting in an official capacity. In particular, the obligations contained in articles 10, 11, 12 and 13 shall apply with the substitution for references to torture or references to other forms of cruel, inhuman or degrading treatment or punishment.

2. The provisions of this Convention are without prejudice to the provisions of any other international instrument or national law which prohibit cruel, inhuman or degrading treatment or punishment or which relate to extradition or expulsion.

Part II

Article 17. 1. There shall be established a Committee against Torture (hereinafter referred to as the Committee) which shall carry out the functions hereinafter provided. The Committee shall consist of 10 experts of high moral standing and recognized competence in the field of human rights, who shall serve in their personal capacity. The experts shall be elected by the States Parties, consideration being given to equitable geographical distribution and to the usefulness of the participation of some persons having legal experience.

. . . .

Article 20. 1. If the Committee receives reliable information which appears to it to contain well-founded indications that torture is being systematically practised in the territory of a State Party, the Committee shall invite that State Party to co-operate in the examination of the information and to this end to submit observations with regard to the information concerned.

2. Taking into account any observations which may have been submitted by the State Party concerned as well as any other relevant information available to it, the Committee may, if it decides that this is warranted, designate one or more of its members to make a confidential inquiry and to report to the Committee urgently.

3. If an inquiry is made in accordance with paragraph 2, the Committee shall seek the co-operation of the State Party concerned. In agreement with that State Party, such an inquiry may include a visit to its territory.

4. After examining the findings of its member or members submitted in accordance with paragraph 2, the Committee shall transmit these findings to the State Party concerned together with any comments or suggestions which seem appropriate in view of the situation.

5. All the proceedings of the Committee referred to in paragraphs 1 to 4 of this article shall be confidential, and at all stages of the proceedings the co-operation of the State Party shall be sought. After such proceedings have been completed with regard to an inquiry made in accordance with paragraph 2, the Committee may, after consultations with the State Party concerned, decide to include a summary account of the results of the proceedings in its annual report made in accordance with article 24.

....

Part III

....

Article 29. 1. Any State Party to this Convention may propose an amendment and file it with the Secretary-General of the United Nations. The Secretary-General shall thereupon communicate the proposed amendment to the States Parties to this Convention with a request that they notify him whether they favour a conference of States Parties for the purpose of considering and voting upon the proposal. In the event that within four months from the date of such communication at least one third of the State Parties favours such a conference, the Secretary-General shall convene the conference under the auspices of the United Nations. Any amendment adopted by a majority of the States Parties present and voting at the conference shall be submitted by the Secretary-General to all the States Parties for acceptance.

2. An amendment adopted in accordance with paragraph 1 shall enter into force when two thirds of the States Parties to this Convention have notified the Secretary-General of the United Nations that they have accepted it in accordance with their respective constitutional processes.

3. When amendments enter into force, they shall be binding on those States Parties which have accepted them, other States Parties still being bound by the provisions of this Convention and any earlier amendments which they have accepted.

Article 30. 1. Any dispute between two or more States Parties concerning the interpretation or application of this Convention which cannot be settled through negotiation, shall, at the request of one of them, be submitted to arbitration. If within six months from the date of the request for arbitration the Parties are unable to agree on the organization of the arbitration, any one of those Parties may refer the dispute to the International Court of Justice by request in conformity with the Statute of the Court.

2. Each State may at the time of signature or ratification of this Convention or accession thereto, declare that it does not consider itself bound by the preceding paragraph. The other States Parties shall not be bound by the preceding paragraph with respect to any State Party having made such a reservation.

3. Any State Party having made a reservation in accordance with the preceding paragraph may at any time withdraw this reservation by notification to the Secretary-General of the United Nations.

Article 31. 1. A State Party may denounce this Convention by written notification to the Secretary-General of the United Nations. Denunciation becomes effective one year after the date of receipt of the notification by the Secretary-General.

2. Such a denunciation shall not have the effect of releasing the State Party from its obligations under this Convention in regard to any act or omission which occurs prior to the date at which the denunciation becomes effective. Nor shall denunciation prejudice in any way the continued consideration of any matter which is already under consideration by the Committee prior to the date at which the denunciation becomes effective.

3. Following the date at which the denunciation of a State Party becomes effective, the Committee shall not commence consideration of any new matter regarding that State.

. . . .

DOCUMENT OF THE COPENHAGEN MEETING OF THE CONFERENCE ON THE HUMAN DIMENSION OF CSCE*

The representatives of the participating States of the Conference on Security and Co-operation in Europe (CSCE), Austria, Belgium, Bulgaria, Canada, Cyprus, Czechoslovakia, Denmark, Finland, France, the German Democratic Republic, the Federal Republic of Germany, Greece, the Holy See, Hungary, Iceland, Ireland, Italy, Liechtenstein, Luxembourg, Malta, Monaco, the Netherlands, Norway, Poland, Portugal, Romania, San Marino, Spain, Sweden, Switzerland, Turkey, the Union of Soviet Socialist Republics, the United Kingdom, the United States of America and Yugoslavia, met in Copenhagen from 5 to 29 June 1990, in accordance with the provisions relating to the Conference on the Human Dimension of the CSCE contained in the Concluding Document of the Vienna Follow-up Meeting of the CSCE.

....

At a special meeting of the Ministers for Foreign Affairs of the participating States of the CSCE on 5 June 1990, convened on the invitation of the Minister for Foreign Affairs of Denmark, it was agreed to convene a Preparatory Committee in Vienna on 10 July 1990 to prepare a Summit Meeting in Paris of their Heads of State or Government.

The participating States welcome with great satisfaction the fundamental political changes that have occurred in Europe since the first Meeting of the Conference on the Human Dimension of the CSCE in Paris in 1989. They note that the CSCE process has contributed significantly to bringing about these changes and that these developments in turn have greatly advanced the implementation of the provisions of the Final Act and of the other CSCE documents.

They recognize that pluralistic democracy and the rule of law are essential for ensuring respect for all human rights and fundamental freedoms, the development of human contacts and the resolution of other issues of a related humanitarian character. They therefore welcome the commitment expressed by all participating States to the ideals of democracy and political pluralism as well as their common determination to build democratic societies based on free elections and the rule of law.

At the Copenhagen Meeting the participating States held a review of the implementation of their commitments in the field of the human dimension. They considered that the degree of compliance with the commitments contained in the relevant provisions of the CSCE documents had shown a fundamental improvement since the Paris Meeting. They also expressed the view, however, that further steps are required for the full realization of their commitments relating to the human dimension.

The participating States express their conviction that full respect for human rights and fundamental freedoms and the development of societies based on pluralistic democracy and the rule of law are prerequisites for progress in setting up the lasting order of peace, security, justice and co-operation that they seek to establish in Europe. They therefore reaffirm their commitment to implement fully all provisions of the Final

---

* 29 I.L.M. 1305 (1990), *available at* http://www.osce.org/documents/odihr/1990/06/13992_en.pdf.

Act and of the other CSCE documents relating to the human dimension and undertake to build on the progress they have made.

They recognize that co-operation among themselves, as well as the active involvement of persons, groups, organizations and institutions, will be essential to ensure continuing progress towards their shared objectives.

In order to strengthen respect for, and enjoyment of, human rights and fundamental freedoms, to develop human contacts and to resolve issues of a related humanitarian character, the participating States agree on the following:

I

(1) The participating States express their conviction that the protection and promotion of human rights and fundamental freedoms is one of the basic purposes of government, and reaffirm that the recognition of these rights and freedoms constitutes the foundation of freedom, justice and peace.

(2) They are determined to support and advance those principles of justice which form the basis of the rule of law. They consider that the rule of law does not mean merely a formal legality which assures regularity and consistency in the achievement and enforcement of democratic order, but justice based on the recognition and full acceptance of the supreme value of the human personality and guaranteed by institutions providing a framework for its fullest expression.

(3) They reaffirm that democracy is an inherent element of the rule of law. They recognize the importance of pluralism with regard to political organizations.

(4) They confirm that they will respect each other's right freely to choose and develop, in accordance with international human rights standards, their political, social, economic and cultural systems. In exercising this right, they will ensure that their laws, regulations, practices and policies conform with their obligations under international law and are brought into harmony with the provisions of the Declaration on Principles and other CSCE commitments.

(5) They solemnly declare that among those elements of justice which are essential to the full expression of the inherent dignity and of the equal and inalienable rights of all human beings are the following:

(5.1) - free elections that will be held at reasonable intervals by secret ballot or by equivalent free voting procedure, under conditions which ensure in practice the free expression of the opinion of the electors in the choice of their representatives;

(5.2) - a form of government that is representative in character, in which the executive is accountable to the elected legislature or the electorate;

(5.3) - the duty of the government and public authorities to comply with the constitution and to act in a manner consistent with law;

(5.4) - a clear separation between the State and political parties; in particular, political parties will not be merged with the State;

(5.5) - the activity of the government and the administration as well as that of the judiciary will be exercised in accordance with the system established by law. Respect for that system must be ensured;

(5.6) - military forces and the police will be under the control of, and accountable to, the civil authorities;

(5.7) - human rights and fundamental freedoms will be guaranteed by law and in accordance with their obligations under international law;

(5.8) - legislation, adopted at the end of a public procedure, and regulations will be published, that being the condition for their applicability. Those texts will be accessible to everyone;

(5.9) - all persons are equal before the law and are entitled without any discrimination to the equal protection of the law. In this respect, the law will prohibit any discrimination and guarantee to all persons equal and effective protection against discrimination on any ground;

(5.10) - everyone will have an effective means of redress against administrative decisions, so as to guarantee respect for fundamental rights and ensure legal integrity;

(5.11) - administrative decisions against a person must be fully justifiable and must as a rule indicate the usual remedies available;

(5.12) - the independence of judges and the impartial operation of the public judicial service will be ensured;

(5.13) - the independence of legal practitioners will be recognized and protected, in particular as regards conditions for recruitment and practice;

(5.14) - the rules relating to criminal procedure will contain a clear definition of powers in relation to prosecution and the measures preceding and accompanying prosecution;

(5.15) - any person arrested or detained on a criminal charge will have the right, so that the lawfulness of his arrest or detention can be decided, to be brought promptly before a judge or other officer authorized by law to exercise this function;

(5.16) - in the determination of any criminal charge against him, or of his rights and obligations in a suit at law, everyone will be entitled to a fair and public hearing by a competent, independent and impartial tribunal established by law;

(5.17) - any person prosecuted will have the right to defend himself in person or through prompt legal assistance of his own choosing or, if he does not have sufficient means to pay for legal assistance, to be given it free when the interests of justice so require;

(5.18) - no one will be charged with, tried for or convicted of any criminal offence unless the offence is provided for by a law which defines the elements of the offence with clarity and precision;

(5.19) - everyone will be presumed innocent until proved guilty according to law;

(5.20) - considering the important contribution of international instruments in the field of human rights to the rule of law at a national level, the participating States reaffirm that they will consider acceding to the International Covenant on Civil and Political Rights, the International Covenant on Economic, Social and Cultural Rights and other relevant international instruments, if they have not yet done so;

(5.21) - in order to supplement domestic remedies and better to ensure that the participating States respect the international obligations they have undertaken, the participating States will consider acceding to a regional or global international convention concerning the protection of human rights, such as the European Convention on Human Rights or the Optional Protocol to the International Covenant on Civil and Political Rights, which provide for procedures of individual recourse to international bodies.

(6) The participating States declare that the will of the people, freely and fairly expressed through periodic and genuine elections, is the basis of the authority and legitimacy of all government. The participating States will accordingly respect the right of

their citizens to take part in the governing of their country, either directly or through representatives freely chosen by them through fair electoral processes. They recognize their responsibility to defend and protect, in accordance with their laws, their international human rights obligations and their international commitments, the democratic order freely established through the will of the people against the activities of persons, groups or organizations that engage in or refuse to renounce terrorism or violence aimed at the overthrow of that order or of that of another participating State.

(7) To ensure that the will of the people serves as the basis of the authority of government, the participating States will

(7.1) - hold free elections at reasonable intervals, as established by law;

(7.2) - permit all seats in at least one chamber of the national legislature to be freely contested in a popular vote;

(7.3) - guarantee universal and equal suffrage to adult citizens;

(7.4) - ensure that votes are cast by secret ballot or by equivalent free voting procedure, and that they are counted and reported honestly with the official results made public;

(7.5) - respect the right of citizens to seek political or public office, individually or as representatives of political parties or organizations, without discrimination;

(7.6) - respect the right of individuals and groups to establish, in full freedom, their own political parties or other political organizations and provide such political parties and organizations with the necessary legal guarantees to enable them to compete with each other on a basis of equal treatment before the law and by the authorities;

(7.7) - ensure that law and public policy work to permit political campaigning to be conducted in a fair and free atmosphere in which neither administrative action, violence nor intimidation bars the parties and the candidates from freely presenting their views and qualifications, or prevents the voters from learning and discussing them or from casting their vote free of fear of retribution;

(7.8) - provide that no legal or administrative obstacle stands in the way of unimpeded access to the media on a non-discriminatory basis for all political groupings and individuals wishing to participate in the electoral process;

(7.9) - ensure that candidates who obtain the necessary number of votes required by law are duly installed in office and are permitted to remain in office until their term expires or is otherwise brought to an end in a manner that is regulated by law in conformity with democratic parliamentary and constitutional procedures.

(8) The participating States consider that the presence of observers, both foreign and domestic, can enhance the electoral process for States in which elections are taking place. They therefore invite observers from any other CSCE participating States and any appropriate private institutions and organizations who may wish to do so to observe the course of their national election proceedings, to the extent permitted by law. They will also endeavour to facilitate similar access for election proceedings held below the national level. Such observers will undertake not to interfere in the electoral proceedings.

II

(9) The participating States reaffirm that:

(9.1) - everyone will have the right to freedom of expression including the right to communication. This right will include freedom to hold opinions and to receive and impart information and ideas without interference by public authority and regardless of frontiers. The exercise of this right may be subject only to such restrictions as are prescribed by law and are consistent with international standards. In particular, no limitation will be imposed on access to, and use of, means of reproducing documents of any kind, while respecting, however, rights relating to intellectual property, including copyright;

(9.2) - everyone will have the right of peaceful assembly and demonstration. Any restrictions which may be placed on the exercise of these rights will be prescribed by law and consistent with international standards;

(9.3) - the right of association will be guaranteed. The right to form and - subject to the general right of a trade union to determine its own membership - freely to join a trade union will be guaranteed. These rights will exclude any prior control. Freedom of association for workers, including the freedom to strike, will be guaranteed, subject to limitations prescribed by law and consistent with international standards;

(9.4) - everyone will have the right to freedom of thought, conscience and religion. This right includes freedom to change one's religion or belief and freedom to manifest one's religion or belief, either alone or in community with others, in public or in private, through worship, teaching, practice and observance. The exercise of these rights may be subject only to such restrictions as are prescribed by law and are consistent with international standards;

(9.5) - they will respect the right of everyone to leave any country, including his own, and to return to his country, consistent with a State's international obligations and CSCE commitments. Restrictions on this right will have the character of very rare exceptions, will be considered necessary only if they respond to a specific public need, pursue a legitimate aim and are proportionate to that aim, and will not be abused or applied in an arbitrary manner;

(9.6) - everyone has the right peacefully to enjoy his property either on his own or in common with others. No one may be deprived of his property except in the public interest and subject to the conditions provided for by law and consistent with international commitments and obligations.

(10) In reaffirming their commitment to ensure effectively the rights of the individual to know and act upon human rights and fundamental freedoms, and to contribute actively, individually or in association with others, to their promotion and protection, the participating States express their commitment to:

(10.1) - respect the right of everyone, individually or in association with others, to seek, receive and impart freely views and information on human rights and fundamental freedoms, including the rights to disseminate and publish such views and information;

(10.2) - respect the rights of everyone, individually or in association with others, to study and discuss the observance of human rights and fundamental freedoms and to develop and discuss ideas for improved protection of human rights and better means for ensuring compliance with international human rights standards;

(10.3) - ensure that individuals are permitted to exercise the right to association, including the right to form, join and participate effectively in non-governmental organizations which seek the promotion and protection of human rights and fundamental freedoms, including trade unions and human rights monitoring groups;

(10.4) - allow members of such groups and organizations to have unhindered access to and communication with similar bodies within and outside their countries and with international organizations, to engage in exchanges, contacts and co-operation with such groups and organizations and to solicit, receive and utilize for the purpose of promoting and protecting human rights and fundamental freedoms voluntary financial contributions from national and international sources as provided for by law.

(11) The participating States further affirm that, where violations of human rights and fundamental freedoms are alleged to have occurred, the effective remedies available include:

(11.1) - the right of the individual to seek and receive adequate legal assistance;

(11.2) - the right of the individual to seek and receive assistance from others in defending human rights and fundamental freedoms, and to assist others in defending human rights and fundamental freedoms;

(11.3) - the right of individuals or groups acting on their behalf to communicate with international bodies with competence to receive and consider information concerning allegations of human rights abuses.

....

III

(26) The participating States recognize that vigorous democracy depends on the existence as an integral part of national life of democratic values and practices as well as an extensive range of democratic institutions. They will therefore encourage, facilitate and, where appropriate, support practical co-operative endeavours and the sharing of information, ideas and expertise among themselves and by direct contacts and co-operation between individuals, groups and organizations in areas including the following:

— constitutional law, reform and development,

— electoral legislation, administration and observation,

— establishment and management of courts and legal systems,

— the development of an impartial and effective public service where recruitment and advancement are based on a merit system,

— law enforcement,

— local government and decentralization,

— access to information and protection of privacy,

— developing political parties and their role in pluralistic societies,

— free and independent trade unions,

— co-operative movements,

— developing other forms of free associations and public interest groups

— journalism, independent media, and intellectual and cultural life

— the teaching of democratic values, institutions and practices in educational institutions and the fostering of an atmosphere of free enquiry.

Such endeavours may cover the range of co-operation encompassed in the human dimension of the CSCE, including training, exchange of information, books and instructional materials, co-operative programmes and projects, academic and professional exchanges and conferences, scholarships, research grants, provision of expertise and advice, business and scientific contacts and programmes.

(27) The participating States will also facilitate the establishment and strengthening of independent national institutions in the area of human rights and the rule of law, which may also serve as focal points for co-ordination and collaboration between such institutions in the participating States. They propose that co-operation be encouraged between parliamentarians from participating States, including through existing inter-parliamentary associations and, *inter alia,* through joint commissions, television debates involving parliamentarians, meetings and round-table discussions. They will also encourage existing institutions, such as organizations within the United Nations system and the Council of Europe, to continue and expand the work they have begun in this area.

....

IV

(30) The participating States recognize that the questions relating to national minorities can only be satisfactorily resolved in a democratic political framework based on the rule of law, with a functioning independent judiciary. This framework guarantees full respect for human rights and fundamental freedoms, equal rights and status for all citizens, the free expression of all their legitimate interests and aspirations, political pluralism, social tolerance and the implementation of legal rules that place effective restraints on the abuse of governmental power.

They also recognize the important role of non-governmental organizations, including political parties, trade unions, human rights organizations and religious groups, in the promotion of tolerance, cultural diversity and the resolution of questions relating to national minorities.

They further reaffirm that respect for the rights of persons belonging to national minorities as part of universally recognized human rights is an essential factor for peace, justice, stability and democracy in the participating States.

(31) Persons belonging to national minorities have the right to exercise fully and effectively their human rights and fundamental freedoms without any discrimination and in full equality before the law.

The participating States will adopt, where necessary, special measures for the purpose of ensuring to persons belonging to national minorities full equality with the other citizens in the exercise and enjoyment of human rights and fundamental freedoms.

(32) To belong to a national minority is a matter of a person's individual choice and no disadvantage may arise from the exercise of such choice.

Persons belonging to national minorities have the right freely to express, preserve and develop their ethnic, cultural, linguistic or religious identity and to maintain and develop their culture in all its aspects, free of any attempts at assimilation against their will. In particular, they have the right

(32.1) - to use freely their mother tongue in private as well as in public;

(32.2) - to establish and maintain their own educational, cultural and religious institutions, organizations or associations, which can see voluntary financial and other contributions as well as public assistance, in conformity with national legislation;

(32.3) - to profess and practise their religion, including the acquisition, possession and use of religious materials, and to conduct religious educational activities in their mother tongue;

(32.4) - to establish and maintain unimpeded contacts among themselves within their country as well as contacts across frontiers with citizens of other States with whom they share a common ethnic or national origin, cultural heritage or religious beliefs;

(32.5) - to disseminate, have access to and exchange information in their mother tongue;

(32.6) - to establish and maintain organizations or associations within their country and to participate in international non-governmental organizations.

Persons belonging to national minorities can exercise and enjoy their rights individually as well as in community with other members of their group. No disadvantage may arise for a person belonging to a national minority on account of the exercise or non-exercise of any such rights.

(33) The participating States will protect the ethnic, cultural, linguistic and religious identity of national minorities on their territory and create conditions for the promotion of that identity. They will take the necessary measures to that effect after due consultations, including contacts with organizations or associations of such minorities, in accordance with the decision-making procedures of each State.

Any such measures will be in conformity with the principles of equality and non-discrimination with respect to the other citizens of the participating State concerned.

(34) The participating States will endeavour to ensure that persons belonging to national minorities, notwithstanding the need to learn the official language or languages of the State concerned, have adequate opportunities for instruction of their mother tongue or in their mother tongue, as well as, wherever possible and necessary, for its use before public authorities, in conformity with applicable national legislation.

In the context of the teaching of history and culture in educational establishments, they will also take account of the history and culture of national minorities.

(35) The participating States will respect the right of persons belonging to national minorities to effective participation in public affairs, including participation in the affairs relating to the protection and promotion of the identity of such minorities.

The participating States note the efforts undertaken to protect and create conditions for the promotion of the ethnic, cultural, linguistic and religious identity of certain national minorities by establishing, as one of the possible means to achieve these aims, appropriate local or autonomous administrations corresponding to the specific historical and territorial circumstances of such minorities and in accordance with the policies of the State concerned.

(36) The participating States recognize the particular importance of increasing constructive co-operation among themselves on questions relating to national minorities. Such co-operation seeks to promote mutual understanding and confidence, friendly and good-neighbourly relations, international peace, security and justice.

Every participating State will promote a climate of mutual respect, understanding, co-operation and solidarity among all persons living on its territory, without distinction as to ethnic or national origin or religion, and will encourage the solution of problems through dialogue based on the principles of the rule of law.

(37) None of these commitments may be interpreted as implying any right to engage in any activity or perform any action in contravention of the purposes and principles of the Charter of the United Nations, other obligations under international law or the provisions of the Final Act, including the principle of territorial integrity of States.

(38) The participating States, in their efforts to protect and promote the rights of persons belonging to national minorities, will fully respect their undertakings under existing human rights conventions and other relevant international instruments and consider adhering to the relevant conventions, if they have not yet done so, including those providing for a right of complaint by individuals.

(39) The participating States will co-operate closely in the competent international organizations to which they belong, including the United Nations and, as appropriate, the Council of Europe, bearing in mind their on-going work with respect to questions relating to national minorities.

They will consider convening a meeting of experts for a thorough discussion of the issue of national minorities.

(40) The participating States clearly and unequivocally condemn totalitarianism, racial and ethnic hatred, anti-semitism, xenophobia and discrimination against anyone as well as persecution on religious and ideological grounds. In this context, they also recognize the particular problems of Roma (gypsies).

....

TORTURE VICTIM PROTECTION ACT OF 1991*

An Act

To carry out obligations of the United States under the United nations Charter and other international agreements pertaining to the protection of human rights by establishing a civil action for recovery of damages from an individual who engages in torture or extrajudicial killing.

....

Sec. 2. Establishment of Civil Action

(a) Liability.—An individual who, under actual or apparent authority, or color of law, of any foreign nation—

(1) subjects an individual to torture shall, in a civil action, be liable for damages to that individual; or

(2) subjects an individual to extrajudicial killing shall, in a civil action, be liable for damages to the individual's legal representative, or to any person who may be a claimant in an action for wrongful death.

(b) Exhaustion of Remedies.—A court shall decline to hear a claim under this section if the claimant has not exhausted adequate and available remedies in the place in which the conduct giving rise to the claim occurred.

(c) Statute of Limitations.—No action shall be maintained under this section unless it is commenced within 10 years after the cause of action arose.

Sec. 3. Definitions

(a) Extrajudicial Killing.—For the purposes of this Act, the term "extrajudicial killing" means a deliberated killing not authorized by a previous judgment pronounced by a regularly constituted court affording all the judicial guarantees which are recognized as indispensable by civilized peoples. Such term, however, does not include any such killing that, under international law, is lawfully carried out under the authority of a foreign nation.

(b) Torture.—For the purposes of this Act—

(1) the term "torture" means any act, directed against an individual in the offender's custody or physical control, by which severe pain or suffering (other than pain or suffering arising from or inherent or incidental to, lawful sanctions), whether physical or mental, is intentionally inflicted on that individual for such purposes as obtaining that individual or a third person information or confession, punish that individual for an act that individual or third person has committed or is suspected of having committed, intimidating or coercing that individual or third person, or for any reason based on discrimination of any kind; and

(2) mental pain or suffering refers to prolonged mental harm caused by or resulting from—

(A) the intentional infliction or threatened infliction of severe physical pain or suffering;

---

* Pub. L. No. 102-256, 106 Stat. 73 (1992), *available at* http://thomas.loc.gov/cgi-bin/query/z?c102:H.R.2092.ENR.

(B) the administration or application, or threatened administration or application, of mind altering substances or other procedures calculated to disrupt profoundly the senses or the personality;

(C) the threat of imminent death; or

(D) the threat that another individual will imminently be subject to death, severe physical pain or suffering, or the administration or application of mind altering substances or other procedures calculated to disrupt profoundly the senses or personality.

FINAL WARSAW DECLARATION: TOWARD A COMMUNITY OF DEMOCRACIES[1]

Note

Origin of the Community of Democracies

By the late 1990s, the evidence supporting superior performance of democracies across a crucial spectrum of goals, from war avoidance to human rights and economic development was clear. Yet programmatic efforts by democratic governments to encourage development of democracy and the rule of law were rudimentary and uncoordinated. When John Norton Moore raised the need at a Freedom House Board meeting for more effective governmental efforts at democracy building he was asked by the then-Chairman of Freedom House, Ambassador Max Kampelman, to prepare a programmatic initiative that Freedom House might then support. The result was a proposal prepared by Ambassador John Norton Moore, Ambassador Mark Palmer and The Honorable Peter W. Rodman entitled "The Community of Democracies." This proposal called for a United States initiative to "mobilize a shared effort among the world's democracies to promote democratic values and institutions."[2] The proposal also called for a caucus of democratic member states at the United Nations. Subsequent efforts by Freedom House to promote this approach led to a United States initiative in 1999 to create a "Community of Democracies." A convening group, led by the governments of Chile, India, Poland, the Czech Republic, the United States, Mali, Mexico, Portugal, South Africa and South Korea, then took the initiative in formation of the new Community of Democracies.

The first ministerial meeting of what became the new Community was held in Warsaw, Poland, in 2000. More than 100 countries participated. A declaration that emerged on June 27, 2000, called for democracy and the rule of law and for creation of "A Community of Democracies." A second meeting was held in Seoul, South Korea, in November 2002. At the Seoul meeting ninety-five participating governments agreed on a "Plan of Action" for promotion of democracy. Subsequently, pursuant to this initiative, as had been a feature of the first draft proposal, a democratic nation caucusing group was set up at the United Nations. A third meeting of the Community of Democracies was held in Santiago, Chile, April 28–30, 2005.

The Community of Democracies has emerged as one of the most important international institutions for the promotion of democracy, human rights, the rule of law and human freedom. It seems destined to continue to become more influential through time. It recently has been described by Secretary of State Condoleezza Rice as a forum to discuss "the responsibilities and the opportunities of democratic governance."—Eds.

---

1. June 27, 2000, (signed in Warsaw, Poland), *available at* http://www.state.gov/g/drl/rls/26811.htm.

2. John Norton Moore, Mark Palmer & Peter W. Rodman, "The Community of Democracies" (a preliminary concept paper prepared for Freedom House, January 1997). A first draft prepared by John Norton Moore was entitled "Partnership for Democracy." *See* John Norton Moore & Mark Palmer, "Partnership for Democracy" (a preliminary concept paper prepared for Freedom House, September 19, 1996).

Warsaw, Poland, June 27, 2000

We the participants from:

Republic of Albania, People's Democratic Republic of Algeria, Argentine Republic, Republic of Armenia, Australia, Republic of Austria, Azerbaijani Republic, People's Republic of Bangladesh, Kingdom of Belgium, Belize, Republic of Benin, Republic of Bolivia, Bosnia and Herzegovina, Republic of Botswana, Federative Republic of Brazil, Republic of Bulgaria, Burkina Faso, Canada, Republic of Cape Verde, Republic of Chile, Republic of Colombia, Republic of Costa Rica, Republic of Croatia, Republic of Cyprus, Czech Republic, Kingdom of Denmark, Commonwealth of Dominica, Dominican Republic, Republic of Ecuador, Arab Republic of Egypt, Republic of El Salvador, Republic of Estonia, Republic of Finland, Georgia, Federal Republic of Germany, Republic of Guatemala, Republic of Haiti, Hellenic Republic, Republic of Hungary, Republic of Iceland, Republic of India, Republic of Indonesia, Ireland, State of Israel, Italian Republic, Japan, Hashemite Kingdom of Jordan, Republic of Kenya, Republic of Korea, State of Kuwait, Republic of Latvia, Kingdom of Lesotho, Principality of Liechtenstein, Republic of Lithuania, Grand Duchy of Luxembourg, former Yugoslav Republic of Macedonia, Republic of Madagascar, Republic of Malawi, Republic of Mali, Republic of Malta, Republic of Mauritius, Mexico, Republic of Moldova, Principality of Monaco, Mongolia, Kingdom of Morocco, Republic of Mozambique, Republic of Namibia, Kingdom of Nepal, Kingdom of the Netherlands, New Zealand, Republic of Nicaragua, Republic of the Niger, Federal Republic of Nigeria, Kingdom of Norway, Republic of Panama, Papua New Guinea, Republic of Paraguay, Republic of Peru, Republic of the Philippines, Republic of Poland, Portuguese Republic, State of Qatar, Romania, Russian Federation, Saint Lucia, Democratic Republic of Sao Tome and Principe, Republic of Senegal, Republic of Seychelles, Slovak Republic, Republic of Slovenia, Republic of South Africa, Kingdom of Spain, Democratic Socialist Republic of Sri Lanka, Kingdom of Sweden, Swiss Confederation, United Republic of Tanzania, Kingdom of Thailand, Republic of Tunisia, Republic of Turkey, Ukraine, United Kingdom of Great Britain and Northern Ireland, United States of America, Eastern Republic of Uruguay, Bolivarian Republic of Venezuela, Republic of Yemen, in the Community of Democracies Ministerial Meeting convened in Warsaw, 26–27 June 2000:

Expressing our common adherence to the purposes and principles set forth in the Charter of the United Nations and the Universal Declaration of Human Rights,

Reaffirming our commitment to respect relevant instruments of international law,

Emphasizing the interdependence between peace, development, human rights and democracy,

Recognizing the universality of democratic values,

Hereby agree to respect and uphold the following core democratic principles and practices:

- The will of the people shall be the basis of the authority of government, as expressed by exercise of the right and civic duties of citizens to choose their representatives through regular, free and fair elections with universal and equal suffrage, open to multiple parties, conducted by secret ballot, monitored by independent electoral authorities, and free of fraud and intimidation.

- The right of every person to equal access to public service and to take part in the conduct of public affairs, directly or through freely chosen representatives.

• The right of every person to equal protection of the law, without any discrimination as to race, color, sex, language, religion, political or other opinion, national or social origin, property, birth or other status.

• The right of every person to freedom of opinion and of expression, including to exchange and receive ideas and information through any media, regardless of frontiers.

• The right of every person to freedom of thought, conscience and religion.

• The right of every person to equal access to education.

• The right of the press to collect, report and disseminate information, news and opinions, subject only to restrictions necessary in a democratic society and prescribed by law, while bearing in mind evolving international practices in this field.

• The right of every person to respect for private family life, home, correspondence, including electronic communications, free of arbitrary or unlawful interference.

• The right of every person to freedom of peaceful assembly and association, including to establish or join their own political parties, civic groups, trade unions or other organizations with the necessary legal guarantees to allow them to operate freely on a basis of equal treatment before the law.

• The right of persons belonging to minorities or disadvantaged groups to equal protection of the law, and the freedom to enjoy their own culture, to profess and practice their own religion, and use their own language.

• The right of every person to be free from arbitrary arrest or detention; to be free from torture and other cruel, inhumane or degrading treatment or punishment; and to receive due process of law, including to be presumed innocent until proven guilty in a court of law.

• That the aforementioned rights, which are essential to full and effective participation in a democratic society, be enforced by a competent, independent and impartial judiciary open to the public, established and protected by law.

• That elected leaders uphold the law and function strictly in accordance with the constitution of the country concerned and procedures established by law.

• The right of those duly elected to form a government, assume office and fulfill the term of office as legally established.

• The obligation of an elected government to refrain from extra-constitutional actions, to allow the holding of periodic elections and to respect their results, and to relinquish power when its legal mandate ends.

• That government institutions be transparent, participatory and fully accountable to the citizenry of the country and take steps to combat corruption, which corrodes democracy.

• That the legislature be duly elected and transparent and accountable to the people.

• That civilian, democratic control over the military be established and preserved.

• That all human rights—civil, cultural, economic, political and social—be promoted and protected as set forth in the Universal Declaration of Human Rights and other relevant human rights instruments.

The Community of Democracies affirms our determination to work together to promote and strengthen democracy, recognizing that we are at differing stages in our democratic development. We will cooperate to consolidate and strengthen democratic institutions, with due respect for sovereignty and the principle of non-interference in internal affairs. Our goal is to support adherence to common democratic values and standards, as outlined above. To that end, our governments hereby agree to abide by these principles in practice, and to support one another in meeting these objectives which we set for ourselves today.

We will seek to strengthen institutions and processes of democracy. We appreciate the value of exchanging experiences in the consolidation of democracy and identifying best practices. We will promote discussions and, where appropriate, create forums on subjects relevant to democratic governance for the purpose of continuing and deepening our dialogue on democratization. We would focus our deliberations on our common principles and values rather than extraneous bilateral issues between members. We resolve jointly to cooperate to discourage and resist the threat to democracy posed by the overthrow of constitutionally elected governments. We resolve to strengthen cooperation to face the transnational challenges to democracy, such as state-sponsored, cross-border and other forms of terrorism; organized crime; corruption; drug trafficking; illegal arms trafficking; trafficking in human beings and money laundering, and to do so in accordance with respect for human rights of all persons and for the norms of international law.

We will encourage political leaders to uphold the values of tolerance and compromise that underpin effective democratic systems, and to promote respect for pluralism so as to enable societies to retain their multi-cultural character, and at the same time maintain stability and social cohesion. We reject ethnic and religious hatred, violence and other forms of extremism. We will also promote civil society, including women's organizations, non-governmental organizations, labor and business associations, and independent media in their exercise of their democratic rights. Informed participation by all elements of society, men and women, in a country's economic and political life, including by persons belonging to minority groups, is fundamental to a vibrant and durable democracy.

We will help to promote government-to-government and people-to-people linkages and promote civic education and literacy, including education for democracy. In these ways we will strengthen democratic institutions and practices and support the diffusion of democratic norms and values.

We will work with relevant institutions and international organizations, civil society and governments to coordinate support for new and emerging democratic societies.

We recognize the importance our citizens place on the improvement of living conditions. We also recognize the mutually-reinforcing benefits the democratic process offers to achieving sustained economic growth. To that end, we will seek to assist each other in economic and social development, including eradication of poverty, as an essential contributing factor to the promotion and preservation of democratic development.

We will collaborate on democracy-related issues in existing international and regional institutions, forming coalitions and caucuses to support resolutions and other international activities aimed at the promotion of democratic governance. This will help to create an external environment conducive to democratic development.

C. Cyber Threats

CONVENTION ON CYBERCRIME* (CYBER CRIME)

Preamble

The member States of the Council of Europe and the other States signatory hereto,

. . . .

Convinced of the need to pursue, as a matter of priority, a common criminal policy aimed at the protection of society against cybercrime, *inter alia,* by adopting appropriate legislation and fostering international co-operation;

Conscious of the profound changes brought about by the digitalisation, convergence and continuing globalisation of computer networks;

Concerned by the risk that computer networks and electronic information may also be used for committing criminal offences and that evidence relating to such offences may be stored and transferred by these networks;

. . . .

Mindful of the need to ensure a proper balance between the interests of law enforcement and respect for fundamental human rights as enshrined in the 1950 Council of Europe Convention for the Protection of Human Rights and Fundamental Freedoms, the 1966 United Nations International Covenant on Civil and Political Rights and other applicable international human rights treaties, which reaffirm the right of everyone to hold opinions without interference, as well as the right to freedom of expression, including the freedom to seek, receive, and impart information and ideas of all kinds, regardless of frontiers, and the rights concerning the respect for privacy;

. . . .

Have agreed as follows:

. . . .

Chapter II—Measures to be Taken at the National Level

Section 1—Substantive Criminal Law

Title 1—Offences Against the Confidentiality, Integrity and Availability of Computer Data and Systems

Article 2. *Illegal access.* Each Party shall adopt such legislative and other measures as may be necessary to establish as criminal offences under its domestic law, when committed intentionally, the access to the whole or any part of a computer system without right. A Party may require that the offence be committed by infringing security measures, with the intent of obtaining computer data or other dishonest intent, or in relation to a computer system that is connected to another computer system.

Article 3. *Illegal interception.* Each Party shall adopt such legislative and other measures as may be necessary to establish as criminal offences under its domestic

---

* Nov. 23, 2001, Europ. T.S. 185, *available at* http://conventions.coe.int/Treaty/en/Treaties/html/185.htm.

law, when committed intentionally, the interception without right, made by technical means, of non-public transmissions of computer data to, from or within a computer system, including electromagnetic emissions from a computer system carrying such computer data. A Party may require that the offence be committed with dishonest intent, or in relation to a computer system that is connected to another computer system.

Article 4. *Data interference.* 1. Each Party shall adopt such legislative and other measures as may be necessary to establish as criminal offences under its domestic law, when committed intentionally, the damaging, deletion, deterioration, alteration or suppression of computer data without right.

2. A Party may reserve the right to require that the conduct described in paragraph 1 result in serious harm.

Article 5. *System interference.* Each Party shall adopt such legislative and other measures as may be necessary to establish as criminal offences under its domestic law, when committed intentionally, the serious hindering without right of the functioning of a computer system by inputting, transmitting, damaging, deleting, deteriorating, altering or suppressing computer data.

Article 6. *Misuse of devices.* 1. Each Party shall adopt such legislative and other measures as may be necessary to establish as criminal offences under its domestic law, when committed intentionally and without right:

a. the production, sale, procurement for use, import, distribution or otherwise making available of:

i. a device, including a computer program, designed or adapted primarily for the purpose of committing any of the offences established in accordance with the above Articles 2 through 5;

ii. a computer password, access code, or similar data by which the whole or any part of a computer system is capable of being accessed,

with intent that it be used for the purpose of committing any of the offences established in Articles 2 through 5;

. . . .

Title 2—Computer-Related Offences

Article 7. *Computer-related forgery.* Each Party shall adopt such legislative and other measures as may be necessary to establish as criminal offences under its domestic law, when committed intentionally and without right, the input, alteration, deletion, or suppression of computer data, resulting in inauthentic data with the intent that it be considered or acted upon for legal purposes as if it were authentic, regardless whether or not the data is directly readable and intelligible. A Party may require an intent to defraud, or similar dishonest intent, before criminal liability attaches.

Article 8. *Computer-related fraud.* Each Party shall adopt such legislative and other measures as may be necessary to establish as criminal offences under its domestic law, when committed intentionally and without right, the causing of a loss of property to another person by:

a. any input, alteration, deletion or suppression of computer data;

b. any interference with the functioning of a computer system, with fraudulent or dishonest intent of procuring, without right, an economic benefit for oneself or for another person.

....

Section 3—Jurisdiction

Article 22. Jurisdiction. 1. Each Party shall adopt such legislative and other measures as may be necessary to establish jurisdiction over any offence established in accordance with Articles 2 through 11 of this Convention, when the offence is committed:

a. in its territory; or

b. on board a ship flying the flag of that Party; or

c. on board an aircraft registered under the laws of that Party; or

d. by one of its nationals, if the offence is punishable under criminal law where it was committed or if the offence is committed outside the territorial jurisdiction of any State.

....

Chapter III—International Co-operation

Section 1—General Principles

Title 1—General Principles Relating to International Co-operation

Article 23. *General principles relating to international co-operation.* The Parties shall co-operate with each other, in accordance with the provisions of this chapter, and through the application of relevant international instruments on international co-operation in criminal matters, arrangements agreed on the basis of uniform or reciprocal legislation, and domestic laws, to the widest extent possible for the purposes of investigations or proceedings concerning criminal offences related to computer systems and data, or for the collection of evidence in electronic form of a criminal offence.

Title 2—Principles relating to extradition

Article 24. *Extradition.*

....

2. The criminal offences described in paragraph 1 of this article shall be deemed to be included as extraditable offences in any extradition treaty existing between or among the Parties. The Parties undertake to include such offences as extraditable offences in any extradition treaty to be concluded between or among them.

3. If a Party that makes extradition conditional on the existence of a treaty receives a request for extradition from another Party with which it does not have an extradition treaty, it may consider this Convention as the legal basis for extradition with respect to any criminal offence referred to in paragraph 1 of this article.

....

Title 3—General Principles Relating to Mutual Assistance

Article 25. *General principles relating to mutual assistance.* 1. The Parties shall afford one another mutual assistance to the widest extent possible for the purpose of investigations or proceedings concerning criminal offences related to computer systems and data, or for the collection of evidence in electronic form of a criminal offence.

. . . .

Article 41. *Federal clause.* 1. A federal State may reserve the right to assume obligations under Chapter II of this Convention consistent with its fundamental principles governing the relationship between its central government and constituent States or other similar territorial entities provided that it is still able to co-operate under Chapter III.

. . . .

Part V

Domestic Law and National Security

A. The National Security Process

NATIONAL SECURITY ACT OF 1947*

AN ACT

To promote the national security by providing for a Secretary of Defense; for a National Military Establishment; for a Department of the Army, a Department of the Navy, and a Department of the Air Force; and for the coordination of the activities of the National Military Establishment with other departments and agencies of the Government concerned with the national security.

Be it enacted by the Senate and House of Representatives of the United States of America in Congress assembled,

SHORT TITLE

That this Act may be cited as the "National Security Act of 1947".

. . . .

DECLARATION OF POLICY

SEC. 2. In enacting this legislation, it is the intent of Congress to provide a comprehensive program for the future security of the United States; to provide for the establishment of integrated policies and procedures for the departments, agencies, and functions of the Government relating to the national security; to provide three military departments for the operation and administration of the Army, the Navy (including naval aviation and the United States Marine Corps), and the Air Force, with their assigned combat and service components; to provide for their authoritative coordination and unified direction under civilian control but not to merge them; to provide for the effective strategic direction of the armed forces and for their operation under unified control and for their integration into an efficient team of land, naval, and air forces.

TITLE I—COORDINATION FOR NATIONAL SECURITY
NATIONAL SECURITY COUNCIL

SEC. 101. (a) There is hereby established a council to be known as the National Security Council (hereinafter in this section referred to as the "Council").

The President of the United States shall preside over meetings of the Council:

Provided, That in his absence he may designate a member of the Council to preside in his place.

The function of the Council shall be to advise the President with respect to the integration of domestic, foreign, and military policies relating to the national security so as to enable the military services and the other departments and agencies of the Government to cooperate more effectively in matters involving the national security.

The Council shall be composed of the President; the Secretary of State; the Secretary of Defense, appointed under section 202; the Secretary of the Army, referred to in sec-

* National Security Act of 1947, ch. 343, 61 Stat. 495 (codified as amended in scattered sections of 5, 10 & 50 U.S.C.), *available at* http://www.law.cornell.edu/uscode/html/uscode50/usc_sup_01_50_10_15.html.

tion 205; the Secretary of the Navy; the Secretary of the Air Force, appointed under section 207; the Chairman of the National Security Resources Board, appointed under section 103; and such of the following named officers as the President may designate from time to time: The Secretaries of the executive departments, the Chairman of the Munitions Board appointed under section 213, and the Chairman of the Research and Development Board appointed under section 214; but no such additional member shall be designated until the advice and consent of the Senate has been given to his appointment to the office the holding of which authorizes his designation as a member of the Council.

(b) In addition to performing such other functions as the President may direct, for the purpose of more effectively coordinating the policies and functions of the departments and agencies of the Government relating to the national security, it shall, subject to the direction of the President, be the duty of the Council—

(1) to assess and appraise the objectives, commitments, and risks of the United States in relation to our actual and potential military power, in the interest of national security, for the purpose of making recommendations to the President in connection therewith; and

(2) to consider policies on matters of common interest to the departments and agencies of the Government concerned with the national security, and to make recommendations to the President in connection therewith.

(c) The Council shall have a staff to be headed by a civilian executive secretary who shall be appointed by the President,...

(d) The Council shall, from time to time, make such recommendations, and such other reports to the President as it deems appropriate or as the President may require.

CENTRAL INTELLIGENCE AGENCY

SEC.102. (a) There is hereby established under the National Security Council a Central Intelligence Agency with a Director of Central Intelligence, who shall be the head thereof. The Director shall be appointed by the President, by and with the advice and consent of the Senate, from among the commissioned officers of the armed services or from among individuals in civilian life....

....

(d) For the purpose of coordinating the intelligence activities of the several Government departments and agencies in the interest of national security, it shall be the duty of the Agency, under the direction of the National Security Council—

(1) to advise the National Security Council in matters concerning such intelligence activities of the Government departments and agencies as relate to national security;

(2) to make recommendations to the National Security Council for the coordination of such intelligence activities of the departments and agencies of the Government as relate to the national security;

(3) to correlate and evaluate intelligence relating to the national security, and provide for the appropriate dissemination of such intelligence within the Government using where appropriate existing agencies and facilities: *Provided,* That the Agency shall have no police, subpoena, law-enforcement powers, or internal-security functions: *Provided further,* That the departments and other agencies of the Government shall continue to collect, evaluate, correlate, and disseminate depart-

mental intelligence: *And provided further,* That the Director of Central Intelligence shall be responsible for protecting intelligence sources and methods from unauthorized disclosure;

(4) to perform, for the benefit of the existing intelligence agencies, such additional services of common concern as the National Security Council determines can be more efficiently accomplished centrally;

(5) to perform such other functions and duties related to intelligence affecting the national security as the National Security Council may from time to time direct.

(e) To the extent recommended by the National Security Council and approved by the President, such intelligence of the departments and agencies of the Government, except as hereinafter provided, relating to the national security shall be open to the inspection of the Director of Central Intelligence, and such intelligence as relates to the national security and is possessed by such departments and other agencies of the Government, except as hereinafter provided, shall be made available to the Director of Central Intelligence for correlation, evaluation, and dissemination: *Provided, however,* That upon the written request of the Director of Central Intelligence, the Director of the Federal Bureau of Investigation shall make available to the Director of Central Intelligence such information for correlation, evaluation, and dissemination as may be essential to the national security.

....

NATIONAL SECURITY RESOURCES BOARD

SEC. 103. (a) There is hereby established a National Security Resources Board (hereinafter in this section referred to as the "Board") to be composed of the Chairman of the Board and such heads or representatives of the various executive departments and independent agencies as may from time to time be designated by the President to be members of the. Board. The Chairman of the Board shall be appointed from civilian life by the President, by and with the advice and consent of the Senate, and shall receive compensation at the rate of $14,000 a year.

(b) The Chairman of the Board, subject to the direction of the President, is authorized, subject to the civil-service laws and the Classification Act of 1923, as amended, to appoint and fix the compensation of such personnel as may be necessary to assist the Board in carrying out its functions.

(c) It shall be the function of the Board to advise the President concerning the coordination of military, industrial, and civilian mobilization, including—

(1) policies concerning industrial and civilian mobilization in order to assure the most effective mobilization and maximum utilization of the Nation's manpower in the event of war;

(2) programs for the effective use in time of war of the Nation's natural and industrial resources for military and civilian needs, for the maintenance and stabilization of the civilian economy in time of war, and for the adjustment of such economy to war needs and conditions;

(3) policies for unifying, in time of war, the activities of Federal agencies and departments engaged in or concerned with production, procurement, distribution, or transportation of military or civilian supplies, materials, and products;

(4) the relationship between potential supplies of, and potential requirements for, manpower, resources, and productive facilities in time of war;

(5) policies for establishing adequate reserves of strategic and critical material, and for the conservation of these reserves;

(6) the strategic relocation of industries, services, government, and economic activities, the continuous operation of which is essential to the Nation's security.

(d) In performing its functions, the Board shall utilize to the maximum extent the facilities and resources of the departments and agencies of the Government.

TITLE II—THE NATIONAL MILITARY ESTABLISHMENT

ESTABLISHMENT OF THE NATIONAL MILITARY ESTABLISHMENT

SEC. 201. (a) There is hereby established the National Military Establishment, and the Secretary of Defense shall be the head thereof.

(b) The National Military Establishment shall consist of the Department of the Army, the Department of the Navy, and the Department of the Air Force, together with all other agencies created under title II of this Act.

SECRETARY OF DEFENSE

SEC. 202. (a) There shall be a Secretary of Defense, who shall be appointed from civilian life by the President, by and with the advice and consent of the Senate: *Provided,* That a person who has within ten years been on active duty as a commissioned officer in a Regular component of the armed services shall not be eligible for appointment as Secretary of Defense. The Secretary of Defense shall be the principal assistant to the President in all matters relating to the national security. Under the direction of the President and subject to the provisions of this Act he shall perform the following duties:

(1) Establish general policies and programs for the National Military Establishment and for all of the departments and agencies therein;

(2) Exercise general direction, authority, and control over such departments and agencies;

(3) Take appropriate steps to eliminate unnecessary duplication or overlapping in the fields of procurement, supply, transportation, storage, health, and research;

(4) Supervise and coordinate the preparation of the budget estimates of the departments and agencies comprising the National Military Establishment; formulate and determine the budget estimates for submittal to the Bureau of the Budget; and supervise the budget programs of such departments and agencies under the applicable appropriation Act:

....

DEPARTMENT OF THE ARMY

SEC. 205. (a) The Department of War shall hereafter be designated the Department of the Army, and the title of the Secretary of War shall be changed to Secretary of the Army. Changes shall be made in the titles of other officers and activities of the Department of the Arm as the Secretary of the Army may determine.

....

(c) The term "Department of the Army" as used in this Act shall be construed to mean the Department of the Army at the seat of government and all field headquarters, forces, reserve components, installations, activities, and functions under the control or supervision of the Department of the Army.

....

(e) In general the United States Army, within the Department of the Army, shall include land combat and service forces and such aviation and water transport as may be organic therein. It shall be organized, trained, and equipped primarily for prompt and sustained combat incident to operations on land. It shall be responsible for the preparation of land forces necessary for the effective prosecution of war except as otherwise assigned and, in accordance with integrated joint mobilization plans, for the expansion of peacetime components of the Army to meet the needs of war.

DEPARTMENT OF THE NAVY

SEC. 206. (a) The term "Department of the Navy" as used in this Act shall be construed to mean the Department of the Navy at the seat of government; the headquarters, United States Marine Corps; the entire operating forces of the United States Navy, including naval aviation, and of the United States Marine Corps, including the reserve components of such forces; all field activities, headquarters, forces, bases, installations, activities, and functions under the control or supervision of the Department of the Navy; and the United States Coast Guard when operating as a part of the Navy pursuant to law.

(b) In general the United States Navy, within the Department of the Navy, shall include naval combat and services forces and such aviation as may be organic therein. It shall be organized, trained, and equipped primarily for prompt and sustained combat incident to operations at sea. It shall be responsible for the preparation of naval forces necessary for the effective prosecution of war except as otherwise assigned, and, in accordance with integrated joint mobilization plans, for the expansion of the peacetime components of the Navy to meet the needs of war.

All naval aviation shall be integrated with the naval service as part thereof within the Department of the Navy. Naval aviation shall consist of combat and service and training forces, and shall include land-based naval aviation, air transport essential for naval operations, all air weapons and air techniques involved in the operations and activities of the United States Navy, and the entire remainder of the aeronautical organization of the United States Navy, together with the personnel necessary therefor.

The Navy shall be generally responsible for naval reconnaissance, antisubmarine warfare, and protection of shipping.

The Navy shall develop aircraft, weapons, tactics, technique, organization and equipment of naval combat and service elements; matters of joint concern as to these functions shall be coordinated between the Army, the Air Force, and the Navy.

(c) The United States Marine Corps, within the Department of the Navy, shall include land combat and service forces and such aviation as may be organic therein. The Marine Corps shall be organized, trained, and equipped to provide fleet marine forces of combined arms, together with supporting air components, for service with the fleet in the seizure or defense of advanced naval bases and for the conduct of such land operations as may be essential to the prosecution of a naval campaign. It shall be the duty of the Marine Corps to develop, in coordination with the Army and the Air Force, those phases of amphibious operations which pertain to the tactics, technique, and equipment employed by landing forces. In addition, the Marine Corps shall provide detachments and organizations for service on armed vessels of the Navy, shall provide security detachments for the protection of naval property at naval stations and bases, and shall perform such other duties as the President may direct: *Provided,* That such additional duties shall not detract from or interfere with the operations for which the Marine Corps is primarily organized. The Marine Corps shall be responsible, in accordance with integrated joint mobilization plans, for the expansion of peacetime components of the Marine Corps to meet the needs of war.

DEPARTMENT OF THE AIR FORCE

SEC. 207. (a) Within the National Military Establishment there is hereby established an executive department to be known as the Department of the Air Force, and a Secretary of the Air Force, who shall be the head thereof. The Secretary of the Air Force shall be appointed from civilian life by the President, by and with the advice and consent of the Senate.

....

(c) The term "Department of the Air Force" as used in this Act shall be construed to mean the Department of the Air Force at the seat of government and all field headquarters, forces, reserve components, installations, activities, and functions under the control or supervision of the Department of the Air Force.

....

UNITED STATES AIR FORCE

SEC. 208. (a) The United States Air Force is hereby established under the Department of the Air Force. The Army Air Forces, the Air Corps, United States Army, and the General Headquarters Air Force (Air Force Combat Command), shall be transferred to the United States Air Force.

(b) There shall be a Chief of Staff, United States Air Force, who shall be appointed by the President, by and with the advice and consent of the Senate, for a term of four years from among the officers of general rank who are assigned to or commissioned in the United States Air Force. Under the direction of the Secretary of the Air Force, the Chief of Staff, United States Air Force, shall exercise command over the United States Air Force and shall be charged with the duty of carrying into execution all lawful orders and directions which may be transmitted to him. The functions of the Commanding General, General Headquarters Air Force (Air Force Combat Command), and of the Chief of the Air Corps and of the Commanding General, Army Air Forces, shall be transferred to the Chief of Staff, United States Air Force....

....

(f) In general the United States Air Force shall include aviation forces both combat and service not otherwise assigned. It shall be organized, trained and equipped primarily for prompt and sustained offensive and defensive air operations. The Air Force shall be responsible for the preparation of the air forces necessary for the effective prosecution of war except as otherwise assigned and, in accordance with integrated joint mobilization plans, for the expansion of the peacetime components of the Air Force to meet the needs of war.

....

WAR COUNCIL

SEC. 210. There shall be within the National Military Establishment a War Council composed of the Secretary of Defense, as Chairman, who shall have power of decision;

the Secretary of the Army; the Secretary of the Navy; the Secretary of the Air Force; the Chief of Staff, United States Army; the Chief of Naval Operations; and the Chief of Staff, United States Air Force. The War Council shall advise the Secretary of Defense on matters of broad policy relating to the armed forces, and shall consider and report on such other matters as the Secretary of Defense may direct.

JOINT CHIEFS OF STAFF

SEC. 211. (a) There is hereby established within the National Military Establishment the Joint Chiefs of Staff, which shall consist of the Chief of Staff, United States Army; the Chief of Naval Operations; the Chief of Staff, United States Air Force; and the Chief of Staff to the Commander in Chief, if there be one.

(b) Subject to the authority and direction of the President and the Secretary of Defense, it shall be the duty of the Joint Chiefs of Staff—

(1) to prepare strategic plans and to provide for the strategic direction of the military forces;

(2) to prepare joint logistic plans and to assign to the military services logistic responsibilities in accordance with such plans;

(3) to establish unified commands in strategic areas when such unified commands are in the interest of national security;

(4) to formulate policies for joint training of the military forces;

(5) to formulate policies for coordinating the education of members of the military forces ;

(6) to review major material and personnel requirements of the military forces, in accordance with strategic and logistic plans; and

(7) to provide United States representation on the Military Staff Committee of the United Nations in accordance with the provisions of the Charter of the United Nations.

(c) The Joint Chiefs of Staff shall act as the principal military advisers to the President and the Secretary of Defense and shall perform such other duties as the President and the Secretary of Defense may direct or as may be prescribed by law.

JOINT STAFF

SEC. 212. There shall be, under the Joint Chiefs of Staff, a Joint Staff to consist of not to exceed one hundred officers and to be composed of approximately equal numbers of officers from each of the three armed services. The Joint Staff, operating under a Director thereof appointed by the Joint Chiefs of Staff, shall perform such duties as may be directed by the Joint Chiefs of Staff. The Director shall be an officer junior in grade to all members of the Joint Chiefs of Staff.

MUNITIONS BOARD

SEC. 213. (a) There is hereby established in the National Military Establishment a Munitions Board (hereinafter in this section referred to as the "Board").

(b) The Board shall be composed of a Chairman, who shall be the head thereof, and an Under Secretary or Assistant Secretary from each of the three military departments, to be designated in each case by the Secretaries of their respective departments. The Chairman shall be appointed from civilian life by the President, by and with the advice and consent of the Senate, and shall receive compensation at the rate of $14,000 a year.

(c) It shall be the duty of the Board under the direction of the Secretary of Defense and in support of strategic and logistic plans prepared by the Joint Chiefs of Staff—

(1) to coordinate the appropriate activities within the National Military Establishment with regard to industrial matters, including the procurement, production, and distribution plans of the departments and agencies comprising the Establishment;

(2) to plan for the military aspects of industrial mobilization;

(3) to recommend assignment of procurement responsibilities among the several military services and to plan for standardization of specifications and for the greatest practicable allocation of purchase authority of technical equipment and common use items on the basis of single procurement;

(4) to prepare estimates of potential production, procurement, and personnel for use in evaluation of the logistic feasibility of strategic operations;

(5) to determine relative priorities of the various segments of the military procurement programs;

(6) to supervise such subordinate agencies as are or may be created to consider the subjects falling within the scope of the Board's responsibilities;

(7) to make recommendations to regroup, combine, or dissolve existing interservice agencies operating in the fields of procurement, production, and distribution in such manner as to promote efficiency and economy;

(8) to maintain liaison with other departments and agencies for the proper correlation of military requirements with the civilian economy, particularly in regard to the procurement or disposition of strategic and critical material and the maintenance of adequate reserves of such material, and to make recommendations as to policies in connection therewith;

(9) to assemble and review material and personnel requirements presented by the Joint Chiefs of Staff and those presented by the production, procurement, and distribution agencies assigned to meet military needs, and to make recommendations thereon to the Secretary of Defense; and

(10) to perform such other duties as the Secretary of Defense may direct.

....

RESEARCH AND DEVELOPMENT BOARD

SEC. 214. (a) There is hereby established in the National Military Establishment a Research and Development Board (hereinafter in this section referred to as the "Board"). The Board shall be composed of a Chairman, who shall be the head thereof, and two representatives from each of the Departments of the Army, Navy, and Air Force, to be designated by the Secretaries of their respective Departments. The Chairman shall be appointed from civilian life by the President, by and with the advice and consent of the Senate, and shall receive compensation at the rate of $14,000 a year. The purpose of the Board shall be to advise the Secretary of Defense as to the status of scientific research relative to the national security, and to assist him in assuring adequate provision for research and development on scientific problems relating to the national security.

(b) It shall be the duty of the Board, under the direction of the Secretary of Defense—

(1) to prepare a complete and integrated program of research and development for military purposes;

(2) to advise with regard to trends in scientific research relating to national security and the measures necessary to assure continued and increasing progress;

(3) to recommend measures of coordination of research and development among the military departments, and allocation among them of responsibilities for specific programs of joint interest;

(4) to formulate policy for the National Military Establishment in connection with research and development matters involving agencies outside the National Military Establishment;

(5) to consider the interaction of research and development and strategy, and to advise the Joint Chiefs of Staff in connection therewith; and

(6) to perform such other duties as the Secretary of Defense may direct.

....

TITLE III—MISCELLANEOUS

....

ADVISORY COMMITTEES AND PERSONNEL

SEC. 303. (a) The Secretary of Defense, the Chairman of the National Security Resources Board, and the Director of Central Intelligence are authorized to appoint such advisory committees and to employ, consistent with other provisions of this Act, such part-time advisory personnel as they may deem necessary in carrying out their respective functions and the functions of agencies under their control. Persons holding other offices or positions under the United States for which they receive compensation while serving as members of such committees shall receive no additional compensation for such service. Other members of such committees and other part-time advisory personnel so employed may serve without compensation or may receive compensation at a rate not to exceed $35 for each day of service, as determined by the appointing authority.

NATIONAL SECURITY ACT AMENDMENTS OF 1949*

AN ACT

To reorganize fiscal management in the National Military Establishment to promote economy and efficiency, and for other purposes.

Be it enacted by the Senate and House of Representatives of the United States of America in Congress assembled,

SHORT TITLE

SEC. 1. This Act may be cited as the "National Security Act Amendments of 1949".

SEC. 2. Section 2 of the National Security Act of 1947 is amended to read as follows:

"**SEC. 2.** In enacting this legislation, it is the intent of Congress to provide a comprehensive program for the future security of the United States; to provide for the establishment of integrated policies and procedures for the departments, agencies, and functions of the Government relating to the national security; to provide three military departments, separately administered, for the operation and administration of the Army, the Navy (including naval aviation and the United States Marine Corps), and the Air Force, with their assigned combat and service components; to provide for their authoritative coordination and unified direction under civilian control of the Secretary of Defense but not to merge them; to provide for the effective strategic direction of the armed forces and for their operation under unified control and for their integration into an efficient team of land, naval, and air forces but not to establish a single Chief of Staff over the armed forces nor an armed forces general staff (but this is not to be interpreted as applying to the Joint Chiefs of Staff or Joint Staff)."

CHANGE IN COMPOSITION OF THE NATIONAL SECURITY COUNCIL

SEC. 3. The fourth paragraph of section 101 (a) of the National Security Act of 1947 is amended to read as follows:

"The Council shall be composed of—

"(1) the President;

"(2) the Vice President;

"(3) the Secretary of State;

"(4) the Secretary of Defense;

"(5) the Chairman of the National Security Resources Board; and

* National Security Act Amendments of 1949, ch. 412, 63 Stat. 578 (codified as amended in scattered sections of 5, 10 & 50 U.S.C.).

"(6) The Secretaries and Under Secretaries of other executive departments and of the military departments, the Chairman of the Munitions Board, and the Chairman of the Research and Development Board, when appointed by the President by and with the advice and consent of the Senate, to serve at his pleasure."

CONVERSION OF THE NATIONAL MILITARY ESTABLISHMENT INTO AN EXECUTIVE DEPARTMENT

SEC. 4. Section 201 of the National Security Act of 1947 is amended to read as follows:

"**SEC. 201.** (a) There is hereby established, as an Executive Department of the Government, the Department of Defense, and the Secretary of Defense shall be the head thereof.

"(b) There shall be within the Department of Defense (1) the Department of the Army, the Department of the Navy, and the Department of the Air Force, and each such department shall on and after the date of enactment of the National Security Act Amendments of 1949 be military departments in lieu of their prior status as Executive Departments, and (2) all other agencies created under title II of this Act.

"(c) Section 158 of the Revised Statutes, as amended, is amended to read as follows:

"'**SEC. 158.** The provisions of this title shall apply to the following Executive Departments:

"'First. The Department of State.

"'Second. The Department of Defense.

"'Third. The Department of the Treasury.

"'Fourth. The Department of Justice.

"'Fifth. The Post Office Department.

"'Sixth. The Department of the Interior.

"'Seventh. The Department of Agriculture.

"'Eighth. The Department of Commerce.

"'Ninth. The Department of Labor.'

"(d) Except to the extent inconsistent with the provisions of this Act, the provisions of title IV of the Revised Statutes as now or hereafter amended shall be applicable to the Department of Defense."

THE SECRETARY OF DEFENSE

SEC. 5. Section 202 of the National Security Act of 1947, as amended, is further amended to read as follows:

"**SEC. 202.** (a) There shall be a Secretary of Defense, who shall be appointed from civilian life by the President, by and with the advice and consent of the Senate: *Provided,* That a person who has within ten years been on active duty as a commissioned officer in a Regular component of the armed services shall not be eligible for appointment as Secretary of Defense.

"(b) The Secretary of Defense shall be the principal assistant to the President in all matters relating to the Department of Defense. Under the direction of the President, and subject to the provisions of this Act, he shall have direction, authority, and control over the Department of Defense.

"(c) (1) Notwithstanding any other provision of this Act, the combatant functions assigned to the military services by sections 205 (e), 206 (b), 206 (c), and 208 (f) hereof shall not be transferred, reassigned, abolished, or consolidated.

"(2) Military personnel shall not be so detailed or assigned as to impair such combatant functions.

"(3) The Secretary of Defense shall not direct the use and expenditure of funds of the Department of Defense in such manner as to effect the results prohibited by paragraphs (1) and (2) of this subsection.

"(4) The Departments of the Army, Navy, and Air Force shall be separately administered by their respective Secretaries under the direction, authority, and control of the Secretary of Defense.

"(5) Subject to the provisions of paragraph (1) of this subsection no function which has been or is hereafter authorized by law to be performed by the Department of Defense shall be substantially transferred, reassigned, abolished or consolidated until after a report in regard to all pertinent details shall have been made by the Secretary of Defense to the Committees on Armed Services of the Congress.

"(6) No provision of this Act shall be so construed as to prevent a Secretary of a military department or a member of the Joint Chiefs of Staff from presenting to the Congress, on his own initiative, after first so informing the Secretary of Defense, any recommendation relating to the Department of Defense that he may deem proper.

"(d) The Secretary of Defense shall not less often than semiannually submit written reports to the President and the Congress covering expenditures, work and accomplishments of the Department of Defense, accompanied by:

"(1) such recommendations as he shall deem appropriate,

"(2) separate reports from the military departments covering their expenditures, work and accomplishments, and

"(3) itemized statements showing the savings of public funds and the eliminations of unnecessary duplications and overlappings that have been accomplished pursuant to the provisions of this Act.

....

CREATING THE POSITION OF CHAIRMAN OF THE JOINT CHIEFS OF STAFF AND PRESCRIBING HIS POWERS AND DUTIES

SEC. 7. (a) Section 210 of the National Security Act of 1947 is amended to read as follows:

"**SEC. 210.** There shall be within the Department of Defense an Armed Forces Policy Council composed of the Secretary of Defense, as Chairman, who shall have power of decision; the Deputy Secretary of Defense; the Secretary of the Army; the Secretary of the Navy; the Secretary of the Air Force; the Chairman of the Joint Chiefs of Staff; the Chief of Staff, United States Army; the Chief of Naval Operations; and the Chief of Staff, United States Air Force. The Armed Forces Policy Council shall advise the Secretary of Defense on matters of broad policy relating to the armed forces and shall consider and report on such other matters as the Secretary of Defense may direct."

(b) Section 211 of the National Security Act of 1947 is amended to read as follows:

"**SEC. 211.** (a) There is hereby established within the Department of Defense the Joint Chiefs of Staff, which shall consist of the Chairman, who shall be the presiding officer thereof but who shall have no vote; the Chief of Staff, United States Army, the Chief of Naval Operations; and the Chief of Staff, United States Air Force. The Joint Chiefs of Staff shall be the principal military advisers to the President, the National Security Council, and the Secretary of Defense,

"(b) Subject to the authority and direction of the President and the Secretary of Defense, the Joint Chiefs of Staff shall perform the following duties, in addition to such other duties as the President or the Secretary of Defense may direct:

"(1) preparation of strategic plans and provision for the strategic direction of the military forces;

"(2) preparation of joint logistic plans and assignment to the military services of logistic responsibilities in accordance with such plans;

"(3) establishment of unified commands in strategic areas;

"(4) review of major material and personnel requirements of the military forces in accordance with strategic and logistic plans;

"(5) formulation of policies for joint training of the military forces;

"(6) formulation of policies for coordinating the military education of members of the military forces; and

"(7) providing United States representation on the Military Staff Committee of the United Nations in accordance with the provisions of the Charter of the United Nations.

"(c) The Chairman of the Joint Chiefs of Staff (hereinafter referred to as the 'Chairman') shall be appointed by the President, by and with the advice and consent of the Senate, from among the Regular officers of the armed services to serve at the pleasure of the President for a term of two years and shall be eligible for one reappointment, by and with the advice and consent of the Senate, except in time of war hereafter declared by the Congress when there shall be no limitation on the number of such reappointments. The Chairman shall receive the basic pay and basic and personal money allowances prescribed by law for the Chief of Staff, United States Army, and such special pays and hazardous duty pays to which he may be entitled under other provisions of law.... ."(e) In addition to participating as a member of the Joint Chiefs of Staff in the performance of the duties assigned in subsection (b) of this section, the Chairman shall, subject to the authority and direction of the President and the Secretary of Defense, perform the following duties:

"(1) serve as the presiding officer of the Joint Chiefs of Staff;

"(2) provide agenda for meetings of the Joint Chiefs of Staff and assist the Joint Chiefs of Staff to prosecute their business as promptly as practicable; and

"(3) inform the Secretary of Defense and, when appropriate as determined by the President or the Secretary of Defense, the President, of those issues upon which agreement among the Joint Chiefs of Staff has not been reached."

(c) Section 212 of the National Security Act of 1947 is amended to read as follows:

"**SEC. 212.** There shall be, under the Joint Chiefs of Staff, a Joint Staff to consist of not to exceed two hundred and ten officers and to be composed of approximately equal numbers of officers appointed by the Joint Chiefs of Staff from each of the three armed services. The Joint Staff, operating under a Director thereof appointed by the Joint Chiefs of Staff, shall perform such duties as may be directed by the Joint Chiefs of Staff. The Director shall be an officer junior in grade to all members of the Joint Chiefs of Staff."

CHANGING THE RELATIONSHIP OF THE SECRETARY OF DEFENSE TO THE MUNITIONS BOARD

SEC. 8. Section 213 of the National Security Act of 1947 is amended to read as follows:

"**SEC. 213.** (a) There is hereby established in the Department of Defense a Munitions Board (hereinafter in this section referred to as the 'Board').

"(b) The Board shall be composed of a Chairman, who shall be the head thereof and who shall, subject to the authority of the Secretary of Defense and in respect to such matters authorized by him, have the power of decision upon matters falling within the jurisdiction of the Board, and an Under Secretary or Assistant Secretary from each of the three military departments, to be designated in each case by the Secretaries of their respective departments. The Chairman shall be appointed from civilian life by the President, by and with the advice and consent of the Senate, and shall receive compensation at the rate of $14,000 a year.

"(c) Subject to the authority and direction of the Secretary of Defense, the Board shall perform the following duties in support of strategic and logistic plans and in consonance with guidance in those fields provided by the Joint Chiefs of Staff, and such other duties as the Secretary of Defense may prescribe:

"(1) coordination of the appropriate activities with regard to industrial matters, including the procurement, production, and distribution plans of the Department of Defense;

"(2) planning for the military aspects of industrial mobilization;

"(3) assignment of procurement responsibilities among the several military departments and planning for standardization of specifications and for the greatest practicable allocation of purchase authority of technical equipment and common use items on the basis of single procurement;

"(4) preparation of estimates of potential production, procurement, and personnel for use in evaluation of the logistic feasibility of strategic operations;

"(5) determination of relative priorities of the various segments of the military procurement programs;

"(6) supervision of such subordinate agencies as are or may be created to consider the subjects falling within the scope of the Board's responsibilities;

"(7) regrouping, combining, or dissolving of existing interservice agencies operating in the fields of procurement, production, and distribution in such manner as to promote efficiency and economy;

"(8) maintenance of liaison with other departments and agencies for the proper correlation of military requirements with the civilian economy, particularly in regard to the procurement or disposition of strategic and critical material and the maintenance of adequate reserves of such material, and making of recommendations as to policies in connection therewith; and

"(9) assembly and review of material and personnel requirements presented by the Joint Chiefs of Staff and by the production, procurement, and distribution agencies assigned to meet military needs, and making of recommendations thereon to the Secretary of Defense."

. . . .

CHANGING THE RELATIONSHIP OF SECRETARY OF DEFENSE TO THE RESEARCH AND DEVELOPMENT BOARD

SEC. 9. Section 214 of the National Security Act of 1947 is amended to read as follows:

"**SEC. 214.** (a) There is hereby established in the Department of Defense a Research and Development Board (hereinafter in this section referred to as the 'Board'). The Board shall be composed of a Chairman, who shall be the head thereof and who shall, subject to the authority of the Secretary of Defense and in respect to such matters authorized by him, have the power of decision on matters falling within the jurisdiction of the Board, and two representatives from each of the Departments of the Army, Navy, and Air Force, to be Chairman designated by the Secretaries of their respective Departments. The Chairman shall be appointed from civilian life by the President, by and with the advice and consent of the Senate, and shall receive compensation at the rate of $14,000 a year. The purpose of the Board shall be to advise the Secretary of Defense as to the status of scientific research relative to the national security, and to assist him in assuring adequate provision for research and development on scientific problems relating to the national security.

"(b) Subject to the authority and direction of the Secretary of Defense, the Board shall perform the following duties and such other duties as the Secretary of Defense may prescribe:

"(1) preparation of a complete and integrated program of research and development for military purposes;

"(2) advising with regard to trends in scientific research relating to national security and the measures necessary to assure continued and increasing progress;

"(3) coordination of research and development among the military departments, and allocation among them of responsibilities for specific programs;

"(4) formulation of policy for the Department of Defense in connection with research and development matters involving agencies outside the Department of Defense; and

"(5) consideration of the interaction of research and development and strategy, and advising the Joint Chiefs of Staff in connection therewith."

. . . .

REORGANIZATION OF FISCAL MANAGEMENT TO PROMOTE ECONOMY AND EFFICIENCY

SEC. 11. The National Security Act of 1947 is amended by inserting at the end thereof the following new title:

"TITLE IV

"PROMOTION OF ECONOMY AND EFFICIENCY THROUGH ESTABLISHMENT OF UNIFORM BUDGETARY AND FISCAL PROCEDURES AND ORGANIZATIONS

"COMPTROLLER OF DEPARTMENT OF DEFENSE

"**SEC. 401.** (a) There is hereby established in the Department of Defense the Comptroller of the Department of Defense, who shall be one of the Assistant Secretaries of Defense.

"(b) The Comptroller shall advise and assist the Secretary of Defense in performing such budgetary and fiscal functions as may be required to carry out the powers conferred upon the Secretary of Defense by this Act, including but not limited to those specified in this subsection. Subject to the authority, direction, and control of the Secretary of Defense, the Comptroller shall—

"(1) supervise and direct the preparation of the budget estimates of the Department of Defense; and

"(2) establish, and supervise the execution of—

"(A) principles, policies, and procedures to be followed in connection with organizational and administrative matters relating to—

"(i) the preparation and execution of the budgets,

"(ii) fiscal, cost, operating, and capital property accounting,

"(iii) progress and statistical reporting,

"(iv) internal audit, and

"(B) policies and procedures relating to the expenditure and collection of funds administered by the Department of Defense; and

"(3) establish uniform terminologies, classifications, and procedures in all such matters."

....

GOLDWATER-NICHOLS DEPARTMENT OF DEFENSE REORGANIZATION ACT OF 1986*

....

CHAPTER 5—JOINT CHIEFS OF STAFF

SEC. 151. Joint Chiefs of Staff: Composition; Functions.

SEC. 152. Chairman: Appointment; Grade and Rank.

SEC. 153. Chairman: Functions.

SEC. 154. Vice Chairman.

SEC. 155. Joint Staff.

SEC. 151. Joint Chiefs of Staff: Composition; Functions

(a) *Composition.* There are in the Department of Defense the Joint Chiefs of Staff, headed by the Chairman of the Joint Chiefs of Staff. The Joint Chiefs of Staff consist of the following:

(1) The Chairman.

(2) The Vice Chairman.

(3) The Chief of Staff of the Army.

(4) The Chief of Naval Operations.

(5) The Chief of Staff of the Air Force.

(6) The Commandant of the Marine Corps.

(b) *Function as Military Advisers.*

(1) The Chairman of the Joint Chiefs of Staff is the principal military adviser to the President, the National Security Council, and the Secretary of Defense.

(2) The other members of the Joint Chiefs of Staff are military advisers to the President, the National Security Council, and the Secretary of Defense as specified in subsections (d) and (e).

(c) *Consultation by Chairman.*

(1) In carrying out his functions, duties, and responsibilities, the Chairman shall, as he considers appropriate, consult with and seek the advice of:

(A) the other members of the Joint Chiefs of Staff; and

(B) the commanders of the unified and specified combatant commands.

(2) Subject to subsection (d), in presenting advice with respect to any matter to the President, the National Security Council, or the Secretary of Defense, the Chairman shall, as he considers appropriate, inform the President, the National Security Council, or the Secretary of Defense, as the case may be, of the range of military advice and opinion with respect to that matter.

---

* Goldwater-Nichols Department of Defense Reorganization Act of 1986 §§ 151–155, Pub. L. No. 99-433, 100 Stat. 992, 1005–12 (codified as amended at 10 U.S.C. §§ 151–155 (2000)), *available at* http://www.ndu.edu/library/goldnich/goldnich.html#97.

(d) *Advice and Opinions of Members Other Than Chairman.*

(1) A member of the Joint Chiefs of Staff (other than the Chairman) may submit to the Chairman advice or an opinion in disagreement with, or advice or an opinion in addition to, the advice presented by the Chairman to the President, the National Security Council, or the Secretary of Defense. If a member submits such advice or opinion, the Chairman shall present the advice or opinion of such member at the same time he presents his own advice to the President, the National Security Council, or the Secretary of Defense, as the case may be.

(2) The Chairman shall establish procedures to ensure that the presentation of his own advice to the President, the National Security Council, or the Secretary of Defense is not unduly delayed by reason of the submission of the individual advice or opinion of another member of the Joint Chiefs of Staff.

(e) *Advice on Request.* The members of the Joint Chiefs of Staff, individually or collectively, in their capacity as military advisers, shall provide advice to the President, the National Security Council, or the Secretary of Defense on a particular matter when the President, the National Security Council, or the Secretary requests such advice.

(f) *Recommendations to Congress.* After first informing the Secretary of Defense, a member of the Joint Chiefs of Staff may make such recommendations to Congress relating to the Department of Defense as he considers appropriate.

(g) *Meetings of JCS.*

(1) The Chairman shall convene regular meetings of the Joint Chiefs of Staff.

(2) Subject to the authority, direction, and control of the President and the Secretary of Defense, the Chairman shall:

(A) preside over the Joint Chiefs of Staff;

(B) provide agenda for the meetings of the Joint Chiefs of Staff (including, as the Chairman considers appropriate, any subject for the agenda recommended by any other member of the Joint Chiefs of Staff);

(C) assist the Joint Chiefs of Staff in carrying on their business as promptly as practicable; and

(D) determine when issues under consideration by the Joint Chiefs of Staff shall be decided.

SEC. 152. Chairman: Appointment; Grade and Rank

(a) *Appointment; Term of Office.*

(1) There is a Chairman of the Joint Chiefs of Staff, appointed by the President, by and with the advice and consent of the Senate, from the officers of the regular components of the armed forces. The Chairman serves at the pleasure of the President for a term of two years, beginning on October 1 of odd-numbered years. Subject to paragraph (3), an officer serving as Chairman may be reappointed in the same manner for two additional terms. However, in time of war there is no limit on the number of reappointments.

(2) In the event of the death, retirement, resignation, or reassignment of the officer serving as Chairman before the end of the term for which the officer was appointed, an officer appointed to fill the vacancy shall serve as Chairman only for the remainder of the original term, but may be reappointed as provided in paragraph (1).

(3) An officer may not serve as Chairman or Vice Chairman of the Joint Chiefs of Staff if the combined period of service of such officer in such positions exceeds six years. However, the President may extend to eight years the combined period of service an officer may serve in such positions if he determines such action is in the national interest. The limitations of this paragraph do not apply in time of war.

(b) *Requirement for Appointment.*

(1) The President may appoint an officer as Chairman of the Joint Chiefs of Staff only if the officer has served as:

(A) the Vice Chairman of the Joint Chiefs of Staff;

(B) the Chief of Staff of the Army, the Chief of Naval Operations, the Chief of Staff of the Air Force, or the Commandant of the Marine Corps; or

(C) the commander of a unified or specified combatant command.

(2) The President may waive paragraph (1) in the case of an officer if the President determines such action is necessary in the national interest.

(c) *Grade and Rank.* The Chairman, while so serving, holds the grade of general or, in the case of an officer of the Navy, admiral and outranks all other officers of the armed forces. However, he may not exercise military command over the Joint Chiefs of Staff or any of the armed forces.

SEC. 153. Chairman: Functions

(a) *Planning; Advice; Policy Formulation.* Subject to the authority, direction, and control of the President and the Secretary of Defense, the Chairman of the Joint Chiefs of Staff shall be responsible for the following:

(1) Strategic Direction. Assisting the President and the Secretary of Defense in providing for the strategic direction of the armed forces.

(2) Strategic Planning.

(A) Preparing strategic plans, including plans which conform with resource levels projected by the Secretary of Defense to be available for the period of time for which the plans are to be effective.

(B) Preparing joint logistic and mobility plans to support those strategic plans and recommending the assignment of logistic and mobility responsibilities to the armed forces in accordance with those logistic and mobility plans.

(C) Performing net assessments to determine the capabilities of the armed forces of the United States and its allies as compared with those of their potential adversaries.

(3) Contingency Planning; Preparedness.

(A) Providing for the preparation and review of contingency plans which conform to policy guidance from the President and the Secretary of Defense.

(B) Preparing joint logistic and mobility plans to support those contingency plans and recommending the assignment of logistic and mobility responsibilities to the armed forces in accordance with those logistic and mobility plans.

(C) Advising the Secretary on critical deficiencies and strengths in force capabilities (including manpower, logistic, and mobility support) identified during the preparation and review of contingency plans and assessing the effect of such deficiencies and strengths on meeting national security objectives and policy and on strategic plans.

(D) Establishing and maintaining, after consultation with the commanders of the unified and specified combatant commands, a uniform system of evaluating the preparedness of each such command to carry out missions assigned to the command.

(4) Advice on Requirements, Programs, and Budget.

(A) Advising the Secretary, under section 163(b)(2) of this title, on the priorities of the requirements identified by the commanders of the unified and specified combatant commands.

(B) Advising the Secretary on the extent to which the program recommendations and budget proposals of the military departments and other components of the Department of Defense for a fiscal year conform with the priorities established in strategic plans and with the priorities established for the requirements of the unified and specified combatant commands.

(C) Submitting to the Secretary alternative program recommendations and budget proposals, within projected resource levels and guidance provided by the Secretary, in order to achieve greater conformance with the priorities referred to in clause (B).

(D) Recommending to the Secretary, in accordance with section 166 of this title, a budget proposal for activities of each unified and specified combatant command.

(E) Advising the Secretary on the extent to which the major programs and policies of the armed forces in the area of manpower conform with strategic plans.

(F) Assessing military requirements for defense acquisition programs.

(5) Doctrine, Training, and Education.

(A) Developing doctrine for the joint employment of the armed forces.

(B) Formulating policies for the joint training of the armed forces.

(C) Formulating policies for coordinating the military education and training of members of the armed forces.

(6) Other Matters.

(A) Providing for representation of the United States on the Military Staff Committee of the United Nations in accordance with the Charter of the United Nations.

(B) Performing such other duties as may be prescribed by law or by the President or the Secretary of Defense.

(b) *Report on Assignment of Roles and Missions.*

(1) Not less than once every three years, or upon the request of the President or the Secretary of Defense, the Chairman shall submit to the Secretary of Defense a report containing such recommendations for changes in the assignment of functions (or roles and missions) to the armed forces as the Chairman considers necessary to achieve maximum effectiveness of the armed forces. In prepar-

ing each such report, the Chairman shall consider (among other matters) the following:

(A) Changes in the nature of the threats faced by the United States.

(B) Unnecessary duplication of effort among the armed forces.

(C) Changes in technology that can be applied effectively to warfare.

(2) The Chairman shall include in each such report recommendations for such changes in policies, directives, regulations, and legislation as may be necessary to achieve the changes in the assignment of functions recommended by the Chairman.

SEC. 154. Vice Chairman.

(a) *Appointment.*

(1) There is a Vice Chairman of the Joint Chiefs of Staff, appointed by the President, by and with the advice and consent of the Senate, from the officers of the regular components of the armed forces.

(2) The Chairman and Vice Chairman may not be members of the same armed force. However, the President may waive the restriction in the preceding sentence for a limited period of time in order to provide for the orderly transition of officers appointed to serve in the positions of Chairman and Vice Chairman.

(3) The Vice Chairman serves at the pleasure of the President for a term of two years and may be reappointed in the same manner for two additional terms. However, in time of war there is no limit on the number of reappointments.

(b) *Requirement for Appointment.*

(1) The President may appoint an officer as Vice Chairman of the Joint Chiefs of Staff only if the officer:

(A) has the joint specialty under section 661 of this title; and

(B) has completed a full tour of duty in a joint duty assignment (as defined in section 664(f) of this title) as a general or flag officer.

(2) The President may waive paragraph (1) in the case of an officer if the President determines such action is necessary in the national interest.

(c) *Duties.* The Vice Chairman performs the duties prescribed for him as a member of the Joint Chiefs of Staff and such other duties as may be prescribed by the Chairman with the approval of the Secretary of Defense.

(d) *Function as Acting Chairman.* When there is a vacancy in the office of Chairman or in the absence or disability of the Chairman, the Vice Chairman acts as Chairman and performs the duties of the Chairman until a successor is appointed or the absence or disability ceases.

(e) *Succession After Chairman and Vice Chairman.* When there is a vacancy in the offices of both Chairman and Vice Chairman or in the absence or disability of both the Chairman and the Vice Chairman, or when there is a vacancy in one such office and in the absence or disability of the officer holding the other, the President shall designate a member of the Joint Chiefs of Staff to act as and perform the duties of the Chairman until a successor to the Chairman or Vice Chairman is appointed or the absence or disability of the Chairman or Vice Chairman ceases.

. . . .

(g) *Grade and Rank.* The Vice Chairman, while so serving, holds the grade of general or, in the case of an officer of the Navy, admiral and outranks all other officers of the armed forces except the Chairman. The Vice Chairman may not exercise military command over the Joint Chiefs of Staff or any of the armed forces.

SEC. 155. Joint Staff

(a) *Appointment of Officers to Joint Staff.*

(1) There is a Joint Staff under the Chairman of the Joint Chiefs of Staff. The Joint Staff assists the Chairman and, subject to the authority, direction, and control of the Chairman, the other members of the Joint Chiefs of Staff in carrying out their responsibilities.

(2) Officers of the armed forces (other than the Coast Guard) assigned to serve on the Joint Staff shall be selected by the Chairman in approximately equal numbers from:

(A) the Army;

(B) the Navy and the Marine Corps; and

(C) the Air Force.

(3) Selection of officers of an armed force to serve on the Joint Staff shall be made by the Chairman from a list of officers submitted by the Secretary of the military department having jurisdiction over that armed force. Each officer whose name is submitted shall be among those officers considered to be the most outstanding officers of that armed force. The Chairman may specify the number of officers to be included on any such list.

(b) *Director.* The Chairman of the Joint Chiefs of Staff, after consultation with the other members of the Joint Chiefs of Staff and with the approval of the Secretary of Defense, may select an officer to serve as Director of the Joint Staff.

(c) *Management of Joint Staff.* The Chairman of the Joint Chiefs of Staff manages the Joint Staff and the Director of the Joint Staff. The Joint Staff shall perform such duties as the Chairman prescribes and shall perform such duties under such procedures as the Chairman prescribes.

(d) *Operation of Joint Staff.* The Secretary of Defense shall ensure that the Joint Staff is independently organized and operated so that the Joint Staff supports the Chairman of the Joint Chiefs of Staff in meeting the congressional purpose set forth in the last clause of section 2 of the National Security Act of 1947 (50 U.S.C. 401) to provide:

(1) for the unified strategic direction of the combatant forces;

(2) for their operation under unified command; and

(3) for their integration into an efficient team of land, naval, and air forces.

(e) *Prohibition of Function as Armed Forces General Staff.* The Joint Staff shall not operate or be organized as an overall Armed Forces General Staff and shall have no executive authority. The Joint Staff may be organized and may operate along conventional staff lines.

(f) *Tour of Duty of Joint Staff Officers.*

(1) An officer who is assigned or detailed to permanent duty on the Joint Staff may not serve for a tour of duty of more than four years. However, such a tour of duty may be extended with the approval of the Secretary of Defense.

(2) In accordance with procedures established by the Secretary of Defense, the Chairman of the Joint Chiefs of Staff may suspend from duty and recommend the reassignment of any officer assigned to the Joint Staff. Upon receipt of such a recommendation, the Secretary concerned shall promptly reassign the officer.

(3) An officer completing a tour of duty with the Joint Staff may not be assigned or detailed to permanent duty on the Joint Staff within two years after relief from that duty except with the approval of the Secretary.

(4) Paragraphs (1) and (3) do not apply:

(A) in time of war; or

(B) during a national emergency declared by the President or Congress.

....

(h) *Composition of Joint Staff.*

(1) The Joint Staff is composed of all members of the armed forces and civilian employees assigned or detailed to permanent duty in the executive part of the Department of Defense to perform the functions and duties prescribed under subsections (a) and (c).

(2) The Joint Staff does not include members of the armed forces or civilian employees assigned or detailed to permanent duty in a military department.

NATIONAL SECURITY DECISION DIRECTIVE 266[1] (IMPLEMENTING NSC REFORMS PROPOSED BY TOWER COMMISSION FOLLOWING IRAN-CONTRA)

THE WHITE HOUSE
Washington

March 31, 1987

IMPLEMENTATION OF THE RECOMMENDATIONS OF

THE PRESIDENT'S SPECIAL REVIEW BOARD

The President's Special Review Board submitted its Report on February 26, 1987. I addressed the Nation on March 4 and announced first, that I endorse the Board's recommendations; and second, that I intend to go beyond the Board's recommendations to put the National Security Council (NSC) process in even better order. This Directive spells out the specific steps I have approved to implement the letter and spirit of the Board's recommendations.

Many steps were taken even prior to the issuance of the Board's Report. The NSC staff was rebuilt and made subject to proper management discipline. A directive was issued on my instruction to prohibit the NSC staff itself from undertaking covert operations. A comprehensive legal and policy review of such operations, ordered by me, was already far advanced. Proper procedures for consultation with the Congress were reaffirmed and are being observed.

In light of the Board's Report, additional measures are required. This Directive sets forth the specific timetable according to which I expect all such measures to be completed. It is of utmost importance that the NSC—including all members of, and advisors to, the NSC, the Assistant to the President for National Security Affairs, and NSC staff, and all other participants in the NSC process—act decisively to accomplish my objectives fully.

I shall inform Congress of the nature and progress of these Executive branch efforts prior to the end of March; I also shall call upon Congress to heed the balance of the Board's recommendations, namely:

— that no substantive change be made in the provisions of the National Security Act dealing with the structure and operation of the NSC system;

— that the position of Assistant to the President for National Security Affairs not be made subject to Senate confirmation; and

1. Nat'l Sec. Decision Directive No. 266, Implementation of the Recommendations of the President's Special Review Board (Mar. 31, 1987), *reprinted in* Christopher Simpson, National Security Directives of the Reagan and Bush Administrations: The Declassified History of U.S. Political and Military Policy, 1981–1991, at 789–96 (1995), *available at* http://www.fas.org/irp/offdocs/nsdd/nsdd-266.htm.

— that Congress replace the existing Intelligence Committees of the Senate and House of Representatives with a new joint committee with a restricted staff to oversee the intelligence community.

These recommendations of the Board, which are addressed to Congress, I also strongly endorse.

I. Model for the National Security Council System

The structure and procedures of the National Security Council shall incorporate all aspects of the model of the NSC system described in the Report of the President's Special Review Board as the Board's principal recommendation. This directive implements that recommendation in each of the following respects:

— organizing for national security, including provisions of appropriate guidelines to participants in the NSC process;

— the role and functions of the Assistant to the President for National Security Affairs;

— the nature and responsibilities of the NSC staff; and

— the NSC and interagency process.

A. Organizing for National Security

The National Security Council shall be the principal forum for consideration of national security policy issues requiring presidential decision. The function of the NSC shall be as set forth in the National Security Act of 1947, as amended. Broadly speaking, the NSC shall advise the President with respect to the integration of domestic, foreign, and military policies relating to the national security so as to enable Executive departments and agencies to cooperate more effectively in matters involving the national security.

Participation in the NSC shall be as provided by law and this Directive. Statutory members of the NSC are the President, the Vice President, the Secretary of State, and the Secretary of Defense. Other heads of Executive departments and agencies and senior officials within the Executive Office of the President shall participate in the NSC as provided in this Directive.

The Director of Central Intelligence and the Chairman of the Joint Chiefs of Staff are statutory advisors to the NSC. The Director of Central Intelligence shall advise the NSC with respect to coordinating intelligence activities of Executive departments and agencies in the interest of national security and as otherwise provided by law. The Chairman of the Joint Chiefs of Staff shall be principal military advisor to the President, the Secretary of Defense, and the NSC.

The Directors of the United States Arms Control and Disarmament Agency and United States Information Agency are special statutory advisors to the NSC. The Director of the Arms Control and Disarmament Agency shall be principal advisor to the President, the Secretary of State, and the NSC on arms control and disarmament matters. The Director of the United States Information Agency shall be principal advisor to the President, the Secretary of State, and the NSC on international informational, educational, and cultural matters.

The Secretary of State shall be the President's principal foreign policy advisor. As such, the Secretary shall be responsible for the formulation of foreign policy, subject to review within the NSC process and the President's guidance as appropriate, and for the execution of approved policy. I assign to the Secretary of State authority and responsibility, to the extent permitted by law and this Directive, for the overall direction, coordination, and supervision of the interdepartmental activities incident to foreign policy formulation, and the activities of Executive departments and agencies of the United States overseas. Such activities shall not include those of United States military forces operating in the field under the command of a United States area military commander, and such other military activities as I elect, as Commander in Chief, to conduct exclusively through military or other channels. Activities that are internal to the execution and administration of the approved programs of a single department or agency and that are not of such nature as to affect significantly the overall United States overseas program in a country or region are not considered to be activities covered within the meaning of this Directive.

The Secretary of Defense shall be the President's principal defense policy advisor. As such, the Secretary shall be responsible for the formulation of general defense policy, subject to review within the NSC process and the President's guidance as appropriate, for policy related to all matters of direct and primary concern to the Department of Defense, and for the execution of approved policy. I assign to the Secretary of Defense authority and responsibility, to the extent permitted by law and this Directive, for the overall direction, coordination, and supervision of the interdepartmental activities incident to defense policy formulation.

The Director of Central Intelligence shall be the President's principal advisor on intelligence matters. As such, the Director shall be responsible for the formulation of intelligence activities, policy and proposals, subject to review within the NSC process and the President's guidance as appropriate, as set forth in law and relevant Executive orders. I assign to the Director of Central Intelligence authority and responsibility, to the extent permitted by law, Executive order, and this Directive, for the overall direction, coordination, and supervision of the interdepartmental activities incident to intelligence matters.

Although taking part in the NSC system by virtue of official positions as heads of Executive departments or agencies or as senior officials within the Executive departments or agencies or as senior officials within the Executive Office of the President, all NSC participants shall sit as advisors to the President in connection with the President's exercise of authority under the Constitution and laws of the United States. In their capacity as department and agency heads, NSC participants shall ensure the effective and expeditious execution and implementation of overall national security policies established by the President for National Security Affairs or of the NSC staff except as the President specifically directs.

B. The Assistant to the President for National Security Affairs

The Assistant to the President for National Security Affairs ("National Security Advisor") shall have primary responsibility for day-to-day management of the National Security Council process, and shall serve as principal advisor on the President's staff with respect to all national security affairs. The National Security Advisor shall have access and report directly to the President, and shall keep the President and the Chief of Staff to the President fully and currently informed on all matters of substance.

As manager of the NSC process, the National Security Advisor shall ensure the following: that matters submitted for consideration by the NSC cover the full range of issues on which review is required; that those issues are fully analyzed; that a full range of options is considered; that the prospects and risks of each are examined; that all relevant intelligence and other information is available to NSC participants; that legal matters are addressed; and that policies are executed in conformity with the intent of presidential decisions. He shall initiate periodic reassessments of policies and operations, in light of changed circumstances or United States interests. The National Security Advisor shall keep NSC participants currently informed of presidential decisions. He shall ensure that NSC consultations and presidential decisions are adequately recorded, and that appropriate and timely preparations are made with respect to meetings convened under NSC auspices.

As the President's principal staff advisor on national security affairs, the National Security Advisor shall present his own views and advice and, at the same time, faithfully represent the views of other NSC participants.

C. The National Security Council Staff

The functions and responsibilities of the Executive Secretary of the National Security Council shall be as provided by the National Security Act of 1947, as amended. The Executive Secretary heads the NSC staff, and, in accordance with applicable laws and regulations, appoints and fixes the compensation of personnel required to perform such duties as may be prescribed by the President, the NSC, or the National Security Advisor. The Executive Secretary shall establish procedures within the NSC Executive Secretariat for maximum effective support of the NSC and the National Security Advisor in performance of responsibilities assigned by the President. With the guidance and under the instruction of the National Security Advisor, the Executive Secretary shall develop and implement appropriate policies with respect to the overall size of the NSC staff, the background and experience of its members, and duration of their service, and the organization of staff offices. The objectives shall be twofold: first, an NSC staff that is small, highly competent, broadly experienced in the making of national security policy, and properly balanced from among Executive departments and agencies and persons drawn from within and outside government; and second, an NSC staff organization that imposes clear, vertical lines of control and accountability.

The Executive Secretary, through the National Security Advisor, shall recommend for my consideration specific measures designed to enhance the continuity of the functioning of the NSC, including measures to ensure adequate institutional recordkeeping from administration to administration. Specific recommendations for these purposes shall be made not later than June 30, 1987.

The NSC staff, through the Executive Secretary, shall assist the National Security Advisor in each aspect of his roles both as manager of the NSC process and as my principal staff advisor on national security affairs.

The NSC staff shall include a Legal Advisor whose particular responsibility it will be to provide legal counsel to the National Security Advisor, the Executive Secretary, and the NSC staff with respect to the full range of their activities, and to assist the National Security Advisor in ensuring that legal considerations are fully addressed in the NSC process and in interagency deliberations. The NSC Legal Advisor shall be accorded access to all information and deliberations as may be required for these purposes, and shall advise the National Security Advisor and Executive Secretary as appropriate on all matters within his responsibility. He shall work cooperatively with the Counsel to the President, the Legal Adviser of the Department of State, and with senior counsel to all other NSC members, advisors, and participants.

D. The National Security Council and Interagency Process

1. National Security Council Meetings

The National Security Council shall meet regularly to consider matters directed by the President or recommended by the National Security Advisor or by the other NSC members. The National Security Advisor shall attend all NSC meetings and shall be responsible for the agenda and conduct of such meetings under my direction. The statutory members of the NSC, and the Director of Central Intelligence and Chairman of the Joint Chiefs of Staff as statutory advisors to the NSC, shall attend NSC meetings. In addition, the Attorney General, the Secretary of the Treasury, and the Chief of Staff to the President at my invitation small attend NSC meetings. The special statutory advisors to the NSC, the Director of the Office of Management and Budget, and the heads of other Executive departments and agencies shall be invited to attend such NSC meetings as relate to matters vested under their authority.

The National Security Advisor shall provide NSC participants advance notice of all NSC meetings and agenda therefor. To the extent practicable, the National Security Advisor shall circulate decision documents in advance of such meetings. The Executive Secretary of the NSC and the NSC staff shall assist the National Security Advisor in connection with appropriate preparations for, and follow-up to, NSC meetings, as directed by the President. Such assistance shall include preparation of meeting minutes and the development and dissemination of decision documents and, as appropriate, study directives. All decision documents shall be submitted for the President's review and action by the National Security Advisor. The National Security Advisor shall transmit decision documents to the President through the Chief of Staff to the President. National Security Decision Directives, intelligence findings, and similar decision documents shall be coordinated, in advance of their submission to the President, by the NSC Legal Advisor with the Counsel to the President.

2. The Interagency Process

To assist the NSC at large and its individual members and advisors in fulfilling their responsibilities, I previously directed or authorized the establishment of senior interagency groups and regional and functional interagency groups. The purpose of such groups was to establish policy objectives, develop policy options, make appropriate recommendations, consider the implications of agency programs for foreign policy or overall national security policy, and undertake such other activities as may be assigned by the NSC.

The NSC, through the National Security Advisor, shall review the structure of senior interagency groups and regional and functional interagency groups established pursuant to, or under authority of, presidential directives or applicable memoranda, and shall recommend all such changes thereto as may be necessary or desirable to realize fully and promptly in practice the Special Review Board's recommended model for the NSC system, as well as all of the Board's other recommendations. These include establishment of an interagency process in which the National Security Advisor chairs the senior level committees of the NSC. The National Security Advisor shall present, for consideration by the NSC, a draft National Security Decision Directive for this purpose not later than April 30, 1987.

II. Covert Actions and Use of Non-Government Personnel

I have directed the National Security Council's Planning and Coordination Group (PCG) to review all covert action programs. This review is designed to ensure that such programs are commenced and pursued in accordance with law and are consistent with United States policy. The PCG shall complete this review on an expedited basis. It shall report its findings to the NSC on or before April 30, 1987. The NSC promptly shall review all such programs and seek my concurrence in their continuation as appropriate. The NSC, through the National Security Advisor, shall review current procedures for covert action policy approval and coordination and shall recommend such changes as may be necessary or desirable to ensure, among other things, the following:

— that proposed covert actions will be coordinated with NSC participants, including the Attorney General, and their respective recommendations communicated to the President;

— that all requirements of law concerning covert activities, including those requirements relating to presidential authorization and congressional notification, will be addressed in a timely manner and complied with fully;

— consistent with the foregoing, that covert activities will be subject to tightly restricted consideration, and measures to protect the security of all information concerning such activities will be enhanced;

— that the NSC staff itself will not undertake the conduct of covert activities; and

— that the use of private individuals and organizations as intermediaries to conduct covert activities will be appropriately limited and subject in every case to close observation and supervision by appropriate Executive departments and agencies.

This review shall take fully into account such changes as I have authorized by this Directive to the structure of the NSC. The National Security Advisor shall present, for consideration by the NSC, a revised National Security Decision Directive on procedures for covert action policy approval and coordination not later than April 30, 1987.

III. Intelligence Process

Maintaining the integrity and objectivity of the intelligence process is an important goal of the United States intelligence effort. It demands, as the President's Special Review Board has stated, careful differentiation between the respective roles of foreign intelligence, on the one hand, and policy advocacy, on the other. The Director of Central Intelligence shall provide such additional review of, guidance for, and direction to, the conduct of national foreign intelligence estimates as may be required to accomplish fully this objective. The Director of Central Intelligence shall review established procedures for the production of national foreign intelligence estimates and, not later than July 31, 1987, shall inform the NSC, through the National Security Advisor, of any modifications or additions thereto he may deem appropriate for this purpose.

IV. Reporting

The National Security Advisor shall keep me fully informed of progress on all aspects of the implementation of the recommendations of the President's Special Review Board.

TO THE CONGRESS OF THE UNITED STATES:[2]

In my address to the American people on March 4, I promised that I would report to the Congress by the end of March on all the steps I have taken to implement the

2. Ronald Reagan, Message to the Congress Transmitting the Directive Implementing the Recommendations of the President's Special Review Board for the National Security Council, 1 Pub. Papers 310, 310–11 (Mar. 31, 1987).

recommendations of the President's Special Review Board chaired by former Senator John Tower.

I hereby submit to the Congress for its information the text of the decision directive I issued to implement the Special Review Board's recommendations. This directive mandates certain actions to put the National Security Council (NSC) process in better order and to avoid any recurrence of the deficiencies and abuses that the Special Review Board described. Many of these remedial measures—including the prohibition of NSC staff engagement in covert activities—were implemented before the Special Review Board reported to me on February 26. The remaining steps have been taken or will be completed shortly.

The President and the Congress share a significant responsibility for safeguarding and advancing the interests of the United States in the world at large. When our two branches of government are at odds, we weaken ourselves as a force for international peace and freedom; when our two branches work in harmony, there is little our Nation cannot accomplish. Each branch is jealous of its constitutional prerogatives; yet, each must also respect the prerogatives of the other.

In this regard, I endorse the Special Review Board's recommendation that the structure and procedures of the National Security Council system not be the subject of further legislation. The NSC and NSC system have traditionally been a flexible instrument for presidential management of national security affairs. Every President since 1947 has used this instrument in a different way; as my successors, too, will discover, its flexibility is an important part of its usefulness. Similarly, the Special Review Board found that it was not the present structure or procedures that were at fault; rather, the problem was that the properly established structure and procedures were not properly used.

The reforms and changes I have made are evident of my determination to return to proper procedures, including consultation with the Congress. I will do my share, as I said on March 4, "to make the congressional oversight process work."

I look to the Congress to do its share, as well. In the intelligence field, I welcome the Congress's oversight role as it has developed in the last decade. At the same time, this is a sphere of policy that requires a strong Executive role—for constitutional, historical, and practical reasons—as well as a special spirit of close cooperation between our two branches.

The Special Review Board recommended that the existing Intelligence Committees of the House and Senate be merged into a new Joint Committee, with a restricted staff, to oversee the intelligence community. This is a recommendation that deserves to be enacted as it would help ensure the necessary secrecy of deliberations in this sensitive area. In addition, I must make clear that I will strongly oppose legislation that would attempt to encroach further on what I regard as the President's independent constitutional authority in the intelligence field.

I pledge to the American people and to the Congress that I will follow through on all the commitments set forth in the decision directive that I am transmitting. I intend, as well, to move ahead on the pressing agenda of foreign policy challenges and opportunities that lie before us. This agenda will not wait. I was elected to carry forward this Nation's vital role of leadership in the world, and I intend to do so.

Ronald Reagan

THE WHITE HOUSE,
March 31, 1987

NATIONAL SECURITY PRESIDENTIAL DIRECTIVE - 1* (ORGANIZATION OF NATIONAL SECURITY COUNCIL SYSTEM)

THE WHITE HOUSE
Washington

February 13, 2001

....

SUBJECT: Organization of the National Security Council System

This document is the first in a series of National Security Presidential Directives. National Security Presidential Directives shall replace both Presidential Decision Directives and Presidential Review Directives as an instrument for communicating presidential decisions about the national security policies of the United States.

National security includes the defense of the United States of America, protection of our constitutional system of government, and the advancement of United States interests around the globe. National security also depends on America's opportunity to prosper in the world economy. The National Security Act of 1947, as amended, established the National Security Council to advise the President with respect to the integration of domestic, foreign, and military policies relating to national security. That remains its purpose. The NSC shall advise and assist me in integrating all aspects of national security policy as it affects the United States—domestic, foreign, military, intelligence, and economics (in conjunction with the National Economic Council (NEC)). The National Security Council system is a process to coordinate executive departments and agencies in the effective development and implementation of those national security policies.

The National Security Council (NSC) shall have as its regular attendees (both statutory and non-statutory) the President, the Vice President, the Secretary of State, the Secretary of the Treasury, the Secretary of Defense, and the Assistant to the President for National Security Affairs. The Director of Central Intelligence and the Chairman of the Joint Chiefs of Staff, as statutory advisors to the NSC, shall also attend NSC meetings. The Chief of Staff to the President and the Assistant to the President for Economic Policy are invited to attend any NSC meeting. The Counsel to the President shall be consulted regarding the agenda of NSC meetings, and shall attend any meeting when, in consultation with the Assistant to the President for National Security Affairs, he deems it appropriate. The Attorney General and the Director of the Office of Management and Budget shall be invited to attend meetings pertaining to their responsibilities. For the Attorney General, this includes both those matters within the Justice Department's jurisdiction and those matters implicating the Attorney General's responsibility under 28 U.S.C. 511 to give his advice and opinion on questions of law when required by the President. The heads of other executive departments and agencies, as well as other senior officials, shall be invited to attend meetings of the NSC when appropriate.

* Nat'l Sec. Presidential Directive No. 1, Organization of the National Security Council System (Feb. 13, 2001), *available at* http://www.fas.org/irp/offdocs/nspd/nspd-1.htm.

The NSC shall meet at my direction. When I am absent from a meeting of the NSC, at my direction the Vice President may preside. The Assistant to the President for National Security Affairs shall be responsible, at my direction and in consultation with the other regular attendees of the NSC, for determining the agenda, ensuring that necessary papers are prepared, and recording NSC actions and Presidential decisions. When international economic issues are on the agenda of the NSC, the Assistant to the President for National Security Affairs and the Assistant to the President for Economic Policy shall perform these tasks in concert.

The NSC Principals Committee (NSC/PC) will continue to be the senior interagency forum for consideration of policy issues affecting national security, as it has since 1989. The NSC/PC shall have as its regular attendees the Secretary of State, the Secretary of the Treasury, the Secretary of Defense, the Chief of Staff to the President, and the Assistant to the President for National Security Affairs (who shall serve as chair). The Director of Central Intelligence and the Chairman of the Joint Chiefs of Staff shall attend where issues pertaining to their responsibilities and expertise are to be discussed. The Attorney General and the Director of the Office of Management and Budget shall be invited to attend meetings pertaining to their responsibilities. For the Attorney General, this includes both those matters within the Justice Department's jurisdiction and those matters implicating the Attorney General's responsibility under 28 U.S.C. 511 to give his advice and opinion on questions of law when required by the President. The Counsel to the President shall be consulted regarding the agenda of NSC/PC meetings, and shall attend any meeting when, in consultation with the Assistant to the President for National Security Affairs, he deems it appropriate. When international economic issues are on the agenda of the NSC/PC, the Committee's regular attendees will include the Secretary of Commerce, the United States Trade Representative, the Assistant to the President for Economic Policy (who shall serve as chair for agenda items that principally pertain to international economics), and, when the issues pertain to her responsibilities, the Secretary of Agriculture. The Chief of Staff and National Security Adviser to the Vice President shall attend all meetings of the NSC/PC, as shall the Assistant to the President and Deputy National Security Advisor (who shall serve as Executive Secretary of the NSC/PC). Other heads of departments and agencies, along with additional senior officials, shall be invited where appropriate.

The NSC/PC shall meet at the call of the Assistant to the President for National Security Affairs, in consultation with the regular attendees of the NSC/PC. The Assistant to the President for National Security Affairs shall determine the agenda in consultation with the foregoing, and ensure that necessary papers are prepared. When international economic issues are on the agenda of the NSC/PC, the Assistant to the President for National Security Affairs and the Assistant to the President for Economic Policy shall perform these tasks in concert.

The NSC Deputies Committee (NSC/DC) will also continue to serve as the senior sub-Cabinet interagency forum for consideration of policy issues affecting national security. The NSC/DC can prescribe and review the work of the NSC interagency groups discussed later in this directive. The NSC/DC shall also help ensure that issues being brought before the NSC/PC or the NSC have been properly analyzed and prepared for decision. The NSC/DC shall have as its regular members the Deputy Secretary of State or Under Secretary of the Treasury or Under Secretary of the Treasury for International Affairs, the Deputy Secretary of Defense or Under Secretary of Defense for Policy, the Deputy Attorney General, the Deputy Director of the Office of Management and Budget, the Deputy Director of Central Intelligence, the Vice Chairman of the Joint Chiefs of Staff, the Deputy Chief of Staff to the President for Policy, the Chief of Staff and National Security Adviser to the Vice President, the Deputy Assistant to the President for International Economic Affairs, and the Assistant to the President and Deputy National Security Advisor (who shall serve as chair). When international economic issues are on the agenda, the NSC/DC's regular membership will include the Deputy Secretary of Commerce, a Deputy United States Trade Representative, and, when the issues pertain to his responsibilities, the Deputy Secretary of Agriculture, and the NSC/DC shall be chaired by the Deputy Assistant to the President for International Economic Affairs for agenda items that principally pertain to international economics. Other senior officials shall be invited where appropriate.

The NSC/DC shall meet at the call of its chair, in consultation with the other regular members of the NSC/DC. Any regular member of the NSC/DC may also request a meeting of the Committee for prompt crisis management. For all meetings the chair shall determine the agenda in consultation with the foregoing, and ensure that necessary papers are prepared.

The Vice President and I may attend any and all meetings of any entity established by or under this directive.

Management of the development and implementation of national security policies by multiple agencies of the United States Government shall usually be accomplished by the NSC Policy Coordination Committees (NSC/PCCs). The NSC/PCCs shall be the main day-to-day fora for interagency coordination of national security policy. They shall provide policy analysis for consideration by the more senior committees of the NSC system and ensure timely responses to decisions made by the President. Each NSC/PCC shall include representatives from the executive departments, offices, and agencies represented in the NSC/DC.

Six NSC/PCCs are hereby established for the following regions: Europe and Eurasia, Western Hemisphere, East Asia, South Asia, Near East and North Africa, and Africa. Each of the NSC/PCCs shall be chaired by an official of Under Secretary or Assistant Secretary rank to be designated by the Secretary of State.

Eleven NSC/PCCs are hereby also established for the following functional topics, each to be chaired by a person of Under Secretary or Assistant Secretary rank designated by the indicated authority:

Democracy, Human Rights, and International Operations (by the Assistant to the President for National Security Affairs);

International Development and Humanitarian Assistance (by the Secretary of State);

Global Environment (by the Assistant to the President for National Security Affairs and the Assistant to the President for Economic Policy in concert);

International Finance (by the Secretary of the Treasury);

Transnational Economic Issues (by the Assistant to the President for Economic Policy);

Counter-Terrorism and National Preparedness (by the Assistant to the President for National Security Affairs);

Defense Strategy, Force Structure, and Planning (by the Secretary of Defense);

Arms Control (by the Assistant to the President for National Security Affairs);

Proliferation, Counterproliferation, and Homeland Defense (by the Assistant to the President for National Security Affairs);

Intelligence and Counterintelligence (by the Assistant to the President for National Security Affairs); and

Records Access and Information Security (by the Assistant to the President for National Security Affairs).

The Trade Policy Review Group (TPRG) will continue to function as an interagency coordinator of trade policy. Issues considered within the TPRG, as with the PCCs, will flow through the NSC and/or NEC process, as appropriate.

Each NSC/PCC shall also have an Executive Secretary from the staff of the NSC, to be designated by the Assistant to the President for National Security Affairs. The Executive Secretary shall assist the Chairman in scheduling the meetings of the NSC/PCC, determining the agenda, recording the actions taken and tasks assigned, and ensuring timely responses to the central policymaking committees of the NSC system. The Chairman of each NSC/PCC, in consultation with the Executive Secretary, may invite representatives of other executive departments and agencies to attend meetings of the NSC/PCC where appropriate.

The Assistant to the President for National Security Affairs, at my direction and in consultation with the Vice President and the Secretaries of State, Treasury, and Defense, may establish additional NSC/PCCs as appropriate.

The Chairman of each NSC/PCC, with the agreement of the Executive Secretary, may establish subordinate working groups to assist the PCC in the performance of its duties.

. . . .

This Directive shall supersede all other existing presidential guidance on the organization of the National Security Council system. With regard to application of this document to economic matters, this document shall be interpreted in concert with any Executive Order governing the National Economic Council and with presidential decision documents signed hereafter that implement either this directive or that Executive Order.

[signed: George W. Bush]
cc: The Executive Clerk

B. Homeland Security and Counterterrorism

POSSE COMITATUS ACT*

Background Note

The Posse Comitatus Act was passed in 1878 in response to the use of federal troops for law enforcement purposes in the south during the Reconstruction period. Not only were soldiers not trained to respect the rights of citizens, but there was concern that the use of soldiers at polling stations and similar settings was politicizing the military. Although the statute does not mention the Navy or Marine Corps, under Department of Defense Directive 5525.5 they are precluded along with the Army and Air Force from direct participation in a search, seizure, arrest, or other similar activity unless participation in such activity is authorized by law. The act does not apply to the Coast Guard or to the National Guard when under the control of state governors. Several exceptions have been enacted over recent years to permit some involvement by federal military personnel in areas of special concern like counter-drug assistance (10 U.S.C. §371-381). When the Attorney General and Secretary of Defense jointly determine the existence of an "emergency situation" that poses a serious threat and is beyond the capabilities of civilian law enforcement, the military may assist law enforcement in the case of crimes involving nuclear materials (18 U.S.C. §831) or chemical or biological weapons of mass destructions (10 U.S.C. § 382). State governors and legislators may also request military assistance under the Civil Disturbance Statutes (10 U.S.C. §331-334) in settings where local law enforcement is unable to protect civil rights and property (such as in the 1992 Los Angeles riots). Limited use of the military is also authorized for immigration control and tariff enforcement. Courts have generally distinguished between "active" and "passive" forms of military involvement, barring the military (save for the Coast Guard, which has important statutory law enforcement responsibilities and is trained to be sensitive to individual rights) from making arrests or participating directly in law enforcement activities but permitting certain types of logistical support.—Eds.

SEC. 1385. *Use of Army and Air Force as posse comitatus.*

Whoever, except in cases and under circumstances expressly authorized by the Constitution or Act of Congress, willfully uses any part of the Army or the Air Force as a posse comitatus or otherwise to execute the laws shall be fined under this title or imprisoned not more than two years, or both.

---

* Posse Comitatus Act, ch. 263, § 15, 20 Stat. 152 (1878), *amended by* Amendments to Title 18, Crimes and Criminal Procedure § 18, 70A Stat. 626 (1956) (codified as amended at 18 U.S.C. § 1385 (2000)).

EXECUTIVE ORDER 13228* (ESTABLISHING OFFICE OF HOMELAND SECURITY)

By the authority vested in me as President by the Constitution and the laws of the United States of America, it is hereby ordered as follows:

Section 1. *Establishment.* I hereby establish within the Executive Office of the President an Office of Homeland Security (the "Office") to be headed by the Assistant to the President for Homeland Security.

Section 2. *Mission.* The mission of the Office shall be to develop and coordinate the implementation of a comprehensive national strategy to secure the United States from terrorist threats or attacks. The Office shall perform the functions necessary to carry out this mission, including the functions specified in section 3 of this order.

Section 3. *Functions.* The functions of the Office shall be to coordinate the executive branch's efforts to detect, prepare for, prevent, protect against, respond to, and recover from terrorist attacks within the United States.

(a) National Strategy. The Office shall work with executive departments and agencies, State and local governments, and private entities to ensure the adequacy of the national strategy for detecting, preparing for, preventing, protecting against, responding to, and recovering from terrorist threats or attacks within the United States and shall periodically review and coordinate revisions to that strategy as necessary.

(b) Detection. The Office shall identify priorities and coordinate efforts for collection and analysis of information within the United States regarding threats of terrorism against the United States and activities of terrorists or terrorist groups within the United States. The Office also shall identify, in coordination with the Assistant to the President for National Security Affairs, priorities for collection of intelligence outside the United States regarding threats of terrorism within the United States.

(i) In performing these functions, the Office shall work with Federal, State, and local agencies, as appropriate, to:

(A) facilitate collection from State and local governments and private entities of information pertaining to terrorist threats or activities within the United States;

(B) coordinate and prioritize the requirements for foreign intelligence relating to terrorism within the United States of executive departments and agencies responsible for homeland security and provide these requirements and priorities to the Director of Central Intelligence and other agencies responsible collection of foreign intelligence;

(C) coordinate efforts to ensure that all executive departments and agencies that have intelligence collection responsibilities have sufficient

* Exec. Order No. 13,228, 3 C.F.R. 796 (2001), *reprinted in* 50 U.S.C.A. §402 note (West 2003), *available at* http://www.yale.edu/lawweb/avalon/sept_11/execord_100801.htm.

technological capabilities and resources to collect intelligence and data relating to terrorist activities or possible terrorist acts within the United States, working with the Assistant to the President for National Security Affairs, as appropriate;

(D) coordinate development of monitoring protocols and equipment for use in detecting the release of biological, chemical, and radiological hazards; and

(E) ensure that, to the extent permitted by law, all appropriate and necessary intelligence and law enforcement information relating to homeland security is disseminated to and exchanged among appropriate executive departments and agencies responsible for homeland security and, where appropriate for reasons of homeland security, promote exchange of such information with and among State and local governments and private entities.

(ii) Executive departments and agencies shall, to the extent permitted by law, make available to the Office all information relating to terrorist threats and activities within the United States.

(c) Preparedness. The Office of Homeland Security shall coordinate national efforts to prepare for and mitigate the consequences of terrorist threats or attacks within the United States. In performing this function, the Office shall work with Federal, State, and local agencies, and private entities, as appropriate, to:

(i) review and assess the adequacy of the portions of all Federal emergency response plans that pertain to terrorist threats or attacks within the United States;

(ii) coordinate domestic exercises and simulations designed to assess and practice systems that would be called upon to respond to a terrorist threat or attack within the United States and coordinate programs and activities for training Federal, State, and local employees who would be called upon to respond to such a threat or attack;

(iii) coordinate national efforts to ensure public health preparedness for a terrorist attack, including reviewing vaccination policies and reviewing the adequacy of and, if necessary, increasing vaccine and pharmaceutical stockpiles and hospital capacity;

(iv) coordinate Federal assistance to State and local authorities and nongovernmental organizations to prepare for and respond to terrorist threats or attacks within the United States;

(v) ensure that national preparedness programs and activities for terrorist threats or attacks are developed and are regularly evaluated under appropriate standards and that resources are allocated to improving and sustaining preparedness based on such evaluations; and

(vi) ensure the readiness and coordinated deployment of Federal response teams to respond to terrorist threats or attacks, working with the Assistant to the President for National Security Affairs, when appropriate.

(d) Prevention. The Office shall coordinate efforts to prevent terrorist attacks within the United States. In performing this function, the Office shall work with Federal, State, and local agencies, and private entities, as appropriate, to:

(i) facilitate the exchange of information among such agencies relating to immigration and visa matters and shipments of cargo; and, working with the

Assistant to the President for National Security Affairs, ensure coordination among such agencies to prevent the entry of terrorists and terrorist materials and supplies into the United States and facilitate removal of such terrorists from the United States, when appropriate;

(ii) coordinate efforts to investigate terrorist threats and attacks within the United States; and

(iii) coordinate efforts to improve the security of United States borders, territorial waters, and airspace in order to prevent acts of terrorism within the United States, working with the Assistant to the President for National Security Affairs, when appropriate.

(e) Protection. The Office shall coordinate efforts to protect the United States and its critical infrastructure from the consequences of terrorist attacks. In performing this function, the Office shall work with Federal, State, and local agencies, and private entities, as appropriate, to:

(i) strengthen measures for protecting energy production, transmission, and distribution services and critical facilities; other utilities; telecommunications; facilities that produce, use, store, or dispose of nuclear material; and other critical infrastructure services and critical facilities within the United States from terrorist attack;

(ii) coordinate efforts to protect critical public and privately owned information systems within the United States from terrorist attack;

(iii) develop criteria for reviewing whether appropriate security measures are in place at major public and privately owned facilities within the United States;

(iv) coordinate domestic efforts to ensure that special events determined by appropriate senior officials to have national significance are protected from terrorist attack;

(v) coordinate efforts to protect transportation systems within the United States, including railways, highways, shipping, ports and waterways, and airports and civilian aircraft, from terrorist attack;

(vi) coordinate efforts to protect United States livestock, agriculture, and systems for the provision of water and food for human use and consumption from terrorist attack; and

(vii) coordinate efforts to prevent unauthorized access to, development of, and unlawful importation into the United States of, chemical, biological, radiological, nuclear, explosive, or other related materials that have the potential to be used in terrorist attacks.

(f) Response and Recovery. The Office shall coordinate efforts to respond to and promote recovery from terrorist threats or attacks within the United States. In performing this function, the Office shall work with Federal, State, and local agencies, and private entities, as appropriate, to:

(i) coordinate efforts to ensure rapid restoration of transportation systems, energy production, transmission, and distribution systems; telecommunications; other utilities; and other critical infrastructure facilities after disruption by a terrorist threat or attack;

(ii) coordinate efforts to ensure rapid restoration of public and private critical information systems after disruption by a terrorist threat or attack;

(iii) work with the National Economic Council to coordinate efforts to stabilize United States financial markets after a terrorist threat or attack and manage the immediate economic and financial consequences of the incident;

(iv) coordinate Federal plans and programs to provide medical, financial, and other assistance to victims of terrorist attacks and their families; and

(v) coordinate containment and removal of biological, chemical, radiological, explosive, or other hazardous materials in the event of a terrorist threat or attack involving such hazards and coordinate efforts to mitigate the effects of such an attack.

(g) Incident Management. The Assistant to the President for Homeland Security shall be the individual primarily responsible for coordinating the domestic response efforts of all departments and agencies in the event of an imminent terrorist threat and during and in the immediate aftermath of a terrorist attack within the United States and shall be the principal point of contact for and to the President with respect to coordination of such efforts. The Assistant to the President for Homeland Security shall coordinate with the Assistant to the President for National Security Affairs, as appropriate.

(h) Continuity of Government. The Assistant to the President for Homeland Security, in coordination with the Assistant to the President for National Security Affairs, shall review plans and preparations for ensuring the continuity of the Federal Government in the event of a terrorist attack that threatens the safety and security of the United States Government or its leadership.

(i) Public Affairs. The Office, subject to the direction of the White House Office of Communications, shall coordinate the strategy of the executive branch for communicating with the public in the event of a terrorist threat or attack within the United States. The Office also shall coordinate the development of programs for educating the public about the nature of terrorist threats and appropriate precautions and responses.

(j) Cooperation with State and Local Governments and Private Entities. The Office shall encourage and invite the participation of State and local governments and private entities, as appropriate, in carrying out the Office's functions.

(k) Review of Legal Authorities and Development of Legislative Proposals. The Office shall coordinate a periodic review and assessment of the legal authorities available to executive departments and agencies to permit them to perform the functions described in this order. When the Office determines that such legal authorities are inadequate, the Office shall develop, in consultation with executive departments and agencies, proposals for presidential action and legislative proposals for submission to the Office of Management and Budget to enhance the ability of executive departments and agencies to perform those functions. The Office shall work with State and local governments in assessing the adequacy of their legal authorities to permit them to detect, prepare for, prevent, protect against, and recover from terrorist threats and attacks.

(l) Budget Review. The Assistant to the President for Homeland Security, in consultation with the Director of the Office of Management and Budget (the "Director") and the heads of executive departments and agencies, shall identify programs that contribute to the Administration's strategy for homeland security and, in the development of the President's annual budget submission, shall review and provide advice to the heads of departments and agencies for such programs. The

Assistant to the President for Homeland Security shall provide advice to the Director on the level and use of funding in departments and agencies for homeland security-related activities and, prior to the Director's forwarding of the proposed annual budget submission to the President for transmittal to the Congress, shall certify to the Director the funding levels that the Assistant to the President for Homeland Security believes are necessary and appropriate for the homeland security-related activities of the executive branch.

Section 4. *Administration.* (a) The Office of Homeland Security shall be directed by the Assistant to the President for Homeland Security.

(b) The Office of Administration within the Executive Office of the President shall provide the Office of Homeland Security with such personnel, funding, and administrative support, to the extent permitted by law and subject to the availability of appropriations, as directed by the Chief of Staff to carry out the provisions of this order.

(c) Heads of executive departments and agencies are authorized, to the extent permitted by law, to detail or assign personnel of such departments and agencies to the Office of Homeland Security upon request of the Assistant to the President for Homeland Security, subject to the approval of the Chief of Staff.

Section 5. *Establishment of Homeland Security Council.* (a) I hereby establish a Homeland Security Council (the "Council"), which shall be responsible for advising and assisting the President with respect to all aspects of homeland security. The Council shall serve as the mechanism for ensuring coordination of homeland security-related activities of executive departments and agencies and effective development and implementation of homeland security policies.

(b) The Council shall have as its members the President, the Vice President, the Secretary of the Treasury, the Secretary of Defense, the Attorney General, the Secretary of Health and Human Services, the Secretary of Transportation, the Director of the Federal Emergency Management Agency, the Director of the Federal Bureau of Investigation, the Director of Central Intelligence, the Assistant to the President for Homeland Security, and such other officers of the executive branch as the President may from time to time designate. The Chief of Staff, the Chief of Staff to the Vice President, the Assistant to the President for National Security Affairs, the Counsel to the President, and the Director of the Office of Management and Budget also are invited to attend any Council meeting. The Secretary of State, the Secretary of Agriculture, the Secretary of the Interior, the Secretary of Energy, the Secretary of Labor, the Secretary of Commerce, the Secretary of Veterans Affairs, the Administrator of the Environmental Protection Agency, the Assistant to the President for Economic Policy, and the Assistant to the President for Domestic Policy shall be invited to attend meetings pertaining to their responsibilities. The heads of other executive departments and agencies and other senior officials shall be invited to attend Council meetings when appropriate.

(c) The Council shall meet at the President's direction. When the President is absent from a meeting of the Council, at the President's direction the Vice President may preside. The Assistant to the President for Homeland Security shall be responsible, at the President's direction, for determining the agenda, ensuring that necessary papers are prepared, and recording Council actions and Presidential decisions.

Section 6. *Original Classification Authority.* I hereby delegate the authority to classify information originally as Top Secret, in accordance with Executive Order 12958 or any successor Executive Order, to the Assistant to the President for Homeland Security.

Section 7. *Continuing Authorities.* This order does not alter the existing authorities of United States Government departments and agencies. All executive departments and agencies are directed to assist the Council and the Assistant to the President for Homeland Security in carrying out the purposes of this order.

Section 8. *General Provisions.* (a) This order does not create any right or benefit, substantive or procedural, enforceable at law or equity by a party against the United States, its departments, agencies or instrumentalities, its officers or employees, or any other person.

(b) References in this order to State and local governments shall be construed to include tribal governments and United States territories and other possessions.

(c) References to the "United States" shall be construed to include United States territories and possessions.

Section 9. *Amendments to Executive Order 12656.* Executive Order 12656 of November 18, 1988, as amended, is hereby further amended as follows:

(a) Section 101(a) is amended by adding at the end of the fourth sentence: ", except that the Homeland Security Council shall be responsible for administering such policy with respect to terrorist threats and attacks within the United States."

(b) Section 104(a) is amended by adding at the end: ", except that the Homeland Security Council is the principal forum for consideration of policy relating to terrorist threats and attacks within the United States."

(c) Section 104(b) is amended by inserting the words "and the Homeland Security Council" after the words "National Security Council."

(d) The first sentence of section 104(c) is amended by inserting the words "and the Homeland Security Council" after the words "National Security Council."

(e) The second sentence of section 104(c) is replaced with the following two sentences: "Pursuant to such procedures for the organization and management of the National Security Council and Homeland Security Council processes as the President may establish, the Director of the Federal Emergency Management Agency also shall assist in the implementation of and management of those processes as the President may establish. The Director of the Federal Emergency Management Agency also shall assist in the implementation of national security emergency preparedness policy by coordinating with the other Federal departments and agencies and with State and local governments, and by providing periodic reports to the National Security Council and the Homeland Security Council on implementation of national security emergency preparedness policy."

(f) Section 201(7) is amended by inserting the words "and the Homeland Security Council" after the words "National Security Council."

(g) Section 206 is amended by inserting the words "and the Homeland Security Council" after the words "National Security Council."

(h) Section 208 is amended by inserting the words "or the Homeland Security Council" after the words "National Security Council."

GEORGE W. BUSH
THE WHITE HOUSE,
October 8, 2001.

USA PATRIOT ACT[1]

Note

Both because of its great length and the need to have access to several other statutes to fully understand its technical language,[2] we have elected not to attempt to include even short excerpts from this 2001 statute. However, to provide a general overview of the statute's provisions, we reprint below a brief summary prepared by the Congressional Research Service of the Library of Congress.[3]—Eds.

Uniting and Strengthening America by Providing Appropriate Tools Required to Intercept and Obstruct Terrorism (USA PATRIOT ACT) Act of 2001.

Title I: Enhancing Domestic Security Against Terrorism—Establishes in the Treasury the Counterterrorism Fund.

(Sec. 102) Expresses the sense of Congress that:

(1) the civil rights and liberties of all Americans, including Arab Americans, must be protected, and that every effort must be taken to preserve their safety;

(2) any acts of violence or discrimination against any Americans be condemned; and

(3) the Nation is called upon to recognize the patriotism of fellow citizens from all ethnic, racial, and religious backgrounds.

(Sec. 103) Authorizes appropriations for the Federal Bureau of Investigation's (FBI) Technical Support Center.

(Sec. 104) Authorizes the Attorney General to request the Secretary of Defense to provide assistance in support of Department of Justice (DOJ) activities relating to the enforcement of Federal criminal code (code) provisions regarding the use of weapons of mass destruction during an emergency situation involving a weapon (currently, chemical weapon) of mass destruction.

(Sec. 105) Requires the Director of the U.S. Secret Service to take actions to develop a national network of electronic crime task forces throughout the United States to prevent, detect, and investigate various forms of electronic crimes, including potential terrorist attacks against critical infrastructure and financial payment systems.

(Sec. 106) Modifies provisions relating to presidential authority under the International Emergency Powers Act to:

---

1. Uniting and Strengthening America by Providing Appropriate Tools Required to Intercept and Obstruct Terrorism (USA PATRIOT ACT) Act of 2001, Pub. L. No. 107-56, 115 Stat. 272 (codified as amended in scattered sections of U.S.C.A.).

2. For example, Section 104 of the Patriot Act provides: "Section 2332e of title 18, United States Code, is amended—(1) by striking '2332c' and inserting '2332a'; and (2) by striking 'chemical'." *See id.* § 104, 115 Stat. at 277. Such provisions can only be understood by examining the various prior statutes that are referenced.

3. Library of Cong., Cong. Research Serv., Bill Summary & Status [for H.R. 3162, 107th Cong. (2001) (enacted)], *available at* http://thomas.loc.gov/cgi-bin/bdquery/z?d107:HR03162:@@@L&summ2=m&#summary.

(1) authorize the President, when the United States is engaged in armed hostilities or has been attacked by a foreign country or foreign nationals, to confiscate any property subject to U.S. jurisdiction of a foreign person, organization, or country that he determines has planned, authorized, aided, or engaged in such hostilities or attacks (the rights to which shall vest in such agency or person as the President may designate); and

(2) provide that, in any judicial review of a determination made under such provisions, if the determination was based on classified information such information may be submitted to the reviewing court ex parte and in camera.

Title II: Enhanced Surveillance Procedures—Amends the Federal criminal code to authorize the interception of wire, oral, and electronic communications for the production of evidence of:

(1) specified chemical weapons or terrorism offenses; and

(2) computer fraud and abuse.

(Sec. 203) Amends rule 6 of the Federal Rules of Criminal Procedure (FRCrP) to permit the sharing of grand jury information that involves foreign intelligence or counterintelligence with Federal law enforcement, intelligence, protective, immigration, national defense, or national security officials (such officials), subject to specified requirements.

Authorizes an investigative or law enforcement officer, or an attorney for the Government, who, by authorized means, has obtained knowledge of the contents of any wire, oral, or electronic communication or evidence derived therefrom to disclose such contents to such officials to the extent that such contents include foreign intelligence or counterintelligence.

Directs the Attorney General to establish procedures for the disclosure of information (pursuant to the code and the FRCrP) that identifies a United States person, as defined in the Foreign Intelligence Surveillance Act of 1978 (FISA).

Authorizes the disclosure of foreign intelligence or counterintelligence obtained as part of a criminal investigation to such officials.

(Sec. 204) Clarifies that nothing in code provisions regarding pen registers shall be deemed to affect the acquisition by the Government of specified foreign intelligence information, and that procedures under FISA shall be the exclusive means by which electronic surveillance and the interception of domestic wire and oral (current law) and electronic communications may be conducted.

(Sec. 205) Authorizes the Director of the FBI to expedite the employment of personnel as translators to support counter-terrorism investigations and operations without regard to applicable Federal personnel requirements. Requires: (1) the Director to establish such security requirements as necessary for such personnel; and (2) the Attorney General to report to the House and Senate Judiciary Committees regarding translators.

(Sec. 206) Grants roving surveillance authority under FISA after requiring a court order approving an electronic surveillance to direct any person to furnish necessary information, facilities, or technical assistance in circumstances where the Court finds that the actions of the surveillance target may have the effect of thwarting the identification of a specified person.

(Sec. 207) Increases the duration of FISA surveillance permitted for non-U.S. persons who are agents of a foreign power.

(Sec. 208) Increases (from seven to 11) the number of district court judges designated to hear applications for and grant orders approving electronic surveillance. Requires that no fewer than three reside within 20 miles of the District of Columbia.

(Sec. 209) Permits the seizure of voice-mail messages under a warrant.

(Sec. 210) Expands the scope of subpoenas for records of electronic communications to include the length and types of service utilized, temporarily assigned network addresses, and the means and source of payment (including any credit card or bank account number).

(Sec. 211) Amends the Communications Act of 1934 to permit specified disclosures to Government entities, except for records revealing cable subscriber selection of video programming from a cable operator.

(Sec. 212) Permits electronic communication and remote computing service providers to make emergency disclosures to a governmental entity of customer electronic communications to protect life and limb.

(Sec. 213) Authorizes Federal district courts to allow a delay of required notices of the execution of a warrant if immediate notice may have an adverse result and under other specified circumstances.

(Sec. 214) Prohibits use of a pen register or trap and trace devices in any investigation to protect against international terrorism or clandestine intelligence activities that is conducted solely on the basis of activities protected by the first amendment to the U.S. Constitution.

(Sec. 215) Authorizes the Director of the FBI (or designee) to apply for a court order requiring production of certain business records for foreign intelligence and international terrorism investigations. Requires the Attorney General to report to the House and Senate Intelligence and Judiciary Committees semi-annually.

(Sec. 216) Amends the code to:

(1) require a trap and trace device to restrict recoding or decoding so as not to include the contents of a wire or electronic communication;

(2) apply a court order for a pen register or trap and trace devices to any person or entity providing wire or electronic communication service in the United States whose assistance may facilitate execution of the order;

(3) require specified records kept on any pen register or trap and trace device on a packet-switched data network of a provider of electronic communication service to the public; and

(4) allow a trap and trace device to identify the source (but not the contents) of a wire or electronic communication.

(Sec. 217) Makes it lawful to intercept the wire or electronic communication of a computer trespasser in certain circumstances.

(Sec. 218) Amends FISA to require an application for an electronic surveillance order or search warrant to certify that a significant purpose (currently, the sole or main purpose) of the surveillance is to obtain foreign intelligence information.

(Sec. 219) Amends rule 41 of the FRCrP to permit Federal magistrate judges in any district in which terrorism-related activities may have occurred to issue search warrants for searches within or outside the district.

(Sec. 220) Provides for nationwide service of search warrants for electronic evidence.

(Sec. 221) Amends the Trade Sanctions Reform and Export Enhancement Act of 2000 to extend trade sanctions to the territory of Afghanistan controlled by the Taliban.

(Sec. 222) Specifies that:

(1) nothing in this Act shall impose any additional technical obligation or requirement on a provider of a wire or electronic communication service or other person to furnish facilities or technical assistance; and

(2) a provider of such service, and a landlord, custodian, or other person who furnishes such facilities or technical assistance, shall be reasonably compensated for such reasonable expenditures incurred in providing such facilities or assistance.

(Sec. 223) Amends the Federal criminal code to provide for administrative discipline of Federal officers or employees who violate prohibitions against unauthorized disclosures of information gathered under this Act. Provides for civil actions against the United States for damages by any person aggrieved by such violations.

(Sec. 224) Terminates this title on December 31, 2005, except with respect to any particular foreign intelligence investigation beginning before that date, or any particular offense or potential offense that began or occurred before it.

(Sec. 225) Amends the Foreign Intelligence Surveillance Act of 1978 to prohibit a cause of action in any court against a provider of a wire or electronic communication service, landlord, custodian, or any other person that furnishes any information, facilities, or technical assistance in accordance with a court order or request for emergency assistance under such Act (for example, with respect to a wiretap).

Title III: International Money Laundering Abatement and Anti-Terrorist Financing Act of 2001—International Money Laundering Abatement and Financial Anti-Terrorism Act of 2001—Sunsets this Act after the first day of FY 2005 if Congress enacts a specified joint resolution to that effect.

Subtitle A: International Counter Money Laundering and Related Measures—Amends Federal law governing monetary transactions to prescribe procedural guidelines under which the Secretary of the Treasury (the Secretary) may require domestic financial institutions and agencies to take specified measures if the Secretary finds that reasonable grounds exist for concluding that jurisdictions, financial institutions, types of accounts, or transactions operating outside or within the United States, are of primary money laundering concern. Includes mandatory disclosure of specified information relating to certain correspondent accounts.

(Sec. 312) Mandates establishment of due diligence mechanisms to detect and report money laundering transactions through private banking accounts and correspondent accounts.

(Sec. 313) Prohibits U.S. correspondent accounts with foreign shell banks.

(Sec. 314) Instructs the Secretary to adopt regulations to encourage further cooperation among financial institutions, their regulatory authorities, and law enforcement authorities, with the specific purpose of encouraging regulatory authorities and law enforcement authorities to share with financial institutions information regarding individuals, entities, and organizations engaged in or reasonably suspected (based on credible evidence) of engaging in terrorist acts or money laundering activities. Authorizes such regulations to create procedures for cooperation and information sharing on matters specifically related to the finances of terrorist groups as well as their relationships with international narcotics traffickers.

Requires the Secretary to distribute annually to financial institutions a detailed analysis identifying patterns of suspicious activity and other investigative insights derived from suspicious activity reports and investigations by Federal, State, and local law enforcement agencies.

(Sec. 315) Amends Federal criminal law to include foreign corruption offenses as money laundering crimes.

(Sec. 316) Establishes the right of property owners to contest confiscation of property under law relating to confiscation of assets of suspected terrorists.

(Sec. 317) Establishes Federal jurisdiction over:

(1) foreign money launderers (including their assets held in the United States); and

(2) money that is laundered through a foreign bank.

(Sec. 319) Authorizes the forfeiture of money laundering funds from interbank accounts. Requires a covered financial institution, upon request of the appropriate Federal banking agency, to make available within 120 hours all pertinent information related to anti-money laundering compliance by the institution or its customer. Grants the Secretary summons and subpoena powers over foreign banks that maintain a correspondent bank in the United States. Requires a covered financial institution to terminate within ten business days any correspondent relationship with a foreign bank after receipt of written notice that the foreign bank has failed to comply with certain judicial proceedings. Sets forth civil penalties for failure to terminate such relationship.

(Sec. 321) Subjects to record and report requirements for monetary instrument transactions:

(1) any credit union; and

(2) any futures commission merchant, commodity trading advisor, and commodity pool operator registered, or required to register, under the Commodity Exchange Act.

(Sec. 323) Authorizes Federal application for restraining orders to preserve the availability of property subject to a foreign forfeiture or confiscation judgment.

(Sec. 325) Authorizes the Secretary to issue regulations to ensure that concentration accounts of financial institutions are not used to prevent association of the identity of an individual customer with the movement of funds of which the customer is the direct or beneficial owner.

(Sec. 326) Directs the Secretary to issue regulations prescribing minimum standards for financial institutions regarding customer identity in connection with the opening of accounts.

Requires the Secretary to report to Congress on:

(1) the most timely and effective way to require foreign nationals to provide domestic financial institutions and agencies with appropriate and accurate information;

(2) whether to require foreign nationals to obtain an identification number (similar to a Social Security or tax identification number) before opening an account with a domestic financial institution; and

(3) a system for domestic financial institutions and agencies to review Government agency information to verify the identities of such foreign nationals.

(Sec. 327) Amends the Bank Holding Company Act of 1956 and the Federal Deposit Insurance Act to require consideration of the effectiveness of a company or companies in combating money laundering during reviews of proposed bank shares acquisitions or mergers.

(Sec. 328) Directs the Secretary take reasonable steps to encourage foreign governments to require the inclusion of the name of the originator in wire transfer instructions sent to the United States and other countries, with the information to remain with the transfer from its origination until the point of disbursement. Requires annual progress reports to specified congressional committees.

(Sec. 329) Prescribes criminal penalties for Federal officials or employees who seek or accept bribes in connection with administration of this title.

(Sec. 330) Urges U.S. negotiations for international cooperation in investigations of money laundering, financial crimes, and the finances of terrorist groups, including record sharing by foreign banks with U.S. law enforcement officials and domestic financial institution supervisors.

Subtitle B: Bank Secrecy Act Amendments and Related Improvements—Amends Federal law known as the Bank Secrecy Act to revise requirements for civil liability immunity for voluntary financial institution disclosure of suspicious activities. Authorizes the inclusion of suspicions of illegal activity in written employment references.

(Sec. 352) Authorizes the Secretary to exempt from minimum standards for anti-money laundering programs any financial institution not subject to certain regulations governing financial recordkeeping and reporting of currency and foreign transactions.

(Sec. 353) Establishes civil penalties for violations of geographic targeting orders and structuring transactions to evade certain recordkeeping requirements. Lengthens the effective period of geographic targeting orders from 60 to 180 days.

(Sec. 355) Amends the Federal Deposit Insurance Act to permit written employment references to contain suspicions of involvement in illegal activity.

(Sec. 356) Instructs the Secretary to:

(1) promulgate regulations requiring registered securities brokers and dealers, futures commission merchants, commodity trading advisors, and commodity pool operators, to file reports of suspicious financial transactions;

(2) report to Congress on the role of the Internal Revenue Service in the administration of the Bank Secrecy Act; and

(3) share monetary instruments transactions records upon request of a U.S. intelligence agency for use in the conduct of intelligence or counterintelligence activities, including analysis, to protect against international terrorism.

(Sec. 358) Amends the Right to Financial Privacy Act to permit the transfer of financial records to other agencies or departments upon certification that the records are relevant to intelligence or counterintelligence activities related to international terrorism.

Amends the Fair Credit Reporting Act to require a consumer reporting agency to furnish all information in a consumer's file to a government agency upon certification that the records are relevant to intelligence or counterintelligence activities related to international terrorism.

(Sec. 359) Subjects to mandatory records and reports on monetary instruments transactions any licensed sender of money or any other person who engages as a business in the transmission of funds, including through an informal value transfer banking system or network (e.g., hawala) of people facilitating the transfer of money domestically or internationally outside of the conventional financial institutions system.

(Sec. 360) Authorizes the Secretary to instruct the United States Executive Director of each international financial institution to use his or her voice and vote to: (1) support the use of funds for a country (and its institutions) which contributes to U.S. efforts against international terrorism; and (2) require an auditing of disbursements to ensure that no funds are paid to persons who commit or support terrorism.

(Sec. 361) Makes the existing Financial Crimes Enforcement Network a bureau in the Department of the Treasury.

(Sec. 362) Directs the Secretary to establish a highly secure network in the Network that allows financial institutions to file certain reports and receive alerts and other information regarding suspicious activities warranting immediate and enhanced scrutiny.

(Sec. 363) Increases to $1 million the maximum civil penalties (currently $10,000) and criminal fines (currently $250,000) for money laundering. Sets a minimum civil penalty and criminal fine of double the amount of the illegal transaction.

(Sec. 364) Amends the Federal Reserve Act to provide for uniform protection authority for Federal Reserve facilities, including law enforcement officers authorized to carry firearms and make warrantless arrests.

(Sec. 365) Amends Federal law to require reports relating to coins and currency of more than $10,000 received in a nonfinancial trade or business.

(Sec. 366) Directs the Secretary to study and report to Congress on:

(1) the possible expansion of the currency transaction reporting requirements exemption system; and

(2) methods for improving financial institution utilization of the system as a way of reducing the submission of currency transaction reports that have little or no value for law enforcement purposes.

Subtitle C: Currency Crimes—Establishes as a bulk cash smuggling felony the knowing concealment and attempted transport (or transfer) across U.S. borders of currency and monetary instruments in excess of $10,000, with intent to evade specified currency reporting requirements.

(Sec. 372) Changes from discretionary to mandatory a court's authority to order, as part of a criminal sentence, forfeiture of all property involved in certain currency reporting offenses. Leaves a court discretion to order civil forfeitures in money laundering cases.

(Sec. 373) Amends the Federal criminal code to revise the prohibition of unlicensed (currently, illegal) money transmitting businesses.

(Sec. 374) Increases the criminal penalties for counterfeiting domestic and foreign currency and obligations.

(Sec. 376) Amends the Federal criminal code to extend the prohibition against the laundering of money instruments to specified proceeds of terrorism.

(Sec. 377) Grants the United States extraterritorial jurisdiction where:

(1) an offense committed outside the United States involves an access device issued, owned, managed, or controlled by a financial institution, account issuer, credit card system member, or other entity within U.S. jurisdiction; and

(2) the person committing the offense transports, delivers, conveys, transfers to or through, or otherwise stores, secrets, or holds within U.S. jurisdiction any article used to assist in the commission of the offense or the proceeds of such offense or property derived from it.

Title IV: Protecting the Border—Subtitle A: Protecting the Northern Border— Authorizes the Attorney General to waive certain Immigration and Naturalization Service (INS) personnel caps with respect to ensuring security needs on the Northern border.

(Sec. 402) Authorizes appropriations to:

(1) triple the number of Border Patrol, Customs Service, and INS personnel (and support facilities) at points of entry and along the Northern border; and

(2) INS and Customs for related border monitoring technology and equipment.

(Sec. 403) Amends the Immigration and Nationality Act to require the Attorney General and the Federal Bureau of Investigation (FBI) to provide the Department of State and INS with access to specified criminal history extracts in order to determine whether or not a visa or admissions applicant has a criminal history. Directs the FBI to provide periodic extract updates. Provides for confidentiality.

Directs the Attorney General and the Secretary of State to develop a technology standard to identify visa and admissions applicants, which shall be the basis for an electronic system of law enforcement and intelligence sharing system available to consular, law enforcement, intelligence, and Federal border inspection personnel.

(Sec. 404) Amends the Department of Justice Appropriations Act, 2001 to eliminate certain INS overtime restrictions.

(Sec. 405) Directs the Attorney General to report on the feasibility of enhancing the Integrated Automated Fingerprint Identification System and other identification systems to better identify foreign individuals in connection with U.S. or foreign criminal investigations before issuance of a visa to, or permitting such person's entry or exit from, the United States. Authorizes appropriations.

Subtitle B: Enhanced Immigration Provisions—Amends the Immigration and Nationality Act to broaden the scope of aliens ineligible for admission or deportable due to terrorist activities to include an alien who:

(1) is a representative of a political, social, or similar group whose political endorsement of terrorist acts undermines U.S. antiterrorist efforts;

(2) has used a position of prominence to endorse terrorist activity, or to persuade others to support such activity in a way that undermines U.S. antiterrorist efforts (or the child or spouse of such an alien under specified circumstances); or

(3) has been associated with a terrorist organization and intends to engage in threatening activities while in the United States.

(Sec. 411) Includes within the definition of "terrorist activity" the use of any weapon or dangerous device.

Redefines "engage in terrorist activity" to mean, in an individual capacity or as a member of an organization, to:

(1) commit or to incite to commit, under circumstances indicating an intention to cause death or serious bodily injury, a terrorist activity;

(2) prepare or plan a terrorist activity;

(3) gather information on potential targets for terrorist activity;

(4) solicit funds or other things of value for a terrorist activity or a terrorist organization (with an exception for lack of knowledge);

(5) solicit any individual to engage in prohibited conduct or for terrorist organization membership (with an exception for lack of knowledge); or

(6) commit an act that the actor knows, or reasonably should know, affords material support, including a safe house, transportation, communications, funds, transfer of funds or other material financial benefit, false documentation or identification, weapons (including chemical, biological, or radiological weapons), explosives, or training for the commission of a terrorist activity; to any individual who the actor knows or reasonably should know has committed or plans to commit a terrorist activity; or to a terrorist organization (with an exception for lack of knowledge).

Defines "terrorist organization" as a group:

(1) designated under the Immigration and Nationality Act or by the Secretary of State; or

(2) a group of two or more individuals, whether related or not, which engages in terrorist-related activities.

Provides for the retroactive application of amendments under this Act. Stipulates that an alien shall not be considered inadmissible or deportable because of a relationship to an organization that was not designated as a terrorist organization prior to enactment of this Act. States that the amendments under this section shall apply to all aliens in exclusion or deportation proceedings on or after the date of enactment of this Act.

Directs the Secretary of State to notify specified congressional leaders seven days prior to designating an organization as a terrorist organization. Provides for organization redesignation or revocation.

(Sec. 412) Provides for mandatory detention until removal from the United States (regardless of any relief from removal) of an alien certified by the Attorney General as a suspected terrorist or threat to national security. Requires release of such alien after seven days if removal proceedings have not commenced, or the alien has not been charged with a criminal offense. Authorizes detention for additional periods of up to six months of an alien not likely to be deported in the reasonably foreseeable future only if release will threaten U.S. national security or the safety of the community or any person. Limits judicial review to habeas corpus proceedings in the U.S. Supreme Court, the U.S. Court of Appeals for the District of Columbia, or any district court with jurisdiction to entertain a habeas corpus petition. Restricts to the U.S. Court of Appeals for the District of Columbia the right of appeal of any final order by a circuit or district judge.

(Sec. 413) Authorizes the Secretary of State, on a reciprocal basis, to share criminal- and terrorist-related visa lookout information with foreign governments.

(Sec. 414) Declares the sense of Congress that the Attorney General should:

(1) fully implement the integrated entry and exit data system for airports, seaports, and land border ports of entry with all deliberate speed; and

(2) begin immediately establishing the Integrated Entry and Exit Data System Task Force. Authorizes appropriations.

Requires the Attorney General and the Secretary of State, in developing the integrated entry and exit data system, to focus on the use of biometric technology and the development of tamper-resistant documents readable at ports of entry.

(Sec. 415) Amends the Immigration and Naturalization Service Data Management Improvement Act of 2000 to include the Office of Homeland Security in the Integrated Entry and Exit Data System Task Force.

(Sec. 416) Directs the Attorney General to implement fully and expand the foreign student monitoring program to include other approved educational institutions like air flight, language training, or vocational schools.

(Sec. 417) Requires audits and reports on implementation of the mandate for machine readable passports.

(Sec. 418) Directs the Secretary of State to:

(1) review how consular officers issue visas to determine if consular shopping is a problem; and

(2) if it is a problem, take steps to address it, and report on them to Congress.

Subtitle C: Preservation of Immigration Benefits for Victims of Terrorism—Authorizes the Attorney General to provide permanent resident status through the special immigrant program to an alien (and spouse, child, or grandparent under specified circumstances) who was the beneficiary of a petition filed on or before September 11, 2001, to grant the alien permanent residence as an employer-sponsored immigrant or of an application for labor certification if the petition or application was rendered null because of the disability of the beneficiary or loss of employment due to physical damage to, or destruction of, the business of the petitioner or applicant as a direct result of the terrorist attacks on September 11, 2001 (September attacks), or because of the death of the petitioner or applicant as a direct result of such attacks.

(Sec. 422) States that an alien who was legally in a nonimmigrant status and was disabled as a direct result of the September attacks may remain in the United States until his or her normal status termination date or September, 11, 2002. Includes in such extension the spouse or child of such an alien or of an alien who was killed in such attacks. Authorizes employment during such period.

Extends specified immigration-related deadlines and other filing requirements for an alien (and spouse and child) who was directly prevented from meeting such requirements as a result of the September attacks respecting:

(1) nonimmigrant status and status revision;

(2) diversity immigrants;

(3) immigrant visas;

(4) parolees; and

(5) voluntary departure.

(Sec. 423) Waives, under specified circumstances, the requirement that an alien spouse (and child) of a U.S. citizen must have been married for at least two years prior to such citizen's death in order to maintain immediate relative status if such citizen died as a direct result of the September attacks. Provides for:

(1) continued family-sponsored immigrant eligibility for the spouse, child, or unmarried son or daughter of a permanent resident who died as a direct result of such attacks; and

(2) continued eligibility for adjustment of status for the spouse and child of an employment-based immigrant who died similarly.

(**Sec. 424**) Amends the Immigration and Nationality Act to extend the visa categorization of "child" for aliens with petitions filed on or before September 11, 2001, for aliens whose 21st birthday is in September 2001 (90 days), or after September 2001 (45 days).

(**Sec. 425**) Authorizes the Attorney General to provide temporary administrative relief to an alien who, as of September, 10, 2001, was lawfully in the United States and was the spouse, parent, or child of an individual who died or was disabled as a direct result of the September attacks.

(**Sec. 426**) Directs the Attorney General to establish evidentiary guidelines for death, disability, and loss of employment or destruction of business in connection with the provisions of this subtitle.

(**Sec. 427**) Prohibits benefits to terrorists or their family members.

Title V: Removing Obstacles to Investigating Terrorism—Authorizes the Attorney General to pay rewards from available funds pursuant to public advertisements for assistance to DOJ to combat terrorism and defend the Nation against terrorist acts, in accordance with procedures and regulations established or issued by the Attorney General, subject to specified conditions, including a prohibition against any such reward of $250,000 or more from being made or offered without the personal approval of either the Attorney General or the President.

(**Sec. 502**) Amends the State Department Basic Authorities Act of 1956 to modify the Department of State rewards program to authorize rewards for information leading to: (1) the dismantling of a terrorist organization in whole or significant part; and (2) the identification or location of an individual who holds a key leadership position in a terrorist organization. Raises the limit on rewards if the Secretary State determines that a larger sum is necessary to combat terrorism or defend the Nation against terrorist acts.

(**Sec. 503**) Amends the DNA Analysis Backlog Elimination Act of 2000 to qualify a Federal terrorism offense for collection of DNA for identification.

(**Sec. 504**) Amends FISA to authorize consultation among Federal law enforcement officers regarding information acquired from an electronic surveillance or physical search in terrorism and related investigations or protective measures.

(**Sec. 505**) Allows the FBI to request telephone toll and transactional records, financial records, and consumer reports in any investigation to protect against international terrorism or clandestine intelligence activities only if the investigation is not conducted solely on the basis of activities protected by the first amendment to the U.S. Constitution.

(**Sec. 506**) Revises U.S. Secret Service jurisdiction with respect to fraud and related activity in connection with computers. Grants the FBI primary authority to investigate specified fraud and computer related activity for cases involving espionage, foreign counter-intelligence, information protected against unauthorized disclosure for reasons of national defense or foreign relations, or restricted data, except for offenses affecting Secret Service duties.

(**Sec. 507**) Amends the General Education Provisions Act and the National Education Statistics Act of 1994 to provide for disclosure of educational records to the Attorney General in a terrorism investigation or prosecution.

Title VI: Providing for Victims of Terrorism, Public Safety Officers, and Their Families—Subtitle A: Aid to Families of Public Safety Officers—Provides for expedited payments for:

(1) public safety officers involved in the prevention, investigation, rescue, or recovery efforts related to a terrorist attack; and

(2) heroic public safety officers. Increases Public Safety Officers Benefit Program payments.

Subtitle B: Amendments to the Victims of Crime Act of 1984—Amends the Victims of Crime Act of 1984 to:

(1) revise provisions regarding the allocation of funds for compensation and assistance, location of compensable crime, and the relationship of crime victim compensation to means-tested Federal benefit programs and to the September 11th victim compensation fund; and

(2) establish an antiterrorism emergency reserve in the Victims of Crime Fund.

Title VII: Increased Information Sharing for Critical Infrastructure Protection—Amends the Omnibus Crime Control and Safe Streets Act of 1968 to extend Bureau of Justice Assistance regional information sharing system grants to systems that enhance the investigation and prosecution abilities of participating Federal, State, and local law enforcement agencies in addressing multi-jurisdictional terrorist conspiracies and activities. Authorizes appropriations.

Title VIII: Strengthening the Criminal Laws Against Terrorism—Amends the Federal criminal code to prohibit specific terrorist acts or otherwise destructive, disruptive, or violent acts against mass transportation vehicles, ferries, providers, employees, passengers, or operating systems.

(**Sec. 802**) Amends the Federal criminal code to:

(1) revise the definition of "international terrorism" to include activities that appear to be intended to affect the conduct of government by mass destruction; and

(2) define "domestic terrorism" as activities that occur primarily within U.S. jurisdiction, that involve criminal acts dangerous to human life, and that appear to be intended to intimidate or coerce a civilian population, to influence government policy by intimidation or coercion, or to affect government conduct by mass destruction, assassination, or kidnapping.

(**Sec. 803**) Prohibits harboring any person knowing or having reasonable grounds to believe that such person has committed or to be about to commit a terrorism offense.

(**Sec. 804**) Establishes Federal jurisdiction over crimes committed at U.S. facilities abroad.

(**Sec. 805**) Applies the prohibitions against providing material support for terrorism to offenses outside of the United States.

(**Sec. 806**) Subjects to civil forfeiture all assets, foreign or domestic, of terrorist organizations.

(**Sec. 808**) Expands:

(1) the offenses over which the Attorney General shall have primary investigative jurisdiction under provisions governing acts of terrorism transcending national boundaries; and

(2) the offenses included within the definition of the Federal crime of terrorism.

(Sec. 809) Provides that there shall be no statute of limitations for certain terrorism offenses if the commission of such an offense resulted in, or created a foreseeable risk of, death or serious bodily injury to another person.

(Sec. 810) Provides for alternative maximum penalties for specified terrorism crimes.

(Sec. 811) Makes:

(1) the penalties for attempts and conspiracies the same as those for terrorism offenses;

(2) the supervised release terms for offenses with terrorism predicates any term of years or life; and

(3) specified terrorism crimes Racketeer Influenced and Corrupt Organizations statute predicates.

(Sec. 814) Revises prohibitions and penalties regarding fraud and related activity in connection with computers to include specified cyber-terrorism offenses.

(Sec. 816) Directs the Attorney General to establish regional computer forensic laboratories, and to support existing laboratories, to develop specified cyber-security capabilities.

(Sec. 817) Prescribes penalties for knowing possession in certain circumstances of biological agents, toxins, or delivery systems, especially by certain restricted persons.

Title IX: Improved Intelligence—Amends the National Security Act of 1947 to require the Director of Central Intelligence (DCI) to establish requirements and priorities for foreign intelligence collected under the Foreign Intelligence Surveillance Act of 1978 and to provide assistance to the Attorney General (AG) to ensure that information derived from electronic surveillance or physical searches is disseminated for efficient and effective foreign intelligence purposes. Requires the inclusion of international terrorist activities within the scope of foreign intelligence under such Act.

(Sec. 903) Expresses the sense of Congress that officers and employees of the intelligence community should establish and maintain intelligence relationships to acquire information on terrorists and terrorist organizations.

(Sec. 904) Authorizes deferral of the submission to Congress of certain reports on intelligence and intelligence-related matters until:

(1) February 1, 2002; or

(2) a date after February 1, 2002, if the official involved certifies that preparation and submission on February 1, 2002, will impede the work of officers or employees engaged in counterterrorism activities. Requires congressional notification of any such deferral.

(Sec. 905) Requires the AG or the head of any other Federal department or agency with law enforcement responsibilities to expeditiously disclose to the DCI any foreign intelligence acquired in the course of a criminal investigation.

(Sec. 906) Requires the AG, DCI, and Secretary of the Treasury to jointly report to Congress on the feasibility and desirability of reconfiguring the Foreign Asset Tracking Center and the Office of Foreign Assets Control to provide for the analysis and dissemination of foreign intelligence relating to the financial capabilities and resources of international terrorist organizations.

(Sec. 907) Requires the DCI to report to the appropriate congressional committees on the establishment and maintenance of the National Virtual Translation Center for timely and accurate translation of foreign intelligence for elements of the intelligence community.

(Sec. 908) Requires the AG to provide a program of training to Government officials regarding the identification and use of foreign intelligence.

Title X: Miscellaneous—Directs the Inspector General of the Department of Justice to designate one official to review allegations of abuse of civil rights, civil liberties, and racial and ethnic profiling by government employees and officials.

(Sec. 1002) Expresses the sense of Congress condemning acts of violence or discrimination against any American, including Sikh-Americans. Calls upon local and Federal law enforcement authorities to prosecute to the fullest extent of the law all those who commit crimes.

(Sec. 1004) Amends the Federal criminal code with respect to venue in money laundering cases to allow a prosecution for such an offense to be brought in:

(1) any district in which the financial or monetary transaction is conducted; or

(2) any district where a prosecution for the underlying specified unlawful activity could be brought, if the defendant participated in the transfer of the proceeds of the specified unlawful activity from that district to the district where the financial or monetary transaction is conducted.

States that:

(1) a transfer of funds from one place to another, by wire or any other means, shall constitute a single, continuing transaction; and

(2) any person who conducts any portion of the transaction may be charged in any district in which the transaction takes place.

Allows a prosecution for an attempt or conspiracy offense to be brought in the district where venue would lie for the completed offense, or in any other district where an act in furtherance of the attempt or conspiracy took place.

(Sec. 1005) First Responders Assistance Act—Directs the Attorney General to make grants to State and local governments to improve the ability of State and local law enforcement, fire department, and first responders to respond to and prevent acts of terrorism. Authorizes appropriations.

(Sec. 1006) Amends the Immigration and Nationality Act to make inadmissible into the United States any alien engaged in money laundering. Directs the Secretary of State to develop a money laundering watchlist which:

(1) identifies individuals worldwide who are known or suspected of money laundering; and

(2) is readily accessible to, and shall be checked by, a consular or other Federal official before the issuance of a visa or admission to the United States.

(Sec. 1007) Authorizes FY 2002 appropriations for regional antidrug training in Turkey by the Drug Enforcement Administration for police, as well as increased precursor chemical control efforts in South and Central Asia.

(Sec. 1008) Directs the Attorney General to conduct a feasibility study and report to Congress on the use of a biometric identifier scanning system with access to the FBI integrated automated fingerprint identification system at overseas consular posts and points of entry to the United States.

(Sec. 1009) Directs the FBI to study and report to Congress on the feasibility of providing to airlines access via computer to the names of passengers who are suspected of terrorist activity by Federal officials. Authorizes appropriations.

(Sec. 1010) Authorizes the use of Department of Defense funds to contract with local and State governments, during the period of Operation Enduring Freedom, for the performance of security functions at U.S. military installations.

(Sec. 1011) Crimes Against Charitable Americans Act of 2001—Amends the Telemarketing and Consumer Fraud and Abuse Prevention Act to cover fraudulent charitable solicitations. Requires any person engaged in telemarketing for the solicitation of charitable contributions, donations, or gifts to disclose promptly and clearly the purpose of the telephone call.

(Sec. 1012) Amends the Federal transportation code to prohibit States from licensing any individual to operate a motor vehicle transporting hazardous material unless the Secretary of Transportation determines that such individual does not pose a security risk warranting denial of the license. Requires background checks of such license applicants by the Attorney General upon State request.

(Sec. 1013) Expresses the sense of the Senate on substantial new U.S. investment in bioterrorism preparedness and response.

(Sec. 1014) Directs the Office for State and Local Domestic Preparedness Support of the Office of Justice Programs to make grants to enhance State and local capability to prepare for and respond to terrorist acts. Authorizes appropriations for FY 2002 through 2007.

(Sec. 1015) Amends the Crime Identification Technology Act of 1998 to extend it through FY 2007 and provide for antiterrorism grants to States and localities. Authorizes appropriations.

(Sec. 1016) Critical Infrastructures Protection Act of 2001—Declares it is U.S. policy:

(1) that any physical or virtual disruption of the operation of the critical infrastructures of the United States be rare, brief, geographically limited in effect, manageable, and minimally detrimental to the economy, human and government services, and U.S. national security;

(2) that actions necessary to achieve this policy be carried out in a public-private partnership involving corporate and non-governmental organizations; and

(3) to have in place a comprehensive and effective program to ensure the continuity of essential Federal Government functions under all circumstances.

Establishes the National Infrastructure Simulation and Analysis Center to serve as a source of national competence to address critical infrastructure protection and continuity through support for activities related to counterterrorism, threat assessment, and risk mitigation.

Defines critical infrastructure as systems and assets, whether physical or virtual, so vital to the United States that their incapacity or destruction would have a debilitating impact on security, national economic security, national public health or safety, or any combination of those matters.

Authorizes appropriations.

HOMELAND SECURITY ACT OF 2002*

AN ACT

To establish the Department of Homeland Security, and for other purposes.

Be it enacted by the Senate and House of Representatives of the United States of America in Congress assembled,

SECTION 1. SHORT TITLE; TABLE OF CONTENTS.

(a) SHORT TITLE.—This Act may be cited as the "Homeland Security Act of 2002".

. . . .

SEC. 2. DEFINITIONS.

In this Act, the following definitions apply:

. . . .

(15) The term "terrorism" means any activity that—

(A) involves an act that—

(i) is dangerous to human life or potentially destructive of critical infrastructure or key resources; and

(ii) is a violation of the criminal laws of the United States or of any State or other subdivision of the United States; and

(B) appears to be intended—

(i) to intimidate or coerce a civilian population;

(ii) to influence the policy of a government by intimidation or coercion; or

(iii) to affect the conduct of a government by mass destruction, assassination, or kidnapping.

. . . .

TITLE I—DEPARTMENT OF HOMELAND SECURITY

SEC. 101. EXECUTIVE DEPARTMENT; MISSION.

(a) ESTABLISHMENT.—There is established a Department of Homeland Security, as an executive department of the United States within the meaning of title 5, United States Code.

(b) MISSION.—

(1) IN GENERAL.—The primary mission of the Department is to—

(A) prevent terrorist attacks within the United States;

* Pub. L. No. 107-296, 116 Stat. 2135 (2002), *available at* http://www.dhs.gov/interweb/assetlibrary/hr_5005_enr.pdf.

(B) reduce the vulnerability of the United States to terrorism;

(C) minimize the damage, and assist in the recovery, from terrorist attacks that do occur within the United States;

(D) carry out all functions of entities transferred to the Department, including by acting as a focal point regarding natural and manmade crises and emergency planning;

(E) ensure that the functions of the agencies and subdivisions within the Department that are not related directly to securing the homeland are not diminished or neglected except by a specific explicit Act of Congress;

(F) ensure that the overall economic security of the United States is not diminished by efforts, activities, and programs aimed at securing the homeland; and

(G) monitor connections between illegal drug trafficking and terrorism, coordinate efforts to sever such connections, and otherwise contribute to efforts to interdict illegal drug trafficking.

(2) RESPONSIBILITY FOR INVESTIGATING AND PROSECUTING TERRORISM.—Except as specifically provided by law with respect to entities transferred to the Department under this Act, primary responsibility for investigating and prosecuting acts of terrorism shall be vested not in the Department, but rather in Federal, State, and local law enforcement agencies with jurisdiction over the acts in question.

....

SUBTITLE D—OFFICE OF SCIENCE AND TECHNOLOGY

SEC. 231. ESTABLISHMENT OF OFFICE; DIRECTOR.

(a) ESTABLISHMENT.—

(1) IN GENERAL.—There is hereby established within the Department of Justice an Office of Science and Technology (hereinafter in this title referred to as the "Office").

(2) AUTHORITY.—The Office shall be under the general authority of the Assistant Attorney General, Office of Justice Programs, and shall be established within the National Institute of Justice.

(b) DIRECTOR.—The Office shall be headed by a Director, who shall be an individual appointed based on approval by the Office of Personnel Management of the executive qualifications of the individual.

SEC. 232. MISSION OF OFFICE; DUTIES.

(a) MISSION.—The mission of the Office shall be—

(1) to serve as the national focal point for work on law enforcement technology; and

(2) to carry out programs that, through the provision of equipment, training, and technical assistance, improve the safety and effectiveness of law enforcement technology and improve access to such technology by Federal, State, and local law enforcement agencies.

....

TITLE IV—DIRECTORATE OF BORDER AND TRANSPORTATION SECURITY

SUBTITLE A—UNDER SECRETARY FOR BORDER AND TRANSPORTATION SECURITY

SEC. 401. UNDER SECRETARY FOR BORDER AND TRANSPORTATION SECURITY.

There shall be in the Department a Directorate of Border and Transportation Security headed by an Under Secretary for Border and Transportation Security.

SEC. 402. RESPONSIBILITIES.

The Secretary, acting through the Under Secretary for Border and Transportation Security, shall be responsible for the following:

(1) Preventing the entry of terrorists and the instruments of terrorism into the United States.

(2) Securing the borders, territorial waters, ports, terminals, waterways, and air, land, and sea transportation systems of the United States, including managing and coordinating those functions transferred to the Department at ports of entry.

(3) Carrying out the immigration enforcement functions vested by statute in, or performed by, the Commissioner of Immigration and Naturalization (or any officer, employee, or component of the Immigration and Naturalization Service) immediately before the date on which the transfer of functions specified under section 441 takes effect.

(4) Establishing and administering rules, in accordance with section 428, governing the granting of visas or other forms of permission, including parole, to enter the United States to individuals who are not a citizen or an alien lawfully admitted for permanent residence in the United States.

(5) Establishing national immigration enforcement policies and priorities.

(6) Except as provided in subtitle C, administering the customs laws of the United States.

(7) Conducting the inspection and related administrative functions of the Department of Agriculture transferred to the Secretary of Homeland Security under section 421.

(8) In carrying out the foregoing responsibilities, ensuring the speedy, orderly, and efficient flow of lawful traffic and commerce.

....

SUBTITLE B—UNITED STATES CUSTOMS SERVICE

SEC. 411. ESTABLISHMENT; COMMISSIONER OF CUSTOMS.

(a) ESTABLISHMENT.—There is established in the Department the United States Customs Service, under the authority of the Under Secretary for Border and Transportation Security, which shall be vested with those functions including, but not limited to those set forth in section 415(7), and the personnel, assets, and liabilities attributable to those functions.

....

SUBTITLE D—IMMIGRATION ENFORCEMENT FUNCTIONS

SEC. 441. TRANSFER OF FUNCTIONS TO UNDER SECRETARY FOR BORDER AND TRANSPORTATION SECURITY.

In accordance with title XV (relating to transition provisions), there shall be transferred from the Commissioner of Immigration and Naturalization to the Under Secretary for Border and Transportation Security all functions performed under the following programs, and all personnel, assets, and liabilities pertaining to such programs, immediately before such transfer occurs:

(1) The Border Patrol program.

(2) The detention and removal program.

(3) The intelligence program.

(4) The investigations program.

(5) The inspections program.

....

SUBTITLE E—CITIZENSHIP AND IMMIGRATION SERVICES

SEC. 451. ESTABLISHMENT OF BUREAU OF CITIZENSHIP AND IMMIGRATION SERVICES.

(a) ESTABLISHMENT OF BUREAU.—

(1) IN GENERAL.—There shall be in the Department a bureau to be known as the "Bureau of Citizenship and Immigration Services".

(2) DIRECTOR.—The head of the Bureau of Citizenship and Immigration Services shall be the Director of the Bureau of Citizenship and Immigration Services, who—

(A) shall report directly to the Deputy Secretary;

....

SUBTITLE F—GENERAL IMMIGRATION PROVISIONS

SEC. 471. ABOLISHMENT OF INS.

(a) IN GENERAL.—Upon completion of all transfers from the Immigration and Naturalization Service as provided for by this Act, the Immigration and Naturalization Service of the Department of Justice is abolished.

(b) PROHIBITION.—The authority provided by section 1502 may be used to reorganize functions or organizational units within the Bureau of Border Security or the Bureau of Citizenship and Immigration Services, but may not be used to recombine the two bureaus into a single agency or otherwise to combine, join, or consolidate functions or organizational units of the two bureaus with each other.

....

TITLE V—EMERGENCY PREPAREDNESS AND RESPONSE

SEC. 501. UNDER SECRETARY FOR EMERGENCY PREPAREDNESS AND RESPONSE.

There shall be in the Department a Directorate of Emergency Preparedness and Response headed by an Under Secretary for Emergency Preparedness and Response.

SEC. 502. RESPONSIBILITIES.

The Secretary, acting through the Under Secretary for Emergency Preparedness and Response, shall include—

(1) helping to ensure the effectiveness of emergency response providers to terrorist attacks, major disasters, and other emergencies;

(2) with respect to the Nuclear Incident Response Team (regardless of whether it is operating as an organizational unit of the Department pursuant to this title)—

(A) establishing standards and certifying when those standards have been met;

(B) conducting joint and other exercises and training and evaluating performance; and

(C) providing funds to the Department of Energy and the Environmental Protection Agency, as appropriate, for homeland security planning, exercises and training, and equipment;

(3) providing the Federal Government's response to terrorist attacks and major disasters, including—

(A) managing such response;

(B) directing the Domestic Emergency Support Team, the Strategic National Stockpile, the National Disaster Medical System, and (when operating as an organizational unit of the Department pursuant to this title) the Nuclear Incident Response Team;

(C) overseeing the Metropolitan Medical Response System; and

(D) coordinating other Federal response resources in the event of a terrorist attack or major disaster;

(4) aiding the recovery from terrorist attacks and major disasters;

(5) building a comprehensive national incident management system with Federal, State, and local government personnel, agencies, and authorities, to respond to such attacks and disasters;

(6) consolidating existing Federal Government emergency response plans into a single, coordinated national response plan; and

(7) developing comprehensive programs for developing interoperative communications technology, and helping to ensure that emergency response providers acquire such technology.

....

SUBTITLE C—UNITED STATES SECRET SERVICE

SEC. 821. FUNCTIONS TRANSFERRED.

In accordance with title XV, there shall be transferred to the Secretary the functions, personnel, assets, and obligations of the United States Secret Service, which shall be maintained as a distinct entity within the Department, including the functions of the Secretary of the Treasury relating thereto.

....

SUBTITLE H—MISCELLANEOUS PROVISIONS

....

SEC. 876. MILITARY ACTIVITIES.

Nothing in this Act shall confer upon the Secretary any authority to engage in warfighting, the military defense of the United States, or other military activities, nor shall anything in this Act limit the existing authority of the Department of Defense or the Armed Forces to engage in warfighting, the military defense of the United States, or other military activities.

....

SEC. 880. PROHIBITION OF THE TERRORISM INFORMATION AND PREVENTION SYSTEM.

Any and all activities of the Federal Government to implement the proposed component program of the Citizen Corps known as Operation TIPS (Terrorism Information and Prevention System) are hereby prohibited.

....

SEC. 886. SENSE OF CONGRESS REAFFIRMING THE CONTINUED IMPORTANCE AND APPLICABILITY OF THE POSSE COMITATUS ACT.

(a) FINDINGS.—Congress finds the following:

(1) Section 1385 of title 18, United States Code (commonly known as the "Posse Comitatus Act"), prohibits the use of the Armed Forces as a posse comitatus to execute the laws except in cases and under circumstances expressly authorized by the Constitution or Act of Congress.

(2) Enacted in 1878, the Posse Comitatus Act was expressly intended to prevent United States Marshals, on their own initiative, from calling on the Army for assistance in enforcing Federal law.

(3) The Posse Comitatus Act has served the Nation well in limiting the use of the Armed Forces to enforce the law.

(4) Nevertheless, by its express terms, the Posse Comitatus Act is not a complete barrier to the use of the Armed Forces for a range of domestic purposes, including law enforcement functions, when the use of the Armed Forces is authorized by Act of Congress or the President determines that the use of the Armed Forces is required to fulfill the President's obligations under the Constitution to respond promptly in time of war, insurrection, or other serious emergency.

(5) Existing laws, including chapter 15 of title 10, United States Code (commonly known as the "Insurrection Act"), and the Robert T. Stafford Disaster Relief and Emergency Assistance Act (42 U.S.C. 5121 et seq.), grant the President broad powers that may be invoked in the event of domestic emergencies, including an attack against the Nation using weapons of mass destruction, and these laws specifically authorize the President to use the Armed Forces to help restore public order.

(b) SENSE OF CONGRESS.—Congress reaffirms the continued importance of section 1385 of title 18, United States Code, and it is the sense of Congress that nothing in this Act should be construed to alter the applicability of such section to any use of the Armed Forces as a posse comitatus to execute the laws.

....

SEC. 888. PRESERVING COAST GUARD MISSION PERFORMANCE.

(a) DEFINITIONS.—In this section:

(1) NON-HOMELAND SECURITY MISSIONS.—The term "non-homeland security missions" means the following missions of the Coast Guard:

(A) Marine safety.

(B) Search and rescue.

(C) Aids to navigation.

(D) Living marine resources (fisheries law enforcement).

(E) Marine environmental protection.

(F) Ice operations.

(2) HOMELAND SECURITY MISSIONS.—The term "homeland security missions" means the following missions of the Coast Guard:

(A) Ports, waterways and coastal security.

(B) Drug interdiction.

(C) Migrant interdiction.

(D) Defense readiness.

(E) Other law enforcement.

(b) TRANSFER.—There are transferred to the Department the authorities, functions, personnel, and assets of the Coast Guard, which shall be maintained as a distinct entity within the Department, including the authorities and functions of the Secretary of Transportation relating thereto.

(c) MAINTENANCE OF STATUS OF FUNCTIONS AND ASSETS.—Notwithstanding any other provision of this Act, the authorities, functions, and capabilities of the Coast Guard to perform its missions shall be maintained intact and without significant reduction after the transfer of the Coast Guard to the Department, except as specified in subsequent Acts.

(d) CERTAIN TRANSFERS PROHIBITED.—No mission, function, or asset (including for purposes of this subsection any ship, aircraft, or helicopter) of the Coast Guard may be diverted to the principal and continuing use of any other organization, unit, or entity of the Department, except for details or assignments that do not reduce the Coast Guard's capability to perform its missions.

(e) CHANGES TO MISSIONS.—

(1) PROHIBITION.—The Secretary may not substantially or significantly reduce the missions of the Coast Guard or the Coast Guard's capability to perform those missions, except as specified in subsequent Acts.

(2) WAIVER.—The Secretary may waive the restrictions under paragraph (1) for a period of not to exceed 90 days upon a declaration and certification by the Secretary to Congress that a clear, compelling, and immediate need exists for such a waiver. A certification under this paragraph shall include a detailed justification for the declaration and certification, including the reasons and specific information that demonstrate that the Nation and the Coast Guard cannot respond effectively if the restrictions under paragraph (1) are not waived.

....

SUBTITLE I—INFORMATION SHARING

SEC. 891. SHORT TITLE; FINDINGS; AND SENSE OF CONGRESS.

(a) SHORT TITLE.—This subtitle may be cited as the "Homeland Security Information Sharing Act".

(b) FINDINGS.—Congress finds the following:

(1) The Federal Government is required by the Constitution to provide for the common defense, which includes terrorist attack.

(2) The Federal Government relies on State and local personnel to protect against terrorist attack.

(3) The Federal Government collects, creates, manages, and protects classified and sensitive but unclassified information to enhance homeland security.

(4) Some homeland security information is needed by the State and local personnel to prevent and prepare for terrorist attack.

(5) The needs of State and local personnel to have access to relevant homeland security information to combat terrorism must be reconciled with the need to preserve the protected status of such information and to protect the sources and methods used to acquire such information.

(6) Granting security clearances to certain State and local personnel is one way to facilitate the sharing of information regarding specific terrorist threats among Federal, State, and local levels of government.

(7) Methods exist to declassify, redact, or otherwise adapt classified information so it may be shared with State and local personnel without the need for granting additional security clearances.

(8) State and local personnel have capabilities and opportunities to gather information on suspicious activities and terrorist threats not possessed by Federal agencies.

(9) The Federal Government and State and local governments and agencies in other jurisdictions may benefit from such information.

(10) Federal, State, and local governments and intelligence, law enforcement, and other emergency preparation and response agencies must act in partnership to maximize the benefits of information gathering and analysis to prevent and respond to terrorist attacks.

(11) Information systems, including the National Law Enforcement Telecommunications System and the Terrorist Threat Warning System, have been established for rapid sharing of classified and sensitive but unclassified information among Federal, State, and local entities.

(12) Increased efforts to share homeland security information should avoid duplicating existing information systems.

(c) SENSE OF CONGRESS.—It is the sense of Congress that Federal, State, and local entities should share homeland security information to the maximum extent practicable, with special emphasis on hard-to-reach urban and rural communities.

. . . .

(c) SHARING OF CLASSIFIED INFORMATION AND SENSITIVE BUT UNCLASSIFIED INFORMATION WITH STATE AND LOCAL PERSONNEL.—

(1) The President shall prescribe procedures under which Federal agencies may, to the extent the President considers necessary, share with appropriate State and local personnel homeland security information that remains classified or otherwise protected after the determinations prescribed under the procedures set forth in subsection (a).

(2) It is the sense of Congress that such procedures may include 1 or more of the following means:

(A) Carrying out security clearance investigations with respect to appropriate State and local personnel.

(B) With respect to information that is sensitive but unclassified, entering into nondisclosure agreements with appropriate State and local personnel.

(C) Increased use of information-sharing partnerships that include appropriate State and local personnel, such as the Joint Terrorism Task Forces of the Federal Bureau of Investigation, the Anti-Terrorism Task Forces of the Department of Justice, and regional Terrorism Early Warning Groups.

....

SEC. 896. AUTHORITY TO SHARE ELECTRONIC, WIRE, AND ORAL INTERCEPTION INFORMATION.

Section 2517 of title 18, United States Code, is amended by adding at the end the following:

"(7) Any investigative or law enforcement officer, or other Federal official in carrying out official duties as such Federal official, who by any means authorized by this chapter, has obtained knowledge of the contents of any wire, oral, or electronic communication, or evidence derived therefrom, may disclose such contents or derivative evidence to a foreign investigative or law enforcement officer to the extent that such disclosure is appropriate to the proper performance of the official duties of the officer making or receiving the disclosure, and foreign investigative or law enforcement officers may use or disclose such contents or derivative evidence to the extent such use or disclosure is appropriate to the proper performance of their official duties."

....

EXECUTIVE ORDER 13354* (NATIONAL COUTERTERRORISM CENTER)

By the authority vested in me as President by the Constitution and laws of the United States of America, including section 103(c)(8) of the National Security Act of 1947, as amended (Act), and to protect the security of the United States through strengthened intelligence analysis and strategic planning and intelligence support to operations to counter transnational terrorist threats against the territory, people, and interests of the United States of America, it is hereby ordered as follows:

Section 1. Policy. (a) To the maximum extent consistent with applicable law, agencies shall give the highest priority to (i) the detection, prevention, disruption, preemption, and mitigation of the effects of transnational terrorist activities against the territory, people, and interests of the United States of America, (ii) the interchange of terrorism information among agencies, (iii) the interchange of terrorism information between agencies and appropriate authorities of States and local governments, and (iv) the protection of the ability of agencies to acquire additional such information.

(b) Agencies shall protect the freedom, information privacy, and other legal rights of Americans in the conduct of activities implementing section 1(a) of this order.

Sec. 2. Establishment of National Counterterrorism Center. (a) There is hereby established a National Counterterrorism Center (Center).

(b) A Director of the Center shall supervise the Center.

(c) The Director of the Center shall be appointed by the Director of Central Intelligence with the approval of the President.

(d) The Director of Central Intelligence shall have authority, direction, and control over the Center and the Director of the Center.

Sec. 3. Functions of the Center. The Center shall have the following functions:

(a) serve as the primary organization in the United States Government for analyzing and integrating all intelligence possessed or acquired by the United States Government pertaining to terrorism and counterterrorism, excepting purely domestic counterterrorism information. The Center may, consistent with applicable law, receive, retain, and disseminate information from any Federal, State, or local government, or other source necessary to fulfill its responsibilities concerning the policy set forth in section 1 of this order; and agencies authorized to conduct counterterrorism activities may query Center data for any information to assist in their respective responsibilities;

(b) conduct strategic operational planning for counterterrorism activities, integrating all instruments of national power, including diplomatic, financial, military, intelligence, homeland security, and law enforcement activities within and among agencies;

(c) assign operational responsibilities to lead agencies for counterterrorism activities that are consistent with applicable law and that support strategic plans to counter terrorism. The Center shall ensure that agencies have access to and receive intelligence needed to accomplish their assigned activities. The Center shall not direct the execution

* Exec. Order No. 13,354, 3 C.F.R. 214 (2005), *available at* http://www.fas.org/irp/offdocs/eo/eo-13354.htm.

of operations. Agencies shall inform the National Security Council and the Homeland Security Council of any objections to designations and assignments made by the Center in the planning and coordination of counterterrorism activities;

(d) serve as the central and shared knowledge bank on known and suspected terrorists and international terror groups, as well as their goals, strategies, capabilities, and networks of contacts and support; and

(e) ensure that agencies, as appropriate, have access to and receive all-source intelligence support needed to execute their counterterrorism plans or perform independent, alternative analysis.

Sec. 4. Duties of the Director of Central Intelligence. The Director of Central Intelligence shall:

(a) exercise the authority available by law to the Director of Central Intelligence to implement this order, including, as appropriate, the authority set forth in section 102(e)(2)(H) of the Act;

(b) report to the President on the implementation of this order, within 120 days after the date of this order and thereafter not less often than annually, including an assessment by the Director of Central Intelligence of:

(1) the effectiveness of the United States in implementing the policy set forth in section 1 of this order, to the extent execution of that policy is within the responsibilities of the Director of Central Intelligence;

(2) the effectiveness of the Center in the implementation of the policy set forth in section 1 of this order, to the extent execution of that policy is within the responsibilities of the Director of Central Intelligence; and

(3) the cooperation of the heads of agencies in the implementation of this order; and

(c) ensure the performance of all-source intelligence analysis that, among other qualities, routinely considers and presents alternative analytical views to the President, the Vice President in the performance of executive functions, and other officials of the executive branch as appropriate.

Sec. 5. Duties of the Director of the Center. In implementing the policy set forth in section 1 of this order and ensuring that the Center effectively performs the functions set forth in section 3 of this order, the Director of the Center shall:

(a) access, as deemed necessary by the Director of the Center for the performance of the Center's functions, information to which the Director of the Center is granted access by section 6 of this order;

(b) correlate, analyze, evaluate, integrate, and produce reports on terrorism information;

(c) disseminate transnational terrorism information, including current terrorism threat analysis, to the President, the Vice President in the performance of Executive functions, the Secretaries of State, Defense, and Homeland Security, the Attorney General, the Director of Central Intelligence, and other officials of the executive branch as appropriate;

(d) support the Department of Homeland Security, and the Department of Justice, and other appropriate agencies, in fulfillment of their responsibility to disseminate terrorism information, consistent with applicable law, Executive Orders and other Presidential guidance, to State and local government officials, and other entities, and coordinate dissemination of terrorism information to foreign governments when approved by the Director of Central Intelligence;

(e) establish both within the Center, and between the Center and agencies, information systems and architectures for the effective access to and integration, dissemination, and use of terrorism information from whatever sources derived;

(f) undertake, as soon as the Director of Central Intelligence determines it to be practicable, all functions assigned to the Terrorist Threat Integration Center;

(g) consistent with priorities approved by the President, assist the Director of Central Intelligence in establishing requirements for the Intelligence Community for the collection of terrorism information, to include ensuring military force protection requirements are met;

(h) under the direction of the Director of Central Intelligence, and in consultation with heads of agencies with organizations in the Intelligence Community, identify, coordinate, and prioritize counterterrorism intelligence requirements for the Intelligence Community; and

(i) identify, together with relevant agencies, specific counterterrorism planning efforts to be initiated or accelerated to protect the national security.

Sec. 6. Duties of the Heads of Agencies. (a) To implement the policy set forth in section 1 of this order:

(i) the head of each agency that possesses or acquires terrorism information:

(A) shall promptly give access to such information to the Director of the Center, unless prohibited by law (such as section 103(c)(7) of the Act or Executive Order 12958, as amended) or otherwise directed by the President;

(B) shall cooperate in and facilitate the production of reports based on terrorism information with contents and formats that permit dissemination that maximizes the utility of the information in protecting the territory, people, and interests of the United States; and

(C) shall cooperate with the Director of Central Intelligence in the preparation of the report to the President required by section 4 of this order; and

(ii) the head of each agency that conducts diplomatic, financial, military, homeland security, intelligence, or law enforcement activities relating to counterterrorism shall keep the Director of the Center fully and currently informed of such activities, unless prohibited by law (such as section 103(c)(7) of the Act or Executive Order 12958, as amended) or otherwise directed by the President.

(b) The head of each agency shall, consistent with applicable law, make available to the Director of the Center such personnel, funding, and other resources as the Director of Central Intelligence, after consultation with the head of the agency and with the approval of the Director of the Office of Management and Budget, may request. In order to ensure maximum information sharing consistent with applicable law, each agency representative to the Center, unless otherwise specified by the Director of Central Intelligence, shall operate under the authorities of the representative's agency.

Sec. 7. Definitions. As used in this order:

(a) the term "agency" has the meaning set forth for the term "executive agency" in section 105 of title 5, United States Code, together with the Department of Homeland

Security, but includes the Postal Rate Commission and the United States Postal Service and excludes the Government Accountability Office;

(b) the term "Intelligence Community" has the meaning set forth for that term in section 3.4(f) of Executive Order 12333 of December 4, 1981, as amended;

(c) the terms "local government", "State", and, when used in a geographical sense, "United States" have the meanings set forth for those terms in section 2 of the Homeland Security Act of 2002 (6 U.S.C. 101); and

(d) the term "terrorism information" means all information, whether collected, produced, or distributed by intelligence, law enforcement, military, homeland security, or other United States Government activities, relating to (i) the existence, organization, capabilities, plans, intentions, vulnerabilities, means of finance or material support, or activities of foreign or international terrorist groups or individuals, or of domestic groups or individuals involved in transnational terrorism; (ii) threats posed by such groups or individuals to the United States, United States persons, or United States interests, or to those of other nations; (iii) communications of or by such groups or individuals; or (iv) information relating to groups or individuals reasonably believed to be assisting or associated with such groups or individuals.

Sec. 8. General Provisions. (a) This order:

(i) shall be implemented in a manner consistent with applicable law, including Federal law protecting the information privacy and other legal rights of Americans, and subject to the availability of appropriations;

(ii) shall be implemented in a manner consistent with the authority of the principal officers of agencies as heads of their respective agencies, including under section 199 of the Revised Statutes (22 U.S.C. 2651), section 201 of the Department of Energy Reorganization Act (42 U.S.C. 7131), section 102(a) of the Homeland Security Act of 2002 (6 U.S.C. 112(a)), and sections 301 of title 5, 113(b) and 162(b) of title 10, 503 of title 28, and 301(b) of title 31, United States Code; and

(iii) shall not be construed to impair or otherwise affect the functions of the Director of the Office of Management and Budget relating to budget, administrative, and legislative proposals.

(b) This order and amendments made by this order are intended only to improve the internal management of the Federal Government and are not intended to, and do not, create any rights or benefits, substantive or procedural, enforceable at law or in equity by a party against the United States, its departments, agencies, instrumentalities, or entities, its officers, employees, or agents, or any other person.

[signed:] George W. Bush
THE WHITE HOUSE,
August 27, 2004.

EXECUTIVE ORDER 13356* (STRENGTHENING THE SHARING OF TERRORISM INFORMATION TO PROTECT AMERICANS)

By the authority vested in me as President by the Constitution and laws of the United States of America, and in order to further strengthen the effective conduct of United States intelligence activities and protect the territory, people, and interests of the United States of America, including against terrorist attacks, it is hereby ordered as follows:

Section 1. Policy. To the maximum extent consistent with applicable law, agencies shall, in the design and use of information systems and in the dissemination of information among agencies:

(a) give the highest priority to (i) the detection, prevention, disruption, preemption, and mitigation of the effects of terrorist activities against the territory, people, and interests of the United States of America, (ii) the interchange of terrorism information among agencies, (iii) the interchange of terrorism information between agencies and appropriate authorities of States and local governments, and (iv) the protection of the ability of agencies to acquire additional such information; and

(b) protect the freedom, information privacy, and other legal rights of Americans in the conduct of activities implementing subsection (a).

Sec. 2. Duty of Heads of Agencies Possessing or Acquiring Terrorism Information. To implement the policy set forth in section 1 of this order, the head of each agency that possesses or acquires terrorism information:

(a) shall promptly give access to the terrorism information to the head of each other agency that has counterterrorism functions, and provide the terrorism information to each such agency in accordance with the standards and information sharing guidance issued pursuant to this order, unless otherwise directed by the President, and consistent with (i) the statutory responsibilities of the agencies providing and receiving the information, (ii) any guidance issued by the Attorney General to fulfill the policy set forth in subsection 1(b) of this order, and (iii) other applicable law, including section 103(c)(7) of the National Security Act of 1947, section 892 of the Homeland Security Act of 2002, Executive Order 12958 of April 17, 1995, as amended, and Executive Order 13311 of July 29, 2003;

(b) shall cooperate in and facilitate production of reports based on terrorism information with contents and formats that permit dissemination that maximizes the utility of the information in protecting the territory, people, and interests of the United States; and

(c) shall facilitate implementation of the plan developed by the Information Systems Council established by section 5 of this order.

Sec. 3. Preparing Terrorism Information for Maximum Distribution within Intelligence Community. To assist in expeditious and effective implementation by agencies

---

* Exec. Order No. 13,356, 3 C.F.R. 223 (2005), *available at* http://www.fas.org/irp/offdocs/eo/eo-13356.htm.

within the Intelligence Community of the policy set forth in section 1 of this order, the Director of Central Intelligence shall, in consultation with the Attorney General and the other heads of agencies within the Intelligence Community, set forth not later than 90 days after the date of this order, and thereafter as appropriate, common standards for the sharing of terrorism information by agencies within the Intelligence Community with (i) other agencies within the Intelligence Community, (ii) other agencies having counterterrorism functions, and (iii) through or in coordination with the Department of Homeland Security, appropriate authorities of State and local governments. These common standards shall improve information sharing by such methods as:

(a) requiring, at the outset of the intelligence collection and analysis process, the creation of records and reporting, for both raw and processed information including, for example, metadata and content, in such a manner that sources and methods are protected so that the information can be distributed at lower classification levels, and by creating unclassified versions for distribution whenever possible;

(b) requiring records and reports related to terrorism information to be produced with multiple versions at an unclassified level and at varying levels of classification, for example on an electronic tearline basis, allowing varying degrees of access by other agencies and personnel commensurate with their particular security clearance levels and special access approvals;

(c) requiring terrorism information to be shared free of originator controls, including, for example, controls requiring the consent of the originating agency prior to the dissemination of the information outside any other agency to which it has been made available, to the maximum extent permitted by applicable law, Executive Orders, or Presidential guidance;

(d) minimizing the applicability of information compartmentalization systems to terrorism information, to the maximum extent permitted by applicable law, Executive Orders, and Presidential guidance; and

(e) ensuring the establishment of appropriate arrangements providing incentives for, and holding personnel accountable for, increased sharing of terrorism information, consistent with requirements of the Nation's security and with applicable law, Executive Orders, and Presidential guidance.

Sec. 4. Requirements for Collection of Terrorism Information Inside the United States.

(a) The Attorney General, the Secretary of Homeland Security, and the Director of Central Intelligence shall, not later than 90 days after the date of this order, jointly submit to the President, through the Assistants to the President for National Security Affairs and Homeland Security, their recommendation on the establishment of executive branch-wide collection and sharing requirements, procedures, and guidelines for terrorism information to be collected within the United States, including, but not limited to, from publicly available sources, including nongovernmental databases.

(b) The recommendation submitted under subsection (a) of this section shall also:

(i) address requirements and guidelines for the collection and sharing of other information necessary to protect the territory, people, and interests of the United States; and

(ii) propose arrangements for ensuring that officers of the United States with responsibilities for protecting the territory, people, and interests of the United States are provided with clear, understandable, consistent, effective, and lawful procedures and guidelines for the collection, handling, distribution, and retention of information.

Sec. 5. Establishment of Information Systems Council.

(a) There is established an Information Systems Council (Council), chaired by a designee of the Director of the Office of Management and Budget, and composed exclusively of designees of: the Secretaries of State, the Treasury, Defense, Commerce, Energy, and Homeland Security; the Attorney General; the Director of Central Intelligence; the Director of the Federal Bureau of Investigation; the Director of the National Counterterrorism Center, once that position is created and filled (and until that time the Director of the Terrorism Threat Integration Center); and such other heads of departments or agencies as the Director of the Office of Management and Budget may designate.

(b) The mission of the Council is to plan for and oversee the establishment of an interoperable terrorism information sharing environment to facilitate automated sharing of terrorism information among appropriate agencies to implement the policy set forth in section 1 of this order.

(c) Not later than 120 days after the date of this order, the Council shall report to the President through the Assistants to the President for National Security Affairs and Homeland Security, on a plan, with proposed milestones, timetables for achieving those milestones, and identification of resources, for the establishment of the proposed interoperable terrorism information sharing environment. The plan shall, at a minimum:

(i) describe and define the parameters of the proposed interoperable terrorism information sharing environment, including functions, capabilities, and resources;

(ii) identify and, as appropriate, recommend the consolidation and elimination of current programs, systems, and processes used by agencies to share terrorism information, and recommend as appropriate the redirection of existing resources to support the interoperable terrorism information sharing environment;

(iii) identify gaps, if any, between existing technologies, programs, and systems used by agencies to share terrorism information and the parameters of the proposed interoperable terrorism information sharing environment;

(iv) recommend near-term solutions to address any such gaps until the interoperable terrorism information sharing environment can be established;

(v) recommend a plan for implementation of the interoperable terrorism information sharing environment, including roles and responsibilities, measures of success, and deadlines for the development and implementation of functions and capabilities from the initial stage to full operational capability;

(vi) recommend how the proposed interoperable terrorism information sharing environment can be extended to allow interchange of terrorism information between agencies and appropriate authorities of States and local governments; and

(vii) recommend whether and how the interoperable terrorism information sharing environment should be expanded, or designed so as to allow future expansion, for purposes of encompassing other categories of intelligence and information.

Sec. 6. Definitions. As used in this order:

(a) the term "agency" has the meaning set forth for the term "executive agency" in section 105 of title 5, United States Code, together with the Department of Homeland

Security, but includes the Postal Rate Commission and the United States Postal Service and excludes the Government Accountability Office;

(b) the terms "Intelligence Community" and "agency within the Intelligence Community" have the meanings set forth for those terms in section 3.4(f) of Executive Order 12333 of December 4, 1981, as amended;

(c) the terms "local government," "State," and, when used in a geographical sense, "United States," have the meanings set forth for those terms in section 2 of the Homeland Security Act of 2002 (6 U.S.C. 101); and

(d) the term "terrorism information" means all information, whether collected, produced, or distributed by intelligence, law enforcement, military, homeland security, or other United States Government activities, relating to (i) the existence, organization, capabilities, plans, intentions, vulnerabilities, means of finance or material support, or activities of foreign or international terrorist groups or individuals, or of domestic groups or individuals involved in transnational terrorism; (ii) threats posed by such groups or individuals to the United States, United States persons, or United States interests, or to those of other nations; (iii) communications of or by such groups or individuals; or (iv) information relating to groups or individuals reasonably believed to be assisting or associated with such groups or individuals.

Sec. 7. General Provisions.

(a) This order:

(i) shall be implemented in a manner consistent with applicable law, including Federal law protecting the information privacy and other legal rights of Americans, and subject to the availability of appropriations;

(ii) shall be implemented in a manner consistent with the authority of the principal officers of agencies as heads of their respective agencies, including under section 199 of the Revised Statutes (22 U.S.C. 2651), section 201 of the Department of Energy Reorganization Act (42 U.S.C. 7131), section 102(a) of the National Security Act of 1947 (50 U.S.C. 403(a)), section 102(a) of the Homeland Security Act of 2002 (6 U.S.C. 112(a)), and sections 301 of title 5, 113(b) and 162(b) of title 10, 1501 of title 15, 503 of title 28, and 301(b) of title 31, United States Code; and

(iii) shall not be construed to impair or otherwise affect the functions of the Director of the Office of Management and Budget relating to budget, administrative, and legislative proposals.

(b) This order is intended only to improve the internal management of the Federal Government and is not intended to, and does not, create any rights or benefits, substantive or procedural, enforceable at law or in equity by a party against the United States, its departments, agencies, instrumentalities, or entities, its officers, employees, or agents, or any other person.

[signed:] George W. Bush
THE WHITE HOUSE,
August 27, 2004.

PROVIDING MATERIAL SUPPORT OR RESOURCES TO DESIGNATED FOREIGN TERRORIST ORGANIZATIONS*

§2339B. Providing material support or resources to designated foreign terrorist organizations.

(a) Prohibited activities.

(1) Unlawful conduct. Whoever knowingly provides material support or resources to a foreign terrorist organization, or attempts or conspires to do so, shall be fined under this title or imprisoned not more than 15 years, or both, and, if the death of any person results, shall be imprisoned for any term of years or for life. To violate this paragraph, a person must have knowledge that the organization is a designated terrorist organization (as defined in subsection (g)(6)), that the organization has engaged or engages in terrorist activity (as defined in section 212(a)(3)(B) of the Immigration and Nationality Act [8 USCS §1182(a)(3)(B)]), or that the organization has engaged or engages in terrorism (as defined in section 140(d)(2) of the Foreign Relations Authorization Act, Fiscal Years 1988 and 1989 [22 USCS §2656f(d)(2)]).

(2) Financial institutions. Except as authorized by the Secretary, any financial institution that becomes aware that it has possession of, or control over, any funds in which a foreign terrorist organization, or its agent, has an interest, shall—

(A) retain possession of, or maintain control over, such funds; and

(B) report to the Secretary the existence of such funds in accordance with regulations issued by the Secretary.

(b) Civil penalty. Any financial institution that knowingly fails to comply with subsection (a)(2) shall be subject to a civil penalty in an amount that is the greater of—

(A) $ 50,000 per violation; or

(B) twice the amount of which the financial institution was required under subsection (a)(2) to retain possession or control.

(c) Injunction. Whenever it appears to the Secretary or the Attorney General that any person is engaged in, or is about to engage in, any act that constitutes, or would constitute, a violation of this section, the Attorney General may initiate civil action in a district court of the United States to enjoin such violation.

(d) Extraterritorial jurisdiction.

(1) In general. There is jurisdiction over an offense under subsection (a) if—

(A) an offender is a national of the United States (as defined in section 101(a)(22) of the Immigration and Nationality Act (8 U.S.C. 1101(a)(22))) or

---

* 18 U.S.C.A. §2239B (2000 & Supp. 2004).

an alien lawfully admitted for permanent residence in the United States (as defined in section 101(a)(20) of the Immigration and Nationality Act (8 U.S.C. 1101(a)(20)));

(B) an offender is a stateless person whose habitual residence is in the United States;

(C) after the conduct required for the offense occurs an offender is brought into or found in the United States, even if the conduct required for the offense occurs outside the United States;

(D) the offense occurs in whole or in part within the United States;

(E) the offense occurs in or affects interstate or foreign commerce; or

(F) an offender aids or abets any person over whom jurisdiction exists under this paragraph in committing an offense under subsection (a) or conspires with any person over whom jurisdiction exists under this paragraph to commit an offense under subsection (a).

(2) Extraterritorial jurisdiction. There is extraterritorial Federal jurisdiction over an offense under this section.

(e) Investigations.

(1) In general. The Attorney General shall conduct any investigation of a possible violation of this section, or of any license, order, or regulation issued pursuant to this section.

(2) Coordination with the department of the treasury. The Attorney General shall work in coordination with the Secretary in investigations relating to—

(A) the compliance or noncompliance by a financial institution with the requirements of subsection (a)(2); and

(B) civil penalty proceedings authorized under subsection (b).

(3) Referral. Any evidence of a criminal violation of this section arising in the course of an investigation by the Secretary or any other Federal agency shall be referred immediately to the Attorney General for further investigation. The Attorney General shall timely notify the Secretary of any action taken on referrals from the Secretary, and may refer investigations to the Secretary for remedial licensing or civil penalty action.

(f) Classified information in civil proceedings brought by the United States.

(1) Discovery of classified information by defendants.

(A) Request by United States. In any civil proceeding under this section, upon request made ex parte and in writing by the United States, a court, upon a sufficient showing, may authorize the United States to—

(i) redact specified items of classified information from documents to be introduced into evidence or made available to the defendant through discovery under the Federal Rules of Civil Procedure;

(ii)substitute a summary of the information for such classified documents; or

(iii) substitute a statement admitting relevant facts that the classified information would tend to prove.

(B) Order granting request. If the court enters an order granting a request under this paragraph, the entire text of the documents to which the request relates shall be sealed and preserved in the records of the court to be made available to the appellate court in the event of an appeal.

(C) Denial of request. If the court enters an order denying a request of the United States under this paragraph, the United States may take an immediate, interlocutory appeal in accordance with paragraph (5). For purposes of such an appeal, the entire text of the documents to which the request relates, together with any transcripts of arguments made ex parte to the court in connection therewith, shall be maintained under seal and delivered to the appellate court.

(2) Introduction of classified information; precautions by court.

(A) Exhibits. To prevent unnecessary or inadvertent disclosure of classified information in a civil proceeding brought by the United States under this section, the United States may petition the court ex parte to admit, in lieu of classified writings, recordings, or photographs, one or more of the following:

(i) Copies of items from which classified information has been redacted.

(ii) Stipulations admitting relevant facts that specific classified information would tend to prove.

(iii) A declassified summary of the specific classified information.

(B) Determination by court. The court shall grant a request under this paragraph if the court finds that the redacted item, stipulation, or summary is sufficient to allow the defendant to prepare a defense.

(3) Taking of trial testimony.

(A) Objection. During the examination of a witness in any civil proceeding brought by the United States under this subsection, the United States may object to any question or line of inquiry that may require the witness to disclose classified information not previously found to be admissible.

(B) Action by court. In determining whether a response is admissible, the court shall take precautions to guard against the compromise of any classified information, including—

(i) permitting the United States to provide the court, ex parte, with a proffer of the witness's response to the question or line of inquiry; and

(ii) requiring the defendant to provide the court with a proffer of the nature of the information that the defendant seeks to elicit.

(C) Obligation of defendant. In any civil proceeding under this section, it shall be the defendant's obligation to establish the relevance and materiality of any classified information sought to be introduced.

(4) Appeal. If the court enters an order denying a request of the United States under this subsection, the United States may take an immediate interlocutory appeal in accordance with paragraph (5).

(5) Interlocutory appeal.

(A) Subject of appeal. An interlocutory appeal by the United States shall lie to a court of appeals from a decision or order of a district court—

(i) authorizing the disclosure of classified information;

(ii) imposing sanctions for nondisclosure of classified information; or

(iii) refusing a protective order sought by the United States to prevent the disclosure of classified information.

(B) Expedited consideration.

(i) In general. An appeal taken pursuant to this paragraph, either before or during trial, shall be expedited by the court of appeals.

(ii) Appeals prior to trial. If an appeal is of an order made prior to trial, an appeal shall be taken not later than 10 days after the decision or order appealed from, and the trial shall not commence until the appeal is resolved.

(iii) Appeals during trial. If an appeal is taken during trial, the trial court shall adjourn the trial until the appeal is resolved, and the court of appeals—

(I) shall hear argument on such appeal not later than 4 days after the adjournment of the trial;

(II) may dispense with written briefs other than the supporting materials previously submitted to the trial court;

(III) shall render its decision not later than 4 days after argument on appeal; and

(IV) may dispense with the issuance of a written opinion in rendering its decision.

(C) Effect of ruling. An interlocutory appeal and decision shall not affect the right of the defendant, in a subsequent appeal from a final judgment, to claim as error reversal by the trial court on remand of a ruling appealed from during trial.

(6) Construction. Nothing in this subsection shall prevent the United States from seeking protective orders or asserting privileges ordinarily available to the United States to protect against the disclosure of classified information, including the invocation of the military and State secrets privilege.

(g) Definitions. As used in this section—

(1) the term "classified information" has the meaning given that term in section 1(a) of the Classified Information Procedures Act (18 U.S.C. App.);

(2) the term "financial institution" has the same meaning as in section 5312(a)(2) of title 31, United States Code [31 USCS § 5312(a)(2)];

(3) the term "funds" includes coin or currency of the United States or any other country, traveler's checks, personal checks, bank checks, money orders, stocks, bonds, debentures, drafts, letters of credit, any other negotiable instrument, and any electronic representation of any of the foregoing;

(4) the term "material support or resources" has the same meaning given that term in section 2339A [18 USCS § 2339A] (including the definitions of "training" and "expert advice or assistance" in that section);

(5) the term "Secretary" means the Secretary of the Treasury; and

(6) the term "terrorist organization" means an organization designated as a terrorist organization under section 219 of the Immigration and Nationality Act [8 USCS § 1189].

(h) Provision of personnel. No person may be prosecuted under this section in connection with the term "personnel" unless that person has knowingly provided, attempted to provide, or conspired to provide a foreign terrorist organization with 1 or more individuals (who may be or include himself) to work under that terrorist organization's direction or control or to organize, manage, supervise, or otherwise direct the operation of that organization. Individuals who act entirely independently of the foreign terrorist organization to advance its goals or objectives shall not be considered to be working under the foreign terrorist organization's direction and control.

(i) Rule of construction. Nothing in this section shall be construed or applied so as to abridge the exercise of rights guaranteed under the First Amendment to the Constitution of the United States.

(j) Exception. No person may be prosecuted under this section in connection with the term "personnel", "training", or "expert advice or assistance" if the provision of that material support or resources to a foreign terrorist organization was approved by the Secretary of State with the concurrence of the Attorney General. The Secretary of State may not approve the provision of any material support that may be used to carry out terrorist activity (as defined in section 212(a)(3)(B)(iii) of the Immigration and Nationality Act [8 USCS § 1182(a)(3)(B)(iii)]).

DESIGNATION OF FOREIGN TERRORIST ORGANIZATIONS*

§ **1189.** Designation of foreign terrorist organizations

(a) Designation.

(1) In general. The Secretary is authorized to designate an organization as a foreign terrorist organization in accordance with this subsection if the Secretary finds that—

(A) the organization is a foreign organization;

(B) the organization engages in terrorist activity (as defined in section 212(a)(3)(B) [8 USCS § 1182(a)(3)(B)]) or terrorism (as defined in section 140(d)(2) of the Foreign Relations Authorization Act, Fiscal Years 1988 and 1989 (22 U.S.C. 2656f(d)(2)), or retains the capability and intent to engage in terrorist activity or terrorism; and

(C) the terrorist activity or terrorism of the organization threatens the security of United States nationals or the national security of the United States.

(2) Procedure.

(A) Notice.

(i) To congressional leaders. Seven days before making a designation under this subsection, the Secretary shall, by classified communication, notify the Speaker and Minority Leader of the House of Representatives, the President pro tempore, Majority Leader, and Minority Leader of the Senate, and the members of the relevant committees of the House of Representatives and the Senate, in writing, of the intent to designate an organization under this subsection, together with the findings made under paragraph (1) with respect to that organization, and the factual basis therefor.

(ii) Publication in Federal Register. The Secretary shall publish the designation in the Federal Register seven days after providing the notification under clause (i).

(B) Effect of designation.

(i) For purposes of section 2339B of title 18, United States Code, a designation under this subsection shall take effect upon publication under subparagraph (A)(ii).

(ii) Any designation under this subsection shall cease to have effect upon an Act of Congress disapproving such designation.

(C) Freezing of assets. Upon notification under paragraph (2)(A)(i), the Secretary of the Treasury may require United States financial institutions possessing or controlling any assets of any foreign organization included in the notification to block all financial transactions involving those assets until further directive from either the Secretary of the Treasury, Act of Congress, or order of court.

---

* 8 U.S.C.S § 1189 (LexisNexis 1997 & Supp. 2005).

(3) Record.

(A) In general. In making a designation under this subsection, the Secretary shall create an administrative record.

(B) Classified information. The Secretary may consider classified information in making a designation under this subsection. Classified information shall not be subject to disclosure for such time as it remains classified, except that such information may be disclosed to a court ex parte and in camera for purposes of judicial review under subsection (c).

(4) Period of designation.

(A) In general. A designation under this subsection shall be effective for all purposes until revoked under paragraph (5) or (6) or set aside pursuant to subsection (c).

(B) Review of designation upon petition.

(i) In general. The Secretary shall review the designation of a foreign terrorist organization under the procedures set forth in clauses (iii) and (iv) if the designated organization files a petition for revocation within the petition period described in clause (ii).

(ii) Petition period. For purposes of clause (i)—

(I) if the designated organization has not previously filed a petition for revocation under this subparagraph, the petition period begins 2 years after the date on which the designation was made; or

(II) if the designated organization has previously filed a petition for revocation under this subparagraph, the petition period begins 2 years after the date of the determination made under clause (iv) on that petition.

(iii) Procedures. Any foreign terrorist organization that submits a petition for revocation under this subparagraph must provide evidence in that petition that the relevant circumstances described in paragraph (1) are sufficiently different from the circumstances that were the basis for the designation such that a revocation with respect to the organization is warranted.

(iv) Determination.

(I) In general. Not later than 180 days after receiving a petition for revocation submitted under this subparagraph, the Secretary shall make a determination as to such revocation.

(II) Classified information. The Secretary may consider classified information in making a determination in response to a petition for revocation. Classified information shall not be subject to disclosure for such time as it remains classified, except that such information may be disclosed to a court ex parte and in camera for purposes of judicial review under subsection (c).

(III) Publication of determination. A determination made by the Secretary under this clause shall be published in the Federal Register.

(IV) Procedures. Any revocation by the Secretary shall be made in accordance with paragraph (6).

(C) Other review of designation.

(i) In general. If in a 5-year period no review has taken place under subparagraph (B), the Secretary shall review the designation of the foreign terrorist organization in order to determine whether such designation should be revoked pursuant to paragraph (6).

(ii) Procedures. If a review does not take place pursuant to subparagraph (B) in response to a petition for revocation that is filed in accordance with that subparagraph, then the review shall be conducted pursuant to procedures established by the Secretary. The results of such review and the applicable procedures shall not be reviewable in any court.

(iii) Publication of results of review. The Secretary shall publish any determination made pursuant to this subparagraph in the Federal Register.

(5) Revocation by Act of Congress. The Congress, by an Act of Congress, may block or revoke a designation made under paragraph (1).

(6) Revocation based on change in circumstances.

(A) In general. The Secretary may revoke a designation made under paragraph (1) at any time, and shall revoke a designation upon completion of a review conducted pursuant to subparagraphs (B) and (C) of paragraph (4) if the Secretary finds that—

(i) the circumstances that were the basis for the designation have changed in such a manner as to warrant revocation; or

(ii) the national security of the United States warrants a revocation.

(B) Procedure. The procedural requirements of paragraphs (2) and (3) shall apply to a revocation under this paragraph. Any revocation shall take effect on the date specified in the revocation or upon publication in the Federal Register if no effective date is specified.

(7) Effect of revocation. The revocation of a designation under paragraph (5) or (6) shall not affect any action or proceeding based on conduct committed prior to the effective date of such revocation.

(8) Use of designation in trial or hearing. If a designation under this subsection has become effective under paragraph (2)(B) a defendant in a criminal action or an alien in a removal proceeding shall not be permitted to raise any question concerning the validity of the issuance of such designation as a defense or an objection at any trial or hearing.

(b) Amendments to a designation.

(1) In general. The Secretary may amend a designation under this subsection if the Secretary finds that the organization has changed its name, adopted a new alias, dissolved and then reconstituted itself under a different name or names, or merged with another organization.

(2) Procedure. Amendments made to a designation in accordance with paragraph (1) shall be effective upon publication in the Federal Register. Subparagraphs (B) and (C) of subsection (a)(2) shall apply to an amended designation upon such publication. Paragraphs (2)(A)(i), (4), (5), (6), (7), and (8) of subsection (a) shall also apply to an amended designation.

(3) Administrative record. The administrative record shall be corrected to include the amendments as well as any additional relevant information that supports those amendments.

(4) Classified information. The Secretary may consider classified information in amending a designation in accordance with this subsection. Classified information shall not be subject to disclosure for such time as it remains classified, except that such information may be disclosed to a court ex parte and in camera for purposes of judicial review under subsection (c).

(c) Judicial review of designation.

(1) In general. Not later than 30 days after publication in the Federal Register of a designation, an amended designation, or a determination in response to a petition for revocation, the designated organization may seek judicial review in the United States Court of Appeals for the District of Columbia Circuit.

(2) Basis of review. Review under this subsection shall be based solely upon the administrative record, except that the Government may submit, for ex parte and in camera review, classified information used in making the designation, amended designation, or determination in response to a petition for revocation.

(3) Scope of review. The Court shall hold unlawful and set aside a designation, amended designation, or determination in response to a petition for revocation the court finds to be—

(A) arbitrary, capricious, an abuse of discretion, or otherwise not in accordance with law;

(B) contrary to constitutional right, power, privilege, or immunity;

(C) in excess of statutory jurisdiction, authority, or limitation, or short of statutory right;

(D) lacking substantial support in the administrative record taken as a whole or in classified information submitted to the court under paragraph (2), or

(E) not in accord with the procedures required by law.

(4) Judicial review invoked. The pendency of an action for judicial review of a designation, amended designation, or determination in response to a petition for revocation shall not affect the application of this section, unless the court issues a final order setting aside the designation, amended designation, or determination in response to a petition for revocation.

(d) Definitions. As used in this section—

(1) the term "classified information" has the meaning given that term in section 1(a) of the Classified Information Procedures Act (18 U.S.C. App.);

(2) the term "national security" means the national defense, foreign relations, or economic interests of the United States;

(3) the term "relevant committees" means the Committees on the Judiciary, Intelligence, and Foreign Relations of the Senate and the Committees on the Judiciary, Intelligence, and International Relations of the House of Representatives; and

(4) the term "Secretary" means the Secretary of State, in consultation with the Secretary of the Treasury and the Attorney General.

C. The Constitutional Framework for the Division of Powers between the Congress and the President

U.S. CONSTITUTION ARTICLES I, II, III, VI AND AMENDMENT XIV*

ARTICLE I

Section 1. All legislative Powers herein granted shall be vested in a Congress of the United States, which shall consist of a Senate and House of Representatives.

. . . .

Section 7. Clause 1: All Bills for raising Revenue shall originate in the House of Representatives; but the Senate may propose or concur with Amendments as on other Bills.

Clause 2: Every Bill which shall have passed the House of Representatives and the Senate, shall, before it become a Law, be presented to the President of the United States; If he approve he shall sign it, but if not he shall return it, with his Objections to that House in which it shall have originated, who shall enter the Objections at large on their Journal, and proceed to reconsider it. If after such Reconsideration two thirds of that House shall agree to pass the Bill, it shall be sent, together with the Objections, to the other House, by which it shall likewise be reconsidered, and if approved by two thirds of that House, it shall become a Law. But in all such Cases the Votes of both Houses shall be determined by yeas and Nays, and the Names of the Persons voting for and against the Bill shall be entered on the Journal of each House respectively. If any Bill shall not be returned by the President within ten Days (Sundays excepted) after it shall have been presented to him, the Same shall be a Law, in like Manner as if he had signed it, unless the Congress by their Adjournment prevent its Return, in which Case it shall not be a Law.

Clause 3: Every Order, Resolution, or Vote to which the Concurrence of the Senate and House of Representatives may be necessary (except on a question of Adjournment) shall be presented to the President of the United States; and before the Same shall take Effect, shall be approved by him, or being disapproved by him, shall be repassed by two thirds of the Senate and House of Representatives, according to the Rules and Limitations prescribed in the Case of a Bill.

Section 8. Clause 1: The Congress shall have Power To lay and collect Taxes, Duties, Imposts and Excises, to pay the Debts and provide for the common Defence and general Welfare of the United States; but all Duties, Imposts and Excises shall be uniform throughout the United States;

Clause 2: To borrow Money on the credit of the United States;

Clause 3: To regulate Commerce with foreign Nations, and among the several States, and with the Indian Tribes;

Clause 4: To establish an uniform Rule of Naturalization, and uniform Laws on the subject of Bankruptcies throughout the United States;

Clause 5: To coin Money, regulate the Value thereof, and of foreign Coin, and fix the Standard of Weights and Measures;

* U.S. Const. arts. I–III, VI & amend. XIV, *available at* http://www.gpoaccess.gov/constitution/browse.html#1992.

Clause 6: To provide for the Punishment of counterfeiting the Securities and current Coin of the United States;

Clause 7: To establish Post Offices and post Roads;

Clause 8: To promote the Progress of Science and useful Arts, by securing for limited Times to Authors and Inventors the exclusive Right to their respective Writings and Discoveries;

Clause 9: To constitute Tribunals inferior to the supreme Court;

Clause 10: To define and punish Piracies and Felonies committed on the high Seas, and Offences against the Law of Nations;

Clause 11: To declare War, grant Letters of Marque and Reprisal, and make Rules concerning Captures on Land and Water;

Clause 12: To raise and support Armies, but no Appropriation of Money to that Use shall be for a longer Term than two Years;

Clause 13: To provide and maintain a Navy;

Clause 14: To make Rules for the Government and Regulation of the land and naval Forces;

Clause 15: To provide for calling forth the Militia to execute the Laws of the Union, suppress Insurrections and repel Invasions;

Clause 16: To provide for organizing, arming, and disciplining, the Militia, and for governing such Part of them as may be employed in the Service of the United States, reserving to the States respectively, the Appointment of the Officers, and the Authority of training the Militia according to the discipline prescribed by Congress;

Clause 17: To exercise exclusive Legislation in all Cases whatsoever, over such District (not exceeding ten Miles square) as may, by Cession of particular States, and the Acceptance of Congress, become the Seat of the Government of the United States, and to exercise like Authority over all Places purchased by the Consent of the Legislature of the State in which the Same shall be, for the Erection of Forts, Magazines, Arsenals, dock-Yards, and other needful Buildings;—And

Clause 18: To make all Laws which shall be necessary and proper for carrying into Execution the foregoing Powers, and all other Powers vested by this Constitution in the Government of the United States, or in any Department or Officer thereof.

Section 9. Clause 1: The Migration or Importation of such Persons as any of the States now existing shall think proper to admit, shall not be prohibited by the Congress prior to the Year one thousand eight hundred and eight, but a Tax or duty may be imposed on such Importation, not exceeding ten dollars for each Person.

Clause 2: The Privilege of the Writ of Habeas Corpus shall not be suspended, unless when in Cases of Rebellion or Invasion the public Safety may require it.

Clause 3: No Bill of Attainder or ex post facto Law shall be passed.

Clause 4: No Capitation, or other direct, Tax shall be laid, unless in Proportion to the Census or Enumeration herein before directed to be taken. *(See Note 7)*

Clause 5: No Tax or Duty shall be laid on Articles exported from any State.

Clause 6: No Preference shall be given by any Regulation of Commerce or Revenue to the Ports of one State over those of another: nor shall Vessels bound to, or from, one State, be obliged to enter, clear, or pay Duties in another.

Clause 7: No Money shall be drawn from the Treasury, but in Consequence of Appropriations made by Law; and a regular Statement and Account of the Receipts and Expenditures of all public Money shall be published from time to time.

Clause 8: No Title of Nobility shall be granted by the United States: And no Person holding any Office of Profit or Trust under them, shall, without the Consent of the Congress, accept of any present, Emolument, Office, or Title, of any kind whatever, from any King, Prince, or foreign State.

Section 10. Clause 1: No State shall enter into any Treaty, Alliance, or Confederation; grant Letters of Marque and Reprisal; coin Money; emit Bills of Credit; make any Thing but gold and silver Coin a Tender in Payment of Debts; pass any Bill of Attainder, ex post facto Law, or Law impairing the Obligation of Contracts, or grant any Title of Nobility.

Clause 2: No State shall, without the Consent of the Congress, lay any Imposts or Duties on Imports or Exports, except what may be absolutely necessary for executing it's inspection Laws: and the net Produce of all Duties and Imposts, laid by any State on Imports or Exports, shall be for the Use of the Treasury of the United States; and all such Laws shall be subject to the Revision and Control of the Congress.

Clause 3: No State shall, without the Consent of Congress, lay any Duty of Tonnage, keep Troops, or Ships of War in time of Peace, enter into any Agreement or Compact with another State, or with a foreign Power, or engage in War, unless actually invaded, or in such imminent Danger as will not admit of delay.

ARTICLE II

Section 1. Clause 1: The executive Power shall be vested in a President of the United States of America. He shall hold his Office during the Term of four Years, and, together with the Vice President, chosen for the same Term, be elected, as follows:

....

Section 2. Clause 1: The President shall be Commander in Chief of the Army and Navy of the United States, and of the Militia of the several States, when called into the actual Service of the United States; he may require the Opinion, in writing, of the principal Officer in each of the executive Departments, upon any Subject relating to the Duties of their respective Offices, and he shall have Power to grant Reprieves and Pardons for Offences against the United States, except in Cases of Impeachment.

Clause 2: He shall have Power, by and with the Advice and Consent of the Senate, to make Treaties, provided two thirds of the Senators present concur; and he shall nominate, and by and with the Advice and Consent of the Senate, shall appoint Ambassadors, other public Ministers and Consuls, Judges of the supreme Court, and all other Officers of the United States, whose Appointments are not herein otherwise provided for, and which shall be established by Law: but the Congress may by Law vest the Appointment of such inferior Officers, as they think proper, in the President alone, in the Courts of Law, or in the Heads of Departments.

Clause 3: The President shall have Power to fill up all Vacancies that may happen during the Recess of the Senate, by granting Commissions which shall expire at the End of their next Session.

Section 3. He shall from time to time give to the Congress Information of the State of the Union, and recommend to their Consideration such Measures as he shall judge necessary and expedient; he may, on extraordinary Occasions, convene both Houses, or either of them, and in Case of Disagreement between them, with Respect to the Time of Adjournment, he may adjourn them to such Time as he shall think proper; he shall receive Ambassadors and other public Ministers; he shall take Care that the Laws be faithfully executed, and shall Commission all the Officers of the United States.

....

ARTICLE III

Section 1. The judicial Power of the United States, shall be vested in one supreme Court, and in such inferior Courts as the Congress may from time to time ordain and establish. The Judges, both of the supreme and inferior Courts, shall hold their Offices during good Behaviour, and shall, at stated Times, receive for their Services, a Compensation, which shall not be diminished during their Continuance in Office.

Section 2. Clause 1: The judicial Power shall extend to all Cases, in Law and Equity, arising under this Constitution, the Laws of the United States, and Treaties made, or which shall be made, under their Authority;—to all Cases affecting Ambassadors, other public Ministers and Consuls;—to all Cases of admiralty and maritime Jurisdiction;—to Controversies to which the United States shall be a Party;—to Controversies between two or more States;—between a State and Citizens of another State;—between Citizens of different States,—between Citizens of the same State claiming Lands under Grants of different States, and between a State, or the Citizens thereof, and foreign States, Citizens or Subjects.

Clause 2: In all Cases affecting Ambassadors, other public Ministers and Consuls, and those in which a State shall be Party, the supreme Court shall have original Jurisdiction. In all the other Cases before mentioned, the supreme Court shall have appellate Jurisdiction, both as to Law and Fact, with such Exceptions, and under such Regulations as the Congress shall make.

....

ARTICLE VI

....

Clause 2: This Constitution, and the Laws of the United States which shall be made in Pursuance thereof; and all Treaties made, or which shall be made, under the Authority of the United States, shall be the supreme Law of the Land; and the Judges in every State shall be bound thereby, any Thing in the Constitution or Laws of any State to the Contrary notwithstanding.

....

AMENDMENT XIV [1868]

Section 1. All persons born or naturalized in the United States, and subject to the jurisdiction thereof, are citizens of the United States and of the State wherein they reside. No State shall make or enforce any law which shall abridge the privileges or immunities of citizens of the United States; nor shall any State deprive any person of life, liberty, or property, without due process of law; nor deny to any person within its jurisdiction the equal protection of the laws.

....

ACT CREATING DEPARTMENT OF FOREIGN AFFAIRS*

An Act for Establishing an Executive Department, to be denominated the Department of Foreign Affairs

Section 1. *Be it enacted by the Senate and House of Representatives of the United States of America in Congress assembled,* That there shall be an Executive department, to be denominated the Department of Foreign Affairs, and that there shall be a principal officer therein, to be called the Secretary for the Department of Foreign Affairs, who shall perform and execute such duties as shall from time to time be enjoined on or intrusted to him by the President of the United States, agreeable to the Constitution, relative to correspondences, commissions or instructions to or with public ministers or consuls, from the United States, or to negotiations with public ministers from foreign public ministers or other foreigners, or to such other matters respecting foreign affairs, as the President of the United States shall assign to the said department; and furthermore, that the said principal officer shall conduct the business of the said department in such manner as the President of the United States shall from time to time order or instruct.

Section 2. *And be it further enacted,* That there shall be in the said department, an inferior officer, to be appointed by the said principal officer, and to be employed therein as he shall deem proper, and to be called the chief Clerk in the Department of Foreign Affairs, and who, whenever the said principal officer shall be removed from office by the President of the United States, or in any other case of vacancy, shall during such vacancy have the charge and custody of all records, books and papers appertaining to the said department.

Section 3. *And be it further enacted,* That the said principal officer, and every other person to be appointed or employed in the said department, shall, before he enters on the execution of his office or employment, take an oath or affirmation, well and faithfully to execute the trust committed to him.

Section 4. *And be it further enacted,* That the Secretary for the Department of Foreign Affairs, to be appointed in consequence of this act, shall forthwith after his appointment, be entitled to have the custody and charge of all records, books and papers in the office of Secretary for the Department of Foreign Affairs, heretofore established by the United States in Congress assembled.

Approved, July 27, 1789.

---

* An Act for Establishing an Executive Department, to Be Denominated the Department of Foreign Affairs, ch. IV, 1 Stat. 28, 28–29 (1789). This department was redesignated as the Department of State soon thereafter.

FIRST APPROPRIATIONS ACT FOR FOREIGN AFFAIRS*

Section 1. *Be it enacted by the Senate and House of Representatives of the United States of America in Congress assembled,* That the President of the United States shall be, and he hereby is authorized to draw from the treasury of the United States, a sum not exceeding forty thousand dollars annually, to be paid out of the monies arising from the duties on imports and tonnage, for the support of such persons as he shall commission to serve the United States in foreign parts, and for the expense incident to the business in which they may be employed: *Provided,* That exclusive of an outfit, which shall in no case exceed the amount of one year's full salary to the minister plenipotentiary or charge des affaires to whom the same may be allowed, the President shall not allow to any minister plenipotentiary a greater sum than at the rate of nine thousand dollars per annum, as a compensation for all his personal services and other expenses; nor a greater sum for the same, than four thousand five hundred dollars per annum to a charge des affaires; nor a greater sum for the same, than one thousand three hundred and fifty dollars per annum to the secretary of any minister plenipotentiary: *And provided also*, That the President shall account specifically for all such expenditures of the said money as in his judgment may be made public, and also for the amount of such expenditures as he may think it advisable not to specify, and cause a regular statement and account thereof to be laid before Congress annually, and also lodged in the proper office of the treasury department.

Section 2. *And be it further enacted,* That this act shall continue and be in force for the space of two years, and from thence until the end of the next session of Congress thereafter, and no longer.

APPROVED, July 1, 1790.

* An Act Providing the Means of Intercourse Between the United States and Foreign Nations, ch. XXII, 1 Stat. 128, 128–29 (1790).

1. Treaty Power

CASE-ZABLOCKI ACT*

§ 112b. United States international agreements; transmission to Congress

(a) The Secretary of State shall transmit to the Congress the text of any international agreement (including the text of any oral international agreement, which agreement shall be reduced to writing), other than a treaty, to which the United States is a party as soon as practicable after such agreement has entered into force with respect to the United States but in no event later than sixty days thereafter. However, any such agreement the immediate public disclosure of which would, in the opinion of the President, be prejudicial to the national security of the United States shall not be so transmitted to the Congress but shall be transmitted to the Committee on Foreign Relations of the Senate and the Committee on International Relations of the House of Representatives under an appropriate injunction of secrecy to be removed only upon due notice from the President. Any department or agency of the United States Government which enters into any international agreement on behalf of the United States shall transmit to the Department of State the text of such agreement not later than twenty days after such agreement has been signed.

(b) Not later than March 1, 1979, and at yearly intervals thereafter, the President shall, under his own signature, transmit to the Speaker of the House of Representatives and the chairman of the Committee on Foreign Relations of the Senate a report with respect to each international agreement which, during the preceding year, was transmitted to the Congress after the expiration of the 60-day period referred to in the first sentence of subsection (a), describing fully and completely the reasons for the late transmittal.

(c) Notwithstanding any other provision of law, an international agreement may not be signed or otherwise concluded on behalf of the United States without prior consultation with the Secretary of State. Such consultation may encompass a class of agreements rather than a particular agreement.

(d) (1) The Secretary of State shall annually submit to Congress a report that contains an index of all international agreements, listed by country, date, title, and summary of each such agreement (including a description of the duration of activities under the agreement and the agreement itself), that the United States—

(A) has signed, proclaimed, or with reference to which any other final formality has been executed, or that has been extended or otherwise modified, during the preceding calendar year; and

(B) has not been published, or is not proposed to be published, in the compilation entitled "United States Treaties and Other International Agreements".

(2) The report described in paragraph (1) may be submitted in classified form.

(e) (1) Subject to paragraph (2), the Secretary of State shall determine for and within the executive branch whether an arrangement constitutes an international agreement within the meaning of this section.

(2) (A) An arrangement shall constitute an international agreement within the meaning of this section (other than subsection (c)) irrespective of the duration of activities under the arrangement or the arrangement itself.

---

* Case-Zablocki Act, Pub. L. No. 92-403, 86 Stat. 619 (1972) (codified as amended at 1 U.S.C.A § 112b (West 2005 & Supp. 2005)), *available at* http://www.state.gov/g/oes/rls/rpts/175/1447.htm.

(B) Arrangements that constitute an international agreement within the meaning of this section (other than subsection (c)) include the following:

(i) A bilateral or multilateral counterterrorism agreement.

(ii) A bilateral agreement with a country that is subject to a determination under section 6(j)(1)(A) of the Export Administration Act of 1979 *(50 U.S.C. App. 2405*(j)(1)(A)), section 620A(a) of the Foreign Assistance Act of 1961 *(22 U.S.C. 2371*(a)), or section 40(d) of the Arms Export Control Act *(22 U.S.C. 2780*(d)).

(f) The President shall, through the Secretary of State, promulgate such rules and regulations as may be necessary to carry out this section.

CIRCULAR 175*
(DEPARTMENT OF STATE)

TREATIES AND OTHER INTERNATIONAL AGREEMENTS

Guidelines or information to be followed to facilitate the application of orderly procedures in the negotiation, signature, publication, and registration of treaties and other international agreements of the United States are provided in revised chapter 700.

. . . .

710 PURPOSE AND DISCLAIMER

711 PURPOSE

a. The purpose of this chapter is to facilitate the application of orderly and uniform measures and procedures for the negotiation, signature, publication, and registration of treaties and other international agreements of the United States. It is also designed to facilitate the maintenance of complete and accurate records on treaties and agreements and the publication of authoritative information regarding them.

b. The chapter is not a catalog of all the essential guidelines or information pertaining to the making and application of international agreements. It is limited to guidelines or information necessary for general guidance.

712 DISCLAIMER

This chapter is intended solely as a general outline of measures and procedures ordinarily followed which, it is recognized, cannot anticipate all circumstances or situations that may arise. Deviation or derogation from the provisions of this chapter will not invalidate actions taken by officers nor affect the validity of negotiations engaged in or of treaties or other agreements concluded.

713 THROUGH 719 UNASSIGNED

720 NEGOTIATION AND SIGNATURE

720.1 Circular 175 Procedure

This subchapter is a codification of the substance of Department Circular No. 175, December 13, 1955, as amended, on the negotiation and signature of treaties and other international agreements. It may be referred to for convenience and continuity as the "Circular 175 Procedure."

720.2 General Objectives

The objectives are:

a. That the making of treaties and other international agreements for the United States is carried out within constitutional and other appropriate limits;

b. That the objectives to be sought in the negotiation of particular treaties and other international agreements are approved by the Secretary or an officer specifically authorized by him or her for that purpose;

---

* 11 U.S. Dep't of State, Foreign Affairs Manual §§ 700–750.5 (1985), *available at* http://foia.state.gov/REGS/fams.asp?level=2&id=12&fam=0.

c. That timely and appropriate consultation is had with congressional leaders and committees on treaties and other international agreements;

d. That where, in the opinion of the Secretary of State or a designee, the circumstances permit, the public be given an opportunity to comment on treaties and other international agreements;

e. That firm positions departing from authorized positions are not undertaken without the approval of the Legal Adviser and interested Assistant Secretaries or their deputies;

f. That the final texts developed are approved by the Legal Adviser and the interested assistant secretaries or their deputies and, when required, brought a reasonable time before signature to the attention of the Secretary or an officer specifically designated by the Secretary for that purpose;

g. That authorization to sign the final text is obtained and appropriate arrangements for signature are made; and

h. That there is compliance with the requirements of *1 U.S.C. 112b, as amende*d, on the transmission of the texts of international agreements other than treaties to the Congress (see section 724); the law on the publication of treaties and other international agreements (see section 725); and treaty provisions on registration (see section 750.3-3).

721 EXERCISE OF THE INTERNATIONAL AGREEMENT POWER

721.1 Determination of Type of Agreement

The following considerations will be taken into account along with other relevant factors in determining whether an international agreement shall be dealt with by the United States as a treaty to be brought into force with the advice and consent of the Senate or as an agreement to be brought into force on some other constitutional basis.

721.2 Constitutional Requirements

There are two procedures under the Constitution through which the United States becomes a party to international agreement. Those procedures and the constitutional parameters of each are:

a. Treaties

International agreements (regardless of their title, designation, or form) whose entry into force with respect to the United States takes place only after the Senate has given its advice and consent are "treaties." The President, with the advice and consent of two-thirds of the Senators present, may enter into an international agreement on any subject genuinely of concern in foreign relations, so long as the agreement does not contravene the United States Constitution; and

b. International Agreements Other Than Treaties

International agreements brought into force with respect to the United States on a constitutional basis other than with the advice and consent of the Senate are "international agreements other than treaties." (The term "executive agreement" is appropriately reserved for agreements made solely on the basis of the constitutional authority of the President.) There are three constitutional bases for international agreements other than treaties as set forth below. An international agreement may be concluded pursuant to one or more of these constitutional bases:

(1) Agreements Pursuant to Treaty

The President may conclude an international agreement pursuant to a treaty brought into force with the advice and consent of the Senate, the provisions of which constitute authorization for the agreement by the Executive without subsequent action by the Congress;

(2) Agreements Pursuant to Legislation

The President may conclude an international agreement on the basis of existing legislation or subject to legislation to be enacted by the Congress; and

(3) Agreements Pursuant to the Constitutional Authority of the President

The President may conclude an international agreement on any subject within his constitutional authority so long as the agreement is not inconsistent with legislation enacted by the Congress in the exercise of its constitutional authority. The constitutional sources of authority for the President to conclude international agreements include:

(a) The President's authority as Chief Executive to represent the nation in foreign affairs;

(b) The President's authority to receive ambassadors and other public ministers;

(c) The President's authority as "Commander-in-Chief"; and

(d) The President's authority to "take care that the laws be faithfully executed."

721.3 Considerations for Selecting among Constitutionally Authorized Procedures

In determining a question as to the procedure which should be followed for any particular international agreement, due consideration is given to the following factors along with those in 721.2:

a. The extent to which the agreement involves commitments or risks affecting the nation as a whole;

b. Whether the agreement is intended to affect State laws;

c. Whether the agreement can be given effect without the enactment of subsequent legislation by the Congress;

d. Past U.S. practice as to similar agreements;

e. The preference of the Congress as to a particular type of agreement;

f. The degree of formality desired for an agreement;

g. The proposed duration of the agreement, the need for prompt conclusion of an agreement, and the desirability of concluding a routine or short-term agreement; and

h. The general international practice as to similar agreements.

In determining whether any international agreement should be brought into force as a treaty or as an international agreement other than a treaty, the utmost care is to be exercised to avoid any invasion or compromise of the constitutional powers of the Senate, the Congress as a whole, or the President.

721.4 Questions as to Type of Agreement to Be Used; Consultation with Congress

a. All legal memorandums accompanying Circular 175 requests (see section 722.3, paragraph h) will discuss thoroughly the bases for the type of agreement recommended.

b. When there is any question whether an international agreement should be concluded as a treaty or as an international agreement other than a treaty, the matter is brought to the attention of the Legal Adviser of the Department. If the Legal Adviser considers the question to be a serious one that may warrant congressional consultation, a memorandum will be transmitted to the Assistant Secretary for Legislative and Intergovernmental Affairs and other officers concerned. Upon receiving their views on the subject, the Legal Adviser shall, if the matter has not been resolved, transmit a memorandum thereon to the Secretary for a decision. Every practicable effort will be made to identify such questions at the earliest possible date so that consultations may be completed in sufficient time to avoid last-minute consideration.

c. Consultations on such questions will be held with congressional leaders and committees as may be appropriate. Arrangements for such consultations shall be made by the Assistant Secretary for Legislative and Intergovernmental Affairs and shall be held with the assistance of the Office of the Legal Adviser and such other offices as may be determined. Nothing in this section shall be taken as derogating from the requirement of appropriate consultations with the Congress in accordance with section 723.1, paragraph e, in connection with the initiation of, and developments during negotiations for international agreements, particularly where the agreements are of special interest to the Congress.

722 ACTION REQUIRED IN NEGOTIATION AND/OR SIGNATURE OF TREATIES AND AGREEMENTS

722.1 Authorization Required to Undertake Negotiations

Negotiations of treaties, or other international agreements on matters of substance, or for their extension or revision, are not to be undertaken, nor any exploratory discussions undertaken with representatives of another government, until authorized in writing by the Secretary or an officer specifically authorized by the Secretary for that purpose. Notification of the termination of any treaty or other international agreement on matters of substance requires similar authorization.

722.2 Scope of Authorization

Approval of a request for authorization to negotiate a treaty or other international agreement does not constitute advance approval of the text nor authorization to agree upon a date for signature or to sign the treaty or agreement. Authorization to agree upon a given date for, and to proceed with, signature must be specifically requested in writing, as provided in section 722.3. This applies to treaties and other agreements to be signed abroad as well as those to be signed at Washington. Special instructions may be required, because of the special circumstances involved, for multilateral conventions or agreements to be signed at international conferences.

722.3 Request for Authorization to Negotiate and/or Sign Action Memorandum

a. A request for authorization to negotiate and/or sign a treaty or other international agreement takes the form of an action memorandum addressed to the Secretary *or other principal to whom such authority has been delegated, as appropriate, and cleared with the Office of the Legal Adviser (including the Assistant Legal Adviser for Treaty Affairs)*, the Office of the Assistant Secretary for Legislative and Intergovernmental Affairs, other appropriate bureaus, and any other agency (such as Defense, Commerce, etc.) which has primary responsibility or a substantial interest in the subject matter. It is submitted through the Executive Secretariat.

b. The action memorandum may request one of the following:

(1) authority to negotiate,

(2) authority to sign, or

(3) authority to negotiate and sign.

The request in each instance states that any substantive changes in the draft text will be cleared with the Office of the Legal Adviser and other specified regional and/or functional bureaus before definitive agreement is reached. Drafting offices should consult closely with the Office of the Legal Adviser to insure that all legal requirements are met.

c. The action memorandum indicates what arrangements are planned as to:

(1) congressional consultation and

(2) opportunity for public comment on the treaty or agreement being negotiated, signed, or acceded to.

....

f. Where it appears that there may be obstacles to the immediate public disclosure of the text upon its entry into force, the action memorandum shall include an explanation thereof (see sections 723.2 and 723.3).

....

h. The action memorandum is accompanied by:

(1) *the U.S. draft, if available, of any agreement or other instrument intended to be negotiated; or*

(2) *the text of any agreement and related exchange of notes, agreed minutes, or other document to be signed (with appropriate clearances, including the Assistant Legal Adviser for Treaty affairs)*; and

(3) a memorandum of law prepared in the Office of the Legal Adviser.

....

722.4 Separate Authorizations

When authorization is sought for a particular treaty or other agreement, either multilateral or bilateral, the action memorandum for this purpose outlines briefly and clearly the principal features of the proposed treaty or other agreement, indicates any special problems which may be encountered and, if possible, the contemplated solutions of those problems.

722.5 Blanket Authorizations

....

722.6 Certification of Foreign Language Text

....

722.7 Transmission of Texts to the Secretary

....

723 RESPONSIBILITY OF OFFICE OR OFFICER CONDUCTING NEGOTIATIONS

723.1 Conduct of Negotiations

The office or officer responsible for any negotiations keeps in mind:

a. That during the negotiations no position is communicated to a foreign government or to an international organization as a U.S. position that goes beyond any existing authorization or instructions;

b. That no proposal is made or position is agreed to beyond the original authorization without appropriate clearance (see section 722.3, paragraph a);

c. That all significant policy-determining memorandums and instructions to the field on the subject of the negotiations have appropriate clearance (see section 722.3, paragraph a);

d. That the Secretary *or other principal, as appropriate*, is kept informed in writing of important policy decisions and developments, including any particularly significantly departures from substantially standard drafts that have been evolved;

e. That with the advice and assistance of the Assistant Secretary for Legislative and Intergovernmental Affairs, the appropriate congressional leaders and committees are advised of the intention to negotiate significant new international agreements, consulted concerning such agreements, and kept informed of developments affecting them, including especially whether any legislation is considered necessary or desirable for the implementation of the new treaty or agreement. Where the proposal for any especially important treaty or other international agreement is contemplated, the Office of the Assistant Secretary for Legislative and Intergovernmental Affairs will be informed as early as possible by the office responsible for the subjects;

f. That the interest of the public be taken into account and, where in the opinion of the Secretary of State or his or her designee the circumstances permit, the public be given an opportunity to comment;

g. That in no case, after accord has been reached on the substance and wording of the texts to be signed, do the negotiators sign an agreement or exchange notes constituting an agreement until a request under section 722.3 for authorization to sign has been approved and, if at a post abroad, until finally Instructed by the Department to do so as stated in section 730.3. If an agreement is to be signed in two languages, each language text must be cleared in full with the Language Services Division or, if at a post abroad, with the Department before signature, as stated in section 722.6;

h. That due consideration is given also to the provisions of section 723.2 through section 723.9, section 730.3, and section 731 of this chapter; and

i. That, in any case where any other department or agency is to play a primary or significant role or has a major interest in negotiation of an international agreement, the appropriate official or officials in such department or agency are informed of the provisions of this subchapter.

723.2 Avoiding Obstacles to Publications and Registration

The necessity of avoiding any commitment incompatible with the law requiring publication (1 U.S.C. 112a) and with the treaty provisions requiring registration (see section 750.3-3) should be borne in mind by U.S. negotiators. Although negotiations may be conducted on a confidential basis, every practicable effort must be made to assure that any definitive agreement or commitment entered into will be devoid of any aspect which would prevent the publication and registration of the agreement.

723.3 Questions on Immediate Public Disclosure

In any instance where it appears to the officer or office in the Department responsible for the negotiations or to the U.S. representatives that the immediate public disclosure upon its entry into force of an agreement under negotiations would be prejudicial to the national security of the United States, the pertinent circumstances shall be reported to the Secretary of State and his or her decision awaited before any further action is taken. Where such circumstances are known before authorization to negotiate or to sign is requested, they shall be included in the request for authorization. All such reports and requests are to be cleared with the Office of the Legal Adviser.

723.4 Public Statements

No public statement is to be made indicating that agreement on a text has been reached, or that negotiations have been successfully completed, before authorization is granted to sign the treaty or other agreement. If such authorization has been granted subject to a condition that no substantive change in the proposed text is made without appropriate clearance (see section 722.3, paragraph a), no such public statement is to be made until definitive agreement on the text has been reached and such clearance has been received. Normally, such a public statement is made only at the time a treaty or other agreement is actually signed, inasmuch as it remains possible that last-minute changes will be made in the text. Any such statement prior to that time must have the appropriate clearance, and the approval of the Secretary or the Department principal who originally approved the action memorandum request under "Circular 175 Procedure."

723.5 English-Language Text

Negotiators will assure that every bilateral treaty or other international agreement to be signed for the United States contains an English-language text. If the language of the other country concerned is one other than English, the text is done in English and, if desired by the other country, in the language of that country. A U.S. note that constitutes part of an international agreement effected by exchange of notes is always in the English language. If it quotes a foreign *government* note, the quotation is to be rendered in English translation. A U.S. note is not in any language in addition to English, unless specifically authorized *(with the clearance of the Assistant Legal Adviser for Treaty Affairs)*. The note of the other government concerned may be in whatever language that government desires.

723.6 Transmission of Signed Texts to Assistant Legal Adviser for Treaty Affairs

a. The officer responsible for the negotiation of a treaty or other agreement at any post is responsible for insuring the most expeditious transmission of the signed original text, together with all accompanying papers such as agreed minutes, exchanges of notes, plans, etc. *(indicating full names of persons who signed)*, to the Department for the attention of the Assistant Legal Adviser for Treaty Affairs; *provided*, that where originals are *not* available, accurate certified copies are obtained and transmitted as in the case of the original. (See sections 723.7, 723.8, and 723.9.). The transmittal is by airgram, *not* by transmittal slip or operations memorandum.

....

724 TRANSMISSION OF INTERNATIONAL AGREEMENTS OTHER THAN TREATIES TO CONGRESS: COMPLIANCE WITH THE CASE-ZABLOCKI ACT

All officers will be especially diligent in cooperating to assure compliance with Pub. L. 92-403 "An Act to require that international agreements other than treaties, hereafter entered into by the United States, be transmitted to the Congress within sixty days after the execution thereof." That Act, *popularly known as the Case-Zablocki Act*, approved August 22, 1972 (86 Stat. 619; 1 U.S.C. 112b), provides as follows:

> The Secretary of State shall transmit to the Congress the text of any international agreement other than a treaty, to which the United States is a party as soon as practicable after such agreement has entered into force with respect to the United States but in no event later than sixty days thereafter. However, any such agreement the immediate public disclosure of which would in the opinion of the President, be prejudicial to the national security of the United States shall not be so transmitted to the Congress but shall be transmitted to the Committee on Foreign Relations of the Senate and the Committee on Foreign Affairs of the House of Representatives under an appropriate injunction of secrecy to be removed only upon due notice from the President.

....

725 PUBLICATION OF TREATIES AND OTHER INTERNATIONAL AGREEMENTS OF THE UNITED STATES

....

726 THROUGH 729 UNASSIGNED

730 GUIDELINES FOR CONCLUDING INTERNATIONAL AGREEMENTS

730.1 Method of Concluding Bilateral and Multilateral Agreements

An agreement may be concluded (entered into) by the process of bilateral negotiations which result either in the signing of a single instrument in duplicate or in exchange of diplomatic notes, or by the process of multilateral negotiations, usually at an international conference to which the governments concerned send official delegations for the purpose of formulating and signing an instrument of agreement.

730.2 Bilateral Treaties and Agreements

730.2-1 Negotiation and Background Assistance

Whenever the negotiation of a new international agreement is under consideration, the Department office or the post having primary responsibility informs the Legal Adviser and may, if considered necessary, request background material and advice regarding relevant provisions in existing treaties and agreements, the general treaty relations of this Government with the government or governments concerned, and other pertinent information.

730.2-2 Role of Office of the Legal Adviser

a. Legal Review of Draft Agreements

As soon as tentative provisions for an agreement are considered or drafted, the Office of the Legal Adviser is requested to make available the services of an attorney-adviser to insure that the agreement is properly drafted and agreed policy is expressed clearly and fully. The Office of the Legal Adviser prepares a draft in the first instance upon the request of another office.

b. Legal Clearance Required

Any draft of a proposed treaty or agreement, or any outgoing correspondence regarding the negotiation, signature, and ratification or approval, as well as the existence, status, and application, of any international agreement to which the United States is or may become a party, is cleared with the Office of the Legal Adviser and with other appropriate bureaus or offices and, as appropriate, with any other agency concerned with the reply.

730.3 Instructions to Negotiators

When an agreement is to be concluded at a foreign capital, the Department designates the *United States* negotiator or negotiators, and the negotiator or negotiators are given appropriate instructions. If the agreement to be negotiated is a treaty which will be referred to the Senate, the Secretary of State may at some time prior to or during the negotiations issue or request the President to issue or request the President to issue a "full power" (see section 732) constituting formal authorization for the *United States* negotiators to sign the agreement. Such a "full power" is not customary with respect to an international agreement other than a treaty. The receipt or possession of a "full power" is never to be considered as a final authorization to sign. That authorization is given by the Department by a written or telegraphic instruction, and no signature is affixed in the absence of such instruction. If the proposal for an agreement originates with the United States, the *U.S.* negotiators as a rule furnish a tentative draft of the proposed agreement for submission to the other government for its consideration. The negotiators submit to the Department any modification of the draft or any counterproposal made by the other government and await instructions from the Department. If the original proposal emanates from a foreign government, the mission forwards the proposal to the Department and awaits its instructions.

. . . .

731 CONFORMITY OF TEXTS

. . . .

732 EXCHANGE OR EXHIBITION OF FULL POWERS

. . . .

733 SIGNATURE AND SEALING

. . . .

734 EXCHANGE OF RATIFICATIONS

. . . .

735 THROUGH 739 UNASSIGNED

740 MULTILATERAL TREATIES AND AGREEMENTS

740.1 General Procedures

The procedures for the making of multilateral agreements are in many respects the same as those for the making of bilateral agreements; for example, the general requirements in regard to full powers, ratification, proclamation, and publication. This subchapter covers those procedures which are at variance with bilateral procedures.

740.2 Negotiation

740.2-1 Function of International Conference

The international conference is the device usually employed for the negotiation of multilateral agreements. The greater the number of countries involved, the greater the necessity for such a conference. If only three or four countries are involved, it may be convenient to carry on the preliminary negotiations through correspondence and have a joint meeting of plenipotentiaries to complete the negotiations and to sign the document.

740.2-2 Invitation

Traditionally, the international conference was convened by one government's extending to other interested governments an invitation (acceptance usually assured beforehand) to participate, the host government bearing most, if not all, of the expense incident to the physical aspects of the conference. This is still often the practice, but increasing numbers of conferences have been convened under the auspices, and at the call of international organizations.

740.2-3 Statement of Purpose

When a call is made or invitations are extended for a conference for the formulation of a multilateral agreement, it is customary for a precise statement of purpose to accompany the call or the invitations. Sometimes, the invitation is also accompanied by a draft agreement to be used as a basis for negotiations. If the conference is called under the auspices of an international organization, the precise statement of purpose or the draft agreement may be prepared in preliminary sessions of the organization or by the secretariat of the organization.

740.2-4 Instructions to Negotiators

The U.S. delegation to a conference may be comprised of one or more representatives. As a rule, the U.S. delegation is furnished written instructions by the Department prior to the conference in the form of a position paper for the U.S. delegation cleared with the Secretary or an officer specifically authorized by him or her and other appropriate Department officers for that purpose, under the procedures described in section 722.3. The Office of the Legal Adviser in all instances reviews drafts of international conventions to be considered in meetings of an international organization of which the United States is a member; when necessary, it also provides legal assistance at international conferences and meetings.

740.2-5 Final Acts of Conference

The "Final Act" of a conference must not contain international commitments. A Final Act must be limited to such matters as a statement or summary of the proceedings of the conference, the names of the states that participated, the organization of the conference and the committees established, resolutions adopted, the drafts of international agreements formulated for consideration by governments concerned, and the like. If an international agreement is to be opened for signature at the close of the conference, a text thereof may be annexed to the Final Act but must not be incorporated in the body thereof; the text to be signed must be prepared and bound separately for that purpose. Where a Final Act appears to embody international commitments, the U.S. representative reports the same to the Department and awaits specific instruments before taking any further action.

741 OFFICIAL AND WORKING LANGUAGES

a. General Procedures

The working languages of the conference and the official languages of the conference documents are determined by the conference. A conference does not necessarily adopt all of the same languages for both purposes. It is customary and preferable for all the officials' languages in which the final document is prepared for signature to be designated as having equal authenticity. It is possible, however, for the conference to determine, because of special circumstances, that in the event of dispute one of the languages is to prevail and to include in the text of the agreement a provision to that effect. Before a U.S. delegation concurs in any such proposal, it must request instructions from the Department.

b. English Language Text

Negotiators will use every practicable effort to assure that an English-language text is part of the authentic text of any multilateral treaty negotiated for the United

States. Where any question exists on this subject, the negotiators should seek further instructions.

. . . .

742 ENGROSSING

. . . .

743 FULL POWERS

. . . .

744 SIGNATURE AND SEALING

. . . .

745 DISPOSITION OF FINAL DOCUMENTS OF CONFERENCE

. . . .

746 PROCEDURE FOLLOWING SIGNATURE

746.1 Understandings or Reservations

If it is necessary to inform other governments concerned, and perhaps obtain their consent, with respect to an understanding, interpretation, or reservation included by the Senate in its resolution of advice and consent, this Government communicates with the depositary, which then carries on the necessary correspondence with the other governments concerned.

746.2 Deposit of Ratification

When the depositary for a multilateral agreement is a foreign government or an international organization, the U.S. instrument of ratification (or adherence, accession, acceptance, etc.) is sent by the *Office of Assistant Legal Adviser for Treaty Affairs* to the appropriate Foreign Service mission or to the U.S. representative to the organization if there is a permanent representative. The mission or the representative deposits it with the depositary authority in accordance with the terms of the accompanying instruction from the Department concerning the time of deposit. When this Government is depositary for a multilateral agreement, posts are not authorized to accept instruments of ratification of foreign governments; that is, the foreign government cannot deposit its instrument with the post. If a post is requested to transmit an instrument of ratification to the Department, it must make clear to the foreign government that the post is acting only as a transmitting agent and that the ratification cannot be considered as accepted for deposit until received and examined by the Department.

746.3 Registration (See also section 750.3-3.)

It is generally recognized that the depositary for a multilateral agreement has a primary responsibility for its registration. Normally, the depositary has custody not only of the original document of agreement but also of instruments of ratification and other formal documents. Consequently, the depositary is the most authoritative source of information and documentation.

747 THROUGH 749 UNASSIGNED

750 RESPONSIBILITIES OF THE ASSISTANT LEGAL ADVISER FOR TREATY AFFAIRS

750.1 Preparation of Documents, Ceremonies, and Instructions

. . . .

750.3 Publication and Registration

750.3-1 Publication of Texts

After the necessary action has been taken to bring into force the treaty or other international agreement concluded by the United States, it is published promptly in the Treaties and Other International Acts Series issued by the Department. After publication in that series, the text of the treaty or other agreement is printed in the annual volume(s) (which may consist of two or more bindings) of *United States Treaties and Other International Agreements*, as required by law (see section 725). Treaties and other agreements concluded prior to January 1, 1950, were published in the United States Statutes at Large and for easy reference were reprinted in Bevans, *Treaties and Other International Agreements of the United States of America, 1776–1949*.

750.3-2 Responsibility for Other Treaty Publications

The Office of the Assistant Legal Adviser for Treaty Affairs prepares and maintains the annual publication, *Treaties in Force*, an authoritative guide to the text and status of treaties and other international agreements currently in force for the United States. It also compiles and has published, in addition to the text referred to in 750.3-1, other volumes containing texts of treaties and other agreements as required or authorized by law. The "Treaty Information" section of the *Department of State Bulletin* is compiled by that office.

750.3-3 Registration

Article 102 of the United Nations Charter requires that every treaty and every international agreement entered into by a member of the United Nations be registered, as soon as possible, with the Secretariat and published by it. Article 83 of the Chicago Aviation Convention of 1944 requires registration of aviation agreements with the Council of the International Civil Aviation Organization.

750.4 United States as Depositary

a. Inquiries from foreign diplomatic missions at Washington and from U.S. diplomatic missions abroad with respect to the preparation or deposit of instruments relating to any multilateral agreement of which the United States is depositary are referred to the Assistant Legal Adviser for Treaty Affairs. That officer is to be notified immediately of the receipt of any such document anywhere in the Department, inasmuch as a depositary is required to ascertain whether those documents are properly executed before accepting them for deposit, to keep accurate records regarding them, and to inform other governments concerned of the order and date of receipt of such documents.

b. Before any arrangements are proposed or agreed to for the United States to serve as depositary for any international agreement, the views of the Assistant Legal Adviser for Treaty Affairs will be obtained.

750.5 Records and Correspondence Custody

a. The Assistant Legal Adviser for Treaty Affairs compiles and maintains authoritative records regarding the negotiation, signature, transmission to the Senate, and ratification or approval, as well as the existence, status, and application, of all international agreements to which the United States is or may become a party and, so far as information is available, of agreements between other countries to which the United States is not a party. Inquiries on these subjects are addressed to, and outgoing communications cleared with, the Office of the Legal Adviser.

. . . .

SENATE RESOLUTION OF RATIFICATION OF THE INF TREATY*

Resolution: Text of Resolution of advice and consent to ratification as reported by the Committee on Foreign Relations:

Resolved, (two-thirds of the Senators present concurring therein), That the Senate advise and consent to ratification of the Treaty between the United States of America and the Union of Soviet Socialist Republics on the Elimination of Their Intermediate-Range and Shorter-Range Missiles, together with the Memorandum of Understanding and the two Protocols thereto, collectively referred to as the INF Treaty, all signed at Washington on December 8, 1987 (Treaty Doc. 100-11), provided that the Senate's advice and consent to ratification of the INF Treaty is subject to the following condition, which shall be binding on the Executive:

That this Treaty shall be subject to the following principles, which derive, as a necessary implication, from the provisions of the Constitution (Article II, section 2, clause 2) for the making of treaties:

(a) the United States shall interpret this Treaty in accordance with the understanding of the Treaty shared by the Executive and the Senate at the time of Senate consent to ratification;

(b) such common understanding is:

(i) based on the text of the Treaty; and

(ii) reflected in the authoritative representations provided by the Executive branch to the Senate and its committees in seeking Senate consent to ratification, insofar as such representations are directed to the meaning and legal effect of the text of the Treaty;

(c) the United States shall not agree to or adopt an interpretation different from that common understanding except pursuant to Senate advice and consent to a subsequent treaty or protocol, or the enactment of a statute.

This understanding shall not be incorporated in the instruments of ratification of this Treaty or otherwise officially conveyed to the other contracting Party.

---

* S. Res. 167, 100th Cong. (1988), *in* U.S. SENATE, COMM. ON FOREIGN RELATIONS, THE INF TREATY: REPORT, S. EXEC. REP. NO. 100-15, at 436 (1988). For a discussion of this resolution and a challenge to its constitutionality, see JOHN NORTON MOORE, TREATY INTERPRETATION, THE CONSTITUTION AND THE RULE OF LAW 654–95 (2001), and JOHN NORTON MOORE, THE NATIONAL LAW OF TREATY IMPLEMENTATION 4 n.11, 4–30 (2001).

2. War Powers

DECLARATION OF WAR—WAR OF 1812*

An Act Declaring War Between the United Kingdom of Great Britain and Ireland and the Dependencies Thereof and the United States of America and Their Territories.

Be it enacted by the Senate and House of Representatives of the United States of America in Congress assembled, That war be and the same is hereby declared to exist between the United Kingdom of Great Britain and Ireland and the dependencies thereof, and the United States of America and their territories; and that the President of the United States is hereby authorized to use the whole land and naval force of the United States to carry the same into effect, and to issue to private armed vessels of the United States commissions or letters of marque and general reprisal, in such form as he shall think proper, and under the seal of the United States, against the vessels, goods, and effects of the government of the said United Kingdom of Great Britain and Ireland, and the subjects thereof.

APPROVED, June 18, 1812.

* An Act Declaring War Between the United Kingdom of Great Britain and Ireland and the Dependencies Thereof, and the United States of America and Their Territories, ch. CII, 2 Stat. 755 (1812), *available at* http://www.yale.edu/lawweb/avalon/statutes/1812-01.htm.

DECLARATION OF WAR— MEXICAN-AMERICAN WAR* (AN ACT PROVIDING FOR PROSECUTION OF THE WAR BETWEEN THE UNITED STATES AND THE REPUBLIC OF MEXICO)

Chap. XVI.—*An Act providing for the Prosecution of the existing War between the United States and the Republic of Mexico.*

Whereas, by the act of the Republic of Mexico, a state of war exists between that Government and the United States:

Be it enacted by the Senate and the House of Representatives of the United States of America in Congress assembled, That, for the purpose of enabling the government of the United States to prosecute said war to a speedy and successful termination, the President be, and he is hereby, authorized to employ the militia, naval, and military forces of the United States, and to call for and accept the services of any number of volunteers, not exceeding fifty thousands, who may offer their services, either as cavalry, artillery, infantry, or riflemen, to serve twelve months after they shall have arrived at the place of rendezvous, or to the end of the war, unless sooner discharged, according to the time for which they shall have been mustered into service; and that the sum of ten million dollars, out of any moneys in the treasury, or to come into the treasury, not otherwise appropriated, be, and the same is hereby, appropriated for the purpose of carrying the provisions of this act into effect.

Sec. 2. *And be it further enacted,* That the militia, when called into the service of the United States by virtue of this act, may, if in the opinion of the President of the United States the public interest requires it, be compelled to serve for a term not exceeding six months after their arrival at the place of rendezvous, in any one year, unless sooner discharged.

Sec. 3. *And be it further enacted,* That the said volunteers shall furnish their own clothes, and if cavalry, their own horses and horse equipments; and when mustered into service shall be armed at the expense of the United States.

Sec. 4. *And be it further enacted,* That said volunteers shall, when called into actual service, and while remaining therein, be subject to the rules and articles of war, and shall be, in all respects except as to clothing and pay, placed on the same footing with similar corps of the United States army: and in lieu of clothing every non-commissioned officer and privacy in any company, who may thus offer himself, shall be entitled, when called into actual service, to receive in money a sum equal to the cost of clothing of a non-commissioned officer or private (as the case may be) in regular troops of the United States.

Sec. 5. *And be it further enacted,* That the said volunteers so offering their services shall be accepted by the President in companies, battalions, squadrons, and regiments, whose offices shall be appointed in the manner prescribed by law in the several states

* An Act Providing for the Prosecution of the Existing War Between the United States and the Republic of Mexico, ch. XVI, 9 Stat. 9, 9–10 (1846).

and Territories to which such companies, battalions, squadrons, and regiments, shall respectively belong.

Sec. 6. *And be it further enacted,* That the President of the United States be, and he is hereby, authorized to organize companies so tendering their services into battalions or squadrons, battalions and squadrons into regiments, regiments into brigades, and brigades into divisions, as soon as the number of volunteers shall render such organization, in his judgment, expedient; and the President shall, if necessary, apportion the staff, field, and general officers among the respective States and Territories from which the volunteers shall tender their services or he may deem proper.

Sec. 7. *And be it further enacted,* That the volunteers who may be received into the service of the United States by virtue of the provisions of this act, and who shall be wounded or otherwise disabled in the service, shall be entitled to all the benefit which may be conferred or persons wounded in the service of the United States.

Sec. 8. *And be it further enacted,* That the President of the United States be, and he is hereby, authorized forthwith to complete all the public armed vessels now authorized by law, and to purchase or charter, arm, equip, and man, such merchant vessels and steam boats as, upon examination, may be found fit, or easily converted into armed vessels fit for the public service, and in such number as he may deem necessary for the protection of the seaboard, lake coast, and the general defense of the country.

Sec. 9. *And be it further enacted,* That whenever the militia or volunteers are called and received into the service of the United States, under the provision of this act, they shall have the organization of the army of the United States, and shall have the same pay and allowances; and all mounted privates, non-commissioned officers, musicians, and artificers, shall be allowed 40 cents pay per day for the use and risk of their horses, except of horses actually killed in action; and if any mounted volunteer, private, non-commissioned officer, musician, or artificer, shall not keep himself provided with a serviceable horse, the said volunteer shall serve on foot.

APPROVED, May 13, 1846.

DECLARATION OF WAR— SPANISH-AMERICAN WAR* (BILL (H.R. 10086) DECLARING WAR BETWEEN THE UNITED STATES OF AMERICA AND THE KINGDOM OF SPAIN)

Be it enacted by the Senate and House of Representatives of the United States of America in Congress assembled, First, That war be, and the same is hereby, declared to exist, and that war has existed since the 21st day of April, A. D. 1898, including said day, between the United States of America and the Kingdom of Spain.

Second, That the President of the United States be, and he hereby is, directed and empowered to use the entire land and naval forces of the United States and to call into the actual service of the United States the militia of the several States to such extent as may be necessary to carry this act into effect.

Approved, April 25, 1898.

---

* An Act Declaring that War Exists Between the United States of America and the Kingdom of Spain, H.R. 10086, 55th Cong., ch. 189, 30 Stat. 364 (2d Sess. 1898), *available at* http://www.spanamwar.com/McKinleywardec.htm.

DECLARATION OF WAR—WORLD WAR I*

Joint Resolution Declaring that a state of war exists between the Imperial German Government and the Government and the people of the United States and making provision to prosecute the same.

Whereas the Imperial German Government has committed repeated acts of war against the Government and the people of the United States of America;

Therefore be it

Resolved by the Senate and the House of Representatives of the United States of America in Congress Assembled, that the state of war between the United States and the Imperial German Government which has thus been thrust upon the United States is hereby formally declared; and that the President be, and he is hereby, authorized and directed to employ the entire naval and military forces of the United States and the resources of the Government to carry on war against the Imperial German Government; and to bring the conflict to a successful termination all of the resources of the country are hereby pledged by the Congress of the United States.

Approved, April 6, 1917

* S.J. Res. 1, 65th Cong., ch. 1, 40 Stat. 1 (1917), *available at* http://www.firstworldwar.com/source/usofficialawardeclaration.htm.

DECLARATION OF WAR—WORLD WAR II*

JOINT RESOLUTION

Declaring that a state of war exists between the Imperial Government of Japan and the Government and the people of the United States and making provisions to prosecute the same.

Whereas the Imperial Government of Japan has committed unprovoked acts of war against the Government and the people of the United States of America: Therefore be it

Resolved by the Senate and House of Representatives of the United States of America in Congress assembled, That the state of war between the United states and the Imperial Government of Japan which has thus been thrust upon the United States is hereby formally declared; and the President is hereby authorized and directed to employ the entire naval and military forces of the United States and the resources of the Government to carry on war against the Imperial Government of Japan; and to bring the conflict to a successful termination, all of the resources of the country are hereby pledged by the Congress of the United States.

Approved, December 8, 1941, 4:10 p.m., E.S.T.

* S.J. Res. 116, 77th Cong., ch. 561, 55 Stat. 795 (1941), *available at* http://www.ibiblio.org/pha/77-1-148/77-1-148.html#pro-1.

FORMOSA RESOLUTION*

JOINT RESOLUTION

Authorizing the President to employ the Armed Forces of the United States for protecting the security of Formosa, the Pescadores and related positions and territories of that area.

Whereas the primary purpose of the United States, in its relations with all other nations, is to develop and sustain a just and enduring peace for all; and

Whereas certain territories in the West Pacific under the jurisdiction of the Republic of China are now under armed attack, and threats and declarations have been and are being made by the Chinese Communists that such armed attack is in aid of and in preparation for armed attack on Formosa and the Pescadores,

Whereas such armed attack if continued would gravely endanger the peace and security of the West Pacific Area and particularly of Formosa and the Pescadores; and

Whereas the secure possession by friendly governments of the Western Pacific Island chain, of which Formosa is a part, is essential to the vital interests of the United States and all friendly nations in or bordering upon the Pacific Ocean; and

Whereas the President of the United States on January 6, 1955, submitted to the Senate for its advice and consent to ratification a Mutual Defense Treaty between the United States of America and the Republic of China, which recognizes that an armed attack in the West Pacific area directed against territories, therein described, in the region of Formosa and the Pescadores, would be dangerous to the peace and safety of the parties to the treaty: Therefore be it

Resolved by the Senate and House of Representatives of the United States of America in Congress assembled, That the President of the United States be and he hereby is authorized to employ the Armed Forces of the United States as he deems necessary for the specific purpose of securing and protecting Formosa and the Pescadores against armed attack, this authority to include the securing and protection of such related positions and territories of that area now in friendly hands and the taking of such other measures as he judges to be required or appropriate in assuring the defense of Formosa and the Pescadores.

This resolution shall expire when the President shall determine that the peace and security of the area is reasonably assured by international conditions created by action of the United Nations or otherwise, and shall so report to the Congress.

APPROVED JANUARY 29, 1955, 8:42 a.m.

* H.R.J. Res. 159, 84th Cong., ch. 4, 69 Stat. 7 (1955), *repealed by* Pub. L. No. 93-475, § 3, 88 Stat. 1439 (1974), *available at* http://cns.miis.edu/straittalk/Appendix%2016.htm.

JOINT RESOLUTION TO PROMOTE PEACE AND STABILITY IN THE MIDDLE EAST*

JOINT RESOLUTION

To promote peace and stability in the Middle East.

Resolved by the Senate and House of Representatives of the United States of America in Congress assembled, That the President be and hereby is authorized to cooperate with and assist any nation or group of nations in the general area of the Middle East desiring such assistance in the development of economic strength dedicated to the maintenance of national independence.

Sec. 2. The President is authorized to undertake, in the general area of the Middle East, military assistance programs with any nation or group of nations of that area desiring such assistance. Furthermore, the United States regards as vital to the national interest and world peace the preservation of the independence and integrity of the nations of the Middle East. To this end, if the President determines the necessity thereof, the United States is prepared to use armed forces to assist any such nation or group of such nations requesting assistance against armed aggression from any country controlled by international communism: *Provided,* That such employment shall be consonant with the treaty obligations of the United States and with the Constitution of the United States.

Sec. 3. The President is hereby authorized to use during the balance of fiscal year 1957 for economic and military assistance under this joint resolution not to exceed $200,000,000 from any appropriation now available for carrying out the provisions of the Mutual Security Act of 1954, as amended, in accord with the provisions of such Act:

*Provided,*That, whenever the President determines it to be important to the security of the United States, such use may be under the authority of section 401 (a) of the Mutual Security Act of 1954, as amended (except that the provisions of section 105 (a) thereof shall not be waived), and without regard to the provisions of section 105 of the Mutual Security Appropriation Act, 1957: *Provided further,* That obligations incurred in carrying out the purposes of the first sentence of section 2 of this joint resolution shall be paid only out of appropriations for military assistance, and obligations incurred in carrying out the purposes of the first section of this joint resolution shall be paid only out of appropriations other than those for military assistance. This authorization is in addition to other existing authorizations with respect to the use of such appropriations. None of the additional authorization contained in this section shall be used until fifteen days after the Committee on Foreign Relations of the Senate, the Committee on Foreign Affairs of the House of Representatives, the Committees on Appropriations of the Senate and the House of Representatives and, when military assistance is involved, the Committees on Armed Services of the Senate and the House of Representatives have been furnished a report showing the object of the proposed use, the country for the benefit of which such use is intended and the particular appropriation or appropriations for carrying out the provisions of the Mutual Security Act of 1954, as amended,

* H.R.J. Res. 117, 85th Cong., Pub. L. No. 85-7, 71 Stat. 5, 5–6 (1957), *amended by* Foreign Assistance Act of 1961 §705, S. 1983, 87th Cong., Pub. L. No. 87-195, 75 Stat. 424, 463 (1961) (codified as amended at 22 U.S.C.A. §§1961–1965 (West 2004 & Supp. 2005)).

from which the funds are proposed to be derived: *Provided,* That funds available under this section during the balance of fiscal year 1957 shall, in the case of any such report submitted during the last fifteen days of the fiscal year, remain available for use under this section for the purposes stated in such report for a period of twenty days following the date of submission of such report. Nothing contained in this joint resolution shall be construed as itself authorizing the appropriation of additional funds for the purpose of carrying out the provisions of the first section or of the first sentence of section 2 of this joint resolution.

Sec. 4. The President should continue to furnish facilities and military assistance, within the provisions of applicable law and established policies, to the United Nations Emergency Force in the Middle East, with a view to maintaining the truce in that region.

Sec. 5. The President shall within the months of January and July of each year report to the Congress his action hereunder.

Sec. 6. This joint resolution shall expire when the President shall determine that the peace and security of the nations in the general area of the Middle East are reasonably assured by international conditions created by action of the United Nations or otherwise except that it may be terminated earlier by a concurrent resolution of the two Houses of Congress.

Approved March 9, 1957.

CUBAN RESOLUTION*

JOINT RESOLUTION Expressing the determination of the united States with respect to the situation in Cuba.

Whereas President James Monroe, announcing the Monroe Doctrine in 1823, declared that the United States would consider any attempt on the part of European powers "to extend their system to any portion of this hemisphere as dangerous to our peace and safety"; and

Whereas in the Rio Treaty of 1947 the parties agreed that "an armed attack by any State against an American State shall be considered as an attack against all the American States, and, consequently, each one of the said contracting parties undertakes to assist in meeting the attack in the exercise of the inherent right of individual or collective self-defense recognized by article 51 of the Charter of the United Nations"; and

Whereas the Foreign Ministers of the Organization of American States at Punta del Este in January 1962 declared: "The present Government of Cuba has identified itself with the principles of Marxist-Leninist ideology, has established a political, economic, and social system based on that doctrine, and accepts military assistance from extracontinental Communist powers, including even the threat of military intervention in America on the part of the Soviet Union"; and

Whereas the international Communist movement has increasingly extended into Cuba its political, economic, and military sphere of influence; Now, therefore, be it

Resolved by the Senate and House of Representatives of the United States of America in Congress assembled, That the United States is determined—

(a) to prevent by whatever means may be necessary, including the use of arms, the Marxist-Leninist regime in Cuba from extending, by force or the threat of force, its aggressive or subversive activities to any part of this hemisphere;

(b) to prevent in Cuba the creation or use of an externally supported military capability endangering the security of the United States; and

(c) to work with the Organization of American States and with freedom-loving Cubans to support the aspirations of the Cuban people for self-determination.

Approved October 3, 1962.

* S.J. Res. 230, 87th Cong., Pub. L. No. 87-733, 76 Stat. 697 (1962).

SOUTHEAST ASIA RESOLUTION* (GULF OF TONKIN)

JOINT RESOLUTION To promote the maintenance of international peace and security in southeast Asia.

Whereas naval units of the Communist regime in Vietnam, in violation of the principles of the Charter of the United Nations and of international law, have deliberately and repeatedly attacked United States naval vessels lawfully present in international waters, and have thereby created a serious threat to international peace; and

Whereas these attacks are part of a deliberate and systematic campaign of aggression that the Communist regime in North Vietnam has been waging against its neighbors and the nations joined with them in the collective defense of their freedom; and

Whereas the United States is assisting the peoples of southeast Asia to protect their freedom and has no territorial, military or political ambitions in that area, but desires only that these peoples should be left in peace to work out their own destinies in their own way: Now, therefore, be it

Resolved by the Senate and House of Representatives of the United States of America in Congress assembled, That the Congress approves and supports the determination of the President, as Commander in Chief, to take all necessary measures to repel any armed attack against the forces of the United States and to prevent further aggression.

Sec. 2. The United States regards as vital to its national interest and to world peace the maintenance of international peace and security in southeast Asia. Consonant with the Constitution of the United States and the Charter of the United Nations and in accordance with its obligations under the Southeast Asia Collective Defense Treaty, the United States is, therefore, prepared, as the President determines, to take all necessary steps, including the use of armed force, to assist any member or protocol state of the Southeast Asia Collective Defense Treaty requesting assistance in defense of its freedom.

Sec. 3. This resolution shall expire when the President shall determine that the peace and security of the area is reasonably assured by international conditions created by action of the United Nations or otherwise, except that it may be terminated earlier by concurrent resolution of the Congress.

* H.R.J. Res. 1145, 88th Cong., Pub. L. No. 88-408, 78 Stat. 384 (1964).

NATIONAL COMMITMENTS RESOLUTION*

Whereas accurate definition of the term "national commitment" in recent years has become obscured: Now, therefore, be it

Resolved, That (1) a national commitment for the purpose of this resolution means the use of the Armed Forces of the United States on foreign territory, or a promise to assist a foreign country, government, or people by the use of the Armed Forces or financial resources of the United States, either immediately or upon the happening of certain events, and (2) it is the sense of the Senate that a national commitment by the United States results only from affirmative action taken by the executive and legislative branches of the United States Government by means of a treaty, statute, or concurrent resolution of both Houses of Congress specifically providing for such commitment.

---

* S. Res. 85, 91st Cong., 115 Cong. Rec. 17,245 (1969) (enacted).

WAR POWERS RESOLUTION*

. . . .

PURPOSE AND POLICY

Sec. 2. (a) It is the purpose of this joint resolution to fulfill the intent of the framers of the Constitution of the United States and insure that the collective judgment of both the Congress and the President will apply to the introduction of United States Armed Forces into hostilities, or into situations where imminent involvement in hostilities is clearly indicated by the circumstances, and to the continued use of such forces in hostilities or in such situations.

(b) Under article I, section 8, of the Constitution, it is specifically provided that the Congress shall have the power to make all laws necessary and proper for carrying into execution, not only its own powers but also all other powers vested by the Constitution in the Government of the United States, or in any department or officer thereof.

(c) The constitutional powers of the President as Commander-in-Chief to introduce United States Armed Forces into hostilities, or into situations where imminent involvement in hostilities is clearly indicated by the circumstances, are exercised only pursuant to (1) a declaration of war, (2) specific statutory authorization, or (3) a national emergency created by attack upon the United States, its territories or possessions, or its armed forces.

CONSULTATION

Sec. 3. The President in every possible instance shall consult with Congress before introducing United States Armed Forces into hostilities or into situations where imminent involvement in hostilities is clearly indicated by the circumstances, and after every such introduction shall consult regularly with the Congress until United States Armed Forces are no longer engaged in hostilities or have been removed from such situations.

REPORTING

Sec. 4. (a) In the absence of a declaration of war, in any case in which United States Armed Forces are introduced—

(1) into hostilities or into situations where imminent involvement in hostilities is clearly indicated by the circumstances;

(2) into the territory, airspace or waters of a foreign nation, while equipped for combat, except for deployments which relate solely to supply, replacement, repair, or training of such forces; or

(3) in numbers which substantially enlarge United States Armed Forces equipped for combat already located in a foreign nation;

the President shall submit within 48 hours to the Speaker of the House of Representatives and to the President pro tempore of the Senate a report, in writing, setting forth—

* H.R.J. Res. 542, 93d Cong. §§2–9, Pub. L. No. 93-148, 87 Stat. 555, 555–59 (1973).

(A) the circumstances necessitating the introduction of United States Armed Forces;

(B) the constitutional and legislative authority under which such introduction took place; and

(C) the estimated scope and duration of the hostilities or involvement.

(b) The President shall provide such other information as the Congress may request in the fulfillment of its constitutional responsibilities with respect to committing the Nation to war and to the use of United States Armed Forces abroad.

(c) Whenever United States Armed Forces are introduced into hostilities or into any situation described in subsection (a) of this section, the President shall so long as such armed forces continue to be engaged in such hostilities or situation, report to the Congress periodically on the status of such hostilities or situation as well as on the scope and duration of such hostilities or situation, but in no event shall lie report to the Congress less often than once every six months.

CONGRESSIONAL ACTION

Sec. 5. (a) Each report submitted pursuant to section 4 (a) (1) shall be transmitted to the Speaker of the House of Representatives and to the President pro tempore of the Senate on the same calendar day. Each report so transmitted shall be referred to the Committee on Foreign Affairs of the House of Representatives and to the Committee on Foreign Relations of the Senate for appropriate action. If, when the report is transmitted, the Congress has adjourned sine die or has adjourned for any period in excess of three calendar days, the Speaker of the House of Representatives and the President pro tempore of the Senate, if they deem it advisable (or if petitioned by at least 30 percent of the membership of their respective Houses) shall jointly request the President to convene Congress in order that it may consider the report and take appropriate action pursuant to this section.

(b) Within sixty calendar days after a report is submitted or is required to be submitted pursuant to section 4(a) (1), whichever is earlier, the President shall terminate any use of United States Armed Forces with respect to which such report was submitted (or required to be submitted), unless the Congress (1) has declared war or has enacted a specific authorization for such use of United States Armed Forces, (2) has extended by law such sixty-day period, or (3) is physically unable to meet as a result of an armed attack upon the United States. Such sixty-day period shall be extended for not more than an additional thirty days if the President determines and certifies to the Congress in writing that unavoidable military necessity respecting the safety of United States Armed Forces requires the continued use of such armed forces in the course of bringing about a prompt removal of such forces.

(c) Notwithstanding subsection (b), at any time that United States Armed Forces are engaged in hostilities outside the territory of the United States, its possessions and territories without a declaration of war or specific statutory authorization, such forces shall be removed by the President if the Congress so directs by concurrent resolution.

CONGRESSIONAL PRIORITY PROCEDURES FOR JOINT RESOLUTION OR BILL

Sec. 6. (a) Any joint resolution or bill introduced pursuant to section 5(b) at least thirty calendar days before the expiration of the sixty-day period specified in such section shall be referred to the Committee on Foreign Affairs of the House of Representatives or the Committee on Foreign Relations of the Senate, as the case may be, and such committee shall report one such joint resolution or bill, together with its recommendations, not later than twenty-four calendar days before the expiration of the sixty-day period specified in such section unless such House shall otherwise determine by the yeas and nays.

(b) Any joint resolution or bill so reported shall become the pending business of the House in question (in the case of the Senate the time for debate shall be equally divided between the proponents and the opponents) , and shall be voted on within three calendar days thereafter, unless such House shall otherwise determine by yeas and nays.

(c) Such a joint resolution or bill passed by one House shall be referred to the committee of the other House named in subsection (a) and shall be reported out not later than fourteen calendar days before the expiration of the sixty-day period specified in section 5(b). The joint resolution or bill so reported shall become the pending business of the House in question and shall be voted on within three calendar days after it has been reported, unless such House shall otherwise determine by yeas and nays.

(d) In the case of any disagreement between the two Houses of Congress with respect to a joint resolution or bill passed by both Houses, conferees shall be promptly appointed and the committee of conference shall make and file a report with respect to such resolution or bill not later than four calendar days before the expiration of the sixty-day period specified in section 5(b). In the event the conferees are unable to agree within 48 hours, they shall report back to their respective Houses in disagreement. Notwithstanding any rule in either House concerning the printing of conference reports in the Record or concerning any delay in the consideration of such reports. such report shall be acted on by both Houses not later than the expiration of such sixty-day period.

CONGRESSIONAL PRIORITY PROCEDURES FOR CONCURRENT RESOLUTION

Sec. 7. (a) Any concurrent resolution introduced pursuant to section 5 (c) shall be referred to the Committee on Foreign Affairs of the House of Representatives or the Committee on Foreign Relations of the Senate, as the case may be, and one such concurrent resolution shall be reported out by such committee together with its recommendations within fifteen calendar days, unless such House shall otherwise determine by the yeas and nays.

(b) Any concurrent resolution so reported shall become the pending business of the House in question (in the case of the Senate the time for debate shall be equally divided between the proponents and the opponents) and shall be voted on within three calendar days thereafter, unless such House shall otherwise determine by yeas and nays.

(c) Such a concurrent resolution passed by one House shall be referred to the committee of the other House named in subsection (a) and shall be reported out by such committee together with its recommendations within fifteen calendar days and shall thereupon become the pending business of such House and shall be voted upon within three calendar days, unless such House shall otherwise determine by yeas and nays.

(d) In the case of any disagreement between the two Houses of Congress with respect to a concurrent resolution passed by both Houses, conferees shall be promptly appointed and the committee of conference shall make and file a report with respect to such concurrent resolution within six calendar days after the legislation is referred to the committee of conference. Notwithstanding any rule in either House concerning the printing of conference reports in the Record or concerning any delay in the consideration of such reports, such report shall be acted on by both Houses not later than six calendar days after the conference report is filed. In the event the conferees are unable to agree within 48 hours, they shall report back to their respective Houses in disagreement.

INTERPRETATION OF JOINT RESOLUTION

Sec. 8. (a) Authority to introduce United States Armed Forces into hostilities or into situations wherein involvement in hostilities is clearly indicated by the circumstances shall not be inferred—

(1) from any provision of law (whether or not in effect before the date of the enactment of this joint resolution), including any provision contained in any appropriation Act, unless such provision specifically authorizes the introduction of United States Armed Forces into hostilities or into such situations and states that it is intended to constitute specific statutory authorization within the meaning of this joint resolution; or

(2) from any treaty heretofore or hereafter ratified unless such treaty is implemented by legislation specifically authorizing the introduction of United States Armed Forces into hostilities or into such situations and stating that it is intended to constitute specific statutory authorization within the meaning of this joint resolution.

(b) Nothing in this joint resolution shall be construed to require any further specific statutory authorization to permit members of United States Armed Forces to participate jointly with members of the armed forces of one or more foreign countries in the headquarters operations of high-level military commands which were established prior to the date of enactment of this joint resolution and pursuant to the United Nations Charter or any treaty ratified by the United States prior to such date.

(c) For purposes of this joint resolution, the term "introduction of United States Armed Forces" includes the assignment of members of such armed forces to command, coordinate, participate in the movement of, or accompany the regular or irregular military forces of any foreign country or government when such military forces are engaged, or there exists an imminent threat that such forces will become engaged, in hostilities.

(d) Nothing in this joint resolution—

(1) is intended to alter the constitutional authority of the Congress or of the President, or the provisions of existing treaties; or

(2) shall be construed as granting any authority to the President with respect to the introduction of United States Armed Forces into hostilities or into situations wherein involvement in hostilities is clearly indicated by the circumstances which authority he would not have had in the absence of this joint resolution.

SEPARABILITY CLAUSE

Sec. 9. If any provision of this joint resolution or the application thereof to any person or circumstance is held invalid, the remainder of the joint resolution and the application of such provision to any other person or circumstance shall not be affected thereby.

. . . .

NIXON'S VETO OF THE WAR POWERS RESOLUTION*

311 Veto of the War Powers Resolution.

October 24, 1973

To the House of Representatives:

I hereby return without my approval House Joint Resolution 542—the War Powers Resolution. While I am in accord with the desire of the Congress to assert its proper role in the conduct of our foreign affairs, the restrictions which this resolution would impose upon the authority of the President are both unconstitutional and dangerous to the best interests of our Nation.

The proper roles of the Congress and the Executive in the conduct of foreign affairs have been debated since the founding of our country. Only recently, however has there been a serious challenge to the wisdom of the Founding Fathers in choosing not to draw a precise and detailed line of demarcation between the foreign policy powers of the two branches.

The Founding Fathers understood the impossibility of foreseeing every contingency that might arise in this complex area. They acknowledged the need for flexibility in responding to changing circumstances. They recognized that foreign policy decisions must be made through close cooperation between the two branches and not through rigidly codified procedures.

These principles remain as valid today as they were when our Constitution was written. Yet House Joint Resolution 542 would violate those principles by defining the President's powers in ways which would strictly limit his constitutional authority.

CLEARLY UNCONSTITUTIONAL

House Joint Resolution 542 would attempt to take away, by a mere legislative act, authorities which the President has properly exercised under the Constitution for almost 200 years. One of its provisions would automatically cut off certain authorities after sixty days unless the Congress extended them. Another would allow the Congress to eliminate certain authorities merely by the passage of a concurrent resolution an action which does not normally have the force of law, since it denies the President his constitutional role in approving legislation.

I believe that both these provisions are unconstitutional. The only way in which the constitutional powers of a branch of the Government can be altered is by amending the Constitution and any attempt to make such alterations by legislation alone is clearly without force.

UNDERMINING OUR FOREIGN POLICY

While I firmly believe that a veto of House Joint Resolution 542 is warranted solely on constitutional grounds, I am also deeply disturbed by the practical consequences of this resolution. For it would seriously undermine this Nation's ability to act decisively

* Richard Nixon, Veto of the War Powers Resolution, PUB. PAPERS 893–95 (Oct. 24, 1973), *available at* http://lostlaws.tripod.com/Nixveet.htm.

and convincingly in times of international crisis. As a result, the confidence of our allies in our ability to assist them could be diminished and the respect of our adversaries for our deterrent posture could decline. A permanent and substantial element of unpredictability would be injected into the world's assessment of American behavior, further increasing the likelihood of miscalculation and war.

If this resolution had been in operation, America's effective response to a variety of challenges in recent years would have been vastly complicated or even made impossible. We may well have been unable to respond in the way we did during the Berlin crisis of 1961, the Cuban missile crisis of 1962, the Congo rescue operation in 1964, and the Jordanian crisis of 1970 to mention just a few examples. In addition, our recent actions to bring about a peaceful settlement of the hostilities in the Middle East would have been seriously impaired if this resolution had been in force.

While all the specific consequences of House Joint Resolution 542 cannot yet be predicted, it is clear that it would undercut the ability of the United States to act as an effective influence for peace. For example, the provision automatically cutting off certain authorities after 60 days unless they are extended by the Congress could work to prolong or intensify a crisis. Until the Congress suspended the deadline, there would be at least a chance of United States withdrawal and an adversary would be tempted therefore to postpone serious negotiations until the 60 days were up. Only after the Congress acted would there be a strong incentive for an adversary to negotiate. In addition, the very existence of a deadline could lead to an escalation of hostilities in order to achieve certain objectives before the 60 days expired.

The measure would jeopardize our role as a force for peace in other ways as well. It would, for example, strike from the President's hand a wide range of important peacekeeping tools by eliminating his ability to exercise quiet diplomacy backed by subtle shifts in our military deployments. It would also cast into doubt authorities which Presidents have used to undertake certain humanitarian relief missions in conflict areas, to protect fishing boats from seizure, to deal with ship or aircraft hijackings, and to respond to threats of attack. Not the least of the adverse consequences of this resolution would be the prohibition contained in section 8 against fulfilling our obligations Under the NATO treaty as ratified by the Senate.

Finally, since the bill is somewhat vague as to when the 60 day rule would apply, it could lead to extreme confusion and dangerous disagreements concerning the prerogatives of the two branches, seriously damaging our ability to respond to international crises.

FAILURE TO REQUIRE POSITIVE CONGRESSIONAL ACTION

I am particularly disturbed by the fact that certain of the President's constitutional powers as Commander in Chief of the Armed Forces would terminate automatically under this resolution 60 days after they were invoked. No overt Congressional action would be required to cut off these powers—they would disappear automatically unless the Congress extended them. In effect, the Congress is here attempting to increase its policymaking role through a provision which requires it to take absolutely no action at all.

In my view, the proper way for the Congress to make known its will on such foreign policy questions is through a positive action, with full debate on the merits of the issue and with each member taking the responsibility of casting a yes or no vote after considering those merits. The authorization and appropriations process represents one of the ways in which such influence can be exercised. I do not, however, believe that the Congress can responsibly contribute its considered, collective judgment on such grave questions without full debate and without a yes or no vote. Yet this is precisely what the joint resolution would allow. It would give every future Congress the ability to handcuff every future President merely by doing nothing and sitting still. In my view, one cannot become a responsible partner unless one is prepared to take responsible action.

STRENGTHENING COOPERATION BETWEEN THE CONGRESS AND THE EXECUTIVE BRANCHES

The responsible and effective exercise of the war powers requires the fullest cooperation between the Congress and the Executive and the prudent fulfillment by each branch of its constitutional responsibilities. House Joint Resolution 542 includes certain constructive measures which would foster this process by enhancing the flow of information from the executive branch to the Congress. Section 3, for example, calls for consultations with the Congress before and during the involvement of the United States forces in hostilities abroad. This provision is consistent with the desire of this Administration for regularized consultations with the Congress in an even wider range of circumstances.

I believe that full and cooperative participation in foreign policy matters by both the executive and the legislative branches could be enhanced by a careful and dispassionate study of their constitutional roles. Helpful proposals for such a study have already been made in the Congress. I would welcome the establishment by a non-partisan commission on the constitutional roles of the Congress and the President in the conduct of foreign affairs. This commission could make a thorough review of the principal constitutional issues in Executive-Congressional relations, including the war powers, the international agreement powers, and the question of Executive privilege, and then submit its recommendations to the President and the Congress. The members of such a commission could be drawn from both parties—and could represent many perspectives including those of the Congress, the executive branch, the legal profession, and the academic community.

This Administration is dedicated to strengthening cooperation between the Congress and the President in the conduct of foreign affairs and to preserving the constitutional prerogatives of both branches of our Government. I know that the Congress shares that goal. A commission on the constitutional roles of the Congress and the President would provide a useful opportunity for both branches to work together toward that common objective.

RICHARD NIXON

The White House,
October 24, 1973.

NOTE: On November 7, 1973, the House of Representatives and the Senate voted to over-ride the President's veto. As enacted, H. J. Res. 542 is public Law 93-148 (87 Stat. 555), which became law without the President's signature on November 7.

FULBRIGHT [COOPER-CHURCH] AMENDMENT*

Background Note

This was one of a number of amendments designed to prohibit the expenditure of appropriated funds for military operations in Indochina. Although often referred to as the "Cooper-Church" Amendment (for sponsors Republican John Sherman Cooper and Democrat Frank Church, both members of the Foreign Relations Committee), this particular amendment is more accurately identified as the "Fulbright Amendment," for Foreign Relations Committee Chairman J. William Fulbright.—Eds.

Sec. 108. Notwithstanding any other provision of law, on or after August 15, 1973, no funds herein or heretofore appropriated may be obligated or expended to finance directly or indirectly combat activities by United States military forces in or over or from off the shores of North Vietnam, South Vietnam, Laos or Cambodia.

---

* Joint Resolution Making Continuing Appropriations for the Fiscal Year 1974, and for Other Purposes § 108, Pub. L. No. 93-52, 87 Stat. 130, 134 (1973).

BOLAND AMENDMENT[*] (LIMITING AID TO NICARAGUAN CONTRAS)

Background Note

In 1979 the "Sandinista National Liberation Front" took power in Nicaragua and soon began providing training, weapons, and assistance to other Marxist revolutionary groups seeking to overthrow the governments of neighboring countries. As part of a defensive response the United States began secretly providing support to a group of Nicaraguan guerrillas known as the "Contras." In late 1982, after the existence of the covert CIA assistance to the Contras was disclosed in the press, Representative Tom Harkin (D-IOWA) introduced an amendment to the FY 1983 Intelligence Authorization Act to prohibit further funding. Representative Edward Boland (D-MASS), chair of the House Permanent Select Committee on Intelligence, then introduced a substitute amendment (known as the "Boland Amendment") designed to permit the covert assistance to continue so long as the Administration's "purpose" was not to overthrow the Government of Nicaragua or provoke a military conflict between Nicaragua and Honduras. In the years which followed, the program continued to be controversial and Congress would bar all support or appropriate additional funds at various times. Some critics later argued that the Boland Amendment had been violated by giving any money to the Contras because their clear purpose had been to overthrow the Government of Nicaragua. But the clear understanding of the original amendment was that it was the "purpose" of the United States that controlled.—Eds.

Section 793. None of the funds provided in this Act may be used by the Central Intelligence Agency or the Department of Defense to furnish military equipment, military training or advice, or other support for military activities, to any group or individual, not part of a country's armed forces, for the purposes of overthrowing the Government of Nicaragua or provoking a military exchange between Nicaragua and Honduras.

---

* Pub. L. No. 97-377, § 793, 96 Stat. 1830, 1865 (1982).

AUTHORIZATION FOR USE OF MILITARY FORCE AGAINST IRAQ RESOLUTION [1991]*

To authorize the use of United States Armed Forces pursuant to United Nations Security Council Resolution 678.

Whereas the Government of Iraq without provocation invaded and occupied the territory of Kuwait on August 2, 1990;

Whereas both the House of Representatives (in H.J. Res. 658 of the 101st Congress) and the Senate (in S. Con. Res. 147 of the 101st Congress) have condemned Iraq's invasion of Kuwait and declared their support for international action to reverse Iraq's aggression;

Whereas, Iraq's conventional, chemical, biological, and nuclear weapons and ballistic missile programs and its demonstrated willingness to use weapons of mass destruction pose a grave threat to world peace;

Whereas the international community has demanded that Iraq withdraw unconditionally and immediately from Kuwait and that Kuwait's independence and legitimate government be restored;

Whereas the United Nations Security Council repeatedly affirmed the inherent right of individual or collective self-defense in response to the armed attack by Iraq against Kuwait in accordance with Article 51 of the United Nations Charter;

Whereas, in the absence of full compliance by Iraq with its resolutions, the United Nations Security Council in Resolution 678 has authorized member states of the United Nations to use all necessary means, after January 15, 1991, to uphold and implement all relevant Security Council resolutions and to restore international peace and security in the area; and

Whereas Iraq has persisted in its illegal occupation of, and brutal aggression against Kuwait: Now, therefore, be it

Resolved by the Senate and House of Representatives of the United States of America in Congress assembled,

SECTION 1. SHORT TITLE.

This joint resolution may be cited as the "Authorization for Use of Military Force Against Iraq Resolution".

SECTION 2. AUTHORIZATION FOR USE OF UNITED STATES ARMED FORCES.

(a) AUTHORIZATION. The President is authorized, subject to subsection (b), to use United States Armed Forces pursuant to United Nations Security Council Resolution 678 (1990) in order to achieve implementation of Security Council Resolutions 660, 661, 662, 664, 665, 666, 667, 669, 670, 674, and 677.

---

* Joint Resolution to Authorize the Use of United States Armed Forces Pursuant to United Nations Security Council Resolution 678, H.R.J. Res. 77, 102d Cong., Pub. L. No. 102-1, 105 Stat. 3, 3–4 (1991) (codified at 50 U.S.C. § 1541 note (2000)), *available at* http://www.fas.org/news/iraq/1991/910113-168336.htm. The resolutions passed in the House by a vote of 250 for to 183 against and two not voting. In the Senate, as S.J. Res. 2, 102d Cong. (1991) (enacted), it was passed by a vote of 52 to 47.

(b) REQUIREMENT FOR DETERMINATION THAT USE OF MILITARY FORCE IS NECESSARY. Before exercising the authority granted in subsection (a), the President shall make available to the Speaker of the House of Representatives and the President pro tempore of the Senate his determination that—

(1) the United States has used all appropriate diplomatic and other peaceful means to obtain compliance by Iraq with the United Nations Security Council resolutions cited in subsection (a); and

(2) that those efforts have not been and would not be successful in obtaining such compliance.

(c) WAR POWERS RESOLUTION REQUIREMENTS.

(1) SPECIFIC STATUTORY AUTHORIZATION. Consistent with section 8(a)(1) of the War Powers Resolution, the Congress declares that this section is intended to constitute specific statutory authorization within the meaning of section 5(b) of the War Powers Resolution.

(2) APPLICABILITY OF OTHER REQUIREMENTS. Nothing in this resolution supersedes any requirement of the War Powers Resolution.

SECTION 3. REPORTS TO CONGRESS.

At least once every 60 days, the President shall submit to the Congress a summary on the status of efforts to obtain compliance by Iraq with the resolutions adopted by the United Nations Security Council in response to Iraq's aggression.

IRAQ LIBERATION ACT OF 1998*

AN ACT

To establish a program to support a transition to democracy in Iraq.

Be it enacted by the Senate and House of Representatives of the United States of America in Congress assembled,

SECTION 1. SHORT TITLE

This Act may be cited as the "Iraq Liberation Act of 1998".

SECTION 2. FINDINGS.

The Congress makes the following findings:

(1) On September 22, 1980, Iraq invaded Iran, starting an 8 year war in which Iraq employed chemical weapons against Iranian troops and ballistic missiles against Iranian cities.

(2) In February 1988, Iraq forcibly relocated Kurdish civilians from their home villages in the Anfal campaign, killing an estimated 50,000 to 180,000 Kurds.

(3) On March 16, 1988, Iraq used chemical weapons against Iraqi Kurdish civilian opponents in the town of Halabja, killing an estimated 5,000 Kurds and causing numerous birth defects that affect the town today.

(4) On August 2, 1990, Iraq invaded and began a 7 month occupation of Kuwait, killing and committing numerous abuses against Kuwaiti civilians, and setting Kuwait's oil wells ablaze upon retreat.

(5) Hostilities in Operation Desert Storm ended on February 28, 1991, and Iraq subsequently accepted the ceasefire conditions specified in United Nations Security Council Resolution 687 (April 3, 1991) requiring Iraq, among other things, to disclose fully and permit the dismantlement of its weapons of mass destruction programs and submit to long-term monitoring and verification of such dismantlement.

(6) In April 1993, Iraq orchestrated a failed plot to assassinate former President George Bush during his April 14–16, 1993, visit to Kuwait.

(7) In October 1994, Iraq moved 80,000 troops to areas near the border with Kuwait, posing an imminent threat of a renewed invasion of or attack against Kuwait.

(8) On August 31, 1996, Iraq suppressed many of its opponents by helping one Kurdish faction capture Irbil, the seat of the Kurdish regional government.

(9) Since March 1996, Iraq has systematically sought to deny weapons inspectors from the United Nations Special Commission on Iraq (UNSCOM) access to key facilities and documents, has on several occasions endangered the safe operation of UNSCOM helicopters transporting UNSCOM personnel in Iraq, and has persisted in a pattern of deception and concealment regarding the history of its weapons of mass destruction programs.

* Iraq Liberation Act of 1998, Pub. L. No. 105-338, 112 Stat. 3178 (codified as amended at 22 U.S.C. §2151 note (2000)), *available at* http://news.findlaw.com/hdocs/docs/iraq/libact103198.pdf.

(10) On August 5, 1998, Iraq ceased all cooperation with UNSCOM, and subsequently threatened to end long-term monitoring activities by the International Atomic Energy Agency and UNSCOM.

(11) On August 14, 1998, President Clinton signed Public Law 105-235, which declared that "the Government of Iraq is in material and unacceptable breach of its international obligations" and urged the President "to take appropriate action, in accordance with the Constitution and relevant laws of the United States, to bring Iraq into compliance with its international obligations".

(12) On May 1, 1998, President Clinton signed Public Law 105-174, which made $5,000,000 available for assistance to the Iraqi democratic opposition for such activities as organization, training, communication and dissemination of information, developing and implementing agreements among opposition groups, compiling information to support the indictment of Iraqi officials for war crimes, and for related purposes.

SECTION 3. SENSE OF THE CONGRESS REGARDING UNITED STATES POLICY TOWARD IRAQ.

It should be the policy of the United States to support efforts to remove the regime headed by Saddam Hussein from power in Iraq and to promote the emergence of a democratic government to replace that regime.

SECTION 4. ASSISTANCE TO SUPPORT A TRANSITION TO DEMOCRACY IN IRAQ.

(a) AUTHORITY TO PROVIDE ASSISTANCE.—The President may provide to the Iraqi democratic opposition organizations designated in accordance with section 5 the following assistance:

. . . .

(2) MILITARY ASSISTANCE—

(A) The President is authorized to direct the drawdown of defense articles from the stocks of the Department of Defense, defense services of the Department of Defense, and military education and training for such organizations.

(B) The aggregate value (as defined in section 644(m) of the Foreign Assistance Act of 1961) of assistance provided under this paragraph may not exceed $97,000,000.

(b) HUMANITARIAN ASSISTANCE—The Congress urges the President to use existing authorities under the Foreign Assistance Act of 1961 to provide humanitarian assistance to individuals living in areas of Iraq controlled by organizations designated in accordance with section 5, with emphasis on addressing the needs of individuals who have fled to such areas from areas under the control of the Saddam Hussein regime.

(c) RESTRICTION ON ASSISTANCE—No assistance under this section shall be provided to any group within an organization designated in accordance with section 5 which group is, at the time the assistance is to be provided, engaged in military cooperation with the Saddam Hussein regime.

. . . .

(g) AUTHORITY TO PROVIDE ASSISTANCE—Activities under this section (including activities of the nature described in subsection (b)) may be undertaken notwithstanding any other provision of law.

....

SECTION 5 DESIGNATION OF IRAQI DEMOCRATIC OPPOSITION ORGANIZATION.

....

SECTION 6. WAR CRIMES TRIBUNAL FOR IRAQ.

Consistent with section 301 of the Foreign Relations Authorization Act, Fiscal Years 1992 and 1993 (Public Law 102-138), House Concurrent Resolution 137, 105th Congress (approved by the House of Representatives on November 13, 1997), and Senate Concurrent Resolution 78, 105th Congress (approved by the Senate on March 13, 1998), the Congress urges the President to call upon the United Nations to establish an international criminal tribunal for the purpose of indicting, prosecuting, and imprisoning Saddam Hussein and other Iraqi officials who are responsible for crimes against humanity, genocide, and other criminal violations of international law.

SECTION 7. ASSISTANCE FOR IRAQ UPON REPLACEMENT OF SADDAM HUSSEIN REGIME.

It is the sense of the Congress that once the Saddam Hussein regime is removed from power in Iraq, the United States should support Iraq's transition to democracy by providing immediate and substantial humanitarian assistance to the Iraqi people, by providing democracy transition assistance to Iraqi parties and movements with democratic goals, and by convening Iraq's foreign creditors to develop a multilateral response to Iraq's foreign debt incurred by Saddam Hussein's regime.

SECTION 8. RULE OF CONSTRUCTION.

Nothing in this Act shall be construed to authorize or otherwise speak to the use of United States Armed Forces (except as provided in section 4(a)(2)) in carrying out this Act.

Approved October 31, 1998.

AUTHORIZATION FOR USE OF MILITARY FORCE* (AGAINST 9/11 TERRORISTS)

JOINT RESOLUTION To authorize the use of United States Armed Forces against those responsible for the recent attacks launched against the United States.

Whereas, on September 11, 2001, acts of treacherous violence were committed against the United States and its citizens; and

Whereas, such acts render it both necessary and appropriate that the United States exercise its rights to self-defense and to protect United States citizens both at home and abroad; and

Whereas, in light of the threat to the national security and foreign policy of the United States posed by these grave acts of violence; and

Whereas, such acts continue to pose an unusual and extraordinary threat to the national security and foreign policy of the United States; and

Whereas, the President has authority under the Constitution to take action to deter and prevent acts of international terrorism against the United States: Now, therefore, be it

Resolved by the Senate and House of Representatives of the United States of America in Congress assembled,

SECTION 1. SHORT TITLE.

This joint resolution may be cited as the "Authorization for Use of Military Force".

SECTION 2. AUTHORIZATION FOR USE OF UNITED STATES ARMED FORCES.

(a) IN GENERAL.—That the President is authorized to use all necessary and appropriate force against those nations, organizations, or persons he determines planned, authorized, committed, or aided the terrorist attacks that occurred on September 11, 2001, or harbored such organizations or persons, in order to prevent any future acts of international terrorism against the United States by such nations, organizations or persons.

(b) War Powers Resolution Requirements—

(1) SPECIFIC STATUTORY AUTHORIZATION.—Consistent with section 8(a)(1) of the War Powers Resolution, the Congress declares that this section is intended to constitute specific statutory authorization within the meaning of section 5(b) of the War Powers Resolution.

(2) APPLICABILITY OF OTHER REQUIREMENTS.—Nothing in this resolution supercedes any requirement of the War Powers Resolution.

Approved September 18, 2001.

---

* Authorization for Use of Military Force, S.J. Res. 23, 107th Cong., Pub. L. No. 107-40, 115 Stat. 224 (2001) (codified at 50 U.S.C.A. §1541 note (West 2003)), *available at* http://usgovinfo.about.com/library/bills/blsjres23.htm.

AUTHORIZATION FOR THE USE OF MILITARY FORCE AGAINST IRAQ [RESOLUTION OF 2002]*

Whereas in 1990 in response to Iraq's war of aggression against and illegal occupation of Kuwait, the United States forged a coalition of nations to liberate Kuwait and its people in order to defend the national security of the United States and enforce United Nations Security Council resolutions relating to Iraq;

Whereas after the liberation of Kuwait in 1991, Iraq entered into a United Nations sponsored cease-fire agreement pursuant to which Iraq unequivocally agreed, among other things, to eliminate its nuclear, biological, and chemical weapons programs and the means to deliver and develop them, and to end its support for international terrorism;

Whereas the efforts of international weapons inspectors, United States intelligence agencies, and Iraqi defectors led to the discovery that Iraq had large stockpiles of chemical weapons and a large scale biological weapons program, and that Iraq had an advanced nuclear weapons development program that was much closer to producing a nuclear weapon than intelligence reporting had previously indicated;

Whereas Iraq, in direct and flagrant violation of the cease-fire, attempted to thwart the efforts of weapons inspectors to identify and destroy Iraq's weapons of mass destruction stockpiles and development capabilities, which finally resulted in the withdrawal of inspectors from Iraq on October 31, 1998;

Whereas in 1998 Congress concluded that Iraq's continuing weapons of mass destruction programs threatened vital United States interests and international peace and security, declared Iraq to be in "material and unacceptable breach of its international obligations" and urged the President "to take appropriate action, in accordance with the Constitution and relevant laws of the United States, to bring Iraq into compliance with its international obligations" (Public Law 105-235);

Whereas Iraq both poses a continuing threat to the national security of the United States and international peace and security in the Persian Gulf region and remains in material and unacceptable breach of its international obligations by, among other things, continuing to possess and develop a significant chemical and biological weapons capability, actively seeking a nuclear weapons capability, and supporting and harboring terrorist organizations;

Whereas Iraq persists in violating resolutions of the United Nations Security Council by continuing to engage in brutal repression of its civilian population thereby threatening international peace and security in the region, by refusing to release, repatriate, or account for non-Iraqi citizens wrongfully detained by Iraq, including an American serviceman, and by failing to return property wrongfully seized by Iraq from Kuwait;

Whereas the current Iraqi regime has demonstrated its capability and willingness to use weapons of mass destruction against other nations and its own people;

---

* Authorization for Use of Military Force Against Iraq Resolution of 2002, Pub. L. No. 107-243, 116 Stat. 1498 (codified at 50 U.S.C.A. § 1541 note (West Supp. 2005)), *available at* http://www.whitehouse.gov/news/releases/2002/10/20021002-2.html.

Whereas the current Iraqi regime has demonstrated its continuing hostility toward, and willingness to attack, the United States, including by attempting in 1993 to assassinate former President Bush and by firing on many thousands of occasions on United States and Coalition Armed Forces engaged in enforcing the resolutions of the United Nations Security Council;

Whereas members of Al-Qaida, an organization bearing responsibility for attacks on the United States, its citizens, and interests, including the attacks that occurred on September 11, 2001, are known to be in Iraq;

Whereas Iraq continues to aid and harbor other international terrorist organizations, including organizations that threaten the lives and safety of American citizens;

Whereas the attacks on the United States of September 11, 2001 underscored the gravity of the threat posed by the acquisition of weapons of mass destruction by international terrorist organizations;

Whereas Iraq's demonstrated capability and willingness to use weapons of mass destruction, the risk that the current Iraqi regime will either employ those weapons to launch a surprise attack against the United States or its Armed Forces or provide them to international terrorists who would do so, and the extreme magnitude of harm that would result to the United States and its citizens from such an attack, combine to justify action by the United States to defend itself;

Whereas United Nations Security Council Resolution 678 authorizes the use of all necessary means to enforce United Nations Security Council Resolution 660 and subsequent relevant resolutions and to compel Iraq to cease certain activities that threaten international peace and security, including the development of weapons of mass destruction and refusal or obstruction of United Nations weapons inspections in violation of United Nations Security Council Resolution 687, repression of its civilian population in violation of United Nations Security Council Resolution 688, and threatening its neighbors or United Nations operations in Iraq in violation of United Nations Security Council Resolution 949;

Whereas Congress in the Authorization for Use of Military Force Against Iraq Resolution (Public Law 102-1) has authorized the President "to use United States Armed Forces pursuant to United Nations Security Council Resolution 678 (1990) in order to achieve implementation of Security Council Resolutions 660, 661, 662, 664, 665, 666, 667, 669, 670, 674, and 677";

Whereas in December 1991, Congress expressed its sense that it "supports the use of all necessary means to achieve the goals of United Nations Security Council Resolution 687 as being consistent with the Authorization of Use of Military Force Against Iraq Resolution (Public Law 102-1)," that Iraq's repression of its civilian population violates United Nations Security Council Resolution 688 and "constitutes a continuing threat to the peace, security, and stability of the Persian Gulf region," and that Congress, "supports the use of all necessary means to achieve the goals of United Nations Security Council Resolution 688";

Whereas the Iraq Liberation Act (Public Law 105-338) expressed the sense of Congress that it should be the policy of the United States to support efforts to remove from power the current Iraqi regime and promote the emergence of a democratic government to replace that regime;

Whereas on September 12, 2002, President Bush committed the United States to "work with the United Nations Security Council to meet our common challenge" posed by

Iraq and to "work for the necessary resolutions," while also making clear that "the Security Council resolutions will be enforced, and the just demands of peace and security will be met, or action will be unavoidable";

Whereas the United States is determined to prosecute the war on terrorism and Iraq's ongoing support for international terrorist groups combined with its development of weapons of mass destruction in direct violation of its obligations under the 1991 cease-fire and other United Nations Security Council resolutions make clear that it is in the national security interests of the United States and in furtherance of the war on terrorism that all relevant United Nations Security Council resolutions be enforced, including through the use of force if necessary;

Whereas Congress has taken steps to pursue vigorously the war on terrorism through the provision of authorities and funding requested by the President to take the necessary actions against international terrorists and terrorist organizations, including those nations, organizations or persons who planned, authorized, committed or aided the terrorist attacks that occurred on September 11, 2001 or harbored such persons or organizations;

Whereas the President and Congress are determined to continue to take all appropriate actions against international terrorists and terrorist organizations, including those nations, organizations or persons who planned, authorized, committed or aided the terrorist attacks that occurred on September 11, 2001, or harbored such persons or organizations;

Whereas the President has authority under the Constitution to take action in order to deter and prevent acts of international terrorism against the United States, as Congress recognized in the joint resolution on Authorization for Use of Military Force (Public Law 107-40); and

Whereas it is in the national security of the United States to restore international peace and security to the Persian Gulf region:

Now, therefore, be it

Resolved by the Senate and House of Representatives of the United States of America in Congress assembled,

SECTION 1. SHORT TITLE.

This joint resolution may be cited as the "Authorization for the Use of Military Force Against Iraq".

SECTION 2. SUPPORT FOR UNITED STATES DIPLOMATIC EFFORTS.

The Congress of the United States supports the efforts by the President to—

(a) strictly enforce through the United Nations Security Council all relevant Security Council resolutions applicable to Iraq and encourages him in those efforts; and

(b) obtain prompt and decisive action by the Security Council to ensure that Iraq abandons its strategy of delay, evasion and noncompliance and promptly and strictly complies with all relevant Security Council resolutions.

SECTION 3. AUTHORIZATION FOR USE OF UNITED STATES ARMED FORCES.

(a) AUTHORIZATION—The President is authorized to use the Armed Forces of the United States as he determines to be necessary and appropriate in order to—

(1) defend the national security of the United States against the continuing threat posed by Iraq; and

(2) enforce all relevant United Nations Security Council Resolutions regarding Iraq.

(b) PRESIDENTIAL DETERMINATION—In connection with the exercise of the authority granted in subsection (a) to use force the President shall, prior to such exercise or as soon there after as may be feasible, but no later than 48 hours after exercising such authority, make available to the Speaker of the House of Representatives and the President pro tempore of the Senate his determination that—

(1) reliance by the United States on further diplomatic or other peaceful means alone either—

(A) will not adequately protect the national security of the United States against the continuing threat posed by Iraq or

(B) is not likely to lead to enforcement of all relevant United Nations Security Council resolutions regarding Iraq, and

(2) acting pursuant to this resolution is consistent with the United States and other countries continuing to take the necessary actions against international terrorists and terrorist organizations, including those nations, organizations or persons who planned, authorized, committed or aided the terrorists attacks that occurred on September 11, 2001.

(c) WAR POWERS RESOLUTION REQUIREMENTS—

(1) SPECIFIC STATUTORY AUTHORIZATION—Consistent with section 8(a)(1) of the War Powers Resolution, the Congress declares that this section is intended to constitute specific statutory authorization within the meaning of section 5(b) of the War Powers Resolution.

(2) APPLICABILITY OF OTHER REQUIREMENTS—Nothing in this resolution supersedes any requirement of the War Powers Resolution.

SECTION 4. REPORTS TO CONGRESS.

(a) The President shall, at least once every 60 days, submit to the Congress a report on matters relevant to this joint resolution, including actions taken pursuant to the exercise of authority granted in section 2 and the status of planning for efforts that are expected to be required after such actions are completed, including those actions described in section 7 of Public Law 105-338 (the Iraq Liberation Act of 1998).

(b) To the extent that the submission of any report described in subsection (a) coincides with the submission of any other report on matters relevant to this joint resolution otherwise required to be submitted to Congress pursuant to the reporting requirements of Public Law 93-148 (the War Powers Resolution), all such reports may be submitted as a single consolidated report to the Congress.

(c) To the extent that the information required by section 3 of Public Law 102-1 is included in the report required by this section, such report shall be considered as meeting the requirements of section 3 of Public Law 102-1.

Approved October 16, 2002.

3. Executive Privilege

WASHINGTON, MESSAGE TO THE HOUSE REGARDING DOCUMENTS RELATIVE TO THE JAY TREATY, MARCH 30, 1796*

Background Note

Many members of the House were shocked by this message, not so much because of the President's refusal to provide the requested documents, but because of the grounds given for the refusal. The President had not justified his denial on the basis of a need to protect national security secrets, but rather because of his judgment of the proper constitutional role of the House of Representatives. One week after the President's message was received—a week spent in almost constant debate over the matter—Representative James Madison spoke at great length about what later became known as the "Executive Privilege" to refuse to provide information to the Legislative Branch.—Eds.

March 30, 1796.

To the House of Representatives of the United States:

With the utmost attention I have considered your resolution of the with instant, requesting me to lay before your House a copy of the instructions to the minister of the United States who negotiated the treaty with the King of Great Britain,...

In deliberating upon this subject it was impossible for me to lose sight of the principle which some have avowed in its discussion, or to avoid extending my views to the consequences which must flow from the admission of that principle.

I trust that no part of my conduct has ever indicated a disposition to withhold any information which the Constitution has enjoined upon the President as a duty to give, or which could be required of him by either House of Congress as a right; and with truth I affirm that it has been, as it will continue to be while I have the honor to preside in the Government, my constant endeavor to harmonize with the other branches thereof so far as the trust delegated to me by the people of the United States and my sense of the obligation it imposes to "preserve, protect, and defend the Constitution" will permit.

The nature of foreign negotiations requires caution, and their success must often depend on secrecy; and even when brought to a conclusion a full disclosure of all the measures, demands, or eventual concessions which may have been proposed or contemplated would be extremely impolitic; for this might have a pernicious influence on future negotiations, or produce immediate inconveniences, perhaps danger and mischief, in relation to other powers. The necessity of such caution and secrecy was one cogent reason for vesting the power of making treaties in the President, with the advice and consent of the Senate, the principle on which that body was formed confining it to a small number of members. To admit, then, a right in the House of Representatives to

---

* George Washington, Message to the House of Representatives of the United States (Mar. 30, 1796), *in* 1 A Compilation of the Messages and Papers of the Presidents 1789–1897, at 194-96 (James D. Richardson ed., 1896), *available at* http://www.yale.edu/lawweb/avalon/presiden/messages/gw003.htm.

demand and to have as a matter of course all the papers respecting a negotiation with a foreign power would be to establish a dangerous precedent.

. . . .

If other proofs than these and the plain letter of the Constitution itself be necessary to ascertain the point under consideration, they may be found in the journals of the General Convention, which I have deposited in the office of the Department of State. In those journals it will appear that a proposition was made "that no treaty should be binding on the United States which was not ratified by a law," and that the proposition was explicitly rejected.

As, therefore, it is perfectly clear to my understanding that the assent of the House of Representatives is not necessary to the validity of a treaty; as the treaty with Great Britain exhibits in itself all the objects requiring legislative provision, and on these the papers called for can throw no light, and as it is essential to the due administration of the Government that the boundaries fixed by the Constitution between the different departments should be preserved, a just regard to the Constitution and to the duty of my office, under all the circumstances of this case, forbids a compliance with your request.

G° WASHINGTON

MADISON, SPEECH TO THE HOUSE OF REPRESENTATIVES ON THE JAY TREATY, APRIL 6, 1796*

....

...He thought it clear that the house must have a right, in all cases, to ask for information, which might assist their deliberations on subjects submitted to them by the Constitution; being responsible nevertheless for the propriety of the measure. He was as ready to admit, that the Executive had a right under a due responsibility also, to withhold information, when of a nature that did not permit a disclosure of it at the time. And if the refusal of the President had been founded simply on a representation, that the state of the business within his department, and the contents of the Papers asked for, required it, although he might have regretted the refusal, he should have been little disposed to criticise it....

....

...It belonged, he said, to each department to judge for itself.

If the Executive conceived that in relation to his own department, papers could not be safely communicated, he might on that ground refuse them, because he was the competent though a responsible judge within his own department. If the papers could be communicated, without injury to the objects of his department, he ought not to refuse them as irrelative to the objects of the House of Representatives; because the House was, in such cases, the only proper judge of its own objects.

....

* James Madison, Speech to the House of Representatives on the Treaty with Great Britain (Apr. 6, 1796), *in* 5 Annals of Cong. 772, 773 (1796), *available at* http://www.constitution.org/jm/17960406_jaytreaty.htm.

NIXON, STATEMENT ON EXECUTIVE PRIVILEGE, MARCH 12, 1973, WITH RELATED MEMORANDUM ESTABLISHING A PROCEDURE TO GOVERN COMPLIANCE WITH CONGRESSIONAL DEMANDS FOR INFORMATION*

During my press conference of January 31, 1973, I stated that I would issue a statement outlining my views on executive privilege.

The doctrine of executive privilege is well established. It was first invoked by President Washington, and it has been recognized and utilized by our Presidents for almost 200 years since that time. The doctrine is rooted in the Constitution, which vests "the Executive Power" solely in the President, and it is designed to protect communications within the executive branch in a variety of circumstances in time of both war and peace. Without such protection, our military security, our relations with other countries, our law enforcement procedures, and many other aspects of the national interest could be significantly damaged and the decisionmaking process of the executive branch could be impaired.

The general policy of this Administration regarding the use of executive privilege during the next 4 years will be the same as the one we have followed during the past 4 years and which I outlined in my press conference: Executive privilege will not be used as a shield to prevent embarrassing information from being made available but will be exercised only in those particular instances in which disclosure would harm the public interest.

I first enunciated this policy in a memorandum of March 24, 1969, which I sent to Cabinet officers and heads of agencies. The memorandum read in part:

> "The policy of this Administration is to comply to the fullest extent possible with Congressional requests for information. While the Executive branch has the responsibility of withholding certain information the disclosure of which would be incompatible with the public interest, this Administration will invoke this authority only in the most compelling circumstances and after a rigorous inquiry into the actual need for its exercise. For those reasons Executive privilege will not be used without specific Presidential approval."

In recent weeks, questions have been raised about the availability of officials in the executive branch to present testimony before committees of the Congress. As my 1969 memorandum dealt primarily with guidelines for providing information to the Congress and did not focus specifically on appearances by officers of the executive branch and members of the President's personal staff, it would be useful to outline my policies concerning the latter question.

During the first 4 years of my Presidency, hundreds of Administration officials spent thousands of hours freely testifying before committees of the Congress. Secretary of De-

---

* Richard Nixon, Statement About Executive Privilege, PUB. PAPERS 184–87 (Mar. 12, 1973), *available at* http://www.nixonfoundation.org/clientuploads/directory/archive/1973_pdf_files/1973_0076.pdf.

fense Laird, for instance, made 86 separate appearances before Congressional committees, engaging in over 327 hours of testimony. By contrast, there were only three occasions during the first term of my Administration when executive privilege was invoked anywhere in the executive branch in response to a Congressional request for information. These facts speak not of a closed Administration but of one that is pledged to openness and is proud to stand on its record.

Requests for Congressional appearances by members of the President's personal staff present a different situation and raise different considerations. Such requests have been relatively infrequent through the years, and in past administrations they have been routinely declined. I have followed that same tradition in my Administration, and I intend to continue it during the remainder of my term.

Under the doctrine of separation of powers, the manner in which the President personally exercises his assigned executive powers is not subject to questioning by another branch of Government. If the President is not subject to such questioning, it is equally appropriate that members of his staff not be so questioned, for their roles are in effect an extension of the Presidency.

This tradition rests on more than Constitutional doctrine: It is also a practical necessity. To insure the effective discharge of the executive responsibility, a President must be able to place absolute confidence in the advice and assistance offered by the members of his staff. And in the performance of their duties for the President, those staff members must not be inhibited by the possibility that their advice and assistance will ever become a matter of public debate, either during their tenure in Government or at a later date. Otherwise, the candor with which advice is rendered and the quality of such assistance will inevitably be compromised and weakened. What is at stake, therefore, is not simply a question of confidentiality but the integrity of the decisionmaking process at the very highest levels of our Government.

The considerations I have just outlined have been and must be recognized in other fields, in and out of government. A law clerk, for instance, is not subject to interrogation about the factors or discussions that preceded a decision of the judge.

For these reasons, just as I shall not invoke executive privilege lightly, I shall also look to the Congress to continue this proper tradition in asking for executive branch testimony only from the officers properly constituted to provide the information sought, and only when the eliciting of such testimony will serve a genuine legislative purpose.

As I stated in my press conference on January 31, the question of whether circumstances warrant the exercise of executive privilege should be determined on a case-by-case basis. In making such decisions, I shall rely on the following guidelines:

1. In the case of a department or agency, every official shall comply with a reasonable request for an appearance before the Congress, provided that the performance of the duties of his office will not be seriously impaired thereby. If the official believes that a Congressional request for a particular document or for testimony on a particular point raises a substantial question as to the need for invoking executive privilege, he shall comply with the procedures set forth in my memorandum of March 24, 1969. Thus executive privilege will not be invoked until the compelling need for its exercise has been clearly demonstrated and the request has been approved first by the Attorney General and then by the President.

2. A Cabinet officer or any other Government official who also holds a position as a member of the President's personal staff shall comply with any reasonable request to

testify in his non-White House capacity, provided that the performance of his duties will not be seriously impaired thereby. If the official believes that the request raises a substantial question as to the need for invoking executive privilege, he shall comply with the procedures set forth in my memorandum of March 24, 1969.

3. A member or former member of the President's personal staff normal shall follow the well-established precedent and decline a request for a formal appearance before a committee of the Congress. At the same time, it will continue to be my policy to provide all necessary and relevant information through informal contacts between my present staff and committees of the Congress in ways which preserve intact the Constitutional separation of the branches.

Note: The text of the memorandum to which the statement refers was also made available by the White House Press Office, as follows:

March 24, 1969

MEMORANDUM FOR THE HEADS OF EXECUTIVE DEPARTMENTS AND AGENCIES

SUBJECT: ESTABLISHING A PROCEDURE TO GOVERN COMPLIANCE WITH CONGRESSIONAL DEMANDS FOR INFORMATION

The policy of this Administration is to comply to the fullest extent possible with Congressional requests for information. While the Executive branch has the responsibility of withholding certain information the disclosure of which would be incompatible with the public interest, this Administration will invoke this authority only in the most compelling circumstances and after a rigorous inquiry into the actual need for its exercise. For those reasons Executive privilege will not be used without specific Presidential approval. The following procedural steps will govern the invocation of Executive privilege:

1. If the head of an Executive department or agency (hereafter referred to as "department head") believes that compliance with a request for information from a Congressional agency addressed to his department or agency raises substantial question as to the need for invoking Executive privilege, he should consult the Attorney General through the Office of Legal Counsel of the Department of Justice.

2. If the department head and the Attorney General agree, in accordance with the policy set forth above, that Executive privilege shall not be invoked in the circumstances, the information shall be released to the inquiring Congressional agency.

3. If the department head and the Attorney General agree that the circumstances justify the invocation of Executive privilege, or if either of them believes that the issue should be submitted to the President, the matter shall be transmitted to the Counsel to the President, who will advise the department head of the President's decision.

4. In the event of a Presidential decision to invoke Executive privilege, the department head should advise the Congressional agency that the claim of Executive privilege is being made with the specific approval of the President.

5. Pending a final determination of the matter, the department head should request the Congressional agency to hold its demand for the information in abeyance until such determination can be made. Care shall be taken to indicate that the purpose of this request is to protect the privilege pending the determination, and that the request does not constitute a claim of privilege.

Richard Nixon

D. Access to Information

FREEDOM OF INFORMATION ACT*

§ 552. Public information; agency rules, opinions, orders, records, and proceedings

(a) Each agency shall make available to the public information as follows:

(1) Each agency shall separately state and currently publish in the Federal Register for the guidance of the public—

(A) descriptions of its central and field organization and the established places at which, the employees (and in the case of a uniformed service, the members) from whom, and the methods whereby, the public may obtain information, make submittals or requests, or obtain decisions;

(B) statements of the general course and method by which its functions are channeled and determined, including the nature and requirements of all formal and informal procedures available;

(C) rules of procedure, descriptions of forms available or the places at which forms may be obtained, and instructions as to the scope and contents of all papers, reports, or examinations;

(D) substantive rules of general applicability adopted as authorized by law, and statements of general policy or interpretations of general applicability formulated and adopted by the agency; and

(E) each amendment, revision, or repeal of the foregoing.

Except to the extent that a person has actual and timely notice of the terms thereof, a person may not in any manner be required to resort to, or be adversely affected by, a matter required to be published in the Federal Register and not so published. For the purpose of this paragraph, matter reasonably available to the class of persons affected thereby is deemed published in the Federal Register when incorporated by reference therein with the approval of the Director of the Federal Register.

(2) Each agency, in accordance with published rules, shall make available for public inspection and copying—

(A) final opinions, including concurring and dissenting opinions, as well as orders, made in the adjudication of cases;

(B) those statements of policy and interpretations which have been adopted by the agency and are not published in the Federal Register;

(C) administrative staff manuals and instructions to staff that affect a member of the public;

(D) copies of all records, regardless of form or format, which have been released to any person under paragraph (3) and which, because of the nature of their subject matter, the agency determines have become or are likely to become the subject of subsequent requests for substantially the same records; and

(E) a general index of the records referred to under subparagraph (D);

---

* Freedom of Information Act, Pub. L. No. 89-554, 80 Stat. 383 (1966) (codified as amended at 5 U.S.C.A. § 552 (West 1996 & Supp. 2005)), *available at* http://www.usdoj.gov/oip/foia_updates/Vol_XVII_4/page2.htm.

unless the materials are promptly published and copies offered for sale. For records created on or after November 1, 1996, within one year after such date, each agency shall make such records available, including by computer telecommunications or, if computer telecommunications means have not been established by the agency, by other electronic means. To the extent required to prevent a clearly unwarranted invasion of personal privacy, an agency may delete identifying details when it makes available or publishes an opinion, statement of policy, interpretation, staff manual, instruction, or copies of records referred to in subparagraph (D). However, in each case the justification for the deletion shall be explained fully in writing, and the extent of such deletion shall be indicated on the portion of the record which is made available or published, unless including that indication would harm an interest protected by the exemption in subsection (b) under which the deletion is made. If technically feasible, the extent of the deletion shall be indicated at the place in the record where the deletion was made. Each agency shall also maintain and make available for public inspection and copying current indexes providing identifying information for the public as to any matter issued, adopted, or promulgated after July 4, 1967, and required by this paragraph to be made available or published. Each agency shall make the index referred to in subparagraph (E) available by computer telecommunications by December 31, 1999. Each agency shall promptly publish, quarterly or more frequently, and distribute (by sale or otherwise) copies of each index or supplements thereto unless it determines by order published in the Federal Register that the publication would be unnecessary and impracticable, in which case the agency shall nonetheless provide copies of such index on request at a cost not to exceed the direct cost of duplication. A final order, opinion, statement of policy, interpretation, or staff manual or instruction that affects a member of the public may be relied on, used, or cited as precedent by an agency against a party other than an agency only if—

(i) it has been indexed and either made available or published as provided by this paragraph; or

(ii) the party has actual and timely notice of the terms thereof.

(3) (A) Except with respect to the records made available under paragraphs (1) and (2) of this subsection, and except as provided in subparagraph (E), each agency, upon any request for records which (i) reasonably describes such records and (ii) is made in accordance with published rules stating the time, place, fees (if any), and procedures to be followed, shall make the records promptly available to any person.

(B) In making any record available to a person under this paragraph, an agency shall provide the record in any form or format requested by the person if the record is readily reproducible by the agency in that form or format. Each agency shall make reasonable efforts to maintain its records in forms or formats that are reproducible for purposes of this section.

(C) In responding under this paragraph to a request for records, an agency shall make reasonable efforts to search for the records in electronic form or format, except when such efforts would significantly interfere with the operation of the agency's automated information system.

(D) For purposes of this paragraph, the term "search" means to review, manually or by automated means, agency records for the purpose of locating those records which are responsive to a request.

(E) An agency, or part of an agency, that is an element of the intelligence community (as that term is defined in section 3(4) of the National Security Act of 1947 (50 U.S.C. 401a(4))) shall not make any record available under this paragraph to—

(i) any government entity, other than a State, territory, commonwealth, or district of the United States, or any subdivision thereof; or

(ii) a representative of a government entity described in clause (i).

(4) (A) (i) In order to carry out the provisions of this section, each agency shall promulgate regulations, pursuant to notice and receipt of public comment, specifying the schedule of fees applicable to the processing of requests under this section and establishing procedures and guidelines for determining when such fees should be waived or reduced. Such schedule shall conform to the guidelines which shall be promulgated, pursuant to notice and receipt of public comment, by the Director of the Office of Management and Budget and which shall provide for a uniform schedule of fees for all agencies.

(ii) Such agency regulations shall provide that—

(I) fees shall be limited to reasonable standard charges for document search, duplication, and review, when records are requested for commercial use;

(II) fees shall be limited to reasonable standard charges for document duplication when records are not sought for commercial use and the request is made by an educational or noncommercial scientific institution, whose purpose is scholarly or scientific research; or a representative of the news media; and

(III) for any request not described in (I) or (II), fees shall be limited to reasonable standard charges for document search and duplication.

(iii) Documents shall be furnished without any charge or at a charge reduced below the fees established under clause (ii) if disclosure of the information is in the public interest because it is likely to contribute significantly to public understanding of the operations or activities of the government and is not primarily in the commercial interest of the requester.

(iv) Fee schedules shall provide for the recovery of only the direct costs of search, duplication, or review. Review costs shall include only the direct costs incurred during the initial examination of a document for the purposes of determining whether the documents must be disclosed under this section and for the purposes of withholding any portions exempt from disclosure under this section. Review costs may not include any costs incurred in resolving issues of law or policy that may be raised in the course of processing a request under this section. No fee may be charged by any agency under this section—

(I) if the costs of routine collection and processing of the fee are likely to equal or exceed the amount of the fee; or

(II) for any request described in clause (ii)(II) or (III) of this subparagraph for the first two hours of search time or for the first one hundred pages of duplication.

(v) No agency may require advance payment of any fee unless the requester has previously failed to pay fees in a timely fashion, or the agency has determined that the fee will exceed $250.

(vi) Nothing in this subparagraph shall supersede fees chargeable under a statute specifically providing for setting the level of fees for particular types of records.

(vii) In any action by a requester regarding the waiver of fees under this section, the court shall determine the matter de novo: Provided, That the court's review of the matter shall be limited to the record before the agency.

(B) On complaint, the district court of the United States in the district in which the complainant resides, or has his principal place of business, or in which the agency records are situated, or in the District of Columbia, has jurisdiction to enjoin the agency from withholding agency records and to order the production of any agency records improperly withheld from the complainant. In such a case the court shall determine the matter de novo, and may examine the contents of such agency records in camera to determine whether such records or any part thereof shall be withheld under any of the exemptions set forth in subsection (b) of this section, and the burden is on the agency to sustain its action. In addition to any other matters to which a court accords substantial weight, a court shall accord substantial weight to an affidavit of an agency concerning the agency's determination as to technical feasibility under paragraph (2)(C) and subsection (b) and reproducibility under paragraph (3)(B).

(C) Notwithstanding any other provision of law, the defendant shall serve an answer or otherwise plead to any complaint made under this subsection within thirty days after service upon the defendant of the pleading in which such complaint is made, unless the court otherwise directs for good cause shown.

(D) [Repealed]

(E) The court may assess against the United States reasonable attorney fees and other litigation costs reasonably incurred in any case under this section in which the complainant has substantially prevailed.

(F) Whenever the court orders the production of any agency records improperly withheld from the complainant and assesses against the United States reasonable attorney fees and other litigation costs, and the court additionally issues a written finding that the circumstances surrounding the withholding raise questions whether agency personnel acted arbitrarily or capriciously with respect to the withholding, the Special Counsel shall promptly initiate a proceeding to determine whether disciplinary action is warranted against the officer or employee who was primarily responsible for the withholding. The Special Counsel, after investigation and consideration of the evidence submitted, shall submit his findings and recommendations to the administrative authority of the agency concerned and shall send copies of the findings and recommendations to the officer or employee or his representative. The administrative authority shall take the corrective action that the Special Counsel recommends.

(G) In the event of noncompliance with the order of the court, the district court may punish for contempt the responsible employee, and in the case of a uniformed service, the responsible member.

(5) Each agency having more than one member shall maintain and make available for public inspection a record of the final votes of each member in every agency proceeding.

(6) (A) Each agency, upon any request for records made under paragraph (1), (2), or (3) of this subsection, shall—

(i) determine within 20 days (excepting Saturdays, Sundays, and legal public holidays) after the receipt of any such request whether to comply with such request and shall immediately notify the person making such request of such determination and the reasons therefor, and of the right of such person to appeal to the head of the agency any adverse determination; and

(ii) make a determination with respect to any appeal within twenty days (excepting Saturdays, Sundays, and legal public holidays) after the receipt of such appeal. If on appeal the denial of the request for records is in whole or in part upheld, the agency shall notify the person making such request of the provisions for judicial review of that determination under paragraph (4) of this subsection.

(B) (i) In unusual circumstances as specified in this subparagraph, the time limits prescribed in either clause (i) or clause (ii) of subparagraph (A) may be extended by written notice to the person making such request setting forth the unusual circumstances for such extension and the date on which a determination is expected to be dispatched. No such notice shall specify a date that would result in an extension for more than ten working days, except as provided in clause (ii) of this subparagraph.

(ii) With respect to a request for which a written notice under clause (i) extends the time limits prescribed under clause (i) of subparagraph (A), the agency shall notify the person making the request if the request cannot be processed within the time limit specified in that clause and shall provide the person an opportunity to limit the scope of the request so that it may be processed within that time limit or an opportunity to arrange with the agency an alternative time frame for processing the request or a modified request. Refusal by the person to reasonably modify the request or arrange such an alternative time frame shall be considered as a factor in determining whether exceptional circumstances exist for purposes of subparagraph (C).

(iii) As used in this subparagraph, "unusual circumstances" means, but only to the extent reasonably necessary to the proper processing of the particular requests—

(I) the need to search for and collect the requested records from field facilities or other establishments that are separate from the office processing the request;

(II) the need to search for, collect, and appropriately examine a voluminous amount of separate and distinct records which are demanded in a single request; or

(III) the need for consultation, which shall be conducted with all practicable speed, with another agency having a substantial interest in the determination of the request or among two or more components of the agency having substantial subject-matter interest therein.

(iv) Each agency may promulgate regulations, pursuant to notice and receipt of public comment, providing for the aggregation of certain requests by the same requestor, or by a group of requestors acting in concert, if the agency reasonably believes that such requests actually constitute a single request, which would otherwise satisfy the unusual circumstances specified in this subparagraph, and the requests involve clearly related matters. Multiple requests involving unrelated matters shall not be aggregated.

(C) (i) Any person making a request to any agency for records under paragraph (1), (2), or (3) of this subsection shall be deemed to have exhausted his administrative remedies with respect to such request if the agency fails to comply with the applicable time limit provisions of this paragraph. If the Government can show exceptional circumstances exist and that the agency is exercising due diligence in responding to the request, the court may retain jurisdiction and allow the agency additional time to complete its review of the records. Upon any determination by an agency to comply with a request for records, the records shall be made promptly available to such person making such request. Any notification of denial of any request for records under this subsection shall set forth the names and titles or positions of each person responsible for the denial of such request.

(ii) For purposes of this subparagraph, the term "exceptional circumstances" does not include a delay that results from a predictable agency workload of requests under this section, unless the agency demonstrates reasonable progress in reducing its backlog of pending requests.

(iii) Refusal by a person to reasonably modify the scope of a request or arrange an alternative time frame for processing a request (or a modified request) under clause (ii) after being given an opportunity to do so by the agency to whom the person made the request shall be considered as a factor in determining whether exceptional circumstances exist for purposes of this subparagraph.

(D) (i) Each agency may promulgate regulations, pursuant to notice and receipt of public comment, providing for multitrack processing of requests for records based on the amount of work or time (or both) involved in processing requests.

(ii) Regulations under this subparagraph may provide a person making a request that does not qualify for the fastest multitrack processing an opportunity to limit the scope of the request in order to qualify for faster processing.

(iii) This subparagraph shall not be considered to affect the requirement under subparagraph (C) to exercise due diligence.

(E) (i) Each agency shall promulgate regulations, pursuant to notice and receipt of public comment, providing for expedited processing of requests for records—

(I) in cases in which the person requesting the records demonstrates a compelling need; and

(II) in other cases determined by the agency.

(ii) Notwithstanding clause (i), regulations under this subparagraph must ensure—

(I) that a determination of whether to provide expedited processing shall be made, and notice of the determination shall be provided to the person making the request, within 10 days after the date of the request; and

(II) expeditious consideration of administrative appeals of such determinations of whether to provide expedited processing.

(iii) An agency shall process as soon as practicable any request for records to which the agency has granted expedited processing under this subparagraph. Agency action to deny or affirm denial of a request for expedited processing pursuant to this subparagraph, and failure by an agency to respond in a timely manner to such a request shall be subject to judicial review under paragraph (4), except that the judicial review shall be based on the record before the agency at the time of the determination.

(iv) A district court of the United States shall not have jurisdiction to review an agency denial of expedited processing of a request for records after the agency has provided a complete response to the request.

(v) For purposes of this subparagraph, the term "compelling need" means—

(I) that a failure to obtain requested records on an expedited basis under this paragraph could reasonably be expected to pose an imminent threat to the life or physical safety of an individual; or

(II) with respect to a request made by a person primarily engaged in disseminating information, urgency to inform the public concerning actual or alleged Federal Government activity.

(vi) A demonstration of a compelling need by a person making a request for expedited processing shall be made by a statement certified by such person to be true and correct to the best of such person's knowledge and belief.

(F) In denying a request for records, in whole or in part, an agency shall make a reasonable effort to estimate the volume of any requested matter the provision of which is denied, and shall provide any such estimate to the person making the request, unless providing such estimate would harm an interest protected by the exemption in subsection (b) pursuant to which the denial is made.

(b) This section does not apply to matters that are—

(1) (A) specifically authorized under criteria established by an Executive order to be kept secret in the interest of national defense or foreign policy and

(B) are in fact properly classified pursuant to such Executive order;

(2) related solely to the internal personnel rules and practices of an agency;

(3) specifically exempted from disclosure by statute (other than section 552b of this title) provided that such statute (A) requires that the matters be withheld from the public in such a manner as to leave no discretion on the issue, or (B) establishes particular criteria for withholding or refers to particular types of matters to be withheld;

(4) trade secrets and commercial or financial information obtained from a person and privileged or confidential;

(5) inter-agency or intra-agency memorandums or letters which would not be available by law to a party other than an agency in litigation with the agency;

(6) personnel and medical files and similar files the disclosure of which would constitute a clearly unwarranted invasion of personal privacy;

(7) records or information compiled for law enforcement purposes, but only to the extent that the production of such law enforcement records or information

(A) could reasonably be expected to interfere with enforcement proceedings,

(B) would deprive a person of a right to a fair trial or an impartial adjudication,

(C) could reasonably be expected to constitute an unwarranted invasion of personal privacy,

(D) could reasonably be expected to disclose the identity of a confidential source, including a State, local, or foreign agency or authority or any private institution which furnished information on a confidential basis, and, in the case of a record or information compiled by criminal law enforcement authority in the course of a criminal investigation or by an agency conducting a lawful national security intelligence investigation, information furnished by a confidential source,

(E) would disclose techniques and procedures for law enforcement investigations or prosecutions, or would disclose guidelines for law enforcement investigations or prosecutions if such disclosure could reasonably be expected to risk circumvention of the law, or

(F) could reasonably be expected to endanger the life or physical safety of any individual;

(8) contained in or related to examination, operating, or condition reports prepared by, on behalf of, or for the use of an agency responsible for the regulation or supervision of financial institutions; or

(9) geological or geophysical information and data, including maps, concerning wells.

Any reasonably segregable portion of a record shall be provided to any person requesting such record after deletion of the portions which are exempt under this subsection. The amount of information deleted shall be indicated on the released portion of the record, unless including that indication would harm an interest protected by the exemption in this subsection under which the deletion is made. If technically feasible, the amount of the information deleted shall be indicated at the place in the record where such deletion is made.

(c) (1) Whenever a request is made which involves access to records described in subsection (b)(7)(A) and—

(A) the investigation or proceeding involves a possible violation of criminal law; and

(B) there is reason to believe that

(i) the subject of the investigation or proceeding is not aware of its pendency, and

(ii) disclosure of the existence of the records could reasonably be expected to interfere with enforcement proceedings, the agency may, during only such time as that circumstance continues, treat the records as not subject to the requirements of this section.

(2) Whenever informant records maintained by a criminal law enforcement agency under an informant's name or personal identifier are requested by a third party according to the informant's name or personal identifier, the agency may treat the records as not subject to the requirements of this section unless the informant's status as an informant has been officially confirmed.

(3) Whenever a request is made which involves access to records maintained by the Federal Bureau of Investigation pertaining to foreign intelligence or counterintelligence, or international terrorism, and the existence of the records is classified information as provided in subsection (b)(1), the Bureau may, as long as the existence of the records remains classified information, treat the records as not subject to the requirements of this section.

(d) This section does not authorize withholding of information or limit the availability of records to the public, except as specifically stated in this section. This section is not authority to withhold information from Congress.

(e) (1) On or before February 1 of each year, each agency shall submit to the Attorney General of the United States a report which shall cover the preceding fiscal year and which shall include—

(A) the number of determinations made by the agency not to comply with requests for records made to such agency under subsection (a) and the reasons for each such determination;

(B) (i) the number of appeals made by persons under subsection (a)(6), the result of such appeals, and the reason for the action upon each appeal that results in a denial of information; and

(ii) a complete list of all statutes that the agency relies upon to authorize the agency to withhold information under subsection (b)(3), a description of whether a court has upheld the decision of the agency to withhold information under each such statute, and a concise description of the scope of any information withheld;

(C) the number of requests for records pending before the agency as of September 30 of the preceding year, and the median number of days that such requests had been pending before the agency as of that date;

(D) the number of requests for records received by the agency and the number of requests which the agency processed;

(E) the median number of days taken by the agency to process different types of requests;

(F) the total amount of fees collected by the agency for processing requests; and

(G) the number of full-time staff of the agency devoted to processing requests for records under this section, and the total amount expended by the agency for processing such requests.

(2) Each agency shall make each such report available to the public including by computer telecommunications, or if computer telecommunications means have not been established by the agency, by other electronic means.

(3) The Attorney General of the United States shall make each report which has been made available by electronic means available at a single electronic access point. The Attorney General of the United States shall notify the Chairman and ranking minority member of the Committee on Government Reform and Oversight of the House of Representatives and the Chairman and ranking minority member of the Committees on Governmental Affairs and the Judiciary of the Senate, no later than April 1 of the year in which each such report is issued, that such reports are available by electronic means.

(4) The Attorney General of the United States, in consultation with the Director of the Office of Management and Budget, shall develop reporting and performance guidelines in connection with reports required by this subsection by October 1, 1997, and may establish additional requirements for such reports as the Attorney General determines may be useful.

(5) The Attorney General of the United States shall submit an annual report on or before April 1 of each calendar year which shall include for the prior calendar year a listing of the number of cases arising under this section, the exemption involved in each case, the disposition of such case, and the cost, fees, and penalties assessed under subparagraphs (E), (F), and (G) of subsection (a)(4). Such report shall also include a description of the efforts undertaken by the Department of Justice to encourage agency compliance with this section.

(f) For purposes of this section, the term—

(1) "agency" as defined in section 551(1) of this title [5 USCS § 551(1)] includes any executive department, military department, Government corporation, Government controlled corporation, or other establishment in the executive branch of the Government (including the Executive Office of the President), or any independent regulatory agency; and

(2) "record" and any other term used in this section in reference to information includes any information that would be an agency record subject to the requirements of this section when maintained by an agency in any format, including an electronic format.

(g) The head of each agency shall prepare and make publicly available upon request, reference material or a guide for requesting records or information from the agency, subject to the exemptions in subsection (b), including—

(1) an index of all major information systems of the agency;

(2) a description of major information and record locator systems maintained by the agency; and

(3) a handbook for obtaining various types and categories of public information from the agency pursuant to chapter 35 of title 44 [44 USCS §§ 3501 et seq.], and under this section.

(Sept. 6, 1966, P.L. 89-554, § 1, 80 Stat. 383; June 5, 1967, P.L. 90-23 § 1, 81 Stat. 54; Nov. 21, 1974, P.L. 93-502, §§ 1–3, 88 Stat. 1561, 1563, 1564; Sept. 13, 1976, P.L. 94-409, § 5(b), 90 Stat. 1247; Oct. 13, 1978, P.L. 95-454, Title IX, § 906(a)(10), 92 Stat. 1225; Nov. 8, 1984, P.L. 98-620, Title IV, Subtitle A, § 402(2), 98 Stat. 3357; Oct. 27, 1986, P.L. 99-570, Title I, Subtitle N, §§ 1802, 1803, 100 Stat. 3207-48, 3207-49.)

(As amended Oct. 2, 1996, P.L. 104-231, §§ 3–11, 110 Stat. 3049; Nov. 27, 2002, P.L. 107-306, Title III, Subtitle B, § 312, 116 Stat. 2390.)

PRIVACY ACT OF 1974*

§ 552a. Records maintained on individuals

(a) Definitions. For purposes of this section—

(1) the term "agency" means agency as defined in section 552[(f)](e) of this title;

(2) the term "individual" means a citizen of the United States or an alien lawfully admitted for permanent residence;

(3) the term "maintain" includes maintain, collect, use, or disseminate;

(4) the term "record" means any item, collection, or grouping of information about an individual that is maintained by an agency, including, but not limited to, his education, financial transactions, medical history, and criminal or employment history and that contains his name, or the identifying number, symbol, or other identifying particular assigned to the individual, such as a finger or voice print or a photograph;

....

(8) the term "matching program"—

....

(B) but does not include—

....

(vi) matches performed for foreign counterintelligence purposes or to produce background checks for security clearances of Federal personnel or Federal contractor personnel;

....

(b) Conditions of disclosure. No agency shall disclose any record which is contained in a system of records by any means of communication to any person, or to another agency, except pursuant to a written request by, or with the prior written consent of, the individual to whom the record pertains, unless disclosure of the record would be—

....

(7) to another agency or to an instrumentality of any governmental jurisdiction within or under the control of the United States for a civil or criminal law enforcement activity if the activity is authorized by law, and if the head of the agency or instrumentality has made a written request to the agency which maintains the record specifying the particular portion desired and the law enforcement activity for which the record is sought;

....

(e) Agency requirements. Each agency that maintains a system of records shall—

(1) maintain in its records only such information about an individual as is relevant and necessary to accomplish a purpose of the agency required to be accomplished by statute or by executive order of the President;

* Privacy Act of 1974, Pub. L. No. 93-579, 88 Stat. 1897 (codified as amended at 5 U.S.C.A. § 552a (West 1996 & Supp. 2005)), *available at* http://www.usdoj.gov/04foia/privstat.htm.

....

(7) maintain no record describing how any individual exercises rights guaranteed by the First Amendment unless expressly authorized by statute or by the individual about whom the record is maintained or unless pertinent to and within the scope of an authorized law enforcement activity;

(8) make reasonable efforts to serve notice on an individual when any record on such individual is made available to any person under compulsory legal process when such process becomes a matter of public record;

....

(10) establish appropriate administrative, technical, and physical safeguards to insure the security and confidentiality of records and to protect against any anticipated threats or hazards to their security or integrity which could result in substantial harm, embarrassment, inconvenience, or unfairness to any individual on whom information is maintained;

....

(f) Agency Rules. In order to carry out the provisions of this section, each agency that maintains a system of records shall promulgate rules, in accordance with the requirements (including general notice) of section 553 of this title [5 USCS § 553], which shall—

(1) establish procedures whereby an individual can be notified in response to his request if any system of records named by the individual contains a record pertaining to him;

....

(i) Criminal penalties.

(1) Any officer or employee of an agency, who by virtue of his employment or official position, has possession of, or access to, agency records which contain individually identifiable information the disclosure of which is prohibited by this section or by rules or regulations established thereunder, and who knowing that disclosure of the specific material is so prohibited, willfully discloses the material in any manner to any person or agency not entitled to receive it, shall be guilty of a misdemeanor and fined not more than $5,000.

(2) Any officer or employee of any agency who willfully maintains a system of records without meeting the notice requirements of subsection (e)(4) of this section shall be guilty of a misdemeanor and fined not more than $5,000.

(3) Any person who knowingly and willfully requests or obtains any record concerning an individual from an agency under false pretenses shall be guilty of a misdemeanor and fined not more than $5,000.

(j) General exemptions. The head of any agency may promulgate rules, in accordance with the requirements (including general notice) of sections 553(b)(1), (2), and (3), (c), and (e) of this title [5 USCS §§ 553(b)(1), (2), and (3), (c), and (e)], to exempt any system of records within the agency from any part of this section except subsections (b), (c)(1) and (2), (e)(4)(A) through (F), (e)(6), (7), (9), (10), and (11), and (i) if the system of records is—

(1) maintained by the Central Intelligence Agency; or

(2) maintained by an agency or component thereof which performs as its principal function any activity pertaining to the enforcement of criminal laws, includ-

ing police efforts to prevent, control, or reduce crime or to apprehend criminals, and the activities of prosecutors, courts, correctional, probation, pardon, or parole authorities, and which consists of

(A) information compiled for the purpose of identifying individual criminal offenders and alleged offenders and consisting only of identifying data and notations of arrests, the nature and disposition of criminal charges, sentencing, confinement, release, and parole and probation status;

(B) information compiled for the purpose of a criminal investigation, including reports of informants and investigators, and associated with an identifiable individual; or

(C) reports identifiable to an individual compiled at any stage of the process of enforcement of the criminal laws from arrest or indictment through release from supervision.

....

(k) Specific exemptions. The head of any agency may promulgate rules, in accordance with the requirements (including general notice) of sections 553(b)(1), (2), and (3), (c), and (e) of this title [5 USCS §§553(b)(1), (2), and (3), (c), and (e)], to exempt any system of records within the agency from subsections (c)(3), (d), (e)(1), (e)(4)(G), (H), and (I) and (f) of this section if the system of records is—

(1) subject to provisions of section 552(b)(1) of this title *[5 USCS §552*(b)(1)];

(2) investigatory material compiled for law enforcement purposes, other than material within the scope of subsection (j)(2) of this section: *Provided, however,* That if any individual is denied any right, privilege, or benefit that he would otherwise be entitled by Federal law, or for which he would otherwise be eligible, as a result of the maintenance of such material, such material shall be provided to such individual, except to the extent that the disclosure of such material would reveal the identity of a source who furnished information to the Government under an express promise that the identity of the source would be held in confidence, or, prior to the effective date of this section, under an implied promise that the identity of the source would be held in confidence;

(3) maintained in connection with providing protective services to the President of the United States or other individuals pursuant to section 3056 of title 18;

....

(5) investigatory material compiled solely for the purpose of determining suitability, eligibility, or qualifications for Federal civilian employment, military service, Federal contracts, or access to classified information, but only to the extent that the disclosure of such material would reveal the identity of a source who furnished information to the Government under an express promise that the identity of the source would be held in confidence, or, prior to the effective date of this section, under an implied promise that the identity of the source would be held in confidence;

....

(7) evaluation material used to determine potential for promotion in the armed services, but only to the extent that the disclosure of such material would reveal the identity of a source who furnished information to the Government under an express promise that the identity of the source would be held in confidence, or, prior

to the effective date of this section, under an implied promise that the identity of the source would be held in confidence.

. . . .

(Added Dec. 31, 1974, P.L. 93-579, § 3, 88 Stat. 1897; Dec. 31, 1975, P.L. 94-183, § 2(2), 89 Stat 1057; Oct. 25, 1982, P.L. 97-365, § 2, 96 Stat. 1749; Dec. 21, 1982, P.L. 97-375, Title II, § 201(a), (b), 96 Stat. 1821; Jan. 12, 1983, P.L. 97-452, § 2(a)(1), 96 Stat. 2478; Oct. 15, 1984, P.L. 98-477, § 2(c), 98 Stat. 2211; Oct. 19, 1984, P.L. 98-497, Title I, § 107(g), 98 Stat. 2292; Oct. 18, 1988, P.L. 100-503, §§ 2–5, 6(a), 7, 8, 102 Stat. 2507-2514.)

(As amended Nov. 5, 1990, P.L. 101-508, Title VII, Subtitle C, § 7201(b)(1), 104 Stat. 1388-334; Aug. 10, 1993, P.L. 103-66, Title XIII, Ch 2, Subch A, Part V, § 13581(c), 107 Stat. 611; Aug. 22, 1996, P.L. 104-193, Title I, § 110(w), 110 Stat. 2175; Oct. 2, 1996, P.L. 104-226, § 1(b)(3), 110 Stat. 3033; Oct. 19, 1996, P.L. 104-316, Title I, § 115(g)(2)(B), 110 Stat. 3835; Aug. 5, 1997, P.L. 105-34, Title IX, Subtitle C, § 1026(b)(2), 111 Stat. 925; Nov. 10, 1998, P.L. 105-362, Title XIII, § 1301(d), 112 Stat. 3293; Dec. 17, 1999, P.L. 106-170, Title IV, § 402(a)(2), 113 Stat. 1908.)

GOVERNMENT IN THE SUNSHINE ACT*

§ 552b. Open meetings

....

(b) Members [of a collegial body heading an agency] shall not jointly conduct or dispose of agency business other than in accordance with this section. Except as provided in subsection (c), every portion of every meeting of an agency shall be open to public observation.

(c) Except in a case where the agency finds that the public interest requires otherwise, the second sentence of subsection (b) shall not apply to any portion of an agency meeting, and the requirements of subsections (d) and (e) shall not apply to any information pertaining to such meeting otherwise required by this section to be disclosed to the public, where the agency properly determines that such portion or portions of its meeting or the disclosure of such information is likely to—

(1) disclose matters that are (A) specifically authorized under criteria established by an Executive order to be kept secret in the interests of national defense or foreign policy and (B) in fact properly classified pursuant to such Executive order;

....

(3) disclose matters specifically exempted from disclosure by statute (other than section 552 of this title [5 USCS § 552]), provided that such statute (A) requires that the matters be withheld from the public in such a manner as to leave no discretion on the issue, or (B) establishes particular criteria for withholding or refers to particular types of matters to be withheld;

....

(7) disclose investigatory records compiled for law enforcement purposes, or information which if written would be contained in such records, but only to the extent that the production of such records or information would:....

(D) disclose the identity of a confidential source and, in the case of a record compiled by a criminal law enforcement authority in the course of a criminal investigation, or by an agency conducting a lawful national security intelligence investigation, confidential information furnished only by the confidential source,

(E) disclose investigative techniques and procedures, or

(F) endanger the life or physical safety of law enforcement personnel;

....

(d) (1) Action under subsection (c) shall be taken only when a majority of the entire membership of the agency...votes to take such action.

....

* Government in the Sunshine Act, Pub. L. No. 94-409, 90 Stat. 1241 (1976) (codified as amended at 5 U.S.C. § 552b (2000)), *available at* http://www.usdoj.gov/foia/gisastat.pdf.

(e) (1) In the case of each meeting, the agency shall make public announcement, at least one week before the meeting, of the time, place, and subject matter of the meeting, whether it is to be open or closed to the public, and the name and phone number of the official designated by the agency to respond to requests for information about the meeting....

....

(f) (1) For every meeting closed pursuant to paragraphs (1) through (10) of subsection (c), the General Counsel or chief legal officer of the agency shall publicly certify that, in his or her opinion, the meeting may be closed to the public and shall state each relevant exemptive provision....

....

(2) The agency shall make promptly available to the public, in a place easily accessible to the public, the transcript, electronic recording, or minutes (as required by paragraph (1)) of the discussion of any item on the agenda, or of any item of the testimony of any witness received at the meeting, except for such item or items of such discussion or testimony as the agency determines to contain information which may be withheld under subsection (c)....

....

(g) Each agency subject to the requirements of this section shall, within 180 days after the date of enactment of this section [enacted Sept. 13, 1976], following consultation with the Office of the Chairman of the Administrative Conference of the United States and published notice in the Federal Register of at least thirty days and opportunity for written comment by any person, promulgate regulations to implement the requirements of subsections (b) through (f) of this section....

....

(h) (1) The district courts of the United States shall have jurisdiction to enforce the requirements of subsections (b) through (f) of this section by declaratory judgment, injunctive relief, or other relief as may be appropriate....

....

(j) Each agency subject to the requirements of this section shall annually report to the Congress regarding the following:

(1) The changes in the policies and procedures of the agency under this section that have occurred during the preceding 1-year period.

(2) A tabulation of the number of meetings held, the exemptions applied to close meetings, and the days of public notice provided to close meetings.

(3) A brief description of litigation or formal complaints concerning the implementation of this section by the agency.

(4) A brief explanation of any changes in law that have affected the responsibilities of the agency under this section.

....

(l) This section does not constitute authority to withhold any information from Congress, and does not authorize the closing of any agency meeting or portion thereof required by any other provision of law to be open.

....

CLASSIFIED INFORMATION PROCEDURES ACT*

....

DEFINITIONS

Sec. 1. (a) "Classified information", as used in this Act, means any information or material that has been determined by the United States Government pursuant to an Executive order, statute, or regulation, to require protection against unauthorized disclosure for reasons of national security and any restricted data, as defined in paragraph r. of section 11 of the Atomic Energy Act of 1954 (42 U.S.C. 2014(y)).

(b) "National security", as used in this Act, means the national defense and foreign relations of the United States.

PRETRIAL CONFERENCE

Sec. 2. At any time after the filing of the indictment or information, any party may move for a pretrial conference to consider matters relating to classified information that may arise in connection with the prosecution. Following such motion, or on its own motion, the court shall promptly hold a pretrial conference to establish the timing of requests for discovery, the provision of notice required by section 5 of this Act, and the initiation of the procedure established by section 6 of this Act. In addition, at the pretrial conference the court may consider any matters which relate to classified information or which may promote a fair and expeditious trial. No admission made by the defendant or by any attorney for the defendant at such a conference may be used against the defendant unless the admission is in writing and is signed by the defendant and by the attorney for the defendant.

PROTECTIVE ORDERS

Sec. 3. Upon motion of the United States, the court shall issue an order to protect against the disclosure of any classified information disclosed by the United States to any defendant in any criminal case in a district court of the United States.

DISCOVERY OF CLASSIFIED INFORMATION BY DEFENDANTS

Sec. 4. The court, upon a sufficient showing, may authorize the United States to delete specified items of classified information from documents to be made available to the defendant through discovery under the Federal Rules of Criminal Procedure, to substitute a summary of the information for such classified documents, or to substitute a statement admitting relevant facts that the classified information would tend to prove. The court may permit the United States to make a request for such authorization in the form of a written statement to be inspected by the court alone. If the court enters an

* Classified Information Procedures Act, Pub. L. No. 96-456, 94 Stat. 2025 (1980) (codified as amended at 18 U.S.C.A. app. 3 (West 2000 & Supp. 2005)), *available at* http://www.fas.org/irp/offdocs/laws/pl096456.htm.

order granting relief following such an ex parte showing, the entire text of the statement of the United States shall be sealed and preserved in the records of the court to be made available to the appellate court in the event of an appeal.

NOTICE OF DEFENDANT'S INTENTION TO DISCLOSE CLASSIFIED INFORMATION

Sec. 5. (a) **Notice by defendant.**—If a defendant reasonably expects to disclose or to cause the disclosure of classified information in any manner in connection with any trial or pretrial proceeding involving the criminal prosecution of such defendant, the defendant shall, within the time specified by the court or, where no time is specified, within thirty days prior to trial, notify the attorney for the United States and the court in writing. Such notice shall include a brief description of the classified information. Whenever a defendant learns of additional classified information he reasonably expects to disclose at any such proceeding, he shall notify the attorney for the United States and the court in writing as soon as possible thereafter and shall include a brief description of the classified information. No defendant shall disclose any information known or believed to be classified in connection with a trial or pretrial proceeding until notice has been given under this subsection and until the United States has been afforded a reasonable opportunity to seek a determination pursuant to the procedure set forth in section 6 of this Act, and until the time for the United States to appeal such determination under section 7 has expired or any appeal under section 7 by the United States is decided.

(b) **Failure to comply.**—If the defendant fails to comply with the requirements of subsection (a) the court may preclude disclosure of any classified information not made the subject of notification and may prohibit the examination by the defendant of any witness with respect to any such information.

PROCEDURE FOR CASES INVOLVING CLASSIFIED INFORMATION

Sec. 6. (a) **Motion for hearing.**—Within the time specified by the court for the filing of a motion under this section, the United States may request the court to conduct a hearing to make all determinations concerning the use, relevance, or admissibility of classified information that would otherwise be made during the trial or pretrial proceeding. Upon such a request, the court shall conduct such a hearing. Any hearing held pursuant to this subsection (or any portion of such hearing specified in the request of the Attorney General) shall be held in camera if the Attorney General certifies to the court in such petition that a public proceeding may result in the disclosure of classified information. As to each item of classified information, the court shall set forth in writing the basis for its determination. Where the United States' motion under this subsection is filed prior to the trial or pretrial proceeding, the court shall rule prior to the commencement of the relevant proceeding.

(b) **Notice.**—(1) Before any hearing is conducted pursuant to a request by the United States under subsection (a), the United States shall provide the defendant with notice of the classified information that is at issue. Such notice shall identify the specific classified information at issue whenever that information previously has been made available to the defendant by the United States. When the United States has not previously made the information available to the defendant in connection with the case, the information may be described by generic category, in such form as the court may approve, rather than by identification of the specific information of concern to the United States.

(2) Whenever the United States requests a hearing under subsection (a), the court, upon request of the defendant, may order the United States to provide the defendant, prior to trial, such details as to the portion of the indictment or information at issue in the hearing as are needed to give the defendant fair notice to prepare for the hearing.

(c) **Alternative procedure for disclosure of classified information.**—(1) Upon any determination by the court authorizing the disclosure of specific classified information under the procedures established by this section, the United States may move that, in lieu of the disclosure of such specific classified information, the court order—

(A) the substitution for such classified information of a statement admitting relevant facts that the specific classified information would tend to prove; or

(B) the substitution for such classified information of a summary of the specific classified information.

The court shall grant such a motion of the United States if it finds that the statement or summary will provide the defendant with substantially the same ability to make his defense as would disclosure of the specific classified information. The court shall hold a hearing on any motion under this section. Any such hearing shall be held in camera at the request of the Attorney General.

(2) The United States may, in connection with a motion under paragraph (1), submit to the court an affidavit of the Attorney General certifying that disclosure of classified information would cause identifiable damage to the national security of the United States and explaining the basis for the classification of such information. If so requested by the United States, the court shall examine such affidavit in camera and ex parte.

(d) **Sealing of records of in camera hearings.**—If at the close of an in camera hearing under this Act (or any portion of a hearing under this Act that is held in camera) the court determines that the classified information at issue may not be disclosed or elicited at the trial or pretrial proceeding, the record of such in camera hearing shall be sealed and preserved by the court for use in the event of an appeal. The defendant may seek reconsideration of the court's determination prior to or during trial.

(e) **Prohibition on disclosure of classified information by defendant, relief for defendant when United States opposes disclosure.**—(1) Whenever the court denies a motion by the United States that it issue an order under subsection (c) and the United States files with the court an affidavit of the Attorney General objecting to disclosure of the classified information at issue, the court shall order that the defendant not disclose or cause the disclosure of such information.

(2) Whenever a defendant is prevented by an order under paragraph (1) from disclosing or causing the disclosure of classified information, the court shall dismiss the indictment or information; except that, when the court determines that the interests of justice would not be served by dismissal of the indictment or information, the court shall order such other action, in lieu of dismissing the indictment or information, as the court determines is appropriate. Such action may include, but need not be limited to—

(A) dismissing specified counts of the indictment or information;

(B) finding against the United States on any issue as to which the excluded classified information relates; or

(C) striking or precluding all or part of the testimony of a witness.

An order under this paragraph shall not take effect until the court has afforded the United States an opportunity to appeal such order under section 7, and thereafter to withdraw its objection to the disclosure of the classified information at issue.

(f) **Reciprocity.**—Whenever the court determines pursuant to subsection (a) that classified information may be disclosed in connection with a trial or pretrial proceeding, the court shall, unless the interests of fairness do not so require, order the United States to provide the defendant with the information it expects to use to rebut the classified information. The court may place the United States under a continuing duty to disclose such rebuttal information. If the United States fails to comply with its obligation under this subsection, the court may exclude any evidence not made the subject of a required disclosure and may prohibit the examination by the United States of any witness with respect to such information.

INTERLOCUTORY APPEAL

Sec. 7. (a) An interlocutory appeal by the United States taken before or after the defendant has been placed in jeopardy shall lie to a court of appeals from a decision or order of a district court in a criminal case authorizing the disclosure of classified information, imposing sanctions for nondisclosure of classified information, or refusing a protective order sought by the United States to prevent the disclosure of classified information.

(b) An appeal taken pursuant to this section either before or during trial shall be expedited by the court of appeals. Prior to trial, an appeal shall be taken within ten days after the decision or order appealed from and the trial shall not commence until the appeal is resolved. If an appeal is taken during trial, the trial court shall adjourn the trial until the appeal is resolved and the court of appeals—

(1) shall hear argument on such appeal within four days of the adjournment of the trial,

(2) may dispense with written briefs other than the supporting materials previously submitted to the trial court,

(3) shall render its decision within four days of argument on appeal, and

(4) may dispense with the issuance of a written opinion in rendering its decision.

Such appeal and decision shall not affect the right of the defendant, in a subsequent appeal from a judgment of conviction, to claim as error reversal by the trial court on remand of a ruling appealed from during trial.

INTRODUCTION OF CLASSIFIED INFORMATION

Sec. 8. (a) **Classification status.**—Writings, recordings, and photographs containing classified information may be admitted into evidence without change in their classification status.

(b) **Precautions by court.**—The court, in order to prevent unnecessary disclosure of classified information involved in any criminal proceeding, may order admission into evidence of only part of a writing, recording, or photograph, or may order admission into evidence of the whole writing, recording, or photograph with excision of some or all of the classified information contained therein, unless the whole ought in fairness be considered.

(c) **Taking of testimony.**—During the examination of a witness in any criminal proceeding, the United States may object to any question or line of inquiry that may require the witness to disclose classified information not previously found to be admissible. Following such an objection, the court shall take such suitable action to determine whether the response is admissible as will safeguard against the compromise of any classified information. Such action may include requiring the United States to provide the court with a proffer of the witness' response to the question or line of inquiry and requiring the defendant to provide the court with a proffer of the nature of the information he seeks to elicit.

. . . .

PRESIDENTIAL DECISION DIRECTIVE 39* (POLICY ON COUNTERTERRORISM)

Presidential Decision Directive 39

June 21, 1995

SUBJECT: U.S. Policy on Counterterrorism

It is the policy of the United States to deter, defeat and respond vigorously to all terrorist attacks on our territory and against our citizens, or facilities, whether they occur domestically, in international waters or airspace or on foreign territory. The United States regards all such terrorism as a potential threat to national security as well as a criminal act and will apply all appropriate means to combat it. In doing so, the U.S. shall pursue vigorously efforts to deter and preempt, apprehend and prosecute, or assist other governments to prosecute, individuals who perpetrate or plan to perpetrate such attacks.

We shall work closely with friendly governments in carrying out our counterterrorism policy and will support Allied and friendly governments in combating terrorist threats against them.

Furthermore, the United States shall seek to identify groups or states that sponsor or support such terrorists, isolate them and extract a heavy price for their actions.

It is the policy of the United States not to make concessions to terrorists.

To ensure that the United States is prepared to combat domestic and international terrorism in all its forms, I direct the following steps be taken.

1. *Reducing our Vulnerabilities*

The United States shall reduce its vulnerabilities to terrorism, at home and abroad.

It shall be the responsibility of all Department and Agency heads to ensure that their personnel and facilities, and the people and facilities under their jurisdiction, are fully protected against terrorism. With regard to ensuring security:

— The Attorney General, as the chief law enforcement officer, shall chair a Cabinet Committee to review the vulnerability to terrorism of government facilities in the United States and critical national infrastructure and make recommendations to me and the appropriate Cabinet member or Agency head;

— The Director, FBI, as head of the investigative agency for terrorism, shall reduce vulnerabilities by an expanded program of counterterrorism;

— The Secretary of State shall reduce vulnerabilities affecting the security of all personnel and facilities at non-military U.S. Government installations abroad and affecting the general safety of American citizens abroad);

— The Secretary of Defense shall reduce vulnerabilities affecting the security of all U.S. military personnel (except those assigned to diplomatic missions and facilities);

---

* Presidential Decision Directive No. 39, U.S. Policy on Counterterrorism (June 21, 1995), *available at* http://www.fas.org/irp/offdocs/pdd39.htm.

— The Secretary of Transportation shall reduce vulnerabilities affecting the security of all airports in the U.S. and all aircraft and passengers and all maritime shipping under U.S. flag or registration or operating within the territory of the United States and shall coordinate security measures for rail, highway, mass transit and pipeline facilities);

— The Secretary of State and the Attorney General, in addition to the latter's overall responsibilities as the chief law enforcement official, shall use all legal means available to exclude from the United States persons who pose a terrorist threat and deport or otherwise remove from the United States any such aliens;

— The Secretary of the Treasury shall reduce vulnerabilities by preventing unlawful traffic in firearms and explosives, by protecting the President and other officials against terrorist attack and through enforcement of laws controlling movement of assets, and export from or import into the United States of goods and services, subject to jurisdiction of the Department of the Treasury;

— The Director, Central Intelligence shall lead the efforts of the Intelligence Community to reduce U.S. vulnerabilities to international terrorism through an aggressive program of foreign intelligence collection, analysis, counterintelligence and covert action in accordance with the National Security Act of 1947 and E.O. 12333.

2. *Deterring Terrorism*

The United States shall seek to deter terrorism through a clear public position that our policies will not be affected by terrorist acts and that we will act vigorously to deal with terrorists and their sponsors. Our actions will reduce the capabilities and support available to terrorists.

[CLASSIFIED MATERIAL DELETED]

Within the United States, we shall vigorously apply U.S. laws and seek new legislation to prevent terrorist groups from operating in the United States or using it as a base for recruitment, training, fund raising or other related activities.

- *Return of Indicted Terrorists to the U.S. for Prosecution:* We shall vigorously apply extraterritorial statutes to counter acts of terrorism and apprehend terrorists outside of the United States. When terrorists wanted for violation of U.S. law are at large overseas, their return for prosecution shall be a matter of the highest priority and shall be a continuing central issue in bilateral relations with any state that harbors or assists them. Where we do not have adequate arrangements, the Departments of State and Justice shall work to resolve the problem, where possible and appropriate, through negotiation and conclusion of new extradition treaties.

  If we do not receive adequate cooperation from a state that harbors a terrorist whose extradition we are seeking, we shall take appropriate measures to induce cooperation. Return of suspects by force may be effected without the cooperation of the host government, consistent with the procedures outlined in NSD-77, which shall remain in effect.

- *State Support and Sponsorship:* Foreign governments assist terrorists in a variety of ways.

[CLASSIFIED MATERIAL DELETED]

C. *Enhancing Counterterrorism Capabilities:* The Secretaries of State, Defense, Treasury, Energy and Transportation, the Attorney General, the Director of Central Intelligence and the Director, FBI shall ensure that their organizations' counterterrorism capabilities within their present areas of responsibility are well managed, funded and exercised.

[CLASSIFIED MATERIAL DELETED]

3. *Responding to Terrorism*

We shall have the ability to respond rapidly and decisively to terrorism directed against us wherever it occurs, to protect Americans, arrest or defeat the perpetrators, respond with all appropriate instruments against the sponsoring organizations and governments and provide recovery relief to victims, as permitted by law.

[CLASSIFIED MATERIAL DELETED]

D. *Lead Agency Responsibilities:* This directive validates and reaffirms existing lead agency responsibilities for all facets of the United States counterterrorism effort. Lead agencies are those that have the most direct role in and responsibility for implementation of U.S. counterterrorism policy, as set forth in this Directive. Lead agencies will normally be designated as follows:

The Department of State is the lead agency for international terrorist incidents that take place outside of U.S. territory, other than incidents on U.S. flag vessels in international waters. The State Department shall act through U.S. ambassadors as the on-scene coordinators for the U.S. Government. Once military force has been directed, however, the National Command Authority shall exercise control of the U.S. military force.

[CLASSIFIED MATERIAL DELETED]

F. *Interagency Support:* To ensure that the full range of necessary expertise and capabilities are available to the on-scene coordinator, there shall be a rapidly deployable interagency Emergency Support Team (EST). The State Department shall be responsible for leading and managing the Foreign Emergency Support Team (FEST) in foreign incidents. The FBI shall be responsible for the Domestic Emergency Support Team (DEST) in domestic incidents. The DEST shall consist only of those agencies needed to respond to the specific requirements of the incident. Membership in the two teams shall include modules for specific types of incidents such as nuclear, biological or chemical threats. The Defense Department shall provide timely transportation for ESTs.

G. *Transportation-related terrorism:* The Federal Aviation Administration has exclusive responsibility in instances of air piracy for the coordination of any law enforcement activity affecting the safety of persons aboard aircraft within the special aircraft jurisdiction of the UPS as defined in public law. The Department of Justice, acting through the FBI, shall establish and maintain procedures, in coordination with the Departments of State, Defense, and Transportation, to ensure the efficient resolution of terrorist hijackings. These procedures shall be based on the principle of lead agency responsibility for command, control and rules of engagement.

H. *Consequence Management:* The Director of the Federal Emergency Management Agency shall ensure that the Federal Response Plan is adequate to respond to the consequences of terrorism directed against large populations in the United States, including terrorism involving weapons of mass destruction. FEMA shall ensure that States' response plans are adequate and their capabilities are tested. The State Department shall develop a plan with the Office of Foreign Disaster Assistance and DOD to Provide assistance to foreign populations so victimized.

[CLASSIFIED MATERIAL DELETED]

K. *Costs:* Agencies directed to participate in the resolution of terrorist incidents or conduct of counterterrorist operations shall bear the costs of their participation, unless otherwise directed by me.

4. *Weapons of Mass Destruction*

The United States shall give the highest priority to developing effective capabilities to detect, prevent, defeat and manage the consequences of nuclear, biological or chemical (NBC) materials or weapons use by terrorists.

The acquisition of weapons of mass destruction by a terrorist group, through theft or manufacture, is unacceptable. There is no higher priority than preventing the acquisition of this capability or removing this capability from terrorist groups potentially opposed to the U.S.

[CLASSIFIED MATERIAL DELETED]

Signed
William J. Clinton

EXECUTIVE ORDER 12968* (EMPLOYEE ACCESS TO CLASSIFIED INFORMATION)

ACCESS TO CLASSIFIED INFORMATION

The national interest requires that certain information be maintained in confidence through a system of classification in order to protect our citizens, our democratic institutions, and our participation within the community of nations. The unauthorized disclosure of information classified in the national interest can cause irreparable damage to the national security and loss of human life.

Security policies designed to protect classified information must ensure consistent, cost effective, and efficient protection of our Nation's classified information, while providing fair and equitable treatment to those Americans upon whom we rely to guard our national security.

This order establishes a uniform Federal personnel security program for employees who will be considered for initial or continued access to classified information.

NOW, THEREFORE, by the authority vested in me as President by the Constitution and the laws of the United States of America, it is hereby ordered as follows:

PART 1—DEFINITIONS, ACCESS TO CLASSIFIED INFORMATION, FINANCIAL DISCLOSURE, AND OTHER ITEMS

Sec. 1.1. Definitions.

For the purposes of this order:

(a) "Agency" means any "Executive agency," as defined in 5 U.S.C. 105, the "military departments," as defined in 5 U.S.C. 102, and any other entity within the executive branch that comes into the possession of classified information, including the Defense Intelligence Agency, National Security Agency, and the National Reconnaissance Office.

(b) "Applicant" means a person other than an employee who has received an authorized conditional offer of employment for a position that requires access to classified information.

(c) "Authorized investigative agency" means an agency authorized by law or regulation to conduct a counterintelligence investigation or investigation of persons who are proposed for access to classified information to ascertain whether such persons satisfy the criteria for obtaining and retaining access to such information.

(d) "Classified information" means information that has been determined pursuant to Executive Order No. 12958, or any successor order, Executive Order No. 12951, or any successor order, or the Atomic Energy Act of 1954 (42 U.S.C. 2011), to require protection against unauthorized disclosure.

(e) "Employee" means a person, other than the President and Vice President, employed by, detailed or assigned to, an agency, including members of the Armed Forces;

* Exec. Order No. 12968, 3 C.F.R. 391 (1995), *reprinted in* 50 U.S.C. § 435 note (2000), *available at* http://www.fas.org/sgp/clinton/eo12968.html.

an expert or consultant to an agency; an industrial or commercial contractor, licensee, certificate holder, or grantee of an agency, including all subcontractors; a personal services contractor; or any other category of person who acts for or on behalf of an agency as determined by the appropriate agency head.

(f) "Foreign power" and "agent of a foreign power" have the meaning provided in 50 U.S.C. 1801.

(g) "Need for access" means a determination that an employee requires access to a particular level of classified information in order to perform or assist in a lawful and authorized governmental function.

(h) "Need-to-know" means a determination made by an authorized holder of classified information that a prospective recipient requires access to specific classified information in order to perform or assist in a lawful and authorized governmental function.

(i) "Overseas Security Policy Board" means the Board established by the President to consider, develop, coordinate and promote policies, standards and agreements on overseas security operations, programs and projects that affect all United States Government agencies under the authority of a Chief of Mission.

(j) "Security Policy Board" means the Board established by the President to consider, coordinate, and recommend policy directives for U.S. security policies, procedures, and practices.

(k) "Special access program" has the meaning provided in section 4.1 of Executive Order No. 12958, or any successor order.

Sec. 1.2. Access to Classified Information.

(a) No employee shall be granted access to classified information unless that employee has been determined to be eligible in accordance with this order and to possess a need-to-know.

(b) Agency heads shall be responsible for establishing and maintaining an effective program to ensure that access to classified information by each employee is clearly consistent with the interests of the national security.

(c) Employees shall not be granted access to classified information unless they:

(1) have been determined to be eligible for access under section 3.1 of this order by agency heads or designated officials based upon a favorable adjudication of an appropriate investigation of the employee's background;

(2) have a demonstrated need-to-know; and

(3) have signed an approved nondisclosure agreement.

(d) All employees shall be subject to investigation by an appropriate government authority prior to being granted access to classified information and at any time during the period of access to ascertain whether they continue to meet the requirements for access.

(e) (1) All employees granted access to classified information shall be required as a condition of such access to provide to the employing agency written consent permitting access by an authorized investigative agency, for such time as access to classified information is maintained and for a period of 3 years thereafter, to:

(A) relevant financial records that are maintained by a financial institution as defined in 31 U.S.C. 5312(a) or by a holding company as defined in section 1101(6) of the Right to Financial Privacy Act of 1978 (12 U.S.C. 3401);

(B) consumer reports pertaining to the employee under the Fair Credit Reporting Act (15 U.S.C. 1681a); and

(C) records maintained by commercial entities within the United States pertaining to any travel by the employee outside the United States.

(2) Information may be requested pursuant to employee consent under this section where:

(A) there are reasonable grounds to believe, based on credible information, that the employee or former employee is, or may be, disclosing classified information in an unauthorized manner to a foreign power or agent of a foreign power;

(B) information the employing agency deems credible indicates the employee or former employee has incurred excessive indebtedness or has acquired a level of affluence that cannot be explained by other information; or

(C) circumstances indicate the employee or former employee had the capability and opportunity to disclose classified information that is known to have been lost or compromised to a foreign power or an agent of a foreign power.

(3) Nothing in this section shall be construed to affect the authority of an investigating agency to obtain information pursuant to the Right to Financial Privacy Act, the Fair Credit Reporting Act or any other applicable law.

Sec. 1.3. Financial Disclosure.

(a) Not later than 180 days after the effective date of this order, the head of each agency that originates, handles, transmits, or possesses classified information shall designate each employee, by position or category where possible, who has a regular need for access to classified information that, in the discretion of the agency head, would reveal:

(1) the identity of covert agents as defined in the Intelligence Identities Protection Act of 1982 (50 U.S.C. 421);

(2) technical or specialized national intelligence collection and processing systems that, if disclosed in an unauthorized manner, would substantially negate or impair the effectiveness of the system;

(3) the details of:

(A) the nature, contents, algorithm, preparation, or use of any code, cipher, or cryptographic system or;

(B) the design, construction, functioning, maintenance, or repair of any cryptographic equipment; but not including information concerning the use of cryptographic equipment and services;

(4) particularly sensitive special access programs, the disclosure of which would substantially negate or impair the effectiveness of the information or activity involved; or

(5) especially sensitive nuclear weapons design information (but only for those positions that have been certified as being of a high degree of importance or sensitivity, as described in section 145(f) of the Atomic Energy Act of 1954, as amended).

(b) An employee may not be granted access, or hold a position designated as requiring access, to information described in subsection (a) unless, as a condition of access to such information, the employee:

(1) files with the head of the agency a financial disclosure report, including information with respect to the spouse and dependent children of the employee, as part of all background investigations or reinvestigations;

(2) is subject to annual financial disclosure requirements, if selected by the agency head; and

(3) files relevant information concerning foreign travel, as determined by the Security Policy Board.

(c) Not later than 180 days after the effective date of this order, the Security Policy Board shall develop procedures for the implementation of this section, including a standard financial disclosure form for use by employees under subsection (b) of this section, and agency heads shall identify certain employees, by position or category, who are subject to annual financial disclosure.

....

PART 2—ACCESS ELIGIBILITY POLICY AND PROCEDURE

Sec. 2.1. Eligibility Determinations.

(a) Determinations of eligibility for access to classified information shall be based on criteria established under this order. Such determinations are separate from suitability determinations with respect to the hiring or retention of persons for employment by the government or any other personnel actions.

....

PART 5—REVIEW OF ACCESS DETERMINATIONS

Sec. 5.1. Determinations of Need for Access.

A determination under section 2.1(b)(4) of this order that an employee does not have, or no longer has, a need for access is a discretionary determination and shall be conclusive.

Sec. 5.2. Review Proceedings for Denials or Revocations of Eligibility for Access.

(a) Applicants and employees who are determined to not meet the standards for access to classified information established in section 3.1 of this order shall be:

(1) provided as comprehensive and detailed a written explanation of the basis for that conclusion as the national security interests of the United States and other applicable law permit;

(2) provided within 30 days, upon request and to the extent the documents would be provided if requested under the Freedom of Information Act (5 U.S.C. 552) or the Privacy Act (3 U.S.C. 552a), as applicable, any documents, records, and reports upon which a denial or revocation is based;

(3) informed of their right to be represented by counsel or other representative at their own expense; to request any documents, records, and reports as described in section 5.2(a)(2) upon which a denial or revocation is based; and to request the entire investigative file, as permitted by the national security and other applicable law, which, if requested, shall be promptly provided prior to the time set for a written reply;

(4) provided a reasonable opportunity to reply in writing to, and to request a review of, the determination;

(5) provided written notice of and reasons for the results of the review, the identity of the deciding authority, and written notice of the right to appeal;

(6) provided an opportunity to appeal in writing to a high level panel, appointed by the agency head, which shall be comprised of at least three members, two of whom shall be selected from outside the security field. Decisions of the panel shall be in writing, and final except as provided in subsection (b) of this section; and

(7) provided an opportunity to appear personally and to present relevant documents, materials, and information at some point in the process before an adjudicative or other authority, other than the investigating entity, as determined by the agency head. A written summary or recording of such appearance shall be made part of the applicant's or employee's security record, unless such appearance occurs in the presence of the appeals panel described in subsection (a)(6) of this section.

....

PART 7—GENERAL PROVISIONS

Sec. 7.1. Classified Information Procedures Act.

Nothing in this order is intended to alter the procedures established under the Classified Information Procedures Act (18 U.S.C. App. 1).

Sec. 7.2. General.

(a) Information obtained by an agency under sections 1.2(e) or 1.3 of this order may not be disseminated outside the agency, except to:

(1) the agency employing the employee who is the subject of the records or information;

(2) the Department of Justice for law enforcement or counterintelligence purposes; or

(3) any agency if such information is clearly relevant to the authorized responsibilities of such agency.

(b) The Attorney General, at the request of the head of an agency, shall render an interpretation of this order with respect to any question arising in the course of its administration.

(c) No prior Executive orders are repealed by this order. To the extent that this order is inconsistent with any provision of any prior Executive order, this order shall control, except that this order shall not diminish or otherwise affect the requirements of Executive Order No. 10450, the denial and revocation procedures provided to individuals covered by Executive Order No. 10865, as amended, or access by historical researchers and former presidential appointees under Executive Order No. 12958 or any successor order.

....

(f) This order is effective immediately.

William J. Clinton
The White House,
August 2, 1995.

DEPARTMENT OF DEFENSE DIRECTIVE 5230.9 CLEARANCE OF DOD INFORMATION FOR PUBLIC RELEASE*

SUBJECT: Clearance of DoD Information for Public Release

References: (a) DoD Directive 5230.9, subject as above, April 2, 1982 (hereby canceled)

(b) *DoD Directive 5110.4,* "Washington Headquarters Services (WHS)," May 10, 1999

(c) DoD Directive 5400.4, "Provision of Information to Congress," January 30, 1978

(d) DoD Directive 5220.22, "DoD Industrial Security Program," December 8, 1980

(e) through (u), see enclosure 1

1. REISSUANCE AND PURPOSE

This Directive reissues reference (a) to update policy and responsibilities for the security and policy review and clearance of official DoD information proposed for official public release by the Department of Defense and its employees under reference (b).

2. APPLICABILITY AND SCOPE

2.1. This Directive applies to:

2.1.1. The Office of the Secretary of Defense (OSD), the Military Departments, the Chairman of the Joint Chiefs of Staff, the Combatant Commands, the Defense Agencies, and the DoD Field Activities (hereafter referred to collectively as "the DoD Components").

2.1.2. All DoD employees.

2.2. For provisions governing review of:

2.2.1. Prepared statements, transcripts of testimony, and other material provided to congressional committees that may be included in the published records, reference (c) applies.

2.2.2. Information before publication or disclosure by DoD contractors, DoD Directive 5220.22 and DoD 5220.22-M (references (d) and (e)) apply.

2.2.3. Release of official information in litigation, DoD Directive 5405.2 (reference (f)) applies.

3. DEFINITIONS

Terms used in this Directive are defined in enclosure 2.

4. POLICY

It is DoD policy that:

---

* (Nov. 21, 2003), http://www.dtic.mil/whs/directives/corres/pdf/d52309wch1_040996/d52309p.pdf.

4.1. Accurate and timely information is made available to the public, the Congress, and the news media to help the analysis and understanding of defense strategy and national security issues.

4.2. Any official DoD information intended for public release that pertains to military matters, national security issues, or subjects of significant concern to the Department of Defense shall be reviewed for clearance by appropriate security review and public affairs offices prior to release.

4.3. The public release of official DoD information is limited only as necessary to safeguard information requiring protection in the interest of national security or other legitimate governmental interest, as authorized by references (g) through (t).

4.4. Information released officially is consistent with established national and DoD policies and programs.

4.5. The Inspector General of the Department of Defense, as an independent and objective office in the Department of Defense, is exempt from the policy review provisions of this Directive. As necessary, information may be submitted for security review prior to public release.

4.6. To ensure a climate of academic freedom and to encourage intellectual expression, students (including midshipmen and cadets) and faculty members (DoD civilian or military) of an academy, college, university or DoD school are not required to submit for review papers or materials that are prepared in response to academic requirements and not intended for release outside the academic institution. Information that is intended for public release or made available in libraries to which the public has access shall be submitted for review. Clearance shall be granted if classified information is not disclosed, the DoD interests in non-classified areas are not jeopardized, and the author accurately portrays official policy, even if the author takes issue with that policy.

4.7. Retired personnel, former DoD employees, and non-active duty members of the Reserve components may use the review services to ensure that the information intended for public release does not compromise national security.

4.8. DoD personnel, while acting in a private capacity and not in connection with their official duties, have the right to prepare information for public release through non-DoD forums or media. Such activity is authorized if:

4.8.1. No laws or regulations are violated.

4.8.2. Ethical standards and compliance with DoD Directive 5500.7 and DoD 5500.7-R (references (q) and (r)) are maintained.

4.8.3. The preparation activities are not done during normal duty hours or with the use of DoD facilities, property, or personnel except as authorized by references (q) and (r).

4.8.4. The author does not use official DoD information generally not available to the public and which would not be released under DoD 5400.7-R (reference (m)).

5. <u>RESPONSIBILITIES</u>

5.1. The Director, Washington Headquarters Services, shall:

5.1.1. Monitor compliance with this Directive.

5.1.2. Develop procedures and review guidelines for the security and policy review of information intended for public release in coordination with offices of the OSD Principal Staff Assistants.

5.2. The Heads of the DoD Components shall:

5.2.1. Provide prompt guidance and assistance to the Director, Washington Headquarters Services (WHS), when requested, for the security or policy implications of information proposed for public release.

5.2.2. Establish policies and procedures to implement this Directive in their Components.

5.2.3. Forward official DoD information proposed for public release that is determined to require clearance by the Director, WHS, to the Director, Freedom of Information and Security Review, for review, including recommendation on the releasability of the information being forwarded.

6. EFFECTIVE DATE

This Directive is effective immediately.

[Signed]
John P. White
Deputy Secretary of Defense

E1. ENCLOSURE 1

REFERENCES, continued

(e) DoD 5220.22-M, "National Industrial Security Program Operating Manual," January 1995

(f) DoD Directive 5405.2, "Release of Official Information in Litigation and Testimony of DoD Personnel as Witnesses," July 23, 1985

(g) DoD Directive 5200.1, "DoD Information Security Program," December 13, 1996

(h) DoD 5200.1-R, "Information Security Program Regulation," January 1997

(i) DoD Directive 5230.24, "Distribution Statements on Technical Documents," March 18, 1987

(j) DoD Directive 5230.25, "Withholding of Unclassified Technical Data from Public Disclosure," November 6, 1984

(k) DoD Instruction 5230.27, "Presentation of DoD-Related Scientific and Technical Papers at Meetings," October 6, 1987

(l) DoD Directive 5400.7, "DoD Freedom of Information Act Program," September 29, 1997

(m) DoD 5400.7-R, "DoD Freedom of Information Act Program," September 1998

(n) DoD Directive 5400.11, "Department of Defense Privacy Program," June 9, 1982

(o) DoD 5400.11-R, "Department of Defense Privacy Program," August 1983

(p) DoD Directive 5205.2, "DoD Operations Security Program," July 7, 1983

(q) DoD Directive 5500.7, "Standards of Conduct," August 30, 1993

(r) DoD 5500.7-R, "Joint Ethics Regulation (JER)," August 1993

(s) International Traffic in Arms Regulations (ITAR), Department of State, November 1989

(t) Executive Order 12958, "Classified National Security Information," April 20, 1995

(u) Title 10, United States Code

E2. ENCLOSURE 2

DEFINITIONS

E2.1.1. DoD Employee:

E2.1.1.1. Any DoD civilian officer or employee (including special Government employees) of any DoD Component (including any nonappropriated fund activity).

E2.1.1.2. Any active duty Regular or Reserve military officer, warrant officer, and active duty enlisted member of the Army, the Navy, the Air Force, or the Marine Corps.

E2.1.1.3. Any Reserve or National Guard member on active duty under orders issued pursuant to 10 U.S.C. (reference (u)).

E2.1.1.4. Any Reserve or National Guard member performing official duties, including while on inactive duty for training or while earning retirement points, pursuant to reference (u), or while engaged in any activity related to the performance of a Federal duty or function.

E2.1.1.5. Any faculty member in a civil service position or hired pursuant to reference (u), and any student (including a cadet or midshipman) of an academy, college, university, or school of the Department of Defense.

E2.1.1.6. Consistent with labor agreements and international treaties and agreements, and host-country laws, any foreign national working for a DoD Component except those hired pursuant to a defense contract.

E2.1.2. Information. Any communication or representation of knowledge such as facts, data, or opinions in any medium or form.

E2.1.3. Official DoD Information. All information that is in the custody and control of the Department of Defense, relates to information in the custody and control of the Department, or was acquired by DoD employees as part of their official duties or because of their official status within the Department.

DEPARTMENT OF DEFENSE INSTRUCTION 5230.29 SECURITY AND POLICY REVIEW OF DOD INFORMATION FOR PUBLIC RELEASE*

References: (a) DOD Directive 5230.9, "Clearance of DOD Information for Public Release," April 9, 1996.

(b) DOD Directive 5400.4, "Provision of Information to Congress," January 30, 1978.

(c) DOD Directive 5230.24, "Distribution Statements on Technical Documents," March 18, 1987.

(d) DOD Directive 5230.25, "Withholding of Unclassified Technical Data from Public Disclosure," November 6, 1984.

(e) International Traffic in Arms Regulation (ITAR),Department of State, November 1989.

A. PURPOSE

This Instruction implements policy, assigns responsibilities, identifies information that must be cleared before public release, and prescribes procedures under reference (a) to carry out security and policy review of DOD information for public release.

B. APPLICABILITY

This Instruction applies to the Office of the Secretary of Defense, the Military Departments, the Chairman of the Joint Chiefs of Staff, the Unified Combatant Commands, the Defense Agencies, and the DOD FieldActivities (hereafter referred to collectively as "the DOD Components").

C. DEFINITIONS

Terms used in this Instruction are defined in enclosure 2 of reference (a).

D. POLICY

It is DOD policy under reference (a) that a security and policy review shall be done on all official DOD information intended for public release that pertains to military matters, national security issues, or subjectsof significant concern to the Department of Defense.

E. RESPONSIBILITIES

1. The Assistant Secretary of Defense for Public Affairs shall:

a. Monitor compliance with the procedures established in section F., below, for the security and policy review of official DOD information.

b. Provide for the prompt security and policy review of official DOD information proposed for public release that is originated by, in, or for the Department of Defense, to include statements intended for openpresentation before the Congress and other material submitted to the Congress in accordance with DOD Directive 5400.4 (reference (b)). The review is made to ensure that properly classified information is notdisclosed

* (May 6, 1996), https://sites.defenselink.mil/523029.html.

and no conflict exists with established policies or programs of the Department of Defense or the U.S. Government.

c. Coordinate, as necessary, with the staffs of the DOD Components when reviewing official DOD information for public release clearance to ensure accuracy and currency of existing policy and security guidance.

d. Respond to requests for review of information submitted voluntarily by non-DOD sources or DOD personnel acting in a private capacity to ensure that such material does not contain classified information. This review shall also address technology transfer and public releasability of technical data under DOD Directives 5230.24 and .5230.25, and the ITAR (references (c) through (e)).

2. The General Counsel of the Department of Defense shall conduct legal reviews, as needed, to ensure compliance with applicable laws and regulations to protect DOD rights and interests.

3. The Heads of the DOD Components shall:

a. Ensure compliance with this Instruction and issue any guidance necessary for the internal administration of the requirements prescribed in section F., below.

b. Forward official DOD information specified under subsection F.1., below, which is proposed for public release to the Assistant Secretary of Defense for Public Affairs, ATTN: Director for Freedom of Information and Security Review (DFOISR), for review and clearance, as prescribed in subsection F.2., below, with specific recommendation on the releasability of the information being forwarded.

c. Provide prompt guidance and assistance to the ASD(PA), when requested, on any information proposed for public release.

d. Exercise clearance authority for information not specified under subsection F.1., below. This authority may be delegated to the lowest level competent to evaluate the content and implications of public release of the information.

F. PROCEDURES

1. Clearance Requirements. Official DOD information that is prepared by or for DOD personnel and is proposed for public release shall be submitted to the ASD(PA), ATTN: DFOISR, 1400 Defense Pentagon, Room 2C757, Washington DC 20301-1400, for review and clearance, if the information:

a. Originates or is proposed for release in the Washington D.C. area;

b. Is or has the potential to become an item of national or international interest;

c. Affects national security policy or foreign relations;

d. Concerns a subject of potential controversy among the DOD Components or with other Federal Agencies;

e. Is presented by a DOD employee, who by virtue of rank, position, or expertise would be considered an official DOD spokesperson;

f. Contains technical data, including data developed under contract or independently developed and controlled by the ITAR (reference (e)) that may be militarily critical and subject to limited distribution, but on which a distribution determination has not been made; or,

g. Bears on any of the following subjects:

(1) New weapons or weapons systems, or significant modifications or improvements to existing weapons or weapons systems, equipment, or techniques.

(2) Military operations, significant exercises, and operations security.

(3) National Command Authorities; command, control, communications, computers, and intelligence; information warfare and computer security.

(4) Military activities or application in space; nuclear weapons, including nuclear weapons effects research; chemical warfare and defensive biological warfare; and arms control treaty implementation.

(5) Any other contemporary topic that is designated by the ASD(PA).

2. Submission for Review. The following procedures apply to all information required to be submitted to DFOISR for clearance:

a. A minimum of five copies of material, in its final form, shall be submitted, together with DD Form 1910, "Clearance Request for Public Release of Department of Defense Information," to DFOISR.

b. Any material submitted for review shall be initialed by the speaker, author, or other authorized individual acting for the principal to indicate approval of the text.

c. All information submitted for review to DFOISR must first be coordinated within the originating DOD Component to ensure that it reflects the organization's policy position and does not containclassified information requiring withholding.

d. Only the full and final text of material proposed for release shall be submitted for review. Notes, outlines, briefing charts, etc., may not be submitted as a substitute for a complete text.

e. Abstracts to be published in advance of a complete paper, manuscript, etc., require clearance. Clearance of an abstract does not fulfill the requirement to submit the full text for clearance before its publication. If an abstract is cleared in advance, that fact, and the DFOISR case number assigned to the abstract, shall be noted on the DD Form 1910 or other transmittal when the full text is submitted.

f. The requirements of DOD Directive 5400.4 (reference (b)) shall apply to the processing of information proposed for submission to Congress.

g. Information intended for placement on electronic bulletin boards accessible through the INTERNET, or other publicly accessible computer servers, requires review and clearance for public release if, it meets the requirements of subsection F.l., above.

3. Time Limits

a. Submit speeches and briefings a minimum of 3 working days before the event. Additional time may be needed for complex or potentially controversial speeches.

b. Papers, articles, and other material shall be submitted a minimum of 5 working days before the date needed. The length, complexity, and content shall determine the number of reviewing Agencies and, consequently, the time required for the complete review process.

c. Technical papers shall require a minimum of 10 working days. The majority of papers are processed in that time-frame. Occasionally, more time is needed if the material is complex or requires review by several agencies.

4. Effect of Review Actions and Appeals

a. Information reviewed for public release clearance shall result in one of the following actions:

(1) Cleared for Open Publication. The information may be released without restriction by the originating Component or its authorized official. DFOISR may require a disclaimer to accompany the information, as follows:

"The views expressed are those of the author and do not reflect the official policy or position of the Department of Defense or the U.S. Government."

(2) Cleared "as amended" for omen publication Amendments, made in red, are binding on the submitter. Red brackets identify information that must be deleted. When possible, alternative wording is provided to substitute for the deleted material. Occasionally, wording will be included that shall be added to the text before public release. A disclaimer, as in subparagraph F.4.a.(1), above, may also be required.

(3) Not Cleared. The information submitted for review may not be released.

b. Although DFOISR has no responsibility for correcting errors of fact or making editorial changes, obvious errors may be identified in the text and noted as "recommended." Those corrections are not binding on the author or submitter.

c. All amendments or "not cleared" determinations may be appealed through DFOISR to the ASD(PA). All appeals shall be resolved at the lowest practical level and as quickly as possible.

G. EFFECTIVE DATE

This Instruction is effective immediately.

Clifford H. Bernath
Principal Deputy Assistant
Secretary of Defense
for Public Affairs

EXECUTIVE ORDER 13292* (CLASSIFIED NATIONAL SECURITY INFORMATION)

FURTHER AMENDMENT TO EXECUTIVE ORDER 12958, AS AMENDED, CLASSIFIED NATIONAL SECURITY INFORMATION

By the authority vested in me as President by the Constitution and the laws of the United States of America, and in order to further amend Executive Order 12958, as amended, it is hereby ordered that Executive Order 12958 is amended to read as follows:

Classified National Security Information

This order prescribes a uniform system for classifying, safeguarding, and declassifying national security information, including information relating to defense against transnational terrorism. Our democratic principles require that the American people be informed of the activities of their Government. Also, our Nations progress depends on the free flow of information. Nevertheless, throughout our history, the national defense has required that certain information be maintained in confidence in order to protect our citizens, our democratic institutions, our homeland security, and our interactions with foreign nations. Protecting information critical to our Nations security remains a priority.

NOW, THEREFORE, by the authority vested in me as President by the Constitution and the laws of the United States of America, it is hereby ordered as follows:

PART 1—ORIGINAL CLASSIFICATION

Sec. 1.1. Classification Standards.

(a) Information may be originally classified under the terms of this order only if all of the following conditions are met:

(1) an original classification authority is classifying the information;

(2) the information is owned by, produced by or for, or is under the control of the United States Government;

(3) the information falls within one or more of the categories of information listed in section 1.4 of this order; and

(4) the original classification authority determines that the unauthorized disclosure of the information reasonably could be expected to result in damage to the national security, which includes defense against transnational terrorism, and the original classification authority is able to identify or describe the damage.

(b) Classified information shall not be declassified automatically as a result of any unauthorized disclosure of identical or similar information.

(c) The unauthorized disclosure of foreign government information is presumed to cause damage to the national security.

---

* Exec. Order No. 13292, 3 C.F.R. 196 (2003), *reprinted in* 50 U.S.C.A. §435 note (West Supp. 2005) (amending Exec. Order No. 12958, 3 C.F.R. 333 (1995)), *available at* http://www.fas.org/sgp/bush/eoamend.html.

Sec. 1.2. Classification Levels.

(a) Information may be classified at one of the following three levels:

(1) "Top Secret" shall be applied to information, the unauthorized disclosure of which reasonably could be expected to cause exceptionally grave damage to the national security that the original classification authority is able to identify or describe.

(2) "Secret" shall be applied to information, the unauthorized disclosure of which reasonably could be expected to cause serious damage to the national security that the original classification authority is able to identify or describe.

(3) "Confidential" shall be applied to information, the unauthorized disclosure of which reasonably could be expected to cause damage to the national security that the original classification authority is able to identify or describe.

(b) Except as otherwise provided by statute, no other terms shall be used to identify United States classified information.

Sec. 1.3. Classification Authority.

(a) The authority to classify information originally may be exercised only by:

(1) the President and, in the performance of executive duties, the Vice President;

(2) agency heads and officials designated by the President in the Federal Register; and

(3) United States Government officials delegated this authority pursuant to paragraph (c) of this section.

(b) Officials authorized to classify information at a specified level are also authorized to classify information at a lower level.

(c) Delegation of original classification authority.

(1) Delegations of original classification authority shall be limited to the minimum required to administer this order. Agency heads are responsible for ensuring that designated subordinate officials have a demonstrable and continuing need to exercise this authority.

....

Sec. 1.4. Classification Categories. Information shall not be considered for classification unless it concerns:

(a) military plans, weapons systems, or operations;

(b) foreign government information;

(c) intelligence activities (including special activities), intelligence sources or methods, or cryptology;

(d) foreign relations or foreign activities of the United States, including confidential sources;

(e) scientific, technological, or economic matters relating to the national security, which includes defense against transnational terrorism;

(f) United States Government programs for safeguarding nuclear materials or facilities;

(g) vulnerabilities or capabilities of systems, installations, infrastructures, projects, plans, or protection services relating to the national security, which includes defense against transnational terrorism; or

(h) weapons of mass destruction.

Sec. 1.5. Duration of Classification.

(a) At the time of original classification, the original classification authority shall attempt to establish a specific date or event for declassification based upon the duration of the national security sensitivity of the information. Upon reaching the date or event, the information shall be automatically declassified. The date or event shall not exceed the time frame established in paragraph (b) of this section.

(b) If the original classification authority cannot determine an earlier specific date or event for declassification, information shall be marked for declassification 10 years from the date of the original decision, unless the original classification authority otherwise determines that the sensitivity of the information requires that it shall be marked for declassification for up to 25 years from the date of the original decision.

. . . .

Sec. 1.7. Classification Prohibitions and Limitations.

(a) In no case shall information be classified in order to:

(1) conceal violations of law, inefficiency, or administrative error;

(2) prevent embarrassment to a person, organization, or agency;

(3) restrain competition; or

(4) prevent or delay the release of information that does not require protection in the interest of the national security.

(b) Basic scientific research information not clearly related to the national security shall not be classified.

(c) Information may be reclassified after declassification and release to the public under proper authority only in accordance with the following conditions:

(1) the reclassification action is taken under the personal authority of the agency head or deputy agency head, who determines in writing that the reclassification of the information is necessary in the interest of the national security;

(2) the information may be reasonably recovered; and

(3) the reclassification action is reported promptly to the Director of the Information Security Oversight Office.

(d) Information that has not previously been disclosed to the public under proper authority may be classified or reclassified after an agency has received a request for it under the Freedom of Information Act (5 U.S.C. 552) or the Privacy Act of 1974 (5 U.S.C. 552a), or the mandatory review provisions of section 3.5 of this order only if such classification meets the requirements of this order and is accomplished on a document-by-document basis with the personal participation or under the direction of the agency head, the deputy agency head, or the senior agency official designated under section 5.4 of this order.

. . . .

Sec. 1.8. Classification Challenges.

. . . .

(b) In accordance with implementing directives issued pursuant to this order, an agency head or senior agency official shall establish procedures under which authorized holders of information are encouraged and expected to challenge the classification of information that they believe is improperly classified or unclassified. These procedures shall ensure that:

(1) individuals are not subject to retribution for bringing such actions;

(2) an opportunity is provided for review by an impartial official or panel; and

(3) individuals are advised of their right to appeal agency decisions to the Interagency Security Classification Appeals Panel (Panel) established by section 5.3 of this order.

PART 2—DERIVATIVE CLASSIFICATION

....

PART 3—DECLASSIFICATION AND DOWNGRADING

Sec. 3.1. Authority for Declassification.

(a) Information shall be declassified as soon as it no longer meets the standards for classification under this order.

(b) It is presumed that information that continues to meet the classification requirements under this order requires continued protection. In some exceptional cases, however, the need to protect such information may be outweighed by the public interest in disclosure of the information, and in these cases the information should be declassified. When such questions arise, they shall be referred to the agency head or the senior agency official. That official will determine, as an exercise of discretion, whether the public interest in disclosure outweighs the damage to the national security that might reasonably be expected from disclosure. This provision does not:

(1) amplify or modify the substantive criteria or procedures for classification; or

(2) create any substantive or procedural rights subject to judicial review.

....

Sec. 3.3. Automatic Declassification.

(a) Subject to paragraphs (b)–(e) of this section, on December 31, 2006, all classified records that (1) are more than 25 years old and (2) have been determined to have permanent historical value under title 44, United States Code, shall be automatically declassified whether or not the records have been reviewed. Subsequently, all classified records shall be automatically declassified on December 31 of the year that is 25 years from the date of its original classification, except as provided in paragraphs (b)–(e) of this section.

(b) An agency head may exempt from automatic declassification under paragraph (a) of this section specific information, the release of which could be expected to:

(1) reveal the identity of a confidential human source, or a human intelligence source, or reveal information about the application of an intelligence source or method;

(2) reveal information that would assist in the development or use of weapons of mass destruction;

(3) reveal information that would impair U.S. cryptologic systems or activities;

(4) reveal information that would impair the application of state of the art technology within a U.S. weapon system;

(5) reveal actual U.S. military war plans that remain in effect;

(6) reveal information, including foreign government information, that would seriously and demonstrably impair relations between the United States and a foreign government, or seriously and demonstrably undermine ongoing diplomatic activities of the United States;

(7) reveal information that would clearly and demonstrably impair the current ability of United States Government officials to protect the President, Vice President, and other protectees for whom protection services, in the interest of the national security, are authorized;

(8) reveal information that would seriously and demonstrably impair current national security emergency preparedness plans or reveal current vulnerabilities of systems, installations, infrastructures, or projects relating to the national security; or

(9) violate a statute, treaty, or international agreement.

....

PART 4—SAFEGUARDING

Sec. 4.1. General Restrictions on Access.

(a) A person may have access to classified information provided that:

(1) a favorable determination of eligibility for access has been made by an agency head or the agency heads designee;

(2) the person has signed an approved nondisclosure agreement; and

(3) the person has a need-to-know the information.

(b) Every person who has met the standards for access to classified information in paragraph (a) of this section shall receive contemporaneous training on the proper safeguarding of classified information and on the criminal, civil, and administrative sanctions that may be imposed on an individual who fails to protect classified information from unauthorized disclosure.

(c) Classified information shall remain under the control of the originating agency or its successor in function. An agency shall not disclose information originally classified by another agency without its authorization. An official or employee leaving agency service may not remove classified information from the agency's control.

(d) Classified information may not be removed from official premises without proper authorization.

(e) Persons authorized to disseminate classified information outside the executive branch shall ensure the protection of the information in a manner equivalent to that provided within the executive branch.

(f) Consistent with law, directives, and regulation, an agency head or senior agency official shall establish uniform procedures to ensure that automated information systems, including networks and telecommunications systems, that collect, create, communicate, compute, disseminate, process, or store classified information have controls that:

(1) prevent access by unauthorized persons; and

(2) ensure the integrity of the information.

(g) Consistent with law, directives, and regulation, each agency head or senior agency official shall establish controls to ensure that classified information is used, processed, stored, reproduced, transmitted, and destroyed under conditions that provide adequate protection and prevent access by unauthorized persons.

(h) Consistent with directives issued pursuant to this order, an agency shall safeguard foreign government information under standards that provide a degree of protection at least equivalent to that required by the government or international organization of governments that furnished the information. When adequate to achieve equivalency, these standards may be less restrictive than the safeguarding standards that ordinarily apply to United States "Confidential" information, including modified handling and transmission and allowing access to individuals with a need-to-know who have not otherwise been cleared for access to classified information or executed an approved nondisclosure agreement.

(i) Except as otherwise provided by statute, this order, directives implementing this order, or by direction of the President, classified information originating in one agency shall not be disseminated outside any other agency to which it has been made available without the consent of the originating agency. An agency head or senior agency official may waive this requirement for specific information originated within that agency. For purposes of this section, the Department of Defense shall be considered one agency. Prior consent is not required when referring records for declassification review that contain information originating in several agencies.

....

Sec. 4.3. Special Access Programs.

(a) Establishment of special access programs. Unless otherwise authorized by the President, only the Secretaries of State, Defense, and Energy, and the Director of Central Intelligence, or the principal deputy of each, may create a special access program. For special access programs pertaining to intelligence activities (including special activities, but not including military operational, strategic, and tactical programs), or intelligence sources or methods, this function shall be exercised by the Director of Central Intelligence. These officials shall keep the number of these programs at an absolute minimum, and shall establish them only when the program is required by statute or upon a specific finding that:

(1) the vulnerability of, or threat to, specific information is exceptional; and

(2) the normal criteria for determining eligibility for access applicable to information classified at the same level are not deemed sufficient to protect the information from unauthorized disclosure.

....

PART 5—IMPLEMENTATION AND REVIEW

....

PART 6—GENERAL PROVISIONS

Sec. 6.1. Definitions. For purposes of this order:

(a) "Access" means the ability or opportunity to gain knowledge of classified information.

(b) "Agency" means any "Executive agency," as defined in 5 U.S.C. 105; any "Military department" as defined in 5 U.S.C. 102; and any other entity within the executive branch that comes into the possession of classified information.

(c) "Automated information system" means an assembly of computer hardware, software, or firmware configured to collect, create, communicate, compute, disseminate, process, store, or control data or information.

(d) "Automatic declassification" means the declassification of information based solely upon:

(1) the occurrence of a specific date or event as determined by the original classification authority; or

(2) the expiration of a maximum time frame for duration of classification established under this order.

(e) "Classification" means the act or process by which information is determined to be classified information.

....

(h) "Classified national security information" or "classified information" means information that has been determined pursuant to this order or any predecessor order to require protection against unauthorized disclosure and is marked to indicate its classified status when in documentary form.

(i) "Confidential source" means any individual or organization that has provided, or that may reasonably be expected to provide, information to the United States on matters pertaining to the national security with the expectation that the information or relationship, or both, are to be held in confidence.

(j) "Damage to the national security" means harm to the national defense or foreign relations of the United States from the unauthorized disclosure of information, taking into consideration such aspects of the information as the sensitivity, value, utility, and provenance of that information.

(k) "Declassification" means the authorized change in the status of information from classified information to unclassified information.

(l) "Declassification authority" means:

(1) the official who authorized the original classification, if that official is still serving in the same position;

(2) the originators current successor in function;

(3) a supervisory official of either; or

(4) officials delegated declassification authority in writing by the agency head or the senior agency official.

....

(p) "Downgrading" means a determination by a declassification authority that information classified and safeguarded at a specified level shall be classified and safeguarded at a lower level.

....

(s) "Information" means any knowledge that can be communicated or documentary material, regardless of its physical form or characteristics, that is owned by, produced by or for, or is under the control of the United States Government. "Control" means the authority of the agency that originates information, or its successor in function, to regulate access to the information.

. . . .

(x) "Multiple sources" means two or more source documents, classification guides, or a combination of both.

(y) "National security" means the national defense or foreign relations of the United States.

(z) "Need-to-know" means a determination made by an authorized holder of classified information that a prospective recipient requires access to specific classified information in order to perform or assist in a lawful and authorized governmental function.

. . . .

(dd) "Records" means the records of an agency and Presidential papers or Presidential records, as those terms are defined in title 44, United States Code, including those created or maintained by a government contractor, licensee, certificate holder, or grantee that are subject to the sponsoring agency's control under the terms of the contract, license, certificate, or grant.

(ee) "Records having permanent historical value" means Presidential papers or Presidential records and the records of an agency that the Archivist has determined should be maintained permanently in accordance with title 44, United States Code.

. . . .

(ii) "Senior agency official" means the official designated by the agency head under section 5.4(d) of this order to direct and administer the agency's program under which information is classified, safeguarded, and declassified.

(jj) "Source document" means an existing document that contains classified information that is incorporated, paraphrased, restated, or generated in new form into a new document.

(kk) "Special access program" means a program established for a specific class of classified information that imposes safeguarding and access requirements that exceed those normally required for information at the same classification level.

(ll) "Systematic declassification review" means the review for declassification of classified information contained in records that have been determined by the Archivist to have permanent historical value in accordance with title 44, United States Code.

. . . .

(nn) "Unauthorized disclosure" means a communication or physical transfer of classified information to an unauthorized recipient.

(oo) "Violation" means:

(1) any knowing, willful, or negligent action that could reasonably be expected to result in an unauthorized disclosure of classified information;

(2) any knowing, willful, or negligent action to classify or continue the classification of information contrary to the requirements of this order or its implementing directives; or

(3) any knowing, willful, or negligent action to create or continue a special access program contrary to the requirements of this order.

(pp) "Weapons of mass destruction" means chemical, biological, radiological, and nuclear weapons.

....

Sec. 6.2. General Provisions.

....

(c) Nothing in this order limits the protection afforded any information by other provisions of law, including the Constitution, Freedom of Information Act exemptions, the Privacy Act of 1974, and the National Security Act of 1947, as amended. This order is not intended to and does not create any right or benefit, substantive or procedural, enforceable at law by a party against the United States, its departments, agencies, officers, employees, or agents. The foregoing is in addition to the specific provisos set forth in sections 3.1(b) and 5.3(e) of this order.

....

Sec. 6.3. Effective Date.

This order is effective immediately, except for section 1.6, which shall become effective 180 days from the date of this order.

George W. Bush
The White House,
March 25, 2003.

EXECUTIVE ORDER 13381* (ELIGIBILITY FOR ACCESS TO CLASSIFIED INFORMATION)

By the authority vested in me as President by the Constitution and the laws of the United States of America, and in order to assist in determining eligibility for access to classified national security information, while taking appropriate account of title III of Public Law 108-458, it is hereby ordered as follows:

Sec. 1. Policy. To the extent consistent with safeguarding the security of the United States and protecting classified national security information from unauthorized disclosure, agency functions relating to determining eligibility for access to classified national security information shall be appropriately uniform, centralized, efficient, effective, timely, and reciprocal.

Sec. 2. Functions of the Office of Management and Budget. The Director of the Office of Management and Budget (Director):

a. may, to ensure the effective implementation of the policy set forth in section 1 of this order, assign, in whole or in part, to the head of any agency (solely or jointly) any process relating to determinations of eligibility for access to classified national security information, with the agency's exercise of such assigned process to be subject to the Director's supervision and to such terms and conditions (including approval by the Office of Management and Budget) as the Director determines appropriate;

b. shall carry out any process that the Director does not assign to another agency (or agencies) under subsection (a);

c. may, after consultation with the Secretary of State, Secretary of Defense, the Attorney General, the Secretary of Energy, the Secretary of Homeland Security, the Director of National Intelligence (DNI), and the Director of the Office of Personnel Management, issue guidelines and instructions to the heads of agencies to ensure appropriate uniformity, centralization, efficiency, effectiveness, and timeliness in processes relating to determinations by agencies of eligibility for access to classified national security information;

d. may, with regard to determining eligibility for access to Sensitive Compartmented Information (SCI) and "special access programs pertaining to intelligence activities; including special activities, but not including military operational, strategic, and tactical programs" (Intelligence SAPs) under section 4.3(a) of Executive Order 12958 of April 17, 1995, as amended, issue guidelines and instructions with the concurrence of the DNI to the heads of agencies to ensure appropriate uniformity, centralization, efficiency, effectiveness, and timeliness in making such determinations relating to those programs;

e. may, with regard to determining eligibility for access to special access programs (SAP) as defined in Executive Order 12958 other than Intelligence SAPs, issue guidelines and instructions with the concurrence of the agency head with responsibility for the SAP to ensure appropriate uniformity, centralization, efficiency, effectiveness, and timeliness in making such determinations relating to those programs;

---

* Exec. Order No. 13381, 70 Fed. Reg. 37,953 (June 27, 2005), *available at* http://www.whitehouse.gov/news/releases/2005/06/20050628-4.html.

f. may report periodically to the President on implementation by agencies of the policy set forth in section 1; and

g. shall submit reports to the Congress relating to the subject matter of this order to the extent required by law.

Sec. 3. Functions of the Heads of Agencies.

a. Heads of agencies shall:

i. carry out any process assigned to the agency head by the Director under subsection 2(a) of this order, and shall assist the Director in carrying out any process under subsection 2(b);

ii. implement guidelines and instructions issued by the Director under subsections 2(c), 2(d), and 2(e) of this order;

iii. to the extent permitted by law, make available to the Director such information as the Director may request to implement this order;

iv. ensure that all actions taken under this order take appropriate account of the counterintelligence interests of the United States; and

v. ensure that all actions taken under this order are consistent with the DNI's responsibility to protect intelligence sources and methods.

b. The Director and other heads of agencies shall ensure that all actions taken under this order are consistent with the President's constitutional authority to (i) conduct the foreign affairs of the United States, (ii) withhold information the disclosure of which could impair the foreign relations, the national security, the deliberative processes of the Executive, or the performance of the Executive's constitutional duties, (iii) recommend for congressional consideration such measures as the President may judge necessary or expedient, and (iv) supervise the unitary executive branch.

Sec. 4. Definitions. As used in this order:

a. the term "agencies" means: (i) any "executive department" as defined in section 101 of title 5, United States Code, as well as the Department of Homeland Security; (ii) any "military department" as defined in section 102 of title 5, United States Code; (iii) any "government corporation" as defined in section 103 of title 5, United States Code; and (iv) any "independent establishment" as defined in section 104 of title 5, United States Code, but excluding the Government Accountability Office and including the United States Postal Service and the Postal Rate Commission.

b. the term "classified national security information" means information that is classified pursuant to Executive Order 12958;

c. the term "counterintelligence" has the meaning specified for that term in section 3 of the National Security Act of 1947 (50 U.S.C. 401a); and

d. the term "process" means: (i) oversight of determinations of eligibility for access to classified national security information, including for SCI and SAPs made by any agency, as well as the acquisition of information through investigation or other means upon which such determinations are made; (ii) developing and implementing uniform and consistent policies and procedures to ensure the effective, efficient, and timely completion of access eligibility determinations, to include for SAPs; (iii) designating an authorized agency for making access eligibility determinations and an authorized agency for collecting information through investigation upon which such determinations are made; (iv) ensuring reciprocal recognition of determinations of eligibility for access to classified information among the agencies of the United States Government, including resolution of disputes involving the reciprocity of security clearances and access to SCI and SAPs; (v) ensuring the availability of resources to achieve clearance and investigative program goals regarding the making of access determinations as well as the collection of information through investigation and other means upon which such determinations are made; and (vi) developing tools and techniques for enhancing the making of access eligibility determinations as well as the collection of information through investigation and other means upon which such determinations are made.

Sec. 5. General Provisions.

a. Nothing in this order shall be construed to supersede, impede, or otherwise affect:

1. Executive Order 10865 of February 20, 1960, as amended;

2. Executive Order 12333 of December 4, 1981, as amended;

3. Executive Order 12958, as amended;

4. Executive Order 12968 of August 2, 1995;

5. Executive Order 12829 of January 6, 1993, as amended;

6. subsections 102A(i) and (j) of the National Security Act of 1947 (50 U.S.C. 403-1(i) and (j)); and

7. sections 141 through 146 of the Atomic Energy Act of 1954 (42 U.S.C. 2161 through 2166).

b. Executive Order 12171 of November 19, 1979, as amended, is further amended by inserting after section 1-215 the following new section: "1-216. The Center for Federal Investigative Services, Office of Personnel Management."

c. Nothing in this order shall be construed to impair or otherwise affect any authority of the Director, including with respect to budget, legislative, or administrative proposals. The Director may use any authority of the Office of Management and Budget in carrying out this order.

d. Existing delegations of authority to any agency relating to granting access to classified information and conducting investigations shall remain in effect, subject to the authority of the Office of Management and Budget under section 2 of this order to revise or revoke such delegation.

e. This order is intended solely to improve the internal management of the executive branch and is not intended to, and does not, create any right or benefit, substantive or procedural, enforceable at law or in equity by a party against the United States, its departments, agencies, entities, officers, employees, or agents, or any other person.

Sec. 6. Submission of Report and Expiration of Order.

a. The Director shall submit a report to the President, on or before April 1, 2006, on the implementation of this order and the policy set forth in section 1 of this order.

b. Unless extended by the President, this order shall expire on July 1, 2006.

GEORGE W. BUSH
THE WHITE HOUSE,
June 27, 2005.

E. Intelligence and Counter-Intelligence

SENATE STANDING ORDER 79.13 (SENATE SELECT COMMITTEE ON INTELLIGENCE)[1]

[79.13] **Select Committee on Intelligence**

Resolved, That it is the purpose of this resolution to establish a new select committee of the Senate, to be known as the Select Committee on Intelligence, to oversee and make continuing studies of the intelligence activities and programs of the United States Government, and to submit to the Senate appropriate proposals for legislation and report to the Senate concerning such intelligence activities and programs. In carrying out this purpose, the Select Committee on Intelligence shall make every effort to assure that the appropriate departments and agencies of the United States provide informed and timely intelligence necessary for the executive and legislative branches to make sound decisions affecting the security and vital interests of the Nation. It is further the purpose of this resolution to provide vigilant legislative oversight over the intelligence activities of the United States to assure that such activities are in conformity with the Constitution and laws of the United States.

Sec. 2. (a)(1) There is hereby established a select committee to be known as the Select Committee on Intelligence (hereinafter in this resolution referred to as the "select committee"). The select committee shall be composed of fifteen members appointed as follows:

(A) two members from the Committee on Appropriations;

(B) two members from the Committee on Armed Services;

(C) two members from the Committee on Foreign Relations;

(D) two members from the Committee on the Judiciary; and

(E) seven members to be appointed from the Senate at large.

(2) Members appointed from each committee named in clauses (A) through (D) of paragraph (1) shall be evenly divided between the two major political parties and shall be appointed by the President pro tempore of the Senate upon the recommendations of the majority and minority leaders of the Senate. Four of the members appointed under clause (E) of paragraph (1) shall be appointed by the President pro tempore of the Senate upon the recommendation of the majority leader of the Senate and three shall be appointed by the President pro tempore of the Senate upon the recommendation of the minority leader of the Senate.

(3) The majority leader of the Senate and the minority leader of the Senate shall be ex officio members of the select committee but shall have no vote in the committee and shall not be counted for purposes of determining a quorum.

(b) No Senator may serve on the select committee for more than eight years of continuous service, exclusive of service by any Senator on such committee during the

1. Standing Order 79.13 was first adopted in 1976 as S. Res. 400, 94th Cong. (1976) (enacted), and has been reprinted as amended in U.S. Senate Comm. On Rules & Admin., Authority and Rules of Senate Committees, 2003–2004: A Compilation of the Authority and Rules of Senate and Joint Committees, and Related Materials, S. Doc. No. 108-6, at 141–49 (2003), *available at* http://cryptome.org/senate-sci.txt.

Ninety-fourth Congress. To the greatest extent practicable, one-third of the Members of the Senate appointed to the select committee at the beginning of the Ninety-seventh Congress and each Congress thereafter shall be Members of the Senate who did not serve on such committee during the preceding Congress.

(c) At the beginning of each Congress, the Members of the Senate who are members of the majority party of the Senate shall elect a chairman for the select committee, and the Members of the Senate who are from the minority party of the Senate shall elect a vice chairman for such committee. The vice chairman shall act in the place and stead of the chairman in the absence of the chairman. Neither the chairman nor the vice chairman of the select committee shall at the same time serve as chairman or ranking minority member of any other committee referred to in paragraph 4(e)(1) of rule XXV of the Standing Rules of the Senate.

Sec. 3. (a) There shall be referred to the select committee all proposed legislation, messages, petitions, memorials, and other matters relating to the following:

(1) The Central Intelligence Agency and the Director of Central Intelligence.

(2) Intelligence activities of all other departments and agencies of the Government, including, but not limited to, the intelligence activities of the Defense Intelligence Agency, the National Security Agency, and other agencies of the Department of Defense; the Department of State; the Department of Justice; and the Department of the Treasury.

(3) The organization or reorganization of any department or agency of the Government to the extent that the organization or reorganization relates to a function or activity involving intelligence activities.

(4) Authorizations for appropriations, both direct and indirect, for the following:

(A) The Central Intelligence Agency and Director of Central Intelligence.

(B) The Defense Intelligence Agency.

(C) The National Security Agency.

(D) The intelligence activities of other agencies and subdivisions of the Department of Defense.

(E) The intelligence activities of the Department of State.

(F) The intelligence activities of the Federal Bureau of Investigation, including all activities of the Intelligence Division.

(G) Any department, agency, or subdivision which is the successor to any agency named in clause (A), (B), or (C); and the activities of any department, agency, or subdivision which is the successor to any department, agency, bureau, or subdivision named in clause (D), (E), or (F) to the extent that the activities of such successor department, agency, or subdivision are activities described in clause (D), (E), or (F).

(b) Any proposed legislation reported by the select committee, except any legislation involving matters specified in clause (1) or (4)(A) of subsection (a), containing any matter otherwise within the jurisdiction of any standing committee shall, at the request of the chairman of such standing committee, be referred to such standing committee for its consideration of such matter and be reported to the Senate by such standing committee within thirty days after the day on which such proposed legislation is referred to such standing committee; and any proposed legislation reported by any committee, other than the select committee, which contains any matter within the jurisdiction of the select committee shall, at the request of the chairman of the select committee, be referred to the select committee for its consideration of such matter and be reported to the Senate by the select committee within thirty days after the day on which such proposed legislation is referred to such committee. In any case in which a committee fails to report any proposed legislation referred to it within the time limit prescribed herein, such committee shall be automatically discharged from further consideration of such proposed legislation on the thirtieth day following the day on which such proposed legislation is referred to such committee unless the Senate provides otherwise. In computing any thirty-day period under this paragraph there shall be excluded from such computation any days on which the Senate is not in session.

(c) Nothing in this resolution shall be construed as prohibiting or otherwise restricting the authority of any other committee to study and review any intelligence activity to the extent that such activity directly affects a matter otherwise within the jurisdiction of such committee.

(d) Nothing in this resolution shall be construed as amending, limiting, or otherwise changing the authority of any standing committee of the Senate to obtain full and prompt access to the product of the intelligence activities of any department or agency of the Government relevant to a matter otherwise within the jurisdiction of such committee.

. . . .

Sec. 5. (a) For the purposes of this resolution, the select committee is authorized in its discretion

(1) to make investigations into any matter within its jurisdiction,

(2) to make expenditures from the contingent fund of the Senate,

(3) to employ personnel,

(4) to hold hearings,

(5) to sit and act at any time or place during the sessions, recesses, and adjourned periods of the Senate,

(6) to require, by subpoena or otherwise, the attendance of witnesses and the production of correspondence, books, papers, and documents,

(7) to take depositions and other testimony,

(8) to procure the service of individual consultants or organizations thereof, in accordance with the provisions of section 202(i) of the Legislative Reorganization Act of 1946, and

(9) with the prior consent of the Government department or agency concerned and the Committee on Rules and Administration, to use on a reimbursable basis the services of personnel of any such department or agency.

(b) The chairman of the select committee or any member thereof may administer oaths to witnesses.

(c) Subpoenas authorized by the select committee may be issued over the signature of the chairman, the vice chairman or any member of the select committee designated by the chairman, and may be served by any person designated by the chairman or any member signing the subpoenas.

. . . .

Sec. 7. The select committee shall formulate and carry out such rules and procedures as it deems necessary to prevent the disclosure, without the consent of the person or persons concerned, of information in the possession of such committee which unduly infringes upon the privacy or which violates the constitutional rights of such person or persons. Nothing herein shall be construed to prevent such committee from publicly disclosing any such information in any case in which such committee determines the national interest in the disclosure of such information clearly outweighs any infringement on the privacy of any person or persons.

Sec. 8. (a) The select committee may, subject to the provisions of this section, disclose publicly any information in the possession of such committee after a determination by such committee that the public interest would be served by such disclosure. Whenever committee action is required to disclose any information under this section, the committee shall meet to vote on the matter within five days after any member of the committee requests such a vote. No member of the select committee shall disclose any information, the disclosure of which requires a committee vote, prior to a vote by the committee on the question of the disclosure of such information or after such vote except in accordance with this section.

(b) (1) In any case in which the select committee votes to disclose publicly any information which has been classified under established security procedures, which has been submitted to it by the executive branch, and which the executive branch requests be kept secret, such committee shall notify the President of such vote.

(2) The select committee may disclose publicly such information after the expiration of a five-day period following the day on which notice of such vote is transmitted to the President, unless, prior to the expiration of such five-day period, the President, personally in writing, notifies the committee that he objects to the disclosure of such information, provides his reasons therefor, and certifies that the threat to the national interest of the United States posed by such disclosure is of such gravity that it outweighs any public interest in the disclosure.

(3) If the President, personally in writing, notifies the select committee of his objections to the disclosure of such information as provided in paragraph (2), such committee may, by majority vote, refer the question of the disclosure of such information to the Senate for consideration. The committee shall not publicly disclose such information without leave of the Senate.

(4) Whenever the select committee votes to refer the question of disclosure of any information to the Senate under paragraph (3), the chairman shall not later than the first day on which the Senate is in session following the day on which the vote occurs, report the matter to the Senate for its consideration.

(5) One hour after the Senate convenes on the fourth day on which the Senate is in session following the day on which any such matter is reported to the Senate, or at such earlier time as the majority leader and the minority leader of the Senate jointly agree upon in accordance with paragraph 5 of rule XVII of the Standing Rules of the Senate, the Senate shall go into closed session and the matter shall be the pending business. In considering the matter in closed session the Senate may—

(A) approve the public disclosure of all or any portion of the information in question, in which case the committee shall publicly disclose the information ordered to be disclosed,

(B) disapprove the public disclosure of all or any portion of the information in question, in which case the committee shall not publicly disclose the information ordered not to be disclosed, or

(C) refer all or any portion of the matter back to the committee, in which case the committee shall make the final determination with respect to the public disclosure of the information in question.

Upon conclusion of the consideration of such matter in closed session, which may not extend beyond the close of the ninth day on which the Senate is in session following the day on which such matter was reported to the Senate, or the close of the fifth day following the day agreed upon jointly by the majority and minority leaders in accordance with paragraph 5 of rule XVII of the Standing Rules of the Senate (whichever the case may be), the Senate shall immediately vote on the disposition of such matter in open session, without debate, and without divulging the information with respect to which the vote is being taken. The Senate shall vote to dispose of such matter by one or more of the means specified in clauses (A), (B), and (C) of the second sentence of this paragraph. Any vote of the Senate to disclose any information pursuant to this paragraph shall be subject to the right of a Member of the Senate to move for reconsideration of the vote within the time and pursuant to the procedures specified in rule XIII of the Standing Rules of the Senate, and the disclosure of such information shall be made consistent with that right.

(c) (1) No information in the possession of the select committee relating to the lawful intelligence activities of any department or agency of the United States which has been classified under established security procedures and which the select committee, pursuant to subsection (a) or (b) of this section, has determined should not be disclosed shall be made available to any person by a Member, officer, or employee of the Senate except in a closed session of the Senate or as provided in paragraph (2).

(2) The select committee may, under such regulations as the committee shall prescribe to protect the confidentiality of such information, make any information described in paragraph (1) available to any other committee or any other Member of the Senate. Whenever the select committee makes such information available, the committee shall keep a written record showing, in the case of any particular information, which committee or which Members of the Senate received such information. No Member of the Senate who, and no committee which, receives any information under this subsection, shall disclose such information except in a closed session of the Senate.

(d) It shall be the duty of the Select Committee on Standards and Conduct[2] to investigate any unauthorized disclosure of intelligence information by a Member, officer or employee of the Senate in violation of subsection (c) and to report to the Senate concerning any allegation which it finds to be substantiated.

(e) Upon the request of any person who is subject to any such investigation, the Select Committee on Standards and Conduct shall release to such individual at the conclusion of its investigation a summary of its investigation together with its findings. If, at the conclusion of its investigation, the Select Committee on Standards and Conduct determines that there has been a significant breach of confidentiality or unauthorized disclosure by a Member, officer, or employee of the Senate, it shall report its findings to the Senate and recommend appropriate action such as censure, removal from committee membership, or expulsion from the Senate, in the case of a Member, or removal from office or employment or punishment for contempt, in the case of an officer or employee.

2. Name changed to the Select Committee on Ethics by S.Res. 4, 95-1, Feb. 4, 1977.

. . . .

Sec. 11. (a) It is the sense of the Senate that the head of each department and agency of the United States should keep the select committee fully and currently informed with respect to intelligence activities, including any significant anticipated activities, which are the responsibility of or engaged in by such department or agency: Provided, That this does not constitute a condition precedent to the implementation of any such anticipated intelligence activity.

(b) It is the sense of the Senate that the head of any department or agency of the United States involved in any intelligence activities should furnish any information or document in the possession, custody, or control of the department or agency, or person paid by such department or agency, whenever requested by the select committee with respect to any matter within such committee's jurisdiction.

(c) It is the sense of the Senate that each department and agency of the United States should report immediately upon discovery to the select committee any and all intelligence activities which constitute violations of the constitutional rights of any person, violations of law, or violations of Executive orders, presidential directives, or departmental or agency rules or regulations; each department and agency should further report to such committee what actions have been taken or are expected to be taken by the departments or agencies with respect to such violations.

. . . .

Sec. 14. (a) As used in this resolution, the term "intelligence activities" includes:

(1) the collection, analysis, production, dissemination, or use of information which relates to any foreign country, or any government, political group, party, military force, movement, or other association in such foreign country, and which relates to the defense, foreign policy, national security, or related policies of the United States, and other activity which is in support of such activities;

(2) activities taken to counter similar activities directed against the United States;

(3) covert or clandestine activities affecting the relations of the United States with any foreign government, political group, party, military force, movement or other association;

(4) the collection, analysis, production, dissemination, or use of information about activities of persons within the United States, its territories and possessions, or nationals of the United States abroad whose political and related activities pose, or may be considered by any department, agency, bureau, office, division, instrumentality, or employee of the United States to pose, a threat to the internal security of the United States, and covert or clandestine activities directed against such persons. Such term does not include tactical foreign military intelligence serving no national policymaking function.

(b) As used in this resolution, the term "department or agency" includes any organization, committee, council, establishment, or office within the Federal Government.

(c) For purposes of this resolution, reference to any department, agency, bureau, or subdivision shall include a reference to any successor department, agency, bureau, or subdivision to the extent that such successor engages in intelligence activities now conducted by the department, agency, bureau, or subdivision referred to in this resolution.

. . . .

HOUSE OF REPRESENTATIVES RULE XLVIII, PERMANENT SELECT COMMITTEE ON INTELLIGENCE*

1. (a) There is hereby established a permanent select committee to be known as the Permanent Select Committee on Intelligence (hereinafter in this rule referred to as the "select committee"). The select committee shall be composed of not more than sixteen Members, of whom not more than nine may be from the same party. The select committee shall include at least one Member from:

(1) the Committee on Appropriations;

(2) the Committee on National Security;

(3) the Committee on International Relations; and

(4) the Committee on the Judiciary.

(b) (1) The Speaker of the House and the Minority Leader of the House shall be ex officio members of the select committee, but shall have no vote in the committee and shall not be counted for purposes of determining a quorum.

(2) The Speaker and Minority Leader each may designate a member of their leadership staff to assist them in their capacity as ex officio members, with the same access to committee meetings, hearings, briefings, and materials as if employees of the select committee, and subject to the same security clearance and confidentiality requirements as employees of the select committee under this rule.

(c) No Member of the House other than the Speaker and the Minority

Leader may serve on the select committee during more than four Congresses in any period of six successive Congresses (disregarding for this purpose any service for less than a full session in any Congress), except that the incumbent chairman or ranking minority member having served on the select committee for four Congresses and having served as chairman or ranking minority member for not more than one Congress shall be eligible for reappointment to the select committee as chairman or ranking minority member for one additional Congress.

2. (a) There shall be referred to the select committee all proposed legislation, messages, petitions, memorials, and other matters relating to the following:

(1) The Central Intelligence Agency and Director of Central Intelligence, and the National Foreign Intelligence Program as defined in section 3(6) of the National Security Act of 1947.

(2) Intelligence and intelligence-related activities of all other departments and agencies of the Government, including, but not limited to, the tactical intelligence and intelligence-related activities of the Department of Defense.

(3) The organization or reorganization of any department or agency of the Government to the extent that the organization or reorganization relates to a function or activity involving intelligence or intelligence-related activities.

---

* House Rule XLVIII, §§ 1–2, 6–7, 10, Charles W. Johnson, Constitution, Jefferson's Manual, and Rules of the House of Representatives, H.R. Doc. No. 104-272, at 842–46, 848–55 (1997), *available at* http://bernie.house.gov/research/house_documents_rules.asp.

(4) Authorizations for appropriations, both direct and indirect, for the following:

(A) The Central Intelligence Agency, Director of Central Intelligence, and the National Foreign Intelligence Program as defined in section 3(6) of the National Security Act of 1947.

(B) Intelligence and intelligence-related activities of all other departments and agencies of the Government, including, but not limited to, the tactical intelligence and intelligence-related activities of the Department of Defense.

(C) Any department, agency, or subdivision, or program that is a successor to any agency or program named or referred to in subdivision (A) or (B).

....

6. The select committee shall formulate and carry out such rules and procedures as it deems necessary to prevent the disclosure, without the consent of the person or persons concerned, of information in the possession of such committee which unduly infringes upon the privacy or which violates the constitutional rights of such person or persons. Nothing herein shall be construed to prevent such committee from publicly disclosing any such information in any case in which such committee determines that national interest in the disclosure of such information clearly outweighs any infringement on the privacy of any person or persons.

7. (a) The select committee may, subject to the provisions of this clause, disclose publicly any information in the possession of such committee after a determination by such committee that the public interest would be served by such disclosure. Whenever committee action is required to disclose any information under this clause, the committee shall meet to vote on the matter within five days after any member of the committee requests such a vote. No member of the select committee shall disclose any information, the disclosure of which requires a committee vote, prior to a vote by the committee on the question of the disclosure of such information or after such vote except in accordance with this clause.

(b) (1) In any case in which the select committee votes to disclose publicly any information which has been classified under established security procedures, which has been submitted to it by the executive branch, and which the executive branch requests be kept secret, such committee shall notify the President of such vote.

(2) The select committee may disclose publicly such information after the expiration of a five-day period following the day on which notice of such vote is transmitted to the President, unless, prior to the expiration of such five-day period, the President, personally in writing, notifies the committee that he objects to the disclosure of such information, provides his reasons therefor, and certifies that the threat to the national interest of the United States posed by such disclosure is of such gravity that it outweighs any public interest in the disclosure.

(3) If the President, personally, in writing, notifies the select committee of his objections to the disclosure of such information as provided in subparagraph (2), such committee may, by majority vote, refer the question of this disclosure of such information with a recommendation thereon to the House for consideration. The committee shall not publicly disclose such information without leave of the House.

(4) Whenever the select committee votes to refer the question of disclosure of any information to the House under subparagraph (3), the chairman shall, not later than the first day on which the House is in session following the day on which the vote occurs, report the matter to the House for its consideration.

(5) If within four calendar days on which the House is in session, after such recommendation is reported, no motion has been made by the chairman of the select committee to consider, in closed session, the matter reported under subparagraph (4), then such a motion will be deemed privileged and may be made by any Member. The motion under this subparagraph shall not be subject to debate or amendment. When made, it shall be decided without intervening motion, except one motion to adjourn.

(6) If the House adopts a motion to resolve into closed session, the Speaker shall then be authorized to declare a recess subject to the call of the Chair. At the expiration of such recess, the pending question, in closed session, shall be, "Shall the House approve the recommendation of the select committee?".

(7) After not more than two hours of debate on the motion, such debate to be equally divided and controlled by the chairman and ranking minority member of the select committee, or their designees, the previous question shall be considered as ordered and the House, without intervening motion except one motion to adjourn, shall immediately vote on the question, in open session but without divulging the information with respect to which the vote is being taken. If the recommendation of the select committee is not agreed to, the question shall be deemed recommitted to the select committee for further recommendation.

(c) (1) No information in the possession of the select committee relating to the lawful intelligence or intelligence-related activities of any department or agency of the United States which has been classified under established security procedures and which the select committee, pursuant to paragraphs (a) or (b) of this clause, has determined should not be disclosed shall be made available to any person by a Member, officer, or employee of the House except as provided in subparagraphs (2) and (3).

(2) The select committee shall, under such regulations as the committee shall prescribe, make any information described in subparagraph (1) available to any other committee or any other Member of the House and permit any other Member of the House to attend any hearing of the committee which is closed to the public. Whenever the select committee makes such information available (other than to the Speaker), the committee shall keep a written record showing, in the case of any particular information, which committee or which Members of the House received such information. No Member of the House who, and no committee which, receives any information under this subparagraph, shall disclose such information except in a closed session of the House.

(d) The Committee on Standards of Official Conduct shall investigate any unauthorized disclosure of intelligence or intelligence-related information by a Member, officer, or employee of the House in violation of paragraph (c) and report to the House concerning any allegation which it finds to be substantiated.

(e) Upon the request of any person who is subject to any such investigation, the Committee on Standards of Official Conduct shall release to such individual at the conclusion of its investigation a summary of its investigation, together with its findings. If, at the conclusion of its investigation, the Committee on Standards of Official Conduct determines that there has been a significant breach of confidentiality or unauthorized disclosure by a Member, officer, or employee of the House, it shall report its findings to the House and recommend appropriate action such as censure, removal from committee membership, or expulsion from the House, in the case of a Member, or removal from office or employment or punishment for contempt, in the case of an officer or employee.

. . . .

10. (a) As used in this rule, the term "intelligence and intelligence-related activities" includes:

> (1) the collection, analysis, production, dissemination, or use of information which relates to any foreign country, or any government, political group, party, military force, movement or other association in such foreign country, and which relates to the defense, foreign policy, national security, or related policies of the United States, and other activity which is in support of such activities;
>
> (2) activities taken to counter similar activities directed against the United States;
>
> (3) covert or clandestine activities affecting the relations of the United States with any foreign government, political group, party, military force, movement, or other association;
>
> (4) the collection, analysis, production, dissemination, or use of information about activities of persons within the United States, its territories and possessions, or nationals of the United States abroad whose political and related activities pose, or may be considered by any department, agency, bureau, office, division, instrumentality, or employee of the United States to pose, a threat to the internal security of the United States, and covert or clandestine activities directed against such persons.

(b) As used in this rule, the term "department or agency" includes any organization, committee, council, establishment, or office within the Federal Government.

(c) For purposes of this rule, reference to any department, agency, bureau, or subdivision shall include a reference to any successor department, agency, bureau, or subdivision to the extent that such successor engages in intelligence or intelligence-related activities now conducted by the department, agency, bureau, or subdivision referred to in this rule.

. . . .

FOREIGN INTELLIGENCE SURVEILLANCE ACT*

§ 1801. Definitions

As used in this title [50 USCS §§ 1801 et seq.]:

(a) "Foreign power" means—

(1) a foreign government or any component thereof whether or not recognized by the United States;

(2) a faction of a foreign nation or nations, not substantially composed of United States persons;

(3) an entity that is openly acknowledged by a foreign government or governments to be directed and controlled by such foreign government or governments;

(4) a group engaged in international terrorism or activities in preparation therefor;

(5) a foreign-based political organization, not substantially composed of United States persons; or

(6) an entity that is directed and controlled by a foreign government or governments.

(b) "Agent of a foreign power" means—

(1) any person other than a United States person, who—

(A) acts in the United States as an officer or employee of a foreign power, or as a member of a foreign power as defined in subsection (a)(4);

(B) acts for or on behalf of a foreign power which engages in clandestine intelligence activities in the United States contrary to the interests of the United States, when the circumstances of such person's presence in the United States indicate that such person may engage in such activities in the United States, or when such person knowingly aids or abets any person in the conduct of such activities or knowingly conspires with any person to engage in such activities; or

(C) engages in international terrorism or activities in preparation therefore; or

(2) any person who—

(A) knowingly engages in clandestine intelligence gathering activities for or on behalf of a foreign power, which activities involve or may involve a violation of the criminal statutes of the United States;

(B) pursuant to the direction of an intelligence service or network of a foreign power, knowingly engages in any other clandestine intelligence activities for or on behalf of such foreign power, which activities involve or are about to involve a violation of the criminal statues of the United States;

(C) knowingly engages in sabotage or international terrorism, or activities that are in preparation therefor, for or on behalf of a foreign power;

* Foreign Intelligence Surveillance Act of 1978, Pub. L. No. 95-511, 92 Stat. 1783 (codified as amended at 18 U.S.C.A. §§ 2511, 2518–2519 (West. 2000 & Supp. 2005) and 50 U.S.C.A. §§ 1801–1811 (West 2003 & Supp. 2005))., *available at* http://www4.law.cornell.edu/uscode/html/uscode50/usc_sup_01_50_10_36.html.

(D) knowingly enters the United States under a false or fraudulent identity for or on behalf of a foreign power or, while in the United States, knowingly assumes a false or fraudulent identity for or on behalf of a foreign power; or

(E) knowingly aids or abets any person in the conduct of activities described in subparagraph (A), (B), or (C) or knowingly conspires with any person to engage in activities described in subparagraph (A), (B), or (C).

(c) "International terrorism" means activities that—

(1) involve violent acts or acts dangerous to human life that are a violation of the criminal laws of the United States or of any State, or that would be a criminal violation if committed within the jurisdiction of the United States or any State;

(2) appear to be intended—

(A) to intimidate or coerce a civilian population;

(B) to influence the policy of a government by intimidation or coercion; or

(C) to affect the conduct of a government by assassination or kidnapping; and

(3) occur totally outside the United States or transcend national boundaries in terms of the means by which they are accomplished, the persons they appear intended to coerce or intimidate, or the locale in which their perpetrators operate or seek asylum.

(d) "Sabotage" means activities that involve a violation of chapter 105 of title 18, United States Code [18 USCS §§ 2151 et seq.], or that would involve such a violation if committed against the United States.

(e) "Foreign intelligence information" means—

(1) information that relates to, and if concerning a United States person is necessary to, the ability of the United States to protect against—

(A) actual or potential attack or other grave hostile acts of a foreign power or an agent of a foreign power;

(B) sabotage or international terrorism by a foreign power or an agent of a foreign power; or

(C) clandestine intelligence activities by an intelligence service or network of a foreign power or by an agent of a foreign power; or

(2) information with respect to a foreign power or foreign territory that relates to, and if concerning a United States person is necessary to—

(A) the national defense or the security of the United States; or

(B) the conduct of the foreign affairs of the United States.

(f) "Electronic surveillance" means—

(1) the acquisition by an electronic, mechanical, or other surveillance device of the contents of any wire or radio communication sent by or intended to be received by a particular, known United States person who is in the United States, if the contents are acquired by intentionally targeting that United States person, under circumstances in which a person has a reasonable expectation of privacy and a warrant would be required for law enforcement purposes;

(2) the acquisition by an electronic, mechanical, or other surveillance device of the contents of any wire communication to or from a person in the United States,

without the consent of any party thereto, if such acquisition occurs in the United States, but does not include the acquisition of those communications of computer trespassers that would be permissible under section 2511(2)(i) of title 18, United States Code;

(3) the intentional acquisition by an electronic, mechanical, or other surveillance device of the contents of any radio communication, under circumstances in which a person has a reasonable expectation of privacy and a warrant would be required for law enforcement purposes, and if both the sender and all intended recipients are located within the United States; or

(4) the installation or use of an electronic, mechanical, or other surveillance device in the United States for monitoring to acquire information, other than from a wire or radio communication, under circumstances in which a person has a reasonable expectation of privacy and a warrant would be required for law enforcement purposes.

(g) "Attorney General" means the Attorney General of the United States (or Acting Attorney General) or the Deputy Attorney General.

(h) "Minimization procedures", with respect to electronic surveillance, means—

(1) specific procedures, which shall be adopted by the Attorney General, that are reasonably designed in light of the purpose and technique of the particular surveillance, to minimize the acquisition and retention, and prohibit the dissemination, of nonpublicly available information concerning unconsenting United States persons consistent with the need of the United States to obtain, produce, and disseminate foreign intelligence information;

(2) procedures that require that nonpublicly available information, which is not foreign intelligence information, as defined in subsection (e)(1), shall not be disseminated in a manner that identifies any United States person, without such person's consent, unless such person's identity is necessary to understand foreign intelligence information or assess its importance;

(3) notwithstanding paragraphs (1) and (2), procedures that allow for the retention and dissemination of information that is evidence of a crime which has been, is being, or is about to be committed and that is to be retained or disseminated for law enforcement purposes; and

(4) notwithstanding paragraphs (1), (2), and (3), with respect to any electronic surveillance approved pursuant to section 102(a) [50 USCS § 1802(a)], procedures that require that no contents of any communication to which a United States person is a party shall be disclosed, disseminated, or used for any purpose or retained for longer than 72 hours unless a court order under section 105 [50 USCS § 1805] is obtained or unless the Attorney General determines that the information indicates a threat of death or serious bodily harm to any person.

(i) "United States person" means a citizen of the United States, an alien lawfully admitted for permanent residence (as defined in section 101(a)(20) of the Immigration and Nationality Act [8 USCS § 1101(a)(20)]), an unincorporated association a substantial number of members of which are citizens of the United States or aliens lawfully admitted for permanent residence, or a corporation which is incorporated in the United States, but does not include a corporation or an association which is a foreign power, as defined in subsection (a)(1), (2), or (3).

....

§ 1802. Electronic surveillance authorization without court order; certification by Attorney General; reports to congressional committees; transmittal under seal; duties and compensation of communication common carrier; applications; jurisdiction of court

(a) (1) Notwithstanding any other law, the President, through the Attorney General, may authorize electronic surveillance without a court order under this title [50 USCS §§ 1801 et seq.] to acquire foreign intelligence information for periods of up to one year if the Attorney General certifies in writing under oath that—

(A) the electronic surveillance is solely directed at—

(i) the acquisition of the contents of communications transmitted by means of communications used exclusively between or among foreign powers, as defined in section 101(a) (1), (2), or (3) [50 USCS § 1801(a)(1), (2), or (3)]; or

(ii) the acquisition of technical intelligence, other than the spoken communications of individuals, from property or premises under the open and exclusive control of a foreign power, as defined in section 101(a) (1), (2), or (3) [50 USCS § 1801(a)(1), (2), or (3)];

(B) there is no substantial likelihood that the surveillance will acquire the contents of any communication to which a United States person is a party; and

(C) the proposed minimization procedures with respect to such surveillance meet the definition of minimization procedures under section 101(h) [50 USCS § 1801(h)]; and if the Attorney General reports such minimization procedures and any changes thereto to the House Permanent Select Committee on Intelligence and the Senate Select Committee on Intelligence at least thirty days prior to their effective date, unless the Attorney General determines immediate action is required and notifies the committees immediately of such minimization procedures and the reason for their becoming effective immediately.

....

§ 1804. Applications for court orders

(a) Submission by Federal officer; approval of Attorney General; contents. Each application for an order approving electronic surveillance under this title [50 USCS §§ 1801 et seq.] shall be made by a Federal officer in writing upon oath or affirmation to a judge having jurisdiction under section 103 [50 USCS § 1803]. Each application shall require the approval of the Attorney General based upon his finding that it satisfies the criteria and requirements of such application as set forth in this title [50 USCS §§ 1801 et seq.]. It shall include—

(1) the identity of the Federal officer making the application;

(2) the authority conferred on the Attorney General by the President of the United States and the approval of the Attorney General to make the application;

(3) the identity, if known, or a description of the target of the electronic surveillance;

(4) a statement of the facts and circumstances relied upon by the applicant to justify his belief that—

(A) the target of the electronic surveillance is a foreign power or an agent of a foreign power; and

(B) each of the facilities or places at which the electronic surveillance is directed is being used, or is about to be used, by a foreign power or an agent of a foreign power;

(5) a statement of the proposed minimization procedures;

(6) a detailed description of the nature of the information sought and the type of communications or activities to be subjected to the surveillance;

(7) a certification or certifications by the Assistant to the President for National Security Affairs or an executive branch official or officials designated by the President from among those executive officers employed in the area of national security or defense and appointed by the President with the advice and consent of the Senate—

(A) that the certifying official deems the information sought to be foreign intelligence information;

(B) that a significant purpose of the surveillance is to obtain foreign intelligence information;

(C) that such information cannot reasonably be obtained by normal investigative techniques;

(D) that designates the type of foreign intelligence information being sought according to the categories described in section 101(e) [50 USCS § 1801(e)]; and

(E) including a statement of the basis for the certification that—

(i) the information sought is the type of foreign intelligence information designated; and

(ii) such information cannot reasonably be obtained by normal investigative techniques;

(8) a statement of the means by which the surveillance will be effected and a statement whether physical entry is required to effect the surveillance;

(9) a statement of the facts concerning all previous applications that have been made to any judge under this title [50 USCS §§ 1801 et seq.] involving any of the persons, facilities, or places specified in the application, and the action taken on each previous application;

(10) a statement of the period of time for which the electronic surveillance is required to be maintained, and if the nature of the intelligence gathering is such that the approval of the use of electronic surveillance under this title [50 USCS §§ 1801 et seq.] should not automatically terminate when the described type of information has first been obtained, a description of facts supporting the belief that additional information of the same type will be obtained thereafter; and

(11) whenever more than one electronic, mechanical or other surveillance device is to be used with respect to a particular proposed electronic surveillance, the coverage of the devices involved and what minimization procedures apply to information acquired by each device.

(b) Exclusion of certain information respecting foreign power targets. Whenever the target of the electronic surveillance is a foreign power, as defined in section 101(a)(1), (2), or (3) [50 USCS § 1801(a)(1), (2) or (3)], and each of the facilities or places at which the surveillance is directed is owned, leased, exclusively used by that foreign power, the application need not contain the information required by paragraphs (6), (7)(E), (8), and (11) of subsection (a), but shall state whether physical entry is required to effect the surveillance and shall contain such information about the surveillance techniques and communications or other information concerning United States persons likely to be obtained as may be necessary to assess the proposed minimization procedures.

....

§ 1805. Issuance of order

(a) Necessary findings. Upon an application made pursuant to section 104 [50 USCS § 1804], the judge shall enter an ex parte order as requested or as modified approving the electronic surveillance if he finds that—

(1) the President has authorized the Attorney General to approve applications for electronic surveillance for foreign intelligence information;

(2) the application has been made by a Federal officer and approved by the Attorney General;

(3) on the basis of the facts submitted by the applicant there is probable cause to believe that—

(A) the target of the electronic surveillance is a foreign power or agent of a foreign power: *Provided,* That no United States person may be considered a foreign power or an agent of a foreign power solely upon the basis of activities protected by the first amendment to the Constitution of the United States; and

(B) each of the facilities or places at which the electronic surveillance is directed is being used, or is about to be used, by a foreign power or an agent of a foreign power;

(4) the proposed minimization procedures meet the definition of minimization procedures under section 101(h) [50 USCS § 1804(h)]; and

(5) the application which has been filed contains all statements and certifications required by section 104 [50 USCS § 1804] and, if the target is a United States person, the certification or certifications are not clearly erroneous on the basis of the statement made under section 104(a)(7)(E) [50 USCS § 1804(a)(7)(E)] and any other information furnished under section 104(d) [50 USCS § 1804(d)].

....

(f) Emergency orders. Notwithstanding any other provision of this title [50 USCS §§ 1801 et seq.], when the Attorney General reasonably determines that—

(1) an emergency situation exists with respect to the employment of electronic surveillance to obtain foreign intelligence information before an order authorizing such surveillance can with due diligence be obtained; and

(2) the factual basis for issuance of an order under this title [50 USCS §§ 1801 et seq.] to approve such surveillance exists;

he may authorize the emergency employment of electronic surveillance if a judge having jurisdiction under section 103 [50 USCS § 1803] is informed by the Attorney General or his designee at the time of such authorization that the decision has been made to employ emergency electronic surveillance and if an application in accordance with this title [50 USCS §§ 1801 et seq.] is made to that judge as soon as practicable, but no more than 72 hours after the Attorney General authorizes such surveillance. If the Attorney General authorizes such emergency employment of electronic surveillance, he shall require that the minimization procedures required by this title [50 USCS §§ 1801 et seq.] for the issuance of a judicial order be followed. In the absence of a judicial order approving such electronic surveillance, the surveillance shall terminate when the information sought is obtained, when the application for the order is denied, or after the expiration of 72 hours from the time of authorization by the Attorney General, whichever is earliest....

....

§ 1806. Use of information

(a) Compliance with minimization procedures; privileged communications; lawful purposes. Information acquired from an electronic surveillance conducted pursuant to this title [50 USCS §§ 1801 et seq.] concerning any United States person may be used and disclosed by Federal officers and employees without the consent of the United States person only in accordance with the minimization procedures required by this title [50 USCS §§ 1801 et seq.]. No otherwise privileged communication obtained in accordance with, or in violation of, the provisions of this title [50 USCS §§ 1801 et seq.] shall lose its privileged character. No information acquired from an electronic surveillance pursuant to this title [50 USCS §§ 1801 et seq.] may be used or disclosed by Federal officers or employees except for lawful purposes.

(b) Statement for disclosure. No information acquired pursuant to this title [50 USCS §§ 1801 et seq.] shall be disclosed for law enforcement purposes unless such disclosure is accompanied by a statement that such information, or any information derived therefrom, may only be used in a criminal proceeding with the advance authorization of the Attorney General.

(c) Notification by United States. Whenever the Government intends to enter into evidence or otherwise use or disclose in any trial, hearing, or other proceeding in or before any court, department, officer, agency, regulatory body, or other authority of the United States, against an aggrieved person, any information obtained or derived from an electronic surveillance of that aggrieved person pursuant to the authority of this title [50 USCS §§ 1801 et seq.], the Government shall, prior to the trial, hearing, or other proceeding or at a reasonable time prior to an effort to so disclose or so use that information or submit it in evidence, notify the aggrieved person and the court or other authority in which the information is to be disclosed or used that the Government intends to so disclose or so use such information.

....

(e) Motion to suppress. Any person against whom evidence obtained or derived from an electronic surveillance to which he is an aggrieved person is to be, or has been, introduced or otherwise used or disclosed in any trial, hearing, or other proceeding in or before any court, department, officer, agency, regulatory body, or other authority of the United States, a State, or a political subdivision thereof, may move to suppress the evidence obtained or derived from such electronic surveillance on the grounds that—

(1) the information was unlawfully acquired; or

(2) the surveillance was not made in conformity with an order of authorization or approval.

Such a motion shall be made before the trial, hearing, or other proceeding unless there was no opportunity to make such a motion or the person was not aware of the grounds of the motion.

(f) In camera and ex parte review by district court. Whenever a court or other authority is notified pursuant to subsection (c) or (d), or whenever a motion is made pursuant to subsection (e), or whenever any motion or request is made by an aggrieved person pursuant to any other statute or rule of the United States of any State before any court or other authority of the United States or any state to discover or obtain applications or orders or other materials relating to electronic surveillance or to discover, obtain, or suppress evidence or information obtained or derived from electronic surveillance under this Act, the United States district court or, where the motion is made before another authority, the United States district court in the same district as the authority, shall, notwithstanding any other law, if the Attorney General files an affidavit under oath that disclosure or an adversary hearing would harm the national security of the United States, review in camera and ex parte the application, order, and such other materials relating to the surveillance as may be necessary to determine whether the surveillance of the aggrieved person was lawfully authorized and conducted. In making this determination, the court may disclose to the aggrieved person, under appropriate security procedures and protective orders, portions of the application, order, or other materials relating to the surveillance only where such disclosure is necessary to make an accurate determination of the legality of the surveillance.

(g) Suppression of evidence; denial of motion. If the United States district court pursuant to subsection (f) determines that the surveillance was not lawfully authorized or conducted, it shall, in accordance with the requirements of law, suppress the evidence which was unlawfully obtained or derived from electronic surveillance of the aggrieved person or otherwise grant the motion of the aggrieved person. If the court determines that the surveillance was lawfully authorized and conducted, it shall deny the motion of the aggrieved person except to the extent that due process requires discovery or disclosure.

....

§ 1809. Criminal sanctions

(a) Prohibited activities. A person is guilty of an offense if he intentionally—

(1) engages in electronic surveillance under color of law except as authorized by statute; or

(2) discloses or uses information obtained under color of law by electronic surveillance, knowing or having reason to know that the information was obtained through electronic surveillance not authorized by statute.

(b) Defense. It is a defense to a prosecution under subsection (a) that the defendant was a law enforcement or investigative officer engaged in the course of his official duties and the electronic surveillance was authorized by and conducted pursuant to a search warrant or court order of a court of competent jurisdiction.

(c) Penalties. An offense described in this section is punishable by a fine of not more than $ 10,000 or imprisonment for not more than five years, or both.

(d) Federal jurisdiction. There is Federal jurisdiction over an offense under this section if the person committing the offense was an officer or employee of the United States at the time the offense was committed.

§ 1810. Civil liability

An aggrieved person, other than a foreign power or an agent of a foreign power, as defined in section 101(a) or (b)(1)(A) [50 USCS § 1801(a) or (b)(1)(A)], respectively, who has been subjected to an electronic surveillance or about whom information obtained by electronic surveillance of such person has been disclosed or used in violation of section 109 [50 USCS § 1809] shall have a cause of action against any person who committed such violation and shall be entitled to recover—

(a) actual damages, but not less than liquidated damages of $ 1,000 or $ 100 per day for each day of violation, whichever is greater;

(b) punitive damages; and

(c) reasonable attorney's fees and other investigation and litigation costs reasonably incurred.

§ 1811. Authorization during time of war

Notwithstanding any other law, the President, through the Attorney General, may authorize electronic surveillance without a court order under this title [50 USCS §§ 1801 et seq.] to acquire foreign intelligence information for a period not to exceed fifteen calendar days following a declaration of war by the Congress.

EXECUTIVE ORDER 12333[1] (UNITED STATES INTELLIGENCE ACTIVITIES AS AMENDED BY EXECUTIVE ORDERS 13284 AND 13355)

....

Part 1

Goals, Direction, Duties and Responsibilities With Respect to the National Intelligence Effort

1.1 *Goals.* The United States intelligence effort shall provide the President and the National Security Council with the necessary information on which to base decisions concerning the conduct and development of foreign, defense and economic policy, and the protection of United States national interests from foreign security threats. All departments and agencies shall cooperate fully to fulfill this goal.

(a) Maximum emphasis should be given to fostering analytical competition among appropriate elements of the Intelligence Community.

(b) All means, consistent with applicable United States law and this Order, and with full consideration of the rights of United States persons, shall be used to develop intelligence information for the President and the National Security Council. A balanced approach between technical collection efforts and other means should be maintained and encouraged.

(c) Special emphasis should be given to detecting and countering espionage and other threats and activities directed by foreign intelligence services against the United States Government, or United States corporations, establishments, or persons.

(d) To the greatest extent possible consistent with applicable United States law and this Order, and with full consideration of the rights of United States persons, all agencies and departments should seek to ensure full and free exchange of information in order to derive maximum benefit from the United States intelligence effort.

1.2 *The National Security Council.*

(a) *Purpose.* The National Security Council (NSC) was established by the National Security Act of 1947 to advise the President with respect to the integration of domestic, foreign and military policies relating to the national security. The NSC shall act as the highest Executive Branch entity that provides review of, guidance for and direction to the conduct of all national foreign intelligence, counterintelligence, and special activities, and attendant policies and programs.

....

1.4 *The Intelligence Community.* The agencies within the Intelligence Community shall, in accordance with applicable United States law and with the other provisions of

1. Exec. Order No. 12333, 3 C.F.R. 200 (1981), *reprinted as amended in* 50 U.S.C.A. §401 note (West 2003 & Supp. 2005), *available at* http://www.cia.gov/cia/information/eo12333.html.

this Order, conduct intelligence activities necessary for the conduct of foreign relations and the protection of the national security of the United States, including:

(a) Collection of information needed by the President, and, in the performance of Executive functions, the Vice President,[2] the National Security Council, the Secretaries of State and Defense, and other Executive Branch officials for the performance of their duties and responsibilities;

(b) Production and dissemination of intelligence;

(c) Collection of information concerning, and the conduct of activities to protect against, intelligence activities directed against the United States, international terrorist and international narcotics activities, and other hostile activities directed against the United States by foreign powers, organizations, persons, and their agents;

(d) Special activities;

(e) Administrative and support activities within the United States and abroad necessary for the performance of authorized activities; and

(f) Such other intelligence activities as the President may direct from time to time.

....

1.7 *Senior Officials of the Intelligence Community.* The heads of departments and agencies with organizations in the Intelligence Community or the heads of such organizations, as appropriate, shall:

(a) Report to the Attorney General possible violations of federal criminal laws by employees and of specified federal criminal laws by any other person as provided in procedures agreed upon by the Attorney General and the head of the department or agency concerned, in a manner consistent with the protection of intelligence sources and methods, as specified in those procedures;

(b) In any case involving serious or continuing breaches of security, recommend to the Attorney General that the case be referred to the FBI for further investigation;

(c) Furnish the NSC, in accordance with applicable law and procedures approved by the Attorney General under this Order, the information required for the performance of its duties;[3]

(d) Report to the Intelligence Oversight Board, and keep the Director of Central Intelligence appropriately informed, concerning any intelligence activities of their organizations that they have reason to believe may be unlawful or contrary to Executive order or Presidential directive;

(e) Protect intelligence and intelligence sources and methods from unauthorized disclosure consistent with guidance from the Director of Central Intelligence;

(f) Disseminate intelligence to cooperating foreign governments under arrangements established or agreed to by the Director of Central Intelligence;

---

2. Subsection 1.4(a) is amended by President George W. Bush in Executive Order 13355 of August 27, 2004, to insert, "and, in the performance of Executive functions, the Vice President,". *See* Exec. Order No. 13355, 69 F.R. 53,593 (August 27, 2004).

3. Subsection 1.7(c) is amended by President George W. Bush in Executive Order 13355 of August 27, 2004, by striking "the Director of Central Intelligence and" and by striking "their respective" and inserting "its". *See* Exec. Order No. 13355, 69 F.R. 53,593 (August 27, 2004).

....

1.8 *The Central Intelligence Agency.* All duties and responsibilities of the CIA shall be related to the intelligence functions set out below. As authorized by this Order; the National Security Act of 1947, as amended; the CIA Act of 1949, as amended; appropriate directives or other applicable law, the CIA shall:

(a) Collect, produce and disseminate foreign intelligence and counterintelligence, including information not otherwise obtainable. The collection of foreign intelligence or counterintelligence within the United States shall be coordinated with the FBI as required by procedures agreed upon by the Director of Central Intelligence and the Attorney General;

(b) Collect, produce and disseminate intelligence on foreign aspects of narcotics production and trafficking;

(c) Conduct counterintelligence activities outside the United States and, without assuming or performing any internal security functions, conduct counterintelligence activities within the United States in coordination with the FBI as required by procedures agreed upon by[4] the Director of Central Intelligence and the Attorney General;

(d) Coordinate counterintelligence activities and the collection of information not otherwise obtainable when conducted outside the United States by other departments and agencies;

(e) Conduct special activities approved by the President. No agency except the CIA (or the Armed Forces of the United States in time of war declared by Congress or during any period covered by a report from the President to the Congress under the War Powers Resolution (87 Stat. 855)) may conduct any special activity unless the President determines that another agency is more likely to achieve a particular objective;

....

Part 2

Conduct of Intelligence Activities

2.1 *Need.* Accurate and timely information about the capabilities, intentions and activities of foreign powers, organizations, or persons and their agents is essential to informed decisionmaking in the areas of national defense and foreign relations. Collection of such information is a priority objective and will be pursued in a vigorous, innovative and responsible manner that is consistent with the Constitution and applicable law and respectful of the principles upon which the United States was founded.

2.2 *Purpose.* This Order is intended to enhance human and technical collection techniques, especially those undertaken abroad, and the acquisition of significant foreign intelligence, as well as the detection and countering of international terrorist activities and espionage conducted by foreign powers. Set forth below are certain general principles that, in addition to and consistent with applicable laws, are intended to achieve the proper balance between the acquisition of essential information and protection of indi-

---

4. Subsection 1.8(c) is amended by President George W. Bush in Executive Order 13355 of August 27, 2004, by inserting "by" after "agreed upon". *See* Exec. Order No. 13355, 69 F.R. 53,593 (August 27, 2004).

vidual interests. Nothing in this Order shall be construed to apply to or interfere with any authorized civil or criminal law enforcement responsibility of any department or agency.

2.3 *Collection of Information.* Agencies within the Intelligence Community are authorized to collect, retain or disseminate information concerning United States persons only in accordance with procedures established by the head of the agency concerned and approved by the Attorney General, consistent with the authorities provided by Part 1 of this Order. Those procedures shall permit collection, retention and dissemination of the following types of information:

(a) Information that is publicly available or collected with the consent of the person concerned;

(b) Information constituting foreign intelligence or counterintelligence, including such information concerning corporations or other commercial organizations. Collection within the United States of foreign intelligence not otherwise obtainable shall be undertaken by the FBI or, when significant foreign intelligence is sought, by other authorized agencies of the Intelligence Community, provided that no foreign intelligence collection by such agencies may be undertaken for the purpose of acquiring information concerning the domestic activities of United States persons;

(c) Information obtained in the course of a lawful foreign intelligence, counterintelligence, international narcotics or international terrorism investigation;

(d) Information needed to protect the safety of any persons or organizations, including those who are targets, victims or hostages of international terrorist organizations;

(e) Information needed to protect foreign intelligence or counterintelligence sources or methods from unauthorized disclosure. Collection within the United States shall be undertaken by the FBI except that other agencies of the Intelligence Community may also collect such information concerning present or former employees, present or former intelligence agency contractors or their present or former employees, or applicants for any such employment or contracting;

(f) Information concerning persons who are reasonably believed to be potential sources or contacts for the purpose of determining their suitability or credibility;

(g) Information arising out of a lawful personnel, physical or communications security investigation;

(h) Information acquired by overhead reconnaissance not directed at specific United States persons;

(i) Incidentally obtained information that may indicate involvement in activities that may violate federal, state, local or foreign laws; and

(j) Information necessary for administrative purposes.

In addition, agencies within the Intelligence Community may disseminate information, other than information derived from signals intelligence, to each appropriate agency within the Intelligence Community for purposes of allowing the recipient agency to determine whether the information is relevant to its responsibilities and can be retained by it.

2.4 *Collection Techniques.* Agencies within the Intelligence Community shall use the least intrusive collection techniques feasible within the United States or directed against United States persons abroad. Agencies are not authorized to use such techniques as electronic surveillance, unconsented physical search, mail surveillance, physical surveillance, or monitoring devices unless they are in accordance with procedures established by the head of the agency concerned and approved by the Attorney General. Such procedures shall protect constitutional and other legal rights and limit use of such information to lawful governmental purposes. These procedures shall not authorize:

(a) The CIA to engage in electronic surveillance within the United States except for the purpose of training, testing, or conducting countermeasures to hostile electronic surveillance;

(b) Unconsented physical searches in the United States by agencies other than the FBI, except for:

(1) Searches by counterintelligence elements of the military services directed against military personnel within the United States or abroad for intelligence purposes, when authorized by a military commander empowered to approve physical searches for law enforcement purposes, based upon a finding of probable cause to believe that such persons are acting as agents of foreign powers; and

(2) Searches by CIA of personal property of non-United States persons lawfully in its possession.

(c) Physical surveillance of a United States person in the United States by agencies other than the FBI, except for:

(1) Physical surveillance of present or former[5] employees, present or former intelligence agency contractors or their present of former employees, or applicants for any such employment or contracting; and

(2) Physical surveillance of a military person employed by a nonintelligence element of a military service.

(d) Physical surveillance of a United States person abroad to collect foreign intelligence, except to obtain significant information that cannot reasonably be acquired by other means.

2.5 *Attorney General Approval.* The Attorney General hereby is delegated the power to approve the use for intelligence purposes, within the United States or against a United States person abroad, of any technique for which a warrant would be required if undertaken for law enforcement purposes, provided that such techniques shall not be undertaken unless the Attorney General has determined in each case that there is probable cause to believe that the technique is directed against a foreign power or an agent of a foreign power. Electronic surveillance, as defined in the Foreign Intelligence Surveillance Act of 1978, shall be conducted in accordance with that Act, as well as this Order.

. . . .

2.8 *Consistency With Other Laws.* Nothing in this Order shall be construed to authorize any activity in violation of the Constitution or statutes of the United States.

2.9 *Undisclosed Participation in Organizations Within the United States.* No one acting on behalf of agencies within the Intelligence Community may join or otherwise partici-

5. Subsection 2.4(c)(1) is amended by President George W. Bush in Executive Order 13355 of August 27, 2004, by striking "present of former" and inserting in lieu thereof "present or former". *See* Exec. Order No. 13355, 69 F.R. 53,593 (August 27, 2004).

pate in any organization in the United States on behalf of any agency within the Intelligence Community without disclosing his intelligence affiliation to appropriate officials of the organization, except in accordance with procedures established by the head of the agency concerned and approved by the Attorney General. Such participation shall be authorized only if it is essential to achieving lawful purposes as determined by the agency head or designee. No such participation may be undertaken for the purpose of influencing the activity of the organization or its members except in cases where:

(a) The participation is undertaken on behalf of the FBI in the course of a lawful investigation; or

(b) The organization concerned is composed primarily of individuals who are not United States persons and is reasonably believed to be acting on behalf of a foreign power.

2.10 *Human Experimentation.* No agency within the Intelligence Community shall sponsor, contract for or conduct research on human subjects except in accordance with guidelines issued by the Department of Health and Human Services. The subject's informed consent shall be documented as required by those guidelines.

2.11 *Prohibition on Assassination.* No person employed by or acting on behalf of the United States Government shall engage in, or conspire to engage in, assassination.

2.12 *Indirect Participation.* No agency of the Intelligence Community shall participate in or request any person to undertake activities forbidden by this Order.

Part 3

General Provisions

3.1 *Congressional Oversight.* The duties and responsibilities of the Director of Central Intelligence and the heads of other departments, agencies, and entities engaged in intelligence activities to cooperate with the Congress in the conduct of its responsibilities for oversight of intelligence activities shall be implemented in accordance with applicable law, including title V of the Act.[6] The requirements of applicable law, including title V of the Act[7] shall apply to all special activities as defined in this Order.

. . . .

3.4 *Definitions.* For the purposes of this Order, the following terms shall have these meanings:

(a) *Counterintelligence* means information gathered and activities conducted to protect against espionage, other intelligence activities, sabotage, or assassinations conducted for or on behalf of foreign powers, organizations or persons, or international terrorist activities, but not including personnel, physical, document or communications security programs.

---

6. Subsection 3.1 is amended by President George W. Bush in Executive Order 13355 of August 27, 2004, by striking "as provided in title 50, United States Code, section 413" and inserting in lieu thereof "implemented in accordance with applicable law, including title V of the Act". *See* Exec. Order No. 13355, 69 F.R. 53,593 (August 27, 2004).

7. Subsection 3.1 is amended by President George W. Bush in Executive Order 13355 of August 27, 2004, by striking "section 662 of the Foreign Assistance Act of 1961 as amended (22 U.S.C. 2422), and section 501 of the National Security Act of 1947, as amended (50 U.S.C. 413)," and inserting in lieu thereof "applicable law, including title V of the Act,". *See* Exec. Order No. 13355, 69 F.R. 53,593 (August 27, 2004).

....

(e) *Intelligence activities* means all activities that agencies within the Intelligence Community are authorized to conduct pursuant to this Order.

(f) *Intelligence Community and agencies within the Intelligence Community or organizations within the Intelligence Community*[8] refer to the following agencies or organizations:

(1) The Central Intelligence Agency (CIA);

(2) The National Security Agency (NSA);

(3) The Defense Intelligence Agency (DIA);

(4) The offices within the Department of Defense for the collection of specialized national foreign intelligence through reconnaissance programs;

(5) The Bureau of Intelligence and Research of the Department of State;

(6) The intelligence elements of the Army, Navy, Air Force, and Marine Corps, the Federal Bureau of Investigation (FBI), the Department of the Treasury, and the Department of Energy;[9]

(7) The staff elements of the Director of Central Intelligence;[10]

(8) The intelligence elements of the Coast Guard and those elements of the Department of Homeland Security that are supervised by the Department's Under Secretary for Information Analysis and Infrastructure Protection through the Department's Assistant Secretary for Information Analysis, with the exception of those functions that involve no analysis of foreign intelligence information.[11]

(9) National Geospatial-Intelligence Agency.

....

(h) *Special activities* means activities conducted in support of national foreign policy objectives abroad which are planned and executed so that the role of the United States Government is not apparent or acknowledged publicly, and functions in support of such activities, but which are not intended to influence United States political processes, public opinion, policies, or media and do not include diplomatic activities or the collection and production of intelligence or related support functions.

(i) *United States person* means a United States citizen, an alien known by the intelligence agency concerned to be a permanent resident alien, an unincorporated

---

8. Subsection 3.4(f) is amended by President George W. Bush in Executive Order 13355 of August 27, 2004, by inserting ", *or organizations within the Intelligence Community*". *See* Exec. Order No. 13355, 69 F.R. 53,593 (August 27, 2004).

9. Subsection 3.4(f)(6) is amended by President George W. Bush in Executive Order 13284 of January 23, 2003, by striking "and" at the end of this subsection. *See* Exec. Order No. 13284, 68 F.R. 4075 (January 23, 2003).

10. Subsection 3.4(f)(7) is amended by President George W. Bush in Executive Order 13355 of August 27, 2004, by striking the "and" at the end of this subsection. *See* Exec. Order No. 13355, 69 F.R. 53,593 (August 27, 2004).

11. Subsection 3.4(f)(8) is amended by President George W. Bush in Executive Order 13284 of January 23, 2003, by inserting this entire subsection. *See* Exec. Order No. 13284, 68 F.R. 4075 (January 23, 2003) and in Executive Order 13355 of August 27, 2004, by striking "those" and inserting in lieu thereof "The intelligence elements of the Coast Guard and those" , and by striking the period at the end of paragraph (8) and inserting in lieu thereof "and", and adding at the end thereof "(9) National Geospatial-Intelligence Agency".

association substantially composed of United States citizens or permanent resident aliens, or a corporation incorporated in the United States, except for a corporation directed and controlled by a foreign government or governments.

3.5 *Purpose and Effect.* This Order is intended to control and provide direction and guidance to the Intelligence Community. Nothing contained herein or in any procedures promulgated hereunder is intended to confer any substantive or procedural right or privilege on any person or organization.

3.6 *Revocation.* Executive Order No. 12036 of January 24, 1978, as amended, entitled "United States Intelligence Activities," is revoked.

RONALD REAGAN

THE WHITE HOUSE,
December 4, 1981.

INTELLIGENCE IDENTITIES PROTECTION ACT OF 1982*

§421. Protection of identities of certain United States undercover intelligence officers, agents, informants, and sources

(a) Disclosure of information by persons having or having had access to classified information that identifies covert agent.

Whoever, having or having had authorized access to classified information that identifies a covert agent, intentionally discloses any information identifying such covert agent to any individual not authorized to receive classified information, knowing that the information disclosed so identifies such covert agent and that the United States is taking affirmative measures to conceal such covert agent's intelligence relationship to the United States, shall be fined under title 18, United States Code, or imprisoned not more than ten years, or both.

(b) Disclosure of information by persons who learn identity of covert agent as result of having access to classified information.

Whoever, as a result of having authorized access to classified information, learns the identity of a covert agent and intentionally discloses any information identifying such covert agent to any individual not authorized to receive classified information, knowing that the information disclosed so identifies such covert agent and that the United States is taking affirmative measures to conceal such covert agent's intelligence relationship to the United States, shall be fined under title 18, United States Code, or imprisoned not more than five years, or both.

....

§422. Defenses and exceptions

(a) Disclosure by United States of identity of covert agent.

It is a defense to a prosecution under section 601 [50 USCS §421] that before the commission of the offense with which the defendant is charged, the United States had publicly acknowledged or revealed the intelligence relationship to the United States of the individual the disclosure of whose intelligence relationship to the United States is the basis for the prosecution.

(b) Conspiracy, misprision of felony, aiding and abetting, etc.

(1) Subject to paragraph (2), no person other than a person committing an offense under section 601 shall be subject to prosecution under such section by virtue of section 2 or 4 of title 18, United States Code, or shall be subject to prosecution for conspiracy to commit an offense under such section.

(2) Paragraph (1) shall not apply (A) in the case of a person who acted in the course of a pattern of activities intended to identify and expose covert agents and with reason to believe that such activities would impair or impede the foreign intelligence activities

---

* Intelligence Identities Protection Act of 1982, Pub. L. No. 97-200, 96 Stat. 122 (codified as amended at 50 U.S.C.A. §§421–426 (West 2003 & Supp. 2005))., *available at* http://www4.law.cornell.edu/uscode/html/uscode50/usc_sup_01_50_10_15_20_IV.html.

of the United States, or (B) in the case of a person who has authorized access to classified information.

(c) Disclosure to select Congressional committees on intelligence.

It shall not be an offense under section 601 [50 USCS § 421] to transmit information described in such section directly to either congressional intelligence committee.

(d) Disclosure by agent of own identity.

It shall not be an offense under section 601 [50 USCS § 421] for an individual to disclose information that solely identifies himself as a covert agent.

§ 423. Report

(a) Annual report by President to Congress on measures to protect identities of covert agents.

The President, after receiving information from the Director of National Intelligence, shall submit to the congressional intelligence committees an annual report on measures to protect the identities of covert agents, and on any other matter relevant to the protection of the identities of covert agents. The date for the submittal of the report shall be the date provided in section 507 [50 USCS § 415b].

(b) Exemption from disclosure; date of initial submission.

The report described in subsection (a) shall be exempt from any requirement for publication or disclosure.

§ 424. Extraterritorial jurisdiction

There is jurisdiction over an offense under section 601 [50 USCS § 421] committed outside the United States if the individual committing the offense is a citizen of the United States or an alien lawfully admitted to the United States for permanent residence (as defined in section 101(a)(20) of the Immigration and Nationality Act) [8 USCS § 1101(a)(20)].

§ 425. Providing information to Congress

Nothing in this title [50 USCS §§ 421 et seq.] may be construed as authority to withhold information from the Congress or from a committee of either House of Congress.

§ 426. Definitions

For the purposes of this title [50 USCS §§ 421 et seq.]:

(1) The term "classified information" means information or material designated and clearly marked or clearly represented, pursuant to the provisions of a statute or Executive order (or a regulation or order issued pursuant to a statute or Executive order), as requiring a specific degree of protection against unauthorized disclosure for reasons of national security.

(2) The term "authorized", when used with respect to access to classified information, means having authority, right, or permission pursuant to the provisions of a statute, Executive order, directive of the head of any department or agency engaged in foreign intelligence or counterintelligence activities, order of any United States court, or provisions of any Rule of the House of Representatives or resolution of the Senate which assigns responsibility within the respective House of Congress for the oversight of intelligence activities.

(3) The term "disclose" means to communicate, provide, impart, transmit, transfer, convey, publish, or otherwise make available.

(4) The term "covert agent" means—

(A) a present or retired officer or employee of an intelligence agency or a present or retired member of the Armed Forces assigned to duty with an intelligence agency—

(i) whose identity as such an officer, employee, or member is classified information, and

(ii) who is serving outside the United States or has within the last five years served outside the United States; or

(B) a United States citizen whose intelligence relationship to the United States is classified information, and—

(i) who resides and acts outside the United States as an agent of, or informant or source of operational assistance to, an intelligence agency, or

(ii) who is at the time of the disclosure acting as an agent of, or informant to, the foreign counterintelligence or foreign counterterrorism components of the Federal Bureau of Investigation; or

(C) an individual, other than a United States citizen, whose past or present intelligence relationship to the United States is classified information and who is a present or former agent of, or a present or former informant or source of operational assistance to, an intelligence agency.

(5) The term "intelligence agency" means the Central Intelligence Agency, a foreign intelligence component of the Department of Defense, or the foreign counterintelligence or foreign counterterrorism components of the Federal Bureau of Investigation.

(6) The term "informant" means any individual who furnishes information to an intelligence agency in the course of a confidential relationship protecting the identity of such individual from public disclosure.

....

(10) The term "pattern of activities" requires a series of acts with a common purpose or objective.

HUGHES-RYAN AMENDMENT* (INTELLIGENCE OVERSIGHT)

§ 413. General congressional oversight provisions

(a) Reports to Congressional committees of intelligence activities and anticipated activities.

(1) The President shall ensure that the congressional intelligence committees are kept fully and currently informed of the intelligence activities of the United States, including any significant anticipated intelligence activity as required by this title [50 USCS §§ 413 et seq.].

(2) Nothing in this title [50 USCS §§ 413 et seq.] shall be construed as requiring the approval of the congressional intelligence committees as a condition precedent to the initiation of any significant anticipated intelligence activity.

(b) Reports concerning illegal intelligence activities. The President shall ensure that any illegal intelligence activity is reported promptly to the congressional intelligence committees, as well as any corrective action that has been taken or is planned in connection with such illegal activity.

(c) Procedures for reporting information. The President and the congressional intelligence committees shall each establish such procedures as may be necessary to carry out the provision of this title [50 USCS §§ 413 et seq.].

(d) Procedures to protect from unauthorized disclosure. The House of Representatives and the Senate shall each establish, by rule or resolution of such House, procedures to protect from unauthorized disclosure all classified information, and all information relating to intelligence sources and methods, that is furnished to the congressional intelligence committees or to Members of Congress under this title [50 USCS §§ 413 et seq.]. Such procedures shall be established in consultation with the Director of National Intelligence. In accordance with such procedures, each of the congressional intelligence committees shall promptly call to the attention of its respective House, or to any appropriate committee or committees of its respective House, any matter relating to intelligence activities requiring the attention of such House or such committee or committees.

(e) Construction of authority conferred. Nothing in this Act shall be construed as authority to withhold information from the congressional intelligence committees on the grounds that providing the information to the intelligence committees would constitute the unauthorized disclosure of classified information or information relating to intelligence sources and methods.

(f) "Intelligence activities" defined. As used in this section, the term "intelligence activities" includes covert actions as defined in section 503(e) [50 USCS § 413b(e)], and includes financial intelligence activities.

* Pub. L. No. 102-88, § 602(a)(2), 105 Stat. 441 (1991) (codified as amended at 50 U.S.C.S. § 413 (LexisNexis 2004 & Supp. 2005)).

EXECUTIVE ORDER 12863[1] (PRESIDENT'S FOREIGN INTELLIGENCE ADVISORY BOARD, AS AMENDED BY EXECUTIVE ORDERS 13070, 13301, 13376)

By the authority vested in me as President by the Constitution and the laws of the United States of America, and in order to enhance the security of the United States by improving the quality and effectiveness of intelligence available to the United States, and to assure the legality of activities of the Intelligence Community, it is ordered as follows:

Part I. Assessment of Intelligence Activities

Section 1.1. There is hereby established within the White House Office, Executive Office of the President, the President's Foreign Intelligence Advisory Board (PFIAB). The PFIAB shall consist of not more than 16 members, who shall serve at the pleasure of the President and shall be appointed by the President from among trustworthy and distinguished citizens outside the Government who are qualified on the basis of achievement, experience and independence. The President shall establish the terms of the members upon their appointment. To the extent practicable, one-third of the PFIAB at any one time shall be comprised of members whose term of service does not exceed 2 years. The President shall designate a Chairman and Vice Chairman from among the members. The PFIAB shall utilize full-time staff and consultants as authorized by the President. Such staff shall be headed by an Executive Director, appointed by the President.

Sec. 1.2. The PFIAB shall assess the quality, quantity, and adequacy of intelligence collection, of analysis and estimates, and of counterintelligence and other intelligence activities. The PFIAB shall have the authority to review continually the performance of all agencies of the Federal Government that are engaged in the collection, evaluation, or production of intelligence or the execution of intelligence policy. The PFIAB shall further be authorized to assess the adequacy of management, personnel and organization in the intelligence agencies. The heads of departments and agencies of the Federal Government, to the extent permitted by law, shall provide the PFIAB with access to all information that the PFIAB deems necessary to carry out its responsibilities.

Sec. 1.3. The PFIAB shall report directly to the President and advise him concerning the objectives, conduct, management and coordination of the various activities of the agencies of the Intelligence Community. The PFIAB shall report periodically, but at least semiannually, concerning its findings and appraisals and shall make appropriate recommendations for the improvement and enhancement of the intelligence efforts of the United States.

Sec. 1.4. The PFIAB shall consider and recommend appropriate action with respect to matters, identified to the PFIAB by the Director of National[2] Intelligence, the Central Intelligence Agency, or other Government agencies engaged in intelligence or related ac-

1. Exec. Order No. 12863, 3 C.F.R. 632 (1993), *reprinted as amended in* 50 U.S.C.A. § 401 note (West Supp. 2006), *available at* http://www.fas.org/irp/offdocs/eo12863.htm.

2. Amended by President George W. Bush in Executive Order 13376 of April 13, 2005, to change "director of Central Intelligence" to "Director of National Intelligence." *See* Exec. Order No. 13376, 70 F.R. 20,261 (Apr. 13, 2005).

tivities, in which the advice of the PFIAB will further the effectiveness of the national intelligence effort. With respect to matters deemed appropriate by the President, the PFIAB shall advise and make recommendations to the Director of National[3] Intelligence, the Central Intelligence Agency, and other Government agencies engaged in intelligence and related activities, concerning ways to achieve increased effectiveness in meeting national intelligence needs.

Part II. Oversight of Intelligence Activities

Sec. 2.1. The Intelligence Oversight Board (IOB) is hereby established as a standing committee of the PFIAB. The IOB shall consist of no more than five[4] members designated by the President from among the membership of the PFIAB. The Chairman of the PFIAB may also serve as the Chairman or a member of the IOB if so designated by the President. The IOB shall utilize such full-time staff and consultants as authorized by the Chairman of the IOB with the concurrence of the Chairman of the PFIAB.[5]

Sec. 2.2. The IOB shall:

(a) prepare for the President reports of intelligence activities that the IOB believes may be unlawful or contrary to Executive order or Presidential directive;

(b) forward to the Attorney General reports received concerning intelligence activities that the IOB believes may be unlawful or contrary to Executive order or Presidential directive;

(c) review the internal guidelines of each agency within the Intelligence Community that concern the lawfulness of intelligence activities;

(d) review the practices and procedures of the Inspectors General and General Counsel of the Intelligence Community for discovering and reporting intelligence activities that may be unlawful or contrary to Executive order or Presidential directive; and

(e) conduct such investigations as the IOB deems necessary to carry out its functions under this order.

Sec. 2.3. The IOB shall report to the President.[6] The IOB shall consider and take appropriate action with respect to matters identified by the Director of National Intelligence,[7] the Central Intelligence Agency or other agencies of the Intelligence Community. With respect to matters deemed appropriate by the President, the IOB shall advise and make appropriate recommendations to the Director of National Intelligence, the Central Intelligence Agency and other agencies of the Intelligence Community.

Sec. 2.4. The heads of departments and agencies of the Intelligence Community, to the extent permitted by law, shall provide the IOB with all information that the IOB deems necessary to carry out its responsibilities. Inspectors General and General Counsel of the Intelligence Community, to the extent permitted by law, shall report to the IOB, at least on a quarterly basis and from time to time as necessary or appropriate,

---

3. *Id.*

4. Amended by President Bush by Executive Order 13301 of May 14, 2003 to increase membership from four to five. *See* Exec. Order No. 13301, 3 C.F.R. 226 (2003).

5. Amended by President Clinton in Executive Order 13070 of December 15, 1997 "in order to emphasize the role of the Intelligence Oversight Board in providing executive branch oversight...." *See* Exec. Order No. 13070, 3 C.F.R. 234 (1997).

6. Amended by President Clinton by Executive Order 13070 of December 15, 1997. *See id.* In the original the IOB reported to the President "through" the PFIAB Chairman.

7. *See supra,* note 1.

concerning intelligence activities that they have reason to believe may be unlawful or contrary to Executive order or Presidential directive.

Part III. General Provisions

Sec. 3.1. Information made available to the PFIAB, or members of the PFIAB acting in their IOB capacity, shall be given all necessary security protection in accordance with applicable laws and regulations. Each member of the PFIAB, each member of the PFIAB's staff and each of the PFIAB's consultants shall execute an agreement never to reveal any classified information obtained by virtue of his or her services with the PFIAB except to the President or to such persons as the President may designate.

Sec. 3.2. Members of the PFIAB shall serve without compensation but may receive transportation expenses and per diem allowance as authorized by law. Staff and consultants to the PFIAB shall receive pay and allowances as authorized by the President.

Sec. 3.3. Executive Order No. 12334 of December 4, 1981, as amended, and Executive Order No. 12537 of October 28, 1985, as amended,[8] are revoked.

Sec. 3.4. This order is intended only to improve the internal management of the executive branch of the Federal Government, and is not intended to, and does not, create any right or benefit, substantive or procedural, enforceable at law or in equity, against the United States, its departments, agencies, or other entities, its officers or employees, or any other person.

William J. Clinton

The White House,
September 13, 1993.

---

8. Amended by President George W. Bush by Exec. Order No. 13376, 70 F.R. 20,261 (Apr. 13, 2005).

EXECUTIVE ORDER 12949* (FOREIGN INTELLIGENCE PHYSICAL SEARCHES AS AMENDED BY EXECUTIVE ORDER 13383)

By the authority vested in me as President by the Constitution and the laws of the United States, including sections 302 and 303 of the Foreign Intelligence Surveillance Act of 1978 ("Act") *(50 U.S.C. 1801,* et seq.), as amended by Public Law 103-359, and in order to provide for the authorization of physical searches for foreign intelligence purposes as set forth in the Act, it is hereby ordered as follows:

Section 1. Pursuant to section 302(a)(1) of the Act, the Attorney General is authorized to approve physical searches, without a court order, to acquire foreign intelligence information for periods of up to one year, if the Attorney General makes the certifications required by that section.

Section 2. Pursuant to section 302(b) of the Act, the Attorney General is authorized to approve applications to the Foreign Intelligence Surveillance Court under section 303 of the Act to obtain orders for physical searches for the purpose of collecting foreign intelligence information.

Section 3. Pursuant to section 303(a)(7) of the Act, the following officials, each of whom is employed in the area of national security or defense, is designated to make the certifications required by section 303(a)(7) of the Act in support of applications to conduct physical searches:

(a) Secretary of State;

(b) Secretary of Defense;

(c) Director of National Intelligence;

(d) Director of the Federal Bureau of Investigation;

(e) Deputy Secretary of State;

(f) Deputy Secretary of Defense;

(g) Director of the Central Intelligence Agency; and

(h) Principal Deputy Director of National Intelligence.

None of the above officials, nor anyone officially acting in that capacity, may exercise the authority to make the above certifications, unless that official has been appointed by the President, by and with the advice and consent of the Senate.

WILLIAM J. CLINTON
THE WHITE HOUSE,
February 9, 1995

---

* Exec. Order No. 12949, 3 C.F.R. 321 (1995), *reprinted as amended in* 50 U.S.C. § 1822 note (2000), *available at* http://frwebgate.access.gpo.gov/cgi-bin/getdoc.cgi?dbname=1995_register&docid=fr13fe95-85.pdf.

ECONOMIC ESPIONAGE ACT OF 1996*

. . . .

Section 1831. *Economic espionage.* (a) In General.—Whoever, intending or knowing that the offense will benefit any foreign government, foreign instrumentality, or foreign agent, knowingly—

(1) steals, or without authorization appropriates, takes, carries away, or conceals, or by fraud, artifice, or deception obtains a trade secret;

(2) without authorization copies, duplicates, sketches, draws, photographs, downloads, uploads, alters, destroys, photocopies, replicates, transmits, delivers, sends, mails, communicates, or conveys a trade secret;

(3) receives, buys, or possesses a trade secret, knowing the same to have been stolen or appropriated, obtained, or converted without authorization;

(4) attempts to commit any offense described in any of paragraphs (1) through (3); or

(5) conspires with one or more other persons to commit any offense described in any of paragraphs (1) through (3), and one or more of such persons do any act to effect the object of the conspiracy, shall, except as provided in subsection (b), be fined not more than $ 500,000 or imprisoned not more than 15 years, or both.

(b) Organizations.—Any organization that commits any offense described in subsection (a) shall be fined not more than $ 10,000,000.

Section 1832. *Theft of trade secrets.* (a) Whoever, with intent to convert a trade secret, that is related to or included in a product that is produced for or placed in interstate or foreign commerce, to the economic benefit of anyone other than the owner thereof, and intending or knowing that the offense will, injure any owner of that trade secret, knowingly—

(1) steals, or without authorization appropriates, takes, carries away, or conceals, or by fraud, artifice, or deception obtains such information;

(2) without authorization copies, duplicates, sketches, draws, photographs, downloads, uploads, alters, destroys, photocopies, replicates, transmits, delivers, sends, mails, communicates, or conveys such information;

(3) receives, buys, or possesses such information, knowing the same to have been stolen or appropriated, obtained, or converted without authorization;

(4) attempts to commit any offense described in paragraphs (1) through (3); or

(5) conspires with one or more other persons to commit any offense described in paragraphs (1) through (3), and one or more of such persons do any act to effect the object of the conspiracy, shall, except as provided in subsection (b), be fined under this title or imprisoned not more than 10 years, or both.

(b) Any organization that commits any offense described in subsection (a) shall be fined not more than $ 5,000,000.

---

* Economic Espionage Act of 1996, Pub. L. No. 104-294, 110 Stat. 3488 (codified as amended at 18 U.S.C.A. §§ 1831–1839 (West 2000 & Supp. 2005)), *available at* http://www.tscm.com/USC18_90.html.

Section 1833. *Exceptions to prohibitions.* This chapter does not prohibit—

(1) any otherwise lawful activity conducted by a governmental entity of the United States, a State, or a political subdivision of a State; or

(2) the reporting of a suspected violation of law to any governmental entity of the United States, a State, or a political subdivision of a State, if such entity has lawful authority with respect to that violation.

Section 1834. *Criminal forfeiture.* (a) The court, in imposing sentence on a person for a violation of this chapter, shall order, in addition to any other sentence imposed, that the person forfeit to the United States—

(1) any property constituting, or derived from, any proceeds the person obtained, directly or indirectly, as the result of such violation; and

(2) any of the person's property used, or intended to be used, in any manner or part, to commit or facilitate the commission of such violation, if the court in its discretion so determines, taking into consideration the nature, scope, and proportionality of the use of the property in the offense.

(b) Property subject to forfeiture under this section, any seizure and disposition thereof, and any administrative or judicial proceeding in relation thereto, shall be governed by section 413 of the Comprehensive Drug Abuse Prevention and Control Act of 1970, except for subsections (d) and (j) of such section, which shall not apply to forfeitures under this section.

Section 1835. *Orders to preserve confidentiality.* In any prosecution or other proceeding under this chapter, the court shall enter such orders and take such other action as may be necessary and appropriate to preserve the confidentiality of trade secrets, consistent with the requirements of the Federal Rules of Criminal and Civil Procedure, the Federal Rules of Evidence, and all other applicable laws. An interlocutory appeal by the United States shall lie from a decision or order of a district court authorizing or directing the disclosure of any trade secret.

Section 1836. *Civil proceedings to enjoin violations.* (a) The Attorney General may, in a civil action, obtain appropriate injunctive relief against any violation of this section.

(b) The district courts of the United States shall have exclusive original jurisdiction of civil actions under this subsection.

Section 1837. *Applicability to conduct outside the United States.* This chapter also applies to conduct occurring outside the United States if—

(1) the offender is a natural person who is a citizen or permanent resident alien of the United States, or an organization organized under the laws of the United States or a State or political subdivision thereof; or

(2) an act in furtherance of the offense was committed in the United States.

Section 1838. *Construction with other laws.* This chapter shall not be construed to preempt or displace any other remedies, whether civil or criminal, provided by United States Federal, State, commonwealth, possession, or territory law for the misappropriation of a trade secret, or to affect the otherwise lawful disclosure of information by any Government employee under section 552 of title 5 (commonly known as the Freedom of Information Act).

Section 1839. *Definitions.* As used in this chapter—

(1) the term "foreign instrumentality" means any agency, bureau, ministry, component, institution, association, or any legal, commercial, or business organi-

zation, corporation, firm, or entity that is substantially owned, controlled, sponsored, commanded, managed, or dominated by a foreign government;

(2) the term "foreign agent" means any officer, employee, proxy, servant, delegate, or representative of a foreign government;

(3) the term "trade secret" means all forms and types of financial, business, scientific, technical, economic, or engineering information, including patterns, plans, compilations, program devices, formulas, designs, prototypes, methods, techniques, processes, procedures, programs, or codes, whether tangible or intangible, and whether or how stored, compiled, or memorialized physically, electronically, graphically, photographically, or in writing if—

(A) the owner thereof has taken reasonable measures to keep such information secret; and

(B) the information derives independent economic value, actual or potential, from not being generally known to, and not being readily ascertainable through proper means by, the public; and

(4) the term "owner", with respect to a trade secret, means the person or entity in whom or in which rightful legal or equitable title to, or license in, the trade secret is reposed.

(b) Clerical Amendment.—The table of chapters at the beginning part I of title 18, United States Code, is amended by inserting after the item relating to chapter 89 the following:

"90. Protection of trade secrets 1831".

(c) Reports.—Not later than 2 years and 4 years after the date of the enactment of this Act, the Attorney General shall report to Congress on the amounts received and distributed from fines for offenses under this chapter deposited in the Crime Victims Fund established by section 1402 of the Victims of Crime Act of 1984 (42 U.S.C. 10601).

....

ATTORNEY GENERAL'S GUIDELINES FOR FBI NATIONAL SECURITY INVESTIGATIONS AND FOREIGN INTELLIGENCE COLLECTION*

Background Note

Following congressional investigations of reported intelligence abuses in the aftermath of Watergate and the Vietnam War, in 1976 Attorney General Edward Levy issued classified guidelines for FBI national security investigations and foreign intelligence collection. The most recent version of these guidelines was issued in October, 2003, by Attorney General John Ashcroft. While substantial portions of the guidelines remain classified, some provisions have been made public and are excerpted here.—Eds.

....

A. NATIONAL SECURITY INVESTIGATIONS

These Guidelines authorize the investigation by the FBI of threats to the national security. Matters constituting threats to the national security, including international terrorism and espionage, are identified in Part 1.A1. Parts II and V of the Guidelines contain the specific provisions governing the conduct of investigations of these threats.

The investigations authorized by these Guidelines serve to protect the national security by providing the basis for, and informing decisions concerning, a variety of measures to deal with threats to the national security. These measures may include, for example, recruitment of double agents and other assets; excluding or removing persons involved in terrorism or espionage from the United States; freezing assets of organizations that engage in or support terrorism; securing targets of terrorism or espionage; providing threat information and warnings to other federal agencies and officials, state and local governments, and private entities; diplomatic or military actions; and actions by other intelligence agencies to counter international terrorism or other national security threats. In addition, the matters identified by these Guidelines as threats to the national security, including international terrorism and espionage, almost invariably involve possible violations of criminal statutes. Detecting, solving, and preventing these crimes—and in many cases, arresting and prosecuting the perpetrators—are crucial objectives of national security investigations under these Guidelines. Thus, these investigations are usually both "counterintelligence" investigations and "criminal" investigations.

The authority to conduct national security investigations under these Guidelines does not supplant or limit the authority to carry out activities under other Attorney General guidelines or pursuant to other lawful authorities of the FBI. Thus, matters within the scope of these Guidelines, such as crimes involved in international terrorism and the activities of groups and organizations that aim to commit such crimes, may

---

* JOHN ASHCROFT, U.S. ATT'Y GEN., THE ATTORNEY GENERAL'S GUIDELINES FOR FBI NATIONAL SECURITY INVESTIGATIONS AND FOREIGN INTELLIGENCE COLLECTION (Oct. 31, 2003), *available at* http://www.fas.org/irp/agency/doj/fbi/nsiguidelines.pdf.

also be investigated under the guidelines for general crimes investigations and criminal intelligence investigations....

....

[CLASSIFIED LANGUAGE OMITTED]

....

D. RETENTION AND DISSEMINATION OF INFORMATION

Part VII of these Guidelines requires the maintenance of adequate records and information relating to investigations and other activities under these Guidelines, and provides standards for the sharing and dissemination of information obtained in such investigations and activities.

Part VII includes, in Subpart B.2, provisions for sharing of information and consultation with other Department of Justice components, which reflect legal reforms and policies adopted by the Attorney General following the September 11, 2001, terrorist attack. Consistent with legal norms and standards of effective management, all relevant components, including the Criminal Division, relevant United States Attorneys' offices and the Office of Intelligence Policy and Review, must be fully informed about the nature, scope, and conduct of national security investigations and other activities under these Guidelines....

I. <u>GENERAL AUTHORITIES AND PRINCIPLES</u>

A. GENERAL AUTHORITIES

1. The FBI is authorized to conduct investigations to obtain information concerning or to protect against threats to the national security, including investigations of crimes involved in or related to threats to the national security, as provided in Parts II and V of these Guidelines. Threats to the national security are:

a. International terrorism.

b. Espionage and other intelligence activities, sabotage, or assassination, conducted by, for, or on behalf of foreign powers, organizations, or persons.

c. Foreign computer intrusions.

d. Other matters as determined by the Attorney General, consistent with Executive Order 12333 or a successor order.

....

B. USE OF AUTHORITIES AND METHODS

1. Protection of National Security

The FBI shall fully utilize the authorities provided and the methods authorized by these Guidelines to protect the national security of the United States.

2. Choice of Methods

The conduct of investigations and other activities authorized by these Guidelines may present choices between the use of information collection methods that are more or less intrusive, considering such factors as the effect on the privacy of individuals and potential damage to reputation. As Executive Order 12333 § 2.4 provides, "the least intrusive collection techniques feasible" are to be used in such situations. It is recognized, however, that the choice of techniques is a matter of judgment. The FBI shall not hesitate to use any lawful techniques consistent with these Guidelines, even if intrusive, where the degree of intrusiveness is warranted in light of the seriousness of a threat to the national security or the strength of the information indicating its existence. This point is to be particularly observed in investigations relating to terrorism.

3. Respect for Legal Rights

These Guidelines do not authorize investigating or maintaining information on United States persons solely for the purpose of monitoring activities protected by the First Amendment or the lawful exercise of other rights secured by the Constitution or laws of the United States. Rather, all activities under these Guidelines must have a valid purpose consistent with these Guidelines, and must be carried out in conformity with the Constitution and all applicable statutes, executive orders, Department of Justice regulations and policies, and Attorney General guidelines.

. . . .

C. DETERMINATION OF UNITED STATES PERSON STATUS

In some contexts, these Guidelines provide different standards or rules depending on whether investigations or other activities relate to a United States person or to a non-United States person. This Subpart shall be applied in determining whether an individual, group, or organization is a United States person.

1. Meaning of United States Person

A United States person is:

a. an individual who is a United States citizen or an alien lawfully admitted for permanent residence;

b. an unincorporated association substantially composed of individuals who are United States persons; or

c. a corporation incorporated in the United States.

Notwithstanding the foregoing, a foreign power as defined in Part VIII.L.1.-3. of these Guidelines is never to be considered a United States person, including any foreign government or component thereof, any faction of a foreign nation or nations not substantially composed of individuals who are United States persons, or any entity that is openly acknowledged by a foreign government or governments to be directed and controlled by such foreign government or governments.

[CLASSIFIED LANGUAGE OMITTED]

3. Determination Whether Certain Groups are Substantially Composed of United States Persons

In determining whether a group or organization in the United States that is affiliated with a foreign-based international organization is substantially composed of United States persons, the relationship between the two shall be considered. If the U.S.-based group or organization operates directly under the control of the international organization and has no independent program or activities in the United States, the membership of the entire international organization shall be considered in determining if it is substantially composed of United States persons. If, however, the U.S.-based group or organization has programs or activities separate from, or in addition to, those directed by the international organization, only its membership in the United States shall be considered in determining whether it is substantially composed of United States persons.

D. NATURE AND APPLICATION OF THE GUIDELINES

1. Status as Internal Guidance

These Guidelines are set forth solely for the purpose of internal Department of Justice guidance. They are not intended to, do not, and may not be relied upon to create any rights, substantive or procedural, enforceable by law by any party in any matter, civil or criminal, nor do they place any limitation on otherwise lawful investigative and litigative prerogatives of the Department of Justice.

....

II. NATIONAL SECURITY INVESTIGATIONS

The levels of investigative activity in national security investigations are: (1) threat assessments; (2) preliminary investigations; and (3) full investigations. If the available information shows at any point that the threshold standard for a preliminary investigation or full investigation is satisfied, then. that level of investigative activity may be initiated immediately, without progressing through more limited investigative stages.

....

[CLASSIFIED LANGUAGE OMITTED]

B. COMMON PROVISIONS FOR PRELIMINARY AND FULL INVESTIGATIONS

l. Circumstances for Opening an Investigation

[CLASSIFIED LANGUAGE OMITTED]

2. Authorization and Notice

a. An FBI field office or FBI Headquarters may initiate a preliminary or full investigation. A field office shall notify FBI Headquarters within ten working days of the initiation by the field office of a preliminary or full investigation. The notice of initiation of a preliminary or full investigation, whether the investigation is initiated by a field office or FBI Headquarters, shall identify the grounds for the investigation [CLASSIFIED LANGUAGE OMITTED].

....

3. Investigations of Groups and Organizations

a. Preliminary and full investigations of groups and organizations should focus on activities related to threats to the national security, not on unrelated First Amendment activities [CLASSIFIED LANGUAGE OMITTED].

....

[CLASSIFIED LANGUAGE OMITTED]

....

III. INVESTIGATIVE ASSISTANCE TO STATE, LOCAL, AND FOREIGN GOVERNMENTS

....

B. FOREIGN GOVERNMENTS

1. The FBI may conduct, background inquiries concerning consenting individuals when requested by foreign governments or agencies.

2. At the request of foreign law enforcement, intelligence, or security agencies, the FBI may, within the United States, conduct intelligence or security related investigations or provide assistance to such investigations by such agencies, consistent with the national security interests of the United States and with due consideration of the effect on any identifiable United States person. Such requests must be in writing and must identify the information sought and specify the purpose of the investigation. investigations or assistance under this paragraph must be approved by FBI Headquarters [CLASSIFIED LANGUAGE OMITTED].

....

[CLASSIFIED LANGUAGE OMITTED]

....

B. INFORMATION SHARING

Legal rules and Department of Justice policies regarding information sharing and interagency coordination have been significantly modified since the September 11, 2001, terrorist attack by statutory reforms and new Attorney General guidelines. The general principle reflected in current laws and policies is that information should be shared as consistently and fully as possible among agencies with relevant responsibilities to protect the United States and its people from terrorism and other threats to the national security, except as limited by specific constraints on such sharing. Under this general principle, the FBI shall provide information expeditiously to other agencies in the Intelligence Community, so that these agencies can take action in a timely manner to protect the national security in accordance with their lawful functions. This Subpart provides standards and procedures for the sharing and dissemination of information obtained in national security investigations, foreign intelligence collection, and other activities under these Guidelines.

1. General

a. Information may be disseminated with the consent of the person whom the information concerns, or where necessary to protect life or property from threatened force or violence, otherwise necessary for the safety or security of persons or property or for the prevention of crime, or necessary to obtain information for the conduct of a lawful investigation by the FBI.

b. Information that is publicly available or does not identify United States persons may be disseminated for any lawful purpose.

c. Dissemination of information provided to the FBI by other Intelligence Community agencies is subject to applicable agreements and understandings with such agencies concerning the dissemination of such information.

....

C. SPECIAL STATUTORY REQUIREMENTS

1. Dissemination of information acquired under the Foreign Intelligence Surveillance Act is subject to minimization procedures approved by the Foreign Intelligence Surveillance Court and other requirements specified in that Act.

2. Information obtained through the use of National Security Letters under 15 U.S.C. 1681 v may be disseminated in conformity with the general standards of this Part....

VIII. DEFINITIONS

A. AGENT OF A FOREIGN POWER:

1. any person who is not a United States person and who:

a. acts in the United States as an officer or employee of a foreign power, or as a member of a group engaged in international terrorism or activities in preparation therefor; or

b. acts for or on behalf of a foreign power which engages in clandestine intelligence activities in the United States contrary to the interests of the United States, when the circumstances of such person's presence in the United States indicate that such person may engage in such activities in the United States, or when such person knowingly aids or abets any person in the conduct of such activities or knowingly conspires with any person to engage in such activities; or

2. any person who:

a. knowingly engages in clandestine intelligence gathering activities for or on behalf of a foreign power, which activities involve or may involve a violation of the criminal statutes of the United States;

b. pursuant to the direction of an intelligence service or network of a foreign power, knowingly engages in any other clandestine intelligence activities for or on behalf of such foreign power, which activities involve or are about to involve a violation of the criminal statutes of the United States;

c. knowingly engages in sabotage or international terrorism, or activities that are in preparation therefor, for of, on behalf of a foreign power;

d. knowingly enters the United States under a false or fraudulent identity for or on behalf of a foreign power or, while in the United States, knowingly assumes a false or fraudulent identity for or on behalf of a foreign power; or

e. knowingly aids or abets any person in the conduct of activities described in subparagraph a., b., or c., or knowingly conspires with any person to engage in such activities.

....

[CLASSIFIED LANGUAGE OMITTED]

....

O. INTERNATIONAL TERRORISM:

Activities that:

1. involve violent acts or acts dangerous to human life that are a violation of the criminal laws of the United States or of any State, or that would be a criminal violation if committed within the jurisdiction of the United States or any State;

2. appear to be intended:

a. to intimidate or coerce a civilian population;

b. to influence the policy of a government by intimidation or coercion;

c. to affect the conduct of a government by assassination or kidnapping; and

3. occur totally outside the United States, or transcend national boundaries in terms of the means by which they are accomplished, the persons they appear to be intended to coerce or intimidate, or the locale in which their perpetrators operate or seek asylum.

....

[CLASSIFIED LANGUAGE OMITTED]

....

Y. UNDISCLOSED PARTICIPATION:

Joining or participating in the activities of an organization by an FBI asset or employee without disclosure of FBI affiliation, but not including participation with the knowledge and approval of an official of the organization authorized to act in relation to the activities in question, attendance at an activity open to the public or to acknowledged U.S. Government employees, personal activities not related to FBI employment, or attendance at an academic institution to obtain education or training relevant to FBI employment or to a future undercover role.

....

[signed]
John Ashcroft
Attorney General
Date: October 31, 2003

INTELLIGENCE REFORM AND TERRORISM PREVENTION ACT OF 2004*

An Act

To reform the intelligence community and the intelligence and intelligence-related activities of the United States Government, and for other purposes.

Be it enacted by the Senate and House of Representatives of the United States of America in Congress assembled,

SECTION 1. SHORT TITLE; TABLE OF CONTENTS.

(a) Short Title.—This Act may be cited as the "Intelligence Reform and Terrorism Prevention Act of 2004".

(b) Table of Contents.—The table of contents for this Act is as follows:

* Intelligence Reform and Terrorism Prevention Act of 2004, Pub. L. No. 108-458, 118 Stat. 3638 (codified as amended in scattered sections of U.S.C.A.), *available at* http://www.c-span.org/resources/pdf/2004IntelAct.pdf.

Since the Intelligence Reform and Terrorism Prevention Act of 2004 is 236 pages, and only a short portion is reprinted here, the Table of Contents of the Act has been included here in full.

Sec. 4020. Checked baggage screening area monitoring.
Sec. 4021. Wireless communication.
Sec. 4022. Improved pilot licenses.
Sec. 4023. Aviation security staffing.
Sec. 4024. Improved explosive detection systems.
Sec. 4025. Prohibited items list.
Sec. 4026. Man-Portable Air Defense Systems (MANPADs).
Sec. 4027. Technical corrections.
Sec. 4028. Report on secondary flight deck barriers.
Sec. 4029. Extension of authorization of aviation security funding.

Subtitle C—Air Cargo Security

Sec. 4051. Pilot program to evaluate use of blast resistant cargo and baggage containers.
Sec. 4052. Air cargo security.
Sec. 4053. Air cargo security regulations.
Sec. 4054. Report on international air cargo threats.

Subtitle D—Maritime Security

Sec. 4071. Watch lists for passengers aboard vessels.
Sec. 4072. Deadlines for completion of certain plans, reports, and assessments.

Subtitle E—General Provisions

Sec. 4081. Definitions.
Sec. 4082. Effective date.

TITLE V—BORDER PROTECTION, IMMIGRATION, AND VISA MATTERS

Subtitle A—Advanced Technology Northern Border Security Pilot Program

Sec. 5101. Establishment.
Sec. 5102. Program requirements.
Sec. 5103. Administrative provisions.
Sec. 5104. Report.
Sec. 5105. Authorization of appropriations.

Subtitle B—Border and Immigration Enforcement

Sec. 5201. Border surveillance.
Sec. 5202. Increase in full-time Border Patrol agents.
Sec. 5203. Increase in full-time immigration and customs enforcement investigators.
Sec. 5204. Increase in detention bed space.

TITLE I—REFORM OF THE INTELLIGENCE COMMUNITY

SEC. 1001. SHORT TITLE.

This title may be cited as the "National Security Intelligence Reform Act of 2004".

Subtitle A—Establishment of Director of National Intelligence

SEC. 1011. REORGANIZATION AND IMPROVEMENT OF MANAGEMENT OF INTELLIGENCE COMMUNITY.

(a) In General.—Title I of the National Security Act of 1947 (50 U.S.C. 402 et seq.) is amended by striking sections 102 through 104 and inserting the following new sections:

"DIRECTOR OF NATIONAL INTELLIGENCE

"Sec. 102. (a) Director of National Intelligence.—(1) There is a Director of National Intelligence who shall be appointed by the President, by and with the advice and consent of the Senate. Any individual nominated for appointment as Director of National Intelligence shall have extensive national security expertise.

"(2) The Director of National Intelligence shall not be located within the Executive Office of the President.

"(b) Principal Responsibility.—Subject to the authority, direction, and control of the President, the Director of National Intelligence shall—

"(1) serve as head of the intelligence community;

"(2) act as the principal adviser to the President, to the National Security Council, and the Homeland Security Council for intelligence matters related to the national security; and

"(3) consistent with section 1018 of the National Security Intelligence Reform Act of 2004, oversee and direct the implementation of the National Intelligence Program.

"(c) Prohibition on Dual Service.—The individual serving in the position of Director of National Intelligence shall not, while so serving, also serve as the Director of the Central Intelligence Agency or as the head of any other element of the intelligence community.

"RESPONSIBILITIES AND AUTHORITIES OF THE DIRECTOR OF NATIONAL INTELLIGENCE

"SEC. 102A. (a) PROVISION OF INTELLIGENCE.—(1) The Director of National Intelligence shall be responsible for ensuring that national intelligence is provided—

"(A) to the President;

"(B) to the heads of departments and agencies of the executive branch;

"(C) to the Chairman of the Joint Chiefs of Staff and senior military commanders;

"(D) to the Senate and House of Representatives and the committees thereof; and

"(E) to such other persons as the Director of National Intelligence determines to be appropriate.

"(2) Such national intelligence should be timely, objective, independent of political considerations, and based upon all sources available to the intelligence community and other appropriate entities.

"(b) ACCESS TO INTELLIGENCE.—Unless otherwise directed by the President, the Director of National Intelligence shall have access to all national intelligence and intelligence related to the national security which is collected by any Federal department, agency, or other entity, except as otherwise provided by law or, as appropriate, under guidelines agreed upon by the Attorney General and the Director of National Intelligence.

"(c) BUDGET AUTHORITIES.—(1) With respect to budget requests and appropriations for the National Intelligence Program, the Director of National Intelligence shall—

"(A) based on intelligence priorities set by the President, provide to the heads of departments containing agencies or organizations within the intelligence community, and to the heads of such agencies and organizations, guidance for developing the National Intelligence Program budget pertaining to such agencies and organizations;

"(B) based on budget proposals provided to the Director of National Intelligence by the heads of agencies and organizations within the intelligence community and the heads of their respective departments and, as appropriate, after obtaining the advice of the Joint Intelligence Community Council, develop and determine an annual consolidated National Intelligence Program budget; and

"(C) present such consolidated National Intelligence Program budget, together with any comments from the heads of departments containing agencies or organizations within the intelligence community, to the President for approval.

"(2) In addition to the information provided under paragraph (1)(B), the heads of agencies and organizations within the intelligence community shall provide the Director of National Intelligence such other information as the Director shall request for the purpose of determining the annual consolidated National Intelligence Program budget under that paragraph.

"(3) (A) The Director of National Intelligence shall participate in the development by the Secretary of Defense of the annual budgets for the Joint Military Intelligence Program and for Tactical Intelligence and Related Activities.

"(B) The Director of National Intelligence shall provide guidance for the development of the annual budget for each element of the intelligence community that is not within the National Intelligence Program.

"(4) The Director of National Intelligence shall ensure the effective execution of the annual budget for intelligence and intelligence-related activities.

"(5) (A) The Director of National Intelligence shall be responsible for managing appropriations for the National Intelligence Program by directing the allotment or allocation of such appropriations through the heads of the departments containing agencies or organizations within the intelligence community and the Director of the Central Intelligence Agency, with prior notice (including the provision of appropriate supporting information) to the head of the department containing an agency or organization receiving any such allocation or allotment or the Director of the Central Intelligence Agency.

"(B) Notwithstanding any other provision of law, pursuant to relevant appropriations Acts for the National Intelligence Program, the Director of the Office of Management and Budget shall exercise the authority of the Director of the Office of Management and Budget to apportion funds, at the exclusive direction of the Director of National Intelligence, for allocation to the elements of the intelligence community through the relevant host executive departments and the Central Intelligence Agency. Department comptrollers or appropriate budget execution officers shall allot, allocate, reprogram, or transfer funds appropriated for the National Intelligence Program in an expeditious manner.

"(C) The Director of National Intelligence shall monitor the implementation and execution of the National Intelligence Program by the heads of the elements of the intelligence community that manage programs and activities that are part of the National Intelligence Program, which may include audits and evaluations.

"(6) Apportionment and allotment of funds under this sub-section shall be subject to chapter 13 and section 1517 of title 31, United States Code, and the Congressional Budget and Impoundment Control Act of 1974 (2 U.S.C. 621 et seq.).

"(7) (A) The Director of National Intelligence shall provide a semi-annual report, beginning April 1, 2005, and ending April 1, 2007, to the President and the Congress regarding implementation of this section.

"(B) The Director of National Intelligence shall report to the President and the Congress not later than 15 days after learning of any instance in which a departmental comptroller acts in a manner inconsistent with the law (including permanent statutes, authorization Acts, and appropriations Acts), or the direction of the Director of National Intelligence, in carrying out the National Intelligence Program.

"(d) ROLE OF DIRECTOR OF NATIONAL INTELLIGENCE IN TRANSFER AND REPROGRAMMING OF FUNDS.—(1) (A) No funds made available under the National Intelligence Program may be transferred or reprogrammed without the prior approval of the Director of National Intelligence, except in accordance with procedures prescribed by the Director of National Intelligence.

"(B) The Secretary of Defense shall consult with the Director of National Intelligence before transferring or reprogramming funds made available under the Joint Military Intelligence Program.

"(2) Subject to the succeeding provisions of this subsection, the Director of National Intelligence may transfer or reprogram funds appropriated for a program within the National Intelligence Program to another such program.

"(3) The Director of National Intelligence may only transfer or reprogram funds referred to in subparagraph (A)—

"(A) with the approval of the Director of the Office of Management and Budget; and

"(B) after consultation with the heads of departments containing agencies or organizations within the intelligence community to the extent such agencies or organizations are affected, and, in the case of the Central Intelligence Agency, after consultation with the Director of the Central Intelligence Agency.

"(4) The amounts available for transfer or reprogramming in the National Intelligence Program in any given fiscal year, and the terms and conditions governing such transfers and reprogrammings, are subject to the provisions of annual appropriations Acts and this subsection.

"(5) (A) A transfer or reprogramming of funds or personnel may be made under this subsection only if—

"(i) the funds are being transferred to an activity that is a higher priority intelligence activity;

"(ii) the transfer or reprogramming supports an emergent need, improves program effectiveness, or increases efficiency;

"(iii) the transfer or reprogramming does not involve a transfer or reprogramming of funds to a Reserve for Contingencies of the Director of National Intelligence or the Reserve for Contingencies of the Central Intelligence Agency;

"(iv) the transfer or reprogramming results in a cumulative transfer or reprogramming of funds out of any department or agency, as appropriate, funded in the National Intelligence Program in a single fiscal year—

"(I) that is less than $150,000,000, and

"(II) that is less than 5 percent of amounts available to a department or agency under the National Intelligence Program; and

"(v) the transfer or reprogramming does not terminate an acquisition program.

"(B) A transfer or reprogramming may be made without regard to a limitation set forth in clause (iv) or (v) of subparagraph (A) if the transfer has the concurrence of the head of the department involved or the Director of the Central Intelligence Agency (in the case of the Central Intelligence Agency). The authority to provide such concurrence may only be delegated by the head of the department or agency involved to the deputy of such officer.

"(6) Funds transferred or reprogrammed under this subsection shall remain available for the same period as the appropriations account to which transferred or reprogrammed.

"(7) Any transfer or reprogramming of funds under this subsection shall be carried out in accordance with existing procedures applicable to reprogramming notifications for the appropriate congressional committees. Any proposed transfer or reprogramming for which notice is given to the appropriate congressional committees shall be accompanied by a report explaining the nature of the proposed transfer or reprogramming and how it satisfies the requirements of this subsection. In addition, the congressional intelligence committees shall be promptly notified of any transfer or reprogramming of funds made pursuant to this subsection in any case in which the transfer or reprogramming would not have otherwise required reprogramming notification under procedures in effect as of the date of the enactment of this subsection.

"(e) TRANSFER OF PERSONNEL.—(1)(A) In addition to any other authorities available under law for such purposes, in the first twelve months after establishment of a new national intelligence center, the Director of National Intelligence, with the approval of the Director of the Office of Management and Budget and in consultation with the congressional committees of jurisdiction referred to in subparagraph (B), may transfer not more than 100 personnel authorized for elements of the intelligence community to such center.

"(B) The Director of National Intelligence shall promptly provide notice of any transfer of personnel made pursuant to this paragraph to—

"(i) the congressional intelligence committees;

"(ii) the Committees on Appropriations of the Senate and the House of Representatives;

"(iii) in the case of the transfer of personnel to or from the Department of Defense, the Committees on Armed Services of the Senate and the House of Representatives; and

"(iv) in the case of the transfer of personnel to or from the Department of Justice, to the Committees on the Judiciary of the Senate and the House of Representatives.

"(C) The Director shall include in any notice under subparagraph (B) an explanation of the nature of the transfer and how it satisfies the requirements of this subsection.

"(2) (A) The Director of National Intelligence, with the approval of the Director of the Office of Management and Budget and in accordance with procedures to be developed by the Director of National Intelligence and the heads of the departments and agencies concerned, may transfer personnel authorized for an element of the intelligence community to another such element for a period of not more than 2 years.

"(B) A transfer of personnel may be made under this paragraph only if—

"(i) the personnel are being transferred to an activity that is a higher priority intelligence activity; and

"(ii) the transfer supports an emergent need, improves program effectiveness, or increases efficiency.

"(C) The Director of National Intelligence shall promptly provide notice of any transfer of personnel made pursuant to this paragraph to—

"(i) the congressional intelligence committees;

"(ii) in the case of the transfer of personnel to or from the Department of Defense, the Committees on Armed Services of the Senate and the House of Representatives; and "(iii) in the case of the transfer of personnel to or from the Department of Justice, to the Committees on the Judiciary of the Senate and the House of Representatives.

"(D) The Director shall include in any notice under subparagraph (C) an explanation of the nature of the transfer and how it satisfies the requirements of this paragraph.

"(3) It is the sense of Congress that—

"(A) the nature of the national security threats facing the United States will continue to challenge the intelligence community to respond rapidly and flexibly to bring analytic resources to bear against emerging and unforeseen requirements;

"(B) both the Office of the Director of National Intelligence and any analytic centers determined to be necessary should be fully and properly supported with appropriate levels of personnel resources and that the President's yearly budget requests adequately support those needs; and

"(C) the President should utilize all legal and administrative discretion to ensure that the Director of National Intelligence and all other elements of the intelligence community have the necessary resources and procedures to respond promptly and effectively to emerging and unforeseen national security challenges.

"(f) Tasking and Other Authorities.—(1)(A) The Director of National Intelligence shall—

"(i) establish objectives, priorities, and guidance for the intelligence community to ensure timely and effective collection, processing, analysis, and dissemination (including access by users to collected data consistent with applicable law and, as appropriate, the guidelines referred to in subsection (b) and analytic products generated by or within the intelligence community) of national intelligence;

"(ii) determine requirements and priorities for, and manage and direct the tasking of, collection, analysis, production, and dissemination of national intelligence by elements of the intelligence community, including—

"(I) approving requirements (including those requirements responding to needs provided by consumers) for collection and analysis; and

"(II) resolving conflicts in collection requirements and in the tasking of national collection assets of the elements of the intelligence community; and

"(iii) provide advisory tasking to intelligence elements of those agencies and departments not within the National Intelligence Program.

"(B) The authority of the Director of National Intelligence under subparagraph (A) shall not apply—

"(i) insofar as the President so directs;

"(ii) with respect to clause (ii) of subparagraph (A), insofar as the Secretary of Defense exercises tasking authority under plans or arrangements agreed upon by the Secretary of Defense and the Director of National Intelligence; or "(iii) to the direct dissemination of information to State government and local government officials and private sector entities pursuant to sections 201 and 892 of the Homeland Security Act of 2002 (6 U.S.C. 121, 482).

"(2) The Director of National Intelligence shall oversee the National Counterterrorism Center and may establish such other national intelligence centers as the Director determines necessary.

"(3) (A) The Director of National Intelligence shall prescribe, in consultation with the heads of other agencies or elements of the intelligence community, and the heads of their respective departments, personnel policies and programs applicable to the intelligence community that—

"(i) encourage and facilitate assignments and details of personnel to national intelligence centers, and between elements of the intelligence community;

"(ii) set standards for education, training, and career development of personnel of the intelligence community;

"(iii) encourage and facilitate the recruitment and retention by the intelligence community of highly qualified individuals for the effective conduct of intelligence activities;

"(iv) ensure that the personnel of the intelligence community are sufficiently diverse for purposes of the collection and analysis of intelligence through the recruitment and training of women, minorities, and individuals with diverse ethnic, cultural, and linguistic backgrounds;

"(v) make service in more than one element of the intelligence community a condition of promotion to such positions within the intelligence community as the Director shall specify; and

"(vi) ensure the effective management of intelligence community personnel who are responsible for intelligence community-wide matters.

"(B) Policies prescribed under subparagraph (A) shall not be inconsistent with the personnel policies otherwise applicable to members of the uniformed services.

"(4) The Director of National Intelligence shall ensure compliance with the Constitution and laws of the United States by the Central Intelligence Agency and shall ensure such compliance by other elements of the intelligence community through the host executive departments that manage the programs and activities that are part of the National Intelligence Program.

"(5) The Director of National Intelligence shall ensure the elimination of waste and unnecessary duplication within the intelligence community.

"(6) The Director of National Intelligence shall establish requirements and priorities for foreign intelligence information to be collected under the Foreign Intelligence Surveillance Act of 1978 (50 U.S.C. 1801 et seq.), and provide assistance to the Attorney General to ensure that information derived from electronic surveillance or physical searches under that Act is disseminated so it may be used efficiently and effectively for national intelligence purposes, except that the Director shall have no authority to direct or undertake electronic surveillance or physical search operations pursuant to that Act unless authorized by statute or Executive order.

"(7) The Director of National Intelligence shall perform such other functions as the President may direct.

"(8) Nothing in this title shall be construed as affecting the role of the Department of Justice or the Attorney General under the Foreign Intelligence Surveillance Act of 1978.

"(g) Intelligence Information Sharing.—(1) The Director of National Intelligence shall have principal authority to ensure maximum availability of and access to intelligence information within the intelligence community consistent with national security requirements. The Director of National Intelligence shall—

"(A) establish uniform security standards and procedures;

"(B) establish common information technology standards, protocols, and interfaces;

"(C) ensure development of information technology systems that include multi-level security and intelligence integration capabilities;

"(D) establish policies and procedures to resolve conflicts between the need to share intelligence information and the need to protect intelligence sources and methods;

"(E) develop an enterprise architecture for the intelligence community and ensure that elements of the intelligence community comply with such architecture; and

"(F) have procurement approval authority over all enterprise architecture-related information technology items funded in the National Intelligence Program.

"(2) The President shall ensure that the Director of National Intelligence has all necessary support and authorities to fully and effectively implement paragraph (1).

"(3) Except as otherwise directed by the President or with the specific written agreement of the head of the department or agency in question, a Federal agency or official shall not be considered to have met any obligation to provide any information, report, assessment, or other material (including unevaluated intelligence information) to that department or agency solely by virtue of having provided that information, report, assessment, or other material to the Director of National Intelligence or the National Counterterrorism Center.

"(4) Not later than February 1 of each year, the Director of National Intelligence shall submit to the President and to the Congress an annual report that identifies any statute, regulation, policy, or practice that the Director believes impedes the ability of the Director to fully and effectively implement paragraph (1).

"(h) Analysis.—To ensure the most accurate analysis of intelligence is derived from all sources to support national security needs, the Director of National Intelligence shall—

"(1) implement policies and procedures—

"(A) to encourage sound analytic methods and tradecraft throughout the elements of the intelligence community;

"(B) to ensure that analysis is based upon all sources available; and

"(C) to ensure that the elements of the intelligence community regularly conduct competitive analysis of analytic products, whether such products are produced by or disseminated to such elements;

"(2) ensure that resource allocation for intelligence analysis is appropriately proportional to resource allocation for intelligence collection systems and operations in order to maximize analysis of all collected data;

"(3) ensure that differences in analytic judgment are fully considered and brought to the attention of policymakers; and

"(4) ensure that sufficient relationships are established between intelligence collectors and analysts to facilitate greater understanding of the needs of analysts.

"(i) PROTECTION OF INTELLIGENCE SOURCES AND METHODS.—(1) The Director of National Intelligence shall protect intelligence sources and methods from unauthorized disclosure.

"(2) Consistent with paragraph (1), in order to maximize the dissemination of intelligence, the Director of National Intelligence shall establish and implement guidelines for the intelligence community for the following purposes:

"(A) Classification of information under applicable law, Executive orders, or other Presidential directives.

"(B) Access to and dissemination of intelligence, both in final form and in the form when initially gathered.

"(C) Preparation of intelligence products in such a way that source information is removed to allow for dissemination at the lowest level of classification possible or in unclassified form to the extent practicable.

"(3) The Director may only delegate a duty or authority given the Director under this subsection to the Principal Deputy Director of National Intelligence.

"(j) UNIFORM PROCEDURES FOR SENSITIVE COMPARTMENTED INFORMATION.—The Director of National Intelligence, subject to the direction of the President, shall—

"(1) establish uniform standards and procedures for the grant of access to sensitive compartmented information to any officer or employee of any agency or department of the United States and to employees of contractors of those agencies or departments;

"(2) ensure the consistent implementation of those standards and procedures throughout such agencies and departments;

"(3) ensure that security clearances granted by individual elements of the intelligence community are recognized by all elements of the intelligence community, and under contracts entered into by those agencies; and

"(4) ensure that the process for investigation and adjudication of an application for access to sensitive compartmented information is performed in the most expeditious manner possible consistent with applicable standards for national security.

"(k) COORDINATION WITH FOREIGN GOVERNMENTS.—Under the direction of the President and in a manner consistent with section 207 of the Foreign Service Act of 1980 (22 U.S.C. 3927), the Director of National Intelligence shall oversee the coordination of the relationships between elements of the intelligence community and the intelligence or security services of foreign governments or international organizations on all matters involving intelligence related to the national security or involving intelligence acquired through clandestine means.

"(l) ENHANCED PERSONNEL MANAGEMENT.—(1)(A) The Director of National Intelligence shall, under regulations prescribed by the Director, provide incentives for personnel of elements of the intelligence community to serve—

"(i) on the staff of the Director of National Intelligence;

"(ii) on the staff of the national intelligence centers;

"(iii) on the staff of the National Counterterrorism Center; and

"(iv) in other positions in support of the intelligence community management functions of the Director.

"(B) Incentives under subparagraph (A) may include financial incentives, bonuses, and such other awards and incentives as the Director considers appropriate.

"(2) (A) Notwithstanding any other provision of law, the personnel of an element of the intelligence community who are assigned or detailed under paragraph (1)(A) to service under the Director of National Intelligence shall be promoted at rates equivalent to or better than personnel of such element who are not so assigned or detailed.

"(B) The Director may prescribe regulations to carry out this section.

"(3) (A) The Director of National Intelligence shall prescribe mechanisms to facilitate the rotation of personnel of the intelligence community through various elements of the intelligence community in the course of their careers in order to facilitate the widest possible understanding by such personnel of the variety of intelligence requirements, methods, users, and capabilities.

"(B) The mechanisms prescribed under subparagraph (A) may include the following:

"(i) The establishment of special occupational categories involving service, over the course of a career, in more than one element of the intelligence community.

"(ii) The provision of rewards for service in positions undertaking analysis and planning of operations involving two or more elements of the intelligence community.

"(iii) The establishment of requirements for education, training, service, and evaluation for service involving more than one element of the intelligence community.

"(C) It is the sense of Congress that the mechanisms prescribed under this subsection should, to the extent practical, seek to duplicate for civilian personnel within the intelligence community the joint officer management policies established by chapter 38 of title 10, United States Code, and the other amendments made by title IV of the Goldwater-Nichols Department of Defense Reorganization Act of 1986 (Public Law 99-433).

"(4) (A) Except as provided in subparagraph (B) and subparagraph (D), this subsection shall not apply with respect to personnel of the elements of the intelligence community who are members of the uniformed services.

"(B) Mechanisms that establish requirements for education and training pursuant to paragraph (3)(B)(iii) may apply with respect to members of the uniformed services who are assigned to an element of the intelligence community funded through the National Intelligence Program, but such mechanisms shall not be inconsistent with personnel policies and education and training requirements otherwise applicable to members of the uniformed services.

"(C) The personnel policies and programs developed and implemented under this subsection with respect to law enforcement officers (as that term is defined in section 5541(3) of title 5, United States Code) shall not affect the ability of law enforcement entities to conduct operations or, through the applicable chain of command, to control the activities of such law enforcement officers.

"(D) Assignment to the Office of the Director of National Intelligence of commissioned officers of the Armed Forces shall be considered a joint-duty assignment for purposes of the joint officer management policies prescribed by chapter 38 of title 10, United States Code, and other provisions of that title.

"(m) Additional Authority with Respect to Personnel.—(1) In addition to the authorities under subsection (f)(3), the Director of National Intelligence may exercise with respect to the personnel of the Office of the Director of National Intelligence any authority of the Director of the Central Intelligence Agency with respect to the personnel of the Central Intelligence Agency under the Central Intelligence Agency Act of 1949 (50 U.S.C. 403a et seq.), and other applicable provisions of law, as of the date of the enactment of this subsection to the same extent, and subject to the same conditions and limitations, that the Director of the Central Intelligence Agency may exercise such authority with respect to personnel of the Central Intelligence Agency.

"(2) Employees and applicants for employment of the Office of the Director of National Intelligence shall have the same rights and protections under the Office of the Director of National Intelligence as employees of the Central Intelligence Agency have under the Central Intelligence Agency Act of 1949, and other applicable provisions of law, as of the date of the enactment of this subsection.

"(n) Acquisition Authorities.—(1) In carrying out the responsibilities and authorities under this section, the Director of National Intelligence may exercise the acquisition and appropriations authorities referred to in the Central Intelligence Agency Act of 1949 (50 U.S.C. 403a et seq.) other than the authorities referred to in section 8(b) of that Act (50 U.S.C. 403j(b)).

"(2) For the purpose of the exercise of any authority referred to in paragraph (1), a reference to the head of an agency shall be deemed to be a reference to the Director of National Intelligence or the Principal Deputy Director of National Intelligence.

"(3) (A) Any determination or decision to be made under an authority referred to in paragraph (1) by the head of an agency may be made with respect to individual purchases and contracts or with respect to classes of purchases or contracts, and shall be final.

"(B) Except as provided in subparagraph (C), the Director of National Intelligence or the Principal Deputy Director of National Intelligence may, in such official's discretion, delegate to any officer or other official of the Office of the Director of National Intelligence any authority to make a determination or decision as the head of the agency under an authority referred to in paragraph (1).

"(C) The limitations and conditions set forth in section 3(d) of the Central Intelligence Agency Act of 1949 (50 U.S.C. 403c(d)) shall apply to the exercise by the Director of National Intelligence of an authority referred to in paragraph (1).

"(D) Each determination or decision required by an authority referred to in the second sentence of section 3(d) of the Central Intelligence Agency Act of 1949 shall be based upon written findings made by the official making such determination or decision, which findings shall be final and shall be available within the Office of the Director of National Intelligence for a period of at least six years following the date of such determination or decision.

"(o) Consideration of Views of Elements of Intelligence Community.—In carrying out the duties and responsibilities under this section, the Director of National Intelligence shall take into account the views of a head of a department containing an element of the intelligence community and of the Director of the Central Intelligence Agency.

"(p) Responsibility of Director of National Intelligence Regarding National Intelligence Program Budget Concerning the Department of Defense.—Subject to the direction of the President, the Director of National Intelligence shall, after consultation with the Secretary of Defense, ensure that the National Intelligence Program budgets for the elements of the intelligence community that are within the Department of Defense are adequate to satisfy the national intelligence needs of the Department of Defense, including the needs of the Chairman of the Joint Chiefs of Staff and the commanders of the unified and specified commands, and wherever such elements are performing Government-wide functions, the needs of other Federal departments and agencies.

"(q) Acquisitions of Major Systems.—(1) For each intelligence program within the National Intelligence Program for the acquisition of a major system, the Director of National Intelligence shall—

"(A) require the development and implementation of a program management plan that includes cost, schedule, and performance goals and program milestone criteria, except that with respect to Department of Defense programs the Director shall consult with the Secretary of Defense;

"(B) serve as exclusive milestone decision authority, except that with respect to Department of Defense programs the Director shall serve as milestone decision authority jointly with the Secretary of Defense or the designee of the Secretary; and

"(C) periodically—

"(i) review and assess the progress made toward the achievement of the goals and milestones established in such plan; and

"(ii) submit to Congress a report on the results of such review and assessment.

"(2) If the Director of National Intelligence and the Secretary of Defense are unable to reach an agreement on a milestone decision under paragraph (1)(B), the President shall resolve the conflict.

"(3) Nothing in this subsection may be construed to limit the authority of the Director of National Intelligence to delegate to any other official any authority to perform the responsibilities of the Director under this subsection.

"(4) In this subsection:

"(A) The term 'intelligence program', with respect to the acquisition of a major system, means a program that—

"(i) is carried out to acquire such major system for an element of the intelligence community; and

"(ii) is funded in whole out of amounts available for the National Intelligence Program.

"(B) The term 'major system' has the meaning given such term in section 4(9) of the Federal Property and Administrative Services Act of 1949 (41 U.S.C. 403(9)).

"(r) PERFORMANCE OF COMMON SERVICES.—The Director of National Intelligence shall, in consultation with the heads of departments and agencies of the United States Government containing elements within the intelligence community and with the Director of the Central Intelligence Agency, coordinate the performance by the elements of the intelligence community within the National Intelligence Program of such services as are of common concern to the intelligence community, which services the Director of National Intelligence determines can be more efficiently accomplished in a consolidated manner.

"OFFICE OF THE DIRECTOR OF NATIONAL INTELLIGENCE

"SEC. 103. (a) OFFICE OF DIRECTOR OF NATIONAL INTELLIGENCE.—There is an Office of the Director of National Intelligence.

"(b) FUNCTION.—The function of the Office of the Director of National Intelligence is to assist the Director of National Intelligence in carrying out the duties and responsibilities of the Director under this Act, the National Security Act of 1947 (50 U.S.C. 401 et seq.), and other applicable provisions of law, and to carry out such other duties as may be prescribed by the President or by law.

"(c) COMPOSITION.—The Office of the Director of National Intelligence is composed of the following:

"(1) The Director of National Intelligence.

"(2) The Principal Deputy Director of National Intelligence.

"(3) Any Deputy Director of National Intelligence appointed under section 103A.

"(4) The National Intelligence Council.

"(5) The General Counsel.

"(6) The Civil Liberties Protection Officer.

"(7) The Director of Science and Technology.

"(8) The National Counterintelligence Executive (including the Office of the National Counterintelligence Executive).

"(9) Such other offices and officials as may be established by law or the Director may establish or designate in the Office, including national intelligence centers.

"(d) STAFF.—(1) To assist the Director of National Intelligence in fulfilling the duties and responsibilities of the Director, the Director shall employ and utilize in the Office of the Director of National Intelligence a professional staff having an expertise in matters relating to such duties and responsibilities, and may establish permanent positions and appropriate rates of pay with respect to that staff.

"(2) The staff of the Office of the Director of National Intelligence under paragraph (1) shall include the staff of the Office of the Deputy Director of Central Intelligence for Community Management that is transferred to the Office of the Director of National Intelligence under section 1091 of the National Security Intelligence Reform Act of 2004.

"(e) LIMITATION ON CO-LOCATION WITH OTHER ELEMENTS OF INTELLIGENCE COMMUNITY.—Commencing as of October 1, 2008, the Office of the Director of National Intelligence may not be co-located with any other element of the intelligence community.

"DEPUTY DIRECTORS OF NATIONAL INTELLIGENCE

"SEC. 103A. (a) PRINCIPAL DEPUTY DIRECTOR OF NATIONAL INTELLIGENCE.—(1) There is a Principal Deputy Director of National Intelligence who shall be appointed by the President, by and with the advice and consent of the Senate.

"(2) In the event of a vacancy in the position of Principal Deputy Director of National Intelligence, the Director of National Intelligence shall recommend to the President an individual for appointment as Principal Deputy Director of National Intelligence.

"(3) Any individual nominated for appointment as Principal Deputy Director of National Intelligence shall have extensive national security experience and management expertise.

"(4) The individual serving as Principal Deputy Director of National Intelligence shall not, while so serving, serve in any capacity in any other element of the intelligence community.

"(5) The Principal Deputy Director of National Intelligence shall assist the Director of National Intelligence in carrying out the duties and responsibilities of the Director.

"(6) The Principal Deputy Director of National Intelligence shall act for, and exercise the powers of, the Director of National Intelligence during the absence or disability of the Director of National Intelligence or during a vacancy in the position of Director of National Intelligence.

"(b) DEPUTY DIRECTORS OF NATIONAL INTELLIGENCE.—(1) There may be not more than four Deputy Directors of National Intelligence who shall be appointed by the Director of National Intelligence.

"(2) Each Deputy Director of National Intelligence appointed under this subsection shall have such duties, responsibilities, and authorities as the Director of National Intelligence may assign or are specified by law.

"(c) MILITARY STATUS OF DIRECTOR OF NATIONAL INTELLIGENCE AND PRINCIPAL DEPUTY DIRECTOR OF NATIONAL INTELLIGENCE.—(1) Not more than one of the individuals serving in the positions specified in paragraph (2) may be a commissioned officer of the Armed Forces in active status.

"(2) The positions referred to in this paragraph are the following:

"(A) The Director of National Intelligence.

"(B) The Principal Deputy Director of National Intelligence.

"(3) It is the sense of Congress that, under ordinary circumstances, it is desirable that one of the individuals serving in the positions specified in paragraph (2)—

"(A) be a commissioned officer of the Armed Forces, in active status; or

"(B) have, by training or experience, an appreciation of military intelligence activities and requirements.

"(4) A commissioned officer of the Armed Forces, while serving in a position specified in paragraph (2)—

"(A) shall not be subject to supervision or control by the Secretary of Defense or by any officer or employee of the Department of Defense;

"(B) shall not exercise, by reason of the officer's status as a commissioned officer, any supervision or control with respect to any of the military or civilian personnel of the Department of Defense except as otherwise authorized by law; and

"(C) shall not be counted against the numbers and percentages of commissioned officers of the rank and grade of such officer authorized for the military department of that officer.

"(5) Except as provided in subparagraph (A) or (B) of paragraph (4), the appointment of an officer of the Armed Forces to a position specified in paragraph (2) shall not affect the status, position, rank, or grade of such officer in the Armed Forces, or any emolument, perquisite, right, privilege, or benefit incident to or arising out of such status, position, rank, or grade.

"(6) A commissioned officer of the Armed Forces on active duty who is appointed to a position specified in paragraph (2), whilc serving in such position and while remaining on active duty, shall continue to receive military pay and allowances and shall not receive the pay prescribed for such position. Funds from which such pay and allowances are paid shall be reimbursed from funds available to the Director of National Intelligence.

"NATIONAL INTELLIGENCE COUNCIL

"SEC. 103B. (a) NATIONAL INTELLIGENCE COUNCIL.—There is a National Intelligence Council.

"(b) COMPOSITION.—(1) The National Intelligence Council shall be composed of senior analysts within the intelligence community and substantive experts from the public and private sector, who shall be appointed by, report to, and serve at the pleasure of, the Director of National Intelligence.

"(2) The Director shall prescribe appropriate security requirements for personnel appointed from the private sector as a condition of service on the Council, or as contractors of the Council or employees of such contractors, to ensure the protection of intelligence sources and methods while avoiding, wherever possible, unduly intrusive requirements which the Director considers to be unnecessary for this purpose.

"(c) DUTIES AND RESPONSIBILITIES.—(1) The National Intelligence Council shall—

"(A) produce national intelligence estimates for the United States Government, including alternative views held by elements of the intelligence community and other information as specified in paragraph (2);

"(B) evaluate community-wide collection and production of intelligence by the intelligence community and the requirements and resources of such collection and production; and

"(C) otherwise assist the Director of National Intelligence in carrying out the responsibilities of the Director under section 102A.

"(2) The Director of National Intelligence shall ensure that the Council satisfies the needs of policymakers and other consumers of intelligence.

"(d) SERVICE AS SENIOR INTELLIGENCE ADVISERS.—Within their respective areas of expertise and under the direction of the Director of National Intelligence, the members of the National Intelligence Council shall constitute the senior intelligence advisers of the intelligence community for purposes of representing the views of the intelligence community within the United States Government.

"(e) AUTHORITY TO CONTRACT.—Subject to the direction and control of the Director of National Intelligence, the National Intelligence Council may carry out its responsibilities under this section by contract, including contracts for substantive experts necessary to assist the Council with particular assessments under this section.

"(f) STAFF.—The Director of National Intelligence shall make available to the National Intelligence Council such staff as may be necessary to permit the Council to carry out its responsibilities under this section.

"(g) AVAILABILITY OF COUNCIL AND STAFF.—(1) The Director of National Intelligence shall take appropriate measures to ensure that the National Intelligence Council and its staff satisfy the needs of policymaking officials and other consumers of intelligence.

"(2) The Council shall be readily accessible to policymaking officials and other appropriate individuals not otherwise associated with the intelligence community.

"(h) SUPPORT.—The heads of the elements of the intelligence community shall, as appropriate, furnish such support to the National Intelligence Council, including the preparation of intelligence analyses, as may be required by the Director of National Intelligence.

"(i) NATIONAL INTELLIGENCE COUNCIL PRODUCT.—For purposes of this section, the term 'National Intelligence Council product' includes a National Intelligence Estimate and any other intelligence community assessment that sets forth the judgment of the intelligence community as a whole on a matter covered by such product.

"GENERAL COUNSEL

"SEC. 103C. (a) GENERAL COUNSEL.—There is a General Counsel of the Office of the Director of National Intelligence who shall be appointed by the President, by and with the advice and consent of the Senate.

"(b) PROHIBITION ON DUAL SERVICE AS GENERAL COUNSEL OF ANOTHER AGENCY.—The individual serving in the position of General Counsel may not, while so serving, also serve as the General Counsel of any other department, agency, or element of the United States Government.

"(c) SCOPE OF POSITION.—The General Counsel is the chief legal officer of the Office of the Director of National Intelligence.

"(d) FUNCTIONS.—The General Counsel shall perform such functions as the Director of National Intelligence may prescribe.

"CIVIL LIBERTIES PROTECTION OFFICER

"SEC. 103D. (a) CIVIL LIBERTIES PROTECTION OFFICER.—(1) Within the Office of the Director of National Intelligence, there is a Civil Liberties Protection Officer who shall be appointed by the Director of National Intelligence.

"(2) The Civil Liberties Protection Officer shall report directly to the Director of National Intelligence.

"(b) Duties.—The Civil Liberties Protection Officer shall—

"(1) ensure that the protection of civil liberties and privacy is appropriately incorporated in the policies and procedures developed for and implemented by the Office of the Director of National Intelligence and the elements of the intelligence community within the National Intelligence Program;

"(2) oversee compliance by the Office and the Director of National Intelligence with requirements under the Constitution and all laws, regulations, Executive orders, and implementing guidelines relating to civil liberties and privacy;

"(3) review and assess complaints and other information indicating possible abuses of civil liberties and privacy in the administration of the programs and operations of the Office and the Director of National Intelligence and, as appropriate, investigate any such complaint or information;

"(4) ensure that the use of technologies sustain, and do not erode, privacy protections relating to the use, collection, and disclosure of personal information;

"(5) ensure that personal information contained in a system of records subject to section 552a of title 5, United States Code (popularly referred to as the 'Privacy Act'), is handled in full compliance with fair information practices as set out in that section;

"(6) conduct privacy impact assessments when appropriate or as required by law; and

"(7) perform such other duties as may be prescribed by the Director of National Intelligence or specified by law.

"(c) Use of Agency Inspectors General.—When appropriate, the Civil Liberties Protection Officer may refer complaints to the Office of Inspector General having responsibility for the affected element of the department or agency of the intelligence community to conduct an investigation under paragraph (3) of subsection (b).

"DIRECTOR OF SCIENCE AND TECHNOLOGY

"Sec. 103E. (a) Director of Science and Technology.—There is a Director of Science and Technology within the Office of the Director of National Intelligence who shall be appointed by the Director of National Intelligence.

"(b) Requirement Relating to Appointment.—An individual appointed as Director of Science and Technology shall have a professional background and experience appropriate for the duties of the Director of Science and Technology.

"(c) Duties.—The Director of Science and Technology shall—

"(1) act as the chief representative of the Director of National Intelligence for science and technology;

"(2) chair the Director of National Intelligence Science and Technology Committee under subsection (d);

"(3) assist the Director in formulating a long-term strategy for scientific advances in the field of intelligence;

"(4) assist the Director on the science and technology elements of the budget of the Office of the Director of National Intelligence; and

"(5) perform other such duties as may be prescribed by the Director of National Intelligence or specified by law.

"(d) Director of National Intelligence Science and Technology Committee.—(1) There is within the Office of the Director of Science and Technology a Director of National Intelligence Science and Technology Committee.

"(2) The Committee shall be composed of the principal science officers of the National Intelligence Program.

"(3) The Committee shall—

"(A) coordinate advances in research and development related to intelligence; and

"(B) perform such other functions as the Director of Science and Technology shall prescribe.

"NATIONAL COUNTERINTELLIGENCE EXECUTIVE

"Sec. 103F. (a) National Counterintelligence Executive.—The National Counterintelligence Executive under section 902 of the Counterintelligence Enhancement Act of 2002 (title IX of Public Law 107-306; 50 U.S.C. 402b et seq.) is a component of the Office of the Director of National Intelligence.

"(b) Duties.—The National Counterintelligence Executive shall perform the duties provided in the Counterintelligence Enhancement Act of 2002 and such other duties as may be prescribed by the Director of National Intelligence or specified by law.

"CENTRAL INTELLIGENCE AGENCY

"Sec. 104. (a) Central Intelligence Agency.—There is a Central Intelligence Agency.

"(b) Function.—The function of the Central Intelligence Agency is to assist the Director of the Central Intelligence Agency in carrying out the responsibilities specified in section 104A(c).

"DIRECTOR OF THE CENTRAL INTELLIGENCE AGENCY

"Sec. 104A. (a) Director of Central Intelligence Agency.—There is a Director of the Central Intelligence Agency who shall be appointed by the President, by and with the advice and consent of the Senate.

"(b) Supervision.—The Director of the Central Intelligence Agency shall report to the Director of National Intelligence regarding the activities of the Central Intelligence Agency.

"(c) Duties.—The Director of the Central Intelligence Agency shall—

"(1) serve as the head of the Central Intelligence Agency; and

"(2) carry out the responsibilities specified in subsection (d).

"(d) Responsibilities.—The Director of the Central Intelligence Agency shall—

"(1) collect intelligence through human sources and by other appropriate means, except that the Director of the Central Intelligence Agency shall have no police, subpoena, or law enforcement powers or internal security functions;

"(2) correlate and evaluate intelligence related to the national security and provide appropriate dissemination of such intelligence;

"(3) provide overall direction for and coordination of the collection of national intelligence outside the United States through human sources by elements of the intelligence community authorized to undertake such collection and, in coordination with other departments, agencies, or elements of the United States Government which are authorized to undertake such collection, ensure that the most effective use is made of resources and that appropriate account is taken of the risks to the United States and those involved in such collection; and

"(4) perform such other functions and duties related to intelligence affecting the national security as the President or the Director of National Intelligence may direct.

"(e) Termination of Employment of CIA Employees.—(1) Notwithstanding the provisions of any other law, the Director of the Central Intelligence Agency may, in the discretion of the Director, terminate the employment of any officer or employee of the Central Intelligence Agency whenever the Director deems the termination of employment of such officer or employee necessary or advisable in the interests of the United States.

"(2) Any termination of employment of an officer or employee under paragraph (1) shall not affect the right of the officer or employee to seek or accept employment in any other department, agency, or element of the United States Government if declared eligible for such employment by the Office of Personnel Management.

"(f) Coordination with Foreign Governments.—Under the direction of the Director of National Intelligence and in a manner consistent with section 207 of the Foreign Service Act of 1980 (22 U.S.C. 3927), the Director of the Central Intelligence Agency shall coordinate the relationships between elements of the intelligence community and the intelligence or security services of foreign governments or international organizations on all matters involving intelligence related to the national security or involving intelligence acquired through clandestine means.".

(b) Sense of Congress.—It is the sense of Congress that—

(1) the human intelligence officers of the intelligence community have performed admirably and honorably in the face of great personal dangers;

(2) during an extended period of unprecedented investment and improvements in technical collection means, the human intelligence capabilities of the United States have not received the necessary and commensurate priorities;

(3) human intelligence is becoming an increasingly important capability to provide information on the asymmetric threats to the national security of the United States;

(4) the continued development and improvement of a robust and empowered and flexible human intelligence work force is critical to identifying, understanding, and countering the plans and intentions of the adversaries of the United States; and

(5) an increased emphasis on, and resources applied to, enhancing the depth and breadth of human intelligence capabilities of the United States intelligence community must be among the top priorities of the Director of National Intelligence.

(c) Transformation of Central Intelligence Agency.—The Director of the Central Intelligence Agency shall, in accordance with standards developed by the Director in consultation with the Director of National Intelligence—

(1) enhance the analytic, human intelligence, and other capabilities of the Central Intelligence Agency;

(2) develop and maintain an effective language program within the Agency;

(3) emphasize the hiring of personnel of diverse backgrounds for purposes of improving the capabilities of the Agency;

(4) establish and maintain effective relationships between human intelligence and signals intelligence within the Agency at the operational level; and

(5) achieve a more effective balance within the Agency with respect to unilateral operations and liaison operations.

(d) Report.—(1) Not later than 180 days after the date of the enactment of this Act, the Director of the Central Intelligence Agency shall submit to the Director of National Intelligence and the congressional intelligence committees a report setting forth the following:

(A) A strategy for improving the conduct of analysis (including strategic analysis) by the Central Intelligence Agency, and the progress of the Agency in implementing that strategy.

(B) A strategy for improving the human intelligence and other capabilities of the Agency, and the progress of the Agency in implementing that strategy.

(2) (A) The information in the report under paragraph (1) on the strategy referred to in paragraph (1)(B) shall—

(i) identify the number and types of personnel required to implement that strategy;

(ii) include a plan for the recruitment, training, equipping, and deployment of such personnel; and

(iii) set forth an estimate of the costs of such activities.

(B) If as of the date of the report under paragraph (1), a proper balance does not exist between unilateral operations and liaison operations, such report shall set forth the steps to be taken to achieve such balance.

SEC. 1012. REVISED DEFINITION OF NATIONAL INTELLIGENCE.

Paragraph (5) of section 3 of the National Security Act of 1947 (50 U.S.C. 401a) is amended to read as follows:

"(5) The terms 'national intelligence' and 'intelligence related to national security' refer to all intelligence, regardless of the source from which derived and including information gathered within or outside the United States, that—

"(A) pertains, as determined consistent with any guidance issued by the President, to more than one United States Government agency; and

"(B) that involves—

"(i) threats to the United States, its people, property, or interests;

"(ii) the development, proliferation, or use of weapons of mass destruction; or

"(iii) any other matter bearing on United States national or homeland security.".

SEC. 1013. JOINT PROCEDURES FOR OPERATIONAL COORDINATION BETWEEN DEPARTMENT OF DEFENSE AND CENTRAL INTELLIGENCE AGENCY.

(a) Development of Procedures.—The Director of National Intelligence, in consultation with the Secretary of Defense and the Director of the Central Intelligence Agency, shall develop joint procedures to be used by the Department of Defense and the Central Intelligence Agency to improve the coordination and deconfliction of operations that involve elements of both the Armed Forces and the Central Intelligence Agency consistent with national security and the protection of human intelligence sources and methods. Those procedures shall, at a minimum, provide the following:

(1) Methods by which the Director of the Central Intelligence Agency and the Secretary of Defense can improve communication and coordination in the planning, execution, and sustainment of operations, including, as a minimum—

(A) information exchange between senior officials of the Central Intelligence Agency and senior officers and officials of the Department of Defense when planning for such an operation commences by either organization; and

(B) exchange of information between the Secretary and the Director of the Central Intelligence Agency to ensure that senior operational officials in both the Department of Defense and the Central Intelligence Agency have knowledge of the existence of the ongoing operations of the other.

(2) When appropriate, in cases where the Department of Defense and the Central Intelligence Agency are conducting separate missions in the same geographical area, a mutual agreement on the tactical and strategic objectives for the region and a clear delineation of operational responsibilities to prevent conflict and duplication of effort.

(b) Implementation Report.—Not later than 180 days after the date of the enactment of the Act, the Director of National Intelligence shall submit to the congressional defense committees (as defined in section 101 of title 10, United States Code) and the congressional intelligence committees (as defined in section 3(7) of the National Security Act of 1947 (50 U.S.C. 401a(7))) a report describing the procedures established pursuant to sub-section (a) and the status of the implementation of those procedures.

....

SEC. 1016. INFORMATION SHARING.

(a) Definitions.—In this section:

(1) Information Sharing Council.—The term "Information Sharing Council" means the Information Systems Council established by Executive Order 13356, or any successor body designated by the President, and referred to under subsection (g).

(2) Information Sharing Environment; ISE.—The terms "information sharing environment" and "ISE" mean an approach that facilitates the sharing of terrorism information, which approach may include any methods determined necessary and appropriate for carrying out this section.

(3) Program Manager.—The term "program manager" means the program manager designated under subsection (f).

(4) Terrorism Information.—The term "terrorism information" means all information, whether collected, produced, or distributed by intelligence, law enforcement, military, homeland security, or other activities relating to—

(A) the existence, organization, capabilities, plans, intentions, vulnerabilities, means of finance or material support, or activities of foreign or international terrorist groups or individuals, or of domestic groups or individuals involved in transnational terrorism;

(B) threats posed by such groups or individuals to the United States, United States persons, or United States interests, or to those of other nations;

(C) communications of or by such groups or individuals; or

(D) groups or individuals reasonably believed to be assisting or associated with such groups or individuals.

(b) Information Sharing Environment.—

(1) Establishment.—The President shall—

(A) create an information sharing environment for the sharing of terrorism information in a manner consistent with national security and with applicable legal standards relating to privacy and civil liberties;

(B) designate the organizational and management structures that will be used to operate and manage the ISE; and

(C) determine and enforce the policies, directives, and rules that will govern the content and usage of the ISE.

(2) Attributes.—The President shall, through the structures described in subparagraphs (B) and (C) of paragraph (1), ensure that the ISE provides and facilitates the means for sharing terrorism information among all appropriate Federal, State, local, and tribal entities, and the private sector through the use of policy guidelines and technologies. The President shall, to the greatest extent practicable, ensure that the ISE provides the functional equivalent of, or otherwise supports, a decentralized, distributed, and coordinated environment that—

(A) connects existing systems, where appropriate, provides no single points of failure, and allows users to share information among agencies, between levels of government, and, as appropriate, with the private sector;

(B) ensures direct and continuous online electronic access to information;

(C) facilitates the availability of information in a form and manner that facilitates its use in analysis, investigations and operations;

(D) builds upon existing systems capabilities currently in use across the Government;

(E) employs an information access management approach that controls access to data rather than just systems and networks, without sacrificing security;

(F) facilitates the sharing of information at and across all levels of security;

(G) provides directory services, or the functional equivalent, for locating people and information;

(H) incorporates protections for individuals' privacy and civil liberties; and

(I) incorporates strong mechanisms to enhance accountability and facilitate oversight, including audits, authentication, and access controls.

....

SEC. 1017. ALTERNATIVE ANALYSIS OF INTELLIGENCE BY THE INTELLIGENCE COMMUNITY.

(a) In General.—Not later than 180 days after the effective date of this Act, the Director of National Intelligence shall establish a process and assign an individual or entity the responsibility for ensuring that, as appropriate, elements of the intelligence community conduct alternative analysis (commonly referred to as "red-team analysis") of the information and conclusions in intelligence products.

(b) Report.—Not later than 270 days after the effective date of this Act, the Director of National Intelligence shall provide a report to the Select Committee on Intelligence of the Senate and the Permanent Select Committee of the House of Representatives on the implementation of subsection (a).

....

SEC. 1019. ASSIGNMENT OF RESPONSIBILITIES RELATING TO ANALYTIC INTEGRITY.

(a) Assignment of Responsibilities.—For purposes of carrying out section 102A(h) of the National Security Act of 1947 (as added by section 1011(a)), the Director of National Intelligence shall, not later than 180 days after the date of the enactment of this Act, assign an individual or entity to be responsible for ensuring that finished intelligence products produced by any element or elements of the intelligence community are timely, objective, independent of political considerations, based upon all sources of avail-able intelligence, and employ the standards of proper analytic tradecraft.

(b) Responsibilities.—(1) The individual or entity assigned responsibility under subsection (a)—

(A) may be responsible for general oversight and management of analysis and production, but may not be directly responsible for, or involved in, the specific production of any finished intelligence product;

(B) shall perform, on a regular basis, detailed reviews of finished intelligence product or other analytic products by an element or elements of the intelligence community covering a particular topic or subject matter;

(C) shall be responsible for identifying on an annual basis functional or topical areas of analysis for specific review under subparagraph (B); and

(D) upon completion of any review under subparagraph (B), may draft lessons learned, identify best practices, or make recommendations for improvement to the analytic tradecraft employed in the production of the reviewed product or products.

(2) Each review under paragraph (1)(B) should—

(A) include whether the product or products concerned were based on all sources of available intelligence, properly describe the quality and reliability of underlying sources, properly caveat and express uncertainties or confidence in analytic judgments, properly distinguish between underlying intelligence and the assumptions and judgments of analysts, and incorporate, where appropriate, alternative analyses; and

(B) ensure that the analytic methodologies, tradecraft, and practices used by the element or elements concerned in the production of the product or products concerned meet the standards set forth in subsection (a).

(3) Information drafted under paragraph (1)(D) should, as appropriate, be included in analysis teaching modules and case studies for use throughout the intelligence community.

(c) ANNUAL REPORTS.—Not later than December 1 each year, the Director of National Intelligence shall submit to the congressional intelligence committees, the heads of the relevant elements of the intelligence community, and the heads of analytic training departments a report containing a description, and the associated findings, of each review under subsection (b)(1)(B) during such year.

(d) CONGRESSIONAL INTELLIGENCE COMMITTEES DEFINED.—In this section, the term "congressional intelligence committees" means—

(1) the Select Committee on Intelligence of the Senate; and

(2) the Permanent Select Committee on Intelligence of the House of Representatives.

SEC. 1020. SAFEGUARD OF OBJECTIVITY IN INTELLIGENCE ANALYSIS.

(a) IN GENERAL.—Not later than 180 days after the effective date of this Act, the Director of National Intelligence shall identify an individual within the Office of the Director of National Intelligence who shall be available to analysts within the Office of the Director of National Intelligence to counsel, conduct arbitration, offer recommendations, and, as appropriate, initiate inquiries into real or perceived problems of analytic tradecraft or politicization, biased reporting, or lack of objectivity in intelligence analysis.

(b) REPORT.—Not later than 270 days after the effective date of this Act, the Director of National Intelligence shall provide a report to the Select Committee on Intelligence of the Senate and the Permanent Select Committee on Intelligence of the House of Representatives on the implementation of subsection (a).

Subtitle B—National Counterterrorism

Center, National Counter Proliferation Center, and National Intelligence Centers

SEC. 1021. NATIONAL COUNTERTERRORISM CENTER.

Title I of the National Security Act of 1947 (50 U.S.C. 402 et seq.) is amended by adding at the end the following new section:

"NATIONAL COUNTERTERRORISM CENTER

"SEC. 119. (a) ESTABLISHMENT OF CENTER.—There is within the Office of the Director of National Intelligence a National Counterterrorism Center.

"(b) DIRECTOR OF NATIONAL COUNTERTERRORISM CENTER.—(1) There is a Director of the National Counterterrorism Center, who shall be the head of the National Counterterrorism Center, and who shall be appointed by the President, by and with the advice and consent of the Senate.

"(2) The Director of the National Counterterrorism Center may not simultaneously serve in any other capacity in the executive branch.

"(c) REPORTING.—(1) The Director of the National Counterterrorism Center shall report to the Director of National Intelligence with respect to matters described in paragraph (2) and the President with respect to matters described in paragraph (3).

"(2) The matters described in this paragraph are as follows:

"(A) The budget and programs of the National Counterterrorism Center.

"(B) The activities of the Directorate of Intelligence of the National Counterterrorism Center under subsection (h).

"(C) The conduct of intelligence operations implemented by other elements of the intelligence community; and

"(3) The matters described in this paragraph are the planning and progress of joint counterterrorism operations (other than intelligence operations).".

"(d) Primary Missions.—The primary missions of the National Counterterrorism Center shall be as follows:

"(1) To serve as the primary organization in the United States Government for analyzing and integrating all intelligence possessed or acquired by the United States Government pertaining to terrorism and counterterrorism, excepting intelligence pertaining exclusively to domestic terrorists and domestic counterterrorism.

"(2) To conduct strategic operational planning for counterterrorism activities, integrating all instruments of national power, including diplomatic, financial, military, intelligence, homeland security, and law enforcement activities within and among agencies.

"(3) To assign roles and responsibilities as part of its strategic operational planning duties to lead Departments or agencies, as appropriate, for counterterrorism activities that are consistent with applicable law and that support counterterrorism strategic operational plans, but shall not direct the execution of any resulting operations.

"(4) To ensure that agencies, as appropriate, have access to and receive all-source intelligence support needed to execute their counterterrorism plans or perform independent, alternative analysis.

"(5) To ensure that such agencies have access to and receive intelligence needed to accomplish their assigned activities.

"(6) To serve as the central and shared knowledge bank on known and suspected terrorists and international terror groups, as well as their goals, strategies, capabilities, and networks of contacts and support.

"(e) Domestic Counterterrorism Intelligence.—(1) The Center may, consistent with applicable law, the direction of the President, and the guidelines referred to in section 102A(b), receive intelligence pertaining exclusively to domestic counterterrorism from any Federal, State, or local government or other source necessary to fulfill its responsibilities and retain and disseminate such intelligence.

"(2) Any agency authorized to conduct counterterrorism activities may request information from the Center to assist it in its responsibilities, consistent with applicable law and the guidelines referred to in section 102A(b).

"(f) Duties and Responsibilities of Director.—(1) The Director of the National Counterterrorism Center shall—

"(A) serve as the principal adviser to the Director of National Intelligence on intelligence operations relating to counterterrorism;

"(B) provide strategic operational plans for the civilian and military counterterrorism efforts of the United States Government and for the effective integration of counterterrorism intelligence and operations across agency boundaries, both inside and outside the United States;

"(C) advise the Director of National Intelligence on the extent to which the counterterrorism program recommendations and budget proposals of the departments, agencies, and elements of the United States Government conform to the priorities established by the President;

"(D) disseminate terrorism information, including current terrorism threat analysis, to the President, the Vice President, the Secretaries of State, Defense, and Homeland Security, the Attorney General, the Director of the Central Intelligence Agency, and other officials of the executive branch as appropriate, and to the appropriate committees of Congress;

"(E) support the Department of Justice and the Department of Homeland Security, and other appropriate agencies, in fulfillment of their responsibilities to disseminate terrorism information, consistent with applicable law, guidelines referred to in section 102A(b), Executive orders and other Presidential guidance, to State and local government officials, and other entities, and coordinate dissemination of terrorism information to foreign governments as approved by the Director of National Intelligence;

"(F) develop a strategy for combining terrorist travel intelligence operations and law enforcement planning and operations into a cohesive effort to intercept terrorists, find terrorist travel facilitators, and constrain terrorist mobility;

"(G) have primary responsibility within the United States Government for conducting net assessments of terrorist threats;

"(H) consistent with priorities approved by the President, assist the Director of National Intelligence in establishing requirements for the intelligence community for the collection of terrorism information; and

"(I) perform such other duties as the Director of National Intelligence may prescribe or are prescribed by law.

"(2) Nothing in paragraph (1)(G) shall limit the authority of the departments and agencies of the United States to conduct net assessments.

"(g) LIMITATION.—The Director of the National Counterterrorism Center may not direct the execution of counterterrorism operations.

"(h) RESOLUTION OF DISPUTES.—The Director of National Intelligence shall resolve disagreements between the National Counterterrorism Center and the head of a department, agency, or element of the United States Government on designations, assignments, plans, or responsibilities under this section. The head of such a department, agency, or element may appeal the resolution of the disagreement by the Director of National Intelligence to the President.

"(i) DIRECTORATE OF INTELLIGENCE.—The Director of the National Counterterrorism Center shall establish and maintain within the National Counterterrorism Center a Directorate of Intelligence which shall have primary responsibility within the United States Government for analysis of terrorism and terrorist organizations (except for purely domestic terrorism and domestic terrorist organizations) from all sources of intelligence, whether collected inside or outside the United States.

"(j) DIRECTORATE OF STRATEGIC OPERATIONAL PLANNING.—(1) The Director of the National Counterterrorism Center shall establish and maintain within the National

Counterterrorism Center a Directorate of Strategic Operational Planning which shall provide strategic operational plans for counterterrorism operations conducted by the United States Government.

"(2) Strategic operational planning shall include the mission, objectives to be achieved, tasks to be performed, interagency coordination of operational activities, and the assignment of roles and responsibilities.

"(3) The Director of the National Counterterrorism Center shall monitor the implementation of strategic operational plans, and shall obtain information from each element of the intelligence community, and from each other department, agency, or element of the United States Government relevant for monitoring the progress of such entity in implementing such plans.".

SEC. 1022. NATIONAL COUNTER PROLIFERATION CENTER.

Title I of the National Security Act of 1947, as amended by section 1021 of this Act, is further amended by adding at the end the following new section:

"NATIONAL COUNTER PROLIFERATION CENTER

"SEC. 119A. (a) ESTABLISHMENT.—Not later than 18 months after the date of the enactment of the National Security Intelligence Reform Act of 2004, the President shall establish a National Counter Proliferation Center, taking into account all appropriate government tools to prevent and halt the proliferation of weapons of mass destruction, their delivery systems, and related materials and technologies.

"(b) MISSIONS AND OBJECTIVES.—In establishing the National Counter Proliferation Center, the President shall address the following missions and objectives to prevent and halt the proliferation of weapons of mass destruction, their delivery systems, and related materials and technologies:

"(1) Establishing a primary organization within the United States Government for analyzing and integrating all intelligence possessed or acquired by the United States pertaining to proliferation.

"(2) Ensuring that appropriate agencies have full access to and receive all-source intelligence support needed to execute their counter proliferation plans or activities, and perform independent, alternative analyses.

"(3) Establishing a central repository on known and suspected proliferation activities, including the goals, strategies, capabilities, networks, and any individuals, groups, or entities engaged in proliferation.

"(4) Disseminating proliferation information, including proliferation threats and analyses, to the President, to the appropriate departments and agencies, and to the appropriate committees of Congress.

"(5) Conducting net assessments and warnings about the proliferation of weapons of mass destruction, their delivery systems, and related materials and technologies.

"(6) Coordinating counter proliferation plans and activities of the various departments and agencies of the United States Government to prevent and halt the proliferation of weapons of mass destruction, their delivery systems, and related materials and technologies.

"(7) Conducting strategic operational counter proliferation planning for the United States Government to prevent and halt the proliferation of weapons of mass destruction, their delivery systems, and related materials and technologies.

"(c) NATIONAL SECURITY WAIVER.—The President may waive the requirements of this section, and any parts thereof, if the President determines that such requirements do not materially improve the ability of the United States Government to prevent and halt the proliferation of weapons of mass destruction, their delivery systems, and related materials and technologies. Such waiver shall be made in writing to Congress and shall include a description of how the missions and objectives in subsection (b) are being met.

"(d) REPORT TO CONGRESS.—(1) Not later than nine months after the implementation of this Act, the President shall submit to Congress, in classified form if necessary, the findings and recommendations of the President's Commission on Weapons of Mass Destruction established by Executive Order in February 2004, together with the views of the President regarding the establishment of a National Counter Proliferation Center.

"(2) If the President decides not to exercise the waiver authority granted by subsection (c), the President shall submit to Congress from time to time updates and plans regarding the establishment of a National Counter Proliferation Center.

"(e) SENSE OF CONGRESS.—It is the sense of Congress that a central feature of counter proliferation activities, consistent with the President's Proliferation Security Initiative, should include the physical interdiction, by air, sea, or land, of weapons of mass destruction, their delivery systems, and related materials and technologies, and enhanced law enforcement activities to identify and disrupt proliferation networks, activities, organizations, and persons.".

SEC. 1023. NATIONAL INTELLIGENCE CENTERS.

Title I of the National Security Act of 1947, as amended by section 1022 of this Act, is further amended by adding at the end the following new section:

"NATIONAL INTELLIGENCE CENTERS

"SEC. 119B. (a) AUTHORITY TO ESTABLISH.—The Director of National Intelligence may establish one or more national intelligence centers to address intelligence priorities, including, but not limited to, regional issues.

"(b) RESOURCES OF DIRECTORS OF CENTERS.—(1) The Director of National Intelligence shall ensure that the head of each national intelligence center under subsection (a) has appropriate authority, direction, and control of such center, and of the personnel assigned to such center, to carry out the assigned mission of such center.

"(2) The Director of National Intelligence shall ensure that each national intelligence center has appropriate personnel to accomplish effectively the mission of such center.

"(c) INFORMATION SHARING.—The Director of National Intelligence shall, to the extent appropriate and practicable, ensure that each national intelligence center under subsection (a) and the other elements of the intelligence community share information in order to facilitate the mission of such center.

"(d) MISSION OF CENTERS.—Pursuant to the direction of the Director of National Intelligence, each national intelligence center under subsection (a) may, in the area of intelligence responsibility assigned to such center—

"(1) have primary responsibility for providing all-source analysis of intelligence based upon intelligence gathered both domestically and abroad;

"(2) have primary responsibility for identifying and proposing to the Director of National Intelligence intelligence collection and analysis and production requirements; and

"(3) perform such other duties as the Director of National Intelligence shall specify.

"(e) REVIEW AND MODIFICATION OF CENTERS.—The Director of National Intelligence shall determine on a regular basis whether—

"(1) the area of intelligence responsibility assigned to each national intelligence center under subsection (a) continues to meet appropriate intelligence priorities; and

"(2) the staffing and management of such center remains appropriate for the accomplishment of the mission of such center.

"(f) TERMINATION.—The Director of National Intelligence may terminate any national intelligence center under subsection (a).

"(g) SEPARATE BUDGET ACCOUNT.—The Director of National Intelligence shall, as appropriate, include in the National Intelligence Program budget a separate line item for each national intelligence center under subsection (a).".

Subtitle C—Joint Intelligence Community Council

SEC. 1031. JOINT INTELLIGENCE COMMUNITY COUNCIL.

Title I of the National Security Act of 1947 (50 U.S.C. 402 et seq.) is amended by inserting after section 101 the following new section:

"JOINT INTELLIGENCE COMMUNITY COUNCIL

"SEC. 101A. (a) JOINT INTELLIGENCE COMMUNITY COUNCIL.—There is a Joint Intelligence Community Council.

"(b) MEMBERSHIP.—The Joint Intelligence Community Council shall consist of the following:

"(1) The Director of National Intelligence, who shall chair the Council.

"(2) The Secretary of State.

"(3) The Secretary of the Treasury.

"(4) The Secretary of Defense.

"(5) The Attorney General.

"(6) The Secretary of Energy.

"(7) The Secretary of Homeland Security.

"(8) Such other officers of the United States Government as the President may designate from time to time.

"(c) FUNCTIONS.—The Joint Intelligence Community Council shall assist the Director of National Intelligence in developing and implementing a joint, unified national intelligence effort to protect national security by—

"(1) advising the Director on establishing requirements, developing budgets, financial management, and monitoring and evaluating the performance of the intelligence community, and on such other matters as the Director may request; and

"(2) ensuring the timely execution of programs, policies, and directives established or developed by the Director.

"(d) MEETINGS.—The Director of National Intelligence shall convene regular meetings of the Joint Intelligence Community Council.

"(e) ADVICE AND OPINIONS OF MEMBERS OTHER THAN CHAIRMAN.—(1) A member of the Joint Intelligence Community Council (other than the Chairman) may submit to the Chairman advice or an opinion in disagreement with, or advice or an opinion in addition to, the advice presented by the Director of National Intelligence to the President or the National Security Council, in the role of the Chairman as Chairman of the Joint Intelligence Community Council. If a member submits such advice or opinion, the Chairman shall present the advice or opinion of such member at the same time the Chairman presents the advice of the Chairman to the President or the National Security Council, as the case may be.

"(2) The Chairman shall establish procedures to ensure that the presentation of the advice of the Chairman to the President or the National Security Council is not unduly delayed by reason of the submission of the individual advice or opinion of another member of the Council.

"(f) RECOMMENDATIONS TO CONGRESS.—Any member of the Joint Intelligence Community Council may make such recommendations to Congress relating to the intelligence community as such member considers appropriate.".

....

Subtitle F—Privacy and Civil Liberties

SEC. 1061. PRIVACY AND CIVIL LIBERTIES OVERSIGHT BOARD.

(a) FINDINGS.—Consistent with the report of the National Commission on Terrorist Attacks Upon the United States, Congress makes the following findings:

(1) In conducting the war on terrorism, the Federal Government may need additional powers and may need to enhance the use of its existing powers.

(2) This potential shift of power and authority to the Federal Government calls for an enhanced system of checks and balances to protect the precious liberties that are vital to our way of life.

(b) ESTABLISHMENT OF BOARD.—There is established within the Executive Office of the President a Privacy and Civil Liberties Oversight Board (referred to in this section as the "Board").

(c) FUNCTIONS.—

(1) ADVICE AND COUNSEL ON DEVELOPMENT AND IMPLEMENTATION OF POLICY.—For the purpose of providing advice to the President or to the head of any department or agency of the executive branch, the Board shall—

(A) review proposed regulations and executive branch policies related to efforts to protect the Nation from terrorism, including the development and adoption of information sharing guidelines under subsections (d) and (f) of section 1016;

(B) review the implementation of laws, regulations, and executive branch policies related to efforts to protect the Nation from terrorism, including the implementation of information sharing guidelines under subsections (d) and (f) of section 1016;

(C) advise the President and the head of any department or agency of the executive branch to ensure that privacy and civil liberties are appropriately considered in the development and implementation of such regulations and executive branch policies; and

(D) in providing advice on proposals to retain or enhance a particular governmental power, consider whether the department, agency, or element of the executive branch concerned has explained—

(i) that there is adequate supervision of the use by the executive branch of the power to ensure protection of privacy and civil liberties;

(ii) that there are adequate guidelines and oversight to properly confine the use of the power; and

(iii) that the need for the power, including the risk presented to the national security if the Federal Government does not take certain actions, is balanced with the need to protect privacy and civil liberties.

(2) Oversight.—The Board shall continually review—

(A) regulations, executive branch policies, and procedures (including the implementation of such regulations, policies, and procedures), related laws pertaining to efforts to protect the Nation from terrorism, and other actions by the executive branch related to efforts to protect the Nation from terrorism to ensure that privacy and civil liberties are protected; and

(B) the information sharing practices of the departments, agencies, and elements of the executive branch to determine whether or not such practices appropriately protect privacy and civil liberties and adhere to the information sharing guidelines under subsections (d) and (f) of section 1016 and to other applicable laws, regulations, and executive branch policies regarding the protection of privacy and civil liberties.

(3) Scope.—The Board shall ensure that concerns with respect to privacy and civil liberties are appropriately considered in the implementation of laws, regulations, and executive branch policies related to efforts to protect the Nation against terrorism.

(4) Reports to Congress.—Not less frequently than annually, the Board shall prepare a report to Congress, unclassified to the greatest extent possible (with a classified annex, if necessary), on the Board's major activities during the preceding period.

(d) Access to Information.—

(1) Authorization.—If determined by the Board to be necessary to carry out its responsibilities under this section, the Board is authorized, to the extent permitted by law, to—

(A) have access from any department or agency of the executive branch, or any Federal officer or employee of any such department or agency, to all relevant records, reports, audits, reviews, documents, papers, recommendations, or other relevant material, including classified information consistent with applicable law;

(B) interview or take statements from officers of any department or agency of the executive branch;

(C) request information or assistance from any State, tribal, or local government; and

(D) (i) request that persons (other than departments, agencies, and elements of the executive branch) produce for the Board relevant information, documents, reports, answers, records, accounts, papers, and other documentary and testimonial evidence; and

(ii) if the person to whom such a request is directed does not comply with the request within 45 days of receipt of such request, notify the Attorney General of such person's failure to comply with such request, which notice shall include all relevant information.

(2) PRODUCTION OF INFORMATION AND EVIDENCE.—

(A) EXPLANATION OF NONCOMPLIANCE.—Upon receiving notification under paragraph (1)(D)(ii) regarding a request, the Attorney General shall provide an opportunity for the person subject to the request to explain the reasons for not complying with the request.

(B) ACTION BY ATTORNEY GENERAL.—Upon receiving notification under paragraph (1)(D)(ii) regarding a request, the Attorney General shall review the request and may take such steps as appropriate to ensure compliance with the request for the information, documents, reports, answers, records, accounts, papers, and other documentary and testimonial evidence covered by the request.

(3) AGENCY COOPERATION.—Whenever information or assistance requested under subparagraph (A) or (B) of paragraph (1) is, in the judgment of the Board, unreasonably refused or not provided, the Board shall report the circumstances to the head of the department or agency concerned without delay. If the requested information or assistance may be provided to the Board in accordance with applicable law, the head of the department or agency concerned shall ensure compliance with such request.

(4) EXCEPTIONS FOR NATIONAL SECURITY.—

(A) IN GENERAL.—If the National Intelligence Director, in consultation with the Attorney General, determines that it is necessary to withhold information requested under paragraph (3) to protect the national security interests of the United States, the head of the department or agency concerned shall not furnish such information to the Board.

(B) CERTAIN INFORMATION.—If the Attorney General determines that it is necessary to withhold information requested under paragraph (3) from disclosure to protect sensitive law enforcement or counterterrorism information or ongoing operations, the head of the department or agency concerned shall not furnish such information to the Board.

(e) MEMBERSHIP.—

(1) MEMBERS.—

(A) IN GENERAL.—The Board shall be composed of a chairman, a vice chairman, and three additional members appointed by the President.

(B) CHAIRMAN AND VICE CHAIRMAN.—The chairman and vice chairman shall each be appointed by the President, by and with the advice and consent of the Senate.

(C) Appointment Requirements.—Any individual appointed to the Board shall be appointed from among trustworthy and distinguished citizens outside the Federal Government who are qualified on the basis of achievement, experience, and independence.

(D) Full-Time Service of Chairman.—The chairman may serve on a full-time basis.

(E) Service at Pleasure of President.—The chairman, vice chairman, and other members of the Board shall each serve at the pleasure of the President.

(2) Incompatible Office.—An individual appointed to the Board may not, while serving on the Board, be an elected official, officer, or employee of the Federal Government, other than in the capacity as a member of the Board.

(3) Quorum and Meetings.—The Board shall meet upon the call of the chairman or a majority of its members. Three members of the Board shall constitute a quorum.

(f) Compensation and Travel Expenses.—

(1) Compensation.—

(A) Chairman on Full-Time Basis.—If the chairman serves on a full-time basis, the rate of pay for the chairman shall be the annual rate of basic pay in effect for a position at level III of the Executive Schedule under section 5314 of title 5, United States Code.

(B) Chairman and Vice Chairman on Part-Time Basis.—The chairman, if serving on a part-time basis, and the vice chairman shall be compensated at a rate equal to the daily equivalent of the annual rate of basic pay in effect for a position at level III of the Executive Schedule under section 5314 of title 5, United States Code, for each day during which such official is engaged in the actual performance of the duties of the Board.

(C) Members.—Each member of the Board shall be compensated at a rate equal to the daily equivalent of the annual rate of basic pay in effect for a position at level IV of the Executive Schedule under section 5315 of title 5, United States Code, for each day during which that member is engaged in the actual performance of the duties of the Board.

(2) Travel Expenses.—Members of the Board shall be allowed travel expenses, including per diem in lieu of subsistence, at rates authorized for persons employed intermittently by the Federal Government under section 5703(b) of title 5, United States Code, while away from their homes or regular places of business in the performance of services for the Board.

(g) Staff.—

(1) Appointment and Compensation.—The chairman, in accordance with rules agreed upon by the Board, shall appoint and fix the compensation of an executive director and such other personnel as may be necessary to enable the Board to carry out its functions, without regard to the provisions of title 5, United States Code, governing appointments in the competitive service, and without regard to the provisions of chapter 51 and subchapter III of chapter 53 of such title relating to classification and General Schedule pay rates, except that no rate of pay fixed under this subsection may exceed the equivalent of that payable for a position at level V of the Executive Schedule under section 5316 of title 5, United States Code.

(2) Detailees.—Federal employees may be detailed to the Board without reimbursement from the Board, and such detailee shall retain the rights, status, and privileges of the detailee's regular employment without interruption.

(3) Consultant Services.—The Board may procure the temporary or intermittent services of experts and consultants in accordance with section 3109 of title 5, United States Code, at rates that do not exceed the daily rate paid a person occupying a position at level IV of the Executive Schedule under section 5315 of such title.

(h) Security Clearances.—The appropriate departments and agencies of the executive branch shall cooperate with the Board to expeditiously provide Board members and staff with appropriate security clearances to the extent possible under applicable procedures and requirements. Promptly upon commencing its work, the Board shall adopt, after consultation with the Secretary of Defense, the Attorney General, and the National Intelligence Director, rules and procedures of the Board for physical, communications, computer, document, personnel, and other security in relation to the work of the Board.

(i) Applicability of Certain Laws.—

(1) Federal Advisory Committee Act.—The Federal Advisory Committee Act (5 U.S.C. App.) shall not apply with respect to the Board and its activities.

(2) Freedom of Information Act.—For purposes of the Freedom of Information Act, the Board shall be treated as an agency (as that term is defined in section 551(1) of title 5, United States Code).

(j) Construction.—Except as otherwise provided in this section, nothing in this section shall be construed to require any consultation with the Board by any department or agency of the executive branch or any Federal officer or employee, or any waiting period that must be observed by any department or agency of the executive branch or any Federal officer or employee, before developing, proposing, or implementing any legislation, law, regulation, policy, or guideline related to efforts to protect the Nation from terrorism.

(k) Presidential Responsibility.—The Board shall perform its functions within the executive branch and under the general supervision of the President.

(l) Authorization of Appropriations.—There are authorized to be appropriated such sums as may be necessary to carry out this section.

SEC. 1062. SENSE OF CONGRESS ON DESIGNATION OF PRIVACY AND CIVIL LIBERTIES OFFICERS.

It is the sense of Congress that each executive department or agency with law enforcement or antiterrorism functions should designate a privacy and civil liberties officer.

....

TITLE II—FEDERAL BUREAU OF INVESTIGATION

SEC. 2001. IMPROVEMENT OF INTELLIGENCE CAPABILITIES OF THE FEDERAL BUREAU OF INVESTIGATION.

(a) Findings.—Congress makes the following findings:

(1) The National Commission on Terrorist Attacks Upon the United States in its final report stated that, under Director Robert Mueller, the Federal Bureau of Investigation has made significant progress in improving its intelligence capabilities.

(2) In the report, the members of the Commission also urged that the Federal Bureau of Investigation fully institutionalize the shift of the Bureau to a preventive counterterrorism posture.

(b) Improvement of Intelligence Capabilities.—The Director of the Federal Bureau of Investigation shall continue efforts to improve the intelligence capabilities of the Federal Bureau of Investigation and to develop and maintain within the Bureau a national intelligence workforce.

(c) National Intelligence Workforce.—(1) In developing and maintaining a national intelligence workforce under subsection (b), the Director of the Federal Bureau of Investigation shall, develop and maintain a specialized and integrated national intelligence workforce consisting of agents, analysts, linguists, and surveillance specialists who are recruited, trained, and rewarded in a manner which ensures the existence within the Federal Bureau of Investigation an institutional culture with substantial expertise in, and commitment to, the intelligence mission of the Bureau.

(2) Each agent employed by the Bureau after the date of the enactment of this Act shall receive basic training in both criminal justice matters and national intelligence matters.

(3) Each agent employed by the Bureau after the date of the enactment of this Act shall, to the maximum extent practicable, be given the opportunity to undergo, during such agent's early service with the Bureau, meaningful assignments in criminal justice matters and in national intelligence matters.

(4) The Director shall—

(A) establish career positions in national intelligence matters for agents, analysts, and related personnel of the Bureau; and

(B) in furtherance of the requirement under subparagraph (A) and to the maximum extent practicable, afford agents, analysts, and related personnel of the Bureau the opportunity to work in the career specialty selected by such agents, analysts, and related personnel over their entire career with the Bureau.

(5) The Director shall carry out a program to enhance the capacity of the Bureau to recruit and retain individuals with backgrounds in intelligence, international relations, language, technology, and other skills relevant to the intelligence mission of the Bureau.

(6) The Director shall, to the maximum extent practicable, afford the analysts of the Bureau training and career opportunities commensurate with the training and career opportunities afforded analysts in other elements of the intelligence community.

(7) Commencing as soon as practicable after the date of the enactment of this Act, each direct supervisor of a Field Intelligence Group, and each Bureau Operational Manager at the Section Chief and Assistant Special Agent in Charge (ASAC) level and above, shall be a certified intelligence officer.

(8) The Director shall, to the maximum extent practicable, ensure that the successful discharge of advanced training courses, and of one or more assignments to another element of the intelligence community, is a precondition to advancement to higher level intelligence assignments within the Bureau.

(d) Field Office Matters.—(1) In improving the intelligence capabilities of the Federal Bureau of Investigation under subsection (b), the Director of the Federal

Bureau of Investigation shall ensure that each Field Intelligence Group reports directly to a field office senior manager responsible for intelligence matters.

(2) The Director shall provide for such expansion of the secure facilities in the field offices of the Bureau as is necessary to ensure the discharge by the field offices of the intelligence mission of the Bureau.

(3) The Director shall require that each Field Intelligence Group manager ensures the integration of analysts, agents, linguists, and surveillance personnel in the field.

(e) Discharge of Improvements.—(1) The Director of the Federal Bureau of Investigation shall carry out subsections (b) through (d) through the head of the Directorate of Intelligence of the Federal Bureau of Investigation.

(2) The Director of the Federal Bureau of Investigation shall carry out subsections (b) through (d) under the joint guidance of the Attorney General and the National Intelligence Director in a manner consistent with section 112(e).

(f) Budget Matters.—The Director of the Federal Bureau of Investigation shall, establish a budget structure of the Federal Bureau of Investigation to reflect the four principal missions of the Bureau as follows:

(1) Intelligence.

(2) Counterterrorism and counterintelligence.

(3) Criminal Enterprises/Federal Crimes.

(4) Criminal justice services.

(g) Reports.—(1) Not later than 180 days after the date of the enactment of this Act, the Director of the Federal Bureau of Investigation shall submit to Congress a report on the progress made as of the date of such report in carrying out the requirements of this section.

(2) The Director shall include in each annual program review of the Federal Bureau of Investigation that is submitted to Congress a report on the progress made by each field office of the Bureau during the period covered by such review in addressing Bureau and national program priorities.

(3) Not later than 180 days after the date of the enactment of this Act, and every 12 months thereafter, the Director shall submit to Congress a report assessing the qualifications, status, and roles of analysts at Bureau headquarters and in the field offices of the Bureau.

(4) Not later than 180 days after the date of the enactment of this Act, and every 12 months thereafter, the Director shall submit to Congress a report on the progress of the Bureau in implementing information-sharing principles.

SEC. 2002. DIRECTORATE OF INTELLIGENCE OF THE FEDERAL BUREAU OF INVESTIGATION.

(a) Directorate of Intelligence of Federal Bureau of Investigation.—The element of the Federal Bureau of Investigation known as of the date of the enactment of this Act as the Office of Intelligence is hereby redesignated as the Directorate of Intelligence of the Federal Bureau of Investigation.

(b) Head of Directorate.—The head of the Directorate of Intelligence shall be the Executive Assistant Director for Intelligence of the Federal Bureau of Investigation.

(c) RESPONSIBILITIES.—The Directorate of Intelligence shall be responsible for the following:

(1) Supervision of all national intelligence programs, projects, and activities of the Bureau.

(2) The discharge by the Bureau of the requirements in section 105B of the National Security Act of 1947 (50 U.S.C. 403-5b).

(3) The oversight of Bureau field intelligence operations.

(4) Coordinating human source development and management by the Bureau.

(5) Coordinating collection by the Bureau against nationally-determined intelligence requirements.

(6) Strategic analysis.

(7) Intelligence program and budget management.

(8) The intelligence workforce.

(9) Any other responsibilities specified by the Director of the Federal Bureau of Investigation or specified by law.

(d) STAFF.—The Directorate of Intelligence shall consist of such staff as the Director of the Federal Bureau of Investigation considers appropriate for the activities of the Directorate.

....

F. Foreign Assistance

FOREIGN ASSISTANCE ACT OF 1961, AS AMENDED*

AN ACT To promote the foreign policy, security, and general welfare of the United States by assisting peoples of the world in their efforts toward economic development and internal and external security, and for other purposes.

Be it enacted by the Senate and House of Representatives of the United States of America in Congress assembled, That this Act may be cited as "The Foreign Assistance Act of 1961."

PART I

Chapter 1 — Policy; Development Assistance Authorizations

Sec. 101. General Policy. — (a) The Congress finds that fundamental political, economic, and technological changes have resulted in the interdependence of nations. The Congress declares that the individual liberties, economic prosperity, and security of the people of the United States are best sustained and enhanced in a community of nations which respect individual civil and economic rights and freedoms and which work together to use wisely the world's limited resources in an open and equitable international economic system. Furthermore, the Congress reaffirms the traditional humanitarian ideals of the American people and renews its commitment to assist people in developing countries to eliminate hunger, poverty, illness, and ignorance.

Therefore, the Congress declares that a principal objective of the foreign policy of the United States is the encouragement and sustained support of the people of developing countries in their efforts to acquire the knowledge and resources essential to development and to build the economic, political, and social institutions which will improve the quality of their lives.

United States development cooperation policy should emphasize five principal goals:

(1) the alleviation of the worst physical manifestations of poverty among the world's poor majority;

(2) the promotion of conditions enabling developing countries to achieve self-sustaining economic growth with equitable distribution of benefits;

(3) the encouragement of development processes in which individual civil and economic rights are respected and enhanced;

(4) the integration of the developing countries into an open and equitable international economic system; and

(5) the promotion of good governance through combating corruption and improving transparency and accountability.

---

* Foreign Assistance Act of 1961, Pub. L. No. 87-195, §§ 101–461, 75 Stat. 424, 424–34 (codified as amended in scattered sections of 7, 20, 22 & 42 U.S.C.); International Peace and Security Act of 1961, Pub. L. No. 87-195, §§ 501–710, 75 Stat. 434–65 (codified as amended in scattered sections of 7, 20, 22 & 42 U.S.C.), *available at* http://www.usaid.gov/policy/ads/faa.pdf.

The Congress declares that pursuit of these goals requires that development concerns be fully reflected in United States foreign policy and that United States development resources be effectively and efficiently utilized.

(b) Under the policy guidance of the Secretary of State, the agency primarily responsible for administering this part should have the responsibility for coordinating all United States development-related activities.

Sec. 102. Development Assistance Policy.—(a) The Congress finds that the efforts of developing countries to build and maintain the social and economic institutions necessary to achieve self-sustaining growth and to provide opportunities to improve the quality of life for their people depend primarily upon successfully marshalling their own economic and human resources. The Congress recognizes that the magnitude of these efforts exceeds the resources of developing countries and therefore accepts that there will be a long-term need for wealthy countries to contribute additional resources for development purposes. The United States should take the lead in concert with other nations to mobilize such resources from public and private sources.

....

(8) United States cooperation in development should be carried out to the maximum extent possible through the private sector, including those institutions which already have ties in the developing areas, such as educational institutions, cooperatives, credit unions, free labor unions, and private and voluntary agencies.

(9) To the maximum extent practicable, United States private investment should be encouraged in economic and social development programs to which the United States lends support.

(10) Assistance shall be planned and utilized to encourage regional cooperation by developing countries in the solution of common problems and the development of shared resources.

(11) Assistance efforts of the United States shall be planned and furnished to the maximum extent practicable in coordination and cooperation with assistance efforts of other countries, including the planning and implementation of programs and projects on a multilateral and multidonor basis.

(12) United States bilateral development assistance should be concentrated on projects which do not involve large-scale capital transfers. However, to the extent that such assistance does involve large-scale capital transfers, it should be furnished in association with contributions from other countries working together in a multilateral framework.

(13) United States encouragement of policy reforms is necessary if developing countries are to achieve economic growth with equity.

(14) Development assistance should, as a fundamental objective, promote private sector activity in open and competitive markets in developing countries, recognizing such activity to be a productive and efficient means of achieving equitable and long-term economic growth.

(15) United States cooperation in development should recognize as essential the need of developing countries to have access to appropriate technology in order to improve food and water, health and housing, education and employment, and agriculture and industry.

(16) United States assistance should focus on establishing and upgrading the institutional capacities of developing countries in order to promote long-term development. An important component of institution building involves training to expand the human resource potential of people in developing countries.

(17) Economic reform and development of effective institutions of democratic governance are mutually reinforcing. The successful transition of a developing country is dependent upon the quality of its economic and governance institutions. Rule of law, mechanisms of accountability and transparency, security of person, property, and investments, are but a few of the critical governance and economic reforms that underpin the sustainability of broad-based economic growth. Programs in support of such reforms strengthen the capacity of people to hold their governments accountable and to create economic opportunity.

....

Chapter 3—International Organizations and Programs

Sec. 301. General Authority.—(a) When he determines it to be in the national interest, the President is authorized to make voluntary contributions on a grant basis to international organizations and to programs administered by such organizations, and in the case of the Indus Basin Development Fund administered by the International Bank for Reconstruction and Development to make grants and loans payable as to principal and interest in United States dollars and subject to the provisions of section 122(b), on such terms and conditions as he may determine, in order to further the purposes of this part.

....

(c) No contributions by the United States shall be made to the United Nations Relief and Works Agency for Palestine Refugees in the Near East except on the condition that the United Nations Relief and Works Agency take all possible measures to assure that no part of the United States contribution shall be used to furnish assistance to any refugee who is receiving military training as a member of the so-called Palestine Liberation Army or any other guerrilla type organization or who has engaged in any act of terrorism.

....

PART II

Chapter 1—Policy

Sec. 501. Statement of Policy.—The Congress of the United States reaffirms the policy of the United States to achieve international peace and security through the United Nations so that armed force shall not be used except for individual or collective self-defense. The Congress hereby finds that the efforts of the United States and other friendly countries to promote peace and security continue to require measures of support based upon the principle of effective self-help and mutual aid. It is the purpose of this part to authorize measures in the common defense against internal and external aggression, including the furnishing of military assistance, upon request, to friendly countries and international organizations. In furnishing such military assistance, it remains the policy of the United States to continue to exert maximum efforts to achieve universal control of weapons of mass destruction and universal regulation and reduction of armaments, including armed forces, under adequate safeguards to protect complying countries against violation and invasion.

The Congress recognizes that the peace of the world and the security of the United States are endangered so long as hostile countries continue by threat of military action, by the use of economic pressure, and by internal subversion, or other means to attempt to bring under their domination peoples now free and independent and continue to deny the rights of freedom and self-government to peoples and countries once free but now subject to such domination.

It is the sense of the Congress that an important contribution toward peace would be made by the establishment under the Organization of American States of an international military force.

In enacting this legislation, it is therefore the intention of the Congress to promote the peace of the world and the foreign policy, security, and general welfare of the United States by fostering an improved climate of political independence and individual liberty, improving the ability of friendly countries and international organizations to deter or, if necessary, defeat aggression, facilitating arrangements for individual and collective security, assisting friendly countries to maintain internal security, and creating an environment of security and stability in the developing friendly countries essential to their more rapid social, economic, and political progress. The Congress urges that all other countries able to contribute join in a common undertaking to meet the goals stated in this part.

It is the sense of the Congress that in the administration of this part priority shall be given to the needs of those countries in danger of becoming victims of aggression or in which the internal security is threatened by internal subversion inspired or supported by hostile countries.

Finally, the Congress reaffirms its full support of the progress of the members of the North Atlantic Treaty Organization toward increased cooperation in political, military, and economic affairs. In particular, the Congress welcomes the steps which have been taken to promote multilateral programs of coordinated procurement, research, development, and production of defense articles and urges that such programs be expanded to the fullest extent possible to further the defense of the North Atlantic area.

Sec. 502. Utilization of Defense Articles and Services.—Defense articles and defense services to any country shall be furnished solely for internal security (including for antiterrorism and nonproliferation purposes), for legitimate self-defense, to permit the recipient country to participate in regional or collective arrangements or measures consistent with the Charter of the United Nations, or otherwise to permit the recipient country to participate in collective measures requested by the United Nations for the purpose of maintaining or restoring international peace and security, or for the purpose of assisting foreign military forces in less developed friendly countries (or the voluntary efforts of personnel of the Armed Forces of the United States in such countries) to construct public works and to engage in other activities helpful to the economic and social development of such friendly countries. It is the sense of the Congress that such foreign military forces should not be maintained or established solely for civic action activities and that such civic action activities not significantly detract from the capability of the military forces to perform their military missions and be coordinated with and form part of the total economic and social development effort.

Sec. 502B. Human Rights.—(a)(1) The United States shall, in accordance with its international obligations as set forth in the Charter of the United Nations and in keeping with the constitutional heritage and traditions of the United States, promote and encourage increased respect for human rights and fundamental freedoms throughout the world without distinction as to race, sex, language, or religion. Accordingly, a principal goal of the foreign policy of the United States shall be to promote the increased observance of internationally recognized human rights by all countries.

(2) Except under circumstances specified in this section, no security assistance may be provided to any country the government of which engages in a consistent pattern of gross violations of internationally recognized human rights. Security assistance may not be provided to the police, domestic intelligence, or similar law enforcement forces of a country, and licenses may not be issued under the Export Administration Act of 1979 for the export of crime control and detection instruments and equipment to a country, the government of which engages in a consistent pattern of gross violations of internationally recognized human rights unless the President certifies in writing to the Speaker of the House of Representatives and the chairman of the Committee on Foreign Relations of the Senate and the chairman of the Committee on Banking, Housing, and Urban Affairs of the Senate (when licenses are to be issued pursuant to the Export Administration Act of 1979), that extraordinary circumstances exist warranting provision of such assistance and issuance of such licenses. Assistance may not be provided under chapter 5 of this part to a country the government of which engages in a consistent pattern of gross violations of internationally recognized human rights unless the President certifies in writing to the Speaker of the House of Representatives and the chairman of the Committee on Foreign Relations of the Senate that extraordinary circumstances exist warranting provision of such assistance.

(3) In furtherance of paragraphs (1) and (2), the President is directed to formulate and conduct international security assistance programs of the United States in a manner which will promote and advance human rights and avoid identification of the United States, through such programs, with governments which deny to their people internationally recognized human rights and fundamental freedoms, in violation of international law or in contravention of the policy of the United States as expressed in this section or otherwise.

(4) In determining whether the government of a country engages in a consistent pattern of gross violations of internationally recognized human rights, the President shall give particular consideration to whether the government—

(A) has engaged in or tolerated particularly severe violations of religious freedom, as defined in section 3 of the International Religious Freedom Act of 1998; or

(B) has failed to undertake serious and sustained efforts to combat particularly severe violations of religious freedom when such efforts could have been reasonably undertaken.

....

(d) For the purposes of this section—

(1) the term "gross violations of internationally recognized human rights" includes torture or cruel, inhuman, or degrading treatment or punishment, prolonged detention without charges and trial, causing the disappearance of persons by the abduction and clandestine detention of those persons, and other flagrant denial of the right to life, liberty, or the security of person; and

(2) the term "security assistance" means—

(A) assistance under chapter 2 (military assistance) or chapter 4 (economic support fund) or chapter 5 (military education and training) or chapter 6 (peacekeeping operations) or chapter 8 (antiterrorism assistance) of this part;

(B) sales of defense articles or services, extensions of credits (including participations in credits), and guaranties of loans under the Arms Export Control Act; or

(C) any license in effect with respect to the export of defense articles or defense services to or for the armed forces, police, intelligence, or other internal security forces of a foreign country under section 38 of the Arms Export Control Act.

(e) Notwithstanding any other provision of law, funds authorized to be appropriated under part I of this Act may be made available for the furnishing of assistance to any country with respect to which the President finds that such a significant improvement in its human rights record has occurred as to warrant lifting the prohibition on furnishing such assistance in the national interest of the United States.

(f) In allocating the funds authorized to be appropriated by this Act and the Arms Export Control Act, the President shall take into account significant improvements in the human rights records of recipient countries, except that such allocations may not contravene any other provision of law.

....

Chapter 2—Military Assistance

Sec. 503. General Authority.—(a) The President is authorized to furnish military assistance, on such terms and conditions as he may determine, to any friendly country or international organization, the assisting of which the President finds will strengthen the security of the United States and promote world peace and which is otherwise eligible to receive such assistance, by—

(1) acquiring from any source and providing (by loan or grant) any defense article or defense service;

(2) assigning or detailing members of the Armed Forces of the United States and other personnel of the Department of Defense to perform duties of a noncombatant nature; or

(3) transferring such of the funds appropriated or otherwise made available under this chapter as the President may determine for assistance to a recipient country, to the account in which funds for the procurement of defense articles and defense services under section 21 and section 22 of the Arms Export Control Act have been deposited for such recipient, to be merged with such deposited funds, and to be used solely to meet obligations of the recipient for payment for sales under that Act. Sales which are wholly paid from funds transferred under paragraph (3) or from funds made available on a non-repayable basis under section 23 of the Arms Export Control Act shall be priced to exclude the costs of salaries of members of the Armed Forces of the United States (other than the Coast Guard).

....

Sec. 505. Conditions of Eligibility.—(a) In addition to such other provisions as the President may require, no defense articles or related training or other defense service shall be furnished to any country on a grant basis unless it shall have agreed that—

(1) it will not, without the consent of the President—

(A) permit any use of such articles or related training or other defense service by anyone not an officer, employee, or agent of that country,

(B) transfer, or permit any officer, employee, or agent of that country to transfer such articles or related training or other defense service by gift, sale, or otherwise, or

(C) use or permit the use of such articles or related training or other defense service for purposes other than those for which furnished;

(2) it will maintain the security of such articles or related training or other defense service, and will provide substantially the same degree of security protection afforded to such articles or related training or other defense service by the United States Government;

(3) it will, as the President may require, permit continuous observation and review by, and furnish necessary information to, representatives of the United States Government with regard to the use of such articles or related training or other defense service; and

(4) unless the President consents to other disposition, it will return to the United States Government for such use or disposition as the President considers in the best interests of the United States, such articles or related training or other defense service which are no longer needed for the purposes for which furnished.

(b) No defense articles shall be furnished on a grant basis to any country at a cost in excess of $3,000,000 in any fiscal year unless the President determines—

(1) that such country conforms to the purposes and principles of the Charter of the United Nations;

(2) that such defense articles will be utilized by such country for the maintenance of its own defensive strength, or the defensive strength of the free world;

(3) that such country is taking all reasonable measures, consistent with its political and economic stability, which may be needed to develop its defense capacities; and

(4) that the increased ability of such country to defend itself is important to the security of the United States.

Sec. 506. Special Authority.—(a)(1) If the President determines and reports to the Congress in accordance with section 652 of this Act that—

(A) an unforeseen emergency exists which requires immediate military assistance to a foreign country or international organization; and

(B) the emergency requirement cannot be met under the authority of the Arms Export Control Act or any other law except this section;

he may direct, for the purposes of this part, the drawdown of defense articles from the stocks of the Department of Defense, defense services of the Department of Defense, and military education and training, of an aggregate value of not to exceed $100,000,000 in any fiscal year.

(2) (A) If the President determines and reports to the Congress in accordance with section 652 of this Act that it is in the national interest of the United States to draw down articles and services from the inventory and resources of any agency of the United States Government and military education and training from the Depart-

ment of Defense, the President may direct the drawdown of such articles, services, and military education and training—

(i) for the purposes and under the authorities of—

(I) chapter 8 of part I (relating to international narcotics control assistance);

(II) chapter 9 of part I (relating to international disaster assistance);

(III) chapter 8 of part II (relating to antiterrorism assistance);

(IV) chapter 9 of part II (relating to nonproliferation assistance); or

(V) the Migration and Refugee Assistance Act of 1962; or

(ii) for the purpose of providing such articles, services, and military education and training to Vietnam, Cambodia, and Laos as the President determines are necessary—

(I) to support cooperative efforts to locate and repatriate members of the United States Armed Forces and civilians employed directly or indirectly by the United States Government who remain unaccounted for from the Vietnam War; and

(II) to ensure the safety of United States Government personnel engaged in such cooperative efforts and to support Department of Defense-sponsored humanitarian projects associated with such efforts.

(B) An aggregate value of not to exceed $200,000,000 in any fiscal year of such articles, services, and military education and training may be provided pursuant to subparagraph (A) of this paragraph—

(i) not more than $75,000,000 of which may be provided from the drawdown from the inventory and resources of the Department of Defense;

(ii) not more than $75,000,000 of which may be provided pursuant to clause (i)(I) of such subparagraph; and

(iii) not more than $15,000,000 of which may be provided to Vietnam, Cambodia, and Laos pursuant to clause (ii) of such subparagraph.

(b) (1) The authority contained in this section shall be effective for any such emergency only upon prior notification to the Committee on Foreign Affairs of the House of Representatives, the Committee on Foreign Relations of the Senate, and the Committee on Appropriations of each House of Congress. In the case of drawdowns authorized by subclauses (I) and (III) of subsection (a)(2)(A)(i), notifications shall be provided to those committees at least 15 days in advance of the drawdowns in accordance with the procedures applicable to reprogramming notifications under section 634A.

(2) The President shall keep the Congress fully and currently informed of all defense articles, defense services, and military education and training provided under this section, including providing the Congress with a report detailing all defense articles, defense services, and military education and training delivered to the recipient country or international organization upon delivery of such articles or upon completion of such services or education and training. Such report shall also include whether any savings were realized by utilizing commercial transport services rather than acquiring those services from United States Government transport assets.

(c) For the purposes of any provision of law that authorizes the drawdown of defense or other articles or commodities, or defense or other services from an agency of the United States Government, such drawdown may include the supply of commercial transportation and related services that are acquired by contract for the purposes of the drawdown in question if the cost to acquire such commercial transportation and related services is less than the cost to the United States Government of providing such services from existing agency assets.

(d) There are authorized to be appropriated to the President such sums as may be necessary to reimburse the applicable appropriation, fund, or account for defense articles, defense services, and military education and training provided under this section.

....

Chapter 8—Antiterrorism Assistance

Sec. 571. General Authority.—Notwithstanding any other provision of law that restricts assistance to foreign countries (other than sections 502B and 620A of this Act), the President is authorized to furnish, on such terms and conditions as the President may determine, assistance to foreign countries in order to enhance the ability of their law enforcement personnel to deter terrorists and terrorist groups from engaging in international terrorist acts such as bombing, kidnapping, assassination, hostage taking, and hi-jacking. Such assistance may include training services and the provision of equipment and other commodities related to bomb detection and disposal, management of hostage situations, physical security, and other matters relating to the detection, deterrence, and prevention of acts of terrorism, the resolution of terrorist incidents, and the apprehension of those involved in such acts.

Sec. 572. Purposes.—Activities conducted under this chapter shall be designed—

(1) to enhance the antiterrorism skills of friendly countries by providing training and equipment to deter and counter terrorism;

(2) to strengthen the bilateral ties of the United States with friendly governments by offering concrete assistance in this area of great mutual concern; and

(3) to increase respect for human rights by sharing with foreign civil authorities modern, humane, and effective antiterrorism techniques.

Sec. 573. Limitations.—(a) Whenever the President determines it to be consistent with and in furtherance of the purposes of this chapter, and on such terms and conditions consistent with this Act as he may determine, any agency of the United States Government is authorized to furnish services and commodities, without charge to funds available to carry out this chapter, to an eligible foreign country, subject to payment in advance of the value thereof (within the meaning of section 644(m)) in United States dollars by the foreign country. Credits and the proceeds of guaranteed loans made available to such countries pursuant to the Arms Export Control Act shall not be used for such payments. Collections under this chapter shall be credited to the currently applicable appropriation, account, or fund of the agency providing such services and commodities and shall be available for the purposes for which such appropriation, account, or fund is authorized to be used.

(b) The Assistant Secretary of State for Democracy, Human Rights, and Labor shall be consulted in the determinations of the foreign countries that will be furnished assistance under this chapter and determinations of the nature of assistance to be furnished to each such country.

(c) (1) Arms and ammunition may be provided under this chapter only if they are directly related to antiterrorism assistance.

(2) The value (in terms of original acquisition cost) of all equipment and commodities provided under this chapter in any fiscal year shall not exceed 30 percent of the funds made available to carry out this chapter for that fiscal year.

....

Chapter 9—Nonproliferation and Export Control Assistance

Sec. 581. Purposes. The purposes of assistance under this chapter are to halt the proliferation of nuclear, chemical, and biological weapons, and conventional weaponry, through support of activities designed—

(1) to enhance the nonproliferation and export control capabilities of friendly countries by providing training and equipment to detect, deter, monitor, interdict, and counter proliferation;

(2) to strengthen the bilateral ties of the United States with friendly governments by offering concrete assistance in this area of vital national security interest;

(3) to accomplish the activities and objectives set forth in sections 503 and 504 of the FREEDOM Support Act (22 U.S.C. 5853, 5854), without regard to the limitation of those sections to the independent states of the former Soviet Union; and
(4) to promote multilateral activities, including cooperation with international organizations, relating to nonproliferation.

Sec. 582. Authorization of Assistance. Notwithstanding any other provision of law (other than section 502B or section 620A of this Act), the President is authorized to furnish, on such terms and conditions as the President may determine, assistance in order to carry out the purposes of this chapter. Such assistance may include training services and the provision of funds, equipment, and other commodities related to the detection, deterrence, monitoring, interdiction, and prevention or countering of proliferation, the establishment of effective nonproliferation laws and regulations, and the apprehension of those individuals involved in acts of proliferation of such weapons.

Sec. 583. Transit Interdiction.

(a) ALLOCATION OF FUNDS.—In providing assistance under this chapter, the President should ensure that not less than one-quarter of the total of such assistance is expended for the purpose of enhancing the capabilities of friendly countries to detect and interdict proliferation-related shipments of cargo that originate from, and are destined for, other countries.

(b) PRIORITY TO CERTAIN COUNTRIES.—Priority shall be given in the apportionment of the assistance described under subsection (a) to any friendly country that has been determined by the Secretary of State to be a country frequently transited by proliferation-related shipments of cargo.

....

PART III

Chapter 1—General Provisions

Sec. 601. Encouragement of Free Enterprise and Private Participation.—(a) The Congress of the United States recognizes the vital role of free enterprise in achieving rising levels of production and standards of living essential to economic progress and development. Accordingly, it is declared to be the policy of the United States to encourage the efforts of other countries to increase the flow of international trade, to foster private initiative and competition, to encourage the development and use of cooperatives, credit unions, and savings and loan associations, to discourage monopolistic practices, to improve the technical efficiency of their industry, agriculture, and commerce, and to strengthen free labor unions; and to encourage the contribution of United States enterprise toward economic strength of less developed friendly countries, through private trade and investment abroad, private participation in programs carried out under this Act (including the use of private trade channels to the maximum extent practicable in carrying out such programs), and exchange of ideas and technical information on the matters covered by this subsection.

(b) In order to encourage and facilitate participation by private enterprise to the maximum extent practicable in achieving any of the purposes of this Act, the President shall—

(1) make arrangements to find, and draw the attention of private enterprise to opportunities for investment and development in less developed countries and areas;

(2) establish an effective system for obtaining adequate information with respect to the activities of, and opportunities for, nongovernmental participation in the development process, and for utilizing such information in the planning, direction, and execution of programs carried out under this Act, and in the coordination of such programs with the ever-increasing developmental activities of nongovernmental United States institutions;

(3) accelerate a program of negotiating treaties for commerce and trade, including tax treaties, which shall include provisions to encourage and facilitate the flow of private in vestment to, and its equitable treatment in, friendly countries and areas participating in programs under this Act;

(4) seek, consistent with the national interest, compliance by other countries or areas with all treaties for commerce and trade and taxes, and take all reasonable measures under this Act or other authority to secure compliance therewith and to assist United States citizens in obtaining just compensation for losses sustained by them or payments exacted from them as a result of measures taken or imposed by any country or area thereof in violation of any such treaty;

(5) to the maximum extent practicable carry out programs of assistance through private channels and to the extent practicable in conjunction with local private or governmental participation, including loans under the authority of section 122 to any individual, corporation, or other body of persons;

....

Sec. 620A. Prohibition on Assistance to Governments Supporting International Terrorism.

(a) PROHIBITION.—The United States shall not provide any assistance under this Act, the Agricultural Trade Development and Assistance Act of 1954, the Peace Corps Act, or the Export-Import Bank Act of 1945 to any country if the Secretary of State determines that the government of that country has repeatedly provided support for acts of international terrorism.

(b) PUBLICATION OF DETERMINATIONS.—Each determination of the Secretary of State under subsection (a), including each determination in effect on the date of the enactment of the Antiterrorism and Arms Export Amendments Act of 1989, shall be published in the Federal Register.

(c) RESCISSION.—A determination made by the Secretary of State under subsection (a) may not be rescinded unless the President submits to the Speaker of the House of Representatives and the Chairman of the Committee on Foreign Relations of the Senate—

(1) before the proposed rescission would take effect, a report certifying that—

(A) there has been a fundamental change in the leadership and policies of the government of the country concerned;

(B) that government is not supporting acts of international terrorism;

(C) that government has provided assurances that it will not support acts of international terrorism in the future; or

(2) at least 45 days before the proposed rescission would take effect, a report justifying the rescission and certifying that—

(A) the government concerned has not provided any support for international terrorism during the preceding 6-month period; and

(B) the government concerned has provided assurances that it will not support acts of international terrorism in the future.

(d) WAIVER.—Assistance prohibited by subsection (a) may be provided to a country described in that subsection if—

(1) the President determines that national security interests or humanitarian reasons justify a waiver of subsection (a), except that humanitarian reasons may not be used to justify assistance under part II of this Act (including chapter 4, chapter 6, and chapter 8), or the Export-Import Bank Act of 1945; and

(2) at least 15 days before the waiver takes effect, the President consults with the Committee on Foreign Affairs 915 of the House of Representatives and the Committee on Foreign Relations of the Senate regarding the proposed waiver and submits a report to the Speaker of the House of Representatives and the chairman of the Committee on Foreign Relations of the Senate containing—

(A) the name of the recipient country;

(B) a description of the national security interests or humanitarian reasons which require the waiver;

(C) the type and amount of and the justification for the assistance to be provided pursuant to the waiver; and

(D) the period of time during which such waiver will be effective.

The waiver authority granted in this subsection may not be used to provide any assistance under the Foreign Assistance Act of 1961 which is also prohibited by section 40 of the Arms Export Control Act.

....

Sec. 622. Coordination With Foreign Policy.—(a) Nothing contained in this Act shall be construed to infringe upon the powers or functions of the Secretary of State.

(b) The President shall prescribe appropriate procedures to assure coordination among representatives of the United States Government in each country, under the leadership of the Chief of the United States Diplomatic Mission. The Chief of the

Diplomatic Mission shall make sure that recommendations of such representatives pertaining to military assistance (including civic action) and military education and training programs are coordinated with political and economic considerations, and his comments shall accompany such recommendations if he so desires.

(c) Under the direction of the President, the Secretary of State shall be responsible for the continuous supervision and general direction of economic assistance, military assistance, and military education and training programs, including but not limited to determining whether there shall be a military assistance (including civic action) or a military education and training program for a country and the value thereof, to the end that such programs are effectively integrated both at home and abroad and the foreign policy of the United States is best served thereby.

Sec. 623. The Secretary of Defense.—(a) In the case of assistance under part II of this Act, the Secretary of Defense shall have primary responsibility for—

(1) the determination of military end-item requirements;

(2) the procurement of military equipment in a manner which permits its integration with service programs;

(3) the supervision of end-item use by the recipient countries;

(4) the supervision of the training of foreign military and related civilian personnel;

(5) the movement and delivery of military end-items; and

(6) within the Department of Defense, the performance of any other functions with respect to the furnishing of military assistance, education and training.

(b) The establishment of priorities in the procurement, delivery, and allocation of military equipment shall be determined by the Secretary of Defense.

....

G. Emergency Preparedness

DEFENSE PRODUCTION ACT OF 1950*

....

DECLARATION OF POLICY

Sec. 2. It is the policy of the United States to oppose acts of aggression and to promote peace by insuring respect for world law and the peaceful settlement of differences among nations. To that end this Government is pledged to support collective action through the United Nations and through regional arrangements for mutual defense in conformity with the Charter of the United Nations. The United States is determined to develop and maintain whatever military and economic strength is found to be necessary to carry out this purpose. Under present circumstances, this task requires diversion of certain materials and facilities from civilian use to military and related purposes. It requires expansion of productive facilities beyond the levels needed to meet the civilian demand. In order that this diversion and expansion may proceed at once, and that the national economy may be maintained with the maximum effectiveness and the least hardship normal civilian production and purchases must be curtailed and redirected.

It is the objective of this Act to provide the President with authority to accomplish these adjustments in the operation of the economy. It is the intention of the Congress that the President shall use the powers conferred by this Act to promote the national defense, by meeting, promptly and effectively, the requirements of military programs in support of our national security and foreign policy objectives, and by preventing undue strains and dislocations upon wages, prices, and production or distribution of materials for civilian use, within the framework, as far as practicable, of the American system of competitive enterprise.

TITLE I—PRIORITIES AND ALLOCATIONS

Sec. 101. The President is hereby authorized (1) to require that performance under contracts or orders (other than contracts of employment) which he deems necessary or appropriate to promote the national defense shall take priority over performance under any other contract or order, and, for the purpose of assuring such priority, to require acceptance and performance of such contracts or orders in preference to other contracts or orders by any person he finds to be capable of their performance, and (2) to allocate materials and facilities in such manner, upon such conditions, and to such extent as he shall deem necessary or appropriate to promote the national defense.

Sec. 102. In order to prevent hoarding, no person shall accumulate (1) in excess of the reasonable demands of business, personal, or home consumption, or (2) for the purpose of resale at prices in excess of prevailing market prices, materials which have been designated by the President as scarce materials or materials the supply of which would be threatened by such accumulation. The President shall order published in the Federal Register, and in such other manner as he may deem appropriate, every designa-

* Pub. L. No. 81-774, 64 Stat. 798. (1950).

tion of materials the accumulation of which is unlawful and any withdrawal of such designation. This section shall not be construed to limit the authority contained in section 101 of this Act.

Sec. 103. Any person who willfully performs any act prohibited, or willfully fails to perform any act required, by the provisions of this title or any rule, regulation, or order thereunder, shall, upon conviction, be fined not more than $10,000 or imprisoned for not more than one year, or both.

TITLE II—AUTHORITY TO REQUISITION

Sec. 201. (a) Whenever the President determines (1) that the use of any equipment, supplies, or component parts thereof, or materials or facilities necessary for the manufacture, servicing, or operation of such equipment, supplies, or component parts, is needed for the national defense, (2) that such need is immediate and impending and such as will not admit of delay or resort to any other source of supply, and (3) that all other means of obtaining the use of such property for the defense of the United States upon fair and reasonable terms have been exhausted, he is authorized to requisition such property or the use thereof for the defense of the United States upon the payment of just compensation for such property or the use thereof to be determined as hereinafter provided. The President shall promptly determine the amount of the compensation to be paid for any property or the use thereof requisitioned pursuant to this title but each such determination shall be made as of the time it is requisitioned in accordance with the provision for just compensation in the fifth amendment to the Constitution of the United States. If the person entitled to receive the amount so determined by the President as just compensation is unwilling to accept the same as full and complete compensation for such property or the use thereof, he shall be paid promptly 75 per centum of such amount and shall be entitled to recover from the United States, in an action brought in the Court of Claims or, without regard to whether the amount involved exceeds $10,000, in any district court of the United States, within three years after the date of the President's award, an additional amount which, when added to the amount so paid to him, shall be just compensation.

....

TITLE III—EXPANSION OF PRODUCTIVE CAPACITY AND SUPPLY

Sec. 301. (a) In order to expedite production and deliveries or services under Government contracts, the President may authorize, subject to such regulations as he may prescribe, the Department of the Army, the Department of the Navy, the Department of the Air Force, the Department of Commerce, and such other agencies of the United States engaged in procurement for the national defense as he may designate (hereinafter referred to as "guaranteeing agencies"), without regard to provisions of law relating to the making, performance, amendment, or modification of contracts, to guarantee in whole or in part any public or private financing institution (including any Federal Reserve bank), by commitment to purchase, agreement to share losses, or otherwise, against loss of principal or interest on any loan, discount, or advance, or on any commitment in connection therewith, which may be made by such financing institution for the purpose of financing any contractor, subcontractor, or other person in connection with the performance, or in connection with or in contemplation of the termination, of any contract or other operation deemed by the guaranteeing agency to be necessary to expedite production and deliveries or services under Government contracts for the procurement of materials or the performance of services for the national defense.

....

TITLE IV—PRICE AND WAGE STABILIZATION

Sec. 401. It is the intent of Congress to provide authority necessary to achieve the following purposes in order to promote the national defense: To prevent inflation and preserve the value of the national currency; to assure that defense appropriations are not dissipated by excessive costs and prices; to stabilize the cost of living for workers and other consumers and the costs of production for farmers and businessmen; to eliminate and prevent profiteering, hoarding, manipulation, speculation, and other disruptive practices resulting from abnormal market conditions or scarcities; to protect consumers, wage earners, investors, and persons with relatively fixed or limited incomes from undue impairment of their living standards; to prevent economic disturbances, labor disputes, interferences with the effective mobilization of national resources, and impairment of national unity and morale; to assist in maintaining a reasonable balance between purchasing power and the supply of consumer goods and services; to protect the national economy against future loss of needed purchasing power by the present dissipation of individual savings; and to prevent a future collapse of values. It is the intent of Congress that the authority conferred by this title shall be exercised in accordance with the policies set forth in section 2 of this Act, and in particular with full consideration and emphasis, so far as practicable, on the maintenance and furtherance of the American system of competitive enterprise, including independent small-business enterprises, the maintenance and furtherance of a sound agricultural industry, the maintenance and furtherance of sound working relations, including collective bargaining, and the maintenance and furtherance of the American way of life. Whenever the authority granted by this title is exercised, all agencies of the Government dealing with the subject matter of this title, within the limits of their authority and jurisdiction, shall cooperate in carrying out these purposes.

Sec. 402. (a) In order to carry out the objectives of this title, the President may encourage and promote voluntary action by business, agriculture, labor and consumers. In proceeding under this subsection the President may exercise the authority to approve voluntary programs and agreements conferred on him under section 708, and may utilize the services of persons and agencies as provided in section 710.

(b) (1) To the extent that the objectives of this title cannot be attained by action under subsection (a), the President may issue regulations and orders establishing a ceiling or ceilings on the price, rental, commission, margin, rate, fee, charge, or allowance paid or received on the sale or delivery, or the purchase or receipt, by or to any person, of any material or service, and at the same time shall issue regulations and orders stabilizing wages, salaries, and other compensation in accordance with the provisions of this subsection.

(2) Action under this subsection may be taken either with respect to individual materials and services and to individual types of employment, or with respect to materials, services, and types of employment generally. A ceiling may be established with respect to an individual material or service only when the President finds that (i) the price of the material or service has risen or threatens to rise unreasonably above the price prevailing during the period from May 24, 1950 to June 24, 1950, (ii) such price increase will materially affect the cost of living or the national defense, (iii) the imposition of such ceiling is necessary to effectuate the purposes

of this Act, (iv) it is practicable and feasible to impose such ceiling, and (v) such ceiling will be generally fair and equitable to sellers and buyers of such material or service and to sellers and buyers of related or competitive materials and services.

(3) Whenever a ceiling has been imposed with respect to a particular material or service, the President shall stabilize wages, salaries, and other compensation in the industry or business producing the material or performing the service.

(4) Whenever ceilings on prices have been established on materials and services comprising a substantial part of all sales at retail and materially affecting the cost of living, the President (i) shall impose ceilings on prices and services generally, and (ii) shall stabilize wages, salaries, and other compensation generally.

(5) In stabilizing wages under paragraph (3) of this subsection, the President shall issue regulations prohibiting increases in wages, salaries, and other compensation which he deems would require an increase in the price ceiling or impose hardships or inequities on sellers operating under the price ceiling.

....

TITLE V—SETTLEMENT OF LABOR DISPUTES

Sec. 501. It is the intent of Congress, in order to provide for effective price and wage stabilization pursuant to title IV of this Act and to maintain uninterrupted production, that there be effective procedures for the settlement of labor disputes affecting national defense.

Sec. 502. The national policy shall be to place primary reliance upon the parties to any labor dispute to make every effort through negotiation and collective bargaining and the full use of mediation and conciliation facilities to effect a settlement in the national interest. To this end, the President is authorized (1) to initiate voluntary conferences between management, labor, and such persons as the President may designate to represent government and the public, and (2) subject to the provisions of section 503, to take such action as may be agreed upon in any such conference and appropriate to carry out the provisions of this title. The President may designate such persons or agencies as he may deem appropriate to carry out the provisions of this title.

Sec. 503. In any such conference, due regard shall be given to terms and conditions of employment established by prevailing collective bargaining practice which will be fair to labor and management alike, and will be consistent with stabilization policies established under this Act. No action inconsistent with the provisions of the Fair Labor Standards Act of 1938, as amended, other Federal labor standards statutes, the Labor Management Relations Act, 1947, or with other applicable laws shall be taken under this title.

....

STRATEGIC AND CRITICAL MATERIALS STOCKPILING ACT*

....

§ 98a. Congressional findings and declaration of purpose

....

(b) It is the purpose of this Act [50 USCS §§ 98 et seq.] to provide for the acquisition and retention of stocks of certain strategic and critical materials and to encourage the conservation and development of sources of such materials within the United States and thereby to decrease and to preclude, when possible, a dangerous and costly dependence by the United States upon foreign sources for supplies of such materials in times of national emergency.

(c) The purpose of the National Defense Stockpile is to serve the interest of national defense only. The National Defense Stockpile is not to be used for economic or budgetary purposes.

§ 98b. National Defense Stockpile

(a) Determination of materials; quantities. Subject to subsection (c), the President shall determine from time to time:

(1) which materials are strategic and critical materials for the purposes of this Act, and

(2) the quality and quantity of each such material to be acquired for the purposes of this Act and the form in which each such material shall be acquired and stored.

Such materials when acquired, together with the other materials described in section 4 of this Act [50 USCS § 98c], shall constitute and be collectively known as the National Defense Stockpile (hereinafter in this Act referred to as the "stockpile").

(b) Guidelines for exercise of Presidential authority. The President shall make the determinations required to be made under subsection (a) on the basis of the principles stated in section 2(c) [50 USCS § 98a(c)].

(c) Quantity change; notification to Congress.

(1) The quantity of any material to be stockpiled under this Act, as in effect on September 30, 1987, may be changed only as provided in this subsection or as otherwise provided by law enacted after December 4, 1987.

(2) The President shall notify Congress in writing of any change proposed to be made in the quantity of any material to be stockpiled. The President may make the change after the end of the 45-day period beginning on the date of the notification. The President shall include a full explanation and justification for the proposed change with the notification.

§ 98c. Materials constituting the National Defense Stockpile

(a) Contents. The stockpile consists of the following materials:

---

* Strategic and Critical Materials Stock Piling Revision Act of 1979, Pub. L. No. 96-41, 93 Stat. 319 (codified as amended at 50 U.S.C.A. §§ 98 to 98h-7 (West 2003 & Supp. 2005)).

(1) Materials acquired under this Act [50 USCS §§ 98 et seq.] and contained in the national stockpile on July 29, 1979.

(2) Materials acquired under this Act [50 USCS §§ 98 et seq.] after July 29, 1979.

(3) Materials in the supplemental stockpile established by section 104(b) of the Agricultural Trade Development and Assistance Act of 1954 [7 USCS § 1704(b)] (as in effect from September 21, 1959, through December 31, 1966) on July 29, 1979.

(4) Materials acquired by the United States under the provisions of section 303 of the Defense Production Act of 1950 (50 U.S.C. App. 2093) and transferred to the stockpile by the President pursuant to subsection (f) of such section.

(5) Materials transferred to the United States under section 663 of the Foreign Assistance Act of 1961 (22 U.S.C. 2423) that have been determined to be strategic and critical materials for the purposes of this Act [50 USCS §§ 98 et seq.] and that are allocated by the President under subsection (b) of such section for stockpiling in the stockpile.

(6) Materials acquired by the Commodity Credit Corporation and transferred to the stockpile under section 4(h) of the Commodity Credit Corporation Charter Act (15 U.S.C. 714b(h)).

(7) Materials acquired by the Commodity Credit Corporation under paragraph (2) of section 103(a) of the Act entitled "An Act to provide for greater stability in agriculture; to augment the marketing and disposal of agricultural products; and for other purposes", approved August 28, 1954 (7 U.S.C. 1743(a)), and transferred to the stockpile under the third sentence of such section.

(8) Materials transferred to the stockpile by the President under paragraph (4) of section 103(a) of such Act of August 28, 1954 [7 USCS § 1743(a)(4)].

(9) Materials transferred to the stockpile under subsection (b).

(10) Materials transferred to the stockpile under subsection (c).

(b) Transfer and reimbursement. Notwithstanding any other provision of law, any material that (1) is under the control of any department or agency of the United States, (2) is determined by the head of such department or agency to be excess to its needs and responsibilities, and (3) is required for the stockpile shall be transferred to the stockpile. Any such transfer shall be made without reimbursement to such department or agency, but all costs required to effect such transfer shall be paid or reimbursed from funds appropriated to carry out this Act [50 USCS §§ 98 et seq.].

....

INTERNATIONAL EMERGENCY ECONOMIC POWERS ACT[1] (IEEPA)

Sec. 1701. Unusual and extraordinary threat; declaration of national emergency; exercise of Presidential authorities

(a) Any authority granted to the President by section 1702 of this title may be exercised to deal with any unusual and extraordinary threat, which has its source in whole or substantial part outside the United States, to the national security, foreign policy, or economy of the United States, if the President declares a national emergency with respect to such threat.

(b) The authorities granted to the President by section 1702 of this title may only be exercised to deal with an unusual and extraordinary threat with respect to which a national emergency has been declared for purposes of this chapter and may not be exercised for any other purpose. Any exercise of such authorities to deal with any new threat shall be based on a new declaration of national emergency which must be with respect to such threat.

Sec. 1702. Presidential authorities

(a) (1) At the times and to the extent specified in section 1701 of this title, the President may, under such regulations as he may prescribe, by means of instructions, licenses, or otherwise—

(A) investigate, regulate, or prohibit—

(i) any transactions in foreign exchange,

(ii) transfers of credit or payments between, by, through, or to any banking institution, to the extent that such transfers or payments involve any interest of any foreign country or a national thereof,

(iii) the importing or exporting of currency or securities; and

(B) investigate, regulate, direct and compel, nullify, void, prevent or prohibit, any acquisition, holding, withholding, use, transfer, withdrawal, transportation, importation or exportation of, or dealing in, or exercising any right, power, or privilege with respect to, or transactions involving, any property in which any foreign country or a national thereof has any interest; by any person, or with respect to any property, subject to the jurisdiction of the United States.[2]

---

1. International Emergency Economic Powers Act, Pub. L. No. 95-223, §§ 201–208, 91 Stat. 1625, 1626–29 (1977), *amended by* Omnibus Trade and Competitiveness Act of 1988, Pub. L. No. 100-418, § 2502(b), 102 Stat. 1371, 1371–72 (codified as amended at 50 U.S.C.A. §§ 1701–1706 (West 2003 & Supp. 2005), 50 U.S.C. app. §§ 1–44, 2401–2413 (2000)). Except for the provisions printed herein, this Act consists of amendments to the Trading with the Enemy Act, ch. 106, 40 Stat. 411 (1917) (codified as amended at 50 U.S.C. app. §§ 1–44 (2000)), and the Export Administration Act of 1969, Pub. L. No. 91-184, 83 Stat. 841 (codified as amended at 50 U.S.C. app. §§ 2401–2413 (2000)), *available at* http://www4.law.cornell.edu/uscode/html/uscode50/usc_sup_01_50_10_35.html. For Trading with the EnemyAct and its amendments, see below Document 5:69.

2. Concerning the President's exercising authority under this subsection, see Exec. Order No. 12,170, 3 C.F.R. 457 (1979), *reprinted as amended in* 50 U.S.C.A. § 1701 note (West 2003 & Supp.

(2) In exercising the authorities granted by paragraph (1), the President may require any person to keep a full record of, and to furnish under oath, in the form of reports or otherwise, complete information relative to any act or transaction referred to in paragraph (1) either before, during, or after the completion thereof, or relative to any interest in foreign property, or relative to any property in which any foreign country or any national thereof has or has had any interest, or as may be otherwise necessary to enforce the provisions of such paragraph. In any case in which a report by a person could be required under this paragraph, the President may require the production of any books of account, records, contracts, letters, memoranda, or other papers, in the custody or control of such person.

(3) Compliance with any regulation, instruction, or direction issued under this chapter shall to the extent thereof be a full acquittance and discharge for all purposes of the obligation of the person making the same. No person shall be held liable in any court for or with respect to anything done or omitted in good faith in connection with the administration of, or pursuant to and in reliance on, this chapter, or any regulation, instruction, or direction issued under this chapter.

(b) The authority granted to the President by this section does not include the authority to regulate or prohibit, directly or indirectly—

(1) any postal, telegraphic, telephonic, or other personal communication, which does not involve a transfer of anything of value;[3]

(2) donations, by persons subject to the jurisdiction of the United States, of articles, such as food, clothing, and medicine, intended to be used to relieve human suffering, except to the extent that the President determines that such donations—

(A) would seriously impair his ability to deal with any national emergency declared under section 1701 of this title,

(B) are in response to coercion against the proposed recipient or donor, or

(C) would endanger Armed Forces of the United States which are engaged in hostilities or are in a situation where imminent involvement in hostilities is clearly indicated by the circumstances; or

(3) the importation from any country, or the exportation to any country, whether commercial or otherwise, regardless of format or medium of transmission, of any information or informational materials, including but not limited to, publications, films, posters, phonograph records, photographs, microfilms, microfiche, tapes, compact disks, CD ROMs, artworks, and news wire feeds. The exports exempted from regulation or prohibition by this paragraph do not include those which are otherwise controlled for export under section 2404 of the Appendix to this title, or under section 2405 of the Appendix to this title to the extent that such

---

2005); Exec. Order No. 12,205, 3 C.F.R. 248 (1980), *reprinted as amended in* 50 U.S.C. § 1701 note (2000); Exec. Order No. 12,211, 3 C.F.R. 253 (1980), *reprinted in* 50 U.S.C. § 1701 note (2000).

3. Section 203(b) was amended by section 2502(b)(1) of Pub. L. No. 100-418, 102 Stat. 1371 (1988), which struck out "or" in para. (1); struck out the period and inserted "; or" in para. (2) and added new para. (3). Section 2502(b)(2) of that Act also stated that:

> (2) The amendments made by paragraph (1) apply to actions by the President under section 203 of the International Emergency Economic Powers Act before the date of the enactment of this Act which are in effect on such date of enactments, and to actions taken under such section on or after such date of enactment.

102 Stat. at 1372.

controls promote the nonproliferation or antiterrorism policies of the United States, or with respect to which acts are prohibited by chapter 37 of title 18; or

(4) any transactions ordinarily incident to travel to or from any country, including importation of accompanied baggage for personal use, maintenance within any country including payment of living expenses and acquisition of goods or services for personal use, and arrangement or facilitation of such travel including non-scheduled air, sea, or land voyages.

Sec. 1703. Consultation and reports

(a) *Consultation with Congress.*

The President, in every possible instance, shall consult with the Congress before exercising any of the authorities granted by this chapter and shall consult regularly with the Congress so long as such authorities are exercised.

(b) *Report to Congress upon exercise of Presidential authorities.*

Whenever the President exercises any of the authorities granted by this chapter, he shall immediately transmit to the Congress a report[4] specifying—

(1) the circumstances which necessitate such exercise of authority;

(2) why the President believes those circumstances constitute an unusual and extraordinary threat, which has its source in whole or substantial part outside the United States, to the national security, foreign policy, or economy of the United States;

(3) the authorities to be exercised and the actions to be taken in the exercise of those authorities to deal with those circumstances;

(4) why the President believes such actions are necessary to deal with those circumstances; and

(5) any foreign countries with respect to which such actions are to be taken and why such actions are to be taken with respect to those countries.

(c) *Periodic follow-up reports.*

At least once during each succeeding six-month period after transmitting a report pursuant to subsection (b) of this section with respect to an exercise of authorities under this chapter, the President shall report to the Congress with respect to the actions taken, since the last such report, in the exercise of such authorities, and with respect to any changes which have occurred concerning any information previously furnished pursuant to paragraphs (1) through (5) of subsection (b) of this section.

(d) *Supplemental requirements.*

The requirements of this section are supplemental to those contained in title IV of the National Emergencies Act (50 U.S.C. 1641).

Sec. 1704. Authority to issue regulations

The President may issue such regulations, including regulations prescribing definitions, as may be necessary for the exercise of the authorities granted by this chapter.

4. Such reports were transmitted to Congress regarding the authority exercised by the President as discussed in Exec. Order Nos. 12,170, 12,205, and 12,211, *supra* note 8, *reprinted infra* pp. 950–51, 953.

Sec. 1705. Penalties

(a) A civil penalty of not to exceed $10,000 may be imposed on any person who violates any license, order, or regulation issued under this chapter.

(b) Whoever willfully violates any license, order, or regulation issued under this chapter shall, upon conviction, be fined not more than $50,000, or, if a natural person, may be imprisoned for not more than ten years, or both; and any officer, director, or agent of any corporation who knowingly participates in such violation may be punished by a like fine, imprisonment, or both.

Sec. 1706. Savings provisions

(a) *Termination of national emergencies pursuant to National Emergencies Act.*

(1) Except as provided in subsection (b) of this section, notwithstanding the termination pursuant to the National Emergencies Act (50 U.S.C. 1601 et seq.) of a national emergency declared for purposes of this chapter, any authorities granted by this chapter, which are exercised on the date of such termination on the basis of such national emergency to prohibit transactions involving property in which a foreign country or national thereof has any interest, may continue to be so exercised to prohibit transactions involving that property if the President determines that the continuation of such prohibition with respect to that property is necessary on account of claims involving such country or its nationals.

(2) Notwithstanding the termination of the authorities described in section 101(b) of this Act, any such authorities, which are exercised with respect to a country on the date of such termination to prohibit transactions involving any property in which such country or any national thereof has any interest, may continue to be exercised to prohibit transactions involving that property if the President determines that the continuation of such prohibition with respect to that property is necessary on account of claims involving such country or its nationals.

(b) *Congressional termination of national emergencies by concurrent resolution.*

The authorities described in subsection (a)(1) of this section may not continue to be exercised under this section if the national emergency is terminated by the Congress by concurrent resolution pursuant to section 202 of the National Emergencies Act (50 U.S.C. 1622) and if the Congress specifies in such concurrent resolution that such authorities may not continue to be exercised under this section.

(c) *Supplemental savings provisions; supersedure of inconsistent provisions.*

(1) The provisions of this section are supplemental to the savings provisions of paragraphs (1), (2), and (3) of section 101(a) (50 U.S.C. 1601(a)(1), (2), (3)) and of paragraphs (A), (B), and (C) of section 202(a) (50 U.S.C. 1622(a)(A), (B), and (C)) of the National Emergencies Act.

(2) The provisions of this section supersede the termination provisions of section 101(a) (50 U.S.C. 1601(a)) and of title II (50 U.S.C. 1621 et seq.) of the National Emergencies Act to the extent that the provisions of this section are inconsistent with these provisions.

(d) *Periodic reports to Congress.*

If the President uses the authority of this section to continue prohibitions on transactions involving foreign property interests, he shall report to the Congress every six months on the use of such authority.

EXECUTIVE ORDER 12472* (ASSIGNMENT OF NATIONAL SECURITY AND EMERGENCY PREPAREDNESS TELECOMMUNICATIONS FUNCTIONS)

By the authority vested in me as President by the Constitution and laws of the United States of America, including the Communications Act of 1934, as amended (47 U.S.C. 151), the National Security Act of 1947, as amended, the Defense Production Act of 1950, as amended (50 U.S.C. App. 2061), the Federal Civil Defense Act of 1950, as amended (50 U.S.C. App. 2251), the Disaster Relief Act of 1974 (42 U.S.C. 5121), Section 5 of Reorganization Plan No. 1 of 1977 (3 C.F.R. 197, 1978 Comp.), and Section 203 of Reorganization Plan No. 3 of 1978 (3 C.F.R. 389, 1978 Comp.), and in order to provide for the consolidation of assignment and responsibility for improved execution of national security and emergency preparedness telecommunications functions, it is hereby ordered as follows:

Section 1. The National Communications System.

(a) There is hereby established the National Communications System (NCS). The NCS shall consist of the telecommunications assets of the entities represented on the NCS Committee of Principals and an administrative structure consisting of the Executive Agent, the NCS Committee of Principals and the Manager. The NCS Committee of Principals shall consist of representatives from those Federal departments, agencies or entities, designated by the President, which lease or own telecommunications facilities or services of significance to national security or emergency preparedness, and, to the extent permitted by law, other Executive entities which bear policy, regulatory or enforcement responsibilities of importance to national security or emergency preparedness telecommunications capabilities.

(b) The mission of the NCS shall be to assist the President, the National Security Council, the Homeland Security Council, the Director of the Office of Science and Technology Policy and the Director of the Office of Management and Budget in:

1. the exercise of the telecommunications functions and responsibilities set forth in Section 2 of this Order; and
2. the coordination of the planning for and provision of national security and emergency preparedness communications for the Federal government under all circumstances, including crisis or emergency, attack, recovery and reconstitution.

(c) The NCS shall seek to ensure that a national telecommunications infrastructure is developed which:

1. Is responsive to the national security and emergency preparedness needs of the President and the Federal departments, agencies and other entities, including telecommunications in support of national security leadership and continuity of government;

---

* Exec. Order No. 12472, 3 C.F.R. 193 (1984), *reprinted as amended in* 42 U.S.C.A. § 5195 note (West 2003), *available at* http://www.ncs.gov/library/policy_docs/eo_12472.html.

2. Is capable of satisfying priority telecommunications requirements under all circumstances through use of commercial, government and privately owned telecommunications resources;

3. Incorporates the necessary combination of hardness, redundancy, mobility, connectivity, interoperability, restorability and security to obtain, to the maximum extent practicable, the survivability of national security and emergency preparedness telecommunications in all circumstances, including conditions of crisis or emergency; and

4. Is consistent, to the maximum extent practicable, with other national telecommunications policies.

(d) To assist in accomplishing its mission, the NCS shall:

1. serve as a focal point for joint industry-government national security and emergency preparedness telecommunications planning; and

2. establish a joint industry-government National Coordinating Center which is capable of assisting in the initiation, coordination, restoration and reconstitution of national security or emergency preparedness telecommunications services or facilities under all conditions of crisis or emergency.

(e) The Secretary of Homeland Security is designated as the Executive Agent for the NCS....

....

Ronald Reagan

EXECUTIVE ORDER 12656* (ASSIGNMENT OF EMERGENCY PREPAREDNESS RESPONSIBILITIES)

WHEREAS our national security is dependent upon our ability to assure continuity of government, at every level, in any national security emergency situation that might confront the Nation; and

WHEREAS effective national preparedness planning to meet such an emergency, including a massive nuclear attack, is essential to our national survival; and

WHEREAS effective national preparedness planning requires the identification of functions that would have to be performed during such an emergency, the assignment of responsibility for developing plans for performing these functions, and the assignment of responsibility for developing the capability to implement those plans; and

WHEREAS the Congress has directed the development of such national security emergency preparedness plans and has provided funds for the accomplishment thereof;

NOW, THEREFORE, by virtue of the authority vested in me as President by the Constitution and laws of the United States of America, and pursuant to Reorganization Plan No. 1 of 1958 (72 Stat. 1799), the National Security Act of 1947, as amended, the Defense Production Act of 1950, as amended, and the Federal Civil Defense Act, as amended, it is hereby ordered that the responsibilities of the Federal departments and agencies in national security emergencies shall be as follows:

Part 1—Preamble

Section 101. National Security Emergency Preparedness Policy.

(a) The policy of the United States is to have sufficient capabilities at all levels of government to meet essential defense and civilian needs during any national security emergency. A national security emergency is any occurrence, including natural disaster, military attack, technological emergency, or other emergency, that seriously degrades or seriously threatens the national security of the United States. Policy for national security emergency preparedness shall be established by the President. Pursuant to the President's direction, the National Security Council shall be responsible for developing and administering such policy. All national security emergency preparedness activities shall be consistent with the Constitution and

* Exec. Order No. 12,656, 3 C.F.R. 585 (1988), *reprinted as amended in* 42 U.S.C.A. § 5195 note (West 2003), *available at* http://www.archives.gov/federal-register/codification/executive-order/12656.html..As amended by E.O. 13286 of February 28, 2003 which also states, "Without prejudice to subsections (a) through (i) of this section, all responsibilities assigned to specific Federal officials pursuant to Executive Order 12656 that are substantially the same as any responsibility assigned to, or function transferred to, the Secretary of Homeland Security pursuant to the Homeland Security Act of 2002 (regardless of whether such responsibility or function is expressly required to be carried out through another official of the Department of Homeland Security or not pursuant to such Act), or intended or required to be carried out by an agency or an agency component transferred to the Department of Homeland Security pursuant to such Act, are hereby assigned to the Secretary of Homeland Security."

laws of the United States and with preservation of the constitutional government of the United States.

(b) Effective national security emergency preparedness planning requires: identification of functions that would have to be performed during such an emergency; development of plans for performing these functions; and development of the capability to execute those plans.

Sec. 102. Purpose.

(a) The purpose of this Order is to assign national security emergency preparedness responsibilities to Federal departments and agencies. These assignments are based, whenever possible, on extensions of the regular missions of the departments and agencies.

(b) This Order does not constitute authority to implement the plans prepared pursuant to this Order. Plans so developed may be executed only in the event that authority for such execution is authorized by law.

Sec. 103. Scope.

(a) This Order addresses national security emergency preparedness functions and activities. As used in this Order, preparedness functions and activities include, as appropriate, policies, plans, procedures, and readiness measures that enhance the ability of the United States Government to mobilize for, respond to, and recover from a national security emergency.

(b) This Order does not apply to those natural disasters, technological emergencies, or other emergencies, the alleviation of which is normally the responsibility of individuals, the private sector, volunteer organizations, State and local governments, and Federal departments and agencies unless such situations also constitute a national security emergency.

(c) This Order does not require the provision of information concerning, or evaluation of, military policies, plans, programs, or states of military readiness.

(d) This Order does not apply to national security emergency preparedness telecommunications functions and responsibilities that are otherwise assigned by Executive Order 12472.

Sec. 104. Management of National Security Emergency Preparedness.

(a) The National Security Council is the principal forum for consideration of national security emergency preparedness policy.

(b) The National Security Council shall arrange for Executive branch liaison with, and assistance to, the Congress and the Federal judiciary on national security-emergency preparedness matters.

(c) The Secretary of Homeland Security shall serve as an advisor to the National Security Council on issues of national security emergency preparedness, including mobilization preparedness, civil defense, continuity of government, technological disasters, and other issues, as appropriate. Pursuant to such procedures for the organization and management of the National Security Council process as the President may establish, the Secretary of Homeland Security also shall assist in the implementation of and management of the National Security Council process as the President may establish, the Secretary of Homeland Security also shall assist in the implementation of national security emergency preparedness policy by coordinating with the other Federal departments and agencies and with State and local governments, and by providing periodic reports to the National Security Council on implementation of national security emergency preparedness policy.

(d) National security emergency preparedness functions that are shared by more than one agency shall be coordinated by the head of the Federal department or agency having primary responsibility and shall be supported by the heads of other departments and agencies having related responsibilities.

(e) There shall be a national security emergency exercise program that shall be supported by the heads of all appropriate Federal departments and agencies.

(f) Plans and procedures will be designed and developed to provide maximum flexibility to the President for his implementation of emergency actions.

Sec. 105. Interagency Coordination.

(a) All appropriate Cabinet members and agency heads shall be consulted regarding national security emergency preparedness programs and policy issues. Each department and agency shall support interagency coordination to improve preparedness and response to a national security emergency and shall develop and maintain decentralized capabilities wherever feasible and appropriate.

....

Part 4—Department of Commerce

Sec. 401. Lead Responsibilities. In addition to the applicable responsibilities covered in Parts 1 and 2, the Secretary of Commerce shall:

(1) Develop control systems for priorities, allocation, production, and distribution of materials and other resources that will be available to support both national defense and essential civilian programs in a national security emergency;

(2) In cooperation with the Secretary of Defense and other departments and agencies, identify those industrial products and facilities that are essential to mobilization readiness, national defense, or post-attack survival and recovery;

(3) In cooperation with the Secretary of Defense and other Federal departments and agencies, analyze potential effects of national security emergencies on actual production capability, taking into account the entire production complex, including shortages of resources, and develop preparedness measures to strengthen capabilities for production increases in national security emergencies;

(4) In cooperation with the Secretary of Defense, perform industry analyses to assess capabilities of the commercial industrial base to support the national defense, and develop policy alternatives to improve the international competitiveness of specific domestic industries and their abilities to meet defense program needs;

(5) In cooperation with the Secretary of the Treasury, develop plans for providing emergency assistance to the private sector through direct or participation loans for the financing of production facilities and equipment;

(6) In cooperation with the Secretaries of State, Defense, Transportation, and the Treasury, prepare plans to regulate and control exports and imports in national security emergencies;

(7) Provide for the collection and reporting of census information on human and economic resources, and maintain a capability to conduct emergency surveys to provide information on the status of these resources as required for national security purposes;

(8) Develop overall plans and programs to ensure that the fishing industry continues to produce and process essential protein in national security emergencies;

(9) Develop plans to provide meteorological, hydrologic, marine weather, geodetic, hydrographic, climatic, seismic, and oceanographic data and services to Federal, State, and local agencies, as appropriate;

(10) In coordination with the Secretary of State and the Secretary of Homeland Security, represent the United States in industry-related international (NATO and allied) civil emergency preparedness planning and related activities.

Sec. 402. Support Responsibilities. The Secretary of Commerce shall:

(1) Assist the Secretary of Defense in formulating and carrying out plans for stockpiling strategic and critical materials;

(2) Support the Secretary of Agriculture in planning for the national security management, production, and processing of forest and fishery products;

(3) Assist, in consultation with the Secretaries of State and Defense, the Secretary of the Treasury in the formulation and execution of economic measures affecting other nations.

Part 5—Department of Defense

Sec. 501. Lead Responsibilities. In addition to the applicable responsibilities covered in Parts 1 and 2, the Secretary of Defense shall:

(1) Ensure military preparedness and readiness to respond to national security emergencies;

(2) In coordination with the Secretary of Commerce, develop, with industry, government, and the private sector, reliable capabilities for the rapid increase of defense production to include industrial resources required for that production;

(3) Develop and maintain, in cooperation with the heads of other departments and agencies, national security emergency plans, programs, and mechanisms to ensure effective mutual support between and among the military, civil government, and the private sector;

(4) Develop and maintain damage assessment capabilities and assist the Secretary of Homeland Security and the heads of other departments and agencies in developing and maintaining capabilities to assess attack damage and to estimate the effects of potential attack on the Nation;

(5) Arrange, through agreements with the heads of other Federal departments and agencies, for the transfer of certain Federal resources to the jurisdiction and/or operational control of the Department of Defense in national security emergencies;

(6) Acting through the Secretary of the Army, develop, with the concurrence of the heads of all affected departments and agencies, overall plans for the management, control, and allocation of all usable waters from all sources within the jurisdiction of the United States. This includes:

(a) Coordination of national security emergency water resource planning at the national, regional, State, and local levels;

(b) Development of plans to assure emergency provision of water from public works projects under the jurisdiction of the Secretary of the Army to public water supply utilities and critical defense production facilities during national security emergencies;

(c) Development of plans to assure emergency operation of waterways and harbors; and

(d) Development of plans to assure the provision of potable water;

(7) In consultation with the Secretaries of State and Energy, the Secretary of Homeland Security, and others, as required, develop plans and capabilities for identifying, analyzing, mitigating, and responding to hazards related to nuclear weapons, materials, and devices; and maintain liaison, as appropriate, with the Secretary of Energy and the Members of the Nuclear Regulatory Commission to ensure the continuity of nuclear weapons production and the appropriate allocation of scarce resources, including the recapture of special nuclear materials from Nuclear Regulatory Commission licensees when appropriate;

(8) Coordinate with the Administrator of the National Aeronautics and Space Adminstration and the Secretary of Energy, as appropriate, to prepare for the use, maintenance, and development of technologically advanced aerospace and aeronautical-related systems, equipment, and methodologies applicable to national security emergencies;

(9) Develop, in coordination with the Secretaries of Labor and Homeland Security, the Directors of the Selective Service System, the Office of Personnel Management, and the Federal Emergency Management Agency, plans and systems to ensure that the Nation's human resources are available to meet essential military and civilian needs in national security emergencies;

(10) Develop national security emergency operational procedures, and coordinate with the Secretary of Housing and Urban Development with respect to residential property, for the control, acquisition, leasing, assignment and priority of occupancy of real property within the jurisdiction of the Department of Defense;

(11) Review the priorities and allocations systems developed by other departments and agencies to ensure that they meet Department of Defense needs in a national security emergency; and develop and maintain the Department of Defense programs necessary for effective utilization of all priorities and allocations systems;

(12) Develop, in coordination with the Attorney General of the United States, specific procedures by which military assistance to civilian law enforcement authorities may be requested, considered, and provided;

(13) In cooperation with the Secretary of Commerce and other departments and agencies, identify those industrial products and facilities that are essential to mobilization readiness, national defense, or post-attack survival and recovery;

(14) In cooperation with the Secretary of Commerce and other Federal departments and agencies, analyze potential effects of national security emergencies on actual production capability, taking into account the entire production complex, including shortages of resources, and develop preparedness measures to strengthen capabilities for production increases in national security emergencies;

(15) With the assistance of the heads of other Federal departments and agencies, provide management direction for the stockpiling of strategic and critical materials, conduct storage, maintenance, and quality assurance operations for the stockpile of strategic and critical materials, and formulate plans, programs, and reports relating to the stockpiling of strategic and critical materials.

Sec. 502. Support Responsibilities. The Secretary of Defense shall:

(1) Advise and assist the heads of other Federal departments and agencies in the development of plans and programs to support national mobilization. This includes providing, as appropriate:

(a) Military requirements, prioritized and time-phased to the extent possible, for selected end-items and supporting services, materials, and components;

(b) Recommendations for use of financial incentives and other methods to improve defense production as provided by law; and

(c) Recommendations for export and import policies;

(2) Advise and assist the Secretary of State and the heads of other Federal departments and agencies, as appropriate, in planning for the protection, evacuation, and repatriation of United States citizens in threatened areas overseas;

(3) Support the Secretary of Housing and Urban Development and the heads of other agencies, as appropriate, in the development of plans to restore community facilities;

(4) Support the Secretary of Energy in international liaison activities pertaining to nuclear materials facilities;

(5) In consultation with the Secretaries of State and Commerce, assist the Secretary of the Treasury in the formulation and execution of economic measures that affect other nations;

(6) Support the Secretary of State and the heads of other Federal departments and agencies as appropriate in the formulation and implementation of foreign policy, and the negotiation of contingency and post-emergency plans, intergovernmental agreements, and arrangements with allies and friendly nations, which affect national security;

(7) Coordinate with the Secretary of Homeland Security the development of plans for mutual civil-military support during national security emergencies;

(8) Develop plans to support the Secretary of Labor in providing education and training to overcome shortages of critical skills.

....

Part 13—Department of State

Sec. 1301. Lead Responsibilities. In addition to the applicable responsibilities covered in Parts 1 and 2, the Secretary of State shall:

(1) Provide overall foreign policy coordination in the formulation and execution of continuity of government and other national security emergency preparedness activities that affect foreign relations;

(2) Prepare to carry out Department of State responsibilities in the conduct of the foreign relations of the United States during national security emergencies, under the direction of the President and in consultation with the heads of other appropriate Federal departments and agencies, including, but not limited to:

(a) Formulation and implementation of foreign policy and negotiation regarding contingency and post-emergency plans, intergovernmental agreements, and arrangements with United States' allies;

(b) Formulation, negotiation, and execution of policy affecting the relationships of the United States with neutral states;

(c) Formulation and execution of political strategy toward hostile or enemy states;

(d) Conduct of mutual assistance activities;

(e) Provision of foreign assistance, including continuous supervision and general direction of authorized economic and military assistance programs;

(f) Protection or evacuation of United States citizens and nationals abroad and safeguarding their property abroad, in consultation with the Secretaries of Defense and Health and Human Services;

(g) Protection of international organizations and foreign diplomatic, consular, and other official personnel and property, or other assets, in the United States, in coordination with the Attorney General and the Secretary of the Treasury;

(h) Formulation of policies and provisions for assistance to displaced persons and refugees abroad;

(i) Maintenance of diplomatic and consular representation abroad; and

(j) Reporting of and advising on conditions overseas that bear upon national security emergencies.

Sec. 1302. Support Responsibilities. The Secretary of State shall:

(1) Assist appropriate agencies in developing planning assumptions concerning accessibility of foreign sources of supply;

(2) Support the Secretary of the Treasury, in consultation, as appropriate, with the Secretaries of Commerce and Defense, in the formulation and execution of economic measures with respect to other nations;

(3) Support the Secretary of Energy in international liaison activities pertaining to nuclear materials facilities;

(4) Support the Secretary of Homeland Security in the coordination and integration of United States policy regarding the formulation and implementation of civil emergency resources and preparedness planning;

(5) Assist the Attorney General of the United States in the formulation of national security emergency plans for the control of persons entering or leaving the United States.

....

Ronald Reagan

STAFFORD DISASTER RELIEF AND EMERGENCY ASSISTANCE ACT*

§5121. CONGRESSIONAL FINDINGS AND DECLARATIONS {Sec. 101}

a. The Congress hereby finds and declares that—

1. because disasters often cause loss of life, human suffering, loss of income, and property loss and damage; and

2. because disasters often disrupt the normal functioning of governments and communities, and adversely affect individuals and families with great severity;

special measures, designed to assist the efforts of the affected States in expediting the rendering of aid, assistance, and emergency services, and the reconstruction and rehabilitation of devastated areas, are necessary.

b. It is the intent of the Congress, by this Act, to provide an orderly and continuing means of assistance by the Federal Government to State and local governments in carrying out their responsibilities to alleviate the suffering and damage which result from such disasters by—

1. revising and broadening the scope of existing disaster relief programs;

2. encouraging the development of comprehensive disaster preparedness and assistance plans, programs, capabilities, and organizations by the States and by local governments;

3. achieving greater coordination and responsiveness of disaster preparedness and relief programs;

4. encouraging individuals, States, and local governments to protect themselves by obtaining insurance coverage to supplement or replace governmental assistance;

5. encouraging hazard mitigation measures to reduce losses from disasters, including development of land use and construction regulations; and

6. providing Federal assistance programs for both public and private losses sustained in disasters.

. . . .

TITLE II—DISASTER PREPAREDNESS AND MITIGATION ASSISTANCE

§5131. FEDERAL AND STATE DISASTER PREPAREDNESS PROGRAMS {Sec. 201}

a. Utilization of services of other agencies.

The President is authorized to establish a program of disaster preparedness that utilizes services of all appropriate agencies and includes—

1. preparation of disaster preparedness plans for mitigation, warning, emergency operations, rehabilitation, and recovery;

2. training and exercises;

---

* Robert T. Stafford Disaster Relief and Emergency Assistance Act §§101, 201, 203 note, 302, 401–403, 413, 417–418, 42 U.S.C. §§5121, 5131, 5133 note, 5143, 5170–5170b, 5180, 5184–5185 (2000 & Supp. II 2002), *available at* http://www.fema.gov/library/stafact.shtm.

3. postdisaster critiques and evaluations;
4. annual review of programs;
5. coordination of Federal, State, and local preparedness programs;
6. application of science and technology;
7. research.

....

SEC. 101. FINDINGS AND PURPOSE.

a. FINDINGS—Congress finds that—

1. natural disasters, including earthquakes, tsunamis, tornadoes, hurricanes, flooding, and wildfires, pose great danger to human life and to property throughout the United States;

2. greater emphasis needs to be placed on—

A. identifying and assessing the risks to States and local governments (including Indian tribes) from natural disasters;

B. implementing adequate measures to reduce losses from natural disasters; and

C. ensuring that the critical services and facilities of communities will continue to function after a natural disaster;

3. expenditures for postdisaster assistance are increasing without commensurate reductions in the likelihood of future losses from natural disasters;

4. in the expenditure of Federal funds under the Robert T. Stafford Disaster Relief and Emergency Assistance Act (42 U.S.C. 5121 et seq.), high priority should be given to mitigation of hazards at the local level; and

5. with a unified effort of economic incentives, awareness and education, technical assistance, and demonstrated Federal support, States and local governments (including Indian tribes) will be able to—

A. form effective community-based partnerships for hazard mitigation purposes;

B. implement effective hazard mitigation measures that reduce the potential damage from natural disasters;

C. ensure continued functionality of critical services;

D. leverage additional non-Federal resources in meeting natural disaster resistance goals; and

E. make commitments to long-term hazard mitigation efforts to be applied to new and existing structures.

b. PURPOSE—The purpose of this title is to establish a national disaster hazard mitigation program—

1. to reduce the loss of life and property, human suffering, economic disruption, and disaster assistance costs resulting from natural disasters; and

2. to provide a source of predisaster hazard mitigation funding that will assist States and local governments (including Indian tribes) in implementing effective

hazard mitigation measures that are designed to ensure the continued functionality of critical services and facilities after a natural disaster.

....

§ 5143. COORDINATING OFFICERS {Sec. 302}

a. Appointment of Federal coordinating officer

Immediately upon his declaration of a major disaster or emergency, the President shall appoint a Federal coordinating officer to operate in the affected area.

b. Functions of Federal coordinating officer

In order to effectuate the purposes of this Act, the Federal coordinating officer, within the affected area, shall—

1. make an initial appraisal of the types of relief most urgently needed;
2. establish such field offices as he deems necessary and as are authorized by the President;
3. coordinate the administration of relief, including activities of the State and local governments, the American National Red Cross, the Salvation Army, the Mennonite Disaster Service, and other relief or disaster assistance organizations, which agree to operate under his advice or direction, except that nothing contained in this Act shall limit or in any way affect the responsibilities of the American National Red Cross under the Act of January 5, 1905, as amended (33 Stat. 599) [36 U.S.C. §§ 1 et seq.]; and;
4. take such other action, consistent with authority delegated to him by the President, and consistent with the provisions of this Act, as he may deem necessary to assist local citizens and public officials in promptly obtaining assistance to which they are entitled.;
5. State coordinating officer When the President determines assistance under this Act is necessary, he shall request that the Governor of the affected State designate a State coordinating officer for the purpose of coordinating State and local disaster assistance efforts with those of the Federal Government.

....

SUBCHAPTER IV—MAJOR DISASTER ASSISTANCE PROGRAMS

§ 5170. PROCEDURE FOR DECLARATION {Sec. 401}

All requests for a declaration by the President that a major disaster exists shall be made by the Governor of the affected State. Such a request shall be based on a finding that the disaster is of such severity and magnitude that effective response is beyond the capabilities of the State and the affected local governments and that Federal assistance is necessary. As part of such request, and as a prerequisite to major disaster assistance under this Act, the Governor shall take appropriate response action under State law and direct execution of the State's emergency plan. The Governor shall furnish information on the nature and amount of State and local resources which have been or will be committed to alleviating the results of the disaster, and shall certify that, for the current disaster, State and local government obligations and expenditures (of which State commitments must be a significant proportion) will comply with all applicable cost-sharing requirements of this Act. Based on the request of a Governor under this section, the President may declare under this Act that a major disaster or emergency exists.

§ 5170a. GENERAL FEDERAL ASSISTANCE {Sec. 402}

In any major disaster, the President may—

1. direct any Federal agency, with or without reimbursement, to utilize its authorities and the resources granted to it under Federal law (including personnel, equipment, supplies, facilities, and managerial, technical, and advisory services) in support of State and local assistance efforts;

2. coordinate all disaster relief assistance (including voluntary assistance) provided by Federal agencies, private organizations, and State and local governments;

3. provide technical and advisory assistance to affected State and local governments for—

   A. the performance of essential community services;

   B. issuance of warnings of risks and hazards;

   C. public health and safety information, including dissemination of such information;

   D. provision of health and safety measures; and

   E. management, control, and reduction of immediate threats to public health and safety; and

4. assist State and local governments in the distribution of medicine, food, and other consumable supplies, and emergency assistance.

§ 5170b. ESSENTIAL ASSISTANCE {Sec. 403}

a. In general

Federal agencies may on the direction of the President, provide assistance essential to meeting immediate threats to life and property resulting from a major disaster, as follows:

1. Federal resources, generally

Utilizing, lending, or donating to State and local governments Federal equipment, supplies, facilities, personnel, and other resources, other than the extension of credit, for use or distribution by such governments in accordance with the purposes of this Act.

2. Medicine, food, and other consumables

Distributing or rendering through State and local governments, the American National Red Cross, the Salvation Army, the Mennonite Disaster Service, and other relief and disaster assistance organizations medicine, food, and other consumable supplies, and other services and assistance to disaster victims.

3. Work and services to save lives and protect property

Performing on public or private lands or waters any work or services essential to saving lives and protecting and preserving property or public health and safety, including—

   A. debris removal;

   B. search and rescue, emergency medical care, emergency mass care, emergency shelter, and provision of food, water, medicine, and other essential needs, including movement of supplies or persons;

   C. clearance of roads and construction of temporary bridges necessary to the performance of emergency tasks and essential community services;

D. provision of temporary facilities for schools and other essential community services;

E. demolition of unsafe structures which endanger the public;

F. warning of further risks and hazards;

G. dissemination of public information and assistance regarding health and safety measures;

H. provision of technical advice to State and local governments on disaster management and control; and

I. reduction of immediate threats to life, property, and public health and safety.

4. Contributions

Making contributions to State or local governments or owners or operators of private nonprofit facilities for the purpose of carrying out the provisions of this subsection.

b. Federal share

The Federal share of assistance under this section shall be not less than 75 percent of the eligible cost of such assistance.

c. Utilization of DOD resources

1. General rule

During the immediate aftermath of an incident which may ultimately qualify for assistance under this title or title V of this Act [42 U.S.C. §§5170 et seq. or 5191 et seq.], the Governor of the State in which such incident occurred may request the President to direct the Secretary of Defense to utilize the resources of the Department of Defense for the purpose of performing on public and private lands any emergency work which is made necessary by such incident and which is essential for the preservation of life and property. If the President determines that such work is essential for the preservation of life and property, the President shall grant such request to the extent the President determines practicable. Such emergency work may only be carried out for a period not to exceed 10 days.

....

§5180. FOOD COMMODITIES {Sec. 413}

a. Emergency mass feeding

The President is authorized and directed to assure that adequate stocks of food will be ready and conveniently available for emergency mass feeding or distribution in any area of the United States which suffers a major disaster or emergency.

b. Funds for purchase of food commodities

The Secretary of Agriculture shall utilize funds appropriated under section 32 of the Act of August 24, 1935 (7 U.S.C. 612c), to purchase food commodities necessary to provide adequate supplies for use in any area of the United States in the event of a major disaster or emergency in such area.

....

§5184. COMMUNITY DISASTER LOANS {Sec. 417}

a. In General.—The President is authorized to make loans to any local government which may suffer a substantial loss of tax and other revenues as a result of a major disaster, and has demonstrated a need for financial assistance in order to perform its governmental functions.

a. Amount.—The amount of any such loan shall be based on need, shall not exceed 25 per centum of the annual operating budget of that local government for the fiscal year in which the major disaster occur, and shall not exceed $5,000,000.

....

§ 5185. EMERGENCY COMMUNICATIONS {Sec. 418}

The President is authorized during, or in anticipation of an emergency or major disaster to establish temporary communications systems and to make such communications available to State and local government officials and other persons as he deems appropriate.

....

H. Trade and Technology Transfer

TRADING WITH THE ENEMY ACT OF 1917[1] (WITH AMENDMENTS)

....

Be it enacted by the Senate and House of Representatives of the United States of America in Congress assembled,

That this Act shall be known as the "Trading with the Enemy Act."

Sec. 2. That the word "enemy," as used herein, shall be deemed to mean, for the purposes of such trading and of this Act—

(a) Any individual, partnership, or other body of individuals, of any nationality, resident within the territory (including that occupied by the military and naval forces) of any nation with which the United States is at war, or resident outside the United States and doing business within such territory, and any corporation incorporated within such territory of any nation with which the United States is at war or incorporated within any country other than the United States and doing business within such territory.

(b) The government of any nation with which the United States is at war, or any political or municipal subdivision thereof, or any officer, official, agent, or agency thereof.

(c) Such other individuals, or body or class of individuals, as may be natives, citizens, or subjects of any nation with which the United States is at war, other than citizens of the United States, wherever resident or wherever doing business, as the President, if he shall find the safety of the United States or the successful prosecution of the war shall so require, may, by proclamation, include within the term "enemy."

The words "ally of enemy," as used herein, shall be deemed to mean—

(a) Any individual, partnership, or other body of individuals, of any nationality, resident within the territory (including that occupied by the military and naval forces) of any nation which is an ally of a nation with which the United States is at war, or resident outside the United States and doing business within such territory of such ally nation, or incorporated within any country other than the United States and doing business within such territory.

(b) The government of any nation which is an ally of a nation with which the United States is at war, or any political or municipal subdivision of such ally nation, or any officer, official, agent, or agency thereof.

(c) Such other individuals, or body or class of individuals, as may be natives, citizens, or subjects of any nation which is an ally of a nation with which the United States is at war, other than citizens of the United States, wherever resident or wherever doing business, as the President, if he shall find the safety of the United States or the successful prosecution of the war shall so require, may, by proclamation, include within the term "ally of enemy."

The word "person," as used herein, shall be deemed to mean an individual, partnership, association, company, or other unincorporated body of individuals, or corporation or body politic.

---

1. Trading with the Enemy Act, ch. 106, 40 Stat. 411, *available at* http://www4.law.cornell.edu/uscode/html/uscode50a/usc_sup_05_50_10_sq1.html.

The words "United States," as used herein, shall be deemed to mean all land and water, continental or insular, in any way within the jurisdiction of the United States or occupied by the military or naval forces thereof.

The words "the beginning of the war," as used herein, shall be deemed to mean midnight ending the day on which Congress has declared or shall declare war or the existence of a state of war.

The words "end of the war," as used herein, shall be deemed to mean the date of proclamation of exchange of ratifications of the treaty of peace, unless the President shall, by proclamation, declare a prior date, in which case the date so proclaimed shall be deemed to be the "end of the war" within the meaning of this Act.

The words "bank or banks," as used herein, shall be deemed to mean and include national banks, State banks, trust companies, or other banks or banking associations doing business under the laws of the United States, or of any State of the United States.

The words "to trade," as used herein, shall be deemed to mean—

(a) Pay, satisfy, compromise, or give security for the payment or satisfaction of any debt or obligation.

(b) Draw, accept, pay, present for acceptance or payment, or indorse any negotiable instrument or chose in action.

(c) Enter into, carry on, complete, or perform any contract, agreement, or obligation.

(d) Buy or sell, loan or extend credit, trade in, deal with, exchange, transmit, transfer, assign, or otherwise dispose of, or receive any form of property.

(e) To have any form of business or commercial communication or intercourse with.

Sec. 3. That it shall be unlawful—

(a) For any person in the United States, except with the license of the President, granted to such person, or to the enemy, or ally of enemy, as provided in this Act, to trade, or attempt to trade, either directly or indirectly, with, to, or from, or for, or on account of, or on behalf of, or for the benefit of, any other person, with knowledge or reasonable cause to believe that such other person is an enemy or ally of enemy, or is conducting or taking part in such trade, directly or indirectly, for, or on account of, or on behalf of, or for the benefit of, an enemy or ally of enemy.

(b) For any person, except with the license of the President, to transport or attempt to transport into or from the United States, or for any owner, master, or other person in charge of a vessel of American registry to transport or attempt to transport from any place to any other place, any subject or citizen of an enemy or ally of enemy nation, with knowledge or reasonable cause to believe that the person transported or attempted to be transported is such subject or citizen.

(c) For any person (other than a person in the service of the United States Government or of the Government of any nation, except that of an enemy or ally of enemy nation, and other than such persons or classes of persons as may be exempted hereunder by the President or by such person as he may direct), to send, or take out of, or bring into, or attempt to send, or take out of, or bring into the United States, any letter or other writing or tangible form of communication, except in the regular course of the mail; and it shall be unlawful for any person to send, take, or transmit, or attempt to send, take, or transmit out of the United States, any letter or other writing, book, map, plan, or other paper, picture, or any telegram, cablegram, or wireless message, or other form of communication intended for or to be delivered, directly or indirectly, to an enemy or ally of enemy: *Provided, however,* That any person may send, take, or transmit out of the United States anything herein forbidden if he shall first submit the same to the President, or to such officer as the President may direct, and shall obtain the license or consent of the President, under such rules and regulations, and with such exemptions, as shall be prescribed by the President.

(d) Whenever, during the present war, the President shall deem that the public safety demands it, he may cause to be censored under such rules and regulations as he may from time to time establish, communications by mail, cable, radio, or other means of transmission passing between the United States and any foreign country he may from time to time specify, or which may be carried by any vessel or other means of transportation touching at any port, place, or territory of the United States and bound to or from any foreign country. Any person who willfully evades or attempts to evade the submission of any such communication to such censorship or willfully uses or attempts to use any code or other device for the purpose of concealing from such censorship the intended meaning of such communication shall be punished as provided in section sixteen of this Act.

....

Sec. 17. That the district courts of the United States are hereby given jurisdiction to make and enter all such rules as to notice and otherwise, and all such orders and decrees, and to issue such process as may be necessary and proper in the premises to enforce the provisions of this Act, with a right of appeal from the final order or decree of such court as provided in sections one hundred and twenty-eight and two hundred and thirty-eight of the Act of March third, nineteen hundred and eleven, entitled "An Act to codify, revise, and amend the laws relating to the judiciary."

....

AMENDMENTS TO THE TRADING WITH THE ENEMY ACT[2]

REMOVAL OF NATIONAL EMERGENCY POWERS UNDER THE TRADING WITH THE ENEMY ACT

Sec. 101.

....

(b)[3] Notwithstanding the amendment made by subsection (a), the authorities conferred upon the President by section 5(b) of the Trading With the Enemy Act, which were being exercised with respect to a country on July 1, 1977, as a result of a national emergency declared by the President before such date, may continue to be exercised with respect to such country, except that, unless extended, the exercise of such authorities shall terminate (subject to the savings provisions of the second sentence of section 101 (a) of the National Emergencies Act) at the end of the two-year period beginning on the date of enactment of the National Emergencies Act. The President may extend the exercise of such authorities for one-year periods upon a determination for each such extension that the exercise of such authorities with respect to such country for another year is in the national interest of the United States.[4]

---

2. International Emergency Economic Powers Act, Pub. L. No. 95-223, § 101, 91 Stat. 1625 (1977).

3. 50 U.S.C. app. § 5 note (2000).

4. Since 1977, the President has utilized this provision each year to extend certain authorities being exercised prior to July 1, 1977, under section 5(b) of the Trading with the Enemy Act. The most recent action, a memorandum of Sept. 13, 2002, extended until Sept. 14, 2003 the exercise of

(c) The termination and extension provisions of subsection (b) of this section supersede the provisions of section 101 (a) and of title II of the National Emergencies Act to the extent that the provisions of subsection (b) of this section are inconsistent with those provisions.

(d) Paragraph (1) of section 502 (a) of the National Emergencies Act is repealed.

those authorities with respect to countries affected by the Foreign Assets Control Regulations, the Transaction Control Regulations, and the Cuban Assets Control Regulations. For the complete text of this memorandum see Presidential Determination No. 2002-31, Continuation of the Exercise of Certain Authorities Under the Trading with the Enemies Act, 67 Fed. Reg. 58,681, 3 C.F.R. 308 (2002), *reprinted in* 50 U.S.C.A. app. § 5 note (West Supp. 2005).

EXPORT ADMINISTRATION ACT OF 1979

Background Note

The Export Administration Act of 1979 expired on August 20, 1994, however the Export Administration Regulations under the act were kept in force by President Clinton through Executive Order 12924 (August 19, 1994) and were renewed annually until the act was reauthorized by Pub. L. 106-508 (November 13, 2000). When that authorization expired in August 2001, President Bush acted to keep the regulations in force under the International Emergency Economic Powers Act by Executive Order 13222, which was most recently extended for one year by presidential notice dated August 2, 2005. See: http://www.whitehouse.gov/news/releases/2005/08/20050802-10.html.—Eds.

Sec. 2401.[1] Congressional findings.

The Congress makes the following findings:

(1) The ability of United States citizens to engage in international commerce is a fundamental concern of United States policy.

(2) Exports contribute significantly to the economic well-being of the United States and the stability of the world economy by increasing employment and production in the United States, and by earning foreign exchange, thereby contributing favorably to the trade balance. The restriction of exports from the United States can have serious adverse effects on the balance of payments and on domestic employment, particularly when restrictions applied by the United States are more extensive than those imposed by other countries.

(3) It is important for the national interest of the United States that both the private sector and the Federal Government place a high priority on exports, consistent with the economic, security, and foreign policy objectives of the United States.

(4) The availability of certain materials at home and abroad varies so that the quantity and composition of United States exports and their distribution among importing countries may affect the welfare of the domestic economy and may have an important bearing upon fulfillment of the foreign policy of the United States.

(5) Exports of goods or technology without regard to whether they make a significant contribution to the military potential of individual countries or combinations of countries may adversely affect the national security of the United States.

(6) Uncertainty of export control policy can inhibit the efforts of United States business and work to the detriment of the overall attempt to improve the trade balance of the United States.

(7) Unreasonable restrictions on access to world supplies can cause worldwide political and economic instability, interfere with free international trade, and retard the growth and development of nations.

(8) It is important that the administration of export controls imposed for national security purposes give special emphasis to the need to control exports of technology

---

1. 50 U.S.C.S. app. § 2401 (LexisNexis 1996 & Supp. 2005) (original footnotes included as endnotes).

(and goods which contribute significantly to the transfer of such technology) which could make a significant contribution to the military potential of any country or combination of countries which would be detrimental to the national security of the United States.

(9) Minimization of restrictions on exports of agricultural commodities and products is of critical importance to the maintenance of a sound agricultural sector, to a positive contribution to the balance of payments, to reducing the level of Federal expenditures for agricultural support programs, and to United States cooperation in efforts to eliminate malnutrition and world hunger.

(10) It is important that the administration of export controls imposed for foreign policy purposes give special emphasis to the need to control exports of goods and substances hazardous to the public health and the environment which are banned or severely restricted for use in the United States, and which, if exported, could affect the international reputation of the United States as a responsible trading partner.

(11) Availability to controlled countries of goods and technology from foreign sources is a fundamental concern of the United States and should be eliminated through negotiations and other appropriate means whenever possible.[i]

(12) Excessive dependence of the United States, its allies, or countries sharing common strategic objectives with the United States, on energy and other critical resources from potential adversaries can be harmful to the mutual and individual security of all those countries.

(13) [Redesignated].

Sec. 2402.[2] Congressional declaration of policy.

The Congress makes the following declarations:

(1) It is the policy of the United States to minimize uncertainties in export control policy and to encourage trade with all countries with which the United States has diplomatic or trading relations, except those countries with which such trade has been determined by the President to be against the national interest.

(2) It is the policy of the United States to use export controls only after full consideration of the impact on the economy of the United States and only to the extent necessary—

(A) to restrict the export of goods and technology which would make a significant contribution to the military potential of any other country or combination of countries which would prove detrimental to the national security of the United States;

(B) to restrict the export of goods and technology where necessary to further significantly the foreign policy of the United States or to fulfill its declared international obligations; and

(C) to restrict the export of goods where necessary to protect the domestic economy from the excessive drain of scarce materials and to reduce the serious inflationary impact of foreign demand.

(3) It is the policy of the United States—

(A) to apply any necessary controls to the maximum extent possible in cooperation with all nations, and

2. Id. § 2402.

(B) to encourage observance of a uniform export control by all nations with which the United States has defense treaty commitments or common strategic directives.

(4) It is the policy of the United States to use its economic resources and trade potential to further the sound growth and stability of its economy as well as to further its national security and foreign policy objectives.

(5) It is the policy of the United States—

(A) to oppose restrictive trade practices or boycotts fostered or imposed by foreign countries against other countries friendly to the United States or against any United States person;

(B) to encourage and, in specified cases, require United States persons engaged in the export of goods or technology or other information to refuse to take actions, including furnishing information or entering into or implementing agreements, which have the effect of furthering or supporting the restrictive trade practices or boycotts fostered or imposed by any foreign country against a country friendly to the United States or against any United States person; and

(C) to foster international cooperation and the development of international rules and institutions to assure reasonable access to world supplies.

(6) It is the policy of the United States that the desirability of subjecting, or continuing to subject, particular goods or technology or other information to United States export controls should be subjected to review by and consultation with representatives of appropriate United States Government agencies and private industry.

(7) It is the policy of the United States to use export controls, including license fees, to secure the removal by foreign countries of restrictions on access to supplies where such restrictions have or may have a serious domestic inflationary impact, have caused or may cause a serious domestic shortage, or have been imposed for purposes of influencing the foreign policy of the United States. In effecting this policy, the President shall make reasonable and prompt efforts to secure the removal or reduction of such restrictions, policies, or actions through international cooperation and agreement before imposing export controls. No action taken in fulfillment of the policy set forth in this paragraph shall apply to the export of medicine or medical supplies.

(8) It is the policy of the United States to use export controls to encourage other countries to take immediate steps to prevent the use of their territories or resources to aid, encourage, or give sanctuary to those persons involved in directing, supporting, or participating in acts of international terrorism. To achieve this objective, the President shall make reasonable and prompt efforts to secure the removal or reduction of such assistance to international terrorists through international cooperation and agreement before imposing export controls.

(9) It is the policy of the United States to cooperate with other countries with which the United States has defense treaty commitments or common strategic objectives in restricting the export of goods and technology which would make a significant contribution to the military potential of any country or combination of countries which would prove detrimental to the security of the United States and of those countries with which the United States has defense treaty commitments or common strategic objectives, and to encourage other friendly countries to cooperate in restricting the sale of goods and technology that can harm the security of the United States.

(10) It is the policy of the United States that export trade by United States citizens be given a high priority and not be controlled except when such controls—

(A) are necessary to further fundamental national security, foreign policy, or short supply objectives,

(B) will clearly further such objectives, and

(C) are administered consistent with basic standards of due process.

(11) It is the policy of the United States to minimize restrictions on the export of agricultural commodities and products.

(12) It is the policy of the United States to sustain vigorous scientific enterprise. To do so involves sustaining the ability of scientists and other scholars freely to communicate research findings, in accordance with applicable provisions of law, by means of publication, teaching, conferences, and other forms of scholarly exchange.

(13) It is the policy of the United States to control the export of goods and substances banned or severely restricted for use in the United States in order to foster public health and safety and to prevent injury to the foreign policy of the United States as well as to the credibility of the United States as a responsible trading partner.

(14) It is the policy of the United States to cooperate with countries which are allies of the United States and countries which share common strategic objectives with the United States in minimizing dependence on imports of energy and other critical resources from potential adversaries and in developing alternative supplies of such resources in order to minimize strategic threats posed by excessive hard currency earnings derived from such resource exports by countries with policies adverse to the security interests of the United States.

(15) [Repealed].[ii]

Sec. 2403.[3] General provisions.

(a) TYPES OF LICENSES. Under such conditions as may be imposed by the Secretary which are consistent with the provisions of this Act, the Secretary may require any of the following types of export licenses:

(1) A validated license, authorizing a specific export, issued pursuant to an application by the exporter.

(2) Validated licenses authorizing multiple exports, issued pursuant to an application by the exporter, in lieu of an individual validated license for each such export, including, but not limited to, the following:

(A) A distribution license, authorizing exports of goods to approved distributors or users of the goods in countries other than controlled countries, except that the Secretary may establish a type of distribution license appropriate for consignees in the People's Republic of China....

(B) A comprehensive operations license, authorizing exports and reexports of technology and related goods, including items from the list of military critical technologies developed pursuant to section 5(d) of this Act which are included on the control list in accordance with that section, from a domestic concern to and among its foreign subsidiaries, affiliates, joint venturers, and licensees that have long-term, contractually defined relations with the exporter,

3. Id. § 2403.

are located in countries other than controlled countries except the People's Republic of China, and are approved by the Secretary. The Secretary shall grant the license to manufacturing, laboratory, or related operations on the basis of approval of the exporter's systems of control, including internal proprietary controls, applicable to the technology and related goods to be exported rather than approval of individual export transactions....

(C) A project license, authorizing exports of goods or technology for a specified activity.

(D) A service supply license, authorizing exports of spare or replacement parts for goods previously exported.

(3) A general license, authorizing exports, without application by the exporter.

(4) Such other licenses as may assist in the effective and efficient implementation of this Act.

(b) CONTROL LIST. The Secretary shall establish and maintain a list (hereinafter in this Act referred to as the "control list") stating license requirements (other than for general licenses) for exports of goods and technology under this Act.

(c) FOREIGN AVAILABILITY. In accordance with the provisions of this Act, the President shall not impose export controls for foreign policy or national security purposes on the export from the United States of goods or technology which he determines are available without restriction from sources outside the United States in sufficient quantities and comparable in quality to those produced in the United States so as to render the controls ineffective in achieving their purposes, unless the President determines that adequate evidence has been presented to him demonstrating that the absence of such controls would prove detrimental to the foreign policy or national security of the United States. In complying with the provisions of this subsection, the President shall give strong emphasis to bilateral or multilateral negotiations to eliminate foreign availability. The Secretary and the Secretary of Defense shall cooperate in gathering information relating to foreign availability, including the establishment and maintenance of a jointly operated computer system.

....

(e) DELEGATION OF AUTHORITY. The President may delegate the power, authority, and discretion conferred upon him by this Act to such departments, agencies, or officials of the Government as he may consider appropriate, except that no authority under this Act may be delegated to, or exercised by, any official of any department or agency the head of which is not appointed by the President, by and with the advice and consent of the Senate. The President may not delegate or transfer his power, authority, and discretion to overrule or modify any recommendation or decision made by the Secretary, the Secretary of Defense, or the Secretary of State pursuant to the provisions of this Act.

(f) NOTIFICATION OF THE PUBLIC; CONSULTATION WITH BUSINESS. The Secretary shall keep the public fully apprised of changes in export control policy and procedures instituted in conformity with this Act with a view to encouraging trade. The Secretary shall meet regularly with representatives of a broad spectrum of enterprises, labor organizations, and citizens interested in or affected by export controls, in order to obtain their views on United States export control policy and the foreign availability of goods and technology.

....

Sec. 2404.[4] National Security Controls.

(a) AUTHORITY. (1) In order to carry out the policy set forth in section 3(2)(A) of this Act, the President may, in accordance with the provisions of this section, prohibit or curtail the export of any goods or technology subject to the jurisdiction of the United States or exported by any person subject to the jurisdiction of the United States. The authority contained in this subsection includes the authority to prohibit or curtail the transfer of goods or technology within the United States to embassies and affiliates of controlled countries. For purposes of the preceding sentence, the term "affiliates" includes both governmental entities and commercial entities that are controlled in fact by controlled countries. The authority contained in this subsection shall be exercised by the Secretary, in consultation with the Secretary of Defense, and such other departments and agencies as the Secretary considers appropriate, and shall be implemented by means of export licenses described in section 4(a) of this Act.

(2) Whenever the Secretary makes any revision with respect to any goods or technology, or with respect to the countries or destinations, affected by export controls imposed under this section, the Secretary shall publish in the Federal Register a notice of such revision and shall specify in such notice that the revision relates to controls imposed under the authority contained in this section.

(3) In issuing regulations to carry out this section, particular attention shall be given to the difficulty of devising effective safeguards to prevent a country that poses a threat to the security of the United States from diverting critical technologies to military use, the difficulty of devising effective safeguards to protect critical goods, and the need to take effective measures to prevent the reexport of critical technologies from other countries to countries that pose a threat to the security of the United States.

(4) (A) No authority or permission may be required under this section to reexport any goods or technology subject to the jurisdiction of the United States to any country which maintains export controls on such goods or technology cooperatively with the United States pursuant to the agreement of the group known as the Coordinating Committee, or pursuant to an agreement described in subsection (k) of this section. The Secretary may require any person reexporting any goods or technology under this subparagraph to notify the Secretary of such reexports.

(B) Notwithstanding subparagraph (A), the Secretary may require authority or permission to reexport the following:

(i) supercomputers;

(ii) goods or technology for sensitive nuclear uses (as defined by the Secretary);

(iii) devices for surreptitious interception of wire or oral communications; and

(iv) goods or technology intended for such end users as the Secretary may specify by regulation.

. . . .

(b) POLICY TOWARD INDIVIDUAL COUNTRIES. (1) In administering export controls for national security purposes under this section, the President shall

4. Id. § 2404.

establish as a list of controlled countries those countries set forth in section 620(f) of the Foreign Assistance Act of 1961, except that the President may add any country to or remove any country from such list of controlled countries if he determines that the export of goods or technology to such country would or would not (as the case may be) make a significant contribution to the military potential of such country or a combination of countries which would prove detrimental to the national security of the United States. In determining whether a country is added to or removed from the list of controlled countries, the President shall take into account—

(A) the extent to which the country's policies are adverse to the national security interests of the United States;

(B) the country's Communist or non-Communist status;

(C) the present and potential relationship of the country with the United States;

(D) the present and potential relationships of the country with countries friendly or hostile to the United States;

(E) the country's nuclear weapons capability and the country's compliance record with respect to multilateral nuclear weapons agreements to which the United States is a party; and

(F) such other factors as the President considers appropriate.

Nothing in the preceding sentence shall be interpreted to limit the authority of the President provided in this Act to prohibit or curtail the export of any goods or technology to any country to which exports are controlled for national security purposes other than countries on the list of controlled countries specified in this paragraph. The President shall review not less frequently than every three years in the case of controls maintained cooperatively with other nations, and annually in the case of all other controls, United States policy toward individual countries to determine whether such policy is appropriate in light of the factors set forth in this paragraph.

(2) (A) Except as provided in subparagraph (B), no authority or permission may be required under this section to export goods or technology to a country which maintains export controls on such goods or technology cooperatively with the United States pursuant to the agreement of the group known as the Coordinating Committee or pursuant to an agreement described in subsection (k) of this section, if the export of such goods or technology to the People's Republic of China or a controlled country on the date of the enactment of the Export Enhancement Act of 1988 [enacted Aug. 23, 1988] would require only notification of the participating governments of the Coordinating Committee.

(B) (i) The Secretary may require a license for the export of goods or technology described in subparagraph (A) to such end users as the Secretary may specify by regulation.

(ii) The Secretary may require any person exporting goods or technology under this paragraph to notify the Secretary of those exports.

(C) The Secretary shall, within 3 months after the date of the enactment of the Export Enhancement Act of 1988 [enacted Aug. 23, 1988], determine which countries referred to in subparagraph (A) are implementing an effective export control system consistent with principles agreed to in the Coordinating Committee, including the following:

(i) national laws providing appropriate civil and criminal penalties and statutes of limitations sufficient to deter potential violations;

(ii) a program to evaluate export license applications that includes sufficient technical expertise to assess the licensing status of exports and ensure the reliability of end-users;

(iii) an enforcement mechanism that provides authority for trained enforcement officers to investigate and prevent illegal exports;

(iv) a system of export control documentation to verify the movement of goods and technology; and

(v) procedures for the coordination and exchange of information concerning violations of the agreement of the Coordinating Committee.

The Secretary shall, at least once each year, review the determinations made under the preceding sentence with respect to all countries referred to in subparagraph (A). The Secretary may, as appropriate, add countries to, or remove countries from, the list of countries that are implementing an effective export control system in accordance with this subparagraph. No authority or permission to export may be required for the export of goods or technology to a country on such list.

(3) (A) No authority or permission may be required under this section to export to any country, other than a controlled country, any goods or technology if the export of the goods or technology to controlled countries would require only notification of the participating governments of the Coordinating Committee.

(B) The Secretary may require any person exporting any goods or technology under subparagraph (A) to notify the Secretary of those exports.

(c) CONTROL LIST. (1) The Secretary shall establish and maintain, as part of the control list, a list of all goods and technology subject to export controls under this section. Such goods and technology shall be clearly identified as being subject to controls under this section.

(2) The Secretary of Defense and other appropriate departments and agencies shall identify goods and technology for inclusion on the list referred to in paragraph (1). Those items which the Secretary and the Secretary of Defense concur shall be subject to export controls under this section shall comprise such list.[5] If the Secretary and the Secretary of Defense are unable to concur on such items, as determined by the Secretary, the Secretary of Defense may, within 20 days after receiving notification of the Secretary's determination, refer the matter to the President for resolution. The Secretary of Defense shall notify the Secretary of any such referral. The President shall, not later than 20 days after such referral, notify the Secretary of his determination with respect to the inclusion of such items on the list. Failure of the Secretary of Defense to notify the President or the Secretary, or

5. Section 2404(c)(2) was amended and restated by sec. 2416(a) of Pub. L. No. 100-418, 102 Stat. 1107, 1349 (1988), which inserted the text following this point in lieu of "If the Secretary and the Secretary of Defense are unable to concur on such items, the matter shall be referred to the President for resolution."

failure of the President to notify the Secretary, in accordance with this paragraph, shall be deemed by the Secretary to constitute concurrence in the implementation of the actions proposed by the Secretary regarding the inclusion of such items on the list.

(3) The Secretary shall conduct partial reviews of the list established pursuant to this subsection at least once each calendar quarter in order to carry out the policy set forth in section 3(2)(A) of this Act and the provisions of this section, and shall promptly make such revisions of the list as may be necessary after each such review. Before beginning each quarterly review, the Secretary shall publish notice of that review in the Federal Register. The Secretary shall provide a 30-day period during each review for comment and the submission of data, with or without oral presentation, by interested Government agencies and other affected or potentially affected parties. After consultation with appropriate Government agencies, the Secretary shall make a determination of any revisions in the list within 30 days after the end of the review period. The concurrence or approval of any other department or agency is not required before any such revision is made. The Secretary shall publish in the Federal Register any revisions in the list, with an explanation of the reasons for the revisions....

(4) The appropriate technical advisory committee appointed under subsection (h) of this section shall be consulted by the Secretary with respect to changes, pursuant to paragraph (2) or (3), in the list established pursuant to this subsection, and such technical advisory committee may submit recommendations to the Secretary with respect to such changes. The Secretary shall consider the recommendations of the technical advisory committee and shall inform the committee of the disposition of its recommendations.

....

(6) (A) Notwithstanding subsection (f) or (h)(6) of this section, any export control imposed under this section which is maintained unilaterally by the United States shall expire 6 months after the date of the enactment of this paragraph [enacted Aug. 23, 1988], or 6 months after the export control is imposed, whichever date is later, except that—

(i) any such export controls on those goods or technology for which a determination of the Secretary that there is no foreign availability has been made under subsection (f) or (h)(6) of this section before the end of the applicable 6-month period and is in effect may be renewed for periods of not more than 6 months each, and

(ii) any such export controls on those goods or technology with respect to which the President, by the end of the applicable 6-month period, is actively pursuing negotiations with other countries to achieve multilateral export controls on those goods or technology may be renewed for 2 periods of not more than 6 months each.

(B) Export controls on goods or technology described in clause (i) or (ii) of subparagraph (A) may be renewed only if, before each renewal, the President submits to the Congress a report setting forth all the controls being renewed and stating the specific reasons for such renewal.

(7) Notwithstanding any other provision of this subsection, after 1 year has elapsed since the last review in the Federal Register on any item within a category

on the control list the export of which to the People's Republic of China would require only notification of the members of the group known as the Coordinating Committee, an export license applicant may file an allegation with the Secretary that such item has not been so reviewed within such 1-year period. Within 90 days after receipt of such allegation, the Secretary—

(A) shall determine the truth of the allegation;

(B) shall, if the allegation is confirmed, commence and complete the review of the item; and

(C) shall, pursuant to such review, submit a finding for publication in the Federal Register.

In such finding, the Secretary shall identify those goods or technology which shall remain on the control list and those goods or technology which shall be removed from the control list. If such review and submission for publication are not completed within that 90-day period, the goods or technology encompassed by such item shall immediately be removed from the control list.

(d) MILITARILY CRITICAL TECHNOLOGIES. (1) The Secretary, in consultation with the Secretary of Defense, shall review and revise the list established pursuant to subsection (c), as prescribed in paragraph (3) of such subsection, for the purpose of insuring that export controls imposed under this section cover and (to the maximum extent consistent with the purposes of this Act) are limited to militarily critical goods and technologies and the mechanisms through which such goods and technologies may be effectively transferred.

(2) The Secretary of Defense shall bear primary responsibility for developing a list of militarily critical technologies. In developing such list, primary emphasis shall be given to—

(A) arrays of design and manufacturing know-how,

(B) keystone manufacturing, inspection, and test equipment,

(C) goods accompanied by sophisticated operation, application, or maintenance know-how, and

(D) keystone equipment which would reveal or give insight into the design and manufacture of a United States military system, which are not possessed by, or available in fact from sources outside the United States to, controlled countries and which, if exported, would permit a significant advance in a military system of any such country.

(3) The list referred to in paragraph (2) shall be sufficient by specific to guide the determinations of any official exercising export licensing responsibilities under this Act.

....

(5) The Secretary of Defense shall establish a procedure for reviewing the goods and technology on the list of militarily critical technologies on an ongoing basis for the purpose of removing from the list of militarily critical technologies any goods or technology that are no longer militarily critical. The Secretary of Defense may add to the list of militarily critical technologies any good or technology that the Secretary of Defense determines is militarily critical, consistent with the provisions

of paragraph (2) of this subsection. If the Secretary and the Secretary of Defense disagree as to whether any change in the list of militarily critical technologies by the addition or removal of a good or technology should also be made in the control list, consistent with the provisions of the fourth sentence of paragraph (4) of this subsection, the President shall resolve the disagreement.

....

(e) EXPORT LICENSES. (1) The Congress finds that the effectiveness and efficiency of the process of making export licensing determinations under this section is severely hampered by the large volume of validated export license applications required to be submitted under this Act. Accordingly, it is the intent of Congress in this subsection to encourage the use of the multiple validated export licenses described in section 4(a)(2) of this Act in lieu of individual validated licenses.

(2) To the maximum extent practicable, consistent with the national security of the United States, the Secretary shall require a validated license under this section for the export of goods or technology only if—

(A) the export of such goods or technology is restricted pursuant to a multilateral agreement, formal or informal, to which the United States is a party and, under the terms of such multilateral agreement, such export requires the specific approval of the parties to such multilateral agreement;

(B) with respect to such goods or technology, other nations do not possess capabilities comparable to those possessed by the United States; or

(C) the United States is seeking the agreement of other suppliers to apply comparable controls to such goods or technology and, in the judgment of the Secretary, United States export controls on such goods or technology, by means of such license, are necessary pending the conclusion of such agreement.

....

(f) FOREIGN AVAILABILITY. (1) Foreign availability to controlled countries.

(A) The Secretary, in consultation with the Secretary of Defense and other appropriate Government agencies and with appropriate technical advisory committees established pursuant to subsection (h) of this section, shall review, on a continuing basis, the availability to controlled countries, from sources outside the United States, including countries which participate with the United States in multilateral export controls, of any goods or technology the export of which requires a validated license under this section. In any case in which the Secretary determines, in accordance with procedures and criteria which the Secretary shall by regulation establish, that any such goods or technology are available in fact to controlled countries from such sources in sufficient quantity and of comparable quality so that the requirement of a validated license for the export of such goods or technology is or would be ineffective in achieving the purpose set forth in subsection (a) of this section, the Secretary may not, after the determination is made, require a validated license for the export of such goods or technology during the period of such foreign availability, unless the President determines that the absence of export controls under this section on the goods or technology would prove detrimental to the national security of the United States. In any case in which the President determines under this paragraph that export controls under this section must be maintained notwithstanding foreign availability, the Secretary shall publish that determination, together with a concise statement of its basis and the estimated economic impact of the decision.

(B) The Secretary shall approve any application for a validated license which is required under this section for the export of any goods or technology to a controlled country and which meets all other requirements for such an application, if the Secretary determines that such goods or technology will, if the license is denied, be available in fact to such country from sources outside the United States, including countries which participate with the United States in multilateral export controls, in sufficient quantity and of comparable quality so that denial of the license would be ineffective in achieving the purpose set forth in subsection (a) of this section, unless the President determines that approving the license application would prove detrimental to the national security of the United States. In any case in which the Secretary makes a determination of foreign availability under this subparagraph with respect to any goods or technology, the Secretary shall determine whether a determination of foreign availability under subparagraph (A) with respect to such goods or technology is warranted.

(2) Foreign availability to other than controlled countries.

(A) The Secretary shall review, on a continuing basis, the availability to countries other than controlled countries, from sources outside the United States, of any goods or technology the export of which requires a validated license under this section. If the Secretary determines, in accordance with procedures which the Secretary shall establish, that any goods or technology in sufficient quantity and of comparable quality are available in fact from sources outside the United States (other than availability under license from a country which maintains export controls on such goods or technology cooperatively with the United States pursuant to the agreement of the group known as the Coordinating Committee or pursuant to an agreement described in subsection (i) of this section), the Secretary may not, after the determination is made and during the period of such foreign availability, require a validated license for the export of such goods or technology to any country (other than a controlled country) to which the country from which the goods or technology is available does not place controls on the export of such goods or technology. The requirement with respect to a validated license in the preceding sentence shall not apply if the President determines that the absence of export controls under this section on the goods or technology would prove detrimental to the national security of the United States. In any case in which the President determines under this paragraph that export controls under this section must be maintained notwithstanding foreign availability, the Secretary shall publish that determination, together with a concise statement of its basis and the estimated economic impact of the decision.

. . . .

(6) OFFICE OF FOREIGN AVAILABILITY. The Secretary shall establish in the Department of Commerce an Office of Foreign Availability, which shall be under the direction of the Under Secretary of Commerce for Export Administration. The Office shall be responsible for gathering and analyzing all the necessary information in order for the Secretary to make determinations of foreign availability under this Act. The Secretary shall make available to the Committee on Foreign Affairs of

the House of Representatives and the Committee on Banking, Housing, and Urban Affairs of the Senate at the end of each 6-month period during a fiscal year information on the operations of the Office, and on improvements in the Government's ability to assess foreign availability, during that 6-month period, including information on the training of personnel, the use of computers, and the use of Commercial Service Officers of the United States and Foreign Commercial Service. Such information shall also include a description of representative determinations made under this Act during that 6-month period that foreign availability did or did not exist (as the case may be), together with an explanation of such determinations.

(7) SHARING OF INFORMATION. Each department or agency of the United States, including any intelligence agency, and all contractors with any such department or agency, shall, upon the request of the Secretary and consistent with the protection of intelligence sources and methods, furnish information to the Office of Foreign Availability concerning foreign availability of goods and technology subject to export controls under this Act. Each such department or agency shall allow the Office of Foreign Availability access to any information from a laboratory or other facility within such department or agency.

....

(10) AVAILABILITY DEFINED. For purposes of this subsection and subsections (f) and (h), the term "available in fact to controlled countries" includes production or availability of any goods or technology in any country—

(A) from which the goods or technology is not restricted for export to any controlled country; or

(B) in which such export restrictions are determined by the Secretary to be ineffective.

For purposes of subparagraph (B), the mere inclusion of goods or technology on a list of goods or technology subject to bilateral or multilateral national security export controls shall not alone constitute credible evidence that a country provides an effective means of controlling the export of such goods or technology to controlled countries.

....

(i) MULTILATERAL EXPORT CONTROLS. Recognizing the ineffectiveness of unilateral controls and the importance of uniform enforcement measures to the effectiveness of multilateral controls, the President shall enter into negotiations with the governments participating in the group known as the Coordinating Committee (hereinafter in this subsection referred to as the "Committee") wit ha view toward accomplishing the following objectives:

(1) Enhanced public understanding of the Committee's purpose and procedures, including publication of the list of items controlled for export by agreement of the Committee, together with all notes, understandings, and other aspects of such agreement of the Committee, and all changes thereto.

(2) Periodic meetings of high-level representatives of participating governments for the purpose of coordinating export control policies and issuing policy guidance to the Committee.

(3) Strengthened legal basis for each government's export control system, including, as appropriate, increased penalties and statutes of limitations.

(4) Harmonization of export control documentation by the participating governments to verify the movement of goods and technology subject to controls by the Committee.

(5) Improved procedures for coordination and exchange of information concerning violations of the agreement of the Committee.

(6) Procedures for effective implementation of the agreement through uniform and consistent interpretations of export controls agreed to by the governments participating in the Committee.

(7) Coordination of national licensing and enforcement efforts by governments participating in the Committee, including sufficient technical expertise to assess the licensing status of exports and to ensure end-use verification.

(8) More effective procedures for enforcing export controls, including adequate training, resources, and authority for enforcement officers to investigate and prevent illegal exports.

(9) Agreement to provide adequate resources to enhance the functioning of individual national export control systems and of the Committee.

(10) Improved enforcement and compliance with the agreement through elimination of unnecessary export controls and maintenance of an effective control list.

(11) Agreement to enhance cooperation among members of the Committee in obtaining the agreement of governments outside the Committee to restrict the export of goods and technology on the International Control List, to establish an ongoing mechanism in the Committee to coordinate planning and implementation of export control measures related to such agreements, and to remove items from the International Control List if such items continue to be available to controlled countries or if the control of the items no longer serves the common strategic objectives of the members of the Committee.

For purposes of reviews of the International Control List, the President may include as advisors to the United States delegation to the Committee representatives of industry who are knowledgeable with respect to the items being reviewed.

(j) COMMERCIAL AGREEMENTS WITH CERTAIN COUNTRIES. (1) Any United States firm, enterprise, or other nongovernmental entity which enters into an agreement with any agency of the government of a controlled country, that calls for the encouragement of technical cooperation and that is intended to result in the export from the United States to the other party of unpublished technical data of United States origin, shall report to the Secretary the agreement with such agency in sufficient detail.

(2) The provisions of paragraph (1) shall not apply to colleges, universities, or other educational institutions.

(k) NEGOTIATIONS WITH OTHER COUNTRIES. The Secretary of State, in consultation with the Secretary of Defense, the Secretary of Commerce, and the heads of other appropriate departments and agencies, shall be responsible for conducting negotiations with other countries, including those countries not participating in the group known as the Coordinating Committee, regarding their cooperation in restricting the export of goods and technology in order to carry out the policy set forth in section 3(9) of this Act, as authorized by subsection (a) of this section, including negotiations with respect to which goods and technology should be subject to multilaterally agreed export restrictions and what conditions should apply for exceptions from those restrictions. In cases where such negotiations produce agreements on export restrictions comparable in practice to those maintained by the Coordinating Committee, the Secretary shall treat exports, whether by individual or multiple licenses, to countries party to such agreements in the same manner as exports to members of the Coordinating Committee are treated, including the same manner as exports are treated under subsection (b)(2) of this section and section 10(o) of this Act.

(l) DIVERSION OF CONTROLLED GOODS OR TECHNOLOGY. (1) Whenever there is reliable evidence, as determined by the Secretary, that goods or technology which were exported subject to national security controls under this section to a controlled country have been diverted to an unauthorized use or consignee in violation of the conditions of an export license, the Secretary for as long as that diversion continues—

(A) shall deny all further exports, to or by the party or parties responsible for that diversion or who conspired in that diversion, of any goods or technology subject to national security controls under this section, regardless of whether such goods or technology are available from sources outside the United States; and

(B) may take such additional actions under this Act with respect to the party or parties referred to in subparagraph (A) as the Secretary determines are appropriate in the circumstances to deter the further unauthorized use of the previously exported goods or technology.

(2) As used in this subsection, the term "unauthorized use" means the use of United States goods or technology in the design, production, or maintenance of any item on the United States Munitions List, or the military use of any item on the International Control List of the Coordinating Committee.

....

Sec. 2405.[6] Foreign policy controls.

(a) AUTHORITY. (1) In order to carry out the policy set forth in paragraph (2)(B), (7), (8), or (13) of section 3 of this Act, the President may prohibit or curtail the exportation of any goods, technology, or other information subject to the jurisdiction of the United States or exported by any person subject to the jurisdiction of the United States, to the extent necessary to further significantly the foreign policy of the United States or to fulfill its declared international obligations. The authority granted by this subjection shall be exercised by the Secretary, in consultation with the Secretary of State, the Secretary of Defense, the Secretary of Agriculture, the Secretary of the Treasury, the United States Trade Representative, and such other departments and agencies as the Secretary considers appropriate, and shall be implemented by means of export licenses issued by the Secretary.

....

(b) CRITERIA. (1) Subject to paragraph (2) of this subsection, the President may impose, extend, or expand export controls under this section only if the President determines that—

(A) such controls are likely to achieve the intended foreign policy purpose, in light of other factors, including the availability from other countries of the

6. 50 U.S.C.S. § app. 2405 (LexisNexis 1996 & Supp. 2005).

goods or technology proposed for such controls, and that foreign policy purpose cannot be achieved through negotiations or other alternative means;

(B) the proposed controls are compatible with the foreign policy objectives of the United States and with overall United States policy toward the country to which exports are to be subject to the proposed controls;

(C) the reaction of other countries to the imposition, extension, or expansion of such export controls by the United States is not likely to render the controls ineffective in achieving the intended foreign policy purpose or to be counterproductive to United States foreign policy interests;

(D) the effect of the proposed controls on the export performance of the United States, the competitive position of the United States in the international economy, the international reputation of the United States as a supplier of goods and technology, or on the economic well-being of individual United States companies and their employees and communities does not exceed the benefit to United States foreign policy objectives; and

(E) the United States has the ability to enforce the proposed controls effectively.

(2) With respect to those export controls in effect under this section on the date of the enactment of the Export Administration Amendments Act of 1985 [enacted July 12, 1985], the President, in determining whether to extend those controls, as required by subsection (a)(3) of this section, shall consider the criteria set forth in paragraph (1) of this subsection and shall consider the foreign policy consequences of modifying the export controls.

....

(j) COUNTRIES SUPPORTING INTERNATIONAL TERRORISM. (1) A validated license shall be required for the export of goods or technology to a country if the Secretary of State has made the following determinations:

(A) The government of such country has repeatedly provided support for acts of international terrorism.

(B) The export of such goods or technology could make a significant contribution to the military potential of such country, including its military logistics capability, or could enhance the ability of such country to support acts of international terrorism.

(2) The Secretary and the Secretary of State shall notify the Committee on Foreign Affairs of the House of Representatives and the Committee on Banking, Housing, and Urban Affairs and the Committee on Foreign Relations of the Senate at least 30 days before issuing any validated license required by paragraph (1).

(3) Each determination of the Secretary of State under paragraph (1)(A), including each determination in effect on the date of the enactment of the Antiterrorism and Arms Export Amendments Act of 1989 [enacted Dec. 12, 1989], shall be published in the Federal Register.

(4) A determination made by the Secretary of State under paragraph (1)(A) may not be rescinded unless the President submits to the Speaker of the House of Representatives and the chairman of the Committee on Banking, Housing, and Urban Affairs and the chairman of the Committee on Foreign Relations of the Senate—

(A) before the proposed rescission would take effect, a report certifying that—

(i) there has been a fundamental change in the leadership and policies of the government of the country concerned;

(ii) that government is not supporting acts of international terrorism; and

(iii) that government has provided assurances that it will not support acts of international terrorism in the future; or

(B) at least 45 days before the proposed rescission would take effect, a report justifying the rescission and certifying that—

(i) the government concerned has not provided any support for international terrorism during the preceding 6-month period; and

(ii) the government concerned has provided assurances that it will not support acts of international terrorism in the future.

....

Sec. 2407.[7] Foreign boycotts.

(a) PROHIBITIONS AND EXCEPTIONS. (1) For the purpose of implementing the policies set forth in subparagraph (A) or (B) of paragraph (5) of section 3 of this Act, the President shall issue regulations prohibiting any United States person, with respect to his activities in the interstate or foreign commerce of the United States, from taking or knowingly agreeing to take any of the following actions with intent to comply with, further, or support any boycott fostered or imposed by a foreign country against a country which is friendly to the United States and which is not itself the object of any form of boycott pursuant to United States law or regulation:

(A) Refusing, or requiring any other person to refuse, to do business with or in the boycotted country, with any business concern organized under the laws of the boycotted country, with any national or resident of the boycotted country, or with any other person, pursuant to an agreement with, a requirement of, or a request from or on behalf of the boycotting country. The mere absence of a business relationship with or in the boycotted country with any business concern organized under the laws of the boycotted country, with any national or resident of the boycotted country, or with any other person, does not indicate the existence of the intent required to establish a violation of regulations issued to carry out this subparagraph.

(B) Refusing, or requiring any other person to refuse, to employ or otherwise discriminating against any United States person on the basis of race, religion, sex, or national origin of that person or of any owner, officer, director, or employee of such person.

(C) Furnishing information with respect to the race, religion, sex, or national origin of any United States person or of any owner, officer, director, or employee of such person.

(D) Furnishing information about whether any person has, has had, or proposes to have any business relationship (including a relationship by way of

7. Id. § 2407.

sale, purchase, legal or commercial representation, shipping or other transport, insurance, investment, or supply) with or in the boycotted country, with any business concern organized under the laws of the boycotted country, with any national or resident of the boycotted country, or with any other person which is known or believed to be restricted from having any business relationship with or in the boycotting country. Nothing in this paragraph shall prohibit the furnishing of normal business information in a commercial context as defined by the Secretary.

(E) Furnishing information about whether any person is a member of, has made contributions to, or is otherwise associated with or involved in the activities of any charitable or fraternal organization which supports the boycotted country.

(F) Paying, honoring, confirming, or otherwise implementing a letter of credit which contains any condition or requirement compliance with which is prohibited by regulations issued pursuant to this paragraph, and no United States person shall, as a result of the application of this paragraph, be obligated to pay or otherwise honor or implement such letter of credit.

(2) Regulations issued pursuant to paragraph (1) shall provide exceptions for—

(A) complying or agreeing to comply with requirements—

(i) prohibiting the import of goods or services from the boycotted country or goods produced or services provided by any business concern organized under the laws of the boycotted country or by nationals or residents of the boycotted country, or

(ii) prohibiting the shipment of goods to the boycotting country on a carrier of the boycotted country, or by a route other than that prescribed by the boycotting country or the recipient of the shipment;

(B) complying or agreeing to comply with import and shipping document requirements with respect to the country of origin, the name of the carrier and route of shipment, the name of the supplier of the shipment or the name of the provider of other services, except that no information knowingly furnished or conveyed in response to such requirements may be stated in negative, blacklisting, or similar exclusionary terms, other than with respect to carriers or route of shipment as may be permitted by such regulations in order to comply with precautionary requirements protecting against war risks and confiscation;

(C) complying or agreeing to comply in the normal course of business with the unilateral and specific selection by a boycotting country, or national or resident thereof, of carriers, insurers, suppliers of services to be performed within the boycotting country or specific goods which, in the normal course of business, are identifiable by source when imported into the boycotting country;

(D) complying or agreeing to comply with export requirements of the boycotting country relating to shipments or transshipments of exports to the boycotted country, to any business concern of or organized under the laws of the boycotted country, or to any national or resident of the boycotted country;

(E) compliance by an individual or agreement by an individual to comply with the immigration or passport requirements of any country with respect to such individual or any member of such individual's family or with requests for information regarding requirements of employment of such individual within the boycotting country; and

(F) compliance by a United States person resident in a foreign country or agreement by such person to comply with the laws of that country with respect to his activities exclusively therein, and such regulations may contain exceptions for such resident complying with the laws or regulations of that foreign country governing imports into such country of trademarked, trade named, or similarly specifically identifiable products, or components of products for his own use, including the performance of contractual services within that country, as may be defined by such regulations.

(3) Regulations issued pursuant to paragraphs (2)(C) and (2)(F) shall not provide exceptions from paragraphs (1)(B) and (1)(C).

(4) Nothing in this subsection may be construed to supersede or limit the operation of the antitrust or civil rights laws of the United States.

(5) This section shall apply to any transaction or activity undertaken, by or through a United States person or any other person, with intent to evade the provisions of this section as implemented by the regulations issued pursuant to this subsection, and such regulations shall expressly provide that the exceptions set forth in paragraph (2) shall not permit activities or agreements (expressed or implied by a course of conduct, including a pattern of responses) otherwise prohibited, which are not within the intent of such exceptions.

....

---

i. FRIENDSHIP Act, Pub. L. No. 103-199, §201(a), 107 Stat. 2317, 2320 (1993), deleted para. (11), which read: "The acquisition of national security sensitive goods and technology by the Soviet Union and other countries the actions or policies of which run counter to the national security interests of the United States, has led to the significant enhancement of Soviet bloc military-industrial capabilities. This enhancement poses a threat to the security of the United States, its allies, and other friendly nations, and places additional demands on the defense budget of the United States.", and redesignated paras. (12) and (13) as paras. (11) and (12), respectively.

ii. FRIENDSHIP Act, Pub. L. No. 103-188, §201(b)(2), 107 Stat. 2317, 2321 (1993), repealed para. (15), which read: "It is the policy of the United States, particularly in light of the Soviet massacre of innocent men, women, and children aboard Korean Air Lines flight 7, to continue to object to exceptions to the International Control List for the Union of Soviet Socialist Republics, subject to periodic review by the President.".

OFFICE OF EXPORT ADMINISTRATION ENFORCEMENT REGULATIONS*

§764.3 Sanctions.

(a) *Administrative.*[i] Violations of the EAA, the EAR, or any order, license or authorization issued thereunder are subject to the administrative sanctions described in this section and to any other liability, sanction, or penalty available under law. The protective administrative measures that are described in §764.6 of this part are distinct from administrative sanctions.

(1) *Civil penalty.* (i) A civil penalty not to exceed $10,000 may be imposed for each violation, except that a civil penalty not to exceed $100,000 may be imposed for each violation involving national security controls imposed under section 5 of the EAA.

(ii) The payment of any civil penalty may be made a condition, for a period not exceeding one year after the imposition of such penalty, to the granting, restoration, or continuing validity of any export license, License Exception, permission, or privilege granted or to be granted to the person upon whom such penalty is imposed.

(iii) The payment of any civil penalty may be deferred or suspended in whole or in part during any probation period that may be imposed. Such deferral or suspension shall not bar the collection of the penalty if the conditions of the deferral, suspension, or probation are not fulfilled.

(2) *Denial of export privileges.* An order may be issued that restricts the ability of the named persons to engage in export and reexport transactions involving items subject to the EAR, or that restricts access by named persons to items subject to the EAR. An order denying export privileges may be imposed either as a sanction for a violation specified in this part or as a protective administrative measure described in §764.6(c) or (d) of this part. An order denying export privileges may suspend or revoke any or all outstanding licenses issued under the EAR to a person named in the denial order or in which such person has an interest, may deny or restrict exports and reexports by or to such person of any item subject to the EAR, and may restrict dealings in which that person may benefit from any export or reexport of such items. The standard terms of a denial order are set forth in Supplement No. 1 to this part. A non-standard denial order, narrower in scope, may be issued. Authorization to engage in actions otherwise prohibited by a denial order may be given by the Office of Exporter Services, in consultation with the Office of Export Enforcement, following application by a person named in the denial order or by a person seeking permission to deal with a named person.

(3) *Exclusion from practice.* Any person acting as an attorney, accountant, consultant, freight forwarder, or in any other representative capacity for any license application or other matter before BIS may be excluded by order from any or all such activities before BIS.

---

* 15 C.F.R. §764.3 (2005) (original version at 61 Fed. Reg. 12,902 (Mar. 25, 1996)), *available at* http://www.washingtonwatchdog.org/documents/cfr/title15/part764.html#764.3. (Original footnotes included as endnotes).

(b) *Criminal.*[ii] (1) *General.* Except as provided in paragraph (b)(2) of this section, whoever knowingly violates or conspires to or attempts to violate the EAA, EAR, or any order or license issued thereunder, shall be fined not more than five times the value of the exports or reexports involved or $50,000, whichever is greater, or imprisoned not more than five years, or both.

(2) *Willful violations.* (i) Whoever willfully violates or conspires to or attempts to violate any provision of the EAA, the EAR, or any order or license issued thereunder, with knowledge that the exports involved will be used for the benefit of, or that the destination or intended destination of items involved is, any controlled country or any country to which exports or reexports are controlled for foreign policy purposes, except in the case of an individual, shall be fined not more than five times the value of the export or reexport involved or $1,000,000, whichever is greater; and, in the case of an individual, shall be fined not more than $250,000, or imprisoned not more than 10 years, or both.

(ii) Any person who is issued a license under the EAA or the EAR for the export or reexport of any items to a controlled country and who, with knowledge that such export or reexport is being used by such controlled country for military or intelligence gathering purposes contrary to the conditions under which the license was issued, willfully fails to report such use to the Secretary of Defense, except in the case of an individual, shall be fined not more than five times the value of the exports or reexports involved or $1,000,000, whichever is greater; and in the case of an individual, shall be fined not more than $250,000, or imprisoned not more than five years or both.

(iii) Any person who possesses any item with the intent to export or reexport such item in violation of an export control imposed under sections 5 or 6 of the EAA, the EAR, or any order or license issued thereunder, or knowing or having reason to believe that the item would be so exported or reexported, shall, in the case of a violation of an export control imposed under section 5 of the EAA (or the EAR, or any order or license issued thereunder with respect to such control), be subject to the penalties set forth in paragraph (b)(2)(i) of this section and shall in the case of a violation of an export control imposed under section 6 of the EAA (or the EAR, or any order or license issued thereunder with respect to such control), be subject to the penalties set forth in paragraph (b)(1) of this section.

(iv) Any person who takes any action with intent to evade the provisions of the EAA, the EAR, or any order or license issued thereunder, shall be subject to the penalties set forth in paragraph (b)(1) of this section, except that in the case of an evasion of an export control imposed under sections 5 or 6 of the EAA (or the EAR, or any order or license issued thereunder with respect to such control), such person shall be subject to the penalties set forth in paragraph (b)(2)(i) of this section.

(3) *Other criminal sanctions.* Conduct that constitutes a violation of the EAA, the EAR, or any order, license or authorization issued thereunder, or that occurs in connection with such a violation, may also be prosecuted under other provisions of law, including 18 U.S.C. 371 (conspiracy), 18 U.S.C. 1001 (false statements), 18 U.S.C. 1341, 1343, and 1346 (mail and wire fraud), and 18 U.S.C. 1956 and 1957 (money laundering).

(c) *Other sanctions.* Conduct that violates the EAA, the EAR, or any order, license or authorization issued thereunder, and other conduct specified in the EAA may be subject to sanctions or other measures in addition to criminal and administrative sanctions under the EAA or EAR. These include, but are not limited to, the following:

(1) *Statutory sanctions.* Statutorily-mandated sanctions may be imposed on account of specified conduct related to weapons proliferation. Such statutory sanctions are not civil or criminal penalties, but restrict imports and procurement (See section 11A of the EAA, Multilateral Export Control Violations, and section 11C of the EAA, Chemical and Biological Weapons Proliferation), or restrict export licenses (See section 11B of the EAA, Missile Proliferation Violations, and the Iran-Iraq Arms Non-Proliferation Act of 1992).

(2) *Other sanctions and measures*—(i) *Seizure and forfeiture.* Items that have been, are being, or are intended to be, exported or shipped from or taken out of the United States in violation of the EAA, the EAR, or any order, license or authorization issued thereunder, are subject to being seized and detained as are the vessels, vehicles, and aircraft carrying such items. Seized items are subject to forfeiture. (50 U.S.C. app. 2411(g); 22 U.S.C. 401.)

(ii) *Cross-debarment.* (A) The Department of State may deny licenses or approvals for the export or reexport of defense articles and defense services controlled under the Arms Export Control Act to persons indicted or convicted of specified criminal offenses, including violations of the EAA, or to persons denied export privileges by BIS or another agency. (22 CFR 126.7(a) and 127.11(a).)

(B) The Department of Defense, among other agencies, may suspend the right of any person to contract with the United States Government based on export control violations. (Federal Acquisition Regulations 9.407-2.)

---

i. In the event that any part of the EAR is not under the authority of the EAA, sanctions shall be limited to those provided for by such other authority, but the provisions of this part and of part 766 of the EAR shall apply insofar as not inconsistent with that other authority.

ii. In the event that any part of the EAR is not under the authority of the EAA, sanctions shall be limited to those provided for by such other authority or by 18 U.S.C. 3571, a criminal code provision that establishes a maximum criminal fine for a felony that is the greater of the amount provided by the statute that was violated, or an amount not more than $500,000 for an organization. The Federal Sentencing Guidelines found in §2M5.1 of Appendix 4 to Title 18 of the United States Code apply, to the extent followed by the court, to sentencing for convictions for violating the EAA.

KNOW YOUR CUSTOMER GUIDANCE and RED FLAG INDICATORS*

Certain provisions in the Export Administration Regulations (EAR) require an exporter to submit an individual validated license application if the exporter "knows" that an export that is otherwise exempt from the validated licensing requirements is for end-uses involving nuclear, chemical, and biological weapons (CBW), or related missile delivery systems, in named destinations listed in the regulations.

The Bureau of Industry and Security (BIS) has issued the following guidance on how individuals and firms should act under this knowledge standard. This guidance does not change or revise the EAR.

Decide whether there are "red flags"

Take into account any abnormal circumstances in a transaction that indicate that the export may be destined for an inappropriate end-use, end-user, or destination. Such circumstances are referred to as "red flags." Included among examples of red flags are orders for items which are inconsistent with the needs of the purchaser, a customer's declining installation and testing when included in the sales price or when normally requested, or requests for equipment configurations which are incompatible with the stated destination (e.g.—120 volts in a country with a standard of 220 volts). Commerce has developed lists of such "red flags" which are not all-inclusive but are intended to illustrate the types of circumstances that should cause reasonable suspicion that a transaction will violate the EAR.

If there are "red flags"

If there are no "red flags" in the information that comes to your firm, you should be able to proceed with a transaction in reliance on information you have received. That is, absent "red flags" (or an express requirement in the EAR), there is no affirmative duty upon exporters to inquire, verify, or otherwise "go behind" the customer's representations. However, when "red flags" are raised in the information that comes to your firm, you have a duty to check out the suspicious circumstances and inquire about the end-use, end-user, or ultimate country of destination.

The duty to check out "red flags" is not confined to the use of general licenses affected by the "know" or "reason to know" language in the EAR. Applicants for validated licenses are required by the EAR to obtain documentary evidence concerning the transaction, and misrepresentation or concealment of material facts is prohibited, both in the licensing process and in all export control documents. You can rely upon representations from your customer and repeat them in the documents you file unless "red flags" oblige you to take verification steps.

Do not self-blind

Do not cut off the flow of information that comes to your firm in the normal course of business. For example, do not instruct the sales force to tell potential customers to

---

* 15 C.F.R. pt. 732, Supp. 3 (1999), *available at* http://www.bxa.doc.gov/ComplianceAndEnforcement/KnowYourCustomerGuidance.htm *and* http://www.bxa.doc.gov/enforcement/redflags.htm.

refrain from discussing the actual end-use, end-user and ultimate country of destination for the product your firm is seeking to sell. Do not put on blinders that prevent the learning of relevant information. An affirmative policy of steps to avoid "bad" information would not insulate a company from liability, and it would usually be considered an aggravating factor in an enforcement proceeding.

Employees need to know how to handle "red flags." Knowledge possessed by an employee of a company can be imputed to a firm so as to make it liable for a violation. This makes it important for firms to establish clear policies and effective compliance procedures to ensure that such knowledge about transactions can be evaluated by responsible senior officials. Failure to do so could be regarded as a form of self-blinding.

Reevaluate all the information after the inquiry

The purpose of this inquiry and reevaluation is to determine whether the "red flags" can be explained or justified. If they can, you may proceed with the transaction. If the "red flags" cannot be explained or justified and you proceed, you run the risk of having had "knowledge" that would make your action a violation of the EAR.

Refrain from the transaction, disclose the information to BIS and wait

If you continue to have reason for concern after your inquiry, then you should either refrain from the transaction or submit all the relevant information to BIS in the form of an application for a validated license or in such other form as BIS may specify.

Industry has an important role to play in preventing exports and reexports contrary to the national security and foreign policy interests of the United States. BIS will continue to work in partnership with industry to make this front line of defense effective, while minimizing the regulatory burden on exporters. If you have any question about whether you have encountered a "red flag," you may contact BIS's Office of Export Enforcement or use this Confidential Enforcement Lead/Tip Form to submit a confidential tip.

RED FLAG INDICATORS

Use this as a check list to discover possible violations of the Export Administration Regulations. You may also wish to visit our page that provides "Know Your Customer Guidance".

- The customer or its address is similar to one of the parties found on the Commerce Department's [BIS's] list of denied persons.
- The customer or purchasing agent is reluctant to offer information about the end-use of the item.
- The product's capabilities do not fit the buyer's line of business, such as an order for sophisticated computers for a small bakery.
- The item ordered is incompatible with the technical level of the country to which it is being shipped, such as semiconductor manufacturing equipment being shipped to a country that has no electronics industry.
- The customer is willing to pay cash for a very expensive item when the terms of sale would normally call for financing.
- The customer has little or no business background.
- The customer is unfamiliar with the product's performance characteristics but still wants the product.
- Routine installation, training, or maintenance services are declined by the customer.

- Delivery dates are vague, or deliveries are planned for out of the way destinations.
- A freight forwarding firm is listed as the product's final destination.
- The shipping route is abnormal for the product and destination.
- Packaging is inconsistent with the stated method of shipment or destination.
- When questioned, the buyer is evasive and especially unclear about whether the purchased product is for domestic use, for export, or for reexport.

ARMS EXPORT CONTROL ACT*

§ 2751. Need for international defense cooperation and military export controls; Presidential waiver; report to Congress; arms sales policy

As declared by the Congress in the Arms Control and Disarmament Act [22 U.S.C. 2551 et seq.], an ultimate goal of the United States continues to be a world which is free from the scourge of war and the dangers and burdens of armaments; in which the use of force has been subordinated to the rule of law; and in which international adjustments to a changing world are achieved peacefully. In furtherance of that goal, it remains the policy of the United States to encourage regional arms control and disarmament agreements and to discourage arms races.

The Congress recognizes, however, that the United States and other free and independent countries continue to have valid requirements for effective and mutually beneficial defense relationships in order to maintain and foster the environment of international peace and security essential to social, economic, and political progress. Because of the growing cost and complexity of defense equipment, it is increasingly difficult and uneconomic for any country, particularly a developing country, to fill all of its legitimate defense requirements from its own design and production base. The need for international defense cooperation among the United States and those friendly countries to which it is allied by mutual defense treaties is especially important, since the effectiveness of their armed forces to act in concert to deter or defeat aggression is directly related to the operational compatibility of their defense equipment.

Accordingly, it remains the policy of the United States to facilitate the common defense by entering into international arrangements with friendly countries which further the objective of applying agreed resources of each country to programs and projects of cooperative exchange of data, research, development, production, procurement, and logistics support to achieve specific national defense requirements and objectives of mutual concern. To this end, this chapter authorizes sales by the United States Government to friendly countries having sufficient wealth to maintain and equip their own military forces at adequate strength, or to assume progressively larger shares of the costs thereof, without undue burden to their economies, in accordance with the restraints and control measures specified herein and in furtherance of the security objectives of the United States and of the purposes and principles of the United Nations Charter.

It is the sense of the Congress that all such sales be approved only when they are consistent with the foreign policy interests of the United States, the purposes of the foreign assistance program of the United States as embodied in the Foreign Assistance Act of 1961, as amended [22 U.S.C. 2551 et seq.], the extent and character of the military requirement, and the economic and financial capability of the recipient country, with particular regard being given, where appropriate, to proper balance among such sales, grant military assistance, and economic assistance as well as to the impact of the sales on programs of social and economic development and on existing or incipient arms races.

It shall be the policy of the United States to exert leadership in the world community to bring about arrangements for reducing the international trade in implements of war

* Arms Export Control Act, 22 U.S.C.A. §§ 2751–2756, 2770a, 2780–2781, 2785, 2797–2798, 2799aa–2799aa-1 (West 2004), *available at* http://www.fas.org/asmp/resources/govern/aeca01.pdf.

and to lessen the danger of outbreak of regional conflict and the burdens of armaments. United States programs for or procedures governing the export, sale, and grant of defense articles and defense services to foreign countries and international organizations shall be administered in a manner which will carry out this policy.

It is the sense of the Congress that the President should seek to initiate multilateral discussions for the purpose of reaching agreements among the principal arms suppliers and arms purchasers and other countries with respect to the control of the international trade in armaments. It is further the sense of Congress that the President should work actively with all nations to check and control the international sale and distribution of conventional weapons of death and destruction and to encourage regional arms control arrangements. In furtherance of this policy, the President should undertake a concerted effort to convene an international conference of major arms-supplying and arms-purchasing nations which shall consider measures to limit conventional arms transfers in the interest of international peace and stability.

....

It is the sense of the Congress that the President maintain adherence to a policy of restraint in conventional arms transfers and that, in implementing this policy worldwide, a balanced approach should be taken and full regard given to the security interests of the United States in all regions of the world and that particular attention should be paid to controlling the flow of conventional arms to the nations of the developing world. To this end, the President is encouraged to continue discussions with other arms suppliers in order to restrain the flow of conventional arms to less developed countries.

§ 2752. Coordination with foreign policy

(a) Noninfringement of powers or functions of the Secretary of State

Nothing contained in this chapter shall be construed to infringe upon the powers or functions of the Secretary of State.

(b) Responsibility for supervision and direction of sales, leases, financing, cooperative projects, and exports

Under the direction of the President, the Secretary of State (taking into account other United States activities abroad, such as military assistance, economic assistance, and the food for peace program) shall be responsible for the continuous supervision and general direction of sales, leases, financing, cooperative projects, and exports under this chapter, including, but not limited to, determining—

(1) whether there will be a sale to or financing for a country and the amount thereof;

(2) whether there will be a lease to a country;

(3) whether there will be a cooperative project and the scope thereof; and

(4) whether there will be delivery or other performance under such sale, lease, cooperative project, or export,

to the end that sales, financing, leases, cooperative projects, and exports will be integrated with other United States activities and to the end that the foreign policy of the United States would be best served thereby.

....

§ 2753. Eligibility for defense services or defense articles

(a) Prerequisites for consent by President; report to Congress

No defense article or defense service shall be sold or leased by the United States Government under this chapter to any country or international organization, and no agreement shall be entered into for a cooperative project (as defined in section 2767 of this title), unless—

(1) the President finds that the furnishing of defense articles and defense services to such country or international organization will strengthen the security of the United States and promote world peace;

(2) the country or international organization shall have agreed not to transfer title to, or possession of, any defense article or related training or other defense service so furnished to it, or produced in a cooperative project (as defined in section 2767 of this title), to anyone not an officer, employee, or agent of that country or international organization (or the North Atlantic Treaty Organization or the specified member countries (other than the United States) in the case of a cooperative project) and not to use or permit the use of such article or related training or other defense service for purposes other than those for which furnished unless the consent of the President has first been obtained:

(3) the country or international organization shall have agreed that it will maintain the security of such article or service and will provide substantially the same degree of security protection afforded to such article or service by the United States Government; and

(4) the country or international organization is otherwise eligible to purchase or lease defense articles or defense services.

....

(c) Termination of credits, guaranties or sales; report of violation by President; national security exception; conditions for reinstatement

(1) (A) No credits (including participations in credits) may be issued and no guaranties may be extended for any foreign country under this chapter as hereinafter provided, if such country uses defense articles or defense services furnished under this chapter, or any predecessor Act, in substantial violation (either in terms of quantities or in terms of the gravity of the consequences regardless of the quantities involved) of any agreement entered into pursuant to any such Act

(i) by using such articles or services for a purpose not authorized under section 2754 of this title or, if such agreement provides that such articles or services may only be used for purposes more limited than those authorized under section 2754 of this title for a purpose not authorized under such agreement;

(ii) by transferring such articles or services to, or permitting any use of such articles or services by, anyone not an officer, employee, or agent of the recipient country without the consent of the President; or

(iii) by failing to maintain the security of such articles or services.

(B) No cash sales or deliveries pursuant to previous sales may be made with respect to any foreign country under this chapter as hereinafter provided, if such country uses defense articles or defense services furnished under this chapter, or any predecessor Act, in substantial violation (either in terms of quantity or in terms of the gravity of the consequences regardless of the quantities involved) of any agreement entered into pursuant to any such Act by using such articles or services for a purpose not authorized....

(2) The President shall report to the Congress promptly upon the receipt of information that a violation described in paragraph (1) of this subsection may have occurred.

(3) (A) A country shall be deemed to be ineligible under subparagraph (A) of paragraph (1) of this subsection, or both subparagraphs (A) and (B) of such paragraph in the case of a violation described in both such paragraphs, if the President so determines and so reports in writing to the Congress, or if the Congress so determines by joint resolution.

(B) Notwithstanding a determination by the President of ineligibility under subparagraph (B) of paragraph (1) of this subsection, cash sales and deliveries pursuant to previous sales may be made if the President certifies in writing to the Congress that a termination thereof would have significant adverse impact on United States security, unless the Congress adopts or has adopted a joint resolution pursuant to subparagraph (A) of this paragraph with respect to such ineligibility.

(4) A country shall remain ineligible in accordance with paragraph (1) of this subsection until such time as—

(A) the President determines that the violation has ceased; and

(B) the country concerned has given assurances satisfactory to the President that such violation will not recur.

....

(f) Sales and leases to countries in breach of nuclear nonproliferation agreements and treaties

No sales or leases shall be made to any country that the President has determined is in material breach of its binding commitments to the United States under international treaties or agreements concerning the nonproliferation of nuclear explosive devices (as defined in section 6305 (4) of this title) and unsafeguarded special nuclear material (as defined in section 6305 (8) of this title).

(g) Unauthorized use of articles

Any agreement for the sale or lease of any article on the United States Munitions List entered into by the United States Government after November 29, 1999, shall state that the United States Government retains the right to verify credible reports that such article has been used for a purpose not authorized under section 2754 of this title or, if such agreement provides that such article may only be used for purposes more limited than those authorized under section 2754 of this title, for a purpose not authorized under such agreement.

§ 2754. Purposes for which military sales or leases by the United States are authorized; report to Congress

Defense articles and defense services shall be sold or leased by the United States Government under this chapter to friendly countries solely for internal security, for legitimate self-defense, for preventing or hindering the proliferation of weapons of mass destruction and of the means of delivering such weapons, to permit the recipient country to participate in regional or collective arrangements or measures consistent with the Charter of the United Nations, or otherwise to permit the recipient country to participate in collective measures requested by the United Nations for the purpose of maintaining or restoring international peace and security, or for the purpose of enabling foreign military forces in less developed friendly countries to construct public works and to engage in other activities helpful to the economic and social development of such friendly countries. It is the sense of the Congress that such foreign military forces should not be maintained or established solely for civic action activities and that such civic action activities not significantly detract from the capability of the military forces to perform their military missions and be coordinated with and form part of the total economic and social development effort: Provided, That none of the funds contained in this authorization shall be used to guarantee, or extend credit, or participate in an extension of credit in connection with any sale of sophisticated weapons systems, such as missile systems and jet aircraft for military purposes, to any underdeveloped country other than Greece, Turkey, Iran, Israel, the Republic of China, the Philippines and Korea unless the President determines that such financing is important to the national security of the United States and reports within thirty days each such determination to the Congress.

§ 2755. Discrimination prohibited if based on race, religion, national origin, or sex

(a) Congressional declaration of policy

It is the policy of the United States that no sales should be made, and no credits (including participations in credits) or guaranties extended to or for any foreign country, the laws, regulations, official policies, or governmental practices of which prevent any United States person (as defined in section 7701 (a) (30) of title 26) from participating in the furnishing of defense articles or defense services under this chapter on the basis of race, religion, national origin, or sex.

....

§ 2756. Foreign intimidation and harassment of individuals in United States

No letters of offer may be issued, no credits or guarantees may be extended, and no export licenses may be issued under this chapter with respect to any country determined by the President to be engaged in a consistent pattern of acts of intimidation or harassment directed against individuals in the United States. The President shall report any such determination promptly to the Speaker of the House of Representatives and to the chairman of the Committee on Foreign Relations of the Senate.

....

SUBCHAPTER II-C—EXCHANGE OF TRAINING AND RELATED SUPPORT

§ 2770a. Exchange of training and related support

(a) Authorization; eligibility; scope

Subject to subsection (b) of this section, the President may provide training and related support to military and civilian defense personnel of a friendly foreign country or an international organization. Such training and related support shall be provided by a

Secretary of a military department and may include the provision of transportation, food services, health services, and logistics and the use of facilities and equipment.

....

SUBCHAPTER III—MILITARY EXPORT CONTROLS

....

§ 2780. Transactions with countries supporting acts of international terrorism

(a) Prohibited transactions by United States Government

The following transactions by the United States Government are prohibited:

(1) Exporting or otherwise providing (by sale, lease or loan, grant, or other means), directly or indirectly, any munitions item to a country described in subsection (d) of this section under the authority of this chapter, the Foreign Assistance Act of 1961 [22 U.S.C. 2151 et seq.], or any other law (except as provided in subsection (h) of this section). In implementing this paragraph, the United States Government—

(A) shall suspend delivery to such country of any such item pursuant to any such transaction which has not been completed at the time the Secretary of State makes the determination described in subsection (d) of this section, and

(B) shall terminate any lease or loan to such country of any such item which is in effect at the time the Secretary of State makes that determination.

(2) Providing credits, guarantees, or other financial assistance under the authority of this chapter, the Foreign Assistance Act of 1961 [22 U.S.C. 2151 et seq.], or any other law (except as provided in subsection (h) of this section), with respect to the acquisition of any munitions item by a country described in subsection (d) of this section. In implementing this paragraph, the United States Government shall suspend expenditures pursuant to any such assistance obligated before the Secretary of State makes the determination described in subsection (d) of this section. The President may authorize expenditures otherwise required to be suspended pursuant to the preceding sentence if the President has determined, and reported to the Congress, that suspension of those expenditures causes undue financial hardship to a supplier, shipper, or similar person and allowing the expenditure will not result in any munitions item being made available for use by such country.

(3) Consenting under section 2753a of this title, under section 505(a) of the Foreign Assistance Act of 1961 [22 U.S.C. 2314 (a)], under the regulations issued to carry out section 2778 of this title, or under any other law (except as provided in subsection (h) of this section), to any transfer of any munitions item to a country described in subsection (d) of this section. In implementing this paragraph, the United States Government shall withdraw any such consent which is in effect at the time the Secretary of State makes the determination described in subsection (d) of this section, except that this sentence does not apply with respect to any item that has already been transferred to such country.

(4) Providing any license or other approval under section 2778 of this title for any export or other transfer (including by means of a technical assistance agreement, manufacturing licensing agreement, or coproduction agreement) of any munitions item to a country described in subsection (d) of this section. In implement-

ing this paragraph, the United States Government shall suspend any such license or other approval which is in effect at the time the Secretary of State makes the determination described in subsection (d) of this section, except that this sentence does not apply with respect to any item that has already been exported or otherwise transferred to such country.

(5) Otherwise facilitating the acquisition of any munitions item by a country described in subsection (d) of this section. This paragraph applies with respect to activities undertaken—

(A) by any department, agency, or other instrumentality of the Government,

(B) by any officer or employee of the Government (including members of the United States Armed Forces), or

(C) by any other person at the request or on behalf of the Government.

The Secretary of State may waive the requirements of the second sentence of paragraph (1), the second sentence of paragraph (3), and the second sentence of paragraph (4) to the extent that the Secretary determines, after consultation with the Congress, that unusual and compelling circumstances require that the United States Government not take the actions specified in that sentence.

(b) Prohibited transactions by United States persons

(1) In general—

A United States person may not take any of the following actions:

(A) Exporting any munitions item to any country described in subsection (d) of this section.

(B) Selling, leasing, loaning, granting, or otherwise providing any munitions item to any country described in subsection (d) of this section.

(C) Selling, leasing, loaning, granting, or otherwise providing any munitions item to any recipient which is not the government of or a person in a country described in subsection (d) of this section if the United States person has reason to know that the munitions item will be made available to any country described in subsection (d) of this section.

(D) Taking any other action which would facilitate the acquisition, directly or indirectly, of any munitions item by the government of any country described in subsection (d) of this section, or any person acting on behalf of that government, if the United States person has reason to know that that action will facilitate the acquisition of that item by such a government or person.

(2) Liability for actions of foreign subsidiaries, etc.

A United States person violates this subsection if a corporation or other person that is controlled in fact by that United States person (as determined under regulations, which the President shall issue) takes an action described in paragraph (1) outside the United States.

(3) Applicability to actions outside the United States

Paragraph (1) applies with respect to actions described in that paragraph which are taken either within or outside the United States by a United States person described in subsection (l)(3)(A) or (B) of this section. To the extent provided in regulations issued under subsection (l)(3)(D) of this section, paragraph (1) applies with respect to actions described in that paragraph which are taken outside the United States by a person designated as a United States person in those regulations.

(c) Transfers to governments and persons covered

This section applies with respect to—

(1) the acquisition of munitions items by the government of a country described in subsection (d) of this section; and

(2) the acquisition of munitions items by any individual, group, or other person within a country described in subsection (d) of this section, except to the extent that subparagraph (D) of subsection (b)(1) of this section provides otherwise.

(d) Countries covered by prohibition

The prohibitions contained in this section apply with respect to a country if the Secretary of State determines that the government of that country has repeatedly provided support for acts of international terrorism. For purposes of this subsection, such acts shall include all activities that the Secretary determines willfully aid or abet the international proliferation of nuclear explosive devices to individuals or groups, willfully aid or abet an individual or groups in acquiring unsafeguarded special nuclear material, or willfully aid or abet the efforts of an individual or group to use, develop, produce, stockpile, or otherwise acquire chemical, biological, or radiological weapons.

....

(g) Waiver

The President may waive the prohibitions contained in this section with respect to a specific transaction if—

(1) the President determines that the transaction is essential to the national security interests of the United States; and

(2) not less than 15 days prior to the proposed transaction, the President—

(A) consults with the Committee on Foreign Affairs of the House of Representatives and the Committee on Foreign Relations of the Senate; and

(B) submits to the Speaker of the House of Representatives and the chairman of the Committee on Foreign Relations of the Senate a report containing—

(i) the name of any country involved in the proposed transaction, the identity of any recipient of the items to be provided pursuant to the proposed transaction, and the anticipated use of those items;

(ii) a description of the munitions items involved in the proposed transaction (including their market value) and the actual sale price at each step in the transaction (or if the items are transferred by other than sale, the manner in which they will be provided);

(iii) the reasons why the proposed transaction is essential to the national security interests of the United States and the justification for such proposed transaction;

(iv) the date on which the proposed transaction is expected to occur; and

(v) the name of every United States Government department, agency, or other entity involved in the proposed transaction, every foreign government involved in the proposed transaction, and every private party with significant participation in the proposed transaction.

To the extent possible, the information specified in subparagraph (B) of paragraph (2) shall be provided in unclassified form, with any classified information provided in an addendum to the report.

....

(j) Criminal penalty

Any person who willfully violates this section shall be fined for each violation not more than $1,000,000, imprisoned not more than 10 years, or both.

(k) Civil penalties; enforcement

In the enforcement of this section, the President is authorized to exercise the same powers concerning violations and enforcement which are conferred upon departments, agencies, and officials by sections 11(c), 11(e), 11(g), and 12(a) of the Export Administration Act of 1979....and further may commence a civil action to recover such civil penalties, and except further that, notwithstanding section 11(c) of that Act, the civil penalty for each violation of this section may not exceed $500,000.

(l) Definitions

As used in this section—

(1) the term "munitions item" means any item enumerated on the United States Munitions list (without regard to whether the item is imported into or exported from the United States);

(2) the term "United States", when used geographically, means the several States, the District of Columbia, the Commonwealth of Puerto Rico, the Commonwealth of the Northern Mariana Islands, and any territory or possession of the United States;

(3) the term "United States person" means—

(A) any citizen or permanent resident alien of the United States;

(B) any sole proprietorship, partnership, company, association, or corporation having its principal place of business within the United States or organized under the laws of the United States, any State, the District of Columbia, the Commonwealth of Puerto Rico, the Commonwealth of the Northern Mariana Islands, or any territory or possession of the United States;

(C) any other person with respect to that person's actions while in the United States; and

(D) to the extent provided in regulations issued by the Secretary of State, any person that is not described in subparagraph (A), (B), or (C) but—

(i) is a foreign subsidiary or affiliate of a United States person described in subparagraph (B) and is controlled in fact by that United States person (as determined in accordance with those regulations), or

(ii) is otherwise subject to the jurisdiction of the United States, with respect to that person's actions while outside the United States;

(4) the term "nuclear explosive device" has the meaning given that term in section 6305(4) of this title; and

(5) the term "unsafeguarded special nuclear material" has the meaning given that term in section 6305(8) of this title.

§2781. Transactions with countries not fully cooperating with United States antiterrorism efforts

(a) Prohibited transactions

No defense article or defense service may be sold or licensed for export under this chapter in a fiscal year to a foreign country that the President determines and certifies to Congress, by May 15 of the calendar year in which that fiscal year begins, is not cooperating fully with United States antiterrorism efforts.

(b) Waiver

The President may waive the prohibition set forth in subsection (a) of this section with respect to a specific transaction if the President determines that the transaction is important to the national interests of the United States.

SUBCHAPTER III-A—END USE MONITORING OF DEFENSE ARTICLES AND DEFENSE SERVICES

§2785. End-use monitoring of defense articles and defense services

(a) Establishment of monitoring program

(1) In general

In order to improve accountability with respect to defense articles and defense services sold, leased, or exported under this chapter or the Foreign Assistance Act of 1961 (22 U.S.C. 2151 et seq.), the President shall establish a program which provides for the end-use monitoring of such articles and services.

....

SUBCHAPTER VII—CONTROL OF MISSILES AND MISSILE EQUIPMENT OR TECHNOLOGY

§2797. Licensing

(a) Establishment of list of controlled items

The Secretary of State, in consultation with the Secretary of Defense and the heads of other appropriate departments and agencies, shall establish and maintain, as part of the United States Munitions List, a list of all items on the MTCR Annex the export of which is not controlled under section 2405 (l) of title 50, Appendix.

(b) Referral of license applications

(1) A determination of the Secretary of State to approve a license for the export of an item on the list established under subsection (a) of this section may be made only after the license application is referred to the Secretary of Defense.

(2) Within 10 days after a license is issued for the export of an item on the list established under subsection (a) of this section, the Secretary of State shall provide to the Secretary of Defense and the Secretary of Commerce the license application and accompanying documents issued to the applicant, to the extent that the relevant Secretary indicates the need to receive such application and documents.

(c) Information sharing

The Secretary of State shall establish a procedure for sharing information with appropriate officials of the intelligence community, as determined by the Director of Central Intelligence, and with other appropriate Government agencies, that will ensure effective monitoring of transfers of MTCR equipment or technology and other missile technology.

....

§ 2797a. Denial of transfer of missile equipment or technology by United States persons

(a) Sanctions

(1) If the President determines that a United States person knowingly—

(A) exports, transfers, or otherwise engages in the trade of any item on the MTCR Annex, in violation of the provisions of section 2778 of this title, section 2404 or 2405 of title 50, Appendix, or any regulations or orders issued under any such provisions,

(B) conspires to or attempts to engage in such export, transfer, or trade, or

(C) facilitates such export, transfer, or trade by any other person,

then the President shall impose the applicable sanctions described in paragraph (2).

(2) The sanctions which apply to a United States person under paragraph (1) are the following:

(A) If the item on the MTCR Annex involved in the export, transfer, or trade is missile equipment or technology within category II of the MTCR Annex, then the President shall deny to such United States person for a period of 2 years—

(i) United States Government contracts relating to missile equipment or technology; and

(ii) licenses for the transfer of missile equipment or technology controlled under this chapter.

(B) If the item on the MTCR Annex involved in the export, transfer, or trade is missile equipment or technology within category I of the MTCR, then the President shall deny to such United States person for a period of not less than 2 years—

(i) all United States Government contracts, and

(ii) all export licenses and agreements for items on the United States Munitions List.

(b) Discretionary sanctions

In the case of any determination made pursuant to subsection (a) of this section, the President may pursue any penalty provided in section 2778(c) of this title.

(c) Presumption

In determining whether to apply sanctions under subsection (a) of this section to a United States person involved in the export, transfer, or trade of an item on the MTCR Annex, it should be a rebuttable presumption that such item is designed for use in a missile listed in the MTCR Annex if the President determines that the final destination of the item is a country the government of which the Secretary of State has determined, for purposes of 2405(j)(1)(A) of title 50, Appendix, has repeatedly provided support for acts of international terrorism.

(d) Waiver

The President may waive the imposition of sanctions under subsection (a) of this section with respect to a product or service if the President certifies to the Congress that—

(1) the product or service is essential to the national security of the United States; and

(2) such person is a sole source supplier of the product or service, the product or service is not available from any alternative reliable supplier, and the need for the product or service cannot be met in a timely manner by improved manufacturing processes or technological developments.

§ 2797b. Transfers of missile equipment or technology by foreign persons

(a) Sanctions

(1) Subject to subsections (c) through (g) of this section, if the President determines that a foreign person, after November 5, 1990, knowingly—

(A) exports, transfers, or otherwise engages in the trade of any MTCR equipment or technology that contributes to the acquisition, design, development, or production of missiles in a country that is not an MTCR adherent and would be, if it were United States-origin equipment or technology, subject to the jurisdiction of the United States under this chapter,

(B) conspires to or attempts to engage in such export, transfer, or trade, or

(C) facilitates such export, transfer, or trade by any other person,

or if the President has made a determination with respect to a foreign person under section 2410b (b)(1) of title 50, Appendix, then the President shall impose on that foreign person the applicable sanctions under paragraph (2).

(2) The sanctions which apply to a foreign person under paragraph (1) are the following:

(A) If the item involved in the export, transfer, or trade is within category II of the MTCR Annex, then the President shall deny, for a period of 2 years—

(i) United States Government contracts relating to missile equipment or technology; and

(ii) licenses for the transfer to such foreign person of missile equipment or technology controlled under this chapter.

(B) If the item involved in the export, transfer, or trade is within category I of the MTCR Annex, then the President shall deny, for a period of not less than 2 years—

(i) all United States Government contracts with such foreign person; and

(ii) licenses for the transfer to such foreign person of all items on the United States Munitions List.

(C) If, in addition to actions taken under subparagraphs (A) and (B), the President determines that the export, transfer, or trade has substantially contributed to the design, development, or production of missiles in a country that is not an MTCR adherent, then the President shall prohibit, for a period of not less than 2 years, the importation into the United States of products produced by that foreign person.

(b) Inapplicability with respect to MTCR adherents

(1) **In general**

Except as provided in paragraph (2), subsection (a) of this section does not apply with respect to—

(A) any export, transfer, or trading activity that is authorized by the laws of an MTCR adherent, if such authorization is not obtained by misrepresentation or fraud; or

(B) any export, transfer, or trade of an item to an end user in a country that is an MTCR adherent.

....

(d) Advisory opinions

The Secretary of State, in consultation with the Secretary of Defense and the Secretary of Commerce, may, upon the request of any person, issue an advisory opinion to that person as to whether a proposed activity by that person would subject that person to sanctions under this section. Any person who relies in good faith on such an advisory opinion which states that the proposed activity would not subject a person to such sanctions, and any person who thereafter engages in such activity, may not be made subject to such sanctions on account of such activity.

(e) Waiver and report to Congress

(1) In any case other than one in which an advisory opinion has been issued under subsection (d) of this section stating that a proposed activity would not subject a person to sanctions under this section, the President may waive the application of subsection (a) of this section to a foreign person if the President determines that such waiver is essential to the national security of the United States.

(2) In the event that the President decides to apply the waiver described in paragraph (1), the President shall so notify the Committee on Armed Services and the Committee on Foreign Relations of the Senate and the Committee on National Security and the Committee on International Relations of the House of Representatives not less than 45 working days before issuing the waiver. Such notification shall include a report fully articulating the rationale and circumstances which led the President to apply the waiver.

....

(h) Exceptions

The President shall not apply the sanction under this section prohibiting the importation of the products of a foreign person—

(1) in the case of procurement of defense articles or defense services—

(A) under existing contracts or subcontracts, including the exercise of options for production quantities to satisfy requirements essential to the national security of the United States;

(B) if the President determines that the person to which the sanctions would be applied is a sole source supplier of the defense articles and services, that the defense articles or services are essential to the national security of the United States, and that alternative sources are not readily or reasonably available; or

(C) if the President determines that such articles or services are essential to the national security of the United States under defense coproduction agreements or NATO Programs of Cooperation;

(2) to products or services provided under contracts entered into before the date on which the President publishes his intention to impose the sanctions; or

(3) to—

(A) spare parts,

(B) component parts, but not finished products, essential to United States products or production,

(C) routine services and maintenance of products, to the extent that alternative sources are not readily or reasonably available, or

(D) information and technology essential to United States products or production.

....

§ 2797c. Definitions

(a) In general

For purposes of this subchapter—

(1) the term "missile" means a category I system as defined in the MTCR Annex, and any other unmanned delivery system of similar capability, as well as the specially designed production facilities for these systems;

(2) the term "Missile Technology Control Regime" or "MTCR" means the policy statement, between the United States, the United Kingdom, the Federal Republic of Germany, France, Italy, Canada, and Japan, announced on April 16, 1987, to restrict sensitive missile-relevant transfers based on the MTCR Annex, and any amendments thereto;

(3) the term "MTCR adherent" means a country that participates in the MTCR or that, pursuant to an international understanding to which the United States is a party, controls MTCR equipment or technology in accordance with the criteria and standards set forth in the MTCR;

(4) the term "MTCR Annex" means the Guidelines and Equipment and Technology Annex of the MTCR, and any amendments thereto;

(5) the terms "missile equipment or technology" and "MTCR equipment or technology" mean those items listed in category I or category II of the MTCR Annex;

(6) the term "United States person" has the meaning given that term in section 2415 (2) of title 50, Appendix;

(7) the term "foreign person" means any person other than a United States person;

(8) (A) the term "person" means a natural person as well as a corporation, business association, partnership, society, trust, any other nongovernmental entity, organization, or group, and any governmental entity operating as a business enterprise, and any successor of any such entity; and

(B) in the case of countries with non-market economies (excluding former members of the Warsaw Pact), the term "person" means—

(i) all activities of that government relating to the development or production of any missile equipment or technology; and

(ii) all activities of that government affecting the development or production of electronics, space systems or equipment, and military aircraft; and

(9) the term "otherwise engaged in the trade of" means, with respect to a particular export or transfer, to be a freight forwarder or designated exporting agent, or a consignee or end user of the item to be exported or transferred.

(b) International understanding defined

For purposes of subsection (a)(3) of this section, as it relates to any international understanding concluded with the United States after January 1, 2000, the term "international understanding" means—

(1) any specific agreement by a country not to export, transfer, or otherwise engage in the trade of any MTCR equipment or technology that contributes to the acquisition, design, development, or production of missiles in a country that is not an MTCR adherent and would be, if it were United States-origin equipment or technology, subject to the jurisdiction of the United States under this chapter; or

....

SUBCHAPTER VIII—CHEMICAL OR BIOLOGICAL WEAPONS PROLIFERATION

§ 2798. Sanctions against certain foreign persons

(a) Imposition of sanctions

(1) Determination by the President

Except as provided in subsection (b)(2) of this section, the President shall impose both of the sanctions described in subsection (c) of this section if the President determines that a foreign person, on or after October 28, 1991, has knowingly and materially contributed—

(A) through the export from the United States of any goods or technology that are subject to the jurisdiction of the United States,

(B) through the export from any other country of any goods or technology that would be, if they were United States goods or technology, subject to the jurisdiction of the United States, or

(C) through any other transaction not subject to sanctions pursuant to the Export Administration Act of 1979 [50 App. U.S.C. 2401 et seq.],

to the efforts by any foreign country, project, or entity described in paragraph (2) to use, develop, produce, stockpile, or otherwise acquire chemical or biological weapons.

(2) Countries, projects, or entities receiving assistance

Paragraph (1) applies in the case of—

(A) any foreign country that the President determines has, at any time after January 1, 1980—

(i) used chemical or biological weapons in violation of international law;

(ii) used lethal chemical or biological weapons against its own nationals; or

(iii) made substantial preparations to engage in the activities described in clause (i) or (ii);

(B) any foreign country whose government is determined for purposes of section 6(j) of the Export Administration Act of 1979 [50 App. U.S.C. 2405 (j)] to be a government that has repeatedly provided support for acts of international terrorism; or

(C) any other foreign country, project, or entity designated by the President for purposes of this section.

(3) **Persons against whom sanctions are to be imposed**

Sanctions shall be imposed pursuant to paragraph (1) on—

(A) the foreign person with respect to which the President makes the determination described in that paragraph;

(B) any successor entity to that foreign person;

(C) any foreign person that is a parent or subsidiary of that foreign person if that parent or subsidiary knowingly assisted in the activities which were the basis of that determination; and

(D) any foreign person that is an affiliate of that foreign person if that affiliate knowingly assisted in the activities which were the basis of that determination and if that affiliate is controlled in fact by that foreign person.

....

(c) **Sanctions**

(1) **Description of sanctions**

The sanctions to be imposed pursuant to subsection (a)(1) of this section are, except as provided in paragraph (2) of this subsection, the following:

(A) **Procurement sanction**

The United States Government shall not procure, or enter into any contract for the procurement of, any goods or services from any person described in subsection (a)(3) of this section.

(B) **Import sanctions**

The importation into the United States of products produced by any person described in subsection (a)(3) of this section shall be prohibited.

(2) **Exceptions**

The President shall not be required to apply or maintain sanctions under this section—

(A) in the case of procurement of defense articles or defense services—

(i) under existing contracts or subcontracts, including the exercise of options for production quantities to satisfy United States operational military requirements;

(ii) if the President determines that the person or other entity to which the sanctions would otherwise be applied is a sole source supplier of the defense articles or services, that the defense articles or services are essential, and that alternative sources are not readily or reasonably available; or

(iii) if the President determines that such articles or services are essential to the national security under defense coproduction agreements;

(B) to products or services provided under contracts entered into before the date on which the President publishes his intention to impose sanctions;

(C) to—

(i) spare parts,

(ii) component parts, but not finished products, essential to United States products or production, or

(iii) routine servicing and maintenance of products, to the extent that alternative sources are not readily or reasonably available;

(D) to information and technology essential to United States products or production; or

(E) to medical or other humanitarian items.

(d) Termination of sanctions

The sanctions imposed pursuant to this section shall apply for a period of at least 12 months following the imposition of sanctions and shall cease to apply thereafter only if the President determines and certifies to the Congress that reliable information indicates that the foreign person with respect to which the determination was made under subsection (a)(1) of this section has ceased to aid or abet any foreign government, project, or entity in its efforts to acquire chemical or biological weapons capability as described in that subsection.

(e) Waiver

(1) Criterion for waiver

The President may waive the application of any sanction imposed on any person pursuant to this section, after the end of the 12-month period beginning on the date on which that sanction was imposed on that person, if the President determines and certifies to the Congress that such waiver is important to the national security interests of the United States.

(2) Notification of and report to Congress

If the President decides to exercise the waiver authority provided in paragraph (1), the President shall so notify the Congress not less than 20 days before the waiver takes effect. Such notification shall include a report fully articulating the rationale and circumstances which led the President to exercise the waiver authority.

(f) "Foreign person" defined

For the purposes of this section, the term "foreign person" means—

(1) an individual who is not a citizen of the United States or an alien admitted for permanent residence to the United States; or

(2) a corporation, partnership, or other entity which is created or organized under the laws of a foreign country or which has its principal place of business outside the United States.

. . . .

SUBCHAPTER X—NUCLEAR NONPROLIFERATION CONTROLS

§ 2799aa. Nuclear enrichment transfers

(a) Prohibitions; safeguards and management

Except as provided in subsection (b) of this section, no funds made available to carry out the Foreign Assistance Act of 1961 [22 U.S.C. 2151 et seq.] or this chapter may be used for the purpose of providing economic assistance (including assistance under chapter 4 of part II of the Foreign Assistance Act of 1961, providing military assistance or grant military education and training, providing assistance under chapter 6 of part II of that Act or extending military credits or making guarantees, to any country which the President determines delivers nuclear enrichment equipment, materials, or technology to any other country on or after August 4, 1977, or receives such equipment, materials, or technology from any other country on or after August 4, 1977, unless before such delivery—

(1) the supplying country and receiving country have reached agreement to place all such equipment, materials, or technology, upon delivery, under multilateral auspices and management when available; and

(2) the recipient country has entered into an agreement with the International Atomic Energy Agency to place all such equipment, materials, technology, and all nuclear fuel and facilities in such country under the safeguards system of such Agency.

(b) Certification by President of necessity of continued assistance; disapproval by Congress

(1) Notwithstanding subsection (a) of this section, the President may furnish assistance which would otherwise be prohibited under such subsection if he determines and certifies in writing to the Speaker of the House of Representatives and the Committee on Foreign Relations of the Senate that—

(A) the termination of such assistance would have a serious adverse effect on vital United States interests; and

(B) he has received reliable assurances that the country in question will not acquire or develop nuclear weapons or assist other nations in doing so.

Such certification shall set forth the reasons supporting such determination in each particular case.

....

§ 2799aa-1. Nuclear reprocessing transfers, illegal exports for nuclear explosive devices, transfers of nuclear explosive devices, and nuclear detonation

(a) Prohibitions on assistance to countries involved in transfer of nuclear reprocessing equipment, materials, or technology; exceptions; procedures applicable

(1) Except as provided in paragraph (2) of this subsection, no funds made available to carry out the Foreign Assistance Act of 1961 or this chapter may be used for the purpose of providing economic assistance.... providing military assistance or grant military education and training... to any country which the President determines—

(A) delivers nuclear reprocessing equipment, materials, or technology to any other country on or after August 4, 1977, or receives such equipment, materials, or technology from any other country on or after August 4, 1977 (except for the transfer of reprocessing technology associated with the investigation, under international evaluation programs in which the United States participates, of technologies which are alternatives to pure plutonium reprocessing), or

(B) is a non-nuclear-weapon state which, on or after August 8, 1985, exports illegally (or attempts to export illegally) from the United States any material, equipment, or technology which would contribute significantly to the ability of such country to manufacture a nuclear explosive device, if the President determines that the material, equipment, or technology was to be used by such country in the manufacture of a nuclear explosive device.

For purposes of clause (B), an export (or attempted export) by a person who is an agent of, or is otherwise acting on behalf of or in the interests of, a country shall be considered to be an export (or attempted export) by that country.

(2) Notwithstanding paragraph (1) of this subsection, the President in any fiscal year may furnish assistance which would otherwise be prohibited under that paragraph if he determines and certifies in writing during that fiscal year to the Speaker of the House of Representatives and the Committee on Foreign Relations of the Senate that the termination of such assistance would be seriously prejudicial to the achievement of United States nonproliferation objectives or otherwise jeopardize the common defense and security. The President shall transmit with such certification a statement setting forth the specific reasons therefor.

....

(b) Prohibitions on assistance to countries involved in transfer or use of nuclear explosive devices; exceptions; procedures applicable

(1) Except as provided in paragraphs (4), (5), and (6), in the event that the President determines that any country, after the effective date of part B of the Nuclear Proliferation Prevention Act of 1994—

(A) transfers to a non-nuclear-weapon state a nuclear explosive device,

(B) is a non-nuclear-weapon state and either—

(i) receives a nuclear explosive device, or

(ii) detonates a nuclear explosive device,

(C) transfers to a non-nuclear-weapon state any design information or component which is determined by the President to be important to, and known by the transferring country to be intended by the recipient state for use in, the development or manufacture of any nuclear explosive device, or

(D) is a non-nuclear-weapon state and seeks and receives any design information or component which is determined by the President to be important to, and intended by the recipient state for use in, the development or manufacture of any nuclear explosive device,

then the President shall forthwith report in writing his determination to the Congress and shall forthwith impose the sanctions described in paragraph (2) against that country.

(2) The sanctions referred to in paragraph (1) are as follows:

(A) The United States Government shall terminate assistance to that country under the Foreign Assistance Act of 1961 [22 U.S.C. 2151 et seq.], except for humanitarian assistance or food or other agricultural commodities.

(B) The United States Government shall terminate—

(i) sales to that country under this chapter of any defense articles, defense services, or design and construction services, and

(ii) licenses for the export to that country of any item on the United States Munitions List.

(C) The United States Government shall terminate all foreign military financing for that country under this chapter.

(D) The United States Government shall deny to that country any credit, credit guarantees, or other financial assistance by any department, agency, or instrumentality of the United States Government, except that the sanction of this subparagraph shall not apply—

(i) to any transaction subject to the reporting requirements of title V of the National Security Act of 1947 [50 U.S.C. 413 et seq.] (relating to congressional oversight of intelligence activities),

(ii) to medicines, medical equipment, and humanitarian assistance, or

(iii) to any credit, credit guarantee, or financial assistance provided by the Department of Agriculture to support the purchase of food or other agricultural commodity.

(E) The United States Government shall oppose, in accordance with section 262d of this title, the extension of any loan or financial or technical assistance to that country by any international financial institution.

(F) The United States Government shall prohibit any United States bank from making any loan or providing any credit to the government of that country, except for loans or credits for the purpose of purchasing food or other agricultural commodities, which includes fertilizer.

(G) The authorities of section 2405 of title, Appendix, shall be used to prohibit exports to that country of specific goods and technology (excluding food and other agricultural commodities), except that such prohibition shall not apply to any transaction subject to the reporting requirements of title V of the National Security Act of 1947 (relating to congressional oversight of intelligence activities).

(3) As used in this subsection—

(A) the term "design information" means specific information that relates to the design of a nuclear explosive device and that is not available to the public; and

(B) the term "component" means a specific component of a nuclear explosive device.

....

I. Immigration and Refugees

IMMIGRATION AND NATIONALITY ACT*

§ 1101. Definitions

....

(13) (A) The terms "admission" and "admitted" mean, with respect to an alien, the lawful entry of the alien into the United States after inspection and authorization by an immigration officer.

....

(42) The term "refugee" means (A) any person who is outside any country of such person's nationality or, in the case of a person having no nationality, is outside any country in which such person last habitually resided, and who is unable or unwilling to return to, and is unable or unwilling to avail himself or herself of the protection of, that country because of persecution or a well-founded fear of persecution on account of race, religion, nationality, membership in a particular social group, or political opinion, or (B) in such special circumstances as the President after appropriate consultation (as defined in section 1157(e) of this title) may specify, any person who is within the country of such person's nationality or, in the case of a person having no nationality, within the country in which such person is habitually residing, and who is persecuted or who has a well-founded fear of persecution on account of race, religion, nationality, membership in a particular social group, or political opinion. The term "refugee" does not include any person who ordered, incited, assisted, or otherwise participated in the persecution of any person on account of race, religion, nationality, membership in a particular social group, or political opinion. For purposes of determinations under this chapter, a person who has been forced to abort a pregnancy or to undergo involuntary sterilization, or who has been persecuted for failure or refusal to undergo such a procedure or for other resistance to a coercive population control program, shall be deemed to have been persecuted on account of political opinion, and a person who has a well founded fear that he or she will be forced to undergo such a procedure or subject to persecution for such failure, refusal, or resistance shall be deemed to have a well founded fear of persecution on account of political opinion.

....

§ 1157. Annual admission of refugees and admission of emergency situation refugees

(a) Maximum number of admissions; increases for humanitarian concerns; allocations

(1) Except as provided in subsection (b) of this section, the number of refugees who may be admitted under this section in fiscal year 1980, 1981, or 1982, may not exceed fifty thousand unless the President determines, before the beginning of the fiscal year and after appropriate consultation (as defined in subsection (e) of this section), that admission of a specific number of refugees in excess of such number is justified by humanitarian concerns or is otherwise in the national interest.

---

* Immigration and Nationality Act, 8 U.S.C.A. §§ 1101, 1157–1159, 1182 (West 1999 & Supp. 2005), *available at* http://uscis.gov/lpBin/lpext.dll/inserts/slb/slb-1/slb-22?f=templates&fn=document-frame.htm#slb-act.

(2) Except as provided in subsection (b) of this section, the number of refugees who may be admitted under this section in any fiscal year after fiscal year 1982 shall be such number as the President determines, before the beginning of the fiscal year and after appropriate consultation, is justified by humanitarian concerns or is otherwise in the national interest.

(3) Admissions under this subsection shall be allocated among refugees of special humanitarian concern to the United States in accordance with a determination made by the President after appropriate consultation.

(4) In the determination made under this subsection for each fiscal year (beginning with fiscal year 1992), the President shall enumerate, with the respective number of refugees so determined, the number of aliens who were granted asylum in the previous year.

....

(b) Determinations by President respecting number of admissions for humanitarian concerns.

If the President determines, after appropriate consultation, that (1) an unforeseen emergency refugee situation exists, (2) the admission of certain refugees in response to the emergency refugee situation is justified by grave humanitarian concerns or is otherwise in the national interest, and (3) the admission to the United States of these refugees cannot be accomplished under subsection (a) of this section, the President may fix a number of refugees to be admitted to the United States during the succeeding period (not to exceed twelve months) in response to the emergency refugee situation and such admissions shall be allocated among refugees of special humanitarian concern to the United States in accordance with a determination made by the President after the appropriate consultation provided under this subsection.

(c) Admission by Attorney General of refugees; criteria; admission status of spouse or child; applicability of other statutory requirements; termination of refugee status of alien, spouse or child.

(1) Subject to the numerical limitations established pursuant to subsections (a) and (b) of this section, the Attorney General may, in the Attorney General's discretion and pursuant to such regulations as the Attorney General may prescribe, admit any refugee who is not firmly resettled in any foreign country, is determined to be of special humanitarian concern to the United States, and is admissible (except as otherwise provided under paragraph (3)) as an immigrant under this chapter.

(2) (A) A spouse or child (as defined in section 1101(b)(1)(A), (B), (C), (D), or (E) of this title) of any refugee who qualifies for admission under paragraph (1) shall, if not otherwise entitled to admission under paragraph (1) and if not a person described in the second sentence of section 1101(a)(42) of this title, be entitled to the same admission status as such refugee if accompanying, or following to join, such refugee and if the spouse or child is admissible (except as otherwise provided under paragraph (3)) as an immigrant under this chapter. Upon the spouse's or child's admission to the United States, such admission shall be charged against the numerical limitation established in accordance with the appropriate subsection under which the refugee's admission is charged.

(B) An unmarried alien who seeks to accompany, or follow to join, a parent granted admission as a refugee under this subsection, and who was under 21 years of age on the date on which such parent applied for refugee status under this section, shall continue to be classified as a child for purposes of this paragraph, if the alien attained 21 years of age after such application was filed but while it was pending.

(3) The provisions of paragraphs (4), (5), and (7)(A) of section 1182(a) of this title shall not be applicable to any alien seeking admission to the United States under this subsection, and the Attorney General may waive any other provision of such section (other than paragraph (2)(C) or subparagraph (A), (B), (C), or (E) of paragraph (3)) with respect to such an alien for humanitarian purposes, to assure family unity, or when it is otherwise in the public interest. Any such waiver by the Attorney General shall be in writing and shall be granted only on an individual basis following an investigation. The Attorney General shall provide for the annual reporting to Congress of the number of waivers granted under this paragraph in the previous fiscal year and a summary of the reasons for granting such waivers.

(4) The refugee status of any alien (and of the spouse or child of the alien) may be terminated by the Attorney General pursuant to such regulations as the Attorney General may prescribe if the Attorney General determines that the alien was not in fact a refugee within the meaning of section 1101(a)(42) of this title at the time of the alien's admission.

(d) Oversight reporting and consultation requirements.

(1) Before the start of each fiscal year the President shall report to the Committees on the Judiciary of the House of Representatives and of the Senate regarding the foreseeable number of refugees who will be in need of resettlement during the fiscal year and the anticipated allocation of refugee admissions during the fiscal year. The President shall provide for periodic discussions between designated representatives of the President and members of such committees regarding changes in the worldwide refugee situation, the progress of refugee admissions, and the possible need for adjustments in the allocation of admissions among refugees.

(2) As soon as possible after representatives of the President initiate appropriate consultation with respect to the number of refugee admissions under subsection (a) of this section or with respect to the admission of refugees in response to an emergency refugee situation under subsection (b) of this section, the Committees on the Judiciary of the House of Representatives and of the Senate shall cause to have printed in the Congressional Record the substance of such consultation.

(3) (A) After the President initiates appropriate consultation prior to making a determination under subsection (a) of this section, a hearing to review the proposed determination shall be held unless public disclosure of the details of the proposal would jeopardize the lives or safety of individuals.

(B) After the President initiates appropriate consultation prior to making a determination, under subsection (b) of this section, that the number of refugee admissions should be increased because of an unforeseen emergency refugee situation, to the extent that time and the nature of the emergency refugee situation permit, a hearing to review the proposal to increase refugee admissions shall be held unless public disclosure of the details of the proposal would jeopardize the lives or safety of individuals.

(e) "Appropriate consultation" defined.

For purposes of this section, the term "appropriate consultation" means, with respect to the admission of refugees and allocation of refugee admissions, discussions in person by designated Cabinet-level representatives of the President with members of the Committees on the Judiciary of the Senate and of the House of Representatives to review the refugee situation or emergency refugee situation, to project the extent of possible participation of the United States therein, to discuss the reasons for believing that the proposed admission of refugees is justified by humanitarian concerns or grave humanitarian concerns or is otherwise in the national interest, and to provide such members with the following information:

(1) A description of the nature of the refugee situation.

(2) A description of the number and allocation of the refugees to be admitted and an analysis of conditions within the countries from which they came.

(3) A description of the proposed plans for their movement and resettlement and the estimated cost of their movement and resettlement.

(4) An analysis of the anticipated social, economic, and demographic impact of their admission to the United States.

(5) A description of the extent to which other countries will admit and assist in the resettlement of such refugees.

(6) An analysis of the impact of the participation of the United States in the resettlement of such refugees on the foreign policy interests of the United States.

(7) Such additional information as may be appropriate or requested by such members.

To the extent possible, information described in this subsection shall be provided at least two weeks in advance of discussions in person by designated representatives of the President with such members.

. . . .

§ 1158. Asylum

(a) Authority to apply for asylum

(1) In general

Any alien who is physically present in the United States or who arrives in the United States (whether or not at a designated port of arrival and including an alien who is brought to the United States after having been interdicted in international or United States waters), irrespective of such alien's status, may apply for asylum in accordance with this section or, where applicable, section 1225(b) of this title.

. . . .

(3) Treatment of spouse and children.

(A) In general

A spouse or child (as defined in section 1101(b)(1) (A), (B), (C), (D), or (E) of this title) of an alien who is granted asylum under this subsection may, if not otherwise eligible for asylum under this section, be granted the same status as the alien if accompanying, or following to join, such alien.

. . . .

(2) Termination of asylum.

Asylum granted under subsection (b) of this section does not convey a right to remain permanently in the United States, and may be terminated if the Attorney General determines that—

(A) the alien no longer meets the conditions described in subsection (b)(1) of this section owing to a fundamental change in circumstances;

(B) the alien meets a condition described in subsection (b)(2) of this section;

(C) the alien may be removed, pursuant to a bilateral or multilateral agreement, to a country (other than the country of the alien's nationality or, in the case of an alien having no nationality, the country of the alien's last habitual residence) in which the alien's life or freedom would not be threatened on account of race, religion, nationality, membership in a particular social group, or political opinion, and where the alien is eligible to receive asylum or equivalent temporary protection;

. . . .

(d) Asylum procedure.

(1) Applications.

The Attorney General shall establish a procedure for the consideration of asylum applications filed under subsection (a) of this section. The Attorney General may require applicants to submit fingerprints and a photograph at such time and in such manner to be determined by regulation by the Attorney General.

. . . .

§ 1159. Adjustment of status of refugees

(a) Criteria and procedures applicable for admission as immigrant; effect of adjustment

(1) Any alien who has been admitted to the United States under section 1157 of this title—

(A) whose admission has not been terminated by the Secretary of Homeland Security or the Attorney General pursuant to such regulations as the Secretary of Homeland Security or the Attorney General may prescribe,

(B) who has been physically present in the United States for at least one year, and

(C) who has not acquired permanent resident status,

shall, at the end of such year period, return or be returned to the custody of the Department of Homeland Security for inspection and examination for admission to the United States as an immigrant in accordance with the provisions of sections 1225, 1229a, and 1231 of this title.

(2) Any alien who is found upon inspection and examination by an immigration officer pursuant to paragraph (1) or after a hearing before an immigration judge to be admissible (except as otherwise provided under subsection (c) of this section) as an immigrant under this chapter at the time of the alien's inspection and examination shall, notwithstanding any numerical limitation specified in this chap-

ter, be regarded as lawfully admitted to the United States for permanent residence as of the date of such alien's arrival into the United States.

(b) Maximum number of adjustments; recordkeeping.

The Secretary of Homeland Security or the Attorney General, in the Secretary's or the Attorney General's discretion and under such regulations as the Secretary or the Attorney General may prescribe, may adjust to the status of an alien lawfully admitted for permanent residence the status of any alien granted asylum who—

(1) applies for such adjustment,

(2) has been physically present in the United States for at least one year after being granted asylum,

(3) continues to be a refugee within the meaning of section 1101(a)(42)(A) of this title or a spouse or child of such a refugee,

(4) is not firmly resettled in any foreign country, and

(5) is admissible (except as otherwise provided under subsection (c) of this section) as an immigrant under this chapter at the time of examination for adjustment of such alien.

Upon approval of an application under this subsection, the Secretary of Homeland Security or the Attorney General shall establish a record of the alien's admission for lawful permanent residence as of the date one year before the date of the approval of the application.

(c) Applicability of other Federal statutory requirements.

The provisions of paragraphs (4), (5), and (7)(A) of section 1182(a) of this title shall not be applicable to any alien seeking adjustment of status under this section, and the Secretary of Homeland Security or the Attorney General may waive any other provision of such section (other than paragraph (2)(C) or subparagraph (A), (B), (C), or (E) of paragraph (3)) with respect to such an alien for humanitarian purposes, to assure family unity, or when it is otherwise in the public interest.

....

§ 1182. Inadmissible aliens

(a) Classes of aliens ineligible for visas or admission.

Except as otherwise provided in this chapter, aliens who are inadmissible under the following paragraphs are ineligible to receive visas and ineligible to be admitted to the United States:

(1) Health-related grounds.

....

(2) Criminal and related grounds.

(A) Conviction of certain crimes.

(i) In general.

Except as provided in clause (ii), any alien convicted of, or who admits having committed, or who admits committing acts which constitute the essential elements of—

(I) a crime involving moral turpitude (other than a purely political offense) or an attempt or conspiracy to commit such a crime, or

(II) a violation of (or a conspiracy or attempt to violate) any law or regulation of a State, the United States, or a foreign country relating to a controlled substance (as defined in section 802 of Title 21),

is inadmissible.

(ii) Exception.

Clause (i)(I) shall not apply to an alien who committed only one crime if—

(I) the crime was committed when the alien was under 18 years of age, and the crime was committed (and the alien released from any confinement to a prison or correctional institution imposed for the crime) more than 5 years before the date of application for a visa or other documentation and the date of application for admission to the United States, or

(II) the maximum penalty possible for the crime of which the alien was convicted (or which the alien admits having committed or of which the acts that the alien admits having committed constituted the essential elements) did not exceed imprisonment for one year and, if the alien was convicted of such crime, the alien was not sentenced to a term of imprisonment in excess of 6 months (regardless of the extent to which the sentence was ultimately executed).

(B) Multiple criminal convictions.

Any alien convicted of 2 or more offenses (other than purely political offenses), regardless of whether the conviction was in a single trial or whether the offenses arose from a single scheme of misconduct and regardless of whether the offenses involved moral turpitude, for which the aggregate sentences to confinement were 5 years or more is inadmissible.

(C) Controlled substance traffickers.

Any alien who the consular officer or the Attorney General knows or has reason to believe—

(i) is or has been an illicit trafficker in any controlled substance or in any listed chemical (as defined in section 802 of title 21), or is or has been a knowing aider, abettor, assister, conspirator, or colluder with others in the illicit trafficking in any such controlled or listed substance or chemical, or endeavored to do so; or

(ii) is the spouse, son, or daughter of an alien inadmissible under clause (i), has, within the previous 5 years, obtained any financial or other benefit from the illicit activity of that alien, and knew or reasonably should have known that the financial or other benefit was the product of such illicit activity,

is inadmissible.

....

(H) Significant traffickers in persons.

(i) In general

Any alien who is listed in a report submitted pursuant to section 7108(b) of Title 22, or who the consular officer or the Attorney General knows or has reason to believe is or has been a knowing aider, abettor, assister, conspirator, or colluder with such a trafficker in severe forms of trafficking in persons, as defined in the section 7102 of Title 22, is inadmissible.

....

(3) Security and related grounds.

(A) In general

Any alien who a consular officer or the Attorney General knows, or has reasonable ground to believe, seeks to enter the United States to engage solely, principally, or incidentally in—

(i) any activity (I) to violate any law of the United States relating to espionage or sabotage or (II) to violate or evade any law prohibiting the export from the United States of goods, technology, or sensitive information,

(ii) any other unlawful activity, or

(iii) any activity a purpose of which is the opposition to, or the control or overthrow of, the Government of the United States by force, violence, or other unlawful means,

is inadmissible.

(B) Terrorist activities.

(i) In general

Any alien who—

(I) has engaged in a terrorist activity;

(II) a consular officer, the Attorney General, or the Secretary of Homeland Security knows, or has reasonable ground to believe, is engaged in or is likely to engage after entry in any terrorist activity (as defined in clause (iv));

(III) has, under circumstances indicating an intention to cause death or serious bodily harm, incited terrorist activity;

(IV) is a representative (as defined in clause (v)) of—

(aa) a terrorist organization (as defined in clause (vi)); or

(bb) a political, social, or other group that endorses or espouses terrorist activity;

(V) is a member of a terrorist organization described in subclause (I) or (II) of clause (vi);

(VI) is a member of a terrorist organization described in clause (vi) (III), unless the alien can demonstrate by clear and convincing evidence that the alien did not know, and should not reasonably have known, that the organization was a terrorist organization;

(VII) endorses or espouses terrorist activity or persuades others to endorse or espouse terrorist activity or support a terrorist organization;

(VIII) has received military-type training (as defined in section 2339D(c)(1) of Title 18) from or on behalf of any organization that, at the time the training was received, was a terrorist organization (as defined in clause (vi)); or

(IX) is the spouse or child of an alien who is inadmissible under this subparagraph, if the activity causing the alien to be found inadmissible occurred within the last 5 years, is inadmissible.

....

(iii) "Terrorist activity" defined.

As used in this chapter, the term "terrorist activity" means any activity which is unlawful under the laws of the place where it is committed (or which, if it had been committed in the United States, would be unlawful under the laws of the United States or any State) and which involves any of the following:

(I) The highjacking or sabotage of any conveyance (including an aircraft, vessel, or vehicle).

(II) The seizing or detaining, and threatening to kill, injure, or continue to detain, another individual in order to compel a third person (including a governmental organization) to do or abstain from doing any act as an explicit or implicit condition for the release of the individual seized or detained.

(III) A violent attack upon an internationally protected person (as defined in section 1116(b)(4) of Title 18) or upon the liberty of such a person.

(IV) An assassination.

(V) The use of any—

(aa) biological agent, chemical agent, or nuclear weapon or device, or

(bb) explosive, firearm, or other weapon or dangerous device (other than for mere personal monetary gain),

with intent to endanger, directly or indirectly, the safety of one or more individuals or to cause substantial damage to property.

(VI) A threat, attempt, or conspiracy to do any of the foregoing.

(iv) Engage in terrorist activity defined.

As used in this chapter, the term "engage in terrorist activity" means, in an individual capacity or as a member of an organization—

(I) to commit or to incite to commit, under circumstances indicating an intention to cause death or serious bodily injury, a terrorist activity;

(II) to prepare or plan a terrorist activity;

(III) to gather information on potential targets for terrorist activity;

(IV) to solicit funds or other things of value for—

(aa) a terrorist activity;

(bb) a terrorist organization described in clause (vi)(I) or (vi)(II); or

(cc) a terrorist organization described in clause (vi)(III), unless the solicitor can demonstrate by clear and convincing evidence that he did not know, and should not reasonably have known, that the organization was a terrorist organization;

(V) to solicit any individual—

(aa) to engage in conduct otherwise described in this subsection;

(bb) for membership in a terrorist organization described in clause (vi)(I) or (vi)(II); or

(cc) for membership in a terrorist organization described in clause (vi)(III) unless the solicitor can demonstrate by clear and convincing evidence that he did not know, and should not reasonably have known, that the organization was a terrorist organization; or

(VI) to commit an act that the actor knows, or reasonably should know, affords material support, including a safe house, transportation, communications, funds, transfer of funds or other material financial benefit, false documentation or identification, weapons (including chemical, biological, or radiological weapons), explosives, or training—

(aa) for the commission of a terrorist activity;

(bb) to any individual who the actor knows, or reasonably should know, has committed or plans to commit a terrorist activity;

(cc) to a terrorist organization described in subclause (I) or (II) of clause (vi) or to any member of such an organization; or

(dd) to a terrorist organization described in clause (vi)(III), or to any member of such an organization, unless the actor can demonstrate by clear and convincing evidence that the actor did not know, and should not reasonably have known, that the organization was a terrorist organization.

....

(C) Foreign policy.

(i) In general.

An alien whose entry or proposed activities in the United States the Secretary of State has reasonable ground to believe would have potentially serious adverse foreign policy consequences for the United States is inadmissible.

....

(D) Immigrant membership in totalitarian party.

(i) In general

Any immigrant who is or has been a member of or affiliated with the Communist or any other totalitarian party (or subdivision or affiliate thereof), domestic or foreign, is inadmissible.

....

(E) Participants in Nazi persecution, genocide, or the commission of any act of torture or extrajudicial killing.

(i) Participation in Nazi persecutions.

....

(ii) Participation in genocide.

Any alien who ordered, incited, assisted, or otherwise participated in conduct outside the United States that would, if committed in the United States or by a United States national, be genocide, as defined in section 1091(a) of Title 18, is inadmissible.

(iii) Commission of acts of torture or extrajudicial killings.

Any alien who, outside the United States, has committed, ordered, incited, assisted, or otherwise participated in the commission of—

(I) any act of torture, as defined in section 2340 of Title 18; or

(II) under color of law of any foreign nation, any extrajudicial killing, as defined in section 3(a) of the Torture Victim Protection Act of 1991 (28 U.S.C. 1350 note),

is inadmissible.

(F) Association with terrorist organizations.

Any alien who the Secretary of State, after consultation with the Attorney General, or the Attorney General, after consultation with the Secretary of State, determines has been associated with a terrorist organization and intends while in the United States to engage solely, principally, or incidentally in activities that could endanger the welfare, safety, or security of the United States is inadmissible.

....

CONVENTION RELATING TO THE STATUS OF REFUGEES*

....

CHAPTER I. GENERAL PROVISIONS

Article 1. Definition of the term "Refugee"

A. For the purposes of the present Convention, the term "refugee" shall apply to any person who:

(1) Has been considered a refugee under the Arrangements of 12 May 1926 and 30 June 1928 or under the Conventions of 28 October 1933 and 10 February 1938, the Protocol of 14 September 1939 or the Constitution of the International Refugee Organization;

Decisions of non-eligibility taken by the International Refugee Organization during the period of its activities shall not prevent the status of refugee being accorded to persons who fulfill the conditions of paragraph 2 of this section;

(2) As a result of events occurring before I January 1951 and owing to well-founded fear of being persecuted for reasons of race, religion, nationality, membership of a particular social group or political opinion, is outside the country of his nationality and is unable, or owing to such fear, is unwilling to avail himself of the protection of that country; or who, not having a nationality and being outside the country of his former habitual residence as a result of such events, is unable or, owing to such fear, is unwilling to return to it.

In the case of a person who has more than one nationality, the term "the country of his nationality" shall mean each of the countries of which he is a national, and a person shall not be deemed to be lacking the protection of the country of his nationality if, without any valid reason based on well-founded fear, he has not availed himself of the protection of one of the countries of which he is a national.

B. (1) For the purposes of this Convention, the words "events occurring before I January 1951" in article 1, section A, shall be understood to mean either:

(a) "events occurring in Europe before 1 January 1951"; or

(b) "events occurring in Europe or elsewhere before 1 January 1951"; and each Contracting State shall make a declaration at the time of signature, ratification or accession, specifying which of these meanings it applies for the purpose of its obligations under this Convention.

(2) Any Contracting State which has adopted alternative (a) may at any time extend its obligations by adopting alternative (b) by means of a notification addressed to the Secretary-General of the United Nations.

C. This Convention shall cease to apply to any person falling under the terms of section A if:

(1) He has voluntarily re-availed himself of the protection of the country of his nationality; or

---

* July 28, 1951, 189 U.N.T.S. 150 (entered into force on Apr. 22, 1954), *available at* http://www.unhchr.ch/html/menu3/b/o_c_ref.htm.

(2) Having lost his nationality, he has voluntarily reacquired it; or

(3) He has acquired a new nationality, and enjoys the protection of the country of his new nationality; or

(4) He has voluntarily re-established himself in the country which he left or outside which he remained owing to fear of persecution; or

(5) He can no longer, because the circumstances in connection with which he has been recognized as a refugee have ceased to exist, continue to refuse to avail himself of the protection of the country of his nationality;

Provided that this paragraph shall not apply to a refugee falling under section A (I) of this article who is able to invoke compelling reasons arising out of previous persecution for refusing to avail himself of the protection of the country of nationality;

(6) Being a person who has no nationality he is, because the circumstances in connection with which he has been recognized as a refugee have ceased to exist, able to return to the country of his former habitual residence;

Provided that this paragraph shall not apply to a refugee falling under section A (I) of this article who is able to invoke compelling reasons arising out of previous persecution for refusing to return to the country of his former habitual residence.

D. This Convention shall not apply to persons who are at present receiving from organs or agencies of the United Nations other than the United Nations High Commissioner for Refugees protection or assistance.

When such protection or assistance has ceased for any reason, without the position of such persons being definitively settled in accordance with the relevant resolutions adopted by the General Assembly of the United Nations, these persons shall ipso facto be entitled to the benefits of this Convention.

E. This Convention shall not apply to a person who is recognized by the competent authorities of the country in which he has taken residence as having the rights and obligations which are attached to the possession of the nationality of that country.

F. The provisions of this Convention shall not apply to any person with respect to whom there are serious reasons for considering that:

(a) He has committed a crime against peace, a war crime, or a crime against humanity, as defined in the international instruments drawn up to make provision in respect of such crimes;

(b) He has committed a serious non-political crime outside the country of refuge prior to his admission to that country as a refugee;

(c) He has been guilty of acts contrary to the purposes and principles of the United Nations.

Article 2. General obligations

Every refugee has duties to the country in which he finds himself, which require in particular that he conform to its laws and regulations as well as to measures taken for the maintenance of public order.

Article 3. Non-discrimination

The Contracting States shall apply the provisions of this Convention to refugees without discrimination as to race, religion or country of origin.

. . . .

Article 7. Exemption from reciprocity

1. Except where this Convention contains more favourable provisions, a Contracting State shall accord to refugees the same treatment as is accorded to aliens generally.

2. After a period of three years' residence, all refugees shall enjoy exemption from legislative reciprocity in the territory of the Contracting States.

3. Each Contracting State shall continue to accord to refugees the rights and benefits to which they were already entitled, in the absence of reciprocity, at the date of entry into force of this Convention for that State.

4. The Contracting States shall consider favourably the possibility of according to refugees, in the absence of reciprocity, rights and benefits beyond those to which they are entitled according to paragraphs 2 and 3, and to extending exemption from reciprocity to refugees who do not fulfill the conditions provided for in paragraphs 2 and 3.

5. The provisions of paragraphs 2 and 3 apply both to the rights and benefits referred to in articles 13, 18, 19, 21 and 22 of this Convention and to rights and benefits for which this Convention does not provide.

....

Article 9. Provisional measures

Nothing in this Convention shall prevent a Contracting State, in time of war or other grave and exceptional circumstances, from taking provisionally measures which it considers to be essential to the national security in the case of a particular person, pending a determination by the Contracting State that that person is in fact a refugee and that the continuance of such measures is necessary in his case in the interests of national security.

....

CHAPTER II. JURIDICAL STATUS

Article 12. Personal status

1. The personal status of a refugee shall be governed by the law of the country of his domicile or, if he has no domicile, by the law of the country of his residence.

2. Rights previously acquired by a refugee and dependent on personal status, more particularly rights attaching to marriage, shall be respected by a Contracting State, subject to compliance, if this be necessary, with the formalities required by the law of that State, provided that the right in question is one which would have been recognized by the law of that State had he not become a refugee.

....

Article 16. Access to courts

1. A refugee shall have free access to the courts of law on the territory of all Contracting States.

2. A refugee shall enjoy in the Contracting State in which he has his habitual residence the same treatment as a national in matters pertaining to access to the courts, including legal assistance and exemption from *cautio judicatum solvi*.

3. A refugee shall be accorded in the matters referred to in paragraph 2 in countries other than that in which he has his habitual residence the treatment granted to a national of the country of his habitual residence.

CHAPTER III. GAINFUL EMPLOYMENT

Article 17. Wage-earning employment

1. The Contracting States shall accord to refugees lawfully staying in their territory the most favourable treatment accorded to nationals of a foreign country in the same circumstances, as regards the right to engage in wage-earning employment.

2. In any case, restrictive measures imposed on aliens or the employment of aliens for the protection of the national labour market shall not be applied to a refugee who was already exempt from them at the date of entry into force of this Convention for the Contracting State concerned, or who fulfils one of the following conditions:

(a) He has completed three years' residence in the country;

(b) He has a spouse possessing the nationality of the country of residence. A refugee may not invoke the benefit of this provision if he has abandoned his spouse;

(c) He has one or more children possessing the nationality of the country of residence.

3. The Contracting States shall give sympathetic consideration to assimilating the rights of all refugees with regard to wage-earning employment to those of nationals, and in particular of those refugees who have entered their territory pursuant to programmes of labour recruitment or under immigration schemes.

. . . .

CHAPTER IV. WELFARE

. . . .

Article 22. Public education

1. The Contracting States shall accord to refugees the same treatment as is accorded to nationals with respect to elementary education.

2. The Contracting States shall accord to refugees treatment as favourable as possible, and, in any event, not less favourable than that accorded to aliens generally in the same circumstances, with respect to education other than elementary education and, in particular, as regards access to studies, the recognition of foreign school certificates, diplomas and degrees, the remission of fees and charges and the award of scholarships.

Article 23. Public relief

The Contracting States shall accord to refugees lawfully staying in their territory the same treatment with respect to public relief and assistance as is accorded to their nationals.

Article 24. Labour legislation and social security

1. The Contracting States shall accord to refugees lawfully staying in their territory the same treatment as is accorded to nationals in respect of the following matters;

(a) In so far as such matters are governed by laws or regulations or are subject to the control of administrative authorities: remuneration, including family allowances where these form part of remuneration, hours of work, overtime arrangements, holidays with pay, restrictions on home work, minimum age of employment, apprenticeship and training, women's work and the work of young persons, and the enjoyment of the benefits of collective bargaining;

(b) Social security (legal provisions in respect of employment injury, occupational diseases, maternity, sickness, disability, old age, death, unemployment, family responsibilities and any other contingency which, according to national laws or regulations, is covered by a social security scheme), subject to the following limitations:

(i) There may be appropriate arrangements for the maintenance of acquired rights and rights in course of acquisition;

(ii) National laws or regulations of the country of residence may prescribe special arrangements concerning benefits or portions of benefits which are payable wholly out of public funds, and concerning allowances paid to persons who do not fulfill the contribution conditions prescribed for the award of a normal pension.

2. The right to compensation for the death of a refugee resulting from employment injury or from occupational disease shall not be affected by the fact that the residence of the beneficiary is outside the territory of the Contracting State.

3. The Contracting States shall extend to refugees the benefits of agreements concluded between them, or which may be concluded between them in the future, concerning the maintenance of acquired rights and rights in the process of acquisition in regard to social security, subject only to the conditions which apply to nationals of the States signatory to the agreements in question.

4. The Contracting States will give sympathetic consideration to extending to refugees so far as possible the benefits of similar agreements which may at any time be in force between such Contracting States and non-contracting States.

CHAPTER V. ADMINISTRATIVE MEASURES

....

Article 26. Freedom of movement

Each Contracting State shall accord to refugees lawfully in its territory the right to choose their place of residence and to move freely within its territory subject to any regulations applicable to aliens generally in the same circumstances.

Article 27. Identity papers

The Contracting States shall issue identity papers to any refugee in their territory who does not possess a valid travel document.

Article 28. Travel documents

1. The Contracting States shall issue to refugees lawfully staying in their territory travel documents for the purpose of travel outside their territory, unless compelling reasons of national security or public order otherwise require, and the provisions of the Schedule to this Convention shall apply with respect to such documents. The Contracting States may issue such a travel document to any other refugee in their territory; they

shall in particular give sympathetic consideration to the issue of such a travel document to refugees in their territory who are unable to obtain a travel document from the country of their lawful residence.

2. Travel documents issued to refugees under previous international agreements by Parties thereto shall be recognized and treated by the Contracting States in the same way as if they had been issued pursuant to this article.

....

Article 31. Refugees unlawfully in the country of refuge

1. The Contracting States shall not impose penalties, on account of their illegal entry or presence, on refugees who, coming directly from a territory where their life or freedom was threatened in the sense of article 1, enter or are present in their territory without authorization, provided they present themselves without delay to the authorities and show good cause for their illegal entry or presence.

2. The Contracting States shall not apply to the movements of such refugees restrictions other than those which are necessary and such restrictions shall only be applied until their status in the country is regularized or they obtain admission into another country. The Contracting States shall allow such refugees a reasonable period and all the necessary facilities to obtain admission into another country.

Article 32. Expulsion

1. The Contracting States shall not expel a refugee lawfully in their territory save on grounds of national security or public order.

2. The expulsion of such a refugee shall be only in pursuance of a decision reached in accordance with due process of law. Except where compelling reasons of national security otherwise require, the refugee shall be allowed to submit evidence to clear himself, and to appeal to and be represented for the purpose before competent authority or a person or persons specially designated by the competent authority.

3. The Contracting States shall allow such a refugee a reasonable period within which to seek legal admission into another country. The Contracting States reserve the right to apply during that period such internal measures as they may deem necessary.

Article 33. Prohibition of expulsion or return ("refoulement")

1. No Contracting State shall expel or return ("refouler") a refugee in any manner whatsoever to the frontiers of territories where his life or freedom would be threatened on account of his race, religion, nationality, membership of a particular social group or political opinion.

2. The benefit of the present provision may not, however, be claimed by a refugee whom there are reasonable grounds for regarding as a danger to the security of the country in which he is, or who, having been convicted by a final judgment of a particularly serious crime, constitutes a danger to the community of that country.

Article 34. Naturalization

The Contracting States shall as far as possible facilitate the assimilation and naturalization of refugees. They shall in particular make every effort to expedite naturalization proceedings and to reduce as far as possible the charges and costs of such proceedings.

....

PROTOCOL RELATING TO THE STATUS OF REFUGEES*

The States Parties to the present Protocol,

Considering that the Convention relating to the Status of Refugees done at Geneva on 28 July 1951 (hereinafter referred to as the Convention) covers only those persons who have become refugees as a result of events occurring before 1 January 1951,

Considering that new refugee situations have arisen since the Convention was adopted and that the refugees concerned may therefore not fall within the scope of the Convention,

Considering that it is desirable that equal status should be enjoyed by all refugees covered by the definition in the Convention irrespective of the dateline 1 January 1951,

Have agreed as follows:

Article 1. General provision

1. The States Parties to the present Protocol undertake to apply articles 2 to 34 inclusive of the Convention to refugees as hereinafter defined.

2. For the purpose of the present Protocol, the term "refugee" shall, except as regards the application of paragraph 3 of this article, mean any person within the definition of article I of the Convention as if the words "As a result of events occurring before 1 January 1951 and..." and the words "...as a result of such events", in article 1 A (2) were omitted.

3. The present Protocol shall be applied by the States Parties hereto without any geographic limitation, save that existing declarations made by States already Parties to the Convention in accordance with article I B (I) (a) of the Convention, shall, unless extended under article I B (2) thereof, apply also under the present Protocol.

Article 2. Co-operation of the national authorities with the United Nations

1. The States Parties to the present Protocol undertake to co-operate with the Office of the United Nations High Commissioner for Refugees, or any other agency of the United Nations which may succeed it, in the exercise of its functions, and shall in particular facilitate its duty of supervising the application of the provisions of the present Protocol.

2. In order to enable the Office of the High Commissioner or any other agency of the United Nations which may succeed it, to make reports to the competent organs of the United Nations, the States Parties to the present Protocol undertake to provide them with the information and statistical data requested, in the appropriate form, concerning:

(a) The condition of refugees;

---

* Jan. 31, 1967, 19 U.S.T. 6223, 606 U.N.T.S. 267, *available at* http://www.unhchr.ch/html/menu3/b/o_p_ref.htm.

The Protocol was taken note of with approval by the Economic and Social Council in resolution 1186 (XLI) of 18 November 1966 and was taken note of by the General Assembly in resolution 2198 (XXI) of 16 December 1966. In the same resolution the General Assembly requested the Secretary-General to transmit the text of the Protocol to the States mentioned in article V thereof, with a view to enabling them to accede to the Protocol.

(b) The implementation of the present Protocol;

(c) Laws, regulations and decrees which are, or may hereafter be, in force relating to refugees.

Article 3. Information on national legislation

The States Parties to the present Protocol shall communicate to the Secretary-General of the United Nations the laws and regulations which they may adopt to ensure the application of the present Protocol.

Article 4. Settlement of dispute

Any dispute between States Parties to the present Protocol which relates to its interpretation or application and which cannot be settled by other means shall be referred to the International Court of Justice at the request of any one of the parties to the dispute.

. . . .

EXECUTIVE ORDER 12807* (INTERDICTION OF ILLEGAL ALIENS, AS AMENDED BY EXECUTIVE ORDER 13286)

By the authority vested in me as President by the Constitution and the laws of the United States of America, including sections 212(f) and 215(a)(1) of the Immigration and Nationality Act, as amended (8 U.S.C. 1182(f) and 1185(a)(1)), and whereas:

(1) The President has authority to suspend the entry of aliens coming by sea to the United States without necessary documentation, to establish reasonable rules and regulations regarding, and other limitations on, the entry or attempted entry of aliens into the United States, and to repatriate aliens interdicted beyond the territorial sea of the United States;

(2) The international legal obligations of the United States under the United Nations Protocol Relating to the Status of Refugees (U.S. T.I.A.S. 6577; 19 U.S.T. 6223) to apply Article 33 of the United Nations Convention Relating to the Status of Refugees do not extend to persons located outside the territory of the United States;

(3) Proclamation No. 4865 suspends the entry of all undocumented aliens into the United States by the high seas; and

(4) There continues to be a serious problem of persons attempting to come to the United States by sea without necessary documentation and otherwise illegally.

I, GEORGE BUSH, President of the United States of America, hereby order as follows:

Sec. 1. The Secretary of State shall undertake to enter into, on behalf of the United States, cooperative arrangements with appropriate foreign governments for the purpose of preventing illegal migration to the United States by sea.

Sec. 2. (a) The Secretary of the Department in which the Coast Guard is operating, in consultation, where appropriate, with the Secretary of Defense, the Attorney General, and the Secretary of State, shall issue appropriate instruction to the Coast Guard in order to enforce the suspension of the entry of undocumented aliens by sea and the interdiction of any defined vessel carrying such aliens.

(b) Those instructions shall apply to any of the following defined vessels:

(1) Vessels of the United States, meaning any vessel documented or numbered pursuant to the laws of the United States, or owned in whole or in part by the United States, a citizen of the United States, or a corporation incorporated under the laws of the United States or any State, Territory, District, Commonwealth, or possession thereof, unless the vessel has been granted nationality by a foreign nation in accord with Article 5 of the Convention on the High Seas of 1958 (U.S. T.I.A.S. 5200; 13 U.S.T. 2312).

(2) Vessels without nationality or vessels assimilated to vessels without nationality in accordance with paragraph (2) of Article 6 of the Convention on the High Seas of 1958 (U.S. T.I.A.S. 5200; 13 U.S.T. 2312).

---

* Exec. Order No. 12807, 3 C.F.R. 303 (1993) (signed May 24, 1992), *amended by* Exec. Order No. 13286 (2003).

(3) Vessels of foreign nations with whom we have arrangements authorizing the United States to stop and board such vessels.

(c) Those instructions to the Coast Guard shall include appropriate directives providing for the Coast Guard:

(1) To stop and board defined vessels, when there is reason to believe that such vessels are engaged in the irregular transportation of persons or violations of United States law or the law of a country with which the United States has an arrangement authorizing such action.

(2) To make inquiries of those on board, examine documents and take such actions as are necessary to carry out this order.

(3) To return the vessel and its passengers to the country from which it came, or to another country, when there is reason to believe that an offense is being committed against the United States immigration laws, or appropriate laws of a foreign country with which we have an arrangement to assist; provided, however, that the Secretary of Homeland Security, in his unreviewable discretion, may decide that a person who is a refugee will be returned without his consent.

(d) These actions, pursuant to this section, are authorized to be undertaken only beyond the territorial sea of the United States.

Sec. 3. This order is intended only to improve the internal management of the Executive Branch. Neither this order nor any agency guidelines, procedures, instructions, directives, rules or regulations implementing this order shall create, or shall be construed to create, any right or benefit, substantive or procedural (including without limitation any right or benefit under the Administrative Procedure Act), legally enforceable by any party against the United States, its agencies or instrumentalities, officers, employees, or any other person. Nor shall this order is construed to require any procedures to determine whether a person is a refugee.

Sec. 4. Executive Order No. 12324 is hereby revoked and replaced by this order.

Sec. 5. This order shall be effective immediately.

[signed:] George Bush
THE WHITE HOUSE
May 24, 1992.

J. The Environment

NATIONAL ENVIRONMENTAL POLICY ACT OF 1969*

AN ACT to establish a national policy for the environment, to provide for the establishment of a Council on Environmental Quality, and for other purposes.

....

Purpose

Sec. 2. The purposes of this Act are: To declare a national policy which will encourage productive and enjoyable harmony between man and his environment; to promote efforts which will prevent or eliminate damage to the environment and biosphere and stimulate the health and welfare of man; to enrich the understanding of the ecological systems and natural resources important to the Nation; and to establish a Council on Environmental Quality.

TITLE I
CONGRESSIONAL DECLARATION OF NATIONAL ENVIRONMENTAL POLICY

Sec. 101. (a) The Congress, recognizing the profound impact of man's activity on the interrelations of all components of the natural environment, particularly the profound influences of population growth, high-density urbanization, industrial expansion, resource exploitation, and new and expanding technological advances and recognizing further the critical importance of restoring and maintaining environmental quality to the overall welfare and development of man, declares that it is the continuing policy of the Federal Government, in cooperation with State and local governments, and other concerned public and private organizations, to use all practicable means and measures, including financial and technical assistance, in a manner calculated to foster and promote the general welfare, to create and maintain conditions under which man and nature can exist in productive harmony, and fulfill the social, economic, and other requirements of present and future generations of Americans.

(b) In order to carry out the policy set forth in this Act, it is the continuing responsibility of the Federal Government to use all practicable means, consistent with other essential considerations of national policy, to improve and coordinate Federal plans, functions, programs, and resources to the end that the Nation may—

1. fulfill the responsibilities of each generation as trustee of the environment for succeeding generations;
2. assure for all Americans safe, healthful, productive, and aesthetically and culturally pleasing surroundings;
3. attain the widest range of beneficial uses of the environment without degradation, risk to health or safety, or other undesirable and unintended consequences;

---

* National Environmental Policy Act of 1969 §§2, 101–102, Pub. L. No. 91-190, 83 Stat. 852, 852-53 (codified as amended at 42 U.S.C. §§4321, 4331–4332 (2000)), *available at* http://ceq.eh.doe.gov/nepa/regs/nepa/nepaeqia/htm.

4. preserve important historic, cultural, and natural aspects of our national heritage, and maintain, wherever possible, an environment which supports diversity, and variety of individual choice;

5. achieve a balance between population and resource use which will permit high standards of living and a wide sharing of life's amenities; and

6. enhance the quality of renewable resources and approach the maximum attainable recycling of depletable resources.

(c) The Congress recognizes that each person should enjoy a healthful environment and that each person has a responsibility to contribute to the preservation and enhancement of the environment.

Sec. 102. The Congress authorizes and directs that, to the fullest extent possible:

(1) the policies, regulations, and public laws of the United States shall be interpreted and administered in accordance with the policies set forth in this Act, and (2) all agencies of the Federal Government shall—

(A) utilize a systematic, interdisciplinary approach which will insure the integrated use of the natural and social sciences and the environmental design arts in planning and in decisionmaking which may have an impact on man's environment;

(B) identify and develop methods and procedures, in consultation with the Council on Environmental Quality established by title II of this Act, which will insure that presently unquantified environmental amenities and values may be given appropriate consideration in decisionmaking along with economic and technical considerations;

(C) include in every recommendation or report on proposals for legislation and other major Federal actions significantly affecting the quality of the human environment, a detailed statement by the responsible official on—

(i) the environmental impact of the proposed action,

(ii) any adverse environmental effects which cannot be avoided should the proposal be implemented,

(iii) alternatives to the proposed action,

(iv) the relationship between local short-term uses of man's environment and the maintenance and enhancement of long-term productivity, and

(v) any irreversible and irretrievable commitments of resources which would be involved in the proposed action should it be implemented.

Prior to making any detailed statement, the responsible Federal official shall consult with and obtain the comments of any Federal agency which has jurisdiction by law or special expertise with respect to any environmental impact involved. Copies of such statement and the comments and views of the appropriate Federal, State, and local agencies, which are authorized to develop and enforce environmental standards, shall be made available to the President, the Council on Environmental Quality and to the public as provided by section 552 of title 5, United States Code, and shall accompany the proposal through the existing agency review processes;

. . . .

CLEAN AIR ACT*

TITLE I—AIR POLLUTION PREVENTION AND CONTROL

Part A—Air Quality and Emission Limitations

FINDINGS AND PURPOSES

Sec. 101. (a) The Congress finds—

(1) that the predominant part of the Nation's population is located in its rapidly expanding metropolitan and other urban areas, which generally cross the boundary lines of local jurisdictions and often extend into two or more States;

(2) that the growth in the amount and complexity of air pollution brought about by urbanization, industrial development, and the increasing use of motor vehicles, has resulted in mounting dangers to the public health and welfare, including injury to agricultural crops and livestock, damage to and the deterioration of property, and hazards to air and ground transportation;

(3) that air pollution prevention (that is, the reduction or elimination, through any measures, of the amount of pollutants produced or created at the source) and air pollution control at its source is the primary responsibility of States and local governments; and

(4) that Federal financial assistance and leadership is essential for the development of cooperative Federal, State, regional, and local programs to prevent and control air pollution.

(b) The purposes of this title are—

(1) to protect and enhance the quality of the Nation's air resources so as to promote the public health and welfare and the productive capacity of its population;

(2) to initiate and accelerate a national research and development program to achieve the prevention and control of air pollution;

(3) to provide technical and financial assistance to State and local governments in connection with the development and execution of their air pollution prevention and control programs; and

(4) to encourage and assist the development and operation of regional air pollution prevention and control programs.

(c) Pollution Prevention.—A primary goal of this Act is to encourage or otherwise promote reasonable Federal, State, and local governmental actions, consistent with the provisions of this Act, for pollution prevention.

COOPERATIVE ACTIVITIES AND UNIFORM LAWS

Sec. 102. (a) The Administrator shall encourage cooperative activities by the States and local governments for the prevention and control of air pollution; encourage the

---

* Clean Air Act §§101–102, 107–110, 115, 118, 173, 203, 246, 42 U.S.C.A. §§7401–7402, 7407–7410, 7415, 7418, 7503, 7522, 7586 (West 2003 & Supp. 2005), *available at* http://www.epa.gov/oar/caa/caa.txt.

enactment of improved and, so far as practicable in the light of varying conditions and needs, uniform State and local laws relating to the prevention and control of air pollution; and encourage the making of agreements and compacts between States for the prevention and control of air pollution.

(b) The Administrator shall cooperate with and encourage cooperative activities by all Federal departments and agencies having functions relating to the prevention and control of air pollution, so as to assure the utilization in the Federal air pollution control program of all appropriate and available facilities and resources within the Federal Government.

(c) The consent of the Congress is hereby given to two or more States to negotiate and enter into agreements or compacts, not in conflict with any law or treaty of the United States, for (1) cooperative effort and mutual assistance for the prevention and control of air pollution and the enforcement of their respective laws relating thereto, and (2) the establishment of such agencies, joint or otherwise, as they may deem desirable for making effective such agreements or compacts. No such agreement or compact shall be binding or obligatory upon any State a party thereto unless and until it has been approved by Congress. It is the intent of Congress that no agreement or compact entered into between States after the date of enactment of the Air Quality Act of 1967, which relates to the control and abatement of air pollution in an air quality control region, shall provide for participation by a State which is not included (in whole or in part) in such air quality control region.

. . . .

AIR QUALITY CONTROL REGIONS

Sec. 107. (a) Each State shall have the primary responsibility for assuring air quality within the entire geographic area comprising such State by submitting an implementation plan for such State which will specify the manner in which national primary and secondary ambient air quality standards will be achieved and maintained within each air quality control region in such State.

(b) For purposes of developing and carrying out implementation plans under section 110—

(1) an air quality control region designated under this section before the date of enactment of the Clean Air Amendments of 1970, or a region designated after such date under subsection (c), shall be an air quality control region; and

(2) the portion of such State which is not part of any such designated region shall be an air quality control region, but such portion may be subdivided by the State into two or more air quality control regions with the approval of the Administrator.

. . . .

AIR QUALITY CRITERIA AND CONTROL TECHNIQUES

Sec. 108. (a) (1) For the purpose of establishing national primary and secondary ambient air quality standards, the Administrator shall within 30 days after the date of enactment of the Clean Air Amendments of 1970 publish, and shall from time to time thereafter revise, a list which includes each air pollutant—

(A) emissions of which, in his judgment, cause or contribute to air pollution which may reasonably be anticipated to endanger public health or welfare;

(B) the presence of which in the ambient air results from numerous or diverse mobile or stationary sources; and

(C) for which air quality criteria had not been issued before the date of enactment of the Clean Air Amendments of 1970, but for which he plans to issue air quality criteria under this section.

(2) The Administrator shall issue air quality criteria for an air pollutant within 12 months after he has included such pollutant in a list under paragraph (1). Air quality criteria for an air pollutant shall accurately reflect the latest scientific knowledge useful in indicating the kind and extent of all identifiable effects on public health or welfare which may be expected from the presence of such pollutant in the ambient air, in varying quantities. The criteria for an air pollutant, to the extent practicable, shall include information on—

(A) those variable factors (including atmospheric conditions) which of themselves or in combination with other factors may alter the effects on public health or welfare of such air pollutant;

(B) the types of air pollutants which, when present in the atmosphere, may interact with such pollutant to produce an adverse effect on public health or welfare; and

(C) any known or anticipated adverse effects on welfare.

....

NATIONAL AMBIENT AIR QUALITY STANDARDS

Sec. 109. (a)(1) The Administrator—

(A) within 30 days after the date of enactment of the Clean Air Amendments of 1970, shall publish proposed regulations prescribing a national primary ambient air quality standard and a national secondary ambient air quality standard for each air pollutant for which air quality criteria have been issued prior to such date of enactment;

....

IMPLEMENTATION PLANS

Sec. 110. (a)(1) Each State shall, after reasonable notice and public hearings, adopt and submit to the Administrator, within 3 years (or such shorter period as the Administrator may prescribe) after the promulgation of a national primary ambient air quality standard (or any revision thereof) under section 109 for any air pollutant, a plan which provides for implementation, maintenance, and enforcement of such primary standard in each air quality control region (or portion thereof) within such State. In addition, such State shall adopt and submit to the Administrator (either as a part of a plan submitted under the preceding sentence or separately) within 3 years (or such shorter period as the Administrator may prescribe) after the promulgation of a national ambient air quality secondary standard (or revision thereof), a plan which provides for implementation, maintenance, and enforcement of such secondary standard in each air quality control region (or portion thereof) within such State.

....

INTERNATIONAL AIR POLLUTION

Sec. 115. (a) Whenever the Administrator, upon receipt of reports, surveys or studies from any duly constituted international agency has reason to believe that any air pollutant or pollutants emitted in the United States cause or contribute to air pollution which may reasonably be anticipated to endanger public health or welfare in a foreign country or whenever the Secretary of State requests him to do so with respect to such pollution which the Secretary of State alleges is of such a nature, the Administrator shall give formal notification thereof to the Governor of the State in which such emissions originate.

(b) The notice of the Administrator shall be deemed to be a finding under section 110(a)(2)(H)(ii) which requires a plan revision with respect to so much of the applicable implementation plan as is inadequate to prevent or eliminate the endangerment referred to in subsection (a). Any foreign country so affected by such emission of pollutant or pollutants shall be invited to appear at any public hearing associated with any revision of the appropriate portion of the applicable implementation plan.

(c) This section shall apply only to a foreign country which the Administrator determines has given the United States essentially the same rights with respect to the prevention or control of air pollution occurring in that country as is given that country by this section.

....

CONTROL OF POLLUTION FROM FEDERAL FACILITIES

Sec. 118. (a) General Compliance.—Each department, agency, and instrumentality of executive, legislative, and judicial branches of the Federal Government (1) having jurisdiction over any property or facility, or (2) engaged in any activity resulting, or which may result, in the discharge of air pollutants, and each officer, agent, or employee thereof, shall be subject to, and comply with, all Federal, State, interstate, and local requirements, administrative authority, and process and sanctions respecting the control and abatement of air pollution in the same manner, and to the same extent as any nongovernmental entity. The preceding sentence shall apply (A) to any requirement whether substantive or procedural (including any recordkeeping or reporting requirement, any requirement respecting permits and any other requirement whatsoever), (B) to any requirement to pay a fee or charge imposed by any State or local agency to defray the costs of its air pollution regulatory program, (C) to the exercise of any Federal, State, or local administrative authority, and (D) to any process and sanction, whether enforced in Federal, State, or local courts, or in any other manner. This subsection shall apply notwithstanding any immunity of such agencies, officers, agents, or employees under any law or rule of law. No officer, agent, or employee of the United States shall be personally liable for any civil penalty for which he is not otherwise liable.

(b) The President, may exempt any emission source of any department, agency, or instrumentality in the executive branch from compliance with such a requirement if he determines it to be in the paramount interest of the United States to do so, except that no exemption may be granted from section 111, and an exemption from section 112 may be granted only in accordance with section 112(i)(4). No such exemption shall be granted due to lack of appropriation unless the President shall have specifically requested such appropriation as a part of the budgetary process and the Congress shall have failed to make available such requested appropriation. Any exemption shall be for a period not in excess of one year, but additional exemptions may be granted for periods of not to exceed one year upon the President's making a new determination. In addition to any such exemption of a particular emission source, the President may, if he determines it to be in the paramount interest of the United States to do so, issue regulations exempting from compliance with the requirements of this section any weaponry, equipment, aircraft, vehicles, or other classes or categories of property which are owned or operated by the Armed Forces of the United States (including the Coast Guard) or by the National Guard of any State and which are uniquely military in nature. The President shall reconsider the need for such regulations at three-year intervals. The President shall report each January to the Congress all exemptions from the requirements of this section granted during the preceding calendar year, together with his reason for granting each such exemption.

....

PERMIT REQUIREMENTS

Sec. 173. (a) In General.—The permit program required by section 172(b)(6) shall provide that permits to construct and operate may be issued if—

(1) in accordance with regulations issued by the Administrator for the determination of baseline emissions in a manner consistent with the assumptions underlying the applicable implementation plan approved under section 110 and this part, the permitting agency determines that—

(A) by the time the source is to commence operation, sufficient offsetting emissions reductions have been obtained, such that total allowable emissions from existing sources in the region, from new or modified sources which are not major emitting facilities, and from the proposed source will be sufficiently less than total emissions from existing sources (as determined in accordance with the regulations under this paragraph) prior to the application for such permit to construct or modify so as to represent (when considered together with the plan provisions required under section 172) reasonable further progress (as defined in section 171); or

(B) in the case of a new or modified major stationary source which is located in a zone (within the nonattainment area) identified by the Administrator, in consultation with the Secretary of Housing and Urban Development, as a zone to which economic development should be targeted, that emissions of such pollutant resulting from the proposed new or modified major stationary source will not cause or contribute to emissions levels which exceed the allowance permitted for such pollutant for such area from new or modified major stationary sources under section 172(c);

(2) the proposed source is required to comply with the lowest achievable emission rate;

(3) the owner or operator of the proposed new or modified source has demonstrated that all major stationary sources owned or operated by such person (or by any entity controlling, controlled by, or under common control with such person) in such State are subject to emission limitations and are in compliance, or on a schedule for compliance, with all applicable emission limitations and standards under this Act;

(4) the Administrator has not determined that the applicable implementation plan is not being adequately implemented for the nonattainment area in which the proposed source is to be constructed or modified in accordance with the requirements of this part; and

(5) an analysis of alternative sites, sizes, production processes, and environmental control techniques for such proposed source demonstrates that benefits of the

proposed source significantly outweigh the environmental and social costs imposed as a result of its location, construction, or modification.

Any emission reductions required as a precondition of the issuance of a permit under paragraph (1) shall be federally enforceable before such permit may be issued.

(b) Prohibition on Use of Old Growth Allowances.—Any growth allowance included in an applicable implementation plan to meet the requirements of section 172(b)(5) (as in effect immediately before the date of the enactment of the Clean Air Act Amendments of 1990) shall not be valid for use in any area that received or receives a notice under section 110(a)(2)(H)(ii) (as in effect immediately before the date of the enactment of the Clean Air Act Amendments of 1990) or under section 110(k)(1) that its applicable implementation plan containing such allowance is substantially inadequate.

(c) Offsets.—(1) The owner or operator of a new or modified major stationary source may comply with any offset requirement in effect under this part for increased emissions of any air pollutant only by obtaining emission reductions of such air pollutant from the same source or other sources in the same nonattainment area, except that the State may allow the owner or operator of a source to obtain such emission reductions in another nonattainment area if (A) the other area has an equal or higher nonattainment classification than the area in which the source is located and (B) emissions from such other area contribute to a violation of the national ambient air quality standard in the nonattainment area in which the source is located. Such emission reductions shall be, by the time a new or modified source commences operation, in effect and enforceable and shall assure that the total tonnage of increased emissions of the air pollutant from the new or modified source shall be offset by an equal or greater reduction, as applicable, in the actual emissions of such air pollutant from the same or other sources in the area.

(2) Emission reductions otherwise required by this Act shall not be creditable as emissions reductions for purposes of any such offset requirement. Incidental emission reductions which are not otherwise required by this Act shall be creditable as emission reductions for such purposes if such emission reductions meet the requirements of paragraph (1).

(d) Control Technology Information.—The State shall provide that control technology information from permits issued under this section will be promptly submitted to the Administrator for purposes of making such information available through the RACT/BACT/LAER clearinghouse to other States and to the general public.

(e) Rocket Engines or Motors.—The permitting authority of a State shall allow a source to offset by alternative or innovative means emission increases from rocket engine and motor firing, and cleaning related to such firing, at an existing or modified major source that tests rocket engines or motors under the following conditions:

(1) Any modification proposed is solely for the purpose of expanding the testing of rocket engines or motors at an existing source that is permitted to test such engines on the date of enactment of this subsection.

(2) The source demonstrates to the satisfaction of the permitting authority of the State that it has used all reasonable means to obtain and utilize offsets, as determined on an annual basis, for the emissions increases beyond allowable levels, that all available offsets are being used, and that sufficient offsets are not available to the source.

(3) The source has obtained a written finding from the Department of Defense, Department of Transportation, National Aeronautics and Space Administration or

other appropriate Federal agency, that the testing of rocket motors or engines at the facility is required for a program essential to the national security.

(4) The source will comply with an alternative measure, imposed by the permitting authority, designed to offset any emission increases beyond permitted levels not directly offset by the source. In lieu of imposing any alternative offset measures, the permitting authority may impose an emissions fee to be paid to such authority of a State which shall be an amount no greater than 1.5 times the average cost of stationary source control measures adopted in that area during the previous 3 years. The permitting authority shall utilize the fees in a manner that maximizes the emissions reductions in that area.

PROHIBITED ACTS

Sec. 203. (a) The following acts and the causing thereof are prohibited—

(1) in the case of a manufacturer of new motor vehicles or new motor vehicle engines for distribution in commerce, the sale, or the offering for sale, or the introduction, or delivery for introduction, into commerce, or (in the case of any person, except as provided by regulation of the Administrator), the importation into the United States, of any new motor vehicle or new motor vehicle engine, manufactured after the effective date of regulations under this part which are applicable to such vehicle or engine unless such vehicle or engine is covered by a certificate of conformity issued (and in effect) under regulations prescribed under this part or part C in the case of clean-fuel vehicles (except as provided in subsection (b));

(2) (A) for any person to fail or refuse to permit access to or copying of records or to fail to make reports or provide information required under section 208;

(B) for any person to fail or refuse to permit entry, testing or inspection authorized under section 206(c) or section 208;

(C) for any person to fail or refuse to perform tests, or have tests performed as required under section 208;

(D) for any manufacturer to fail to make information available as provided by regulation under section 202(m)(5);

(3) (A) for any person to remove or render inoperative any device or element of design installed on or in a motor vehicle or motor vehicle engine in compliance with regulations under this title prior to its sale and delivery to the ultimate purchaser, or for any person knowingly to remove or render inoperative any such device or element of design after such sale and delivery to the ultimate purchaser; or

(B) for any person to manufacture or sell, or offer to sell, or install, any part or component intended for use with, or as part of, any motor vehicle or motor vehicle engine, where a principal effect of the part or component is to bypass, defeat, or render inoperative any device or element of design installed on or in a motor vehicle or motor vehicle engine in compliance with regulations under this title, and where the person knows or should know that such part or component is being offered for sale or installed for such use or put to such use; or

(4) for any manufacturer of a new motor vehicle or new motor vehicle engine subject to standards prescribed under section 202 or Part C—

(A) to sell or lease any such vehicle or engine unless such manufacturer has complied with (i) the requirements of section 207 (a) and (b) with respect to such vehicle or engine, and unless a label or tag is affixed to such vehicle or engine in accordance with section 207(c)(3), or (ii) the corresponding requirements of part C in the case of clean fuel vehicles unless the manufacturer has complied with the corresponding requirements of part C

(B) to fail or refuse to comply with the requirements of section 207 (c) or (e), or the corresponding requirements of part C in the case of clean fuel vehicles

(C) except as provided in subsection (c)(3) of section 207 and the corresponding requirements of part C in the case of clean fuel vehicles, to provide directly or indirectly in any communication to the ultimate purchaser or any subsequent purchaser that the coverage of any warranty under this Act is conditioned upon use of any part, component, or system manufactured by such manufacturer or any person acting for such manufacturer or under his control, or conditioned upon service performed by any such person, or

(D) to fail or refuse to comply with the terms and conditions of the warranty under section 207 (a) or (b) or the corresponding requirements of part C in the case of clean fuel vehicles with respect to any vehicle; or

(5) for any person to violate section 218, 219, or part C of this title or any regulations under section 218, 219, or part C.

No action with respect to any element of design referred to in paragraph (3) (including any adjustment or alteration of such element) shall be treated as a prohibited act under such paragraph (3) if such action is in accordance with section 215. Nothing in paragraph (3) shall be construed to require the use of manufacturer parts in maintaining or repairing any motor vehicle or motor vehicle engine. For the purposes of the preceding sentence, the term "manufacturer parts" means, with respect to a motor vehicle engine, parts produced or sold by the manufacturer of the motor vehicle or motor vehicle engine. No action with respect to any device or element of design referred to in paragraph (3) shall be treated as a prohibited act under that paragraph if (i) the action is for the purpose of repair or replacement of the device or element, or is a necessary and temporary procedure to repair or replace any other item and the device or element is replaced upon completion of the procedure, and (ii) such action thereafter results in the proper functioning of the device or element referred to in paragraph (3). No action with respect to any device or element of design referred to in paragraph (3) shall be treated as a prohibited act under that paragraph if the action is for the purpose of a conversion of a motor vehicle for use of a clean alternative fuel (as defined in this title) and if such vehicle complies with the applicable standard under section 202 when operating on such fuel, and if in the case of a clean alternative fuel vehicle (as defined by rule by the Administrator), the device or element is replaced upon completion of the conversion procedure and such action results in proper functioning of the device or element when the motor vehicle operates on conventional fuel.

(b) (1) The Administrator may exempt any new motor vehicle or new motor vehicle engine from subsection (a), upon such terms and conditions as he may find necessary for the purpose of research, investigations, studies, demonstrations, or training, or for reasons of national security.

....

CENTRALLY FUELED FLEETS

Sec. 246. (a) Fleet Program Required for Certain Nonattainment Areas.—

(1) SIP revision.—Each State in which there is located all or part of a covered area (as defined in paragraph (2)) shall submit, within 42 months after the enactment of the Clean Air Act Amendments of 1990, a State implementation plan revision under section 110 and part D of title I to establish a clean-fuel vehicle program for fleets under this section.

....

(g) Availability to the Public.—At any facility owned or operated by a department, agency, or instrumentality of the United States where vehicles subject to this subsection are supplied with clean alternative fuel, such fuel shall be offered for sale to the public for use in other vehicles during reasonable business times and subject to national security concerns, unless such fuel is commercially available for vehicles in the vicinity of such Federal facilities.

....

CLEAN WATER ACT*

AN ACT To provide for water pollution control activities in the Public Health Service of the Federal Security Agency and in the Federal Works Agency, and for other purposes.

Be it enacted by the Senate and House of Representatives of the United States of America in Congress assembled,

TITLE I—RESEARCH AND RELATED PROGRAMS

DECLARATION OF GOALS AND POLICY

SEC. 101. (a) The objective of this Act is to restore and maintain the chemical, physical, and biological integrity of the Nation's waters. In order to achieve this objective it is hereby declared that, consistent with the provisions of this Act—

(1) it is the national goal that the discharge of pollutants into the navigable waters be eliminated by 1985;

(2) it is the national goal that wherever attainable, an interim goal of water quality which provides for the protection and propagation of fish, shellfish, and wildlife and provides for recreation in and on the water be achieved by July 1, 1983;

(3) it is the national policy that the discharge of toxic pollutants in toxic amounts be prohibited;

(4) it is the national policy that Federal financial assistance be provided to construct publicly owned waste treatment works;

(5) it is the national policy that areawide treatment management planning processes be developed and implemented to assure adequate control of sources of pollutants in each State;

(6) it is the national policy that a major research and demonstration effort be made to develop technology necessary to eliminate the discharge of pollutants into the navigable waters, waters of the contiguous zone and the oceans; and

(7) it is the national policy that programs for the control of nonpoint sources of pollution be developed and implemented in an expeditious manner so as to enable the goals of this Act to be met through the control of both point and nonpoint sources of pollution.

(b) It is the policy of the Congress to recognize, preserve, and protect the primary responsibilities and rights of States to prevent, reduce, and eliminate pollution, to plan the development and use (including restoration, preservation, and enhancement) of land and water resources, and to consult with the Administrator in the exercise of his authority under this Act. It is the policy of Congress that the States manage the con-

---

* Federal Water Pollution Control Act Amendments of 1972 §§ 101–102, 312, Pub. L. No. 92-500, 86 Stat. 816, 816–17, 871 (codified as amended at 33 U.S.C. §§ 1251–1252, 1322 (West 2001 & Supp. 2005)), *available at* http://www.epa.gov/region5/water/pdf/ecwa.pdf.

struction grant program under this Act and implement the permit programs under sections 402 and 404 of this Act. It is further the policy of the Congress to support and aid research relating to the prevention, reduction, and elimination of pollution, and to provide Federal technical services and financial aid to State and interstate agencies and municipalities in connection with the prevention, reduction, and elimination of pollution.

(c) It is further the policy of Congress that the President, acting through the Secretary of State and such national and international organizations as he determines appropriate, shall take such action as may be necessary to insure that to the fullest extent possible all foreign countries shall take meaningful action for the prevention, reduction, and elimination of pollution in their waters and in international waters and for the achievement of goals regarding the elimination of discharge of pollutants and the improvement of water quality to at least the same extent as the United States does under its laws.

(d) Except as otherwise expressly provided in this Act, the Administrator of the Environmental Protection Agency (hereinafter in this Act called "Administrator") shall administer this Act.

(e) Public participation in the development, revision, and enforcement of any regulation, standard, effluent limitation, plan, or program established by the Administrator or any State under this Act shall be provided for, encouraged, and assisted by the Administrator and the States. The Administrator, in cooperation with the States, shall develop and publish regulations specifying minimum guidelines for public participation in such processes.

(f) It is the national policy that to the maximum extent possible the procedures utilized for implementing this Act shall encourage the drastic minimization of paperwork and interagency decision procedures, and the best use of available manpower and funds, so as to prevent needless duplication and unnecessary delays at all levels of government.

(g) It is the policy of Congress that the authority of each State to allocate quantities of water within its jurisdiction shall not be superseded, abrogated or otherwise impaired by this Act. It is the further policy of Congress that nothing in this Act shall be construed to supersede or abrogate rights to quantities of water which have been established by any State. Federal agencies shall co-operate with State and local agencies to develop comprehensive solutions to prevent, reduce and eliminate pollution in concert with programs for managing water resources.

COMPREHENSIVE PROGRAMS FOR WATER POLLUTION CONTROL

Sec. 102. (a) The Administrator shall, after careful investigation, and in cooperation with other Federal agencies, State water pollution control agencies, interstate agencies, and the municipalities and industries involved, prepare or develop comprehensive programs for preventing, reducing, or eliminating the pollution of the navigable waters and ground waters and improving the sanitary condition of surface and underground waters. In the development of such comprehensive programs due regard shall be given to the improvements which are necessary to conserve such waters for the protection and propagation of fish and aquatic life and wildlife, recreational purposes, and the withdrawal of such waters for public water supply, agricultural, industrial, and other purposes.

....

MARINE SANITATION DEVICES

Sec. 312. (a) For the purpose of this section, the term—

....

(14) "vessel of the Armed Forces" means—

(A) any vessel owned or operated by the Department of Defense, other than a time or voyage chartered vessel; and

(B) any vessel owned or operated by the Department of Transportation that is designated by the Secretary of the department in which the Coast Guard is operating as a vessel equivalent to a vessel described in subparagraph (A).

(b) (1) As soon as possible, after the enactment of this section and subject to the provisions of section 104(j) of this Act, the Administrator, after consultation with the Secretary of the department in which the Coast Guard is operating, after giving appropriate consideration to the economic costs involved, and within the limits of available technology, shall promulgate Federal standards of performance for marine sanitation devices (hereinafter in this section referred to as "standards") which shall be designed to prevent the discharge of untreated or inadequately treated sewage into or upon the navigable waters from new vessels and existing vessels, except vessels not equipped with installed toilet facilities. Such standards and standards established under subsection (c)(1)(B) of this section shall be consistent with maritime safety and the marine and navigation laws and regulations and shall be coordinated with the regulations issued under this subsection by the Secretary of the department in which the Coast Guard is operating. The Secretary of the department in which the Coast Guard is operating shall promulgate regulations, which are consistent with standards promulgated under this subsection and subsection (c) of this section and with maritime safety and the marine and navigation laws and regulations governing the design, construction, installation, and operation of any marine sanitation device on board such vessels.

....

(d) The provisions of this section and the standards and regulations promulgated hereunder apply to vessels owned and operated by the United States unless the Secretary of Defense finds that compliance would not be in the interest of national security. With respect to vessels owned and operated by the Department of Defense, regulations under the last sentence of subsection (b)(1) of this section and certifications under subsection (g)(2) of this section shall be promulgated and issued by the Secretary of Defense.

....

(n) Uniform National Discharge Standards for Vessels of the Armed Forces.—

(1) Applicability.—This subsection shall apply to vessels of the Armed Forces and discharges, other than sewage, incidental to the normal operation of a vessel of the Armed Forces, unless the Secretary of Defense finds that compliance with this subsection would not be in the national security interests of the United States.

....

ENDANGERED SPECIES ACT OF 1973*

FINDINGS, PURPOSES, AND POLICY

SEC. 2. (a) FINDINGS.—The Congress finds and declares that—

(1) various species of fish, wildlife, and plants in the United States have been rendered extinct as a consequence of economic growth and development untempered by adequate concern and conservation;

(2) other species of fish, wildlife, and plants have been so depleted in numbers that they are in danger of or threatened with extinction;

(3) these species of fish, wildlife, and plants are of esthetic, ecological, educational, historical, recreational, and scientific value to the Nation and its people;

(4) the United States has pledged itself as a sovereign state in the international community to conserve to the extent practicable the various species of fish or wildlife and plants facing extinction, pursuant to—

(A) migratory bird treaties with Canada and Mexico;

(B) the Migratory and Endangered Bird Treaty with Japan;

(C) the Convention on Nature Protection and Wildlife Preservation in the Western Hemisphere;

(D) the International Convention for the Northwest Atlantic Fisheries;

(E) the International Convention for the High Seas Fisheries of the North Pacific Ocean;

(F) the Convention on International Trade in Endangered Species of Wild Fauna and Flora; and

(G) other international agreements; and

(5) encouraging the States and other interested parties, through Federal financial assistance and a system of incentives, to develop and maintain conservation programs which meet national and international standards is a key to meeting the Nation's international commitments and to better safeguarding, for the benefit of all citizens, the Nation's heritage in fish, wildlife, and plants.

(b) PURPOSES.—The purposes of this Act are to provide a means whereby the ecosystems upon which endangered species and threatened species depend may be conserved, to provide a program for the conservation of such endangered species and threatened species, and to take such steps as may be appropriate to achieve the purposes of the treaties and conventions set forth in subsection (a) of this section.

(c) POLICY.—(1) It is further declared to be the policy of Congress that all Federal departments and agencies shall seek to conserve endangered species and threatened species and shall utilize their authorities in furtherance of the purposes of this Act.

---

* Endangered Species Act of 1973 §§2, 4, 16 U.S.C.A. §§1531, 1533 (West 2000 & Supp. 2005), *available at* http://www.fws.gov/endangered/esaall.pdf.

(2) It is further declared to be the policy of Congress that Federal agencies shall cooperate with State and local agencies to resolve water resource issues in concert with conservation of endangered species.

....

DETERMINATION OF ENDANGERED SPECIES AND THREATENED SPECIES

SEC. 4. (a) GENERAL.—(1) The Secretary shall by regulation promulgated in accordance with subsection (b) determine whether any species is an endangered species or a threatened species because of any of the following factors:

(A) the present or threatened destruction, modification, or curtailment of its habitat or range;

(B) overutilization for commercial, recreational, scientific, or educational purposes;

(C) disease or predation;

(D) the inadequacy of existing regulatory mechanisms; or

(E) other natural or manmade factors affecting its continued existence.

(2) With respect to any species over which program responsibilities have been vested in the Secretary of Commerce pursuant to Reorganization Plan Numbered 4 of 1970—

(A) in any case in which the Secretary of Commerce determines that such species should—

(i) be listed as an endangered species or a threatened species, or

(ii) be changed in status from a threatened species to an endangered species, he shall so inform the Secretary of the Interior, who shall list such species in accordance with this section;

(B) in any case in which the Secretary of Commerce determines that such species should—

(i) be removed from any list published pursuant to subsection (c) of this section, or

(ii) be changed in status from an endangered species to a threatened species, he shall recommend such action to the Secretary of the Interior, and the Secretary of the Interior, if he concurs in the recommendation, shall implement such action; and

(C) the Secretary of the Interior may not list or remove from any list any such species, and may not change the status of any such species which are listed, without a prior favorable determination made pursuant to this section by the Secretary of Commerce.

....

(i) REVIEW BY SECRETARY OF STATE.—Notwithstanding any other provision of this Act, the Committee shall be prohibited from considering for exemption any application made to it, if the Secretary of State, after a review of the proposed agency action and its potential implications, and after hearing, certifies, in writing, to the Committee within 60 days of any application made under this section that the granting of any such exemption and the carrying out of such action would be in violation of an international treaty obligation or other international obligation of the United States. The Secretary of State shall, at the time of such certification, publish a copy thereof in the Federal Register.

(j) Notwithstanding any other provision of this Act, the Committee shall grant an exemption for any agency action if the Secretary of Defense finds that such exemption is necessary for reasons of national security.

(k) Special Provisions.—An exemption decision by the Committee under this section shall not be a major Federal action for purposes of the National Environmental Policy Act of 1969 (42 U.S.C. 4321 et seq.): *Provided,* That an environmental impact statement which discusses the impacts upon endangered species or threatened species or their critical habitats shall have been previously prepared with respect to any agency action exempted by such order.

. . . .

(p) Exemptions in Presidentially Declared Disaster Areas.—In any area which has been declared by the President to be a major disaster area under the Disaster Relief and Emergency Assistance Act, the President is authorized to make the determinations required by subsections (g) and (h) of this section for any project for the repair or replacement of a public facility substantially as it existed prior to the disaster under section 405 or 406 of the Disaster Relief and Emergency Assistance Act, and which the President determines (1) is necessary to prevent the recurrence of such a natural disaster and to reduce the potential loss of human life, and (2) to involve an emergency situation which does not allow the ordinary procedures of this section to be followed. Notwithstanding any other provision of this section, the Committee shall accept the determinations of the President under this subsection.

. . . .

EXECUTIVE ORDER 12114*
(ENVIRONMENTAL EFFECTS ABROAD OF MAJOR FEDERAL ACTIONS)

By virtue of the authority vested in me by the Constitution and the laws of the United states, and as President of the United States, in order to further environmental objectives consistent with the foreign policy and national security policy of the United States, it is ordered as follows:

Section 1

1-1. Purpose and Scope. The purpose of this Executive Order is to enable responsible officials of Federal agencies having ultimate responsibility for authorizing and approving actions encompassed by this Order to be informed of pertinent environmental considerations and to take such considerations into account, with other pertinent considerations of national policy, in making decisions regarding such actions. While based on independent authority, this Order furthers the purpose of the National Environmental Policy Act and the Marine Protection Research and Sanctuaries Act and the Deepwater Port Act consistent with the foreign policy and national security policy of the United States, and represents the United States government's exclusive and complete determination of the procedural and other actions to be taken by Federal agencies to further the purpose of the National Environmental Policy Act, with respect to the environment outside the United States, its territories and possessions.

Section 2

2-1. Agency Procedures. Every Federal agency taking major Federal actions encompassed hereby and not exempted herefrom having significant effects on the environment outside the geographical borders of the United States and its territories and possessions shall within eight months after the effective date of this Order have in effect procedures to implement this Order. Agencies shall consult with the Department of State and the Council on Environmental Quality concerning such procedures prior to placing them in effect.

2-2. Information Exchange. To assist in effectuating the foregoing purpose, the Department of State and the Council on Environmental Quality in collaboration with other interested Federal agencies and other nations shall conduct a program for exchange on a continuing basis of information concerning the environment. The objectives of this program shall be to provide information for use by decisionmakers, to heighten awareness of and interest in environmental concerns and, as appropriate, to facilitate environmental cooperation with foreign nations.

2-3. Actions Included. Agencies in their procedures under Section 2-1 shall establish procedures by which their officers having ultimate responsibility for authority and approving actions in one of the following categories encompassed by this Order, take into consideration in making decisions concerning such actions, a document described in Section 2-4(a):

---

* Exec. Order No. 12,114, 3 C.F.R. 356 (1979), *reprinted in* 42 U.S.C. §4321 note (2000), *available at* http://www.archives.gov/federal-register/codification/executive-order/12114.html.

(a) major Federal actions significantly affecting the environment of the global commons outside the jurisdiction of any nation (e.g., the oceans or Antarctica);

(b) major Federal actions significantly affecting the environment of a foreign nation not participating with the United States and not otherwise involved in the action;

(c) major Federal actions significantly affecting the environment of a foreign nation which provide to that nation:

(1) a product, or physical project producing a principal product or an emission or effluent, which is prohibited or strictly regulated by Federal law in the United States because its toxic effects on the environment create a serious public health risk; or

(2) a physical project which in the United States is prohibited or strictly regulated by Federal law to protect the environment against radioactive substances.

(d) major Federal actions outside the United States, its territories and possessions which significantly affect natural or ecological resources of global importance designated for protection under this subsection by the President, or, in the case of such a resource protected by international agreement binding on the United States, by the Secretary of State. Recommendations to the President under this subsection shall be accompanied by the views of the Council on Environmental Quality and the Secretary of State.

2-4. Applicable Procedures. (a) There are the following types of documents to be used in connection with actions described in Section 2-3:

(i) environmental impact statements (including generic, program and specific statements);

(ii) bilateral or multilateral environmental studies, relevant or related to the proposed action, by the United States and one or more foreign nations, or by an international body or organization in which the United States is a member or participant; or

(iii) concise reviews of the environmental issues involved, including environmental assessments, summary environmental analyses or other appropriate documents.

(b) Agencies shall in their procedures provide for preparation of documents described in Section 2-4(a), with respect to actions described in Section 2-3, as follows:

(i) for effects described in Section 2-3(a), an environmental impact statement described in Section 2-4(a)(i);

(ii) for effects described in Section 2-3(b), a document described in Section 2-4(a)(ii) or (iii), as determined by the agency;

(iii) for effects described in Section 2-3(c), a document described in Section 2-4(a)(ii) or (iii), as determined by the agency;

(iv) for effects described in Section 2-3(d), a document described in Section 2-4(a)(i), (ii) or (iii), as determined by the agency.

Such procedures may provide that an agency need not prepare a new document when a document described in Section 2-4(a) already exists.

(c) Nothing in this Order shall serve to invalidate any existing regulations of any agency which have been adopted pursuant to court order or pursuant to judicial settlement of any case or to prevent any agency from providing in its procedures for measures in addition to those provided for herein to further the purpose of the National Environmental Policy Act and other environmental laws, including the Marine Protection Research and Sanctuaries Act and the Deepwater Port Act, consistent with the foreign and national security policies of the United States.

(d) Except as provided in Section 2-5(b), agencies taking action encompassed by this Order shall, as soon as feasible, inform other Federal agencies with relevant expertise of the availability of environmental documents prepared under this Order.

Agencies in their procedures under Section 2-1 shall make appropriate provision for determining when an affected nation shall be informed in accordance with Section 3-2 of this Order of the availability of environmental documents prepared pursuant to those procedures.

In order to avoid duplication of resources, agencies in their procedures shall provide for appropriate utilization of the resources of other Federal agencies with relevant environmental jurisdiction or expertise.

2-5. Exemptions and Considerations. (a) Notwithstanding Section 2-3, the following actions are exempt from this Order:

(i) actions not having a significant effect on the environment outside the United States as determined by the agency;

(ii) actions taken by the President;

(iii) actions taken by or pursuant to the direction of the President or Cabinet officer when the national security or interest is involved or when the action occurs in the course of an armed conflict;

(iv) intelligence activities and arms transfers;

(v) export licenses or permits or export approvals, and actions relating to nuclear activities except actions providing to a foreign nation a nuclear production or utilization facility as defined in the Atomic Energy Act of 1954, as amended, or a nuclear waste management facility;

(vi) votes and other actions in international conferences and organizations;

(vii) disaster and emergency relief action.

(b) Agency procedures under Section 2-1 implementing Section 2-4 may provide for appropriate modifications in the contents, timing and availability of documents to other affected Federal agencies and affected nations, where necessary to:

(i) enable the agency to decide and act promptly as and when required;

(ii) avoid adverse impacts on foreign relations or infringement in fact or appearance of other nations' sovereign responsibilities, or

(iii) ensure appropriate reflection of:

(1) diplomatic factors;

(2) international commercial, competitive and export promotion factors;

(3) needs for governmental or commercial confidentiality;

(4) national security considerations;

(5) difficulties of obtaining information and agency ability to analyze meaningfully environmental effects of a proposed action; and

(6) the degree to which the agency is involved in or able to affect a decision to be made.

(c) Agency procedure under Section 2-1 may provide for categorical exclusions and for such exemptions in addition to those specified in subsection (a) of this Section as may be necessary to meet emergency circumstances, situations involving exceptional foreign policy and national security sensitivities and other such special circumstances. In utilizing such additional exemptions agencies shall, as soon as feasible, consult with the Department of State and the Council on Environmental Quality.

(d) The provisions of Section 2-5 do not apply to actions described in Section 2-3(a) unless permitted by law.

Section 3

3-1. Rights of Action. This Order is solely for the purpose of establishing internal procedures for Federal agencies to consider the significant effects of their actions on the environment outside the United States, its territories and possessions, and nothing in this Order shall be construed to create a cause of action.

3-2. Foreign Relations. The Department of State shall coordinate all communications by agencies with foreign governments concerning environmental agreements and other arrangements in implementation of this Order.

3-3. Multi-Agency Actions. Where more than one Federal agency is involved in an action or program, a lead agency, as determined by the agencies involved, shall have responsibility for implementation of this Order.

3-4. Certain Terms. For purposes of this Order, "environment" means the natural and physical environment and excludes social, economic and other environments; and an action significantly affects the environment if it does significant harm to the environment even though on balance the agency believes the action to be beneficial to the environment. The term "export approvals" in Section 2-5(a)(v) does not mean or include direct loans to finance exports.

3-5. Multiple Impacts. If a major Federal action having effects on the environment of the United States or the global commons requires preparation of an environmental impact statement, and if the action also has effects on the environment of a foreign nation, an environmental impact statement need not be prepared with respect to the effects on the environment of the foreign nation.

JIMMY CARTER

The White House.
January 4, 1979.

COMPREHENSIVE ENVIRONMENTAL RESPONSE, COMPENSATION, AND LIABILITY ACT OF 1980* (CERCLA)

....

REPORTABLE QUANTITIES AND ADDITIONAL DESIGNATIONS

SEC. 102. (a) The Administrator shall promulgate and revise as may be appropriate, regulations designating as hazardous substances, in addition to those referred to in section 101(14) of this title, such elements, compounds, mixtures, solutions, and substances which, when released into the environment may present substantial danger to the public health or welfare or the environment, and shall promulgate regulations establishing that quantity of any hazardous substance the release of which shall be reported pursuant to section 103 of this title. The Administrator may determine that one single quantity shall be the reportable quantity for any hazardous substance, regardless of the medium into which the hazardous substance is released.

For all hazardous substances for which proposed regulations establishing reportable quantities were published in the Federal Register under this subsection on or before March 1, 1986, the Administrator shall promulgate under this subsection final regulations establishing reportable quantities not later than December 31, 1986. For all hazardous substances for which proposed regulations establishing reportable quantities were not published in the Federal Register under this subsection on or before March 1, 1986, the Administrator shall publish under this subsection proposed regulations establishing reportable quantities not later than December 31, 1986, and promulgate final regulations under this subsection establishing reportable quantities not later than April 30, 1988.

(b) Unless and until superseded by regulations establishing a reportable quantity under subsection (a) of this section for any hazardous substance as defined in section 101(14) of this title, (1) a quantity of one pound, or (2) for those hazardous substances for which reportable quantities have been established pursuant to section 311(b)(4) of the Federal Water Pollution Control Act, such reportable quantity, shall be deemed that quantity, the release of which requires notification pursuant to section 103(a) or (b) of this title.

NOTICES, PENALTIES

SEC. 103. (a) Any person in charge of a vessel or an offshore or an onshore facility shall, as soon as he has knowledge of any release (other than a federally permitted release) of a hazardous substance from such vessel or facility in quantities equal to or greater than those determined pursuant to section 102 of this title, immediately notify the National Response Center established under the Clean Water Act of such release.

---

* Comprehensive Environmental Response, Compensation, and Liability Act of 1980 §§ 102–107, 111, 42 U.S.C.A. §§ 9602–9607, 9611 (West 1995 & Supp. 2005), *available at* http://www.uscg.mil/hq/g-m/nmc/response/cercla.pdf.

The National Response Center shall convey the notification expeditiously to all appropriate Government agencies, including the Governor of any affected State.

(b) Any person—

(1) in charge of a vessel from which a hazardous substance is released, other than a federally permitted release, into or upon the navigable waters of the United States, adjoining shorelines, or into or upon the waters of the contiguous zone, or

(2) in charge of a vessel from which a hazardous substance is released, other than a federally permitted release, which may affect natural resources belonging to, appertaining to, or under the exclusive management authority of the United States (including resources under the Magnuson Fishery Conservation and Management Act of 1976), and who is otherwise subject to the jurisdiction of the United States at the time of the release, or

(3) in charge of a facility from which a hazardous substance is released, other than a federally permitted release, in a quantity equal to or greater than that determined pursuant to section 102 of this title who fails to notify immediately the appropriate agency of the United States Government as soon as he has knowledge of such release or who submits in such a notification any information which he knows to be false or misleading shall, upon conviction, be fined in accordance with the applicable provisions of title 18 of the United States Code or imprisoned for not more than 3 years (or not more than 5 years in the case of a second or subsequent conviction), or both. Notification received pursuant to this subsection or information obtained by the exploitation of such notification shall not be used against any such person in any criminal case, except a prosecution for perjury or for giving a false statement.

....

RESPONSE AUTHORITIES

Sec. 104. (a)(1) Whenever (A) any hazardous substance is released or there is a substantial threat of such a release into the environment, or (B) there is a release or substantial threat of release into the environment of any pollutant or contaminant which may present an imminent and substantial danger to the public health or welfare, the President is authorized to act, consistent with the national contingency plan, to remove or arrange for the removal of, and provide for remedial action relating to such hazardous substance, pollutant, or contaminant at any time (including its removal from any contaminated natural resource), or take any other response measure consistent with the national contingency plan which the President deems necessary to protect the public health or welfare or the environment. When the President determines that such action will be done properly and promptly by the owner or operator of the facility or vessel or by any other responsible party, the President may allow such person to carry out the action, conduct the remedial investigation, or conduct the feasibility study in accordance with section 122. No remedial investigation or feasibility study (RI/FS) shall be authorized except on a determination by the President that the party is qualified to conduct the RI/FS and only if the President contracts with or arranges for a qualified person to assist the President in overseeing and reviewing the conduct of such RI/FS and if the responsible party agrees to reimburse the Fund for any cost incurred by the President under, or in connection with, the oversight contract or arrangement. In no event shall a potentially responsible party be subject to a lesser standard of liability, receive preferential treatment, or in any other way, whether direct or indirect, benefit from any such arrangements as a response action contractor, or as a person hired or retained by such a response action contractor, with respect to the release or facility in question. The President shall give primary attention to those releases which the President deems may present a public health threat.

. . . .

NATIONAL CONTINGENCY PLAN

SEC. 105. (a) Revision And Republication.—Within one hundred and eighty days after the enactment of this Act, the President shall, after notice and opportunity for public comments, revise and republish the national contingency plan for the removal of oil and hazardous substances, originally prepared and published pursuant to section 311 of the Federal Water Pollution Control Act, to reflect and effectuate the responsibilities and powers created by this Act, in addition to those matters specified in section 311(c)(2). Such revision shall include a section of the plan to be known as the national hazardous substance response plan which shall establish procedures and standards for responding to releases of hazardous substances, pollutants, and contaminants, which shall include at a minimum:

(1) methods for discovering and investigating facilities at which hazardous substances have been disposed of or otherwise come to be located;

(2) methods for evaluating, including analyses of relative cost, and remedying any releases or threats of releases from facilities which pose substantial danger to the public health or the environment;

(3) methods and criteria for determining the appropriate extent of removal, remedy, and other measures authorized by this Act;

(4) appropriate roles and responsibilities for the Federal, State, and local governments and for interstate and nongovernmental entities in effectuating the plan;

(5) provision for identification, procurement, maintenance, and storage of response equipment and supplies;

(6) a method for and assignment of responsibility for reporting the existence of such facilities which may be located on federally owned or controlled properties and any releases of hazardous substances from such facilities;

(7) means of assuring that remedial action measures are cost-effective over the period of potential exposure to the hazardous substances or contaminated materials;

(8) (A) criteria for determining priorities among releases or threatened releases throughout the United States for the purpose of taking remedial action and, to the extent practicable taking into account the potential urgency of such action, for the purpose of taking removal action. Criteria and priorities under this paragraph shall be based upon relative risk or danger to public health or welfare or the environment, in the judgment of the President, taking into account to the extent possible the population at risk, the hazard potential of the hazardous substances at such facilities, the potential for contamination of drinking water supplies, the potential for direct human contact, the potential for destruction of sensitive ecosystems, the damage to natural resources which may affect the human food chain and which is associated with any release or threatened release, the contamination or potential contamination of the ambient air which is associated with the release or threatened

release, State preparedness to assume State costs and responsibilities, and other appropriate factors;

. . . .

ABATEMENT ACTION

SEC. 106. (a) In addition to any other action taken by a State or local government, when the President determines that there may be an imminent and substantial endangerment to the public health or welfare or the environment because of an actual or threatened release of a hazardous substance from a facility, he may require the Attorney General of the United States to secure such relief as may be necessary to abate such danger or threat, and the district court of the United States in the district in which the threat occurs shall have jurisdiction to grant such relief as the public interest and the equities of the case may require. The President may also, after notice to the affected State, take other action under this section including, but not limited to, issuing such orders as may be necessary to protect public health and welfare and the environment.

(b) (1) Any person who, without sufficient cause, willfully violates, or fails or refuses to comply with, any order of the President under subsection (a) may, in an action brought in the appropriate United States district court to enforce such order, be fined not more than $25,000 for each day in which such violation occurs or such failure to comply continues.

(2) (A) Any person who receives and complies with the terms of any order issued under subsection (a) may, within 60 days after completion of the required action, petition the President for reimbursement from the Fund for the reasonable costs of such action, plus interest. Any interest payable under this paragraph shall accrue on the amounts expended from the date of expenditure at the same rate as specified for interest on investments of the Hazardous Substance Superfund established under subchapter A of chapter 98 of the Internal Revenue Code of 1954.

(B) If the President refuses to grant all or part of a petition made under this paragraph, the petitioner may within 30 days of receipt of such refusal file an action against the President in the appropriate United States district court seeking reimbursement from the Fund.

. . . .

LIABILITY

SEC. 107. (a) Notwithstanding any other provision or rule of law, and subject only to the defenses set forth in subsection (b) of this section—

(1) the owner and operator of a vessel or a facility,

(2) any person who at the time of disposal of any hazardous substance owned or operated any facility at which such hazardous substances were disposed of,

(3) any person who by contract, agreement, or otherwise arranged for disposal or treatment, or arranged with a transporter for transport for disposal or treatment, of hazardous substances owned or possessed by such person, by any other party or entity, at any facility or incineration vessel owned or operated by another party or entity and containing such hazardous substances, and

(4) any person who accepts or accepted any hazardous substances for transport to disposal or treatment facilities, incineration vessels or sites selected by such per-

son, from which there is a release, or a threatened release which causes the incurrence of response coats, of a hazardous substance, shall be liable for—

(A) all costs of removal or remedial action incurred by the United States Government or a State or an Indian tribe not inconsistent with the national contingency plan;

(B) any other necessary costs of response incurred by any other person consistent with the national contingency plan;

(C) damages for injury to, destruction of, or loss of natural resources, including the reasonable costs of assessing such injury, destruction, or loss resulting from such a release; and

(D) the costs of any health assessment or health effects study carried out under section 104(i).

....

USES OF FUND

Sec. 111. (a) In General.—For the purposes specified in this section there is authorized to be appropriated from the Hazardous Substance Superfund established under subchapter A of chapter 98 of the Internal Revenue Code of 1986 not more than $8,500,000,000 for the 5-year period beginning on the date of enactment of the Superfund Amendments and Reauthorization Act of 1986, and not more than $5,100,000,000 for the period commencing October 1, 1991, and ending September 30, 1994, and such sums shall remain available until expended. The preceding sentence constitutes a specific authorization for the funds appropriated under title II of Public Law 99-160 (relating to payment to the Hazardous Substances Trust Fund). The President shall use the money in the Fund for the following purposes:

(1) Payment of governmental response costs incurred pursuant to section 104 of this title, including costs incurred pursuant to the Intervention on the High Seas Act.

(2) Payment of any claim for necessary response costs incurred by any other person as a result of carrying out the national contingency plan established under section 311(c) of the Clean Water Act and amended by section 105 of this title: Provided, however, That such costs must be approved under said plan and certified by the responsible Federal official.

(3) Payment of any claim authorized by subsection (b) of this section and finally decided pursuant to section 112 of this title, including those costs set out in subsection 112(c)(3) of this title.

(4) Payment of costs specified under subsection (c) of this section.

(5) Grants for technical assistance.—The cost of grants under section 117(e) (relating to public participation grants for technical assistance).

(6) Lead contaminated soil.—Payment of not to exceed $15,000,000 for the costs of a pilot program for removal, decontamination, or other action with respect to lead-contaminated soil in one to three different metropolitan areas.

The President shall not pay for any administrative costs or expenses out of the Fund unless such costs and expenses are reasonably necessary for and incidental to the implementation of this title.

....

K. Space Law

NATIONAL AERONAUTICS AND SPACE ACT OF 1958*

....

TITLE I

....

DECLARATION OF POLICY AND PURPOSE

Sec. 102. (a) The Congress hereby declares that it is the policy of the United States that activities in space should be devoted to peaceful purposes for the benefit of all mankind.

(b) The Congress declares that the general welfare and security of the United States require that adequate provision be made for aeronautical and space activities. The Congress further declares that such activities shall be the responsibility of, and shall be directed by, a civilian agency exercising control over aeronautical and space activities sponsored by the United States, except that activities peculiar to or primarily associated with the development of weapons systems, military operations, or the defense of the United States (including the research and development necessary to make effective provision for the defense of the United States) shall be the responsibility of, and shall be directed by, the Department of Defense; and that determination as to which such agency has responsibility for and direction of any such activity shall be made by the President in conformity with section 201(e).

(c) The Congress declares that the general welfare of the United States requires that the National Aeronautics and Space Administration (as established by title II of this Act) seek and encourage, to the maximum extent possible, the fullest commercial use of space.

(d) The aeronautical and space activities of the United States shall be conducted so as to contribute materially to one or more of the following objectives:

(1) The expansion of human knowledge of the Earth and of phenomena in the atmosphere and space;

(2) The improvement of the usefulness, performance, speed, safety, and efficiency of aeronautical and space vehicles;

(3) The development and operation of vehicles capable of carrying instruments, equipment, supplies, and living organisms through space;

(4) The establishment of long-range studies of the potential benefits to be gained from, the opportunities for, and the problems involved in the utilization of aeronautical and space activities for peaceful and scientific purposes;

(5) The preservation of the role of the United States as a leader in aeronautical and space science and technology and in the application thereof to the conduct of peaceful activities within and outside the atmosphere;

(6) The making available to agencies directly concerned with national defense of discoveries that have military value or significance, and the furnishing by such

* National Aeronautics and Space Act of 1958 § 102, Pub. L. No. 85-568, § 102, 72 Stat. 426, 426–27 (codified as amended at 42 U.S.C. § 2451 (2000 & Supp. I 2001)), *available at* http://www.hq.nasa.gov/ogc/spaceact.html.

agencies, to the civilian agency established to direct and control nonmilitary aeronautical and space activities, of information as to discoveries which have value or significance to that agency;

(7) Cooperation by the United States with other nations and groups of nations in work done pursuant to this Act and in the peaceful application of the results thereof;

(8) The most effective utilization of the scientific and engineering resources of the United States, with close cooperation among all interested agencies of the United States in order to avoid unnecessary duplication of effort, facilities, and equipment; and

(9) The preservation of the United States preeminent position in aeronautics and space through research and technology development related to associated manufacturing processes.

(e) The Congress declares that the general welfare of the United States requires that the unique competence in scientific and engineering systems of the National Aeronautics and Space Administration also be directed toward ground propulsion systems research and development. Such development shall be conducted so as to contribute to the objectives of developing energy- and petroleum-conserving ground propulsion systems, and of minimizing the environmental degradation caused by such systems.

(f) The Congress declares that the general welfare of the United States requires that the unique competence of the National Aeronautics and Space Administration in science and engineering systems be directed to assisting in bioengineering research, development, and demonstration programs designed to alleviate and minimize the effects of disability.

(g) It is the purpose of this Act to carry out and effectuate the policies declared in subsections (a), (b), (c), (d), (e), and (f).

. . . .

TREATY ON PRINCIPLES GOVERNING THE ACTIVITIES OF STATES IN THE EXPLORATION AND USE OF OUTER SPACE, INCLUDING THE MOON AND OTHER CELESTIAL BODIES[1]

The States Parties to this Treaty,

Inspired by the great prospects opening up before mankind as a result of man's entry into outer space,

Recognizing the common interest of all mankind in the progress of the exploration and use of outer space for peaceful purposes,

Believing that the exploration and use of outer space should be carried on for the benefit of all peoples irrespective of the degree of their economic or scientific development,

Desiring to contribute to broad international co-operation in the scientific as well as the legal aspects of the exploration and use of outer space for peaceful purposes,

Believing that such co-operation will contribute to the development of mutual understanding and to the strengthening of friendly relations between States and peoples,

Recalling resolution 1962 (XVIII), entitled 'Declaration of Legal Principles Governing the Activities of States in the Exploration and Use of Outer Space', which was adopted unanimously by the United Nations General Assembly on 13 December 1963,

Recalling resolution 1884 (XVIII), calling upon States to refrain from placing in orbit around the Earth any objects carrying nuclear weapons or any other kinds of weapons of mass destruction or from installing such weapons on celestial bodies, which was adopted unanimously by the United Nations General Assembly on 17 October 1963,

Taking account of United Nations General Assembly resolution 110 (II) of 3 November 1947, which condemned propaganda designed or likely to provoke or encourage any threat to the peace, breach of the peace or act of aggression, and considering that the aforementioned resolution is applicable to outer space,

Convinced that a Treaty on Principles Governing the Activities of States in the Exploration and Use of Outer Space, including the Moon and Other Celestial Bodies, will further the purposes and principles of the Charter of the United Nations,[2]

Have agreed on the following:

Article 1. The exploration and use of outer space, including the Moon and other celestial bodies, shall be carried out for the benefit and in the interests of all countries, irrespective of their degree of economic or scientific development, and shall be the province of all mankind.

Outer space, including the Moon and other celestial bodies, shall be free for exploration and use by all States without discrimination of any kind, on a basis of equality

---

1. Treaty on Principles Governing the Activities of States in the Exploration and Use of Outer Space, Including the Moon and Other Celestial Bodies, Jan. 27, 1967, 18 U.S.T. 2410, 2411, 610 U.N.T.S. 205, 206 (entered into force Oct. 10, 1967), *available at* http://www1.umn.edu/humanrts/peace/docs/treatyouterspace.html.

2. Charter of the United Nations, June 26, 1945, 59 Stat. 1031, 3 Bevans 1153 (entered into force Oct. 24, 1945), *available at* http://www.un.org/aboutun/charter/index.html.

and in accordance with international law, and there shall be free access to all areas of celestial bodies.

There shall be freedom of scientific investigation in outer space, including the Moon and other celestial bodies, and States shall facilitate and encourage international co-operation in such investigation.

....

Article 4. States Parties to the Treaty undertake not to place in orbit around the Earth any object carrying nuclear weapons or any other kind of weapons of mass destruction, install such weapons on celestial bodies, or station such weapons in outer space in any other manner.

The Moon and other celestial bodies shall be used by all States Parties to the Treaty exclusively for peaceful purposes. The establishment of military bases, installations and fortifications, the testing of any type of weapons and the conduct of military manoeuvres on celestial bodies shall be forbidden. The use of military personnel for scientific research or for any other peaceful purposes shall not be prohibited. The use of any equipment or facility necessary for peaceful exploration of the Moon and other celestial bodies shall also not be prohibited.

....

Article 6. States Parties to the Treaty shall bear international responsibility for national activities in outer space, including the Moon and other celestial bodies, whether such activities are carried on by governmental agencies or by non-governmental entities, and for assuring that national activities are carried out in conformity with the provisions set forth in the present Treaty. The activities of nongovernmental entities in outer space, including the Moon and other celestial bodies, shall require authorization and continuing supervision by the appropriate State Party to the Treaty. When activities are carried on in outer space, including the Moon and other celestial bodies, by an international organization, responsibility for compliance with this Treaty shall be borne both by the international organization and by the States Parties to the Treaty participating in such organization.

Article 7. Each State Party to the Treaty that launches or procures the launching of an object into outer space, including the Moon and other celestial bodies, and each State party from whose territory or facility an object is launched, is internationally liable for damage to another State Party to the Treaty or to its natural or juridical persons by such object or its component parts on the Earth, in air space or in outer space, including the Moon and other celestial bodies.

Article 8. A State Party to the Treaty on whose registry an object launched into outer space is carried shall retain jurisdiction and control over such object, and over any personnel thereof, while in outer space or on a celestial body. Ownership of objects launched into outer space including objects landed or constructed on a celestial body, and of their component parts, is not affected by their presence in outer space or on a celestial body or by their return to the Earth. Such objects or component parts found beyond the limits of the State Party to the Treaty on whose registry they are carried shall be returned to that State Party, which shall, upon request, furnish identifying data prior to their return.

....

Appendix

Selected Web Sites Which Publish Documents Concerning National Security Law

Selected Web Sites

Here follows a list of selected Web sites of established government and non-government organizations likely to be maintained for many years. Internet sites are constantly changing, of course, and the editors cannot guarantee the accuracy of the sites listed here. There are also many other relevant sites as well.

American Society of International Law
http://www.asil.org

Central Intelligence Agency
http://www.cia.gov

Cornell University
http://www.cornell.edu/

Federation of American Scientists
http:///www.fas.org

Human Rights Network
http://www.hrni.org

Institute of International Economic Law (John Jackson)
http://www.law.georgetown.edu/iiel/

LexisNexis
http://www.lexisnexis.com/

Library of Congress (legislative information on the Internet)
http://thomas.loc.gov

National Defense University
http://www.ndu.edu

National Security Agency
http://www.nsa.gov

North Atlantic Treaty Organization
http://www.nato.int

Organization for Security and Co-Operation in Europe
http://www.osce.org

United Nations
http://www.un.org

United Nations Treaty Collection
http://www.treaty.un.org

U.S. Courts
http://www.uscourts.gov

U.S. Department of Defense
http://www.defenselink.mil

U.S. Department of State
http://www.state.gov

U.S. National Archives & Records Administration
http://www.archives.gov/

U.S. Institute of Peace
http://www.usip.org/

University of Bologna Research Guide to International Law on the Internet
http://www.spfo.unibo.it/spolfo/ILMAIN.htm

University of Virginia Law Library
http://www.law.virginia.edu

Vinson & Elkins' Government Anti-Terrorism Initiatives web site
http://www.velaw.com

Westlaw
http://www.westlaw.com

White House
http://www.whitehouse.gov

World News Connection
http://wnc.fedworld.gov/

Yale University Avalon Project
http://www.yale.edu/lawweb/avalon